THE
SOCIETIES
OF
EUROPE

The European Population
1850–1945

FRANZ ROTHENBACHER

palgrave
macmillan

THE
SOCIETIES
OF
EUROPE

A series of historical data handbooks on the development
of Europe from the nineteenth to the end of the
twentieth century

Series Editors
Peter Flora, Franz Kraus and Franz Rothenbacher

The European Population
1850–1945

THE SOCIETIES OF EUROPE

A series of publications by the
Mannheim Centre for European Social Research

Elections in Western Europe since 1815

Trade Unions in Western Europe since 1945

The European Population, 1850–1945
The European Population since 1945

The European Labour Force, 1870–1940
The European Labour Force since 1950

European Social Security Systems, 1885–1945
European Social Security Systems since 1945

First published 2002 by
PALGRAVE MACMILLAN
Houndmills, Basingstoke, Hampshire RG21 6XS and
175 Fifth Avenue, New York, N.Y. 10010
Companies and representatives throughout the world

PALGRAVE MACMILLAN is the global academic imprint of Palgrave
Macmillan division of St. Martin's Press, LLC and of Palgrave Macmillan Ltd.
Macmillan® is a registered trademark in the United States, United Kingdom
and other countries. Palgrave® is a registered trademark in the European
Union and other countries.

ISBN 0-333-77705-0 hardback

1003124637

This book is printed on paper suitable for recycling and made from fully
managed and sustained forest sources.

A catalogue record for this book is available from the British Library.

Library of Congress Cataloging-in-Publication Data

Rothenbacher, Franz.
   The European population, 1850–1945 / Franz Rothenbacher.
      p. cm. – (Societies of Europe)
   Includes bibliographical references and index.
      ISBN 0-333-77705-0
      1. Europe–Population–History.   I. Title. II. Series.

HB3581 .A3 R68 2002
304.6′094′09034–dc21   2002025803

10   9   8   7   6   5   4   3   2   1
11   10   09   08   07   06   05   04   03   02

Printed and bound in Great Britain by
Antony Rowe Ltd, Chippenham and Eastbourne

Editorial Introduction
The Unity and Diversity of Europe

by Peter Flora

This handbook on the European population 1850–1945 is the third in a whole series of volumes. With this series we hope to improve the empirical basis for a comparative-historical analysis of the *Societies of Europe* which is also the title chosen for the series.

Unity and diversity

Anyone who is interested in Europe, as a citizen or scientist, faces the basic question of the *unity and diversity* of the European societies. The question itself is characteristic of Europe; for any other region of the world, it would make much less sense. Between unity and diversity, there has been a persistent though varying tension, with productive as well as destructive consequences. This tension was at the very heart of the unique dynamism of European society, of its modern achievements which have spread over the world; but it was also at the root of the unique destructiveness of the Europeans who made their civil wars into world wars.

'Diversity within unity', 'unity of diversity': questions behind such plays on words can only be studied meaningfully in a *long-term historical perspective*. What we call Europe today grew out of the decline of the Roman Empire which was centred on the Mediterranean, superimposed a strong military-administrative structure on the ethnic and cultural diversity of its peoples, and achieved a certain cultural integration through the Latin language, Roman law, and later the Christian religion.

With the breakdown of the Western empire as a political entity and with the Islamic conquests in North Africa and the Iberian peninsula, the centre of gravity shifted to the north-west, and ethnicity became a dominant principle of political organization. This meant increasing diversity. The fragmentation was counteracted, however, by the unifying impact of Western Christianity. The Roman Church had survived the political breakdown and was able to spread its influence over the centuries to the north and east, far beyond the former *limes*.

Through its centralized and bureaucratic structure, the Roman Church had a standardizing effect on the organization of social life across the continent, and through its reliance on canonical law it shaped the specific role law has played in European societies in general and for their social institutions in particular. Thus, the Europe we know today was created first of all as a *cultural and legal entity*.

Cultural unity, however, had to coexist with political fragmentation. The attempt to resurrect the Roman Empire in the Carolingian empire and its successors ultimately failed. The German-Roman Empire never covered all of the then-important territories of Europe, and in the long run its internal structure proved too weak. But nevertheless it kept the *idea of a politically-unified Europe* alive.

The failures of empire-building cleared the way for the development of the modern state with a more compact territory, more clearly-defined boundaries, a more differentiated centre, and closer relationships between centre and territorial population. With these developments, though they varied across time and space, European diversity acquired a clear political *gestalt*: it became a *system of territorial states*.

A *new map of political boundaries* was drawn, overlaying the much *older map of ethnic-linguistic boundaries* which had been the result of successive waves of migration over the centuries. The concurrence or discrepancy of these two types of boundaries set the options for the later transformation of the territorial into *national states*. These conditions greatly varied across Europe, and in general ethnic heterogeneity increased from the west (and north) to the east. Thus, for a long time Europe was divided between Western European nation-states and Eastern European multi-ethnic empires, with the rather different, confederated and consociational political structures of Central Europe in between.

The development of the European nation-state as the predominant form of political organization was closely linked to the earlier rise of vernaculars to languages with written standards and a corresponding decline of Latin as the means of elite communication. It was also facilitated by the establishment of national Protestant churches in northern Europe, as a consequence of the Reformation, whereas the Catholic Church retained its supra-national character. The division of Western Christianity also produced a new map which, as in the case of ethnic-linguistic boundaries, did not always coincide with the political map.

In this way, the diversity of Europe assumed a new shape: it became a diversity of varying relationships between political organization on the one hand and cultural, above all linguistic and religious, heterogeneity or homogeneity on the other. This kind of diversity was rooted in the past, but it developed in full only with the fundamental transformation of European societies since the nineteenth century: with industrialization and urbanization, with the creation of national systems of mass education, and with the democratization of the political systems. Europe became a *system of nation-states* and reached the highest degree of fragmentation in its history, hardly contained within a common cultural frame.

The democratization of the European nation-states and their transformation into welfare states added two new dimensions to the diversity of Europe: *the diversity of public institutions* and the *diversity of intermediary structures*. New institutions were created in the search for national solutions to problems and tasks connected with the development of capitalist industrial societies: not only systems for mass education, but also for social security, for health, and for other areas relevant for the life chances and living conditions of the mass population. And these institutions have greatly varied in many respects, above all in the degree of their 'stateness' as well as in the extent of their fragmentation or unity.

This institutional diversity across Europe largely persists today, as does the diversity of *intermediary structures*. In the process of democratization, older and newer cleavages dividing the people of the nation-states were transformed into a variety of 'intermediary' organizations: political parties, trade unions, co-operatives, voluntary welfare organizations and many others. Many of these organizations emerged from older cleavages resulting from the non-congruence of political and cultural boundaries. Others were related to new cleavages generated by the process of capitalist industrialization. As the structure of these cleavages has greatly varied across Europe, so have the intermediary structures.

In the process of *industrialization*, due to differences in its timing and character, economic diversity was increasing across Europe over a long period of time, and the continent became ever more structured into economic centres and peripheries. This was not a completely new diversity, however, but one that developed out of older divisions. There was, first, the *old city belt* stretching from Northern Italy to the Low Countries and across the Channel, a product of the revival and redirection of long-distance trade in medieval times. Industrialization added new towns and urban areas, but did not replace this dorsal spine of economic Europe with something completely new.

There was, second, the later rise of a mercantilist *Atlantic capitalism* which divided Europe roughly into an advanced economic centre in the north-west, a dependent periphery in the east, and a semi-periphery in the mediterranean south. The diffusion of the process of industrialization and the later rise of other regions such as Scandinavia have somewhat changed and also reduced economic diversity, but older divisions still reappear in the territorial structuring of the more advanced industrial as well as 'post-industrial' activities across Europe today.

Dimensions of variation

Putting together the elements mentioned above, one may try to define *European diversity since the nineteenth century*, the period covered by this series of handbooks, in the following way: it is first of all a diversity of societies politically organized as nation-states varying in at least *three crucial dimensions*:

1. the *varying interrelations between political organization and cultural heterogeneity*, as a result of the different political and cultural boundary-building in the processes of state formation and nation-building;

2. the *variations in public institutions and intermediary organizations*, as a result of the transformation of varying cleavage structures and state–society relationships in the processes of democratization and the building of welfare states;

3. the *varying interrelations between the different positions of the national societies in the European world economy* on the one hand, *and the varying structuring of their internal division of labour* on the other.

Twentieth-century divisions

On the eve of World War I, an observer might have gained the impression that the whole of Europe (except Russia and the Ottoman Empire) was on the road to democracy, that industrial capitalism would sooner or later shape the structure of all

European societies, and that the European nations, although in fierce competition throughout the world, were somewhat held together not only by economic exchange, but also by a common belief in scientific and social progress.

History took another turn, as we know today. After the first great civil war of the Europeans in the twentieth century, democracy broke down in most of Central Europe, and it could not develop in the old South nor in the new nation-states of Central-Eastern Europe emerging from the breakdown of the eastern empires. This divided Europe deeply, between a democratic-liberal and a fascist-authoritarian part, building on existing and much older divisions. In addition, Europe was split even more radically by the Russian October Revolution which led not only to a new, totalitarian, political system, but also to a new form of non-capitalist industrial society. And this new political, economic, and social model was exported after the second great civil war, via the Red Army, to Central-Eastern Europe.

This meant that after 1945, the enfeebled Europe, stripped of its leading role in the world, became more divided than ever before in its history, and this for almost half a century until the breakdown of communism in Eastern Europe. Western Europe, however, increasingly identified with Europe itself, proved able to revive the ancient idea of European unity and to base it on common institutions. Ironically, with the liberation of Eastern Europe, a historical event pointing to the future, we seem to witness the *reappearance of the basic and much older structure of Europe in its unity and diversity.*

'Core' and 'peripheries'

The *core of the (Western) European unification movement* still lies in the territories of the old Carolingian empire and the old central city belt. The success of this core, above all in economic terms, and the not unrealistic hope of the other nations to use the increased strength of a more unified Europe for their own purposes explain the momentum European integration has gained. The success of the core was a precondition for the democratization and economic development of Southern Europe, and it may have the same beneficial effects in Eastern Europe, or at least parts of it.

The core territories have become the heart of European integration not because they have been homogeneous; quite the contrary. One might even say that their strength, beyond sheer demographic and economic weight, simply lies in the combination of a diversity typical of Europe, with roots reaching far back into history: to the *limes* and the great migrations which produced Romanic and Germanic territories with their ethnic and cultural differences; to the division of the Carolingian empire which ultimately led to the antithesis of a centralized French nation-state and a federated German empire with a delayed nation-building; and to the Lotharingian middle zone, the origin of the specific development of city states and confederations in Northern Italy and the Low Countries; and to the Reformation which cut across the whole area.

Around the West European 'core' we find territories that one may call 'peripheries', but for very different reasons. There are first of all the *British Isles*, only briefly and partially incorporated into the Roman Empire, never part of the

German-Roman Empire, breaking with Rome and establishing a national church, building its own overseas empire, on the basis of a strong domestic society as the first industrial nation and with a long-standing democratic tradition. This explains the distance to Europe and many of the specifics of English society. With the loss of the empire and a certain move towards 'Europe' this may change but will certainly not disappear.

The *Iberian powers*, Spain above all, shared with Britain the distance-creating experience of overseas empire-building, but their internal development was rather different. Absolutism and social rigidity set barriers to political modernization, social mobility, and economic innovation. This led to a long-lasting decline and to an isolation from 'Europe', overcome only more recently, and with enduring consequences for the social structure and institutions of the Iberian societies.

Scandinavia may be considered a third 'periphery' which also developed in relative isolation from 'Europe' and took an autonomous road. The early end of empire-building efforts and the successful political centralization of the home territories, the establishment of national Protestant churches, early nation-building, and the relatively high degree of freedom and equality traced out the way to mass democracy and welfare states. The Scandinavian countries were able to develop a specific model in which the state and the community of people do not fall apart and in which egalitarianism is writ large.

Moving to the *'peripheries' in eastern and south-eastern Europe*, things become more complicated, because these territories are very heterogeneous in themselves and because there the question of the boundaries of Europe arises. The diversity has been of course one of ethnic-linguistic differences. But two other divisions have probably been even more important: the demarcation line between the Roman Catholic and the Greek Orthodox Church, and the partition of the area among the various multi-ethnic empires.

Europe was Christianized from two centres: from *Rome*, the fountainhead of Western Christendom, pushing to the north into Scandinavia, to the east into Central-Eastern Europe, and also to the south-east; and from *Byzantium*, the centre of Eastern Christianity, moving through the Balkans into Moravia and Bohemia. Where they met, there was conflict. But around the year 1000 the question was settled, the territory partitioned: Poland, the Czech lands, Hungary and Croatia became Roman Catholic and largely remained so; Serbia, Bulgaria, and the Ukrainian and Russian territories became and stayed Orthodox. This line of division was to isolate these Slavic areas from cultural influences coming from the 'West'.

There were early and successful state-building efforts in all these areas, supported by the various 'national' orthodox churches, but also by the Roman Catholic Church in Poland and Hungary. Ultimately, however, they all failed, partly due to the invasions from Central Asia, partly as a consequence of relative economic decline and increasing dependence on the 'West'. Thus, they all became incorporated into *multi-ethnic empires*: into the absolutist Austrian, the autocratic Russian, and the despotic Ottoman empires.

The boundaries of these empires overlaid religious and ethnic boundaries, thus adding to the heterogeneity of the region. The character of these empires and varying lengths of their dominance were decisive in shaping the social structures and institutions of the various societies—and in setting the boundaries of Europe. The Habsburg empire was the leading German power and a stronghold of Catholicism. It was therefore able to draw its non-German and non-Catholic territories and people within the orbit of 'Europe'. The Ottoman empire, on the other hand, was clearly non-European, and the longer its dominance lasted in the Balkans, the less European these territories became. Turkey has special relations with Europe, but does not belong to it.

Russia is a more complicated case. Long isolated from Western developments, it created an autocratic political system and hierarchical society unknown in 'Europe': and moving to the east as well as the west, it developed not only an empire but its own civilization, much as the Americans did, though of course in different form. To speak of a Europe from the Atlantic to the Urals is as meaningful as to define it as the area between Brest-Litovsk and San Francisco. Europe ends where Russia starts, and where Russia dominated over a long period, the boundaries become unclear.

When we started to plan the series of handbooks in the late 1980s, it still seemed natural to limit it to Western Europe. The revolutionary changes after 1989, however, have also changed our *mental map*. We have tried to extend the coverage of the series towards the east, but these attempts ran up against a variety of difficulties of language, data accessibility, availability of literature and more. Thus, our achievements fell short of our ambitions. In some respects, of course, it would not have been meaningful to include Eastern Europe, because institutions and organizations such as free elections and free trade unions simply did not exist. In other respects such as population, labour force and social security, however, we usually have included Poland, the former Czechoslovakia, and Hungary, but other Eastern European countries much less systematically.

Three developments and eight handbooks

The coverage of the series is limited not only in terms of space, but also in terms of time and substance (see Synopsis 1). As to the substance, we have concentrated on various aspects of *three major developments or growth processes* since the nineteenth century: population growth and demographic transition; industrialization and the changing division of labour; democratization and the growth of welfare states. These developmental processes have shaped the social structures and institutions of the European societies for more than a century. For two or more decades, however, they have been approaching an end, and Europe seems to have entered a new historical phase of structural change and institutional adaptation in all three dimensions: family, employment, and social security.

From the mid-nineteenth century up to World War I, Europe was probably the region with the fastest-growing population in the world. But it was also the first to start the 'demographic transition' from high to low birth and death rates, with a first nadir in the 1930s and a second fall since the 1960s. This process was closely linked to changing family structures. (Western) Europe had been characterized for centuries by a specific marriage pattern with a high age at marriage and a high percentage of unmarried adults. This pattern started to change in the late nineteenth century, until

SYNOPSIS 1   Three major processes of development and eight historical data handbooks

Processes of development	Historical handbooks	Period covered	Inclusion of	
			Eastern Europe	Regions
Population growth and demographic transition	I The European Population	1850–1945	limited	limited
	II The European Population	1945–1995	limited	limited
Industrialization and labour force	I The European Labour Force	1870–1940	limited	limited
	II The European Labour Force	1950–2000	limited	extended
	Trade Unions in Western Europe	since 1945	no	no
Democratization and welfare states	I The European Social Security Systems	1885–1945	limited	no
	II The European Social Security Systems	1945–1995	limited	no
	Elections in Europe	since 1815 (1870)	no	extended

marriage and the nuclear family had become almost universal in the 1950s. But then, from the 1960s, there was a radical turn with increasing marriage instability and family variety, and reforms in family law of historic dimensions.

Two volumes of the series are dedicated to *population and family developments*, one for the period from the nineteenth century to the Second World War, and the second for the time after 1945. Data included in the handbooks are limited to those available from the civil or ecclesiastical registers (mainly births, deaths, marriages, divorces) and from the population censuses (mainly population by age, sex, and civil status, later household composition), and for more recent times from microcensuses and other surveys. The time period covered is defined by the earliest availability of data.

Industrialization is the second major development covered by the handbook series. It can be understood in a broader or narrower sense. In the strict sense, industrialization refers to a process of technological progress used to construct new machinery and to open up new sources of energy, leading to an increase in the productivity of work and the volume of production, and ultimately economic growth. In a broader sense, however, industrialization implies a radical transformation of the *social division of labour*: between household and workplace, within the newly established enterprises, and between the newly emerging social classes.

It is this transformation that stands in the middle of the *two volumes* on the *development of the labour force* in Europe, again divided into one volume for the period until the Second World War, and another for the period after. The data presented come from occupation censuses, usually since the late nineteenth century, and in addition from labour force or other surveys, usually since the 1960s. The volumes and supplementary CD-ROMs provide comparative time series, complex cross-tabulations for each census year (such as industry, employment status and sex; sex, age, marital and activity status) and searchable documentation of concepts, definitions and sources.

Until the Russian Revolution, industrialization was identical with the development of *industrial capitalism*. This implied private property, freedom of contract and free choice of work on the one hand, and the development of national labour markets on the other. For a very long period European societies became '*class societies*' in the sense that life chances and living conditions of the mass population were determined by their market position. Class conflict became a predominant political cleavage and gave rise to working-class parties and trade unions everywhere across Europe. The further development was then characterized by varying attempts to 'institutionalize class conflict' through *mass democracy*, the *welfare state*, and *collective bargaining*.

There have been two major revolutions that transformed European society since the nineteenth century: the *Industrial Revolution* and the *National Revolution*. The second meant striving for a congruence between the state and the 'nation' and with it for the ultimate sovereignty of the 'people'. This led to a change in the political map as well as of the political institutions. Political legitimacy began to require some form of mass participation in the political system, a *democratization* of the state.

The institutionalization of *elections* has been crucial in this respect, and the steps in which the suffrage was extended until it became universal have greatly varied across nations, as have the electoral systems translating votes into parliamentary seats. With the successive enfranchisement of ever larger population groups, the cleavages existing between them became transfigured into parties and sooner or later stabilized into party systems and voter alignments differing from one nation to the other. The volume on elections, published already in 2000, traces in detail the development of electoral law in eighteen Western European states and presents the election results (whenever possible) by party for all general elections to the lower houses of parliament since the nineteenth century. What makes this collection unique is not only its wealth and systematic character, but above all the disaggregation of *election results by constituencies* and/or other sub-national units. Thus, for the first time, it has become possible to systematically investigate the territorial structuring of the vote across Europe.

The development of the *nation-state* has had a standardizing effect on the under-lying society, to be sure, and there has been a tendency of territorial cleavages to give way to 'functional' ones cutting across the whole territory. However, this ten-dency as well as the standardization have been far from complete. As mentioned above, the historical overlaying of ethnic-linguistic, religious, economic, and political boundaries has created a varying *internal heterogeneity* which largely persists until today. The volume on elections opens ways for studying the territorial structure of the European nation-states. I wish we could have done more in this direction also in the other volumes (see Synopsis 1), but this will remain a task for the future.

The development of mass democracy, or rather mass politics, was in general a precondition for transforming the state into a welfare state, as was the emergence of capitalist-industrial society. The development of the welfare state, of course, did not replace the market as the fundamental mechanism of distribution, but it added a new mechanism of a political nature. A great variety of public transfer systems and social services has been built across Europe, not only by social democratic and socialist, but also by Catholic, conservative, and liberal forces. And all these institutions heavily influence the distribution of life chances and living conditions of the mass population, not completely but relatively independent of market differentiations.

Among the variety of welfare state transfers and services, *social insurance*, later expanded into *social security*, was perhaps the major social innovation. Starting in most of Europe during the last three decades before the First World War, it was con-tinuously extended throughout the population and across the continent, and has grown in terms of expenditure to between one-fifth and one-third of GDP today. Again, the enormous growth after the war, especially from the 1960s to the 1970s, has not reduced institutional diversity which originated much earlier: the different bases of entitlement from acknowledged need to insurance contributions to social rights, the varying coverage and differentiation of social risks and population groups, the highly diverse levels of individual benefits and total expenditure, and much more. Within the series, two volumes are dedicated to a detailed institutional and quantitative description of the development of the European social security systems since the late nineteenth century. One volume covers the period up to the Second World War, another the time after 1945.

The European Population 1850–1945: The third volume in the series

After the handbooks on elections and on trade unions, both published in 2000, this is the third volume in the series. It covers the development of the European population from the mid-nineteenth century to World War II. This was an extraordinary period in European history, also in demographic terms. There had been earlier waves of population increases in Europe, in the twelfth and thirteenth centuries, and then in the 'long sixteenth century', but the third upswing, which started in the latter half of the eighteenth century, was exceptional. With the spread of the agricultural and the industrial revolution across Europe it accelerated even further in the nineteenth century. In the half-century prior to World War I, the European population grew faster than ever before or afterwards in its history, and at the same time it experienced a wave of overseas emigration of unprecedented dimensions. After the turn of the century, however, population growth began to slow down, and in the 1930s Europe had already completed its—first—demographic transition.

In a European perspective, the population growth rates prior to 1914 were very high, but by modern standards, in a worldwide perspective, they were relatively modest. This means that in a decisive period of its modernization, European society on the whole had to face fewer problems stemming from population pressures than most other societies which began to modernize later. These favourable conditions were the result of a combination of specific characteristics in all elements of population development: mortality, fertility, and migration.

In the course of industrialization, improvements in food, shelter, clothing and water supply as well as in sanitation gradually brought down death rates, but infant mortality and the ravages of infectious diseases long remained powerful forces in Europe. There probably was a gradual decline of mortality throughout the nineteenth century, but greater advances became visible only after 1870, accelerating around 1900 when modern medical science started to have a more direct and systematic impact on infant mortality and infectious diseases.

While the comparatively slow decline of mortality was a first characteristic of the European vital revolution, the relatively low level of fertility was a second one. In general, birth rates started to decrease later than death rates, but even before they began to decline, the level of fertility was significantly lower in Europe than elsewhere in the world. This was the result of a specific 'European marriage pattern' which combined a high age at marriage with lifelong celibacy of sizeable shares of the population. Given the social control of sexuality outside of marriage, this pattern reduced the average level of fertility. It was closely associated with a tradition of neo-local household formation, and it was used by the Europeans as a mechanism of self-regulation in times of crisis. Although from the late nineteenth century until the 1950s the age at marriage slowly declined and the extent of lifelong celibacy was gradually reduced, the impact of the 'European marriage pattern' remained important throughout the period covered here.

In a worldwide perspective, the slower decline of mortality and the lower average levels of fertility were the main reasons why the European population, even during its period of fastest growth, grew less than the population of most other regions would do later. To this slower increase a third factor contributed, too: overseas emigration. From the mid-nineteenth century to World War I overseas emigration moved in waves of ever increasing heights reaching its climax in the early nineteen-hundreds. Until the 1930s, around fifty million people had moved out of Europe to the Western hemisphere and Australasia.

All these migration movements as well as the changes in mortality and fertility, however, were not distributed evenly across Europe. Instead, and not surprisingly, they were closely linked to the enormous differences in the timing of the industrial take-off and to the variations in the paths of modernization. In most advanced countries of north and west Europe there were important declines in mortality since the second half of the eighteenth century already. Then, from 1870, a trend toward marked declines was set in motion simultaneously not only in the north-west, but also in central Europe, and soon also in Italy and some parts of the east, reaching the south-western and south-eastern ends of Europe only twenty years later. The decline of fertility, which usually started later, followed similar lines of territorial differentiation, spreading from north to south and from west to east, but it took more time to spread across Europe. Except for the very early beginnings in France, fertility started to decline in north-west as well as central Europe almost simultaneously around 1875–80. In contrast to mortality, however, the decline of fertility diffused only later to eastern and southern Europe, and at the south-western and south-eastern ends of Europe it only arrived around 1920.

The variations in the timing and volume of overseas emigration also present a similar picture. Almost all countries participated in the movement across the oceans. Only France was never a country of mass emigration, probably due to its much slower population growth. The United Kingdom was the first and largest of all emigration countries, supplying one third of all overseas emigration from Europe. Germany followed, and then Scandinavia. Up to the middle of the nineteenth century, mass emigration took place almost entirely in north-west Europe. In the 1860s mass emigration started in Italy, which then became the second largest emigration country in Europe after the British Isles. In Spain and Portugal emigration increased as late as the 1880s, and most of the eastern and south-eastern Europe followed even later. Thus, the development of migration prior to World War I was clearly linked both geographically and chronologically to stages of the vital revolution.

The First World War with its military losses, excess civilian deaths and birth deficits distorted the age structure of the European population and reduced its growth, but it did not fundamentally alter the long-term vital trends. Compared to the prewar situation, mortality further declined, but more slowly, and fertility also declined further, but more rapidly, after a brief postwar upswing. However, given the fact that the European population was still rather young, it continued to grow, producing an excess of births over deaths, while in terms of net reproduction rates a sizeable section of Europe was not replacing itself any more at the middle of the interwar period. In this sense, Europe had completed its demographic transition in the 1930s. With respect to migration the impact of the First World War was more significant. The interwar period witnessed the virtual disappearance of mass emigration from Europe. This was not only the result of restrictive legislation, especially in the United States, but also of changing opportunities in the overseas countries and the progress of industrialization and social policies in Europe.

An analysis of migration flows would require the collection of scattered and often unreliable empirical information. It therefore has not been included in the volume by Franz Rothenbacher which is limited to census and vital statistics. Within these limits it provides a very valuable instrument for the study of the long-term development of the European population. Or rather for the comparative analysis of 'national populations' within Europe, because in using this collection one should be aware that the distribution of the population across the European space has almost no relation to political boundaries and that the internal heterogeneity of the political territories with respect to levels of modernization and associated demographic phenomena is usually great.

Mannheim, October 2001

Preface and Acknowledgements

This handbook on *The European Population, 1850–1945* is the third in the series *Societies of Europe—European Society* which is planned to embrace at least eight volumes. More than any of the other volumes in the series, the present data handbook is built on older collections and includes work done by others. At the same time, it goes well beyond these earlier efforts by improving, extending and enriching the data base and by adding longer texts.

A major stock of the data in the book and on the CD-ROM goes back to a project called *HIWED* (*H*istorical *I*ndicators of *W*estern *E*uropean *D*emocracies) which I initiated in the 1970s with the intellectual support of Wolfgang Zapf and the financial support of the Volkswagen Foundation. Longstanding collaborators in this project were Jens Alber, Franz Kraus, Winfried Pfenning, and Kurt Seebohm. Apart from a number of comparative studies, there are two main products of the project:

- the publication of two statistical handbooks, in 1983 and 1987, under the general title *State, Economy, and Society in Western Europe 1815–1975* (Frankfurt: Campus; London: Macmillan; Chicago: St. James);
- the creation of the data archive *WEDA* (*W*est *E*uropean *D*ata *A*rchive).

When I began to set up the *Mannheim Centre for European Social Research* in 1989, the archive was incorporated into the new research institute. It was renamed *EURODATA Research Archive* and Franz Kraus, collaborator from the very beginning, was made managing director of the much enlarged archive. Soon, in 1990, we could recruit Franz Rothenbacher, a sociologist with great experience in working with historical statistics, for the archive. He became responsible for the statistics library, for reviewing the efforts in European Social Reporting,—and for demographic statistics. When we developed the idea of starting a new series of handbooks, it was therefore natural that Franz Rothenbacher was charged with the two volumes on the European population.

A first task was to consolidate the collection of demographic data and indicators which was published in 1987 in the second volume of *State, Economy, and Society in Western Europe 1815–1975* with the subtitle *The Growth of Industrial Societies and Capitalist Economies*. The collection, which was also made machine-readable, presented for altogether 13 Western European countries (Austria, Belgium, Denmark, Finland, France, Germany, Ireland, Italy, The Netherlands, Norway, Sweden, Switzerland, United Kingdom) the same data on population structure and population movements as well as the same demographic indicators which are now given in this book and on the CD-ROM.

However, Franz Rothenbacher has extended the coverage by more than one third. The handbook now also includes the three Southern European countries Greece, Portugal, and Spain, the three Central European countries Czechoslovakia, Hungary, and Poland, and the two smaller Western European countries Iceland and Luxemburg which were missing in the older collection.

Given the number of countries and the time span covered, the indicators used in the older collection as well as in this handbook are mainly simple rates (such as crude birth and death rates, marriage and divorce rates, population growth and net migration rates). In addition, however, we developed a few more refined indicators which were calculated for the first time. For example, we set the number of legitimate and illegitimate births into relation to the group of married or non-married women at the age of 15–44.

In order to calculate such indicators, a major effort had to be made to extract from the population censuses the cross-tabulations of age, sex, and civil status, and to estimate the respective figures for the inter-census periods. It was Winfried Pfenning who did this for more than 200 censuses, establishing a machine-readable data set as early as 1980.

However, to offer the possibility to calculate different population groups for other purposes, during the 1990s a new data set of cross-classifications for all ages was established which can be found on the CD-ROM. This work was initiated and organized by Franz Rothenbacher; Benno Burkhart, one of my student assistants, standardized and integrated the different data sets into machine-readable data files. This new data set includes cross-tabulations of age, sex, and civil status in one-year age groups for all 21 countries from 1850 until the population censuses around 1990. This data base was used for calculating the age-standardized indicators for the countries added (Czechoslovakia, Greece, Hungary, Iceland, Luxemburg, Poland, Portugal, and Spain) as well as for updating the time series from 1970 until 1990 for the countries of the previous data set of 13 countries. Furthermore, it was used to present for the first time the data on the population structure by age, sex, and civil status in a graphical form.

In addition to the national aggregate data on the population structure and population movements, the handbook also contains data on the distribution of the census population by region and the population density by region. These data were collected by Michael Quick in the context of a different project. In the early 1990s, Franz Kraus, Michael Quick and myself started to work on a regional social atlas of Europe. The project was limited to a coverage of the 1980s, but it was our intention to go back to the nineteenth century and to produce a historical atlas on a regional basis. For this plan we produced a book on the territorial structuring of Europe since the late nineteenth century which will be published in 2002. It contains, among other things, a complete list of all regions and the changes in names and boundaries, territory, population, and population density.

Franz Rothenbacher has not only extended the coverage of the older demographic data base from 13 to 21 countries, but has also moved into a new field by collecting data on households and families. This is a true innovation, because such data have never been collected before in a systematic way from national population censuses. In doing this, he could profit from his own contributions to the development of the statistical library of EURODATA. The research archive had inherited from our earlier endeavours a larger stock of micro-fiches and micro-films of historical statistical yearbooks and population censuses, which was continuously extended and supplemented by fotocopies of sources not available in such micro-forms. This way we have established a collection of historical statistics which is probably unique in Europe.

Although Franz Rothenbacher's handbook builds on earlier collections and work done by others, he has achieved a completely new quality which goes far beyond the extensions in coverage and in substance. This is due to the accompanying CD-ROM on the one hand and to his texts on the other hand. The CD-ROM does not only facilitate the use of the data set for comparative statistical analysis, it has also made possible a greatly improved documentation. And while older data collections (including our own) usually present numbers without much interpretation, Franz Rothenbacher has written interpretative country introductions. Furthermore, in a comparative introduction, he gives an overview of main characteristics of population structures and developments, based on the data collection, trying to 'make the numbers speak'.

Unlike history, the social sciences do not have a tradition of editing important sources in a systematic way. For the empirical social sciences, the collection of historical data handbooks can therefore be understood as a general infrastructural task. Franz Rothenbacher's volume is a major contribution to this task.

Mannheim, October 2001 Peter Flora

Many people have been involved in the production of this volume. A large number of student research assistants were occupied with data collection and input. Over several years, the following students worked on the data collection, mainly the age/sex/marital status database: Min Yan, Steffen Walter, Bärbel Pföhler, and Karin Reichert. Benno Burkhart documented and integrated this database. Christian Schäfer worked on the documentation of the population censuses. Christian Berger was occupied with the documentation and the age trees. I am especially grateful to Tatjana Bratina who formatted most of the appendix tables and produced most of the age tree figures. Birgit Becker programmed the CD-ROM. Despite this tremendous help, the responsibility for all remaining errors is assumed by the author alone.

Many officials and librarians from national statistical offices have provided me with statistical data that I could not have obtained any other way, especially those from Statistics Sweden, Statistics Netherlands, and Statistics Belgium. I would also like to express my thanks to the staff of the University of Mannheim Library, who managed my many interlibrary loans of European population censuses that were not available from the census population collection on microfilm. My special thanks also go to Marianne Schneider and the whole staff of the EURODATA Research Archive, who have helped me over the years in acquiring the official statistical data I needed for this data handbook.

Mannheim, October 2001 Franz Rothenbacher

List of Symbols

–	Not applicable
..	Data not available (missing)
%	Percent
‰	Per thousand
$^{o}/_{ooo}$	Per ten thousand
~	Circa
N	Absolute figure
Ø	Arithmetic average
+	Addition
–	Subtraction
*	Multiplication
/	Division
ǀ	Territorial change

Table of Contents

List of Tables

List of Figures

Abbreviations and Acronyms

Bd.	Band, volume
BFS	Bundesamt für Statistik, Neuchâtel
BGB	Bürgerliches Gesetzbuch
CBR	Crude birth rate
CBS	Centraal Bureau voor de Statistiek, Voorburg and Heerlen
CDR	Crude divorce rate
cf.	confer, compare
CSO	Central Statistical Office, London
CSO	Central Statistical Office of Finland, Helsinki
CSO	Central Statistics Office, Dublin and Cork
ed.	Edition, editor, edited
eds.	Editors
e.g.	exempli gratia, for example
EKKE	National Centre for Social Research, Athens
esp.	especially
EU	European Union, Brussels/Luxembourg/Strasbourg
EUROSTAT	Statistical Office of the European Union, Luxemburg
EU12	European Union (of the 12)
EU15	European Union (of the 15)
f.	following page
ff.	following pages
FRG	Federal Republic of Germany
GDP	Gross Domestic Product
GDR	German Democratic Republic
GUS	Główny Urząd Statystycny
HCSO	Hungarian Central Statistical Office, Budapest
HIWED	Historical Indicators of West European Democracies
HMSO	Her Majesty's Stationary Office, London
hrsg.	herausgegeben, edited
i.e.	id est, that means
IISG	International Institute for Social History, Amsterdam
INE	Instituto Nacional de Estadística, Madrid
INE	Instituto Nacional de Estatística, Lisbon
INS	Institut National de Statistique, Brussels
INSEE	Institut National de la Statistique et des Études Économiques, Paris
ISTAT	Istituto Nazionale di Statistica, Rome
K. K.	Kaiserlich Königlich
MZES	Mannheim Centre for European Social Research, Mannheim
NIWI	Netherlands Institute for Scientific Information Services, Amsterdam

no., nos.	number(s)
NOS	Norges Offisielle Statistikk (Norway's Official Statistics)
n.s.	new series
NSSG	National Statistical Service of Greece, Athens
ÖSTAT	Österreichisches Statistisches Zentralamt, Wien
p., pp.	page(s)
resp.	respectively
rev.	revised
s.a.	sine anno
SCB	Statistiska Centralbyrån, now Statistics Sweden, Stockholm and Örebro
ser.	series
SOS	Sveriges Officiella Statistik
SØS	Sosiale og økonomiske Studier
sq. km.	square kilometre
SSB	Statistisk Sentralbyrå, Oslo
STATEC	Service Central de la Statistique et des Études Économiques, Luxemburg
Tav.	Tavola
TPFR	Total Period Fertility Rate
UK	United Kingdom of Great Britain and (Northern) Ireland
UN/ECE	United Nations Economic Commission for Europe, Geneva
US	United States of America
vol.	volume
vs.	versus

Part I
Introduction

1

General Introduction

This handbook on *The European Population, 1850–1945*, (as well as the future second volume covering the period since 1945) was planned as an extension of Chapter VI on Population and Families in the second volume of the earlier handbook *State, Economy, and Society in Western Europe, 1815–1975*, published by Peter Flora, Franz Kraus, and Winfried Pfenning in 1987. At the same time, however, it also became closely linked to the international research project 'Family Change and Family Policies in the West'. This project, financed by the German Science Foundation, was initiated by Peter Flora at the Mannheim Centre for European Social Research (MZES) in the early 1990s and has since been directed by him in cooperation with Alfred Kahn and Sheila Kamerman from the Columbia University. The project covered the main Western and Central European countries: Austria, Belgium, Czechoslovakia, Denmark, Finland, France, Germany, Greece, Hungary, Italy, The Netherlands, Norway, Poland, Portugal, Spain, Sweden, Switzerland, and the United Kingdom. The project also included some non-European countries: Canada, New Zealand, and the United States of America. Iceland, Ireland, and Luxemburg were not included from the beginning, nor were eastern and south-eastern European countries. The project will produce five volumes with standardized case studies for all project countries and two additional comparative volumes: one volume on family change and one on family policies. While the project focused mainly on family policy and used demographic, household, family, and employment structures as a baseline and framework for the national family policy profiles, it soon became clear that in the realm of demography and household and family statistics it could not fulfil the project requirements. The project had a very broad time horizon, reaching back to the nineteenth century. The available project data did not suffice for such an ambitious endeavour: they were mostly national data without long time series. Therefore we decided to set up our own demographic database.

The work originated with a dataset compiled by the HIWED project. This dataset extended up to 1975 and included thirteen industrialized Western European countries: Austria, Belgium, Denmark, Finland, France, Germany, Ireland, Italy, The Netherlands, Norway, Sweden, Switzerland, and the United Kingdom. This dataset was first checked for errors and then updated from 1970/1. As demographic data are increasingly inaccurate the greater the length of time from the last census is, the annual vital statistics data were corrected after the censuses of 1980/1, and these corrected data were used for the period after 1970/1. The annual time series were updated up to the early 1990s. (The same problem occurs with the vital statistics data from the 1990s which will only be corrected after the censuses of 2000/1). Completely new time series have been collected for Czechoslovakia, Greece,

Hungary, Iceland, Luxemburg, Poland, Portugal, and Spain. A new dataset has been compiled for population structure, containing for each census a table combining age in one-year age groups with sex and the marital status, and we have also collected new data on household and family statistics. This field of historical European statistics had been completely untouched thus far: there are national collections as stand-alone products (for Germany see Rothenbacher, 1997a), but household and family statistics are usually only rudimentary additions to general historical-statistical works. For the first time, the main available data have been compiled at the national level for the 21 countries included in this data handbook.

Given the very time-consuming task of compiling annual statistics for 21 countries over 100 years (the number of censuses used for data collection is approximately 200), regionalizing this huge amount of variables, time series, and combinatory tables would have been impossible for only one or a few persons. This is a clear lesson learned from the Princeton Fertility Project, which took more than a decade and a large staff to collect, process, and analyse data at the regional level for the subject of fertility alone.

However, the data presented here (and on the CD-ROM) make it possible to not only compare individual countries, but also to group countries into clusters and to compare them with individual countries or other country clusters. For example, it is possible to create rates for Western Europe, for Central Europe, or for Continental Europe alone. Calculating European rates allows for very instructive comparisons of national rates with the European (weighted) averages. In principle, variation coefficients can be calculated, and convergences and divergences can therefore be analysed.

THIS AND PREVIOUS HANDBOOKS

This historical demographic data handbook is not the only one for the territory of Europe, though it is surely the most specialized. Most historical data compilations use demographic data not in their own right, but as a framework for other subjects such as economic and production statistics, political, election, and social policy statistics; or historical demographic data are included in comprehensive 'Historical Statistics of ...' publications. Examples of the first type are the data handbooks by Mitchell (1980/1981, 1992); examples of the second are most national historical statistics, such as *Historical Statistics of the United States* (U.S. Department of Commerce/Bureau of the Census, 1975) and others.

There is a large amount of historical population statistics at the national level, but these are usually included in more comprehensive handbooks (see Rothenbacher, 1998a for a fairly complete list of national historical data handbooks; see also Etemad, 1990). Specialized historical-demographic data handbooks published after 1945 exist for Ireland (Vaughan and Fitzpatrick, 1978), and Germany (Kraus, 1980 for the nineteenth century; Rothenbacher, 1997a). Several compilations with demographic time series in different countries were published before World War II. The disadvantage of these national collections is that they are not internationally co-ordinated, and therefore they follow idiosyncratic views and purposes. Nevertheless, in a highly standardized field like vital statistics, data from national sources are more comparable than in other fields.

Looking at international historical data handbooks, there are some specialized handbooks and several handbooks that are comprehensive in the sense that they include population statistics, among others. One specialized handbook is Keyfitz's and Flieger's *World Population Growth and Aging: Demographic Trends in the Late Twentieth Century* (Chicago and London, 1990). This volume is the sequel to *World Population: An Analysis of Vital Data* by the same authors (University of Chicago Press, 1968). The more recent handbook covers almost the entire world, contains regional summaries and standardized country profiles, but concentrates exclusively on population structure (age, sex), population growth, mortality, and life expectancy. It does not cover nuptiality and marital breakdown, or il/legitimacy and households and families. The time series are not presented annually. The emphasis of this handbook is more on analysis and projection than on historical documentation.

The data handbook *International Mortality Statistics* (Alderson, 1981) presents mortality data by sex and cause of death from 1901 to 1975. The data are presented for 31 countries of the world and for nearly all Western European countries in quinquennial aggregates (missing are Luxembourg and Germany). The main indicator presented is the standard mortality ratio (derived with a factor of 10,000). This indicator is presented for all 31 countries from 1901–1975 and for a large number of causes of death (more than 150; altogether there are 180 tables, including those summarizing by categories of causes of death). Furthermore, population figures (in 1,000s) are presented for each of the 31 countries in five-year age groups and for the quinquennia from 1901 to 1975. The volume contains extensive documentation of data sources, registration systems, effects of wars and migration on death rates, and methodological discussions of validity.

Population data for European cities from 800–1850 has been collected by Bairoch, Batou, and Chèvre (1988) with the purpose of studying urbanization since the Middle Ages. The study emphasizes the territorial pattern of urbanization in Europe.

There are also comprehensive data handbooks containing sections on demography and population statistics. One early international handbook is Sundbärg's *Aperçus Statistiques Internationaux* (first edition 1908), comprising 150 pages of international and historical population statistics for the nineteenth century.

Mitchell's (1980/81, 1992) three volumes on Europe, the Americas, and Asia and Australasia is a standard work in historical statistics. All three volumes have the same structure: they contain a section on population and demography, presenting the population structure by age and sex, for census points. Furthermore, annual vital statistics rates—crude birth, death, and marriage rate—are included. While population figures are given in absolute terms, for the vital statistics there are no absolute and basic figures.

Another standard source for historical statistics is the volume by Flora, Kraus, and Pfenning (1987), which includes data on population structure and vital statistics from 1815–1975 for the Western and Northern European countries. Southern (except Italy) and Eastern European countries are not included, in contrast to Mitchell's volume on Europe which covers all European countries from 1750–1988 (in the second edition). The population section of the data handbook by Flora, Kraus, and Pfenning is however much more detailed and contains several additional demographic indicators. Neither Mitchell (1992) nor Flora, Kraus, and Pfenning have collected household and family statistics data.

A third standard source in international historical statistics concentrates wholly on Eastern Europe (Shoup, 1981). The time frame is from 1945 to 1975 although data are as well presented for the time before World War II. All the socialist countries of south-eastern and Eastern Europe are included: Albania, Bulgaria, Czechoslovakia, the former German Democratic Republic (GDR), Hungary, Poland, Romania, the former USSR, and Yugoslavia. The demographic chapter contains data on the census population by sex since the 1920s as well as vital statistics and mid-year population from 1950–1975. A third section presents population census data since the 1950s by age groups and sex. Furthermore, urban and rural birth rates are calculated for 1946–1975. Finally, age-specific and total fertility rates and population projections have been included. The handbook has not been updated. The enormous political changes since 1990 would require a different concept.

Other works with minor sections on demography include the handbook by Liesner (1985), *Economic Statistics 1900–1983* for the United Kingdom, the United States of America, France, Germany, Italy, and Japan. For each country there is one table with basic demographics: mid-year population, age distribution in four categories, and the geographical distribution of the population. Other comparative and international handbooks containing population data are the *Comparative World Data* handbook by Müller (1988) and the *World Handbook of Political and Social Indicators* by Taylor and Jodice (1983). *The Economist Book of Vital World Statistics* (Leyland, 1990) also belongs to this group; it is a comprehensive data handbook comprising all main social and economic features. Demographic and population data for all countries of the world are presented on pages 11–28. This book is not a historical international data handbook in the narrow sense, but is reminiscent of the World Bank's *World Development Report* (The World Bank, 1978).

International sources for the post-World War II period include publications from international and supranational organizations, most of which were founded after 1945, but some, like the United Nations and the World Health Organization, with forerunners that collected statistics already in the inter-war period.

The Council of Europe (1978–) publication, *Recent Demographic Developments in Council of Europe Member Countries*, is one of the main sources for international demographic and population statistics. The time frame is from the 1960s to the present, but to some degree statistics prior to 1945 are published. This is especially the case in several titles of the Council of Europe Population Studies Series, in which the statistical appendices document long historical time series on population, fertility, household structures, and others.

The statistical office of the European Union, EUROSTAT, first published in 1977 *Demographic Statistics* for the years 1960–1976 (EUROSTAT, 1977–). This is a very useful publication covering nearly all demographic subject matters. In the early years data were presented for member countries only, but more recently all European countries have been covered. In recent publications only some of the database contents are printed; the complete data are only available from the demographic database of EUROSTAT, or from the *New Cronos* database on CD-ROM.

The United Nations, like its predecessor, the League of Nations, began collecting population statistics immediately after its foundation. The specialized *Demographic Yearbook* was first published in 1949, with reference to 1948 (United Nations,

1949–). The first yearbooks also presented time-series data reaching back before 1945 to the inter-war period. Time series from around 1950 to the early 1970s are collected in the historical supplement to the *Demographic Yearbook 1978* (United Nations, 1979).

This data handbook presents the population, demographic, and household data, collected in a standardized and systematic way for the 21 countries of Western and Central Europe whenever possible from 1850 to 1945. Several general guidelines have shaped the work from the beginning:

1. *Territorially aggregated data*: results have been collected at the level of the nation-states only, and regional data have only been collected for population size and population density.
2. *Complete census coverage*: all the population censuses in the time period have been covered, amounting to nearly 200 individual censuses in the 21 countries.
3. *Disaggregated data collection*: while there was no regional disaggregation, in other respects the data have been collected with as much detail as possible on a disaggregated level. Thus, vital statistics have been collected on an annual basis and have not been aggregated into time periods (quinquennia or decennia). Furthermore, the data on age, sex, and marital status was collected in the most disaggregated way possible. Whenever available, one-year age groups have been chosen, and all the different types and combinations of the marital status were included (there are more detailed types of marital status in some countries than the usual four types, single, married, widowed, and divorced).
4. *Historical perspective*: for all countries the collection starts in the nineteenth century, for some already in the eighteenth. The series are documented from 1850 in this data handbook. Nevertheless, in some cases the data collection reaches much further back into history.
5. *Computerization*: all data in the different data sets have been made completely machine-readable in a standardized way, though the degree of standardization varies: it is highest with respect to vital statistics, lower concerning the age, sex, and civil status structure, and lowest concerning households and families.

COUNTRY CHAPTERS

The 21 country chapters that follow have a standard format. Each chapter consists of eleven text sections and an appendix with tables and figures. The eleven sections are (1) State Formation and Territory; (2) Regional Population Structure; (3) Population Growth; (4) The First Demographic Transition; (5) Mortality and Life Expectancy; (6) Fertility and Legitimacy; (7) Marriage and Divorce; (8) Age, Sex, and Civil Status; (9) Family and Household Structures; (10) The National System of Demographic Statistics; and (11) Boundary Changes. Section 10 is furthermore divided into three subsections, presenting information on the development of official statistics in the fields of a) population structure, b) vital statistics, and c) households and families. Each chapter concludes with a standardized appendix containing tables and figures.

We will now outline the different sections of the country chapters. A short introductory section on *state formation and territory* (1) presents essential background information necessary for understanding, using, and interpreting the statistical information presented thereafter. This section describes the political history of each country in terms of state evolution, date of independence, major changes in political regimes, and essential boundary changes through secession, mergers, or territorial losses. Not only politics, but also the long-term economic development, the economic position of the country in European comparison (the 'wealth of the nation'), and important features of the economic structure are described. In addition, major features of the social structure are highlighted which may have important and explanatory influences on population and demographic developments.

The section on *regional population structure* (2) deals with the internal population distribution of a country. Two indicators are used to describe the regional population structure: the proportion of each region's population in per cent of total population, and the population density (in inhabitants per square kilometre) of each region. The hundred years from 1850 to 1950 reveal major shifts in population distribution which are known as *urbanization* and rural exodus. These data show the main settlement structures of a country and the extent to which this structure changed during modernization.

The section on *population growth* (3) deals with the long-term growth processes during the first demographic transition. The main result of the demographic transition in all European countries was enormous growth in the European population and the population of the individual nation-states. Nevertheless, this development was very different according to the conditions in each country. Not only the long-term growth processes and macro-settings are discussed, but also the impact of wars, economic crises, and epidemics on growth rates. This section also describes major developments in net migration.

The fourth section describes *the first demographic transition* (4) of each country. The 'theory' of the demographic transition is in principle a model describing the development of societies from a state of high population turnover to a state of low population turnover. The model furthermore states that the death rate declined first and the birth rate reacted later also with a decline. The development of individual countries shows that this was not always true, and that in several countries the birth rate declined before the death rate. Nevertheless, the model is an important heuristic device for understanding this long-term process. The section describes the main features of the national process of demographic transition, each country's pre-transition level, start and speed of transition. Explanations or interpretations of the individual characteristics of the demographic transition are given wherever possible.

The section on *mortality and life expectancy* (5) presents and discusses the data on the infant mortality rate. This section is closely related to the section on the first demographic transition because the infant mortality rate strongly influenced the crude mortality rate. Therefore, in a country where the infant mortality rate was high, the crude mortality rate was high as well. The national figures are described with reference to other European countries. The singularities of the national developments are presented and possible explanations are given. A second aspect of mortality is life expectancy which provides a much broader picture of mortality. Men and women are included and mortality is calculated also for higher age groups.

The section on *fertility and legitimacy* (6) presents the data on legitimate and illegitimate fertility and on the proportion of illegitimate births to all births (the illegitimacy rate). The disaggregation of births by legitimacy and the calculation of age-standardized birth ratios by legitimacy reveals interesting and important aspects of family organization (the importance of cohabitation), illegitimacy, and attitudes towards the legal status of children. The causes of illegitimate fertility have been manifold and differ from country to country.

The section on *marriage and divorce* (7) deals with the marriage patterns in a country. Indicators used to describe nuptiality and marriage behaviour are the mean age at marriage, the proportion married at age 20–24, the marriage ratio, and the celibacy rate. The typical configuration of a country concerning these indicators is presented and the country's position with reference to such typologies as the 'European Marriage Pattern' is discussed. This section also deals with the long-term growth of marital instability due to divorce and legal separation.

The section on *age, sex, and civil status* (8) discusses the development of the population in a more disaggregated form, looking at the development of the age structure and population changes in the marital status, all according to sex. Major developments are population ageing, which in most countries was already visible in 1900, the increase of the proportion married until the mid-1930s, the lowering of the age at marriage, and the decline in celibacy.

In the section on *family and household structures* (9) the presentation is solely based on the available official household and family statistics collected by the statistical offices. Historical studies using primary sources such as original population census sheets or early population registers are not reviewed here; nevertheless, important relevant results have been included for explanatory purposes.

The section on *the national system of demographic statistics* (10) is documentary in character. It describes the available statistics concerning the introduction of investigation, the history of data collection, and the definition of statistical concepts for the three fields of *population structure*, *vital statistics*, and *households and families*. Especially important is the documentation of the definitions of statistical concepts, because only knowledge about the way data are collected and processed allows for a meaningful interpretation of the empirical facts. Documentation of the definition of statistical concepts is more important for household and family statistics, which were not standardized until after 1945.

The final section on *boundary changes* (11) provides information on the most important boundary changes necessary for understanding and interpreting the different population sizes and the demographic time series.

After the textual presentation there is a large section with *appendix tables and figures*, comprising six standard tables with statistical data, one documentary table, and several figures. All tables and figures included in this appendix have been standardized as far as possible. *Appendix Table 1* documents the census dates and presents for each population census the most basic statistical information: the population by sex, civil status, and three age groups (0–14, 15–64, and 65+) in absolute and relative terms. *Appendix Table 2* includes the regional population distribution for the different population censuses in relative terms. The proportion of each region in per cent of the total population has been calculated. *Appendix Table 3* presents a different kind of regional data: it gives the population density measured by the number of inhabitants per square kilometre for each region and population census. *Appendix Table 4* comprises demographic time series, if available, for the period 1850–1945. The time series are structured in the same way for all countries. They contain information on mid-year population, two different population growth rates, migration, several fertility indicators, legitimacy, and various mortality, nuptiality, and divorce measures. *Appendix Table 5* presents the development of life expectancy at various ages for both sexes. The *Appendix Tables 6A–6E* on households and families are less highly standardized due to the varying national statistics. But, wherever possible, the table provides information on the main household types such as one-person, family, and institutional households (absolute and per cent) together with the respective population living in these households (*Appendix Table 6A*). A second table presents the distribution of households by size in absolute terms (*Appendix Table 6B*) and a third table in per cent distribution (*Appendix Table 6C*). A fourth table gives average household sizes for different household types (*Appendix Table 6D*). A fifth table—if available—presents information on household composition (*Appendix Table 6E*). These five tables are included—if possible—as standard and are supplemented by additional tables if other interesting statistics are available. Such additional data may include disaggregation of households by socio-economic status of the household head or regional information. *Appendix Table 7* documents the availability of the individual vital statistics and population census variables. *Appendix Figure 8* includes several standardized figures on *population by age, sex, and marital status*. These figures are based on the population censuses. The number of figures varies between countries according to the availability of population census results.

All sources and references have been combined in one *Bibliography* at the end of the volume. This bibliography has two main sections: *sources* and *references*. Sources are all statistical titles that have actually been used for this data handbook, while references are all the literature cited in the texts. The references have been arranged in alphabetical order. The sources have been subdivided for each of the 21 countries. For each country the sources have been further divided into three sections: (1) sources on *vital statistics*, (2) sources on *population structure by age, sex, and marital status*, and (3) sources on *population census results on households and families*.

2

Population and Territory

There have been so many boundary changes over the nearly one hundred years dealt with in this volume that only the main shifts in boundaries in Western and Central Europe will be highlighted here. Different types of boundary changes must be distinguished: *first*, changes in what has been defined as Europe; and *second*, changing boundaries of the individual European nation-states. A *third* and *fourth* dimension could be added: the formation of nation-states through processes of unification, and boundary changes through the breakup of large empires.

The *first* type of boundary changes concerns Europe as a unit in the definition of this data handbook. The countries covered in this data handbook represent the European averages we have calculated. Because boundaries of the European national states have changed, the boundaries of this Europe, defined by the sum of national states, have also changed over time. Only the most important changes can be discussed here. While Europe has natural boundaries in the west, north, and south, its eastern boundary is not clear and open to different perspectives. For the purposes of this handbook and the calculation of European averages, we have decided to include countries according to their historical extension. Therefore, the boundaries of Europe differ by time period: the most dramatic changes occurred before and after World War I with the dissolution of the Austro-Hungarian Empire. Before 1919 Austria-Hungary was included in the average. Czechoslovakia, Hungary, Poland, and the Austrian Republic have been included since 1919. Poland before 1919 has not been included in the European average because of difficulties with differing territorial delimitations (see the documentation on the boundaries for the demographic time series in each of the country chapters below).

Let us now come to the *second* type of boundary changes, those of established national states. These boundary changes are very numerous. There are large mergers and secessions as well as very many small boundary changes with which only historians of the relevant country are familiar. In any case, the nation-state has been taken as a unit, and the data typically refer to the actual territory. Only in some cases have data have been presented for different territories, such as Italy before and after the accession of South Tyrol.

The *third* type of boundary changes concerns the creation of nation-states through unification movements. Two of the countries in this handbook were created from the union of a large number of independent states during the second half of the nineteenth century: Italy in 1861 from more than a dozen states on the Italian peninsula, and Germany in 1871 from more than twenty states. Such unifying processes usually mean an interruption in nearly all statistics. Only for some statistics are calculations made retrospectively for the new territory. Therefore, time series for the Italian nation-state date only from the late 1860s, and for the German Empire from the 1870s. Of course statistics in the individual Italian and German states before unification do exist, but differ in comparability and coherence. Efforts to collect such statistics for historical statistics and to aggregate them in order to extend back into history statistical series for the united country have only been made for important indicators such as total population, births, and deaths.

The United Kingdom was also created from more or less autonomous feudal states (kingdoms). The United Kingdom of Great Britain and Ireland was formed in 1801 by uniting Ireland, Scotland, England, and Wales under the British crown. There were fewer problems with statistical integration due to the smaller number of territorial units—compared with Italy and Germany—but the country was less centralized politically and institutionally, which also led to a less centralized statistical system.

Finally, the *fourth* type of boundary changes are those resulting from the breakup of larger empires and the emergence of newly-independent countries. Although not covered by this handbook in a strict sense, the first half of the nineteenth century saw several empires break up: after 1800, the larger empires of Denmark and Sweden broke up when Denmark was punished for its counter-alliance against Napoleon with the loss of Norway to Sweden, while Sweden lost Finland to Russia. The start of the decline of the Ottoman Empire was marked by the independence of Greece in 1830. Belgium won its independence from the United Netherlands with the support of England on the occasion of the French July Revolution of 1830.

The next wave of breakups came with World War I, when the Austro-Hungarian and the German Empire collapsed. While the former was completely split up into new national states, the latter essentially survived, although with major territorial losses. In the aftermath of World War I the Eastern European states of Poland, Czechoslovakia, and Hungary were created. The southern provinces of Ireland also succeeded in gaining independence from the weakened British Empire in 1921.

WESTERN AND EASTERN EUROPE

This data handbook refers mainly to Western Europe. 'Western Europe' is not used here as a geographic term; after the end of World War II the term became highly politicized due to the division of the European continent into two politically and economically opposed spheres of influence. Since the overthrow of the authoritarian regimes in Southern Europe, and the inclusion of the Mediterranean countries in the European Union, these countries have followed politically and economically in the path of the continental and north-western European countries and can thus be considered part of 'Western Europe'. Nevertheless differences in economic and political organization between Northern, continental, and Southern Europe have remained.

The same is true of demography and population: despite some large differences, the Western European countries show several similarities. There is a clear North–South divide in demographic patterns, which reflect different levels of socio-economic development, religious differences, differences in social structure, and finally also cultural differences.

But taken together, in the field of demography, the Western European countries have more in common with each other than with the Eastern European countries. For several demographic domains there is a clear line of demarcation between East and West, most notably in the division between an Eastern and Western European marriage pattern. This cleavage is not restricted only to marriage behaviour, but is also found with regard to other demographic variables such as birth and death rates—the demographic transition—or births by legitimacy. Because demographic variables are interrelated, the different marriage patterns produce secondary differences in other variables: for example, the low age at marriage together with universal marriage, all things being equal, increases fertility, increases child mortality, reduces illegitimacy, and so on.

The countries covered by this data handbook comprise all larger states of Western Europe with the addition of Poland, Czechoslovakia, and Hungary. Following the demarcation line of the Eastern and Western European marriage pattern, which runs from St. Petersburg to Trieste, all three countries belong to the Eastern European marriage pattern. This demarcation line is obviously part of the Slavic-Germanic boundary. Nevertheless, these three countries have been included in the handbook and in the calculation of European averages mainly for historical and cultural (e.g. religion) reasons. Greece has been included as well: since its independence it clearly belongs to Western Europe, but with respect to demography it reveals traits of the Eastern European marriage pattern and its correlates: early and universal marriage (at least for women) and very few illegitimate births. Marital breakdown obviously has nothing to do with the different European marriage patterns: divorce is rare in Greece but frequent in Eastern European countries.

POPULATION STRUCTURE AND DENSITY

Population density continues to differ greatly by geographic and geo-economic position of the European countries. Already since the Middle Ages the corridor from southern England via The Netherlands and Belgium down the Rhine Valley through Switzerland to Northern Italy was the most economically developed and most densely populated region of Europe. This remained the case in the nineteenth century and was even enhanced by the population revolution; external and internal migration processes added to it. Therefore, there is a supranational system of population distribution in Europe.

It can even be said that since the decline of the Roman Empire, in a very long-term perspective, the centre of European population shifted from the Mediterranean to north of the Alps. But this was only a gradual movement, and until the high Middle Ages, Italy for example was one of the most densely populated countries. Furthermore, the largest cities such as Constantinople, Venice, and Genoa were located on the Mediterranean. From the high Middle Ages to the sixteenth century there was a further shift from the Mediterranean to northern Europe, caused by the rise of the Ottomans and the loss of North Africa, parts of Spain and Portugal, and finally of most of the Balkans to the Muslims. As a result, the Mediterranean region was split between cultures; the trading routes were threatened by the resulting instability and increasingly shifted away from the Mediterranean region to overseas, resulting in the decline of Mediterranean trade and of such trading powers as Venice and Genoa. The major discoveries of new territory in the fifteenth and sixteenth centuries by the Portuguese, Spanish, Dutch, and British finally moved the economic and population centre to continental Europe (Rokkan, 1999).

Starting in the sixteenth century the Southern European powers Portugal and Spain suffered from an economic decline which became very apparent in the seventeenth century, when the powers of the North, mainly the Dutch and the British, became dominant. The South declined not only in terms of economic and military power, but also in terms of population (Pounds, 1979; Catalan, 1995), as can be seen from the number of inhabitants of the European countries (Table 2.1). Germany, although not a seapower, had the largest population in 1870 with 41 million. France came second with 35 million; population growth in France had already been low since the late eighteenth century and continued during the nineteenth. The United Kingdom came third with 28 million inhabitants. Population growth in the British Isles and Ireland was quite vigorous, and the population of the United Kingdom exceeded that of France in the decade 1900–10; by 1930 the UK had six million more inhabitants than France. Italy ranked fourth in population with 27 million in 1870. Population growth was higher than in France, but far lower than in the United Kingdom. In 1930 Italy's population was equal to that of France. While France's population increased by only six million inhabitants, Italy's population went up by 14 million. Spain's population ranked fifth in 1880 with 17 million inhabitants, but population growth was quite strong until the 1930s, with an increase of approximately seven million people. Most other European countries were small or medium-sized in terms of absolute population, though some showed strong growth. Population growth was highest in The Netherlands: 'only' 3.6 million in 1870, the population

TABLE 2.1   Census population in Europe (in 1,000s)

Country	1870	1880	1890	1900	1910	1920	1930	1940
Austria[1]	20,218[2]	22,144	23,895	26,150	28,572	6,527[3]	6,763[4]	6,934[5]
Belgium	4,828[6]	5,520	6,069	6,694	7,424	7,406	8,092	8,512[7]
Czechoslovakia	–	–	–	–	–	13,612[8]	14,730	12,338[9]
Denmark	1,785	1,969	2,172	2,450[10]	2,757[11]	3,268[8]	3,551	3,844
Finland	1,913[12]	2,061	2,380	2,712	3,115	3,364	3,667	3,887
France	35,313[13]	37,672[14]	38,343[15]	38,962[10]	39,602[11]	39,210[8]	41,907[16]	40,503[17]
Germany	41,059[18]	45,234	49,428	56,367	64,926	62,411[19]	66,029[20]	..
Greece	1,458	1,679[21]	2,187[22]	2,434[23]	2,632[24]	5,536	6,205[25]	7,345
Hungary[26]	15,860	15,642[14]	17,464	19,255	20,886	7,980	8,688	9,316[27]
Iceland	..	..	..	78[10]	85	95	109	122
Ireland/Irish Republic	5,412[18]	5,175[14]	4,705[15]	4,459[10]	4,390[11]	2,972[28]	2,968[29]	2,955[17]
Italy	26,801[18]	28,460[14]	..	32,475[10]	35,845[11]	38,711[8]	41,177[16]	42,445[29]
Luxemburg	204[30]	211	211	235	259	262[31]	300	297[32]
The Netherlands	3,580[2]	4,013[21]	4,511[22]	5,104[33]	5,858[34]	6,865	7,936	9,625[35]
Norway	..	1,819[36]	2,001[15]	2,240	2,392	2,650	2,814	3,157[17]
Poland	–	–	–	–	–	27,201[8]	32,107[16]	..
Portugal	..	4,551[37]	5,050	5,447	5,695[11]	6,033	6,809	7,755
Spain	..	16,632[38]	17,560[39]	18,608	19,927	21,303	23,564	25,878
Sweden	4,169	4,566	4,785	5,136	5,522	5,904	6,142	6,371
Switzerland	2,655	2,832	2,918[40]	3,315	3,753	3,880	4,066	4,267[27]
United Kingdom	27,935[18]	31,592[14]	34,919[15]	38,901[10]	42,743[11]	45,946[8]	48,006[16]	..

[1] 1869–1910 Austrian Empire, 1923–51 Austrian Republic; 1951 included for comparative purposes. [2] 1869. [3] 1923. [4] 1934. [5] 1951. [6] 1866. [7] 1947. [8] 1921. [9] 1950. [10] 1901. [11] 1911. [12] 1875. [13] 1872. [14] 1881. [15] 1891. [16] 1931. [17] 1946. [18] 1871. [19] 1925. [20] 1933. [21] 1879. [22] 1889. [23] 1896. [24] 1907. [25] 1928. [26] 1870–1910 Hungarian Empire, 1920–46 Kingdom of Hungary. [27] 1941. [28] 1926. [29] 1936. [30] 1865. [31] 1922. [32] 1935. [33] 1899. [34] 1909. [35] 1957. [36] 1876. [37] 1878. [38] 1877. [39] 1887. [40] 1888.

doubled in the decade 1920–30. Further strong increases occurred in the Nordic countries, especially in Denmark, Finland, and Iceland.

There is no relationship between the size of a country in terms of territory and the size of its population: a large territory does not automatically lead to a large population and vice versa. Table 2.2 shows the different territorial sizes of the European countries in square kilometres. France is the largest, followed in rank order by Germany, Spain, Sweden, Poland, Finland, Italy, Norway, and the United Kingdom. It is obvious from this list that the countries with the largest populations are often those with small territories and that there is only small correlation between population size and size of the territory. Territorial population growth and density therefore follow other laws, which cannot be derived only from the size of the territory.

Population density of the European countries is given in Table 2.3. Population density is defined as inhabitants per square kilometre. In 1870 the most densely populated European country was Belgium with 164 inhabitants per sq. km. The United Kingdom was second, followed by The Netherlands, Italy, France, and Germany. This picture changed only gradually up to 1930: Belgium remained the most densely populated country with 265 inhabitants per sq. km., while The Netherlands moved into second place due to their strong population growth. The United Kingdom fell to third place, followed in order by Germany, Italy, and Luxemburg.

REGIONAL POPULATION DISTRIBUTION

This list clearly shows that population density is not at all high in the countries with the largest territories. On the contrary, it is very high in some of the smallest European countries. Most of the countries with high population density are located in the old Lotharingian zone, stretching along the Rhine Valley to The Netherlands. Other regions with high population densities include southern England, northern and north-western France, and northern Italy. Densely-populated areas outside these regions have developed where coal deposits were found and exploited by industry, such as Birmingham, the French and Belgian steel and coal regions, and Saxony and Silesia in the east (Ilbery, 1986). This European population concentration obviously has something to do with the main trade routes from Italy via Switzerland and the Rhine Valley to Southern England, which developed during the Middle Ages and continue to be significant today. The second major factor for population agglomeration was the presence of natural resources—coal and iron ore—necessary for industrialization. Outside these population centres, population density falls the greater the distance to the European population centre. This population structure, with a densely-populated centre and sparsely-populated periphery, is of course shaped by national centre and periphery structures in the peripheries themselves. Thus, Finland, for example, with a very low population density on the whole shows an internal pattern of higher population density in the south and lower density in the north.

Urbanization reinforced the uneven pattern of European population distribution. Because the fertility of urban populations was low and sometimes fell below natural replacement, the urban population always consisted to a significant extent of

TABLE 2.2 Area (in sq. km.)

Country	1870	1880	1900	1910	1920	1930	1940
Austria[1]	300,004[2]	300,004	300,004	300,004	83,833[3]	83,867[4]	83,850[5]
Belgium	29,451[6]	29,451	29,451	29,451	29,455	30,507	30,507[7]
Czechoslovakia	–	–	–	–	141,394[8]	140,493	127,859[9]
Denmark	38,340	38,340	38,455[10]	38,969[11]	43,017[8]	42,931	42,931
Finland	370,103[12]	370,103	331,944	333,140	343,631	343,378	348,477
France	528,572[13]	528,572[14]	536,464[10]	536,464[11]	536,464[8]	536,464[16]	536,464[17]
Germany	540,561[18]	540,522	540,743	540,858	468,746[19]	470,715[20]	..
Greece	50,211[21]	..	..	..	..	130,199[25]	..
Hungary[26]	335,078	322,285[14]	324,851	325,411	92,916	93,073	92,896[27]
Iceland	..	..	103,000[10]	103,000	103,000	103,000	103,000
Ireland/Irish	81,718[18]	81,718[14]	81,718[10]	81,964[11]	68,897[28]	68,897[29]	68,897[17]
Italy	296,305[18]	296,323[14]	286,682[10]	286,610[11]	310,120[8]	310,150[16]	310,190[29]
Luxemburg	2,586[30]	2,586	2,586	2,586	2,586[31]	2,586	2,586[32]
The Netherlands	32,875[2]	33,000[21]	33,079[33]	32,600[34]	32,603	32,566	32,328[35]
Norway	..	318,192[36]	308,477	308,477	309,900	309,900	308,833[17]
Poland	–	–	–	–	388,390[8]	388,390[16]	..
Portugal	..	92,828[37]	91,944	91,944[11]	91,944	91,767	91,721
Spain	..	504,517[38]	504,517	504,517	504,517	505,720	505,720
Sweden	407,447	405,845	411,195	410,354	410,581	410,540	410,329
Switzerland	41,390	41,390	41,298	41,298	41,298	41,295	41,295[27]
United Kingdom	230,098[18]	229,763[15]	230,139[10]	231,619[11]	243,777[8]	243,784[16]	..

Notes: see Table 2.1.

TABLE 2.3 Population density in Europe (inhabitants per sq. km.)

Country	1850	1860	1870	1880	1890	1900	1910	1920	1930	1940
Austria[1]	..	..	67[2]	74	80	87	95	78[3]	81[4]	83[5]
Belgium	147[6]	154[7]	164[8]	187	206	227	252	251	265	279[9]
Czechoslovakia	–	–	–	–	–	–	–	96[10]	105	96[11]
Denmark	..	..	47	51	57	64[12]	71[13]	76[14]	83	90
Finland	..	..	5[15]	6	7	8	9	10	11	11
France	..	..	67[16]	71[17]	73[18]	73[12]	74[13]	73[14]	78[19]	75[20]
Germany	..	..	76[21]	84	91	104	120	133[22]	140[23]	..
Greece	..	..	29[24]	..	..	..	..	..	48[25]	..
Hungary[26]	..	..	47	49[17]	54	59	64	86	93	100[27]
Iceland	..	..	..	..	..	1[12]	1	1	1	1
Ireland/Irish Republic	..	..	66[21]	63[17]	58[18]	55[12]	54[13]	43[28]	43[29]	43[20]
Italy	..	..	90[21]	96[17]	–	113[12]	125[13]	125[14]	133[19]	137[29]
Luxemburg	75[30]	..	79[31]	81	82	91	100	101[32]	116	115[33]
The Netherlands	..	..	109[2]	122[24]	137[34]	154[35]	180[36]	211	244	298[9]
Norway	..	..	..	6[37]	6[18]	7	8	9	9	10[20]
Poland	–	–	–	–	–	–	–	70[14]	83[19]	..
Portugal	..	..	..	49[38]	55	59	62[13]	66	74	85
Spain	..	..	..	33[39]	35[40]	37	39	42	47	51
Sweden	..	..	10	11	12	12	13	14	15	16
Switzerland	..	..	64	68	71[41]	80	91	94	98	103[27]
United Kingdom	..	..	121[21]	137[17]	152[18]	169[12]	185[13]	188[14]	197[19]	..

[1] 1869–1910 Austrian Empire, 1923–51 Austrian Republic; 1951 included for comparative purposes.
[2] 1869. [3] 1923. [4] 1934. [5] 1951. [6] 1846. [7] 1856. [8] 1866. [9] 1947. [10] 1921. [11] 1950. [12] 1901. [13] 1911. [14] 1921.
[15] 1875. [16] 1872. [17] 1881. [18] 1891. [19] 1931. [20] 1946. [21] 1871. [22] 1925. [23] 1933. [24] 1879. [25] 1928. [26] 1870–
1910 Hungarian Empire, 1920–46 Kingdom of Hungary. [27] 1941. [28] 1926. [29] 1936. [30] 1851. [31] 1865.
[32] 1922. [33] 1935. [34] 1889. [35] 1899. [36] 1909. [37] 1876. [38] 1878. [39] 1877. [40] 1887. [41] 1888.

migrants from rural areas. While rural areas lost population either in absolute or in relative terms, urban regions attracted population. Processes of migration occurred within countries as well as between them. Such international migration was already strong during the nineteenth and first half of the twentieth century. The industrial centre of England around Birmingham attracted many Irish, Scottish, and Welsh workers. Industry in the German Ruhr Valley drew Polish workers from eastern German provinces and the Polish territories under Russian and Austrian rule. Already in the nineteenth century, the French and Belgian regions of heavy industry attracted workers from Italy, Flanders, and southern France. Finally, the northern Italian city-states expanded due to industrial development, pulling many workers from the rural countryside of northern Italy as well as from the Mezzogiorno.

The centres of population gravitation for each country or, in empirical terms, the most densely populated region of each country, are described extensively in the individual country chapters, thus only the European gravitation pattern is discussed here. Table 2.4 helps identify the European centre–periphery structure in terms of population distribution. It shows the most densely-populated European regions in 1880 with over 200 inhabitants per square kilometre, and the least densely-populated European regions in 1880 with less than 10 inhabitants per square kilometre. The figure for 1930 shows the change in population density over 50 years. The capital cities and exclusively urban areas have been left out because of their extreme degree of urbanization. The intent is to identify European-wide population agglomerations that are not caused by a monocephalic population structure, for example, where the capital alone makes up a large part of the national population.

Table 2.4 shows clearly the high population density in many parts of England, in most Belgian provinces, in the two core provinces of The Netherlands, in the *département* Nord of France, and in the German Ruhr (Düsseldorf) and Rhine Valley (Rheinhessen). Outside this main European population centre, areas with high population density can be found in Scotland (Renfrew) and Wales (Glamorgan), in the region of Lyon (Rhône) in France, and the region of Zwickau in Saxony.

The least densely populated regions of Europe are more or less all located in the northern periphery, most of them in the northern territories of the Nordic countries. The whole island of Iceland is the least densely populated region of Europe. Most of Norway, Finland, and to a lesser degree Sweden is very sparsely populated. Outside the Nordic countries there are three Scottish counties with very low population density. In continental and southern Europe there was no region in 1880 with such a low population density other than the Spanish province of Segovia.

The developments from 1880 to 1930 have varied for the densely populated regions. Industrialization was important in increasing population density (Düsseldorf), but there are also cases with a lower increase in population density, such as Liège in Belgium. In the European regions with the lowest population density there was only a small change. If the European population centre and the population periphery are compared, the growing cleavage between them from 1880 to 1930 is evident (see also Pounds, 1979: 309–23; Ilbery, 1986: 12–38)

TABLE 2.4 Most and least densely populated regions in Europe 1880 and 1930
(inhabitants per sq. km.)

No.	Region (excluding city regions)	Country	Most/least densely populated region (over 200/under 10 inhab. per sq. km.)	
			~1880	~1930
1	Surrey	England	734	631
2	Lancaster	England	706	1,037
3	Renfrew	Scotland	424	491
4	Durham	England	331	565
5	Stafford	England	324	479
6	Warwick	England	322	607
7	York West Riding	England	304	478
8	Brabant	Belgium	300	512
9	Flandre Orientale	Belgium	294	387
10	Düsseldorf	Germany	291	742
11	Nord	France	282	351
12	Rhone	France	266	366
13	Zuidholland	The Netherlands	266	669
14	Hainaut	Belgium	263	341
15	Noordholland	The Netherlands	245	551
16	Glamorgan	Wales	244	579
17	Kent	England	243	309
18	Chester/Cheshire	England	242	412
19	Zwickau	Germany	239	345
20	Liège	Belgium	229	246
21	Flandre Occidentale	Belgium	214	279
22	Anvers	Belgium	204	410
23	Rheinhessen	Germany	202	300
1	Inverness	Scotland	8	8
2	Nedenæs	Norway	8	8
3	St. Michels/Mikkelin	Finland	7	13
4	Västernorrlands	Sweden	7	12
5	Buskerud	Norway	7	10
6	Kopparbergs	Sweden	7	9
7	Kuopio/Kuopion	Finland	6	11
8	Søndre Trondhjem	Norway	6	10
9	Bratsberg	Norway	6	9
10	Hedemarken	Norway	5	6
11	Kristians	Norway	5	6
12	Nordre Bergenhus	Norway	5	5
13	Nordre Trondhjem	Norway	4	5
14	Sutherland	Scotland	4	3
15	Nordland	Norway	3	5
16	Tromsø	Norway	2	4
17	Västerbottens	Sweden	2	4
18	Jämtlands	Sweden	2	3
19	Segovia	Spain	2	2
20	Uleåborgs/Oulun	Finland	1	3
21	Norrbottens	Sweden	1	2
22	Finnmarken	Norway	1	1
23	Iceland (whole country)	Iceland	1	1

Sources: Country chapters of this volume.

3
Population Growth and Demographic Transition

POPULATION GROWTH

Population growth is made up of three variables: the number of births, the number of deaths, and the extent of migration, i.e. of net migration. There are very different possibilities of combination (leaving migration aside for the moment): high fertility can go along with high mortality, resulting in medium natural population growth. High fertility can also occur with low mortality; in this case the natural population growth would be highest. Low fertility can be combined with low mortality, in which case natural population growth would also be medium. Finally, low fertility can be combined with high mortality, in which case natural population growth would be lowest.

To these four different combinations can be added the element of net migration (the difference between immigration and emigration) which can be high or low. Thus, a country with high natural population growth could have negative net migration, reducing the overall population growth substantially. By contrast, a country with low natural population growth could have positive net migration, with a similar effect for overall population growth.

It is not possible to determine *a priori* whether these three variables are high or low in a given country, as it depends on many factors related to the social, economic, and value (religious) structure of the population. The birth rate in pre-industrial agrarian countries, for example, depends very much on the type of agricultural organization and the system of inheritance. The death rate depends heavily on the amount of infant mortality, which again depends on factors related to the educational level of the population, development of medicine, and sanitary infrastructure. Migration, finally, also depends on a variety of factors, such as the legal possibility to immigrate or emigrate, the population pressure due to overpopulation, expulsion of parts of the population due to political or religious conflicts (Huguenots, Puritans, Waldensians). Of all these, relative overpopulation (or relative underpopulation in countries receiving immigrants) is probably the most important factor causing migration.

Population growth could furthermore depend on the population density in a country at the start of the demographic transition. It might be postulated that the higher the population density in a country at the pre-transition stage, the lower the population growth during the first demographic transition. The underlying supposition would be that high population density will cause people to limit reproduction due to the difficulties arising from high settlement density.

Table 3.1 presents population growth rates from annual mid-year population figures based on the year 1850 (or 1871, 1919, etc.). The five countries with the highest population growth during the period 1850–1945 are Greece, The Netherlands, Denmark, England and Wales, and Finland. But Greece has to be removed from this list, because of its large territorial gains since independence. The five countries with the lowest population growth (in declining order) are Spain, Switzerland, Luxemburg, France, and Ireland. Ireland is the only European country in which population declined absolutely from 1850 to 1945, mainly caused by emigration. These patterns obviously do not confirm the above hypothesis that population growth will be low in countries that had a low population density already before the start of the first demographic transition. As we can see in the introductory Chapter I.2, 'Population and Territory' (Table 2.3), already in 1870 The Netherlands and The United Kingdom had among the highest population densities in Europe. Nevertheless, Denmark and Finland, which are in the top-five group with the highest population growth, had a remarkably low population density in 1870. Let us now look at the country group with the lowest population growth: these countries by no means belong to the group with a high population density in 1870. In France, Luxemburg, and Switzerland, population density was on a medium level, while Spain's population density was low.

Mere number of people per square kilometre therefore does not explain population developments. Rather, there must have been different 'population regimes' (*Bevölkerungsweisen*, Gerhard Mackenroth) in European countries. These different population regimes are probably strongly related to the different European marriage

TABLE 3.1 Population growth in Europe 1850–1945 (in %; 1850, 1871, etc.=100; based on mid-year population)

Country	1850	1860	1870	1880	1890	1900	1910	1920	1930	1940	1945
Austrian Republic	..	..	100[1]	108	118	131	145	141	147	..	..
Belgium	100	107	115	126	138	153	169	170	183	190	189
Czechoslovakia	–	–	–	–	–	–	100[2]	100	108	114	110
Denmark	100	113	126	139	153	171	192	216	249	269	284
Finland	100	107	108	126	145	166	190	206	224	227	231
France	100	102	108	105	108	109	111	109	117	115	111
Germany	100	107	116	128	139	159	183	175	182	198	..
Greece	100	108	145	169	221	249	267	498	633	728	..
Hungary[3]	–	100[4]	101	106	122	137	152	159	173	185	..
Iceland	100	112	116	121	118	130	141	156	179	202	215
Ireland/Irish Rep.[5]	100	85	79	76	69	65	64	63	43	43	43
Italy	–	100[6]	118	129	139	148	159	164	188	204	210
Luxemburg	100	102	105	110	111	122	135	136	156	155	148
The Netherlands	100	109	118	133	149	169	194	224	259	292	304
Norway	100	115	125	138	143	160	171	189	202	214	222
Poland	–	–	–	–	–	100	104	108	126	..	..
Portugal	100	105	114	122	132	142	155	158	179	203	213
Spain	..	101	104	109	114	119	128	137	145	166	173
Sweden	100	110	120	132	138	148	159	170	177	184	192
Switzerland	100[7]	104	110	118	122	137	155	161	168	175	183
United Kingdom	..	100[8]	105	117	126	139	151	157	155	162	166
England/Wales	100	112	127	145	162	181	201	210	224	236	240

[1] 1871. [2] 1919. [3] Data refer to the territory of the Kingdom of Hungary of 1920–46. [4] 1869. [5] 1850–1921 whole island; 1922–1945 Irish Republic. [6] 1862. [7] 1852. [8] 1864.

patterns, to the unequal economic structure in Europe, leading to early industrialization in one country and persistence of agriculture in another, and to the type of agricultural organization in the countries still strongly dominated by agriculture until the mid-twentieth century.

The differing population growth of course had enormous consequences for the territorial population pattern in Europe. Looking at the population of individual European countries as a proportion of the overall European population of that time, we see that the population of some countries increased relative to the total European population, while that of others decreased. Countries whose population shares increased are The Netherlands, Denmark, Finland, Greece, and the United Kingdom. Countries with severe relative losses are mainly France and Ireland, and to some degree Spain.

THE FIRST DEMOGRAPHIC TRANSITION IN EUROPE

The demographic transition is a model of demographic development during the nineteenth and twentieth centuries based on the observations made for Sweden.

The demographic transition is a long-term demographic process affecting all European countries to differing degrees. Important dimensions of analysis for this process are firstly the starting conditions (Zapf, 1995), that is, the starting level of both central variables mortality and fertility. Furthermore, the dimension of the direction of change can be distinguished, because in many countries an initial increase in mortality and sometimes also in fertility can be seen, before both variables moved in the direction described by the model. Another dimension is the speed of change, which varied greatly. Lastly, we can distinguish as the third dimension the depth of these processes of change: how far society was penetrated and according to which pattern. According to Chesnais (1992), the leading author in this field, the development of both processes, mortality and fertility, is very importance. This is due to the fact that the development of fertility has been a reaction to the decline in mortality. The secular decline in births has to be seen primarily as a process of adapting to declining mortality. The declining mortality is overwhelmingly a decline in infant mortality and less an increase in life expectancy for higher age groups; the increase in life expectancy of the higher age groups was not as high as for the younger age groups. For example, in the nineteenth century thirty-year-olds had very good chances to reach a high age (Rothenbacher, 1982).

For long-term comparisons in principle only the crude death rate is available (see Table 3.4 below). This crude death rate is largely determined by the proportion of infant mortality (see Table 3.3 below). The war against infant mortality from the nineteenth century until immediately after World War II led to a drastic reduction of mortality. The ageing of the population in many countries led the crude death rate to increase or stagnate. The convergence of national rates of infant mortality has caused a fundamental convergence of national mortality levels. For mortality, as for other demographic factors, wars and economic crises were important influences. As late as the nineteenth century, some countries experienced hunger crises typical for the 18th and earlier centuries (Imhof, 1978). Since World War II there has been a completely new development: the crude death rate has been stagnating or rising in some countries. The reason for this pattern is not a factual increase in mortality and therefore a decrease in life expectancy, but the shift in the age structure towards greater representation of the higher age groups. It is also a consequence of the ongoing fertility decline which is increasingly diminishing the lower age groups. Apart from the long-term process of convergence in the crude death rate, a new divergence can be seen, because the change in age structure is proceeding faster in some countries with a strong labour migration, such as the Southern European countries. In these countries, a strong increase in the crude death rate occurred because of strong remigration in these countries: young workers left the country, causing low shares of the younger age groups in the age pyramid, and returned to their country of birth years or even decades later.

Because in the model of demographic transition mortality and fertility are interwoven very neatly, there are visible analogous processes—but only on a higher level, because decline in fertility has to be seen as a reaction to the decline in mortality. For a long-term comparison of over 150 years the crude birth rate is the only comparable and available indicator of fertility development (cf. Chesnais, 1992). In the long run differences between countries have diminished here again, because fertility in most countries has meanwhile fallen well below replacement (Table 3.2). Remarkable are the waves with upswings in the inter-war period and the post-war period until the 1960s. In some countries the crude birth rate appears to be rising again, but this new increase cannot be interpreted as real growth in fertility, because the crude rate essentially depends on the age structure of the population.

A more exact measure of fertility development is given by the Total Period Fertility Rate (TPFR). Calculations of this rate are available for most European countries since 1900. There are significant waves in the long-term development. One very deep crisis of fertility development was World War I for those countries immediately involved, speeding birth decline even more. After the war, the birth rate recovered, but there was instead an essential change in level. Birth decline reached its first record low in the mid-1930s in all Western and Northern European countries. Around 1900 precisely those countries with the lowest fertility today, namely the Southern European countries, still had the highest fertility rates in all of Europe. The Southern European countries were only marginally affected by the fertility crisis of the 1930s. In the post-war period the increase in fertility in the 1960s was significant, leading to the formulation of the hypothesis of a 'second demographic transition'. Since about 1965 a strong decline in TPFR was apparent until the mid-1980s and—for some countries—a new growth in TPFR afterwards. The fertility development of the early 1990s indicates a growing divergence between national fertility patterns in Europe because of continuing below-replacement fertility especially in the Southern European countries. The most remarkable pattern is the long-term convergence of fertility on a very low level between 1900 and 1990.

In 1900 the national differences in Europe were still very high: France had the lowest fertility in all of Europe, while the Southern European countries in general showed very high fertility. The fertility level of the Northern European countries was between these extreme poles (Chesnais, 1992; Coale and Watkins, 1986; Watkins, 1991; Smith, 1991; Rostow, 1998; Caselli, 1994).

TABLE 3.2 Crude birth rate in Europe

Country	1850	1860	1870	1880	1890	1900	1910	1920	1930	1940
Austrian Republic	..	..	33.6[1]	33.5	30.7	31.3	26.7	22.7	16.8	20.7[2]
Belgium	29.8	30.8	32.6	31.1	29.0	28.8	23.7	22.0	18.9	13.5
Czechoslovakia	–	–	–	–	–	–	–	26.4	21.8	20.6
Denmark	31.4	32.6	30.4	31.7	30.5	29.7	27.5	25.4	18.7	18.3
Finland	35.8	36.4	36.3	36.5	32.9	32.0	30.1	25.3	20.6	17.8
France	26.8	26.2	25.9	24.6	21.8	21.2	19.6	21.4	18.0	13.6
Germany	37.2	36.3	38.5	37.6	35.7	35.6	29.8	25.9	17.5	20.1
Greece	..	28.3	28.1	24.4	..	..	..	21.2[3]	31.3	24.5
Hungary[4]	..	..	..	44.2	40.2	39.2	34.9	31.4	25.4	20.0
Iceland	38.1	35.5	31.4	31.4	31.0	28.6	25.6	28.1	26.1	20.5
Ireland/Irish Republic	..	..	27.6	24.6	22.3	22.7	23.3	22.8	19.9	19.1
Italy	..	38.1[5]	37.0	34.0	35.6	33.0	32.9	32.3	26.7	23.4
Luxemburg	34.1	33.8	33.0	31.8	28.2	30.2	27.4	21.6	21.5	13.4
The Netherlands	..	..	36.1	35.5	32.9	31.6	28.6	28.3	23.1	20.8
Norway	31.0	33.3	29.2	30.9	30.4	29.7	25.8	26.3	17.0	16.1
Poland	–	–	–	–	–	–	–	31.8	32.4	24.4[6]
Portugal	..	..	..	..	32.6	30.5	31.6	33.6	29.7	24.2
Spain	..	36.7	36.6	36.0	34.8	34.1	32.6	29.3	29.4	24.4
Sweden	31.9	34.8	28.8	29.4	28.0	27.0	24.7	23.6	15.4	15.1
Switzerland	29.0[7]	31.3	29.8	29.6	26.6	28.6	25.0	20.9	17.2	15.2
United Kingdom	..	..	33.8	32.8	29.3	28.2	25.0	25.7	16.8	14.6
England and Wales	33.4	34.4	35.2	34.3	30.2	28.7	25.1	24.5	16.3	14.1

[1] 1871. [2] 1939. [3] 1921. [4] Data refer to the territory of the Kingdom of Hungary of 1920–46. [5] 1862. [6] 1938. [7] 1852.

CLASS-SPECIFIC DIFFERENCES IN REPRODUCTIVE BEHAVIOUR

Reproductive behaviour is marked not only by national differences, but within a society also by strong class-specific differences. Diffusion theory looks at birth control as an innovation and traces how it spreads through the social structure of a country. Data for Germany show that the better-off strata (such as civil servants) started using birth control first; this innovation spread subsequently to employees, workers, and farmers (Rothenbacher, 1989). This behavioural change is likely associated with the invention of a relatively secure means of birth control and should therefore be seen as a technological innovation that was adopted step by step. The diffusion model predicts as a rule that the introduction of an innovation results in growing inequality, as specific social groups act as pioneers and others are latecomers. In the phase of acceleration, the logistic pattern of diffusion leads to a growing inequality in innovative behaviour.

In his study on social-class pioneers in the European fertility decline, Livi-Bacci (1986) also emphasizes the usefulness of a diffusion approach to class-specific developments in fertility decline. Long before masses of national populations voluntarily and intentionally reduced fertility—thereby causing the first demographic transition—several social classes, although small in number, practised fertility control. Artificial fertility control had been used by the aristocracy, by Jews, and by urban prominent families already since the early eighteenth century. Longitudinal studies including several social classes show that during the seventeenth century social-class differences in fertility were still small. During the eighteenth and nineteenth centuries, however, these socio-economic differences widened. Fertility reduction was clearly related to high income, wealth, and social position.

APPROACHES TO EXPLAINING THE VARIATIONS
IN THE BIRTH DECLINE IN EUROPE

Explanations for the variations in fertility in Europe are numerous. For a discussion of 'ideal typical' hypotheses for the process of birth decline in general see Kaufmann (1995: 90ff.). On the national and international comparative level there are different hypotheses or theoretical approaches. As yet, there is no all-embracing explanation for the fertility decline.

Diffusion of practices and means of birth control

The diffusion model is probably the most valuable approach for understanding fertility decline within a nation as well as in Europe overall. Diffusion occurs on the subnational level between segments (social classes, regions) of a society, but also on the international level in the form of diffusion across national boundaries.

The concept of diffusion includes several elements: there must be an *invention*, that is transformed into an *innovation*. This innovation spreads through *imitation*. However, this ideal sequence does not say anything about the circumstances under which these three elements occur. Not every invention leads to an innovation that is accepted and implemented. And not every innovation spreads throughout a population. The same thing may be invented at different times, or innovations may spread only after a considerable time lag. It is thus essential to investigate the factors conditioning diffusion processes.

Diffusion of fertility control can be investigated on two different levels: on the level of the individual nation-state and on the international level. On the national level there is a clear pattern of diffusion in the stratification system. Fertility control was first introduced by the higher social strata and was successively imitated, the lower the social stratum, the later. Fertility reduction therefore finally spread down the social ladder, eventually including the whole population of a country. In addition, there is also an international stratification system: the wealth of countries differs substantially, and there is also a social hierarchy between countries. It may be posited that on the national aggregate wealthier countries reduce fertility earlier than poorer countries. And if both perspectives are combined, it can be supposed that economic elites in the rich countries are the first to control fertility, and that the lower classes in rich countries are still pioneers compared with the socio-economic elites in poorer countries.

These hypotheses must be tested for Europe historically using indicators such as the wealth of countries at different time points. Historical calculations of the gross domestic product (GDP) for European countries in the nineteenth century (see Catalan, 1995: Table 1, p. 2) offer some support for this hypothesis. There are good reasons to interpret the early fertility decline of France or the low fertility of countries such as Belgium and Switzerland already during the nineteenth century in the light of their higher prosperity at the time, compared with countries such as Italy or Spain with below-average GDP per capita and late fertility decline.

In a broad international context including many countries of the world one finds strong support for the above-mentioned hypotheses. Weinberger's (1994) study of approximately 100 countries shows that while in Europe the poorer social strata currently have fertility rates similar to the wealthier classes, in developing countries of the world, the fertility of the upper classes is still higher than that of the poorer classes in the developed European countries.

The most convincing confirmation of the applicability of the diffusion concept comes from the comparative volume of the Princeton European Fertility Project (Coale and Watkins, 1986), in which especially the appendix figures based on regional data for the European countries clearly show the territorial diffusion of low fertility for successive points in time.

Cultural factors

'Culture' is a social phenomenon that does not explain the process of fertility decline as a universal model, but does account for national differences in this process and persisting fertility differences between countries. Culture and thus the specific history of a country influence fertility in some cases. Culture includes tradition and religion, and the influence of cultural and religious traditions can best be shown in the case of Ireland, which is unique in Europe with regard to fertility level. The value orientation concerning the number of children is above the European average, as is the realized number of children. One of the central factors here is the strong influence of the Catholic–traditional–agrarian milieu. Ireland still has a large primary sector and a strict Catholic value orientation concerning birth control (the selling of contraceptives is forbidden) and abortion. Fewer people in Ireland practise birth control than in any other European country. Divorce was introduced as late as 1997. Another indicator for the strong Catholic value orientation is the rate of church attendance, which also remains very high. In other Catholic countries there is no evidence of the direct influence of religion on the number of children: indeed, the Catholic Mediterranean countries Spain, Portugal, and Italy, along with Orthodox Greece, show the lowest fertility rates. Their low fertility is partly in obvious contradiction to the desired number of children, which is much more a reflection of 'social-moral' milieu models. In most European countries, the cultural factor seems to have had little impact on realized fertility, as opposed to desired fertility, for several decades.

Costs and benefits of children

Population economy uses the microeconomic approach of cost/benefit analysis of children (Becker, 1993). Difficulties with this approach arise from the question of the empirical operationalization of the cost/benefit concept.

But there is also a macro-sociological interpretation of the declining value of children, expressed in the concept of functional differentiation of society. This concept interprets the fertility decline as a decline in the societal value of children in a micro-sociological perspective, looking at individual families and persons. It assumes that the functions of children as work-force (for example, on the family farm), for old-age security and care of the elderly, and as heirs to the family property have declined, because society has taken over these social functions. The nation-state has introduced national pension systems, thereby undermining the task of children as caregivers for the elderly. Modernization has diminished the importance of the family farm and the family businesses in crafts, thereby reducing children's importance as work-force and heirs. In a microscopic perspective therefore children's individual value has been reduced, which has therefore led on the macrosocial level to a decline in fertility. It is argued that in modernized societies children have only an emotional and subjective function for their parents, while their objective and rational functions have been lost.

THE IMPACT OF POPULATION AND FAMILY POLICY

Population and family policy were intended to counter the secular birth decline which in most European countries became most visible after the demographic catastrophe of World War I. France was the pioneer in observing and discussing low birth rates already well before 1900 because of its very small natural population increase already in the nineteenth century. France was the first European country to include questions on marital fertility in its population census during the 1880s. It was therefore a pioneer in the statistical assessment of fertility, not in the atomized form of birth statistics, but as statistics of marital fertility or family-related fertility.

The birth decline after World War I in several European countries culminated in the 1930s when in some countries the birth rate reached a level only slightly above the death rate: the danger of a natural population decline was envisaged in several countries. Though during the 1920s there was much discussion of the birth decline, but few concrete measures to stimulate births, population policies were introduced in the 1930s after the world economic depression. The most notable policies were implemented in Sweden, France, and Germany. All of the measures intended to stimulate reproduction, but they were designed very differently. Although it is difficult to attribute fertility increases directly to population policies, the empirical fact remains that, in Sweden, for example, the birth rate rose remarkably in the late 1930s. In France, the birth rate rose decisively only after 1945.

INFANT MORTALITY IN EUROPE

The development of infant mortality in Europe in the last two centuries is neatly related to the process of the demographic transition. The decline in the overall mortality rate was strongly influenced by the decline in the infant mortality rate, because infant deaths made up the largest proportion of all deaths.

For this reason, an early decline in infant mortality often caused an early decline in the fertility rate, and therefore an early start of the demographic transition. This sequence can be seen in the Nordic countries, for example, where infant mortality started already in the first half of the nineteenth century, and demographic transition also started very early. These early developments in some countries led to high natural population growth. Other countries had a rather late decline in infant mortality and thus much smaller natural population growth.

According to Masuy-Stroobant (1997), European countries can be divided into five different country clusters with regard to infant mortality since the beginning of the twentieth century (Table 3.3). The cluster with the lowest infant mortality is made up of the five Nordic countries plus The Netherlands and Switzerland. Next comes the group of the Western European continental countries and the countries of the British Isles with a moderate infant mortality since 1901. The third cluster, with high infant mortality in the first decades but a rapid decline, is made up of the three Mediterranean countries Italy, Spain, and Greece, along with Austria and Czechoslovakia. The fourth cluster, with high infant mortality and a very small decline until World War II, is composed of the Eastern and south-eastern European countries of Bulgaria, Poland, and Hungary. Finally, the fifth cluster, with very high infant mortality and virtually a stagnation until World War II consists of the Balkan countries Romania and Yugoslavia, but Portugal also fits into this group.

TABLE 3.3 Infant mortality rate in Europe

Country	1850	1860	1870	1880	1890	1900	1910	1920	1930	1940
Austrian Republic	..	..	269.9[1]	236.6	247.3	211.6	184.0	156.8	104.1	74.2
Belgium	140.8	138.7	145.4	186.5	166.4	171.6	134.0	110.2	99.5	93.2
Czechoslovakia	–	–	–	–	–	–	–	174.1	134.5	98.8
Denmark	..	135.6	130.9	150.8	132.7	128.5	102.2	90.7	80.0	56.2
Finland	..	..	136.6	166.9	141.7	153.1	117.7	96.7	75.1	88.3
France	147.0	152.7	201.4	180.1	176.1	160.8	110.5	99.2	78.1	90.5
Germany	..	..	..	..	..	206.8[2]	161.8	131.1	84.6	59.8[3]
Greece	..	..	..	..	..	..	..	..	133.8[4]	118.2[5]
Hungary[6]	..	..	..	..	272.1[7]	225.1	196.1	192.5	152.5	130.1
Iceland	242.1	325.9	198.1	169.8	238.9	127.4	105.5	83.4	45.2	35.9
Ireland/Irish Rep.	..	..	95	112	95	109	95	83	68.0	66.4
Italy	..	231.6[8]	230.2	225.0	198.3	174.1	140.0	126.7	105.5	102.7
Luxemburg	..	..	..	..	..	140.1[9]	144.4	96.6	90.5	65.9
The Netherlands	..	..	..	217.6	171.4	155.2	107.9	72.8	50.9	39.1
Norway	102.0	102.0	100.7	95.3	97.2	90.4	67.2	57.5	45.6	38.7
Poland	–	–	–	–	–	–	–	–	142.7	14.0[10]
Portugal	..	..	..	..	..	..	133.9	164.1	143.6	126.1
Spain	170.9	211.6	..	..	..	185.9[11]	149.3	164.3	117.1	108.7
Sweden	146.2	123.8	131.9	120.7	103.1	98.5	75.1	63.3	54.7	39.2
Switzerland	..	..	..	179.9	156.9	149.7	105.0	83.7	50.8	46.2
United Kingdom	..	..	..	..	..	..	..	..	63.1	61.0
England and Wales	145.6	147.6	159.7	152.8	151	154	105.4	83.9	60.0	57.4

[1] 1871. [2] 1901. [3] 1938. [4] 1931. [5] 1939. [6] Data refer to the territory of the Kingdom of Hungary of 1920–46. [7] 1891. [8] 1863. [9] 1901. [10] 1938. [11] 1901.

This clustering of countries shows some correlation with the different marriage patterns in Europe. The Eastern European marriage pattern with early and universal marriage obviously caused not only a higher fertility rate but also a higher infant mortality rate. By contrast, the Western European marriage pattern with late and non-universal (selective) marriage tended to produce a lower fertility rate and therefore also a lower infant mortality rate. Nevertheless, within what is called Western Europe, Southern Europe included, there is much variation and also something like a North–South gradient with respect to infant mortality. One of the factors influencing this variable could be the Protestantism of the North as a state religion, leading to early introduction of vital statistics (around 1750), and therefore awareness of the high infant mortality of the time. Only on the basis of this knowledge could the absolutist state act in order to enhance population growth, one of the main political objectives of the then 'mercantilist' thinking (see for variations of infant mortality in Europe also Van de Walle, 1986; Corsini and Viazzo, 1993b; Rollet, 1997b).

MORTALITY AND LIFE EXPECTANCY IN EUROPE

The model of the first demographic transition states that the mortality decline is the decisive factor for the fertility decline, because people reduced their fertility according to their children's improved chances of survival (Schofield, Reher, and Bideau, 1991). No matter which declined first in the demographic transition, mortality or fertility, the long-term trend in mortality is similar to that of fertility. The general trend is a decline in mortality at least since the 1880s, with some national variation. There were pioneering countries, in which mortality declined some decades earlier, as well as laggards, in which mortality fell later than the average. Until the 1940s there was a clear convergence in the crude death rate: mortality in those countries with high mortality around 1890/1900 declined faster than in countries where mortality was already low at that time. Already in the 1840s the national differences in the mortality rate had become fairly small (Table 3.4). Nevertheless the structure between countries remained very stable, thus reflecting rather invariable characteristics of European societies such as geographical characteristics, country size, and religion.

TABLE 3.4 Crude death rate in Europe

Country	1850	1860	1870	1880	1890	1900	1910	1920	1930	1940
Austrian Republic	..	..	29.8[1]	27.5	26.9	23.2	19.2	19.0	13.5	15.3[2]
Belgium	21.1	19.8	23.4	22.3	20.8	19.2	15.2	13.7	12.8	15.0
Czechoslovakia	–	–	–	–	–	–	–	18.3	13.9	14.0
Denmark	19.1	20.2	19.0	20.4	19.0	16.8	12.9	12.9	10.8	10.4
Finland	26.3	24.8	18.2	23.9	19.7	21.5	16.5	15.9	13.2	19.4
France	21.4	21.4	28.4	22.9	22.8	21.9	17.8	17.2	15.6	18.0
Germany	25.6	23.2	27.4	26.0	24.4	22.1	16.2	15.1	11.1	12.7
Greece	..	20.3	21.9	17.9	..	..	..	13.6[3]	16.3	12.8
Hungary[4]	..	..	..	38.5	31.5	25.9	22.2	21.3	15.5	14.3
Iceland	24.0	48.4	23.1	20.9	27.7	19.8	15.4	14.5	11.6	9.9
Ireland/Irish Republic	..	..	16.7	19.8	18.2	19.6	17.1	15.3	14.2	14.2
Italy	..	31.2[5]	30.1	30.9	26.2	23.7	19.6	19.0	14.1	13.6
Luxemburg	20.5	20.6	24.8	20.3	22.0	21.9	16.7	13.1	13.0	12.1
The Netherlands	..	..	25.8	23.5	20.5	17.9	13.6	12.0	9.1	9.9
Norway	17.2	17.2	16.2	16.2	18.0	15.8	13.5	12.8	10.5	10.8
Poland	–	–	–	–	–	–	–	26.6	15.5	13.8[6]
Portugal	..	..	..	..	25.5	20.3	19.1	23.7	17.0	15.5
Spain	27.9	32.2	30.6	30.1	28.7[7]	29.1	23.0	23.3	17.6	16.5
Sweden	19.8	17.7	19.8	18.1	17.1	16.8	14.0	13.3	11.7	11.4
Switzerland	23.7[8]	22.0	25.8	21.9	20.9	19.3	15.1	14.4	11.6	12.0
United Kingdom	..	..	21.8	20.4	19.4	18.4	14.0	12.9	11.7	14.0
England and Wales	20.8	21.2	22.9	20.6	19.5	18.2	13.5	12.5	11.4	13.9

[1] 1871. [2] 1939. [3] 1921. [4] Data refer to the territory of the Kingdom of Hungary of 1920–46. [5] 1862. [6] 1938. [7] 1889. [8] 1852.

This surprising progress in mortality reduction cannot be interpreted in the sense that adult people lived much longer than before. Instead, the mortality decline during the first demographic transition was mainly a decline in infant mortality. The greatest progress was made in combating deaths in early childhood, mainly during the first five years, primarily due to the introduction of vaccinations (the first was for smallpox shortly after 1800), sanitation, and breastfeeding, among others. The first stage in the so-called epidemiological transition was therefore the fight against early childhood diseases. The second-most dangerous phase of human life was young adulthood, which was mainly threatened by tuberculosis. Whereas much progress in reducing childhood infectious diseases was already made during the nineteenth century, the fight against tuberculosis began to be won only in the first half of the twentieth century. In the nineteenth century, if people reached age 60 they had a good chance of living to age 70 or more. Mortality reduction for the elderly was rather small until the 1940s; the major decreases in mortality of the elderly were achieved after 1945 and mainly since the 1970s.

In the middle of the nineteenth century life expectancy at birth varied greatly between European countries (Table 3.5A). Pioneers in increased life expectancy at birth were the Nordic countries; the lowest life expectancy at birth was found in Southern Europe and the three Central European countries. In most of the continental countries, life expectancy at birth lay between these extremes. Until the 1940s there was a slight converging tendency in life expectancy at birth. Countries with traditionally low life expectancy at birth were to some degree able to catch up with the pioneers; nevertheless, the differences in level remained quite large.

TABLE 3.5A Life expectancy in Europe (at birth)

Country	1850–69	1870–89	1890–1909	1910–29	1930–45	1850–69	1870–89	1890–1909	1910–29	1930–45
	Males					**Females**				
	Life expectancy at birth									
Austria[1]	..	30.98	37.77	40.69	54.47	..	33.70	39.87	42.08	58.53
Belgium	..	43.84	45.39	..	56.02	..	46.98	48.84	..	59.79
Czechoslovakia	–	–	–	46.41	54.92	–	–	–	49.19	58.66
Denmark	43.6	46.8	52.9	55.8	63.5	45.5	48.9	56.2	58.1	65.8
Finland	..	41.4	45.33	50.68	54.32	..	44.2	48.10	55.14	59.48
France	39.10	40.83	45.74	52.19	55.94	40.55	43.42	49.13	55.87	61.64
Germany	..	35.58	40.56	47.41	59.86	..	38.45	43.97	50.68	62.81
Greece	..	35.96	..	44.95	52.94	..	37.46	..	44.46	55.80
Hungary[2]	..	..	36.56	41.04	54.95	..	..	38.15	43.12	58.24
Iceland	32.9	35.1	44.7	52.6	60.9	38.3	40.9	51.8	57.9	65.6
Ireland/Irish Rep.[3]	..	..	49.3	53.6	58.20	..	..	49.6	54.1	59.62
Italy	..	35.1	42.59	46.57	53.76	..	35.5	43.00	47.33	56.00
Luxemburg	..	..	46.3	50.7	62.9	..	..	49.4	53.2	62.2
The Netherlands	36.44	38.4	46.2	55.1	65.5	38.21	40.7	49.0	57.1	67.2
Norway	47.40	48.33	50.41	55.62	94.08	49.95	51.30	54.14	58.71	67.55
Poland	–	–	–	45.9[4]	48.2	–	–	–	45.9[4]	51.4
Portugal	..	..	..	49.66[4]	51.06	..	..	..	49.66[4]	56.17
Spain	..	..	33.85	40.26	47.12	..	..	35.70	42.05	53.24
Sweden	40.48	45.30	50.94	60.72	64.30	44.15	48.60	53.63	62.95	66.92
Switzerland	..	40.6	45.7	54.48	60.93	..	43.2	48.5	57.50	64.84
United Kingdom	..	..	..	..	..	..	..	..	..	..
England and Wales	39.91	41.92	44.13	51.50	58.74	41.85	45.25	47.77	55.35	62.88

[1] 1870/80–1906/10 Austrian Empire; 1930–33 Austrian Republic. [2] Data refer to the territory of the Kingdom of Hungary of 1920–46. [3] 1900/2–1910/12 whole island; 1925/27–1940/42 Irish Republic.
[4] Average data for both sexes.

Increases in life expectancy for 30-year-olds were considerable, but not as large as for children (Table 3.5B). Women gained more years because of the major reduction in maternal mortality. In most countries life expectancy improved more for women than for men at this age, leading to a growing gap between the sexes. The geographical map is very similar to the one we have seen for life expectancy at birth: a North–South gradient, combined with an East–West gradient. Nevertheless, the differences between countries are smaller than for life expectancy at birth.

As already noted, the higher the age, the smaller the improvements in life expectancy. In most European countries gains in life expectancy for 60-year-olds amounted to only 2–3 years over a 100-year period (Table 3.5C). The geographical pattern is the same as for life expectancy at birth and at age 30. There was obviously some convergence between countries until the 1940s; on the other hand, the gap in life expectancy between the sexes widened.

TABLE 3.5B Life expectancy in Europe (at age 30)

Country	1850 –69	1870 –89	1890 – 1909	1910– 29	1930 –45	1850 –69	1870 –89	1890 – 1909	1910– 29	1930 –45
	Males					**Females**				
	Life expectancy at age 30									
Austria[1]	..	30.53	32.86	33.49	36.86	..	31.52	33.70	34.80	39.59
Belgium	..	33.96	34.22	..	37.78	..	36.36	36.96	..	40.17
Czechoslovakia	–	–	–	35.83	38.25	–	–	–	36.70	40.59
Denmark	34.5	35.9	37.4	38.9	41.2	36.1	37.6	39.6	39.6	42.0
Finland	..	34.3	34.94	35.13	35.33	..	36.0	37.30	38.71	39.69
France	34.65	33.83	34.35	35.50	35.52	35.10	35.50	36.93	38.61	40.46
Germany	..	31.41	33.46	35.29	39.47	..	33.07	35.62	37.30	41.05
Greece	..	32.61	..	36.30	38.46	..	33.39	..	39.33	41.44
Hungary[2]	..	..	33.61	34.93	38.58	..	..	33.38	35.90	40.57
Iceland	..	..	..	..	..	..	..	..	..	..
Ireland/Irish Rep.[3]	..	..	31.0	33.5	38.53	..	..	30.9	33.8	39.22
Italy	..	33.6	35.68	36.70	38.58	..	33.5	36.01	37.30	40.41
Luxemburg	..	..	..	..	..	..	..	..	..	..
The Netherlands	31.44	33.7	35.9	38.8	41.8	32.16	34.3	37.1	39.5	42.3
Norway	36.28	36.82	37.69	38.83	41.48	30.70	31.14	31.31	32.96	34.89
Poland	–	–	–	36.2[4]	36.0	–	–	–	36.2[4]	38.0
Portugal	..	..	..	38.21[4]	36.76	..	..	..	38.21[4]	41.82
Spain	..	..	31.86	33.69	32.82	..	..	33.28	35.75	38.85
Sweden	32.91	35.10	37.50	40.66	41.13	36.06	37.50	39.31	41.68	42.48
Switzerland	..	31.7	32.9	35.56	38.10	..	33.2	34.7	37.79	41.03
United Kingdom	..	..	..	..	..	..	..	..	..	..
England and Wales	32.76	32.47	33.07	35.81	38.21	33.81	34.75	35.39	38.54	41.22

[1] 1870/80–1906/10 Austrian Empire; 1930–33 Austrian Republic. [2] Data refer to the territory of the Kingdom of Hungary of 1920–46. [3] 1900/2–1910/12 whole island; 1925/27–1940/42 Irish Republic. [4] Average data for both sexes.

CLASS-SPECIFIC DIFFERENCES IN MORTALITY

As in fertility, there were important variations in mortality according to social class during the transition process. The upper classes not only reduced their fertility first but were also pioneers in reducing mortality. The neat link between fertility and mortality decline therefore reappears also on a disaggregated level of societal categories.

Longitudinal results for infant mortality are available for Prussia or Germany (Spree, 1980; see also Rothenbacher, 1989: 162–9). Infant mortality was lowest in the upper strata and highest in the lower strata. During the demographic transition infant mortality in the upper strata fell first and much faster than in the lower strata. In effect, differences in infant mortality rates between the upper and the lower strata widened for several decades, that is, inequality in life chances increased. Only after a delay of several decades were the lower strata able to close this gap somewhat.

TABLE 3.5C Life expectancy in Europe (at age 60)

Country	1850 –69	1870 –89	1890 – 1909	1910– 29	1930 –45	1850 –69	1870 –89	1890 – 1909	1910– 29	1930 –45
			Males					**Females**		
					Life expectancy at age 60					
Austria[1]	..	12,20	12.58	12.86	14.15	..	12.37	12.77	13.32	15.42
Belgium	..	13.73	13.43	..	14.53	..	14.70	14.78	..	15.93
Czechoslovakia	–	–	–	13.65	14.95	–	–	–	14.12	16.02
Denmark	13.5	14.4	15.0	15.8	16.0	14.8	15.8	16.3	16.4	16.6
Finland	..	13.2	13.56	13.99	13.60	..	14.3	15.08	15.82	15.79
France	13.55	13.58	13.91	13.84	13.92	13.90	14.58	15.08	15.63	16.50
Germany	..	12.11	12.82	13.18	15.11	..	12.71	13.60	14.17	16.07
Greece	..	12.92	..	14.93	15.67	..	13.06	..	17.32	17.72
Hungary[2]	..	..	12.88	13.44	15.00	..	..	12.79	13.96	16.03
Iceland	9.6[3]	10.5[3]	9.2[3]	12.2[3]	13.3[3]	11.7[3]	11.7[3]	12.2[3]	13.6[3]	15.5[3]
Ireland/Irish Rep.[4]	..	..	10.8	13.0	15.46	..	..	10.6	13.4	16.17
Italy	..	13.1	13.47	14.10	15.16	..	12.1	13.60	14.36	16.13
Luxemburg	..	..	13.0	14.1	14.8	..	..	13.2	14.8	15,7
The Netherlands	12.57	13.3	14.0	15.1	16.2	13.12	14.1	15.0	15.9	16.8
Norway	15.19	15.63	16.39	16.98	17.22	16.24	16.67	17.46	17.78	18.38
Poland	–	–	–	14.4[5]	13.7	–	–	–	14.4[5]	15.1
Portugal	..	..	..	14.65[5]	14.44	..	..	..	14.65[5]	17.18
Spain	..	..	11.74	12.60	12.43	..	..	12.17	13.75	15.20
Sweden	13.12	14.20	15.44	16.70	16.35	14.04	15.40	16.56	17.51	17.19
Switzerland	..	12.2	12.5	13.26	14.29	..	12.5	13.0	14.40	15.95
United Kingdom	..	..	..	..	..	..	..	..	..	..
England and Wales	13.53	13.31	12.93	13.78	14.43	14.34	14.32	14.10	15.48	16.50

[1] 1870/80–1906/10 Austrian Empire; 1930–33 Austrian Republic. [2] Data refer to the territory of the Kingdom of Hungary of 1920–46. [3] Age 65. [4] 1900/2–1910/12 whole island; 1925/27–1940/42 Irish Republic. [5] Average data for both sexes.

4

Marriage, Legitimacy, Divorce

MARRIAGE PATTERNS IN EUROPE

In 1965, John Hajnal distinguished between the 'European Marriage Pattern' and the 'Non-European Marriage Pattern' (Hajnal, 1965), with the dividing line between the two running from St. Petersburg to Trieste. This model claims to be valid for the time period until roughly 1940. The European marriage pattern is defined by a high age at first marriage, low nuptiality, and a large share of people remaining single for life. By contrast, the non-European marriage pattern is defined by a low age at first marriage, high nuptiality, and a small share of the population remaining single. According to this definition, the whole of Eastern and south-eastern Europe belongs to the non-European marriage pattern. Hajnal's data refer to the time period until roughly 1900; in the subsequent time period, Hajnal concedes modernization processes on both sides: the non-European marriage pattern becoming more like the European marriage pattern and the European more like the non-European marriage pattern. The question here is whether this hypothetical convergence of marriage patterns for the time after 1900 can really be proved (see Rothenbacher, 1998b).

THE UNMARRIED 1850–1945

The share of the population married in the age group of 45–54 years is a good indicator for the development of marriage in a society. Further, it says something about the institutional chances of getting married, and implicitly about economic and social barriers to marriage.

The ideal-typical development of the proportion married is different for European and non-European marriage patterns. The Western European marriage pattern before 1900 is characterized by a small share of married people and a large share of people remaining single. The share of married people in Western Europe rose in general until the 1960s and declined afterwards; the postponement of marriage, the increase in cohabitation, and the growth of divorces all contributed to reducing the share of married persons to return to the old Western European marriage pattern.

The same processes can be seen in the territory of the Eastern European marriage pattern, but in the opposite direction. Firstly, in Eastern Europe before 1900 a very high percentage of the population in the higher age groups was married. Marriage was thus a universal institution. In the first decades of the twentieth century, the share of never-married people increased slightly, but after the 1950s the trend was again reversed in favour of universal marriage. The marriage boom of the 1960s was probably caused by the same influences as in the West. But the structural difference between East and West persisted.

According to existing data, important modifications must be made to Hajnal's results: firstly, the boundary Hajnal gave for the European and non-European marriage pattern concerning the share of never-married people has to be modified. The line from St. Petersburg to Trieste lies too far east: probably all of the Baltic states still belong to the eastern pattern. One thing seems certain: that the former German Empire belongs to the western pattern; but there are surely zones of transition, which can only be traced by regionalization. Poland and Czechoslovakia surely belong to the eastern pattern, and the same is clearly true of Hungary. In addition, the Alpine country of Austria unequivocally belongs to the Western European marriage pattern. Furthermore, universal marriage was dominant in the Mediterranean and still is today. Thus, Spain and Greece still show a clear non-western marriage pattern, though Italy on the other hand reveals a western pattern. At this point a regional disaggregation must be carried out, because it can be hypothesized that the Mezzogiorno is much more similar to Spain. Portugal on the other hand is situated in the middle between the Eastern and the Western European marriage pattern and plays a specific role in demographic history also in other respects. Universal and early marriage is the norm not only in Eastern Europe, but also in the Mediterranean. The geographical space of the European marriage pattern is therefore confined to 'Germanic Europe' (important and unexplained exceptions are France and Italy), although obviously the whole Slavic territory forms a unity, and parts of the Romanic/Greek Mediterranean region obviously also have a universalistic marriage pattern (Table 4.1).

TABLE 4.1 Marriage patterns in Europe

Celibacy rate	Age at marriage	
	High	Low
High	Nordic countries: Sweden, Norway, Finland, Denmark Continent: Austria, Germany, Switzerland, Netherlands, Belgium (nineteenth century) Outlier: Ireland	Italy Belgium (twentieth century) France Portugal (intermediate country) Spain (only 1890–1914) England and Wales Finland (to some extent)
Low	Spain (pre-1890 and post-World War I) Greece (male marriage age) Portugal (intermediate country)	Eastern Europe: Greece (partly) Poland Hungary Czechoslovakia Bulgaria, Romania, Baltic countries

Within the region of the Western European marriage pattern, encircled in this way, important country differences can be detected. A very high and similar share of never-married persons is significant for both Alpine republics Austria and Switzerland, which points to a similar Alpine pattern. Switzerland has the highest rates in this respect. A similar level can be found for Ireland (until 1921 the whole of Ireland, afterwards the Irish Republic (Eire)), which is one of the major special cases in Europe because of its completely deviating demographic history in the nineteenth and twentieth centuries. The major break in Ireland was the famine of 1846 following the failure of the potato harvest and leading to mass emigration. In the second half of the nineteenth century, in contrast to most other Western European countries, Ireland experienced a rising birth rate. Ireland experienced its real demographic transition only in the twentieth century after World War II. The high share of never-married women could be due to the following factors: very few young men in relation to young women because of strong emigration, and a bad economic situation because of the peripheral situation of the country, making early family formation very difficult. Thus, indeed, the marriage rate as compared to Western Europe has been very low; the share of illegitimate children was on a very low level as well, which is quite surprising if one looks at the low marriage rate, the high share of never-married women and the rather low age at first marriage. Here the strong Catholic value orientation of the Irish population has to be mentioned.

A deviating development can be detected for Finland too, where the share of never-married women aged 45–54 years in 1940 was the highest in Europe, at roughly 45%. This singular increase can be seen from the birth cohorts of 1855–64 until those of 1885–94. Afterwards, Finland returned to the general European trend of universalization of marriage. What are the reasons for the deviating development of Finland? First of all, only in the course of the twentieth century did Finland begin to change from an almost entirely agrarian country into an industrial society, accompanied by rapid urbanization, internal rural–urban migration, and therefore a rapid creation of the welfare state. In the nineteenth century, Finland was under the hegemony of the Russian tsar, with colonial status. The strong increase in the number of women remaining single therefore points among other things to a major crisis in the agrarian economy which did not allow for setting up one's own farm, and to the agricultural system of latifundia, in which unmarried labourers worked on landed estates owned by the nobility.

Sweden and Norway show very similar figures, starting with a rising trend until the birth cohorts of about 1885–94. In Denmark, on the other hand, there were many more married women. But in Denmark the share of unmarried women also rose until about 1890. In addition to the group of countries with rising shares of unmarried women in the second half of the nineteenth century, there is a group of countries where the shares had already declined around 1850: The Netherlands, Belgium and Germany, along with Italy and more or less France and England/Wales. The Netherlands and Belgium in particular were very fast to reach universality in marriage.

EXPLANATIONS OF THE PROPORTION OF THE UNMARRIED

No truly general explanation of the high proportion of never-married people can be found in the relevant literature. Hajnal (1965) himself posits that the European marriage pattern only emerged in the sixteenth and seventeenth centuries and that in Europe before then early marriage had been widespread. One initial explanation relies on population sociology: the relatively—in relation to the available resources—high population density in Western Europe led to a situation where marriage was used as instrument for population control. Entry into marriage was controlled and fertility was restricted to marriage. In this way, the authorities were able to control population growth effectively. The higher the age at marriage, the lower the fertility, because women have fewer childbearing years left. The punishment of premarital and non-marital sexuality was another instrument for controlling fertility; this control was so extensive that sexuality before marriage was punished even when the partners were engaged, as shown by the fact that fines were imposed on women giving birth to a child less than seven months after marriage (in parts of Germany; see Gröwer, 1998 and 1999; also cf. Mitterauer, 1979 and 1983).

The authorities' control of fertility was neatly bound to the economic system. The relation of production to the household and the restriction of procreation to married people led to a reduction in the number of desired full-time positions (for craftsmen). Both the towns and the country were strongly stratified; there was an important distinction between the craftsman and the day labourer in the towns, and between the propertied farmers (with large farms) and the landless day labourers. The social structure of the country differed furthermore by region: those in which inheritance law favoured a principal heir, resulting in large farms, and those in which the inheritance was divided equally, resulting in small farms. In some regions of southern Europe (Sicily, Portugal, Spain), large latifundia estates owned by the nobility and employing a large number of dependent labourers predominated.

In the cities, the introduction of the guild system was intended to protect the income of craftsmen by regulating access to crafts positions. The institution of vocational education at this time must be seen in this context. Young people were trained in the household via the stages of apprentice, journeyman, and finally master craftsman. The institution of the journey had the intended and unintended consequence of deferring economic self-sufficiency. Another effect, especially because vocational education usually took place in households other than the own family, was the learning and diffusion of new products and technologies of production. The highly developed manufacturing economy of Western Europe has to be seen in relation to these institutions. These institutions taken together with the high age at marriage led to a high qualification of labourers in comparison to all non-European regions. Whether this long period of vocational training was a functional prerequisite of the advanced manufacturing industry in Western Europe or whether family formation should have been postponed, is difficult to decide.

By contrast, in those regions where the principal heir inherited the property (primogeniture), family formation was bound to the transmission of the estate which in some cases occurred very late (not before the heir was 30 or 40 years old), and marriage was linked to the taking over of the farm. The parents retired on the farm (*Altenteil*). Regions where inheritance law called for a principal heir can be found predominantly in areas with extensive monasterial property; thus, the hypothesis is plausible that this agrarian structure was created specially to ensure the efficient supply of goods to the monasteries. In those regions where the Reformation was successful, equal inheritance can be found. Whether this form of economy was created by the secularization of monasterial property or later on by the actions of the authorities influenced by egalitarian Protestantism cannot be decided here. In any case, the difference in population growth between both forms of economic organization is obvious: the regions of equal inheritance show much higher population growth. In regions with a principal heir the illegitimacy rates were much higher, pointing to the high proportion of never-married persons. This argumentation is especially valid for southern Germany; in the old Prussian provinces conditions were very different, because Prussia was only lightly populated until about 1800 (policy of *Peuplement* in the eighteenth century). In addition, Prussia was outside the old city belt and had little manufacturing. One may ask to what extent the argumentation represented by population sociology (Thomas Malthus) is valid for other European countries, too.

A second explanation is provided by Goody (1983), who argues that the Catholic Church was essentially interested in standardizing and monopolizing marriage in order to secure its own power position. Thus, for centuries the Catholic Church tried to influence and monopolize the Christian type of marriage. The following questions emerge: what consequences did the Reformation have for this claim of monopoly? Did the Reformation also have important consequences for the monopoly on marriage? The first birth cohorts for which data are available relate to the year 1800. Here one can see that in most Western European countries unmarried women aged 45–54 amounted to roughly 30%, without any systematic differences between the Protestant North and the Catholic South. On the contrary, in Denmark and Norway a rather higher proportion of women were married than in Catholic Italy and Belgium. If the religious factor plays any role, then Protestantism led rather to egalitarian chances of marrying, while Catholicism led rather to unequal chances of marrying. One should keep in mind that in Catholic countries there was a tendency towards celibate forms of living, as shown by the—at that time still numerous—priests, monks, and nuns. On the whole, the idea of celibacy and asceticism was much more widespread in Catholicism than in egalitarian Protestantism.

AGE AT MARRIAGE

Making the right to marry dependent on certain economic preconditions was one way of regulating marriages; the other was to regulate age at marriage. Age at marriage is directly related to fertility and population growth, because all other things being equal, it defines the period of fertility. There are also relations between nuptiality and the rate of illegitimacy. A long-term analysis of women's age at marriage is limited by data availability; data for age at first marriage are only available for a few countries. In most countries, mean age at marriage tended to decline from the 1930s until the 1960s, with the exception of the period from the 1930s to the 1940s, when age at first marriage increased slightly. Only after the wave of marriages in the course of the 'second demographic transition' did mean age at marriage decline by 2–3 years, followed again after the 1960s by a strong increase. The long-term decline in age at marriage is related to the rising proportion of people married. There was not only a growing universalization of marriage up to the 1960s, but also at the same time a tendency towards marriage at younger ages.

The territorial clustering of European marriage behaviour is in general based on Hajnal (1965); for this variable too, Hajnal found a difference between Western Europe and the other European regions. Looking at the data, already around 1850 the Nordic countries Norway and Sweden in particular had a very high age at marriage, as did Switzerland. A low age at marriage can be found for England/Wales and Italy. One may ask whether these results are reinforced by the alternative indicator of 'married women aged 20–24 years'. Denmark, Belgium, and The Netherlands belong to the group with a high age at marriage and therefore a low ratio with respect to this indicator. The Western European group with a low age at marriage and accordingly a high rate of married women is made up of England/Wales, France, Italy, and Spain. The German Empire, Portugal, and Finland occupy a middle position. The group of countries with a non-European marriage pattern and therefore a low age at marriage and a high proportion of married people emerges again here: it can be very clearly seen for Hungary, Poland, and Greece, as well as Czechoslovakia. The big anomaly in this respect is again Ireland, with an increase in age at marriage and a corresponding decline in the share of married women until the 1930s. A similar pattern can be found for Spain and Finland.

The development since the mid-1960s has to be presented with reference to the 'second demographic transition'. In all European countries the marriage boom— even for those with a non-European marriage pattern—led to a decline in age at marriage or a historically unique increase in the rate of the proportion married. In most countries mean age at marriage was lowest around 1970 and later returned to the old pattern or even exceeded the historical figures. Eastern and Western Europe show a big difference in this respect. In Poland, Hungary, and Czechoslovakia only a small increase in age at marriage or no decrease in the share of married people until the 1990s can be found. Poland and Hungary in particular differ significantly from the general European pattern. One explanation could be that the extreme housing shortages resulted in a higher marriage rate, because only married couples were able to get their own flat. The small flats were probably an incentive for leaving the family of origin at an early age. The patterns from 1850 were still rather stable in 1990. The postponement of marriage has progressed most in the Nordic countries and in Switzerland and Ireland. A continuing low age at marriage is found in the Mediterranean countries Italy, Spain, Greece, and Portugal; France and England/Wales are rather in the middle. All in all, there are signs of a growing divergence within Western Europe.

Until now, the discussion has focused only on women. The marriage pattern of men naturally follows that of women, if one looks at the mean age at first marriage and the proportion of married men aged 20–24, though at a different level. Changes in the sex relation of these variables can be found by calculating the age difference between men and women in age at first marriage or the per cent difference in age of married males and females aged 20–24. The second half of the nineteenth century reveals in principle two country clusters. On the one hand, in Western Europe a very high per cent difference can be found in France, Italy, Spain, and Austria-Hungary. The second cluster with a small age difference is made up of all four Nordic countries, along with England/Wales, Ireland, Belgium, The Netherlands, Switzerland, and Austria. Germany takes an intermediate position. Ireland again reveals a strongly deviating pattern with a decreasing age difference until the 1930s, whereas the general trend for all countries until the 1960s is a growing age difference. The growing age difference of both country clusters until the mid-1960s shows a certain tendency towards convergence; afterwards, the divergence is stronger than before. In the mid-1960s the growing age difference of the marriage partners suddenly became a decreasing age difference, although only for the Nordic countries, England/Wales, Ireland, Germany, Austria, and Switzerland. Portugal, Spain, Italy, and Belgium lagged behind in this respect.

A completely different development is characteristic for the non-European marriage pattern: in Greece, Czechoslovakia, Hungary, and Poland the age difference even increased or the decrease in the age difference was much smaller than in Western Europe. Especially for Greece until 1980 the age at marriage for men and women strongly diverged. Already in 1900, the Greek pattern was known for its great age difference between marriage partners. Women married very early, and an age difference of five to 10 years continues to be nothing unusual in Greece. This surprisingly stable element of Greek society seems to be a structural trait and a cultural pattern of the familistic Greek society, where until recently the power of the paterfamilias and the relatives was strong. The Greek family is known for its emphasis on strategic marriages, thinking of marriage as 'business' and orientated towards enlarging the family fortune. The idea of free choice of marriage partners and a free 'marriage market' is less important. The idea of virginity of women still plays an important role, as demonstrated for Mediterranean societies (Goody, 1983). In addition, the concepts of male honour and the honour of the family together with a strong religious orientation and nearly exclusive monopoly of marriage still have a decisive influence on family formation. Another factor in the early marriage of women is the impossibility of free sexuality and therefore of illegitimate births. The number of illegitimate births is still rather low in Greece. The early marriage of women does not mean that fertility has to be very high; Greece currently has among the lowest fertility in Europe. Men's high age at marriage is based in culture as well as in the economy. A semi-peripheral and for a long time colonial country, Greece has struggled since the formation of the nation-state with severe economic problems, resulting in massive emigration. Measured by the quantity of natural and economic resources, population growth—though moderate compared to other European countries—was still too high for this country. In addition, there was considerable migration to the urban centres, making the metropolis of Athens–Piraeus one of the biggest urban agglomerations of Europe. Nearly every second Greek is now living in the Athens metropolitan area. One decisive factor for men's high age at marriage is the difficulty of making a living; young Greek men often emigrate and return after some years, mainly to set up their own business. Self-employment is important in Greek society; the share of self-employment is very high and small businesses make up a dominant element of the economy. The semi-peripheral position of the country is characterized by an underdeveloped industry, a still strong agricultural sector, and a relatively strong public sector—if one takes the many large state enterprises into consideration. The employment possibilities in industry are limited, and agriculture is still strongly subsistence-oriented and suffers from low productivity. What remains is the flight into the private service sector (of tourism) or employment in the public sector.

Hungary, Poland, and Czechoslovakia also still display the typical low age at marriage for women and the large age difference between marriage partners. In addition to the factors discussed for Greece, these countries are influenced by the former socialist planned economy with serious problems of supply, especially in the housing sector; therefore, claim to a flat was only possible in the case of marriage.

Important factors for the postponement of marriage for both sexes, but especially for women, can be seen in the educational expansion of the 1960s which increased the proportion of women in education and consequently the participation of women in higher education. In all peripheral countries (Ireland, Portugal, and Greece), the proportion of persons in tertiary education is markedly below average; this factor alone would imply a lower age at marriage, because marriage only occurs after getting a degree. Furthermore, it is worth noting that there is apparently a positive relation between a low share of students in tertiary education and a high share of women in this sector. In the peripheral countries alone, the proportion of women in tertiary education clearly exceeds 50%. Obviously men in these countries are looking for a career in other economic sectors. The overall low participation in the tertiary educational sector in peripheral countries has consequences for activity rates, because men's educational participation postpones setting up a business and therefore leads to higher age at marriage. The same is true for most women: one may assume that women with university education not only marry later, but are much more interested in remaining at work for a longer time. In a cross-sectional perspective there is a clear positive bivariate relationship between the global activity rate and the age at first marriage of women in EU12 countries (Rothenbacher, 1997b: 111, Figure 3). The higher women's activity rate, the later they marry. Apart from cultural factors, early marriage of women in the peripheries is therefore also due to economic motives, i.e. fewer economic chances for women and a smaller proportion in tertiary education. Women in peripheral countries are not less interested in participating in the labour market, but there are not enough opportunities for them to work.

To conclude: in a long-term perspective, the European marriage pattern became more similar to the non-European marriage pattern until the mid-1960s, resulting in a certain convergence of marriage patterns until about 1960. After 1960 there was partly a return to the old patterns or levels, and partly a growing divergence.

DEVELOPMENT OF THE MARRIAGE RATE

The liberalization of marriage entry in Western Europe in the second half of the nineteenth century resulted in a steady increase in nuptiality. This proposition, valid in a long-term perspective, has to be differentiated according to historical periods. For nearly all Western European countries, in the second half of the nineteenth century the marriage rate remained at a constant level or showed a slight downward trend (in order to enable long-term comparisons, the marriage rate is defined here as persons marrying per 100 unmarried persons aged 15+). From the First World War until the 1960s the marriage rate increased. During the transition period of the 1960s, the marriage rate fell below the level of the nineteenth century. The major trend up to the 1960s was therefore the generalization of the institution of marriage for the whole population. The decline in nuptiality since the 1960s cannot be explained by family law regulations, because precisely in this domain major liberalization has taken place. On the contrary, this decline in nuptiality has to be related to socio-demographic and socio-economic factors. One of the central factors could be the rising educational participation of women resulting in the postponement of marriage. In general, women's increasing economic autonomy is a central factor, reducing the incentives to marry. Another factor could be the rise in divorces and the declining tendency to remarry. The development of nuptiality is furthermore related to the legal status of cohabitation, which varies considerably throughout Europe. In the Scandinavian countries, especially Sweden, the differences between marriage and cohabitation have largely been removed. In other countries such as Germany there has been no move to make the two legally equivalent, although nuptiality has declined and cohabitation has risen.

Marriage behaviour is highly influenced by exogenous events such as wars and economic crises. These influences can be detected for the Franco-Prussian War of 1870/71, but especially for World War I. The effects of World War II were much smaller, as in other areas too (e.g., food supply). The influence of wars on the marriage rate follows a continuous pattern: a drop in the marriage rate at the beginning and at the end of the war. After the war, the postponed marriages are made up, leading to a peak in the marriage rate. This pattern of war influence is normally repeated for economic crises as well. Thus, the Great Depression of 1929–33 had significant consequences for the marriage rate. In countries seriously affected by the Great Depression, the marriage rate declined in the 1930s, but not to the same degree as in the First World War (cf. on this point Ungern-Sternberg, 1937a).

There is tremendous variation between European countries concerning nuptiality. Firstly, the distinction between the European and non-European marriage pattern should be made. The European marriage pattern is again visible for Hungary, Poland, Czechoslovakia, and in the post-war period also for the German Democratic Republic. In addition, the Mediterranean countries Greece, Portugal, Spain, and Italy (around 1900) show a very high nuptiality. The Nordic countries still have a very low marriage rate. For the period 1850–1900 the marriage rate of Belgium and Switzerland was also very low. There are clear interrelations to the other two variables of the European marriage pattern, the never-married and the age at marriage. The marriage rate is the lower/higher, the higher/lower the share of never-married and the higher/lower the age at first marriage. The outlier in this pattern is again Ireland, whose marriage rate for the whole period was very much below the level of other Western European countries. Ireland has to be discussed as a deviating case on the whole.

FROM UNIVERSALIZATION OF MARRIAGE TO DEINSTITUTIONALIZATION

Until the end of the nineteenth century, in many countries access to marriage was restricted to persons having a certain amount of assets. This regulation did not originate in the *ancien régime*, but was introduced in the first half of the nineteenth century to avoid the pauperization of broad segments of the population. The towns in particular feared the burdens of providing communal care for the aged and the sick caused by the growing population exceeding the positions available in the labour market. Marriage was often the precondition for access to political rights, such as the communal right to vote, and thus was highly valued. Access to marriage was restricted particularly in the southern German states until 1867, whereas Prussia was more liberal in this respect (Matz, 1980). Marriage restrictions were removed in the territory of the Federation of Northern Germany (*Norddeutscher Bund*) with the federal treaty (*Bundesordnung*) of 1867 and for the whole of Germany in 1871. After that it was no longer necessary to have a certain income in order to marry. Marriage restrictions were also found in some other continental countries such as Switzerland. In general, the legal barriers to marriage were removed only in the last third of the nineteenth century. In all German states (Kraus, 1979) and in many European countries, there was a slight increase in the marriage rate in the 1870s (Prinzing, 1902). After the legal barriers to marriage had been removed, social and economic barriers increasingly came to the forefront, as Max Marcuse noted already in 1907 (Marcuse, 1907). Economic and social developments such as the spread of female employment, the increase in educational participation, the growth of employment in the public sector, and longer time spent in education were new checks on the freedom to marry. These factors could be significant for the stagnating or declining nuptiality in Western Europe up to 1914.

The general trend in all European countries over the last 150 years is thus the universalization of the right to marry for all population groups and a declining interest of the state in marriage law. The law still regulates the age at marriage and the sex of the marriage partners and bars incestuous and polygamous marriages (Glendon, 1989: 38ff.). In a long-term perspective, the importance of bourgeois marriage as a model of familial behaviour increased after 1850. Thus, the general tendency can be called universalization of marriage regardless of social status and income position.

Since the 1960s a trend in the opposite direction has appeared, in family sociology called the 'deinstitutionalization of marriage and family' (Tyrell, 1990; Kaufmann, 1990; see also Meyer, 1993). Based on the sociological tradition of institutional analysis, it is claimed that the 'bourgeois' (or middle-class) family as a highly institionalized model was valid until the 1960s, and that since then a reversal of this model has occurred. Institutionalization of marriage as a long-term process should therefore mean the societal acceptance of the model of the 'bourgeois' family, understood as the Parsonian nuclear family consisting of parents and two children.

This problem can be dealt with under different aspects: first, the legal aspect of family and marriage law which create explicit norms. One may ask whether in this domain there are important processes of institutionalization and subsequently processes of deinstitutionalization. Second, the question concerning social structural changes has to be raised, exerting possible effects on these processes. Third, a society cannot be seen as a homogeneous block but must be analysed as a stratified system with class-specific family and related social behaviour.

Starting with the last point of social stratification, it can be argued that the 'bourgeois' ideal of marriage already existed in the nineteenth century in some population groups and was imitated by other social strata. In Germany, the acceptance of bourgeois marriage can be described as a process of diffusion, with the 'bourgeoisie' taking over the leading role; factory workers and employees in particular tried to imitate this ideal, but under the special political and economic circumstances of nineteenth-century Germany it could not be realized until the 1960s on the basis of the historically unique 'economic miracle'. By this time, the old innovators, the 'bourgeoisie' (the intellectuals), had already established other familial patterns; thus, a reversal of the bourgeois marriage model was established.

A second line of argumentation starts with changes in the structure of society and the economy, in Germany enabling the realization of the bourgeois marriage norm only in the 1960s. The robust growth of the welfare state and the later expansion of the educational sector led to new tendencies, questioning the 'bourgeois model' of marriage from the perspective of changes in the social structure. From the perspective of changes in marriage and family law one may argue that family law cannot be separated from changes in the social and economic structure. Whereas in the nineteenth century the bourgeois family model was still to be established (as indicated by the treatment of illegitimate children), in the twentieth century there is an obvious trend towards liberalizing marriage and family law. Here again the treatment of illegitimate children, increasingly destigmatized and directed at equal rights, is indicative. This can be seen furthermore in destigmatizing the mother of the illegitimate child (lone parents); the 'new' lone parents probably no longer come from the lower strata as they did before 1945, but rather from higher income levels (lone parent as 'lifestyle' and not as social problem). The liberalization of divorce law did not begin with the reforms of the 1970s, but is a long-term process with small legal steps. A general tendency is the higher value of the child. An economic interpretation looks at the secular birth decline as a shortage of the commodity 'child'; in economic theory this would lead to a higher value or price of the commodity 'child'. For society the child in itself and each child is becoming more valuable, and the 'price' of a child is rising. Whereas in the nineteenth century illegitimate children had very low chances of survival, the illegitimate child in the course of the twentieth century has been revalued fundamentally, because in times of reduced supply all children are important. The same is true for the mother of an illegitimate child, whose position has improved significantly. Another tendency can be seen on the medical side in the largely successful fight against infant mortality.

Deinstitutionalization can be measured empirically by demographic changes and changes in family structure since the 'second demographic transition', that is, the 'new' demographic and familial behavioural patterns and structures.

MARRIAGE AND LEGITIMACY

According to Goody (1983), in a long-term perspective the conjugal family as it exists today—with the monopoly on reproduction—is a product of Christianity, fighting for centuries against non-marital and extra-marital relationships and thus creating the problem of illegitimacy. A perspective orientated much more in economic history argues that illegitimacy is heavily bound to the respective mode of production. Thus, surprisingly, one of the highest proportions of illegitimacy in history was found in Catholic countries (Bavaria, Austria). The influence of the Church as monocausal factor is therefore not a sufficient explanation. In agricultural societies the extent of illegitimacy was among other things also dependent on the regulations of agriculture. Illegitimacy was fairly high in regions with single farms and inheritance by the principal heir; the structure of the agrarian economy in latifundia or family economies may also have played a role. Other factors, especially since the nineteenth century, are liberalization and the growth of lower strata in the process of industrialization. Another chain of argumentation could be that the extent of illegitimacy mainly depends on other demographic factors. Thus, the lower the age at marriage and/or the proportion of persons married, the lower the share of illegitimate births. Another important factor is probably the legal status of the illegitimate child, which differed greatly from country to country. In some German regions with inheritance law of the principle heir (Hindelang, 1909) and in Austria premarital, non-marital and extra-marital children were highly welcome as labourers and proof of fertility, explaining the very high rates in these regions (Mitterauer and Sieder, 1982; Mitterauer, 1983).

Using the indicator of illegitimate births per 10,000 unmarried women aged 15–44 as an indicator of illegitimacy, in Europe births outside marriage decreased until 1939. This decrease is accompanied by a synchronous convergence. In those countries involved in the Second World War, the rate went up after the war, to stabilize at a higher level. Since the mid-1960s, births outside marriage have risen substantially, leading to new divergences.

The alternative indicator of illegitimate births as percentage of all live births shows a remarkable constancy in the level of illegitimacy from 1850 until the 1960s, only slightly exceeding 20%, with the exception of Austria, whose rate was the highest in

Europe until the 1960s (cf. Mitterauer, 1979). Most recently, in Austria illegitimacy is moving towards the European average (EU12).

The question of illegitimate births is neatly related to the institutional regulation of marriage. In the territory of the European marriage pattern with high age at marriage, out-of-wedlock births were numerous. On the other hand, in the regions of the non-European marriage pattern illegitimate births were rare.

A study by Shorter, Knodel, and van de Walle (1971) on the decline of illegitimate fertility uses an index of fertility which relates the decline of illegitimate births to the number of unmarried women of childbearing age. This index is more exact than the rate of illegitimate births as per cent of all births, which does not reveal the fact that in Europe since the nineteenth century fertility decreased overall. The relative stability of the latter indicator until the 1960s therefore means only that fertility on the whole decreased, both illegitimate and legitimate. The calculations of the 'index of illegitimate fertility' demonstrate clearly that in most European countries, illegitimate fertility increased until the end of the nineteenth century, but then followed the path of legitimate fertility (Shorter, Knodel, and van de Walle, 1971: 377). Hungary, Austria, and Portugal deviate greatly from the level of other countries.

The singular development in Portugal—compared to other Mediterranean countries—is explained by the peculiarities of Portuguese society in the nineteenth century. Portugal's loss of the colony of Brazil created nearly insoluble economic problems. Portugal had been much more densely populated than its neighbour Spain, and population growth in Portugal was one of the highest in nineteenth-century Europe. Portugal in the nineteenth century was characterized by a principal imbalance between demographic and economic development. The consequences of this development were strong emigration, mainly to Brazil, the ageing of the population, a surplus of women, and a low marriage rate. According to a study by Livi-Bacci (1971: 71ff.), Portugal's high illegitimacy rate in the nineteenth century can be related to several factors. In some districts in the north of the country, illegitimacy was as high as in Austria or Sweden, due to the surplus of women as a result of male emigration, the low nuptiality, and the large share of women remaining single. In the south, illegitimacy was high, too, but for different reasons: not emigration, but the system of latifundia with landless farm labourers was the decisive factor. The custom of living together without marriage prevailed and marriage often took place only after the birth of the second child.

Another deviating case is represented by Hungary (and the whole of south-eastern Europe north of the Danube) with a very high illegitimacy rate, which would contradict the non-European marriage pattern. The Hungarian situation was very similar in this respect to the Austrian conditions. Interestingly, marital fertility around 1870 was in a middle range, and total fertility was very high in many provinces of this region. Additionally, the proportion of women married around 1870 was one of the highest in Europe and is therefore compatible with the non-European marriage pattern. The big difference between total fertility and marital fertility leads to the hypothesis of a high illegitimate fertility. The high share of married women only allows for children being born before marriage and being legitimized later through marriage. This interpretation is also presented by Shorter, Knodel, and van de Walle (1971: 388), who suppose that the cultural pattern of consensual unions was responsible for the high rates of illegitimacy.

Deviating from this pattern is Austria, where the 'index of illegitimate fertility' was higher than the legitimate fertility index during the whole demographic transition. In Scandinavia, (especially Sweden) and also England and Wales, the disproportional growth of illegitimate fertility can be seen already before 1960, becoming the dominant feature by 1960 (Shorter, Knodel, and van de Walle, 1971: 378).

GROWTH OF DIVORCES AND LIBERALIZATION OF DIVORCE LAW

The dissolution of marriage was not possible until the beginning of the nineteenth century, when it was only possible in some cases, if at all. The grounds for divorce were very limited. Between 1920 and 1965 there were no fundamental changes in divorce legislation, in contrast to the development in divorce rates. Exceptions can be seen in a longer list of grounds for divorce in England (1937) and the divorce legislation of the National Socialists in Germany and Austria (1938). Northern European divorce law is characterized by its flexibility. In Scandinavia there is a wide range of grounds for divorce and it is possible to get a divorce after a certain phase of marital separation, indicating the existence of the principle of breakdown of a marriage and divorce by mutual consent. In the United Kingdom flexibility is provided by the common-law system, based on case law and the principle of legal precedent, which gives the judge greater autonomy in deciding. In other parts of Europe divorce law is bound much more by legal regulation. The countries with law based on the Napoleonic Code—France, Belgium, Luxemburg, and The Netherlands—can be distinguished from Germany and Austria, with the German law tradition based on the civil code (*Bürgerliches Gesetzbuch* (BGB)); the BGB also exerts its influence on Swiss divorce legislation. The Code Napoléon was in principle valid until the 1970s. Divorce legislation based on the BGB was not as liberal as that based on the Code Napoléon. The BGB allowed for divorce only in case of violation of marital duties, and divorce by mutual consent was accepted only in a few cases.

Divorce reform legislation of the 1970s (Switzerland did not enact any reform legislation) can generally be characterized as a liberalization of divorce law, with the following features:

- an extension of the principle of divorce by mutual consent;
- an extension of the principle of breakdown of marriage after a period of separation varying between countries;
- a weakening of the principle of punishment; need rather than marital fault is used to determine maintenance and the right to child custody;
- strengthening of judges' authority and autonomy.

Two types of reform can be distinguished: general new legal reforms or modifications of existing laws. Countries that enacted general reforms (England 1969, The Netherlands 1971, Sweden 1973, Scotland and the Federal Republic of Germany 1976) often did so before countries that only modified existing laws (France 1975, Luxemburg and Austria 1978). The Mediterranean countries also introduced the whole range of grounds for divorce, from divorce due to marital fault to divorce by mutual consent (Italy 1970 and 1975; Portugal 1975 and 1977; Greece 1976, and Spain 1971) (Festy, 1985: 7ff.).

Until World War I divorce rates (defined as divorcing persons per 10,000 married persons aged 15+) in all European countries were very low, though growing at a slow but continuous pace. Both world wars led to a higher level of divorce. The strongest influence on the divorce rate was exerted by the divorce reforms of the 1970s. The long-term development of the divorce rate reveals a step-by-step increase. The very strong increase in divorce figures in the 1970s was followed in the 1980s and early 1990s by a consolidation at a high level with some small decreases. The increase in divorces is largely caused by the change in divorce law, but cannot be explained sufficiently by this factor. Changes in the levels after both world wars—with almost no modifications in divorce legislation—point to social structural changes with consequences for divorce behaviour.

Differences in divorce law in European countries prior to the reforms of the 1970s determined differences in divorce rates. Divorce rates in the Scandinavian countries were higher already before the reforms due to rather easy access to divorce. Countries with the Code Napoléon were characterized by low divorce rates. Countries with German law based on the German civil code (BGB) had figures lying between those of Scandinavia and the countries of the Code Napoléon. In the Mediterranean countries divorce was not possible for a long time, and divorce rates were very low. In Switzerland divorce rates exceeded the European average already in the 1880s.

The growing divergence in the development of the divorce rate is visible already before 1914, because the Southern European countries did not participate in this development. In Europe there are two country clusters. The one with the lowest divorce rates is composed of Greece, Italy, Portugal, and Spain (for these countries no data are available) and Poland (besides Cyprus, Yugoslavia, Bulgaria, and Romania). The cluster with the highest rates is composed of the Nordic countries and Great Britain. The countries of the continent in general show lower rates than the Northern European countries; Switzerland, Austria, the Federal Republic of Germany, Belgium, Hungary, and The Netherlands display very similar figures.

It is possible to describe the development of the divorce rate using the model of the logistic growth curve. Especially remarkable are the changes in level, interpreted by the model of logistic growth as new growth phases. Within Europe the divorce rate reveals the biggest divergence in a secular perspective.

Explanations of the growth in divorces can be seen on the one hand in the liberalization of divorce. On the other hand, cultural factors such as the importance of religion should not be underestimated. Furthermore, divorces covary according to the general level of wealth in a society, making it possible to afford the higher costs of splitting one household into two separate parts. Furthermore, welfare-state policies may alleviate the consequences of divorce, producing side-effects in the form of divorce incentives.

DIVORCES AND LEGAL SEPARATIONS

The relationship between divorces and legal separations takes the following forms: the first and oldest, in which divorce is forbidden and legal separation is used as a functional equivalent for divorce; the second, in which there is the possibility to choose between divorce and legal separation; and the third, in which a longer period of legal separation must precede divorce.

Type 1. In most Catholic countries, divorce was not allowed in principle until the beginning of the nineteenth century. In the Southern European Catholic countries of Italy, Spain, and Portugal divorce was introduced only in the 1970s. Ireland was the last European country to introduce divorce after a referendum on divorce reform in 1995, in which only a small majority voted to introduce divorce.

Type 2. Catholic France introduced divorce already in 1804 through the Code Napoléon; in 1816 divorce was abolished again and replaced with legal separation. Divorce was not reintroduced until 1884. This type, in which the possibility of legal separation is maintained as an alternative to divorce, is found in Switzerland, France, Belgium, The Netherlands, and also the United Kingdom. The absolute numbers of legal separations are very small in all these countries, and the legal separation rate has not changed significantly since the end of the nineteenth century.

Type 3. The pioneer for this form of regulation was Sweden. Since the Reformation divorce was possible according to the principle of fault. In 1915 divorce in the case of marriage breakdown or by mutual consent was introduced after a certain period of separation. Separation was thus introduced as a first stage of divorce, though it did not lead necessarily to divorce. In 1973 in Sweden divorce law was reformed and the precondition of legal separation was abolished. The Swedish example was imitated in 1918 by Norway and in the 1920s by Denmark, Finland, and Iceland. In Finland legal separation, and thus indirectly the possibility of divorce by mutual consent, was introduced in 1948. In Denmark a similar divorce law reform as in Sweden in 1973 was carried out already in 1969. Legal separation no longer plays an important role. In Norway the divorce law of 1909 is still valid, with minor modifications. Legal separation has to precede divorce. In Italy only legal separation was allowed until the introduction of divorce in 1970; following the Nordic model, a phase of marital separation as a precondition for divorce was introduced.

The empirical development of legal separation as opposed to divorce (indicators: separated versus divorced persons per 10,000 married persons aged 15+) reveals two groups of countries. On the one hand are those countries where separation is the first step to divorce, firstly the Scandinavian countries Norway and Finland. In Sweden this phase was abolished in 1973 through the divorce reform. This pattern is additionally important in Italy, where legal separations greatly exceed divorces and not every legal separation ends in divorce. The rates for legal separations in the Scandinavian countries are on a comparable level with divorces; that is, nearly all separations end in divorce. In addition, in some countries legal separation exists as an alternative to divorce. This group includes Switzerland, France, The Netherlands, and Belgium. The rate of legal separations did not increase very much—in contrast to the divorce rate—since the end of the nineteenth century. Legal separations in these countries are only solutions for specific population groups who do not want a divorce for religious or economic reasons.

In Portugal, legislation on legal separations and divorces is laid down in the Civil Code, articles 1792, 1779, and 1781 (INE, 1984: IX). Between 1940 and 1975 Catholic marriages in Portugal could not be dissolved, which explains the very low divorce rate during this period (see INE, 1995: 38f.).

In the nineteenth century, unmarried cohabitation or relationships were very much more frequent than has been recorded because such relationships were not registered by official statistics. Only in recent years has the phenomenon of frequent cohabitation or unmarried sexual relationships been dealt with by demographers and historians (see Leridon, 1989 and Gröwer, 1998 and 1999 on this topic). The existence of these relationships is one of the main reasons for high illegitimate fertility. Other reasons are the structure of agriculture, legal and social barriers to marriage (e.g. laws against marriage under certain conditions in southern Germany until 1867; social barriers such as marriage bans for civil servants and female teachers; economic crises, long education, emigration of young men (Portugal), etc.).

This is one of the major trends in the field of family and marriage. In 1850, there were more or less no divorces and very few separations. Marriage was *de facto* a lifelong institution. But unlike today, life expectancy was not very high, and many men died already in their 40s, and very many women died in childbirth or afterwards. Therefore, in historical terms, marriages were predominantly dissolved by death of a spouse, and second and third marriages—creating many step-families—were very common.

5

Households and Families

This introductory chapter deals with the micro-level of households and families. Families and households are the smallest social units in a society, apart from individuals. Macro-social changes are seen as the framework and causal factors for changes in household and family. Here, households and families are seen as adaptive social units rather than innovative and active ones ('external approach': see Hoffmann-Nowotny, 1996; Kaufmann, 1995). According to the external approach, impetus for change can come from technological innovations, from a change in the system of production, or from changes in the legal system. Several theoretical approaches try to explain family change: (1) economic theories take the primacy of technology and economic rationality for granted. Accordingly, social changes are seen as being caused by technological innovations that modify the economic system and ultimately exert essential influence on the family structure and the legal system. (2) A more sociological tradition emphasizes ideational factors of culture or ideas and hypothesizes that values and behavioural patterns change and therefore influence changes in the family structure. (3) A third line of theory hypothesizes that autonomous changes in the legal system lead to social and familial change. The economic approach, however, postulates that the legal system only plays a reactive role. (4) The functional differentiation approach (Durkheim, Parsons, Smelser) postulates that with the differentiation of society in the general process of modernization, households became more homogeneous. Since institutions in traditional societies were less differentiated, households were subject to a much stronger functional differentiation. The homogenization of households led to a homogenization of household structure. In the 1960s a counter-trend started, leading to a new pluralization of household and family structures and showing new tendencies towards a further dissolution of the family. Repeated divergence and convergence ('doppelte Schere', Gerhard Mackenroth) can thus be observed, where the older patterns disappear and new patterns or processes of substitution emerge (Wall, 1997, 1998; Rothenbacher, 1995, 1997a, 1998b; Rothenbacher and Putz, 1987; Roussel, 1992; Council of Europe, 1990; Commaille and de Singly, 1996).

FROM THE EXTENDED TO THE NUCLEAR FAMILY:
NUCLEARIZATION UP TO THE 1960s

Here the question arises as to what the term *traditional family* actually means. Essential characteristics of this family type are marriage as the starting point of a family, a high valuation and monopoly of marriage and family (e.g. in electoral law), exclusivity of marriage in the sense that not everyone can marry, i.e. high celibacy rates; no limiting of births, since high mortality reduces fertility. Marriage is principally seen as a lifelong institution, but high mortality rates for both sexes mean that surviving spouses remarry. Planning one's life course and life expectancy are impossible due to 'natural checks' (Thomas Malthus, 1992(1798)); life expectancy is low, and one or both partners usually dies after the sixtieth year of life at the latest. Family relationships are unstable due to the high mortality rate, leading to a high remarriage rate and many step-families, some in which both natural parents have died and children have only social and legal parents. The necessity to take on both parental roles (*Rollenergänzungszwang*, Michael Mitterauer) due to remarriage is very high. The traditional family is thus characterized by a very high level of insecurity and the inability to control environmental influences and social conditions.

By contrast, the *modern family* is characterized by the fact that its living conditions can be planned to a large extent, by a high degree of social security and of safety from life-threatening conditions. The general increase in 'security' has encouraged notions of being able to plan for the future and even the claim to a certain length of life. The social security especially of women, but also of men, has amplified trends towards individualization (Zapf et al., 1987), opened up possibilities for living alone, and destroyed the idea of the indissolubility of marriage. Increased affluence makes possible the concepts of 'enjoying life' and 'having it all', which in turn have repercussions on the family.

FROM LARGE HOUSEHOLDS TO SMALL FAMILIES:
DECLINE IN HOUSEHOLD AND FAMILY SIZE

One of the most obvious processes of change in household and family structures is the trend towards the small modern family. The traditional household was large and often included household members who did not belong to the family (such as servants, boarders, and lodgers) or relatives (lateral relatives or grandparents, i.e. an extended household) and, finally, several children. The households and families of today are rather small, because household members who do not belong to the nuclear family have disappeared as a social category; lateral relatives and the third generation live outside the household. Furthermore, the number of children born to a family has decreased. On average, households[1] and families have become much smaller (Table 5.1). The proportion of small households has grown significantly, while the proportion of larger households has declined substantially. A further decline has occurred due to an increase in the number of childless couples, which did not exist to this extent in the past, and due to a rise in the number and proportion of lone-parent families, which on average have fewer children than married couples.

The decline in family household size was also strongly influenced by the disappearance of non-family members from the households. Such households were rather numerous in history: in Germany, for instance, they amounted to one-quarter of all households in 1910 (in German cities such as Frankfurt and Berlin the proportion of households with non-family members was much higher than the national average and partly exceeded 60%). In the process of modernization in the twentieth century, households with non-family members died out slowly; in Germany they were nearly

---

[1] Interestingly, the Danish Statistical Bureau published an international comparison of mean household size in European countries, including some German *Bundesstaaten* in Statistisk Bureau (1894: CXLI) for the years around 1890.

TABLE 5.1 Decline in mean private household size in Europe 1850–1940

Country	1850	1860	1870	1880	1890	1900	1910	1920	1930	1940
Austrian Republic										
'Wohnpartei'	..	..	5.231[1]	5.08	5.01	4.85	4.72	4.13	3.79[2]	..
Households	..	..	..	..	..	..	4.53	–	3.59[3]	..
Belgium	4.87[4]	4.55[5]	4.65[6]	4.59	4.55	4.30	4.05	3.76	3.41	..
Czecho-slovakia	–	–	–	–	–	–	–	–	3.80	..
Denmark	..	..	..	..	4.59	4.33[7]	4.14[8]	4.00[9]	3.66	3.24
Finland	..	..	..	..	..	4.21	..	..	..	..
France	..	..	..	3.52[10]	3.49[11]	3.46[7]	..	..	..	3.11[12]
Germany	..	..	4.64[13]	4.60	4.55	4.49	4.40	3.98[14]	3.61[15]	3.27[16]
Greece[17]	..	4.40[18]	4.38	4.62[19]	–	–	–	4.44	–	4.34
Hungarian Empire/Kingdom[17]	..	..	4.88	4.56	4.61	4.58	4.52	4.37	4.96	..
Iceland	..	..	..	..	..	..	5.75	5.34	5.13	4.03
Ireland/Irish Republic	5.44[20]	5.14[21]	5.07[13]	5.20[22]	5.04[11]	4.90[7]	4.82[9]	4.48[23]	4.31[24]	4.16[12]
Italy	..	..	4.68[13]	4.47[22]		4.52[7]	4.71[8]	4.38[25]	4.21[26]	4.29[24]
Luxemburg	..	..	4.91[13]	..	..	4.77	4.51	..	4.00	3.79[27]
The Netherlands	..	..	..	4.81[19]	4.33[28]	4.51[29]	4.41[30]	4.28	4.00	3.68[31]
Norway	..	..	..	..	4.64	4.53	4.20	4.13	4.52	4.21[12]
Poland	–	–	–	–	–	–	–	4.75[9]	4.42[26]	..
Portugal	..	..	..	..	4.04	4.17	4.22[8]	4.23	..	4.08
Spain	..	4.35	–	3.93[32]	..	..	3.97	4.08	..	..
Sweden	..	4.28	4.07	3.94	3.76	3.72	3.72	3.64	3.51	2.80[33]
Switzerland	..	..	..	..	..	..	..	4.24	3.92	..
England and Wales	..	..	..	..	..	..	..			..
'Families'[34]	4.83[20]	4.47[21]	4.50[13]	4.61[22]	4.73[11]	4.62[7]	4.51[8]			
Households	..	..	..	..	..	..	4.36[8]	4.14[9]	3.72[26]	..

[1] 1869. [2] 1934 *de facto* population. [3] 1934. [4] 1846. [5] 1856. [6] 1866. [7] 1901; [8] 1911. [9] 1921. [10] 1886. [11] 1891. [12] 1946. [13] 1871. [14] 1925. [15] 1933. [16] 1939. [17] Mean total household size. [18] 1861. [19] 1879. [20] 1851. [21] 1861. [22] 1881. [23] 1926. [24] 1936. [25] 1921 new territory. [26] 1931. [27] 1935. [28] 1889. [29] 1899. [30] 1909. [31] 1947. [32] 1877. [33] 1945. [34] Total present population to families or separate occupiers.
Sources: Country chapters of this volume.

non-existent already by 1970 (Rothenbacher, 1997a).

The third and most important source of decline in family household size was the long-term reduction in fertility, a process described by the model of the demographic transition (see Introductory Chapter I.3).

The general decline in household size due to the disappearance of non-family members and the fertility decline led to a convergence of family size by socio-economic status. In Germany mean household size of employed household heads between 1925 and 1970 (comparison is only possible for these two censuses) declined and converged, while the size structure of occupational groups remained stable (Rothenbacher, 1997a). Thus in 1970, the self-employed (peasants) still had larger households than workers (industry) and employees (white-collar). While the household size for employed household heads converged, the mean household size of heads without profession (pensioners) diverged strongly. This is explained by demographic and socio-economic developments in the segment of pensioners.

Looking only at averages hides other important developments at the household level. The decline in mean household size is largely caused by the decline of larger households, as can be seen for households with five or more persons (Table 5.2). While in 1900 the proportion of these households still varied from one-third to two-thirds, by 1940 the respective proportions had fallen to 14–40%. These proportions are converging in the long run, though some countries (Ireland, Spain, Portugal, and Eastern European countries Poland, Czechoslovakia, and others) still have a large share of big households.

TABLE 5.2 Proportion of households with five or more members in Europe 1850–1940 (%)

Country	1850	1860	1870	1880	1890	1900	1910	1920	1930	1940
Austrian Empire/Rep.	..	..	..	..	..	..	47.42	..	..	..
Belgium	..	..	..	..	..	..	..	..	21.25	14.91[1]
Czecho-slovakia	–	–	–	–	–	–	–	–	31.25	..
Denmark	..	..	..	..	42.36	40.42[2]	37.51[3]	..	28.02	19.83
Finland	..	..	..	42.49	41.66	39.62	..	..	..	..
France	30.89	30.51	..	27.15[4]	26.85[5]	28.24[6]	..	..	..	16.03[7]
Germany	..	..	..	..	..	44.40	42.43	33.36[8]	25.89[9]	18.72[10]
Greece	..	..	..	..	..	..	..	41.88	..	..
Hungarian Kingdom	..	..	..	..	..	..	..	..	..	..
Iceland	..	..	..	..	..	..	59.41	..	53.73	38.06
Ireland/Irish Republic	..	..	..	..	..	..	..	43.97[11]	40.81[12]	38.51[13]
Italy	..	..	..	..	..	43.80[2]	42.36[3]	41.25[14]	38.36[15]	39.63[12]
Luxemburg	..	..	..	..	..	48.27	45.17	..	34.05	29.53[16]
The Netherlands	..	..	..	..	..	..	42.85[17]	..	..	28.61[18]
Norway	..	..	..	..	..	..	..	44.14	39.40	20.41[7]
Poland	–	–	–	–	–	–	–	51.26[14]	45.76[15]	..
Portugal	..	..	..	..	37.08	38.15	40.16[3]	40.21	..	38.74
Spain	..	..	..	..	..	..	..	..	..	..
Sweden	..	41.41	39.09	36.62	..	33.41	32.83	30.77	27.24	13.39[19]
Switzerland	..	..	..	..	..	42.96	..	38.48	32.45	..
England and Wales	..	..	..	..	..	..	41.11[3]	36.81[14]	27.99[15]	..

[1] 1947. [2] 1901. [3] 1911. [4] 1881. [5] 1891. [6] 1901. [7] 1946. [8] 1925. [9] 1933. [10] 1939. [11] 1926. [12] 1936. [13] 1946. [14] 1921. [15] 1931. [16] 1935. [17] 1909. [18] 1947. [19] 1945.
Sources: Country chapters of this volume.

Households with three and four persons follow a different pattern within Europe. In all countries the proportion of households with four persons increased up to the 1940s, as did households with three persons. Thus, households with five or more persons declined constantly since 1850, and households with three and four members increased their share until the 1940s. Households with one and two members show a constant increase since the 1850s (Table 5.3). The relations between countries are remarkably stable in these processes; there are signs of divergence only for one-person households.

TABLE 5.3 Proportion of one-person households in Europe 1850–1940 (%)

Country	1850	1860	1870	1880	1890	1900	1910	1920	1930	1940
Austrian Empire/Republic	..	..	..	..	..	..	6.02	..	..	..
Belgium	..	..	..	..	..	..	..	..	11.01	15.83[1]
Czechoslovakia	–	–	–	–	–	–	–	–	7.28	..
Denmark	..	..	..	..	7.46	8.80[2]	10.01[3]	9.54[4]	10.89	13.53
Finland	..	..	..	3.90	4.49	5.08	..	..	..	..
France	2.54	3.15	..	4.15[5]	4.37[6]	4.38[2]	..	..	..	5.97[7]
Germany	..	..	..	..	..	7.15	7.32	6.72[8]	8.38[9]	9.76[10]
Greece	..	..	..	..	..	..	..	8.51	..	..
Hungarian Kingdom	..	..	..	..	..	..	..	..	..	..
Iceland	..	..	..	..	..	..	4.38	..	2.96	18.29
Ireland/Irish Republic	..	..	..	..	..	..	..	8.28[11]	9.36[12]	10.39[7]
Italy	..	..	..	..	..	8.79[2]	9.24[3]	9.13[13]	9.55[14]	9.10[12]
Luxemburg	..	..	3.75[15]	..	5.94	6.48	6.99	..	5.83	6.72[16]
The Netherlands	..	..	..	..	..	..	9.61[17]	9.73	11.16	9.21[1]
Norway	..	..	..	..	..	..	..	9.43	10.13	17.67[7]
Poland	–	–	–	–	–	–	–	6.06[4]	9.01[14]	..
Portugal	..	..	..	..	11.49	10.76	9.82[3]	8.68	..	7.82
Spain	..	..	..	..	..	..	..	..	..	..
Sweden	–	15.52	17.90	20.00	22.50	23.64	22.56	21.87	18.86	25.17[18]
Switzerland	..	..	..	..	..	9.53	..	8.55	8.50	..
England and Wales	..	..	..	..	..	..	5.33[3]	6.03[4]	6.73[14]	..

[1] 1947. [2] 1901. [3] 1911. [4] 1921. [5] 1881. [6] 1891. [7] 1946. [8] 1925. [9] 1933. [10] 1939. [11] 1926. [12] 1936. [13] 1921 new territory. [14] 1931. [15] 1871. [16] 1935. [17] 1909. [18] 1945.
Sources: Country chapters of this volume.

Therefore, at the level of households we can observe very different processes: first, a clear *nuclearization* of family households in the sense that the nuclear family became the dominant family type due to the disappearance of non-family members, the decline of the extended family, and the universalization of marriage. The decline of large households fits very well into this process of nuclearization. On the other hand, already during the first half of the twentieth century we can see the opposite trends of *individualization* and *pluralization*. Indicators for these counter-trends can be seen in the increase in persons living alone and households consisting of only two persons, but also in the decline of the population living in nuclear families. In addition, at the household level we can see what has been called the *polarization* of private living arrangements into a family sector and a non-family sector. The non-family sector is made up of households with one or two members, which are on the rise, and the family sector is made up of households with three and four members, that is, with one or two children in the family. Families with three or more children in the family—in other words, households with five or more persons—declined by tendency already before 1945, due to the strong fertility decline after World War I.

SUBSTITUTION OF THE EXTENDED FAMILY

Even though it was not dominant in reality due to high mortality and low life expectancy in nineteenth century Europe, the extended family as the model of the traditional family system represented a substantial proportion of all families; the lack of statistics however does not allow for exact figures. The extended family dominated in large regions with an agrarian population, but was not as widespread in the strata of landless labourers. The transition from the agrarian to the industrial and, finally, to the post-industrial society in combination with urbanization reduced the share of extended families to only a few percentage points. A cross-sectional perspective within Europe reveals that during the 1990s the extended family was most common in those countries where the proportion of agrarian population is still high, such as Greece, Portugal, Ireland, and Spain. It can therefore be assumed that extended families in history were mainly found in agricultural households. This thesis is supported by the finding that in the advanced industrialized countries of central Europe still today the share of extended families in agriculture is highest. A rather strong bivariate relationship between employment in the agricultural sector and the proportion of extended families has been found (Rothenbacher, 1996). In addition, the remaining extended families have changed in structure: the extension of the family through lateral relatives such as (unmarried) brothers and sisters of the parental generation has been reduced significantly due to the general birth decline, while the importance of the extension through the grandparent generation has grown in relative terms. The decrease in the number of extended families in Europe (as compared to other world regions, such as Japan) has been made possible due to pension systems and social care services which have reduced old-age poverty dramatically and enabled the elderly to live alone.

Table 5.4 shows the proportion of relatives to all household members. The figures often include people of rather uncertain status and therefore may be overstated in some cases. The few data do not clearly show the stated trend of a decline in relatives and therefore the extended family. This is firstly due to the nature of the data, which are partly inconsistent and given for only a few time points. There are also signs that during the economic crisis years of the 1920s and 1930s more relatives lived with family because of housing shortages and low incomes.

THE PRE-NUCLEAR FAMILY

The term 'pre-nuclear family' is used here to denote the family system preceding the emergence of the nuclear family as social ideal and dominant family type. Historical family research has often pointed out the myth of large households before industrialization. In Western Europe complex family systems were very rare and existed only in certain regions. Empirically, the extended family was also a rare phenomenon. From this empirical evidence researchers concluded that the nuclear family system prevailed in Western Europe already before industrialization. Nevertheless, and in contrast to an interpretation of statistical data alone, two different levels concerning the family must be distinguished: first, the normative level, or what people would do under certain conditions; and second, the empirical level, or what people really do, and what is measured statistically. It can be argued that the 'extended family' was the norm in pre-industrial Europe. The house and the

TABLE 5.4 Proportion of relatives to household members in Europe 1850–1940 (%)[1]

Country	1850	1860	1870	1880	1890	1900	1910	1920	1930	1940
Austrian Republic	..	..	..	..	..	..	6.61[2]	..	7.35[3]	..
Greece	..	..	..	..	..	..	..	..	..	11.40[4]
Hungarian Empire/ Kingdom	..	..	..	7.60[5]	6.44[5]	6.86[5]	..	..	..	..
Ireland/Irish Republic	13.97[6]	..	..	15.34[6]	11.10[6]	14.20[6]	17.11[6]	..	..	..
Luxemburg	..	..	..	..	..	3.78[7]	2.68[8]	..	..	..
Norway	..	..	..	..	..	1.21[9]	..	..	..	..
Poland	–	–	–	–	–	–	–	11.00[10]	..	..
Sweden	..	..	..	..	..	..	..	..	2.97[11]	3.52[12]
Switzerland	..	..	..	..	..	..	..	5.50[13]	6.39[13]	..

[1] For all other countries dealt with in this volume data are not available. [2] Other family members. [3] 1934 Other family members. [4] 1951 Other parents of family household heads. [5] Others (parents, servants). [6] Male and female visitors (includes relatives). [7] 1905 Other persons. [8] Other persons. [9] Sons- and daughters-in-law, grandsons and granddaughters, parents. [10] Near and remote parents. [11] Others. [12] 1935 Other household members. [13] Parents, parents-in-law and other relatives of household head.
Sources: Country chapters of this volume.

household were the primary instance for the inclusion of not only relatives of all grades, but also of a large variety of non-related household members (journeymen, servants, lodgers). Thus, normally houses (or parts of a house) were transferred to one of the children before the parents' death. In many cases, when the widowed mother was too old to carry out the household tasks, she legally transferred the house to the son or son-in-law (*Übergabevertrag*) and remained to live in the same house until death. Very often the time period from property transfer to the death of the parent was short, which is the main reason for the small number of extended families in which the parent lived in the household.

If the house was large enough it was also usual to include lateral relatives in the household, though to much lower extent than parents. It can therefore be argued that the pre-industrial family system in most of Western Europe was extended by norm, but in the majority of cases it was nuclear because of late property transfer and low life expectancy. This situation contrasts greatly with the neolocal family system of today, where almost *all* children leave the parental home to form their own nuclear family. One of the main factors behind these changes is economic independence of both young and old: young people no longer have to inherit property or an occupation, and the elderly receive pensions and care from other sources than their own children.

NUCLEAR FAMILIES:
DYNAMICS OF FORMATION AND DISSOLUTION

Family formation changed from 1850 to 1945. While age at marriage was initially rather high, because of legal, social, or economic marriage restrictions, it declined during the 1920s and 1930s. In the nineteenth century women typically did not have children before age 25, but normally bore children throughout their reproductive years. With the onset of family planning and fertility control, fewer women bore children when in their thirties and forties. Women's reproductive phase was shortened and compressed within a period of five to ten years. With the decline in mean age at marriage, reproduction shifted more to the twenties in a woman's life. Female celibacy started to decline by tendency until the 1940s: many more people were now able to marry than during the second half of the nineteenth century. Nevertheless, celibacy was still rather high and marriage far from universal as in Eastern Europe. When legal marriage barriers were removed, often social and economic ones appeared, rendering marriage and family difficult for many people still in the 1920s and 1930s. After World War I modernizing trends in society, such as the growth in women's participation in education, had a small but growing impact on family formation.

Family growth during the process of the demographic transition was extended to more people because of declining celibacy. On the other hand, the fertility decline reduced the size of families. This reduction was enhanced after World War I, especially in the 1920s and 1930s, when fertility planning affected large segments of the population. Family size and fertility decline were not independent of social class; there is a clear pattern of pioneers and latecomers. The new urban professions such as civil servants and employees in private firms (*Privatbeamte*) limited family size rather early, while factory workers and peasants were latecomers in this process. This pattern more or less recurs in all European countries. Thus in modern urban families family growth was compressed into a few years in women's life cycle, mainly during their twenties and thirties.

Voluntary childlessness of married women was low at that time, because a large proportion (sometimes over 50%) of marriages were entered after conception. In the urban classes women usually stopped working after the birth of a child. Wives of factory workers often continued to work, whereas women in the 'bourgeois classes' did not work: they preferred to stay at home, to travel or study. In the peasantry women did not stop working to bear and raise children.

Lone mothers were not uncommon at that time, although illegitimate fertility declined more than legitimate fertility. The proportion of children born out-of-wedlock declined during the first half of the twentieth century. The trend was in favour of the nuclear family.

The long-term fertility decline started to change the concept of childhood. In some social classes, such as that of civil servants, children started to become a scarce commodity. In the social classes with advanced fertility decline, the reduced number of children meant that childhood as a group experience became less common and children often had a monopoly position. The 'peer groups' of children (siblings and neighbouring children) began to shrink as did the number of lateral relatives such as aunts and uncles.

Family dissolution due to death declined as a result of the long-term process of 'epidemiological transition', while family dissolution due to divorce and separation became a more important factor. Nevertheless, until the 1940s, family dissolution due to death was much more frequent than due to divorce. Therefore social problems resulting from widow(er)hood and orphanhood were much more virulent than those arising from divorce and separation, and social legislation concentrated much more on the poverty of widows and the social situation of orphans.

During the nineteenth century and also during the inter-war period unmarried cohabitation was quite widespread. But there are no data on separation during premarital cohabitation for European countries in official statistics.

The pattern of *family reconstitution* changed during the 'epidemiological transition'. During the nineteenth century death of a spouse was almost the only cause of family dissolution. Widows and widowers therefore often remarried,[2] especially if there were children needing care. Remarriages of widowed people often occurred very soon after the death of a spouse. Second and even third marriages were not unusual, and stepchildren and step-parents were a frequent phenomenon. Since the middle of the nineteenth century the remarriage rate of widowed persons declined by tendency until the 1940s. This has to do with the decline in mortality, but could also be a sign of increasing post-marital cohabitation already at that time. Unfortunately, no official statistics exist to answer this question.

While remarriages of widowed people declined by tendency, remarriages of divorced persons increased from the middle of the nineteenth century to the 1940s. Obviously, people divorced willingly in order to enter a new legal partnership, in contrast to the most recent development in which divorce more often does not lead to new marriage but rather to non-marital cohabitation, resulting in a declining remarriage rate of divorced persons since 1945 (Rothenbacher, 1996, 1997a, 1998b; see also Höpflinger, 1997).

NON-NUCLEAR FAMILIES IN HISTORY

COHABITATION WITHOUT MARRIAGE

Official statistics do not say anything about unmarried cohabitation until the 1950s. The discussion about developments in the family treats cohabitation as a 'new' and recent trend. But looking further back in history we see that cohabitation existed in most historical periods, although to varying degrees.[3] Studies on cohabitation in the nineteenth century are a rather new field in social history. In Germany research into private living arrangements in the nineteenth century has 'discovered' cohabitation as a new research field. Due to availability of sources, such studies deal mainly with the large towns. Karin Gröwer (1998, 1999) studies the three Hanseatic cities Hamburg, Bremen, and Lübeck. Previous research had pointed to the very high illegitimacy rates in Germany and especially in the German cities during the nineteenth centuries. Official individualized population statistics therefore give the impression that there were many single women with illegitimate children, living alone or with their parents. But recent local studies in cohabitation show that it was rather common for people mainly in the lower classes to form a family and live together for a long time, having several children, without the legal consent of the church or the public authorities. This behaviour pattern was especially widespread during the pauperism phase in the first half of the nineteenth century, when legal barriers to marriage were erected in order to relieve the municipalities of having to support the poor: receiving a marriage license was dependent on profession and

---

[2] The remarriage rate of divorced men (women) is defined as marriages of divorced men (women) to 1,000 divorced men (women).

[3] In Catholic southern Germany, still at the end of the sixteenth century (1571–86), most of the local Catholic priests and preachers lived in cohabitation and usually had children as well, a fact that came to light after the resolutions at the Council of Trent in 1545–63 to inspect the parishes (see for example the minutes of visitation in the diocese of Constance, published by G. Bossert in 1891; cf. also Goody, 1983).

income. During the second half of the nineteenth century, cohabitation declined when legal marriage restrictions were abolished. But legal marriage restrictions continued to exist, such as those for civil servants well into the twentieth century, and legal marriage barriers were replaced by economic and social ones. Living together without marriage and forming a family with children can therefore be interpreted as a way of adapting to specific legal, economic, and social circumstances of a historical period. The breakthrough of universal marriage in Western Europe in the twentieth century with declining celibacy, low cohabitation, and early marriage is obviously due to improved living conditions, also among the poorer segments of society.

Studies conducted during the inter-war period in Germany show that people practised cohabitation, probably mainly in the large towns and the lower strata (Baum and Westerkamp, 1931). How common this form of living was in the whole population cannot be determined due to lack of studies.

LONE PARENTS

'Incomplete families' or, in modern terminology, 'lone parents', arise out of different situations: birth to an unmarried woman, death of a spouse, or separation or divorce all result in lone parenthood. These three are evident at different times and in different European countries to varying degrees.

In the nineteenth century the two main reasons for lone parenthood were births to unmarried women and the death of a spouse. Which of the two was more important quantitatively cannot be determined due to lack of family statistics for the time. The third reason was more or less non-existent during the nineteenth century due to very low divorce rates, but increased in importance in the first half of the twentieth century.

Lone parenthood during the nineteenth century was often only temporary. Children born to single women often died very young—infant mortality of illegitimate children was extremely high and higher than legitimate infant mortality. Single mothers often married, not necessarily the father of their child(ren); having an illegitimate child was obviously not a major hindrance to marriage. Lone parenthood resulting from the wife's death was also usually temporary, as widowers frequently remarried in order to provide their children with a step-mother. Remarriage chances of widows with small children were not as good as those of widowers, and older widows with adult children were less likely to remarry due to lack of marriage partners (lower male life expectancy) and less economic necessity (help of adult children in business and household).

For Prussia, a proxy measurement for lone parents has been made by subtracting the number of existing marriages from the number of family households (Rothenbacher, 1997a: 320). The proportion of the resulting figure in per cent of all family households indicates all family households that do not include a couple. Such family households comprise not only incomplete families, but also households of related persons (e.g. brother and sister). Furthermore, *de facto* cohabitation can also be included in this figure. The available data show that in the second half of the nineteenth century, the proportion of incomplete households in Prussia was around 15%. From the 1880s this proportion declined by tendency, reaching its lowest level in 1925 with 11%. During the 1930s however the proportion increased slightly to

12%. Differences between towns and rural areas are significant: in cities with over 20,000 inhabitants the proportion of incomplete households was much higher: 24% in 1867 and 16% in 1905. In the rural areas there were fewer incomplete households, 14% in 1867 and 10% in 1905. The much-higher proportion in the large cities cannot be explained by higher mortality alone; there was probably a widespread pattern of unmarried cohabitation and also a large number of single mothers.

RECONSTITUTED FAMILIES

No direct data from official statistics are available on the subject of reconstituted families during the nineteenth and the first half of the twentieth century, because family statistics in the proper sense of the word started only after 1945. Reconstituted families are defined as nuclear or extended families, formed by a married couple with children, in which one or both parents is absent due to death or divorce, and in which the remaining parent has remarried. By definition therefore such reconstituted families are always step-families as long as children are living in the household.

During the nineteenth century reconstituted families must have been frequent due to high adult mortality. Male mortality involved sickness, accidents, and war, while women faced high risks of death in childbirth. Maternal mortality was very high still in the nineteenth century and its reduction led immediately to a decline in reconstituted families.

Because of the high mortality of both sexes, step-families were rather common during the nineteenth century. When the mother died, the father soon had to marry again in order to provide care for his children and to manage the household. If the father died, it was often more difficult for the widow to find a new husband, partly because of men's preference for marrying younger women. But younger men often married older widows for the financial advantages they could offer, such as access to the position of master craftsman in the trades (*Handwerk*). In any case, remarriage rates of widowers were much higher than those of widows, indicating widowers' better chances of marrying a (younger) woman than of widows marrying a (younger) man (Mitterauer, 1979, 1983).

It was not unusual for men and women to be widowed more than once, thus children may have resulted from two or three different marriages. In some cases, children had no biological parents left: if after one biological parent died, the surviving biological parent remarried and later died, children were left with only step-parents. Such constellations were extremely disadvantageous for children's living conditions, as we know from historical investigations. In principle, step-parents were a bad thing for children, a fact well documented by historical research as well as fairy tales.

The number of reconstituted families after the death of a parent must have declined after the mid-nineteenth century, because the remarriage rate of widowed persons declined. At the same time the remarriage rate of divorced persons increased, but divorces were so rare until World War I that the majority of reconstituted families were formed after the death of a spouse. During the 1920s and 1930s divorces become more frequent, although the economic and social crisis of that time rendered remarriage of divorced persons more difficult. Unmarried cohabitation was probably the solution at least for the lower classes (Rothenbacher, 1997a).

LIVING ALONE AS OPTION AND CONSTRAINT

Demographic and social developments from 1850 to 1945 led to an increase in the number of single persons, a development caused by three factors. First, the difference in life expectancy in favour of women led to an increase in the number of widows, who generally live alone. Second, divorced persons, mainly women, often remain alone after divorce if they have no children or if the children have left the household. Third, young adults, especially young men, live as 'singles' for a longer time period after leaving the parental home.

Official household statistics can tell us something about persons living alone, because they are counted by statistics as one-person households. These statistics show an increasing trend in the proportion of one-person households from 1850 to 1945. The increase was steady but slow until World War I; during the 1920s there was some retardation, but increase of one-person households accelerated during the 1930s and 1940s. That same increase can also be shown for the proportion of the population living alone as per cent of total population.

Nevertheless, the number of people living alone was small when compared with the proportions today. While in most countries from 1850 to 1945 one-person households as a proportion of all households was not above 10%, in the 1990s the proportion ranged from 10% to 40%. When individuals rather than households are considered, people living alone as a per cent of total population were well under 5% in most countries until 1945; in the 1990s this figure ranged from 3% to 18% (Rothenbacher, 1998b).

Theoretically, the proportion of people living alone could have been much higher in history than counted by official statistics. If the many apprentices and journeymen, servants, boarders, and lodgers had been counted as one-person households, we would probably arrive at figures as high as those today. That is why the proportion of people not living with their family of origin and the high celibacy rate led to many people living in foreign households for different reasons. But the traditional concept of household organization was that such non-family persons were socially integrated into the household and counted as household members. Traditional houses and housing were orientated on the concept of 'one house, one household' and therefore did not supply separate housing units for single persons. This situation changed only very gradually, but basically not before the inter-war period when home construction was intensified and small flats were provided.

EASTERN EUROPE AND WESTERN EUROPE

One of the persisting structural differences within Europe is the difference between Eastern and Western Europe. Eastern Europe in this volume is represented by the eastern-central European countries of Czechoslovakia, Hungary, and Poland. This structural difference is long-term by nature and is surprisingly persistent. The structural difference between Eastern and Western Europe can mainly be observed in the field of marriage behaviour, as *John Hajnal* (1965) has demonstrated: in Eastern Europe marriages took place early and were universal; in Western Europe, people married late, and many persons remained unmarried. In Eastern Europe, empirical indicators show a low age at marriage, a high marriage rate, and a high proportion of persons married, while in Western Europe the opposite is true. Although Eastern Europe can be clearly separated from Western Europe in terms of family formation, there is no clear-cut dividing line in the field of household and family structures. Only in those (mainly Balkan) countries where the Zadruga family system prevailed, that is, Bulgaria (Todorova, 1993) and Yugoslavia, can a major difference in the family organization be found. In this region, households were very large and comprised several marital units, mostly the married sons of the household head. The very large size of the households in Bulgaria and Yugoslavia is still visible during the first half of the twentieth century, but after 1945 the nuclear family became the dominant family form in these countries as well. In the countries that did not follow the Zadruga system, including Czechoslovakia, Hungary, and Poland, the family system did not deviate much from the Western European extended family system by norm, but nuclear in empirical reality.

Nevertheless, some modifications have to be made concerning these countries. Mean household size was large in Poland and Hungary, but not in Czechoslovakia: the proportion of five-person households was large, while the proportion of one-person households was low.

To some extent, the differences in household structure between these three countries are based on differences in demographic developments. Demographic transition in Czechoslovakia was similar to the European average, while in Hungary and Poland both the birth and death rates were well above the European average. The large households in Poland and Hungary can thus partly be explained by higher fertility. Corresponding to the Eastern European marriage pattern, the marriage rate was high in all three countries. In contradiction to the Eastern European marriage pattern, however, illegitimate fertility was high in all three countries and legitimate fertility was average when compared with Europe as a whole. Although people married young and marriage was universal, marriages were not very stable: the divorce rate in Hungary was extremely high, and that of Czechoslovakia still above the European average (for Poland no data are available before 1945).

6

Demographic Measures and Demographic Statistics

DEMOGRAPHIC STATISTICS

It is a well-known fact that population statistics are one of the oldest and most reliable type of official statistics. Population censuses have been conducted in growing numbers since the eighteenth century (of course, the history of census-taking is much older), but the first modern census in the sense of being based on scientific criteria and the principle of self-enumeration was carried out in Belgium in 1846.

Thus already in the middle of the nineteenth century population structure and *population censuses* were rather highly standardized instruments. Further improvements were made in the second half of the nineteenth century. Population censuses became more and more detailed with respect to questions asked of the population; in technical terms, the number of variables assessed continuously increased. At the same time, the publishing of population census results increased in volume from census to census. Very often the available data were only exploited to a small degree: for example, data to tabulate age by sex by marital status existed, but this three-dimensional classification was not carried out.

Vital statistics were easier to standardize, and already in the second half of the nineteenth century the international statistical congresses recommended common definitions. Crucial measurement problems in vital statistics concerned the definition of stillbirths and the undercounting of stillbirths and early infant deaths, particularly of girls in some countries. In some countries with a large rural population in the nineteenth century, population registration was often underdeveloped or non-existent, so that no reliable vital statistics could be derived. While in the early nineteenth century only the most important variables of the population process were of interest for official statistics, such as births, deaths, and marriages, the topics covered increased continuously over time. Important disaggregations introduced were marriages by marital status, age, and sex, births by legitimacy and age of mother, and deaths by age (under one year). Completely new topics introduced were statistics on divorce and legal separations, due to the growing importance of these phenomena.

Definitions of households varied widely between European countries. The *household and family statistics* before 1950 were only rudimentary and little information about households is available. The main features are the number and size of households, and sometimes disaggregations by age, sex, and profession of the household head. Household composition (the number of different household members) or household type (according to the existence of different household members) was sometimes processed and published. Until 1945 the household was the more important social unit; that is, while household statistics were emphasized. The nuclear family emerged as distinct from the large household system when relatives started to form their own households, and servants, boarders, and lodgers moved out. Family statistics as we know them today developed with the birth decline after World War I and diffused from the pioneering country France, which was the first European country to face a severe birth decline and the first to investigate marital fertility. For the first time the statistical focus was not the household, but the couple. The other origin of family statistics was in household statistics. Already before 1945 there were some statistics on the structure of the nuclear family; these were extended by official statistics after 1945.

Only since 1945 have general guidelines for internationally comparable household and family statistics been available, with the recommendations of the United Nations Economic Commission for Europe (UN/ECE) in Geneva for the conducting of population censuses (see e.g. United Nations Statistical Commission/Economic Commission for Europe (UN/ECE), 1987).

DEMOGRAPHIC SOURCES

The sources for this data handbook consist exclusively of published official statistics. No unpublished archived source material has been used and normally no data material from historical studies using unpublished archived historical documents has been processed.

In principle two types of statistics are available: secondary statistics (concerning the term see Rothenbacher, 1998a) from other data handbooks or data collections; and primary statistics from the original statistical sources. Very few historical demographic data handbooks or data handbooks including demographic parts for the time period under consideration exist, and most of the existing ones do not present the information in the desired way. The most important data handbooks directly used are comparative: the handbooks by Mitchell (1980/81, 1992), Flora, Kraus, and Pfenning (1987), and Sundbärg (1908). There is basically no genuinely historical and demographic data handbook on Europe for the time since the nineteenth century. All of these data handbooks contain population data and vital statistics, but household and family data have never been covered systematically in a historical-comparative data handbook.

While demographic statistics are either of secondary importance or have only been used as a point of reference in international secondary statistics, for individual nations there are many more of the type of historical demographic statistics. Most of these titles have been listed by Flora (1975) up to the early 1970s, by Etemad (1990), and by Rothenbacher (1998a). In most cases, population, demographic, and household/family statistics are included in general historical statistics such as British Historical Statistics or Icelandic Historical Statistics, or the different volumes for France, Sweden, Norway, and so on. All the titles which have been used are found in the Bibliography. For some countries there are special historical statistics in the realm of demography: the Irish historical population statistics go back very far (Vaughan and Fitzpatrick, 1978); there is a volume for Germany by Antje Kraus (1980) and others. In the field of historical household and family statistics there are almost no specialized historical data handbooks (except Germany, see Rothen-bacher, 1997a), and all that is available is included in more general handbooks.

The compendia of national historical statistics have been widely used mainly for constructing the vital statistics rates, which have been rather well collected by national statistical offices. In addition to these sources, the main source for vital statistics before 1945 was the annual statistical abstract (after 1945 the other main source is annual statistical series on population and demography in nearly every country (cf. Rothenbacher, 1998a)).

To some degree data on household and family statistics were also taken from national historical statistics. But this information basis was too narrow, and it was therefore necessary to go back to the original population census publications for the collection of household and family data. The titles of the population censuses used are documented in the Bibliography.

Finally, the database on age by sex and marital status had to be based entirely on national population census publications. The sources used are also documented in the Bibliography.

DEMOGRAPHIC DATA VALIDITY

The validity of the data stemming from population censuses, vital statistics enumeration, social surveys, and register statistics differs greatly by source, country, and time period. Undercount in population censuses is obviously a serious problem and has been emphasized by Clogg, Massagli, and Eliason (1989) for the United States census. A special point is not general undercount, but underregistration for special population groups according to age, sex, and nationality, among others.

There is no general account of data validity in census-taking, but many individual publications point to inaccuracies and undercount in particular censuses (Chesnais, 1992: 15f.; Fircks, 1898: 7–20). Undercount probably varies not only within a country between population subgroups, but also between countries and historical time points. It can be argued that since the nineteenth century data accuracy has improved everywhere. Furthermore, there are reasons to suppose that poorer and underdeveloped countries—at least during the nineteenth century—faced greater difficulties in producing accurate population counts. Within Europe this is probably the case for most of the Balkan countries, including Greece.

On the other hand, there are good reasons to argue that already in the nineteenth century population figures were rather accurate, when the population number was used for political (allocative) reasons. One example may be the population census figures in the German Tariff Union which were used to allocate customs income.

Still in the twentieth century, undercount of vital statistics rates is obvious in some countries such as Greece, where the vital statistics rates are too low. Several publications have dealt with this problem (cf. National Statistical Service of Greece, 1960 and 1980: 15, 31, 59). Especially stillbirths and neo-natal deaths in rural areas have been underreported. During the nineteenth century, the non-registration of children dying shortly after birth was probably widespread in most European countries.

LONG-TERM DEMOGRAPHIC DEVELOPMENT

For the social sciences, especially economics and sociology, a long-term perspective is needed in order to understand societal and economic processes. Most of the macro-sociological theories embrace a time horizon which extends for decades or even centuries. A few of these long-term processes are modernization (see the modernization theorists), social and functional differentiation (Durkheim), industrialization, and urbanization (Kingsley Davis). Macro-economics is also largely based on a long-term perspective. Theories of economic development and stages of economic growth, among others, refer to long-term developments since the onset of industrialization in the nineteenth century.

There are other reasons that a long-term perspective is necessary. European demography needs a longer historical perspective in order to understand differences and similarities of European countries with respect to demography and other developments. In several respects only a macroscopic view allows for the understanding of major differences between societies.

A second point is that long-term trends and time series allow the study of divergence and convergence processes between European countries, an aspect of central importance for European unification. In the history of the last two centuries, European countries changed their position in varying ways. Countries similar at one point in time become quite different at a later point. Long-term time series allow for the study of processes of divergence and convergence, of pioneers and laggards, of diffusion processes, of long waves, and other things. Long-term processes also lead us to the study of astonishing regularities and permanencies in territorial patterns, such as the return of Western Europeans to their older marital patterns or the striking permanence and stability of the Eastern European marriage pattern.

Long-term datasets allow the study of longitudinal changes and of cohort analysis. In particular the dataset on age, sex, and marital status makes it possible to carry out cohort analysis or the construction of age-dependent indices, such as the marriage ratio or the celibacy rate.

DEMOGRAPHIC INDICATORS AND MEASURES

All the demographic indicators presented in the volume have been calculated from the basic values. This means that the dataset on which the data handbook is based not only comprises demographic indicators but also the absolute values (such as absolute number of live births and deaths).

When collecting the data and defining the demographic indicators, the question arose as to which type of indicators to choose: should they be complex and synthetic according to the requirements of modern demography, based on advanced datasets? Or should they be simple in order to allow for comparisons over time and space?

Like others (cf. Chesnais, 1992: 15f.), we have decided to rely on simple indicators, which can be calculated for most countries already from the demographic material of the nineteenth century. Therefore we omitted synthetic indicators such as the Total Period Fertility Rate, Cohort Fertility Rate, and others.

In order to rely not only on 'crude' rates, several rates have been age-standardized to the population at risk. Thus, for example, we calculated the legitimate birth rate as the number of live births to married women aged 15–44.

Concerning households and families the few data available allowed only the calculation of proportions (size distribution of households) and averages (mean household size) as a standard procedure. Several other country-specific calculations can be found in the country chapters. The definitions of the demographic measures used in this volume are given in Table 6.1.

TABLE 6.1 Definition of demographic measures used in the Appendix Tables and Figures (see also section on Remarks in each Country Chapter)

Variable	Unit	Variable name	Variable definition
Status of population			
CENSPOP	N	Population at census date by age, sex, and marital status	Absolute figure
MIDYPOP	N	Mid-year population	Population as of 30 June
NATPOP-GROWTH	‰	Natural population growth rate	Natural population growth: live births minus deaths; natural population growth rate: natural population growth/mid-year population*1,000
POP-GROWTH	‰	Population growth rate	Population growth: mid-year population(t) minus mid-year population(t–1); population growth rate: population growth/mid-year population*1,000
NMR	‰	Net migration rate	Net migration: population growth minus natural population growth; net migration rate: net migration/mid-year population*1,000
Population movement			
Fertility			
CBR	‰	Crude birth rate	Live births/mid-year population*1,000
LEGR	$^o/_{ooo}$	Legitimacy rate	Legitimate live births/married women aged 15–44*10,000
ILLEGR	$^o/_{ooo}$	Illegitimacy rate	Illegitimate live births/unmarried women aged 15–44*10,000
ILLEG%	%	Illegitimacy rate	Illegitimate live births/legitimate live births*100
Mortality			
CDR	‰	Crude death rate	Deaths/mid-year population*1,000
INFANT	%	Infant mortality rate	Deaths under one year of age/total live births*1,000
STILLB	%	Stillbirth rate	Stillbirths/live births*100
INFANT+ STILLB	%	Infant mortality and still-birth rate	Deaths under one year of age plus stillbirths/live births*1,000
Nuptiality			
CMR	‰	Crude marriage rate	Marriages/mid-year population*1,000
MR15+	$^o/_{ooo}$	Marriage ratio 15+	Persons marrying/unmarried persons aged 15+*10,000
MR15–49	$^o/_{ooo}$	Marriage ratio 15–49	Persons marrying/unmarried persons aged 15–49*10,000
Divorce			
CDR	‰	Crude divorce rate	Divorces/mid-year population*1,000
DIVM	%	Divorce rate	Divorces/marriages*100
DIVR	$^o/_{ooo}$	Divorce ratio	Divorces/married persons*10,000

continued

TABLE 6.1 Definition of demographic measures used in the Appendix Tables and Figures (see also section on Remarks in each Country Chapter) (continued)

Variable	Unit	Variable name	Variable definition
Auxiliary variables, used for creating the age-standardized population movement rates above			
v16	N	Married women age 15–44	Absolute figure, created by linear interpolation between census years
v17	N	Non-married women age 15–44	Absolute figure, created by linear interpolation between census years
v18	N	Married population age 15+	Absolute figure, created by linear interpolation between census years
v19	N	Total population age 15+	Absolute figure, created by linear interpolation between census years
v20	N	Non-married population age 15+	Absolute figure, created by linear interpolation between census years
v21	N	Non-married population age 15–44	Absolute figure, created by linear interpolation between census years
Life expectancy			
	Years	Age-specific life expectancy at age 0, 10, 20, 30, 40, 50, 60, 70, and 80	Male and female life expectancy
Households and families			
ALLHH	N	All households	One-person, family, and institutional households
PHH	N	Private households	
FHH	N	Family households	
OPH	N	One-person households	
IHH	N	Institutional households	
ALLHHM	N	Members of all households	Members in one-person, family, and institutional households
PHHM	N	Members of private households total	
FHHM	N	Members of family households total	
OPHM	N	Members of one-person households total	
IHH	N	Members of institutional households total	
1P	N	Private households with 1 person	
....			
15+P	N	Private households with 15+ persons	
MHHS	Ø	Mean size of all households	Total population/all households
MPHHS	Ø	Mean private household size	Population in private households/private households
MFHHS	Ø	Mean family household size	Population in family households/family households
MIHHS	Ø	Mean institutional household size	Population in institutional households/institutional households

BASIC RESEARCH IN DEMOGRAPHY

One could start with the thesis of Stein Rokkan, that social science requires a solid empirical base and the application of scientific methods to social matters, which he carried out in the 1960s, and ask how far this requirement has become reality.

In the social sciences, historical and comparative data collections serve as sources, just as historical text editions are sources for the historical sciences. The historical sciences are much more advanced concerning the collection of source material than the social sciences. Most of the collected sources in the social sciences lack a coherent framework and are disparate: there are different projects, but there are no series of sources or they are discontinued after some time.

Social science data archives are not a substitute for coherent collections of sources, because they mainly collect the data from completed research projects. If a corpus of historical statistical sources is to be established, data collections will have to be built up using a systematic and comparative perspective.

But this cannot be done by one person or one institution alone and should be organized as a permanent endeavour of all the European social sciences. Nevertheless, up to now neither a research organization nor a network of European research institutes of data archives is in sight to carry out such a comprehensive task. In principle, the accumulation of sources will be an endeavour lasting several decades.

Nevertheless, in several European countries there are specialized demographic research institutes which sometimes also cover the field of historical demographic statistics or historical demography. Specialization in the field of demography has increased during the last decade, as evidenced by the growing number of countries having at least one demographic research centre. An overview of demographic research institutes and their main fields of historical-statistical work in Europe is given in Table 6.2.

TABLE 6.2 Demographic research centres in Europe

Country	Demographic research centre	Major contribution to historical demographic statistics[4]
National		
Austria	Institut für Demographie der Österreichischen Akademie der Wissenschaften, Vienna. Internet: http://www.idemog.oeaw.ac.at/.	*Demographische Informationen*
Belgium	Institut de Démographie, Université Catholique de Louvain (UCL), Louvain. Internet: http://www.demo.ucl.ac.be/.	Occasional titles in Working Papers series
	Centrum voor Bevolkings- en Gezinsstudie (C.B.G.S.), Brussels. Internet: http://www.vlaanderen.be/ned/sites/overheid/mvg/.	Occasional titles
Czech Republic	Czech Statistical Office, Prague. Internet: http://www.czso.cz/.	*Czech Demographic Handbook*
Denmark	The Danish Center for Demographic Research, Odense University, Odense. Internet: http://www.ou.dk/tvf/DemCenter.	Research unit on *Historical Demography* (*Hans Chr. Johansen*)

continued

---

[4] For detailed references see the Bibliography in this volume and Rothenbacher (1998a and 1997b).

TABLE 6.2 Demographic research centres in Europe (continued)

Country	Demographic research centre	Major contribution to historical demographic statistics[5]
Denmark (continued)	Nordic Network for Historical Demography, Odense University, Odense. Internet: http://www.ou.dk/tvf/DemCenter/Nordic/nordic_network.html.	Individual publications
Finland	Population Research Unit, Department of Sociology, University of Helsinki, Helsinki. Internet: http://www.valt.helsinki.fi/sosio/pru/.	Occasional titles
	Population Research Institute, Helsinki. Internet: http://www.vaestoliitto.fi/tlaitos_en.htm.	*Yearbook of Population Research in Finland 19..*
France	Institut National d'Etudes Démographiques (INED), Paris. Internet: http://www.ined.fr.	Several historical demographic handbooks. Articles on historical demography in *Population*.
Germany	Bundesinstitut für Bevölkerungsforschung (BIB) at the Statistischen Bundesamt, Wiesbaden.	Occasional titles
	Bevölkerungswissenschaft, Humboldt Universität, Institut Sozialwissenschaften, Berlin. Internet: http://www.demographie.de/english/index.htm.	Occasional titles
	Max Planck Institute for Demographic Research, Rostock. Internet: http://www.demogr.mpg.de.	Occasional titles
Greece	National Centre for Social Research (EKKE), Athens. Internet: http://www.ekke.gr/index.html.	The scientific work of *Michalis Chouliarakis*
Hungary	Központi Statisztikai Hivatal (Hungarian Central Statistical Office), Budapest. Internet: http://www.ksh.hu/eng/homeng.html.	*Time Series of Historical Statistics 1867–1992. Volume I: Population—Vital Statistics*
Iceland	Hagstofa Íslands (Statistics Iceland), Reykjavik. Internet: http://www.hagstofa.is/.	*Icelandic Historical Statistics*
Ireland	Central Statistics Office (CSO), Dublin. Internet: http://www.cso.ie/.	Occasional titles
Italy	Dipartimento di Scienze Demografiche, Università di Roma La Sapienza, Rome. Internet: http://www.uniroma1.it/scidemo/presentazione.htm.	Occasional titles
Luxemburg	Service National de la Statistique et des Etudes Economiques (STATEC), Luxemburg. Internet: http://statec.gouvernement.lu/.	Historical statistics by STATEC and *Georges Als* (1989, 1991)
The Netherlands	Statistics Netherlands, Voorburg and Herleen. Internet: http://www.cbs.nl.	Different historical statistics published in 1999[6]

continued

---

[5] For detailed references see the Bibliography in this volume and Rothenbacher (1998a and 1997b).
[6] See EURODATA Newsletter No. 10, Autumn 1999: 33–4.

TABLE 6.2 Demographic research centres in Europe (continued)

Country	Demographic research centre	Major contribution to historical demographic statistics[7]
The Netherlands (continued)	Netherlands Interdisciplinary Demographic Institute (N.I.D.I), The Hague. Internet: http://www.nidi.nl/.	Occasional titles
Norway	Statistisk sentralbyrå (SSB), Oslo. Internet: http://www.ssb.no/main.html.	*Historical Statistics*
Poland	Polska Statystyka Publiczna, Warsaw. Internet: http://www.stat.gov.pl/index.htm.	*Historia Polski W Liczbach. Ludność. Terytorium*
Portugal	Instituto Nacional de Estatística (INE), Lisbon. Internet: http://www.ine.pt.	Retrospective statistics series
	Instituto de Ciências Sociais da Universidade de Lisboa (ICS), Lisbon. Internet: http://www.ics.ul.pt/.	Occasional titles
Spain	Centre d'Estudis Demogràfics, Universitat Autonoma de Barcelona, Barcelona. Internet: http://www.ced.uab.es/.	Occasional titles
Sweden	Stockholm University Demography Unit (SUDA), Stockholm. Internet: http://www.suda.su.se.	Occasional titles
	Statistics Sweden, Stockholm and Örebro. Internet: http://www.scb.se.	Historical statistics by Statistics Sweden
Switzerland	Université de Genève, Laboratoire de démographie économique et sociale, Geneva. Internet: http://www.unige.ch/ses/demog/.	Occasional titles
United Kingdom	London School of Economics, Population Investigation Committee, London, Internet: http://www.lse.ac.uk/.	*Population Studies*
	Cambridge Group for the History of Population and Social Structure, Cambridge University. Internet: http://www.cam.ac.uk/.	*Cambridge Studies in Population, Economy and Society in Past Time*
International		
	League of Nations, Geneva	*Statistical Yearbook of the League of Nations*
	United Nations Statistics Division (UNSD), New York. Internet: http://www.un. org/Deps/unsd.	*Demographic Yearbook*
	United Nations Children's Fund (UNICEF), International Child Development Centre, Florence, Italy. Internet: http://www.unicef-icdc.org/.	Occasional titles e.g. on infant mortality

Against this background, this data handbook is intended to enable and strengthen basic demographic research in the fields of national and European demographic developments. It is superior to national efforts in that from the beginning it tries to collect statistical information comparatively or at least documents the definitions of statistical concepts when the data are obviously not comparable.

---

[7] For detailed references see the Bibliography in this volume and Rothenbacher (1998a and 1997b).

What should be the subject of further research? *First*, one of the main desiderata for further research is surely the *scientific exploitation* of the material gathered in this handbook, especially of those statistics which have not been collected until now. While the Princeton European Fertility Project has provided good knowledge about the fertility transition in Europe, even on a regional basis, this is not the case for other demographic variables. For general mortality and infant mortality the database and analysis have not progressed to such a degree, as postulated by authors such as Schofield, Reher, and Bideau (1991). A project like the Princeton European Fertility Project has never been organized on the topic of mortality decline in Europe, nor for one important aspect of mortality, namely infant mortality. There is no consolidated database, but several studies have dealt with the decline of infant mortality in the last years (cf. Corsini and Viazzo, 1993a and 1997). By contrast, Jean-Claude Chesnais (1992) has dealt extensively with the demographic transition, and there are not likely to be any new insights going beyond his fundamental results, typologies, and explanations.

Although the data in this handbook only refer to the national level, new results and insights could result from analysing the data included, particularly concerning topics such as overall mortality, infant mortality, nuptiality and other marriage characteristics, and finally divorce behaviour, on which much less research in a historical-comparative European context has been carried out.

Second, the extension to Eastern Europe. When the data handbook was envisaged before the great changes of 1990, the fall of the Iron Curtain and subsequent developments in Russia and the Balkans could not have been foreseen. Including the whole of Western and Southern Europe was already an advance when compared to other data handbooks. The three east-central European countries were able to be included in this handbook, though most of the Balkans and the states of the former Soviet Union could not. This task would have been exceeded the authors' expertise, first, because of the language problem: for these countries, statistics in the inter-war period are fortunately mostly in two languages, but before World War I and after World War II they are overwhelmingly only in the national language. Second, the availability of statistics is clearly restricted for these countries. Without specialized research projects it will not be possible to cover the Eastern European countries using historical demographic statistics. Very often, the statistics were not available in the microfilm collection, and lending from foreign libraries is more or less impossible. Only through research stays in the respective countries or a network of correspondents with knowledge of the relevant languages would it be possible to collect the necessary information. Neither option was available to the project. Another difficulty arises with the sheer number of countries. While this handbook now comprises 21 countries, the inclusion of all the Eastern European countries would have expanded this figure to 26 (adding Albania, Bulgaria, Romania, the Soviet Union, and Yugoslavia). But figures for such diverse federations would be completely meaningless, and data would have had to be presented for the federal states of the Soviet Union and Yugoslavia. The breakup of the Soviet Union, Czechoslovakia, and Yugoslavia created such a large number of newly independent states that this task would have been impossible, with 38 countries over such a long time period. Since 1990 the following have split up or gained independence to become sovereign nations: the Czech Republic, Slovak Republic; Estonia, Latvia,

Lithuania; Russia, Ukraine, Moldavia, Byelorussia and other former Soviet Republics; Slovenia, Croatia, Macedonia, and Bosnia-Hercegovina.

Third, regionalization of the data. Regional data have been collected by the Princeton European Fertility Project over many years for certain demographic variables, and many researchers have been involved in this work. In the context of the present project it would have been impossible to collect data at the regional level for all the variables involved in this handbook for such a long period of time. Such work can only be done for selected demographic variables such as infant mortality, which would in any case need a large research staff. Concerning the demographic variables included in the Princeton European Fertility Project, no duplication is necessary, and future regionalization of data should build upon this dataset. Further extensions could be the cartographic representation of regional data. This is of course also possible for the national level, but the national averages hide large internal variations. Regional data on population size and area of the countries (in square km.) have been collected by Michael Quick (cf. Quick, 1994; Caramani, Flora, and Quick, 1998) for 18 European countries from the 1870s to the 1990s. This database can be and has been used to describe regional population growth, regional population density, and regional territorial changes. The regional information given in the second section of each country chapter on population density and growth is based on this data collection.

Fourth, this data collection could of course be extended substantially. More refined indicators could be formulated, and much more disaggregated information—not only regionally disaggregated—could be collected. For example, data on perinatal and child mortality could be included, or data on internal migration, emigration, and immigration.

Finally, a systematic *inventory of the family laws* in the different countries could be taken. Family law is surely one important variable for understanding marital behaviour, the development and level of divorce, and legitimate and illegitimate fertility, among others.

Part II
Country Chapters

1

Austria

The Austrian Empire as it existed until the end of World War I was a multinational, multiethnic, and multilingual empire. It was built during centuries of competition with other powers such as the Ottoman Empire, the Russian Empire, France, and Spain. The Congress of Vienna in 1815 let the empire reach its largest extension, encompassing such territories as Poland, Bohemia, Moravia, Silesia, Slovakia, parts of Italy, Slovenia, Croatia (Istria and Dalmatia), Galicia, and Transylvania in addition to present-day Austria and Hungary.

The nineteenth century was mainly shaped by the processes of nation-building by the Germans and the Italians. In Germany the Prussians succeeded in pushing the Austrians out of the new German nation. In Italy, the Habsburg Empire possessed large areas in the North: the Veneto, Trentino and South Tyrol, and Lombardy. These were the fruits of Napoleon's defeat and of Metternich's diplomatic success at the Congress of Vienna. The drive for a national state in the first half of the nineteenth century (Serbia, Greece, Belgium, Poland) also started in Italy. During the Italian wars of unification, the empire lost Lombardy in 1859 and the Veneto in 1866.

In the large eastern territories formerly under Byzantine, Venetian, and later Ottoman rule, nationalist movements started later than in the western parts of the empire. Only with Hungary did the empire reach a compromise: under the terms of the 1867 *Ausgleich*, the empire was split into two halves, with the Leitha River marking the boundary (Cisleithania: 'on this side of the Leith River', i.e. Austria; Transleithania: 'on the other side of the Leitha River', i.e. Hungary). Cisleithania, the Austrian half of the empire, also belonged to the German Union (*Deutscher Bund*). Transleithania, the Hungarian half, included a vast territory of different populations.

The continuing decline of the Ottoman Empire led in 1878 to massive territorial losses for Turkey in the Balkans. The Congress of Berlin in 1881 led to the creation of several new nation-states in the Balkans, such as Serbia, Romania, and Bulgaria, and to the expansion of others, such as Greece. Austria-Hungary occupied Bosnia-Hercegovina, which in 1908 was annexed to Austria.

Growing rivalries between the major powers Russia, Britain, and Austria over the territories of south-eastern Europe ('who will inherit the "sick man on the Bosporus?"') contributed to the 'outbreak' of World War I.

By the end of World War I the Austro-Hungarian Empire was dissolved according to the principle of nationalities. Several national states were created in Eastern and south-eastern Europe: already in 1918 Czechoslovakia, which included the former Austrian territories of Bohemia, Moravia, and Slovakia, was recognized by the main powers. Yugoslavia was created out of the Hungarian territories of Slovenia, Croatia (including the Dalmatian coast), Bosnia-Hercegovina, and the already independent Serbia. Romania was enlarged by adding Bukovina and Transylvania which were transferred from Hungary. Poland was reconstructed as an independent state and received Galicia and Silesia from the Austro-Hungarian Empire. Finally, Italy received the Trentino and South Tyrol up to the Brenner Pass for its participation in the war, as promised by the Allies.

At the end of World War I the first Austrian Republic was founded in several steps: on 21 October 1918 the German-speaking representatives of the former *Reichsrat* formed the Provisional National Assembly of the Autonomous German-Austrian state; on 30 October 1918 the Assembly proclaimed the Austrian Republic; and on 11 November 1918 the emperor abdicated. The only territorial change in the inter-war period was the 1921 addition of the Burgenland, which was mainly German-speaking, from the Hungarian half. The first Austrian Republic ended in 1934 with the founding of the Corporate State under Dollfuss. In 1938 the Germans annexed Austria in violation of the peace treaty of Versailles. With the foundation of the Republic, Austria was divided into nine *Länder* (federal states). The federal structure was inherited from the empire, but was discontinued under the Corporate State and the annexation to the German Empire. The territory remained more or less unchanged from 1921 to the end of World War II (for general literature on Austria see Schwenger, 1999).

REGIONAL POPULATION STRUCTURE

The Austrian Empire as it existed until the end of World War I had a rather large territory. Population in absolute terms was high, but population density was rather low, at least when compared with countries like Belgium or The Netherlands. In 1869 population density was 67 inhabitants per square km.; by 1910 it had increased to 95 inhabitants per square km.

In 1869 regional differences in population density were still rather small. Only Trieste had a very high population density because of the small territory of the city and its hinterland. The industrialized provinces of Lower Austria (Niederösterreich), Moravia, Silesia, and Bohemia also showed higher population density, which increased greatly up to 1910.

With the end of World War I and the loss of large tracts of territory, Austria lost most of its industrial centres to Czechoslovakia and Poland, and was reduced to the Alpine region and the Danube River floodplain. One effect was that population density in the Austrian Republic in 1923 was lower than in the Austrian Empire in 1910. Until 1951 population density increased only marginally, which is understandable from the low natural population growth (see section below). The country became more and more monocephalic with Vienna as its centre. Suburbanization and commuting changed this situation slowly.

POPULATION GROWTH

In 1869 the total population in the Austrian Empire was 20,218,000 inhabitants. By 1910 it had increased to 28,572,000 inhabitants, an absolute increase of over eight million people. The natural population growth in the Austrian Empire was therefore rather high with figures fluctuating around 10 per 1,000. Net migration was mostly negative, but usually in the range of 0 to 3 per 1,000. The existing emigration nevertheless was not strong enough to hinder a rather robust population increase. Population gains showed great regional variations: industrializing regions that attracted labour immigrants and had a higher share of workers showed faster increases than others.

If we look at the figures which have been recalculated for the territory of the later Austrian Republic (Figure A.1), we can detect a major difference to the developments in the Austrian Empire. In the territory of the later Austrian Republic the natural population growth rate was much less than in the Austrian Empire. From the 1870s to the 1890s it only fluctuated at around 5 per 1,000. It increased during the 1890s, peaked in the early 1900s, but declined again until World War I. It did not reach the level of 10 per 1,000 until 1913. Nevertheless and rather surprisingly, the total population growth rate was as high as in the Austrian Empire. The explaining factor is the positive net migration rate in the later territory of the Austrian Republic. From the 1870s to World War I immigration from the eastern and southern parts of the Empire to the territory of the later Austrian Republic was very strong. It was high from the 1870s to the 1890s, but declined from the 1890s to World War I.

Population change during the time of the Austrian Republic in the inter-war period was very different from the time before World War I. Natural population growth peaked immediately after the First World War, then declined during the 1920s and 1930s so much that it became negative in the late 1930s. The strong immigration stopped during the 1920s and was outpaced by emigration. Only during the early 1930s was Austria again a country of—low—immigration. Total population growth during the inter-war period was therefore lower than before World War I. It stagnated during the 1920s and declined during the 1930s, when population growth finally became negative, i.e. the population declined in absolute terms.

THE FIRST DEMOGRAPHIC TRANSITION

There are two different time series on the demographic transition of Austria: one for the Austrian Empire from 1850–1913, and the other for the territory of the Austrian Republic from 1871 onwards. The latter have been recalculated for the territory of the Austrian Republic before 1913. Here we describe the demographic transition of Austria before World War I both for the Austrian Empire from 1850 to 1913 and for the territory of the later Austrian Republic from 1871 to 1913. From 1919 to 1939 we refer to the figures for the Austrian Republic.

Demographic transition in the Austrian Empire was characterized by a high birth rate and a high death rate. The death rate in the nineteenth century was well above the European average, due to the rather high infant mortality in the Austrian Empire at that time. Until the 1880s there were strong fluctuations in the birth rate and the death rate, mainly due to epidemics, wars, and economic crises. Austria was Prussia's ally in its 1864 war against Denmark, and in 1867 it was allied with the Southern German states in their war against the Prussians. It was not directly involved in the Franco-Prussian War of 1870/71, but did fight in the Italian wars of unification. The final and irreversible decline in the birth rate came in 1880 and was paralleled by the decline in the death rate. Until the outbreak of World War I there was a rather smooth and peaceful evolution of both demographic indices, resulting in a high natural population increase. There are no data on vital statistics for the war

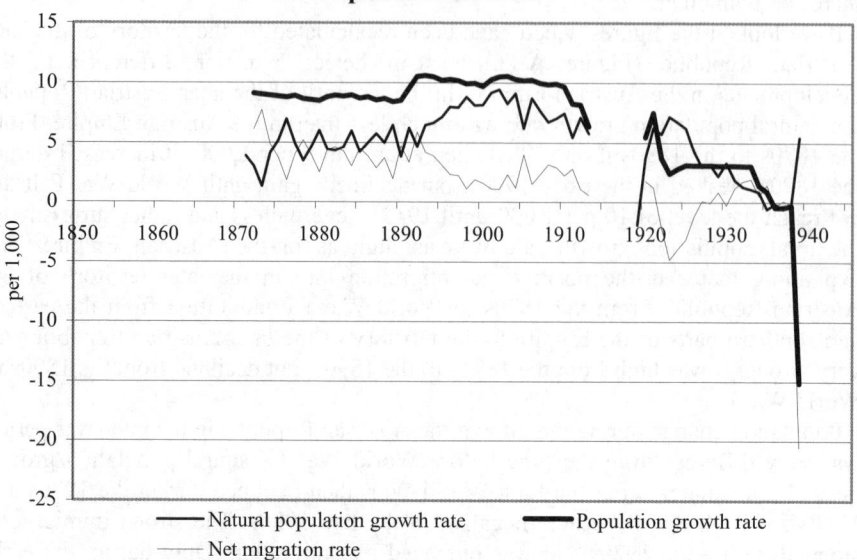

Figure A.1 Population growth and net migration, Austrian Republic 1871-1939

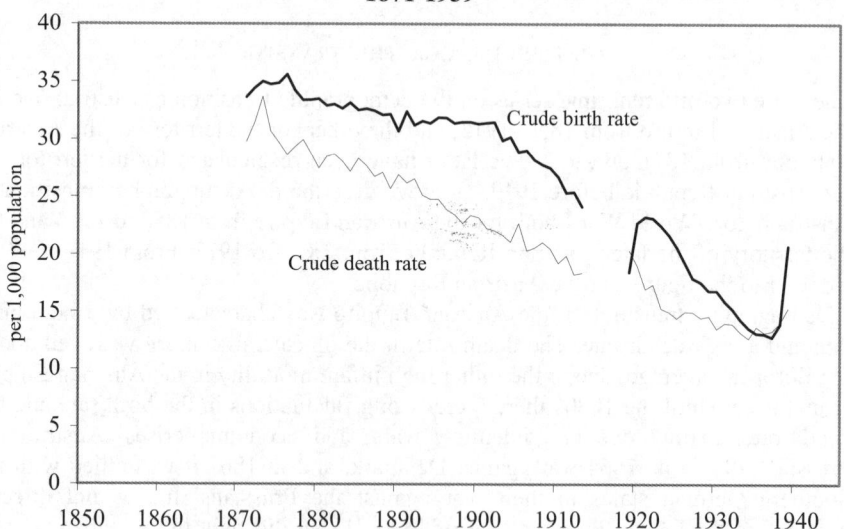

Figure A.2 First demographic transition, Austrian Republic 1871-1939

years, neither for the Austrian Empire nor for the later territory of the Austrian Republic.

The demographic transition in the second half of the nineteenth century in the territory of the later Austrian Republic differs from the demographic transition in the Austrian Empire mainly in one respect: natural population growth was very much lower in the territory of the later Austrian Republic (Figure A.2). This was mainly due to a smaller crude birth rate, which had a structurally lower level and started to decline earlier than in the Austrian Empire. The second difference is the much higher infant mortality rate in the Austrian Republic.

After World War I and the collapse of the Austrian Empire, things changed completely. In the Austrian Republic, marriages and births were recovered, after being postponed because of the war, but in the early 1920s a massive birth decline set in, culminating in a severe demographic crisis in the late 1930s (1938 with the annexation by the Germans), when the birth rate fell below the death rate, resulting in a negative natural population increase. Nevertheless, the following couple of years saw the birth rate recover, mainly due to improved economic and political prospects, but probably also due to population policy measures imported from Germany. Again there are no data for the years of World War II.

Economic crises and wars therefore had a great influence on the demographic transition in Austria. This is apparent already in the 1850s with the world economic crisis in that decade (Rosenberg, 1974), the different wars of the 1860s, World War I, the world economic crisis of the late 1920s and early 1930s, the politically unstable years of the 1930s, and finally World War II.

In a European comparison it can be said that during the Austrian Empire there was a much higher population turnover than on the European average; the birth rate was not so much higher, but the mortality rate and especially the infant mortality rate were very much higher than in Europe. The combined effect was a much lower natural population increase in the Austrian Empire than the European average. The latter continued especially during the Austrian Republic, when the birth rate was a great deal lower than the European average.

MORTALITY AND LIFE EXPECTANCY

Infant mortality in Austria was very high during the nineteenth century compared to Northern and Western Europe (Figure A.3). The infant mortality rate is defined as deaths of children aged under one year per 1,000 live births. According to Masuy-Stroobant (1997) Austria fits into the cluster of the Mediterranean countries comprising Italy, Spain, and Greece (and Czechoslovakia) with rather high child mortality into the first decades of the twentieth century. Austria had one of the highest child mortality rates in this country cluster with over 220 deaths per 1,000 live births. This figure is dramatically higher than for the first cluster with the lowest child mortality of the time, the Nordic countries.

Austria thus does not fit into the Western European pattern of moderate child mortality, but rather into the Eastern and Southern European pattern of high child mortality during the nineteenth and early twentieth century. The main difference in child mortality between Austria and Balkan countries such as Romania, Bulgaria, and Yugoslavia is not the level of child mortality around 1900, which was very similar, but the much faster decline in child mortality in Austria (and the whole

Figure A.3 Infant mortality, Austrian Republic 1871-1945

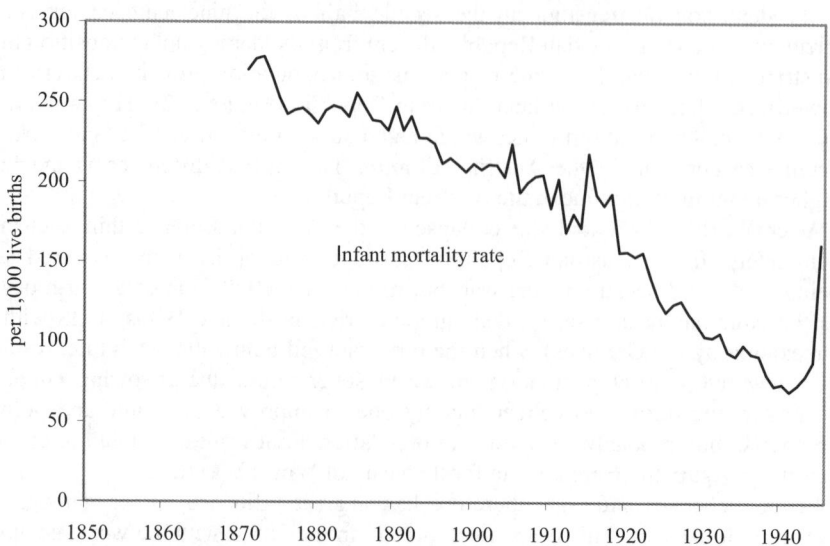

Figure A.4 Life expectancy, Austrian Empire 1870/80-1906/10, Austrian Republic 1930/33

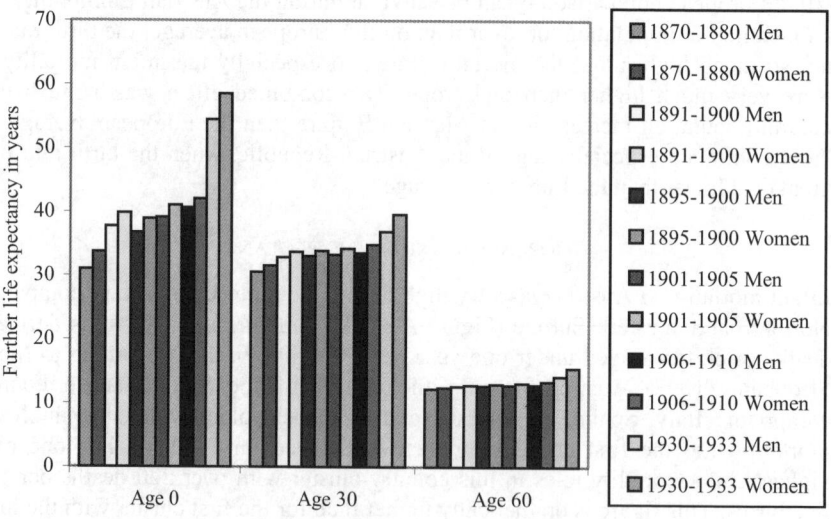

Mediterranean cluster) than in the Balkans, where it took much longer for child mortality to be reduced.

In the nineteenth century child mortality in Austria was very high: around 1850 it amounted to 275 deaths per 1,000 live births. Infant mortality declined substantially only after the 1880s (Kytir and Münz, 1993).

Causes for the high child mortality in Austria are not easily discernible. Regional disparities were rather large in Austria. Infant mortality was much lower in the Alpine regions than in the Austrian lowlands. This difference existed in 1871/75 and was still in existence in 1946/50.

Child mortality also differed between towns and rural districts, and was much higher in towns than in the rural regions. The main difference between the Alpine regions and the non-Alpine regions in child mortality is also stressed by Viazzo (1997).

Life expectancy was very low compared to countries with the best health status at that time, such as Sweden. In Austria in 1870/80 life expectancy for boys at birth was 31 years, compared with 45.3 years in Sweden (1871/80), a difference of 14 years. In 1871/80, life expectancy for 30-year-old male Austrians was 4.5 years less than for male Swedes, and at age 60 the difference was two years (Figure A.4). The same was true for females. Up to the 1930s Austrian life expectancy at birth started to catch up with the Swedish conditions: in 1930/33, male life expectancy at birth in Austria was 54.5 years, compared to 63 years in Sweden (1931/35), thus the difference in life expectancy was cut in half, from 14 to seven years. However, although life expectancy at age 30 and 60 increased in absolute terms, there was no relative improvement (convergence) compared e.g. with Sweden. Sex differences in life expectancy favoured women slightly before World War I, and increased until the 1930s.

FERTILITY AND LEGITIMACY

The Western European marriage pattern *ceteris paribus* favours out-of-wedlock births because it leads many people to remain single or live together without marrying. But the level of illegitimate births in Austria far exceeds anything the model might predict. Illegitimacy in Austria during the nineteenth century in effect was the highest in all of Europe (Figure A.5).

There are several reasons for this phenomenon. Along with southern Portugal, the Austrian province of Carinthia had the highest illegitimacy rates in Europe during the nineteenth century. Illegitimacy in Carinthia was due to a very low propensity to marry, frequent out-of-wedlock births, and widespread unmarried cohabitation. The dominance of agriculture and the law of primogeniture forced young men to wait for a longer period before they could marry. Unmarried cohabitation and having children before marriage was a socially accepted and common pattern of behaviour.

Nevertheless, although Carinthia had the highest illegitimate fertility rates in Austria, illegitimacy was high in other provinces as well. Factors contributing to this pattern were primogeniture throughout the rural and Alpine regions, the extreme proletarianization of the lowland population, and a general laxity concerning whether children were born within or outside marriage.

The diachronic development of the illegitimate fertility rate reveals one master trend, the long-term decline of illegitimate fertility in Austria as well as in Europe generally. In the 1870s there was a major downswing in the rate, the reasons for

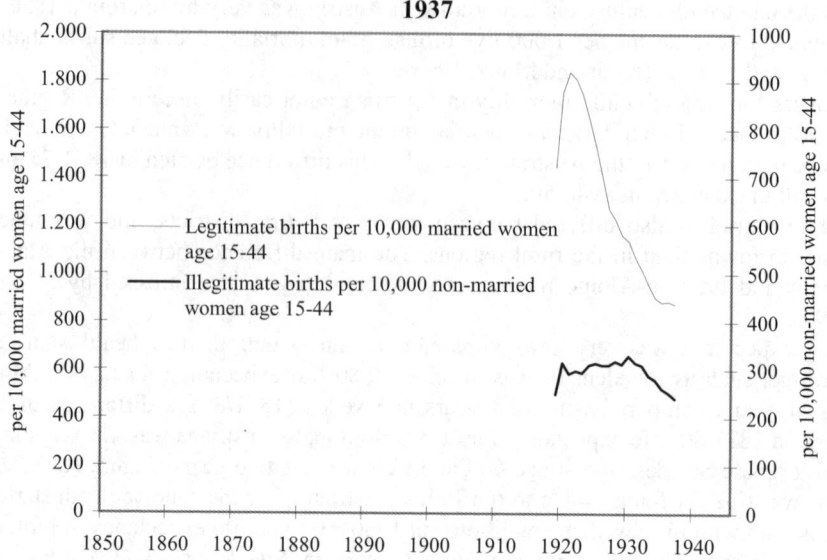

Figure A.5 Fertility and legitimacy, Austrian Republic 1919-1937

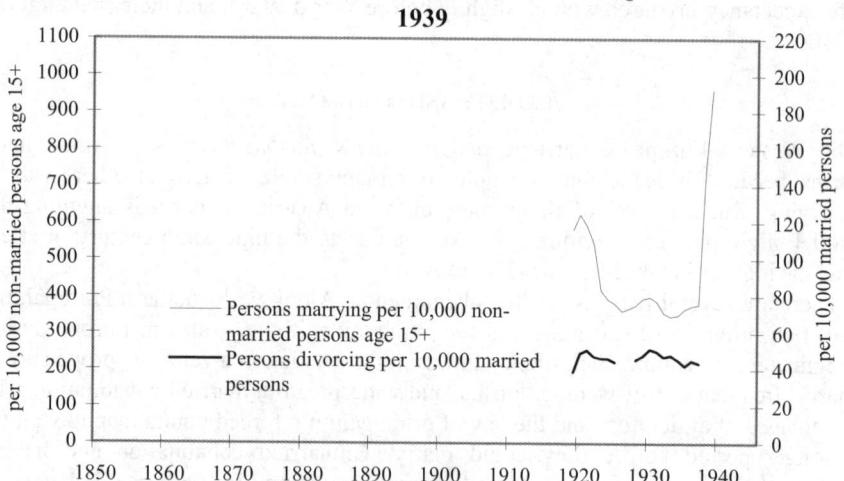

Figure A.6 Marriages and divorces, Austrian Republic 1919-1939

which are not clear. During the inter-war period, in the 1920s, the illegitimacy rate first increased, probably due to the difficult economic situation of that time, and then fell after the end of the world economic recession. After World War II the illegitimacy rate initially rose and then stabilized. At the end of the 1970s there was another downswing in the illegitimate birth rate.

The *legitimate children ratio* is the main indicator for fertility development, because even in Austria most children were born within marriage. The macro-trend in Austria as everywhere in Europe is a decline in marital fertility. But in the Austrian Empire in the second half of the nineteenth century until World War I the legitimate fertility rate was above the European average. Thus, illegitimate fertility and legitimate fertility together add up to the high birth rate of the Austrian Empire at that time. After World War I legitimate births postponed during the war were recovered. The decline in legitimate births during the inter-war period was dramatic, and the Austrian legitimate birth rate was well below the European average. After World War II the legitimate birth rate recovered; there was a rather significant baby boom during the 1960s, when the Austrian legitimate birth rate even exceeded the European rate, but from the 1970s onward the Austrian level was below the European.

If one calculates the ratio between the illegitimate and the legitimate birth rate, then it is clear that for all of the 150 years considered here Austria had disproportional illegitimate fertility, compared with the European average. There was a wave of illegitimate births from the 1920s to the 1940s. Although Austria has been characterized by a high number of out-of-wedlock births, it has participated in the trend towards marriage at higher ages leading to lower marital fertility. The increasing proportion of illegitimate relative to legitimate births is not primarily caused by rising out-of-wedlock births, but by declining marital births.

MARRIAGE AND DIVORCE

Although situated at the eastern periphery of Western Europe, Austria still belongs to the region of the Western European marriage pattern. Some regions in Austria follow a more typically Eastern European marriage pattern, such as Carinthia, with a small Slovene minority, and the Burgenland, but only regional demographic data could reveal such intranational differences. In any case, in the territory of the later Republic of Austria, age at marriage was high, as was the celibacy rate. In the nineteenth century age at marriage was one of the highest in Western Europe; accordingly, the celibacy rate was also one of the highest in Western Europe.

Austria, Germany, Switzerland, and The Netherlands form their own cluster within the Western European marriage pattern. The distinguishing features are an even higher age at marriage for both sexes than in the Nordic cluster, a still higher celibacy rate of women aged 45–54 than in the Nordic countries, and a constantly lower marriage rate, at least during the twentieth century.

Shortly after the turn of the century, in 1910, the proportion of women married at age 20–24 was below 20 per cent, and even decreased slightly until the 1930s. The fall in the mean age at marriage came later in Austria than in the other countries of this cluster, and the 'nuptiality revolution' was not as intense as in other countries of this cluster or the Nordic cluster. In the 1960s the proportion of women married at age 20–24 was only about 45% and was 10 per cent lower than e.g. in Germany. The mean age at marriage declined later than in other countries and also started to rise again later.

Concerning men, the proportion married at age 20–24 in 1910 was at the European extreme, at only 3%. That means a very high age at first marriage for men, which can be explained by a higher legal minimum marriage age, very long military service, or very high economic and social barriers to marriage (e.g. university education; long preparation for a stable and lucrative career as a civil servant; waiting for fathers to retire in order to take over the farm). The proportion of men married at age 20–24 increased to 5% in 1934. In the late 1930s men's age at first marriage fell and the proportion of men married at age 20–24 rose, peaking in 1970 at 26%. After 1970 men's age at first marriage began to rise again, as it did for Austrian women. Interestingly, Austrian women's mean age at first marriage remained comparatively low in the 1980s, indicating that Austrians did not start marrying at higher ages until after the other countries in this cluster.

Marriage intensity as a construct can be measured by the *marriage rate* and the *celibacy rate*. Marriage intensity refers to the availability of marriage, the extent of legal, social, and economic constraints shaping nuptiality, and individual inclination to marry, to remain single, or to cohabit. Marriage intensity also encompasses the urgent need to remarry after widowhood, which was very widespread especially in Austria and was termed 'remarriage need' (*Wiederverheiratungszwang*) by the Austrian family historian Michael Mitterauer. In particular, rural populations in a demographic regime with high mortality (especially mortality of mothers at childbirth, which was very high) were urged to remarry immediately in order to ensure care for the existing children and elderly.

Celibacy of women (measured by the proportion of women never married at age 45–54) was very high in Austria in 1910 with 34% and was only exceeded by Ireland and Finland at that time, both of which were suffering economic hardship and were outliers in the European context. The celibacy of women even increased slightly until 1934 to 35%. In 1951 celibacy of women had declined, but increased again until 1961. The completely new stage of 'universal marriage' came after this time point and was carried by the birth cohorts of the 1920s and 1930s. Celibacy of these birth cohorts remained under 10% of all women in the 45–54 age group.

The second indicator of marriage intensity is the *marriage rate* (Figure A.6). This is an aggregate indicator and includes several different factors, rendering explanations difficult. Austria shows several similarities to Germany concerning demographic behaviour, and the same is true for marriage behaviour. As in the German Empire, in the Austrian Empire the marriage rate was above the European average during the second half of the nineteenth century until the outbreak of World War I (the last census before the war was in 1910). After World War I the marriage rate in the Austrian Republic remained constantly below the European average. After World War I postponed marriages were made up, but during the 1920s and 1930s the marriage rate declined considerably. After 1938, the marriage rate rose strongly, probably due to the official National Socialist population policy, but probably also due to improved economic prospects. After World War II postponed marriages were again recovered as after the previous war, but soon nuptiality reached its low Austrian level again. In the 1980s there were two peaks of the marriage rate due to family policy changes: the first one occurred in 1983, when deduction of the dowry in income tax was abolished and rumours came up on the abolition of the marriage allowance (*'Heiratsbeihilfe'*) by 1 January 1984. Actually the marriage allowance was kept unchanged. A second much stronger increase of the marriage rate occurred in 1987, when the marriage allowance was finally abolished (Statistik Österreich, 2000: 28; Münz, 1984: 95).

To summarize, 'modernization of nuptiality patterns' in Austria was weaker than in the Nordic countries and among the other continental (predominantly) Germanic countries (The Netherlands, Switzerland, and Germany). Modernization started later and was slower. Accordingly, the *'post-modern'* nuptiality pattern was delayed as well. Because modernization of nuptiality (i.e. universal and early marriage) was less dramatic than elsewhere, the return to *pre-modern patterns*, which constitutes the *post-modern pattern*, did not have to be so strong.

Given the high celibacy rates and the pronounced Western European marriage pattern with non-universal marriage and low marriage propensity, it is quite surprising how unstable marriages were in Austria during the twentieth century. But there is a marked contrast to the nineteenth century when the divorce rate was below the European average for the whole time from the 1880s to World War I. The divorce rate during the inter-war period was nowhere so high in Europe as in Austria. During the early 1920s the divorce rate declined somewhat, but increased again around the 1930s, and after 1938 there was a major increase in the divorce rate, probably due to the National Socialist race legislation. It declined in the early 1930s, after the world economic crisis had ended.

After World War II, *divorces* increased strongly, an effect of the war which can be noticed in all the European countries involved in World War II (Figure A.6). In the 1960s the Austrian divorce rate declined to a lower level, but remained well over the European average. In the decades from the 1970s to the 1990s the level of divorce was constantly over the European level. There was obviously no major divorce law reform, and there was no major change in the divorce rate.

Legal separation was possible in Austria and data are available from 1882 to 1935.

AGE, SEX, AND CIVIL STATUS

Appendix Figure A.8 presents the age structure of the population of the Austrian Empire from 1880 to 1910 and the Austrian Republic from 1934 to 1939. From 1880 to 1900 the age structure of the Austrian Empire displayed a rather regular pyramidal form with a concave pattern for the lowest age groups, indicating that the birth rate was rather high, but that infant and child mortality was also high, therefore reducing the age group of 0–4-year-olds strongly. Between the censuses of 1900 and 1910 first signs of a birth decline appeared, reducing the proportions of the lowest age groups. The Austrian wars with Italy in the 1860s had obviously only a minor influence on the age structure of the population. But the impact of World War I was severe: in the Austrian Republic in 1934 the age group of 15–19-year-olds was strongly reduced, caused by the loss of births during World War I. While the birth cohorts of the early 1920s recovered this loss of children to some extent, the birth decline continued during the late 1920s and 1930s. The youngest age group of 0–4 years was very small, probably due to the low incidence of births during the Great Depression 1929/33. In 1939 the age structure became even more bell-shaped because of continued birth decline.

Age at marriage was higher for females than for males, and did not fall significantly for males from 1880 to 1910 in the Austrian Empire. At higher ages the proportion of males married was higher than that of females due to higher male mortality and therefore more widespread widowhood for females. The proportions widowed were rather high in 1880 mainly for females in their 60s, probably caused by the Austrian wars in the nineteenth century; this proportion declined slightly until 1910. Celibacy was slightly higher for females than for males, and a small proportion of both sexes remained unmarried all their lives.

The age structure in the Austrian Republic was deeply disturbed by World War I and the economic and political crises of the inter-war period, which affected Austria more than other European countries. The effects can be seen from the high age at marriage and the high celibacy rates of men and particularly women. Economic difficulties made people postpone or even cancel marriages. The proportion of widows grew strongly in the 1930s due to the major war losses in 1914–18.

FAMILY AND HOUSEHOLD STRUCTURES

Against the background of high celibacy and late marriage, one must ask where the single or widowed people lived. Did they join family households or did they form single-person households? The discussion of this question can only be based on a few indicators, because information on extended households or families is not available.

One indicator could be *mean household size*. In Austria, it should be noted, not households but dwellings (*Wohnparteien*) have been counted. The number of households is normally higher than the number of dwellings, because there may be dwellings with more than one household. A time series for the territory of the later Austrian Republic shows that in 1869 the mean size of a *Wohnpartei* was 5.2 persons. Until 1934 this average shrank to 3.8 persons per *Wohnpartei*. Compared with other countries, the mean number of persons living in a private dwelling was rather high. This is underlined by the rather small proportion of single-person households (6%), the number of which was first available for 1910 for the territory of the Austrian monarchy. Reduction in household size is mainly due to the increase in one-person households and the decrease in very large households.

Data for the nine *Bundesländer* from 1869 to 1934 show that the mean number of persons per private dwelling was largest in Steiermark (5.6) and Vienna (5.5) and smallest in Vorarlberg (4.4). By 1934 the picture had changed completely: the highest number was now in Vorarlberg with 5.3, the lowest in Vienna with 3.5. Vienna, as a large city and capital, had a high number of persons per dwelling in 1869: at that time many servants, boarders, and lodgers were still living in shared dwellings. The differentiation of non-family persons from the households and the extinction of these social categories, accompanied by a significant reduction in urban fertility, led in Vienna to the greatest drop in number of persons per dwelling of all *Bundesländer* (a decrease of 2.0 persons on average). In Vorarlberg, mean household size increased in the years 1910 and 1934. This increase is mainly due to a sudden increase in the population, which must primarily be attributed to immigration.

There are very interesting statistics on household composition for the census years 1910 and 1934, and for all *Bundesländer*. Family members are distinguished, as are non-family members such as foster children, boarders and lodgers, and servants, among others. Inmates of institutions were also counted. On the national level, the percentage of household heads and wives increased, the share of own children declined, boarders and lodgers increased, while other non-family members declined relatively.

Population Structure

The first modern population census in the Austrian Empire was conducted in 1869, after the *Ausgleich* of 1867. But census-taking in Austria has a long tradition and dates back to the mid-eighteenth century (cf. Durdik, 1973). Until 1910 population censuses were held every full decade. World War I interrupted the regular series of population censuses. The addition of the Burgenland in 1921 made it necessary to count the population of the new Republic. Only one further population census was organized by the Austrian statistics in 1934. The 1939 German population census included Austria which had been occupied by Germany in 1938.

Population by age (in one-year age groups), sex, and in combination with marital status was collected in the 1880 census. The 1869 census collected age and marital status separately. All censuses after 1880 maintained the collection of these basic population statistics (Österreichisches Statistisches Zentralamt, 1979a; 1979b). Ladstätter (1973) provides documentation of the contents of the population censuses in Austria from 1869 to 1971.

Vital Statistics

The recording of births, deaths, and marriages in the Austrian Empire was already introduced in the first half of the nineteenth century (1819) and continued until 1913 when most series stop due to World War I. After the war data were collected only for the Austrian Republic.

During the Austrian Empire disaggregations of these basic demographic variables were introduced at later stages: deaths by age (infant mortality), births by legitimacy in 1869, stillbirths in 1881. Divorces and legal separations were introduced in 1882.

There are two different time series of vital statistics available: for the Austrian Empire until 1913 and for the Austrian Republic which have been calculated back for the territory of the Republic until 1871.

Households and Families

Data on households (*Haushaltungen*, later *Haushalte*) were first expressively—using this word—collected in the population census of 1900. The earlier censuses in 1869, 1880, and 1890 used the dwelling (*Wohnpartei*) as unit of investigation. The official report on the 1900 census says that the results for households and for dwellings (*Wohnparteien*) are approximately comparable, although several households may of course live in the same dwelling.

But it must be said that household statistics in Austria before 1900 were only marginally developed: in 1869 only the housing situation in the large cities was investigated; in 1880 household composition with respect to different categories of household members was presented; in 1890 household size by number of persons and household composition was included; the 1900 census again only dealt with the large cities. The first really comprehensive household statistics were published for the 1910 census: households were published by size, by household composition, and combining composition and profession of the household head. In 1934 these extensive household statistics were repeated. In 1939, the German household statistics were used also in Austria (see the chapter on Germany). The 1920 and 1923 censuses did not publish household statistics, but rather statistics on dwellings (*Wohnparteien*).

Disaggregations are available for the individual parts of the Austrian Empire. The censuses during the Austrian Republic presented data for the individual federal states (*Bundesländer*). The German census of 1939 presented household statistics by individual *Bundesländer*.

The definition of a dwelling (*Wohnpartei*) used from 1869 to 1890 deviates from the household definition, insofar as several households can live in one dwelling. The number of dwellings as a rule is smaller than the number of private households, which the 1934 census also demonstrates (Text part, p. 80). (This is the difference between the household-living and the household-dwelling concept, the latter still used in several European countries.)

The introduction to the volume on household statistics of the 1910 census gives a definition of the household and describes the earlier household statistics in Austria (Bureau der K.K. Statistischen Zentralkommission, 1918: 7*f.). The Austrian law of 29 March 1869 on population censuses did not take the household as basic unit instead of the dwelling (*Wohnung* and *Wohnpartei*). 'Unter Wohnpartei (spaced) wird in der Regel die Gesamtheit der Bewohner einer Wohnung verstanden, in einem anderen Sinne aber auch das Oberhaupt dieser Personen' (p. 7*). This definition was used in the censuses of 1889, 1880, and 1890. In 1900 and 1910 Austrian statistics assumed the principles of the German household definition (see chapter on Germany) and defined the household as the basic unit in statistics. A dwelling could contain several households. The household had not been defined in the 1900 and 1910 census, but actually was the same as the German definition:

Unter Haushaltung, wie in der deutschen Reichsstatistik, (sind) die zu einer wohn- und hauswirtschaftlichen Gemeinschaft vereinigten Personen verstanden (...), denen einzeln lebende Personen, sofern sie eine besondere Wohnung innehaben und eine eigene Hauswirtschaft führen, gleich zu halten sind, wogegen andere alleinstehende Personen (Bettgeher) derjenigen Haushaltung zugerechnet werden, bei der sie wohnen und die für sie die Hauswirtschaft führt, auch wenn sie in der Haushaltung keine Beköstigung empfangen (p. 7*).

Since 1910 institutional households (prisons, schools, military barracks, etc.) have also been distinguished. In 1900 institutional households were not explicitly surveyed; instead, family households were divided into those headed by a couple and others, the latter also comprising institutional households.

Household statistics of the censuses since 1910 always used the household definition employed in the 1910 census: the household as the basic unit of investigation and the distinction between the three types of one-person, family, and institutional households.

The censuses of 1920 and 1923 were only limited censuses caused by the events of the war (housing shortage, population changes, new state administration and territorial division of the Austrian Republic, etc.).

In 1934 the definitions of 1910 were applied to distinguish the three household types of one-person, family, and institutional households. The 1939 census was a German census, therefore see the chapter on Germany.

A special investigation on the fertility of married women was first carried out with the 1934 census. The German census of 1939 also contained a question on the children born to families (see the chapter on Germany concerning this census). Family statistics in the modern sense of the word were not implemented before 1950. The 1934 census collected data on marriages contracted since 1890 by the number of children, from 0–10+ children. The results were further differentiated according to period of marriage and region (*Bundesland*, political district, large cities).

Remarks (also see introductory Table 6.1)

A-Austrian Republic
Data from 1930 to 1939 have been created by linear extrapolation using the growth rates of the censuses from 1920 to 1934.

AEMP-Austrian Empire
The marital status for the census of 1869 is only available for the age group 15+ and in relative figures. Estimates of the values for the variables v18, v19, and v20 have been made by reconstructing the absolute figures from the relative ones. For the variables v16–v17 and v21 the relative values from the census of 1880 have been used to estimate the absolute figures for 1869. It is assumed that there have been no changes in the proportion of these relations.

BOUNDARY CHANGES

The Austrian part of the Austro-Hungarian monarchy did not change its territory fundamentally between 1815 and 1918, apart from the loss of Lombardy and the Veneto. In 1878 Bosnia-Hercegovina was occupied and formally annexed in 1908, but its statistics were kept separate. In 1919 the Habsburg monarchy was dissolved and several new nation-states were formed on the former territory of the empire.

The Republic of Austria was founded after the First World War in 1919 from the German-speaking parts of the Habsburg empire. South Tyrol was ceded to Italy in 1919. From 1938 to 1945 Austria was part of the German Empire.

For regional organization see the documentation by Quick (1994) and Caramani, Flora, Kraus, and Quick (1998).

APPENDIX TABLES AND FIGURES

APPENDIX TABLE A.1 Population structure at census dates, Austrian Empire 1869–1910; Austrian Republic 1920–1939

Census number	Census date	Census population			Marital status				Age group		
		Total	Male	Female	Single	Married	Widowed	Divorced	0–14	15–64	65+
		Absolute									
1	31 XII 1869	20,419,683	10,005,601	10,414,082	11,882,636	7,395,181	1,134,774	7,092	6,315,697	14,103,986[2]	..
2	31 XII 1880	22,139,948	10,815,441	11,324,507	13,191,333	7,712,457	1,240,454[1]	..	7,528,207	13,642,080	969,661
3	31 XII 1890	23,895,413	11,689,129	12,206,284	14,521,663	8,038,368	1,335,382[1]	..	8,160,450	14,572,347	1,162,616
4	31 XII 1900	26,150,708	12,852,693	13,298,015	15,724,136	8,969,277	1,457,295[1]	..	8,998,161	15,851,059	1,301,488
5	31 XII 1910	28,570,800	14,032,190	14,538,610	17,050,231	9,885,617	1,634,952[1]	..	9,954,077	17,109,069	1,507,654
6	7 III 1920	6,057,617	2,900,587	3,157,030	3,538,593	2,052,375	466,649[1]	..	1,415,363[3]	4,436,311[4]	205,943[5]
7	22 III 1934	6,760,233	3,248,265	3,511,968	3,530,433	2,627,095	475,014	123,171	1,598,788	4,615,081	534,456
8	17 V 1939	6,881,187	3,289,494	3,591,693	3,298,345	2,969,488	501,269	112,085	1,417,007	4,811,295	652,885
		Per cent									
1	31 XII 1869	100.00	49.00	51.00	58.19	36.22	5.56	0.03	30.93	69.07[2]	..
2	31 XII 1880	100.00	48.85	51.15	59.58	34.84	5.60[1]	..	34.00	61.62	4.38
3	31 XII 1890	100.00	48.92	51.08	60.77	33.64	5.59[1]	..	34.15	60.98	4.87
4	31 XII 1900	100.00	49.15	50.85	60.13	34.30	5.57[1]	..	34.41	60.61	4.98
5	31 XII 1910	100.00	49.11	50.89	59.68	34.60	5.72[1]	..	34.84	59.88	5.28
6	7 III 1920	100.00	47.88	52.12	58.42	33.88	7.70[1]	..	23.37[3]	73.24[4]	3.40[5]
7	22 III 1934	100.00	48.05	51.95	52.22	38.86	7.03	1.82	23.65	68.27	7.91
8	17 V 1939	100.00	47.80	52.20	47.93	43.15	7.28	1.63	20.59	69.92	9.49

Notes: [1] Widowed and separated. [2] 15+. [3] 0–13. [4] 40–69. [5] 70+.

APPENDIX TABLE A.2   Census population and population density by region, Austrian Empire 1866–1910 (per cent and inhabitants per sq. km.)

Province	1866	1880	1890	1900	1910	1866	1880	1890	1900	1910
	Per cent					Per sq. km.				
Nieder-österreich[1]	9.66	10.53	11.14	11.85	12.36	99	118	134	156	178
Oberösterreich[2]	3.62	3.43	3.29	3.10	2.99	61	63	66	68	71
Salzburg	0.75	0.74	0.73	0.74	0.75	21	23	24	27	30
Steiermark	5.59	5.48	5.37	5.19	5.05	50	54	57	60	64
Kärnten	1.66	1.58	1.51	1.40	1.39	33	34	35	36	38
Krain	2.29	2.17	2.09	1.94	1.84	47	48	50	51	53
Küstenland[3]	*2.88*	*2.93*	*2.91*	*2.89*	*3.13*	*73*	*81*	*87*	*95*	*112*
Triest and area	0.61	0.65	0.66	0.68	0.80	1,295	1,526	1,653	1,884	2,421
Görz and Gradisca	1.01	0.95	0.92	0.89	0.91	70	72	75	80	89
Istrien	1.26	1.32	1.33	1.32	1.41	51	59	64	70	82
Tirol and Vorarlberg[3]	*4.35*	*4.12*	*3.89*	*3.76*	*3.82*	*30*	*31*	*32*	*34*	*37*
Tirol	3.84	3.64	3.40	3.26	3.31	29	30	30	32	35
Vorarlberg	0.51	0.48	0.49	0.49	0.51	40	41	45	50	56
Böhmen	25.25	25.11	24.45	24.16	23.69	98	107	112	122	130
Mähren	9.88	9.72	9.53	9.32	9.18	90	97	102	110	118
Schlesien	2.53	2.55	2.54	2.60	2.65	99	110	118	132	147
Galizien	26.80	26.91	27.65	27.98	28.09	69	76	84	93	102
Bukowina	2.53	2.58	2.71	2.79	2.80	49	55	62	70	77
Dalmatien	2.19	2.15	2.21	2.27	2.26	35	37	41	46	50
TOTAL	**100.00**	**100.00**	**100.00**	**100.00**	**100.00**	**67**	**74**	**80**	**87**	**95**

Notes: [1] Named *Oesterreich unter der Enns* in 1869 and *Nieder-Oesterreich* thereafter. [2] Named *Oesterreich ob der Enns* in 1869 and *Ober-Oesterreich* thereafter. [3] *Küstenland* and *Tirol and Vorarlberg* were 'Länder' in 1869. Thereafter both were split, but the aggregate continued to be included in the tables.

APPENDIX TABLE A.3   Census population and population density by region, Austrian Republic 1923–1951 (per cent and inhabitants per sq. km.)

Federal State ('Bundesland')	1923	1934	1951[1]	1923	1934	1951[1]
	Per cent			Per sq. km.		
Wien[2]	28.56	27.50	25.06[3]	6,705	6,691	1,430[3]
Niederösterreich	22.66	22.39	18.08[3]	77	78	68[3]
Oberösterreich	13.39	13.41	15.89	73	76	92
Salzburg	3.42	3.67	4.77	31	35	46
Steiermark	14.97	15.07	15.96	60	62	68
Kärnten	5.67	6.02	6.81	39	43	50
Tirol	4.81	5.19	6.13	25	28	34
Vorarlberg	2.14	2.32	2.80	54	60	75
Burgenland	4.38	4.41	3.74	72	75	65
TOTAL	**100.00**	**100.00**	**100.00**	**78**	**81**	**83**

Notes: [1] 1951 included for comparative purposes. [2] The city of Wien was detached from Niederösterreich in 1920. The population of Wien in 1910 was 2,031,498. [3] Between 1948 and 1939 an area of ca. 930 sq. km. moved from Niederösterreich to Wien.

APPENDIX TABLE A.4A Demographic developments, Austrian Empire 1850–1913
(absolute figures and rates)

Year	Mid-year population	Natural population growth rate	Population growth rate	Net migration rate	Crude birth rate	Legitimate births per 10,000 married women age 15–44	Illegitimate births per 10,000 unmarried women age 15–44	Illeg. births per 100 leg. births
1850	17,540,362	6.6	-0.9	-7.6	39.4	..	..	..
1851	17,600,621	9.4	3.4	-6.0	39.3	..	..	..
1852	17,699,128	6.6	5.6	-1.0	37.7	..	..	..
1853	17,797,635	5.3	5.5	0.2	37.4	..	..	..
1854	17,896,142	1.8	5.5	3.7	36.6	..	..	..
1855	17,994,649	-11.7	5.5	17.2	32.1	..	..	..
1856	18,093,156	6.2	5.4	-0.7	36.1	..	..	..
1857	18,191,663	12.2	5.4	-6.8	39.9	..	..	..
1858	18,332,294	10.7	7.7	-3.1	39.8	..	..	..
1859	18,493,986	11.5	8.7	-2.8	40.8	..	..	..
1860	18,655,678	11.4	8.7	-2.7	38.4	..	..	..
1861	18,817,370	7.7	8.6	0.9	37.6	..	..	..
1862	18,979,062	8.6	8.5	-0.1	38.3	..	..	..
1863	19,140,754	10.7	8.4	-2.3	40.8	..	..	..
1864	19,302,446	10.6	8.4	-2.2	40.9	..	..	..
1865	19,464,138	7.6	8.3	0.7	38.3	..	..	..
1866	19,625,830	-2.9	8.2	11.2	38.0	..	..	..
1867	19,787,522	7.4	8.2	0.8	36.7	..	..	..
1868	19,949,214	9.4	8.1	-1.3	38.0	..	..	..
1869	20,110,909	10.5	8.0	-2.5	39.5	2,835	470	16.0
1870	20,320,000	14.3	10.3	-4.0	43.7	3,214	449	13.5
1871	20,511,666	9.0	9.3	0.3	39.1	2,851	437	14.9
1872	20,665,952	6.4	7.5	1.0	39.2	2,898	412	13.9
1873	20,736,428	0.8	3.4	2.6	39.9	2,967	417	13.8
1874	20,823,333	8.0	4.2	-3.8	39.8	..	..	..
1875	21,005,714	9.9	8.7	-1.2	40.1	3,009	411	13.5
1876	21,214,523	10.3	9.8	-0.5	40.2	3,013	428	14.1
1877	21,396,000	7.2	8.5	1.3	38.8	2,871	463	16.1
1878	21,542,000	6.9	6.8	-0.2	38.7	2,863	468	16.4
1879	21,713,750	9.4	7.9	-1.4	39.4	2,920	486	16.7
1880	21,897,631	7.9	8.4	0.5	37.8	2,802	476	17.1
1881	22,046,750	7.1	6.8	-0.4	37.8	2,826	466	16.8
1882	22,196,053	8.4	6.7	-1.7	39.4	2,955	486	16.8
1883	22,360,000	8.1	7.3	-0.8	38.4	2,897	475	16.9
1884	22,533,947	9.4	7.7	-1.7	39.0	2,951	486	17.1
1885	22,702,894	7.5	7.4	-0.1	37.9	2,881	476	17.3
1886	22,864,800	8.6	7.1	-1.6	38.3	2,928	477	17.2
1887	23,050,000	9.4	8.0	-1.4	38.6	2,963	481	17.2
1888	23,237,368	8.8	8.1	-0.7	38.3	2,958	475	17.1
1889	23,442,500	10.7	8.8	-2.0	38.3	2,975	475	17.2
1890	23,632,863	7.3	8.1	0.8	36.8	2,866	460	17.4
1891	23,808,612	10.3	7.4	-3.0	38.6	3,011	476	17.0
1892	23,976,437	7.4	7.0	-0.4	36.3	2,815	459	17.5
1893	24,152,635	10.9	7.3	-3.6	38.2	2,972	468	16.8
1894	24,349,532	9.0	8.1	-0.9	37.0	2,857	467	17.3
1895	24,543,614	10.5	7.9	-2.6	38.3	2,963	477	16.9
1896	24,774,187	11.8	9.3	-2.5	38.3	2,941	487	17.3
1897	25,025,487	11.9	10.0	-1.9	37.8	2,905	469	16.7

continued

APPENDIX TABLE A.4A Demographic developments, Austrian Empire 1850–1913 (absolute figures and rates)

Crude death rate	Infant mortality rate	Stillbirth rate	Infant mortality and stillbirth rate	Crude marriage rate	Persons marrying per 10,000 unmarried persons age 15+	Persons marrying per 10,000 unmarried persons age 15–49	Crude divorce rate	Divorces per 100 marriages	Divorces per 10,000 married persons	Year
32.8	..	..	..	9.6	..	..	..	..	..	1850
29.9	..	..	..	8.8	..	..	..	..	..	1851
31.1	..	..	..	7.9	..	..	..	..	..	1852
32.1	..	..	..	7.7	..	..	..	..	..	1853
34.8	..	..	..	6.9	..	..	..	..	..	1854
43.8	..	..	..	6.4	..	..	..	..	..	1855
29.9	..	..	..	8.2	..	..	..	..	..	1856
27.7	..	..	..	8.1	..	..	..	..	..	1857
29.1	..	..	..	8.5	..	..	..	..	..	1858
29.2	..	..	..	7.1	..	..	..	..	..	1859
27.0	..	..	..	8.5	..	..	..	..	..	1860
29.9	..	..	..	8.0	..	..	..	..	..	1861
29.7	..	..	..	8.9	..	..	..	..	..	1862
30.1	..	..	..	8.5	..	..	..	..	..	1863
30.3	..	..	..	8.3	..	..	..	..	..	1864
30.8	..	..	..	7.9	..	..	..	..	..	1865
41.0	..	..	..	6.5	..	..	..	..	..	1866
29.3	..	..	..	9.7	..	..	..	..	..	1867
28.7	..	..	..	9.2	..	..	..	..	..	1868
29.0	242.2	21.5	263.7	10.4	632	830	..	..	..	1869
29.5	229.9	20.9	250.9	9.8	599	783	..	..	..	1870
30.1	255.5	24.1	279.6	9.5	583	758	..	..	..	1871
32.8	270.4	23.6	294.0	9.3	575	744	..	..	..	1872
39.1	290.4	24.4	314.7	9.4	583	751	..	..	..	1873
31.8	..	24.1	..	9.1	566	725	..	..	..	1874
30.2	243.2	24.4	267.5	8.6	538	686	..	..	..	1875
29.9	246.9	24.8	271.7	8.3	523	663	..	..	..	1876
31.7	258.3	25.2	283.6	7.5	477	603	..	..	..	1877
31.7	251.6	25.8	277.4	7.6	485	609	..	..	..	1878
30.0	239.7	26.2	265.9	7.8	497	622	..	..	..	1879
29.9	249.9	26.6	276.5	7.6	490	610	..	..	..	1880
30.7	250.0	26.9	276.9	8.0	513	640	..	..	..	1881
30.9	255.9	27.4	283.3	8.3	526	656	0.0	0.4	1.9	1882
30.3	252.9	27.7	280.6	7.9	500	624	0.0	0.4	1.8	1883
29.6	247.1	27.8	275.0	8.0	503	628	0.0	0.4	1.9	1884
30.4	255.3	28.5	283.8	7.7	487	608	0.0	0.4	1.9	1885
29.7	249.6	28.5	278.1	7.9	496	619	0.0	0.4	1.9	1886
29.2	244.1	29.3	273.4	7.9	495	619	0.0	0.4	2.0	1887
29.5	248.8	29.0	277.8	8.0	500	626	0.0	0.4	1.9	1888
27.6	236.3	29.3	265.6	7.6	472	591	0.0	0.5	2.0	1889
29.5	259.2	29.3	288.5	7.6	470	588	0.0	0.5	2.0	1890
28.3	243.0	29.9	272.9	7.8	—488	611	0.0	0.5	2.2	1891
28.9	259.3	29.9	289.2	7.8	489	612	0.0	0.5	2.2	1892
27.3	232.0	29.9	261.9	8.0	501	628	0.0	0.5	2.3	1893
28.0	251.2	30.3	281.6	8.0	501	628	0.0	0.5	2.4	1894
27.8	235.1	29.2	264.3	8.1	512	642	0.0	0.5	2.4	1895
26.5	229.5	29.2	258.8	8.0	506	634	0.0	0.5	2.3	1896
25.8	228.3	28.4	256.8	8.1	516	647	0.0	0.5	2.3	1897

continued

APPENDIX TABLE A.4A Demographic developments, Austrian Empire 1850–1913
(continued)

Year	Mid-year population	Natural population growth rate	Population growth rate	Net migration rate	Crude birth rate	Legitimate births per 10,000 married women age 15–44	Illegitimate births per 10,000 unmarried women age 15–44	Illeg. births per 100 leg. births
1898	25,275,262	11.4	9.9	-1.5	36.5	2,807	452	16.6
1899	25,526,512	11.8	9.8	-2.0	37.6	2,899	452	16.0
1900	25,788,469	12.0	10.2	-1.8	37.5	2,893	444	15.6
1901	26,049,896	12.7	10.0	-2.6	36.9	2,849	432	15.4
1902	26,306,168	12.5	9.7	-2.7	37.4	2,894	433	15.1
1903	26,550,998	11.5	9.2	-2.3	35.6	2,767	393	14.3
1904	26,792,018	11.9	9.0	-2.9	35.9	2,788	403	14.5
1905	26,999,548	8.8	7.7	-1.1	34.1	2,656	379	14.2
1906	27,218,896	12.6	8.1	-4.5	35.3	2,756	385	13.9
1907	27,476,680	11.4	9.4	-2.0	34.3	2,667	381	14.2
1908	27,720,731	11.3	8.8	-2.5	34.0	2,646	373	14.0
1909	27,956,890	10.6	8.4	-2.1	33.7	2,624	368	13.8
1910	28,197,552	11.4	8.5	-2.9	32.8	2,555	358	13.8
1911	28,420,412	9.5	7.8	-1.7	31.6	2,475	335	13.2
1912	28,632,299	10.9	7.4	-3.5	31.6	2,466	339	13.4
1913	28,847,478	9.5	7.5	-2.1	30.0	2,339	325	13.5

APPENDIX TABLE A.4A   Demographic developments, Austrian Empire 1850–1913
(continued)

Crude death rate	Infant mortality rate	Stillbirth rate	Infant mortality and stillbirth rate	Crude marriage rate	Persons marrying per 10,000 unmarried persons age 15+	Persons marrying per 10,000 unmarried persons age 15–49	Crude divorce rate	Divorces per 100 marriages	Divorces per 10,000 married persons	Year
25.1	224.3	29.0	253.3	7.9	502	629	0.1	0.6	2.9	1898
25.8	218.6	29.4	248.0	8.4	534	669	0.1	0.7	3.3	1899
25.5	230.6	28.5	259.1	8.3	531	666	0.1	0.7	3.3	1900
24.2	209.0	28.6	237.5	8.2	525	660	0.1	0.8	3.8	1901
25.0	215.9	27.0	243.0	7.9	504	633	0.1	0.9	4.3	1902
24.0	214.7	27.6	242.2	7.9	507	637	0.1	1.0	4.5	1903
24.0	209.7	27.0	236.7	7.8	506	636	0.1	1.0	4.7	1904
25.4	231.0	26.3	257.3	7.9	510	641	0.1	1.0	4.6	1905
22.7	202.0	27.0	229.0	8.0	517	650	0.1	1.0	4.7	1906
22.9	208.6	26.3	234.9	7.6	495	623	0.1	1.1	5.0	1907
22.6	199.3	25.7	225.0	7.7	502	631	0.1	1.1	5.1	1908
23.1	208.6	25.3	233.9	7.6	498	626	0.1	1.3	5.9	1909
21.4	188.7	25.2	213.9	7.6	499	628	0.1	1.3	5.8	1910
22.1	207.5	24.8	232.2	7.6	502	631	0.1	1.4	6.2	1911
20.7	181.5	24.7	206.1	7.4	487	613	0.1	1.5	6.5	1912
20.4	189.8	25.5	215.3	6.8	448	563	0.1	1.7	6.6	1913

APPENDIX TABLE A.4B Demographic developments, Austrian Republic 1871–1945
(absolute figures and rates)

Year	Mid-year population	Natural population growth rate	Population growth rate	Net migration rate	Crude birth rate	Legitimate births per 10,000 married women age 15–44	Illegitimate births per 10,000 unmarried women age 15–44	Illeg. births per 100 leg. births
1871	4,562,000	3.9	..	..	33.6	..	..	..
1872	4,604,000	3.0	9.1	6.1	34.4	..	..	..
1873	4,646,000	1.3	9.0	7.7	35.0	..	..	..
1874	4,688,000	4.1	9.0	4.9	34.7	..	..	..
1875	4,730,000	5.2	8.9	3.7	34.9	..	..	..
1876	4,772,000	7.0	8.8	1.8	35.6	..	..	..
1877	4,815,000	4.9	8.9	4.0	34.2	..	..	..
1878	4,857,000	3.4	8.6	5.2	33.4	..	..	..
1879	4,899,000	4.6	8.6	3.9	33.4	..	..	..
1880	4,941,000	6.0	8.5	2.5	33.5	..	..	..
1881	4,985,000	4.4	8.8	4.4	32.9	..	..	..
1882	5,030,000	4.3	8.9	4.6	33.0	..	..	..
1883	5,075,000	4.6	8.9	4.3	32.7	..	..	..
1884	5,121,000	6.0	9.0	3.0	33.2	..	..	..
1885	5,166,000	4.2	8.7	4.5	32.5	..	..	..
1886	5,212,000	5.0	8.8	3.8	32.6	..	..	..
1887	5,257,000	5.7	8.6	2.8	32.5	..	..	..
1888	5,303,000	5.0	8.7	3.7	32.1	..	..	..
1889	5,348,000	6.5	8.4	1.9	32.2	..	..	..
1890	5,394,000	3.8	8.5	4.7	30.7	..	..	..
1891	5,446,000	6.2	9.5	3.3	32.4	..	..	..
1892	5,504,000	4.7	10.5	5.9	31.2	..	..	..
1893	5,563,000	6.5	10.6	4.1	31.6	..	..	..
1894	5,622,000	6.6	10.5	3.9	31.4	..	..	..
1895	5,680,000	7.1	10.2	3.1	31.9	..	..	..
1896	5,739,000	8.0	10.3	2.3	31.9	..	..	..
1897	5,798,000	7.9	10.2	2.2	31.4	..	..	..
1898	5,856,000	8.8	9.9	1.1	31.5	..	..	..
1899	5,915,000	8.1	10.0	1.9	31.5	..	..	..
1900	5,973,000	8.1	9.7	1.6	31.3	..	..	..
1901	6,035,000	9.2	10.3	1.1	31.4	..	..	..
1902	6,099,000	9.4	10.5	1.1	31.5	..	..	..
1903	6,164,000	8.2	10.5	2.3	29.9	..	..	..
1904	6,228,000	9.1	10.3	1.2	30.2	..	..	..
1905	6,292,000	6.2	10.2	4.0	28.9	..	..	..
1906	6,357,000	8.7	10.2	1.5	29.0	..	..	..
1907	6,421,000	7.6	10.0	2.3	28.2	..	..	..
1908	6,485,000	6.7	9.9	3.1	27.8	..	..	..
1909	6,550,000	7.0	9.9	2.9	27.5	..	..	..
1910	6,614,000	7.5	9.7	2.2	26.7	..	..	..

continued

APPENDIX TABLE A.4B Demographic developments, Austrian Republic 1871–1945
(absolute figures and rates)

Crude death rate	Infant mortality rate	Stillbirth rate	Infant mortality and stillbirth rate	Crude marriage rate	Persons marrying per 10,000 unmarried persons age 15+	Persons marrying per 10,000 unmarried persons age 15–49	Crude divorce rate	Divorces per 100 marriages	Divorces per 10,000 married persons	Year
29.8	269.9	..	..	8.9	..	..	..	..	..	1871
31.4	276.8	..	..	9.1	..	..	..	..	..	1872
33.7	278.4	..	..	9.0	..	..	..	..	..	1873
30.6	266.9	..	..	8.3	..	..	..	..	..	1874
29.7	252.6	..	..	7.8	..	..	..	..	..	1875
28.6	242.6	..	..	7.6	..	..	..	..	..	1876
29.3	245.0	..	..	6.8	..	..	..	..	..	1877
29.9	246.3	..	..	6.6	..	..	..	..	..	1878
28.8	242.0	..	..	6.9	..	..	..	..	..	1879
27.5	236.6	..	..	6.9	..	..	..	..	..	1880
28.5	244.9	33.5	278.3	7.1	..	..	..	..	..	1881
28.7	247.9	33.7	281.6	7.3	..	..	..	..	..	1882
28.1	246.2	34.5	280.7	7.2	..	..	..	..	..	1883
27.2	241.0	34.1	275.1	7.3	..	..	0.1	1.3	..	1884
28.3	255.9	35.1	291.0	7.2	..	..	0.1	1.3	..	1885
27.6	247.1	35.2	282.3	7.4	..	..	0.1	1.3	..	1886
26.8	238.8	36.1	274.9	7.2	..	..	0.1	1.4	..	1887
27.1	238.1	36.1	274.2	7.2	..	..	0.1	1.3	..	1888
25.7	232.5	37.8	270.3	7.2	..	..	0.1	1.3	..	1889
26.9	247.3	36.7	284.0	7.2	..	..	0.1	1.4	..	1890
26.2	232.6	38.5	271.1	7.4	..	..	0.1	1.4	..	1891
26.6	241.2	40.3	281.6	7.4	..	..	0.1	1.4	..	1892
25.1	227.9	40.6	268.5	7.4	..	..	0.1	1.6	..	1893
24.8	227.7	39.8	267.5	7.6	..	..	0.1	1.6	..	1894
24.8	224.4	37.4	261.8	7.8	..	..	0.1	1.4	..	1895
23.9	212.0	35.0	247.0	7.7	..	..	0.1	1.4	..	1896
23.4	215.2	34.2	249.4	8.0	..	..	0.1	1.4	..	1897
22.7	211.3	35.7	247.0	7.8	..	..	0.1	1.7	..	1898
23.4	206.7	37.0	243.7	8.0	..	..	0.1	1.8	..	1899
23.2	211.6	35.8	247.4	8.0	..	..	0.2	1.9	..	1900
22.2	208.1	36.7	244.8	7.8	..	..	0.2	2.2	..	1901
22.0	211.2	34.2	245.5	7.6	..	..	0.2	2.5	..	1902
21.6	210.9	34.6	245.5	7.5	..	..	0.2	2.6	..	1903
21.1	203.5	35.1	238.6	7.6	..	..	0.2	2.8	..	1904
22.7	224.1	34.5	258.6	7.6	..	..	0.2	2.8	..	1905
20.3	193.7	35.6	229.3	7.7	..	..	0.2	2.9	..	1906
20.6	200.1	34.4	234.5	7.7	..	..	0.2	2.7	..	1907
21.0	204.0	34.0	238.0	7.7	..	..	0.2	2.9	..	1908
20.5	205.0	34.3	239.3	7.8	..	..	0.3	3.3	..	1909
19.2	184.0	34.5	218.6	7.6	..	..	0.2	3.2	..	1910

continued

APPENDIX TABLE A.4B Demographic developments, Austrian Republic 1871–1945
(continued)

Year	Mid-year population	Natural population growth rate	Population growth rate	Net migration rate	Crude birth rate	Legitimate births per 10,000 married women age 15–44	Illegitimate births per 10,000 unmarried women age 15–44	Illeg. births per 100 leg. births
1911	6,669,000	5.4	8.2	2.8	25.3	..	..	..
1912	6,724,000	7.1	8.2	1.1	25.4	..	..	..
1913	6,767,000	5.8	6.4	0.6	24.1	..	..	..
1914	..	..	..	..	..	..	..	30.4
1915	..	..	..	..	..	..	..	30.6
1916	..	..	..	..	..	..	..	32.5
1917	..	..	..	..	..	..	..	35.9
1918	..	..	..	..	..	..	..	36.3
1919	6,419,563	-1.9	..	..	18.5	1,445	249	29.6
1920	6,454,800	3.7	5.5	1.8	22.7	1,758	315	29.9
1921	6,503,567	6.3	7.5	1.2	23.2	1,840	292	25.8
1922	6,527,708	5.7	3.7	-2.0	23.1	1,811	298	26.0
1923	6,543,325	7.2	2.4	-4.8	22.4	1,746	294	26.0
1924	6,561,672	6.7	2.8	-3.9	21.7	1,638	310	28.4
1925	6,582,095	6.2	3.1	-3.1	20.6	1,529	314	30.0
1926	6,602,518	4.3	3.1	-1.2	19.3	1,401	310	31.5
1927	6,622,941	3.0	3.1	0.1	17.9	1,269	310	33.8
1928	6,643,364	3.1	3.1	-0.1	17.6	1,224	318	35.0
1929	6,663,787	2.2	3.1	0.9	16.8	1,161	312	35.4
1930	6,684,210	3.3	3.1	-0.2	16.8	1,137	329	37.1
1931	6,704,633	1.9	3.0	1.2	15.9	1,068	314	36.8
1932	6,725,056	1.3	3.0	1.7	15.2	1,015	309	37.1
1933	6,745,479	1.1	3.0	1.9	14.3	956	288	35.8
1934	6,754,949	0.9	1.4	0.5	13.6	901	279	35.8
1935	6,760,963	-0.6	0.9	1.5	13.1	882	261	33.5
1936	6,758,198	-0.1	-0.4	-0.3	13.1	886	252	31.4
1937	6,755,337	-0.5	-0.4	0.1	12.8	874	241	29.5
1938	6,753,413	-0.1	-0.3	-0.1	13.9	..	..	..
1939	6,652,720	5.4	-15.1	-20.6	20.7	..	..	..
1940	..	..	..	..	..	..	..	..
1941	..	..	..	..	..	..	..	..
1942	..	..	..	..	..	..	..	..
1943	..	..	..	..	..	..	..	..
1944	..	..	..	..	..	..	..	..
1945	..	..	..	..	..	..	..	34.2

APPENDIX TABLE A.4B Demographic developments, Austrian Republic 1871–1945
(continued)

Crude death rate	Infant mortality rate	Stillbirth rate	Infant mortality and stillbirth rate	Crude marriage rate	Persons marrying per 10,000	Persons marrying per 10,000	Crude divorce rate	Divorces per 100 marriages	Divorces per 10,000 married persons	Year
19.9	202.3	..	..	7.6	..	..	0.3	3.4	..	1911
18.3	168.8	..	..	7.7	..	..	0.3	3.5	..	1912
18.4	180.3	..	..	7.0	..	..	0.3	4.1	..	1913
..	171.7	35.2	206.9	..	..	..	..	3.4	..	1914
..	218.1	35.2	253.3	..	..	..	..	3.5	..	1915
..	192.3	38.4	230.7	..	..	..	..	3.8	..	1916
..	185.6	33.0	218.6	..	..	..	..	3.6	..	1917
..	192.9	36.3	229.1	..	..	..	..	4.2	..	1918
20.4	156.4	30.9	187.3	12.5	580	720	0.6	5.2	38.7	1919
19.0	156.8	32.0	188.8	13.3	622	776	0.8	6.2	49.0	1920
17.0	153.8	..	..	12.5	590	740	0.9	7.0	50.7	1921
17.4	156.4	31.4	187.8	11.4	543	684	0.8	7.2	47.3	1922
15.3	140.6	33.2	173.8	8.6	417	528	0.8	9.4	46.2	1923
14.9	127.0	33.3	160.3	8.1	392	499	0.8	10.1	46.1	1924
14.4	119.2	30.4	149.6	7.7	380	486	0.8	10.2	44.1	1925
15.0	124.3	30.7	155.0	7.3	360	463	..	..	..	1926
15.0	126.3	31.0	157.3	7.3	367	475	..	..	..	1927
14.4	118.0	30.3	148.3	7.4	376	488	0.8	11.3	45.5	1928
14.6	111.9	29.1	140.9	7.7	393	514	0.9	11.5	47.7	1929
13.5	104.1	29.0	133.0	7.7	398	523	1.0	12.5	51.2	1930
14.0	103.2	27.9	131.1	7.4	386	510	0.9	12.8	50.1	1931
13.9	106.1	29.4	135.6	6.7	354	471	0.9	13.3	47.1	1932
13.2	94.2	27.9	122.1	6.5	345	462	0.9	14.2	48.0	1933
12.7	91.6	27.5	119.1	6.5	349	469	0.9	13.5	45.1	1934
13.7	98.7	28.0	126.7	6.8	365	494	0.8	12.2	42.1	1935
13.2	93.1	29.0	122.0	6.8	374	508	0.9	12.9	44.9	1936
13.3	91.9	28.3	120.3	6.9	377	516	0.9	12.6	43.5	1937
14.0	80.1	27.0	107.1	13.3	740	1,018	..	..	..	1938
15.3	73.1	27.0	100.1	17.6	962	1,365	1.2	7.0	61.3	1939
..	74.2	25.6	99.9	..	..	..	..	8.4	..	1940
..	69.8	22.7	92.5	..	..	..	..	12.3	..	1941
..	73.6	21.5	95.1	..	..	..	..	12.5	..	1942
..	79.1	20.8	99.9	..	..	..	..	..	..	1943
..	87.8	22.0	109.8	..	..	..	..	..	..	1944
..	161.7	19.9	181.6	..	..	..	..	14.5	..	1945

APPENDIX TABLE A.5 Life expectancy by age 1870/80–1930/33 (in years)

Age	0	10	20	30	40	50	60	70	80
Males									
1870–1880	30.98	44.21	36.80	30.53	..	..	12.20	..	4.42
1891–1900	37.77	48.22	40.08	32.86	25.51	18.64	12.58	7.61	4.39
1895–1900	36.78	48.20	40.17	33.03	..	..	12.69	..	4.45
1901–1905	39.14	48.59	40.50	33.27	..	..	12.78	..	4.39
1906–1910	40.69	49.08	40.90	33.49	26.01	19.04	12.86	7.85	4.41
1930–1933	54.47	54.08	45.18	36.86	28.65	20.96	14.15	8.56	4.60
Females									
1870–1880	33.70	45.52	38.28	31.52	..	..	12.37	..	4.44
1891–1900	39.87	48.54	40.78	33.70	26.64	19.40	12.77	7.65	4.47
1895–1900	38.97	48.55	40.86	33.84	..	..	12.96	..	4.65
1901–1905	41.05	48.81	41.22	34.22	..	..	13.07	..	4.49
1906–1910	42.08	49.71	41.93	34.80	..	..	13.32	..	4.47
1930–1933	58.53	56.96	48.03	39.59	31.13	22.94	15.42	9.21	4.97

Note: 1870/80–1906/10 Austrian Empire; 1930–33 Austrian Republic.

APPENDIX TABLE A.6A Households by type 1910–1934 (absolute and per cent)

Census year	Household types and members									
	Total house-holds	Private house-holds	Family house-holds	One-person house-holds	Institu-tional house-holds	Total household members	Private household members	Family household members	One-person household members	Institu-tional house-hold members
	Absolute									
1910[1]	6,085,915	6,072,157	5,706,648	365,509	13,758	28,031,827	27,492,854	27,127,345	365,509	538,973
1934[2]	1,841,004	1,831,910	1,641,400	190,510	9,094	6,760,233	6,580,307	6,389,797	190,510	179,926
	Per cent									
1910[1]	100.00	99.77	93.77	6.01	0.23	100.00	98.08	96.77	1.30	1.92
1934[2]	100.00	99.51	89.16	10.35	0.49	100.00	97.34	94.52	2.82	2.66

Notes: [1] 1910 Austrian Empire. [2] 1934 Austrian Republic.

APPENDIX TABLE A.6B Households by size and members 1910 (absolute figures)

Census year	Private households total	Households by number of members							
		1 person	2 persons	3 persons	4 persons	5–6 persons	7–8 persons	9–10 persons	10+ persons
		Households							
1910[1]	6,072,157	365,509	844,251	973,396	1,009,472	1,637,086	833,478	298,761	110,204
		Persons							
1910[1]	27,492,854	365,509	1,688,502	2,920,188	4,037,888	9,003,973[2]	6,251,085[3]	2,838,230[4]	387,480[5]

Notes: [1] 1910 Austrian Empire. [2] Calculated using 5.5 persons. [3] Calculated using 7.5 persons. [4] Calculated using 9.5 persons. [5] Calculated by subtraction.

APPENDIX TABLE A.6C Households by size and members 1910 (per cent)

Census year	Private households total	Households by number of members							
		1 person	2 persons	3 persons	4 persons	5–6 persons	7–8 persons	9–10 persons	10+ persons
		Households							
1910[1]	100.00	6.02	13.90	16.03	16.62	26.96	13.73	4.92	1.81
		Persons							
1910[1]	100.00	1.33	6.14	10.62	14.69	32.75[2]	22.74[3]	10.32[4]	1.41[5]

Notes: [1] 1910 Austrian Empire. [2] Calculated using 5.5 persons. [3] Calculated using 7.5 persons. [4] Calculated using 9.5 persons. [5] Calculated by subtraction.

APPENDIX TABLE A.6D Household indicators 1910–1934

Census year	Household indicators			
	Mean total household size	Mean private household size	Mean family household size	Mean institutional household size
1910[1]	4.61	4.53	4.75	39.18
1934[2]	3.67	3.59	3.89	19.79

Notes: [1] 1910 Austrian Empire. [2] 1934 Austrian Republic.

APPENDIX TABLE A.6E Mean household size by region (*Wohnpartei*) 1869–1934

Census year	Wien	Nieder-österreich	Ober-österreich	Salzburg	Steiermark	Kärnten	Tirol	Vorarlberg	Burgen-land	Österreich Total
De facto population										
1869	632,494	1,345,899	736,557	153,159	720,990	315,625	236,931	103,731	254,288	4,498,674
1880	726,105	1,589,338	759,620	163,570	776,735	324,316	244,736	107,373	270,024	4,961,817
1890	1,364,548	1,279,793	785,831	173,510	827,744	336,728	249,984	116,073	282,066	5,416,277
1900	1,728,738	1,351,544	810,246	192,763	888,358	343,144	266,414	129,237	292,261	6,002,705
1910	2,031,498	1,476,952	853,006	214,737	956,899	370,971	304,713	145,408	291,800	6,645,984
1920	1,841,326	1,457,335	858,795	214,200	953,684	366,589	306,304	133,212	294,849	6,426,294
1923	1,865,780	1,480,449	876,074	222,831	978,816	371,227	313,888	139,979	285,698	6,534,742
1934[1]	1,860,308	1,514,252	906,590	248,211	1,018,920	407,371	351,174	157,370	298,491	6,762,687
1934[2]	1,874,130	1,509,076	902,318	245,801	1,015,106	405,129	349,098	155,402	299,447	6,760,233
Number of *Wohnparteien*										
1869	114,383	288,371	163,435	31,894	129,000	61,382	48,952	23,439	–	860,856
1880	141,910	337,778	172,487	34,728	149,685	66,243	50,440	23,351	–	976,622
1890	286,759	274,211	176,357	36,426	165,852	65,589	50,937	24,818	–	1,080,949
1900	399,881	274,378	182,589	41,126	188,024	69,209	56,058	26,785	–	1,238,050
1910	480,476	323,597	189,119	46,141	200,719	76,203	61,006	29,450	–	1,406,711
1920	519,154	336,551	191,103	46,285	202,504	72,480	62,397	28,852	–	1,459,326
1923	534,060	355,923	197,971	49,165	213,185	76,278	65,525	29,858	61,394	1,583,359
1934	605,289	396,333	217,781	58,598	238,147	88,437	77,048	34,958	67,843	1,784,434

continued

APPENDIX TABLE A.6E   Mean household size by region (*Wohnpartei*) 1869–1934 (continued)

Census year	Wien	Nieder-österreich	Ober-österreich	Salzburg	Steiermark	Kärnten	Tirol	Vorarlberg	Burgen-land	Österreich Total
					Persons per *Wohnpartei*					
1869	5.5	4.7	4.5	4.8	5.6	5.1	4.8	4.4	–	5.2
1880	5.1	4.7	4.4	4.7	5.2	4.9	4.9	4.6	–	5.1
1890	4.8	4.7	4.5	4.8	5.0	5.1	4.9	4.7	–	5.0
1900	4.3	4.9	4.4	4.7	4.7	5.0	4.8	4.8	–	4.8
1910	4.2	4.6	4.5	4.7	4.8	4.9	5.0	5.4	–	4.7
1923	3.6	4.2	4.4	4.5	4.6	4.9	4.8	4.9	4.7	4.1
1934[1]	3.5	3.8	4.2	4.2	4.3	4.6	4.6	5.3	4.4	3.8
1934[2]	3.5	4.2	4.6	5.0	4.8	5.3	5.3	5.2	4.9	4.3

Notes: [1] De facto population (*anwesende Bevölkerung*). [2] Resident population (*Wohnbevölkerung*); territory of the Austrian Republic.

APPENDIX TABLE A.6F Household composition 1910 and 1934[1] (absolute and per cent)

Federal State (*Bundesland*)	Year	Population	Household head	Wife of household head	Female companion in life (housekeeper without salary)	Parental child	Adoptive or foster child	Foster child	Other family members	Domestic servants	Sub-tenant without own household	Family members of these sub-tenants	Bed tenant	Other non-family members	Inmates of institutions
						Absolute									
Wien	1910	2,031,421	479,103	313,448		702,919	11,979		113,206	101,364	82,838	10,156	75,423	81,054	59,931
	1934	1,874,130	629,493	386,781	16,603	510,564	15,501	4,717	110,685	49,510	81,731	7,390	2,061	10,501	48,512
Niederösterreich	1910	1,500,153	325,649	233,210		631,990	17,947		98,004	23,568	7,999	1,178	16,266	103,540	40,802
	1934	1,509,076	399,438	286,781	10,701	519,846	20,830	11,196	115,320	14,023	17,641	1,284	1,629	73,146	37,239
Oberösterreich	1910	852,975	177,342	135,417		317,901	5,236		65,131	13,221	3,809	269	5,518	108,764	20,367
	1934	902,318	228,492	146,547	4,119	300,871	19,494	3,704	75,376	9,545	13,332	655	1,402	75,792	22,989
Salzburg	1910	214,737	45,300	30,170		73,650	2,143		14,478	4,722	2,209	162	3,296	30,992	7,615
	1934	245,801	58,804	39,019	1,820	78,623	9,351	1,566	18,611	3,648	6,181	281	533	17,314	10,050
Kärnten	1910	396,228	80,168	46,378		139,365	5,044		39,397	6,184	3,118	371	4,602	58,728	12,873
	1934	405,129	89,524	55,013	5,774	140,279	10,630	2,671	43,859	5,156	6,921	552	7,252	33,201	10,827
Vorarlberg	1910	145,408	29,340	19,743		67,015	961		9,838	1,888	1,648	109	3,692	6,097	5,077
	1934	155,402	35,414	24,039	165	66,952	1,814	476	10,609	2,133	3,676	172	191	3,373	6,388
Austria	1910	5,140,922	1,136,902	778,366		1,932,840	43,310		340,054	150,947	101,621	12,245	108,797	389,175	146,665
	1934	5,091,856	1,441,165	938,180	39,182	1,617,135	77,620	24,330	374,460	84,015	129,482	10,334	13,068	213,327	136,005

continued

APPENDIX TABLE A.6F Household composition 1910 and 1934[1] (absolute and per cent) (continued)

Federal State (*Bundesland*)	Year	Population	House-hold head	Wife of house-hold head	Female compan-ion in life (house-keeper without salary)	Parental child	Adop-tive or foster child	Foster child	Other family mem-bers	Domes-tic servants	Sub-tenant without own house-hold	Family mem-bers of these sub-tenants	Bed tenant	Other non-family mem-bers	Inmates of institu-tions
							Per cent								
Wien	1910	100.00	23.58	15.43		34.60		0.59	5.57	4.99	4.08	0.50	3.71	3.99	2.95
	1934	100.00	33.59	20.64	0.89	27.24	0.83	0.25	5.91	2.64	4.36	0.39	0.11	0.56	2.59
Niederösterreich	1910	100.00	21.71	15.55		42.13		1.20	6.53	1.57	0.53	0.08	1.08	6.90	2.72
	1934	100.00	26.47	19.00	0.71	34.45	1.38	0.74	7.64	0.93	1.17	0.09	0.11	4.85	2.47
Oberösterreich	1910	100.00	20.79	15.88		37.27		0.61	7.64	1.55	0.45	0.03	0.65	12.75	2.39
	1934	100.00	25.32	16.24	0.46	33.34	2.16	0.41	8.35	1.06	1.48	0.07	0.16	8.40	2.55
Salzburg	1910	100.00	21.10	14.05		34.30		1.00	6.74	2.20	1.03	0.08	1.53	14.43	3.55
	1934	100.00	23.92	15.87	0.74	31.99	3.80	0.64	7.57	1.48	2.51	0.11	0.22	7.04	4.09
Kärnten	1910	100.00	20.23	11.70		35.17		1.27	9.94	1.56	0.79	0.09	1.16	14.82	3.25
	1934	100.00	22.10	13.58	1.43	34.63	2.62	0.66	10.83	1.27	1.71	0.14	1.79	8.20	2.67
Vorarlberg	1910	100.00	20.18	13.58		46.09		0.66	6.77	1.30	1.13	0.07	2.54	4.19	3.49
	1934	100.00	22.79	15.47	0.11	43.08	1.17	0.31	6.83	1.37	2.37	0.11	0.12	2.17	4.11
Austria	1910	100.00	22.11	15.14		37.60		0.84	6.61	2.94	1.98	0.24	2.12	7.57	2.85
	1934	100.00	28.30	18.43	0.77	31.76	1.52	0.48	7.35	1.65	2.54	0.20	0.26	4.19	2.67

Note: [1] Territory of the Austrian Republic. Geographical units selected with only minor territorial changes. Original column titles: *Bevölkerung, Haushaltungsvorstand, Ehefrau, Lebensgefährtin (Wirtschafterin ohne Lohn), Leibliches Kind, Zieh- oder Adoptivkind, Pflegekind, Sonstige Familienangehörige, Hauspersonal, Untermieter, Aftermieter ohne eigenen Haushalt, Familienmitglieder dieser Untermieter, Bettgeher, Sonstige familienfremde Personen, Anstaltsinsassen.*

APPENDIX TABLE A.7 Dates and nature of results on population structure,
households/families, and vital statistics

Topic	Intro-duction	Remarks
Population		
Population at census dates	1869–1910; 1880–	1869–1910: Austro-Hungarian Empire; since 1880–: recalculated for the territory of the Austrian Republic.
Population by age, sex, and marital status	1880–	In 1869 age groups and marital status were given separately, but not combined. In one-year age-groups available since 1880.
Households and families		
Households (Wohnparteien or Haushaltungen; Haushalte)		
Total households	1869–	Households were first expressively recorded in 1900; earlier censuses used the dwelling (*Wohnpartei*) as unit. The results for dwelling units and households are roughly comparable, although several households may live in a single dwelling. In 1869 housing in large cities; household composition. 1880: housing in large cities; household composition. 1890: housing in large cities; household composition, number of persons in flat. 1900: data only for large cities. 1910: first comprehensive household statistics. 1920: number of *Wohnparteien*, housewives! 1923: number of *Wohnparteien*. 1934: second comprehensive household statistics. 1939: see chapter on Germany. *Disaggregation*: by part of monarchy.
Households by size	1890, 1900, 1910, 1939	First time in 1890: flats by number of persons. For 1939 see chapter on Germany.
Households by composition	1869, 1880, 1910, 1934, 1939	In 1869, 1880, and 1890 *household composition* was published with respect to different categories of household members (family members, boarders and lodgers, servants, others). For 1939 see chapter on Germany.
Households by profession of household head	1900, 1910, 1934, 1939	Since 1910 household composition by profession of household head. For 1939 see chapter on Germany.

continued

APPENDIX TABLE A.7 Dates and nature of results on population structure, households/families, and vital statistics (continued)

Topic	Intro-duction	Remarks
Families (Familien)		
Families by number of children	1900, 1934	Family statistics in the large cities: families by number of children. Special investigation of the fertility of married women for the first time in 1934. Marriages contracted since 1890 by number of children: 0–10+.
Population movement		
Mid-year population	1850–1913; 1871–	1850–1913: Austro-Hungarian Empire; 1871–: data recalculated for the territory of the Austrian Republic.
Births		
Live births	1850–1913; 1871–	1850–1913: Austro-Hungarian Empire; 1871–: data recalculated for the territory of the Austrian Republic.
Stillbirths	1881–	1881–: data recalculated for the territory of the Austrian Republic.
Legitimate births	1869–1913; 1914–	1869–1913: Austro-Hungarian Empire; 1914–: data recalculated for the territory of the Austrian Republic.
Illegitimate births	1869–1913; 1914–	1869–1913: Austro-Hungarian Empire; 1914–: data recalculated for the territory of the Austrian Republic.
Deaths		
Total deaths	1850–1913; 1871–	1850–1913: Austro-Hungarian Empire; 1871–: data recalculated for the territory of the Austrian Republic.
Infants (under 1 year)	1869–1913; 1871–	1869–1913: Austro-Hungarian Empire; 1871–: data recalculated for the territory of the Austrian Republic.
Marriages		
Total marriages	1850–1913; 1871–	1850–1913: Austro-Hungarian Empire; 1871–: data recalculated for the territory of the Austrian Republic.
Divorces and separations		
Total divorces	1882–1913; 1884–	1882–1913: Austro-Hungarian Empire; 1884–: data recalculated for the territory of the Austrian Republic.
Legal separations	1882–1935	

APPENDIX FIGURE A.8 Population by age, sex and marital status, Austrian Empire 1880, 1890, 1900 and 1910; Austrian Republic 1934 and 1939 (per 10,000 of total population)

Austrian Empire, 1880

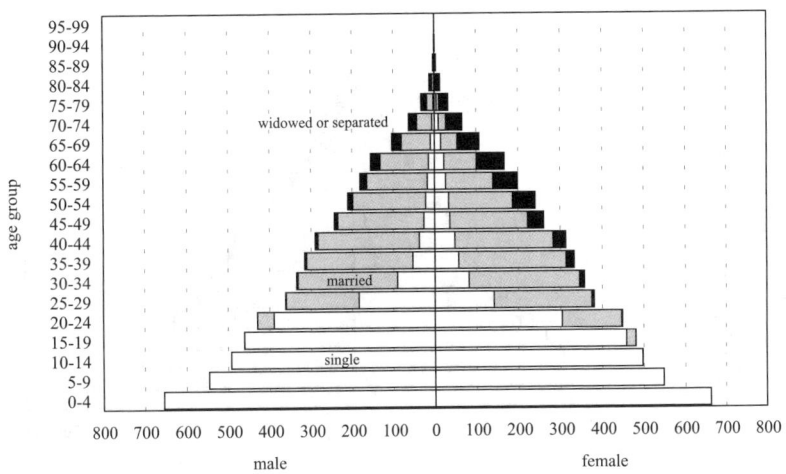

Austrian Empire, 1890

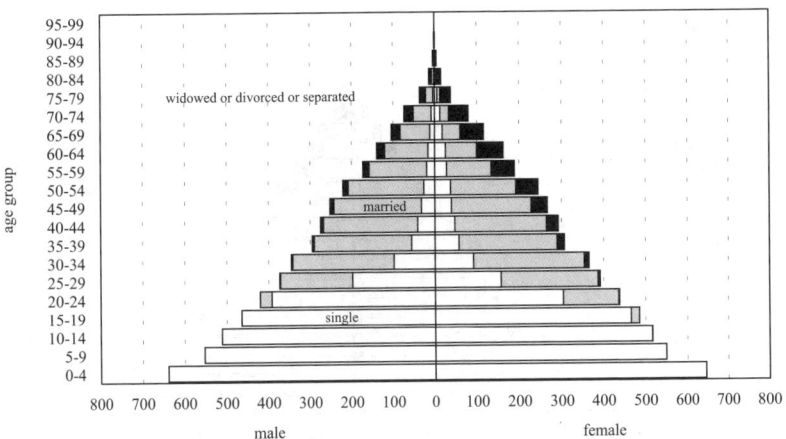

APPENDIX FIGURE A.8 Population by age, sex and marital status, Austrian Empire 1880, 1890, 1900 and 1910; Austrian Republic 1934 and 1939 (per 10,000 of total population) (continued)

Austrian Empire, 1900

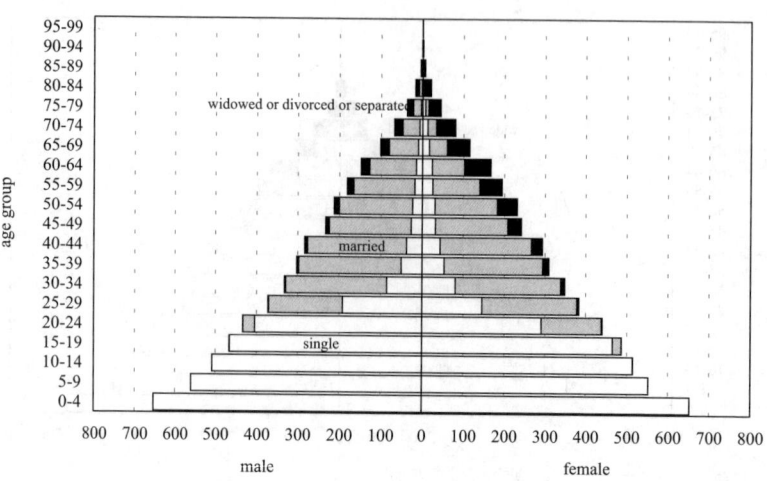

Austrian Empire, 1910

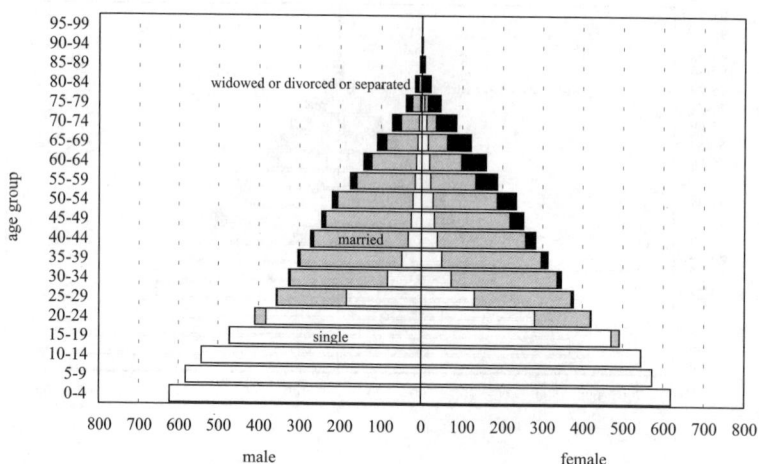

APPENDIX FIGURE A.8 Population by age, sex and marital status, Austrian Empire 1880, 1890, 1900 and 1910; Austrian Republic 1934 and 1939 (per 10,000 of total population) (continued)

Austrian Republic, 1934

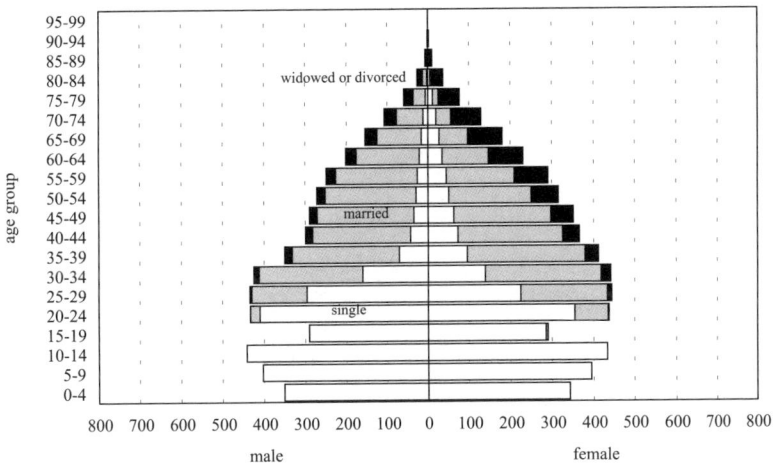

Austrian Republic, 1939

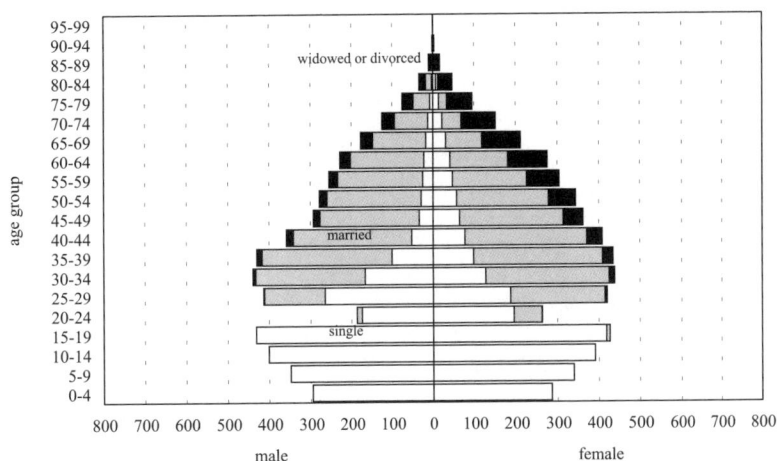

2
Belgium

STATE FORMATION AND TERRITORY

Belgium was established as a national state in 1830 by secession of the southern provinces of the United Kingdom of the Netherlands. In 1839, Belgium annexed the French-speaking western part of the Grand Duchy of Luxemburg and the southern part of the Dutch province of Limburg under the Treaty of London of 19 April. After World War I Belgium gained from Germany the German-speaking parts of Eupen, Malmédy, and surrounding districts. During World War II, from 1940–44, these German-speaking districts were temporarily returned to the German Empire, but given back after the war.

Since independence, Belgium is composed of the northern Flemish part and the southern Wallonian part. Although the country is religiously homogeneous—Catholic—linguistically it is divided between Flemish, a Dutch dialect, and Walloon, a French dialect. Both dialects moved towards the standard language in the last century. The linguistic division of the country coincides with major economic differences. In the nineteenth century Wallonia was industrialized, while Flanders remained mainly agrarian. Coal mining and heavy industry developed in Wallonia, while a weaving industry was established in Flanders. With the decline of heavy industry in Wallonia in the late twentieth century, the centre of economic gravity moved from the south to the north, and Wallonia went into an economic crisis, which continues today.

REGIONAL POPULATION STRUCTURE

Differences in economic development had tremendous effects on the regional population structure, and population growth varied greatly between provinces. The province of Brabant, with the capital, Brussels, is bilingual and shows strong population growth, with the population of Brussels more than doubling since 1866. Between 1866 and 1930 population of Brussels increased from 480,000 to 1,205,000 inhabitants. In Flanders the population of the province of Antwerp more than trebled in the same period, mainly due to the shipping industry and merchandising. Growth in the provinces of western and eastern Flanders was much less: the population here only doubled. The highest rate of population growth can be found in the province of Limburg, where the population was 195,000 inhabitants in 1866 and 750,000 in 1991, an increase of nearly 400%. In Wallonia the largest number of Belgians lived in the province of Hainaut already in 1866, where industrial development came very early. Other Belgian provinces remain very sparsely populated, especially the provinces of Namur and Luxembourg, while the population of Liège nearly doubled.

POPULATION GROWTH

Already at the time of independence in 1830 Belgium was one of the most densely populated regions of Europe, with 128 inhabitants per square kilometre in 1831 and a total population of 3,786,000 inhabitants. This number increased to roughly 10 million inhabitants in 1991, an almost threefold increase over 160 years. This growth constitutes a major difference to most other Western European countries, where the population only doubled.

Both the *natural* and *total population growth rate* during the nineteenth century fluctuated around 10 per 1,000 (Figure B.1). With the fertility decline since about 1900 the population growth rates declined as well, reaching a level of less than 5 per 1,000 in the 1930s. The natural population growth rate developed rather smoothly except in times of economic and mortality crises when growth was negative, in the late 1850s and 1860s, the early 1870s with the impact of the Franco-Prussian War, and during both world wars.

The total population growth rate shows much larger fluctuations due to the impact of emigration. While *net migration* was small but positive during the second half of the nineteenth century, it was nearly zero in the inter-war period. Strong waves of emigration in the late 1850s, the 1860s, and the 1870s interrupted the small movement of population surplus due to migration surplus. The causes for these emigration movements were mainly economic depressions, which occurred repeatedly during the following decades in the early 1880s, 1890s, 1900s, and 1910s. But these waves were small compared to the huge emigration wave following World War I and the inflation of the early 1920s.

THE FIRST DEMOGRAPHIC TRANSITION

Demographic transition in Belgium started around 1870, when the number of deaths began to decline steadily (Figure B.2). The birth rate continued to rise until 1880, and declined slightly afterwards. But around 1900 a very steep decline in Belgian fertility set in, leading to a first reduction in the surplus of natural population growth. This trend towards convergence of the birth and the death rates continued until the end of the 1930s, when the two rates crossed. After World War II, the birth rate rose strongly again and the 'second demographic transition' set in, with a high natural population surplus until the early 1970s. Since that time the birth and death rate have been more or less on the same level and there has been only a small natural population increase.

The population history of Belgium over the last 150 years was strongly influenced by economic crises and wars. Belgium was greatly affected by the world economic crisis of the 1850s (Rosenberg, 1974), as shown by the declining birth rate and the rising death rate in the 1850s. Already the Franco-Prussian War of 1870/71 led to a strong increase in mortality, but no visible decline in births occurred. Belgium was also greatly affected by both world wars, though more so by World War I, in which the front lines went through Belgium, as can be seen by the steep drop in the birth rate and the very strong increase in the death rate. During World War II the same demographic crisis occurred, but to a much lesser degree. The recession during the world wars had some impact on the birth rate, which fell much faster than before.

Figure B.1 Population growth and net migration 1850-1945

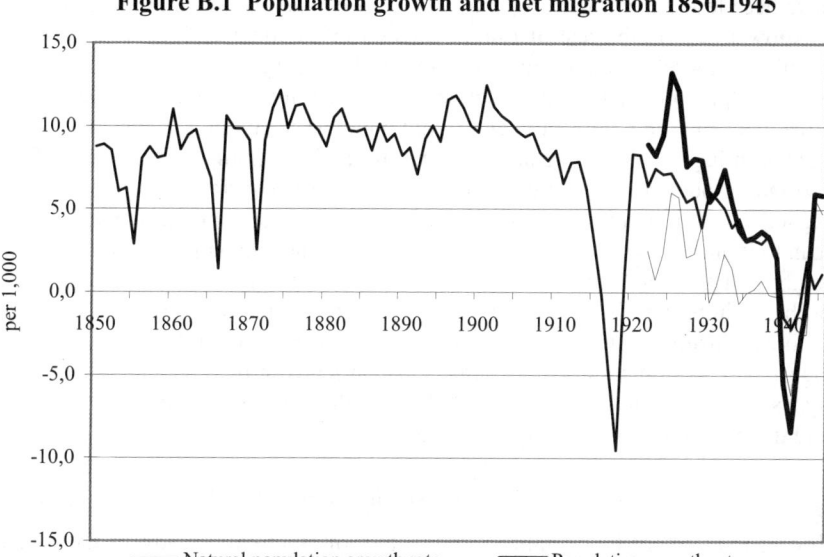

per 1,000

—— Natural population growth rate ■——■Population growth rate
—— Net migration rate

Figure B.2 First demographic transition 1850-1945

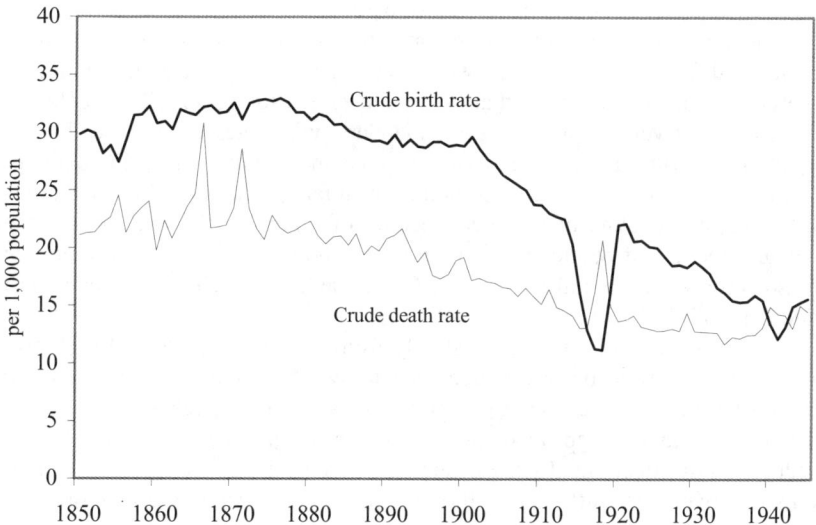

per 1,000 population

Crude birth rate

Crude death rate

Compared with Europe as a whole, in Belgium both the birth and the death rates have been lower than the European rates. This means that in Belgium child mortality was lower than in the rest of Europe already in the nineteenth century. The natural population increase was more or less on the European average. Thus, although half of the Belgian population is French-speaking, fertility control as practised in France already during the nineteenth century did not exist in Belgium. Thus there was little French influence on demographic behaviour, and Belgium, unlike France, faced no substantial population problem during the demographic transition period. It can be argued that Belgium in demographic terms is much more similar to The Netherlands than to France. Causal factors for this interesting phenomenon are not as clear as one might believe. The French Revolution and the introduction of a secular state was probably important in dismantling religious affiliation. Another factor could be the political history: Spain's domination of The Netherlands and the Austrian Habsburgs' domination of the southern Netherlands in the eighteenth century. Both dynasties were strictly Catholic and did not allow the Enlightenment to take hold, and therefore did not face strong anti-clericalism.

MORTALITY AND LIFE EXPECTANCY

The comparatively low infant mortality rate of Belgium already in the nineteenth century is one important factor for explaining the low mortality rate (Figure B.3). In nineteenth-century Europe, the Nordic countries had the lowest infant mortality rate, while in most of Europe infant mortality was rather high. In Belgium some fertility planning was probably in use, combining rather low birth rates with improved care for children. Contributing factors may have been a better system of medical care, or more adequate childraising behaviour of parents.

Although infant mortality was comparatively low in Belgium, there were huge regional differences, mainly between Wallonia and Flanders. In Wallonia infant mortality was much lower than in Flanders (Lesthaeghe, 1977: 171ff.). Infant mortality was very high in western Flanders, with rates often exceeding 200 per 1,000 live births at the end of the nineteenth century, while in many parts of Wallonia the rate was below 100. Studies of infant mortality in Flanders point to the low level and decline of the breastfeeding of infants at the end of the nineteenth century, the use of opiates in sleeping syrup and the pollution of drinking water as reasons for higher mortality (also see Corsini and Viazzo, 1997; Bideau, Desjardins and Brignoli, 1997).

Life expectancy improved only slowly from the 1880s to the 1930s (Figure B.4). For all ages it was lower for men than for women, and the gender gap widened during the period. The greatest improvements in life expectancy were for infants. There were smaller improvements for 30-year-olds, but mainly after 1900, due to reductions of infectious diseases such as tuberculosis. Life expectancy for 60-year-olds improved very little during the time period, increasing less than one year from the 1880s to the 1930s.

FERTILITY AND LEGITIMACY

In Belgium, illegitimate fertility was below the European average (Figure B.5), which is surprising, given the late age at marriage and the high celibacy rate (see next section). The low illegitimate fertility partly explains the rather low overall

Figure B.3 Infant mortality 1850-1945

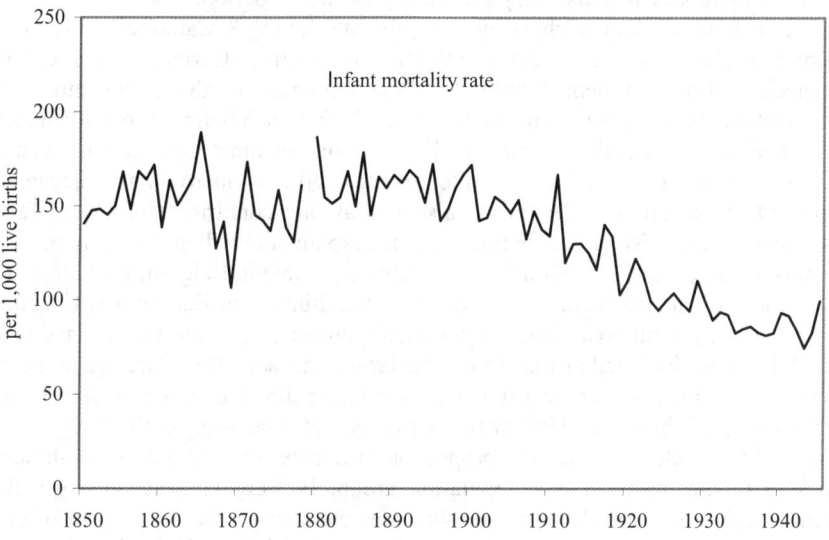

Figure B.4 Life expectancy 1881/90-1928/32

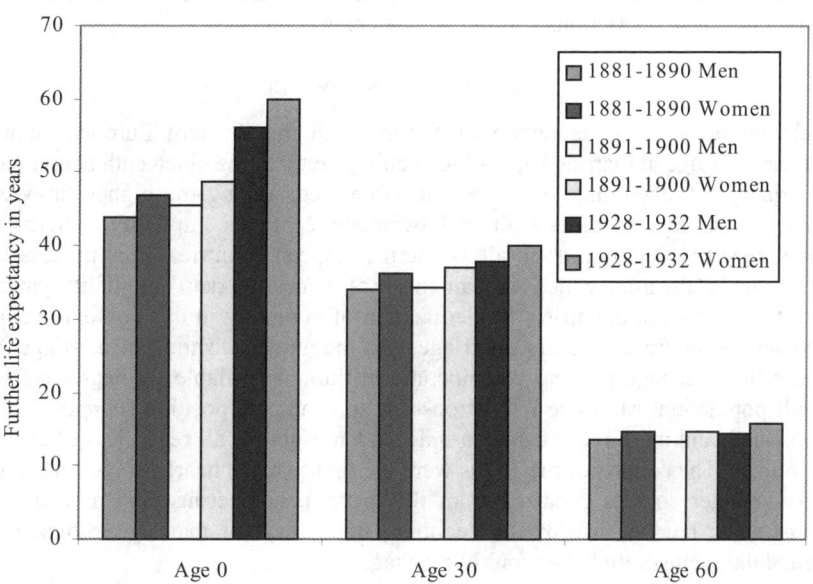

fertility in Belgium, as we have seen from the discussion of the demographic transition. The low Belgian illegitimate fertility is rather similar to the Swiss case, where illegitimacy was also very low during the whole period.

But how to explain such a low illegitimate fertility? Catholicism as such is compatible with a high illegitimacy rate, as Austria (Carinthia) and Germany (especially Bavaria) demonstrate. In these countries in the eighteenth century procreation was restricted to married people. Giving birth before or outside marriage was severely punished. During the first half of the nineteenth century marriage restrictions were retained but illegitimate fertility increasingly became an unavoidable social fact. Therefore, also in Catholic countries illegitimate fertility was high. Catholicism alone therefore cannot explain a low illegitimacy rate.

Another argument to explain the low illegitimacy rate in Belgium could have to do with the economic structure of the country. Illegitimacy in Europe was tolerated in predominantly rural areas with large agricultural estates, where the son had to wait until the father had died or transferred the farm to his son. Therefore age at marriage was very high, and people often had a relationship and children despite being unmarried; children were legitimized regularly after marriage. In these regions very high celibacy rates and the high proportion of female servants led to a high number of illegitimate births in this population group. In Belgium, such an agricultural structure did not exist. Illegitimacy was not tolerated by the public, but of course still occurred. There was no institutionalized system in which illegitimate children were later legitimized within marriage. Illegitimacy was, of course, unavoidable due to the restrictive possibilities of marrying, but it greatly declined as marriage became more universal. Thus, illegitimacy in Belgium can more or less be attributed to the strong marriage restrictions still in the nineteenth century.

MARRIAGE AND DIVORCE

Belgium belongs to the region of Europe with the Western European marriage pattern: late age at marriage and a high celibacy rate. In the nineteenth century age at marriage and, accordingly, the celibacy rate were among the highest in Western Europe. During the nineteenth and twentieth centuries nuptiality patterns were modernized in Belgium as in all Western European countries. This process lasted until the 1960s, after which we can speak of a 'post-modern' nuptiality pattern in Western European countries. Modernization of nuptiality in this context means the secular decline in age at first marriage, and the universalization of marriage in the sense that marriage became a democratic institution available for nearly the whole adult population. Marriage restrictions due to economic position (*pauperism*) were abolished, and marriage became an independent right for all regardless of economic resources. The cohorts of the 1930s were the first to reach nearly universal marriage. The younger cohorts departed from this pattern, not because of 'new' marriage constraints, but because of the declining importance of marriage, which is now called the 'deinstitutionalization' of marriage.

Marriage intensity can be measured by the marriage rate and the celibacy rate (Figure B.6). 'Intensity' means the availability of marriage as well as the urgent need to remarry after widowhood ('*remarriage need*', Michael Mitterauer). A third component is the universality of marriage among the population. The marriage rate refers to all marriages and includes remarriages. From the 1850s to the 1970s the Belgian marriage rate showed a rising tendency, though from 1850 to 1900 the

Figure B.5 Fertility and legitimacy 1864-1939

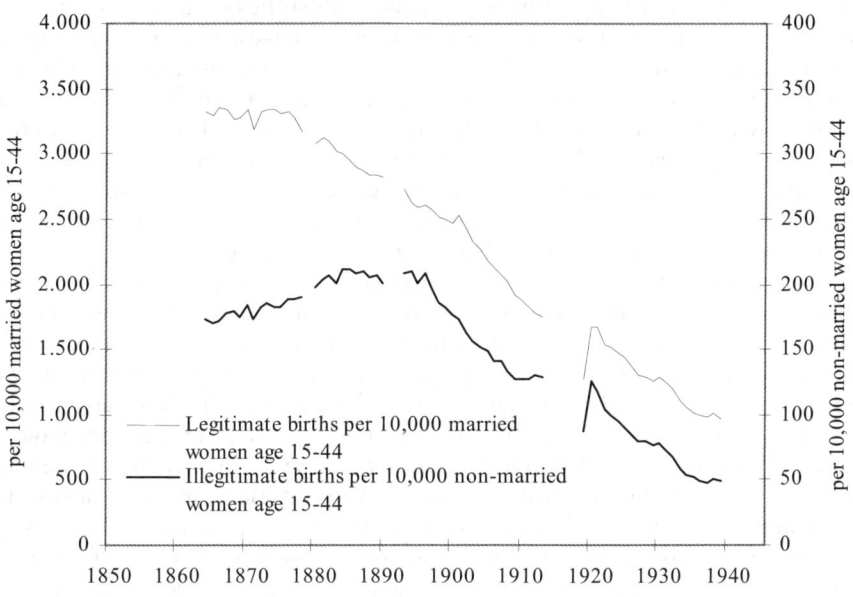

Legitimate births per 10,000 married women age 15-44

Illegitimate births per 10,000 non-married women age 15-44

Figure B.6 Marriages and divorces 1850-1939

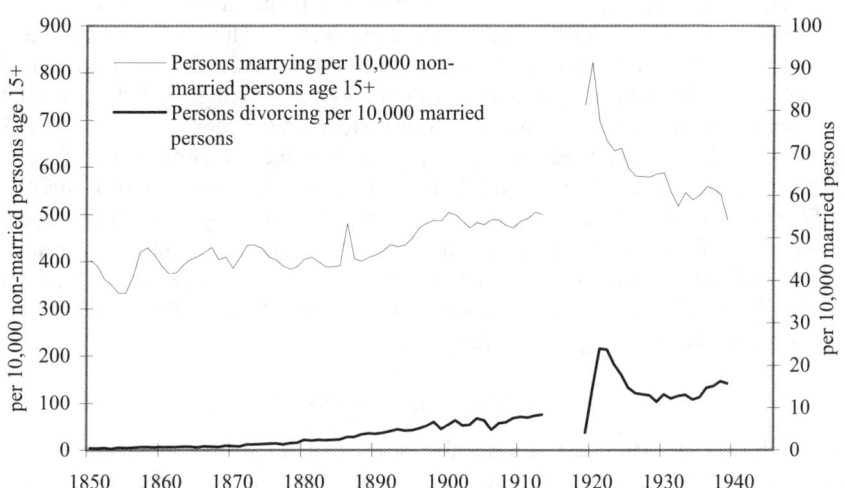

Persons marrying per 10,000 non-married persons age 15+

Persons divorcing per 10,000 married persons

marriage rate was even lower than the European average, clearly demonstrating the very strong marriage barriers in Belgium during the whole nineteenth century. Until 1850 marriage was largely restricted to those with sufficient income to support a family; in trade and in agriculture it was necessary to have a profession or sufficient land to get permission to marry. This Malthusian system of marriage and therefore also fertility control was undermined during the eighteenth century and the first half of the nineteenth century by the proletarianization of parts of the rural and urban population, a process which proved impossible to halt. The population grew during this time, but the economic system did not change in principle. The effects were a pauperization of the masses which finally led to changes in the economic system towards greater liberalism and the abolishing of feudal relationships.

Industrialization finally changed the situation. Belgium was the second European country after England to become industrialized, and industrialization paved the way for the universalization of marriage after 1850. This is clear from comparing the marriage rates for Switzerland and Belgium. In Switzerland, the marriage rate was on the same level as in Belgium, and did not change during the whole period. But in Belgium there was a clear rise in the marriage rate in the direction of universalization. In Switzerland industrialization came much later than in Belgium and was of a completely different nature: while in Belgium coal mining and metallurgy were the dominant sectors during the industrialization process, in Switzerland it was mainly small-scale industry in mechanical engineering. For a long time, the economic resources did not allow for modernization of marriage. In this sense, Switzerland was a latecomer in the modernization of nuptiality.

Concerning marital stability, Belgium participated in the long-term growth in divorce, but for the whole period under consideration the level was under the European average (Figure B.6). Two factors may explain this phenomenon: the low marriage rate and Catholicism. The marriage rate was very low and the marriage age very high, so that marriages on the whole were very stable. It is well-known that marriages are the more unstable the lower the age at marriage and the greater the freedom to choose one's own partner. In a system where people marry at a higher age and are much more likely to marry within the same social class, marriages are said to be more stable. The second factor is Catholicism, which is still one of the unifying factors for all Belgians, given their linguistic heterogeneity. This seems to be a decisive factor when comparing divorce rates in Belgium and Switzerland. In Switzerland the divorce rate was much higher during the whole period, reflecting the religiously mixed structure of this country. Legal separations in Belgium were more or less non-existent during the whole period.

AGE, SEX, AND CIVIL STATUS

The Belgian age structure during the second half of the nineteenth century underlines the rather low birth rate in Belgium already at that time; the lower age groups were rather small compared with other countries, and the bottom of the age pyramid is not concave (Appendix Figure B.8). First signs of birth decline appeared between 1900 and 1910, when the bottom of the age pyramid became convex, indicating that the lowest age groups became smaller. Belgium's strong involvement in World War I is apparent from the age structures of 1920, 1930, and 1947. In 1920 the age structure became bell-shaped, because of the birth losses during the world war. The age groups of the 5–9-year-olds and especially the 0–4-year-olds were greatly reduced. The birth cohorts of the early 1920s were rather strong, but during the 1930s the birth cohorts became small because of increased birth decline. World War II again greatly reduced the number of children born, as can be seen from the age structure for 1947.

During the second half of the nineteenth century, age at marriage was traditionally rather high in Belgium, as was celibacy. While men married later than women, the proportion of married men in higher age groups was higher, because of higher male mortality and therefore higher proportions of widowed women. Until 1910 there was a small tendency towards a lower age at marriage and a higher propensity to marry. World War I obviously did not change this behaviour very much. The only important change was a strong increase in widowed women, most clearly visible in 1947 for women aged 60 and over.

FAMILY AND HOUSEHOLD STRUCTURES

Given the restriction of marriage to a segment of the population because of Malthusian fertility control, the question must be raised as to how the single and widowed people lived. Did they form their own households or did they join a family household and by doing so form extended households? The discussion of this question has to be based mainly on the *mean household size*, as statistics on household composition are not available for Belgium during the nineteenth century. First, the mean size of households in Belgium was rather low compared with other European countries; this must be attributed to the rather low birth rate, but also to the phenomenon that at least in towns, widowed and single people predominantly lived in their own households. But for demographic reasons, as in other Western European countries, the formation of extended households was rather rare and normally did not exceed 10–20% of all households. In the Belgian countryside, mean household size was larger, and the formation of extended households was much more widespread.

THE NATIONAL SYSTEM OF DEMOGRAPHIC STATISTICS

Population structure

The first population census after independence in 1830 and the territorial gains of 1839 was conducted in 1846. This census is famous for being the first modern one, conducted by self-enumeration; it was organized by Adolphe Quételet. Nevertheless, given the limited development of official statistics at that time, relatively few topics were covered. Data collection concentrated on counting the *de facto* population, but already this census collected population data by age, sex, and marital status. All the later censuses continued to collect these basic population statistics. All Belgian censuses counted the whole population, and there were no partial or sample censuses.

Vital statistics

The record of births, deaths, and marriages was introduced with the founding of the Belgian state in 1830. Disaggregation of these basic demographic variables was introduced at later stages: deaths by age and births by legitimacy in 1841. Generally, the more complicated the demographic measures, the later they were introduced.

Households and families

Data on households (*ménages* or *familles*) were already collected in the 1846 census, though it gives only the number of households. Households were disaggregated by size of locality (communes with less than 5,000 inhabitants (*communes rurales*) and communes with more than 5,000 inhabitants (*villes*)) and by provinces. This simple presentation of household statistics was maintained until 1910. Not until 1920 was the presentation enlarged by introducing the number of single-person households and the sex of household heads. In 1930 the first elaborate household statistics were introduced in Belgium: households were presented by size, different types, and household composition. Household heads were disaggregated by sex, age and marital status, and by occupation.

The definition of a household (*ménage*) was more or less the same from 1846 until 1947. The definition principally included all households: households consisting of a single person, households consisting of a family, and institutional households were considered households. The definition of a household included living together in one house; servants living with a family did not count as separate households. A biological family living in the same house could also form several households if family members did not live together or share household income and spending. Examples of institutional households are religious communities or soldiers living in barracks. The first two population censuses of 1846 and 1856 only included the *de facto* population, not persons temporarily absent. Therefore, mean household size is assumed to be underestimated when compared with the later censuses. The Belgian definition of a household clearly states that a *ménage* is not the same as a family (*famille*), because the concept of household does not take into account biological relationships. Thus, we have a very broad definition of a household in the Belgian population census, as compared with German statistics, for example, where already in the 1870s this broad category was split up. Still, when the first more detailed computations for households were made for the 1930 census, the broad household concept was maintained, although it was assumed that the vast majority of all households were family households. The first explicit definition of a household was given in the 1880 census (p. XI); others were presented and discussed for the censuses of 1890 (vol. I, p. XIX), 1900 (vol. I, p. XXIV), 1920 (vol. I, p. 37), and 1930 (vol. I, p. 158).

Family statistics did not start before the census of 1910, when for the first time families were presented by the number of children. These family statistics were maintained and enlarged in the censuses of 1920 and especially in those of 1930 and 1947. In 1910, married couples were distinguished by the duration of marriage (from 0–1, 1–2, 3–4, 5–6, 7–9, 10–14, 15–19, 20–24, and 25+ years of marriage) and the number of children living (from 0–10+). The same question was posed in 1920 (vol. I, pp. 87ff.) and the same presentation of results was carried out. In 1930 (vol. III) the first genuine family statistics were gathered, aimed at measuring the '*productivity of families*'. The number of children born to a married couple was combined with the nationality of the married man, the age of both partners, the duration of marriage, and the mother's occupation.

Remarks (also see introductory Table 6.1)

Data on age structure from 1930 to 1939 have been created by linear extrapolation using the growth rates of the censuses of 1920 to 1930.

BOUNDARY CHANGES

Belgium was established as a national state in 1830 by secession of the southern provinces of the United Kingdom of the Netherlands. In 1839, Belgium annexed the French-speaking western part of the Grand Duchy of Luxemburg and the southern part of the Dutch province of Limburg under the Treaty of London of 19 April. After World War I Belgium gained from Germany the German-speaking parts of Eupen, Malmédy, and surrounding districts. During World War II, from 1940–44, these German-speaking districts were temporarily returned to the German Empire, but given back after the war. For further details on regional organization see Quick (1994) and Caramani, Flora, Kraus, and Quick (1998).

APPENDIX TABLES AND FIGURES

APPENDIX TABLE B.1 Population structure at census dates 1846–1947

Census number	Census date	Census population			Marital status				Age group		
		Total	Male	Female	Single	Married	Widowed	Divorced	0–14	15–64	65+
		Absolute									
1	15 X 1846	4.337.196	2.163.523	2.173.673	2.771.975	1.322.588	242.633	..	1.402.124	2.680.181	254.891
2	31 XII 1856	4.529.560	2.271.783	2.257.777	2.892.895	1.381.997	254.668	..	1.372.678	2.901.104	255.778
3	31 XII 1866	4.827.833	2.419.639	2.408.194	3.011.566	1.528.543	287.724	..	1.529.507	2.993.046	305.280
4	31 XII 1880	5.520.010	2.758.470	2.761.540	3.441.951	1.754.364	321.320	2.375	1.848.764	3.315.335	355.911
5	31 XII 1890	6.069.321	3.026.954	3.042.367	3.780.770	1.932.359	352.506	3.686	1.848.764	3.864.646	355.911
6	31 XII 1900	6.693.546	3.324.834	3.368.712	4.016.007	2.290.238	379.216	8.085	2.122.496	4.156.787	414.263
7	31 XII 1910	7.423.784	3.680.790	3.742.994	4.261.871	2.741.880	405.274	14.759	2.267.019	4.683.871	472.894
8	31 XII 1920	7.406.299	3.644.988	3.761.311	3.956.384	2.991.781	438.203	19.931	1.849.550	5.076.335	480.414
9	31 XII 1930	8.092.004	4.007.418	4.084.586	3.781.206	3.792.907	481.286	36.605	1.859.183	5.618.603	614.218
10	31 XII 1947	8.512.195	4.199.728	4.312.467	3.592.587	4.238.493	610.904	70.211	1.752.493	5.849.813	909.889
		Per cent									
1	15 X 1846	100.00	49.88	50.12	63.91	30.49	5.59	..	32,33	61,80	5,88
2	31 XII 1856	100.00	50.15	49.85	63.87	30.51	5.62	..	30,30	64,05	5,65
3	31 XII 1866	100.00	50.12	49.88	62.38	31.66	5.96	..	31,68	62,00	6,32
4	31 XII 1880	100.00	49.97	50.03	62.35	31.78	5.82	0.04	33,49	60,06	6,45
5	31 XII 1890	100.00	49.87	50.13	62.29	31.84	5.81	0.06	30,46	63,68	5,86
6	31 XII 1900	100.00	49.67	50.33	60.00	34.22	5.67	0.12	31,71	62,10	6,19
7	31 XII 1910	100.00	49.58	50.42	57.41	36.93	5.46	0.20	30,54	63,09	6,37
8	31 XII 1920	100.00	49.21	50.79	53.42	40.40	5.92	0.27	24,97	68,54	6,49
9	31 XII 1930	100.00	49.52	50.48	46.73	46.87	5.95	0.45	22,98	69,43	7,59
10	31 XII 1947	100.00	49.34	50.66	42.21	49.79	7.18	0.82	20,59	68,72	10,69

APPENDIX TABLE B.2 Census population by region 1846–1947 (per cent)

Province/Arrondis-sement	1846	1856	1866	1880	1890	1900	1910	1920	1930	1947
Anvers	**9.37**	**9.59**	**9.65**	**10.45**	**11.53**	**12.23**	**13.05**	**13.73**	**14.50**[2]	**15.05**
Anvers	4.37	4.65	4.87	5.85	6.87	7.53	8.14	8.60	9.21[2]	9.21
Malines	2.68	2.64	2.59	2.59	2.67	2.69	2.75	2.81	2.83	2.93
Turnhout	2.32	2.30	2.17	2.01	1.99	2.02	2.16	2.32	2.47	2.91
Brabant	**15.94**	**16.53**	**16.86**	**17.84**	**18.22**	**18.88**	**19.80**	**20.55**	**20.76**	**21.12**
Bruxelles	8.68	9.42	9.96	11.29	11.91	12.74	13.78	14.56	14.89	15.27
Hal-Vilvorde	..	..	..	..	..	..	..	..	..	..
Louvain	4.01	3.95	3.79	3.70	3.66	3.62	3.62	3.66	3.63	3.72
Nivelles	3.25	3.16	3.09	2.86	2.67	2.51	2.40	2.34	2.24	2.14
Flandre Occidentale	**14.83**	**13.80**	**13.30**	**12.54**	**12.16**	**12.03**	**11.77**	**10.86**	**11.15**	**11.70**
Bruges	2.75	2.62	2.46	2.28	2.24	2.23	2.22	2.27	2.16	2.34
Dixmude	1.08	0.99	0.95	0.89	0.84	0.78	0.73	0.53	0.57	0.56
Ypres	2.39	2.30	2.22	2.05	1.93	1.82	1.74	1.16	1.47	1.45
Courtrai	3.27	3.01	2.94	2.84	2.80	2.90	2.88	2.86	3.03	3.22
Ostende	1.01	1.02	0.97	1.00	1.04	1.17	1.20	1.22	1.21	1.27
Roulers	1.95	1.73	1.74	1.65	1.60	1.55	1.50	1.32	1.35	1.47
Thielt	1.66	1.44	1.39	1.23	1.14	1.06	1.01	0.97	0.85	0.87
Furnes	0.71	0.69	0.64	0.60	0.56	0.52	0.51	0.53	0.51	0.53
Flandre Orientale	**18.29**	**17.15**	**16.69**	**15.98**	**15.65**	**15.39**	**15.09**	**14.95**	**14.20**[2]	**14.30**
Alost	3.19	3.01	2.96	2.77	2.72	2.73	2.79	2.82	2.74	2.80
Termonde	2.23	2.15	2.11	2.01	1.91	1.90	1.89	1.88	1.83[1,4]	1.89
Eeklo	1.29	1.19	1.16	1.11	1.04	1.00	0.96	0.92	0.89[4]	0.93
Gand	6.40	6.03	5.88	5.82	5.83	5.74	5.54	5.47	5.22[1,4]	5.18
Audenarde	2.46	2.11	1.99	1.78	1.68	1.64	1.56	1.51	1.40	1.77
Saint-Nicolas	2.71	2.67	2.61	2.50	2.46	2.38	2.36	2.34	2.13[2]	2.16
Hainaut	**16.48**	**16.98**	**17.50**	**17.72**	**17.28**	**17.07**	**16.61**	**16.47**	**15.69**	**14.39**
Ath	2.16	1.97	1.91	1.70	1.52	1.37	1.23	1.15	1.03	0.93
Charleroi	3.02	3.76	4.39	5.18	5.39	5.20	5.67	5.79	5.59	5.11
Mons	3.66	3.88	3.91	3.88	3.76	3.66	3.52	3.48	3.32	3.04
Mouscron	..	..	..	..	..	..	..	..	..	..
Soignies	2.21	2.14	2.20	2.23	2.21	2.21	2.17	2.17	2.11	1.96
Thuin	1.97	1.97	1.99	1.96	1.88	1.87	1.86	1.81	1.73	1.59
Tournai	3.45	3.26	3.09	2.75	2.52	2.30	2.18	2.05	1.92	1.75
Liège	**10.44**	**11.13**	**11.54**	**12.03**	**12.47**	**12.34**	**11.96**	**11.65**	**12.02**[3]	**11.33**
Huy	1.74	1.60	1.68	1.63	1.58	1.49	1.39	1.32	1.21	1.09
Liège	5.15	5.71	5.92	6.41	6.94	7.13	7.15	7.02	6.96	6.63
Verviers	2.40	2.66	2.78	2.86	2.87	2.66	2.44	2.34	2.97[3]	2.78
Waremme	1.16	1.16	1.14	1.12	1.09	1.05	0.98	0.97	0.89	0.81
Limbourg	**4.29**	**4.23**	**4.04**	**3.82**	**3.67**	**3.60**	**3.72**	**4.05**	**4.55**	**5.40**
Hasselt	1.79	1.77	1.68	1.61	1.57	1.52	1.58	1.77	2.10	2.57
Maaseik	0.85	0.85	0.83	0.76	0.72	0.76	0.82	0.90	0.99	1.23
Tongres	1.64	1.61	1.55	1.45	1.37	1.31	1.31	1.39	1.46	1.60
Luxembourg	**4.29**	**4.28**	**4.14**	**3.79**	**3.49**	**3.27**	**3.11**	**3.02**	**2.73**	**2.50**
Arlon	0.62	0.61	0.58	0.54	0.54	0.55	0.55	0.54	0.52	0.47
Bastogne	0.76	0.75	0.72	0.67	0.63	0.60	0.58	0.58	0.49	0.45
Marche	0.87	0.89	0.89	0.82	0.72	0.66	0.59	0.58	0.52	0.48
Neufchâteau	1.08	1.09	1.06	0.96	0.89	0.82	0.79	0.77	0.69	0.65
Virton	0.97	0.94	0.89	0.80	0.72	0.64	0.59	0.55	0.51	0.47
Namur	**6.08**	**6.32**	**6.28**	**5.85**	**5.52**	**5.18**	**4.89**	**4.70**	**4.40**	**4.18**
Dinant	1.63	1.72	1.72	1.59	1.48	1.36	1.24	1.17	1.08	1.01
Namur	3.25	3.34	3.29	3.15	3.06	2.94	2.83	2.75	2.60	2.51
Philippeville	1.20	1.25	1.24	1.09	0.97	0.87	0.81	0.69	0.73	0.66
TOTAL	**100**	**100**	**100**	**100**	**100**	**100**	**100**	**100**	**100**[3]	**100**[3]

Notes: [1] 20 IV 1921: Arrondissement Termonde lost an area with 1,525 inhabitants to arrondissement Gand. [2] 19 III 1923: Arrondissement Saint Nicolas (Flandre Orientale) lost 2 communes (with 29 sq. km.) to arrondissement Anvers. [3] 6 III 1925: Several communities (e.g. La Calamine, Eupen, Malmédy und St. Vith), with 1,053 sq. km. and 64,000 inhabitants, moved from Germany to the Belgian arrondissement Verviers, following the Treaty of Versaille. [4] 17 III 1927: Termonde and Eeklo lost an area with 442 inhabitants to Gand.

APPENDIX TABLE B.3 Population density by region 1846–1947
(inhabitants per sq. km.)

Province/Arrondissement	1846	1856	1866	1880	1890	1900	1910	1920	1930	1947
Anvers	**143**	**153**	**165**	**204**	**247**	**289**	**342**	**359**	**410**[2]	**448**
Anvers	195	217	242	332	429	519	621	655	744[2]	783
Malines	231	238	248	284	321	357	405	413	454	494
Turnhout	74	77	77	82	89	100	118	127	147	183
Brabant	**211**	**228**	**248**	**300**	**337**	**385**	**448**	**464**	**512**	**548**
Bruxelles	340	386	435	563	653	771	924	974	1.082	1.167
Hal-Vilvorde	..	..	..	..	..	..	..	..	..	..
Louvain	154	159	162	181	197	215	238	240	262	283
Nivelles	135	137	142	151	155	160	170	165	173	174
Flandre Occidentale	**199**	**193**	**199**	**214**	**228**	**249**	**270**	**249**	**279**	**308**
Bruges	182	181	182	192	208	227	252	256	267	303
Dixmude	137	131	134	143	149	152	157	114	134	140
Ypres	170	170	175	185	191	200	211	141	195	201
Courtrai	320	308	321	354	384	438	483	479	553	619
Ostende	149	156	159	186	213	264	301	304	331	365
Roulers	285	263	283	306	327	350	374	330	367	421
Thielt	236	214	220	223	226	233	246	237	227	243
Furnes	108	110	109	116	120	123	134	137	144	158
Flandre Orientale	**264**	**259**	**269**	**294**	**317**	**343**	**373**	**369**	**387**[2]	**410**
Alost	294	289	304	325	350	389	439	444	471	505
Termonde	277	278	291	317	331	363	400	397	433[1,4]	471
Eeklo	155	149	155	169	174	185	196	188	200[4]	219
Gand	306	301	313	354	391	424	454	447	460[1,4]	481
Audenarde	259	232	233	238	248	267	282	272	274	367
Saint-Nicolas	236	243	253	277	299	319	351	347	367[2]	392
Hainaut	**192**	**207**	**227**	**263**	**282**	**307**	**331**	**328**	**341**	**329**
Ath	190	181	187	191	187	187	185	172	168	160
Charleroi	234	304	378	510	583	620	750	765	806	775
Mons	260	287	309	350	373	401	427	422	441	425
Mouscron	..	..	..	..	..	..	..	..	..	..
Soignies	175	177	193	224	245	270	294	294	312	305
Thuin	94	98	106	119	126	138	152	148	154	149
Tournai	249	246	248	253	255	257	270	253	258	248
Liège	**156**	**174**	**192**	**229**	**261**	**285**	**307**	**298**	**246**[3]	**244**
Huy	105	101	112	125	133	139	143	136	136	129
Liège	294	341	377	467	555	629	701	686	743	744
Verviers	104	121	134	158	175	179	182	173	117[3]	115
Waremme	120	125	131	148	158	167	174	172	172	165
Limbourg	**77**	**80**	**81**	**88**	**93**	**100**	**115**	**125**	**153**	**191**
Hasselt	86	88	89	98	105	112	129	144	187	241
Maaseik	43	45	46	49	51	59	71	78	93	122
Tongres	111	115	118	125	130	138	152	161	185	213
Luxembourg	**42**	**44**	**45**	**47**	**48**	**50**	**52**	**51**	**50**	**48**
Arlon	83	86	87	93	103	115	128	125	131	125
Bastogne	33	34	35	37	38	40	43	43	40	38
Marche	40	43	46	48	47	47	47	46	45	44
Neufchâteau	32	34	35	37	37	38	41	39	39	38
Virton	59	59	60	61	61	60	61	57	57	56
Namur	**72**	**78**	**83**	**88**	**92**	**95**	**99**	**95**	**97**	**97**
Dinant	45	50	53	56	57	58	59	55	55	55
Namur	125	135	141	155	165	175	187	181	187	190
Philippeville	54	59	62	62	61	60	62	53	61	58
TOTAL	**147**	**154**	**164**	**187**	**206**	**227**	**252**	**251**	**265**[3]	**279**[3]

Notes: See Appendix Table B.2.

APPENDIX TABLE B.4 Demographic developments 1850–1945 (absolute figures and rates)

Year	Mid-year population[1]	Natural population growth rate	Population growth rate	Net migration rate	Crude birth rate	Legitimate births per 10,000 married women age 15–44	Illegitimate births per 10,000 unmarried women age 15–44	Illeg. births per 100 leg. births
1850	4,403,222	8.8	..	..	29.8	..	..	..
1851	4,449,733	8.9	4.3[2]	-1.2[2]	30.2	..	..	..
1852	4,494,811	8.5	..	..	29.9	..	..	..
1853	4,532,434	6.0	..	..	28.2	..	..	..
1854	4,566,802	6.3	..	..	28.9	..	..	..
1855	4,596,081	2.9	..	..	27.4	..	..	..
1856	4,568,264	8.1	..	..	29.4	..	..	..
1857	4,553,349	8.7	..	..	31.5	..	..	..
1858	4,600,217	8.1	..	..	31.5	..	..	..
1859	4,647,212	8.2	..	..	32.2	..	..	..
1860	4,701,611	11.0	..	..	30.8	..	..	..
1861	4,757,126	8.6	..	..	31.0	..	..	..
1862	4,809,411	9.4	6.4[3]	-1.6[3]	30.3	..	..	..
1863	4,864,794	9.8	..	..	32.0	..	..	..
1864	4,916,796	8.1	..	..	31.7	3.328	173	7.8
1865	4,962,461	6.8	..	..	31.5	3.294	170	7.6
1866	4,906,092	1.4	..	..	32.2	3.355	171	7.4
1867	4,862,814	10.6	..	..	32.3	3.348	177	7.6
1868	4,929,719	9.9	..	..	31.7	3.268	179	7.8
1869	4,991,490	9.8	..	..	31.8	3.278	174	7.5
1870	5,054,581	9.1	..	..	32.6	3.344	183	7.7
1871	5,100,753	2.6	..	..	31.1	3.190	173	7.6
1872	5,144,359	9.2	..	..	32.5	3.326	183	7.6
1873	5,214,416	11.1	9.6[4]	-0.1[4]	32.7	3.335	185	7.6
1874	5,295,214	12.2	..	..	32.9	3.341	183	7.5
1875	5,369,786	9.9	..	..	32.7	3.317	183	7.5
1876	5,369,562	11.2	..	..	32.9	3.327	189	7.6
1877	5,374,458	11.3	..	..	32.6	3.281	188	7.7
1878	5,444,835	10.2	..	..	31.7	3.178	189	7.9
1879	5,506,897	9.7	..	..	31.7	..	..	..
1880	5,528,432	8.8	..	..	31.1	3.084	197	8.4
1881	5,552,928	10.5	..	..	31.6	3.127	203	8.5
1882	5,620,522	11.0	..	..	31.4	3.094	208	8.8
1883	5,688,002	9.7	..	..	30.7	3.021	200	8.7
1884	5,752,883	9.7	..	..	30.7	3.007	212	9.3
1885	5,819,118	9.8	9.5[5]	-0.1[5]	30.1	2.936	211	9.5
1886	5,881,627	8.5	..	..	29.8	2.902	209	9.5
1887	5,942,359	10.1	..	..	29.5	2.871	210	9.7
1888	6,002,393	9.1	..	..	29.3	2.840	206	9.6
1889	6,061,921	9.5	..	..	29.3	2.839	206	9.6
1890	6,081,560	8.2	..	..	29.0	2.816	201	9.4
1891	6,102,883	8.7	..	..	29.8	..	..	..
1892	6,165,900	7.1	..	..	28.8	..	..	..
1893	6,228,814	9.2	..	..	29.4	2.724	208	9.6
1894	6,302,115	10.0	..	..	28.8	2.626	209	9.9
1895	6,376,371	9.1	9.8[6]	0.0[6]	28.7	2.591	201	9.5
1896	6,453,335	11.6	..	..	29.2	2.598	208	9.6
1897	6,541,240	11.8	..	..	29.2	2.574	198	9.1

continued

APPENDIX TABLE B.4 Demographic developments 1850–1945 (absolute figures and rates)

Crude death rate	Infant mortality rate	Stillbirth rate	Infant mortality and stillbirth rate	Crude marriage rate	Persons marrying per 10,000 unmarried persons age 15+	Persons marrying per 10,000 unmarried persons age 15–49	Crude divorce rate	Divorces per 100 marriages	Divorces per 10,000 married persons	Year
21.1	140.8	48.1	188.9	7.7	404	497	0.0	0.1	0.4	1850
21.3	147.6	47.5	195.0	7.5	390	481	0.0	0.1	0.4	1851
21.4	148.4	47.9	196.4	7.0	362	447	0.0	0.1	0.5	1852
22.1	145.3	46.1	191.5	6.8	350	433	0.0	0.1	0.3	1853
22.6	150.2	45.8	195.9	6.5	333	412	0.0	0.1	0.6	1854
24.5	168.3	45.2	213.5	6.5	333	412	0.0	0.1	0.5	1855
21.3	148.3	45.7	194.0	7.2	368	456	0.0	0.1	0.6	1856
22.7	168.4	47.6	215.9	8.2	421	523	0.0	0.1	0.7	1857
23.5	164.0	48.7	212.7	8.3	430	535	0.0	0.1	0.8	1858
24.0	171.9	49.9	221.7	7.9	414	517	0.0	0.1	0.7	1859
19.8	138.7	48.2	186.9	7.5	391	490	0.0	0.2	0.8	1860
22.4	163.6	47.3	210.9	7.1	375	471	0.0	0.2	0.8	1861
20.8	150.4	47.3	197.8	7.1	377	475	0.0	0.2	0.8	1862
22.2	157.2	48.3	205.5	7.4	393	497	0.0	0.2	0.9	1863
23.6	165.1	50.1	215.2	7.5	405	512	0.0	0.2	0.9	1864
24.7	189.1	48.6	237.8	7.6	411	522	0.0	0.1	0.7	1865
30.8	164.4	50.3	214.7	7.7	420	535	0.0	0.2	0.9	1866
21.7	127.5	47.6	175.1	7.9	431	549	0.0	0.2	0.8	1867
21.8	141.6	47.9	189.5	7.4	404	516	0.0	0.2	0.8	1868
22.0	106.5	47.0	153.5	7.4	410	525	0.0	0.2	1.0	1869
23.4	145.4	46.0	191.4	7.0	386	494	0.0	0.2	1.0	1870
28.6	173.4	45.7	219.0	7.4	409	524	0.0	0.2	0.9	1871
23.4	145.1	45.2	190.3	7.8	435	558	0.0	0.3	1.3	1872
21.6	142.2	45.6	187.8	7.8	436	560	0.0	0.3	1.4	1873
20.7	136.9	44.5	181.5	7.6	428	550	0.0	0.3	1.4	1874
22.8	158.4	44.1	202.5	7.3	411	528	0.0	0.3	1.5	1875
21.7	138.6	44.8	183.4	7.1	404	519	0.0	0.4	1.6	1876
21.3	130.8	46.0	176.8	6.9	391	504	0.0	0.3	1.4	1877
21.5	160.9	44.7	205.6	6.7	385	496	0.0	0.4	1.7	1878
22.0	..	46.6	..	6.8	390	503	0.0	0.4	1.7	1879
22.3	186.5	46.9	233.5	7.0	405	524	0.0	0.5	2.4	1880
21.1	154.7	46.8	201.5	7.1	409	528	0.0	0.5	2.3	1881
20.3	151.3	48.0	199.3	7.0	400	516	0.0	0.6	2.4	1882
21.0	154.5	47.8	202.3	6.8	389	502	0.0	0.5	2.3	1883
21.0	168.4	47.2	215.6	6.8	390	501	0.0	0.6	2.4	1884
20.2	149.8	48.7	198.5	6.9	391	503	0.0	0.6	2.5	1885
21.2	178.4	49.3	227.8	8.4	481	618	0.0	0.6	3.1	1886
19.4	145.3	49.7	194.9	7.2	406	522	0.0	0.7	3.1	1887
20.2	165.3	48.0	213.3	7.1	401	514	0.1	0.8	3.7	1888
19.8	159.6	47.4	207.0	7.2	409	524	0.1	0.9	3.9	1889
20.8	166.4	46.6	213.0	7.3	415	530	0.1	0.8	3.9	1890
21.1	162.4	47.2	209.5	7.4	423	541	0.1	0.9	4.1	1891
21.7	168.9	47.9	216.7	7.7	436	558	0.1	0.9	4.4	1892
20.2	164.9	47.2	212.0	7.6	432	553	0.1	1.1	4.9	1893
18.8	151.9	47.2	199.1	7.6	435	557	0.1	1.0	4.6	1894
19.6	172.1	47.1	219.2	7.8	449	575	0.1	1.0	4.7	1895
17.6	142.2	48.7	190.9	8.1	471	604	0.1	1.0	5.1	1896
17.4	148.7	45.9	194.6	8.3	481	616	0.1	1.2	5.7	1897

continued

APPENDIX TABLE B.4 Demographic developments 1850–1945 (continued)

Year	Mid-year population[1]	Natural population growth rate	Population growth rate	Net migration rate	Crude birth rate	Legitimate births per 10,000 married women age 15–44	Illegitimate births per 10,000 unmarried women age 15–44	Illeg. births per 100 leg. births
1898	6,628,163	11.1	..	..	28.8	2,517	186	8.6
1899	6,707,132	10.0	..	..	29.0	2,504	183	8.3
1900	6,719,040	9.6	..	..	28.8	2,467	177	8.0
1901	6,746,774	12.5	..	..	29.7	2,524	174	7.6
1902	6,848,039	11.2	..	..	28.6	2,421	163	7.3
1903	6,940,649	10.6	..	..	27.7	2,327	156	7.2
1904	7,030,065	10.3	..	..	27.3	2,273	151	7.1
1905	7,117,729	9.7	10.4[7]	0.6[7]	26.3	2,176	148	7.1
1906	7,199,585	9.4	..	..	25.9	2,124	142	6.8
1907	7,278,092	9.6	..	..	25.4	2,069	142	6.9
1908	7,352,003	8.4	..	..	25.0	2,023	133	6.6
1909	7,419,174	7.9	..	..	23.8	1,909	127	6.5
1910	7,437,844	8.5	..	..	23.7	1,888	128	6.5
1911	7,457,098	6.6	..	..	23.0	1,818	127	6.7
1912	7,530,899	7.8	..	..	22.7	1,776	131	6.9
1913	7,605,072	7.9	..	..	22.5	1,747	128	6.9
1914[8]	7,661,625	6.2	..	..	20.4	..	..	..
1915[8]	7,696,845	3.1	-0.2[9]	2.9[9]	16.1	..	..	..
1916[8]	7,700,907	-0.2	..	..	12.9	..	..	..
1917[8]	7,667,336	-5.0	..	..	11.3	..	..	..
1918[8]	7,598,815	-9.5	..	..	11.2	..	..	..
1919	7,566,302	1.3	..	..	16.3	1,266	87	7.3
1920	7,491,298	8.3	..	..	22.0	1,676	125	7.6
1921	7,443,851	8.3	..	..	22.1	1,667	118	6.9
1922	7,510,851	6.4	8.9	2.5	20.6	1,534	105	6.4
1923	7,573,194	7.5	8.2	0.8	20.7	1,523	100	6.0
1924	7,645,647	7.1	9.5	2.4	20.2	1,467	94	5.6
1925	7,748,175	7.2	13.2	6.0	20.0	1,443	91	5.3
1926	7,843,239	6.4	12.1	5.7	19.3	1,370	84	4.9
1927	7,903,339	5.5	7.6	2.1	18.5	1,302	79	4.7
1928	7,967,673	5.7	8.1	2.3	18.6	1,292	79	4.6
1929	8,031,729	3.9	8.0	4.1	18.3	1,261	77	4.4
1930	8,076,097	6.1	5.5	-0.6	18.9	1,285	78	4.2
1931	8,125,594	5.6	6.1	0.4	18.4	1,242	72	3.9
1932	8,186,317	5.1	7.4	2.3	17.8	1,190	68	3.7
1933	8,230,699	3.9	5.4	1.5	16.6	1,101	58	3.3
1934	8,261,751	4.4	3.8	-0.7	16.2	1,062	54	3.0
1935	8,287,746	3.2	3.1	0.0	15.5	1,007	53	3.0
1936	8,315,449	3.1	3.3	0.2	15.4	991	49	2.8
1937	8,346,089	2.9	3.7	0.7	15.4	986	47	2.6
1938	8,373,876	3.5	3.3	-0.1	16.0	1,010	50	2.6
1939	8,391,404	2.3	2.1	-0.3	15.5	972	49	2.5
1940[10]	8,345,475	-1.5	-5.5	-4.0	13.5	..	..	3.2
1941[10]	8,276,033	-2.2	-8.4	-6.2	12.2	..	..	3.1
1942[10]	8,246,459	-1.1	-3.6	-2.5	13.2	..	..	2.4
1943[10]	8,241,194	1.9	-0.6	-2.5	15.0	..	..	2.7
1944	8,290,569	0.3	6.0	5.7	15.3	..	..	3.6
1945	8,339,405	1.1	5.9	4.7	15.7	..	..	4.4

Notes: [1] Midyear population figures have been calculated on the basis of population figures at the end of the year. At least up to 1920, the system of population registration was unreliable, and population census figures were used to correct the figures. This procedure produced breaks in the years following the censuses which makes the calculation of annual population growth rates and net migration rates based on the midyear population meaningless. Therefore, from 1846 to 1920, population census figures have been used to calculate these rates. [2] Average 1847–1856. [3] Average 1857–1866. [4] Average 1867–1880. [5] Average 1881–1890. [6] Average 1891–1900. [7] Average 1901–1910. [8] Excluding 50 municipalities. [9] Average 1911–1920. [10] Excluding 41 municipalities under direct German administration.

APPENDIX TABLE B.4 Demographic developments 1850–1945 (continued)

Crude death rate	Infant mortality rate	Stillbirth rate	Infant mortality and stillbirth rate	Crude marriage rate	Persons marrying per 10,000 unmarried persons age 15+	Persons marrying per 10,000 unmarried persons age 15-49	Crude divorce rate	Divorces per 100 marriages	Divorces per 10,000 married persons	Year
17.7	159.8	46.6	206.4	8.4	487	624	0.1	1.3	6.7	1898
18.9	166.6	45.8	212.5	8.3	486	623	0.1	1.0	4.9	1899
19.2	171.6	46.4	218.0	8.6	504	647	0.1	1.2	6.0	1900
17.2	142.2	46.3	188.5	8.5	499	641	0.1	1.4	7.1	1901
17.4	143.9	45.8	189.7	8.2	486	624	0.1	1.3	5.9	1902
17.1	154.9	44.6	199.4	7.9	471	605	0.1	1.3	6.0	1903
17.0	151.7	44.9	196.6	8.1	483	621	0.1	1.6	7.5	1904
16.6	146.2	45.8	192.1	8.0	478	616	0.1	1.6	7.1	1905
16.5	153.1	45.7	198.8	8.1	489	630	0.1	1.1	4.8	1906
15.8	132.5	44.9	177.3	8.1	489	630	0.1	1.4	6.4	1907
16.6	147.2	46.6	193.7	7.8	477	615	0.1	1.5	6.7	1908
15.8	137.6	46.9	184.4	7.7	471	608	0.1	1.8	7.6	1909
15.2	134.0	45.4	179.4	7.9	486	628	0.1	1.9	7.9	1910
16.5	166.5	44.0	210.5	8.0	492	635	0.1	1.8	7.8	1911
14.9	119.9	45.5	165.4	8.1	504	653	0.2	1.9	8.2	1912
14.6	129.9	45.8	175.7	8.0	500	647	0.2	2.0	8.4	1913
14.2	130.0	..	..	5.4	..	..	..	..	..	1914[9]
13.1	125.1	..	..	3.2	..	..	..	..	..	1915[9]
13.1	116.3	..	..	4.0	..	..	..	..	..	1916[9]
16.3	140.1	..	..	4.3	..	..	..	..	..	1917[9]
20.7	133.8	..	..	5.7	..	..	..	..	..	1918[9]
15.0	103.0	46.8	149.8	12.8	732	939	0.1	0.6	4.2	1919
13.7	110.2	41.1	151.2	14.2	823	1061	0.3	2.1	14.5	1920
13.8	122.1	42.3	164.4	11.9	697	904	0.5	4.1	24.0	1921
14.2	113.8	42.7	156.5	11.0	656	855	0.5	4.5	23.7	1922
13.2	99.7	40.8	140.5	10.5	635	833	0.4	4.1	20.3	1923
13.0	94.5	39.4	134.0	10.5	641	844	0.4	3.7	17.9	1924
12.9	99.7	36.2	135.9	9.6	598	793	0.3	3.3	14.8	1925
12.9	103.8	35.6	139.4	9.2	581	775	0.3	3.2	13.5	1926
13.0	98.4	34.9	133.3	9.1	580	778	0.3	3.3	13.2	1927
12.8	94.1	35.0	129.1	9.0	579	782	0.3	3.3	12.9	1928
14.4	110.5	34.5	144.9	8.9	585	795	0.3	3.0	11.5	1929
12.8	99.5	33.7	133.3	8.9	588	804	0.3	3.5	13.2	1930
12.8	89.3	33.8	123.1	8.1	547	753	0.3	3.6	12.2	1931
12.7	93.6	33.3	126.9	7.6	517	716	0.3	4.1	12.8	1932
12.7	92.0	34.2	126.2	7.9	546	761	0.3	4.0	13.1	1933
11.7	82.5	34.0	116.4	7.6	531	745	0.3	3.9	12.0	1934
12.3	84.6	32.6	117.2	7.6	540	763	0.3	4.1	12.5	1935
12.2	86.1	32.3	118.3	7.8	559	795	0.4	4.8	14.8	1936
12.5	82.8	31.1	113.8	7.6	553	792	0.4	5.1	15.1	1937
12.5	81.3	30.8	112.0	7.4	542	782	0.4	5.7	16.3	1938
13.2	82.4	30.1	112.5	6.5	489	710	0.4	6.2	15.7	1939
15.0	93.2	28.7	121.9	4.3	..	..	0.2	5.1	..	1940[10]
14.3	91.6	27.3	118.9	6.4	..	..	0.3	5.0	..	1941[10]
14.2	83.9	25.5	109.4	7.5	..	..	0.4	4.8	..	1942[10]
13.1	74.5	25.2	99.7	6.3	..	..	0.4	6.6	..	1943[10]
15.1	82.6	25.4	108.0	5.5	..	..	0.4	7.5	..	1944
14.5	99.6	25.6	125.2	10.0	..	..	0.4	3.8	..	1945

Notes: [1] Midyear population figures have been calculated on the basis of population figures at the end of the year. At least up to 1920, the system of population registration was unreliable, and population census figures were used to correct the figures. This procedure produced breaks in the years following the censuses which makes the calculation of annual population growth rates and net migration rates based on the midyear population meaningless. Therefore, from 1846 to 1920, population census figures have been used to calculate these rates. [2] Average 1847–1856. [3] Average 1857–1866. [4] Average 1867–1880. [5] Average 1881–1890. [6] Average 1891–1900. [7] Average 1901–1910. [8] Excluding 50 municipalities. [9] Average 1911–1920. [10] Excluding 41 municipalities under direct German administration.

APPENDIX TABLE B.5 Life expectancy by age 1881/90–1928/32 (in years)

Age	0	10	20	30	40	50	60	70	80
Males									
1881–1890	43.84	49.26	40.96	33.96	..	..	13.73	..	4.39
1891–1900	45.39	50.32	41.83	34.22	26.71	19.69	13.43	8.13	4.56
1928–1932	56.02	54.88	46.04	37.78	29.48	21.61	14.53	7.69	4.65
Females									
1881–1890	46.98	51.51	43.56	36.36	..	..	14.70	..	4.86
1891–1900	48.84	52.78	44.44	36.96	29.46	21.87	14.78	8.87	4.91
1928–1932	59.79	57.25	48.43	40.17	31.77	23.55	15.93	9.60	5.20

APPENDIX TABLE B.6A Households by type 1846–1947 (absolute and per cent)

Census year	Household types and members									
	Total house-holds	Private house-holds	Family house-holds	One-person house-holds	Institu-tional house-holds	Total household members	Private household members	Family household members	One-person household members	Institu-tional house-hold members
Absolute										
1846	890,566	..	..	..	..	4,337,196	..	..	..	..
1856	936,284	..	..	..	..	4,259,560	..	..	..	..
1866	1,038,898	..	..	..	..	4,827,833	..	..	..	..
1880	1,202,919	..	..	..	..	5,520,009	..	..	..	..
1890	1,332,796	..	..	..	..	6,069,321	..	..	..	..
1900	1,556,932	..	..	..	..	6,693,548	..	..	..	..
1910	1,831,102	..	..	..	..	7,423,784	..	..	..	..
1920	1,983,192	..	..	..	..	7,465,782	..	..	..	..
1930	2,374,445	2,370,503	2,109,075	261,428	3,942	8,092,004	8,033,031	7,771,603	261,428	58,973
1947	2,836,979	2,833,086	2,383,865	449,221	3,893	8,512,195	8,449,846	8,000,625	449,221	62,349
Per cent										
1846	100.00	..	..	..	..	100.00	..	..	..	..
1856	100.00	..	..	..	..	100.00	..	..	..	..
1866	100.00	..	..	..	..	100.00	..	..	..	..
1880	100.00	..	..	..	..	100.00	..	..	..	..
1890	100.00	..	..	..	..	100.00	..	..	..	..
1900	100.00	..	..	..	..	100.00	..	..	..	..
1910	100.00	..	..	..	..	100.00	..	..	..	..
1920	100.00	..	..	..	..	100.00	..	..	..	..
1930	100.00	99.83	88.82	11.01	0.17	100.00	99.27	96.04	3.23	0.73
1947	100.00	99.86	84.03	15.83	0.14	100.00	99.27	93.99	5.28	0.73

APPENDIX TABLE B.6B Households by size and members 1930–1947 (absolute figures)

Census year	Private households total	1 person	2 persons	3 persons	4 persons	5 persons	6 persons	7 persons	8 persons	9 persons	10 persons	11 persons	12+ persons
						Households							
1930	2,374,445	261,428	607,191	594,172	407,106	230,581	125,175	68,020	37,091	20,257	11,353	5,065	7,006
1947	2,836,979	449,221	873,122	684,668	407,053	204,286	103,540	53,559	28,702	14,447	8,168	4,309	5,904
						Persons							
1930	8,092,004	261,428	1,214,382	1,782,516	1,628,424	1,152,905	751,050	476,140	296,728	182,313	113,530	55,715	176,873
1947	8,512,195	449,221	1,746,244	2,054,004	1,628,212	1,021,430	621,240	374,913	229,616	130,023	81,680	47,399	128,213

APPENDIX TABLE B.6C Households by size and members 1930–1947 (per cent)

Census year	Private households total	1 person	2 persons	3 persons	4 persons	5 persons	6 persons	7 persons	8 persons	9 persons	10 persons	11 persons	12+ persons
						Households							
1930	100.00	11.01	25.57	25.02	17.15	9.71	5.27	2.86	1.56	0.85	0.48	0.21	0.30
1947	100.00	15.83	30.78	24.13	14.35	7.20	3.65	1.89	1.01	0.51	0.29	0.15	0.21
						Persons							
1930	100.00	3.23	15.01	22.03	20.12	14.25	9.28	5.88	3.67	2.25	1.40	0.69	2.19
1947	100.00	5.28	20.51	24.13	19.13	12.00	7.30	4.40	2.70	1.53	0.96	0.56	1.51

APPENDIX TABLE B.6D Household indicators 1846–1947

Census year	Mean total household size	Household indicators		
		Mean private household size	Mean family household size	Mean institutional household size
1846	4.87	:	:	:
1856	4.55	:	:	:
1866	4.65	:	:	:
1880	4.59	:	:	:
1890	4.55	:	:	:
1900	4.30	:	:	:
1910	4.05	:	:	:
1920	3.76	:	:	:
1930	3.41	3.39	3.68	14.96
1947	3.00	2.98	3.36	16.02

APPENDIX TABLE B.6E Household composition 1930–1961 (absolute and per cent)

Census year	Household head									Total	Belgians	Foreigners
	Single	Single with servants	With relatives	With relatives and servants	With foreigners	With foreigners and servants	With relatives, foreigners and without servants	With relatives, foreigners and servants	Household composition unknown			
	Absolute											
1930	261,428	10,146	1,972,597	40,723	32,034	1,816	51,663	4,024	14	2,374,445	2,267,233	107,212
1947	449,221	6,917	2,263,537	25,988	43,052	1,434	44,393	2,430	7	2,836,979	2,720,787	116,192
1961	510,607	..	2,422,820	..	48,804	..	45,470	..	..	3,027,701	2,888,419	139,282
	Per cent											
1930	11.01	0.43	83.08	1.72	1.35	0.08	2.18	0.17	0.00	100.00	95.48	4.52
1947	15.83	0.24	79.79	0.92	1.52	0.05	1.56	0.09	0.00	100.00	95.90	4.10
1961	16.86	..	80.02	..	1.61	..	1.50	..	..	100.00	95.40	4.60

Notes: Household composition including non-family members was conducted for the last time in 1961 and was therefore included. Column heads in the source: *Seuls*: Seuls avec des domestiques; Avec des personnes parentes et avec des domestiques; Sans parents et étrangers; Sans parents et étragers et domestiques; Avec des parents et étrangers sans domestique; Avec des parents et étrangers et domestiques; Avec d'autres personnes (composition du ménage inconnue); Total; Belges; Étrangers.

APPENDIX TABLE B.7 Dates and nature of results on population structure, households/families, and vital statistics

Topic	Intro-duction	Remarks
Population		
Population at census dates	1846	Introduced in 1846. Earlier censuses were conducted in 1801, 1808, 1811 and 1829, but the census of 1846 was the first to cover the whole territory of Belgium after the territorial gains of 1839 (Cf. app. 3, census publication for 1846, p. XX and passim).
Population by age, sex, and marital status	1846	Introduced in 1846.
Households and families		
Households (*ménages* or *familles*)		
Total households	1846	*Disaggregation*: communes with less than 5,000 inhabitants (*communes rurales*) and communes with more than 5,000 inhabitants (*villes*) (1846–at least 1890); communes in 4 (1930: 5) categories by number of inhabitants (1900, 1910, 1920, 1930); household heads living single and heads of family households, total households, all three by sex (1920); household head by sex, age group, marital status, and nationality (1930, 1947).
Households by size	1930, 1947	First time in 1930 in 18 categories and several combinations.
Households by composition	1930, 1947	First time in 1930; with family members and non-family members (servants).
Households by profession of household head	1930, 1947	First time in 1930.
Families (*familles*)		
Families by number of children	1910	Special investigation for the first time in 1910 (vol. 1, pp. 234–238); 1920 (vol. 1, pp. 87–92); 1930 (vol. VIII); 1947 (vol. VII).
Population movement		
Mid-year population	1846	Calculated using census data.
Births		
Live births	1830	
Still births	1841	
Legitimate births	1841	
Illegitimate births	1841	
Deaths		
Total deaths	1830	
Infants (under 1 year)	1841	
Marriages		
Total marriages	1831	
Divorces and separations		
Total divorces	1831	
Total separations	–	Not available for the whole period; of minor importance.

APPENDIX FIGURE B.8 Population by age, sex and marital status, Belgium 1846, 1866, 1890, 1910, 1920 and 1930 (per 10,000 of total population)

Belgium, 1846

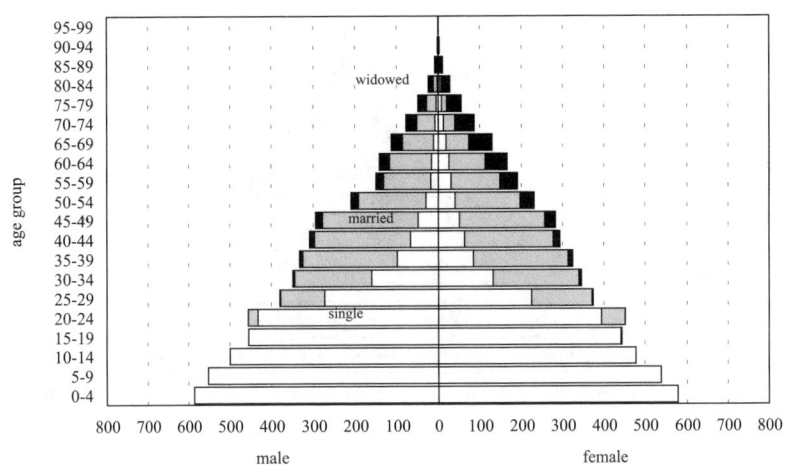

Belgium, 1866

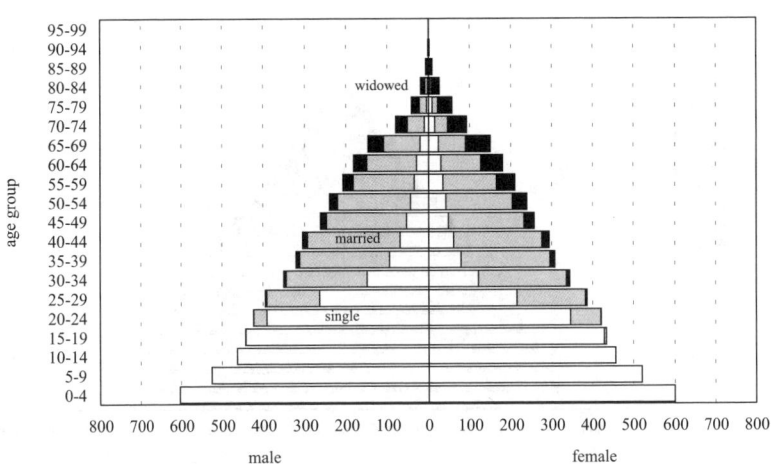

APPENDIX FIGURE B.8 Population by age, sex and marital status, Belgium 1846,
1866, 1890, 1910, 1920 and 1930 (per 10,000 of total population) (continued)

Belgium, 1890

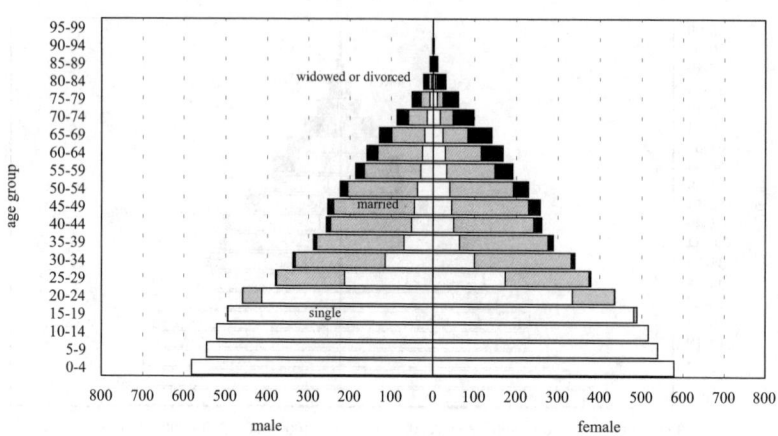

Belgium, 1910

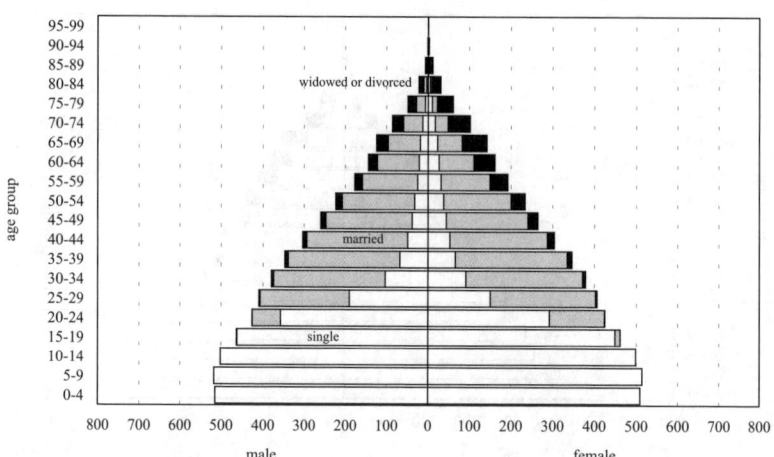

APPENDIX FIGURE B.8 Population by age, sex and marital status, Belgium 1846, 1866, 1890, 1910, 1920 and 1930 (per 10,000 of total population) (continued)

Belgium, 1920

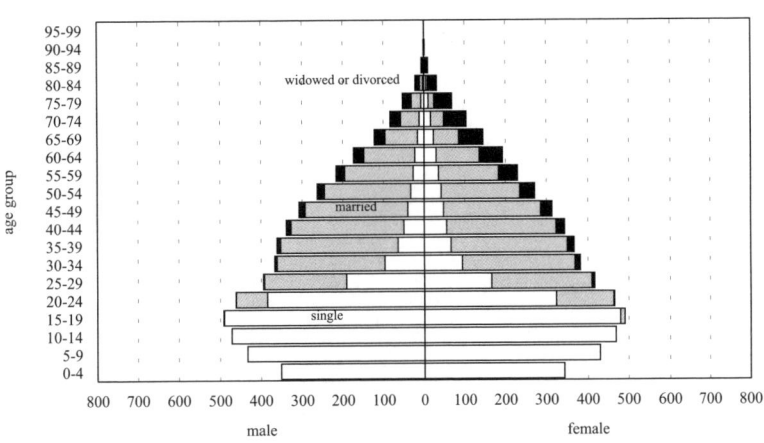

Belgium, 1930

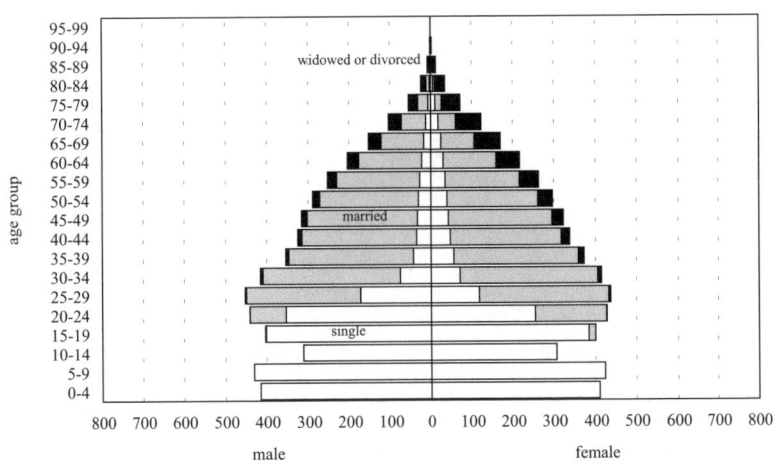

Beijing, 1990

Beijing, 1994

3

Czechoslovakia

STATE FORMATION AND TERRITORY

Czechoslovakia was created in October 1918 by the Treaty of Versailles by uniting the historical territories of Bohemia, Moravia, and Silesia (from the Austrian half of the Austro-Hungarian empire, or Cisleithania) and Slovakia and Ruthenia (from the Hungarian part of the empire, or Transleithania).

The Constitution of 1920 provided for a rather centralized state without federal or proportional elements, although the new state was an amalgamation of different populations, religions, and languages. Czechs and Slovaks made up 64.8% of the population, Germans 23.6%, Hungarians 5.6%, Russians/Ukrainians 3.5%, and the remainder was composed of Jewish, Polish or people of other cultural origin (population census 1921).

This conglomeration of ethnically, religiously, and culturally distinct populations caused severe tensions within the new state. The Slovaks felt oppressed by the Czech majority, and were granted some autonomy in 1927. The economic crisis of the 1930s and the political changes in the neighbouring countries made the latent ethnic conflict manifest: in 1938 the Sudentenland crisis exploded, which finally led to the transfer of the eastern parts of the country (29,000 square kilometres) to Germany. In October 1938 Czechoslovakia had to cede the region of Olsa to Poland and the southern regions of Slovakia to Hungary. The Slovakian population attained more autonomy in November 1938 and Czechoslovakia became a federal state. In March 1939 the state was split and the Czech part annexed by Germany as a 'protectorate'. The Slovak part later became independent under the hegemony of Germany (Hoensch, 1992; Skilling, 1991; Hoesch, 1993).

REGIONAL POPULATION STRUCTURE

At the time of independence in 1920, Czechoslovakia was composed of five provinces (*Územi*): Bohemia, Moravia, Silesia, Slovakia, and Subcarpathian Russia. At the time of the 1930 census, only four republics remained; Silesia was combined with Moravia in one category. The size of the republics was very unequal: in 1921, Bohemia had 6.7 million inhabitants, Slovakia 2.99 million, Moravia 2.7 million, Silesia 670,000, and Subcarpathian Russia 606,000 inhabitants. After World War II Czechoslovakia became a federal republic consisting of only the Czech and the Slovak republic.

Since the foundation of the state there were four levels of territorial organization: republics (*územi*), regions (*kraju*), districts (*okresy*), and communities (*obci*). The number of these territorial units was gradually reduced, mainly for the purpose of administrative simplification.

The different population size and therefore also different population density of the republics shows that the centre of population gravity was in the western part of the country, in Bohemia, Moravia, and Silesia. The reason for this was the regionally disparate economic development of the country: the artisanal, commercial, and industrial centre was located in the west, while the east remained largely agricultural, with some small-scale handicraft in small towns and villages. While Bohemia and Moravia had belonged to the centre of Europe since the Middle Ages, and Prague had been the capital of the medieval German empire for some time, the eastern parts of the country had always been on the periphery (Conze, 1992).

POPULATION GROWTH

Population density was low compared with Western Europe (data available in Czech Statistical Office, 1998: 14). In 1840 population density (inhabitants per square kilometre) was 68 in contrast to Belgium, for example, where population density in 1830 was 128. Czechoslovakia reached the population density of Belgium in 1830 only in 1991 with 122 inhabitants per square kilometre, meaning that Czechoslovakia needed 160 years to reach a population density comparable to Belgium's.

In 1869 the population of the territory which later became Czechoslovakia was 10,099,000 inhabitants. At the time of independence in 1921 the population had only increased to 13 million. In 1930 population had increased another million to 13,998,000 inhabitants. In 1950, the population was 12,338,000 inhabitants, 1.6 million less than in 1930. This drop was due to the expulsion of the Germans from the country during and after the German defeat. In 1991 the population of Czechoslovakia was 15,576,000 inhabitants, an increase of only five million since 1869. In 120 years the population of Czechoslovakia increased by only 50%. This is very low compared with Belgium, for example, where the population tripled in the 160 years after independence; in most other Western European countries the population doubled (data available in Czech Statistical Office, 1998: 14) (Figure CS.1).

THE FIRST DEMOGRAPHIC TRANSITION

For Czechoslovakia only the second or third stage of the demographic transition can be observed, because national data exist only since 1919 (Figure CS.2). Birth and death rates were strongly influenced by World War I, but normalized up to the early 1930s; the rates were nearly the same as the European average, revealing a pattern similar to that in other continental countries (e.g. Belgium). But what is exceptional for Czechoslovakia is the extraordinary shock of the 1930s, starting already with the world economic depression and lasting until the 1940s, for the birth rate, which sank dramatically below the European average. The death rate did not deviate from the European development during this time. Already in the 1940s both rates increased strongly, the birth rate reaching a first peak in the 1950s. During the 1960s the birth rate was rather low. In the 1970s Czechoslovakia experienced its 'second demographic transition'. The 1980s showed a strong birth decline.

Natural population growth was rather high during the whole period since the 1920s, with the exception of the major demographic crisis of the 1930s. It was above the European average during the 1950s and the 1980s.

In general, the Czechoslovak demographic transition could be described as a continental model of demographic transition, with a moderate population increase

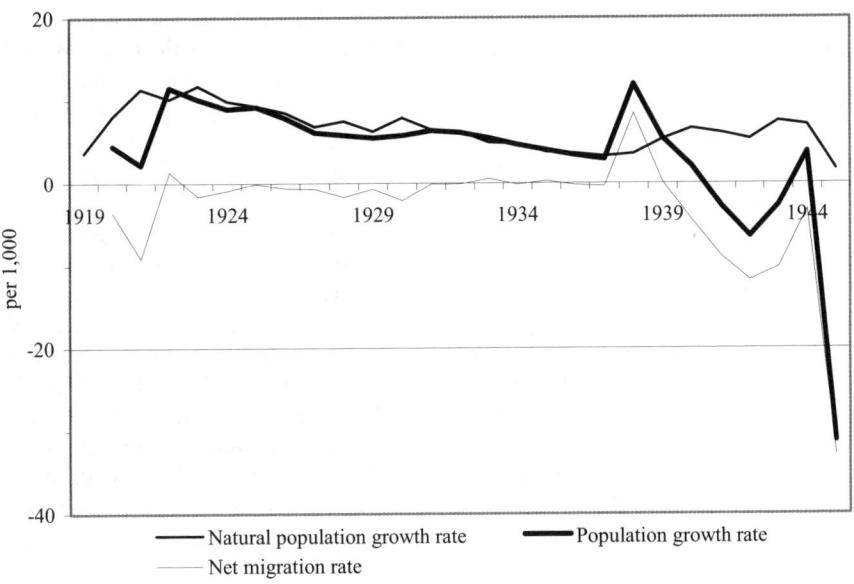

Figure CS.1 Population growth and net migration 1919-1945

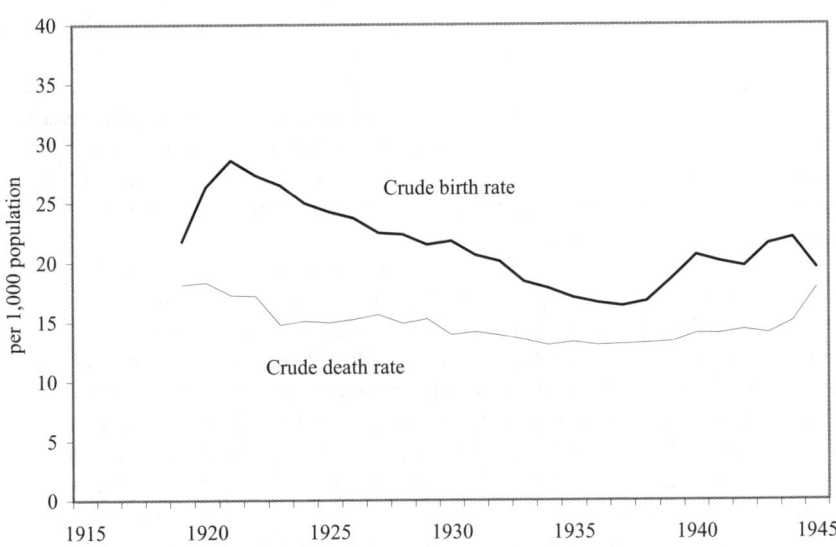

Figure CS.2 First demographic transition 1919-1945

already in the first half of the twentieth century. The second half of the twentieth century is characterized by strong irregularities, particularly in the birth rate, which could be partly explained by political events such as the expulsion and expropriation of the Germans and the subsequent improved living chances for the Czechoslovaks, who became proprietors of all that had been left by the refugees; the Russian intervention of 1968, when the birth rate declined again; the upsurge of the birth rate in the 1980s, which could be a cohort effect of the large birth cohorts of the 1950s. The death rate increased since the 1970s, a sign of birth decline and probably emigration.

Explanations and interpretations of the Czechoslovak pattern could point to the following factors: *ethnicity* (Slavic domination with a strong Germanic minority; the Slavic cultural pattern is important with regard to marriage behaviour; Czechoslovakia already belongs to the Eastern European marriage pattern with universal and early marriage); *religion* (the majority of the population is Catholic; in the sixteenth century it was Protestant, but was conquered by the Catholic Bavarians and Austrians during the Thirty Years' War and subjected to the Counter-Reformation; there are also orthodox Christians); *language* (there are several languages, the major ones Czech and Slovak which are similar; the third most important is German; then Hungarian, Polish, and Russian; the Slavic language is West Slavic); *economic factors* (industry in the west, heavy manufacturing, farming in the east).

MORTALITY AND LIFE EXPECTANCY

In international comparison, Czechoslovakia belongs to the group with rather high infant mortality in the past; it is found in the same cluster as the Mediterranean countries (Italy, Spain, Greece) and Austria (Figure CS.3). In the 1980s Czechoslovakia still had rather high infant mortality which puts it at a level similar to Portugal with a rather poor health infrastructure. It can therefore be assumed that poor health infrastructure and the settlement structure are factors explaining high infant mortality in Czechoslovakia (Masuy-Stroobant, 1997). Interestingly, infant mortality is similar to Austria, perhaps a sign of similar socio-economic features or behavioural patterns in the two countries.

Life expectancy was quite low when compared to more advanced countries in Western and Northern Europe. In 1920/22 life expectancy of boys at birth was only 46.4 years, while in Sweden it was 60.7 in 1921/25, a difference of 14 years. Life expectancy was also lower for higher ages: for 30-year-old men it was 35.8 years (five years less than in Sweden); for 60-year-old men it was 15 years (1.7 years less than in Sweden) (Figure CS.4). Until the late 1930s life expectancy improved in absolute and relative terms. The gap to an advanced country like Sweden became narrower: for males at birth the difference in (lower) life expectancy to Sweden had declined to nine years, for 30-year-old men it was three years and for 60-year-old men it was 1.3 years. Life expectancy of females was higher at all ages, with a diverging tendency until the late 1930s.

FERTILITY AND LEGITIMACY

Surprisingly, illegitimacy in Czechoslovakia was high during the 1920s and 1930s and above the European average. In the 1950s illegitimacy was frequent after World

Figure CS.3 Infant mortality 1919-1945

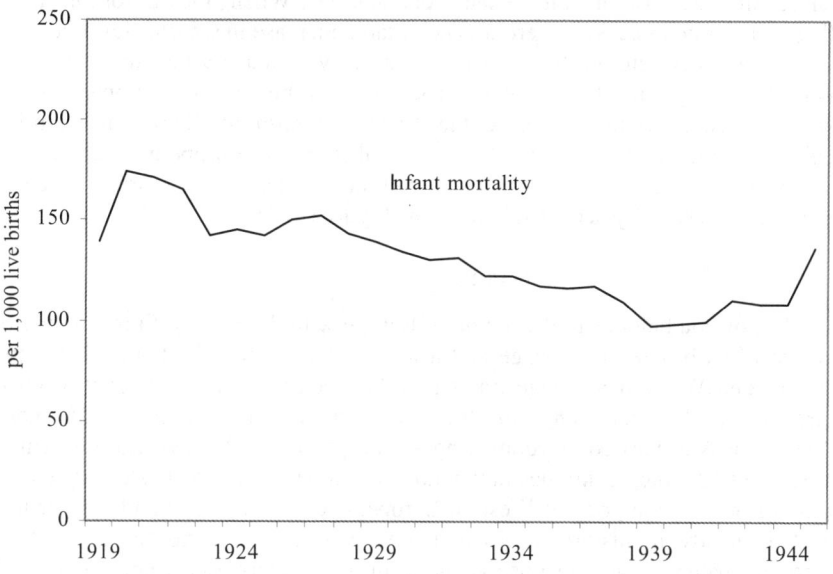

Figure CS.4 Life expectancy 1920/22-1937

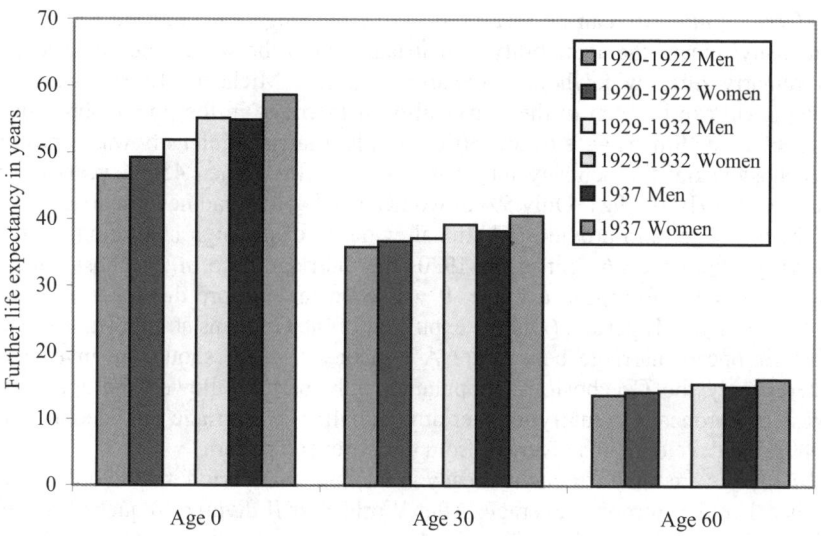

War II. But since 1960 illegitimacy has been rather low in Czechoslovakia, where there was also no deinstitutionalization of marriage in the sense of births outside or before marriage or in unmarried cohabitation. When the European average illegitimacy rate increased, there was no notable increase in Czechoslovakia.

The legitimacy rate on the other hand was very similar to the European average, with the exception of the 1930s when it was below the European average. Nevertheless, from the 1920s to the 1970s the ratio of illegitimate fertility to legitimate fertility was higher in Czechoslovakia than in Europe on average. This is similar to Austria, but in Austria illegitimacy was much more frequent and established as socially accepted behaviour (Figure CS.5).

MARRIAGE AND DIVORCE

Czechoslovakia belongs to the region of Europe with the Eastern European marriage pattern of early age at marriage and a low celibacy rate. The border between the Eastern and Western marriage types runs between Germany and Czechoslovakia. Already at the beginning of the twentieth century women and men in Czechoslovakia married at younger ages than people in Western Europe. This is a structural trait which continues in the most recent decades. Czechoslovakia therefore differs from the countries of Western Europe, because universal and early marriage existed already in historic times and there was therefore no 'modernization of nuptiality patterns' in Czechoslovakia as in all Western European countries. The development of a 'post-modern' nuptiality pattern in Czechoslovakia did not occur; the structures remained more or less stable. It is not clear whether marriage restrictions due to economic situation (pauperism) existed in the territory of Czechoslovakia in the nineteenth century.

Marriage intensity can be measured by the *marriage rate* and the *celibacy rate*. 'Intensity' means the availability of marriage, but at the same time the urgent need to remarry after widowhood ('remarriage need', Michael Mitterauer). A third component can be seen in the universality of marriage in the population. The first rate refers to all marriages of unmarried people. Marriage intensity was very high in Czechoslovakia: the celibacy rate was very low for women 45–54 years old who married in 1910 or 1921. Only 5% of women aged 45–54 had never married.

The marriage ratio provides additional evidence of the high institutionalization of marriage (Figure CS.6). Since the 1920s the marriage ratio in Czechoslovakia was clearly over the European average. It was even much more disproportional in the post-World War II period. (Did the expulsion of the Germans strengthen the 'Slavic' East European marriage behaviour? A hypothesis which should be investigated). Interestingly the Czechoslovak population only partly followed the aggregate of Western Europeans in marrying later or not at all. The marriage ratio declined in the 1980s, but developments diverged from the European pattern.

Divorces were rather frequent already in the inter-war period: the divorce ratio was higher than the European average. After World War II divorce frequency was much higher in Czechoslovakia than in Europe on average. Czechoslovakia thus participated in the long-term growth of divorce but with substantially higher intensity (Figure CS.6).

What factors can explain this phenomenon? A major factor was surely the marriage and divorce law legislation, allowing for much easier divorce in Czechoslovakia. This is in line with legislation in other socialist countries, which

Figure CS.5 Fertility and legitimacy 1919-1939

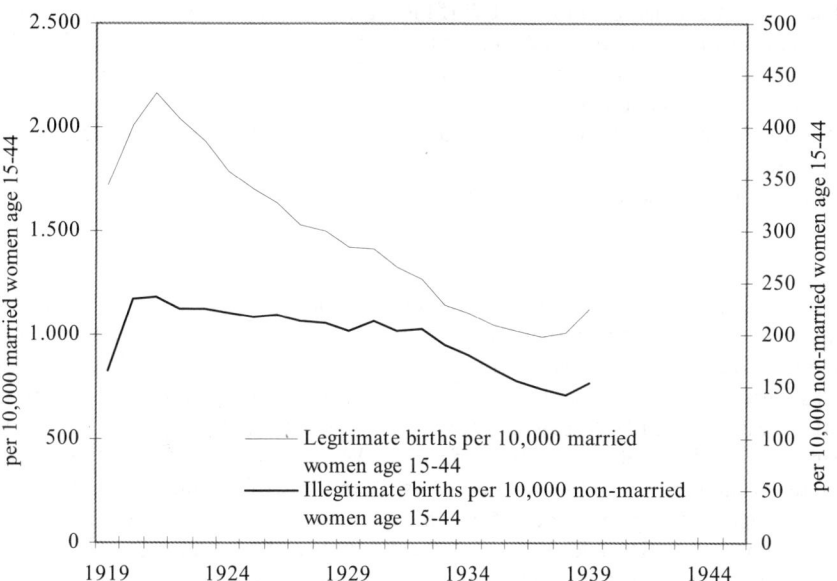

Figure CS.6 Marriages and divorces 1919-1939

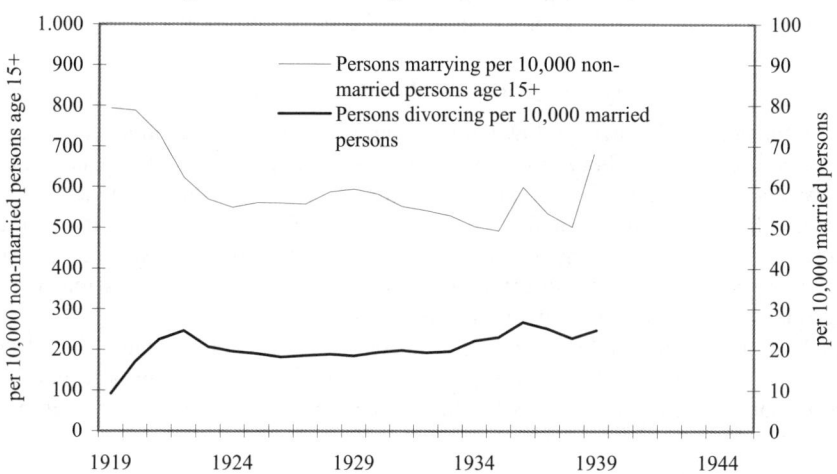

made divorce very easy (see for example divorce frequency in the German Democratic Republic and Hungary).

Did religion also have an influence? If the majority of the population was Catholic before the introduction of socialism, then the divorce rate would have been low. But the introduction of socialism as a secular religion probably destroyed Catholic principles of indissolubility of marriage.

Another factor is the high marriage rate itself and the low age at marriage, both of which increase the propensity to divorce.

Concerning legal separations no statistical data for Czechoslovakia were available.

AGE, SEX, AND CIVIL STATUS

Appendix Figure CS.8 shows the development in the age structure of the population combined with sex and marital status from 1921 to 1930, the only two censuses conducted during the inter-war period. In the age pyramid of 1921 the huge losses of births during World War I and immediately afterwards are apparent. The age cohorts of 0–4-year-olds and 5–9-year-olds are much smaller than the age cohort of 10–14-year-olds, the last cohort not influenced by World War I. Up to 1930 the age structure changed tremendously and shows clear signs of the birth decline and the start of population ageing. The rather large age cohorts of 10–24-year-olds in 1921 had disappeared by 1931 for reasons that are not clear. It may be that emigration of young adults or a change in territorial boundaries caused that change in the age structure.

The distribution of the population by marital status changed between 1921 and 1930. In 1921, fewer people in higher age groups remained unmarried, while in 1930 celibacy was higher in the higher age groups. Age at marriage obviously was lower in 1930 than in 1921, as is evident from the age group 24–29.

FAMILY AND HOUSEHOLD STRUCTURES

Given the universal marriage, low marriage age, and moderate fertility level, it may be hypothesized that households were not very large, that there were fewer unmarried people such as servants and lodgers, and that the widowed elderly probably lived on their own and did not join the households of relatives. It would be interesting to know the number of nuclear and extended family households. But the available statistics provide no information on these topics. The discussion of this question has to be based mainly on the mean household size.

In 1930, mean household size was 3.8 persons per household, a figure that places Czechoslovakia in an intermediate position in Europe. In 1930 the percentage of one-person households was 7.3% , rather low compared with other European countries.

THE NATIONAL SYSTEM OF DEMOGRAPHIC STATISTICS

Population Structure

The first population census after independence in October 1920 was conducted in 1921. This census was based on the law on population censuses of 8 April 1920 (Oberschall 1920). The second census was able to be conducted at a regular interval in 1930. The census of 1940/41 was cancelled due to the war. The next census was only after the war in 1950.

The Czechoslovakian census continued the Austro-Hungarian tradition established by the census law of 29 March 1869. Thus, from the beginning, the quality and extension of the census material was high. All main statistical variables of that time were covered. The results of the first census of 1921 were published in French in three volumes, but the results of the 1930 census were published only in Czech.

Population data were collected for the main parts of the country: Bohemia, Moravia, Silesia, Slovakia, and Subcarpathian Russia.

The population data refer to the *de facto* population. The summary introductions to the first census of 1921 try to compare population figures for 1921 with earlier ones since 1869. Earlier censuses were held in 1869, 1880, 1890, 1900, and 1910.

Vital Statistics

The record of births, deaths, and marriages started with the founding of the Czechoslovak state in 1918. All main demographic aggregates have been published: births by legitimacy, stillbirths, marriages, and divorces. More complicated demographic measures, such as the mean age at marriage and fertility rates, were introduced at later dates.

Households and Families

Data on households were collected in the censuses of 1921 and 1930. Earlier data on households are found in the Austro-Hungarian censuses (see chapter on Austria and Hungary in this book). The 1921 census was still rather limited concerning households and families. But the main elements of household statistics were published: the household composition concerning number of servants and the presence of lodgers; households by the number of children present; heads of households by profession, sex, and ethnic group.

Regional disaggregations have been carried out for the main administrative parts of the country: the five provinces (Bohemia, Moravia, Silesia, Slovakia, and Subcarpathian Russia) as well as the 20 departments.

Households were surveyed on the basis of private dwellings and establishments. The renter or owner of the dwelling (*locataire*) had to provide the required information on the enumeration sheets. Information on persons not belonging to his/her family had to be given separately. It was clearly recognized that several households could live in one dwelling, although this was considered the exception to the rule. Thus the definition of a household (*domácnost*) in the census of 1921 was the 'natural' family including non-family household members, such as servants. The census of 1930 clearly distinguished between households and families (*rodina*), stating that a family was a biological unit, while a household could also comprise members not related by family ties, living in the same dwelling.

In 1921 households were presented by the number of children. In 1930 a special investigation on the fertility (number of children) of married women was carried out, which was continued after the war.

Remarks (also see introductory Table 6.1)

The population census of 1947 was not available for interpolation of v16–v21. In the inter-war period censuses were held in 1921 and 1930. These two censuses were used for linear interpolation back to 1919 and forward to 1945. Boundary changes occurred from 1945 to 1946. Using the census of 1950, linear extrapolations have been performed on the data back to 1946.

BOUNDARY CHANGES

Czechoslovakia was created in October 1918 after World War I from the territories of the Austro-Hungarian Empire. The territory of the population censuses of 1921 and 1930 was identical. A first territorial change came with the Sudentenland crisis in 1938: the eastern parts of the country (29,000 square kilometres) were transferred to Germany. In October 1938 the region of Olsa was given to Poland and the southern regions of Slovakia to Hungary. In March 1939 Czechoslovakia was split; Germany annexed the Czech part as a 'protectorate'. The Slovak part later became independent under the influence of Germany. Thus, the territory of Czechoslovakia remained more or less stable from 1920 until 1938. For regional organization see the documentation by Quick (1994) and Caramani, Flora, Kraus, and Quick (1998).

APPENDIX TABLES AND FIGURES

APPENDIX TABLE CS.1 Population structure at census dates 1921–1930

Census number	Census date	Census population			Marital status				Age group		
		Total	Male	Female	Single	Married	Widowed	Divorced	0–14	15–64	65+
		Absolute									
1	15 II 1921	13,613,172	6,559,503	7,053,669	7,484,168	5,078,361	996,552	52,853[a]	3,988,190	8,828,038	784,613
2	1 XII 1930	14,729,536	7,143,116	7,586,420	7,482,801	6,131,021	1,021,004	91,746[a]	3,873,074	9,870,222	970,533
		Per cent									
1	15 II 1921	100.00	48.18	51.82	54.98	37.30	7.32	0.39[a]	29.30	64.85	5.76
2	1 XII 1930	100.00	48.50	51.50	50.80	41.62	6.93	0.62[a]	26.29	67.01	6.59

Note: a divorced and separated.

APPENDIX TABLE CS.2   Census population by region 1921–1950[1]
(per cent)

Uzemi/Kraj	1921	1930	1950
Cechy	49.01	48.26	72.10
Prazský	–	–	16.47
Hlavni mesto Praha	4.97	5.76	7.55
Ceskobudejovický	–	–	4.04
Plzenský	–	–	4.47
Karlovarský	–	–	2.48
Ustecký	–	–	5.07
Liberecký	–	–	3.89
Hradecký	–	–	4.56
Pardubický	–	–	3.48
Jihlavský	–	–	3.44
Brnenský	–	–	7.68
Olomoucký	–	–	4.87
Gottwaldovský	–	–	4.97
Ostravský	–	–	6.69
Morava a Slezsko	24.53[1]	24.20	–[2]
Slovensko	22.02	22.61	27.90
Bratislavský	–	–	6.88
Nitrianský	–	–	5.58
Banskobystrický	–	–	3.96
Zilinský	–	–	4.23
Kosický	–	–	3.81
Presovský	–	–	3.44
Podkarpatská Rus	4.44	4.92	–[3]
TOTAL	**100.00**	**100.00**	**100.00**

Notes: [1] 1950 included for comparative purposes. [2] Morava and Slezsko were two seperate units in 1921. [3] Territory lost to Poland in 1945. [4] Territory lost to Ukraine in 1945.

APPENDIX TABLE CS.3 Population density by region 1921–1950[1]
(inhabitants per sq. km.)

Uzemi/Kraj	1921	1930	1950
Cechy	128	137	113
Prazský	–	–	209
Hlavni mesto Praha	3,936	4,936	5,419
Ceskobudejovický	–	–	56
Plzenský	–	–	70
Karlovarský	–	–	67
Ustecký	–	–	151
Liberecký	–	–	113
Hradecký	–	–	109
Pardubický	–	–	101
Jihlavský	–	–	64
Brnenský	–	–	127
Olomoucký	–	–	97
Gottwaldovský	–	–	120
Ostravský	–	–	183
Morava a Slezsko	120[1]	133	–[2]
Slovensko	61	68	70
Bratislavský	–	–	112
Nitrianský	–	–	87
Banskobystrický	–	–	53
Zilinský	–	–	63
Kosický	–	–	63
Presovský	–	–	50
Podkarpatská Rus	48	57	–[3]
TOTAL	**96**	**105**	**96**

Notes: See Appendix Table CS.2.

APPENDIX TABLE CS.4 Demographic developments 1919–1945 (absolute figures and rates)

Year	Mid-year population	Natural population growth rate	Population growth rate	Net migration rate	Crude birth rate	Legitimate births per 10,000 married women age 15–44	Illegitimate births per 10,000 unmarried women age 15–44	Illeg. births per 100 leg. births
1919	12,920,970	3.6	..	..	21.8	1,725	165	11.1
1920	12,978,920	8.1	4.5	-3.6	26.4	2,014	234	13.0
1921	13,007,570	11.3	2.2	-9.1	28.6	2,165	237	11.9
1922	13,158,830	10.1	11.5	1.3	27.3	2,036	224	11.6
1923	13,293,070	11.7	10.1	-1.6	26.5	1,935	225	11.9
1924	13,412,970	9.9	8.9	-0.9	25.0	1,786	221	12.3
1925	13,537,360	9.3	9.2	-0.1	24.3	1,706	218	12.3
1926	13,644,110	8.5	7.8	-0.7	23.7	1,638	220	12.6
1927	13,727,640	6.8	6.1	-0.8	22.5	1,526	213	12.8
1928	13,807,349	7.5	5.8	-1.7	22.4	1,498	212	12.6
1929	13,883,515	6.2	5.5	-0.7	21.5	1,422	204	12.5
1930	13,963,516	7.9	5.7	-2.1	21.8	1,418	213	12.7
1931	14,052,366	6.5	6.3	-0.1	20.6	1,322	204	12.7
1932	14,138,342	6.2	5.4	-0.1	20.1	1,267	205	13.1
1933	14,215,715	4.9	75.8	70.9	18.4	1,146	190	13.0
1934	14,282,004	4.8	4.6	-0.2	17.8	1,103	180	12.5
1935	14,339,084	3.7	4.0	0.3	17.0	1,046	168	12.1
1936	14,387,065	3.6	3.3	-0.2	16.6	1,016	156	11.2
1937	14,428,715	3.2	2.9	-0.4	16.3	994	147	10.6
1938	14,603,000	3.5	11.9	8.4	16.7	1,014	142	9.8
1939	14,683,000	5.3	5.4	0.2	18.6	1,121	153	9.4
1940	14,713,000	6.6	2.0	-4.5	20.6	..	..	8.7
1941	14,671,000	6.1	-2.9	-8.9	20.1	..	..	8.3
1942	14,577,000	5.3	-6.4	-11.8	19.7	..	..	8.3
1943	14,538,000	7.5	-2.7	-10.2	21.5	..	..	7.8
1944	14,593,000	7.0	3.8	-3.2	22.1	..	..	8.7
1945	14,151,970	1.7	-31.2	-32.8	19.5	..	..	10.9

APPENDIX TABLE CS.4 Demographic developments 1919–1945 (absolute figures and rates)

Crude death rate	Infant mortality rate	Stillbirth rate	Infant mortality and stillbirth rate	Crude marriage rate	Persons marrying per 10,000 unmarried persons age 15+	Persons marrying per 10,000 unmarried persons age 15–49	Crude divorce rate	Divorces per 100 marriages	Divorces per 10,000 married persons	Year
18.1	139.2	23.0	162.2	13.4	794	985	0.2	1.2	9.2	1919
18.3	174.1	24.9	199.0	13.2	788	981	0.3	2.4	17.0	1920
17.3	171.7	24.1	195.8	12.2	730	912	0.4	3.4	22.5	1921
17.2	165.1	25.1	190.2	10.3	623	780	0.5	4.5	24.7	1922
14.8	142.6	25.9	168.5	9.4	570	716	0.4	4.2	20.7	1923
15.1	145.5	26.5	172.0	9.0	550	692	0.4	4.2	19.6	1924
15.0	142.7	24.3	167.0	9.2	561	708	0.4	4.1	19.0	1925
15.2	150.1	24.1	174.2	9.1	560	709	0.4	4.0	18.1	1926
15.6	152.8	23.6	176.4	9.0	558	708	0.4	4.1	18.5	1927
14.9	143.6	23.1	166.7	9.5	587	748	0.4	4.0	18.9	1928
15.3	139.8	23.1	162.8	9.6	595	759	0.4	4.0	18.5	1929
13.9	134.5	23.2	157.7	9.3	583	746	0.4	4.3	19.3	1930
14.1	130.2	23.1	153.3	8.8	552	709	0.4	4.7	19.8	1931
13.9	131.1	24.0	155.1	8.6	542	697	0.4	4.8	19.3	1932
13.5	122.4	24.1	146.6	8.4	530	684	0.4	5.0	19.6	1933
13.0	122.9	23.8	146.7	7.9	503	651	0.5	6.1	22.2	1934
13.3	117.6	23.7	141.3	7.7	493	639	0.5	6.5	23.1	1935
13.0	116.8	24.4	141.2	9.4	599	779	0.6	6.3	26.7	1936
13.1	117.4	24.3	141.7	8.3	535	698	0.6	6.7	25.2	1937
13.2	109.6	23.7	133.4	7.8	502	656	0.5	6.6	22.8	1938
13.3	97.7	22.3	120.0	10.8	702	920	0.6	5.2	24.8	1939
14.0	98.8	22.4	121.2	9.9	..	..	0.6	6.1	..	1940
14.0	99.9	21.7	121.6	8.6	..	..	0.6	6.8	..	1941
14.3	110.9	19.2	130.1	9.1	..	..	0.6	6.8	..	1942
14.1	108.8	17.6	126.4	7.9	..	..	0.6	8.1	..	1943
15.0	108.8	17.1	125.9	6.8	..	..	0.7	10.5	..	1944
17.8	136.8	15.9	152.7	7.5	..	..	0.7	9.5	..	1945

APPENDIX TABLE CS.5 Life expectancy by age 1920/22–1937 (in years)

Age	0	10	20	30	40	50	60	70	80
				Czechoslovakia					
				Males					
1920–1922	46.41	51.65	43.33	35.83	27.97	20.44	13.65	80.80	4.31
1929–1932	51.92	54.04	45.29	37.15	28.96	21.24	14.35	8.67	4.73
1937	54.92	55.54	46.67	38.25	29.77	21.85	14.95	9.18	5.23
				Females					
1920–1922	49.19	52.53	44.22	36.70	29.04	21.31	14.12	8.30	4.45
1929–1932	55.18	56.10	47.40	39.24	30.98	22.83	15.35	9.24	5.12
1937	58.66	58.00	49.08	40.59	32.00	23.65	16.02	9.76	5.54
				Czech Republic					
				Males					
1909–1912	42.83	53.10	40.83	33.45	26.02	19.11	12.88	7.76	4.26
1920–1922	47.65	57.53	43.38	35.88	28.03	20.50	13.73	8.17	4.30
1929–1932	53.68	60.61	45.39	37.16	28.94	21.23	14.37	8.71	4.77
1937	56.47	62.48	46.74	38.22	29.70	21.79	14.81	9.15	5.23
				Females					
1909–1912	45.90	54.65	42.88	35.78	28.48	20.96	13.94	8.31	4.62
1920–1922	50.79	58.88	44.58	36.99	29.30	21.54	14.31	8.41	4.49
1929–1932	57.52	63.37	47.99	39.71	31.35	23.13	15.58	9.36	5.14
1937	60.48	65.44	49.39	40.80	32.16	23.77	16.11	9.84	5.58
				Slovak Republic					
				Males					
1910–1911	40.16	48.77	39.77	32.62	25.31	18.54	12.53	7.83	4.79
1920–1922	43.38	53.52	43.14	35.66	27.73	20.19	13.31	7.72	4.16
1929–1932	48.88	58.44	45.05	37.17	29.06	21.29	14.33	8.55	4.68
1937	51.84	60.83	46.47	38.39	30.06	22.10	15.05	9.28	5.25
				Females					
1910–1911	42.77	50.20	41.99	34.83	27.32	19.73	12.94	7.93	4.90
1920–1922	45.12	53.38	42.95	35.62	28.12	20.50	13.45	7.81	4.28
1929–1932	50.87	58.95	45.75	37.88	29.90	21.98	14.68	8.89	5.07
1937	54.70	62.29	48.00	39.80	31.41	23.21	15.68	9.53	5.47

APPENDIX TABLE CS.6A Households by type 1921–1950[1] (absolute)

Census Year	Complete families			Composite households		
	Czecho-slovakia	Czech Republik	Slovak Republic	Czecho-slovakia	Czech Republik	Slovak Republic
1921	2,451,000	1,868,000	583,000	3,020,000	2,383,000	637,000
1930	2,952,000	2,273,000	679,000	3,560,000	2,815,000	745,000
1950	2,967,000	2,182,000	785,000	3,642,000	2,767,000	875,000

Note: [1] 1950 included for comparative purposes.

APPENDIX TABLE CS.6B Households by size and members 1930–1950[1] (absolute figures and per cent)

Census year	Households by number of **dwelling persons**							
	Private households total	**1 person**	**2 persons**	**3 persons**	**4 persons**	**5 persons**	**6 persons**	**7+ persons**
	Households absolute							
	Czechoslovakia							
1930	3,559,573	259,025	677,236	801,050	710,004	492,086	299,770	320,402
1950	3,641,507	394,898	853,550	873,153	762,907	407,100	193,553	156,346
	Czech Republic							
1930	2,814,427	213,537	567,999	670,580	572,792	374,312	212,737	202,470
1950	2,766,522	344,323	705,539	687,928	575,000	272,787	111,026	69,919
	Slovak Republic							
1930	745,146	45,488	109,237	130,470	137,212	117,774	87,033	117,932
1950	874,985	50,575	148,011	185,225	187,907	134,313	82,527	86,427
	Households per cent							
	Czechoslovakia							
1930	100.00	7.28	19.03	22.50	19.95	13.82	8.42	9.00
1950	100.00	10.84	23.44	23.98	20.95	11.18	5.32	4.29
	Czech Republic							
1930	100.00	7.59	20.18	23.83	20.35	13.30	7.56	7.19
1950	100.00	12.45	25.50	24.87	20.78	9.86	4.01	2.53
	Slovak Republic							
1930	100.00	6.10	14.66	17.51	18.41	15.81	11.68	15.83
1950	100.00	5.78	16.92	21.17	21.48	15.35	9.43	9.88

Note: [1] 1950 included for comparative purposes.

APPENDIX TABLE CS.6D Household indicators 1930–1950[1]

Census year	**Household indicators**	
	Mean total household size	**Children per household**
Czechoslovakia		
1930	3.80	..
1950	3.33	0.85
Czech Republic		
1930	3.67	..
1950	3.14	0.76
Slovak Republic		
1930	4.29	..
1950	3.96	1.13

Note: [1] 1950 included for comparative purposes.

APPENDIX TABLE CS.7 Dates and nature of results on population structure, households/families, and vital statistics

Topic	Intro-duction	Remarks
Population		
Population at census dates	1921	After the creation of the independent state of Czechoslovakia in 1918 population censuses were conducted in 1921 and 1930. Before World War II there was no further population census. The third census was conducted in 1950. Before World War I Czechoslovakia, as part of Austria-Hungary, participated in the Austro-Hungarian censuses. Census data have been recalculated for the later territory of Czechoslovakia by the CSO (1988: 15).
Population by age, sex, and marital status	1921	Available in one-year age-groups for 1921 and 1930 for the main regional units (Bohemia, Moravia, Silesia, Slovakia, Subcarpathian Russia)
Households and families		
Households (domácnost; pl. domácnosti)		
Total households	1921, 1930	Households and families were first recorded in 1921 and again in 1930. A distinction was made between 'complete' and 'composite' families, a rather strange distinction, making it somewhat difficult to interpret results. *Disaggregation*: the major parts of the country (Bohemia, Moravia, Slovakia, etc.) (cf. CSO 1988).
Households by size	1930	First time in 1930: households by number of persons with 1–7 or more persons.
Households by composition	1921, 1930	In 1921 *household composition* was published with respect to the number of servants and the presence of lodgers (*Bettgeher*). Households by the number of children in 1921. Disaggregations by sex, ethnic group, and profession of household head.
Households by profession of household head	1921	In 1921 household composition by profession of household head.
Families (rodina; pl. rodiny)		
Families by number of children	1930, 1950	Special investigation of the fertility of married women for the first time in 1930 and continued since 1950. Married women by number of children 0–7 or more.

continued

APPENDIX TABLE CS.7 Dates and nature of results on population structure, households/families, and vital statistics (continued)

Topic	Intro-duction	Remarks
Population movement		
Mid-year population	1919	Available since independence.
Births		
Live births	1919	
Stillbirths	1919	
Legitimate births	1919	
Illegitimate births	1919	
Deaths		
Total deaths	1919	
Infants (under 1 year)	1919	
Marriages		
Total marriages	1919	
Divorces and separations		
Total divorces	1919	
Legal separations	–	No calculations available.

APPENDIX FIGURE CS.8 Population by age, sex and marital status, Czechoslovakia
1921 and 1930 (per 10,000 of total population)

Czechoslovakia, 1921

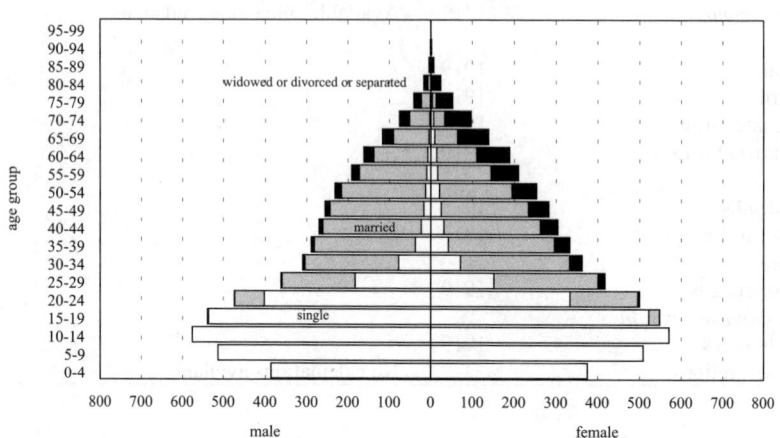

Czechoslovakia, 1930

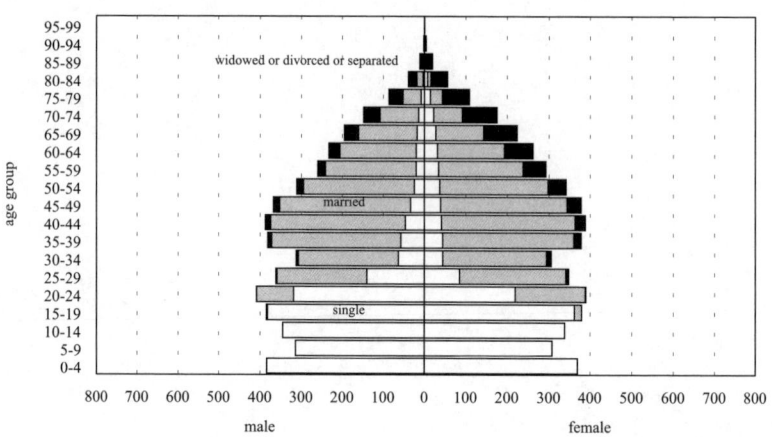

4

Denmark

The territorial history of Denmark is neatly interwoven with its political history, mainly with the relationship to its northern neighbour Norway. Over the centuries, in the northern parts of the European continent, two power centres evolved: one facing the Atlantic, embracing the territories of Norway and Denmark, and one facing the Baltic Sea, embracing Sweden and Finland. The geopolitical location of these two different power centres also shaped the lines of territorial expansion. While Norway–Denmark expanded to the North Sea (including the Channel region— Normandy) and later to the North Atlantic (Faeroe Islands, Iceland and Greenland, North America), as well as the Mediterranean (Norman Sicily, Epirus), Sweden– Finland expanded in the Baltic Sea region mainly to the east and south coast, occupying the region of the Baltic countries and the Baltic Sea coast of Germany during the Thirty Years' War.

In the Middle Ages Norway was much more expansionist than Denmark, and Greenland and Iceland were Norwegian before they came under Danish rule. Denmark only came into possession of these territories by inheriting the Norwegian crown in 1380. In 1397 Denmark formed the Kalmar Union with Norway and Sweden. Sweden left the union in the fifteenth century, which intensified the link between Denmark and Norway. The 1459 Treaty of Bergen gave Norway administrative independence. During the Napoleonic Wars Denmark was allied with Napoleon I; the 1815 Congress of Vienna punished this alliance by annexing Norway to Sweden, though Greenland, Iceland, and the Faeroe Islands remained Danish. During the whole nineteenth century this constellation did not change.

But Denmark became involved in the German states' movement for national unity. The point of conflict was the southern provinces (duchies) of Schleswig, Holstein, and Lauenburg, which had been independent units in changing formation since the Middle Ages and remained so also after 1648 until the Napoleonic era. The Congress of Vienna did not touch the integrity of the three duchies, though Lauenburg and Holstein joined the German Federation (*Deutscher Bund*), while Schleswig did not. Nationalist movements in several European countries in the following decades also influenced the situation in Denmark and the three duchies. In 1848 the Danish king allowed free elections in Denmark and in the duchies, thereby asserting a Danish claim to them. Holstein declared independence from Denmark and Schleswig applied for membership in the German Federation. The 1850s and early 1860s saw serious disputes over the territorial status of the three duchies. Finally, the 1864 war of Prussia and Austria against Denmark decided the conflict, and all three duchies had to be ceded to the German Federation and were administered jointly by the Austrians and Prussians. The next step came with the

1866 war between Prussia and Austria, in which Austria was defeated and Prussia annexed all three duchies as the Prussian province of 'Schleswig-Holstein'.

After World War I, in 1920 northern Schleswig (the four districts (*Ämter*) of Sydlige Jylland) was transferred from Germany to Denmark, and the border was moved to Flensburg. This territorial situation between Denmark and Germany has remained unchanged up to the present.

The next change concerned Iceland, the most densely populated of Denmark's North Sea and Atlantic possessions. In 1903 home rule was established in Iceland, and in 1918 a Danish–Icelandic Act of Union was approved by plebiscite. This was a personal union only in the name of the Danish crown. In 1944 Iceland attained full independence from Denmark through a plebiscite abrogating the 1918 agreement. Iceland became a republic in 1944; it has not joined the European Union.

The Faeroe Islands and Greenland remained with the Danish crown. In the 1920s Norway claimed rights over Greenland for historical reasons, but the International Court of Justice in The Hague denied these claims. Greenland remains with Denmark, although in 1979 greater autonomy was granted and Greenland left the European Community in 1985 (Denmark became a member in 1973). The Faeroe Islands also remained with Denmark (Johansen, 1987; Alestalo, 1986; Alestalo and Kuhnle, 1984).

REGIONAL POPULATION STRUCTURE

Like the other countries of the Northern European periphery, Denmark has a rather low population density when compared with the densely populated regions of continental Europe. Nevertheless, due to Denmark's more favourable geography and climate, the country could support a much higher population in absolute terms. For example, agriculture was possible in the whole of Denmark, which also has the fewest days with snow in all of Scandinavia. Thus, Denmark was a comparatively densely settled country already in the nineteenth century.

Population density in Denmark in 1870 was 47 inhabitants per square kilometre, rising to 71 in 1911 and 90 in 1940. The low population density becomes obvious when contrasted with Belgium which had 128 inhabitants per square kilometre in 1831. Regional diversity in population density did exist, but was not as great as in Finland. In 1870 the *Amter* with the highest population density were those of the larger cities, while western Jutland was the most sparsely populated region. Nevertheless, in terms of geographic population distribution Denmark belongs to the monocephalic type, with Copenhagen and surroundings making up a large proportion of the whole population. The share of city and *Amt* Copenhagen in the Danish population in 1870 amounted to 16%, increasing to 18% in 1901. In 1911 25% of the Danes lived in the capital and its district and finally in 1940 nearly one-third (29%) did so. Thus, other than the capital, Frederiksborg on the Sund and some other larger cities such as Roskilde and Odense, there are no major agglomerations (cf. Caramani, Flora, Kraus, and Quick, 1998).

In the nineteenth century, when the majority of the population made a living from agriculture, this population pattern was related to the possibility of agricultural production throughout the country. With the decline of agriculture, the formation of industrial centres and, later still, of centres offering services, regional heterogeneity increased.

POPULATION GROWTH

In 1870 Denmark had 1.785 million inhabitants. Seventy years later, in 1940, the Danish population had more than doubled to 3.844 million people. By 1991 the population had further increased to 5.146 million inhabitants. Denmark had a rather high natural population growth which already can be seen from the demographic transition, but becomes more clearly visible from the population growth rates (Figure DK.1). From the 1850s to World War I the natural population growth rate ranged between 10 and 15 per 1,000 and only slowed down after the war and the inter-war period of the 1920s and 1930s to a level between 5 and 10 per 1,000.

Total population growth depends on the natural population growth and net migration. Excess of emigration over immigration was strong from the 1870s until World War I. High population pressure was probably the main cause for the high emigration mainly to overseas countries: in Denmark emigration figures peaked in 1881–90 at 82,000 and again in 1931–40 at 100,000 emigrants (Alestalo and Kuhnle, 1984: 27). The pressure to emigrate let up only during the inter-war period with its low population growth, and during the early 1930s immigration was greater than emigration.

THE FIRST DEMOGRAPHIC TRANSITION

Demographic transition in Denmark was very similar to Norway and, to a lesser degree, Sweden (Figure DK.2). Already in the first half of the nineteenth century, all three countries had a very low mortality rate due to their very low infant mortality rates. Thus, the crude mortality rate was well below the European average. The birth rate was rather high, given the low mortality rate and only slightly below the European average. These two time series—fertility and mortality—taken together resulted in very high natural population growth: the product of high fertility and a low mortality rate. This constellation in principle endured during the whole period from 1850 to the 1960s. It was only after the 1970s that the birth rate decreased so strongly that there were more deaths than births for several years.

The period until the end of the 1860s was still a time of major fluctuations due to mortality crises after epidemics or famine. The 1850s and 1860s were dominated by the conflict over the southern three duchies (world economic crisis of the 1850s; cf. Rosenberg, 1974)). In the early 1860s the birth rate declined steeply, and in 1864, the year of the war against Prussia and Austria, the mortality rate rose steeply. The Franco-Prussian War of 1870/71 had only a minor and indirect influence on the birth and death rate. In the early 1890s there was another increase in the mortality rate. Until World War I the rates fluctuated only minimally.

The start of the demographic transition in Denmark can be located in the 1880s when the birth rate definitely began to decline. Denmark fits well into the model of the demographic transition, because the death rate—at least by tendency—started to decline earlier than the birth rate (in the 1870s).

Denmark remained neutral during World War I, but indirect effects on both demographic variables are discernible. Also in this country births were postponed during the war and increased again after the war. The war also had a negative effect on living conditions of the population, as can be seen from the rising death rate during these years.

Figure DK.1 Population growth and net migration 1850-1945

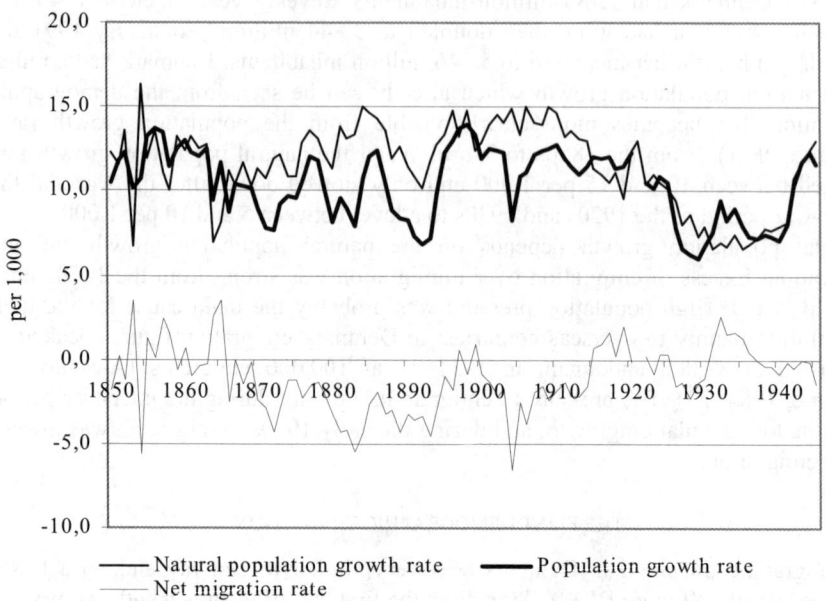

Figure DK.2 First demographic transition 1850-1945

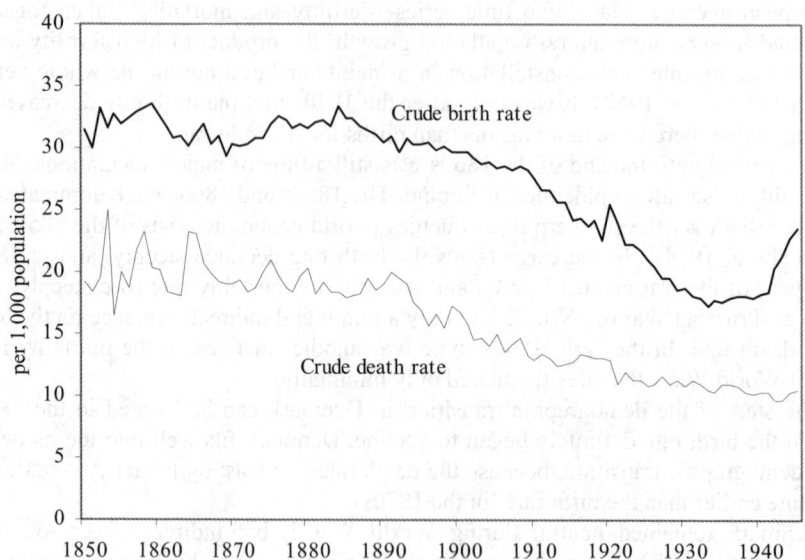

After the war also in Denmark a massive birth decline set in, but did not lead to such a demographic crisis as in Sweden. Yet in the 1930s there was a considerable natural population surplus. Denmark involuntarily became involved in World War II: although declaring itself neutral, it was occupied by Germany. Interestingly, and contrary to usual developments, the number of births and the birth rate increased tremendously during the war years. This, however, was no behavioural change, but an effect of the large cohorts immediately after World War I.

After the war the trend towards *convergence* between the birth rate and the death rate was the dominant pattern and lasted until around 1980, when the birth rate fell below the death rate. There was no clear pattern of a '*second demographic transition*' in Denmark. The remarkable increase in the birth rate in the 1960s again is a cohort effect of the birth wave of the 1940s. Thus, like the United States, Denmark is a good illustration for Richard Easterlin's 'wave theory' (Easterlin 1968, 1987; cf. also Easterlin and Crimmins, 1985).

In the late 1980s Denmark obviously reached a new demographic balance (equilibrium), with very small natural population growth: population growth in Denmark stems now overwhelmingly from a migration surplus.

Compared with Europe as a whole, the demographic history of Denmark together with its two Scandinavian neighbours Norway and Sweden constitutes one type of the transitory process, characterized by the following: early begin of the demographic transition, mostly already in the late eighteenth century, initiated by a declining mortality rate, especially a reduction of the infant mortality rate. Thus the mortality rate of these countries was already rather low in the mid-nineteenth century. Fertility decline came rather late when compared with the mortality decline; but when compared with other European countries, the Nordic countries were the first. Fertility was basically lower in the three Scandinavian countries than on the European average: this is a very clear expression of the Western European marriage pattern, producing low levels of fertility. The distance to the European fertility level was greatest in the second half of the nineteenth century, while from 1910 onwards there was some convergence.

MORTALITY AND LIFE EXPECTANCY

The infant mortality rate is defined as deaths of children aged less than one year per 1,000 live births. Denmark belongs to the group of countries with the lowest infant mortality, the Nordic countries (Figure DK.3). Infant mortality was rather low already in 1900, but it was higher than in Sweden, for instance (Masuy-Stroobant, 1997). During the 1930s and 1940s the decline of infant mortality in Denmark was slower than in other countries of this cluster.

Low infant mortality at the beginning of the twentieth century was due to a very early decline. In Denmark (and very similar in Norway) infant mortality was rather low at a level of approximately 150 deaths per 1,000 live births already in 1840. But unlike in Norway where infant mortality declined continuously after 1840, in Denmark, infant mortality showed only a minor decrease or even stagnated until 1900. A sharp decline occurred only after 1900, but in the inter-war period infant mortality in Denmark was still higher than in Norway, and the catching-up process lasted until the decades after World War II, when a virtual convergence with Norway set in. The comparison with Norway is of special interest, because until

1815 Norway was part of the Danish Kingdom, a fact that could also have influenced demographic conditions.

But there is some support for the hypotheses that the adherence to Sweden from 1815 to 1905 influenced the low level of Norwegian infant mortality, while Denmark developed differently.

Danish infant mortality was low already in the 1840s but did not reach the still lower level of Sweden. Sweden reached an infant mortality rate of 150 deaths per 1,000 live births already around 1780, 60 years before Denmark and Norway (Van de Walle, 1986) (concerning long time series of infant mortality see also Danmarks Statistik, 1964b, 1965a).

Because of the low infant mortality, life expectancy at birth already during the nineteenth century was quite favourable and higher than in most other European countries (Figure DK.4), with the exception of the Nordic neighbours. During the one hundred years from 1840 to 1940 life expectancy for male children at birth increased by 23 years, of males aged 30 for 10 years, and for males aged 60 only for 3.5 years. In Denmark, as elsewhere, the main gains in life expectancy were made by reducing infectious diseases during the early years and decades of life. Surprisingly, there are only minor differences in life expectancy between the sexes. Normally, women at all ages have a higher life expectancy than males, and in many countries there has been a growing divergence between the sexes since the nineteenth century in favour of women. In Denmark in the 1840s female life expectancy was 2.1 years longer than male life expectancy at birth, 1.5 years at age 30, and one year at age 60. Up to the five-year period of 1901/5 these distances increased to 3.3 years at birth, 2.2 years at age 30, and 1.3 years at age 60. From the turn of the century to the five-year period 1941/45 the differences between the sexes again declined to 2.1 years at birth, 0.7 years at age 30, and 0.4 years at age 60. These figures reflect very great improvements in the health situation and a strong levelling-out of health differences between the sexes not found elsewhere.

FERTILITY AND LEGITIMACY

The Western European marriage pattern normally led to high rates of illegitimate births. This was also the case in Denmark. Illegitimate births were structurally above the European average in the last 150 years (Figure DK.5), making Denmark more similar to Sweden than to Norway in this respect. While in Sweden illegitimacy was high as well and above the European average, in Norway it was below the European average. One common trend is the declining tendency of the illegitimacy rate from the nineteenth century until the middle of the twentieth century: the universalization of marriage and the rise of early marriage reduced the propensity to bear children out-of-wedlock. A second common trend for all Scandinavian countries is the change in the meaning of marriage and the legal position of the child, reducing the importance of the legitimate or illegitimate status of the child and explaining why out-of-wedlock births have increased so strongly in Denmark since the 1960s, a trend common to all the Scandinavian countries.

Given Denmark's high illegitimacy rate during the demographic transition it is conceivable that the number of births within marriage (the legitimacy rate) was comparatively low, for example lower than in Norway and Sweden. In the nineteenth century the legitimacy rate was still equal to the European average while after the inter-war period the legitimacy rate fell below the European rate. The

Figure DK.3 Infant mortality 1860-1945

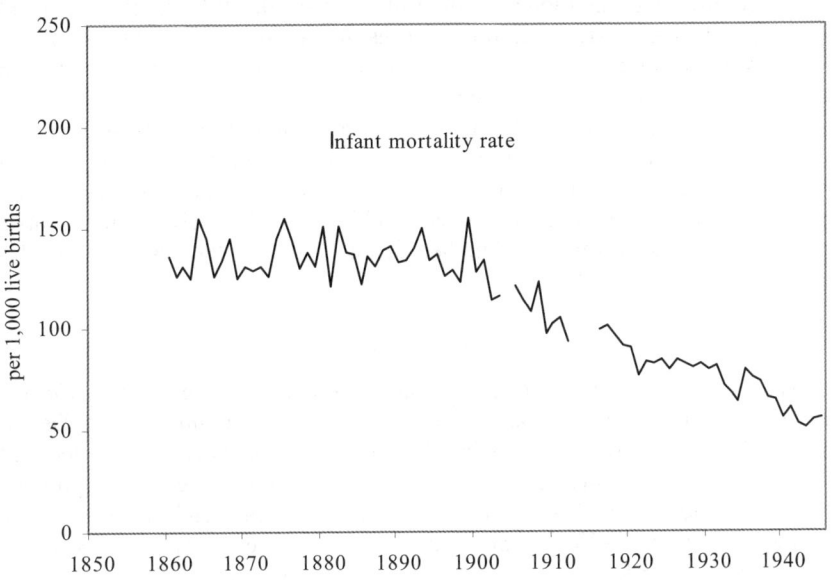

Figure DK.4 Life expectancy 1835/44-1941/45

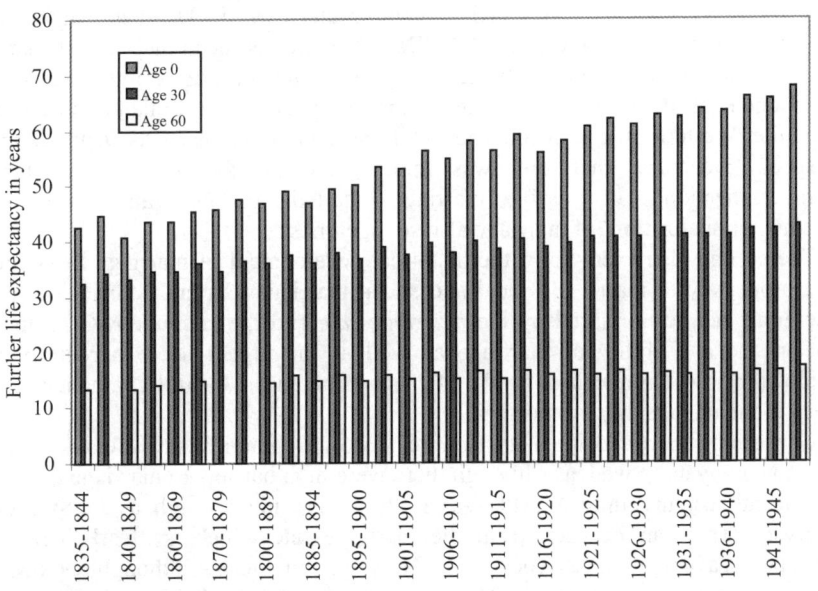

expansion of out-of-wedlock births since the 1970s made childbirth an overwhelmingly pre- and extramarital behaviour.

The large proportion and long tradition of out-of-wedlock births is demonstrated by the ratio of illegitimate to legitimate births: this ratio has constantly been above the European average during the last 150 years as in Sweden, though unlike Norway, where it was below average until the 1960s.

Explanations for the structurally high illegitimacy rate in Denmark must be sought in the structure of the agrarian economy with high proportions of unmarried servants, and the proletarianized landless workers in agriculture. On the other hand legal factors may have played a role; when looking at the high divorce rate, marriage appears as a weak institution. Another factor could be the legal status of the illegitimate child.

MARRIAGE AND DIVORCE

Denmark belongs first of all to the region of Europe with the *Western European marriage pattern* of late *age at marriage* and a high *celibacy rate*. Second, Denmark has much in common with its Scandinavian neighbours Norway and Sweden. In the 1860s and 1870s age at marriage was rather high, when measured by the proportion of people married at age 20–24. But there was a declining trend in age at marriage from the 1870s to the 1930s: the proportion married at age 20–24 increased steadily. Roughly 30% of the females born between 1905–10 were married at age 20–24 (in 1930). Women born after 1910 experienced a marriage boom: age at marriage declined considerably. This pattern of early marriage lasted until the end of World War II. The cohort born afterwards began to marry at later ages.

This process is the same for both sexes, although men's age at marriage was always considerably higher than women's. Data on the mean age at marriage show that the trend towards early marriage came rather early in Denmark, before most European countries. In the mid-1960s Danish women's mean age at first marriage reached its lower limit with 22–23 years. The turning point towards the postponement of marriage came earlier than in Norway and Finland and naturally the other Western European countries. Only Sweden was as early as Denmark in this respect. Denmark therefore was more or less the country where the 'universalization' of early marriage started earliest and where the 'deinstitutionalization' of marriage also set in earliest.

The second characteristic in the historical development of marriage behaviour is the propensity to marry and legal and social marriage barriers. Marriage intensity therefore can be measured by the *marriage rate* and the *celibacy rate*. 'Intensity' means the availability of marriage as well as the urgent need to remarry after widow(er)hood ('remarriage need', Michael Mitterauer). A third component can be seen in the universality of marriage.

Concerning marriage intensity (Figure DK.6), Denmark also differs remarkably from Norway and Sweden. Although there were high barriers to marriage during the nineteenth century until World War I, they were not as high as in Sweden or Norway. This can be seen from the marriage rate which is clearly below the European average in Sweden and Norway, but near—although below—the European average in Denmark. The marriage boom of the 1930s and 1940s, partly due to the strong birth cohorts immediately after World War I, made the marriage

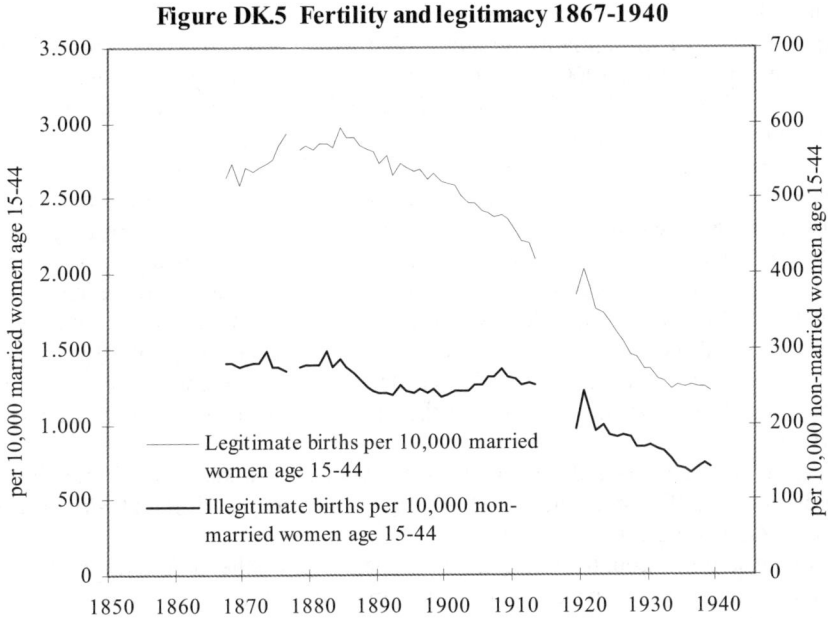

Figure DK.5 Fertility and legitimacy 1867-1940

Legitimate births per 10,000 married women age 15-44

Illegitimate births per 10,000 non-married women age 15-44

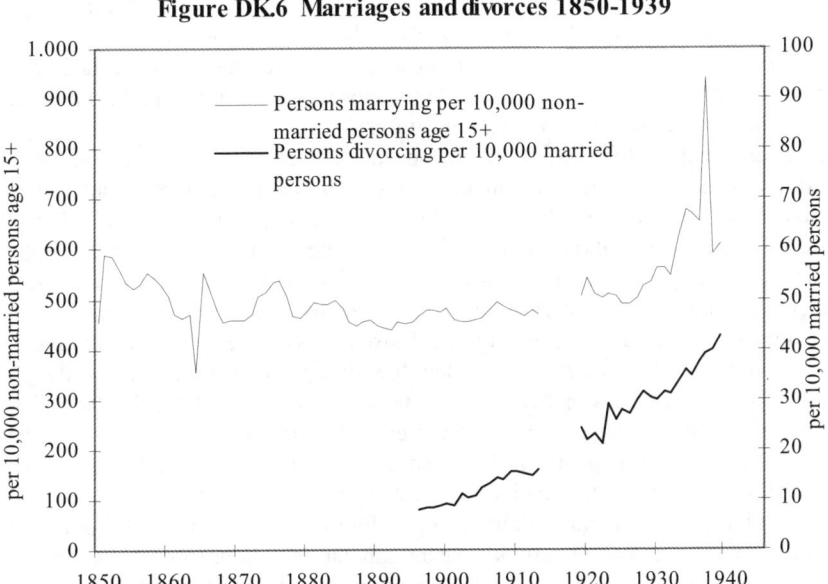

Figure DK.6 Marriages and divorces 1850-1939

Persons marrying per 10,000 non-married persons age 15+

Persons divorcing per 10,000 married persons

rate climb significantly higher than the European average, a sign of the deviating—while early—development of Denmark.

After World War II nuptiality remained high with a declining macro trend. There was a new wave in the 1960s, probably a cohort effect of the marriage wave of the 1930s. Since the late 1960s the deinstitutionalization of marriage was the dominant behavioural pattern in Denmark, with below-average propensity to marry.

The second indicator of marriage intensity, the celibacy rate, puts Denmark in the western pattern, but also this indicator demonstrates the remarkable difference to Norway and Sweden. In Denmark celibacy was lower than its northern neighbours with approximately 25% of women aged 45–54 who never married. In Sweden and Norway this proportion was about 5% higher. There was a slight increase in celibacy until the 1930s and a small decrease afterwards. The birth cohorts of the 1930s finally changed their marriage pattern completely and nearly 95% of all women of these generations married by age 45–54. The post-war generations changed this pattern again and partially returned to the older pattern of non-universal and late marriage.

Reasons for Denmark's difference from Norway and Sweden should probably be sought in its different economic structure, mainly in the different structure of agricultural holdings.

Like most other countries, Denmark participated in the long-term growth of marital breakdown, remarriage, and multiple marriages (Figure DK.6). But the long-term development is characterized by major irregularities when compared with an 'ideal' diffusion curve (logistic curve). Obviously the world wars had a major impact on the level of the divorce rate: after the wars the divorce rate increased (displacement in the level of divorces due to war events which broke up marriages). This is visible after World War I, but dramatically so after World War II. After 1945 the divorce rate started from a very high level and declined until the late 1960s. Divorce law reform at the end of the 1960s caused a steep increase in the divorce rate, which became one of the highest in Europe.

There are major differences to European developments as well as to the Scandinavian countries. Already in the nineteenth century Denmark had a rather liberal divorce law which explains why the Danish divorce rate has been higher than European average throughout the last 150 years. The divergence from the European average is already visible in the last two decades of the nineteenth century, but accelerated in the inter-war period. In Norway, the divorce rate was much lower than in Denmark and remained equal to the European average until the divorce law reforms of the 1970s when it exceeded the European average. In Sweden, the divorce rate remained lower than in Denmark until the end of the 1940s and was near the European average; only since the end of World War II has the level been higher. The steep increase in the Swedish divorce rate, now at a level similar to Denmark's, came only with the divorce law reform of the 1970s.

Explanations for Denmark's rather high divorce rate—compared both to the European average and to Denmark's Scandinavian neighbours—must be sought in the Protestant climate along with earlier urbanization and decline of agriculture than in Sweden and Norway.

Legal separations were non-existent in Denmark during the whole period.

AGE, SEX, AND CIVIL STATUS

Appendix Figure DK.8 reveals interesting developments in the age structure of the population combined with sex and marital status over 80 years, covering the period from 1860–1940. In 1860 the age pyramid still showed the pre-transitional pattern of a population with no birth control. The age structure is concave with very large proportions of the age groups 0–4 and 5–9 years. The cohorts of adults in their twenties were small compared with the age groups of the 35–39-year-olds. During the 1820s the birth rate may have risen following the end of the Napoleonic wars and the hunger crisis of 1816. A very large proportion remained unmarried for much of their life, and age at marriage was rather high. People only started to marry during their twenties and thirties. In 1860 men married later than women. In the higher age groups, most women survived their spouses. There were far fewer widowed men due to lower life expectancy and therefore smaller cohorts and higher chances for men to remarry after the death of a spouse.

During the forty years from 1860 until 1901 this structure changed very little. Nevertheless, first signs of the starting fertility decline can be detected. The concave pattern of the age pyramid became more linear, i.e. the youngest age groups (0–4 and 5–9) declined in size due to the spread of birth control. Age at marriage moved downwards, and the proportions of never-married persons declined. The effect of both was an increasing proportion of the married population.

During the next forty years, until 1940, the picture changed dramatically. The age pyramid now took on a convex shape: the birth decline starting around 1900 reduced the proportion of people under 20 years of age considerably. The cohort of 0–4-year-olds was as large as that of the 15–19-year-olds. Age at marriage declined further, and the proportion of people married increased. Life expectancy improved slightly for persons over 80 years old. Many more women remained single for a longer time, and the proportions of never-married women were higher than in 1901.

FAMILY AND HOUSEHOLD STRUCTURES

Official statistics provide little information on households and families. In Denmark this type of statistics remained underdeveloped until very recently. Only the mere number of households and the size distribution of the households was published. Furthermore, there was no investigation into fertility matters after World War I as in most other countries. Obviously there was a serious lack of interest in all these family matters, which itself is a sociological fact (*fait social*, Emile Durkheim) in need of explanation.

In Denmark, given the predominant agricultural structure of the country in the nineteenth century, households were rather large. There were not only several children in an average family, but also non-family members such as servants, boarders, and lodgers. The fertility decline and the expulsion of non-family members mainly during the century from 1850–1950 reduced the mean size of households dramatically. This reduction of aggregate mean household size hides the shift from a high proportion of larger households to the predominance of smaller households. Another secular trend is the increase of single-person households (*solitarization*). In 1890 (the first available figure) the proportion of one-person households was 7.5% (population living alone making up 1.7% of the total population); by 1950 this proportion had increased to 13.8% (population living alone = 4.4%).

In 1840, the first census giving the number of households, households were still rather large with 5.01 inhabitants per household. This figure includes one-person and institutional households. The mean size of a family household, where a couple formed the nucleus, was constantly much larger: thus, in 1901 the mean size of a family household was 4.56 compared with 4.39 for all households.

There are interesting urban–rural differences concerning household size. In 1840 on average households were largest in the provincial capitals, followed by Copenhagen. In the rural districts the average household size was lowest. This counterintuitive result is caused by the different weight of servants, boarders, and lodgers in the households. In the towns, there were more servants and population density was much higher. Furthermore, the households of the upper classes were larger at that time, not due to the greater number of children, but to servants. The households of the poorer classes were smaller due to the absence of servants. That is why the rural districts had the lowest mean household size (see also Elklit, 1978).

However, this constellation changed rapidly due to the slow disappearance of servants from households and class-specific fertility decline. Already in 1890 Copenhagen had the smallest households; households in the provincial capitals were larger, and the largest households were now found in the rural districts. In only 40 years the picture was completely reversed.

THE NATIONAL SYSTEM OF DEMOGRAPHIC STATISTICS

Population Structure

Population statistics started very early in the Nordic countries in general and in Denmark as well. Already in the eighteenth century censuses and vital statistics were organized and published, mostly taken from the parish registers. Thus, population censuses were conducted on 15 August 1769, 1 July 1787, 1 February 1801, 18 February 1834, and 1 February of the following years: 1840, 1845, 1850, 1855, 1860, 1870, 1880, 1890, 1901, 1911, and 1921. The censuses of 1930 and 1940 were conducted on 5 November.

Population numbers by sex are therefore available since the eighteenth century. Population figures by age and marital status were also combined rather early, but the first combination of population by age, sex, and marital status was made in 1855. The following censuses all published this combination.

A historical introduction concerning population development in the first half of the eighteenth century is found in Statistisk Bureau (1871), and a history of the population censuses from 1769–1890 may be found in Statistisk Bureau (1894: I–XL).

Because the territory of Denmark in the nineteenth century was composed of very different parts (Iceland, Faeroe Islands, Greenland, Schleswig, and Holstein) the government had to produce statistics for all these different territories. For reasons of comparison the data for Denmark proper (without the Faeroe Islands, Iceland, and Greenland, but with Schleswig and Holstein) have been used, although the numbers for Greenland and the Faeroe Islands in particular are very small. Iceland has been left out because it was given its own chapter in this book. Schleswig and Holstein are included for the period they belonged to Denmark.

Vital Statistics

In Denmark as in all Nordic countries the record of vital events was introduced very early, for the most part already in the eighteenth century. For the country, annual time series of the main demographic characteristics of births, deaths, and marriages are documented since 1801 (cf. Statens Statistiske Bureau, 1905). More detailed information became available at later times. Births by legitimacy status have been published since 1867, infant mortality since 1860, and divorces since 1896.

Households and Families

Data on households (*husstande*) have been gathered at least since 1840. But until the census of 1940 no extensive and detailed household statistics were developed in Denmark. Until 1860 only the number of households was published. In 1870 and 1880 the number of households and the persons outside the family were published. In 1890, 1901, and 1991 the number of households, household members, and institutional households plus members was published. In 1921 only the number of households was given. In 1930 and 1940 the number of households, household members, and institutional households plus members was published as from 1890–1911.

The only effort to present more details on private households was the disaggregation of private households by size, introduced in 1890 and repeated in 1901, 1911, 1930, and 1940. Other information such as the composition of households, the profession of household head, or household types was not given.

Comparisons of 1855 household data with those of 1845 were made in Statistisk Bureau (1857). A comparison of the number of households and of mean household size for 1860 and 1870 with regional disaggregation is found in Statistisk Bureau (1871), which also gives some information on servants. The number of households from 1880 back to 1840 (1880, 1870, 1860, 1840) with calculation of mean household size and regional disaggregation is given in Statistisk Bureau (1883: LXVII–LXXI). Statistisk Bureau (1894: CXXXVff.) publishes mean household size for 1840, 1860, 1880, and 1890.

The *definition of a household* (*familie, husstand*) since 1890 distinguished between family and institutional households. Earlier censuses only published one household figure which also included institutional households.

Family statistics as statistics on the fertility of married women were not introduced in the time period under consideration.

Remarks (also see introductory Table 6.1)

No peculiarities.

BOUNDARY CHANGES

In 1864, Denmark ceded the Duchies of Schleswig, Holstein, and Lauenburg to Prussia. In 1920 the northern part of the duchy of Schleswig was returned to Denmark. For regional organization see the documentation by Quick (1994) and Caramani, Flora, Kraus, and Quick (1998).

APPENDIX TABLES AND FIGURES

APPENDIX TABLE DK.1 Population structure at census dates 1855–1940

Census number	Census date	Census population			Marital status				Age group		
		Total	Male	Female	Single	Married	Widowed	Divorced	0–14	15–64	65+
		Absolute									
1	1 II 1855	1,499,850	741,924	757,926	901,625	512,169	80,969	5,087	499,125	922,299	78,426
2	1 II 1860	1,600,551	793,188	807,363	953,232	556,062	85,840	5,417	539,276	978,012	83,263
3	1 II 1870	1,784,741	880,807	903,934	1,062,827	617,252	98,673	5,989	595,532	1,085,564	103,645
4	1 II 1880	1,969,039	967,360	1,001,679	1,167,316	680,904	114,842	5,977	665,049	1,184,753	119,237
5	1 II 1890	2,172,380	1,059,157	1,113,223	1,287,835	748,296	130,384	5,865	755,702	1,265,410	151,268
6	1 II 1901	2,449,540	1,193,448	1,256,092	1,452,867	843,751	144,477	8,445	829,350	1,457,546	162,644
7	1 II 1911	2,757,076	1,337,900	1,419,176	1,620,028	971,222	153,753	12,073	923,841	1,650,961	182,274
8	1 II 1921	3,267,831	1,591,628	1,676,203	1,879,555	1,191,033	177,626	16,764	1,016,070	2,028,830	222,931
9	5 XI 1935	3,706,349	1,824,233	1,882,116	1,921,056	1,535,818	196,997	45,487	940,910	2,487,232	278,207
10	5 XI 1940	3,844,312	1,900,076	1,944,236	1,869,305	1,680,893	205,522	58,305	921,364	2,622,550	300,398
		Per cent									
1	1 II 1855	100.00	49.47	50.53	60.11	34.15	5.40	0.34	33.28	61.49	5.23
2	1 II 1860	100.00	49.56	50.44	59.56	34.74	5.36	0.34	33.69	61.10	5.20
3	1 II 1870	100.00	49.35	50.65	59.55	34.58	5.53	0.34	33.37	60.82	5.81
4	1 II 1880	100.00	49.13	50.87	59.28	34.58	5.83	0.30	33.78	60.17	6.06
5	1 II 1890	100.00	48.76	51.24	59.28	34.45	6.00	0.27	34.79	58.25	6.96
6	1 II 1901	100.00	48.72	51.28	59.31	34.45	5.90	0.34	33.86	59.50	6.64
7	1 II 1911	100.00	48.53	51.47	58.76	35.23	5.58	0.44	33.51	59.88	6.61
8	1 II 1921	100.00	48.71	51.29	57.52	36.45	5.44	0.51	31.09	62.08	6.82
9	5 XI 1935	100.00	49.22	50.78	51.83	41.44	5.32	1.23	25.39	67.11	7.51
10	5 XI 1940	100.00	49.43	50.57	48.63	43.72	5.35	1.52	23.97	68.22	7.81

APPENDIX TABLE DK.2 Census population by region 1870–1901 (per cent
distribution and population density)

Amt	Per cent distribution				Inhabitants per sq. km.			
	1870	1880	1890	1901	1870	1880	1890	1901
Staden	10.14	11.93	14.41	15.431[1]	9.050	11.750	15.650	6.873
Kjöbenhavn								
Kjöbenhavns Amt	5.83	6.15	7.04	7.96[1]	86	100	127	167
Frederiksborg Amt	4.59	4.22	3.91	3.67	61	61	63	67
Holbaek Amt	4.93	4.72	4.33	4.00	52	55	56	57
Sorö Amt	4.76	4.47	4.10	3.84	58	60	60	64
Praestö Amt	5.43	5.13	4.65	4.20	58	60	60	62
Bornholms Amt	1.79	1.78	1.80	1.67	55	60	67	70
Maribo Amt	5.10	4.93	4.65	4.29	54	57	60	60
Svendborg Amt	6.39	5.99	5.57	5.22	69	72	74	78
Odense Amt	6.83	6.55	6.26	6.20	69	73	77	85
Veile Amt	5.77	5.54	6.54	5.14	44	47	61	54
Aarhus Amt	7.00	7.16	7.23	7.59	50	57	63	75
Randers Amt	5.38	5.28	5.06	4.86	39	43	45	49
Aalborg Amt	4.87	4.88	4.83	5.27	30	33	36	44
Hjörring Amt	5.15	5.13	5.06	4.86	33	36	39	42
Thisted Amt	3.42	3.25	3.18	2.90	36	38	41	41
Viborg Amt	4.65	4.72	4.65	4.37	27	31	33	35
Ringkjöbing Amt	4.26	4.42	4.56	4.53	17	19	22	25
Ribe Amt	3.70	3.71	3.64	3.92	22	24	26	32
TOTAL	**100.00**	**100.00**	**100.00**	**100.00**	**47**	**51**	**57**	**64**

Note: [1] 1 I 1901: 31.8 sq. km. move from *Köbenhavn Amt* to *Staden Köbenhavn*.

APPENDIX TABLE DK.3 Census population by region 1911–1940 (per cent distribution and population density)

Amt	Per cent distribution				Inhabitants per sq. km.			
	1911	1921	1930	1940	1911	1921	1930	1940
Staden Kjöbenhavn	16.76	17.17	17.38	18.21	6.507	7.792	8.452	9.589
Kjöbenhavns Amt[1]	7.91	7.93	8.79	10.41	186	221	266	341
Frederiksberg[1]	3.52	3.21	2.99	2.94	10.778	11.667	11.778	12.556
Köbenhavns Amtsrådskreds	–	2.94	4.03	5.70	–	201	300	459
Roskilde Amtsrådskreds	–	1.77	1.77	1.74	–	84	92	97
Frederiksborg Amt	3.52	3.24	3.24	3.23	71	78	85	91
Holbaek Amt	3.92	3.61	3.44	3.12	63	68	70	69
Sorö Amt	3.70	3.37	3.21	3.04	69	74	77	79
Praestö Amt	3.95	3.52	3.32	3.02	64	68	70	69
Bornholms Amt	1.56	1.35	1.30	1.22	73	75	78	80
Maribo Amt	4.17	3.95	3.80	3.46	64	72	75	74
Svendborg Amt	4.97	4.38	4.06	3.69	82	86	86	85
Odense Amt[2]	6.06	5.63	5.74	5.80	92	102	113	123
Odense Amtsrådskreds	–	4.01	4.20	4.37	–	115	130	147
Assens Amtsrådskreds	–	1.62	1.55	1.43	–	79	82	82
Veile Amt	5.08	4.83	4.76	4.66	60	67	72	76
Aarhus Amt[2]	7.65	7.25	7.32	7.49	84	94	103	115
Skanderborg Amtsrådskreds	–	3.24	3.15	3.02	–	62	65	68
Aarhus Amtsrådskreds	–	4.01	4.17	4.47	–	163	184	214
Randers Amt	4.75	4.35	4.22	4.03	53	58	61	63
Aalborg Amt	5.26	5.08	5.27	5.36	49	57	64	70
Hjörring Amt	4.72	4.38	4.22	4.06	46	50	53	55
Thisted Amt	2.76	2.48	2.37	2.21	43	46	47	48
Viborg Amt	4.39	4.07	4.11	3.90	40	44	48	49
Ringkjöbing Amt	4.75	4.47	4.39	4.29	28	31	33	35
Ribe Amt	4.10	3.95	4.03	3.95	37	42	47	50
Haderslev Amt[3]	–	1.71	1.69	1.69	–	41	45	48
Aabenraa-Sönderborg[4]	–	–	–	2.19	–	–	–	68
Aabenraa[3,4]	–	1.07	1.13	1.12	–	45	51	54
Sönderborg[3,4]	–	1.13	1.13	1.07	–	84	91	93
Tönder Amt	–	1.10	1.07	1.04	–	26	–	–
TOTAL	**100.00**	**100.00**	**100.00**	**100.00**	**71**	**76**	**83**	**90**

Notes: [1] 1 IV 1900: *Frederiksberg* was extracted from Köbenhavns Amtsrådskreds. [2] Since 1920 the *Amter Odense* and *Aarhus* have been each split in two Amtsrådskredser. [3] After World War I the territory of *Sydlige Jylland* with four Amter went from Germany to Denmark. [4] Since 1940 *Aabenraa* and *Sonderborg* were united and each got the status of an Amtsrådskreds.

APPENDIX TABLE DK.4 Demographic developments 1850–1945 (absolute figures and rates)

Year	Mid-year population	Natural population growth rate	Population growth rate	Net migration rate	Crude birth rate	Legitimate births per 10,000 married women age 15–44	Illegitimate births per 10,000 unmarried women age 15–44	Illeg. births per 100 leg. births
1850	1,424,000	12.3	10.5	-1.8	31.4	..	..	..
1851	1,441,000	11.6	11.8	0.2	30.1	..	..	..
1852	1,459,000	13.6	12.3	-1.3	33.2	..	..	..
1853	1,474,000	6.7	10.2	3.5	31.6	..	..	..
1854	1,490,000	16.3	10.7	-5.6	32.7	..	..	..
1855	1,510,000	11.9	13.2	1.3	31.9	..	..	..
1856	1,531,000	13.6	13.7	0.1	32.4	..	..	..
1857	1,552,000	11.1	13.5	2.4	32.9	..	..	..
1858	1,570,000	10.0	11.5	1.4	33.2	..	..	..
1859	1,590,000	13.3	12.6	-0.7	33.6	..	..	..
1860	1,611,000	12.4	13.0	0.6	32.6	..	..	..
1861	1,631,000	13.3	12.3	-1.0	31.6	..	..	..
1862	1,651,000	12.6	12.1	-0.4	30.9	..	..	..
1863	1,672,000	12.8	12.6	-0.2	30.9	..	..	..
1864	1,688,000	6.9	9.5	2.5	30.1	..	..	..
1865	1,708,000	8.2	11.7	3.5	31.2	..	..	..
1866	1,723,000	11.3	8.7	-2.6	32.0	..	..	..
1867	1,741,000	10.4	10.3	-0.1	30.3	2,638	282	12.7
1868	1,759,000	11.8	10.2	-1.5	31.0	2,729	282	12.4
1869	1,777,000	10.3	10.1	-0.2	29.3	2,590	275	12.9
1870	1,793,000	11.3	8.9	-2.4	30.4	2,707	278	12.6
1871	1,807,000	10.7	7.7	-2.9	30.1	2,676	282	12.8
1872	1,821,000	12.0	7.7	-4.3	30.3	2,698	280	12.6
1873	1,838,000	12.1	9.2	-2.9	30.8	2,725	296	13.2
1874	1,856,000	10.9	9.7	-1.2	30.9	2,755	277	12.1
1875	1,874,000	10.8	9.6	-1.2	31.9	2,856	275	11.6
1876	1,894,000	12.9	10.6	-2.3	32.6	2,933	271	11.1
1877	1,917,000	13.6	12.0	-1.6	32.3	..	..	..
1878	1,940,000	13.1	11.9	-1.3	31.6	2,825	275	11.6
1879	1,960,000	12.2	10.2	-2.0	31.9	2,846	278	11.6
1880	1,976,000	11.3	8.1	-3.2	31.7	2,825	279	11.7
1881	1,995,000	13.9	9.5	-4.3	32.2	2,868	279	11.5
1882	2,013,000	13.1	8.9	-4.1	32.3	2,866	297	12.2
1883	2,029,000	13.3	7.9	-5.5	31.8	2,834	275	11.4
1884	2,051,000	15.0	10.7	-4.3	33.3	2,975	287	11.3
1885	2,076,000	14.7	12.0	-2.6	32.5	2,905	275	11.1
1886	2,102,000	14.3	12.4	-1.9	32.4	2,900	267	10.8
1887	2,124,000	13.5	10.4	-3.2	31.7	2,845	261	10.7
1888	2,143,000	11.9	8.9	-3.1	31.5	2,828	249	10.3
1889	2,161,000	12.7	8.3	-4.3	31.2	2,808	243	10.0
1890	2,179,000	11.5	8.3	-3.2	30.5	2,736	242	10.2
1891	2,195,000	10.9	7.3	-3.6	31.0	2,780	240	10.0
1892	2,210,000	10.1	6.8	-3.3	29.6	2,647	237	10.4
1893	2,226,000	11.8	7.2	-4.6	30.8	2,737	251	10.6
1894	2,248,000	12.8	9.8	-3.0	30.4	2,698	245	10.5
1895	2,276,000	13.3	12.3	-1.0	30.3	2,685	241	10.4
1896	2,306,000	14.8	13.0	-1.8	30.5	2,693	247	10.6
1897	2,338,000	13.2	13.7	0.5	29.8	2,625	240	10.6

continued

APPENDIX TABLE DK.4 Demographic developments 1850–1945 (absolute figures and rates)

Crude death rate	Infant mortality rate	Stillbirth rate	Infant mortality and stillbirth rate	Crude marriage rate	Persons marrying per 10,000 unmarried persons age 15+	Persons marrying per 10,000 unmarried persons age 15–49	Crude divorce rate	Divorces per 100 marriages	Divorces per 10,000 married persons	Year
19.1	..	47.2	..	7.6	453	547	..	..	..	1850
18.4	..	46.6	..	9.9	591	715	..	..	..	1851
19.6	..	46.9	..	9.7	585	708	..	..	..	1852
25.0	..	48.1	..	9.2	557	674	..	..	..	1853
16.4	..	47.0	..	8.7	532	646	..	..	..	1854
20.0	..	48.2	..	8.5	521	633	..	..	..	1855
18.7	..	46.2	..	8.6	532	646	..	..	..	1856
21.8	..	45.5	..	8.9	555	675	..	..	..	1857
23.2	..	44.4	..	8.7	543	662	..	..	..	1858
20.3	..	45.6	..	8.4	528	644	..	..	..	1859
20.2	135.6	43.0	178.7	8.0	505	618	..	..	..	1860
18.4	126.3	41.3	167.6	7.4	469	574	..	..	..	1861
18.3	131.0	40.6	171.6	7.3	461	564	..	..	..	1862
18.1	125.4	43.3	168.7	7.4	470	576	..	..	..	1863
23.2	154.9	41.1	196.0	5.6	353	433	..	..	..	1864
23.0	144.9	41.6	186.6	8.8	554	681	..	..	..	1865
20.7	126.1	40.1	166.2	8.3	523	643	..	..	..	1866
19.8	134.1	39.1	173.2	7.6	476	586	..	..	..	1867
19.2	144.8	37.7	182.5	7.3	454	560	..	..	..	1868
19.0	125.4	37.4	162.7	7.3	456	562	..	..	..	1869
19.0	130.9	37.7	168.6	7.3	457	564	..	..	..	1870
19.4	129.0	37.0	165.9	7.3	457	565	..	..	..	1871
18.4	131.0	37.2	168.2	7.5	468	580	..	..	..	1872
18.6	126.1	36.1	162.2	8.1	508	631	..	..	..	1873
20.0	145.0	35.7	180.8	8.2	516	642	..	..	..	1874
21.0	154.3	34.2	188.4	8.5	533	665	..	..	..	1875
19.7	143.7	35.3	179.0	8.5	537	671	..	..	..	1876
18.7	129.9	31.2	161.0	8.0	507	634	..	..	..	1877
18.4	137.9	30.2	168.1	7.4	465	582	..	..	..	1878
19.7	130.5	30.5	161.1	7.3	460	578	..	..	..	1879
20.4	150.8	30.6	181.4	7.6	479	602	..	..	..	1880
18.3	120.8	31.1	151.9	7.8	493	622	..	..	..	1881
19.2	150.8	29.3	180.2	7.7	489	618	..	..	..	1882
18.4	138.1	29.8	167.9	7.7	491	622	..	..	..	1883
18.3	136.9	28.3	165.1	7.8	498	631	..	..	..	1884
17.8	121.8	30.4	152.2	7.5	483	613	..	..	..	1885
18.1	135.6	28.9	164.5	7.1	454	577	..	..	..	1886
18.2	131.2	29.7	160.8	6.9	447	569	..	..	..	1887
19.5	138.9	26.6	165.5	7.0	455	581	..	..	..	1888
18.5	140.6	27.5	168.1	7.0	457	584	..	..	..	1889
19.0	132.7	26.1	158.9	6.9	447	572	..	..	..	1890
20.0	134.2	25.4	159.6	6.8	441	565	..	..	..	1891
19.5	139.9	25.9	165.7	6.8	440	563	..	..	..	1892
19.0	149.5	25.5	175.1	7.1	456	583	..	..	..	1893
17.6	134.2	24.6	158.8	7.0	449	574	..	..	..	1894
16.9	136.5	25.0	161.5	7.1	455	582	..	..	..	1895
15.7	125.6	24.5	150.1	7.3	466	597	0.1	1.9	8.0	1896
16.6	129.4	25.9	155.3	7.5	476	609	0.1	2.0	8.5	1897

continued

APPENDIX TABLE DK.4 Demographic developments 1850–1945 (continued)

Year	Mid-year population	Natural population growth rate	Population growth rate	Net migration rate	Crude birth rate	Legitimate births per 10,000 married women age 15–44	Illegitimate births per 10,000 unmarried women age 15–44	Illeg. births per 100 leg. births
1898	2,371,000	14.8	13.9	-0.8	30.2	2,658	246	10.7
1899	2,403,000	12.4	13.3	0.9	29.7	2,610	235	10.4
1900	2,432,000	12.8	11.9	-0.9	29.7	2,599	238	10.6
1901	2,463,000	14.0	12.6	-1.4	29.7	2,579	243	10.8
1902	2,494,000	14.6	12.4	-2.2	29.2	2,520	244	11.1
1903	2,525,000	14.0	12.3	-1.7	28.7	2,461	243	11.2
1904	2,546,000	14.8	8.2	-6.6	28.9	2,470	251	11.5
1905	2,574,000	13.4	10.9	-2.5	28.4	2,410	253	11.8
1906	2,603,000	15.0	11.1	-3.8	28.5	2,401	263	12.2
1907	2,635,000	14.1	12.1	-1.9	28.2	2,368	261	12.3
1908	2,668,000	13.9	12.4	-1.6	28.6	2,385	272	12.6
1909	2,702,000	15.0	12.6	-2.4	28.2	2,355	263	12.3
1910	2,737,000	14.7	12.8	-1.9	27.5	2,285	259	12.4
1911	2,770,000	13.2	11.9	-1.3	26.7	2,210	253	12.5
1912	2,802,000	13.6	11.4	-2.2	26.6	2,196	256	12.6
1913	2,833,000	13.1	10.9	-2.2	25.6	2,097	251	13.0
1914	2,866,000	13.0	11.5	-1.5	25.6	..	..	12.9
1915	2,901,000	11.4	12.1	0.7	24.2	..	..	13.2
1916	2,936,000	11.0	11.9	0.9	24.4	..	..	13.2
1917	2,972,000	10.5	12.1	1.7	23.7	..	..	13.0
1918	3,006,000	11.1	11.3	0.2	24.1	..	..	12.8
1919	3,041,000	9.6	11.5	1.9	22.6	1,855	192	11.7
1920	3,079,000	12.5	12.3	-0.1	25.4	2,031	243	13.2
1921	3,283,000	13.0	62.1	49.2	24.0	1,912	217	12.3
1922	3,318,000	10.4	10.5	0.2	22.3	1,763	192	11.6
1923	3,352,000	11.0	10.1	-0.9	22.3	1,740	200	12.1
1924	3,389,000	10.5	10.9	0.4	21.8	1,688	187	11.4
1925	3,425,000	10.2	10.5	0.3	21.0	1,607	184	11.7
1926	3,452,000	9.5	7.8	-1.6	20.5	1,546	185	12.0
1927	3,475,000	8.0	6.6	-1.4	19.6	1,457	183	12.4
1928	3,497,000	8.6	6.3	-2.3	19.6	1,444	170	12.4
1929	3,518,000	7.3	6.0	-1.4	18.6	1,360	171	12.1
1930	3,542,000	7.9	6.8	-1.2	18.7	1,359	172	12.0
1931	3,569,000	6.6	7.6	0.9	18.0	1,295	166	12.0
1932	3,603,000	6.9	9.4	2.5	17.9	1,282	164	11.8
1933	3,633,000	6.7	8.3	1.5	17.3	1,228	154	11.4
1934	3,666,000	7.4	9.0	1.6	17.8	1,266	143	10.1
1935	3,695,000	6.6	7.8	1.2	17.7	1,249	141	10.0
1936	3,722,000	6.9	7.3	0.4	17.8	1,257	135	9.3
1937	3,749,000	7.2	7.2	0.0	18.0	1,248	143	9.7
1938	3,777,000	7.8	7.4	-0.4	18.1	1,243	149	9.8
1939	3,805,000	7.7	7.4	-0.4	17.8	1,214	143	9.5
1940	3,832,000	7.9	7.0	-0.9	18.3	..	..	9.6
1941	3,863,000	8.2	8.0	-0.1	18.5	..	..	9.4
1942	3,903,000	10.8	10.2	-0.5	20.4	..	..	9.2
1943	3,949,000	11.7	11.6	-0.1	21.4	..	..	9.8
1944	3,998,000	12.4	12.3	-0.1	22.7	..	..	10.1
1945	4,045,000	13.0	11.6	-1.4	23.5	..	..	11.0

APPENDIX TABLE DK.4 Demographic developments 1850–1945 (continued)

Crude death rate	Infant mortality rate	Stillbirth rate	Infant mortality and stillbirth rate	Crude marriage rate	Persons marrying per 10,000 unmarried persons age 15+	Persons marrying per 10,000 unmarried persons age 15–49	Crude divorce rate	Divorces per 100 marriages	Divorces per 10,000 married persons	Year
15.5	122.9	25.7	148.6	7.5	480	614	0.1	2.0	8.5	1898
17.3	154.3	24.8	179.2	7.5	473	605	0.2	2.1	8.9	1899
16.8	128.4	24.2	152.6	7.6	481	615	0.2	2.1	9.1	1900
15.7	134.3	24.8	159.1	7.1	456	579	0.2	2.1	8.8	1901
14.6	113.9	24.2	138.1	7.1	453	575	0.2	2.7	11.1	1902
14.6	115.9	24.1	140.0	7.1	455	578	0.2	2.5	10.2	1903
14.1	..	24.0	..	7.2	460	584	0.2	2.6	10.7	1904
15.0	121.0	24.4	145.4	7.2	462	587	0.2	3.0	12.2	1905
13.5	113.7	23.1	136.9	7.4	479	610	0.2	3.0	13.0	1906
14.1	108.4	24.6	133.0	7.6	493	627	0.3	3.3	14.3	1907
14.6	123.2	24.2	147.4	7.5	485	618	0.2	3.3	13.9	1908
13.3	97.7	23.8	121.5	7.4	478	610	0.3	3.7	15.4	1909
12.9	102.2	23.7	125.9	7.3	474	604	0.3	3.7	15.5	1910
13.4	105.8	23.7	129.5	7.2	467	595	0.3	3.7	15.0	1911
13.0	93.2	23.5	116.7	7.3	477	609	0.3	3.5	14.6	1912
12.5	..	23.9	..	7.2	471	602	0.3	3.9	15.9	1913
12.5	..	23.6	..	6.9	..	..	0.3	4.5	..	1914
12.8	..	25.3	..	6.5	..	..	0.3	4.6	..	1915
13.4	99.0	25.1	124.1	7.2	..	..	0.3	4.4	..	1916
13.2	101.6	25.4	127.0	7.0	..	..	0.3	4.9	..	1917
13.0	96.6	26.0	122.5	7.6	..	..	0.4	4.8	..	1918
13.0	91.6	25.0	116.6	8.2	504	651	0.4	5.2	24.4	1919
12.9	90.7	25.5	116.2	8.8	542	693	0.4	4.4	21.7	1920
11.0	77.0	25.4	102.4	8.2	510	645	0.4	5.2	23.1	1921
11.9	84.1	24.6	108.6	7.9	502	629	0.4	5.0	21.1	1922
11.3	82.9	24.5	107.4	8.0	511	636	0.6	7.0	29.2	1923
11.2	84.5	24.4	108.9	7.8	504	621	0.5	6.4	25.8	1924
10.8	79.9	24.2	104.0	7.5	491	599	0.6	7.3	27.7	1925
11.0	84.4	20.4	104.8	7.5	491	594	0.6	7.4	27.2	1926
11.6	83.2	20.7	103.9	7.5	502	601	0.6	8.1	29.8	1927
11.0	80.8	20.8	101.7	7.8	525	623	0.7	8.5	31.4	1928
11.2	82.9	21.4	104.3	7.9	535	630	0.6	8.2	30.2	1929
10.8	80.0	21.0	100.9	8.2	561	655	0.6	7.9	29.9	1930
11.4	81.4	22.1	103.5	8.1	563	651	0.7	8.5	31.4	1931
11.0	72.0	20.7	92.7	7.8	546	626	0.7	8.9	31.2	1932
10.5	67.5	23.4	90.9	8.8	621	706	0.8	8.6	33.5	1933
10.4	64.4	23.3	87.7	9.5	676	762	0.8	8.7	35.9	1934
11.0	79.5	25.8	105.3	9.3	669	747	0.8	8.7	34.7	1935
11.0	75.9	26.5	102.4	9.3	652	755	0.9	9.3	37.3	1936
10.8	73.4	26.1	99.5	9.1	939	743	0.9	9.8	39.0	1937
10.3	66.2	25.8	91.9	8.9	590	732	0.9	10.1	39.7	1938
10.1	65.2	26.9	92.1	9.4	609	781	1.0	10.2	42.8	1939
10.4	56.2	25.9	82.1	9.2	..	..	0.9	9.8	..	1940
10.3	61.1	23.6	84.7	8.7	..	..	1.0	11.2	..	1941
9.6	53.3	21.3	74.7	9.2	..	..	1.1	12.4	..	1942
9.6	50.9	21.7	72.7	9.3	..	..	1.2	13.4	..	1943
10.3	54.7	20.0	74.7	9.4	..	..	1.3	14.3	..	1944
10.5	56.0	19.8	75.8	9.0	..	..	1.4	16.1	..	1945

APPENDIX TABLE DK.5 Life expectancy by age 1835/44–1941/45 (in years)

Age	0	10	20	30	40	50	60	70	80
				Males					
1835–1844	42.6	47.7	39.8	32.6	..	..	13.2	..	..
1840–1849	40.9	47.8	40.1	33.0	25.8	19.1	13.2	8,0	..
1860–1869	43.6	49.1	41.6	34.5	27.0	19.9	13.5	8.5	4.6
1870–1879	45.6	49.8	..	34.7	..	20.1	..	8.5	..
1880–1889	46.8	51.0	43.2	35.9	..	..	14.4	..	4.8
1885–1894	46.9	51.3	43.6	36.2	..	..	14.6	..	5.0
1895–1900	50.2	52.8	44.5	36.8	28.9	21.5	14.7	9,0	4.9
1901–1905	52.9	54.0	45.4	37.4	29.4	21.8	15.0	9.2	5.0
1906–1910	54.9	55.1	46.3	38.0	29.7	22.1	15.2	9.3	5.1
1911–1915	56.2	55.6	46.7	38.4	30.2	22.4	15.3	9.4	5.1
1916–1920	55.8	54.6	46.1	38.9	31.1	23.1	15.8	9.7	5.1
1921–1925	60.6	58.4	49.4	40.8	32.1	23.7	16.0	9.8	5.2
1926–1930	60.9	58.7	49.6	40.8	32.0	23.6	15.9	9.6	5.1
1931–1935	62.2	59.0	49.8	41.0	32.1	23.6	16.0	9.7	5.2
1936–1940	63.5	59.6	50.3	41.2	32.2	23.7	16.0	9.6	5.2
1941–1945	65.62	60.46	51.12	42.20	33.16	24.51	16.69	10.13	5.40
				Females					
1835–1844	44.7	48.9	41.6	34.2	..	14.3	..	..	..
1840–1849	43.5	49.1	41.8	34.5	27.8	20.8	14.2	8.8	..
1860–1869	45.5	50.2	43.2	36.1	29.1	21.9	14.8	9.0	5.0
1870–1879	47.4	50.6	..	36.3	..	22.0	..	9.2	..
1880–1889	48.9	52.1	44.9	37.6	..	..	15.8	..	5.3
1885–1894	49.2	52.6	45.4	37.9	..	..	15.8	..	5.5
1895–1900	53.2	54.7	46.7	38.9	31.2	23.4	16.0	9.8	5.3
1901–1905	56.2	55.8	47.5	39.6	31.7	23.8	16.3	10.0	5.5
1906–1910	57.9	56.7	48.2	40.1	32.0	24.1	16.5	10.0	5.5
1911–1915	59.2	57.2	48.4	40.2	32.0	24.0	16.4	9.9	5.3
1916–1920	58.1	55.6	47.2	39.6	32.0	24.0	16.4	10.0	5.4
1921–1925	61.9	58.4	49.3	40.8	32.3	24.1	16.5	10.0	5.4
1926–1930	62.6	58.8	49.6	42.0	32.4	24.1	16.3	9.8	5.2
1931–1935	63.8	59.4	50.0	41.2	32.5	24.1	16.4	9.9	5.4
1936–1940	65.8	60.6	51.1	42.0	33.1	24.5	16.6	10.0	5.3
1941–1945	67.70	61.52	52.03	42.91	33.8	25.16	17.14	10.38	5.56

APPENDIX TABLE DK.6A Households by type 1840–1940[1] (absolute and per cent)

Census year	Household types and members									
	Total households	Private households	Family households	One-person households	Institutional households	Total household members	Private household members	Family household members	One-person household members	Institutional household members
Absolute										
1840	256,467	:	:	:	:	1,289,075	:	:	:	:
1845	269,939	:	:	:	:	1,350,327	:	:	:	:
1850	:	:	:	:	:	1,407,747	:	:	:	:
1855	304,440	:	:	:	:	1,499,850	:	:	:	:
1860	330,438	:	:	:	:	1,600,551	:	:	:	:
1870	370,473	:	:	:	:	1,784,741	:	:	:	:
1880	441,692	:	:	:	:	1,969,039	:	:	:	:
1890	474,673	473,345	438,014	35,331	1,328	2,190,547	2,172,380	2,137,049	35,331	18,167
1901	557,493	556,734	507,747	48,987	759	2,449,540	2,408,860	2,359,873	48,987	40,680
1911	651,098	649,432	584,449	64,983	1,666	2,757,076	2,691,542	2,626,559	64,983	65,534
1921	797,257	794,813	719,022	75,791	2,444	3,267,831	3,177,536	3,101,745	75,791	90,295
1930	943,647	940,453	838,054	102,399	3,194	3,550,656	3,440,712	3,338,313	102,399	109,944
1940	1,162,034	1,158,063	1,001,340	156,723	3,971	3,844,312	3,755,766	3,599,043	156,723	88,546
Per cent										
1890	100.00	99.72	92.28	7.44	0.28	100.00	99.17	97.56	1.61	0.83
1901	100.00	99.86	91.08	8.79	0.14	100.00	98.34	96.34	2.00	1.66
1911	100.00	99.74	89.76	9.98	0.26	100.00	97.62	95.27	2.36	2.38
1921	100.00	99.69	90.19	9.51	0.31	100.00	97.24	94.92	2.32	2.76
1930	100.00	99.66	88.81	10.85	0.34	100.00	96.90	94.02	2.88	3.10
1940	100.00	99.66	86.17	13.49	0.34	100.00	97.70	93.62	4.08	2.30

Note: [1] 1840–1890 without Faroer-Islands.

APPENDIX TABLE DK.6B Households by size and members 1890–1940 (absolute figures)

Census year	Private households total	1 person	2 persons	3 persons	4 persons	5 persons	6 persons	7 persons	8 persons	9 persons	10+ persons
Households											
1890	473,345	35,331	78,338	83,864	75,326	63,263	84,624[1]			52,599[2]	
1901	556,734	48,987	95,319	99,251	88,123	72,062	55,081	39,030	25,457	14,672	18,752
1911	649,432	64,983	116,264	119,912	104,703	82,327	60,387	41,379	26,266	15,182	18,029
1921	794,813	75,791	::	::	::	::	::	::	::	::	::
1930	940,453	102,399	205,494	205,280	163,798	109,738	67,229	39,992	22,432	11,849	12,242
1940	1,158,063	156,723	298,961	277,261	195,475	110,988	58,969	30,125	15,230	7,396	6,935
Persons											
1890	2,124,104	35,331	156,676	251,592	301,304	316,315	543,208[1]			519,678[2]	
1901	2,408,860	48,987	190,638	297,753	352,492	360,310	330,486	273,210	203,656	132,048	219,280
1911	2,691,542	64,983	232,528	359,736	418,812	411,635	362,322	289,653	210,128	136,638	205,107
1921	3,177,536	75,791	::	::	::	::	::	::	::	::	::
1930	3,440,712	102,399	410,988	615,840	655,192	548,690	403,374	279,944	179,456	106,641	138,188
1940	3,755,766	156,723	597,922	831,783	781,900	554,940	353,814	210,875	121,840	66,564	79,405

Notes: [1] 6–7 persons. [2] 8 and more persons.

APPENDIX TABLE DK.6C Households by size and members 1890–1940 (per cent)

Census year	Private households total	1 person	2 persons	3 persons	4 persons	5 persons	6 persons	7 persons	8 persons	9 persons	10+ persons
					Households						
1890	100.00	7.46	16.55	17.72	15.91	13.37		17.88[1]		11.11[2]	
1901	100.00	8.80	17.12	17.83	15.83	12.94	9.89	7.01	4.57	2.64	3.37
1911	100.00	10.01	17.90	18.46	16.12	12.68	9.30	6.37	4.04	2.34	2.78
1921	100.00	9.54	..	..	..	..	..	..	..	..	..
1930	100.00	10.89	21.85	21.83	17.42	11.67	7.15	4.25	2.39	1.26	1.30
1940	100.00	13.53	25.82	23.94	16.88	9.58	5.09	2.60	1.32	0.64	0.60
					Persons						
1890	100.00	1.66	7.38	11.84	14.18	14.89		25.57[1]		24.47[2]	
1901	100.00	2.03	7.91	12.36	14.63	14.96	13.72	11.34	8.45	5.48	9.10
1911	100.00	2.41	8.64	13.37	15.56	15.29	13.46	10.76	7.81	5.08	7.62
1921	100.00	2.39	..	..	..	..	..	..	..	..	..
1930	100.00	2.98	11.94	17.90	19.04	15.95	11.72	8.14	5.22	3.10	4.02
1940	100.00	4.17	15.92	22.15	20.82	14.78	9.42	5.61	3.24	1.77	2.11

Notes: [1] 6–7 persons. [2] 8 and more persons.

APPENDIX TABLE DK.6D Household indicators 1840–
1940

Census year	Household indicators			
	Mean total household size	Mean private household size	Mean family household size	Mean institutional household size
1840	5.03	..	..	..
1845	5.00	..	..	..
1850	..	..	..	..
1855	4.93	..	..	..
1860	4.84	..	..	..
1870	4.82	..	..	..
1880	4.46	..	..	..
1890	4.61	4.59	4.88	13.68
1901	4.39	4.33	4.65	53.60
1911	4.23	4.14	4.49	39.34
1921	4.10	4.00	4.31	36.95
1930	3.76	3.66	3.98	34.42
1940	3.31	3.24	3.59	22.30

APPENDIX TABLE DK.6E Mean household size by territorial division 1840–1890
(persons per household)

Territorial division		1840	1860	1880	1890
Det egenlige Danmark	Staden Kjobenhaven	4.98	4.75	4.34	4.15
	Provins-Kjobstaeder	5.22	4.97	4.55	4.43
	Landdistrikter	5.01	4.84	4.86	4.73
	Total	5.03	4.85	4.75	4.59
Faeroerne	Thorshaven By	4.41	4.87	4.80	5.05
	Landdistrikter	5.75	5.52	5.53	5.62
	Total	5.58	5.45	5.45	5.56
Kongeriget Danmark	Staden Kjobenhavn	4.98	4.75	4.34	4.15
	Provins-Kjobstaeder	5.22	4.97	4.55	4.44
	Landdistrikter	5.01	4.84	4.87	4.74
	Total	5.03	4.85	4.75	4.59
Total Danmark		5.03	4.85	4.75	4.60

APPENDIX TABLE DK.6F Households by region and size 1890 (per cent)

Province	Private house-holds	1 per-son	2 per-sons	3 per-sons	4 per-sons	5 per-sons	6–7 per-sons	8+ per-sons
Households								
Kjobenhaven	100.00	10.04	18.17	19.76	16.95	13.09	15.00	6.99
Oernes Kjöbstaeder	100.00	10.33	19.01	18.15	15.34	12.56	15.29	9.33
Jyllands Kjöbstaeder	100.00	9.19	18.45	17.75	16.18	12.78	16.21	9.43
Oernes Landdistrikter	100.00	6.87	16.77	17.97	15.91	13.11	18.07	11.30
Jyllands Landdistrikter	100.00	5.69	14.45	16.36	15.49	14.11	20.14	13.77
Oerne (uden Kbh.)	100.00	7.54	17.20	18.00	15.80	13.01	17.53	10.92
Jylland	100.00	6.40	15.26	16.64	15.63	13.83	19.34	12.89
Faeroerne	100.00	3.30	7.85	11.42	15.41	15.28	26.65	20.09
Total (without Faeroe Is.)	100.00	7.46	16.55	17.72	15.91	13.37	17.88	11.11
Total (with Faeroe Is.)	100.00	7.44	16.51	17.69	15.91	13.37	17.92	11.16
Persons[1]								
Kjobenhaven	100.00	2.42	8.76	14.29	16.33	15.77	23.10	19.33
Oernes Kjöbstaeder	100.00	2.50	9.21	13.19	14.87	15.22	23.71	21.29
Jyllands Kjöbstaeder	100.00	2.18	8.76	12.64	15.36	15.17	24.70	21.19
Oernes Landdistrikter	100.00	1.53	7.44	11.96	14.13	14.55	25.74	24.65
Jyllands Landdistrikter	100.00	1.19	6.03	10.24	12.93	14.72	27.04	27.85
Oerne (uden Kbh.)	100.00	1.70	7.76	12.18	14.26	14.67	25.37	24.04
Jylland	100.00	1.37	6.53	10.69	13.38	14.80	26.61	26.62
Faeroerne	100.00	0.60	2.84	6.20	11.16	13.83	31.05	34.32
Total (without Faeroe Is.)	100.00	1.66	7.38	11.84	14.18	14.89	25.57	24.47
Total (with Faeroe Is.)	100.00	1.66	7.35	11.81	14.17	14.89	25.61	24.53

Note: [1] Persons in households have been calculated using the number of households.

APPENDIX TABLE DK.7 Dates and nature of results on population structure, households/families, and vital statistics

Topic	Intro-duction	Remarks
Population		
Population at census dates	1850	Earlier censuses were carried out in 1801, 1834, 1840, and 1845.
Population by age, sex, and ma-rital status	1855	The earlier censuses present partly grouped data; later one-year age groups were introduced.
Households and families		
Households (*husstande*)		
Total households	1840, 1850, 1855, 1860, 1870, 1880, 1890, 1901, 1911, 1921, 1930, 1940	Number of households: households were counted at least since 1840. 1850: number of households. 1855: number of households. 1860: number of households. 1870: number of households, non-relatives. 1880: number of households, persons outside the family. 1890: private households by members and institutional households by members. 1901: private households by members and institutional households by members. 1911: private households by members and institutional households by members. 1921: number of households only. 1930: private households by members and institutional households by members. 1940: private households by members and institutional households by members. *Disaggregation*: 1840–1880: Copenhagen, towns and rural communities. Distinction between Denmark proper and Denmark including the Faeroe Islands.
Households by size	1890, 1901, 1911, 1930, 1940	For the first time in 1890. Repeated in 1901, 1911, 1930, and 1940. Not available for 1921. Households with 0–10+ persons. Number of household members.
Households by composition	–	Not available.
Households by profession of household head	–	Not available.
Families (*familie*)		
Families by number of children	–	Not available.
Population movement		
Mid-year population	1850	
Births		
Live births	1850	
Stillbirths	1850	
Legitimate births	1867	
Illegitimate births	1867	

continued

APPENDIX TABLE DK.7 Dates and nature of results on population structure, households/families, and vital statistics (continued)

Topic	Intro-duction	Remarks
Deaths		
Total deaths	1850	
Infants (under one year)	1860	
Marriages		
Total marriages	1850	
Divorces and separations		
Total divorces	1896	
Legal separations	–	

APPENDIX FIGURE DK.8 Population by age, sex and marital status, Denmark 1860,
1870, 1880, 1901, 1921, and 1940 (per 10,000 of total population)

Denmark, 1860

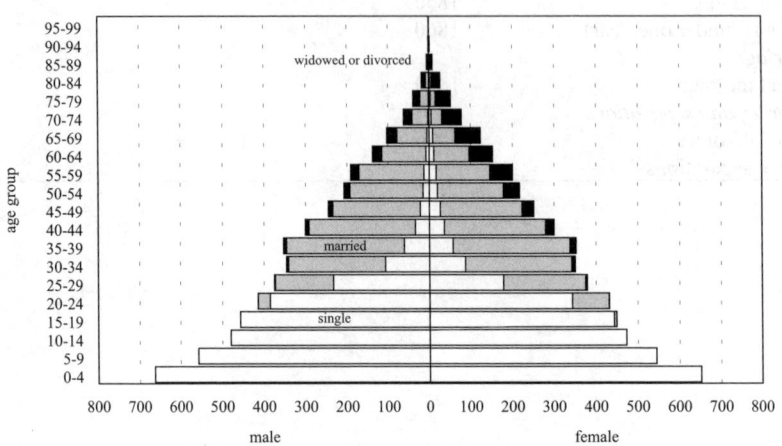

Denmark, 1870

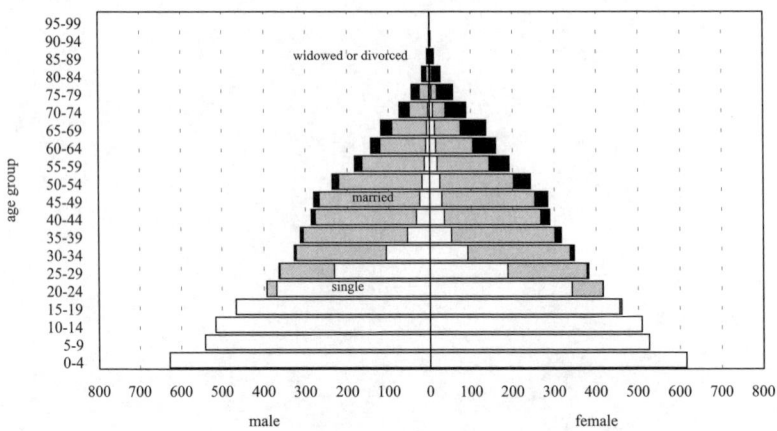

APPENDIX FIGURE DK.8 Population by age, sex and marital status, Denmark 1860, 1870, 1880, 1901, 1921, and 1940 (per 10,000 of total population) (continued)

Denmark, 1880

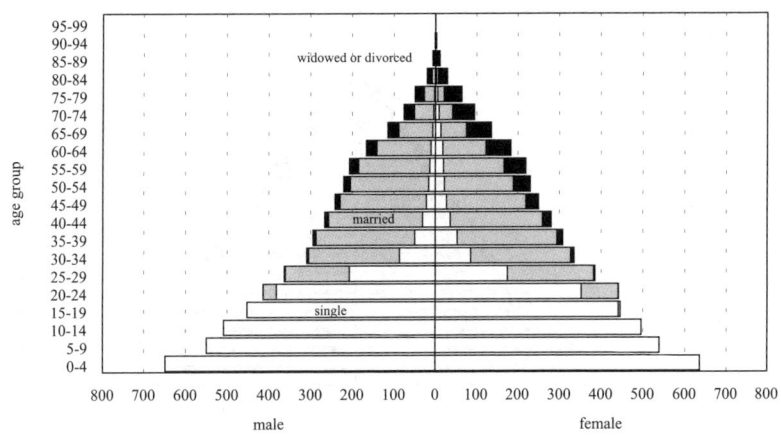

Denmark, 1901

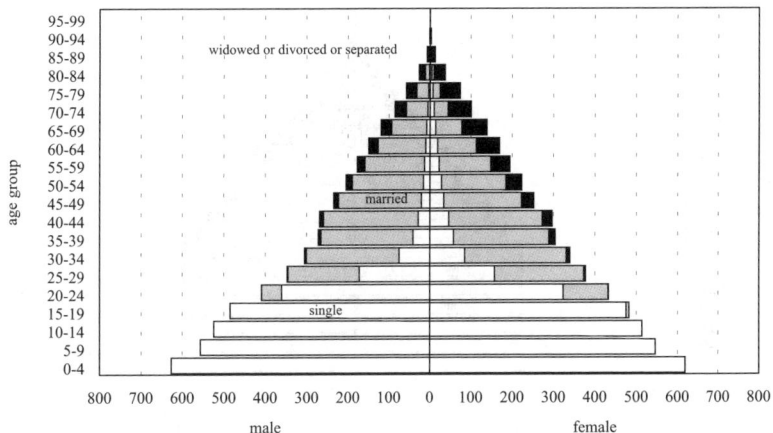

APPENDIX FIGURE DK.8 Population by age, sex and marital status, Denmark 1860, 1870, 1880, 1901, 1921, and 1940 (per 10,000 of total population) (continued)

Denmark, 1921

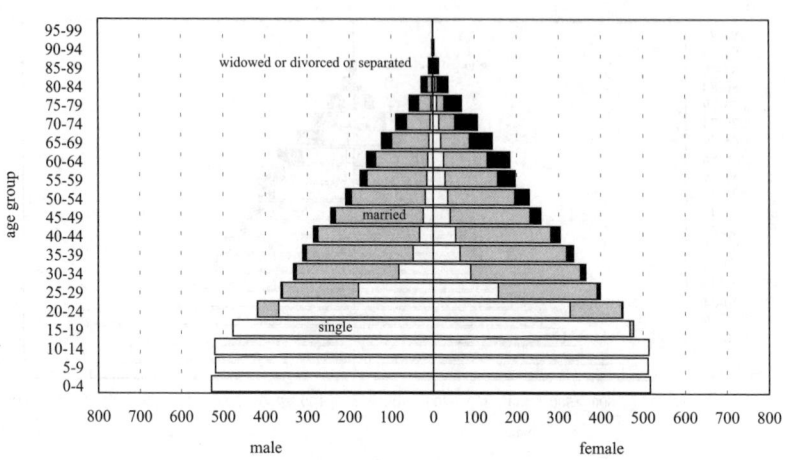

Denmark, 1940

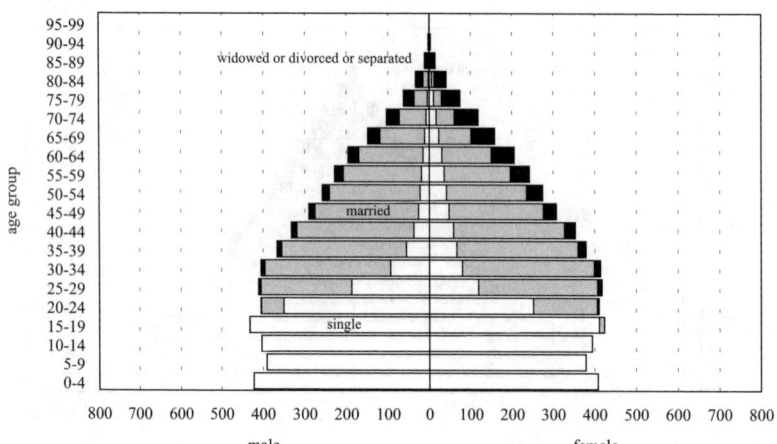

5

Finland

STATE FORMATION AND TERRITORY

The territory of present-day Finland was occupied and settled by the Swedes in the Middle Ages. They introduced the Swedish language, culture, and later Protestantism. The native language of the Finns however remained the spoken language of the people, while Swedish became the official language.

From the sixteenth century onwards Swedish–Finnish expansionism brought the Baltic territories and, in the Thirty Years' War, parts of northern Germany under the Swedish crown. Such expansionism necessarily brought Sweden into conflict with the rising power Russia. In the seventeenth century Peter the Great wanted to modernize and westernize Russia by giving the country a fleet and access to the Baltic Sea. The first major war between Sweden and Russia was the so-called 'Nordic War' which ended with the defeat of Sweden, which had to cede the Baltic territories, south-east Karelia, and the city of Vyborg to Russia in 1721.

The next main territorial conflict between Sweden and Russia came during the Napoleonic period, when Russia defeated Sweden in 1808 and the latter had to cede the whole of Finland to Russia. On the other hand Sweden gained Denmark from Norway in the 1813 battle of Lipsia.

In 1808, Finland came under Russian authority. In 1809 Tsar Alexander I granted the Grand Duchy of Finland some autonomy within the Russian empire. In the same year Finland acquired the Tornie River basin, in 1811 the province of Vyborg, and in 1820 the harbour of Petsano on the north coast. Swedish political and cultural traditions survived during the nineteenth century: the Swedish Constitution of 1772 remained in force, Swedish was still acknowledged as official language, and the official publications (statistics!) were still published in Swedish. In the late nineteenth century Finnish nationalism grew stronger in line with the nationalist movements all over Europe.

But only the Russian revolution of 1905 marked the beginning of a new era. In Finland universal suffrage and the Eduskunta, a single-chamber parliament, were introduced, and the first election was held in 1907. But the end of Russian domination and the birth of independence came only with World War I, Russian capitulation, and the peace treaty with Germany. The October Revolution and the civil war which also raged in Finland finally led to the declaration of Finnish independence from the Soviet Union on 6 December 1917. On 17 July 1919 a constitution was enacted and Finland became a presidential republic. The Constitution is still in force today.

At that time the territory of Finland was much larger than it is today. It included south-east Karelia with the city of Vyborg as well as the port of Petsano on the north coast. Finland and Sweden came to an agreement on the Åland Islands in the Gulf of

Bothnia between the two countries: they were given to Finland in 1921 and remained neutral from 1921 to 1935.

World War II changed this territorial status. In an effort to win back some territories that had belonged to the Russian empire, Soviet forces attacked Finland in 1939. An armistice was granted to Finland only under the condition that it transfer Vyborg and surroundings and the northern part of Karelia (Petsano) to the Soviet Union. After the German attack on the Soviet Union in 1943 Finland tried to regain these territories; in 1944, however, the Russians again attacked the Finns and reconquered them. As a result of the German defeat, the Soviets' territorial gains were secured in the treaty of 1947 between Finland and the Soviet Union (Puntila, 1980; Alestalo, 1986; Alestalo and Kuhnle, 1984; Alestalo, Andorka, and Harcsa, 1987).

REGIONAL POPULATION STRUCTURE

Situated at the north-eastern European periphery, Finland has always been a very sparsely populated country. In 1875 the population was 1.913 million inhabitants, in 1910 it was 3.115 million, and in 1940 it had reached 3.887 million inhabitants. Population density in the respective years (persons per square kilometre) was therefore 5 in 1875, 9 in 1910, and 11 in 1940.

Regional diversity in Finland is great. Urbanization and economic development since the nineteenth century has been concentrated on the southern and western shores of the Baltic Sea, where the main trade and traffic routes start and end: Turku in the west with the connection to Stockholm over the Åland Islands; Helsinki in the south with the connection to the Baltic countries, Poland, and Germany. Industry is concentrated in these regions. The interior of the country is very sparsely settled, and few industries are located there. One of the main ones is the wood industry, delivering raw materials but also all kinds of finished products (furniture).

As a result, the regional population structure follows very clearly the regional distribution of the economic centres of the country. There is a very clear north–south gradient, overlain by an additional east–west gradient. In 1940 more than 1.1 million out of 3.9 million people lived in the two southern provinces around Helsinki and Turku (Uudenman and Turun Porin). If the province of Hämeen is added, then 40% of the Finnish population lived in these three provinces in 1940 (cf. also Caramani, Flora, and Quick 1998). All the interior provinces and the northern tundra regions are very sparsely populated.

POPULATION GROWTH

Industrialization and urbanization came late to Finland, and the welfare state was also late to develop. During the whole nineteenth and the first half of the twentieth century it remained an essentially rural country, the majority of the population living in small villages and towns. There is virtually only one major city, Helsinki; the next major urbanized region is Turku where the sea routes to Sweden and the European continent begin.

Population growth was high when compared with other European countries in the nineteenth century (Figure SF.1). But despite the large territory of the country, the available resources were not sufficient to support the growing number of people, resulting in high emigration, first to Sweden and from Sweden mainly to North America.

Population density in 1875 was very low compared with the very high population density in Western Europe already in the Middle Ages. The population in Finland increased slowly over a period of 75 years and only doubled its size from 1875 to 1950. Population density rose from 5.17 to 13.20 inhabitants per square kilometre, but this disproportional increase is due to territorial losses during World War II. From 1940 to 1950 nearly 50,000 square kilometres had to be ceded to the Soviet Union.

THE FIRST DEMOGRAPHIC TRANSITION

Finland's demographic transition is of the Nordic type, although it shows remarkable peculiarities. Commonalities with the other Nordic countries Sweden, Norway, and Denmark are the early onset of the decline in mortality and the rather low levels of mortality and fertility, together leading to a rather high natural population growth (Figure SF.2).

Differences to the other Nordic countries can be seen mainly in the higher mortality rate, in line with Finland's higher infant mortality rate compared with the other Nordic countries. A consequence of this pattern was a lower natural population growth than in Sweden and especially in Norway where the natural population surplus was very high.

It can be said that the demographic transition set in during the 1870s when both the death and birth rate started to decline continuously. The period from the 1870s to the onset of World War I was a time of large natural population growth in Finland without major demographic crises. There was a relatively large population surplus in the inter-war period and again after World War II with a clear pattern of a 'second demographic transition'.

Unlike for example Sweden, from the 1850s Finland was characterized by strong demographic crises. Still in the second half of the nineteenth century Finland experienced health crises, with an epidemic in the late 1850s (world economic crisis of the 1850s?, cf. Rosenberg, 1974) and late 1860s. There was another demographic shock in the early 1890s with a declining birth rate and rising death rate. The death rate rose once more around 1900 probably due to an epidemic. As a frontier country, Finland, unlike Sweden, was involved in both world wars, and the effects of its involvement were very dramatic. During World War I there was a strong postponement and loss of births, and the death rate also rose strongly. Finland was obviously heavily involved in the economic crisis of the 1930s when the birth rate suddenly declined; it rose again towards the end of the 1930s and during the war years of the 1940s. Although the birth rate did not decline during World War II as it had in World War I, the number of deaths increased dramatically during this period.

After World War II the birth rate rose strongly, as couples began having children postponed during the war years. The birth rate exploded, while the death rate declined, leading to a huge baby boom lasting until 1970. Since the 1970s there seems to be a new equilibrium between births and deaths with a small positive natural population growth (Lutz, 1987; Chesnais, 1992).

Demographic trends prior to 1850 have been studied by Lutz (1987). His study can be perceived as an external contribution to the Princeton European Fertility Project. The demographic transition can be studied on the basis of annual birth and death

Figure SF.1 Population growth and net migration 1850-1945

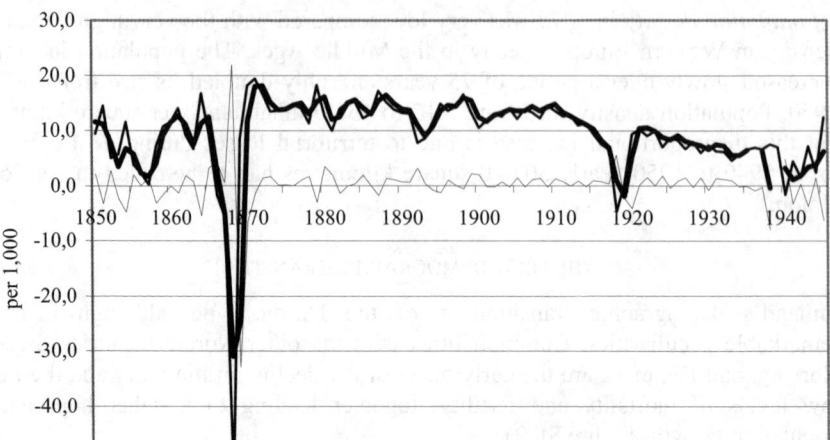

Figure SF.2 First demographic transition 1850-1945

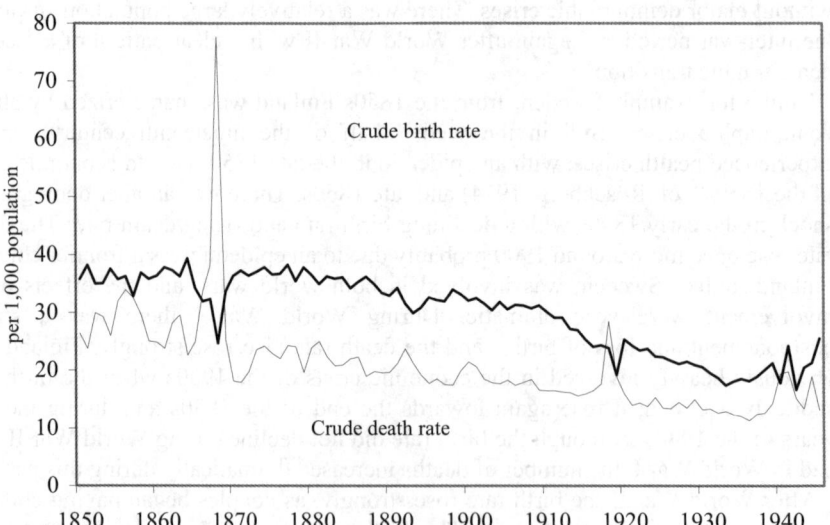

figures since 1722. Finland is unique in that there was already a fertility decline—as in France—before the secular decline at the end of the nineteenth century. Fertility declined from 1776 to 1884 and stagnated until 1900. This fertility decline was caused by a rise in the age at marriage and a rise of the proportion remaining single. Thus, in Finland at the end of the eighteenth century the Western European marriage pattern replaced the Eastern European marriage pattern typical of countries such as Poland and Hungary.

Strong regional variations in fertility existed in Finland until the 1970s, when the rates converged at a very low level. In the last 150 years, the northern provinces had much higher fertility than the southern and western provinces (Lutz, 1987: 37). In addition to this regional variation, there were also urban–rural cleavages: fertility in towns and urban areas was much lower than in villages and rural areas. If fertility in southern urban areas is compared with fertility in rural areas in central Finland, there is not only a large difference in fertility level, but also a rising divergence between these areas until the 1930s, followed by convergence in the subsequent decades. Fertility decline and family planning in Finland obviously spread slowly throughout the country from some pioneering regions and social strata, thus creating the divergence–convergence pattern of diffusion processes (Lutz, 1987: 43).

MORTALITY AND LIFE EXPECTANCY

The infant mortality rate is defined as deaths of children aged under one year per 1,000 live births. Finland belongs to the group of countries with the lowest infant mortality, i.e. the Nordic countries (Figure SF.3). Infant mortality was rather low already in 1900. But within this group of countries, infant mortality was among the highest. In this respect Finland was a latecomer, as infant mortality was higher than for example in Sweden still in the inter-war period (Masuy-Stroobant, 1997).

Infant mortality figures for Finland are available since the introduction of population registration in 1751. During the second half of the eighteenth century the level of infant mortality was very high with over 200 deaths per 1,000 live births. But, interestingly, already since that time there was a declining trend of the logistic curve, accelerating strongly after the decisive turning point of 1860–70 (Lutz, 1987, 65–8, time series data 115–7).

Lutz (1987) emphasizes that there have been large regional variations in infant mortality, which partly coincided with the practice of breastfeeding. Already in the eighteenth century governments were aware of the high infant mortality and tried to reduce it, given the very small Finnish population at that time and the very low population density (cf. Pitkänen, 1983).

Life expectancy at birth—in contrast to other Nordic countries—was very low during the nineteenth and the first half of the twentieth century (Figure SF.4) and remained on a low level also after 1945, as was already apparent from the high infant mortality. Male life expectancy at the age of 30 was 34.3 years in 1881/90 and by 1941/45 had increased only by one year. Male life expectancy at the age of 60 during the same period also increased only slowly from 13.2 years to 13.8 years. Women's life expectancy made much greater progress. Female infants had a life expectancy of 44.2 years in 1881/90, increasing to 61.1 in 1941/45. Women's life expectancies increased also at higher ages: 30-year-old women gained five years during the period (from 36 to 41 years) and 60-year-old women gained 2.3 years (from 14.3 to 16.6 years). From the 1880s to the 1930s the divergence between the

Figure SF.3 Infant mortality 1866-1945

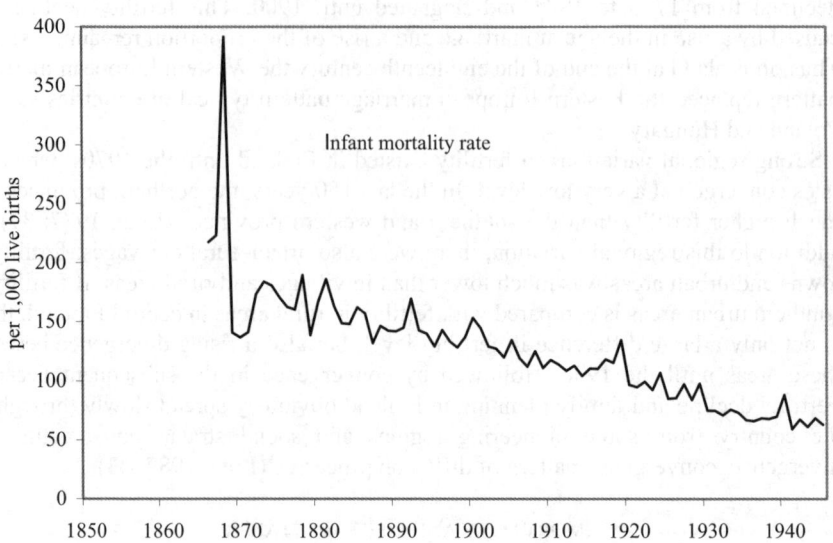

Figure SF.4 Life expectancy 1881/90-1941/45

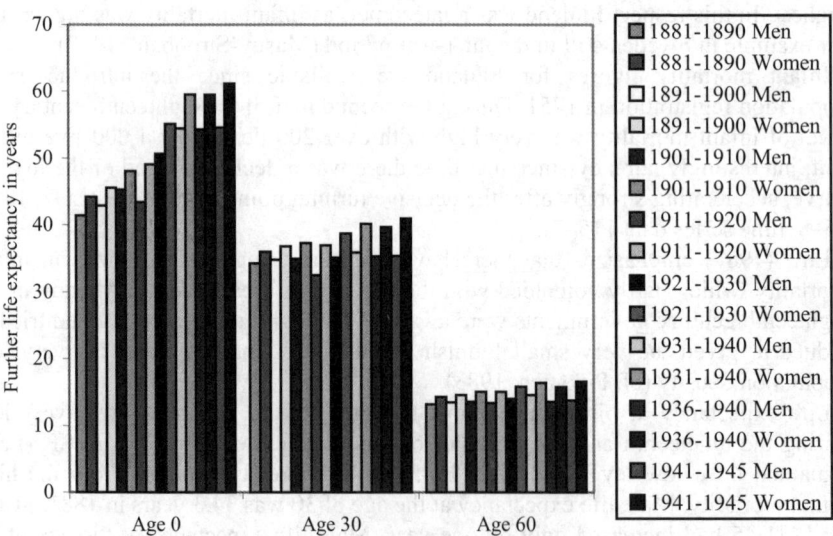

sexes in life expectancy continued to increase for all ages. The divergence in life expectancy between the sexes grew most strongly during both world wars.

FERTILITY AND LEGITIMACY

Structurally, illegitimate fertility in Finland was below the European average until the most recent decades. It was only in the last two decades that a substantial increase over the European level set in (Figure SF.5).

Until World War I illegitimate fertility in Finland was quite low, lower than in the three Scandinavian states Sweden, Norway, and Denmark. It was still below the European average during the inter-war period, but rose strongly during World War II and in the immediate post-war years (until the early 1950s). It was again lower than in Europe during the 1960s and 1970s. Since the mid-1970s there has been a fundamental change in demographic behaviour: childbirth without marriage has become a widespread behavioural pattern.

The other side of the coin is legitimate fertility, but it has not automatically been lower when illegitimate fertility is low. In the case of Finland, legitimate fertility was structurally above the European average during the last 150 years. Only in the last decades has legitimate fertility declined in favour of births out of wedlock. The ratio of illegitimate births to legitimate births in Finland was constantly lower than the European average until the 1970s, when this relationship changed slightly.

The causes of the Finnish pattern of fertility with a comparatively low weight of non-marital fertility must be seen in the rather low age at first marriage, the relatively high marriage rates and the lower celibacy rates, and the lower divorce rate during most of the 100 years from 1850–1950. There are therefore important demographic differences to the Scandinavian countries, which allows Finland only partly to be clustered with the Nordic group. Finland must be seen in some demographic respects as an intermediary between the Western and the Eastern European marriage patterns and demographic regimes.

MARRIAGE AND DIVORCE

Finland belongs to the region of Europe with the Western European marriage pattern of late age at marriage and a high celibacy rate. Finland is in this respect very similar to other Nordic countries like Sweden, Norway, and Denmark; at the same time it is characterized by specific developments and structures.

First, concerning age at marriage, Finland belongs to the group made up of the Nordic countries and the British Isles. At the end of the nineteenth century, women's age at first marriage was lower than in Sweden, Norway, and Denmark, and at a level similar to England and Wales. In other words, the proportion of females in the age group from 20–24 was rather high and higher than in the neighbouring Nordic countries. The development of age at marriage in Finland during the first half of the twentieth century deviates from the other countries of this group because women's age at marriage rose from the 1920s to the 1940s, and the proportion of those married fell dramatically. The inter-war period was therefore obviously a time of diminishing marriage chances and high economic obstacles to starting a family (marriage restrictions). It was only after World War II that the marriage boom set in with very low age at marriage, a very high proportion of people married at young ages (20–24), and a universalization of marriage. This development towards universal

Figure SF.5 Fertility and legitimacy 1865-1939

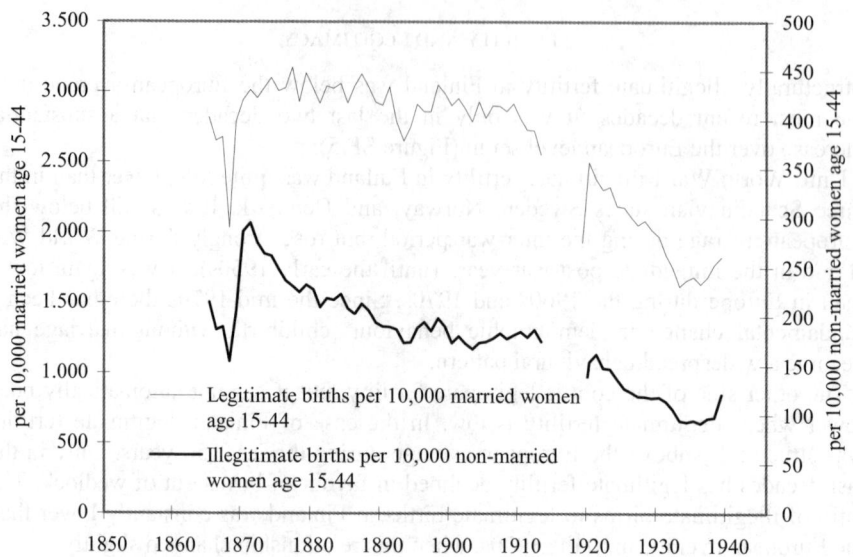

Figure SF.6 Marriages and divorces 1865-1939

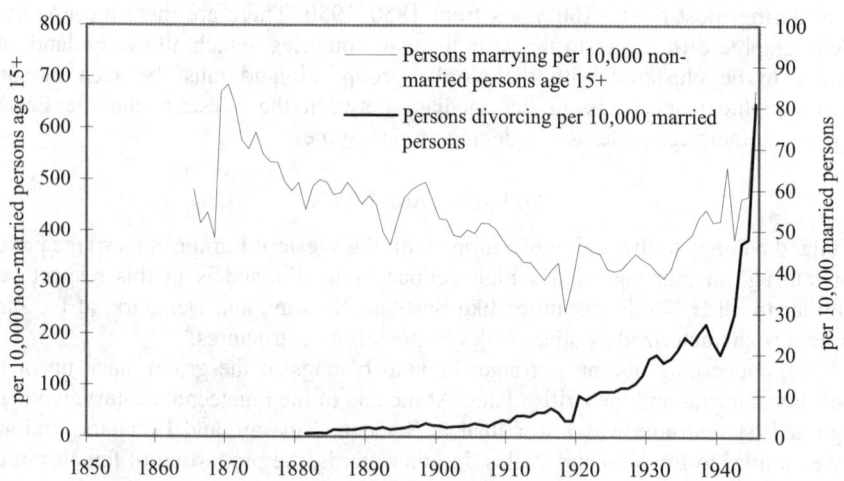

marriage however came later in Finland than in England and Wales or Denmark, for example. This pattern of marriage crisis during the inter-war period and universal marriage afterwards is also visible for men. The curve of the proportion of men married at age 20–24 behaves very similar to the curve of women.

This modernization of nuptiality lasted until the 1970s. Since the 1980s a kind of *postmodern* nuptiality pattern has emerged: marriage is now democratized and available to everyone, but young people have voluntarily returned to the older historical pattern of postponing marriage until later ages (late 20s or the 30s) or not marrying at all. This process has been called the 'deinstitutionalization' of marriage.

Marriage intensity is another aspect of marriage behaviour and can be measured by the *marriage rate* and the *celibacy rate*. 'Intensity' means the availability of marriage, but at the same time the urgent need to remarry after widowhood ('remarriage need', Michael Mitterauer). A third component can be seen in the universality of marriage in the population. The marriage rate includes all marriages of previously unmarried people of age 15 and over.

The Finnish marriage rate (Figure SF.6) is similar to the other Nordic rates in that it was rather low and below the European average. But what is interesting in the case of Finland is the decline of the marriage rate from approximately 1900 to 1940 to well under the European average. This again is in line with the worsening situation with respect to age at marriage and proportion married at age 20–24 and underlines the thesis of a severe national economic crisis in the first half of the twentieth century. After World War II the marriage rate rose steeply, as did fertility and the proportion married (while age at marriage declined), thus illustrating once more the marriage and baby boom of the 1950s and 1960s. Since the 1970s the Finnish marriage rate has declined more strongly than the European one, indicating a pioneering development towards a 'postmodern' marriage behaviour (or the deinstitutionalization of marriage).

The *celibacy rate* (proportion of women never married aged 45–54) of Finnish women clearly puts Finland into the country group with the highest celibacy rates. While the overall development of the celibacy rate follows the other countries in this group, Finland deviates very strongly during the inter-war period. While in most Northern European countries there was only a minor increase (or even a stagnation) of the celibacy rate until the 1940s, in Finland this proportion increased dramatically from roughly 30% of all women in 1910 to over 40% in 1940. Finland was singular in this regard, which again points to the severe economic and demographic crisis of the country during the inter-war period.

Finland participates in the general logistic increase of *divorces* and the divorce rate since the second half of the nineteenth century (Figure SF.6). While data on divorces are already available since the 1880s, legal separation data have been published only since the 1950s. There is a gap in Finnish divorce statistics from 1913 to 1933, when no data were published.

Due to the predominance of agriculture in the nineteenth century, the divorce rate was low in Finland and lower than the European average. This low divorce rate lasted until the start of World War I, when it increased only slightly. In 1934, when data on the divorce rate resume, the Finnish level was above the European level. In the late 1930s the Finnish divorce rate increased at a faster pace than the European rate, perhaps a sign of the economic and demographic crisis of the inter-war period, which we have noted for other demographic developments (see above). While the divorce rate declined during World War II, there was a huge upswing in the number of divorces after 1943 and especially in the years 1945–46, when the divorce rate was more than three times higher than shortly before the war.

With the end of World War II Finland developed rapidly into an industrialized and urbanized welfare state. Rural–urban migration was very high as was overall social mobility. Since 1945 the Finnish divorce rate has constantly been higher than the European level. The country has therefore moved in the same direction as its Nordic neighbours. The growth of the divorce rate was very high during the 1970s, followed by stagnation in the 1980s. A new rise in the divorce rate occurred in the late 1980s and continued during the 1990s. The post-war period seems to be largely influenced by welfare-state development and its demographic consequences: a deinstitutionalization of marriage, high social security benefits enabling people to divorce and remarry, social services for young children, income maintenance, etc.

AGE, SEX, AND CIVIL STATUS

Appendix Figure SF.8 shows the development in the age structure of the Finnish population combined with sex and marital status from 1880 to 1940. The Finnish age structure reveals a clear pyramidal pattern until World War I with a strong concave shape at the bottom. Thus, fertility was rather high, leading to a large age group of 0–4-year-olds. But this high fertility was soon reduced by high infant mortality, causing much smaller proportions for the age groups 5–9 and 10–15. The bad harvests of the 1860s are clearly visible in the Finnish age structure: in 1880 the age group of 10–14 years was much smaller, caused by loss of births and high infant mortality during the 1860s. This small age cohort is visible in all later age structures. Unlike those of other countries, the Finnish age structures do not show any reduction of the proportion of the lowest age group until 1910, the last census before the war. World War I was decisive in reducing fertility in Finland for the first time. But the loss of births was only moderate when compared to the continental countries, and the birth rate recovered greatly in the 1920s. By 1930 the Finnish age structure had become bell-shaped, but the lowest age groups remained stable in size until 1940.

Age at marriage and celibacy were high in Finland during the nineteenth century. Men married later than women, but the proportion of men in the upper age groups was higher because of widespread widowhood. This pattern did not change until 1910. During the inter-war period, it was obviously more difficult to marry than before: the proportions married at early ages became smaller and the proportions remaining unmarried at higher ages increased.

FAMILY AND HOUSEHOLD STRUCTURES

There are few population censuses in Finland covering the field of household statistics. Households were published in 1865, and again from 1880 and 1890 to 1900. There is a gap until the first census after World War II in 1950.

The few materials available reveal some Finnish peculiarities. Households were not very large in Finland. The proportion of households with five or more persons was in a middle field of most Western European countries with approximately 43% in 1880. Interestingly, the proportion of single-person households was high already from 1880–1900 with 18% in 1880 and 21% in 1900.

The twenty-year span from 1880 to 1900 shows the normal developments of households during the demographic transition. There was a shift from large to small households, the stronger the smaller the households. A rather strong increase was for the single-person households. Mean household size declined significantly during this short time: the mean size of all households declined from 4.54 to 4.32 persons per household. Nevertheless, the mean size of family households was much larger and amounted to 5.09 persons per family household.

When compared with data from 1950, it becomes clear that households continued to shrink. The percentage of the population living in single-person households increased further. Households with five or more persons counted now only for 28.31% of all households (against 43% in 1880).

Thus, households in Finland on the average were not as large as in other Nordic countries; this may be due to the demographic regime lying to some degree between the Eastern and Western European marriage patterns.

Obviously, the demarcation line between the two behavioural patterns went through Finnish territory. Thus, in the province of Vyborg in 1865, households were very much larger than in the other Finnish provinces. This would indicate that this eastern province was governed by a different demographic regime than western Finland (after World War II Vyborg was returned to the Soviet Union).

In addition, already in 1865 there was a clear difference between the size of households in towns and the country, with towns having much smaller households than the country (villages).

THE NATIONAL SYSTEM OF DEMOGRAPHIC STATISTICS

Population Structure

As in all the Nordic countries, population statistics in Finland extend back until the mid-eighteenth century. Statistics were introduced by the Swedish administration and are very similar in the eighteenth and nineteenth century for Sweden and Finland. Statistics were mainly taken from the parish registers, but soon independent population censuses were conducted. In the nineteenth century censuses were taken in 1805, 1810, 1820, 1825, 1830, 1840, 1845, 1850, 1855, 1860, and 1865 (see Appendix Table SF.7 for a continuation). Thus, under Russian administration the statistical system remained more or less the Swedish system.

The first combination of the population by age, sex, and marital status was introduced with the 1880 census. In the earlier censuses of 1865 and 1875 age and marital status are given separately and not combined. The marital status of persons 15 years and older is given in a summary figure.

A historical account of the history of population statistics since 1751 is given in Tilastollinen päätoimisto (1870), pp. 5ff. It is continued up to 1890 by Suomenmaan Virallinen Tilasto (1899).

Vital Statistics

Vital statistics also have a long tradition in Finland due to the Swedish administration. Annual time series of the most important demographic variables such as births (by legitimacy), deaths, and marriages are available since 1750.

Stillbirths are available since 1861, infant mortality since 1866, and divorces since 1881.

A historical account of population statistics since 1751 is given in Tilastollinen päätoimisto (1870), pp. 5ff. It is continued until 1890 by Suomenmaan Virallinen Tilasto (1899, 1902, 1909). The most recent historical demographic analysis is Nieminen (1999).

Households and Families

Data on households (*hushåll* in Swedish) were at least collected since the census of 1865, but household statistics remained underdeveloped until the 1950s. Only households by size have been published, but no further disaggregations, such as composition or the profession of the household head.

Households by size were already published by the census of 1865 and repeated in the censuses of 1880, 1890, and 1900. Households were given from 1 to 15 and more members. In 1875 no household figures were published at all. In 1910, 1920, 1930, and 1940 households were collected through a housing census and no special household statistics were kept.

The *definition of a household* (*talouskunta* (Finnish), *hushåll* (Swedish)) was that of the housekeeping-unit concept: a household consisted of those persons who shared meals and lived together (Tilastollinen päätoimisto, 1958: 8f.). Institutional households were only separated in the census of 1900, whereas in 1880 and 1890 all households were classified by size. In the census of 1865 there were some general remarks on households, when data on households were published for the first time:

Den naturligaste grupperingen af befolkningen är den i *familjer* eller *hushåll* (originally spaced). En särskild afdelning är äfven haråt inrymd i tabellverket; ehuru så tillvida bristfällig, att den icke upptager såsom hushåll ensamt boende personer, hvilka bilda egna matlag för sig, eller med andra ord hushåll bestående af en person, utan endast de hushåll, som bestååf två eller flere personer. För öfrigt synes svårigheten att ens få reda på antalet af dessa sistnämda, ha föranledt presterskapet i några församlingar att i sina folkmängdstabeller elldeles utelemna berörde kolumner. Så har skett i 1865 års folkmängdstabeller från helsingfors stads evangeliskt-lutherska svenska och finska församling samt från landsförsamlingarna i Wiborgs prosteri. Antalet hushåll i nyssnämnde, äfvensom i landets samtliga grekisk-ryska församlingar ingår derföre icke i nedanstående tabells uppgifter, som i öfrigt—på sagde undantag när—gälla hela Finland (Tilastollinen päätoimisto, 1870: 22f).

Family statistics in the sense of fertility of married women were not collected during the period under consideration.

Remarks (also see introductory Table 6.1)

For Finland the marital status for the census of 1865 is only available for the age groups 0–14 and 15. Estimates of the values for the variables v18, v19, and v20 could be made by using these data. For the variables v16–v17 and v21 the relative values from the census of 1880 have been used to estimate the absolute figures for 1865. It is assumed that the proportion of these relations has not changed.

BOUNDARY CHANGES

Finland was a province of Sweden until 1811, when it was ceded to the Russian empire. In 1809, Finland acquired the Tornie River basin, in 1811 the province of Vyborg, and in 1820 the harbour of Petsano on the north coast. When in 1917 Finland became an independent state, its territorial status remained the same as under Russian government, thus the territory of Finland was much larger then than it is today. It embraced south-east Karelia with the city of Vyborg as well as the port of Petsano. Finland and Sweden came to an agreement on the Åland Islands in the Gulf of Bothnia between the two countries: they were given to Finland in 1921 and were neutral from 1921 to 1935. This territorial situation remained unchanged until World War II. When Finland was attacked by Soviet forces in 1939, an armistice could only be obtained by transferring Vyborg and its surroundings and the northern part of Karelia (Petsano) to the Soviet Union. This territorial situation was confirmed after the end of World War II (for regional organization see the documentation by Quick (1994) and Caramani, Flora, Kraus, and Quick (1998)).

APPENDIX TABLES AND FIGURES

APPENDIX TABLE SF.1 Population structure at census dates 1865–1940

Census number	Census date	Census population			Marital status				Age group		
		Total	Male	Female	Single	Married	Widowed	Divorced	0–14	15–64	65+
		Absolute									
1	31 XII 1865	1,803,084	878,943	924,141	1,079,535	615,023	108,526	..	630,678	1,172,406[1]	..
2	1 X 1880	2,060,782	1,008,243	1,052,539	1,236,404	700,754	120,482	..	712,030	1,264,271	84,481
3	31 XII 1890	2,380,140	1,171,541	1,208,599	1,444,663	803,059	132,418	..	851,462	1,410,521	118,157
4	31 XII 1900	2,712,562	1,342,082	1,370,480	1,656,569	907,265	147,343	1,385	936,936	1,633,615	142,011
5	7 XII 1910	3,115,247	1,546,744	1,568,503	1,933,637	1,009,602	169,548	2,460	1,067,014	1,871,206	177,027
6	8 XII 1920	3,364,807	1,660,230	1,704,577	2,130,023	1,029,827	200,178	4,779	1,066,545	2,094,453	203,809
7	27 XI 1930	3,667,067	1,809,068	1,857,999	2,274,747	1,159,940	221,357	11,023	1,027,140	2,402,396	237,531
8	31 XII 1940	3,887,217	1,902,303	1,984,914	2,277,939	1,343,597	243,573	22,108	998,254	2,613,084	275,879
		Per cent									
1	31 XII 1865	100.00	48.75	51.25	59.87	34.11	6.02	..	34.98	65.02[1]	..
2	1 X 1880	100.00	48.93	51.07	60.00	34.00	5.85	..	34.55	61.35	4.10
3	31 XII 1890	100.00	49.22	50.78	60.70	33.74	5.56	..	35.77	59.26	4.96
4	31 XII 1900	100.00	49.48	50.52	61.07	33.45	5.43	0.05	34.54	60.22	5.24
5	7 XII 1910	100.00	49.65	50.35	62.07	32.41	5.44	0.08	34.25	60.07	5.68
6	8 XII 1920	100.00	49.34	50.66	63.30	30.61	5.95	0.14	31.70	62.25	6.06
7	27 XI 1930	100.00	49.33	50.67	62.03	31.63	6.04	0.30	28.01	65.51	6.48
8	31 XII 1940	100.00	48.94	51.06	58.60	34.56	6.27	0.57	25.68	67.22	7.10

Note: [1] 15+.

APPENDIX TABLE SF.2 Census population by region 1875–1940 (per cent)

Län[1]	1875	1880	1890[2]	1900	1910	1920	1930	1940
Nylands / Uudenman	9.62	9.85	10.04	10.99	12.07	13.26	13.85	15.49
Åbo-Björneborgs /	16.68	16.74	16.60	16.48	16.02	14.74	14.24	13.79
Turun Porin								
Åland / Ahvenanmaab[3]	–	–	–	–	–	0.80	0.74	0.72
Tavastehus / Hämeen	10.56	10.72	10.84	11.10	10.98	10.73	10.61	10.81
Viborgs / Viipurin	15.05	14.65	14.79	15.56	16.73	16.59	16.99	16.16
(Kymen / Kymmene)[4]								
St. Michels / Mikkelin	8.52	8.10	7.61	6.97	6.39	6.06	5.70	5.25
Kuopio / Kuopion	12.44	12.42	12.23	11.58	10.72	10.58	10.39	10.26
Vasa / Vaasan	16.94	17.37	17.52	16.96	16.53	16.29	15.90	15.44
Uleåborgs / Oulun	10.14	10.09	10.38	10.36	10.53	10.97	11.59	8.41
Lapplands / Lapind[5]	–	–	–	–	–	–	–	3.70
TOTAL	100.00	100.00	100.00	100.00	100.00	100.00	100.00	100.00

Notes: [1] Since 1920 the region names are given in Swedish and Finnish. [2] From 1890 on only the land area (without water surfaces) was considered. The figures are therefore smaller than 1875–1880. [3] 13 VII 1918: Åland (Ahvenanmaa) was separated from Åbo och Björneborgs (Turun Porin). [4] Kymen is the remainder of Viborgs (rest of area was lost to the USSR). [5] 1 I 1938: Lapplands (Lapin) was separated from Uleåborgs (Oulun).

APPENDIX TABLE SF.3 Population density by region 1875–1940 (inhabitants per sq. km.)

Län[1]	1875	1880	1890[a]	1900	1910	1920	1930	1940
Nylands / Uudenman	16	17	21	27	33	39	45	52
Åbo-Björneborgs /	13	14	17	19	21	23	24	24
Turun Porin								
Åland / Ahvenanmaab[2]	–	–	–	–	–	19	19	19
Tavastehus / Hämeen	9	10	14	17	20	21	22	23
Viborgs / Viipurin	8	8	11	13	17	18	20	20
(Kymen / Kymmene)[3]								
St. Michels / Mikkelin	7	7	10	11	12	12	13	12
Kuopio / Kuopion	5	6	8	9	9	10	11	11
Vasa / Vaasan	8	9	11	12	13	14	15	15
Uleåborgs / Oulun	1	1	2	2	2	2	3	6
Lapplands / Lapind[4]	–	–	–	–	–	–	–	1
TOTAL	5	6	7	8	9	10	11	11

Note: See Appendix Table SF.2.

APPENDIX TABLE SF.4 Demographic developments 1850–1945 (absolute figures and rates)

Year	Mid-year population	Natural population growth rate	Population growth rate	Net migration rate	Crude birth rate	Legitimate births per 10,000 married women age 15–44	Illegitimate births per 10,000 unmarried women age 15–44	Illeg. births per 100 leg. births
1850	1,628,883	9.4	11.6	2.1	35.8	..	..	7.6
1851	1,647,262	14.5	11.2	-3.3	38.2	..	..	7.4
1852	1,660,200	5.0	7.8	2.8	35.0	..	..	8.3
1853	1,665,990	5.7	3.5	-2.3	35.1	..	..	7.8
1854	1,677,339	11.6	6.8	-4.8	37.5	..	..	7.5
1855	1,687,096	3.8	5.8	2.0	35.8	..	..	7.8
1856	1,690,994	2.3	2.3	0.0	36.3	..	..	7.7
1857	1,693,865	0.3	1.7	1.4	32.8	..	..	7.4
1858	1,700,610	7.2	4.0	-3.2	36.9	..	..	6.7
1859	1,716,365	10.8	9.2	-1.6	35.8	..	..	7.5
1860	1,736,341	11.6	11.5	-0.1	36.4	..	..	7.6
1861	1,758,684	14.0	12.7	-1.3	37.8	..	..	7.8
1862	1,778,418	9.2	11.1	1.9	37.3	..	..	7.4
1863	1,791,807	6.7	7.5	0.8	36.3	..	..	7.5
1864	1,812,201	16.7	11.3	-5.5	39.3	..	..	7.5
1865	1,835,113	9.3	12.5	3.2	34.2	2,819	215	8.0
1866	1,840,375	-1.7	2.9	4.5	32.0	2,653	187	7.3
1867	1,830,822	-5.8	-5.2	0.6	32.3	2,680	190	7.4
1868	1,775,838	-52.9	-31.0	21.9	24.6	2,033	155	7.9
1869	1,733,549	8.5	-24.4	-32.9	33.7	2,787	206	7.7
1870	1,754,164	18.2	11.8	-6.4	36.3	2,940	286	10.2
1871	1,786,307	19.4	18.0	-1.4	37.3	3,013	295	10.2
1872	1,819,228	16.7	18.1	1.4	36.4	2,956	275	9.7
1873	1,847,293	13.5	15.2	1.7	37.0	3,028	264	9.1
1874	1,873,046	13.7	13.7	0.1	37.8	3,099	262	8.8
1875	1,899,382	13.7	13.9	0.1	36.6	3,006	248	8.6
1876	1,927,651	14.7	14.7	0.0	36.7	3,027	237	8.2
1877	1,957,041	14.0	15.0	1.0	38.2	3,173	231	7.6
1878	1,983,002	11.4	13.1	1.7	35.4	2,929	225	8.0
1879	2,013,621	18.2	15.2	-3.0	37.8	3,134	232	7.7
1880	2,046,726	12.7	16.2	3.5	36.5	3,025	228	7.9
1881	2,071,712	10.0	12.1	2.1	35.0	2,917	210	7.5
1882	2,097,972	13.9	12.5	-1.4	36.3	3,040	219	7.5
1883	2,129,848	15.1	15.0	-0.1	35.9	3,024	217	7.5
1884	2,163,471	15.2	15.5	0.3	36.1	3,060	223	7.6
1885	2,194,532	12.2	14.2	1.9	34.2	2,920	209	7.5
1886	2,223,545	13.1	13.0	0.0	35.3	3,042	203	7.0
1887	2,258,356	17.2	15.4	-1.8	36.2	3,128	213	7.1
1888	2,296,159	15.1	16.5	1.3	34.9	3,035	207	7.1
1889	2,330,940	13.8	14.9	1.1	33.4	2,926	194	6.9
1890	2,363,921	13.3	14.0	0.7	32.9	2,903	190	6.8
1891	2,396,814	13.1	13.7	0.6	34.3	3,035	190	6.6
1892	2,423,580	7.8	11.0	3.2	31.5	2,788	187	7.1
1893	2,445,668	8.6	9.0	0.4	29.9	2,650	173	7.0
1894	2,472,341	11.6	10.8	-0.8	30.8	2,748	174	6.8
1895	2,506,452	14.9	13.6	-1.3	32.6	2,912	189	7.0
1896	2,543,583	13.6	14.6	1.0	32.1	2,860	194	7.4
1897	2,580,820	14.4	14.4	0.1	31.9	2,858	185	7.1

continued

APPENDIX TABLE SF.4 Demographic developments 1850–1945 (absolute figures and rates)

Crude death rate	Infant mortality rate	Stillbirth rate	Infant mortality and stillbirth rate	Crude marriage rate	Persons marrying per 10,000 unmarried persons age 15+	Persons marrying per 10,000 unmarried persons age 15–49	Crude divorce rate	Divorces per 100 marriages	Divorces per 10,000 married persons	Year
26.3	..	..	..	8.1	..	..	..	..	..	1850
23.7	..	..	..	8.3	..	..	..	..	..	1851
30.0	..	..	..	7.2	..	..	..	..	..	1852
29.3	..	..	..	7.4	..	..	..	..	..	1853
25.9	..	..	..	7.8	..	..	..	..	..	1854
32.0	..	..	..	7.9	..	..	..	..	..	1855
34.0	..	..	..	7.9	..	..	..	..	..	1856
32.6	..	..	..	7.1	..	..	..	..	..	1857
29.7	..	..	..	7.7	..	..	..	..	..	1858
25.0	..	..	..	8.0	..	..	..	..	..	1859
24.8	..	..	..	8.9	..	..	..	..	..	1860
23.8	..	28.5	..	8.6	..	..	..	..	..	1861
28.1	..	27.4	..	7.9	..	..	..	..	..	1862
29.6	..	27.9	..	7.4	..	..	..	..	..	1863
22.6	..	26.9	..	7.8	..	..	..	..	..	1864
24.9	..	29.7	..	7.0	482	557	..	..	..	1865
33.6	217.6	33.3	250.9	6.1	415	483	..	..	..	1866
38.1	223.4	35.0	258.4	6.4	437	511	..	..	..	1867
77.6	391.7	43.1	434.8	5.7	386	455	..	..	..	1868
25.2	140.8	30.0	170.8	9.9	670	793	..	..	..	1869
18.2	136.6	29.9	166.5	10.2	685	815	..	..	..	1870
17.9	141.1	29.1	170.2	9.7	647	773	..	..	..	1871
19.7	173.4	30.2	203.6	8.7	576	693	..	..	..	1872
23.6	183.9	29.7	213.6	8.5	559	675	..	..	..	1873
24.1	180.8	30.3	211.1	9.0	591	718	..	..	..	1874
22.9	170.8	29.9	200.7	8.4	549	670	..	..	..	1875
22.0	162.6	29.4	192.0	8.2	534	654	..	..	..	1876
24.2	160.5	26.6	187.2	8.2	534	657	..	..	..	1877
24.1	189.6	29.4	219.0	7.7	496	614	..	..	..	1878
19.6	138.4	28.7	167.2	7.4	478	594	..	..	..	1879
23.9	166.9	28.9	195.8	7.7	494	616	..	..	..	1880
25.0	186.3	28.1	214.4	6.9	441	550	0.0	0.2	0.8	1881
22.3	163.8	28.8	192.6	7.6	487	608	0.0	0.2	0.8	1882
20.8	148.7	28.4	177.1	7.8	500	624	0.0	0.2	0.9	1883
20.9	148.2	29.0	177.1	7.7	495	618	0.0	0.2	0.8	1884
22.0	162.3	28.8	191.0	7.3	471	589	0.0	0.4	1.7	1885
22.3	157.1	28.0	185.1	7.3	474	593	0.0	0.4	1.6	1886
19.0	131.8	29.1	160.9	7.6	495	619	0.0	0.4	1.7	1887
19.8	146.3	29.5	175.8	7.3	476	595	0.0	0.4	1.7	1888
19.6	142.4	29.3	171.7	6.9	452	565	0.0	0.5	2.1	1889
19.7	141.7	27.4	169.1	7.1	469	587	0.0	0.5	2.3	1890
21.2	..	27.4	..	6.9	451	565	0.0	0.5	1.9	1891
23.7	..	27.5	..	6.1	397	497	0.0	0.6	2.4	1892
21.2	..	29.0	..	5.8	372	466	0.0	0.5	1.7	1893
19.2	..	27.7	..	6.5	419	524	0.0	0.5	1.9	1894
17.7	..	27.2	..	7.3	466	583	0.0	0.5	2.2	1895
18.5	..	27.3	..	7.5	481	601	0.0	0.6	2.6	1896
17.5	..	27.2	..	7.7	489	611	0.0	0.5	2.5	1897

continued

APPENDIX TABLE SF.4 Demographic developments 1850–1945 (continued)

Year	Mid-year population	Natural population growth rate	Population growth rate	Net migration rate	Crude birth rate	Legitimate births per 10,000 married women age 15–44	Illegitimate births per 10,000 unmarried women age 15–44	Illeg. births per 100 leg. births
1898	2,622,679	16,5	16.0	-0.6	34,0	3.050	198	7,2
1899	2,663,871	13,3	15.5	2.2	33,2	2.990	190	7,1
1900	2,697,490	10,5	12.5	1.9	32,0	2.904	173	6,7
1901	2,729,419	11,9	11.7	-0.2	32,5	2.955	180	6,9
1902	2,764,971	13,1	12.9	-0.2	31,5	2.881	173	6,9
1903	2,801,968	12,5	13.2	0.7	30,4	2.788	167	6,9
1904	2,841,303	14,1	13.8	-0.2	31,8	2.930	174	6,9
1905	2,880,522	12,2	13.6	1.4	30,5	2.814	175	7,3
1906	2,920,255	13,9	13.6	-0.3	31,3	2.901	178	7,3
1907	2,962,937	13,3	14.4	1.1	31,2	2.899	183	7,5
1908	3,003,758	12,3	13.6	1.3	30,7	2.864	177	7,4
1909	3,047,343	14,6	14.3	-0.3	31,2	2.917	181	7,5
1910	3,093,219	13,6	14.8	1.3	30,1	2.812	185	8,0
1911	3,135,074	12,6	13.4	0.7	29,1	2.732	179	8,0
1912	3,175,387	12,8	12.7	-0.1	29,1	2.726	187	8,5
1913	3,213,500	11,0	11.9	0.9	27,2	2.556	175	8,5
1914	3,249,741	11,4	11.2	-0.2	26,9	..	..	8,5
1915	3,283,795	9,4	10.4	0.9	25,3	..	..	8,7
1916	3,311,323	7,6	8.3	0.7	24,1	..	..	8,6
1917	3,334,511	6,7	7.0	0.3	24,3	..	..	8,7
1918	3,337,643	-4,7	0.9	5.6	23,8	..	..	9,6
1919	3,331,201	0,3	-1.9	-2.2	19,2	1.930	94	7,2
1920	3,348,792	9,4	5.3	-4.1	25,3	2.502	154	9,4
1921	3,384,147	10,3	10.4	0.2	24,3	2.379	162	10,5
1922	3,420,263	9,1	10.6	1.5	23,4	2.302	148	9,7
1923	3,454,561	10,0	9.9	0.0	23,7	2.324	147	9,6
1924	3,485,424	7,1	8.9	1.8	22,4	2.187	137	9,5
1925	3,514,797	8,8	8.4	-0.4	22,3	2.179	127	8,8
1926	3,547,207	8,3	9.1	0.9	21,7	2.112	124	8,8
1927	3,576,125	6,7	8.1	1.4	21,1	2.053	119	8,8
1928	3,603,805	8,0	7.7	-0.3	21,5	2.085	119	8,6
1929	3,630,520	5,9	7.4	1.4	20,9	2.018	118	8,8
1930	3,654,581	7,4	6.6	-0.8	20,6	1.971	118	9,0
1931	3,682,286	6,2	7.5	1.3	19,5	1.842	114	9,1
1932	3,709,129	6,1	7.2	1.1	18,7	1.749	106	8,7
1933	3,729,643	4,6	5.5	0.9	17,4	1.617	95	8,3
1934	3,750,279	5,7	5.5	-0.2	18,1	1.662	93	7,8
1935	3,774,435	6,5	6.4	-0.1	18,5	1.686	95	7,6
1936	3,797,004	6,9	5.9	-0.9	18,1	1.634	92	7,5
1937	3,820,913	6,6	6.3	-0.3	18,9	1.683	97	7,5
1938	3,819,208	7,5	-0.4	-8.0	20,1	1.773	98	7,1
1939[1]	3,685,900	6,9	..ᵃ	..ᵃ	21,2	1.828	121	8,3
1940	3,697,700	-1,6	3.2	4.8	17,8	..	..	10,3
1941	3,701,700	4,4	1.1	-3.3	24,2	..	..	6,4
1942	3,708,300	1,5	1.8	0.3	16,6	..	..	7,4
1943	3,720,700	7,1	3.3	-3.8	20,5	..	..	6,9
1944	3,734,800	2,4	3.8	1.4	21,3	..	..	8,0
1945	3,758,000	12,4	6.2	-6.3	25,5	..	..	7,5

Note: [1] Territorial change.

APPENDIX TABLE SF.4 Demographic developments 1850–1945 (continued)

Crude death rate	Infant mortality rate	Stillbirth rate	Infant mortality and stillbirth rate	Crude marriage rate	Persons marrying per 10,000 unmarried persons age 15+	Persons marrying per 10,000 unmarried persons age 15–49	Crude divorce rate	Divorces per 100 marriages	Divorces per 10,000 married persons	Year
17.4	128,4	27,0	155,4	7.9	496	620	0,1	0,7	3,2	1898
19.9	136,9	27,3	164,2	7.3	460	575	0,0	0,6	2,8	1899
21.5	153,1	26,5	179,6	6.8	424	529	0,0	0,7	2,7	1900
20.6	144,5	25,9	170,4	6.8	422	527	0,0	0,6	2,3	1901
18.4	129,0	26,7	155,7	6.3	392	489	0,0	0,7	2,5	1902
17.8	127,3	25,3	152,6	6.3	388	484	0,0	0,7	2,6	1903
17.7	119,8	25,2	145,0	6.6	403	502	0,0	0,7	2,7	1904
18.3	134,6	25,0	159,6	6.5	395	493	0,1	0,8	3,2	1905
17.4	119,4	25,3	144,7	6.8	416	518	0,0	0,7	2,9	1906
17.9	112,0	23,6	135,6	6.8	415	517	0,0	0,6	2,6	1907
18.4	125,1	24,6	149,7	6.7	404	504	0,1	0,9	3,5	1908
16.6	111,0	26,1	137,1	6.4	384	478	0,1	1,1	4,1	1909
16.5	117,7	25,6	143,3	6.1	364	454	0,1	1,0	3,7	1910
16.5	113,9	26,2	140,1	6.0	357	445	0,1	1,4	5,1	1911
16.3	108,6	25,4	134,0	5.9	340	436	0,1	1,4	5,2	1912
16.1	112,8	25,3	138,1	5.9	340	435	0,1	1,4	5,0	1913
15.6	104,2	26,3	130,5	5.7	322	401	0,1	1,6	6,0	1914
15.9	110,5	26,5	137,0	5.4	305	379	0,1	1,9	6,0	1915
16.5	110,1	26,7	136,8	5.8	324	402	0,1	1,9	7,0	1916
17.7	118,2	26,8	145,0	6.2	339	421	0,1	1,5	6,0	1917
28.5	115,2	25,2	140,4	4.5	244	303	0,1	1,5	4,0	1918
18.9	134,6	26,0	160,6	5.7	302	373	0,1	2,4	4,0	1919
15.9	96,7	26,1	122,8	7.0	374	463	0,2	2,2	10,0	1920
14.0	94,6	27,3	121,9	7.0	369	458	0,1	2,0	9,0	1921
14.4	99,2	27,6	126,8	6.9	360	447	0,1	2,2	10,0	1922
13.8	92,4	27,4	119,8	6.8	355	443	0,2	2,6	11,0	1923
15.3	106,9	26,9	133,8	6.3	326	408	0,2	2,6	11,0	1924
13.5	85,0	26,7	111,7	6.3	322	404	0,2	2,8	11,0	1925
13.4	85,6	28,6	114,2	6.4	326	409	0,2	3,0	12,0	1926
14.5	97,1	27,6	124,7	6.7	341	429	0,2	2,8	12,0	1927
13.5	84,0	25,2	109,2	7.1	356	448	0,2	2,9	13,0	1928
15.0	97,6	26,7	124,3	6.9	344	435	0,2	3,4	15,0	1929
13.2	75,1	27,7	102,8	6.8	337	426	0,3	4,5	19,0	1930
13.3	74,8	28,5	103,3	6.5	321	409	0,3	5,0	20,0	1931
12.6	70,9	26,9	97,8	6.2	309	395	0,3	4,8	18,0	1932
12.9	75,7	26,2	101,8	6.6	327	421	0,3	4,8	19,0	1933
12.4	73,0	27,6	100,6	7.3	366	474	0,3	4,7	21,1	1934
12.0	66,8	26,4	93,1	7.6	380	496	0,4	5,3	24,3	1935
11.3	65,9	25,8	91,8	7.9	393	516	0,4	4,8	22,6	1936
12.3	68,6	24,2	92,8	8.5	426	562	0,4	5,0	25,3	1937
12.5	67,8	24,7	92,5	8.8	441	587	0,5	5,3	27,5	1938
14.3	69,7	22,0	91,7	8.3	417	558	0,4	4,6	23,0	1939[1]
19.4	88,3	21,0	109,3	8.3	419	564	0,4	4,3	20,0	1940
19.8	59,2	21,4	80,6	10.2	524	707	0,4	4,2	24,0	1941
15.1	67,3	22,6	89,9	7.3	383	517	0,5	7,3	30,0	1942
13.3	61,1	21,3	82,4	8.6	464	629	0,9	9,9	47,0	1943
18.9	68,6	20,7	89,3	8.4	468	636	0,9	10,3	48,0	1944
13.1	63,2	21,5	84,7	11.8	672	915	1,5	12,6	81,0	1945

Note: [1] Territorial change.

APPENDIX TABLE SF.5 Life expectancy by age 1881/90–1941/45 (in years)

Age	0	10	20	30	40	50	60	70	80
				Males					
1881–1890	41.4	49.3	41.5	34.3	26.9	19.7	13.2	8.0	4.5
1891–1900	42.9	49.9	42.0	34.8	27.3	20.1	13.5	8.0	4.3
1901–1910	45.33	49.94	42.16	34.94	27.38	20.03	13.56	8.27	4.51
1911–1920	43.41	45.24	37.91	32.49	25.87	19.36	13.37	8.25	4.76
1921–1930	50.68	49.98	41.89	35.13	27.55	20.32	13.99	8.98	5.49
1931–1940	54.45	51.73	43.34	35.89	28.12	20.86	14.57	9.51	5.91
1936–1940	54.32	51.54	42.99	35.33	27.38	19.95	13.60	8.59	5.16
1941–1945	54.62	51.27	42.90	35.36	27.52	20.16	13.78	8.80	5.48
				Females					
1881–1890	44.2	50.9	43.3	36.0	28.8	21.3	14.3	8.6	5.0
1891–1900	45.6	51.6	44.2	36.8	29.5	21.9	14.6	8.7	4.9
1901–1910	48.10	51.74	44.54	37.30	29.92	22.31	15.08	9.00	4.94
1911–1920	49.12	51.11	43.82	36.96	29.73	22.29	15.05	8.92	4.87
1921–1930	55.14	53.78	46.00	38.71	31.01	23.27	15.82	9.61	5.35
1931–1940	59.55	56.24	47.89	40.15	32.07	23.97	16.41	10.06	5.72
1936–1940	59.48	56.03	47.56	39.69	31.57	23.40	15.79	9.50	5.29
1941–1945	61.14	57.42	48.91	40.96	32.68	24.41	16.58	10.03	5.59

APPENDIX TABLE SF.6A Households by type 1865–1900 (absolute and per cent)

Census year	Household types and members									
	Total households	Private households	Family households	One-person households	Institutional households	Total household members	Private household members	Family household members	One-person household members	Institutional household members
Absolute										
1865	::	::	281,253	::	::	1,843,245	::	::	::	::
1880	::	454,339	373,983	80,356	::	2,060,782[1]	::	::	80,356	::
1890	::	539,884	432,980	106,904	::	2,380,140[1]	::	::	106,904	::
1900	::	628,231	493,675	134,556	::	2,712,562	2,646,683	2,512,127	134,556	65,879
Per cent										
1865	::	100.00	::	::	::	100.00[1]	::	::	::	::
1880	::	100.00	82.31	17.69	::	100.00[1]	::	::	3.90	::
1890	::	100.00	80.20	19.80	::	100.00[1]	::	::	4.49	::
1900	::	100.00	78.58	21.42	::	100.00	97.57	92.61	4.96	2.43

Note: [1] Total population.

APPENDIX TABLE SF.6B Households by size and members 1880–1900 (absolute figures)

Census year	Private households total	1 person	2 persons	Households by number of members					
				3 persons	4 persons	5 persons	6 persons	7 persons	8 persons
				Households					
1880	454,339	80,356	65,885	59,570	55,499	50,101	41,324	31,994	22,879
1890	539,884	106,904	77,959	66,869	63,217	58,193	49,499	38,572	27,494
1900	628,231	134,556	91,828	79,838	73,121	64,928	54,778	42,914	31,223
				Persons					
1880	2,060,782[1]	80,356	131,770	178,710	221,996	250,505	247,944	223,958	183,032
1890	2,380,140[1]	106,904	155,918	200,607	252,868	290,965	296,994	270,004	219,952
1900	2,646,683[2]	134,556	183,656	239,514	292,484	324,640	328,668	300,398	249,784

Notes: [1] Total population. [2] Population in private households. Persons in households have been calculated using the number of households.

APPENDIX TABLE SF.6B Households by size and members 1880–1900 (absolute figures) (continued)

Census year	9 persons	10 persons	Households by number of members					
			11 persons	12 persons	13 persons	14 persons	15 persons	16+ persons
			Households					
1880	15,589	10,536	6,803	4,570	3,048	2,130	1,481	2,574
1890	17,926	11,808	7,358	4,829	3,101	2,053	1,466	2,636
1900	20,313	13,038	7,928	4,987	3,048	1,979	1,425	2,327
			Persons					
1880	140,301	105,360	74,833	54,840	39,624	29,820	22,215	75,518
1890	161,334	118,080	80,938	57,948	40,313	28,742	21,990	76,583
1900	182,817	130,380	87,208	59,844	39,624	27,706	21,375	44,029

APPENDIX TABLE SF.6C Households by size and members 1880–1900 (per cent)

Census year	Private households total	Households by number of members							
		1 person	2 persons	3 persons	4 persons	5 persons	6 persons	7 persons	8 persons
		Households							
1880	100.00	17.69	14.50	13.11	12.22	11.03	9.10	7.04	5.04
1890	100.00	19.80	14.44	12.39	11.71	10.78	9.17	7.14	5.09
1900	100.00	21.42	14.62	12.71	11.64	10.34	8.72	6.83	4.97
		Persons							
1880	100.00[1]	3.90	6.39	8.67	10.77	12.16	12.03	10.87	8.88
1890	100.00[1]	4.49	6.55	8.43	10.62	12.22	12.48	11.34	9.24
1900	100.00[2]	5.08	6.94	9.05	11.05	12.27	12.42	11.35	9.44

Notes: See Appendix Table SF.6B.

APPENDIX TABLE SF.6C Households by size and members 1880–1900 (per cent) (continued)

Census year	Households by number of members							
	9 persons	10 persons	11 persons	12 persons	13 persons	14 persons	15 persons	16+ persons
	Households							
1880	3.43	2.32	1.50	1.01	0.67	0.47	0.33	0.57
1890	3.32	2.19	1.36	0.89	0.57	0.38	0.27	0.49
1900	3.23	2.08	1.26	0.79	0.49	0.32	0.23	0.37
	Persons							
1880	6.81	5.11	3.63	2.66	1.92	1.45	1.08	3.66
1890	6.78	4.96	3.40	2.43	1.69	1.21	0.92	3.22
1900	6.91	4.93	3.29	2.26	1.50	1.05	0.81	1.66

APPENDIX TABLE SF.6D Household indicators
1865–1900

Census year	Household indicators		
	Mean total household size	Mean private household size	Mean family household size
1865	..	..	6.55^2
1880	4.54^1	..	..
1890	4.41^1	..	..
1900	4.32^1	4.21	5.09

Notes: [1] Total population per private households. [2] Total population per family households.

APPENDIX TABLE SF.6E Households by region and size 1865 (absolute and per cent)

Region	Family households total	Family households with				
		2 persons	3–5 persons	6–10 persons	11–15 persons	16+ persons
Absolute						
Nylands	25,083	4,741	10,993	7,856	1,215	278
Abo och Björneborgs	58,530	11,171	25,487	18,424	2,906	542
Tavastehus	27,618	4,582	11,539	9,465	1,662	370
Wiborgs (Viborgs)	33,434	3,182	9,860	16,514	3,198	680
St. Michels	25,587	3,862	9,849	9,292	2,120	464
Kuopio	31,131	3,888	12,138	11,298	3,075	732
Wasa (Vasa)	52,159	7,178	21,656	19,663	3,169	493
Uleaborgs	27,711	3,798	10,572	10,610	2,201	530
Total	281,253	42,402	112,094	103,122	19,546	4,089
Towns	18,915	4,998	9,401	3,731	665	120
Whole country	262,338	37,404	102,693	99,391	18,881	3,969
Per cent						
Nylands	100.00	18.90	43.83	31.32	4.84	1.11
Abo och Björneborgs	100.00	19.09	43.55	31.48	4.96	0.93
Tavastehus	100.00	16.59	41.78	34.27	6.02	1.34
Wiborgs (Viborgs)	100.00	9.52	29.49	49.39	9.57	2.03
St. Michels	100.00	15.09	38.49	36.32	8.29	1.81
Kuopio	100.00	12.49	38.99	36.29	9.88	2.35
Wasa (Vasa)	100.00	13.76	41.52	37.70	6.08	0.95
Uleaborgs	100.00	13.71	38.15	38.29	7.94	1.91
Total	100.00	15.08	39.86	36.67	6.95	1.45
Towns	100.00	26.42	49.70	19.73	3.52	0.63
Whole country	100.00	14.26	39.15	37.89	7.20	1.51

APPENDIX TABLE SF.7 Dates and nature of results on population structure, households/families, and vital statistics

Topic	Intro-duction	Remarks
Population		
Population at census dates	1850	Censuses before 1865 were held in 1840, 1845, 1850, 1855, and 1860. Population statistics extends back to 1751 (cf. Tilastollinen päätoimisto (1870), pp. 5ff.).
Population by age, sex, and marital status	1880	In 1865 and 1875 age groups and marital status were given separately, but not combined. Marital status for persons over 15 is given.
Households and families		
Households (talouskunta (Finnish), hushåll (Swedish))		
Total households	1865, 1880, 1890, 1900	Households were counted at least since 1865. 1865: households by size 2–15+ persons. 1870: households by size, but only in the large cities. 1875: no households given. 1880: households by size 1–15+ persons for the country; in addition, a census of the towns was held. Furthermore, a special investigation was carried out in Helsingfors. 1890: households by size 1–15+ persons. 1900: households by size 1–15+ and institutional households. Special survey on the cities: household size and composition. 1910: no households given. A special investigation was carried out in the large cities: household size and composition. 1920: no households given. 1930: no households given. 1940: no households given. *Disaggregation*: 1865–: towns and rural communities.
Households by size	1865, 1880, 1890, 1900	For the first time in 1865 (2, ...). Repeated in 1880, 1890, and 1900 (1, ...). No data given for 1910, 1920, 1930, or 1940.
Households by composition	–	Not available.
Households by profession of household head	–	Not available.
Families (perheet (Finnish), familjer (Swedish))		
Families by number of children	–	Not available.

continued

APPENDIX TABLE SF.7 Dates and nature of results on population structure, households/families, and vital statistics (continued)

Topic	Intro-duction	Remarks
Population movement		
Mid-year population	1850	
Births		
Live births	1850	
Stillbirths	1861	
Legitimate births	1850	
Illegitimate births	1850	
Deaths		
Total deaths	1850	
Infants (under 1 year)	1866	
Marriages		
Total marriages	1850	
Divorces and separations		
Total divorces	1881	
Legal separations	1951	

APPENDIX FIGURE SF.8 Population by age, sex and marital status, Finland 1880, 1900, 1910, 1920, 1930 and 1940 (per 10,000 of total population)

Finland, 1880

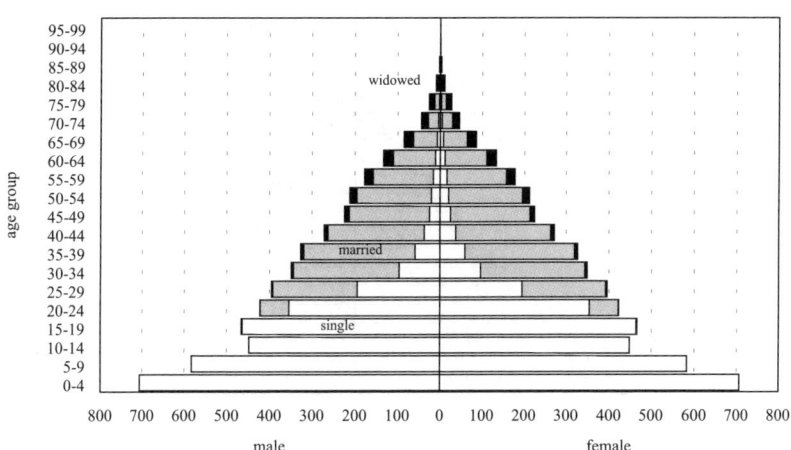

Finland, 1900

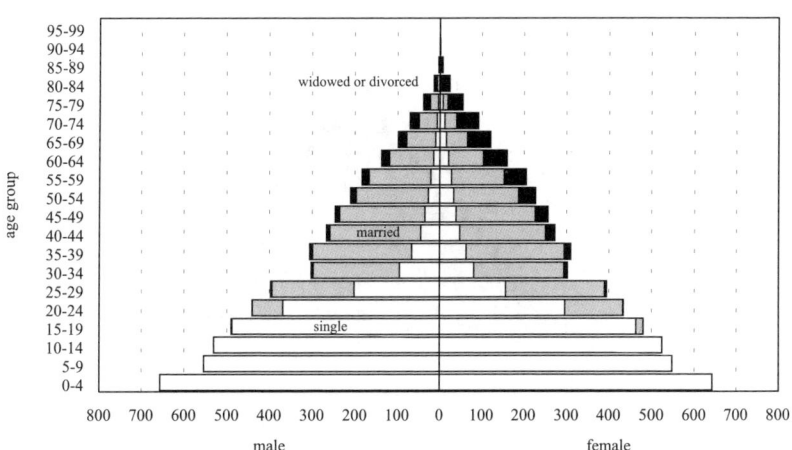

APPENDIX FIGURE SF.8 Population by age, sex and marital status, Finland 1880, 1900, 1910, 1920, 1930 and 1940 (per 10,000 of total population) (continued)

Finland, 1910

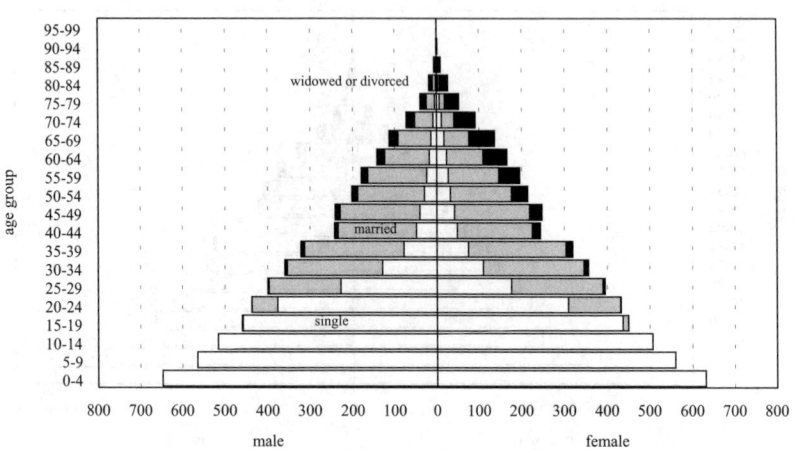

Finland, 1920

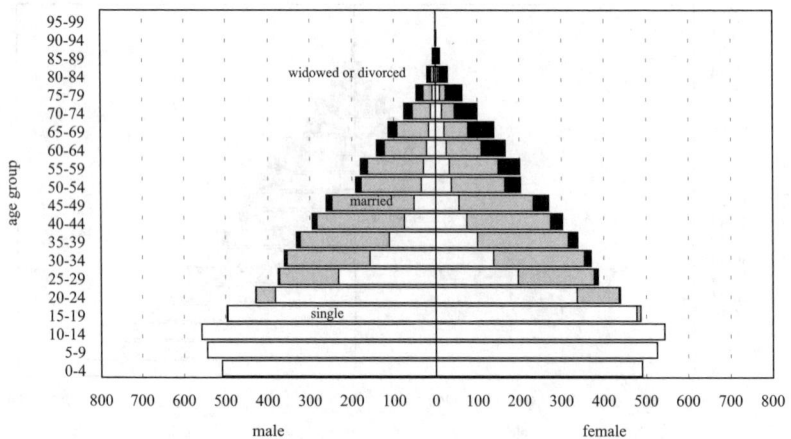

APPENDIX FIGURE SF.8 Population by age, sex and marital status, Finland 1880, 1900, 1910, 1920, 1930 and 1940 (per 10,000 of total population) (continued)

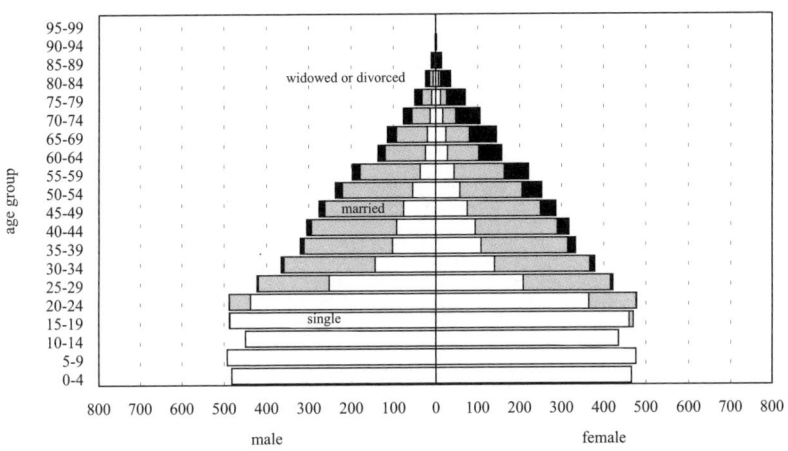

Finland, 1930

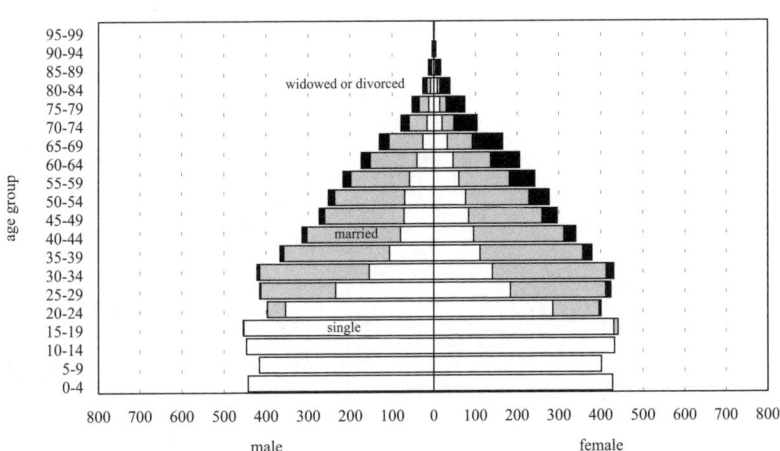

Finland, 1940

6

France

Starting in the late Middle Ages, the French kings had increasing territorial aspirations. In the course of the Hundred Years' War with England, major tracts of France were conquered for the French crown, and since the reign of Louis XIV the explicit aim of French politics was to establish natural borders with its neighbours. In the south, after centuries of struggle the Pyrenees were accepted as the border between France and Spain. In the east and north the Rhine was considered the natural border to the Germanic territories of the Germans and the Dutch.

The French kings were only partly able to achieve this goal. The Thirty Years' War ended successfully for the French king, who was able to add most of Alsace and Lorraine to his kingdom, which then extended to the Rhine from Basle to the Palatinate. After this success the war went on. At the end of the seventeenth century France invaded the Palatinate, causing great destruction (Heidelberg), but was not able to incorporate it into the French kingdom. In the same way France tried to extend its border to the lower Rhine when it invaded the Habsburg Netherlands (Wallonia and Flanders), but it was not able to keep this territory for long.

The next step came with the Napoleonic wars when France made large territorial gains. In particular, the century-old ambition to make the Rhine its eastern border became reality. But after the fall of Napoleon I most of these gains were reversed by the Congress of Vienna in 1815. France kept Alsace and Lorraine, but had to give back the Palatinate, the Rhineland, and The Netherlands which became an independent kingdom. The Grand Duchy of Luxembourg was re-established as well.

Napoleon III tried to profit from the unification of both Italy and Germany, which brought territorial gains and losses for France. First he offered help to Piedmont in the war of unification and was rewarded with Savoy and Nice in 1860. In the 1867 war of unification between Prussia and Austria France made a secret pact with Austria and was promised territorial gains in the case of an Austrian victory. Unfortunately, Austria was defeated at Königgrätz. Bismarck thought that German unification was only possible in direct confrontation with Napoleon III. When Prussia and its allies won the war of 1870/71, France had to cede Alsace-Lorraine.

Until World War I France underwent only marginal territorial changes. Germany's defeat in that war gave Alsace-Lorraine back to France, which also occupied the Rhineland until the 1920s and the Saarland until the 1935 plebiscite in favour of the German Empire. World War II did not change the French boundaries. France again occupied the Saarland but returned it to the Federal Republic of Germany in 1953 after a plebiscite (other general literature about France is included in Rothenbacher, 1998c; Cross and Perry, 1997; Sieburg, 1995; Price, 1993; Loth, 1987; Schultheis, 1988).

REGIONAL POPULATION STRUCTURE

The main characteristics of France's regional population structure are the monocephalic territorial population pattern with the heavy weight of the capital, Paris, and the Île-de-France. There are only a few other centres of high settlement density: the north-eastern region with coal mining and heavy manufacturing; the north sea coast with important ports, the Rhone Valley with the large centre of Lyon, and finally the city and hinterland of Bordeaux. Apart from these centres, in the nineteenth century the population was rather evenly distributed, but rural–urban migration changed this in the twentieth century, and some *départements* experienced severe population losses.

These differences in population structure and density reflect differences in economic development and structure. The population is still fairly evenly distributed across the country, apart from the few centres, due to the still high importance of agriculture. Changes in the industrial and employment structure during the last century, first industrialization and later, tertiarization, also affected the population structure: workers first moved to the industrialized centres of the north and the large cities. With industrial decline after 1945 the industrialized regions faced out-migration to the large cities and the Mediterranean where the service industry is located. These migratory shifts had consequences for the regional age and sex structure of the population (Van de Walle, 1974; Armengaud and Fine, 1988; Dupâquier, 1988).

POPULATION GROWTH

The specific characteristic of France's population history is the early population growth in the seventeenth and eighteenth centuries, building the basis for France's military power at that time. In the eighteenth century France was comparatively densely populated. But during the nineteenth century, birth rates declined so strongly that natural population growth was very small and France became the first country with the 'modern population problem', secular birth decline.

France's population history in the last two centuries is therefore exceptional among Western European countries. During the demographic transition in the nineteenth century population growth was very low due to a rather low birth rate. At a time when other European countries were experiencing a population explosion with all its social and economic consequences, France's population growth fell behind. The population question around 1900 led to the introduction of the first family and population policy measures.

Absolute population in 1872 was 35,313,000 inhabitants. Before World War I, the 1911 census counted 39,602,000 inhabitants, an increase of only 4.3 million people, small when compared e.g. with Great Britain or the German Empire. In 1936, the last census before World War II, the population was 41,907,000 inhabitants; thus from 1911 to 1936, the increase amounted to only 2.3 million inhabitants. During both world wars absolute population losses occurred: in 1946, the population was 40,503,000, less than in 1936 (Figure F.1).

Population density was low in France, compared with densely-populated countries such as Belgium or The Netherlands, mainly due to the very large size of the country. (Today, France has the largest territory in the European Union with 543,965 square km., but it ranks third with regard to population size.) Several

Figure F.1 Population growth and net migration 1850-1945

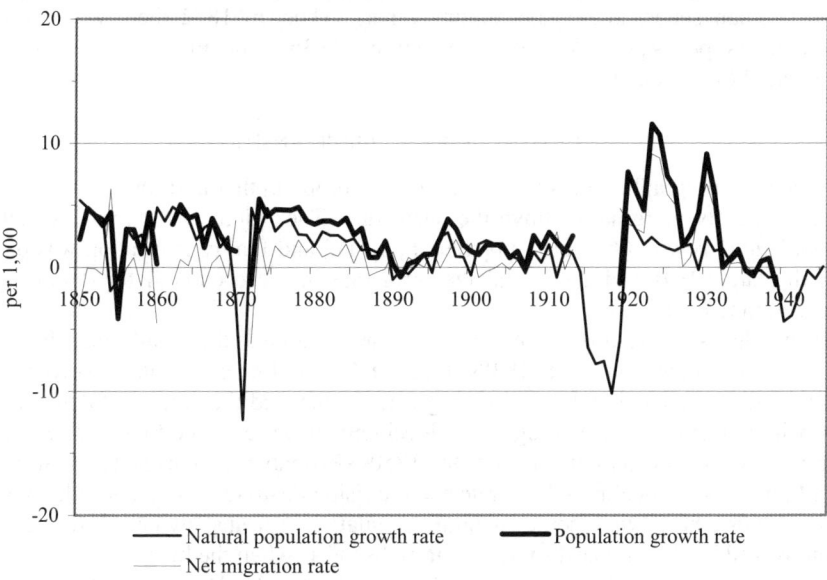

— Natural population growth rate   — Population growth rate
— Net migration rate

Figure F.2 First demographic transition 1850-1945

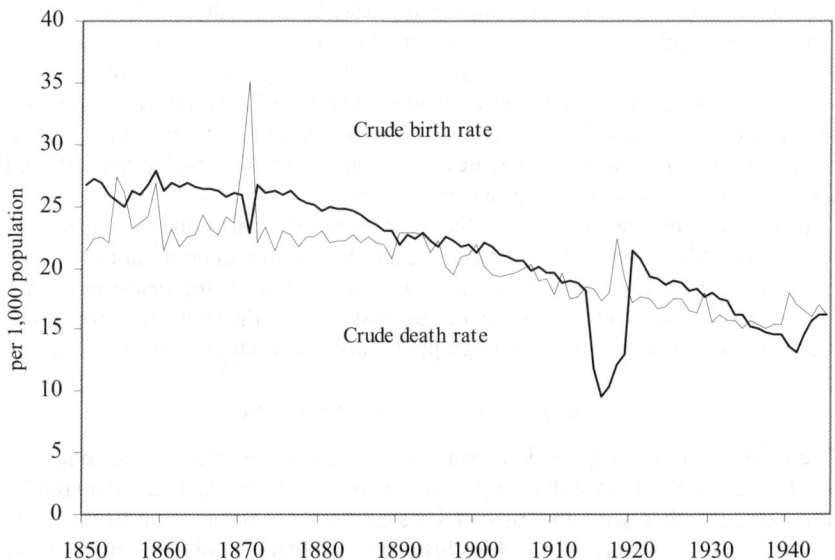

historical circumstances added to this low density: the wars of unification starting in the Middle Ages, the expulsion of the Huguenots, and several wars with England, the German states, and Spain, among others. Thus, in 1872 there were only 67 inhabitants per square km. on average; by 1936 population density had only increased to 78 inhabitants per square km.

THE FIRST DEMOGRAPHIC TRANSITION

France's demographic transition is unique in Europe in that until the 1940s the birth rate was only marginally above the death rate. The result was a very low natural population growth. Only after population, social, and family legislation was passed in the late 1930s and 1940s did the birth rate increase enough for demographic transition to occur.

Nevertheless, the birth rate was structurally above the death rate from the nineteenth century to the late 1930s (Figure F.2). But France's major involvement in nearly all continental and world wars greatly influenced the pattern of demographic transition. Furthermore, demographic development was affected by severe economic crises: the world economic crisis of the 1850s (Rosenberg, 1974) had a great impact on France, as the declining birth rate and the rising death rate in that decade show. In the 1860s there was some natural population surplus, which however was interrupted by the Franco-Prussian War of 1870/71, when the birth rate declined and the death rate surged, greatly exceeding the birth rate. Between 1880 and 1910 several epidemics caused upswings in the mortality rate. France's largest demographic crisis came with World War I, with a heavy loss not only of the population but also of births postponed during the war and not entirely made up after the war. While there was some population growth during the 1920s, the next crisis came in the 1930s, when there was a dramatic drop in the birth rate. During World War II the death rate rose and the birth rate fell, though not as steeply as in World War I. The country's more or less permanent demographic crisis led political leaders before and after World War II to introduce population and family policy measures. In the post-war period, France achieved a rather 'normal' development of the birth and death rate, very near the European average.

Historical demographers argue that demographic transition to a low level of fertility started already in the eighteenth century. But looking only at the time period from 1850, there has been a (possibly second) decline in the death rate since the 1890s. In the case of France one could even argue that the birth rate dropped before the death rate, contrary to the demographic transition model (see Simon 1925).

MORTALITY AND LIFE EXPECTANCY

The infant mortality rate is defined as deaths of children aged under one year per 1,000 live births. France falls into the cluster of countries with moderate infant mortality, together with the British Isles and the European continental countries (Figure F.3). However, within this cluster France had a rather low infant mortality rate already around 1900, which brings it nearer to England than to Germany and Austria, which had rather high infant mortality (Masuy-Stroobant, 1997).

But when looking at the diachronic and historical development of French infant mortality, it becomes clear that France is a unique case in some respects. Already in the eighteenth and nineteenth centuries infant mortality was comparatively low, at

Figure F.3 Infant mortality 1850-1945

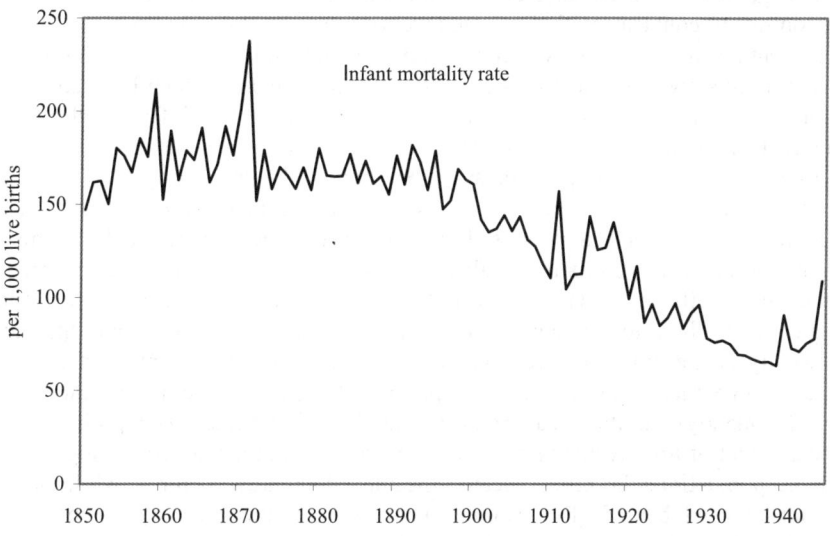

Infant mortality rate

Figure F.4 Life expectancy 1817/31-1933/38

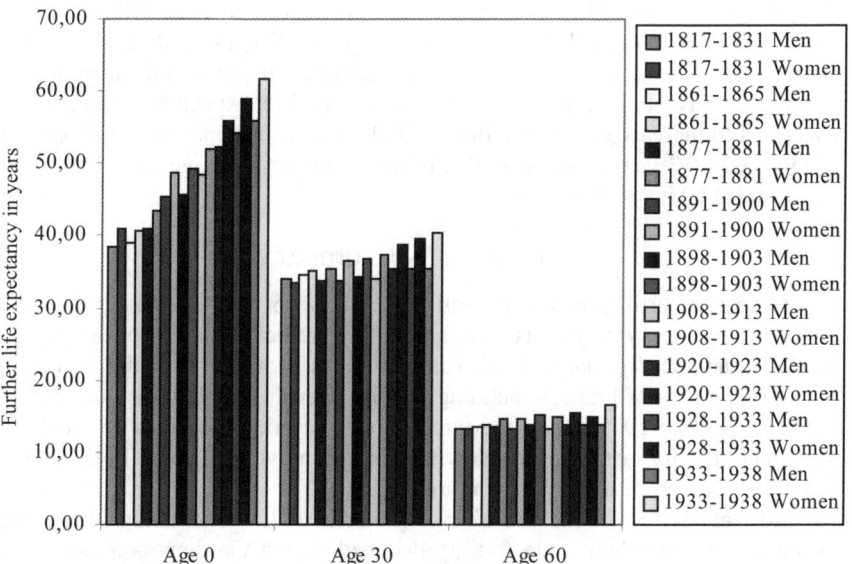

least lower than in neighbouring Germany. But during the second half of the eighteenth and the whole nineteenth century the level of infant mortality more or less stagnated. The decisive decline in infant mortality came shortly before 1900, but in contrast to countries with the same level of infant mortality in the first half of the nineteenth century, such as Sweden and England/Wales, in France this rate fell much more slowly. In the 1920s and 1930s even Germany, which had had a higher infant mortality rate, passed up France, and has had a lower infant death rate ever since. Thus, compared to other countries, France was in a better position at the beginning of the demographic transition but then fell behind.

Due to its large and heterogeneous territory, composed of historically and geographically diverse territories, France showed large geographical variations in infant mortality. First, infant mortality was, as in other countries, higher in urbanized areas, especially in the large industrialized cities (Paris) and regions (coal-mining region of north-eastern France). But this picture changed, as areas with high infant mortality in the nineteenth century became those with low infant mortality in the twentieth century. Now the rural and peripheral regions of the north-west (Brittany and Normandy) and the Mediterranean coast had higher rates. This probably shows the gradient of improvements in sanitary conditions and the general living standards of the population; the cities became the most innovative centres, while the rural regions lagged behind (for example, concerning running water, which was first provided in the large towns) (Rollet and Bourdelais, 1993; see also Bourdelais and Demonet, 1997; Perrenoud, 1997; Rollet, 1997a; Barbieri, 1998).

Life expectancy during the nineteenth century was rather favourable. Compared with Sweden, only life expectancy at birth was lower, while life expectancy at age 30 and age 60 was higher in France (1861/65) than in Sweden (1861/70). By the 1930s, however, France had lost its advantage at all ages relative to Sweden. In particular, life expectancy at birth fell in relative terms, as it did for young adults and the elderly (Figure F.4). Sex differences in life expectancy were high and continued to increase strongly until the 1930s. Life expectancy of new-born girls in 1933/38 was 5.7 years more than that of new-born boys; at age 30 it was 4.9 years more, and at 60 it was 2.6 years.

FERTILITY AND LEGITIMACY

Given the low fertility in France until 1945, it is no wonder that illegitimate and legitimate fertility were low as well, and both were below the European average. It is clear that the *legitimate birth rate* describes more or less the demographic transition process of France: declining fertility over the whole transition, but a shift in the level since 1945 due to the family policy reforms. Whereas before 1945 the legitimate fertility rate was far below the European average, since 1945 it has been exactly at the European average (Figure F.5).

Illegitimate fertility until World War I was also low and below the European average. But while legitimate fertility declined during the demographic transition, the illegitimate fertility rate did not show an obvious decline until World War I. During the inter-war period the strong birth decline also affected illegitimate fertility, but already at that time, the level was higher than in Europe. This continued after 1945, but the strong deinstitutionalization of marriage with the disproportional growth of illegitimate fertility started only in the 1970s.

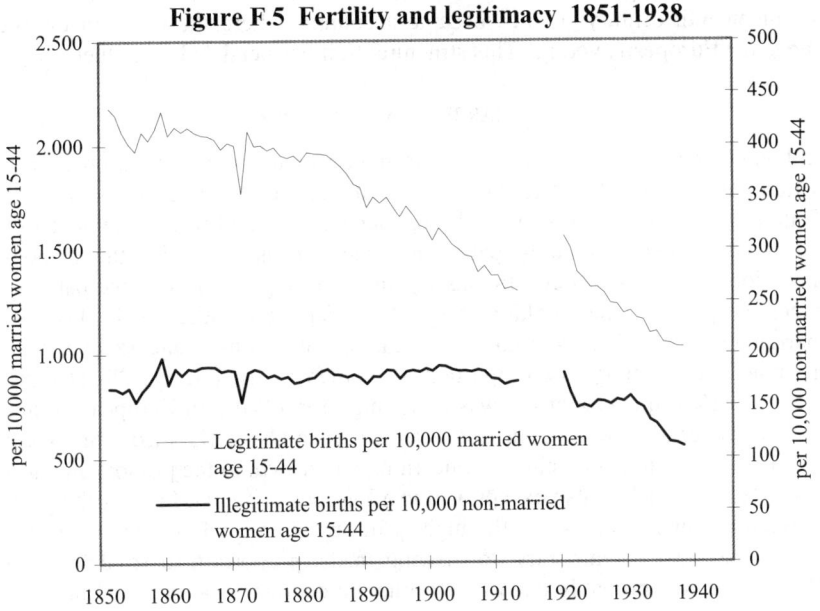

Figure F.5 Fertility and legitimacy 1851-1938

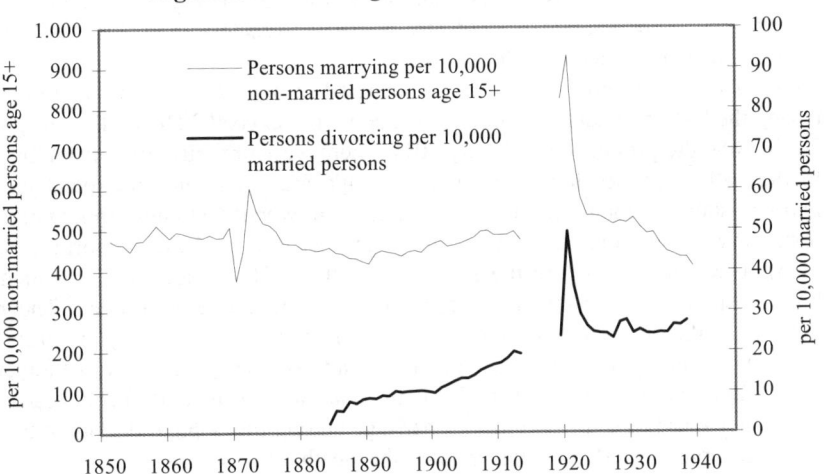

Figure F.6 Marriages and divorces 1851-1939

The ratio of illegitimate to legitimate children changed during the second half of the nineteenth century: France became a country where the illegitimacy rate was above the European average. This structural trait has persisted since then.

MARRIAGE AND DIVORCE

Although France clearly belongs to the region of the Western European marriage pattern, it can be classified into a separate cluster together with other Roman Catholic countries of Romanic culture, such as Italy and to some extent Belgium. But such clustering is only partly accurate because, as with the demographic transition, France is difficult to classify also with regard to marriage patterns. This becomes apparent when looking at age at marriage, one indicator for distinguishing marriage patterns. Because figures on mean age at first marriage are unavailable for the nineteenth century, the proportion of women married at age 20–24 is used. In France in 1850 this proportion was rather high for a Western European country and was only exceeded by England and Wales. France also differs from the Nordic and the Germanic continental cluster concerning the growth in the proportion married up to the 1930s, which is also exceptional in a European context. In 1931 the proportion of women married was 48%, the highest of any Western European country at that time. There was a temporary downswing in the proportion married from 1876 to 1896 which was probably due to the economic depression after the Franco-Prussian War. In France age at first marriage began to rise again already in the 1930s and 1940s (or the proportion married declined), which helps explain the falling birth rate during this time. After World War II the proportion of women married at age 20–24 was around 40%. The most recent trend of 'postponed marriage' started in 1980, and the proportion of women married at age 20–24 was less than 20% in 1990, the lowest level since at least 1850.

Interestingly, the proportion of men married at age 20–24 was structurally low during the last 150 years. The highest value did not exceed 22% of all men aged 20–24. In 1850 the proportion was only 10%. There were obvious crises from the 1870s to the 1890s. Causes for higher marriage age are economic and social marriage barriers such as long military service, long university studies, inheritance law, temporary emigration, etc. Age at marriage was low (and the proportion married high) at two time points: in the 1930s and in the 1950s. Since the 1970s men have been postponing marriage to a degree never seen before in France. The recent deinstutionalization of marriage in France is therefore not only a return to a historically older pattern as in Scandinavia, but to some degree a new phenomenon.

Marriage intensity is measured by the *marriage rate* and the *celibacy rate*. 'Intensity' means the availability of marriage among the population, but at the same time the urgent need to remarry after the death of a spouse ('remarriage need', Michael Mitterauer). The first rate relates all marriages to unmarried people over 15. The second measures the number of women never married at age 45–54 as a proportion of all women in the same age group. As we have already seen for the low age at marriage, marriage intensity in France was structurally rather high, at least higher than in the Nordic countries (Figure F.6). During the second half of the nineteenth century it was near (but slightly below) the European average. While there was no clear pattern during the inter-war period, after World War II France's marriage rate was structurally below the European average. The marriage rate reflected the deep economic crises and especially the involvement in wars. The pattern of these incidences is always the same: a decrease in the marriage rate at the begin of the crisis (war, depression), and a strong recovery after the crisis. This pattern exists for the Franco-Prussian War of 1870/71 with minor amplitude; very strongly for World War I, pointing to the catastrophic effects of this war on the whole French society; and also for the late 1930s and World War II. Importantly, the marriage rate in France had begun declining already in the 1920s so strongly that in the mid-1930s the rate fell below the European average. The world depression of 1930 surely had an important impact.

The celibacy rate during the second half of the nineteenth century was as high as in the Nordic countries, with 30% of all women aged 45–54 never married. Until 1950 there was no change in this proportion: i.e. 30% of the birth cohorts of the 1890/1900s remained unmarried more or less their entire lives. In this respect France is therefore very similar to the Nordic countries. The first decline in the celibacy rate occurred in 1950, that is, for the birth cohorts born after 1900. However, the celibacy rate did not fall from such a high level as in most countries of the Nordic cluster and the Germanic continental cluster. France also experienced universal marriage during the 1970s and a declining tendency to universal marriage since that time.

Already in the nineteenth century the *divorce rate* was very much higher in France than on the European average (Figure F.6). This structural pattern continued in the inter-war period and—to a lesser degree—in the time after World War II. The causes for this comparatively high level of divorce lie in the divorce law (Code Napoleon) which allowed more grounds for divorce than in other countries. The high divorce rate may also explain the rather high marriage rate, because most divorced persons likely remarried.

Surprisingly, relative to the European average France's divorce rate was lower after 1945 than before. The new family legislation with family benefits may have made divorce more difficult or created a completely new family ideology and family orientation. Possibly in line with the new trend of liberalizing divorce laws, the French divorce rate has exceeded the European divorce rate only since the 1970s.

The French divorce rate describes a very clear logistic curve. Only the two world wars interrupted this continuous increase in the well-known pattern: a decline before and during the wars and a rise afterwards. This incidence was strong in France for both world wars.

In addition to divorce, marital separation was also possible in France. Annual data on the number of legal separations have been published since 1865. Divorces (and the different divorce rates) soon outnumbered legal separations, although legal separations continue to be common. In some sense, however, separation is only the first step in the divorce process, so that the number of separations provides a picture of a transitory stage.

AGE, SEX, AND CIVIL STATUS

The age structure of France demonstrates the country's traditionally low fertility during the nineteenth century (Appendix Figure F.8). Already in 1851 France's age structure was bell-shaped rather than pyramidal as in most other countries. The lowest age groups were rather small compared to other countries. Until 1911, the last census before World War I, the pattern changed only slightly. However, World War I had a very strong impact on the French age structure: the losses of births due to the war were very strong and can still be seen in the age structure of 1946, when proportions of young adults aged 15–29 were the smallest. The age cohorts of the 1920s were the same size as those before the war, but during the 1930s the continued fertility decline reduced the youngest age groups further.

During the second half of the nineteenth century, age at marriage was high, as was celibacy. Men remained single longer than women, but many more men were married at higher ages because of widowhood. The proportion of widowed and divorced women in higher age groups was very high already during the second half of the nineteenth century, pointing to high male mortality and probably sex-specific remarriage rates after divorce. The already high proportions of widowed or divorced women grew further in 1911 and again in 1946, probably largely due to the high losses of men during World War I and II.

FAMILY AND HOUSEHOLD STRUCTURES

Information on households and families in France before 1950 is very limited. Only the number and the size distribution of households was published. Much more emphasis was put on the question of marital fertility: already the 1886 census contained a question on the number of children born. This emphasis on the fertility question was in response to France's low population growth. In trying to solve its 'national population question', France became the pioneer in family-related fertility investigations.

Because marital fertility was low until 1945, family households were small. Children are of course one of the major elements in a family household and make up a large proportion of household members. The effect of low fertility was that from the nineteenth century to the 1940s France had the lowest mean private household size in Europe. The share of single people was one of the highest in Europe until the 1940s, exceeded only by Sweden. The proportion of large households (with five or more persons) was the smallest in Europe from the nineteenth century to the 1940s.

Although no data on household composition exist, the existence of non-family household members such as servants, boarders, and lodgers did not strongly affect the picture of small households in France already in the nineteenth century.

THE NATIONAL SYSTEM OF DEMOGRAPHIC STATISTICS

Population Structure

Population censuses in the modern sense of the word have been conducted in France only since the beginning of the nineteenth century. Censuses prior to 1851, documented in Appendix Table F.7, were conducted in 1801, 1806, 1821, 1826, 1831, 1841, and 1846. But these censuses were very limited, intended to cover mainly population number, and did not try to answer social questions by quantitative means.

A good overview of the history of the French census since the beginning is given by Croze (1987). Censuses from 1801 to 1946 are described in the 'Annexe', pp. 33f.

Historical data on population size, dwellings and households from 1801 to 1886 are given in the introduction to *République Française. Ministère du Commerce et de l'Industrie* (1888). The retrospective edition 1966 of the *Annuaire Statistique* also deals with population figures from 1801 onwards (INSEE, 1966).

Population by age, sex, and marital status was published for the first time in 1851 and since that time for almost every subsequent census. The first censuses still used grouped age data, but the more recent censuses gave age in detailed form.

Vital Statistics

Basic variables of population movement such as mid-year population, births (by legitimacy), deaths, infant deaths, and marriages are available since 1806. Stillbirths have been published since 1840, legal separations since 1865, and divorces since 1884 (cf. INSEE, 1966: 66f.). In France, official statistics were organized already early in the country's history, which ensured a good supply of statistical information.

Households and Families

In France information on households (*ménages*) was collected for the first time in the 1851 census. The number of all households and the respective population was given in the same year. In almost every subsequent census households were counted and published. One might take this to mean that France devised elaborate and detailed household statistics, but this is not the case. The only disaggregation which French statistics introduced was households by size (number of household members); no other combinations were made (such as household composition, household types, social status and occupation of household head).

Households were published by size already in 1856; this was repeated in 1861, 1886, 1891, 1896, and in the 1946 housing census. All other censuses presented only the number of households. The 1926 census was not a national census but rather a housing census in towns with more than 5,000 inhabitants.

The rudimentary development of household statistics in France may perhaps be explained by late urbanization and plentiful housing; in other countries (such as Germany) housing shortages were the main stimulus for housing and household statistics. Another interpretation could emphasize the very early introduction of family statistics (see below) in France in response to its extremely low birth rates.

A history of household statistics in France is given in the introduction to the 1946 housing census (République Française. Ministère des Finances et des Affaires Économiques. Institut National de la Statistique et des Études Économiques. Direction de la Statistique Générale, 1949: Vf.).

A definition of household (*ménage*) was given for the first time in the 1856 population census:

Par *ménages,* on a désigné non pas les familles, mais les individus mariés ou non mariés, avec ou sans enfants, habitant un local distinct. Ainsi, aux termes des instructions ministérielles, une personne vivant seule dans un logement séparé a été considérée comme formant un ménage, aussi bien qu'une famille composée du mari, de la femme, d'un ou plusieurs enfants, d'un ou plusieurs domestiques demeurant ensemble dans le même appartement (Bureau de la Statistique Générale, 1859: xxiii).

The same definition of household (*ménage*) was given in the 1861 population census (Bureau de la Statistique Générale, 1864: XXXIX).

France pioneered *family statistics* as family-centred fertility statistics. Already in 1886 a special investigation into the fertility of married women was carried out. Such investigations were repeated in 1891, 1896, and 1901. In 1931 and 1946 extensive investigations into the 'productivity of marriages' were organized. This early and very regular emphasis on fertility measurement in France is caused by the exceptionally low fertility in France already in the nineteenth century, distinguishing France from all other European countries. French fertility measurement was used as a model by other countries, particularly after World War I when births declined on a massive scale in nearly all other European countries.

A history of family statistics in the sense of family-centred fertility statistics in France is given in the introduction to the 1946 family statistics (République Française. Ministère des Finances et des Affaires Économiques. Institut National de la Statistique et des Études Économiques. Direction de la Statistique Générale, 1953: Xff.).

Remarks (also see introductory Table 6.1)

The age*sex*civil status table in the French population censuses of 1921 and 1926 use the age group of 40–49 years instead of 40–44 years. Data for the age group 40–44 have been calculated by splitting this age group into two equal parts. The first post-war census was taken in 1946; the values of the variables v16–v21 have been calculated using linear extrapolation with the growth rates from 1926 to 1931.

BOUNDARY CHANGES

The territory of France did not change fundamentally from 1815 onwards, apart from the loss of Alsace-Lorraine from 1871 to 1918. In 1860 Savoy and Nice were acquired from Piedmont. For regional organization see the documentation by Quick (1994) and Caramani, Flora, Kraus, and Quick (1998).

APPENDIX TABLE F.1 Population structure at census dates 1851–1946

Census number	Census date	Census population			Marital status				Age group		
		Total	Male	Female	Single	Married	Widowed	Divorced	0–14	15–64	65+
						Absolute					
1	IV–V 1851	35,783,170	17,794,964	17,988,206	19,324,027	13,935,051	2,524,092	..	9,763,467	23,674,041	2,316,574
2	V–VI 1856	36,012,669	17,857,439	18,155,230	19,174,867	14,219,160	2,618,642	..	9,886,754	23,755,216	2,297,693
3	V–VI 1861	37,386,313	18,645,276	18,741,037	19,694,457	14,970,707	2,721,149	..	10,120,368	24,709,335	2,498,388
4	IV–V 1866	38,067,064	19,014,079	19,052,985	19,818,265	15,416,096	2,832,703	..	10,247,991	24,998,674	2,742,243
5	IV–V 1872	36,102,921	17,982,511	18,120,410	18,475,224	14,661,249	2,966,448	..	9,760,745	23,640,278	2,675,260
6	XII 1876	36,905,788	18,373,639	18,532,149	18,742,424	15,156,170	3,007,194	..	10,008,465	24,060,637	2,828,752
7	18 XII 1881	37,405,290	18,656,518	18,748,772	19,391,463	15,023,539	2,990,288	..	9,997,596	24,366,727	3,029,942
8	30 V 1886	37,930,759	18,900,312	19,030,447	20,012,498	14,959,335	2,947,511	11,415	10,226,616	24,645,327	3,048,435
9	12 IV 1891	38,133,385	18,932,354	19,201,031	19,706,380	15,296,984	3,093,428	36,593	9,998,152	24,956,376	3,158,203
10	24 III 1901	38,450,788	18,916,889	19,533,899	19,041,534	15,774,282	3,390,781[1]		10,015,141	25,177,855	3,257,792
11	5 III 1911	39,192,133	19,254,444	19,937,689	18,879,303	16,585,596	3,352,941	151,749	10,076,545	25,762,445	3,269,672
12	6 III 1921	38,797,540	18,444,656	20,352,884	17,756,947	16,749,272	3,772,758	211,638	8,805,832	27,823,141[2]	2,094,407[3]
13	7 III 1926	40,228,481	19,309,568	20,918,913	17,862,075	18,134,606	3,652,090	242,493	9,024,175	28,951,152[2]	2,167,492[3]
14	8 III 1931	41,228,466	19,911,676	21,316,790	18,171,594	19,087,896	3,687,944	281,032	9,460,987	29,487,700[2]	2,279,779[3]
15	8 III 1936	41,183,193	19,797,415	21,385,778	17,885,201	19,227,422	3,741,741	328,829	9,446,159	27,350,352	4,386,682
16	10 III 1946	39,848,182	18,878,120	20,970,062	17,269,944	18,179,480	3,781,113	423,417	8,696,138	26,763,407	4,357,334

continued

APPENDIX TABLE F.1 Population structure at census dates 1851–1946 (continued)

Census number	Census date	Census population			Marital status				Age group		
		Total	Male	Female	Single	Married	Widowed	Divorced	0–14	15–64	65+
					Per cent						
1	IV–V 1851	100.00	49.73	50.27	54.00	38.94	7.05	..	27.29	66.16	6.47
2	V–VI 1856	100.00	49.59	50.41	53.24	39.48	7.27	..	27.45	65.96	6.38
3	V–VI 1861	100.00	49.87	50.13	52.68	40.04	7.28	..	27.07	66.09	6.68
4	IV–V 1866	100.00	49.95	50.05	52.06	40.50	7.44	..	26.92	65.67	7.20
5	IV–V 1872	100.00	49.81	50.19	51.17	40.61	8.22	..	27.04	65.48	7.41
6	XII 1876	100.00	49.79	50.21	50.78	41.07	8.15	..	27.12	65.19	7.66
7	18 XII 1881	100.00	49.88	50.12	51.84	40.16	7.99	..	26.73	65.14	8.10
8	30 V 1886	100.00	49.83	50.17	52.76	39.44	7.77	0.03	26.96	64.97	8.04
9	12 IV 1891	100.00	49.65	50.35	51.68	40.11	8.11	0.10	26.22	65.44	8.28
10	24 III 1901	100.00	49.20	50.80	49.52	41.02	8.82[1]		26.05	65.48	8.47
11	5 III 1911	100.00	49.13	50.87	48.17	42.32	8.56	0.39	25.71	65.73	8.34
12	6 III 1921	100.00	47.54	52.46	45.77	43.17	9.72	0.55	22.70	71.71[2]	5.40[3]
13	7 III 1926	100.00	48.00	52.00	44.40	45.08	9.08	0.60	22.43	71.97[2]	5.39[3]
14	8 III 1931	100.00	48.30	51.70	44.08	46.30	8.95	0.68	22.95	71.52[2]	5.53[3]
15	8 III 1936	100.00	48.07	51.93	43.43	46.69	9.09	0.80	22.94	66.41	10.65
16	10 III 1946	100.00	47.38	52.62	43.34	45.62	9.49	1.06	21.82	67.16	10.93

Notes: [1] Widowed and divorced. [2] 15–69. [3] 70+.

APPENDIX TABLE F.2 Census population by region 1872–1946 (per cent)

Département	1872	1881	1891	1901[1]	1911[1]	1921	1931	1936	1946
Seine	6.03	7.43	8.19	9.42	10.49	11.25	11.79	11.84	11.79
Seine-et-Marne	0.94	0.92	0.93	0.92	0.92	0.89	0.97	0.98	1.00
Seine-et-Oise	1.44	1.53	1.64	1.81	2.07	2.35	3.27	3.37	3.49
Ardennes	0.90	0.89	0.85	0.81	0.81	0.71	0.70	0.69	0.60
Aube	0.71	0.68	0.67	0.63	0.61	0.58	0.58	0.57	0.58
Marne	1.08	1.12	1.13	1.11	1.10	0.94	0.98	0.98	0.96
Marne (Haute-)	0.70	0.68	0.64	0.58	0.54	0.51	0.45	0.45	0.45
Aisne	1.54	1.48	1.42	1.38	1.34	1.08	1.17	1.16	1.12
Oise	1.10	1.08	1.05	1.05	1.04	0.99	0.97	0.96	0.98
Somme	1.55	1.46	1.42	1.38	1.31	1.16	1.12	1.11	1.09
Eure	1.05	0.97	0.91	0.86	0.82	0.77	0.73	0.73	0.78
Seine-Inférieure	2.18	2.16	2.26	2.19	2.21	2.25	2.16	2.19	2.09
Cher	0.93	0.93	0.94	0.89	0.85	0.78	0.70	0.69	0.71
Eure-et-Loire	0.79	0.75	0.74	0.71	0.69	0.64	0.61	0.60	0.64
Indre	0.78	0.76	0.76	0.74	0.73	0.67	0.59	0.59	0.62
Indre-et-Loire	0.88	0.87	0.88	0.86	0.86	0.84	0.80	0.82	0.86
Loir-et-Cher	0.75	0.73	0.73	0.71	0.68	0.64	0.58	0.58	0.60
Loiret	0.99	0.98	0.99	0.94	0.92	0.86	0.82	0.82	0.86
Calvados	1.26	1.17	1.12	1.05	1.00	0.98	0.96	0.97	0.99
Manche	1.49	1.40	1.34	1.26	1.20	1.09	1.04	1.05	1.07
Orne	1.12	1.00	0.92	0.84	0.78	0.70	0.65	0.64	0.67
Côte-d'Or	1.04	1.02	0.98	0.93	0.88	0.82	0.80	0.80	0.83
Nièvre	0.95	0.92	0.90	0.83	0.76	0.69	0.61	0.60	0.61
Saône-et-Loire	1.68	1.66	1.59	1.59	1.53	1.42	1.29	1.26	1.25
Yonne	1.02	0.95	0.90	0.82	0.77	0.70	0.66	0.65	0.66
Nord	4.01	4.26	4.53	4.79	4.95	4.56	4.85	4.82	4.73
Pas-de-Calais	2.11	2.17	2.28	2.45	2.70	2.52	2.88	2.81	2.89
Meurthe-et-Moselle[2]	1.02	1.11	1.16	1.24	1.43	1.29	1.42	1.37	1.31
Meuse	0.80	0.77	0.76	0.73	0.70	0.53	0.52	0.52	0.47
Moselle[3]	..	..	..	..	..	1.50	1.66	1.66	1.54
Vosges[2]	1.11	1.08	1.07	1.08	1.10	0.98	0.90	0.90	0.84
Rhin (Bas-)[3]	..	..	..	..	..	1.66	1.64	1.70	1.66
Rhin (Haut-)[3]	..	..	..	..	..	1.20	1.24	1.21	1.17
Doubs	0.80	0.83	0.79	0.77	0.76	0.73	0.73	0.73	0.74
Jura	0.80	0.76	0.71	0.67	0.64	0.58	0.55	0.53	0.53
Saône (Haute-)	0.85	0.79	0.73	0.69	0.65	0.58	0.52	0.51	0.50
Belfort (Territoire de)[2,4]	0.16	0.19	0.22	0.24	0.26	0.24	0.24	0.24	0.21
Loire-Inférieure	1.67	1.66	1.68	1.71	1.69	1.66	1.56	1.57	1.64
Maine-et-Loire	1.44	1.39	1.35	1.32	1.28	1.21	1.14	1.14	1.22
Mayenne	0.98	0.92	0.87	0.80	0.75	0.67	0.61	0.60	0.63
Sarthe	1.25	1.17	1.12	1.09	1.06	0.97	0.92	0.93	1.02
Vendée	1.12	1.12	1.15	1.13	1.11	1.01	0.93	0.93	0.97
Côtes-du-Nord	1.74	1.67	1.61	1.56	1.53	1.42	1.29	1.27	1.30
Finistère	1.76	1.81	1.90	1.98	2.05	1.95	1.78	1.81	1.79
Ille-et-Vilaine	1.63	1.63	1.64	1.58	1.54	1.43	1.35	1.35	1.43
Morbihan	1.35	1.39	1.42	1.44	1.46	1.39	1.29	1.29	1.25
Charente	1.03	0.98	0.94	0.90	0.88	0.81	0.74	0.74	0.77
Charente-Inférieur	1.29	1.24	1.19	1.16	1.14	1.07	0.99	1.00	1.03
Sèvres (Deux-)	0.93	0.93	0.92	0.88	0.85	0.79	0.74	0.74	0.77
Vienne	0.89	0.90	0.90	0.86	0.84	0.78	0.72	0.73	0.78

continued

APPENDIX TABLE F.2 Census population by region 1872–1946 (per cent) (continued)

Département	1872	1881	1891	1901[1]	1911[1]	1921	1931	1936	1946
Dordogne	1.35	1.31	1.25	1.16	1.10	1.01	0.92	0.92	0.96
Gironde	1.96	1.99	2.07	2.11	2.09	2.09	2.04	2.03	2.12
Landes	0.85	0.80	0.78	0.75	0.73	0.67	0.61	0.60	0.61
Lot-et-Garonne	0.89	0.83	0.77	0.72	0.68	0.61	0.59	0.60	0.65
Pyrénées (Basses-)	1.18	1.15	1.11	1.09	1.09	1.03	1.01	0.99	1.03
Ariège	0.69	0.64	0.59	0.54	0.50	0.44	0.38	0.37	0.36
Aveyron	1.13	1.10	1.04	0.98	0.93	0.85	0.77	0.75	0.76
Garonne (Haute-)	1.32	1.27	1.23	1.15	1.09	1.08	1.06	1.10	1.26
Gers	0.80	0.75	0.68	0.61	0.56	0.49	0.46	0.46	0.47
Lot	0.79	0.74	0.66	0.58	0.52	0.45	0.40	0.39	0.38
Pyrénées (Hautes-)	0.66	0.63	0.59	0.55	0.52	0.47	0.45	0.45	0.50
Tarn	0.99	0.95	0.90	0.85	0.82	0.75	0.72	0.71	0.74
Tarn-et-Garonne	0.62	0.58	0.54	0.50	0.46	0.41	0.39	0.39	0.41
Corrèze	0.85	0.84	0.86	0.82	0.78	0.70	0.63	0.63	0.63
Creuse	0.77	0.74	0.74	0.71	0.67	0.58	0.50	0.48	0.47
Vienne (Haute-)	0.90	0.93	0.97	0.98	0.97	0.89	0.80	0.80	0.83
Ain	1.00	0.96	0.93	0.90	0.86	0.81	0.77	0.76	0.76
Ardèche	1.07	1.00	0.97	0.91	0.84	0.75	0.68	0.65	0.63
Drôme	0.89	0.83	0.80	0.76	0.73	0.67	0.64	0.64	0.66
Isère	1.60	1.54	1.49	1.46	1.40	1.34	1.40	1.37	1.42
Loire	1.53	1.59	1.61	1.66	1.62	1.62	1.59	1.55	1.56
Rhône	1.81	1.97	2.10	2.16	2.31	2.44	2.50	2.45	2.27
Savoie	0.74	0.71	0.69	0.65	0.63	0.57	0.56	0.57	0.58
Savoie (Haute-)	0.76	0.73	0.70	0.68	0.64	0.60	0.60	0.62	0.67
Allier	1.09	1.11	1.11	1.08	1.03	0.95	0.89	0.88	0.92
Cantal	0.65	0.63	0.63	0.59	0.56	0.51	0.46	0.46	0.46
Loire (Haute-)	0.86	0.84	0.83	0.81	0.77	0.69	0.60	0.58	0.56
Puy-de-Dôme	1.59	1.50	1.47	1.40	1.33	1.25	1.20	1.16	1.18
Aude	0.79	0.87	0.83	0.81	0.76	0.73	0.71	0.68	0.66
Gard	1.17	1.10	1.09	1.08	1.04	1.01	0.97	0.94	0.94
Hérault	1.18	1.17	1.20	1.26	1.21	1.24	1.23	1.20	1.14
Lozère	0.38	0.38	0.35	0.33	0.31	0.28	0.24	0.23	0.22
Pyrénées-Orientales	0.51	0.55	0.55	0.54	0.54	0.56	0.57	0.56	0.57
Alpes (Basses-)	0.39	0.35	0.32	0.30	0.27	0.23	0.21	0.20	0.20
Alpes (Hautes-)	0.33	0.32	0.30	0.28	0.27	0.23	0.21	0.21	0.21
Alpes-Maritimes[5]	0.55	0.60	0.68	0.75	0.90	0.91	1.18	1.23	1.11
Bouches-du-Rhône	1.50	1.56	1.65	1.88	2.04	2.15	2.63	2.92	2.40
Var[2]	0.78	0.77	0.75	0.84	0.84	0.82	0.90	0.95	0.92
Vaucluse	0.73	0.65	0.61	0.61	0.60	0.56	0.58	0.59	0.62
Corse	0.71	0.72	0.75	0.76	0.73	0.72	0.71	0.77	0.66
TOTAL	**100.00**	**100.00**	**100.00**	**100.00**	**100.00**	**100.00**	**100.00**	**100.00**	**100.00**

Notes: [1] Values not comparable with previous years due to recalculation. [2] Valid only 1881 and 1891.
1872: *Meurthe-et-Moselle* 5,244 sq. km., *Belfort* 605 sq. km., *Var* 6,083 sq. km., *Vosges* 5,877 sq. km.
[3] Départements *Moselle*, *Bas-Rhin* and *Haut-Rhin* gained from Germany after World War I (1918).
[4] The territory of *Belfort* was named *Haut-Rhin* in 1872. This territory is not the same as the Département *Haut-Rhin* that came to existence after 1918. [5] Valid only 1872. 1881: 3,917 sq. km., 1891: 3,743 sq. km.

APPENDIX TABLE F.3 Population density by region 1872–1946 (inhabitants per sq. km.)

Département	1872	1881	1891	1901[1]	1911[1]	1921	1931	1936	1946
Seine	4,449	5,843	6,559	7,646	8,654	9,192	10,279	10,340	9,950
Seine-et-Marne	58	61	62	60	61	59	68	69	69
Seine-et-Oise	91	103	112	125	145	163	241	250	250
Ardennes	61	64	62	60	61	53	56	55	47
Aube	42	42	43	41	40	38	40	40	39
Marne	47	52	53	53	53	45	50	50	47
Marne (Haute-)	40	41	39	36	34	32	30	30	29
Aisne	74	76	74	72	71	57	66	65	61
Oise	66	69	69	69	70	66	69	68	67
Somme	89	89	89	86	83	72	74	74	70
Eure	62	61	59	55	54	50	51	50	52
Seine-Inférieure	128	135	144	135	138	139	143	144	133
Cher	46	49	50	47	46	42	40	40	39
Eure-et-Loire	47	48	49	46	46	42	43	43	43
Indre	40	42	43	42	42	38	36	36	36
Indre-et-Loire	51	54	55	55	55	53	54	56	57
Loir-et-Cher	42	43	44	43	42	39	38	38	38
Loiret	52	54	56	54	53	49	50	50	51
Calvados	81	80	78	72	70	68	70	71	70
Manche	89	89	87	77	74	66	68	68	68
Orne	65	62	58	53	50	45	45	44	44
Côte-d'Or	42	44	43	41	40	37	38	38	38
Nièvre	49	51	50	47	43	39	37	36	36
Saône-et-Loire	69	73	71	72	70	64	62	61	59
Yonne	48	48	46	43	41	37	37	36	36
Nord	249	282	306	323	340	310	351	350	332
Pas-de-Calais	113	124	132	141	158	147	178	175	173
Meurthe-et-Moselle[2]	69	80	85	92	107	95	112	109	100
Meuse	45	47	47	45	45	33	35	35	30
Moselle[3]	..	..	..	..	..	95	111	112	100
Vosges[2]	67	70	70	71	74	65	64	64	58
Rhin (Bas-)[3]	..	..	..	..	..	136	144	149	141
Rhin (Haut-)[3]	..	..	..	..	..	134	147	145	135
Doubs	54	59	58	57	57	54	58	58	57
Jura	57	57	55	52	50	45	45	44	43
Saône (Haute-)	56	55	53	50	48	42	41	40	38
Belfort (Territoire de)[2,4]	93	118	138	151	166	155	163	163	143
Loire-Inférieure	86	91	94	95	96	93	93	94	95
Maine-et-Loire	72	73	73	71	70	66	66	66	69
Mayenne	67	67	64	60	57	50	49	48	49
Sarthe	71	71	69	68	67	61	62	62	66
Vendée	59	63	66	63	63	57	56	55	56
Côtes-du-Nord	89	91	90	84	84	77	75	74	73
Finistère	92	101	108	110	115	109	106	108	103
Ille-et-Vilaine	85	91	93	88	87	80	81	81	83
Morbihan	70	77	80	79	82	77	76	76	71
Charente	61	62	61	59	58	53	52	52	52
Charente-Inférieur	67	68	67	63	62	58	57	58	58
Sèvres (Deux-)	55	58	59	56	56	51	51	51	52
Vienne	45	49	49	48	47	43	43	44	45

continued

APPENDIX TABLE F.3 Population density by region 1872–1946 (inhabitants per sq. km.) (continued)

Département	1872	1881	1891	1901[1]	1911[1]	1921	1931	1936	1946
Dordogne	52	54	52	49	47	43	42	42	42
Gironde	71	77	82	77	77	76	80	79	80
Landes	32	32	32	31	31	28	27	27	26
Lot-et-Garonne	59	58	55	52	50	45	46	47	49
Pyrénées (Basses-)	55	57	56	55	56	52	55	54	54
Ariège	50	49	46	43	41	35	33	32	30
Aveyron	46	47	46	44	42	38	37	36	35
Garonne (Haute-)	74	76	75	70	68	67	69	72	80
Gers	45	45	42	38	35	31	31	31	30
Lot	54	54	49	43	39	34	32	31	30
Pyrénées (Hautes-)	51	52	50	48	45	41	42	42	45
Tarn	61	63	60	57	56	51	52	52	52
Tarn-et-Garonne	59	58	56	53	49	43	44	44	45
Corrèze	51	54	56	54	53	47	45	45	43
Creuse	49	50	51	50	47	41	37	36	34
Vienne (Haute-)	58	63	68	69	69	63	60	60	60
Ain	61	63	62	60	59	54	55	54	53
Ardèche	68	68	67	64	60	53	51	49	46
Drôme	48	48	47	45	44	40	41	41	41
Isère	68	70	69	69	68	64	71	70	70
Loire	114	126	129	135	134	133	139	135	132
Rhône	229	266	289	295	320	335	366	360	321
Savoie	45	46	46	41	40	36	38	39	38
Savoie (Haute-)	63	63	62	57	55	51	55	57	59
Allier	53	57	58	57	55	50	51	50	51
Cantal	40	41	42	40	39	34	34	33	32
Loire (Haute-)	61	64	64	63	61	54	50	49	46
Puy-de-Dôme	70	71	71	68	66	61	63	61	60
Aude	44	52	50	50	47	45	47	45	42
Gard	71	71	72	72	70	67	69	67	65
Hérault	67	71	75	79	77	78	83	81	74
Lozère	26	28	26	25	24	21	20	19	18
Pyrénées-Orientales	44	51	51	51	51	53	58	56	55
Alpes (Basses-)	20	19	18	16	15	13	13	12	12
Alpes (Hautes-)	21	22	21	19	19	16	16	16	15
Alpes-Maritimes[5]	50	59	67	78	95	96	132	138	120
Bouches-du-Rhône	104	115	124	140	154	160	210	233	185
Var[2]	46	48	48	54	55	54	63	66	62
Vaucluse	72	69	66	66	67	61	68	69	70
Corse	29	31	33	34	33	32	34	37	31
TOTAL	**67**	**71**	**73**	**73**	**74**	**73**	**78**	**78**	**75**

Notes: See Appendix Table F.2.

France

APPENDIX TABLE F.4 Demographic developments 1850–1945 (absolute figures and rates)

Year	Mid-year population	Natural population growth rate	Population growth rate	Net migration rate	Crude birth rate	Legitimate births per 10,000 married women age 15–44	Illegitimate births per 10,000 unmarried women age 15–44	Illeg. births per 100 leg. births
1850	35,630,000	5.4	2.2	-3.2	26.8	..	..	7.9
1851	35,800,000	4.8	4.7	-0.1	27.1	2,178	167	7.7
1852	35,950,000	4.3	4.2	-0.1	26.8	2,145	167	7.8
1853	36,070,000	3.9	3.3	-0.6	26.0	2,064	163	7.9
1854	36,230,000	-1.9	4.4	6.3	25.5	2,010	167	8.2
1855	36,080,000	-1.0	-4.2	-3.2	25.0	1,972	154	7.7
1856	36,190,000	3.2	3.0	-0.1	26.3	2,064	164	7.7
1857	36,300,000	2.3	3.0	0.8	25.9	2,024	171	8.2
1858	36,340,000	2.6	1.1	-1.5	26.7	2,078	182	8.3
1859	36,500,000	1.1	4.4	3.3	27.9	2,164	196	8.6
1860	36,510,000	4.8	0.3	-4.5	26.2	2,046	171	7.8
1861[1]	37,390,000	3.7	–	–	26.9	2,088	186	8.3
1862	37,520,000	4.9	3.5	-1.4	26.5	2,063	179	8.0
1863	37,710,000	4.4	5.0	0.6	26.9	2,085	186	8.2
1864	37,860,000	3.8	4.0	0.1	26.6	2,061	185	8.2
1865	38,020,000	2.2	4.2	2.0	26.5	2,048	188	8.3
1866	38,080,000	3.2	1.6	-1.6	26.4	2,045	188	8.3
1867	38,230,000	3.6	3.9	0.3	26.3	2,029	187	8.3
1868	38,330,000	1.6	2.6	1.0	25.7	1,983	183	8.2
1869	38,390,000	2.5	1.6	-0.9	26.0	2,011	185	8.2
1870	38,440,000	-2.5	1.3	3.8	25.9	2,000	184	8.2
1871[1]	36,190,000	-12.3	–	–	22.8	1,768	154	7.7
1872	36,140,000	4.8	-1.4	-6.2	26.7	2,067	182	7.8
1873	36,340,000	2.8	5.5	2.7	26.0	1,997	185	8.1
1874	36,490,000	4.7	4.1	-0.6	26.2	1,999	183	7.8
1875	36,660,000	2.9	4.6	1.7	25.9	1,977	178	7.6
1876	36,830,000	3.6	4.6	1.0	26.2	1,990	180	7.5
1877	37,000,000	3.9	4.6	0.7	25.5	1,951	176	7.6
1878	37,180,000	2.6	4.8	2.2	25.2	1,939	178	7.9
1879	37,320,000	2.6	3.8	1.2	25.1	1,950	172	7.7
1880	37,450,000	1.7	3.5	1.8	24.6	1,921	173	8.0
1881	37,590,000	2.9	3.7	0.8	24.9	1,966	176	8.1
1882	37,730,000	2.6	3.7	1.1	24.8	1,960	177	8.2
1883	37,860,000	2.6	3.4	0.9	24.8	1,958	183	8.6
1884	38,010,000	2.1	3.9	1.9	24.7	1,952	185	8.8
1885	38,110,000	2.3	2.6	0.3	24.3	1,927	180	8.7
1886	38,230,000	1.4	3.1	1.8	23.9	1,899	180	8.9
1887	38,260,000	1.5	0.8	-0.7	23.5	1,861	178	9.0
1888	38,290,000	1.2	0.8	-0.4	23.1	1,812	180	9.3
1889	38,370,000	2.2	2.1	-0.1	22.9	1,797	177	9.1
1890	38,380,000	-1.0	0.3	1.3	21.8	1,701	171	9.3
1891	38,350,000	-0.3	-0.8	-0.5	22.6	1,751	178	9.3
1892	38,360,000	-0.5	0.3	0.8	22.3	1,722	178	9.4
1893	38,380,000	0.2	0.5	0.3	22.8	1,750	184	9.6
1894	38,420,000	1.0	1.0	0.0	22.3	1,701	184	9.8
1895	38,460,000	-0.5	1.0	1.5	21.7	1,654	176	9.6
1896	38,550,000	2.4	2.3	-0.1	22.5	1,706	183	9.7
1897	38,700,000	2.8	3.9	1.1	22.2	1,667	184	9.7

continued

APPENDIX TABLE F.4 Demographic developments 1850–1945 (absolute figures and rates)

Crude death rate	Infant mortality rate	Stillbirth rate	Infant mortality and stillbirth rate	Crude marriage rate	Persons marrying per 10,000 unmarried persons age 15+	Persons marrying per 10,000 unmarried persons age 15–49	Crude divorce rate	Divorces per 100 marriages	Divorces per 10,000 married persons	Year
21.4	147.0	38.9	185.9	8.4			..	..	..	1850
22.3	161.8	38.7	200.6	8.0	475	613	..	..	..	1851
22.6	162.5	38.8	201.2	7.8	466	603	..	..	..	1852
22.1	150.3	41.2	191.5	7.8	465	603	..	..	..	1853
27.4	180.2	43.1	223.3	7.5	449	583	..	..	..	1854
26.0	175.9	42.1	218.0	7.9	473	616	..	..	..	1855
23.1	167.2	42.9	210.1	7.9	475	621	..	..	..	1856
23.7	185.4	44.5	229.9	8.1	493	644	..	..	..	1857
24.1	175.6	45.2	220.8	8.5	512	670	..	..	..	1858
26.8	211.7	45.7	257.4	8.2	496	650	..	..	..	1859
21.4	152.7	46.3	199.0	7.9	481	630	..	..	..	1860
23.2	189.4	44.8	234.2	8.2	496	651	..	..	..	1861[1]
21.7	163.1	45.1	208.2	8.1	493	647	..	..	..	1862
22.5	178.9	44.9	223.8	8.0	488	642	..	..	..	1863
22.7	173.9	46.3	220.2	7.9	484	638	..	..	..	1864
24.2	191.0	46.7	237.7	7.9	482	636	..	..	..	1865
23.2	161.9	47.4	209.3	8.0	489	647	..	..	..	1866
22.7	171.5	46.6	218.2	7.9	482	640	..	..	..	1867
24.1	192.0	47.0	239.0	7.9	483	643	..	..	..	1868
23.6	176.2	47.8	224.0	8.2	508	678	..	..	..	1869
28.4	201.4	47.9	249.3	6.1	375	502	..	..	..	1870
35.1	237.6	48.8	286.4	7.3	448	602	..	..	..	1871[1]
21.9	152.0	45.5	197.5	9.8	604	814	..	..	..	1872
23.2	179.1	47.0	226.1	8.8	549	742	..	..	..	1873
21.4	158.3	46.7	205.0	8.3	518	702	..	..	..	1874
23.1	169.9	46.1	216.0	8.2	513	697	..	..	..	1875
22.6	165.3	46.2	211.5	7.9	497	677	..	..	..	1876
21.7	158.4	45.9	204.3	7.5	469	638	..	..	..	1877
22.6	169.7	46.2	215.9	7.5	465	632	..	..	..	1878
22.5	157.7	46.9	204.6	7.6	465	632	..	..	..	1879
22.9	180.1	45.3	225.4	7.4	454	616	..	..	..	1880
22.0	165.5	46.7	212.3	7.5	453	615	..	..	..	1881
22.2	165.0	47.5	212.5	7.5	449	607	..	..	..	1882
22.2	165.0	46.6	211.6	7.5	451	609	..	..	..	1883
22.6	176.9	48.3	225.2	7.6	456	615	0.0	0.6	2.2	1884
22.0	161.6	47.6	209.2	7.4	444	597	0.1	1.5	5.5	1885
22.5	173.4	47.8	221.2	7.4	441	592	0.1	1.4	5.3	1886
22.0	161.1	47.7	208.8	7.2	431	579	0.2	2.1	7.7	1887
21.9	165.2	47.7	212.9	7.2	430	579	0.1	2.0	7.2	1888
20.7	155.4	48.3	203.6	7.1	423	571	0.2	2.3	8.2	1889
22.8	176.1	48.3	224.4	7.0	417	564	0.2	2.4	8.5	1890
22.9	160.7	49.1	209.7	7.4	442	599	0.2	2.3	8.4	1891
22.8	181.8	49.0	230.8	7.6	449	609	0.2	2.4	9.1	1892
22.6	172.9	48.5	221.3	7.5	444	603	0.2	2.4	9.0	1893
21.2	157.8	49.1	206.9	7.5	443	601	0.2	2.8	10.2	1894
22.2	178.6	49.9	228.5	7.4	436	592	0.2	2.7	9.9	1895
20.0	147.5	49.2	196.7	7.5	446	607	0.2	2.7	10.1	1896
19.4	152.0	49.1	201.1	7.5	450	614	0.2	2.7	10.2	1897

continued

APPENDIX TABLE F.4 Demographic developments 1850–1945 (continued)

Year	Mid-year population	Natural population growth rate	Population growth rate	Net migration rate	Crude birth rate	Legitimate births per 10,000 married women age 15–44	Illegitimate births per 10,000 unmarried women age 15–44	Illeg. births per 100 leg. births
1898	38.820.000	0.9	3.1	2.2	21.7	1.614	182	9.7
1899	38,890,000	0.8	1.8	1.0	21.8	1,600	186	9.7
1900	38,940,000	-0.7	1.3	2.0	21.2	1,542	183	9.7
1901	38,980,000	1.9	1.0	-0.8	22.0	1,600	188	9.5
1902	39,050,000	2.2	1.8	-0.4	21.6	1,566	188	9.6
1903	39,120,000	1.9	1.8	-0.1	21.1	1,522	185	9.6
1904	39,190,000	1.5	1.8	0.3	20.9	1,499	183	9.6
1905	39,220,000	0.9	0.8	-0.2	20.6	1,469	183	9.7
1906	39,270,000	0.7	1.3	0.6	20.5	1,462	183	9.6
1907	39,270,000	-0.5	0.0	0.5	19.7	1,388	184	10.1
1908	39,370,000	1.2	2.5	1.3	20.1	1,419	183	9.8
1909	39,430,000	0.4	1.5	1.2	19.5	1,372	176	9.6
1910	39,540,000	1.8	2.8	1.0	19.6	1,373	175	9.5
1911	39,620,000	-0.8	2.0	2.9	18.7	1,308	170	9.6
1912	39,670,000	1.5	1.3	-0.2	18.9	1,315	172	9.5
1913	39,770,000	1.1	2.5	1.4	18.8	1,298	173	9.6
1914[2]	41,700,000	-0.4	–	–	18.1	..	..	..
1915[2]	40,700,000	-6.5	–	–	11.8	..	..	..
1916[2]	40,100,000	-7.8	–	–	9.5	..	..	..
1917[2]	39,500,000	-7.6	–	–	10.4	..	..	..
1918[2]	38,750,000	-10.2	–	–	12.1	..	..	..
1919	38,700,000	-6.0	-1.3	4.7	13.0	..	..	..
1920	39,000,000	4.2	7.7	3.5	21.4	1,561	181	11.0
1921	39,240,000	3.0	6.1	3.1	20.7	1,505	162	9.9
1922	39,420,000	1.8	4.6	2.7	19.3	1,389	148	9.4
1923	39,880,000	2.4	11.5	9.1	19.1	1,357	150	9.5
1924	40,310,000	1.9	10.7	8.8	18.7	1,314	148	9.3
1925	40,610,000	1.5	7.4	5.9	19.0	1,316	154	9.4
1926	40,870,000	1.3	6.4	5.0	18.8	1,289	154	9.2
1927	40,940,000	1.7	1.7	0.0	18.2	1,239	151	9.1
1928	41,050,000	1.8	2.7	0.8	18.3	1,236	155	9.2
1929	41,230,000	-0.2	4.4	4.6	17.7	1,190	154	9.1
1930	41,610,000	2.4	9.1	6.7	18.0	1,204	159	9.0
1931	41,860,000	1.3	6.0	4.7	17.5	1,168	151	8.6
1932	41,860,000	1.5	0.0	-1.5	17.3	1,158	148	8.4
1933	41,890,000	0.4	0.7	0.3	16.2	1,097	136	8.1
1934	41,950,000	1.0	1.4	0.4	16.2	1,103	132	7.8
1935	41,940,000	-0.4	-0.2	0.2	15.3	1,051	123	7.5
1936	41,910,000	-0.3	-0.7	-0.4	15.1	1,047	115	7.0
1937	41,930,000	-0.3	0.5	0.7	14.7	1,032	114	6.9
1938	41,960,000	-0.8	0.7	1.6	14.6	1,030	111	6.7
1939	41,900,000	-0.7	-1.4	-0.7	14.6	..	..	..
1940[3]	41,000,000	-4.4	-22.0	-17.6	13.6	..	..	..
1941[3]	39,600,000	-3.9	-35.4	-31.5	13.1	..	..	..
1942[3]	39,400,000	-2.1	-5.1	-3.0	14.5	..	..	..
1943[3]	39,000,000	-0.3	-10.3	-10.0	15.7	..	..	..
1944[3]	38,900,000	-1.0	-2.6	-1.6	16.1	..	..	..
1945[3]	39,700,000	0.1	20.2	20.1	16.2	..	..	..

Notes: [1] Territorial change. [2] Present territory. Figures are official estimates based on statistics for 77 departments. The number of deaths excludes military losses (ca. 360,000 in 1914, 320,000 in 1915, 270,000 in 1916, 145,000 in 1917, and 250,000 in 1918). [3] Figures are official estimates based on statistics for 86/87 departments and available information for the other departments. The number of deaths does not include civil or military deaths due to war accidents (ca. 600,000 persons in the period 1939–1945).

APPENDIX TABLE F.4 Demographic developments 1850–1945 (continued)

Crude death rate	Infant mortality rate	Stillbirth rate	Infant mortality and stillbirth rate	Crude marriage rate	Persons marrying per 10,000 unmarried persons age 15+	Persons marrying per 10,000 unmarried persons age 15–49	Crude divorce rate	Divorces per 100 marriages	Divorces per 10,000 married persons	Year
20.9	168.9	47.2	216.0	7.4	445	611	0.2	2.8	10.3	1898
21.0	163.2	47.1	210.2	7.6	460	636	0.2	2.7	10.1	1899
21.9	160.8	47.4	208.1	7.7	468	650	0.2	2.6	9.8	1900
20.1	142.0	47.5	189.4	7.8	473	663	0.2	2.9	11.1	1901
19.5	135.2	47.6	182.8	7.5	460	646	0.2	3.2	11.7	1902
19.3	137.1	47.3	184.3	7.6	463	650	0.3	3.4	12.6	1903
19.4	144.2	47.3	191.5	7.6	468	658	0.3	3.6	13.4	1904
19.6	135.8	46.9	182.7	7.7	475	669	0.3	3.6	13.3	1905
19.9	143.5	46.2	189.8	7.8	482	680	0.3	3.8	14.2	1906
20.2	131.2	47.6	178.9	8.0	496	699	0.3	4.0	15.3	1907
18.9	127.4	47.3	174.7	8.0	499	704	0.3	4.2	16.1	1908
19.1	117.7	46.9	164.6	7.8	487	688	0.4	4.5	16.8	1909
17.8	110.5	46.5	157.0	7.8	487	689	0.4	4.6	17.1	1910
19.6	157.1	45.9	203.0	7.8	488	691	0.4	5.0	18.2	1911
17.5	104.5	46.2	150.7	7.9	496	703	0.4	5.4	19.9	1912
17.7	112.5	46.5	159.0	7.5	475	674	0.4	5.5	19.3	1913
18.5	112.9	43.8	156.7	4.9	..	..	0.2	5.0	..	1914[2]
18.3	143.8	43.8	187.5	2.1	..	..	0.0	2.2	..	1915[2]
17.3	125.7	49.7	175.4	3.1	..	..	0.1	3.9	..	1916[2]
18.0	126.8	48.8	175.6	4.6	..	..	0.2	4.9	..	1917[2]
22.3	140.4	46.8	187.2	5.2	..	..	0.3	4.9	..	1918[2]
19.0	122.5	50.6	173.2	14.3	823	1.172	0.5	3.5	23.8	1919
17.2	99.2	42.5	141.7	16.0	930	1.327	1.1	6.6	49.6	1920
17.7	116.9	42.7	159.6	11.6	683	977	0.8	6.7	36.0	1921
17.4	86.6	42.0	128.6	9.8	580	831	0.6	6.5	29.3	1922
16.7	96.3	40.5	136.7	8.9	534	768	0.6	6.5	26.3	1923
16.8	84.8	38.4	123.2	8.8	535	770	0.5	6.2	24.8	1924
17.4	88.9	37.7	126.6	8.7	532	768	0.5	6.3	24.5	1925
17.4	96.9	36.6	133.6	8.5	523	756	0.5	6.5	24.4	1926
16.5	83.4	35.5	118.8	8.2	513	746	0.5	6.4	23.3	1927
16.4	91.6	35.6	127.2	8.3	521	760	0.6	7.5	27.2	1928
17.9	96.0	34.8	130.8	8.1	517	757	0.6	7.8	27.7	1929
15.6	78.1	34.7	112.8	8.2	529	779	0.6	6.9	24.5	1930
16.2	75.9	35.0	110.9	7.8	508	750	0.6	7.5	25.4	1931
15.8	77.0	35.2	112.1	7.5	491	731	0.6	7.5	24.4	1932
15.8	74.8	35.1	109.9	7.5	493	740	0.6	7.5	24.4	1933
15.1	69.5	34.4	103.9	7.1	466	706	0.6	8.1	24.6	1934
15.7	68.9	34.2	103.0	6.8	446	681	0.6	8.4	24.5	1935
15.3	66.9	34.6	101.5	6.7	440	677	0.6	9.3	26.7	1936
15.0	65.4	34.3	99.7	6.5	432	670	0.6	9.4	26.4	1937
15.4	65.5	36.1	101.6	6.5	432	676	0.6	9.9	27.5	1938
15.3	63.5	35.8	99.3	6.2	409	646	..	..	..	1939
18.0	90.5	32.2	122.7	4.3	..	..	0.3	7.7	..	1940[3]
17.0	72.7	29.8	102.5	5.7	..	..	0.4	7.0	..	1941[3]
16.6	71.0	27.1	98.1	6.8	..	..	0.5	6.7	..	1942[3]
16.0	75.4	25.6	101.0	5.6	..	..	0.5	9.3	..	1943[3]
17.1	77.7	27.0	104.6	5.3	..	..	0.6	10.5	..	1944[3]
16.1	108.9	27.7	136.5	9.9	..	..	1.0	9.6	..	1945[3]

Notes: [1] Territorial change. [2] Present territory. Figures are official estimates based on statistics for 77 departments. The number of deaths excludes military losses (ca. 360,000 in 1914, 320,000 in 1915, 270,000 in 1916, 145,000 in 1917, and 250,000 in 1918). [3] Figures are official estimates based on statistics for 86/87 departments and available information for the other departments. The number of deaths does not include civil or military deaths due to war accidents (ca. 600,000 persons in the period 1939–1945).

APPENDIX TABLE F.5 Life expectancy by age 1817/31–1933/38 (in years)

Age	0	10	20	30	40	50	60	70	80
Males									
1817–1831	38.33	47.00	40.00	34.00	27.00	19.91	13.25	8.08	4.75
1861–1865	39.10	48.70	41.20	34.65	..	..	13.55	..	4.40
1877–1881	40.83	48.25	40.42	33.83	..	20.00	13.58	8.33	4.83
1891–1900	45.35	49.25	41.03	33.86	26.65	19.76	13.31	7.92	4.37
1898–1903	45.74	49.75	41.53	34.35	27.15	20.26	13.91	8.42	4.87
1908–1913	48.49	49.90	41.39	34.03	26.67	19.69	13.34	8.00	4.39
1920–1923	52.19	51.51	42.93	35.50	27.84	20.45	13.84	8.25	4.33
1928–1933	54.30	52.06	43.30	35.42	27.62	20.33	13.76	8.29	4.44
1933–1938	55.94	52.57	43.62	35.52	27.71	20.43	13.92	8.50	4.61
Females									
1817–1831	40.83	47.42	40.08	33.41	26.58	19.58	13.16	8.08	4.75
1861–1865	40.55	48.75	41.60	35.10	..	..	13.90	..	4.66
1877–1881	43.42	49.75	42.25	35.50	..	21.42	14.58	8.83	5.00
1891–1900	48.72	51.53	43.59	36.44	29.10	21.64	14.58	8.72	4.89
1898–1903	49.13	52.03	44.02	36.93	29.60	22.14	15.08	9.21	5.38
1908–1913	52.14	53.08	44.83	37.37	29.75	22.13	14.95	8.95	4.96
1920–1923	55.87	54.49	46.16	38.61	30.82	22.99	15.63	9.33	5.04
1928–1933	59.02	55.95	47.40	39.54	31.37	23.39	14.94	9.58	5.09
1933–1938	61.64	57.50	48.64	40.46	32.10	24.01	16.50	10.06	5.46

APPENDIX TABLE F.6A   Households by type 1851–1946 (absolute and per cent)

Census year	Household types and members									
	Total households	Private households	Family households	One-person households	Institutional households	Total household members	Private household members	Family household members	One-person household members	Institutional household members
	Absolute									
1851	..	9,922,021	..	..	..	35,783,000	..	..	..	..
1856	..	9,387,561	8,472,773	914,788	..	36,039,000	..	..	914,788	..
1861	..	9,747,029	8,567,595	1,179,434	..	37,386,000	..	..	1,179,434	..
1866	..	9,997,360	..	..	..	38,067,000	..	..	..	..
1872	..	9,525,717	..	..	..	36,103,000	..	..	..	789,976
1876	..	10,088,183	..	..	..	36,906,000	..	..	..	860,590
1881	10,761,345	10,399,885	..	..	..	37,672,000	..	..	..	996,945
1886	10,582,251	10,563,782	9,020,120	1,543,662	18,469	38,219,000	37,203,276	35,659,614	1,543,662	1,015,724
1891	10,681,960	10,662,423	9,033,670	1,628,753	19,537	38,343,000	37,251,651	35,622,898	1,628,753	1,091,349
1896	10,812,151	10,797,038	9,109,791	1,687,247	15,113	38,517,000	37,417,269	35,730,022	1,687,247	1,099,731
1901	11,324,471	10,939,994	9,282,248	1,657,746	..	38,962,000	37,822,596	36,164,850	1,657,746	1,139,404
1906¹	..	..	..	..	..	39,252,000	..	..	..	1,069,890
1911	11,858,785	..	..	..	..	39,605,000	..	..	..	1,134,085
1921	11,859,980	..	..	..	..	39,210,000	..	..	..	1,134,370
1926	12,520,498	..	..	..	..	40,744,000	..	..	..	1,003,268
1931	12,982,988	..	..	..	..	41,835,000	..	..	..	1,092,362
1936	13,150,486	..	..	..	..	41,907,000	..	..	..	1,232,822
1946	12,931,000	12,671,657	10,313,927	2,357,730	..	40,503,000	39,461,000	37,103,270	2,357,730	1,042,000

continued

APPENDIX TABLE F.6A   Households by type 1851–1946 (absolute and per cent) (continued)

Census year	Household types and members									
	Total households	Private households	Family households	One-person households	Institutional households	Total household members	Private household members	Family household members	One-person household members	Institutional household members
	Per cent									
1851	..	100.00	..	..	..	100.00	100.00	..	..	..
1856	..	100.00	90.26	9.74	..	100.00	0.00	..	2.54	..
1861	..	100.00	87.90	12.10	..	100.00	0.00	..	3.15	..
1866	..	100.00	..	..	..	100.00	..	..	..	..
1872	..	100.00	..	..	..	100.00	..	..	..	..
1876	..	100.00	..	..	..	100.00	..	..	..	..
1881	100.00	96.64	..	..	..	100.00	..	..	..	..
1886	100.00	99.83	85.24	14.59	0.17	100.00	97.34	93.30	4.04	2.66
1891	100.00	99.82	84.57	15.25	0.18	100.00	97.15	92.91	4.25	2.85
1896	100.00	99.86	84.26	15.61	0.14	100.00	97.14	92.76	4.38	2.86
1901	100.00	96.60	81.97	14.64	..	100.00	97.08	92.82	4.25	2.92
1906[1]	..	..	..	..	..	100.00	..	..	..	2.73
1911	100.00	..	..	..	..	100.00	..	..	..	2.86
1921	100.00	..	..	..	..	100.00	..	..	..	2.89
1926	100.00	..	..	..	..	100.00	..	..	..	2.46
1931	100.00	..	..	..	..	100.00	..	..	..	2.61
1936	100.00	..	..	..	..	100.00	..	..	..	2.94
1946	100.00	97.99	79.76	18.23	..	100.00	97.43	91.61	5.82	2.57

Note: [1] No household data available.

APPENDIX TABLE F.6B Households by size and members 1856–1946 (absolute figures)

Census year	Private households total	Households by number of members							
		1 person	2 persons	3 persons	4 persons	5 persons	6 persons	7+ persons	Unknown
Households									
1856	9,387,561	914,788	1,628,037	1,753,806	1,600,211	1,166,205	786,730	946,499	..
1861	9,747,029	1,179,434	1,935,456	1,953,699	1,704,909	1,223,211	786,116	964,204	..
1886	10,563,782	1,543,662	2,182,294	2,161,167	1,808,191	1,325,936	1,542,532[1]		..
1891	10,662,423	1,628,753	2,285,581	2,133,409	1,752,067	1,235,321	797,217	830,075	..
1896	10,797,038	1,687,247	2,357,183	2,185,179	1,769,155	1,214,206	754,466	829,302	..
1901	10,939,994	1,657,746	2,376,264	2,127,555	1,689,566	1,138,503	689,514	843,195	417,845[2]
1946	12,671,657	2,357,730	3,373,511	2,751,168	1,888,699	1,078,348	575,819	377,677	..
Persons									
1856	36,039,000[3]	914,788	3,256,074	5,261,418	6,400,844	5,831,025	4,720,380	9,654,471	..
1861	37,386,000[3]	1,179,434	3,870,912	5,861,097	6,819,636	6,116,055	4,716,696	8,822,170	..
1886	37,203,276	1,543,662	4,364,588	6,483,501	7,232,764	6,629,680	9,255,192	1,693,889	..
1891	37,251,651	1,628,753	4,571,162	6,400,227	7,008,268	6,176,605	4,783,302	6,683,334	..
1896	37,417,269	1,687,247	4,714,366	6,555,537	7,076,620	6,071,030	4,526,796	6,785,673	..
1901	37,822,596	1,657,746	4,752,528	6,382,665	6,758,264	5,692,515	4,137,084	8,441,794	..
1946	39,461,000	2,357,730	6,747,022	8,253,504	7,554,796	5,391,740	3,454,914	5,701,294	..

Notes: [1] 6 and more persons. [2] Not classified, because of missing information. [3] Total population.

APPENDIX TABLE F.6C Households by size and members 1856–1946 (per cent)

Census year	Private households total	1 person	2 persons	3 persons	4 persons	5 persons	6 persons	7+ persons	Unknown
Households									
1856	100.00[3]	9.74	17.34	18.68	17.05	12.42	8.38	10.08	..
1861	100.00	12.10	19.86	20.04	17.49	12.55	8.07	9.89	..
1886	100.00	14.61	20.66	20.46	17.12	12.55	14.60[1]		..
1891	100.00	15.28	21.44	20.01	16.43	11.59	7.48	7.79	..
1896	100.00	15.63	21.83	20.24	16.39	11.25	6.99	7.68	..
1901	100.00	15.15	21.72	19.45	15.44	10.41	6.30	7.71	3.82[2]
1946	100.00	18.61	26.62	21.71	14.90	8.51	4.54	2.98	..
Persons									
1856	100.00[3]	2.54	9.03	14.60	17.76	16.18	13.10	26.79	..
1861	100.00[3]	3.15	10.35	15.68	18.24	16.36	12.62	23.60	..
1886	100.00	4.15	11.73	17.43	19.44	17.82	24.88	4.55	..
1891	100.00	4.37	12.27	17.18	18.81	16.58	12.84	17.94	..
1896	100.00	4.51	12.60	17.52	18.91	16.23	12.10	18.14	..
1901	100.00	4.38	12.57	16.88	17.87	15.05	10.94	22.32	..
1946	100.00	5.97	17.10	20.92	19.14	13.66	8.76	14.45	..

Notes: See Appendix Table F.6B.

APPENDIX TABLE F.6D Household indicators 1851–
1946

Census year	Household indicators			
	Mean total household size	Mean private household size	Mean family household size	Mean institutional household size
1851[1]	3.61	..	..	..
1856[1]	3.84	..	..	..
1861[1]	3.84	..	..	..
1866[1]	3.81	..	..	..
1872[1]	3.79	..	..	..
1876[1]	3.66	..	..	..
1881[1]	3.50	..	..	..
1886	3.61	3.52	3.95	55.00
1891	3.59	3.49	3.94	55.86
1896	3.56	3.47	3.92	72.77
1901	3.44	3.46	3.90	..
1911	3.34	..	..	..
1921	3.31	..	..	..
1926	3.25	..	..	..
1931	3.22	..	..	..
1936	3.19	..	..	..
1946	3.13	3.11	3.60	..

Note: [1] Total population to private households.

APPENDIX TABLE F.7 Dates and nature of results on population structure, households/families, and vital statistics

Topic	Intro-duction	Remarks
Population		
Population at census dates	1851	Earlier censuses were conducted in 1801, 1806, 1821, 1826, 1831, 1841, and 1846.
Population by age, sex, and marital status	1851	
Households and families		
Households (ménages or familles)		
Total households	1851	Households were first expressly recorded in 1851: 1851: number of households. 1856: households by size. 1861: households by size. 1866: number of households. 1872: number of households. 1876: number of households. 1881: number of households. 1886: households by size. 1891: households by size. 1896: households by size. 1901: number of households; mainly fertility and housing data. 1906: no households. 1911: number of households. 1921: number of households. 1926: special investigation. 1931: number of households. 1936: number of households. 1946: households by size (housing census). *Disaggregation*: 1856: Paris, towns.
Households by size	1856, 1861, 1886, 1891, 1896, 1901, 1926, 1946	First time in 1856: households by number of persons 1–7+. 1861: 1–7+. 1926: housing census; towns with more than 5,000 inhabitants.
Households by composition	–	
Households by profession of household head	–	
Families (familles)		
Families by number of children	1886, 1891, 1896, 1901, 1931, 1946	Special investigation of the fertility of married females for the first time in 1886. Extensive special survey of the 'productivity of marriages' in 1931 and especially in 1946.

continued

APPENDIX TABLE F.7 Dates and nature of results on population structure, households/families, and vital statistics (continued)

Topic	Intro- duction	Remarks
Population movement		
Mid-year population	1850	
Births		
Live births	1850	
Stillbirths	1850	
Legitimate births	1850	
Illegitimate births	1850	
Deaths		
Total deaths	1850	
Infants (under 1 year)	1850	
Marriages		
Total marriages	1850	
Divorces and separations		
Total divorces	1884	
Legal separations	1865	

APPENDIX FIGURE F.8 Population by age, sex and marital status, France 1851,
1872, 1891, 1901, 1911 and 1946 (per 10,000 of total population)

France, 1851

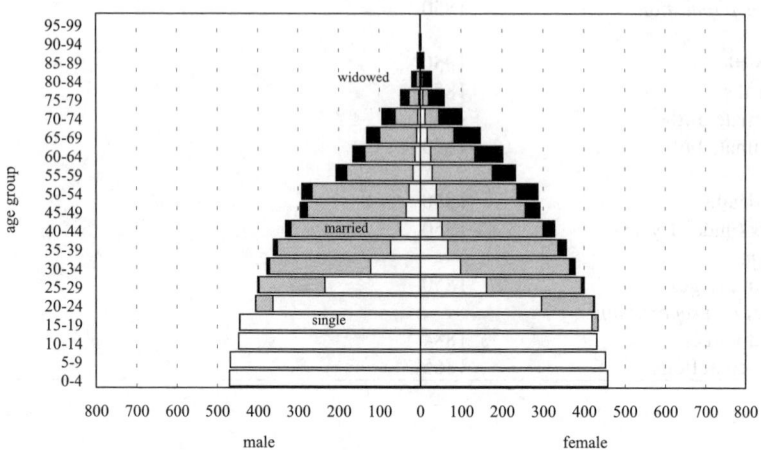

France, 1872

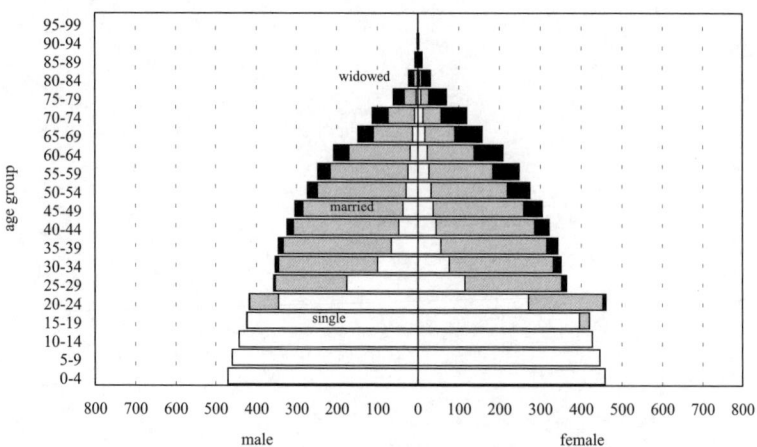

APPENDIX FIGURE F.8 Population by age, sex and marital status, France 1851, 1872, 1891, 1901, 1911 and 1946 (per 10,000 of total population) (continued)

France, 1891

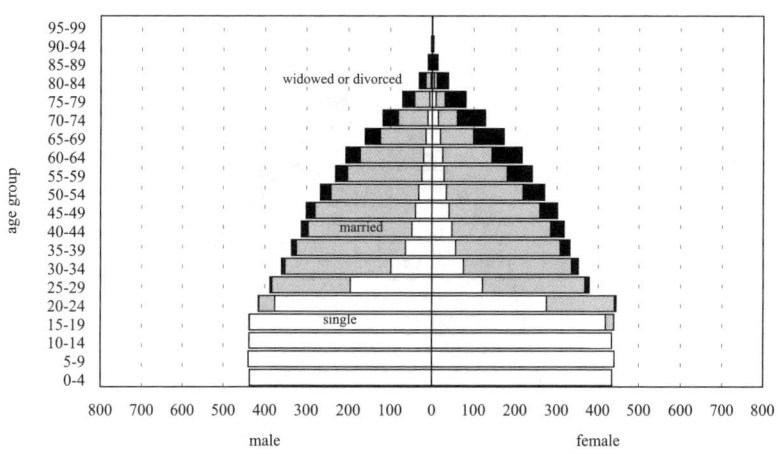

France, 1901

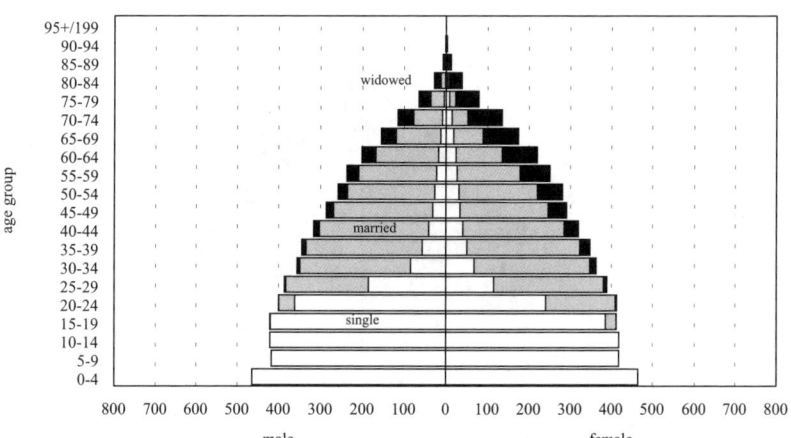

APPENDIX FIGURE F.8 Population by age, sex and marital status, France 1851, 1872, 1891, 1901, 1911 and 1946 (per 10,000 of total population) (continued)

France, 1911

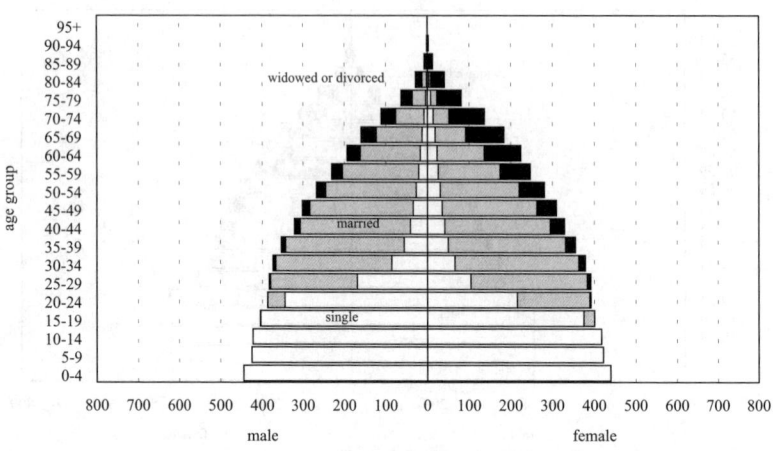

France, 1946

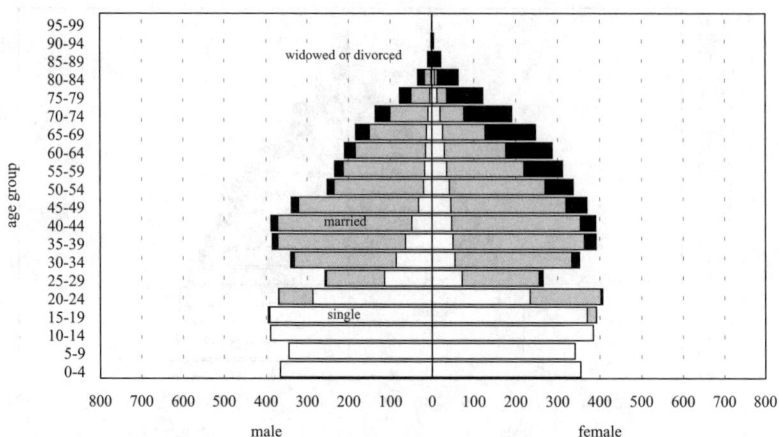

7
Germany

The loose federation of the Holy German Empire was dissolved in 1806 during the Napoleonic wars. The fundamental territorial restructuring was formally agreed on at the 1815 Congress of Vienna which restored the conservative great powers. The several hundred German territories that existed before 1806 were reduced to some 25 more or less sovereign states. These were formally united under the German Federation (*Deutscher Bund*), but this federation had only limited authority and functions. The two major German powers that survived the Napoleonic wars, Prussia and Austria, began striving for territorial integration. There were two different dimensions to integrating the German states: one political and one economic.

During the nineteenth century Prussia increasingly assumed political leadership in Germany, intending to unite Germany under the crown of the Prussian king. The democratic revolution of 1848 was suppressed in line with the principles of the Congress of Vienna. In 1864, Austria and Prussia joined forces against Denmark in the conflict over Schleswig, but in 1866 Prussia went to war with Austria over the issue of German unification, and Prussia's victory led to unification without Austria. In 1867, the North-German Federation (*Norddeutscher Bund*) was founded, a forerunner of the German Empire four years later.

Economic integration became increasingly urgent in the decades following the Napoleonic wars. England, Belgium, and France were more industrialized than Germany, and they all had unified territory. Germany particularly needed to industrialize because severe crises resulting from strong population increase, rising poverty, and proletarianization were causing huge waves of emigration; the whole period from the 1820s to the 1850s was characterized by pauperism. German industry was disadvantaged in several respects: the different states charged tariffs, there was no national railway or other transport system, no postal service, nor a common currency. The first step was therefore the introduction of the German Tariff Union in the 1820s. Friedrich List in particular advocated a national railway system, but did not succeed with his visionary plans. All in all, economic integration was slow and incomplete until political integration.

Finally, Bismarck and the Prussians succeeded in uniting Germany politically through the Franco-Prussian War of 1870/71, in which Germany also won the territory of Alsace-Lorraine. This new federal state was the second imperial formation after the Holy German Empire and is therefore called the second German Empire. The period from 1870 until the outbreak of World War I in 1914 saw the economic, political, cultural, and social integration of Germany. The German economy became one of the strongest in Europe.

World War I ended this promising development. The defeat resulted in major territorial losses: Alsace-Lorraine went back to France, Eupen-Malmedy was ceded to Belgium, part of Schleswig went to Denmark in 1920, and some of eastern Prussia became part of the newly created Polish Republic. The creation of an independent Czechoslovakia, until 1919 part of the Habsburg Empire, left large German minorities in western and northern Bohemia; the same was true for large parts of Poland, Hungary, and Romania. The territorial exchanges were negotiated and regulated by the 1919 Treaty of Versailles.

From the Treaty of Versailles until the end of the Weimar Republic in 1933 the German territory remained unchanged. The 1920s were a time of great turmoil. The early years of the Republic were shaped by the consequences of hyperinflation; many people lost their savings and assets, and the whole class system changed because of the decline of the propertied bourgeoisie and the general proletarianization of large segments of the population. After currency reform brought an end to hyperinflation, economic recovery set in, but the economy and society continued to suffer under reparation payments, restrictions on the steel and coal-mining industries, and disarmament obligations, among others. Nevertheless, the 1920s were a decade of economic growth, new liberalism, and modernity. In 1929, the world economic crisis signalled the end of this hopeful era. Unemployment rose to unprecedented levels, businesses went bankrupt, fortunes were lost, and much of the industrial capacity was shut down. The demographic effects were dramatic: births were postponed, the death rate rose, and marriages declined. The Weimar Republic ended when the National Socialists were voted into government in 1933. Their policies intended to reverse the Treaty of Versailles, to stimulate population growth, and to regain the territories taken away at Versailles. The Saarland, which had been under international administration since 1919, was given back to Germany in 1935. In 1938, the crisis over the Sudetenland was resolved by the Treaty of Munich: western and northern parts of the newly established Czechoslovakia were given to Germany. In the same year, the Republic of Austria was annexed to Germany, which was prohibited by the Versailles Treaty. These were the last territorial gains until the outbreak of World War II in September 1939. During World War II Germany annexed several territories (such as Alsace-Lorraine, Luxembourg, and Eupen-Malmedy), but they were taken away after the war.

In 1945, Germany was subdivided into several zones of occupation. There was no treaty regulation, and the subsequent state and territorial formation was more or less unplanned and in reaction to urgent social, economic, and political needs. The subsequent stand-off between the U.S. and the Soviet Union divided the country into two different spheres of influence which in 1949 were organized as states. The eastern zone became the German Democratic Republic (GDR), the western zones the Federal Republic of Germany (FRG). The eastern parts of the Empire were lost to Poland and the Soviet Union. All other territories acquired in 1938 and during the war had to be given back. The Saarland again came under foreign control.

REGIONAL POPULATION STRUCTURE

Population density and population growth differed greatly between the German regions and administrative units given the strongly heterogeneous character of the German Empire. The population growth index, developed by John Knodel (1974:

32), shows the regional variations, when 1871 is set at 100: along with Berlin, North Rhine-Westphalia had the greatest population increase. Other parts of the country, such as the south, had below-average population increases. Thus internal migration played a major role in regional population growth and population density. The industrializing districts and urban centres attracted the most people. There is no cleavage system along linguistic or religious lines, as in Belgium; industrial development did not overlap with the religious structure of the population or the labour migrants.

POPULATION GROWTH

Population density in Germany was already high in the nineteenth century, though less than in The Netherlands or Belgium. But population density is relative: when seen in relation to the available means of subsistence, in the nineteenth century many parts of Germany were overpopulated, as indicated by the huge streams of emigrants.

At the time of unification in 1871 there were 76 inhabitants per square kilometre. By 1910 population density had increased to 120 inhabitants per sq. km.; in 1925 the figure was 133 and in 1933 it was 140. In 1871 the population was 41,059,000 inhabitants (including Alsace-Lorraine). This number increased to roughly 65 million in 1910. This was the phase of strongest natural population growth (Figure D.1). After World War I population growth was slow, growing from 62.4 million in 1925 to 66 million in 1933. For the whole period from 1871 to 1933, population growth was 182 in 1933 when 1871 is set at 100. Thus, the population of Germany nearly doubled in these 60 years. Therefore, when the whole period is considered, population growth was rather high in Germany (Knodel, 1974: 32).

THE FIRST DEMOGRAPHIC TRANSITION

Compared to Europe, Germany shows a more pronounced pattern of demographic transition, with a significantly higher birth rate, while the death rate equals the European average (Figure D.2). Until the 1880s both the birth rate and the death rate (see infant mortality) increased. The increase in the birth rate was very strong and peaked in the late 1870s, probably due to economic prosperity in that decade. Up to about 1910 the birth rate decreased slightly, while the death rate declined much more strongly already at that time, resulting in a strong natural population growth. Until World War I population growth in Germany was significantly higher than in Europe.

World War I was a major watershed in recent German population history. Due to postponed marriages and births a large number of births was lost. After the war there was a real demographic crisis, when the birth rate fell sharply in the 1920s. The Great Depression of 1929–33 caused the birth rate to drop dramatically, though the birth rate was rising during the 1930s. During the whole inter-war period both the birth rate and the death rate were below the European average, and natural population growth was greatly reduced. The German birth rate rose above the European average only in the late 1930s (Knodel, 1974).

In the Federal Republic of Germany after 1945, the birth rate was constantly below the European average, but the death rate was higher, leading to overall low natural population growth. The birth wave of the 1960s was pronounced for the Federal

Figure D.1 Population growth and net migration 1850-1943

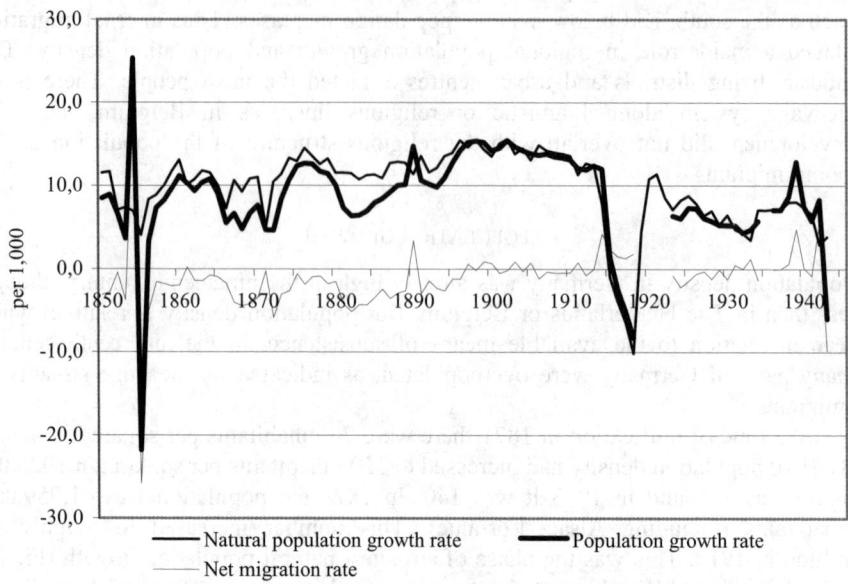

- Natural population growth rate
- Population growth rate
- Net migration rate

Figure D.2 First demographic transition 1850-1943

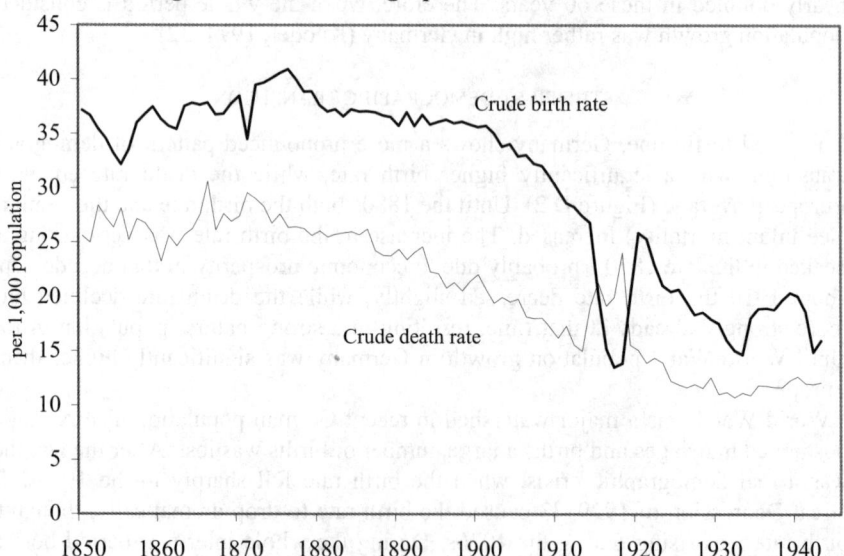

Republic, when seen in the light of the birth decline afterwards. Since the mid-1970s natural population growth has been negative.

The infant mortality rate is defined as deaths of children aged under one year per 1,000 live births. In nineteenth-century Europe, the Nordic countries had the lowest infant mortality rate, while in most of Western Europe infant mortality was rather high. The Nordic countries, The Netherlands, and Switzerland form one cluster of countries with the lowest infant mortality rates in Europe (Eastern Europe included) (Masuy-Stroobant, 1997: 5f.). Germany (until 1945 the German Empire; after 1945 the Federal Republic of Germany and the German Democratic Republic) belongs to the second cluster comprising nearly all Western European countries with the second-lowest infant mortality rates (Figure D.3).

Infant mortality increased from the beginning of the nineteenth century until the 1870/80s, after which it began to decline, although with great regional variations. While in Bavaria there was a clear decline after the 1870s, in Prussia and the whole German Empire the rates from the 1870s to the 1900s fluctuated more or less around the same level. The aggregate of the German Empire began to decline only after 1900. Thus, the highly aggregated figures hide more than they reveal. There were large differences by region, urban/rural settlements, and socio-economic status. In agricultural Bavaria infant mortality was higher than in highly industrialized and urbanized Prussia (Rothenbacher, 1982). In Prussia in the last quarter of the nineteenth century infant mortality was lower in the rural areas, higher in urban Prussia, and highest in towns with more than 15,000 inhabitants (Vögele, 1997: 111). Thus, urbanization and industrialization increased infant mortality, but probably the traditional Bavarian agricultural and inheritance practices contributed even more to infant mortality. By 1910, rural Prussia had lost its 1875 lead in infant mortality to the urban regions and the towns, where sanitary innovations and improvements were introduced first: central water supply, sewer systems, communal refuse disposal, municipal milk supply, hospitals, and so on. This modern health and sanitary infrastructure did not reach the rural areas until decades later. Running water was generally not introduced before 1900, and sewerage even later. That is why in Prussia the infant mortality rates in urban areas fell below those in rural areas after 1910 (Vögele, 1997).

Regional differences in infant mortality were so great in Germany because the country was unified rather late, and central state institutions to make living conditions more homogeneous throughout the country evolved slowly in the decades after unification. Before unification the economic integration of Germany was also rather limited, and the states within the German Federation of that time were largely able to retain their traditional economic structures. During the nineteenth century Bavaria remained largely dependent on agriculture, with lower levels of industrialization and urbanization (except in some centres such as Augsburg, Nuremberg, and Munich) than in other parts of Germany. Infant mortality was furthermore very high in parts of Württemberg (Donaukreis, Jagstkreis), Hohenzollern, and Saxony. More or less all of Southern Germany had high rates in the last quarter of the nineteenth century, as did Saxony and Silesia. Thus, a mixture of factors was responsible for infant mortality: urbanization and industrialization initially raised infant mortality; later the health situation in the cities improved. On

Figure D.3 Infant mortality 1901-1938

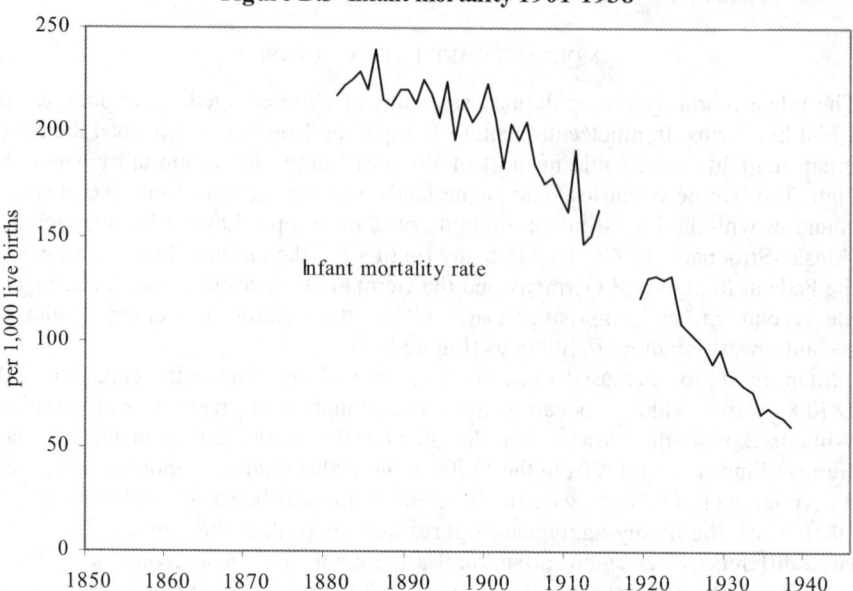

Figure D.4 Life expectancy 1871/81-1932/34

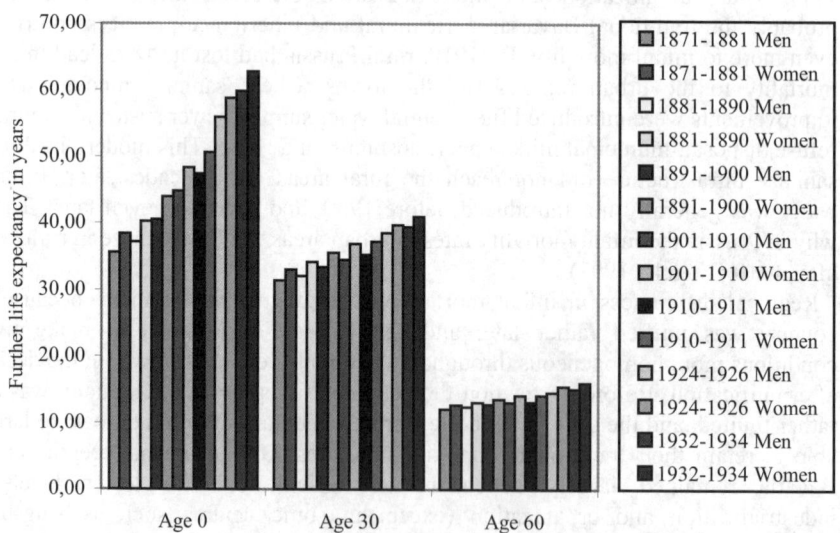

the other hand, specific land structures and agricultural systems, as in Bavaria and parts of Württemberg, resulted in higher infant mortality (Knodel, 1974: 148–87).

Life expectancy in Germany was low for all ages compared with Sweden. In 1871/81 life expectancy of boys at birth was 35.6 in Germany and 45.3 in Sweden (1871/80), a difference of ten years (Figure D.4). For 30-year-old men the difference was five years, and for 60-year-old men it was two years. Up to the 1930s Germany was able to improve the health status of its population in absolute and relative terms and reduce the distance to Sweden: for male infants to 3.5 years, for both 30- and 60-year-old men 1.5 years. Life expectancy of females was better at all ages in Germany. The distance to males increased until World War I, but decreased again until the 1930s.

FERTILITY AND LEGITIMACY

The legitimacy rate can be used as an indicator for the relative importance of *marital fertility* as opposed to non-marital fertility. From the founding of the German Empire in 1871 until World War I this indicator was always above the European average. Nevertheless, the decline in marital births in Germany was faster than in Europe: already in 1913 the German and European curves converged. During the inter-war period and after World War II marital fertility was below the European average. Marital fertility increased again in the mid-1970s, and towards the end of the 1980s the legitimacy rate again exceeded the European average.

The frequency of *illegitimate births* depends on a large number of factors, such as the structure of the agricultural system, legal barriers to marriage, the rigidity of marriage, and a low age at marriage. Between the nation-states of Europe and even within individual countries, the causes of illegitimacy as well as its extent and phenomenology varied considerably (Figure D.5).

In most European countries and on the European average one distinct historical development of illegitimacy can be seen: a long-term decline until the end of the 1960s followed by a new increase. In the 1960s the nuclear family became a more or less universal form of living, and since about 1970 marital and non-marital children have had the same rights in family law, following legislation putting marriage and cohabitation on a similar legal basis. The importance of legitimacy has diminished, and the incentive structure for bearing children within marriage has become weaker. But large variations exist within Europe concerning these changes.

Until recently the illegitimacy rate in Germany was always above the European average, especially from 1870 to 1900. Germany's high illegitimacy rate can be seen on the one hand in connection with widespread industrialization, and on the other hand with legal and later also social barriers to marriage (such as long years of study and on-the-job training for civil servants). In some parts of the German Empire—especially in the rural south (*Anerbengebiete* in Upper Bavaria and Upper Swabia), restricting inheritance to only one heir led to high celibacy rates and many out-of-wedlock births, as in some regions of Austria (mainly Carinthia). The change from a peasant to an industrial society increasingly diminished the importance of such inheritance practices. In the years between the world wars the German illegitimacy rate followed the European pattern, but after 1945 it deviated strongly from the European average. Up to 1980 the illegitimacy rate fell to the lower European level; since then it has increased slightly. The low West German level is related to the

Figure D.5 Fertility and legitimacy 1872-1938

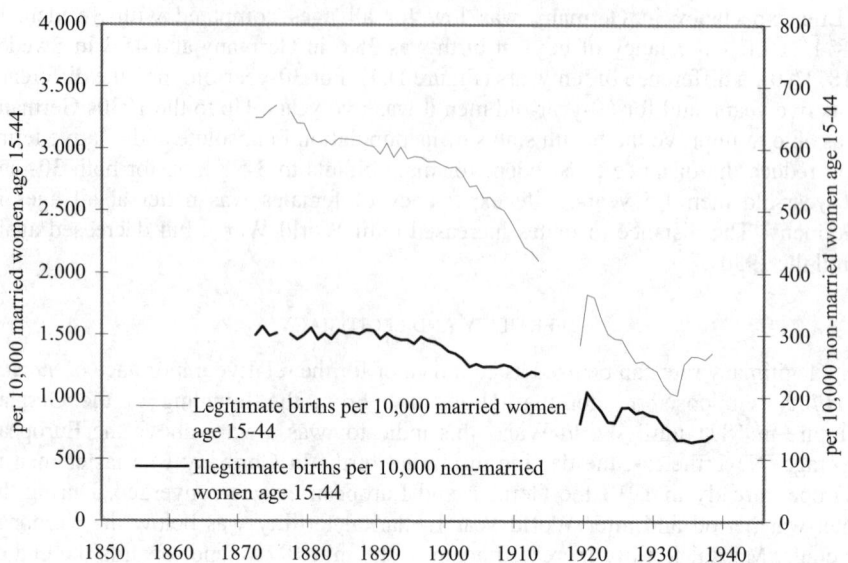

Figure D.6 Marriages and divorces 1871-1939

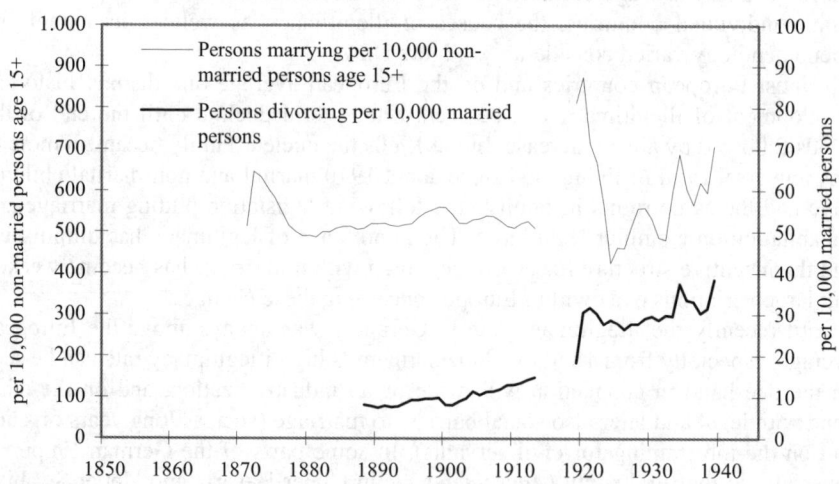

legally privileged status of marriage; the weak position of the illegitimate child and its parents in the legal system has kept the West German illegitimacy rate low.

An even clearer expression of the social acceptance and institutionalization of the social status of the out-of-wedlock child is given by the relationship of illegitimate to legitimate births, the *illegitimacy/legitimacy ratio*. Over the whole period from 1870 to 1990 the relationship was remarkably stable, although with fluctuations. In the 1920s legitimate births declined and illegitimate births increased slightly, increasing the ratio. The same pattern emerged shortly after 1945. Until 1960 there was a trend towards legitimacy: the marriage boom led to a lower number of out-of-wedlock births. The major decline in births during the early 1970s again led to an increase in the illegitimacy/legitimacy ratio. When compared with the European average it seems interesting that the German rate was structurally always over the European average, but did not take part in the 'explosion' of out-of-wedlock births since the 1970s. As they did earlier in history, Germans prefer to have children within marriage or marry when a child is expected.

The *age of the mother at first birth* reveals a similar pattern as the age at marriage, because women overwhelmingly married before the birth of the first child. The age distance between the birth of the first child and the birth of all children diminished steadily. This partly has to do with the rising age at birth, but also with the reduced number of children born, and thus with the reduced procreative phase. The age of West German mothers at first birth is higher than the European average, though mothers' age at all births is near the European average. The very small average time distance between the birth of the first child and all children is related to the very low German fertility rate.

MARRIAGE AND DIVORCE

In history and at present time *marriage* is still the most important basis for family formation. While today increasingly the equalization of marriage and non-marital cohabitation is increasingly discussed, up to the second half of the nineteenth century marriage was a scarce and highly valued commodity which was not available to everyone. Population explosion and pauperism in the early decades after 1800 forced many governments—predominately in the Southern German states—to introduce restrictive legislation concerning marriage. The old policy of marriage restrictions (*Heiratsverbote*) was reintroduced (marriage as the equivalent of subsistence: *Ehe = Nahrung*) and having a secure profession and sufficient income became essential requirements for marriage. Consequently, until the 1850s, age at marriage went up and the share of people remaining single all their lives increased (Figure D.6).

In the decades after 1850 the situation was more favourable; industry expanded after the world economic crisis of the 1850s, the German Tariff Union went into effect, mechanization using steam engines grew, innovative technologies such as telegraphy were introduced, the railways created new jobs and completely new professional groups. The unification of Germany (minus Austria) under Prussian leadership caused a change in ideology: Prussia did not have marriage restrictions, because population density in Prussia had always been low. The North-German Federation therefore abolished marriage restrictions already in 1867, and this was extended to the whole German Empire after 1871. The large French reparation payments after 1871 led to an economic boom in the 1870s (*Gründerjahre*) which coincided with the upswing of the European business cycle. This upswing can be seen in the marriage rate, which started to rise throughout Europe and even more strongly in Germany. Near the end of the 1870s this marriage 'wave' started to normalize, but the marriage rate had a growing tendency until 1900 in both Europe and Germany. It was followed by a decline until the outbreak of World War I. During the forty years from 1870 to 1910 the German marriage rate was above the European average. This can be interpreted as a sign of accelerating industrialization and the expansion of the industrial labour force. During World War I marriages were postponed until after the war, leading to a peak in the marriage rate from 1919–22 (*nachgeholte Ehen*). Marriages tended to increase again during the 1920s, but the world economic crisis from 1929–33 again caused marriages to be postponed. During the 1930s marriage propensity increased further, but this tendency was broken around 1938, probably because of racist marriage legislation and the persecution of the Jews. After World War II there were two marriage booms, one in the 1950s and the second in the 1970s. After that, a new phase of German marriage history set in, when marriage became deinstitutionalized and the marriage rate fell below the European level. But over the whole period from 1880 to 1960 there was a rising marriage propensity.

Germany also participated in the Western European marriage pattern with high celibacy rates and late mean age at marriage. Until the 1960s marriage tended to become universal with declining age at marriage. The birth cohorts of the 1930s married nearly universally and at a very young age, thus causing the marriage boom of the 1960s. The *mean age at first marriage* in West Germany followed the European pattern of a declining age at first marriage until the 1960s and a subsequent increase. In the Federal Republic of Germany this increase was more rapid than in Europe: people in Germany married later than in Europe. Causes for this development can be seen in the socio-structural developments towards higher female employment and greater educational participation of women. On the other hand, the delay of the European average can be understood as the strong weight of countries lagging behind in this process of post-industrial transformation. On average, the difference in age at first marriage between men and women becomes smaller, in the Federal Republic as in the rest of Europe; the later people marry, the lower the mean age difference between the sexes.

The number of *divorces* in Germany was rather low in the second half of the nineteenth century, as in all European countries, but in Germany it exceeded the European average (Figure D.6). A stronger increase in the absolute number of divorces and in the divorce rate set in only at the end of the century (Blasius, 1987). The main reason for this growth was not a liberalization of divorce, but a shift in the social structure. Concerning the divorce rate, World War I caused a shift in the level of the divorce rate (displacement effect[1]). Until 1920, divorces increased to a level previously unknown, declined slightly until the mid-1920s and rose again continuously until 1939. The distance of the German divorce rate to the European rate increased.

World War II was followed by the division of Germany into two states with different societal systems. The processes of family formation must therefore be

---

[1] Peacock, Wiseman and Veverka (1967) have also postulated such 'displacement effects' for the growth in government expenditure in the United Kingdom.

presented separately for each German state until reunification in 1990. After World War II the marriage rate rose significantly in the Federal Republic, predominantly caused by the recovery of many marriages postponed during the war. But remarriages of widowed and divorced persons were very frequent, too, as the extremely high remarriage rates in the first years after the war demonstrate. The steep rise in the divorce rate from shortly after 1945 until 1950 completes this picture. During the 1950s, the situation normalized somewhat again. By the mid-1960s a new marriage boom had set in, followed by a historically singular decline in the marriage rate. In about the early 1970s, the German marriage rate fell below the European level, indicating the pioneering role of Germany in this respect. Up to 1990 nuptiality stabilized on a level below the European average.

By contrast, during the whole post-war period the divorce rate remained above the European average, thus indicating a certain stability of structural patterns. The very high divorce rate immediately after the war fell until approximately 1960, and increased again afterwards. This renewed increase, more or less parallel to the European average, was only disturbed by the 1977 West German reform of the divorce law. Divorces were postponed before the reform and completed after the reform. By the end of the 1980s divorce behaviour in both Europe and Germany stabilized.

The *remarriage rate* of divorced and widowed persons declined steadily after 1945. With the growth in life expectancy and increasing differences in life expectancy between women and men, widowed persons have lower chances of remarrying than divorced persons. The rate of remarriage among widowed persons is significantly lower than that of divorced people. Both widowed and divorced men have a much higher chance of remarrying than widowed or divorced women. The numerical relation of widowers to widows leads to better marriage chances for men; on the other hand, men much more than women prefer younger partners. Similarly, divorced men have a better chance of finding a younger female partner; on the other hand, a second or higher marriage has become less advantageous due to social security regulations. The trend towards post-marital cohabitation and the increasing difficulties of remarrying after divorce, due to the 1977 divorce law reform, led to a decline in the remarriage rate among the divorced population (Rothenbacher, 1997).

AGE, SEX, AND CIVIL STATUS

In the German Empire the age structure of the population kept its pyramidal form until the 1910 census (Appendix Figure D.8). During the second half of the nineteenth century, the age distribution was still slightly concave for the lowest age groups, indicating a persistently high birth rate. During the decade 1900–1910 this pattern became convex for the lowest age groups, pointing to the first massive fertility reduction in Germany during this decade. While the Franco-Prussian War of 1870/71 had only a limited impact on the birth rate and the youngest birth cohorts due to its short duration, the impact of World War I on the German fertility decline and age structure was tremendous, as can be seen from the 1925 census. During the 15 years from 1910 to 1925 the age structure changed to a bell shape, which endured until 1939. The age distribution of the 1925 census shows the loss of births during World War I for the 5–9-year-olds, the smallest age cohort. The cohort of 0–4-year-olds was much larger, but smaller than the last pre-war birth cohort, that of 10–14-year-olds. In 1933 there was a new decline in the youngest age group from 0–4 years due to the Great Depression 1929–33. The age distribution of the 1939 census shows that the youngest group, the 0–4-year-olds, recovered but was very much smaller than the respective pre-World War I age group.

The German age distributions demonstrate that men married later than women, but that celibacy was higher for women than for men. At higher ages more men than women were married because of widespread widowhood. Widowhood increased in importance from the end of World War I to 1939, as did female celibacy. Thus, the German population structure of the first half of the twentieth century was severely affected by the war and the economic crisis of that time.

FAMILY AND HOUSEHOLD STRUCTURES

The developments of households and families in the century from 1850 to 1950 can be described as a movement from large to small, from extended to nuclear, and from three-generational to two- and one-generational households. The most significant shift is the decline in mean household size which hides the change in the composition of households by size: more smaller households and fewer larger households. Compared with Europe, mean household size in Germany was somewhere in the middle, larger than the small French household and smaller than the Irish and Eastern European households. This intermediate position is due to several distinctive features: Germany participated in the Western European marriage pattern with late age at marriage and high celibacy rates, which reduced fertility. On the other hand, in Germany people lived in extended households, thus contributing to larger households and a higher mean household size. Nevertheless, the proportion of extended households was small because of low life expectancy: grandparents only lived for a few years with their children and grandchildren. It was also rather unusual for lateral relatives to live together. Of much greater importance were non-family members such as servants, boarders, and lodgers in the household. The presence of these household members enlarged the households by roughly 10%. The declining household size is therefore due to several factors: the fertility decline, the departure of non-family members, and the disappearance of the extended family or the three-generational households.

It should be emphasized that incomplete families or 'lone parents' were rather common during this time period, probably contrary to the impression we have today when the number of lone parents is rising. But during the nineteenth and the early twentieth centuries incomplete families were caused by high mortality and death of a spouse; on the other hand illegitimate births were rather common due to high celibacy rates and the lack of contraception.

The development of families can more or less be described as a tendency towards the nuclear family model, away from the extended family and the miseries of celibacy, unwanted pregnancy, and illegitimate births. The birth cohorts of the 1930s married very early and almost universally, and their children were mainly legitimate. Until the 1960s the nuclear complete family was the modern family model for young couples; only afterwards did this model begin to be considered 'conservative'.

THE NATIONAL SYSTEM OF DEMOGRAPHIC STATISTICS

Population Structure

The first population census after unification was held in 1871. From 1834 to 1867 population statistics were collected for the German Tariff Union. The Franco-Prussian War prevented the census from being conducted in 1870. From 1875 to 1910 population censuses were held every five years; after that the census dates were very irregular and affected by wars, economic crises, and political decisions. During the German Empire (1871–1919) the censuses in the middle of the decade were often not as extensively published as the decennial censuses at the beginning of each decade. In particular, the censuses of 1895 and 1905 were only partially published.

The territorial changes up to 1938 had consequences for statistics-taking. The 1933 population census referred to the territory of the Treaty of Versailles, i.e. without the Saarland. After it was returned to the Empire in 1935 a special population census was organized for the Saarland that same year. The next general population census in 1939 referred to the German territory including Austria and the Sudetenland. There are no totals given for the territory on 31 December 1937, before the 1938 gains. Nevertheless, for the period since 1938 official statistics after World War II refer to the territory as of 31 December 1937. The population figures presented thereafter also use this convention.

Data on population structure are available for individual German states before 1871, but there are no tabulations concerning age (in small age groups), sex, or marital status. Thus, the age, sex, and civil status structure is only given since 1871. In the censuses of the 1870s and 1880s the age groups are often not one-year but aggregated age groups.

The population in the population censuses and used for the age structure was always the resident population present at the time of census-taking.

Vital Statistics

Vital statistics were introduced in the German Empire in 1872 with the law introducing civil marriage and the registration of births, deaths, and marriages at local offices (*Standesämter*). But this does not mean that data on vital statistics do not exist for earlier times. The different German states had a long tradition of vital statistics and most of them have time series back to the early nineteenth century. This, of course, often mainly concerns the most important variables of vital statistics such as births, deaths, and marriages, while illegitimate births, divorces, and infant mortality are often covered only at later dates. Thus, it was possible for official statistics to calculate the population movement for the territory of the German Empire back to 1840. Several indicators for the Empire also start rather late, such as infant mortality, but data are available for single German states (such as Prussia or Bavaria) back to the early nineteenth century.

Households and Families

Data on households (older term *Haushaltung(en)*; today *Haushalt(e)*) were collected for the German Empire already in the 1871 census. But the published data were still very limited. Only the three basic family types—one-person households, family households, and institutional households—were published. The household statistics were in direct line with earlier developments. Since 1834, the population censuses for the German Tariff Union collected data on the number of households (at this time called 'families' (*Familien*), reflecting older traditions). The collection of the number of households can be traced back to the population censuses of the eighteenth century and before. In 1834 only the number of households (not distinguished by type) was collected. In the following decades the collected items increased constantly; thus, in the course of time, households were split into family households and institutional households, and the family households again disaggregated by size into one-person households and family households with two or more persons. Already before unification some German states were more progressive in household statistics and introduced household composition and households disaggregated by size in the 1860s. Nevertheless, the large cities during urbanization were most innovative and the earliest to extend household statistics.

At the national level household statistics remained rather poor until World War I. Household statistics were not considered the responsibility of the Empire but rather that of the federal states and the large cities. Thus, much more information is to be found in the statistics published by some of the states and large cities. But not all states or large cities emphasized household statistics to the same extent; whereas Prussia was rather comprehensive and innovative, Bavarian statisticians showed little interest in household statistics.

Disaggregations were introduced at the national level after World War I. The 1925 census included disaggregations according to socio-economic characteristics of the household head and according to community size. Disaggregations by community size had previously been introduced in some federal states (e.g. Baden); those by socio-economic status had been introduced e.g. by Württemberg. Other distinctions by type of household, household composition, sex of household members, etc. were also carried out earlier and more extensively by the federal states than by the Empire.

After World War I German statistics became much more centralized: the national censuses became the standard information source, while the information from the federal states declined. This reduction of the federal element is in line with the general centralization of state functions in Germany in the 1920s and 1930s.

The definition of a household (*Haushalt*) since 1871 included two elements: a household was at once a biological unit and a socio-economic unit. For instance, if the people living in the same flat were relatives but did not share resources, then by definition this was not one household. This household definition normally included all those people affiliated with the household, but not biological members; thus, servants, boarders, and lodgers were normally counted as belonging to a family household and not as separate one-person households. One-person households were those living alone and supporting themselves. Institutional households were those households in which persons were not living in a biological family for specific purposes (e.g. educational institutions, monasteries, military barracks, guest houses, etc.). These principal definitions of household were more or less kept for the whole period. Thus, German statistics used the housekeeping concept rather than the household-dwelling concept.

Family statistics (*Familienstatistik*) in Germany before the end of World War II were only rudimentary. Municipal statisticians were the first to put more emphasis on the family (*Familie*) as a biological unit in household statistics. But the attention of social policy-makers and statisticians was focused more on the housing problem (family members and non-family members living together as servants, boarders, and lodgers) than on a value-free assessment of the family structure. The major decline in births after World War I moved public attention in a different direction: family statistics were now viewed as fertility statistics. As in other European countries, in Germany the fertility of couples and women was first assessed systematically in the 1930s, in the censuses of 1933 and 1939. But this type of statistics did not meet the requirements of family statistics concerned with the structure and composition of families. Family statistics were not institutionalized until the 1950 census and the start of the Microcensus in 1957.

Remarks (also see introductory Table 6.1)

The age*sex*civil status table in the 1871 population census of the German Empire includes the age group 40–49 years instead of 40–44 years. Data for the age group 40–44 have been calculated by splitting this age group into two equal parts.

BOUNDARY CHANGES

The data for Germany are based on the territory of the German Empire of 1871. The unification of Germany in 1871 included all countries of the North-German Federation and Southern Germany. Austria, Luxembourg, and The Netherlands were excluded from the German Empire although they belonged to the German Tariff Union. Alsace-Lorraine was annexed by the Empire from France and returned after World War I.

Major territorial changes were made under the Treaty of Versailles: Belgium won Eupen and Malmedy; the newly-established state of Poland took several eastern provinces from the Empire; the Saarland was occupied by France and only returned to Germany in 1935. In 1938 Austria and the Sudetenland were annexed, but the time series data after 1938 do not include these territories.

Thus, the figures represent Germany in the boundaries of 1871 for the period from 1840 to 1919, and in the boundaries of the Treaty of Versailles from 1919 to 1935, when the Saarland returned to Germany. Normally, Austria and the Sudetenland, annexed in 1938, are not included in German population statistics. Thus, the figures since 1938 always refer to the territory as of 31 December 1937.

Concerning regional organization see Quick (1994) and Caramani, Flora, Kraus, and Quick (1998).

APPENDIX TABLES AND FIGURES

APPENDIX TABLE D.1 Population structure at census dates 1871–1939

Census number	Census date	Census population			Marital status				Age group		
		Total	Male	Female	Single	Married	Widowed	Divorced	0–14	15–64	65+
					Absolute						
1	1 XII 1871	41,010,138	20,104,382	20,905,756	24,812,566	13,769,014	2,354,736	69,794	14,088,453	25,880,766[1]	1,010,413[2]
2	1 XII 1880	45,234,061	22,185,433	23,048,628	27,152,376	15,376,685	2,642,779	62,221	16,016,045	27,026,656	2,130,408
3	1 XII 1885	46,855,704	22,933,664	23,922,040	28,144,756	15,855,064	2,788,090	67,794	16,569,733	27,937,575	2,348,396
4	1 XII 1890	49,428,470	24,230,832	25,197,638	29,649,668	16,771,093	2,932,837	74,872	17,372,100	29,535,056	2,521,314
5	1 XII 1900	56,367,178	27,737,247	28,629,931	33,520,123	19,592,879	3,162,159	92,017	19,614,822	34,001,938	2,750,418
6	1 XII 1910	64,925,993	32,040,166	32,885,827	38,107,944	23,229,713	3,450,548	137,788	22,107,930	39,550,991	3,267,072
7	16 VI 1925	62,410,620	30,196,824	32,213,796	33,009,152	25,437,499	3,680,830	283,139	16,071,858	42,745,149	3,593,613
8	16 VI 1933	65,218,461	31,685,562	33,532,899	32,091,072	28,627,849	4,005,018	494,522	14,377,674	45,537,747	5,303,040
9	17 V 1939	68,271,423	32,819,413	35,452,010	30,909,867	32,360,490	4,333,888	667,178	15,526,187	46,996,140	5,749,096
					Per cent						
1	1 XII 1871	100.00	49.02	50.98	60.50	33.57	5.74	0.17	34.35	63.11[1]	2.46[2]
2	1 XII 1880	100.00	49.05	50.95	60.03	33.99	5.84	0.14	35.41	59.75	4.71
3	1 XII 1885	100.00	48.95	51.05	60.07	33.84	5.95	0.14	35.36	59.62	5.01
4	1 XII 1890	100.00	49.02	50.98	59.99	33.93	5.93	0.15	35.15	59.75	5.10
5	1 XII 1900	100.00	49.21	50.79	59.47	34.76	5.61	0.16	34.80	60.32	4.88
6	1 XII 1910	100.00	49.35	50.65	58.69	35.78	5.31	0.21	34.05	60.92	5.03
7	16 VI 1925	100.00	48.38	51.62	52.89	40.76	5.90	0.45	25.75	68.49	5.76
8	16 VI 1933	100.00	48.58	51.42	49.21	43.90	6.14	0.76	22.05	69.82	8.13
9	17 V 1939	100.00	48.07	51.93	45.27	47.40	6.35	0.98	22.74	68.84	8.42

Notes: [1] 15–69. [2] 70+.

APPENDIX TABLE D.2 Census population by region 1871–1933 (per cent)

Bundesstaat Landesteil *Regierungsbezirk*	1871	1880	1890	1900	1910	1925	1933
Preußen	**64.22**	**64.43**	**64.47**	**64.48**	**64.49**	**62.23**	**62.20**
Ostpreußen[1]	6.84	6.84	6.84	6.84	6.84	7.90	7.86
Königsberg	3.90	3.90	3.91	3.90	2.59	2.80	2.79
Gumbinnen	2.94	2.94	2.94	2.94	2.03	2.00	2.00
Allenstein	..	..	..	..	2.22	2.46	2.45
Westpreußen						0.63	0.62
Westpreußen[1]	4.71	4.72	4.72	4.72	4.72	..	..
Danzig	1.47	1.47	1.47	1.47	1.47	..	..
Marienwerder	3.24	3.25	3.25	3.25	3.25	..	..
Berlin (Stadt)	..	..	0.01	0.01	0.01	0.19	0.19
Brandenburg	7.38	7.38	7.37	7.37	7.37	8.33	8.29
Berlin	0.01	0.01	..	..	..	..	..
Potsdam	3.82	3.82	3.82	3.82	3.82	4.23	4.21
Frankfurt	3.55	3.55	3.55	3.55	3.55	4.10	4.08
Pommern	5.57	5.57	5.57	5.57	5.57	6.44	6.43
Stettin	2.23	2.23	2.23	2.23	2.23	2.58	3.43
Köslin	2.60	2.59	2.60	2.59	2.60	3.01	3.00
Stralsund	0.75	0.74	0.74	0.74	0.74	0.86	..
Posen	5.36	5.36	5.36	5.36	5.36	1.64	1.64
Posen	3.24	3.24	3.24	3.24	3.24	..	..
Bromberg	2.12	2.12	2.12	2.12	2.12	..	..
(Nieder-)Schlesien	7.45	7.45	7.46	7.46	7.46	5.68	5.65
Breslau	2.49	2.49	2.49	2.49	2.49	2.77	2.74
Liegnitz	2.52	2.52	2.52	5.85	2.52	2.90	2.91
Oppeln	2.44	2.44	2.45	2.45	2.45	..	..
Oberschlesien (Oppeln)	..	..	..	..	..	2.07	2.06
Sachsen	4.67	4.67	4.67	4.67	4.67	5.39	5.42
Magdeburg	2.13	2.13	2.13	2.13	2.13	2.46	2.46
Merseburg	1.89	1.89	1.89	1.89	1.89	2.18	2.17
Erfurt	0.65	0.65	0.65	0.65	0.65	0.75	0.79
Schleswig-Holstein	3.24	3.49	3.50	3.51	3.52	3.21	3.20
Hannover	7.12	7.11	7.12	7.12	7.12	8.23	8.24
Hannover	1.07	1.07	1.06	1.06	1.06	1.23	1.33
Hildesheim	0.95	0.95	0.98	0.99	0.99	1.14	1.08
Lüneburg	2.15	2.13	2.10	2.10	2.10	2.42	2.42
Stade	1.23	1.24	1.26	1.25	1.25	1.45	1.44
Osnabrück	1.16	1.15	1.15	1.15	1.15	1.32	1.32
Aurich	0.55	0.58	0.57	0.57	0.57	0.66	0.66
Westfalen	3.74	3.74	3.74	3.74	3.74	4.31	4.29
Münster	1.34	1.34	1.34	1.34	1.34	1.55	1.55
Minden	0.97	0.97	0.97	0.97	0.97	1.12	1.12
Arnsberg	1.42	1.42	1.42	1.42	1.42	1.64	1.63
Hessen-Nassau	2.94	2.90	2.90	2.90	2.90	3.35	3.58
Kassel	1.93	1.87	1.86	1.86	1.86	2.15	2.31
Wiesbaden	1.01	1.03	1.04	1.04	1.04	1.20	1.27
Rheinland / Rheinprovinz	4.99	4.99	4.99	4.99	4.99	5.45	5.09
Koblenz	1.15	1.15	1.15	1.15	1.15	1.32	1.21
Düsseldorf	1.01	1.01	1.01	1.01	1.01	1.17	1.17
Köln	0.74	0.74	0.74	0.74	0.74	0.85	0.85
Trier	1.33	1.33	1.33	1.33	1.33	1.22	1.21
Aachen	0.77	0.77	0.77	0.77	0.77	0.68	0.66
Hohenzollern (Sigmaringen)	0.21	0.21	0.21	0.21	0.21	0.24	0.24

continued

APPENDIX TABLE D.2 Census population by region 1871–1933 (cont.) (per cent)

Bundesstaat *Landesteil* *Regierungsbezirk*	1871	1880	1890	1900	1910	1925	1933
Lauenburg[2]	0.22	..	..	..	..	..	..
Bayern	**14.03**	**14.04**	**14.04**	**14.03**	**14.03**	**16.21**	**16.14**
Oberbayern	3.15	3.09	3.09	3.09	3.09	3.56	3.54
Niederbayern	1.99	1.99	1.99	1.99	1.99	2.29	2.28
Pfalz	1.10	1.10	1.10	1.10	1.10	1.17	1.17
Oberpfalz	1.79	1.79	1.79	1.78	1.79	2.06	2.05
Oberfranken	1.29	1.29	1.29	1.29	1.29	1.60	1.59
Mittelfranken	1.40	1.40	1.40	1.40	1.40	1.62	1.68
Unterfranken	1.55	1.55	1.55	1.55	1.55	1.80	1.79
Schwaben	1.76	1.82	1.82	1.82	1.82	2.10	2.10
Sachsen	**2.77**	**2.77**	**2.77**	**2.77**	**2.77**	**3.20**	**3.18**
Dresden (-Bautzen)	0.80	0.80	0.80	0.80	0.80	0.93	1.45
Leipzig	0.66	0.66	0.66	0.66	0.66	0.76	0.76
Chemnitz	..	..	..	0.38	0.38	0.44	0.44
Zwickau	0.86	0.85	0.85	0.47	0.47	0.54	0.54
Bautzen	0.45	0.46	0.46	0.46	0.46	0.53	..
Württemberg	**3.61**	**3.61**	**3.61**	**3.61**	**3.61**	**4.16**	**4.14**
Neckarkreis	0.62	0.62	0.62	0.62	0.62	0.71	0.69
Schwarzwaldkreis	0.88	0.88	0.88	0.88	0.88	1.02	1.01
Jagstkreis	0.95	0.95	0.95	0.95	0.95	1.10	1.11
Donaukreis	1.16	1.16	1.16	1.16	1.16	1.34	1.33
Baden	**2.79**	**2.79**	**2.79**	**2.79**	**2.79**	**3.22**	**3.20**
Konstanz	0.77[4]	0.77[4]	0.77	0.77	0.77	0.82	0.82
Freiburg	0.88[5]	0.88[5]	0.88	0.88	0.88	1.08	1.07
Karlsruhe	0.48[6]	0.48[6]	0.48	0.47	0.48	0.56	0.56
Mannheim	0.66[7]	0.67[7]	0.67	0.67	0.66	0.75	0.75
Hessen	**1.42**	**1.42**	**1.42**	**1.42**	**1.42**	**1.64**	**1.63**
Starkenburg	**0.56**	**0.56**	**0.56**	**0.56**	**0.56**	**0.65**	**0.64**
Oberhessen	**0.61**	**0.61**	**0.61**	**0.61**	**0.61**	**0.70**	**0.70**
Rheinhessen	**0.25**	**0.25**	**0.25**	**0.25**	**0.25**	**0.29**	**0.30**
Thüringen						2.51	2.50
Sachsen-Weimar/Gh.	0.67	0.66	0.67	0.67	0.67	..	..
Sachsen[3]							
Mecklenburg	..	..	..	..	..	..	3.41
Mecklenburg-Schwerin	**2.46**	**2.46**	**2.44**	**2.43**	**2.43**	**2.80**	..
Mecklenburg-Strelitz	**0.54**	**0.54**	**0.54**	**0.54**	**0.54**	**0.63**	..
Oldenburg	**1.18**	**1.19**	**1.19**	**1.19**	**1.19**	**1.37**	**1.37**
Oldenburg	0.99	0.99	1.00	1.00	1.00	1.15	1.14
Lübeck	0.10	0.10	0.10	0.10	0.10	0.12	0.12
Birkenfeld	0.09	0.09	0.09	0.09	0.09	0.11	0.11

continued

APPENDIX TABLE D.2 Census population by region 1871–1933 (cont.) (per cent)

Bundesstaat	1871	1880	1890	1900	1910	1925	1933
Landesteil							
Regierungsbezirk							
Braunschweig	0.68	0.68	0.68	0.68	0.68	0.78	0.78
Sachsen-Meiningen	0.46	0.46	0.46	0.46	0.46	..	..
Sachsen-Altenburg	0.24	0.24	0.24	0.24	0.24	..	..
Sachsen-Koburg-Gotha	0.36	0.36	0.36	0.37	0.37	..	..
Anhalt	0.43	0.43	0.42	0.43	0.43	0.49	0.49
Schwarzburg-Rudolstadt	0.17	0.17	0.17	0.17	0.17	..	..
Schwarzburg-Sondershausen	0.16	0.16	0.16	0.16	0.16	..	..
Waldeck	0.21	0.21	0.21	0.21	0.21	0.23	..
Reuss älterer Linie	0.05	0.06	0.06	0.06	0.06	..	..
Reuss jüngerer Linie	0.15	0.15	0.15	0.15	0.15	..	..
Schaumburg-Lippe	0.08	0.06	0.06	0.06	0.06	0.07	0.07
Lippe	0.21	0.23	0.22	0.22	0.22	0.26	0.26
Lübeck	0.05	0.06	0.06	0.06	0.06	0.06	0.06
Bremen	0.05	0.05	0.05	0.05	0.05	0.05	0.05
Hamburg	0.08	0.08	0.08	0.08	0.08	0.09	0.09
Saarland	..	..	..	..	..	..	0.41
Elsaß-Lothringen	2.68	2.68	2.68	2.68	2.68	..	..
Oberelsaß	0.65	0.65	0.65	0.65	0.65	..	..
Niederelsaß / Unterelsaß	0.88	0.88	0.88	0.88	0.88	..	..
Lothringen	1.15	1.15	1.15	1.15	1.15	..	..
TOTAL	**100.00**	**100.00**	**100.00**	**100.00**	**100.00**	**100.00**	**100.00**

Notes: [1] Only in 1871 the provinces *Ostpreußen* and *Westpreußen* were joined. [2] On 1 VII 1876 *Lauenburg* was incorporated into *Schleswig-Holstein* (Preußen). [3] 1910: *Großherzogthum Sachsen.* [4] Kreise Konstanz, Villingen, Waldshut. [5] Kreise Freiburg, Lörrach, Offenburg. [6] Kreise Baden, Karlsruhe. [7] Kreise Mannheim, Heidelberg, Mosbach.

APPENDIX TABLE D.3 Population density by region 1871–1933 (inhab. per sq. km.)

Bundesstaat Landesteil Regierungsbezirk	1871	1880	1890	1900	1910	1925	1933
Preußen	**71**	**78**	**86**	**99**	**115**	**131**	**136**
Ostpreußen[1]	49	52	53	54	56	61	63
Königsberg	51	55	56	57	65	69	73
Gumbinnen	47	49	50	50	55	57	58
Allenstein	..	..	..	..	45	47	48
Westpreußen	..	..	..	..	..	89	95
Westpreußen[1]	52	55	56	61	67	..	..
Danzig	66	72	74	84	93	..	..
Marienwerder	45	48	48	51	55	..	..
Berlin (Stadt)	..	..	25,063	29,984	32,873	4,583	4,800
Brandenburg	72	57	64	78	103	66	70
Berlin	14,000	18,393	..	..	..	..	..
Potsdam	49	56	68	93	138	66	71
Frankfurt	54	58	59	61	64	67	68
Pommern	48	51	51	54	57	62	63
Stettin	56	61	62	69	72	79	76
Köslin	39	42	40	42	44	48	49
Stralsund	52	54	52	54	56	62	
Posen	55	59	60	65	72	43	44
Posen	58	63	64	68	76	..	..
Bromberg	50	53	55	60	67	..	..
(Nieder-)Schlesien	92	99	105	116	130	118	120
Breslau	105	115	119	126	136	146	152
Liegnitz	72	75	77	35	86	91	91
Oppeln	99	109	119	141	167	..	..
Oberschlesien (Oppeln)	..	..	..	..	..	142	153
Sachsen	83	92	102	112	122	130	133
Magdeburg	74	81	93	102	108	112	113
Merseburg	86	95	105	117	128	138	145
Erfurt	104	114	123	132	150	161	164
Schleswig-Holstein	57	60	65	73	85	101	105
Hannover	51	55	59	67	76	83	87
Hannover	70	80	92	113	131	142	145
Hildesheim	79	85	90	98	106	111	117
Lüneburg	33	35	37	42	48	53	55
Stade	46	48	50	55	63	67	69
Osnabrück	43	47	48	53	61	69	75
Aurich	63	68	70	77	88	94	100
Westfalen	88	101	120	158	204	239	249
Münster	60	65	74	97	136	177	214
Minden	90	96	105	121	140	153	166
Arnsberg	113	139	175	240	312	354	341
Hessen-Nassau	88	99	106	121	141	153	153
Kassel	73	81	81	88	100	108	106
Wiesbaden	116	131	150	179	216	232	241
Rheinland / Rheinprovinz	133	151	174	213	264	284	318
Koblenz	90	97	102	110	121	128	134
Düsseldorf	243	291	360	475	624	703	742
Köln	155	177	208	257	314	361	388
Trier	82	91	99	117	140	83	87
Aachen	118	126	136	148	166	218	239
Hohenzollern (Sigmaringen)	58	59	58	59	62	63	64

continued

APPENDIX TABLE D.3 Population density by region 1871–1933 (cont.) (inhabitants per sq. km.)

Bundesstaat Landesteil Regierungsbezirk	1871	1880	1890	1900	1910	1925	1933
Lauenburg[2]	**43**	..	..	..	..	..	..
Bayern	**64**	**70**	**74**	**81**	**91**	**97**	**101**
Oberbayern	49	57	66	79	92	101	107
Niederbayern	56	60	62	63	67	70	72
Pfalz	104	114	123	140	158	169	179
Oberpfalz	51	55	56	57	62	65	68
Oberfranken	77	82	82	87	95	101	105
Mittelfranken	77	85	93	108	123	131	131
Unterfranken	70	75	74	77	85	90	94
Schwaben	61	65	68	73	80	87	89
Sachsen	**171**	**198**	**234**	**280**	**321**	**333**	**347**
Dresden (-Bautzen)	**156**	**187**	**219**	**280**	**311**	**321**	**281**
Leipzig	**166**	**198**	**244**	**297**	**346**	**367**	**384**
Chemnitz	..	..	..	**382**	**444**	**471**	**505**
Zwickau	**207**	**239**	**284**	**286**	**337**	**336**	**345**
Bautzen	**134**	**142**	**150**	**164**	**180**	**187**	..
Württemberg	**93**	**101**	**104**	**111**	**125**	**132**	**138**
Neckarkreis	165	187	200	224	265	292	320
Schwarzwaldkreis	94	99	101	107	120	125	130
Jagstkreis	75	79	78	78	81	81	82
Donaukreis	70	75	78	82	91	95	97
Baden	**104**	**104**	**110**	**124**	**142**	**153**	**160**
Konstanz	66[4]	68[4]	68	71	78	88	92
Freiburg	92[5]	96[5]	99	107	119	119	125
Karlsruhe	142[6]	158[6]	173	201	238	254	261
Mannheim	107[7]	118[7]	128	151	179	200	210
Hessen	**111**	**122**	**129**	**146**	**167**	**175**	**186**
Starkenburg	116	131	139	162	195	210	222
Oberhessen	77	81	81	86	94	100	104
Rheinhessen	182	202	223	253	278	279	300
Thüringen	..	..	..	..	..	**137**	**142**
Sachsen-Weimar/Gh.	**79**	**86**	**91**	**100**	**116**	..	..
Sachsen[3]							
Mecklenburg	..	..	..	..	..	..	**50**
Mecklenburg-Schwerin	**42**	**43**	**44**	**46**	**49**	**51**	..
Mecklenburg-Strelitz	**33**	**34**	**33**	**35**	**36**	**38**	..
Oldenburg	**49**	**52**	**55**	**62**	**75**	**85**	**89**
Oldenburg	45	49	52	59	73	82	87
Lübeck	66	65	65	68	76	87	89
Birkenfeld	72	78	82	85	99	111	117

continued

APPENDIX TABLE D.3 Population density by region 1871–1933 (cont.) (inhabitants per sq. km.)

Bundesstaat Landesteil Regierungsbezirk	1871	1880	1890	1900	1910	1925	1933
Braunschweig	85	95	110	126	135	137	140
Sachsen-Meiningen	76	84	91	102	113	..	..
Sachsen-Altenburg	107	117	129	147	163	..	..
Sachsen-Koburg-Gotha	88	99	106	116	130	..	..
Anhalt	86	99	119	137	144	152	157
Schwarzburg-Rudolstadt	81	85	91	99	107	..	..
Schwarzburg-Sondershausen	78	82	88	94	104	..	..
Waldeck	49	51	51	52	55	53	..
Reuss älterer Linie	164	161	199	215	231	..	..
Reuss jüngerer Linie	107	122	145	168	185	..	..
Schaumburg-Lippe	72	103	115	126	138	141	147
Lippe	98	98	105	114	124	135	145
Lübeck	184	215	255	326	393	430	456
Bremen	488	613	703	879	1,172	1,324	1,442
Hamburg	833	1,107	1,505	1,851	2,452	2,778	2,935
Saarland	..	..	..	..	..	..	424
Elsaß-Lothringen	107	108	111	118	129	..	..
Oberelsaß	131	132	134	141	148	..	..
Niederelsaß / Unterelsaß	126	128	130	138	146	..	..
Lothringen	79	79	82	91	105	..	..
TOTAL	76	84	91	104	120	133	140

Notes: See Appendix Table D.2.

APPENDIX TABLE D.4 Demographic developments 1850–1945 (absolute figures and rates)

Year	Mid-year population	Natural population growth rate	Population growth rate	Net migration rate	Crude birth rate	Legitimate births per 10,000 married women age 15–44	Illegitimate births per 10,000 unmarried women age 15–44	Illeg. births per 100 leg. births
1850	35,303,000	11.6	8.5	-3.1	37.2	..	..	..
1851	35,620,000	11.7	8.9	-2.8	36.7	..	..	..
1852	35,858,000	7.1	6.6	-0.4	35.5	..	..	..
1853	35,989,000	7.4	3.6	-3.7	34.6	..	..	..
1854	36,923,000	6.9	25.3	18.4	33.2	..	..	..
1855	36,136,000	4.1	-21.8	-25.8	32.2	..	..	..
1856	36,257,000	8.3	3.3	-5.0	33.5	..	..	..
1857	36,524,000	8.9	7.3	-1.5	36.0	..	..	..
1858	36,828,000	10.0	8.3	-1.8	36.8	..	..	..
1859	37,188,000	11.7	9.7	-2.1	37.5	..	..	..
1860	37,609,000	13.1	11.2	-1.9	36.3	..	..	..
1861	38,001,000	10.1	10.3	0.2	35.7	..	..	..
1862	38,360,000	10.8	9.4	-1.4	35.4	..	..	..
1863	38,763,000	11.8	10.4	-1.4	37.5	..	..	..
1864	39,187,000	11.6	10.8	-0.8	37.8	..	..	..
1865	39,545,000	10.0	9.1	-1.0	37.6	..	..	..
1866	39,765,000	7.2	5.5	-1.7	37.9	..	..	..
1867	40,031,000	10.6	6.6	-4.0	36.8	..	..	..
1868	40,223,000	9.2	4.8	-4.5	36.8	..	..	..
1869	40,493,000	10.9	6.7	-4.2	37.8	..	..	..
1870	40,804,000	11.1	7.6	-3.4	38.5	..	..	..
1871	40,995,000	4.9	4.7	-0.3	34.5	..	..	..
1872	41,185,000	10.5	4.6	-5.9	39.5	3,248	299	9.6
1873	41,532,000	11.4	8.4	-3.1	39.7	3,252	314	10.0
1874	41,983,000	13.4	10.7	-2.6	40.1	3,309	298	9.4
1875	42,510,000	13.0	12.4	-0.6	40.6	3,348	303	9.4
1876	43,057,000	14.6	12.7	-1.8	40.9	..	..	..
1877	43,608,000	13.6	12.6	-1.0	40.0	3,301	301	9.4
1878	44,127,000	12.6	11.8	-0.8	38.9	3,206	293	9.4
1879	44,639,000	13.3	11.5	-1.8	38.9	3,205	300	9.6
1880	45,093,000	11.6	10.1	-1.5	37.6	3,080	311	10.3
1881	45,426,000	11.6	7.3	-4.2	37.0	3,053	293	9.9
1882	45,717,000	11.5	6.4	-5.1	37.2	3,071	301	10.1
1883	46,014,000	10.7	6.5	-4.3	36.6	3,031	293	10.0
1884	46,335,000	11.3	6.9	-4.3	37.2	3,083	307	10.4
1885	46,705,000	11.4	7.9	-3.4	37.0	3,077	303	10.3
1886	47,103,000	10.9	8.4	-2.4	37.1	3,076	304	10.4
1887	47,540,000	12.7	9.2	-3.5	37.0	3,066	302	10.3
1888	48,020,000	12.9	10.0	-2.9	36.7	3,033	308	10.7
1889	48,512,000	12.8	10.1	-2.6	36.5	3,019	307	10.6
1890	49,239,000	11.4	14.8	3.4	35.7	2,956	294	10.4
1891	49,767,000	13.6	10.6	-3.0	37.0	3,046	303	10.3
1892	50,279,000	11.6	10.2	-1.4	35.7	2,930	296	10.4
1893	50,778,000	12.2	9.8	-2.3	36.7	3,013	292	10.0
1894	51,339,000	13.6	10.9	-2.6	35.9	2,921	292	10.2
1895	52,001,000	14.0	12.7	-1.2	36.1	2,939	286	9.9
1896	52,753,000	15.5	14.3	-1.2	36.3	2,933	297	10.2
1897	53,569,000	14.6	15.2	0.6	36.0	2,897	291	10.1

continued

APPENDIX TABLE D.4 Demographic developments 1850–1945 (absolute figures and rates)

Crude death rate	Infant mortality rate	Stillbirth rate	Infant mortality and stillbirth rate	Crude marriage rate	Persons marrying per 10,000 unmarried persons age 15+	Persons marrying per 10,000 unmarried persons age 15–49	Crude divorce rate	Divorces per 100 marriages	Divorces per 10,000 married persons	Year
25.6	..		..	8.5	..	..	..	..	..	1850
25.0	..	41.9	..	8.3	..	..	..	..	..	1851
28.4	..	41.6	..	7.7	..	..	..	..	..	1852
27.2	..	41.4	..	7.6	..	..	..	..	..	1853
26.3	..	41.1	..	6.9	..	..	..	..	..	1854
28.1	..	41.0	..	7.0	..	..	..	..	..	1855
25.2	..	41.0	..	7.5	..	..	..	..	..	1856
27.2	..	42.1	..	8.3	..	..	..	..	..	1857
26.8	..	43.7	..	8.5	..	..	..	..	..	1858
25.7	..	43.9	..	8.0	..	..	..	..	..	1859
23.2	..	43.7	..	8.0	..	..	..	..	..	1860
25.6	..	42.9	..	7.8	..	..	..	..	..	1861
24.6	..	43.0	..	8.1	..	..	..	..	..	1862
25.7	..	42.7	..	8.5	..	..	..	..	..	1863
26.2	..	42.6	..	8.5	..	..	..	..	..	1864
27.6	..	42.3	..	8.9	..	..	..	..	..	1865
30.6	..	42.4	..	7.9	..	..	..	..	..	1866
26.1	..	41.5	..	9.1	..	..	..	..	..	1867
27.6	..	42.1	..	8.9	..	..	..	..	..	1868
26.9	..	42.4	..	9.5	..	..	..	..	..	1869
27.4	..	42.3	..	7.7	..	..	..	..	..	1870
29.6	..	41.9	..	8.2	513	638	..	..	..	1871
29.0	..	40.7	..	10.3	647	805	..	..	..	1872
28.3	..	40.8	..	10.0	633	789	..	..	..	1873
26.7	..	41.3	..	9.5	606	756	..	..	..	1874
27.6	..	43.0	..	9.1	581	726	..	..	..	1875
26.3	..	41.8	..	8.5	547	685	..	..	..	1876
26.4	..	40.8	..	8.0	515	645	..	..	..	1877
26.2	..	41.2	..	7.7	500	627	..	..	..	1878
25.6	..	40.8	..	7.5	490	615	..	..	..	1879
26.0	..	40.0	..	7.5	491	616	..	..	..	1880
25.5	218.0	39.6	257.6	7.5	487	613	..	..	..	1881
25.7	222.1	39.4	261.5	7.7	500	629	..	..	..	1882
25.9	225.2	39.3	264.5	7.7	499	628	..	..	..	1883
26.0	228.8	39.6	268.4	7.8	509	639	..	..	..	1884
25.7	220.4	39.7	260.1	7.9	512	643	..	..	..	1885
26.2	239.6	39.2	278.8	7.9	513	643	..	..	..	1886
24.2	215.6	39.0	254.6	7.8	505	633	..	..	..	1887
23.8	213.2	38.0	251.2	7.8	508	637	0.1	1.8	8.1	1888
23.8	220.3	37.2	257.5	8.0	519	651	0.1	1.7	7.9	1889
24.4	220.8	34.7	255.5	8.0	519	650	0.1	1.6	7.4	1890
23.4	213.7	34.2	247.9	8.0	520	651	0.1	1.7	7.9	1891
24.1	224.8	34.0	258.8	7.9	515	644	0.1	1.6	7.6	1892
24.6	218.1	33.5	251.6	7.9	513	642	0.1	1.7	7.7	1893
22.3	207.3	34.3	241.6	7.9	517	646	0.1	1.8	8.5	1894
22.1	223.8	34.3	258.1	8.0	519	649	0.2	2.0	9.3	1895
20.8	196.4	33.9	230.3	8.2	535	668	0.2	2.0	9.3	1896
21.3	215.9	33.4	249.3	8.4	547	682	0.2	2.0	9.6	1897

continued

APPENDIX TABLE D.4 Demographic developments 1850–1945 (continued)

Year	Mid-year population	Natural population growth rate	Population growth rate	Net migration rate	Crude birth rate	Legitimate births per 10,000 married women age 15-44	Illegitimate births per 10,000 unmarried women age 15-44	Illeg. births per 100 leg. births
1898	54,406,000	15.6	15.4	-0.2	36.1	2,900	289	9.9
1899	55,248,000	14.4	15.2	0.8	35.8	2,873	283	9.7
1900	56,046,000	13.6	14.2	0.7	35.6	2,850	274	9.4
1901	56,874,000	15.1	14.6	-0.5	35.7	2,856	270	9.3
1902	57,767,000	15.6	15.5	-0.2	35.1	2,797	262	9.2
1903	58,629,000	13.9	14.7	0.8	33.8	2,694	249	9.0
1904	59,475,000	14.5	14.2	-0.3	34.1	2,704	253	9.1
1905	60,314,000	13.1	13.9	0.8	32.9	2,605	249	9.2
1906	61,153,000	14.9	13.7	-1.2	33.1	2,609	249	9.2
1907	62,013,000	14.2	13.9	-0.4	32.3	2,532	249	9.4
1908	62,863,000	14.0	13.5	-0.5	32.1	2,504	253	9.6
1909	63,717,000	13.9	13.4	-0.5	31.0	2,415	249	9.8
1910	64,568,000	13.6	13.2	-0.4	29.8	2,312	241	9.8
1911	65,359,000	11.3	12.1	0.8	28.6	2,211	234	10.0
1912	66,146,000	12.7	11.9	-0.8	28.3	2,169	241	10.4
1913	66,978,000	12.4	12.4	0.0	27.5	2,100	238	10.6
1914	67,790,000	7.8	12.0	4.2	26.8	..	..	10.7
1915	67,883,000	-1.0	1.4	2.4	20.4	..	..	12.5
1916	67,715,000	-4.0	-2.5	1.5	15.2	..	..	12.3
1917	67,368,000	-6.4	-5.2	1.3	13.5	..	..	12.9
1918	66,811,000	-10.2	-8.3	1.8	13.9	..	..	14.9
1919	62,897,000	4.5	-	-	20.0	1,417	158	12.4
1920[1]	61,794,000	10.8	-	-	25.9	1,829	209	12.6
1921	62,473,000	11.4	10.9	-0.5	25.3	1,806	191	11.6
1922[1]	61,185,000	8.6	-	-	23.0	1,637	178	11.9
1923	61,577,000	7.1	6.4	-0.8	21.1	1,510	160	11.5
1924	61,953,000	8.3	6.1	-2.2	20.5	1,470	159	11.6
1925	62,411,000	8.8	7.3	-1.4	20.7	1,463	184	13.4
1926	62,866,000	7.9	7.2	-0.6	19.5	1,366	184	14.1
1927	63,252,000	6.4	6.1	-0.3	18.4	1,280	174	14.0
1928	63,618,000	7.0	5.8	-1.2	18.6	1,291	177	13.9
1929	63,957,000	5.3	5.3	0.0	17.9	1,243	172	13.7
1930	64,294,000	6.5	5.2	-1.2	17.5	1,211	169	13.6
1931	64,631,000	4.7	5.2	0.5	16.0	1,101	153	13.3
1932	64,911,000	4.3	4.3	0.0	15.1	1,036	145	13.2
1933	65,218,000	3.5	4.7	1.2	14.7	1,016	132	11.9
1934	65,595,000	7.1	5.7	-1.4	18.0	1,268	132	9.3
1935[1]	66,871,000	7.1	19.1	12.0	18.9	1,330	128	8.4
1936	67,349,000	7.2	7.1	-0.1	19.0	1,326	130	8.3
1937	67,831,000	7.1	7.1	0.0	18.8	1,304	131	8.3
1938[2]	68,424,000	8.0[3]	8.7	0.6	19.7	1,356	139	8.2
1939[2]	69,314,000	8.1[3]	12.8	4.8	20.4	..	..	..
1940[2]	69,838,000	7.4[3]	7.5	0.1	20.1	..	..	..
1941[2]	70,244,000	6.6[3]	5.8	-0.8	18.6	..	..	..
1942[2]	70,834,000	2.9[3]	8.3	5.4	14.9	..	..	..
1943[2]	70,411,000	3.9[3]	-6.0	-9.9	16.0	..	..	..
1944	..	..	..	..	..	..	..	..
1945	..	..	..	..	..	..	..	..

Notes: [1] Territorial change. [2] Territory as of December 12, 1937. [3] 1939–1943: excluding military losses.

APPENDIX TABLE D.4 Demographic developments 1850–1945 (continued)

Crude death rate	Infant mortality rate	Stillbirth rate	Infant mortality and stillbirth rate	Crude marriage rate	Persons marrying per 10,000 unmarried persons age 15+	Persons marrying per 10,000 unmarried persons age 15–49	Crude divorce rate	Divorces per 100 marriages	Divorces per 10,000 married persons	Year
20.5	205.6	33.2	238.8	8.4	552	689	0.2	2.0	9.6	1898
21.5	210.8	32.8	243.6	8.5	560	698	0.2	2.0	9.8	1899
22.1	223.1	32.3	255.4	8.5	559	696	0.1	1.7	8.1	1900
20.7	206.8	32.2	239.0	8.2	542	674	0.1	1.7	8.0	1901
19.4	183.1	31.9	215.1	7.9	521	648	0.2	2.0	9.0	1902
20.0	204.0	31.8	235.8	7.9	520	647	0.2	2.1	9.7	1903
19.6	196.4	31.3	227.7	8.0	530	659	0.2	2.5	11.3	1904
19.8	205.3	30.8	236.2	8.1	532	660	0.2	2.3	10.5	1905
18.2	185.2	30.8	216.0	8.2	539	669	0.2	2.4	11.3	1906
18.0	175.5	30.5	206.0	8.1	537	666	0.2	2.5	11.4	1907
18.1	178.2	30.6	208.7	8.0	527	653	0.2	2.7	11.9	1908
17.2	169.6	30.4	199.9	7.8	514	636	0.2	3.0	13.0	1909
16.2	161.8	30.2	192.0	7.7	510	631	0.2	3.0	13.0	1910
17.3	192.2	30.1	222.3	7.8	520	644	0.2	3.1	13.5	1911
15.6	147.4	30.1	177.5	7.9	526	650	0.3	3.2	14.2	1912
15.0	150.8	30.4	181.1	7.7	509	629	0.3	3.5	14.8	1913
19.0	163.5	30.7	194.2	6.8	..	..	0.3	3.9	..	1914
21.4	..	31.1	..	4.1	..	..	0.2	3.9	..	1915
19.2	..	31.9	..	4.1	..	..	0.2	3.8	..	1916
20.0	..	30.5	..	4.6	..	..	0.2	3.8	..	1917
24.0	..	31.8	..	5.3	..	..	0.2	3.8	..	1918
15.6	120.8	30.9	151.6	13.4	813	972	0.4	2.6	18.3	1919
15.1	131.1	32.7	163.8	14.5	875	1,051	0.6	4.1	30.6	1920[1]
13.9	132.1	32.2	164.3	11.9	714	862	0.6	5.2	31.7	1921
14.4	129.7	33.2	163.0	11.1	670	813	0.6	5.4	30.3	1922[1]
13.9	131.8	32.9	164.7	9.4	566	691	0.6	5.8	27.6	1923
12.3	108.6	33.7	142.3	7.1	425	521	0.6	8.2	28.8	1924
11.9	105.2	33.9	139.1	7.7	462	569	0.6	7.3	27.9	1925
11.7	101.6	34.2	135.9	7.7	461	570	0.5	7.1	26.4	1926
12.0	97.0	33.4	130.5	8.5	512	637	0.6	6.8	27.7	1927
11.6	89.3	32.5	121.8	9.2	557	697	0.6	6.3	27.7	1928
12.6	96.4	32.0	128.4	9.2	558	702	0.6	6.7	29.1	1929
11.1	84.6	32.3	116.9	8.8	532	672	0.6	7.2	29.7	1930
11.2	83.0	31.5	114.5	8.0	486	618	0.6	7.8	28.7	1931
10.8	79.2	30.6	109.8	7.9	480	614	0.7	8.3	29.9	1932
11.2	76.6	29.7	106.3	9.7	594	763	0.7	6.7	29.7	1933
10.9	65.8	27.5	93.3	11.2	689	891	0.8	7.4	37.4	1934
11.8	68.6	26.2	94.7	9.7	604	787	0.8	7.7	33.6	1935[1]
11.8	66.2	26.2	92.3	9.1	565	740	0.7	8.3	33.2	1936
11.7	64.4	24.7	89.1	9.9	619	818	0.7	7.0	30.3	1937
11.7	59.8	23.5	83.3	9.4	594	790	0.7	7.7	31.5	1938[2]
12.3[c]	..	23.3	..	11.2	708	948	0.9	8.0	38.5	1939[2]
12.7[c]	..	..	..	8.8	..	..	0.7	8.0	..	1940[2]
12.0[c]	..	..	..	7.2	..	..	0.8	10.5	..	1941[2]
12.0[c]	..	..	..	7.4	..	..	..	..	..	1942[2]
12.1[c]	..	..	..	7.3	..	..	..	..	..	1943[2]
..	..	..	..	..	..	..	..	..	..	1944
..	..	..	..	..	..	..	..	..	..	1945

Notes: [1] Territorial change. [2] Territory as of December 12, 1937. [3] 1939–1943: excluding military losses.

APPENDIX TABLE D.5 Life expectancy by age 1871/81–1932/34 (in years)

Age	0	10	20	30	40	50	60	70	80
				Males					
1871–1881	35.58	46.51	38.45	31.41	24.46	17.98	12.11	7.34	4.10
1881–1890	37.17	47.75	39.52	32.11	25.03	18.41	12.43	7.51	4.11
1891–1900	40.56	49.66	41.23	33.46	25.89	19.00	12.82	7.76	4.23
1901–1910	44.82	51.16	42.56	34.55	26.64	19.43	13.14	7.99	4.38
1910–1911	47.41	52.08	43.43	35.29	27.18	19.71	13.18	7.90	4.25
1924–1926	55.97	55.63	46.70	38.56	30.05	21.89	14.60	8.74	4.77
1932–1934	59.86	57.28	48.16	39.47	30.83	22.54	15.11	9.05	4.84
				Females					
1871–1881	38.45	48.18	40.19	33.07	26.32	19.29	12.71	7.60	4.22
1881–1890	40.25	49.69	41.62	34.21	27.16	19.89	13.14	7.84	4.37
1891–1900	43.97	51.71	43.37	35.62	28.14	20.58	13.60	8.10	4.48
1901–1910	48.33	53.35	44.84	36.94	29.16	21.35	14.17	8.45	4.65
1910–1911	50.68	53.99	45.35	37.30	29.38	21.45	14.17	8.35	4.52
1924–1926	58.82	57.11	48.09	39.76	31.37	23.12	15.51	9.27	5.06
1932–1934	62.81	59.09	49.84	41.05	32.33	23.85	16.07	9.58	5.15

APPENDIX TABLE D.6A Households by type 1871–1939 (absolute and per cent)

Census year	Total households	Private households	Family households	One-person households	Institutional households	Total household members	Private household members	Family household members	One-person household members	Institutional household members
					Absolute					
1871	8,731,919	8,696,806	8,161,298	535,508	35,113	41,058,800	40,309,700	39,774,200	535,500	749,100
1875	9,199,762	9,166,460	8,593,618	572,842	33,302	42,727,400	41,872,000	41,299,200	572,800	855,400
1880	9,652,036	9,608,856	9,004,702	604,154	43,180	45,234,100	44,224,000	43,619,800	604,200	1,010,100
1885	9,999,558	9,966,456	9,288,713	677,743	33,102	46,855,700	45,691,000	45,013,300	677,700	1,164,700
1890	10,617,923	10,584,249	9,836,560	747,689	33,674	49,428,500	48,108,000	47,360,300	747,700	1,320,500
1895	11,256,150	11,206,556	10,417,805	788,751	49,594	52,279,900	50,805,000	50,016,200	788,800	1,474,900
1900	12,260,012	12,178,682	11,308,081	870,601	81,330	56,367,200	54,737,000	53,866,400	870,600	1,630,200
1905	13,274,531	13,213,450	12,247,691	965,759	61,081	60,641,500	58,777,300	57,811,500	965,800	1,864,200
1910	14,346,692	14,283,380	13,238,237	1,045,143	63,312	64,926,000	62,810,200	61,765,100	1,045,100	2,115,800
1925	15,349,247	15,274,894	14,248,847	1,026,047	74,353	62,410,600	60,861,000	59,835,000	1,026,000	1,549,600
1933	17,735,600	17,694,900	16,212,600	1,482,300	40,700	65,218,500	63,945,700	62,463,400	1,482,300	1,272,800
1939	20,411,500	20,334,800	18,351,100	1,983,700	76,700	69,314,100	66,455,900	64,472,200	1,983,700	2,858,200
					Per cent					
1871	100.00	99.60	93.47	6.13	0.40	100.00	98.18	96.87	1.30	1.82
1875	100.00	99.64	93.41	6.23	0.36	100.00	98.00	96.66	1.34	2.00
1880	100.00	99.55	93.29	6.26	0.45	100.00	97.77	96.43	1.34	2.23
1885	100.00	99.67	92.89	6.78	0.33	100.00	97.51	96.07	1.45	2.49
1890	100.00	99.68	92.64	7.04	0.32	100.00	97.33	95.82	1.51	2.67
1895	100.00	99.56	92.55	7.01	0.44	100.00	97.18	95.67	1.51	2.82
1900	100.00	99.34	92.24	7.10	0.66	100.00	97.11	95.56	1.54	2.89
1905	100.00	99.54	92.26	7.28	0.46	100.00	96.93	95.33	1.59	3.07
1910	100.00	99.56	92.27	7.28	0.44	100.00	96.74	95.13	1.61	3.26
1925	100.00	99.52	92.83	6.68	0.48	100.00	97.52	95.87	1.64	2.48
1933	100.00	99.77	91.41	8.36	0.23	100.00	98.05	95.78	2.27	1.95
1939	100.00	99.62	89.91	9.72	0.38	100.00	95.88	93.01	2.86	4.12

APPENDIX TABLE D.6B Households by size and members 1900–1939 (absolute figures)

Census year	Private households total	1 person	2 persons	3 persons	4 persons	5 persons	6 persons	7 persons	8 persons	9 persons	10 persons	11+ persons
Households												
1900	12,178,682	870,601	1,794,046	2,062,342	2,043,850	1,766,442	1,363,416	1,549,926[1]		528,582[2]		199,477
1905	13,213,450	965,759	1,977,726	2,270,590	2,246,846	1,915,099	1,451,004	1,623,530[1]		555,843[2]		207,053
1910	14,283,380	1,045,143	2,167,889	2,529,301	2,480,920	2,056,057	1,523,252	1,038,257	651,367	377,405	203,434	210,355
1925	15,274,894	1,026,047	2,699,067	3,442,178	3,011,588	2,091,016	1,303,922	787,273	441,612	234,288	119,912	117,991
1933	17,694,900	1,482,300	3,840,455	4,390,670	3,400,828	2,097,024	1,185,414	637,287		660,893[3]		
1939	20,334,800	1,983,700	5,539,919	5,362,699	3,642,266	1,921,564	960,120	471,157	231,360	113,642	57,965	50,431
Persons												
1900	54,737,000	870,601	3,588,092	6,187,026	8,175,400	8,832,210	8,180,496	11,449,108[1]		4,940,957[2]		2,513,116
1905	58,777,300	965,759	3,955,452	6,811,770	8,987,384	9,575,495	8,706,024	11,991,494[1]		5,196,544[2]		2,587,332
1910	62,810,200	1,045,143	4,335,778	7,587,903	9,923,680	10,280,285	9,139,512	7,267,799	5,210,936	3,396,645	2,034,340	2,588,187
1925	60,861,000	1,026,047	5,398,134	10,326,534	12,046,352	10,455,080	7,823,532	5,510,911	3,532,896	2,108,592	1,199,120	1,433,830
1933	63,945,700	1,482,300	7,680,910	13,172,010	13,603,312	10,485,120	7,112,484	4,461,009		5,948,459[3]		
1939	66,455,900	1,983,700	11,079,838	16,088,097	14,569,064	9,607,820	5,760,720	3,298,099	1,850,880	1,022,778	579,650	615,282

Notes: [1] 7–8 persons. [2] 9–10 persons. [3] 8 and more persons.

APPENDIX TABLE D.6C Households by size and members 1900–1939 (per cent)

Census year	Private households total	Households by number of members										
		1 person	2 persons	3 persons	4 persons	5 persons	6 persons	7 persons	8 persons	9 persons	10 persons	11+ persons
Households												
1900	100.00	7.15	14.73	16.93	16.78	14.50	11.20	12.73[1]		4.34[2]		1.64
1905	100.00	7.31	14.97	17.18	17.00	14.49	10.98	12.29[1]		4.21[2]		1.57
1910	100.00	7.32	15.18	17.71	17.37	14.39	10.66	7.27	4.56	2.64	1.42	1.47
1925	100.00	6.72	17.67	22.53	19.72	13.69	8.54	5.15	2.89	1.53	0.79	0.77
1933	100.00	8.38	21.70	24.81	19.22	11.85	6.70	3.60		3.73[3]		0.25
1939	100.00	9.76	27.24	26.37	17.91	9.45	4.72	2.32	1.14	0.56	0.29	
Persons												
1900	100.00	1.59	6.56	11.30	14.94	16.14	14.95	20.92[1]		9.03[2]		4.59
1905	100.00	1.64	6.73	11.59	15.29	16.29	14.81	20.40[1]		8.84[2]		4.40
1910	100.00	1.66	6.90	12.08	15.80	16.37	14.55	11.57	8.30	5.41	3.24	4.12
1925	100.00	1.69	8.87	16.97	19.79	17.18	12.85	9.05	5.80	3.46	1.97	2.36
1933	100.00	2.32	12.01	20.60	21.27	16.40	11.12	6.98		9.30[3]		0.93
1939	100.00	2.98	16.67	24.21	21.92	14.46	8.67	4.96	2.79	1.54	0.87	

Notes: See Appendix Table D.6B.

APPENDIX TABLE D.6D Household indicators 1871–1939

Census year	Household indicators			
	Mean total household size	Mean private household size	Mean family household size	Mean institutional household size
1871	4.70	4.64	4.87	21.33
1875	4.64	4.57	4.81	25.69
1880	4.69	4.60	4.84	23.39
1885	4.69	4.58	4.85	35.19
1890	4.66	4.55	4.81	39.21
1895	4.64	4.53	4.80	29.74
1900	4.60	4.49	4.76	20.04
1905	4.57	4.45	4.72	30.52
1910	4.53	4.40	4.67	33.42
1925	4.07	3.98	4.20	20.84
1933	3.68	3.61	3.85	31.27
1939	3.40	3.27	3.51	37.26

APPENDIX TABLE D.6E Household types 1910–1939 (absolute and per cent)

Census Year	Family households total	Family households with only family members	Family households with family members and non-family members, total	Thereof: with domestic servants	Thereof: with journeymen	Thereof: with boarders and lodgers	Thereof: with different combinations
			Absolute				
1910	13,238,237	9,783,401	3,454,836	1,136,441	1,073,095	1,192,261	..
1925	14,894,306	12,291,056	2,603,250	1,465,97[a1]		1,137,280	..
1939	18,351,123	15,878,508	2,472,615	636,550	533,499	1,103,996	198,570
			Per cent				
1910	100.00	73.90	26.10	8.58	8.11	9.01	..
1925	100.00	82.52	17.48	9.84[1]		7.64	..
1939	100.00	86.53	13.47	3.47	2.91	6.02	1.08

Note: [1] With domestic servants and journeymen.

APPENDIX TABLE D.6F Household composition 1910–1925 (absolute and per cent)

Census Year	Persons in family households total	Persons in family households, family members	Persons in family households, non-family members total	Thereof: domestic servants	Thereof: journeymen	Thereof: boarders and lodgers
			Absolute			
1900	53,866,405	47,979,041	5,887,364	1,337,321	4,550,043[1]	..
1905	57,811,495	50,654,994	7,156,501	1,305,915	5,850,586[1]	..
1925	59,968,022	55,751,712	4,216,310	1,052,486	1,631,461	1,532,363
			Per cent			
1900	100.00	89.07	10.93	2.48	8.45[1]	..
1905	100.00	87.62	12.38	2.26	10.12[1]	..
1925	100.00	92.97	7.03	1.76	2.72	2.56

Note: [1] Other persons, includes different non-family members.

APPENDIX TABLE D.7 Dates and nature of results on population structure, households/families, and vital statistics

Topic	Intro- duction	Remarks
Population		
Population at census dates	1871	Introduced in 1871 and held every five years from 1875 to 1910. Earlier censuses were conducted every three years from 1834 in the territory of the German Tariff Union until 1867. The 1870 census was postponed due to the Franco-Prussian War of 1870/71. Before 1834 there were country-specific censuses without national regularity.
Population by age, sex, and marital status	1871	Introduced in 1871, but for federal states already at earlier dates.
Households and families		
Households (*Haushaltungen, Haushalte*)		
Total households	1871	Households and household members. In 1871 the basic distinction was made between single-person households, family households, and institutional households. *Disaggregation*: by region, later sex, size of locality, social status (in 1925), occupational group (in 1925) (for additional information cf. Rothenbacher/Putz 1987).
Households by size	1900	First time in 1900: households with 2–11 or more persons. Higher categories change by putting categories together.
Households by composition	1900, 1910	*Household composition* published since 1900, that is, the number of household members living in the household: family members, servants, boarders, and lodgers. *Household types* since 1910: households with family members only, households with servants, boarders and lodgers, and combinations. *Family composition* in 1910 and 1925. In 1910: household heads by sex, wives, sons, daughters, relatives by sex.
Households by profession of household head		In 1925 and 1939.
Families (Familien)	1933, 1939	Since 1933 separate volumes for family statistics and fertility statistics.
Families by number of children	1933, 1939	Special investigation of the fertility of married couples for the first time in 1933 and repeated in 1939. Couples by children born (1933, 1939), and families by children living in the family (1933).

continued

APPENDIX TABLE D.7 Dates and nature of results on population structure, households/families, and vital statistics (continued)

Topic	Intro-duction	Remarks
Population movement		
Mid-year population	1841	Calculated back until 1841 for the territory of the German Empire of 1871.
Births		
Live births	1841	Calculated back until 1841 for the territory of the German Empire of 1871.
Stillbirths	1872	
Legitimate births	1872	
Illegitimate births	1872	
Deaths		
Total deaths	1841	Calculated back until 1841 for the territory of the German Empire of 1871.
Infants (under 1 year)	1901	
Marriages		
Total marriages	1841	Calculated back until 1841 for the territory of the German Empire of 1871.
Divorces and separations		
Total divorces	1888	
Legal separations	–	

APPENDIX FIGURE D.8 Population by age, sex and marital status, Germany 1880, 1900, 1910, 1925, 1933 and 1939 (per 10,000 of total population)

Germany, 1880

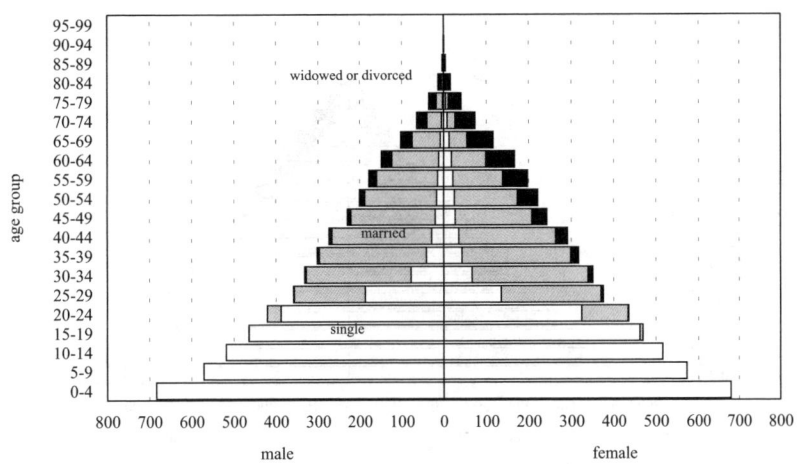

Germany, 1900

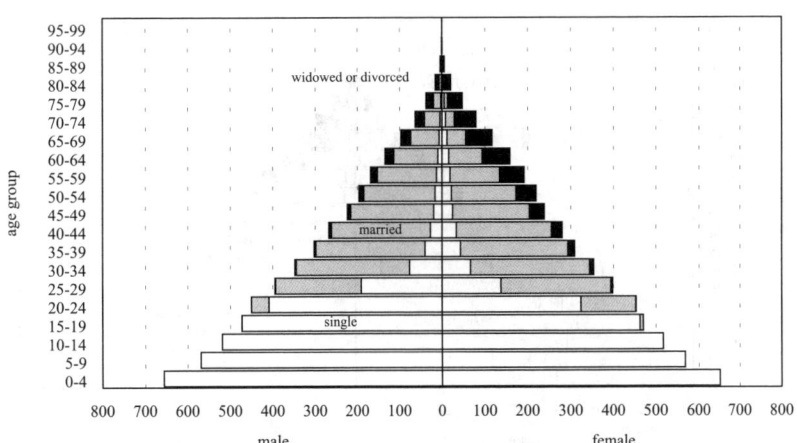

APPENDIX FIGURE D.8 Population by age, sex and marital status, Germany 1880, 1900, 1910, 1925, 1933 and 1939 (per 10,000 of total population) (continued)

Germany, 1910

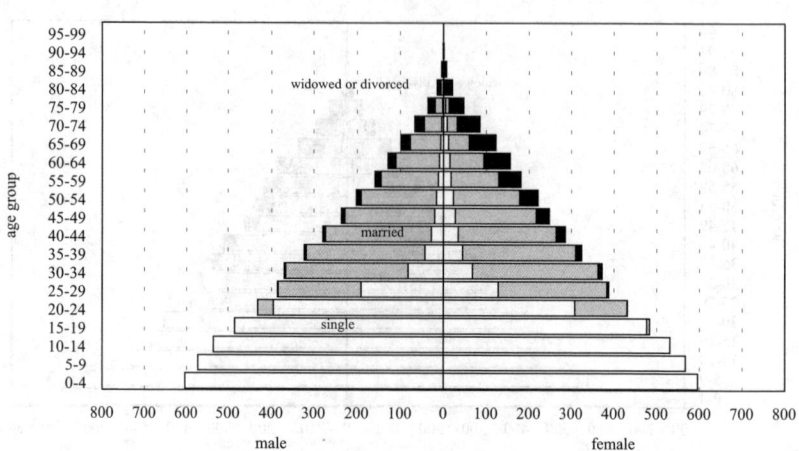

Germany, 1925

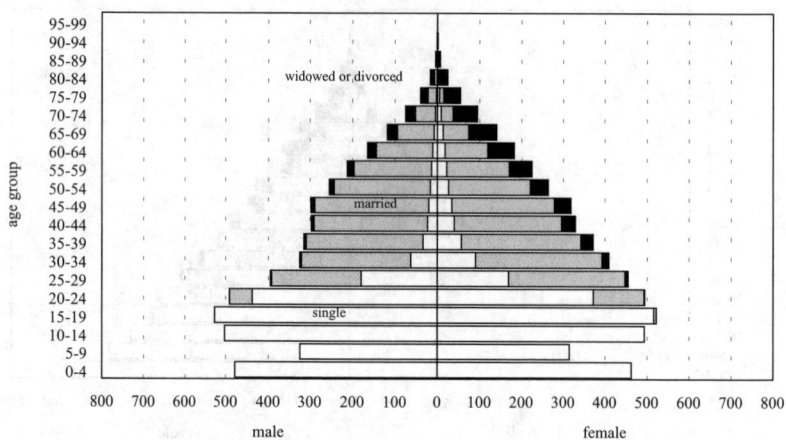

APPENDIX FIGURE D.8 Population by age, sex and marital status, Germany 1880, 1900, 1910, 1925, 1933 and 1939 (per 10,000 of total population) (continued)

Germany, 1933

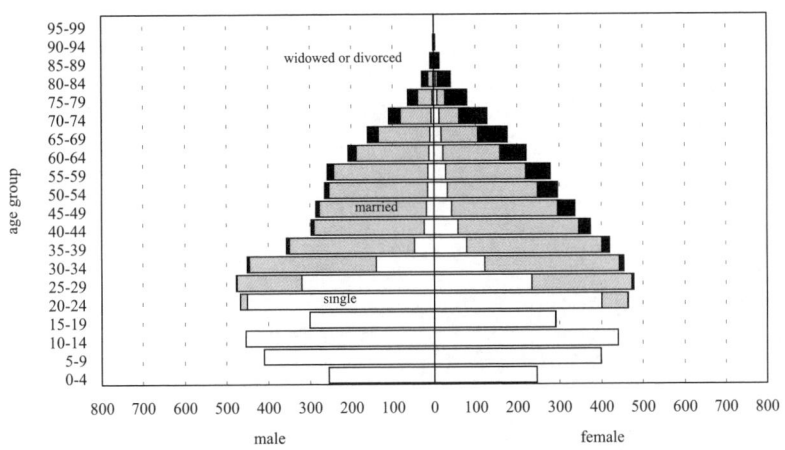

Germany, 1939

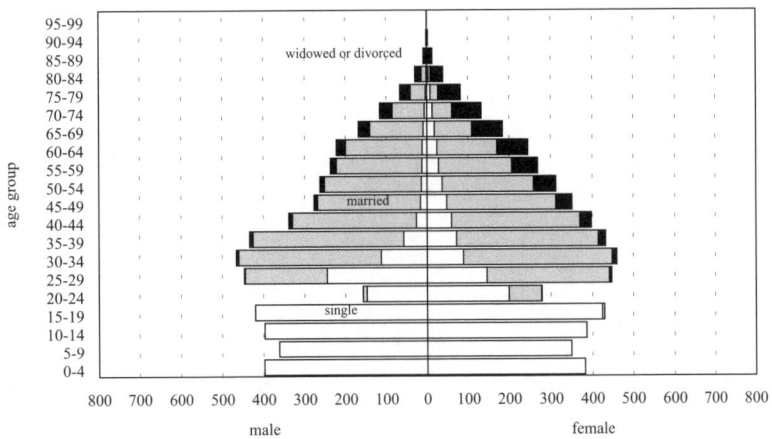

8

Greece

As a nation-state, Greece has a rather short history. The Greek war for independence from the multinational Ottoman Empire began in 1821, and Greek independence was acknowledged on 22 January 1830 with the Treaty of London. For nearly 150 years Greece was able to increase its territory, but the 'megali idea' of uniting all Greek territories and re-establishing Constantinople as the capital ultimately failed with the 1922 defeat in the war against Turkey (Daktoglou, 1980).

Greece's gradual territorial expansion began with the 1830 founding of the Greek national state, which included the Peloponnese, the Cyclades, and mainland Greece with the island of Euboea. In 1864 Great Britain gave Greece the Ionian Islands, the only islands never occupied by Turkey, which had been in the possession of Venice for centuries. In 1881 Thessaly and Arta were acquired from Turkey after the Congress of Berlin. Following the revolt of 1896/97 Crete was administered under Turkish sovereignty by the Greek prince George, the second son of King George, who was appointed High Commissioner (Clogg, 1992).

In 1912/13 Greece participated in the coalition war against the Ottoman Empire together with Serbia and Bulgaria. In 1913, victorious Greece acquired Macedonia, Epirus, and western Thrace, along with Crete and most of the north-eastern Aegean Islands. Participation in World War I led to the acquisition of Thrace and the region of Smyrna, but these territories were lost after the Greek–Turkish war of 1921/22. The last territorial changes occurred after World War II when Italy ceded the Dodecanese islands to Greece in 1947.

Greece's population history since independence has been greatly influenced by political events, wars, and territorial acquisitions; the most dramatic of these was the refugee catastrophe of 1922. As a result of its precarious economic situation, Greece experienced waves of emigration around 1910 mainly to the United States of America and in the 1960s to Western Europe.

The several population exchanges since 1821, especially the one in 1922, made Greece a very homogeneous country with regard to language and religion. More than 90% of the population are Greek Orthodox and nearly all use Greek as their standard language. There are therefore no important cleavage structures along these two cultural lines which could be factors in explaining demographic patterns.

REGIONAL POPULATION STRUCTURE

Overall, the Balkan region has a rather low population density compared with Western Europe. This is also true for Greece, although it belongs partly to the Balkans and partly to the Mediterranean region. Nevertheless the picture for Greece is distorted by major territorial expansion since the founding of the modern Greek state in 1830. From 1861 to 1971 its territory nearly quadrupled, and the population increased by a factor of eight during the same time period. Population density measured in inhabitants per square kilometre was 23.1 in 1861 and increased to 66.4 in 1971 (by comparison, the population density of Belgium in 1831 was 128 inhabitants per square kilometre).

Greece became an independent state through the dissolution of a large empire, a process that began with the 1815 Congress of Vienna and continued during the nineteenth and early twentieth century. As part of the multi-ethnic Ottoman autocracy, Greece had major regional differences already at the time the state was founded and later when new parts were added. That is why already under Ottoman rule the population, economic, and social structures of the regions of Greece differed: densely settled and wealthy regions existed side by side with poor and only sparsely settled ones. The Aegean islanders were seafarers and fishermen, while the mainland Greeks were farmers (raising livestock and grain). The geographic diversity of the country, which is mountainous in the interior, adds to the large regional socio-economic differences. During the second half of the nineteenth and the first half of the twentieth century Greece remained dependent on agriculture, viniculture, animal husbandry, fishing, and shipping. But Greece was not predominantly a country of farmers. Already in the eighteenth century the merchant fleet played an important role, and a large proportion of Greeks were sailors and fishermen. In the nineteenth and early twentieth centuries manufacturing played only a minor role. Industries based on coal mining and steel production did not exist, nor did chemical or textile industries. Olive oil production was one important branch of manufacturing. Thus, a subsistence economy long prevailed in Greece.

Regional population growth and regional population structure were very different during the time period. A strict comparison can only be made for the respective territorial status. But the main tendencies are the following: in the first half of the nineteenth century there were no large cities in Greece. The most densely populated region was the Peloponnese. During the nineteenth century urbanization was still rather slow, and the main population increase was in the rural districts. Greater Athens had 41.3 thousand inhabitants in 1861 and 168.8 thousand in 1907, a small increase compared to later growth. The urbanization process and the formation of the duocephalic population structure of Greece—with Greater Athens and Thessaloniki becoming the dominant centres—only began in the 1920s with the territorial gains and the refugees of 1922, who mostly went to the urban centres of Athens and northern Greece. During the whole twentieth century migration from the rural regions to the two large cities continued. Along with emigration, internal migration caused severe depopulation in rural Greece. For instance, in 1971 the Cyclades had fewer inhabitants (86.3 thousand) than in 1861 (118.1 thousand) (National Statistical Service of Greece, 1980: 10). Thus, over the whole period from 1861 to 1971 the two regions of Thessaloniki and Greater Athens with Attica and Euboea experienced major population growth while the more remote regions faced population decline, especially since World War II (regional population data are also available from Chouliarakis (1973/76) and Caramani, Flora, Kraus, and Quick (1998)).

POPULATION GROWTH

Population growth in Greece was much more the result of territorial gains and the accompanying population gains than natural population growth. But the figures on natural population growth during the nineteenth and the first half of the twentieth century are underestimated. The birth rate in particular seems to be too low because of underregistration of births. Natural population growth was additionally restricted by high emigration in the years from 1900 to 1920 and after World War II. The natural population growth on the other hand was distorted by the influx of 1.1 million refugees and repatriated Greeks from Asia Minor in 1922 and the outflow of 380,000 Muslims to Turkey. Nevertheless, the relative increase in the number of people living in Greece during the time period was one of the highest (or possibly the highest) in Europe.

The available reliable figures on natural population growth from 1921 to 1940 reveal a rather high natural population growth rate of over 10 per 1,000. The major distortion is the influx of refugees from Turkey, which increased the population growth rate to over 150. In 1924 and 1925 population growth became negative because many refugees left the country, mainly for the US. The same tendencies are apparent for the net migration rate; it was positive and high in 1923, but became negative from 1924 to 1926. During the 1930s immigration was stronger than emigration on average, but in the years 1930, 1934, and 1939 there were migratory losses (Figure GR.1).

THE FIRST DEMOGRAPHIC TRANSITION

The demographic transition of Greece since the nineteenth century can only be presented and discussed in a rudimentary fashion because of the lack of data before 1865 and from 1885 to 1920, and because of the underestimation of vital results (Figure GR.2). The birth and death rates for the nineteenth century are probably too low, as can be assumed by comparing the rates of similar countries such as Spain, Italy, or Hungary, which are above the European average during the second half of the nineteenth century. It can nevertheless be supposed that the trend shown by the nineteenth century data is correct. For the short time period from 1860 to 1884 for which data are available it can be argued that there is a small declining tendency, but the data do not indicate when the birth and death rates began to decline definitely. After World War I and the defeat in Asia Minor, the birth rate peaked; this was probably primarily an effect of the integration of the refugees coming from Turkey. Natural population growth in the inter-war years was therefore rather high, and the same can be said for the years following World War II. Mortality was now at a very low level, and fertility declined more or less continuously, leading to a very low reproductive level. While the demographic developments of the inter-war period were unique to Greece because of the refugee catastrophe, the post-war period is very similar to other Southern European countries, starting after the war with a high fertility and low mortality, but rapidly reducing their fertility levels to the lowest in Europe. The high natural population increase since the 1950s led to unprecedented emigration, mainly to Western Europe (Germany).

The crude death rate has been rising since the 1950s, indicating the emigration of young people who often return after some years or after retirement. Therefore the age structure of Greece as a country of strong emigration is 'older' than it would be without emigration. Thus, the rise of the crude death rate does not indicate a rise in mortality levels—life expectancy during the whole period has risen—but only the change in the age structure. This pattern can also be seen in Bulgaria and the Southern European countries.

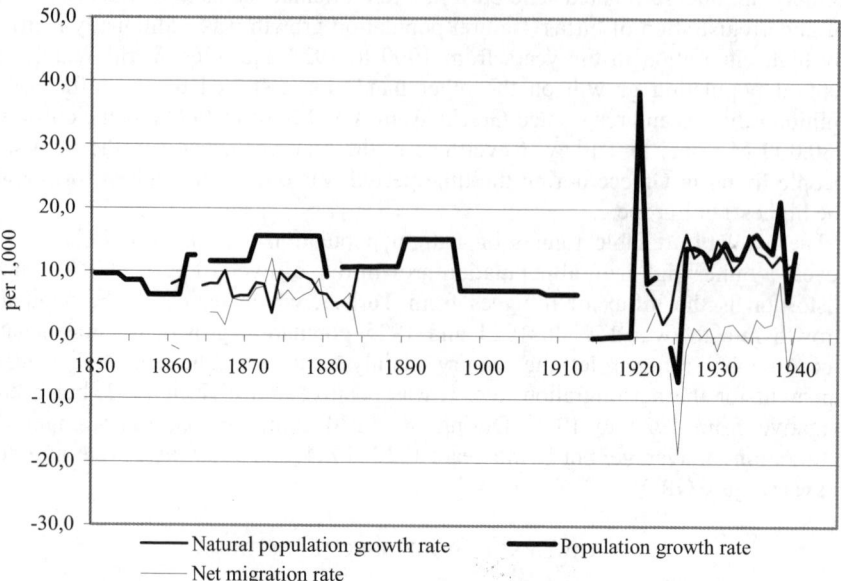

Figure GR.1 Population growth and net migration 1850-1940

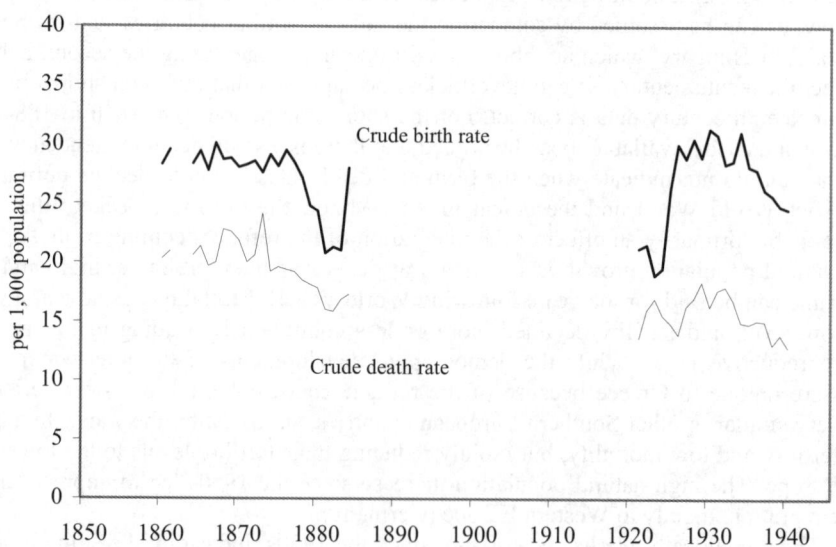

Figure GR.2 First demographic transition 1860-1940

MORTALITY AND LIFE EXPECTANCY

The infant mortality rate is defined as deaths of children aged under one year per 1,000 live births. As outlined below, infant and neonatal mortality in particular were greatly underreported in the nineteenth century and somewhat less so in the first half of the twentieth century (Figure GR.3). Only since the 1950s can it be said that infant mortality has been registered with any accuracy in Greece. The Greek infant mortality level has been rather high as far as valid figures are available. Greek infant mortality therefore belongs to a third cluster of Mediterranean countries with a rather high mortality rate, including Spain and Italy, but also Austria and Czechoslovakia (Masuy-Stroobant, 1997: 5ff.). The data presented by Masuy-Stroobant (1997: 7) clearly show the underreporting during the two world wars, when the infant mortality rate rose, probably only due to better reporting. A slightly growing infant mortality can also be detected in the 1950s, also probably a sign of improved reporting.

Violetta Hionidou's (1997) study of infant mortality on the island of Mykonos for the time period 1859–1959 shows that there was an obvious increase in infant mortality until the 1920s, and only afterwards did infant mortality in Mykonos decline tendentially. The infant mortality rate for Mykonos in the second half of the nineteenth century was lower than for the whole of Greece. Because we know that the Greek rate is too low in the nineteenth century, we can hypothesize that the rate for Mykonos in reality should be much higher. From 1929 to 1959 the Greek infant mortality rate and the Mykonos infant mortality rate do show rather similar levels.

The main conclusion from these observations is that during the nineteenth century the infant mortality rate in Greece increased (as it did also in Prussia and Bavaria). The decrease in infant mortality in Greece came rather late compared to Western Europe.

Life expectancy at birth was rather low in Greece due to the high infant mortality. From 1879 to 1940 life expectancy at birth improved greatly for both sexes. Life expectancy at higher ages was again rather low compared with e.g. the Nordic countries. Because of the low life expectancy in 1879 large gains in life expectancy were made until the 1940s also for higher ages. Divergence in life expectancy between the sexes increased from 1879 to 1940. The comparative gains of women in life expectancy were greater for 60-year-old women than for 30-year-old women or for female newborns (Figure GR.4).

FERTILITY AND LEGITIMACY

Having children outside marriage was very unusual in Greece during the whole twentieth century. Illegitimacy more or less did not exist in Greece, during the period when data are available. Data for the nineteenth century are not available. Illegitimacy was also very low compared with the European average (Figure GR.5).

The low age at first marriage only partly explains the very low illegitimacy rate. Another explanation is the high exclusivity of marriage for procreation and the importance of marriage as an institution; unlike Western Europe, in Greece it was unacceptable for unmarried couples to live together. People 'had' to be married, thus marriage rigidity was very high.

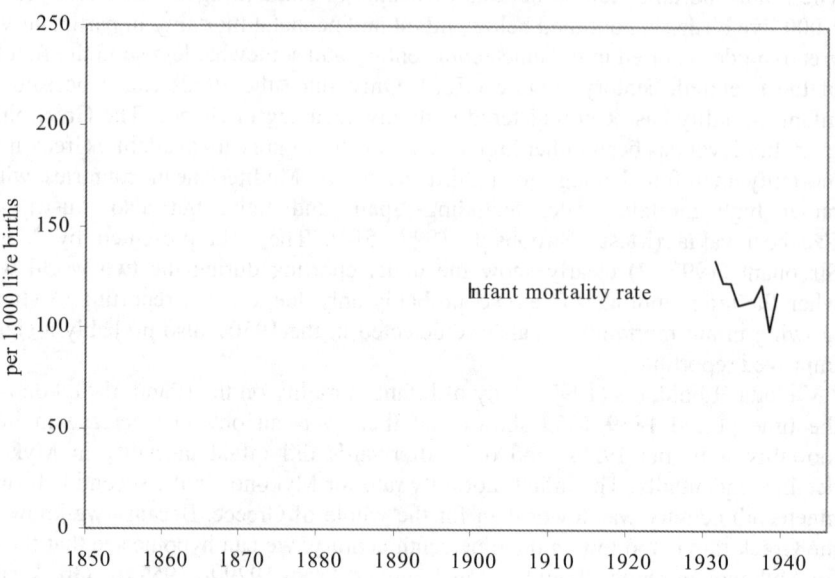

Figure GR.3 Infant mortality 1931-1939

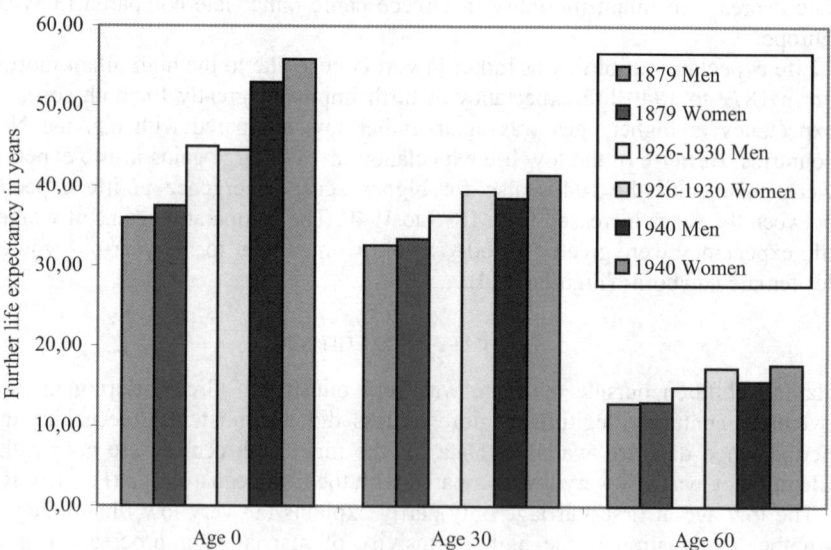

Figure GR.4 Life expectancy 1879-1940

Historically and still today most children in Greece are born within wedlock, and the legitimate birth rate accounts for almost all children born. This can be clearly seen from the legitimacy rate, which shows the relationship between illegitimate and legitimate births: this rate was far below the European average and nearly zero.

In Greece, being an unmarried mother has in principle not been socially acceptable, and there was no place for single women outside the patriarchal family system. Therefore the number of abortions was probably high in the period before reporting began, as it has been in recent times. The institution of non-related servants did not exist in Greece, and young girls were kept at home, a cultural pattern contributing to high legitimacy.

MARRIAGE AND DIVORCE

Greece belongs to the region of Europe with the *Eastern European Marriage Pattern* of early age at marriage and a low celibacy rate. But age at marriage was not stable during the period for which data are available. Concerning age at marriage one could even argue that Greece rather belongs to the group of Southern European countries, though this is not true for the proportion of people ever married, which, with its universalistic pattern, rather fits the Eastern European pattern. Unfortunately, data on the mean age at marriage are only available for some years in the 1920s and 1930s and only for all marriages (not for first marriages). In the inter-war period there is one interesting feature for Greece: mean marriage age for males was nearly as high as in Western Europe, but the marriage age of females was very much lower than in the West. A substitute for missing mean values of marriage age is the proportion of men/women married at age 20–24 as per cent of all males/females in this age group. Data can be calculated for the first time for the census year 1907. Greece at this time shows an intermediate level between the Western and the Eastern pattern. While in 1920 the level of the proportion married was similar to 1907, the proportion was very much higher in the 1928 census, likely because of the refugees from Asia Minor, who probably married at much lower ages. After World War II the proportion of women married at age 20–24 was as low as in 1920; only afterwards did the marriage boom of the 1960s with low mean age at marriage set in, similar to the Western European pattern. A similar development over time can be seen for men. But the proportion of men married at age 20–24 was very low during the whole twentieth century. A similar steep increase can be seen in 1928 (from 1907), probably also due to the impact of the Asia Minor refugees. Very exceptional for Western and Eastern Europe is that the proportion of men married at age 20–24 remained more or less constant in the period following World War II. Thus, Greek men did not participate in the marriage boom of the 1960s or begin to marry at younger ages. The explanation can probably be found in the high emigration of young men during this time period.

Marriage intensity can be measured by the marriage rate and the celibacy rate. 'Intensity' means the availability of marriage, but at the same time the urgent need to remarry after widowhood. A third component can be seen in the universality of marriage in the population. The marriage rate refers to all marriages of unmarried people aged 15 and over (Figure GR.6). From the 1920s to the 1930s nuptiality first recovered from a low level because of World War I, reaching the level of the European marriage rate, but declined during the 1920s and 1930s. Downswings in

Figure GR.5 Fertility and legitimacy 1921-1938

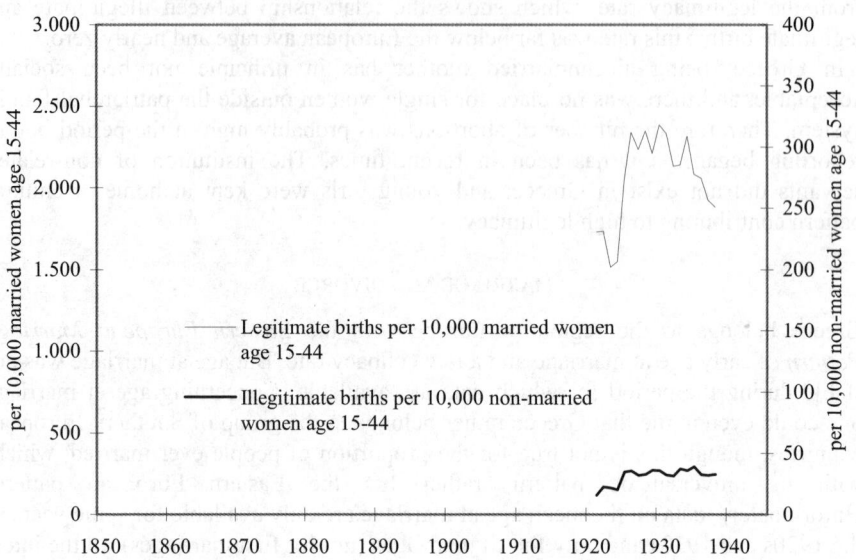

Figure GR.6 Marriages 1921-1939

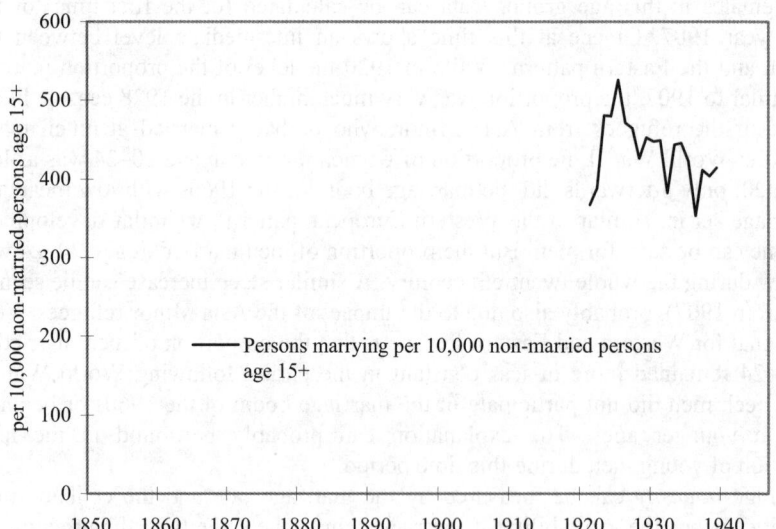

the marriage rate occurred in 1932 and 1936, the first probably caused by the economic depression and the second probably due to the Metaxas dictatorship.

Celibacy was rather low in Greece during the whole twentieth century. Celibacy is measured by the proportion of women never married at age 45–54. During the twentieth century this proportion was always under 10% and therefore very similar to Eastern European countries such as Poland, Czechoslovakia, and Hungary, and in great contrast to Western European countries. In 1920 the proportion was slightly higher than Eastern European countries, and the distance to the Western European country with the lowest proportion—Spain—was small. Thus, there could be some similarities between some Mediterranean countries concerning celibacy for the cohorts born in the nineteenth century. Greece participated in the trend towards universal marriage in the period after World War II, although from a low level of celibacy.

Thus, it can be argued that the institution of marriage was and still is very strong in Greece; before the marriage boom of the 1960s people married rather late. Most significant and unique to Greece is the very large difference between men's and women's ages at marriage, the highest in all of Europe. While Greek women began to marry at younger ages during the second demographic transition, Greek men did not, probably due to emigration, shipping, and the cultural pattern dictating that brothers could not marry until their sisters had married.

No *divorce data* are available for the time period until World War II; data are only available afterwards. The history of vital registration in Greece until 1956 (National Statistical Service of Greece (1960), '*Mouvement Naturel de la Population de la Grèce en 1956*', XXIX–XXXI) does not mention statistics on divorce. But because divorce statistics come from judicial statistics, data are probably included in the early legal judicial statistics.

In any case, the number of divorces must have been very low given the low although rising divorce rate since World War II. Divorce was likely highly restricted or partly forbidden during the Metaxas dictatorship, and the Greek Orthodox Church exerted a great influence by condemning divorce. Given the very low celibacy rate one may assume that divorce was very rare before World War II.

AGE, SEX, AND CIVIL STATUS

For Greece, data are available for the 1907 census prior to the two Balkan wars in 1912 and 1913 and World War I. The 1920 census covers the immediate years after the wars and the territorial acquisitions, while the census of 1928 covers the situation after the Greek-Turkish War of 1921/22 and the repatriation of Greek refugees. In 1907, there were already signs of a birth decline, which is visible in 1920, but in 1928 the youngest age group was again the largest. The Greek population structure reveals strong imbalances between the sexes. The proportion of men remaining single was at all three censuses larger for young men: Greek women married much earlier than Greek men. In higher age groups the proportion of married men was higher than that of married women. This is caused by rather high shares of widowed women, starting with women in the age groups of 30 years and above. Divorce, although also included in these figures, was negligible in Greece at that time. The high incidence of widowhood in Greece during the first three decades of the twentieth century must have been caused by the many wars in which Greece was involved during these years. Another reason for widespread widowhood in

Greece was inherent in the Greek economy, which was heavily concentrated in fishing and the merchant fleet, resulting in many deaths at sea.

Surprisingly, the influx of over one million refugees and repatriated Greeks from Anatolia did not essentially alter the age pyramid, though there are signs that the repatriates changed the age structure by strengthening the youngest age groups. Fertility was probably higher among refugees than among the resident Greeks.

FAMILY AND HOUSEHOLD STRUCTURES

In Greece, the modernization of households and families led to the decline in mean household size as everywhere in Europe. In the last decade of the nineteenth century mean household size was not much greater than in Western Europe. But during the first half of the twentieth century the decline of mean household size slowed, and households remained much larger than in the West. This is due to high fertility during this period, but also to the extended family system with different generations living together, mainly in the rural areas. Thus, the family was a community of three generations and the formation of one-person households was very low.

This observation is confirmed by the distribution of households by size in 1920, where one-person households were rather few when compared with Western European countries. One-person households were probably mainly households of widows and were concentrated in the towns. After World War II, when data are available again, Greece had one of the lowest proportions of one-person households (and persons living alone as percentage of the population) of all European countries.

Mean household size by region can be calculated since 1861. For most regions mean household size increased from 1861 to 1920. There are large regional differences. In 1861 the Cyclades had a very low mean household size with only 3.78 members, while mainland Greece had 4.50. In 1920, the Cyclades again had the lowest average with 4.03 members, while Thessaly and Arta had the highest average with 4.73.

Mean household size by main regions is available for the years 1861, 1870, 1879 (1881 for Thessaly and Arta), and 1920. It shows that, on average, households were much smaller in the Cyclades and Ionian Islands than on the Peloponnese and mainland Greece. In 1920, households were largest in Thessaly and Arta (4.73 persons per household), followed by central Greece and Euboea (4.58), the Peloponnese (4.59), the Ionian Islands (4.26), and the Cyclades (4.03) (République Héllénique, Ministère de l'Économie Nationale 1928: table 89).

Greek household statistics do not give any information on the household composition, servants, boarders and lodgers, and relatives. Only case studies can contribute to the question of household and family composition.

THE NATIONAL SYSTEM OF DEMOGRAPHIC STATISTICS

Population Structure

Population censuses have been taken since the Greek state's declaration of independence in 1821. During the first half of the nineteenth century population censuses were taken at short intervals, sometimes every year. After 1861, the interval was increased to every ten years. The early censuses were mostly published only in rudimentary form, but at least the population figures are available in regional distribution. Beginning with the 1870 census the data were published in more detailed tables with introductory descriptions. For the newly acquired territories a special population census was regularly organized in order to gain reliable information on the topic.

Population by age, sex, marital status, literacy, etc. was first published in 1870. The combination of the population by age, sex, and marital status is available since 1879. The 1907 census was the first to be published very extensively and in great detail. The 1920 population census made considerable innovations. Unfortunately the 1928 census was restricted to a few major topics, and the 1940 population census was never fully analysed due to the war. That is why the 1920 census is the most important census in the inter-war period.

The history of the population censuses is described and documented in several important publications: Chouliarakis (1975a), '*The Statistical Measurement of the Population of Greece 1821–1900*' and Chouliarakis (1975b), '*History of Population Census in Relation to Greece 1900–1971*'. The development of state statistics from 1821–1971, which in the nineteenth century is dominated by the population census, is described in National Centre für Social Research (1972). The population censuses from 1828 to 1981 are described in the publication of the 1981 population census results (NSSG 1994, pp. 11–3). Chouliarakis (1973/76) documents the whole period from 1821 to 1971 by geographical division. The most recent work by Chouliarakis (1988) assesses the agricultural population from 1920 to 1981.

The history of population censuses from 1821 to 1896 is furthermore described in Royaume de Grèce, Ministère de l'Intérieur, Service du Recensement (1909, vol. II: ε'ff.).

Vital Statistics

Vital statistics were introduced rather late in Greece, in 1860 and gathered until 1884, after which vital statistics recording was discontinued until the General Statistical Service of Greece was established in 1925. Only the three major demographic variables, births, deaths, and marriages, are available until the 1920s. More detailed disaggregations for legitimacy, infant mortality, and stillbirths are only available since the 1920s or even only since the 1950s. Statistical data on divorces come from the judicial statistics and are also only available after 1945.

The figures for the nineteenth century are incorrect because of severe underregistration of births and deaths, especially infant and neonatal deaths, and by sex: the registration of girls is too low. This underreporting is obvious in the demographic transition, where both the birth and the death rates are well below the European average. Underreporting was greatest during the nineteenth century, but still had some impact during the inter-war period of the 1930s. Infant and neonatal deaths in particular were prone to underregistration (NSSG, 1966: 37, 53ff., 77). Another analysis by the NSSG (1980: 31, 59) attributes the anomalies in perinatal and infant mortality to the underregistration of both stillbirths and neonatal deaths in rural areas.

Households and Families

Data on households (*oikogéneiai* or *ménages*) were already collected in the census of 1861. But the number of households was long the only item to be collected and published by the population censuses. Not until 1920 were more elaborated household statistics produced. For this census households were published by size from 1 to 16 and more household members, and institutional households were distinguished for the first time. Earlier censuses made no distinction between family households, one-person households, and institutional households, but probably counted private households only.

Some disaggregations have been made according to *nómoi* and lower administrative units. Furthermore, data for the larger cities have been published.

The *definition* of a household (*oikogéneia*) was more or less the same from 1861 until 1940. The definition principally included all private households: households consisting of a single person, and households consisting of a family. Institutional households were not considered households. Most the time household and dwelling were the same, given the low urbanization. Official statistics of household composition are not available for the whole period. There is no information on servants, lodgers and boarders, or relatives in the households, but the 1920 census introduced the occupational status of the household head, rather early in household statistics compared with other countries.

Family statistics were introduced in 1920, but this investigation was the only one during the time period in consideration. Families have been analysed by the number of children born, surviving, and deceased.

Remarks (also see introductory Table 6.1)

Statistics on population movement are only available for the years 1860–1884, 1921–1940, and 1949 to the present. A short history of the Greek statistics on the population movement is given in National Statistical Service of Greece (1960), p. XXIX. The historical data are published in this title on page LXXXIf., in most of the statistical abstracts, and in nearly every edition of the annual '*Mouvement naturel de la population de la Grèce en ...*'. The data on the mid-year population have been taken from Chouliarakis (1973), pp. XXf., where the best estimates for the annual population development have been made. These figures are much more reliable and complete than the figures available from the official statistical sources. In this respect the data are also more complete than those published by Mitchell (1992), who was only able to use the data from the official sources. Chouliarakis (1973) made good estimates for the numerous boundary changes in Greece. The data refer to the period from 1821 to 1971. From 1972 to the present estimates of the mid-year population have been taken from the official sources. The inter- and extrapolation of the variables v16–v21 have been made taking into account these numerous boundary changes, taking the growth rates between censuses and extrapolating forward or back to the time point of the boundary change.

BOUNDARY CHANGES

Modern Greece underwent many boundary changes since gaining independence in 1830. From 1830 to 1947 the territory of Greece was permanently enlarged. Since the acquisition of the Dodecanese islands the territory has remained stable up to the present.

At the time of the Treaty of Constantinople (27 June 1832), the territory was still rather small and consisted of mainland Greece (Sterea Ellada), the Peloponnese,

Euboea, and most of the Cyclades. In 1864, the Treaty of London (17 March 1864), gave Greece the seven Ionian Islands, which had been occupied by Great Britain after defeating Napoleon I. In 1881, with the Treaty of Constantinople (10 May 1881) following the Congress of Berlin, Greece gained Thessaly and Arta (parts of Epirus). The largest territorial acquisition came with the two Balkan wars of 1913, when Greece nearly doubled in size, acquiring Macedonia, Crete, northern Epirus, and the eastern and north-eastern Aegean Islands with the exception of Imbros, Tenedos, and the Dodecanese. With its participation in World War I, Greece gained from the defeated Ottoman Empire eastern and western Thrace, Imbros, and Tenedos, and was given the region of Smyrna by the Treaty of Sèvres in 1920. The Turkish revolution and war with Greece caused the loss of these territories with the exception of western Thrace. More serious however was the expatriation of the Ionian Greeks and therefore the loss of land that had been inhabited by Greeks for nearly 3,000 years. The reality was made complete by the exchange of minorities between Greece and Turkey: Greece had to integrate more than 1.1 million Greeks from Asia Minor, while Turkey received approximately 380,000 Muslims from the Greek territory. The exchange of minorities and the territorial changes were concluded by the 1923 Treaty of Lausanne. Greece was lucky enough to get through World War II without any loss of territory. After its defeat, Italy had to retreat from the Dodecanese, which went to Greece in 1947 (concerning regional organization see Chouliarakis (1973–76), Quick (1994) and Caramani, Flora, Kraus, and Quick (1998)).

APPENDIX TABLE GR.1 Population structure at census dates 1907–1928

Census number	Census date	Census population			Marital status				Age group		
		Total	Male	Female	Single	Married	Widowed	Divorced	0–14	15–64	65+
		Absolute									
1	27 X 1907	2,631,952	1,324,942	1,307,010	1,536,921	917,491	175,405	2,135	940,443	1,581,549[1]	108,389[2]
2	19 XII 1920	5,015,455	2,494,336	2,521,119	2,890,086	1,766,793	352,637	5,939	1,717,864	3,012,443	283,817
3	15 V 1928	6,204,684	3,076,235	3,128,449	3,400,963	2,270,047	466,163	11,513	1,989,701	3,832,473	362,471
		Per cent									
1	27 X 1907	100.00	50.34	49.66	58.39	34.86	6.66	0.08	35.73	60.09[1]	4.12[2]
2	19 XII 1920	100.00	49.73	50.27	57.62	35.23	7.03	0.12	34.25	60.06	5.66
3	15 V 1928	100.00	49.58	50.42	54.81	36.59	7.51	0.19	32.07	61.77	5.84

Notes: [1] 15–65; [2] 66+.

APPENDIX TABLE GR.2 Census population by region 1870–1940 (per cent)

Region/*Nomos*	1870	1879	1889	1896	1907	1920	1928	1940
Central Greece and Euboea	–	–	–	65.45	77.32	41.31	45.51	48.09
Attiki and Viotia	9.40	11.02	11.80	12.86	–[1]	11.25	16.52[2]	18.98
Athens region	–	–	–	–	–	–	–	–
Attiki	–	–	–	–	12.96[1]	–	–	–
Viotia (Béotie)	–	–	–	–	2.51[1]	–	–	–
Etolia and Akarnania	8.37	8.22	7.41	7.03	5.36[3]	3.43	3.55	3.42
Evrytania	–	–	–	–	1.79[3]	–	–	–
Evia (Eubée)	5.69	5.66	4.71	4.77	4.45	2.40	2.48	2.41
Fthiotida and Fokida	7.41	7.62	6.22	6.04	–[1]	3.22	3.13	2.90
Fthiotida	–	–	–	–	4.26[1]	–	–	–
Fokida	–	–	–	–	2.36[1]	–	–	–
Peloponnissos	–	–	–	–	–	–	16.97	15.83
Argolida a. Korinthia	8.78	8.10	6.63	6.49	–[1]	2.94	2.80[2]	2.71
Argolida	–	–	–	–	3.12[1]	–	–	–
Korinthia	–	–	–	–	2.70[1]	–	–	–
Arkadia	9.05	8.87	6.77	6.86	6.16	2.75	2.68	2.31
Achaïa and Ilia	10.29	10.84	9.65	9.70	–[1]	5.00	5.17	–[1]
Achaïa	–	–	–	–	5.74[1]	–	–	3.02[1]
Ilia (Elide)	–	–	–	–	3.95[1]	–	–	2.55[1]
Lakonia	7.27	7.21	5.76	5.55	5.66[4]	2.46	2.32	1.96
Messinia	8.92	9.29	8.37	8.46	8.32[5]	3.92	4.00	3.28
Ionian Islands	–	–	–	–	–	–	3.43	3.00
Zakynthos (Zante)	3.09	2.68	2.01	1.85	1.63	0.67	0.64	0.56
Kerkyra (Corfu)	6.65	6.31	–	5.14	3.80[6]	2.20[7]	1.71[8]	1.52
Kefallinia	5.28	4.76	–	3.41	2.70[6]	1.16[7]	1.06	0.91
Lefkada	–	–	–	–	1.56[6]	–	–	–
Ipiros (Épire)	–	–	–	–	–	–	5.04	4.93
Arta	–	–	1.51[9]	1.60	1.56	0.96	0.85[10]	0.88
Preveza	–	–	–	–	–	0.83[11]	1.29[8]	0.99
Ioannina	–	–	–	–	–	3.02[11]	2.90[10]	–
Thesprotia	–	–	–	–	–	–	–	–
Thessalia	–	–	–	–	–	–	7.95	7.80
Larissa	–	–	7.68[9]	7.48	3.61[12]	4.41[7]	4.48	4.38
Magnissia	–	–	–	–	3.91[12]	–	–	–
Trikala	–	–	6.54[9]	7.27	3.46[13]	3.52[7]	3.46	3.42
Karditsa	–	–	–	–	3.53[13]	–	–	–
Makedonia	–	–	–	–	–	–	22.76	23.93
Grevena	–	–	–	–	–	–	–	–
Drama	–	–	–	–	–	3.31[11]	1.80[14]	1.97
Imathia	–	–	–	–	–	–	–	–
Thessaloniki	–	–	–	–	–	7.35[11]	8.70[14]	7.86
Kavala	–	–	–	–	–	–	1.92[14]	1.88
Kastoria	–	–	–	–	–	–	–	–
Kilkis	–	–	–	–	–	–	–	–
Kozani	–	–	–	–	–	2.94[11]	2.69	2.68
Pella	–	–	–	–	–	1.77[11]	1.56[15]	1.74
Pieria	–	–	–	–	–	–	–	–
Serres	–	–	–	–	–	2.02[11]	2.95	3.16
Florina	–	–	–	–	–	2.31[11]	2.03	2.12
Chalkidiki	–	–	–	–	–	–	1.05[14]	1.10
Agion Oros	–	–	–	–	–	–	0.08[14]	0.07

continued

APPENDIX TABLE GR.2 Census population by region 1870–1940 (per cent)
(continued)

Region/*Nomos*	1870	1879	1889	1896	1907	1920	1928	1940
Thraki	–	–	–	–	–	–	4.88	4.90
Evros	–	–	–	–	–	1.70[11]	1.98[16]	2.11
Xanthi	–	–	–	–	–	–	–	–
Rodopi	–	–	–	–	–	2.11[11]	2.90[17]	2.79
Adrinople	–	–	–	–	–	2.67[11]	–[18]	–
Kallipoli	–	–	–	–	–	1.01[11]	–[18]	–
Rodosto	–	–	–	–	–	2.67[11]	–[18]	–
Saranta Ekklissiae	–	–	–	–	–	2.57[11]	–[18]	–
Aegean Islands	–	–	–	–	–	–	7.06[19]	5.90
Kyklades	8.44	7.86	6.04	5.55	4.94	2.20	2.10	1.76
Lesvos	–	–	–	–	–	2.66[11]	2.61[16]	2.16
Samos	–	–	–	–	–	1.14[11]	1.13	0.94
Chios	–	–	–	–	–	1.14[11]	1.22	1.03
Dodekanissos	–	–	–	–	–	–	–	–
Kriti	–	–	–	–	–	–	6.22	5.96
Iraklio	–	–	–	–	–	2.11[11]	2.24	2.29
Lassithi	–	–	–	–	–	1.12[11]	1.10	0.97
Rethymno	–	–	–	–	–	1.21[11]	1.10[20]	0.99
Chania	–	–	–	–	–	1.81[11]	1.80[20]	1.72
TOTAL	100.00[21]	100.00[21]	100.00	100.00	100.00	100.00	100.00	100.00

Notes: [1] The former region was divided in two. [2] Argolide et Corinthe lost an area with approx. 11,500 inhabitants to Attique et Béotie. [3] Eurytanie was detached from Acarnanie et Étolie. [4] Only in 1907 Laconie comprises the two nomoi Laconie (62,000 inhab.) and Lacedemon (87,000 inhab.). [5] Only in 1907 Messenie comprises the two nomoi Messénie (128,000 inhab.) and Triphylie (91,000 inhab.). [6] Leucade was newly created by joining parts of Corfou and Céphalonie. [7] Definition as in 1896. [8] Corfou lost an area with approx. 26,500 inhabitants to Preveza. [9] Thessalia and part of Epire were annexed by Greece with the treaty of Constantinople (1881) between Greece and Turkey. [10] Arta lost an area with approx. 5.500 inhabitants to Jannina. [11] Annexed from Turkey in 1913. [12] Magnésie was detached from Larissa. [13] Karditsa was detached from Trikala. [14] Chalcidique and Mont Athos were detached from Salonique and Cavalla was detached from Drama. [15] Pella lost an area with approx. 18,000 inhabitants to Salonique. [16] Parts of this area were lost to Turkey in 1922 (Hevros approx.12,000 people, Lesbos approx. 13,000 people). [17] Area grown (approx. 10,000 people). [18] Area lost to Turkey after the Treaty of Lausanne in 1922. [19] Incl. Kyklades, that were shown as a separate Region in the original publications. [20] Canée gained area (approx. 3,500 people) from Réthymnos. [21] Incl. Persons not assigned to a nomos (soldiers etc.) 1870: 20,868; 1879: 25,703.

APPENDIX TABLE GR.3 Population density by region 1870–1951
(inhabitants per sq. km.)

Region/*Nomos*	1870	1928	1951
Central Greece and Euboea	–	**113**	**168**
Attiki & Viotia	21	157[2]	–[22]
Athens region	–	–	3.439[22]
Attiki	–	–	52[22]
Viotia (Béotie)	–	–	34[1]
Etolia & Akarnania	16	28	41[3]
Evrytania	–	–	20[3]
Evia (Eubée)	20	37	43
Fthiotida & Fokida	20	29	–[1]
Fthiotida	–	–	34[1]
Fokida	–	–	24[1]
Peloponnissos	–	**47**	**54**
Argolida & Korinthia	25	35[2]	–[1]
Argolida	–	–	40[1]
Korinthia	–	–	49[1]
Arkadia	30	38	36
Achaïa & Ilia	29	60	–
Achaïa	–	–	73
Ilia (Elide)	–	–	70
Lakonia	28	35	36
Messinia	41	73	78
Ionian Islands	–	**111**	**101**
Zakynthos (Zante)	108	99	95
Kerkyra (Corfu)	92	167[8]	163
Kefallinia	70	74	60[23]
Lefkada	–	–	87[23]
Ipiros (Épire)	–	**33**	**36**
Arta	–	31[10]	46
Preveza	–	50[8]	52
Ioannina	–	30[10]	31
Thesprotia	–	–	31
Thessalia	–	**37**	**45**
Larissa	–	37	38
Magnissia	–	–	60
Trikala	–	37	38[13]
Karditsa	–	–	55[13]
Makedonia	–	**40**	**50**
Grevena	–	–	–
Drama	–	32[14]	34
Imathia	–	–	–
Thessaloniki	–	62[14]	–
Kavala	–	54[14]	66
Kastoria	–	–	27
Kilkis	–	–	34
Kozani	–	26	31
Pella	–	36[15]	47
Pieria	–	–	56
Serres	–	–	56
Florina	–	34	37
Chalkidiki	–	20[14]	25
Agion Oros	–	17[14]	9

continued

APPENDIX TABLE GR.3 Population density by region 1870–1951
(inhabitants per sq. km.) (continued)

Region/*Nomos*	1870	1928	1951
Thraki	–	**35**	**39**
Evros	–	29[16]	34
Xanthi	–	–	–
Rodopi	–	40[17]	–
Aegean Islands	–	**72**[19]	**58**
Kyklades	51	50	49
Lesvos	–	76[16]	73
Samos	–	88	77
Chios	–	83	77
Dodekanissos	–	–	44
Kriti	–	**47**	**55**
Iraklio	–	54	72
Lassithi	–	36	41
Rethymno	–	47[20]	49
Chania	–	47[20]	53
TOTAL	**29**[21]	**48**	**58**

Note: See Appendix Table GR.2. [22] Attique et Beotie was divided in two nomoi. Most census tables extract the Athens region from Attiki. [23] In 1952 Leucade was detached from Céphalonie.

APPENDIX TABLE GR.4 Demographic developments 1850–1945 (absolute figures and rates)

Year	Mid-year population	Natural population growth rate	Population growth rate	Net migration rate	Crude birth rate	Legitimate births per 10,000 married women age 15–44	Illegitimate births per 10,000 unmarried women age 15–44	Illeg. births per 100 leg. births
1850	1,005,966	..	9.6	..	..	..	..	..
1851	1,015,724	..	9.6	..	..	..	..	..
1852	1,025,577	..	9.6	..	..	..	..	..
1853	1,035,527	..	9.6	..	..	..	..	..
1854	1,044,482	..	8.6	..	..	..	..	..
1855	1,053,515	..	8.6	..	..	..	..	..
1856	1,062,627	..	8.6	..	..	..	..	..
1857	1,069,377	..	6.3	..	..	..	..	..
1858	1,076,170	..	6.3	..	..	..	..	..
1859	1,083,006	..	6.3	..	..	..	..	..
1860	1,089,886	8.0	6.3	-1.7	28.3	..	..	..
1861	1,096,810	8.6	6.3	-2.3	29.5	..	..	..
1862	1,110,703	..	12.5	..	..	..	..	..
1863	1,124,772	..	12.5	..	..	..	..	..
1864[1]	1,359,064	7.8	..	..	28.4	..	..	..
1865	1,375,043	8.1	11.6	3.6	29.4	..	..	..
1866	1,391,216	8.1	11.6	3.5	27.8	..	..	..
1867	1,407,585	10.1	11.6	1.5	30.1	..	..	..
1868	1,424,152	5.9	11.6	5.7	28.7	..	..	..
1869	1,440,920	6.2	11.6	5.4	28.8	..	..	..
1870	1,457,894	6.2	11.6	5.4	28.1	..	..	..
1871	1,480,994	8.3	15.6	7.3	28.3	..	..	..
1872	1,504,460	8.0	15.6	7.6	28.6	..	..	..
1873	1,528,298	3.5	15.6	12.1	27.6	..	..	..
1874	1,552,514	9.9	15.6	5.7	29.1	..	..	..
1875	1,577,114	8.5	15.6	7.1	28.1	..	..	..
1876	1,602,103	10.1	15.6	5.5	29.5	..	..	..
1877	1,627,488	9.3	15.6	6.3	28.5	..	..	..
1878	1,653,275	8.7	15.6	6.9	27.2	..	..	..
1879	1,679,470	6.7	15.6	8.9	24.8	..	..	..
1880	1,695,161	6.5	9.3	2.8	24.4	..	..	..
1881[2]	2,004,991	4.7	..	..	20.8	..	..	..
1882	2,026,813	5.4	10.8	5.4	21.3	..	..	..
1883	2,048,901	4.1	10.8	6.7	21.0	..	..	..
1884	2,071,257	10.7	10.8	0.1	28.0	..	..	..
1885	2,093,886	..	10.8	..	..	..	..	..
1886	2,116,792	..	10.8	..	..	..	..	..
1887	2,139,978	..	10.8	..	..	..	..	..
1888	2,163,449	..	10.8	..	..	..	..	..
1889	2,187,208	..	10.9	..	..	..	..	..
1890	2,220,844	..	15.1	..	..	..	..	..
1891	2,254,997	..	15.1	..	..	..	..	..
1892	2,289,675	..	15.1	..	..	..	..	..
1893	2,324,887	..	15.1	..	..	..	..	..
1894	2,360,640	..	15.1	..	..	..	..	..
1895	2,396,943	..	15.1	..	..	..	..	..
1896	2,433,806	..	15.1	..	..	..	..	..
1897	2,451,185	..	7.1	..	..	..	..	..

continued

APPENDIX TABLE GR.4 Demographic developments 1850–1945 (absolute figures and rates)

Crude death rate	Infant mortality rate	Stillbirth rate	Infant mortality and stillbirth rate	Crude marriage rate	Persons marrying per 10,000 unmarried persons age 15+	Persons marrying per 10,000 unmarried persons age 15–49	Crude divorce rate	Divorces per 100 marriages	Divorces per 10,000 married persons	Year
..	..	..	..	..	..	..	..	..	..	1850
..	..	..	..	..	..	..	..	..	..	1851
..	..	..	..	..	..	..	..	..	..	1852
..	..	..	..	..	..	..	..	..	..	1853
..	..	..	..	..	..	..	..	..	..	1854
..	..	..	..	..	..	..	..	..	..	1855
..	..	..	..	..	..	..	..	..	..	1856
..	..	..	..	..	..	..	..	..	..	1857
..	..	..	..	..	..	..	..	..	..	1858
..	..	..	..	..	..	..	..	..	..	1859
20.3	..	..	..	5.6	..	..	..	..	..	1860
20.9	..	..	..	6.5	..	..	..	..	..	1861
..	..	..	..	..	..	..	..	..	..	1862
..	..	..	..	..	..	..	..	..	..	1863
20.6	..	..	..	6.2	..	..	..	..	..	1864[1]
21.4	..	..	..	6.7	..	..	..	..	..	1865
19.7	..	..	..	6.2	..	..	..	..	..	1866
20.0	..	..	..	6.1	..	..	..	..	..	1867
22.8	..	..	..	6.1	..	..	..	..	..	1868
22.6	..	..	..	6.6	..	..	..	..	..	1869
21.9	..	..	..	6.2	..	..	..	..	..	1870
20.0	..	..	..	6.4	..	..	..	..	..	1871
20.6	..	..	..	5.9	..	..	..	..	..	1872
24.1	..	..	..	5.9	..	..	..	..	..	1873
19.2	..	..	..	6.1	..	..	..	..	..	1874
19.6	..	..	..	6.5	..	..	..	..	..	1875
19.4	..	..	..	6.1	..	..	..	..	..	1876
19.2	..	..	..	5.8	..	..	..	..	..	1877
18.5	..	..	..	5.8	..	..	..	..	..	1878
18.2	..	..	..	5.6	..	..	..	..	..	1879
17.9	..	..	..	5.0	..	..	..	..	..	1880
16.1	..	..	..	3.9	..	..	..	..	..	1881[2]
15.9	..	..	..	5.5	..	..	..	..	..	1882
16.9	..	..	..	5.7	..	..	..	..	..	1883
17.3	..	..	..	6.6	..	..	..	..	..	1884
..	..	..	..	..	..	..	..	..	..	1885
..	..	..	..	..	..	..	..	..	..	1886
..	..	..	..	..	..	..	..	..	..	1887
..	..	..	..	..	..	..	..	..	..	1888
..	..	..	..	..	..	..	..	..	..	1889
..	..	..	..	..	..	..	..	..	..	1890
..	..	..	..	..	..	..	..	..	..	1891
..	..	..	..	..	..	..	..	..	..	1892
..	..	..	..	..	..	..	..	..	..	1893
..	..	..	..	..	..	..	..	..	..	1894
..	..	..	..	..	..	..	..	..	..	1895
..	..	..	..	..	..	..	..	..	..	1896
..	..	..	..	..	..	..	..	..	..	1897

continued

APPENDIX TABLE GR.4 Demographic developments 1850–1945 (continued)

Year	Mid-year population	Natural population growth rate	Population growth rate	Net migration rate	Crude birth rate	Legitimate births per 10,000 married women age 15–44	Illegitimate births per 10,000 unmarried women age 15–44	Illeg. births per 100 leg. births
1898	2.468.688	..	7.1	..	..	..	..	..
1899	2,486,316	..	7.1	..	..	..	..	..
1900	2,504,070	..	7.1	..	..	..	..	..
1901	2,521,951	..	7.1	..	..	..	..	..
1902	2,539,960	..	7.1	..	..	..	..	..
1903	2,558,097	..	7.1	..	..	..	..	..
1904	2,576,364	..	7.1	..	..	..	..	..
1905	2,594,761	..	7.1	..	..	..	..	..
1906	2,613,290	..	7.1	..	..	..	..	..
1907	2,631,952	..	7.1	..	..	..	..	..
1908	2,649,218	..	6.5	..	..	..	..	..
1909	2,666,597	..	6.5	..	..	..	..	..
1910	2,684,090	..	6.5	..	..	..	..	..
1911	2,701,698	..	6.5	..	..	..	..	..
1912	2,719,422	..	6.5	..	..	..	..	..
1913[3]	4,819,793	..	..	..	..	..	..	..
1914	4,818,245	..	-0.3	..	..	..	..	..
1915	4,816,998	..	-0.3	..	..	..	..	..
1916	4,816,050	..	-0.2	..	..	..	..	..
1917	4,815,401	..	-0.1	..	..	..	..	..
1918	4,815,049	..	-0.1	..	..	..	..	..
1919	4,814,994	..	0.0	..	..	..	..	..
1920[4]	5,007,500	..	38.4	..	..	..	..	..
1921	5,049,500	7.5	8.3	0.8	21.2	1,730	16	0.8
1922	5,097,000	5.5	9.3	3.8	21.5	1,734	22	1.2
1923[5]	6,010,000	2.0	151.9	149.9	19.0	1,514	22	1.3
1924	6,000,000	3.9	-1.7	-5.6	19.5	1,547	20	1.2
1925	5,957,500	11.4	-7.1	-18.5	26.2	2,059	35	1.5
1926	6,041,500	16.1	13.9	-2.2	30.0	2,341	35	1.3
1927	6,127,000	12.5	14.0	1.5	28.8	2,234	32	1.2
1928	6,210,323	13.5	13.4	0.0	30.5	2,349	33	1.2
1929	6,285,996	10.5	12.0	1.5	28.9	2,212	36	1.4
1930	6,367,149	15.0	12.7	-2.3	31.3	2,386	36	1.3
1931	6,462,772	13.1	14.8	1.7	30.8	2,335	32	1.2
1932	6,543,625	10.4	12.4	2.0	28.4	2,132	31	1.3
1933	6,624,468	11.8	12.2	0.4	28.6	2,141	37	1.4
1934	6,726,891	16.1	15.2	-0.9	31.1	2,316	36	1.3
1935	6,836,984	13.3	16.1	2.8	28.2	2,084	39	1.5
1936	6,936,227	12.7	14.3	1.6	27.9	2,060	32	1.3
1937	7,028,530	11.1	13.1	2.0	26.2	1,924	32	1.3
1938	7,181,753	12.6	21.3	8.7	25.7	1,881	33	1.4
1939	7,221,896	10.9	5.6	-5.3	24.8	..	..	..
1940	7,318,915	11.7	13.3	1.6	24.5	..	..	..
1941	..	..	..	..	..	..	..	..
1942	..	..	..	..	..	..	..	..
1943	..	..	..	..	..	..	..	..
1944	..	..	..	..	..	..	..	..
1945	..	..	..	..	..	..	..	..

Notes: [1] Territorial change: acquisition of the *Ionian islands*. [2] Territorial change: acquisition of *Thessaly* and some parts of *Arta*. [3] Territorial change: acquisition of *Macedonia, Crete, Ipiros, Aegean islands* (without *Imbros, Tenedos, Dodecanesos*). [4] Territorial change: acquisition of *Thraki*. [5] Territorial change. 1923: Population exchange with Turkey: approximately 1.1 million Greeks from Asia Minor came to Greece, while Turkey received 380,000 Muslims from the Greek territory.

APPENDIX TABLE GR.4 Demographic developments 1850–1945 (continued)

Crude death rate	Infant mortality rate	Stillbirth rate	Infant mortality and stillbirth rate	Crude marriage rate	Persons marrying per 10,000 unmarried persons age 15+	Persons marrying per 10,000 unmarried persons age 15–49	Crude divorce rate	Divorces per 100 marriages	Divorces per 10,000 married persons	Year
..	..	..	..	..	..	..	..	..	..	1898
..	..	..	..	..	..	..	..	..	..	1899
..	..	..	..	..	..	..	..	..	..	1900
..	..	..	..	..	..	..	..	..	..	1901
..	..	..	..	..	..	..	..	..	..	1902
..	..	..	..	..	..	..	..	..	..	1903
..	..	..	..	..	..	..	..	..	..	1904
..	..	..	..	..	..	..	..	..	..	1905
..	..	..	..	..	..	..	..	..	..	1906
..	..	..	..	..	..	..	..	..	..	1907
..	..	..	..	..	..	..	..	..	..	1908
..	..	..	..	..	..	..	..	..	..	1909
..	..	..	..	..	..	..	..	..	..	1910
..	..	..	..	..	..	..	..	..	..	1911
..	..	..	..	..	..	..	..	..	..	1912
..	..	..	..	..	..	..	..	..	..	1913[3]
..	..	..	..	..	..	..	..	..	..	1914
..	..	..	..	..	..	..	..	..	..	1915
..	..	..	..	..	..	..	..	..	..	1916
..	..	..	..	..	..	..	..	..	..	1917
..	..	..	..	..	..	..	..	..	..	1918
..	..	..	..	..	..	..	..	..	..	1919
..	..	..	..	..	..	..	..	..	..	1920[4]
13.6	..	..	..	5.6	367	437	..	..	..	1921
16.0	..	..	..	6.0	388	482	..	..	..	1922
17.0	..	..	..	7.4	481	599	..	..	..	1923[5]
15.6	..	..	..	7.4	480	599	..	..	..	1924
14.9	..	..	..	8.1	526	658	..	..	..	1925
13.9	..	..	..	7.3	471	591	..	..	..	1926
16.3	..	..	..	7.2	464	584	..	..	..	1927
17.0	..	..	..	6.6	426	537	..	..	..	1928
18.4	..	..	..	7.1	453	571	..	..	..	1929
16.3	..	..	..	7.0	448	567	..	..	..	1930
17.7	133.8	11.5	145.3	7.0	449	569	..	..	..	1931
18.0	122.8	11.1	133.9	6.0	382	485	..	..	..	1932
16.8	122.7	10.4	133.2	7.0	444	564	..	..	..	1933
15.0	111.7	10.1	121.7	7.0	446	568	..	..	..	1934
14.8	112.8	9.3	122.1	6.7	423	540	..	..	..	1935
15.1	114.2	9.1	123.3	5.6	353	451	..	..	..	1936
15.0	122.2	9.9	132.1	6.5	412	527	..	..	..	1937
13.1	99.4	9.9	109.4	6.4	404	517	..	..	..	1938
13.9	118.2	10.1	128.2	6.6	414	532	..	..	..	1939
12.8	..	..	..	4.5	..	..	..	..	..	1940
..	..	..	..	..	..	..	..	..	..	1941
..	..	..	..	..	..	..	..	..	..	1942
..	..	..	..	..	..	..	..	..	..	1943
..	..	..	..	..	..	..	..	..	..	1944
..	..	..	..	..	..	..	..	..	..	1945

Notes: [1] Territorial change: acquisition of the *Ionian islands*. [2] Territorial change: acquisition of *Thessaly* and some parts of *Arta*. [3] Territorial change: acquisition of *Macedonia, Crete, Ipiros, Aegean islands* (without *Imbros, Tenedos, Dodecanesos*). [4] Territorial change: acquisition of *Thraki*. [5] Territorial change. 1923: Population exchange with Turkey: approximately 1.1 million Greeks from Asia Minor came to Greece, while Turkey received 380,000 Muslims from the Greek territory.

APPENDIX TABLE GR.5 Life expectancy by age 1879–1940 (in years)

Age	0	10	20	30	40	50	60	70	80
				Males					
1879	35.96	46.39	39.53	32.61	25.52	18.61	12.92	8.34	4.68
1926–1930[1]	44.95	51.73	43.62	36.30	28.93	21.66	14.93	9.34	5.34
1940	52.94	54.92	46.42	38.46	30.51	22.74	15.67	9.90	5.70
				Females					
1879	37.46	48.10	40.72	33.39	25.89	19.24	13.06	7.96	4.71
1926–1930[1]	44.46	54.45	46.31	39.33	32.37	24.78	17.32	10.80	5.99
1940	55.80	58.07	49.42	41.44	33.47	25.46	17.72	10.97	6.04

Note: [1] 1928.

APPENDIX TABLE GR.6A Households by type 1861–1951 (absolute and per cent)

Census year	Total households	Private households	Family households	One-person households	Institutional households	Household types and members Total household members	Private household members	Family household members	One-person household members	Institutional household members
					Absolute					
1861	249,399	:	:	:	:	1,096,810	:	:	:	:
1870	327,809	:	:	:	:	1,437,026	:	:	:	:
1879	357,727	:	:	:	:	1,653,767	:	:	:	:
1920	1,131,745	:	:	:	:	5,021,790	:	:	:	:
1940	1,691,006	:	:	:	:	7,344,860	:	:	:	:
1951	1.791.426	:	:	:	:	7.632.801	:	:	:	:
					Per cent					
1861	100.00	:	:	:	:	100.00	:	:	:	:
1870	100.00	:	:	:	:	100.00	:	:	:	:
1879	100.00	:	:	:	:	100.00	:	:	:	:
1920	100.00	:	:	:	:	100.00	:	:	:	:
1940	100.00	:	:	:	:	100.00	:	:	:	:
1951	100.00	:	:	:	:	100.00	:	:	:	:

APPENDIX TABLE GR.6B Households by size and members 1920–1951 (absolute figures)

Census year	Private households total	Households by number of members									
		1 person	2 persons	3 persons	4 persons	5 persons	6 persons	7 persons	8 persons	9 persons	10+ persons
Households											
1920	1,113,340[1]	94,796	168,099	193,847	190,327	164,634	125,190	82,812	46,733	24,292	22,610
1951	1,778,470[2]	154,506	276,781	318,644	332,671	277,911	195,537	114,666	59,418	27,500	20,836
Persons											
1920	4,777,109[1]	94,796	236,198	581,541	761,308	823,170	751,140	579,684	373,864	218,628	256,780
1951	7,309,198[2]	154,506	553,562	955,932	1,330,684	1,389,555	1,173,222	802,662	475,344	247,500	226,231

Notes: [1] Total households. [2] Private households.

APPENDIX TABLE GR.6C Households by size and members 1920–1951 (per cent)

Census year	Private households total	Households by number of members									
		1 person	2 persons	3 persons	4 persons	5 persons	6 persons	7 persons	8 persons	9 persons	10+ persons
Households											
1920	100.00[1]	8.51	15.10	17.41	17.10	14.79	11.24	7.44	4.20	2.18	2.03
1951	100.00[2]	8.69	15.56	17.92	18.71	15.63	10.99	6.45	3.34	1.55	1.17
Persons											
1920	100.00[1]	1.98	4.94	12.17	15.94	17.23	15.72	12.13	7.83	4.58	5.38
1951	100.00[2]	2.11	7.57	13.08	18.21	19.01	16.05	10.98	6.50	3.39	3.10

Notes: [1] Total households. [2] Private households.

APPENDIX TABLE GR.6D
Household indicators 1861–
1951

Census year	Mean total household size
1861	4.40
1870	4.38
1879	4.62
1920	4.44
1940	4.34
1951	4,26

APPENDIX TABLE GR.6E Household composition 1951 (absolute and per cent)

Sex	Total general	Members of family households	Heads of family households	Wives of family household heads	Sons and daughters of family household heads	Other parents of family household heads	Pensioners	Servants	Persons with unknown relationship to family household head	Members of collective households	Heads of collective households	Personnel	Boarders or lodgers
Absolute													
Total	7,632,801	7,309,198	1,699,871	1,239,646	3,268,204	869,790	146,286	64,923	20,478	323,603	6,281	207,543	109,779
Males	3,721,648	3,440,210	1,391,171	–	1,657,751	284,914	78,952	18,498	8,924	281,438	5,456	195,797	80,185
Females	3,911,153	3,368,988	308,700	1,239,646	1,610,453	584,876	67,334	46,425	11,554	42,165	825	11,746	29,594
Per cent													
Total	100.00	95.76	22.27	16.24	42.82	11.40	1.92	0.85	0.27	4.24	0.08	2.72	1.44
Males	100.00	92.44	37.38	–	44.54	7.66	2.12	0.50	0.24	7.56	0.15	5.26	2.15
Females	100.00	86.14	7.89	31.70	41.18	14.95	1.72	1.19	0.30	1.08	0.02	0.30	0.76

Note: Column heads in the source: *Total général; Membres des ménages familiaux; Chefs de ménages familiaux; Épouses des chefs de ménages; Fils et filles des chefs de ménage; Autres parents de chefs de ménage; Pensionnaires; Domestiques; Personnes dont les liens ne sont pas déclarés; Membres des ménages collectifs; Chefs de ménages collectifs; Personnel; Clients ou pensionnaires.*

APPENDIX TABLE GR.7 Dates and nature of results on population structure, households/families, and vital statistics

Topic	Introduction	Remarks
Population		
Population at census dates	1821–	The first population census after the begin of the Greek war of independence was held in 1821. The second followed in 1828. Until 1861 population censuses were held at short intervals, partly annually. From 1861 onwards a census period of approximately ten years was introduced. Special population censuses were held to cover newly-gained territories: in 1881 for Thessaly, Arta, and Crete, in 1900 for Crete (under Greek administration), in 1913 for the territories acquired during the Balkan wars (Macedonia, Crete, Aegean Islands, and northern Epirus), and in 1947 for the newly-acquired Dodecanese islands. The census of 1928 was induced by the Asia Minor refugee catastrophe of 1922. Historical population census data are given by NSSG, 1966: 12 (1839–1961), NSSG, 1980: 10 (1861–1971), Chouliarakis, 1973: XVIIIff., and Statistical Yearbook 1997 (1998), 41.
Population by age, sex, and marital status	1879, 1907–	Not published in 1870; published in the form of relative values in 1879 (1889 and 1896 not clear if published); extensively published for the first time in 1907 for all *nomoi*.
Households and families		
*Households (*ménages* or *oikogeneiai*)*		
Total households	1861, 1870, 1879, 1907, 1920, 1940, 1951	Households (*ménages, oikogeneiai*) and calculation of mean household size is available since 1861. There was no distinction made for one-person households for the whole period; institutional households distinguished in 1920; 1940 population census not extensively published due to World War II. *Disaggregation*: by *départements* (*nomoi*), provinces (*eparchiai*), and communes (*demoi*) in 1870, 1879 (1889 and 1896 vol. not available), and 1920. In 1907 no household data published; household head by sex in 1920; in 1928 no household data published either.
Households by size	1920, 1951	First time in 1920: households with 1–16 and more persons. In 1951 households with 1–20+ persons.
Households by composition	1951	First time in 1951.

continued

APPENDIX TABLE GR.7 Dates and nature of results on population structure, house-
holds/families, and vital statistics (continued)

Topic	Intro-duction	Remarks
Households by profession of household head	1920	For the first time in 1920 for profession of household head by economic sector.
Families (oikogeneiai)	1920	First time in 1920.
Families by number of children	1920	Special investigation of families by number of children born, surviving, and deceased for the first time in 1920.
Population movement		
Mid-year population	1925–40, 1956–	Statistical Yearbook 1997 (1998), 42; historical annual population figures calculated by Chouliarakis from 1821–1971 (1973: XXf.).
Births		
Live births	1860–84, 1921–40, 1949–	Publication of vital statistics started in 1860, but there is a gap from 1885–1919, when statistics were disorganized. Since 1949 the figures have been regularly produced. During the nineteenth century and still in the first half of the twentieth century vital statistics are underreported due to underregistration.
Stillbirths	1931–39, 1949–	Mouvement naturel de la population de la Grèce.
Legitimate births	1927–28, 1936–38, 1956–	Mouvement naturel de la population de la Grèce.
Illegitimate births	1927–28, 1936–38, 1956–	Mouvement naturel de la population de la Grèce.
Deaths		
Total deaths	1860–84, 1921–40, 1949–	See comment on live births.
Infants (under 1 year)	1927–28, 1936–38, 1956–	Mouvement naturel de la population de la Grèce.
Marriages		
Total marriages	1860–84, 1921–40, 1949–	See comment on live births.
Divorces and separations		
Total divorces	1960–	Annuaire Statistique de la Justice 1990; Mouvement naturel de la population de la Grèce; Statistical Yearbook of Greece; Eurostat, Demographic Statistics.
Legal separations	–	Not available.

APPENDIX FIGURE GR.8 Population by age, sex and marital status, Greece 1907, 1920 and 1928 (per 10,000 of total population)

Greece, 1907

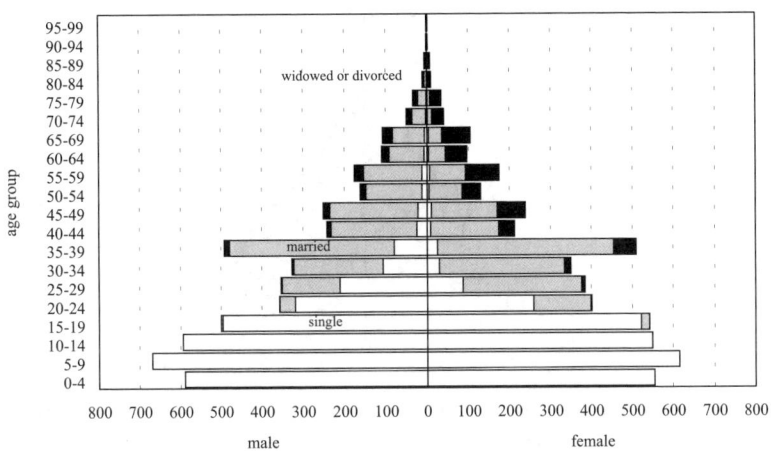

Greece, 1920

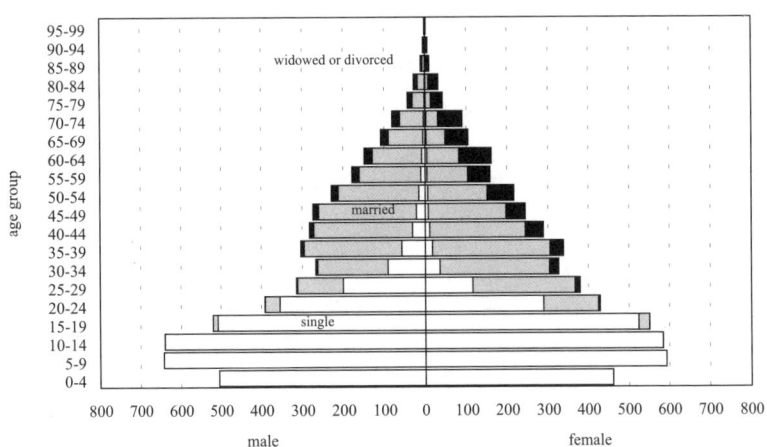

APPENDIX FIGURE GR.8 Population by age, sex and marital status, Greece 1907,
1920 and 1928 (per 10,000 of total population) (continued)

Greece, 1928

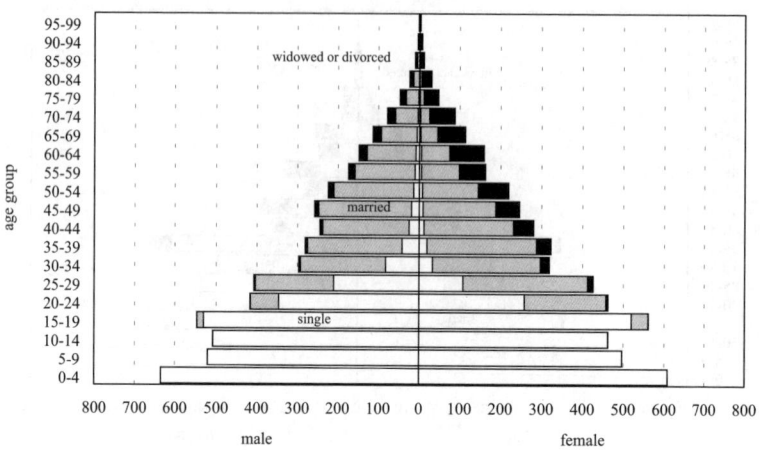

9

Hungary

In the Middle Ages, Hungary was an independent kingdom. Threatened by Ottoman expansion, Hungary was finally defeated by the Turks in 1526. The ruling house of Austria had inherited the Hungarian crown, leading Austria to become involved in the conflict with the Turks; for their part, the Ottomans tried to capture Vienna, the capital of the Holy Roman Empire. The Ottoman defeat in 1683–86 before the walls of Vienna finally marked the beginning of the Ottoman Empire's continuous retreat from the Balkans. In 1699 the Peace of Karlowitz finally freed Hungary from Ottoman rule and brought it under Habsburg rule. The territory of Hungary, known as Transleithania, was the same as before the Turkish occupation in 1526.

Starting in the early eighteenth century Austria introduced a centralized government and the Germanization of the country. The official language, Latin, was superseded by German, and many German-speaking settlers were attracted to the deserted and empty lands of Hungary.

Like many other European countries in the first half of the nineteenth century, Hungary was affected by nationalist and democratic movements which gained momentum especially after the revolution of 1848. After Austria was defeated by Prussia in the Seven Weeks' War of 1866, which solved the conflict of the Austro-Prussian dualism in favour of Prussia, the economic consequences of the war made it necessary to bring to an end the constitutional reorganization of the empire. The *Ausgleich* or compromise of 1867 restored the Hungarian constitution, giving up the idea that Hungary was a mere Austrian province, thereby satisfying the Hungarians' desire for autonomy for several decades.

Hungary in 1867 was larger than it is today. Transleithania was made up of several territories inhabited by different ethnic, linguistic, and religious groups: in addition to Hungarians the population included southern Slavs, Romanians, Germans, Poles, Jews, and Slovakians, among others. Transleithania was composed of Transylvania, Slovenia, Ruthenia, Croatia, Slavonia, Banat, Backa, and the port of Rijeka (Fiume) on the Adriatic coast.

World War I brought an end to this multi-national state. On 30 October 1918 the double monarchy was abolished in the revolutionary upheaval led by Count Mihály Károlyi in Budapest. The republic was proclaimed on 16 November 1918. In 1920 a nominal monarchy was introduced which existed until 1946; from the 1930s until 1944 the country was under the authoritarian rule of Miklós Horthy.

The affinity between the German and the Hungarian fascist regimes in the 1930s allowed Hungary to regain several of its lost territories. The territorial reorganization began with the agreement of Munich in 1938 and continued during the Second World War (1940). But all territorial gains from 1938 onwards had to be returned under the peace treaty of 10 February 1947.

Hungary was occupied by Soviet troops after the war. It was declared a republic on 1 February 1946, and the constitution of 1949 introduced a People's Republic (Andorka and Harcsa, 1990; Hoensch, 1984; Sugar, Hanák and Frank, 1990; Klinger, 1993).

REGIONAL POPULATION STRUCTURE

Hungary's population structure and size differed greatly before and after World War I because of the large population losses and exchanges after the collapse of the Austro-Hungarian Empire. The country was only lightly populated compared with Western European countries: whereas population density in Belgium was 128 inhabitants per square kilometre in 1831, in Hungary in 1870 it was less than 50.

Hungary's regional composition was largely shaped by its economic structure. In the first half of the twentieth century agriculture was still the main subsistence basis for most of the population; industrialization was late and urbanization was low. There were only a few large urban centres: above all the capital, Budapest; other provincial centres were Miskolc, Debrecen, Szeged, Pecs, and Gyor. The low degree of urbanization is reflected in the rather similar population density figures in the counties (cf. Appendix Table H.2).

POPULATION GROWTH

The history of Hungary cannot be separated from the history of its population. Both can be analysed in terms of social modernization and of centre and periphery (or semi-periphery). Ever since the Hungarian people first settled in the Carpathian lowlands, Hungary was on the periphery of the Western European centre.

During the nineteenth century Hungary remained a predominantly agricultural and feudal country. Industrialization was limited and the manufacturing sector was small and mainly based on small-scale crafts. Nevertheless there was a strong population increase, mainly due to immigration of German-speaking settlers. Living standards were very low. The revolution of 1848 and the war of independence did not succeed, but the 1867 *Ausgleich* with Austria realized most of the aims of 1848. Starting in 1867 Hungary experienced a period of social and economic modernization which was interrupted by World War I. Hungary lost two-thirds of its former territory, and its old economic basis and trade relations collapsed. In the inter-war period it became economically dependent on Germany and later also politically dependent. Its relationship to Nazi Germany brought Hungary into World War II, with catastrophic consequences.

Hungary's still-feudal social and economic structures underwent major change during the socialist period after 1945. After the capitalist modernization of the second half of the nineteenth century, this was the second, socialist phase of modernization. Land reform distributed land to the formerly landless serfs of the large estates; public services were introduced in health, education, etc. Educational attainment was improved.

On the territory of present-day Hungary the population at the time of the first census in 1787 was 2.7 million inhabitants; in 1870 it was 5.0 million. Population growth was rather high in comparative terms. Seventy years later, in 1941, the population had nearly doubled in size. Actual population growth was rather different during the whole period. It was strongest in the period from 1880 to 1900, with growth rates between 10 and 12% of the population. Natural population growth was similarly high during these decades, though it was influenced much more by mortality, mainly during World War I. The actual growth rate was furthermore shaped by migration, especially emigration, which was greater than immigration most of the time, resulting in a negative net migration rate (Figure H.1).

THE FIRST DEMOGRAPHIC TRANSITION

The demographic transition of Hungary strongly deviates from that of Western European countries. The main difference is that the demographic transition started from a much higher level; both the crude birth rate and the crude death rate were higher than in Western Europe. In the 1870s the CBR was over 45 live births per 1,000 population, and the CDR was over 35 deaths per 1,000 population. This strongly deviating picture endured until the inter-war period; after 1945 the demographic pattern converged to the European average (Figure H.2).

Starting in the 1870s the CBR and the CDR constantly declined, indicating that both rates had started at a yet higher level. The decline was very steep until World War I, given the very high starting level. The 1880s were shaped by a minor demographic crisis: around 1880 there was a shift in the death rate, followed by a decline which coincided with a rising birth rate. Two additional peaks in the death rate occurred in the late 1880s and the early 1890s, probably due to epidemics.

After the turn of the century, the most important influence on the birth rate was World War I, when the birth rate fell to such a low level that there was a natural population decrease for some years. The rise in the death rate however was of minor importance. The world economic crisis of 1929/30 obviously had no clear effect on the demographic curves, but the 1930s saw a dramatic decline in births. Involvement in World War II led to a peak in the death rate during the war years, with a subsequent decline. The birth rate began to rise already during the war; this trend continued until the mid-1950s, when births declined again until the 1960s. In the 1970s the birth rate rose temporarily, but from the late 1980s the birth rate was lower than the death rate, causing a natural population decrease.

Thus, the two world wars had a major influence on the demographic transition in Hungary, while economic depressions had a minor influence. In the 1880s and 1890s epidemics probably still had some impact. The period since 1945 is influenced by war developments, but probably also by political developments. The major decline in the birth rate in the mid-1950s is probably related to the Soviet invasion, and the rise in the mid-1970s may be an effect of population and family policy measures.

When the Hungarian rates are compared with the European average and even with other Eastern European countries such as Poland and Czechoslovakia, Hungary is clearly an exceptional case, due to the very high level of both the birth and death rates during the second half of the nineteenth century and the even higher level before 1850 (for this time period calculations for the territory of the Kingdom are missing). Infant mortality must have been extremely high in Hungary, and fertility was probably close to the level of completely unrestricted fertility. This high fertility is explained by the very low marriage age and by universal marriage (see below); furthermore, illegitimacy was high in Hungary. These three factors taken together may explain this unique pattern of demographic transition.

Figure H.1 Population growth and net migration, Hungarian Republic 1870-1944

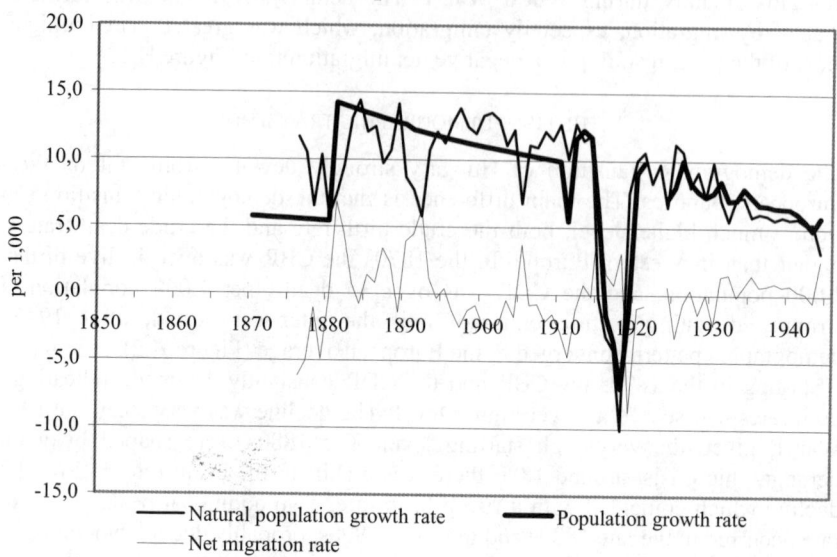

Natural population growth rate   Population growth rate
Net migration rate

Figure H.2 First demographic transition, Hungarian Republic 1876-1944

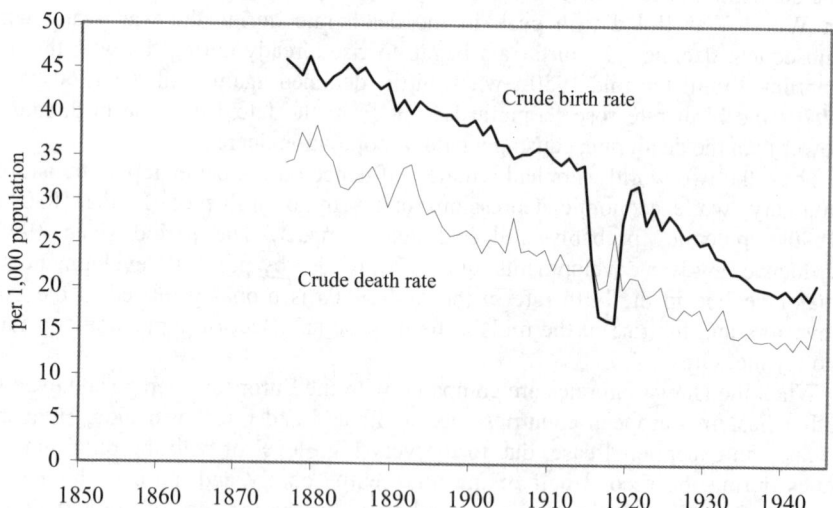

MORTALITY AND LIFE EXPECTANCY

The infant mortality rate is defined as deaths of children aged under one year per 1,000 live births. Hungary belongs to the group of countries with one of the highest infant mortality rates in Europe in the nineteenth and twentieth centuries. Together with Poland and Bulgaria it builds a common cluster. Only Portugal and a few Balkan countries such as Yugoslavia and Romania had higher infant mortality rates during the twentieth century (Figure H.3).

In Hungary in 1900 infant mortality was about 220 deaths per 1,000 live births. The decline in infant mortality in the first half of the twentieth century was slow and late, and there was even a small increase for some years in the 1920s and 1930s. A remarkable and rapid decline came only after World War II (Masuy-Stroobant, 1997).

Prior to 1900 the infant mortality rate was even higher than in 1900. In 1891, the year with the first national results, it was 270. Although the data are incomplete, it can be supposed that in the last decade of the nineteenth century it was constantly over 250.

National figures prior to 1891 are not available from the national statistics, neither for the former Hungarian Empire, nor for the territory of the later Kingdom of Hungary. But the information from the demographic transition in Hungary, based on birth and death rates from the 1870s on, leads to the assumption that infant mortality must have been very high. Both the crude death and birth rates are well over the European average. Because the death rate is highly influenced by the infant mortality rate, the latter must have been at least over 250.

All this taken together suggests a certain interrelation with the demographic pattern of Hungary. Hungary belongs to the region of the Eastern European marriage pattern with early and universal marriage; both led to high fertility as well as high mortality in the first years of life.

Life expectancy was very low compared with more advanced countries of western or northern Europe. In 1900/1 new-born Hungarian boys had a life expectancy of 36.6 years, while new-born Swedish boys had a life expectancy of over 50 years around 1900, a difference of over 15 years. Differences in life expectancy at higher ages were slightly less, though life expectancy was still much lower in Hungary than in Sweden (Figure H.4). By World War II the gap in life expectancy had been reduced somewhat: in 1941 life expectancy of Hungarian new-born boys was ten years lower than that of Swedish new-born boys, a relative improvement of five years. Sex differences in life expectancy were small around 1900 but increased slowly up to World War II in favour of women.

FERTILITY AND LEGITIMACY

Legitimate fertility was at the average level in Hungary, while illegitimate fertility was high and above average. This high illegitimate fertility is quite surprising and in principle contradicts the Eastern European pattern, which—because of early and universal marriage—would predict low illegitimacy. Therefore it is not clear why illegitimate fertility was high in Hungary already in the inter-war period. One possible explanation is the high divorce rate already in the 1920s and 1930s, and a low remarriage rate among divorced people. Another, more general explanation

Figure H.3 Infant mortality, Hungarian Republic 1891-1945

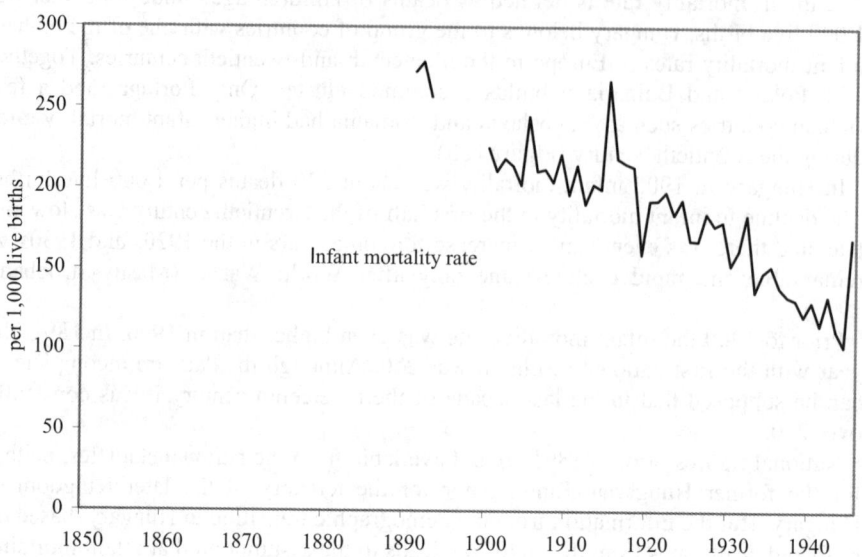

Figure H.4 Life expectancy, Hungarian Republic 1900/01-1941

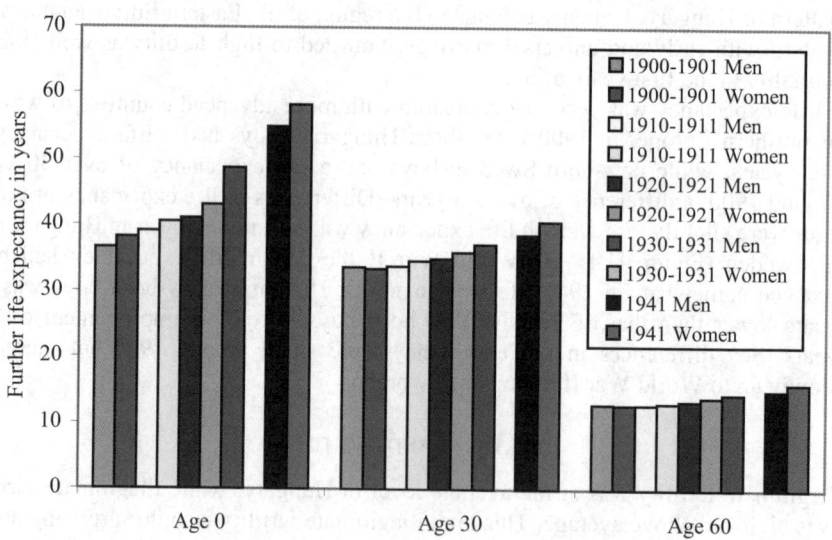

could be the social upheaval in Hungary at the time, leading to high rates of divorce, illegitimacy, and suicide. High suicide rates have often been cited as an indicator of 'anomy' (Emile Durkheim) in Hungary (Figure H.5).

The relationship between illegitimate and legitimate fertility was not stable during the twentieth century. In the inter-war period illegitimate fertility was above the European average while legitimate fertility was at the European average. In the post-war period this pattern changed, as both illegitimate and legitimate fertility declined. Rising after World War II due to the recovery of postponed births, both rates fell dramatically in the 1960s. Since around 1970 both rates have followed the path of the European curve, but at a lower level.

MARRIAGE AND DIVORCE

Hungary belongs to the region of the Eastern European marriage pattern of low age at first marriage and universal marriage. This is in contrast to its western neighbour, Austria, which on the national level is characterized by the Western European marriage pattern. Hungary, Czechoslovakia, and Poland are the three countries in this handbook with the Eastern European marriage pattern. Of course, most of the Balkan countries (Albania, Bulgaria, Romania, and Yugoslavia with its different states) and the Russian territories also fit the Eastern European marriage pattern.

The origins of this pattern are not completely clear: ethnicity may play a role, but also population density, religion, or the rural economy. Interestingly, the Eastern European marriage pattern coincides fairly closely with the settlement area of the Slavic peoples or territories dominated by Slavs or at least Slavic influence (Hungary, Romania, Albania, Greece). On the other hand, territories that were long under Ottoman rule also show this marriage pattern. Therefore one may conclude that not culture or religion, but rather the type and organization of the rural economy and the property distribution and power relations between serf and landlord are the decisive factors for the formation of this system. Another factor is the very low population density and the abundance of land in Eastern Europe, which greatly distinguishes it from Western Europe. Already in the Middle Ages Western Europe was much more densely populated than the East, and relative (!) overpopulation led to eastward migration. Thus, unrestricted marriage and fertility may be caused by the abundance of natural resources.

One indicator for the Eastern European marriage pattern is age at first marriage. But data for this measure became available only after 1945. These data show that in Hungary mean age at first marriage was the lowest of all countries in this handbook and even much lower than in Poland and Greece.

To create an indicator for age at marriage before 1945, we therefore used the proportion of men and women married at age 20–24. The proportion of women married at age 20–24 in 1920 (the first time point for which data are available) was the highest in Europe, with nearly 50% of women married at such a low age. In 1941, in the middle of the war, the proportion was slightly lower, but after World War II the proportion even increased to 55% in 1990.

The results for men aged 20–24 confirm the results obtained for women. In 1910 the proportion of Hungarian men married at age 20–24 was the highest of all European countries in this handbook, with 20%. This proportion fluctuated widely in the following decades. In 1920, the proportion increased, probably because of marriages recovered after World War I. In 1941, during World War II, the

**Figure H.5 Fertility and legitimacy, Hungarian Republic
1919-1939**

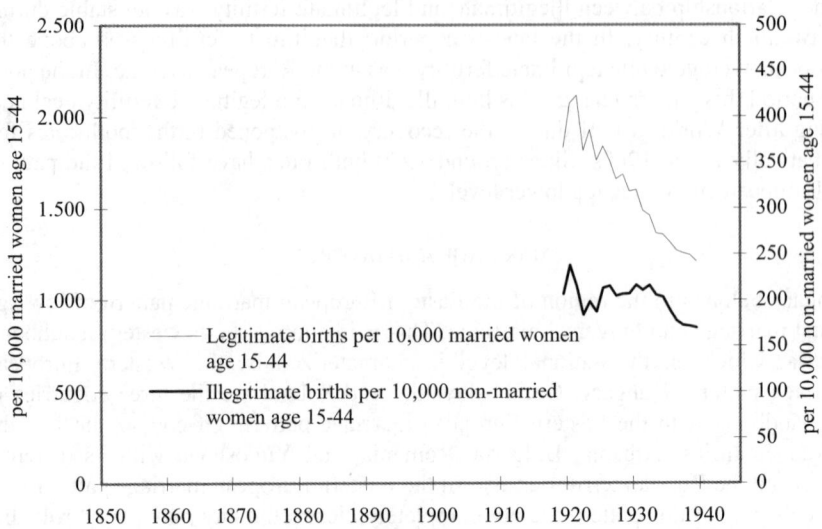

**Figure H.6 Marriages and divorces, Hungarian Republic
1876-1939**

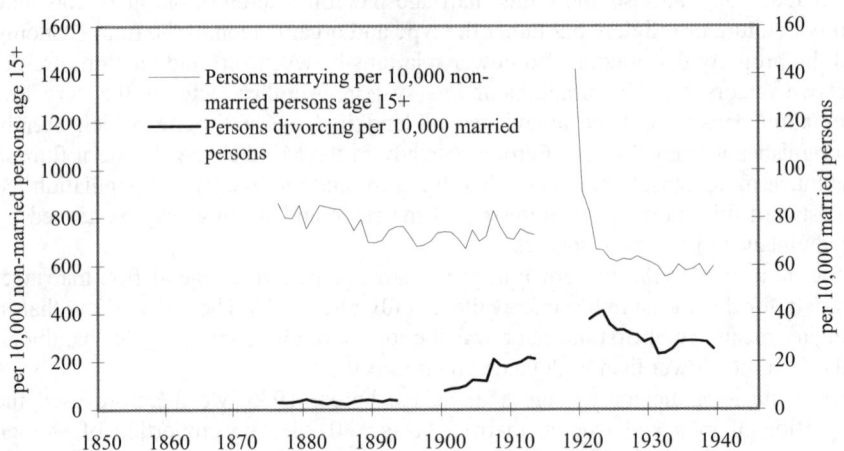

proportion of men married at age 20–24 had declined to only 12%, due to the recruitment of young men into the armed forces. After World War II the proportion increased dramatically until 1980, reaching 25%. From 1980 to 1990 this proportion declined substantially, perhaps as a result of the economic depression during these years.

Although Hungary was a country with a very low age at marriage, the modernization of nuptiality during the twentieth century reduced age at first marriage even further. Hungary therefore also participated in the decline in age at marriage during the 1960s and 1970s, but age did not rise again substantially as in other countries. The whole movement to a lower age at first marriage was weaker in Hungary than in other European countries because age was already so low.

Besides age at first marriage, two other indicators can be used to characterize what can be called *marriage intensity*: the *marriage rate* and the *celibacy rate*. The marriage rate, referring to marriages among the unmarried population, tells us about the frequency of marriages and includes aspects such as early marriage, universal marriage, and the frequency of remarriage after divorce or death of a spouse. It is significant for Hungary that the marriage rate is strongly and structurally above the European average during the whole period since 1870, with only minor fluctuations. Only the distance to the European average was greater in the second half of the nineteenth century than in the twentieth century. After 1945 the marriage rate followed the European average rather neatly, peaking in the 1970s and declining since the 1980s (Figure H.6).

The second indicator concerning marriage intensity, the *celibacy rate*, was under 10% for the cohorts since the 1880s and there was no structural change during the socialist period. Celibacy of women increased from 1920 to 1960 (birth cohorts 1870 to 1910) but declined afterwards. Thus, Hungary did not fundamentally change from being a country of early and universal marriage.

The Hungarian *divorce* rate was high and above the European rate already in the early twentieth century (Figure H.6). During the whole twentieth century divergence from the European level increased. Comparing Hungary to the two other Eastern European countries in this handbook, Poland's divorce rate was lower than average (Catholicism), but Czechoslovakia's was rather similar to Hungary's.

Divorce law reforms obviously came rather early in Hungary. In the post-World War II period no dramatic impact of divorce law reform as in Western European countries during the 1970s can be detected. But what distinguishes Hungary from the European development is the major decline in the divorce rate after 1985, an indication of Hungary's economic decline in the decade before the collapse of socialism. The divorce rate in Hungary fell during the inter-war period as well, also a time of serious economic depression and social problems.

AGE, SEX, AND CIVIL STATUS

The age structures shown in Appendix Figure H.8 refer to the Hungarian Empire from 1880 to 1910 and to the Hungarian Kingdom from 1920 to 1941. Already by 1900 the size of the lowest age groups had shrunk, due to a small fertility decline that continued until 1910. Greater reductions in the lowest age groups are visible during the Hungarian Kingdom, from 1920 to 1941.

In Hungary, as in most European countries, the proportion of men remaining single longer was higher than that of women. While Hungary belongs to the East

European marriage pattern, celibacy on the whole was very low. Interestingly, the differences in celibacy between the sexes were very small and only from the age of 40 were there larger proportions of never-married women than men. The proportion of married was very much in favour of men from the age of 40–50 due to higher male mortality, and widowhood was therefore frequent.

FAMILY AND HOUSEHOLD STRUCTURES

The little information on households and families available from official statistics only allows us to describe the main patterns. Mean size of households was not very large in the second half of the nineteenth century and remained well below five persons per private household (4.9 in 1870 for the territory of the Hungarian Empire). It declined to 4.5 in 1910. In the Hungarian Kingdom mean household size was higher in 1930 than in 1920 (5.0 compared with 4.4 persons per private household). The reason for this pattern is a decline in the number of households and an increase in the population.

Household composition is available from 1880 to 1900 for the old Hungarian Empire. During this 20-year period there was only a minor trend toward strengthening the nuclear family: the dissociation of non-family members is apparent in the decline of the proportion of the residual category 'others' (parents, servants) from 7.6 in 1880 to 6.7% in 1900. In 1930 non-family members made up less than 3% of all household members.

THE NATIONAL SYSTEM OF DEMOGRAPHIC STATISTICS

Population Structure

The first modern population census in Hungary was conducted in 1870. But already in the mid-eighteenth century the Austro-Hungarian Empire began conducting population censuses, Maria Theresa's famous censuses of the 1750s. Thus, until 1870 there were several population censuses which often were not (fully) published at the time of census-taking, however. Censuses (the census dates are identical for Hungary) were taken in 1787, 1801, 1806, 1821, 1826, 1831, 1841, 1846, 1850, and 1857. Material from the censuses of 1787, 1850, and 1857 has been elaborated by the HCSO in recent years.

A principal change came with the end of World War I when Hungary's territorial borders changed significantly. The data for the censuses before and after the war are not really comparable due to these large population changes. This data collection uses the original data for population structure. Data recalculated later by the CSO for the territory of the Hungarian Kingdom reach back to the 1870s.

Population by age, sex, and marital status has become available since the census of 1880, but only for five- to ten-year age groups (cf. Hungarian Central Statistical Office, 1992: 230f.).

Vital Statistics

In Hungary, the regular recording of births (also by legitimacy), deaths, and marriages was introduced in 1865. Additional information was introduced at later dates: infant mortality in 1891 and divorces in 1876. Vital statistics time series for the Hungarian Empire extend up to 1918. From 1919 onwards data are published for the territory of the Hungarian Kingdom. Some more complicated demographic indicators such as the total fertility rate, the cohort fertility rate, age at marriage, and age at childbirth are only available for the Hungarian Kingdom.

Households and Families

Data on *households* (*'Familien/családok'*, *'Haushaltungen/háztartások'*, *'Wohnparteien/lakófelekre'*) were first collected and published for the census of 1870. Nevertheless households were also covered in earlier censuses, but these censuses have only been published very recently and were not exploited fully at the time of census-taking. Earlier censuses including material on households are available for the years 1787, 1850, and 1857. *Wohnparteien* were counted from 1870 to 1910; in 1880 households were also counted. The number of *Wohnparteien* is smaller than the number of households because several households may have lived together in one dwelling. Thus, from 1870 to 1930 only the total number of households or some equivalent is available. Starting in 1890 the institutional households were also counted. Furthermore, household composition by sex was investigated in 1880 and repeated in 1890 and 1900. In 1910 and 1920 no household composition analysis was made. In 1930 a slightly different household composition classification was published.

Data from the original census publications refer to the territory of the Hungarian Empire, from 1870–1919. There are also data recalculated by the Hungarian Central Statistical Office (HCSO) for the territory of the Hungarian Kingdom of 1920.

The *definition of a household* in the census of 1880 and a discussion of comparability with the concept of dwellings (*Wohnparteien*) in the census of 1870 is given in Az Orszagos Magyar Kir, Statisztikai Hivatal (1882), pp. 5–6.

Family statistics started after World War I with the 1920 census when information on the fertility of married and widowed women was collected. This investigation was repeated in the 1930 census.

Remarks (also see introductory Table 6.1)

Population censuses have been used for the years 1920, 1930, 1941 and 1949. In pre-World War I Hungary v16–v21 have been calculated by using the growth rates from 1900 to 1910 and extrapolated to 1918. From 1920–1919 data have been extrapolated linearly backwards from 1920 to 1919 using the growth rates of 1920 to 1930. There were substantial boundary changes in 1919.

BOUNDARY CHANGES

Hungary in 1867 was a multi-national entity comprising the territories of Transylvania, Slovenia, Ruthenia, Croatia, Slavonia, Banat, Backa, and the port of Rijeka (Fiume) on the Adriatic coast. This multi-national state ended as a result of World War I. The Treaty of Trianon of 4 June 1920 made far-reaching territorial changes: Hungary lost more than two-thirds of its territory, and new nation-states were established from the multi-national state. The new Czechoslovakia acquired Slovakia and Ruthenia. Some districts of these countries went to Poland. Romania gained Transylvania (Siebenbürgen) and the eastern Banat. The new Kingdom of Yugoslavia acquired parts of the Banat, the region of Backa, Slovenia, Croatia, and

Slavonia, as well as Bosnia and Hercegovina which had been jointly administered by Austria and Hungary since their annexation in 1908. The German-speaking Burgenland was transferred in 1922 to the new Austrian Republic. In 1924 the city of Fiume (Rijeka) was transferred to fascist Italy. During the 1930s Hungary regained several of its lost territories. But all territorial gains from 1938 onwards had to be returned under the peace treaty of 10 February 1947. For regional organization see the documentation by Quick (1994) and Caramani, Flora, Kraus, and Quick (1998).

APPENDIX TABLES AND FIGURES

APPENDIX TABLE H.1 Population structure at census dates, Hungarian Empire 1880–1910 and Hungarian Kingdom 1920–1941

Census number	Census date	Census population			Marital status				Age group		
		Total	Male	Female	Single	Married	Widowed	Divorced	0–14	15–64	65+
						Absolute					
1	31 XII 1880	13,728,622	6,749,646	6,978,976	7,165,173	5,621,965	908,711	10,809	5,115,627[1]	7,890,433[2]	707,454[3]
2	31 XII 1890	17,463,789	8,668,173	8,795,616	9,236,950	7,104,498	1,087,885	12,496	6,764,504[1]	9,714,848[2]	974,179[3]
3	31 XII 1900	19,252,483	9,580,693	9,671,790	10,312,404	7,744,648	1,176,843	18,474	6,853,869	11,545,899	851,481
4	31 XII 1910	20,886,487	10,345,333	10,541,154	11,159,621	8,399,020	1,288,504	39,342	7,425,864	12,855,490[4]	602,193[5]
5	31 XII 1920	7,980,143	3,870,904	4,109,239	4,153,764	3,235,886	561,368	29,125	2,443,555	5,294,721[4]	238,023[5]
6	31 XII 1930	8,685,109	4,248,452	4,436,657	4,287,688	3,738,476	601,885	57,060	2,392,245	5,743,266	549,598
7	31 I 1941	9,316,074	4,560,875	4,755,199	4,383,949	4,195,034	660,386	76,705	2,420,401	6,244,560	651,113
						Per cent					
1	31 XII 1880	100.00	49.16	50.84	52.19	40.95	6.62	0.08	37.26[1]	57.47[2]	5.15[3]
2	31 XII 1890	100.00	49.64	50.36	52.89	40.68	6.23	0.07	38.73[1]	55.63[2]	5.58[3]
3	31 XII 1900	100.00	49.76	50.24	53.56	40.23	6.11	0.10	35.60	59.97	4.42
4	31 XII 1910	100.00	49.53	50.47	53.43	40.21	6.17	0.19	35.55	61.55[4]	2.88[5]
5	31 XII 1920	100.00	48.51	51.49	52.05	40.55	7.03	0.36	30.62	66.35[4]	2.98[5]
6	31 XII 1930	100.00	48.92	51.08	49.37	43.04	6.93	0.66	27.54	66.13	6.33
7	31 I 1941	100.00	48.96	51.04	47.06	45.03	7.09	0.82	25.98	67.03	6.99

Notes: [1] 0–15. [2] 16–60. [3] 61+. [4] 15–69. [5] 70+.

APPENDIX TABLE H.2 Census population by region, Hungarian Empire 1870–1910 and Hungarian Kingdom 1920–1930 (per cent distribution and inhabitants per sq. km.)

Counties/*Országrész*	1870	1881	1890	1900	1910	1920	1930
	Per cent distribution						
Magyarország	**85.50**	**87.77**	**87.22**	**87.45**	**87.44**	**100.00**	**100.00**
Duna bal partja	..	11.24	10.82	10.65	10.42	3.26	3.28
Duna jobb partja	..	16.38	15.87	15.18	14.75	31.43	30.20
Duna-Tisza köze	..	14.97	15.91	17.06	18.05	41.18	42.16
Tisza-jobb partja	..	9.22	8.76	8.69	8.47	7.17	7.19
Tisza-bal partja	..	11.64	11.89	12.07	12.42	14.87	15.17
Tisza-Maros szöge	..	11.00	10.99	10.61	10.26	2.09	2.00
Erdély / Királyhagón túl	..	13.32	12.99	12.86	12.82	..	..
Fiume[1]	**0.11**	**0.13**	**0.17**	**0.20**	**0.24**	..	..
Horvát-Szlavonország	**11.59**	**12.10**	**12.61**	**12.55**	**12.55**	..	..
Dalmátország	**2.79**	..	..	..	..	..	..
TOTAL	**100.00**	**100.00**	**100.00**	**100.00**	**100.00**	**100.00**	**100.00**

Counties/*Országrész*	1870	1881	1890	1900	1910	1920	1930
	Inhabitants per sq. km.						
Magyarország	**48**	**49**	**54**	**60**	**65**	**86**	**93**
Duna bal partja	..	52	57	62	66	77	82
Duna jobb partja	..	59	62	66	69	69	72
Duna-Tisza köze	..	65	77	91	104	120	134
Tisza-jobb partja	..	46	48	53	56	73	80
Tisza-bal partja	..	41	48	54	60	74	82
Tisza-Maros szöge	..	50	53	56	59	84	87
Erdély / Királyhagón túl	..	37	40	43	46	..	..
Fiume[1]	**900**	**1,050**	**1,429**	**1,857**	**2,381**	..	..
Horvát-Szlavonország	**44**	**45**	**52**	**57**	**62**	..	..
Dalmátország	**35**	..	..	..	..	..	..
TOTAL	**47**	**49**	**54**	**59**	**64**	**86**	**93**

Note: [1] *Fiume* is part of *Magyarorszag* after 1890.

APPENDIX TABLE H.3   Census population by region, Hungarian Kingdom 1930–1949
(per cent distribution and inhabitants per sq. km.)

Városok (Cities)	Per cent distribution			Inhabitants per sq. km.		
Megye (Counties)	1930	1941	1949[1]	1930	1941	1949[1]
Budapest fövaros	*11.58*	*12.51*	*11.49*	*4,860*	*5,628*	*5,111*
Debrecen varos	*1.35*	*1.35*	*1.30*	*122*	*132*	*125*
Miskolc varos	*0.71*	*1.18*	*1.13*	*1,170*	*585*	*553*
Pécs varos	*0.71*	*0.85*	*0.85*	*873*	*940*	*929*
Szeged varos	*1.55*	*1.47*	*1.44*	*165*	*965*	*937*
Baja varos	*0.32*	*0.34*	*0.30*	*140*	*160*	*140*
Békéscsaba varos[2]	*..*	*..*	*0.50*	*..*	*..*	*155*
Györ varos	*0.59*	*0.61*	*0.60*	*944*	*1,056*	*1,019*
Hódmezövásárhely varos	*0.69*	*0.65*	*0.64*	*79*	*82*	*79*
Kaposvár varos	*..*	*0.35*	*0.36*	*..*	*786*	*786*
Kecskemét varos	*0.91*	*0.93*	*0.96*	*84*	*93*	*94*
Sopron varos	*0.41*	*0.45*	*0.36*	*277*	*323*	*254*
Székesfehérvár varos	*0.47*	*0.52*	*0.46*	*342*	*400*	*350*
Szombathely varos	*..*	*0.46*	*0.43*	*..*	*1,132*	*1,053*
Baranya	2.88	2.66	2.72	63	63	64
Fejér	2.65	2.40	2.48	57	58	59
Györ-Moson (-Pozsony)	1.78	1.69	1.72	66	70	70
Komarom-Esztergom	2.06	2.14	2.26	90	101	106
Somogy	4.44	3.77	3.90	58	54	55
Sopron	1.65	1.52	1.51	79	78	77
Tolna	3.10	2.93	2.95	75	75	75
Vas	3.17	2.54	2.56	83	72	72
Veszprem	2.81	3.01	3.02	62	66	65
Zala	4.20	3.90	3.94	75	78	78
Nógrád-Hont	2.57	2.43	2.52	77	807	829
Bács-Bodrog	1.25	1.31	1.42	65	64	69
Csóngrad	1.72	1.64	1.71	79	81	83
Heves	3.65	3.59	3.58	85	86	85
Jasz-Nagykun-Szolnok	4.75	4.72	4.75	79	81	81
Pest-Pilis-Solt-Kiskun	15.72	16.52	16.69	116	133	133
Abauj (-Torna)	1.05	1.00	1.02	54	57	57
Borsod-Gömör (-Kishont)	3.42	2.96	3.07	76	76	78
Zemplén	1.68	1.66	1.63	83	88	85
Békés	3.81	3.74	3.19	90	99	83
Bihar	2.03	1.96	2.03	64	67	68
Hajdu	2.06	2.13	2.20	75	77	79
Szabolcs (-Ung)	4.55	4.54	4.67	85	95	97
Szatmar (-Ugocsa), Bereg	1.73	1.74	1.82	71	75	78
Csanad, Arad, Torontál	2.00	..	..	87	..	..
Csanad	..	1.80	1.80	..	89	88
TOTAL	**100.00**	**100.00**	**100.00**	**93**	**100**	**99**

Notes: [1] The year 1949 has been included in this table because of fundamental regional changes since the 1960 census. [2] 1949 only. This city was part of megye Bekes in 1941.

APPENDIX TABLE H.4A Demographic developments, Hungarian Empire 1865–1918
(absolute figures and rates)

Year	Mid-year population	Natural population growth rate	Population growth rate	Net migration rate	Crude birth rate	Legitimate births per 10,000 married women age 15–44	Illegitimate births per 10,000 unmarried women age 15–44	Illeg. births per 100 leg. births
Hungarian Empire								
1865	..	..	..	..	..	..	..	7.3
1866	..	..	..	..	..	..	..	8.2
1867	..	..	..	..	..	..	..	7.9
1868	..	..	..	..	..	..	..	8.4
1869	..	..	..	..	..	..	..	8.0
1870	13,674,579	9.1	..	..	41.7	..	..	8.3
1871	13,713,751	4.1	2.9	-1.2	43.1	..	..	8.0
1872	13,733,109	-1.2	1.4	2.7	41.0	..	..	8.3
1873	13,570,936	-22.6	-12.0	10.7	41.8	..	..	9.2
1874	13,417,662	0.1	-11.4	-11.5	42.7	..	..	8.2
1875	13,471,740	8.0	4.0	-4.0	45.2	..	..	7.9
1876	13,598,042	8.8	9.3	0.4	45.3	..	..	7.9
1877	13,718,945	6.1	8.8	2.7	42.9	..	..	8.0
1878	13,803,205	4.6	6.1	1.5	42.3	..	..	7.9
1879	13,906,155	9.3	7.4	-1.9	45.0	..	..	8.4
1880	13,903,565	5.5	-0.2	-5.7	42.3	..	..	8.6
1881	13,847,615	7.4	-4.0	-11.4	44.0	..	..	8.6
1882	13,917,096	7.3	5.0	-2.4	44.0	..	..	8.8
1883	14,062,601	12.0	10.3	-1.7	44.8	..	..	8.8
1884	14,257,643	14.0	13.7	-0.4	45.6	..	..	8.7
1885	14,453,581	11.8	13.6	1.8	44.6	..	..	9.1
1886	14,641,053	12.5	12.8	0.3	45.2	..	..	9.1
1887	14,809,804	9.8	11.4	1.6	43.8	..	..	9.2
1888	14,967,397	11.5	10.5	-1.0	43.5	..	..	9.2
1889	15,157,712	13.9	12.6	-1.3	43.3	..	..	9.2
1890	15,262,073	8.1	6.8	-1.3	40.3	..	..	9.8
1891	15,282,002	9.1	1.3	-7.8	42.4	..	..	9.8
1892	15,347,295	5.9	4.3	-1.6	40.5	..	..	8.9
1893	15,484,346	11.9	8.9	-3.0	42.9	..	..	9.5
1894	15,682,768	11.2	12.7	1.5	41.4	..	..	9.8
1895	15,877,069	12.0	12.2	0.2	41.5	..	..	10.1
1896	16,053,264	12.0	11.0	-1.0	40.4	..	..	9.9
1897	16,233,080	12.2	11.1	-1.1	40.1	..	..	10.5
1898	16,395,652	9.6	9.9	0.3	37.5	..	..	10.1
1899	16,557,158	11.8	9.8	-2.1	38.9	..	..	10.3
1900	16,742,871	12.3	11.1	-1.2	39.2	..	..	10.6
1901	16,936,382	12.5	11.4	-1.1	37.6	..	..	10.6
1902	17,125,752	11.5	11.1	-0.5	38.4	..	..	10.7
1903	17,298,895	10.3	10.0	-0.3	36.3	..	..	10.7
1904	17,478,587	12.1	10.3	-1.8	36.7	..	..	11.1
1905	17,636,072	7.6	8.9	1.3	35.2	..	..	10.8
1906	17,785,978	11.0	8.4	-2.6	35.6	..	..	11.6
1907	17,962,148	10.4	9.8	-0.6	35.7	..	..	11.5
1908	18,144,989	11.5	10.1	-1.4	36.1	..	..	10.4
1909	..	..	..	..	..	..	..	10.3

continued

APPENDIX TABLE H.4A Demographic developments, Hungarian Empire 1865–1918
(absolute figures and rates)

Crude death rate	Infant mortality rate	Stillbirth rate	Infant mortality and stillbirth rate	Crude marriage rate	Persons marrying per 10,000 unmarried persons age 15+	Persons marrying per 10,000 unmarried persons age 15–49	Crude divorce rate	Divorces per 100 marriages	Divorces per 10,000 married persons	Year
										Hungarian Empire
..	..	9.9	..	..	..	..	..	..	..	1865
..	..	12.0	..	..	..	..	..	..	..	1866
..	..	12.1	..	..	..	..	..	..	..	1867
..	..	12.0	..	..	..	..	..	..	..	1868
..	..	12.2	..	..	..	..	..	..	..	1869
32.6	..	12.6	..	9.8	..	..	..	..	..	1870
39.0	..	12.3	..	10.4	..	..	..	..	..	1871
42.3	..	13.0	..	10.7	..	..	..	..	..	1872
64.4	..	13.1	..	11.3	..	..	..	..	..	1873
42.6	..	12.9	..	10.7	..	..	..	..	..	1874
37.2	..	12.3	..	10.9	..	..	..	..	..	1875
36.5	..	12.0	..	9.9	..	..	0.1	0.7	..	1876
36.8	..	13.0	..	9.1	..	..	0.1	0.7	..	1877
37.7	..	14.4	..	9.4	..	..	0.1	0.8	..	1878
35.7	..	15.5	..	10.1	..	..	0.1	0.7	..	1879
36.8	..	15.9	..	9.0	..	..	0.1	1.0	..	1880
35.6	..	16.6	..	9.9	..	..	0.1	0.8	..	1881
36.7	..	16.6	..	10.2	..	..	0.1	0.7	..	1882
32.8	..	17.7	..	10.3	..	..	0.1	0.7	..	1883
31.5	..	17.8	..	10.1	..	..	0.1	0.7	..	1884
32.8	..	18.5	..	9.9	..	..	0.1	0.7	..	1885
32.8	..	18.8	..	9.6	..	..	0.1	0.6	..	1886
34.1	..	19.2	..	9.0	..	..	0.1	0.8	..	1887
32.0	..	19.5	..	9.3	..	..	0.1	0.8	..	1888
29.4	..	20.4	..	8.1	..	..	0.1	0.9	..	1889
32.2	..	21.5	..	8.1	..	..	0.1	0.9	..	1890
33.3	259.2	21.7	280.9	8.6	..	..	0.1	0.8	..	1891
34.6	274.7	22.8	297.4	9.2	..	..	0.1	0.9	..	1892
31.0	240.9	22.2	263.0	9.3	..	..	0.1	0.9	..	1893
30.2	247.5	23.3	270.7	9.1	..	..	0.1	1.0	..	1894
29.5	242.0	24.2	266.2	8.5	..	..	0.1	1.0	..	1895
28.4	225.7	25.0	250.6	7.9	..	..	0.0	0.3	..	1896
28.0	222.8	23.4	246.2	8.1	..	..	0.0	0.5	..	1897
27.9	225.5	22.5	248.0	8.2	..	..	0.1	1.0	..	1898
27.1	209.1	21.5	230.5	8.9	..	..	0.1	1.3	..	1899
26.9	222.6	21.1	243.7	8.9	..	..	0.1	1.4	..	1900
25.1	207.2	20.8	228.0	8.8	..	..	0.1	1.7	..	1901
26.9	219.1	16.1	235.1	8.6	..	..	0.2	1.8	..	1902
26.0	212.5	20.7	233.2	8.0	..	..	0.2	2.1	..	1903
24.6	196.7	19.5	216.2	9.0	..	..	0.2	2.3	..	1904
27.5	231.5	18.7	250.2	8.4	..	..	0.2	2.4	..	1905
24.7	206.6	18.7	225.3	8.7	..	..	0.2	2.5	..	1906
25.3	212.4	19.6	232.0	9.9	..	..	0.4	4.0	..	1907
24.6	200.6	19.8	220.4	9.1	..	..	0.3	3.8	..	1908
..	214.3	20.3	234.6	..	..	..	..	4.0	..	1909

continued

APPENDIX TABLE H.4A Demographic developments, Hungarian Empire 1865–1918 (continued)

Year	Mid-year population	Natural population growth rate	Population growth rate	Net migration rate	Crude birth rate	Legitimate births per 10,000 married women aged 15–44	Illegitimate births per 10,000 unmarried women aged 15–44	Illeg. births per 100 leg. births
1910	..	..	..	..	..	..	..	10.5
1911	18,356,071	10.0	..	..	34.8	..	..	10.4
1912	18,514,861	13.0	8.6	-4.4	35.9	..	..	10.3
1913	18,659,565	11.1	7.8	-3.4	34.3	..	..	10.2
1914	18,815,121	11.1	8.3	-2.8	34.5	..	..	9.5
1915	18,852,095	-1.6	2.0	3.5	23.6	..	..	10.7
1916	18,745,687	-4.2	-5.7	-1.5	16.8	..	..	11.0
1917	18,610,241	-4.7	-7.3	-2.6	16.0	..	..	12.2
1918	18,417,690	-10.4	-10.5	0.0	15.3	..	..	13.4

APPENDIX TABLE H.4A Demographic developments, Hungarian Empire 1865–1918
(continued)

Crude death rate	Infant mortality rate	Stillbirth rate	Infant mortality and stillbirth rate	Crude marriage rate	Persons marrying per 10,000 unmarried persons age 15+	Persons marrying per 10,000 unmarried persons age 15–49	Crude divorce rate	Divorces per 100 marriages	Divorces per 10,000 married persons	Year
..	195.0	20.7	215.6	..	..	..	..	4.4	..	1910
24.8	207.5	20.4	227.9	9.3	..	..	0.4	4.7	..	1911
23.0	186.4	21.1	207.4	8.7	..	..	0.4	5.1	..	1912
23.2	201.0	21.1	222.1	9.2	..	..	0.4	4.6	..	1913
23.4	196.9	20.5	217.5	7.2	..	..	0.4	5.1	..	1914
25.2	263.5	20.7	284.2	3.2	..	..	0.1	4.3	..	1915
20.9	218.5	21.9	240.4	3.4	..	..	0.1	3.7	..	1916
20.7	215.5	22.1	237.6	4.1	..	..	0.1	3.6	..	1917
25.7	217.4	24.1	241.5	6.9	..	..	..	..	..	1918

APPENDIX TABLE H.4B Demographic developments, Hungarian Republic 1869–1945 (absolute figures and rates)

Year	Mid-year population	Natural population growth rate	Population growth rate	Net migration rate	Crude birth rate	Legitimate births per 10,000 married women aged 15–44	Illegitimate births per 10,000 unmarried women aged 15–44	Illeg. births per 100 leg. births
Hungarian Republic								
1869	5,011,310	..	..	..	..	..	..	..
1870	5,040,208	..	5.7	..	..	..	..	..
1871	5,069,107	..	5.7	..	..	..	..	..
1872	5,098,005	..	5.7	..	..	..	..	..
1873	5,126,903	..	5.6	..	..	..	..	..
1874	5,155,801	..	5.6	..	..	..	..	..
1875	5,184,700	..	5.6	..	..	..	..	..
1876	5,213,598	11.7	5.5	-6.1	45.9	..	..	..
1877	5,242,496	10.5	5.5	-5.0	45.1	..	..	..
1878	5,271,394	6.5	5.5	-1.0	44.2	..	..	..
1879	5,300,293	10.4	5.5	-4.9	46.3	..	..	..
1880	5,329,191	5.7	5.4	-0.3	44.2	..	..	..
1881	5,406,207	7.4	14.2	6.8	43.0	..	..	..
1882	5,483,223	9.6	14.0	4.5	44.0	..	..	..
1883	5,560,239	13.1	13.9	0.8	44.6	..	..	..
1884	5,637,255	14.4	13.7	-0.7	45.5	..	..	..
1885	5,714,271	12.1	13.5	1.4	44.4	..	..	..
1886	5,791,287	12.5	13.3	0.8	45.1	..	..	..
1887	5,868,303	9.7	13.1	3.4	43.6	..	..	..
1888	5,945,319	10.7	13.0	2.3	42.7	..	..	..
1889	6,022,335	14.2	12.8	-1.4	43.3	..	..	..
1890	6,099,351	8.7	12.6	3.9	40.2	..	..	..
1891	6,174,857	7.8	12.2	4.5	41.4	..	..	..
1892	6,250,364	5.8	12.1	6.3	39.9	..	..	..
1893	6,325,887	10.7	11.9	1.2	41.3	..	..	..
1894	6,401,377	12.1	11.8	-0.3	40.5	..	..	..
1895	6,476,883	11.3	11.7	0.4	40.1	..	..	..
1896	6,552,389	12.8	11.5	-1.2	39.8	..	..	..
1897	6,627,896	13.8	11.4	-2.5	39.8	..	..	..
1898	6,703,402	12.5	11.3	-1.2	38.6	..	..	..
1899	6,778,909	12.0	11.1	-0.8	38.6	..	..	..
1900	6,854,415	13.3	11.0	-2.3	39.2	..	..	..
1901	6,930,185	13.5	10.9	-2.6	37.6	..	..	..
1902	7,005,955	13.0	10.8	-2.2	38.6	..	..	..
1903	7,081,725	11.1	10.7	-0.4	36.5	..	..	..
1904	7,157,495	12.3	10.6	-1.7	36.4	..	..	..
1905	7,233,265	6.8	10.5	3.7	34.9	..	..	..
1906	7,309,034	11.1	10.4	-0.8	35.3	..	..	..
1907	7,384,804	11.0	10.3	-0.7	35.4	..	..	..
1908	7,460,574	12.2	10.2	-2.0	36.0	..	..	..
1909	7,536,344	11.5	10.1	-1.5	36.0	..	..	..
1910	7,612,114	12.7	10.0	-2.7	34.9	..	..	..
1911	7,654,000	10.1	5.5	-4.7	34.2	..	..	..
1912	7,744,000	12.7	11.6	-1.1	35.0	..	..	..
1913	7,840,000	11.5	12.2	0.7	33.7	..	..	..
1914	7,933,000	11.9	11.7	-0.1	34.1	..	..	..

continued

APPENDIX TABLE H.4B Demographic developments, Hungarian Republic 1869–1945 (absolute figures and rates)

Crude death rate	Infant mortality rate	Stillbirth rate	Infant mortality and stillbirth rate	Crude marriage rate	Persons marrying per 10,000 unmarried persons age 15+	Persons marrying per 10,000 unmarried persons age 15–49	Crude divorce rate	Divorces per 100 marriages	Divorces per 10,000 married persons	Year
										Hungarian Republic
..	..	..	..	..	..	..	..	..	..	1869
..	..	..	..	..	..	..	..	..	..	1870
..	..	..	..	..	..	..	..	..	..	1871
..	..	..	..	..	..	..	..	..	..	1872
..	..	..	..	..	..	..	..	..	..	1873
..	..	..	..	..	..	..	..	..	..	1874
..	..	..	..	..	..	..	..	..	..	1875
34.3	..	..	..	10.1	861	..	0.1	0.6	3.0	1876
34.6	..	..	..	9.4	800	..	0.1	0.6	2.9	1877
37.7	..	..	..	9.4	797	..	0.1	0.7	3.1	1878
36.0	..	..	..	10.1	851	..	0.1	0.7	3.6	1879
38.5	..	..	..	9.0	755	..	0.1	1.0	4.4	1880
35.6	..	..	..	9.6	803	..	0.1	0.7	3.5	1881
34.4	..	..	..	10.1	852	..	0.1	0.6	3.1	1882
31.5	..	..	..	10.0	846	..	0.1	0.5	2.6	1883
31.1	..	..	..	9.9	839	..	0.1	0.7	3.2	1884
32.3	..	..	..	9.8	834	..	0.1	0.5	2.6	1885
32.6	..	..	..	9.4	802	..	0.0	0.5	2.3	1886
33.8	..	..	..	8.7	746	..	0.1	0.8	3.3	1887
32.0	..	..	..	9.3	794	..	0.1	0.8	3.8	1888
29.2	..	..	..	8.1	697	..	0.1	1.0	4.1	1889
31.5	..	..	..	8.1	696	..	0.1	0.9	3.7	1890
33.7	272.1	..	..	8.3	705	..	0.1	0.8	3.3	1891
34.1	278.5	..	..	8.8	748	..	0.1	1.0	4.2	1892
30.5	256.6	..	..	9.1	763	..	0.1	0.9	3.9	1893
28.4	..	..	..	9.1	764	..	..	..	..	1894
28.9	..	..	..	8.7	725	..	..	..	..	1895
27.0	..	..	..	8.3	680	..	..	..	..	1896
25.9	224.9	..	..	8.4	685	..	0.1	0.8	3.5	1897
26.2	..	..	..	8.6	701	..	..	..	..	1898
26.6	..	..	..	9.1	737	..	..	..	..	1899
25.9	225.1	..	..	9.0	742	903	0.2	1.7	7.8	1900
24.0	210.6	..	..	8.9	739	905	0.2	2.0	8.7	1901
25.6	218.4	..	..	8.6	711	877	0.2	2.1	8.9	1902
25.3	214.1	..	..	8.1	671	832	0.2	2.5	9.9	1903
24.1	202.3	..	..	9.1	749	934	0.2	2.7	12.3	1904
28.1	244.6	..	..	8.5	702	881	0.2	2.9	12.2	1905
24.2	210.7	..	..	8.7	722	911	0.2	2.7	11.9	1906
24.4	211.9	..	..	10.0	828	1.052	0.4	4.2	21.0	1907
23.8	203.9	..	..	9.2	762	973	0.4	4.0	18.3	1908
24.5	221.1	..	..	8.7	715	918	0.4	4.1	17.8	1909
22.2	196.1	..	..	8.6	708	915	0.4	4.4	18.9	1910
24.0	214.4	..	..	9.1	752	977	0.4	4.3	19.7	1911
22.2	190.5	..	..	8.9	736	961	0.4	4.9	21.7	1912
22.2	202.6	..	..	8.8	728	956	0.4	4.8	21.1	1913
22.3	199.6	..	..	7.3	..	..	0.4	5.0	..	1914
23.7	107.0	..	..	3.4	..	..	0.2	4.6	..	1915

continued

Hungary

APPENDIX TABLE H.4B Demographic developments, Hungarian Republic 1869–1945 (continued)

Year	Mid-year population	Natural population growth rate	Population growth rate	Net migration rate	Crude birth rate	Legitimate births per 10,000 married women aged 15–44	Illegitimate births per 10,000 unmarried women aged 15–44	Illeg. births per 100 leg. births
1915	7,981,000	-0.2	6.0	6.2	23.5	..	..	..
1916	7,969,000	-3.1	-1.5	1.6	17.0	..	..	..
1917	7,942,000	-4.1	-3.4	0.7	16.5	..	..	..
1918	7,887,000	-10.1	-7.0	3.1	16.2	..	..	..
1919	7,878,000	7.6	-1.1	-8.8	27.6	1,831	206	9.0
1920	7,950,000	10.0	9.1	-1.0	31.4	2,071	238	9.1
1921	8,029,000	10.6	9.8	-0.8	31.8	2,113	214	8.0
1922[1]	9,103,000	8.3	..	..	27.4	1,812	183	7.9
1923[1]	8,173,000	9.7	..	..	29.2	1,926	198	7.9
1924	8,232,000	6.5	7.2	0.6	26.9	1,761	187	8.1
1925	8,299,000	11.2	8.1	-3.2	28.4	1,838	213	8.8
1926	8,383,000	10.7	10.0	-0.7	27.4	1,760	215	9.2
1927	8,454,000	8.0	8.4	0.4	25.9	1,656	204	9.2
1928	8,520,000	9.2	7.7	-1.4	26.4	1,684	206	9.0
1929	8,583,000	7.3	7.3	0.0	25.1	1,590	207	9.5
1930	8,649,000	9.9	7.6	-2.2	25.4	1,599	216	9.8
1931	8,723,000	7.1	8.5	1.4	23.7	1,486	210	10.2
1932	8,785,000	5.5	7.1	1.5	23.4	1,459	216	10.5
1933	8,848,000	7.2	7.1	-0.1	21.9	1,364	205	10.6
1934	8,919,000	7.3	8.0	0.6	21.8	1,356	203	10.4
1935	8,985,000	5.8	7.3	1.5	21.1	1,317	190	9.9
1936	9,046,000	6.1	6.7	0.7	20.3	1,269	177	9.5
1937	9,107,000	6.0	6.7	0.7	20.0	1,256	172	9.2
1938	9,167,000	5.6	6.5	0.9	19.9	1,245	171	9.1
1939	9,227,000	5.9	6.5	0.6	19.4	1,210	170	9.2
1940	9,287,000	5.7	6.5	0.8	20.0	..	..	9.1
1941	9,344,000	5.7	6.1	0.4	18.9	..	..	9.1
1942	9,396,000	5.4	5.5	0.2	19.9	..	..	8.9
1943	9,442,000	5.4	4.9	-0.5	18.9	..	..	..
1944	9,497,000	3.2	5.8	2.6	20.6	..	..	9.4
1945	..	..	..	..	..	..	..	12.1

Note: [1] Territorial change.

APPENDIX TABLE H.4B Demographic developments, Hungarian Republic 1869–1945 (continued)

Crude death rate	Infant mortality rate	Stillbirth rate	Infant mortality and stillbirth rate	Crude marriage rate	Persons marrying per 10,000 unmarried persons age 15+	Persons marrying per 10,000 unmarried persons age 15–49	Crude divorce rate	Divorces per 100 marriages	Divorces per 10,000 married persons	Year
20.1	218.6	..	..	3.6	..	..	..	..	..	1916
20.6	215.4	..	..	4.4	..	..	..	..	..	1917
26.3	213.4	..	..	7.5	..	..	..	..	..	1918
20.0	159.3	25.2	184.4	20.4	1.419	1.768	..	..	..	1919
21.3	192.5	27.1	219.6	13.1	910	1.135	..	..	..	1920
21.2	192.7	25.6	218.3	11.9	822	1.028	0.8	6.5	37.8	1921
19.0	198.0	26.4	224.4	9.7	667	835	0.8	8.4	39.7	1922[1]
19.5	183.9	27.5	211.4	9.6	664	833	0.8	8.8	41.0	1923[1]
20.4	193.3	29.8	223.1	9.1	628	788	0.7	8.1	35.7	1924
17.1	167.9	28.3	196.1	9.0	616	774	0.7	7.7	33.1	1925
16.7	167.5	29.6	197.1	9.2	628	791	0.7	7.6	33.2	1926
17.8	184.8	28.5	213.3	9.1	623	786	0.7	7.4	31.7	1927
17.2	176.9	29.5	206.4	9.3	638	806	0.7	7.1	31.0	1928
17.8	179.4	29.1	208.6	9.1	623	788	0.6	6.6	28.1	1929
15.5	152.5	29.0	181.5	9.0	613	776	0.6	7.1	29.5	1930
16.6	161.7	28.9	190.6	8.8	596	758	0.5	5.7	23.1	1931
17.9	183.7	29.2	212.9	8.1	553	706	0.5	6.3	23.5	1932
14.7	136.3	29.2	165.5	8.3	564	723	0.5	6.6	25.0	1933
14.5	147.8	29.4	177.3	8.8	604	778	0.6	7.0	28.2	1934
15.2	152.1	28.6	180.6	8.4	578	748	0.6	7.4	28.6	1935
14.2	139.0	29.0	168.0	8.5	585	760	0.6	7.4	28.7	1936
14.1	133.4	28.4	161.8	8.8	605	789	0.6	7.2	28.5	1937
14.2	131.4	27.8	159.1	8.1	557	729	0.6	7.7	28.2	1938
13.5	121.3	28.6	149.9	8.7	598	786	0.6	6.5	25.1	1939
14.3	130.1	28.1	158.1	7.7	..	..	0.6	7.7	..	1940
13.2	115.6	25.3	140.9	8.5	..	..	0.7	8.7	..	1941
14.6	133.4	24.0	157.4	7.8	..	..	0.7	9.1	..	1942
13.5	112.4	23.2	135.6	8.0	..	..	..	..	..	1943
17.4	102.7	22.6	125.3	7.2	..	..	..	..	..	1944
..	169.1	23.6	192.8	..	..	..	..	2.7	..	1945

Note: [1] Territorial change.

APPENDIX TABLE H.5 Life expectancy by age 1900/1–1941/41 (in years)

Age	0	10	20	30	40	50	60	70	80
				Males					
1900–1901	36.56	48.23	40.61	33.61	26.16	19.20	12.88	7.82	4.42
1910–1911	39.07	48.52	40.79	33.77	26.27	19.19	12.84	7.78	4.26
1920–1921	41.04	49.43	41.78	34.93	27.43	20.11	13.44	7.83	3.99
1930–1931	48.70	53.25	44.77	37.09	29.13	21.48	14.50	8.70	4.40
1941	54.95	55.27	46.65	38.58	30.14	22.15	15.00	8.97	4.64
				Females					
1900–1901	38.15	46.84	39.87	33.38	26.49	19.32	12.79	7.81	4.52
1910–1911	40.48	48.40	41.29	34.60	27.34	19.96	13.07	7.82	4.40
1920–1921	43.12	49.99	42.66	35.90	28.58	21.03	13.96	8.13	4.24
1930–1931	51.80	54.31	46.09	38.64	30.70	22.72	15.38	9.24	4.92
1941	58.24	57.32	48.73	40.57	37.12	23.76	16.03	9.52	5.00

Note: Data have been calculated for the territory of the Hungarian Republic for 1900–1901 and 1910–1911.

APPENDIX TABLE H.6A Households by type 1870–1941 (absolute and per cent)

Census year	Total house-holds	Private house-holds	Family house-holds	One-person house-holds	Institu-tional house-holds	Total household members	Private household members	Family household members	One-person household members	Institu-tional house-hold members
						Household types and members				
					Absolute					
1870	3,179,133[1]	:	:	:	:	15,509,455	:	:	:	:
1880	3,450,855	:	:	:	:	15,738,468	:	:	:	:
1890	3,787,656	:	:	:	3,085	17,463,791	:	:	:	67,262
1900	4,208,341	:	:	:	2,757	19,254,559	:	:	:	194,879
1910	4,619,221	:	:	:	6,689	20,886,487	:	:	:	246,773
1920	1,828,264	:	:	:	2,699	7,986,875	:	:	:	130,845
1930	1,752,716	:	:	:	2,404	8,685,109	:	:	:	61,559
1941	:	:	:	:	:	:	:	:	:	:
					Per cent					
1870	100.00[1]	:	:	:	:	100.00	:	:	:	:
1880	100.00	:	:	:	:	100.00	:	:	:	:
1890	100.00	:	:	:	0.08	100.00	:	:	:	0.39
1900	100.00	:	:	:	0.07	100.00	:	:	:	1.01
1910	100.00	:	:	:	0.14	100.00	:	:	:	1.18
1920	100.00	:	:	:	0.15	100.00	:	:	:	1.64
1930	100.00	:	:	:	0.14	100.00	:	:	:	0.71
1941	:	:	:	:	:	:	:	:	:	:

Note: [1] *Wohnparteien.*

APPENDIX TABLE H.6D Household indicators 1870–1941

Census year	Household indicators			
	Mean total household size	Mean private household size	Mean family household size	Mean institutional household size
1870	4.88	..	..	..
1880	4.56	..	..	..
1890	4.61	..	..	21.80
1900	4.58	..	..	70.69
1910	4.52	..	..	36.89
1920	4.37	..	..	48.48
1930	4.96	..	..	25.61
1941	..	..	..	..

APPENDIX TABLE H.6E Household composition 1880–1900 (absolute and per cent)

| Census year | Civil population | | | Persons living in households | | | | | | | | |
| | | | | Family (household) heads | | | Family members | | | Others (parents, servants) | | |
	Total	Men	Women	Total	Men	Women	Total	Men	Women	Total	Men	Women
							Absolute					
1880	15,642,102	7,702,910	7,939,192	3,604,717	3,072,219	532,498	10,849,000	4,004,371	6,844,629	1,188,385	626,320	562,065
1890	17,282,136	8,506,936	8,775,200	3,926,645	3,419,022	507,623	12,243,302	4,507,157	7,736,145	1,112,189	580,757	531,432
1900	19,042,251	9,400,033	9,642,218	4,389,695	3,806,951	582,744	13,346,055	4,974,549	8,371,506	1,306,501	618,533	687,968
							Per cent					
1880	100.00	49.24	50.76	23.04	19.64	3.40	69.36	25.60	43.76	7.60	4.00	3.59
1890	100.00	49.22	50.78	22.72	19.78	2.94	70.84	26.08	44.76	6.44	3.36	3.08
1900	100.00	49.36	50.64	23.05	19.99	3.06	70.09	26.12	43.96	6.86	3.25	3.61

APPENDIX TABLE H.6F Household composition 1930 (absolute and per cent)

Census year	Total	Family heads	Spouses	Family members (parents)	Domestic servants ('gens de maison')	Family heads of subtenants ('sous-locataires')	Family members of subtenants ('sous-locataires')	Family heads of tenants of a bed ('locataires de lit')	Family members of tenants of a bed ('locataires de lit')	Others and non-permanent residents
				Absolute						
1930	6,943,942	1,672,834	1,311,961	3,688,844	88,386	18,839	15,079	5,150	1,933	140,916
				Per cent						
1930	100.00	24.09	18.89	53.12	1.27	0.27	0.22	0.07	0.03	2.03

Note: Persons present in particular housing units (*logements*).

APPENDIX TABLE H.7 Dates and nature of results on population structure,
households/families, and vital statistics

Topic	Intro-duction	Remarks
Population		
Population at census dates	1870	Earlier censuses were conducted in 1801, 1806, 1821, 1826, 1831, 1841, and 1846. Hungarian Republic: 1870–.
Population by age, sex, and marital status	1870	Hungarian Empire: 1870–1918. Hungarian Republic: 1920–
Households and families		
Households (*Wohnparteien/lakófelekre* or *Haushaltung/háztartások*)		
Total households	1870, 1880, 1890, 1900, 1906, 1910, 1920, 1930, 1941	The Hungarian statistics are similar to the Austrian statistics from 1870–1910. *Wohnparteien* were counted instead of households from 1870–1910. Households were first expressively recorded in 1880. 1870: number of *Wohnparteien*. 1880: number of *Wohnparteien* and households; household composition. 1890: number of households, institutional households; household composition. 1900: number of households, institutional households; household composition. 1906: census of Budapest: extensive household statistics. 1910: number of households, institutional households. 1920: number of households, institutional households. 1930: number of households, institutional households. 1941: no data available. *Disaggregation*: by provinces and smaller units.
Households by size	–	
Households by composition	1880, 1890, 1900, 1930	1880 and 1890: household heads, family members, others, by sex. 1900: household heads, family members, parents, servants, etc., by sex. 1930: household heads, family members, parents, boarders, and lodgers.
Households by profession of household head	–	
Families (családok)		
Families by number of children	1920, 1930	Fertility of married and widowed females for the first time in 1920. Repeated in 1930.

continued

APPENDIX TABLE H.7 Dates and nature of results on population structure, households/families, and vital statistics (continued)

Topic	Intro-duction	Remarks
Population movement		
Mid-year population	1869; 1870–1918	Hungarian Republic: 1869–; Hungarian Empire: 1870–1918.
Births		
Live births	1876; 1865–1918	Hungarian Republic: 1876–; Hungarian Empire: 1865–1918.
Stillbirths	1919	Hungarian Republic
Legitimate births	1919; 1865–1918	Hungarian Republic: 1919–; Hungarian Empire: 1865–1918.
Illegitimate births	1919; 1865–1918	Hungarian Republic: 1919–; Hungarian Empire: 1865–1918.
Deaths		
Total deaths	1876; 1865–1918	Hungarian Republic: 1876–; Hungarian Empire: 1865–1918.
Infants (under 1 year)	1891; 1891–1918	Hungarian Republic: 1891–; Hungarian Empire: 1891–1918.
Marriages		
Total marriages	1876; 1865–1918	Hungarian Republic: 1876–; Hungarian Empire: 1865–1918.
Divorces and separations		
Total divorces	1876; 1876–1918	Hungarian Republic: 1876–; Hungarian Empire: 1876–1918.
Legal separations	–	

Note: Data on vital statistics have been calculated retrospectively for the territory of the Hungarian Republic back to the nineteenth century.

10

Iceland

Iceland was first discovered and settled by Norwegian seafarers in the Middle Ages in their exploration of the North Atlantic and the North American coast. Thus, Greenland and Iceland were initially Norwegian possessions and were only transferred to Denmark in 1380, when Denmark inherited the Norwegian crown. From that time until the early twentieth century Iceland was an overseas territory of Denmark (like Greenland and the Faeroe Islands).

During the nineteenth century Iceland participated in the pan-European wave of nationalism and for the first time a movement for national self-sufficiency came into being. This popular and political movement led to home rule for Iceland in 1903. In 1918 a Danish-Icelandic Act of Union was concluded by plebiscite. This was a personal union only in the name of the Danish crown.

In 1940 Denmark was occupied by German troops, while Iceland was occupied by British and in 1941 by US forces. The British and Americans supported the Icelandic desire for home rule and in 1944 Iceland attained full independence from Denmark through a plebiscite abrogating the 1918 agreement. Iceland became the Republic of Iceland in 1944. It has not joined the European Union (for general literature on Iceland see Lacy, 1998; Hagstofa Íslands/Statistics Iceland, 1997).

REGIONAL POPULATION STRUCTURE

Iceland's population has been always very small. In 1769 the island had 46,000 inhabitants, in 1850 59,000, and in 1940 122,000. Population density was therefore very low. In 1901 it was only 0.76 inhabitants per sq. km. By 1940 it had risen to 1.18 inhabitants per sq. km. Until 1900 population settlement was still rather equally distributed over the country, with a considerable proportion of the total population living in the counties; during the twentieth century, population increase mainly benefited the capital of Reykjavik. Whereas in 1901 the capital had only 8.5% of all inhabitants, in 1940 31.4% of the total Icelandic population lived in the capital. In 1940 nearly 40% of the population lived in the capital and the Reykjanes area taken together, compared to 15% in 1901. All the other counties experienced a relative loss of population from 1901 to 1940. In Austurland the population even declined slightly from 1901 to 1940, and in most of the other counties the absolute population increase was quite low.

Thus, the regional population structure was mainly shaped by the urbanization of the capital during the first half of the twentieth century, and Iceland obtained its monocephalic population structure in this period. In 1901 the capital had 6,667 inhabitants; in 1940 it had 38,196, still a small city in European terms.

POPULATION GROWTH

Population growth in Iceland in the second half of the nineteenth century was still influenced by severe demographic crises, mainly from epidemics (Figure IS.1). Such severe crises occurred in the 1850s and again in the 1860s with downturns in the population growth rate. Until the 1870s the population growth rate was low and did not reach 10 per 1,000; only during the period from 1870 to 1910 was the growth rate higher, at around 10 per 1,000 inhabitants. Population growth became negative during World War I. The rate recovered for some years in the 1920s and during the 1930s declined below a level of 5 per 1,000. Both world wars caused negative growth rates.

From the 1850s to the 1870s the net migration rate oscillated around zero with positive and negative peaks, but from the 1880s to the 1920s the net migration rate became negative, i.e. out-migration was stronger than immigration. The 1880s in particular saw a wave of emigration culminating in the year 1888 with a net migration rate of –25.0‰. Other strong waves of emigration were in the years 1901 and 1912.

THE FIRST DEMOGRAPHIC TRANSITION

Demographic transition in Iceland started in the 1860s, when the birth rate for the first time showed a clear tendency to decline (Figure IS.2). From the 1870s until the 1930s the birth rate generally declined with only minor fluctuations. However, the 1930s saw a major decline in fertility. The nadir was reached in 1940, after which the birth rate started to rise again, constituting the second demographic transition. Iceland remained neutral during both world wars; therefore their impact on demographic developments was not as strong as in most other European countries, though both world wars nevertheless had an indirect impact.

The death rate during the second half of the nineteenth century was fairly high and still influenced by mortality crises due to epidemics. Such peaks in the mortality rate are visible mainly for the 1860s to 1870s, but also in the 1880s. The mortality rate on average increased slightly from the 1850s to the 1870s. Towards the end of the nineteenth century major gains were made in reducing mortality, and the small natural population surplus in the second half of the nineteenth century increased. During the first half of the twentieth century the birth and death rates diverged due to the stronger decrease in the mortality rate. The success in reducing the mortality rate stemmed mainly from the reduction in infant mortality, which was already low in 1900 (see section below).

Both the birth rate and the death rate have been below the European average. The mortality rate was already well below the average during the 1850s and 1860s, mainly due to the low infant mortality rate already at that time. While the mortality rate remained below the European average until the late 1930s, the birth rate exceeded the European birth rate starting in about 1910 and remained higher during the whole inter-war period. With the exception of the late 1930s Iceland had a rather high natural population surplus in the inter-war period, higher than in Europe taken together.

Figure IS.1 Population growth and net migration 1850-1945

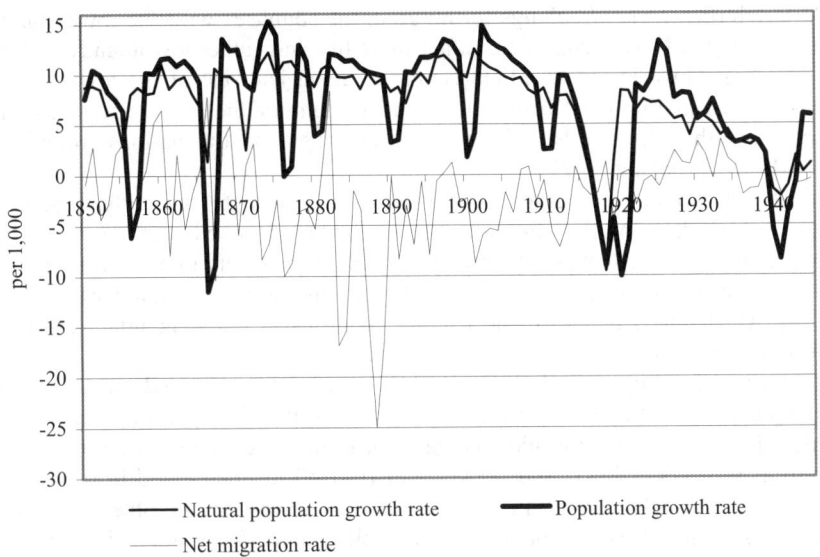

Figure IS.2 First demographic transition 1850-1945

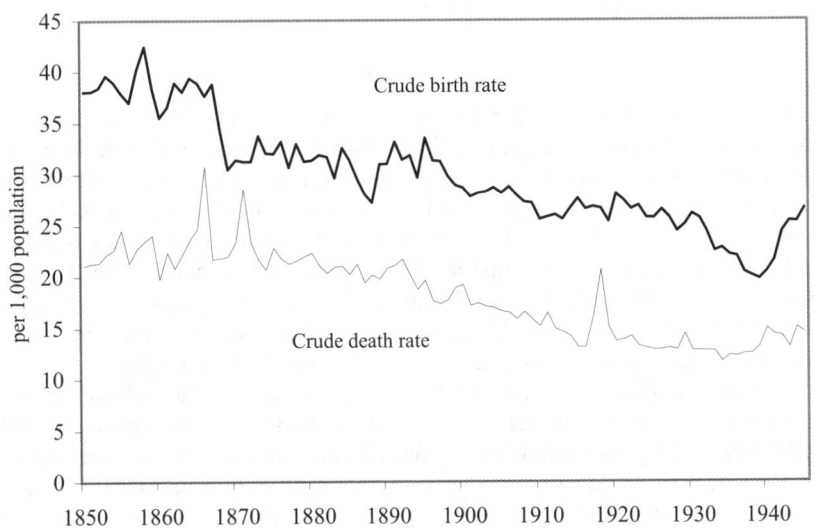

MORTALITY AND LIFE EXPECTANCY

The infant mortality rate is defined as deaths of children aged under one year per 1,000 live births. *Iceland* belongs to the group of countries with the lowest infant mortality, i.e. the Nordic countries. Infant mortality was rather low already in 1900 (Figure IS.3). Thus, in the twentieth century Iceland had one of the lowest infant mortality rates in Europe. During the twentieth century the decline was fast and continuous, although there have been many upswings and fluctuations around this trend (Masuy-Stroobant, 1997).

Although Icelandic demographic statistics extend back to the early eighteenth century (1703), data on infant mortality are available only since 1838. These figures show that in the 1830s Iceland had a very high infant mortality rate of over 300. But during the second half of the nineteenth century mortality in Iceland was greatly reduced, which made it one of the leading countries in reducing infant mortality (Hagstofa Íslands/Statistics Iceland (1997: 50ff.)).

Life expectancy (Figure IS.4) from 1841/50 to 1941/50 increased most for new-born children, from 30 years to over 60 years during this time period for males and females. There were also considerable gains in further life expectancy for 15-year-olds: from 39 years in 1841/50 to 55 years in 1941/50 for males, and from 43 years to 59 years for females. Life expectancy gains were lowest for the oldest age group of 65 years: during these one hundred years males gained 5.1 years and women 5.9 years. Sex differences remained rather stable: life expectancy of women was already higher in the mid-nineteenth century for all ages and remained so in the mid-twentieth century. But there was a temporary divergence in life expectancy between the sexes until the end of the nineteenth century favouring women, followed by a subsequent tendency towards convergence.

FERTILITY AND LEGITIMACY

The development of marital fertility more or less reflects the decline in overall fertility during the period (Figure IS.5). Marital fertility showed a declining trend over the whole time period from 1850 to 1940 from a level of four legitimate births per married woman on average to a level of less than two legitimate births per married woman in the 1940s. Major declines in the marital fertility rate occurred in the 1870s and 1880s while marital fertility recovered during the 1890s and remained—although declining—high during the inter-war period. The decline in marital fertility accelerated in the 1930s and reached its lowest level in 1940 and 1941. During the following war years marital fertility recovered again.

Illegitimate fertility increased slightly during the second half of the nineteenth century, but at the end of the century the illegitimate birth rate also began to decline. It fell faster than legitimate fertility and had already reached low levels before World War I. There was obviously a tendency to give birth within marriage. But already during the 1920s the declining trend in illegitimate fertility was reversed, and since the 1930s illegitimate fertility has shown a very strong increase. In Iceland therefore, the process of the deinstitutionalization of marriage started already in the 1930s, and Iceland now has the highest out-of-wedlock birth rate of all European countries.

In comparative terms, illegitimate fertility in Iceland was far above the European average already in the nineteenth century and was probably the highest of all

Figure IS.3 Infant mortality 1850-1945

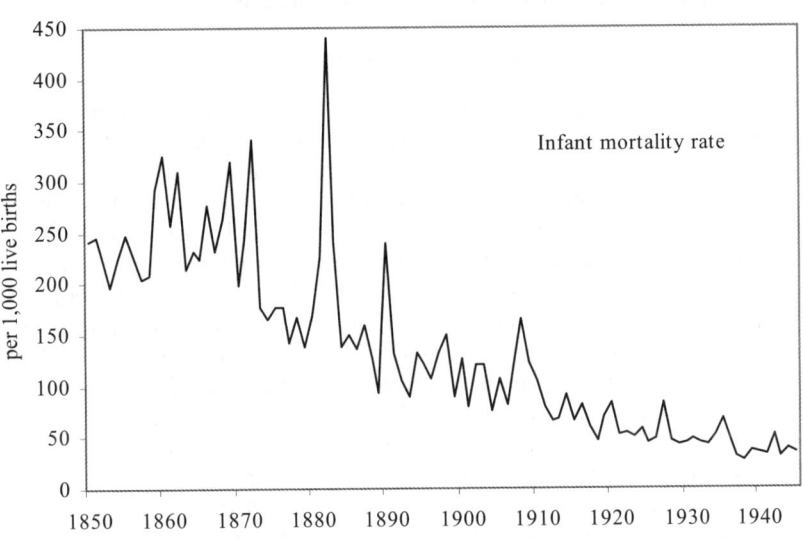

Figure IS.4 Life expectancy 1841/50-1941/50

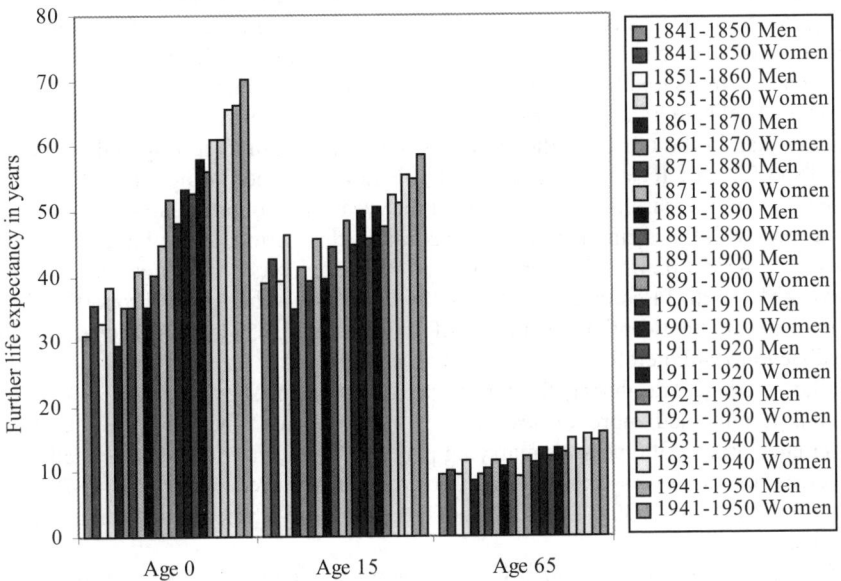

European regions at that time. In the twentieth century, the early growth in illegitimate fertility is also unique in a European context. On the European level, the illegitimate fertility rate only started to rise again during the late 1970s.

MARRIAGE AND DIVORCE

Like all the Nordic countries, Iceland belongs to the European region with the West European marriage pattern: late age at marriage and a high celibacy rate. As in the other Nordic countries, during the nineteenth century *age at marriage* was one of the highest in Western Europe. The proportion of married women aged 20–24 during the second half of the nineteenth century remained low and did not exceed 20% until 1920. From the 1850s to the 1890s there was even a decline in the proportion of women married at age 20–24. Starting from the 1890s there was a tendency towards lower age at marriage. In the inter-war period age at marriage was lowest in 1930 with over 32% of women aged 20–24 having been married. Up to 1940 age at marriage increased again, and the proportion married at age 20–24 declined to 24%.

The age of men at marriage was even higher during the whole time period. The proportion of men married at age 20–24 remained below 10% from 1850–1940. The tendencies and cyclical patterns are the same as for Icelandic women: a rise in age at marriage since the 1850s, a slight increase since the 1890s with the lowest age at marriage in 1920. In contrast to women, whose age at marriage was lowest in 1930, age at marriage for men was highest in 1930. Whether the world economic crisis had an influence remains an open question. Summarizing, the level and development of age at marriage was similar to the Scandinavian countries, particularly Sweden.

Marriage intensity can be measured by the *marriage rate* and the *celibacy rate* (Figure IS.6). 'Intensity' means people's access to marriage, and at the same time the necessity to remarry after widowhood ('remarriage need', Michael Mitterauer). Celibacy is measured by the proportion of women never married at age 45–54. This so-called celibacy rate was very high during the whole time period from 1850–1945, higher than in the other Nordic countries, but not as high as in England and Wales. In 1850 22% of Icelandic women had still never married at age 45–54. Celibacy continued to increase until the 1890s: in that year the proportion attained 30%. This is in line with the rising age at marriage during this period, as we have seen above. After the 1890s the trend reversed towards more universal marriage, but this trend was fairly slight in comparative terms. In 1940 24%—the lowest proportion in the first half of the twentieth century—of women aged 45–45 were never married; celibacy in 1940 therefore was higher than in 1850.

The marriage rate during the whole period does not show a rising or declining trend. It remained more or less stable, but far below the European level, and oscillated around 300 persons marrying per 10,000 non-married persons aged 15 and over. A major downswing in the marriage rate occurred during the 1870s, with another in the late 1930s. The 1940s nevertheless were a time of increasing marriage propensity.

Concerning *marital stability*, Iceland shows a picture very similar to Sweden (Figure IS.6). The divorce rate moved steadily and smoothly upwards beginning in 1904, the year of the first divorce figures, to the 1940s. In 1904 the crude divorce rate (divorces per 1,000 inhabitants) was 0.1. It increased to an average of 0.5 in the five-year period 1941–45. Thus, like most Nordic countries, and especially Sweden and Denmark, Iceland had a rather high divorce propensity already in the first half of

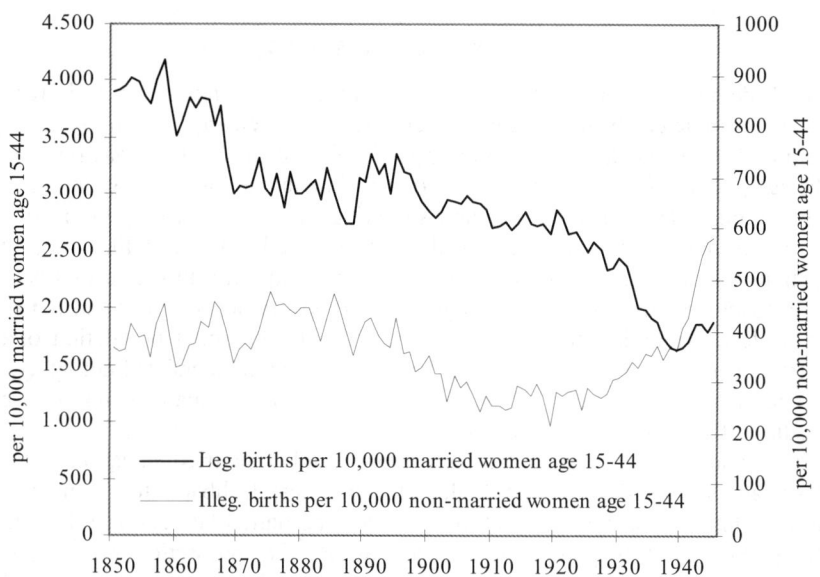

Figure IS.5 Fertility and legitimacy 1850-1945

Leg. births per 10,000 married women age 15-44

Illeg. births per 10,000 non-married women age 15-44

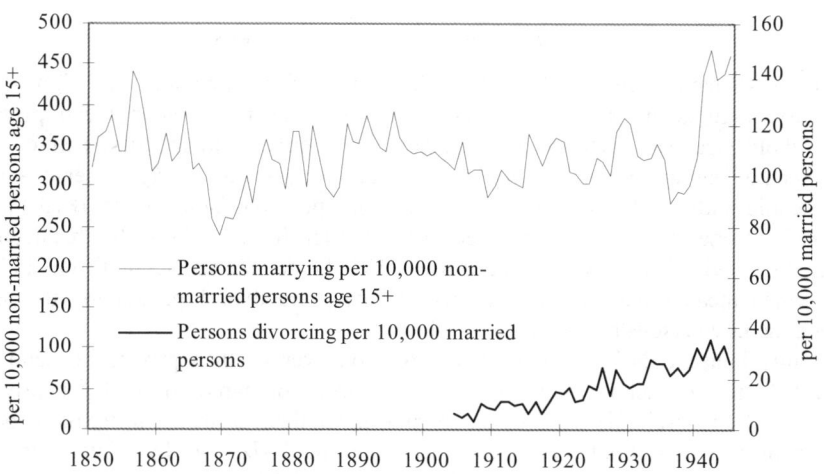

Figure IS.6 Marriages and divorces 1850-1945

Persons marrying per 10,000 non-married persons age 15+

Persons divorcing per 10,000 married persons

the twentieth century. Divorces in Iceland were much more frequent than on the European average.

Iceland's demographic development remained more or less undistorted by European wars in the nineteenth and twentieth centuries, as is clearly shown by the age structure of the Icelandic population (Appendix Figure IS.8). There was no change in the age pyramid from 1910 to 1920 with a decline in the lowest age groups due to fertility decline. Declining fertility and shrinking age groups at the bottom of the pyramid are not visible until between the censuses of 1930 and 1940, though this reduction was fairly small compared to many other countries. In the second half of the nineteenth century the Icelandic age pyramid was rather irregular and deviated from a clear pyramidal shape. This is partly due to the small population of the country at that time, which means that the 'law of large numbers' did not apply; on the other hand, fluctuations in fertility, economic, and climatic conditions had immediate effects on the age structure.

Age at marriage was fairly late in Iceland, and unmarried cohabitation was widespread, statistically causing high celibacy rates. Celibacy for women was constantly higher than for men, but in the long trend until 1940, celibacy fell and a higher proportion of the population entered marriage. The proportion of widowed or divorced (or separated) women already in the nineteenth century was much higher than that of men, caused by higher male mortality and women's lower incidence of remarriage after divorce. The social acceptance of unmarried cohabitation in Iceland made marriage less attractive than in other countries.

FAMILY AND HOUSEHOLD STRUCTURES

Households have been very large in Iceland most of the time since the eighteenth century. Figures are available already for 1703 and 1760, when mean private household size was 6.15 and 6.33 persons, respectively. In the first half of the nineteenth century mean household size had increased to nearly 7 persons per household and in 1870 it peaked at 7.5 persons per household. Since 1870 mean household size has been declining because of the fertility transition. But this decline was slow, and still in 1930 the figure was 5.19. The decline accelerated from 1930–40, when mean private household size fell by more than 1 person in 10 years, reaching 4.09 persons per household in 1940.

Family households have been even larger on average than private households. Mean family household size in 1910 was 5.97 compared to 5.78 for private households. Households were larger in rural areas than in towns, in terms of both mean private household size and family household size. In 1870 mean family household size in rural areas was 7.68 and in towns 5.95, a mean difference of 1.73 persons.

In accordance with the very high mean household size in Iceland from 1850 to 1930, the proportion of one-person households was low. It was higher in 1910, at 4.4% of all private households, than in 1930 at 3%. It climbed rapidly to 18% in 1940. The proportion of the population living alone was therefore also very low, at less than 1% of the population between 1910 and 1930. In 1940 it had risen to 4.5%.

Obviously the 1930s were a decade of demographic crises. We have already seen the severe birth decline during this decade (see section on The First Demographic Transition), and the sudden decline in household size—or the increase in single persons—seems mainly to be an effect of this sudden fertility decline.

Unfortunately there are no data on household composition in Icelandic statistics. It would be very interesting to have information on the composition of these—in European comparison—very large Icelandic households.

THE NATIONAL SYSTEM OF DEMOGRAPHIC STATISTICS

Population structure

Iceland has a very long tradition of population statistics and census-taking. The first census was already held in 1703. This census was analysed according to modern principles in recent decades. There are other early censuses in 1769, 1801, and 1832. From 1840 onwards censuses were taken regularly every five years and later every ten years (cf. Kuhnle, 1989 and Thorsteinsson, 1948).

Population by age, sex, and marital status is available since 1850, first in five-year age groups, but since 1901 for each year.

Vital statistics

The record of vital statistics as well as census-taking dates back very early in history. Most vital statistics time series are covered already since the first half of the eighteenth century.

Households and families

Data on *households* (*heimili*) were already collected in the first census of 1703. This census was elaborated later using modern techniques and research questions. The mere number of households is also available from the censuses of the early nineteenth century. It was not until 1860 that household statistics were extended concerning households by size. This distinction was upheld until the time of World War II.

In 1910 the distinction between private households, family households, and institutional households was introduced.

In 1930 an extension was made by introducing the household composition, which was repeated in 1940. The following household members were distinguished: household heads, dependent children and parents, servants, unrelated workers, children under age 14, adults, and lodgers (*locataires*).

In 1940 households were additionally distinguished by the profession of the household head (household heads by economic sector).

The *definition of a household* (*heimili*) is given by Hagstofa Íslands/Statistics Iceland (1997: 47):

In the censuses of 1910–81 a household is defined as a family, including servants and others boarding in that household. Lodgers who do not board with the family or the household are counted as separate households. These types of households are called one-person or lodger households. Institutions supplying accommodation and boarding for people for long periods of time, such as boarding schools, hospitals, senior citizens' residential care homes, etc., are also classified as households and called institutional households. The third group, which includes households of two and more members, is referred to as a family household. One-person and lodger households and family households are classified together as private households—as opposed to the institutional ones.

Older censuses are based on the same concept as the more recent ones, i.e. that a household is made up of persons sharing their meals, although they do not distinguish between household types. This probably leads to fewer one-person households than would be the case according to the methodology of more recent censuses.

Family-orientated fertility statistics were not gathered before World War II. The same is true for family statistics such as the structure and composition of the biological family. Such data are available after World War II period, first from the censuses, but later, after census-taking had been discontinued following the last census of 1960, from the population registers (cf. Hagstofa Íslands/Statistics Iceland, 1997: 141).

Remarks (also see introductory Table 6.1)

In Iceland the last population census was held in 1960 and was subsequently replaced by register statistics. Thus, the data of the variables v16–v21 have been calculated taking the age*sex*marital status figures for the years 1960, 1974, and 1991 and linearly interpolated between these dates. In Iceland the population censuses of 1840, 1850, 1855, 1860, and 1890 have been used for interpolation of v16–v21.

BOUNDARY CHANGES

As an island with natural borders Iceland has experienced no territorial changes since the Middle Ages. For regional organization see the documentation by Caramani, Flora, Kraus, and Quick (1998) under the heading 'Denmark'.

APPENDIX TABLES AND FIGURES

APPENDIX TABLE IS.1 Population structure at census dates 1840–1940

Census number	Census date	Census population			Marital status				Age group		
		Total	Male	Female	Single	Married	Widowed	Divorced	0–14	15–64	65+
					Absolute						
1	1840	57,094	27,106	29,988	36,596	16,604	3,894	..	20,230	33,056	3,808
2	1 II 1850	59,157	28,234	30,923	38,339	17,287	3,305	226	13,005	41,985	4,167
3	1 X 1855	64,603	30,869	33,734	42,147	18,592	3,580	284	21,644	39,992	2,967
4	1 X 1860	66,987	31,867	35,120	43,558	19,124	4,037	268	22,519	40,887	3,581
5	1 XI 1890	70,927	33,689	37,238	46,903	18,726	4,936	362	22,659	44,519	3,749
6	1 XI 1901	78,470	37,583	40,887	51,421	21,627	5,080	342	27,212	45,936	5,322
7	1 XII 1910	85,183	41,105	44,078	55,753	23,780	5,216	289	28,739	50,906	5,538
8	1 XII 1920	94,690	46,172	48,518	61,160	27,470	5,579	481	31,321	56,803	6,566
9	2 XII 1930	108,861	53,542	55,319	69,568	32,204	6,284	701	35,359	65,206	8,296
10	2 XII 1940	121,474	60,325	61,149	75,797	37,444	6,938	1,279	36,253	75,750	9,471
					Per cent						
1	1840	100.00	47.48	52.52	64.10	29.08	6.82	..	35.43	57.90	6.67
2	1 II 1850	100.00	47.73	52.27	64.81	29.22	5.59	0.38	21.98	70.97	7.04
3	1 X 1855	100.00	47.78	52.22	65.24	28.78	5.54	0.44	33.50	61.90	4.59
4	1 X 1860	100.00	47.57	52.43	65.02	28.55	6.03	0.40	33.62	61.04	5.35
5	1 XI 1890	100.00	47.50	52.50	66.13	26.40	6.96	0.51	31.95	62.77	5.29
6	1 XI 1901	100.00	47.89	52.11	65.53	27.56	6.47	0.44	34.68	58.54	6.78
7	1 XII 1910	100.00	48.25	51.75	65.45	27.92	6.12	0.34	33.74	59.76	6.50
8	1 XII 1920	100.00	48.76	51.24	64.59	29.01	5.89	0.51	33.08	59.99	6.93
9	2 XII 1930	100.00	49.18	50.82	63.91	29.58	5.77	0.64	32.48	59.90	7.62
10	2 XII 1940	100.00	49.66	50.34	62.40	30.82	5.71	1.05	29.84	62.36	7.80

APPENDIX TABLE IS.2 Census population by region 1901–1940 (per cent)

Constituency/*Syslum* (County)	1901	1910	1920	1930	1940
Reykjavik/the capital	**8.50**	**13.62**	**18.67**	**26.00**	**31.37**
Reykjanes/Reykjanes area	**6.77**	**7.04**	**7.02**	**8.16**	**7.61**
Gullbringusysla	..	3.59	3.14	3.05	3.27
Kjosarsysla	..	1.63	1.38	1.81	1.32
Vesturland/West	**12.45**	**12.05**	**10.67**	**8.80**	**8.16**
Borgarfjardarsysla	3.21	3.01	2.62	2.46	2.68
Myrasysla	2.15	2.06	1.99	1.62	1.49
Snaefellsnessysla	4.47	4.62	4.11	3.25	2.84
Dalasysla	2.63	2.37	1.96	1.47	1.16
Vestfirdir/Western Peninsula	**15.73**	**15.71**	**14.15**	**12.01**	**10.64**
Austur-Bardastrandarsysla	1.53	1.34	1.11	0.85	0.72
Vestur-Bardastrandarsysla	2.77	2.63	2.39	2.02	1.74
Vestur-Isafjardarsysla	2.99	2.86	2.73	2.14	1.85
Nordur-Isafjardarsysla	4.72	4.65	3.96	2.99	2.29
Strandasysla	2.31	2.06	1.88	1.68	1.71
Nordurland vestra/Northland west	**10.55**	**9.81**	**10.34**	**9.11**	**8.62**
Vestur-Hunavatnssysla	..	1.95	1.90	1.51	1.25
Austur-Hunavatnssysla	..	2.77	2.61	2.05	1.77
Skagafjardarsysla	5.58	5.09	4.60	3.69	3.24
Siglufjördur	..	..	1.22	1.86	2.37
Nordurland eystra/Northland east	**15.13**	**14.81**	**13.85**	**13.82**	**13.89**
Olafsfjördur	..	..	..	..	..
Eyjafjardarsysla	6.83	6.31	5.28	4.75	4.40
Sudur-pingeyjarsysla	4.81	4.44	4.06	3.60	3.38
Nordur-pingeyjarsysla	1.78	1.61	1.78	1.62	1.54
Austurland/East	**13.21**	**11.40**	**10.79**	**9.61**	**8.31**
Nordur-Mulasysla	4.57	3.54	3.13	2.54	2.19
Sudur-Mulasysla	6.09	5.45	5.51	4.15	3.53
Austur-Skaftafellssysla	1.48	1.32	1.22	1.04	0.94
Sudurland/South	**16.96**	**15.55**	**14.53**	**12.50**	**11.17**
Vestur-Skaftafellssysla	2.48	2.15	1.92	1.58	1.30
Rangarvallasysla	5.56	4.72	4.01	3.22	2.70
Vestmannaeyjar	0.77	1.55	2.56	3.12	2.95
Arnessysla	8.15	7.13	6.03	4.58	4.22
TOTAL	**100.00**	**100.00**	**100.00**	**100.00**	**100.00**

APPENDIX TABLE IS.3 Population density by region 1901–1940 (inhabitants per sq. km.)

Constituency/*Syslum* (County)	1901	1910	1920	1930	1940
Reykjavik/the capital	67	116	177	283	382
Reykjanes/Reykjanes area	3	3	4	5	5
Gullbringusysla	..	3	3	3	4
Kjosarsysla	..	2	2	3	2
Vesturland/West	1	1	1	1	1
Borgarfjardarsysla	1	1	1	1	2
Myrasysla	1	1	1	1	1
Snaefellsnessysla	2	2	2	2	2
Dalasysla	1	1	1	1	1
Vestfirdir/Western Peninsula	1	1	1	1	1
Austur-Bardastrandarsysla	1	1	1	1	1
Vestur-Bardastrandarsysla	1	1	1	1	1
Vestur-Isafjardarsysla	2	2	2	2	2
Nordur-Isafjardarsysla	1	1	1	1	1
Strandasysla	1	1	1	1	1
Nordurland vestra/Northland west	1	1	1	1	1
Vestur-Hunavatnssysla	..	1	1	1	1
Austur-Hunavatnssysla	..	0	1	0	0
Skagafjardarsysla	1	1	1	1	1
Siglufjördur	..	..	8	13	19
Nordurland eystra/Northland east	1	1	1	1	1
Olafsfjördur	..	..	..	..	..
Eyjafjardarsysla	1	1	1	1	1
Sudur-pingeyjarsysla	0	0	0	0	0
Nordur-pingeyjarsysla	0	0	0	0	0
Austurland/East	0	0	0	0	0
Nordur-Mulasysla	0	0	0	0	0
Sudur-Mulasysla	1	1	1	1	1
Austur-Skaftafellssysla	0	0	0	0	0
Sudurland/South	1	1	1	1	1
Vestur-Skaftafellssysla	0	0	0	0	0
Rangarvallasysla	1	0	0	0	0
Vestmannaeyjar	61	132	243	339	359
Arnessysla	1	1	1	1	1
TOTAL	1	1	1	1	1

APPENDIX TABLE IS.4 Demographic developments 1850–1945 (absolute figures and rates)

Year	Mid-year population	Natural population growth rate	Population growth rate	Net migration rate	Crude birth rate	Legitimate births per 10,000 married women age 15–44	Illegitimate births per 10,000 unmarried women age 15–44	Illeg. births per 100 leg. births
1850	60,001	14.0	13.1	-0.9	38.1	3,902	369	17.6
1851	60,645	7.8	10.6	2.9	38.1	3,923	361	16.8
1852	61,375	16.3	11.9	-4.4	38.4	3,962	364	16.6
1853	62,542	21.5	18.7	-2.8	39.6	4,024	413	18.3
1854	63,728	16.4	18.6	2.2	38.9	3,992	387	17.1
1855	64,545	9.4	12.7	3.2	37.9	3,867	389	17.6
1856	65,315	15.2	11.8	-3.4	37.0	3,798	347	15.9
1857	66,308	16.5	15.0	-1.5	40.2	4,015	416	17.9
1858	67,263	13.6	14.2	0.6	42.5	4,177	453	18.6
1859	67,726	1.6	6.8	5.3	38.4	3,790	382	17.2
1860	67,297	-12.9	-6.4	6.5	35.5	3,517	327	15.8
1861	66,901	2.0	-5.9	-7.9	36.5	3,638	332	15.6
1862	66,878	-2.4	-0.3	2.1	38.9	3,857	371	16.5
1863	67,054	7.9	2.6	-5.3	38.0	3,760	375	17.2
1864	67,690	11.2	9.4	-1.8	39.4	3,853	420	18.9
1865	68,388	9.6	10.2	0.6	38.9	3,825	408	18.6
1866	68,490	-6.3	1.5	7.8	37.6	3,604	458	22.3
1867	68,750	14.2	3.8	-10.4	38.8	3,779	443	20.7
1868	69,466	6.9	10.3	3.4	34.2	3,314	403	21.6
1869	69,582	-3.3	1.7	4.9	30.5	3,009	335	19.9
1870	69,747	8.3	2.4	-5.9	31.4	3,079	363	21.2
1871	70,210	5.5	6.6	1.1	31.3	3,052	373	22.1
1872	70,227	-2.9	0.2	3.1	31.3	3,081	363	21.4
1873	70,171	7.6	-0.8	-8.4	33.8	3,324	399	21.9
1874	70,436	10.4	3.8	-6.7	32.1	3,055	441	26.5
1875	70,862	8.4	6.0	-2.4	32.0	2,989	475	29.3
1876	70,964	11.4	1.4	-10.0	33.2	3,189	450	26.1
1877	71,177	11.6	3.0	-8.7	30.7	2,883	455	29.4
1878	71,728	11.2	7.7	-3.6	33.0	3,199	442	25.9
1879	71,941	6.2	3.0	-3.3	31.3	3,013	434	27.1
1880	72,314	10.5	5.2	-5.3	31.4	3,011	447	28.1
1881	72,869	6.8	7.6	0.9	31.9	3,085	446	27.5
1882	72,517	-13.2	-4.9	8.4	31.7	3,128	416	25.4
1883	71,292	-0.3	-17.2	-16.9	29.6	2,948	380	24.8
1884	71,062	12.2	-3.2	-15.5	32.6	3,243	423	25.3
1885	71,862	12.7	11.1	-1.5	31.3	3,006	471	30.5
1886	72,346	10.2	6.7	-3.5	29.5	2,844	441	30.3
1887	71,587	4.3	-10.6	-14.9	28.0	2,743	402	28.8
1888	70,436	8.7	-16.3	-25.0	27.2	2,743	353	25.5
1889	70,364	15.5	-1.0	-16.5	31.0	3,154	391	24.6
1890	70,594	3.3	3.3	-0.1	31.0	3,111	418	26.8
1891	71,093	15.4	7.0	-8.3	33.2	3,361	426	24.8
1892	72,030	16.0	13.0	-3.0	31.4	3,189	392	23.5
1893	72,705	16.2	9.3	-6.9	31.8	3,262	375	21.6
1894	73,079	5.7	5.1	-0.6	29.7	3,000	367	22.6
1895	73,869	18.6	10.7	-7.9	33.5	3,357	425	22.9
1896	75,094	16.9	16.3	-0.6	31.3	3,202	354	19.6
1897	76,149	13.6	13.9	0.3	31.3	3,177	358	19.5

continued

APPENDIX TABLE IS.4 Demographic developments 1850–1945 (absolute figures and rates)

Crude death rate	Infant mortality rate	Stillbirth rate	Infant mortality and stillbirth rate	Crude marriage rate	Persons marrying per 10,000 unmarried persons age 15+	Persons marrying per 10,000 unmarried persons age 15–49	Crude divorce rate	Divorces per 100 marriages	Divorces per 10,000 married persons	Year
24.0	242.1	29.3	271.5	6.6	322	404	..	..	..	1850
30.3	244.6	28.6	273.2	7.3	360	451	..	..	..	1851
22.2	218.3	32.2	250.5	7.3	366	459	..	..	..	1852
18.1	197.3	27.0	224.4	7.5	387	485	..	..	..	1853
22.5	223.2	30.2	253.4	6.6	342	429	..	..	..	1854
28.4	247.0	22.1	269.1	6.5	343	431	..	..	..	1855
21.8	225.5	24.8	250.3	8.3	441	555	..	..	..	1856
23.7	204.6	31.5	236.1	8.0	424	534	..	..	..	1857
28.8	208.3	28.0	236.3	7.2	383	483	..	..	..	1858
36.8	291.9	30.8	322.7	6.0	317	401	..	..	..	1859
48.4	325.9	29.3	355.2	6.2	328	415	..	..	..	1860
34.5	256.9	32.7	289.6	6.9	366	463	..	..	..	1861
41.3	309.3	34.6	343.8	6.3	330	418	..	..	..	1862
30.1	215.2	38.0	253.2	6.5	343	435	..	..	..	1863
28.2	231.3	34.9	266.2	7.5	391	496	..	..	..	1864
29.3	224.5	36.9	261.4	6.2	320	407	..	..	..	1865
44.0	275.8	32.6	308.4	6.3	326	415	..	..	..	1866
24.7	232.0	28.1	260.1	6.0	310	394	..	..	..	1867
27.3	263.4	32.0	295.4	5.0	259	329	..	..	..	1868
33.7	318.7	26.4	345.1	4.7	239	305	..	..	..	1869
23.1	198.1	38.8	236.9	5.1	261	332	..	..	..	1870
25.8	243.3	36.9	280.2	5.0	258	328	..	..	..	1871
34.2	340.6	31.4	372.0	5.4	277	352	..	..	..	1872
26.2	176.4	28.7	205.1	6.1	312	398	..	..	..	1873
21.6	165.6	38.5	204.1	5.5	278	354	..	..	..	1874
23.6	177.7	34.4	212.1	6.4	324	414	..	..	..	1875
21.7	177.5	31.8	209.3	7.1	358	457	..	..	..	1876
19.0	142.9	36.2	179.1	6.6	333	426	..	..	..	1877
21.7	168.2	30.0	198.2	6.5	328	419	..	..	..	1878
25.0	137.4	35.1	172.5	5.9	294	377	..	..	..	1879
20.9	169.8	36.2	205.9	7.3	366	468	..	..	..	1880
25.1	226.3	48.6	275.0	7.4	368	471	..	..	..	1881
44.9	439.3	40.9	480.2	6.0	297	381	..	..	..	1882
29.9	241.0	32.7	273.7	7.6	374	480	..	..	..	1883
20.4	139.1	28.9	168.0	6.7	329	422	..	..	..	1884
18.7	149.2	36.0	185.2	6.1	299	383	..	..	..	1885
19.4	137.1	36.0	173.1	5.8	286	367	..	..	..	1886
23.8	158.9	35.9	194.7	6.1	298	382	..	..	..	1887
18.6	126.8	40.2	166.9	7.8	378	486	..	..	..	1888
15.5	93.6	39.0	132.6	7.3	355	457	..	..	..	1889
27.7	238.9	36.1	275.0	7.3	352	453	..	..	..	1890
17.8	132.7	33.5	166.2	7.9	388	500	..	..	..	1891
15.4	106.1	40.2	146.3	7.4	364	470	..	..	..	1892
15.6	89.5	39.3	128.8	6.9	347	448	..	..	..	1893
24.0	131.9	38.3	170.2	6.8	343	445	..	..	..	1894
14.9	123.5	33.5	157.0	7.7	391	507	..	..	..	1895
14.4	108.0	30.2	138.2	7.0	359	467	..	..	..	1896
17.7	132.8	32.4	165.1	6.7	346	450	..	..	..	1897

continued

APPENDIX TABLE IS.4　Demographic developments 1850–1945 (continued)

Year	Mid-year population	Natural population growth rate	Population growth rate	Net migration rate	Crude birth rate	Legitimate births per 10,000 married women age 15–44	Illegitimate births per 10,000 unmarried women age 15–44	Illeg. births per 100 leg. births
1898	76,898	8.5	9.7	1.2	29.8	3,048	322	18.0
1899	77,572	11.4	8.7	-2.7	28.9	2,927	328	18.7
1900	78,085	8.9	6.6	-2.3	28.6	2,846	351	20.3
1901	78,422	13.1	4.3	-8.8	27.8	2,788	318	18.4
1902	78,911	12.1	6.2	-5.9	28.1	2,840	317	18.1
1903	79,407	11.6	6.2	-5.3	28.3	2,957	260	14.3
1904	80,014	13.1	7.6	-5.5	28.7	2,927	314	17.5
1905	80,711	10.4	8.6	-1.7	28.1	2,915	289	16.3
1906	81,556	14.1	10.4	-3.8	28.8	2,982	301	16.7
1907	82,506	11.0	11.5	0.5	27.9	2,930	277	15.7
1908	83,251	8.1	8.9	0.8	27.3	2,920	241	13.7
1909	84,052	12.1	9.5	-2.6	27.2	2,862	272	15.9
1910	84,875	10.2	9.7	-0.5	25.6	2,712	252	15.6
1911	85,441	12.3	6.6	-5.7	25.8	2,727	255	15.6
1912	85,889	12.4	5.2	-7.2	26.0	2,753	246	14.8
1913	86,627	13.3	8.5	-4.8	25.6	2,683	252	15.4
1914	87,607	10.4	11.2	0.8	26.7	2,740	293	17.5
1915	88,568	12.1	10.9	-1.2	27.6	2,855	286	16.3
1916	89,439	11.8	9.7	-2.1	26.6	2,740	274	16.2
1917	90,594	14.5	12.7	-1.8	26.8	2,721	296	17.5
1918	91,633	10.1	11.3	1.3	26.6	2,734	272	15.9
1919	92,376	12.7	8.0	-4.7	25.4	2,660	217	12.9
1920	93,646	13.5	13.6	0.0	28.1	2,871	280	15.4
1921	94,808	11.8	12.3	0.4	27.4	2,788	274	15.3
1922	95,783	13.2	10.2	-3.0	26.6	2,658	282	16.4
1923	97,045	13.7	13.0	-0.6	26.9	2,672	286	16.5
1924	98,094	10.8	10.7	-0.1	25.7	2,582	245	14.5
1925	99,300	13.3	12.1	-1.2	25.7	2,502	288	17.4
1926	100,924	15.4	16.1	0.7	26.5	2,591	279	16.1
1927	102,529	13.3	15.7	2.4	25.8	2,508	269	16.0
1928	104,070	13.6	14.8	1.2	24.4	2,331	278	17.6
1929	105,586	13.3	14.4	1.0	25.0	2,348	305	19.0
1930	107,495	14.5	17.8	3.2	26.1	2,449	309	18.4
1931	109,237	14.0	15.9	2.0	25.7	2,375	322	19.7
1932	110,700	13.6	13.2	-0.4	24.4	2,198	340	22.4
1933	112,461	12.2	15.7	3.5	22.5	2,006	328	23.7
1934	114,055	12.4	14.0	1.6	22.8	1,994	354	25.6
1935	115,307	10.0	10.9	0.9	22.1	1,923	350	26.3
1936	116,375	11.2	9.2	-2.0	22.0	1,874	371	28.6
1937	117,286	9.2	7.8	-1.4	20.4	1,741	344	28.5
1938	118,290	9.9	8.5	-1.4	20.1	1,658	371	32.2
1939	119,576	10.1	10.8	0.7	19.8	1,641	358	31.4
1940	120,922	10.6	11.1	0.5	20.5	1,649	407	35.4
1941	121,982	10.5	8.7	-1.8	21.6	1,699	426	33.6
1942	123,191	13.9	9.8	-4.1	24.4	1,856	499	33.9
1943	124,982	15.2	14.3	-0.9	25.4	1,862	548	34.8
1944	126,879	15.7	15.0	-0.8	25.3	1,794	575	35.7
1945	129,074	17.5	17.0	-0.5	26.6	1,878	584	32.7

APPENDIX TABLE IS.4 Demographic developments 1850–1945 (continued)

Crude death rate	Infant mortality rate	Stillbirth rate	Infant mortality and stillbirth rate	Crude marriage rate	Persons marrying per 10,000 unmarried persons age 15+	Persons marrying per 10,000 unmarried persons age 15–49	Crude divorce rate	Divorces per 100 marriages	Divorces per 10,000 married persons	Year
21.3	150.7	31.0	181.7	6.5	341	444	..	..	..	1898
17.5	89.6	35.7	125.3	6.5	342	447	..	..	..	1899
19.8	127.4	31.7	159.1	6.3	337	441	..	..	..	1900
14.7	80.8	34.0	114.7	6.4	341	447	..	..	..	1901
16.0	120.3	31.5	151.8	6.2	334	438	..	..	..	1902
16.7	121.7	38.8	160.4	6.1	327	429	..	..	..	1903
15.5	75.9	29.2	105.1	6.0	320	420	0.1	1.5	6.3	1904
17.8	107.0	26.0	133.0	6.7	355	466	0.1	0.9	4.4	1905
14.6	81.8	33.2	115.1	5.9	316	414	0.1	1.4	6.1	1906
16.9	118.9	28.6	147.6	6.0	319	419	0.0	0.8	3.5	1907
19.1	165.6	35.2	200.9	6.0	320	420	0.1	2.4	10.3	1908
15.0	122.2	28.9	151.1	5.4	286	375	0.1	2.2	8.5	1909
15.4	105.5	29.0	134.5	5.7	299	393	0.1	1.9	7.5	1910
13.5	80.7	28.1	108.8	6.1	321	421	0.2	2.5	10.8	1911
13.6	66.7	34.0	100.7	5.8	307	403	0.2	2.6	10.7	1912
12.2	67.2	39.3	106.5	5.7	303	397	0.1	2.4	9.7	1913
16.3	91.1	24.4	115.5	5.6	299	392	0.1	2.6	10.4	1914
15.5	66.2	34.8	101.0	6.9	365	478	0.1	1.3	6.3	1915
14.8	81.2	38.7	119.9	6.4	342	447	0.2	2.4	10.8	1916
12.3	60.6	23.1	83.6	6.1	325	425	0.1	1.4	6.1	1917
16.6	46.3	33.2	79.5	6.5	349	457	0.2	2.5	11.3	1918
12.7	70.5	27.3	97.8	6.7	359	468	0.2	3.2	14.8	1919
14.5	83.4	27.4	110.8	6.6	355	464	0.2	3.1	13.9	1920
15.6	53.1	31.1	84.2	5.9	317	414	0.2	4.1	16.5	1921
13.4	54.6	22.8	77.4	5.9	315	410	0.2	2.7	10.6	1922
13.3	50.9	19.5	70.4	5.7	303	395	0.2	3.1	11.9	1923
14.9	58.6	26.5	85.1	5.7	303	395	0.3	4.5	17.3	1924
12.4	45.0	26.2	71.3	6.3	335	436	0.2	3.7	15.6	1925
11.1	49.0	26.2	75.1	6.2	331	430	0.4	5.8	24.0	1926
12.5	83.3	27.6	110.9	5.8	312	406	0.2	3.3	13.1	1927
10.8	46.0	24.0	70.0	6.9	366	476	0.4	5.2	23.9	1928
11.7	43.1	31.0	74.1	7.2	383	498	0.3	3.7	17.8	1929
11.6	45.2	22.4	67.7	7.1	377	489	0.2	3.4	16.2	1930
11.7	48.9	22.8	71.7	6.4	338	439	0.3	4.3	18.3	1931
10.8	44.9	19.7	64.5	6.3	332	430	0.3	4.3	18.0	1932
10.3	42.3	20.5	62.8	6.4	334	433	0.4	6.6	27.7	1933
10.4	52.4	21.6	73.9	6.7	351	455	0.4	5.9	26.0	1934
12.2	67.8	22.3	90.2	6.4	332	430	0.4	6.1	25.7	1935
10.8	46.9	19.9	66.9	5.4	280	362	0.3	6.1	21.4	1936
11.2	32.1	24.2	56.3	5.7	292	379	0.4	6.6	24.5	1937
10.2	28.2	26.1	54.3	5.7	291	377	0.3	5.8	21.5	1938
9.7	36.8	15.7	52.5	5.9	302	391	0.4	6.1	23.4	1939
9.9	35.9	20.6	56.5	6.6	336	436	0.5	7.5	32.2	1940
11.1	33.0	21.3	54.3	8.4	437	568	0.4	5.3	27.9	1941
10.5	51.9	25.3	77.2	8.7	467	609	0.6	6.6	35.5	1942
10.1	30.3	21.4	51.7	7.9	431	564	0.5	5.8	27.4	1943
9.6	38.9	29.3	68.2	7.8	439	577	0.6	7.3	33.3	1944
9.1	34.4	18.9	53.3	8.0	461	608	0.4	5.6	25.8	1945

APPENDIX TABLE IS.5 Life expectancy by age 1841/50–1941/50
(in years)

Age	0	1	15	50	65	80
Males						
1841–1850	31.1	45.7	38.9	17.3	9.6	4.9
1851–1860	32.9	43.0	39.3	17.6	9.6	4.9
1861–1870	29.5	39.4	34.8	14.7	8.5	4.4
1871–1880	35.1	43.0	39.1	18.0	10.5	4.9
1881–1890	35.4	43.8	39.4	18.3	10.6	5.1
1891–1900	44.7	50.6	41.5	17.8	9.2	5.9
1901–1910	48.2	53.6	44.7	21.1	11.4	4.8
1911–1920	52.6	56.2	45.7	22.0	12.2	5.2
1921–1930	56.2	58.6	47.6	23.0	13.0	6.2
1931–1940	60.9	63.0	51.3	24.1	13.3	6.0
1941–1950	66.1	57.4	54.8	26.0	14.7	6.5
Females						
1841–1850	35.5	49.0	42.6	18.1	10.0	5.1
1851–1860	38.3	48.3	46.2	20.8	11.7	6.1
1861–1870	35.3	44.9	41.5	17.4	9.5	4.5
1871–1880	40.9	48.8	45.8	20.7	11.7	5.4
1881–1890	40.3	48.3	44.5	20.8	11.7	5.5
1891–1900	51.8	57.2	48.3	22.1	12.2	5.9
1901–1910	53.3	58.3	50.0	23.9	13.4	6.3
1911–1920	57.9	60.7	50.7	24.7	13.6	5.9
1921–1930	61.0	63.1	52.4	25.9	14.9	7.2
1931–1940	65.6	67.2	55.4	27.0	15.5	6.8
1941–1950	70.3	71.3	58.5	28.0	15.9	7.0

APPENDIX TABLE IS.6A Households by type 1703–1940 (absolute and per cent)

Census year	Total households	Private households	Family households	One-person households and lodger households	Institutional households	Total household members	Private household members	Family household members	Members in one-person and lodger households	Institutional household members
						Household types and members				
					Absolute					
1703	8,191	8,189	7,622	567	2	50,358	50,205	49,638	567	153
1860	9,607	:	:	:	:	66,987	:	:	:	:
1870	9,306	:	:	:	:	69,763	:	:	:	:
1910	14,725	14,709	14,065	644	16	85,183	84,560	83,916	644	623
1920	17,636	17,620	16,650	970	16	94,690	94,029	93,059	970	661
1930	20,976	20,877	20,259	618	99	108,861	107,048	106,430	618	1,813
1940	29,684	29,619	24,201	5,418	65	121,474	119,269	113,851	5,418	2,205
					Per cent					
1703	100.00	99.98	93.05	6.92	0.02	100.00	99.70	98.57	1.13	0.30
1860	100.00	:	:	:	:	100.00	:	:	:	:
1870	100.00	:	:	:	:	100.00	:	:	:	:
1910	100.00	99.89	95.52	4.37	0.11	100.00	99.27	98.51	0.76	0.73
1920	100.00	99.91	94.41	5.50	0.09	100.00	99.30	98.28	1.02	0.70
1930	100.00	99.53	96.58	2.95	0.47	100.00	98.33	97.77	0.57	1.67
1940	100.00	99.78	81.53	18.25	0.22	100.00	98.18	93.72	4.46	1.82

APPENDIX TABLE IS.6B(1) Family households by size and members 1703–1940 (absolute figures)

Census year	Family households total	Family households by number of members								
		2 persons	3 persons	4 persons	5 persons	6 persons	7 persons	8 persons	9 persons	10+ persons
					Households					
1703	7,622	618	1,093	1,324	1,276	1,077	795	540	358	541
1910	14,065	1,429	1,884	2,013	1,918	1,736	1,424	1,081	858	1,722
1930	20,259	2,532	3,279	3,231	3,033	2,544	2,015	1,391	909	1,325
1940	24,201	3,424	4,963	4,541	3,948	2,828	1,848	1,166	704	779
					Persons					
1703	42,455	1,236	3,279	5,296	6,380	6,462	5,565	4,320	3,222	6,695
1910	83,916	2,858	5,652	8,052	9,590	10,416	9,968	8,648	7,722	21,010
1930	113,851	5,064	9,837	12,924	15,165	15,264	14,105	11,128	8,181	22,183
1940	135,396	6,848	14,889	18,164	19,740	16,968	12,936	9,328	6,336	8,642

APPENDIX TABLE IS.6B(2) Family households by size and members 1703–1940 (per cent)

Census year	Family households total	Family households by number of members								
		2 persons	3 persons	4 persons	5 persons	6 persons	7 persons	8 persons	9 persons	10+ persons
					Households					
1703	100.00	8.11	14.34	17.37	16.74	14.13	10.43	7.08	4.70	7.10
1860[1]	∶	∶			∶					∶
1870[1]	∶	∶			∶					∶
1910	100.00	10.16	13.39	14.31	13.64	12.34	10.12	7.69	6.10	12.24
1930	100.00	12.50	16.19	15.95	14.97	12.56	9.95	6.87	4.49	6.54
1940	100.00	14.15	20.51	18.76	16.31	11.69	7.64	4.82	2.91	3.22
					Persons					
1703	100.00	2.91	7.72	12.47	15.03	15.22	13.11	10.18	7.59	15.77
1860	100.00	5.90			45.10[2]			35.00[3]		14.00
1870	100.00	6.90			37.90[2]			36.60[3]		18.60
1910	100.00	3.41	6.74	9.60	11.43	12.41	11.88	10.31	9.20	25.04
1930	100.00	4.45	8.64	11.35	13.32	13.41	12.39	9.77	7.19	19.48
1940	100.00	6.01	13.08	15.95	17.34	14.90	11.36	8.19	5.57	7.59

Notes: [1] No data available. [2] 3–7 persons. [3] 8–9 persons.

APPENDIX TABLE IS.6C(1) Private households by size and members 1703–1940 (absolute figures)

Census year	Private households total	Households by number of members									
		1 person	2 persons	3 persons	4 persons	5 persons	6 persons	7 persons	8 persons	9 persons	10+ persons
					Households						
1703	8,189	567	618	1,093	1,324	1,276	1,077	795	540	358	541
1910	14,709	644	1,429	1,884	2,013	1,918	1,736	1,424	1,081	858	1,722
1930	20,877	618	2,532	3,279	3,231	3,033	2,544	2,015	1,391	909	1,325
1940	29,619	5,418	3,424	4,963	4,541	3,948	2,828	1,848	1,166	704	779
					Persons						
1703	50,205	567	1,236	3,279	5,296	6,380	6,462	5,565	4,320	3,222	13,878
1910	84,560	644	2,858	5,652	8,052	9,590	10,416	9,968	8,648	7,722	21,010
1930	107,048	618	5,064	9,837	12,924	15,165	15,264	14,105	11,128	8,181	14,762
1940	119,269	5,418	6,848	14,889	18,164	19,740	16,968	12,936	9,328	6,336	8,642

APPENDIX TABLE IS.6C(2) Private households by size and members 1703–1940 (per cent)

Census year	Private households total	Households by number of members									
		1 person	2 persons	3 persons	4 persons	5 persons	6 persons	7 persons	8 persons	9 persons	10+ persons
					Households						
1703	100.00	6.92	7.55	13.35	16.17	15.58	13.15	9.71	6.59	4.37	6.61
1910	100.00	4.38	9.72	12.81	13.69	13.04	11.80	9.68	7.35	5.83	11.71
1930	100.00	2.96	12.13	15.71	15.48	14.53	12.19	9.65	6.66	4.35	6.35
1940	100.00	18.29	11.56	16.76	15.33	13.33	9.55	6.24	3.94	2.38	2.63
					Persons						
1703	100.00	1.13	2.46	6.53	10.55	12.71	12.87	11.08	8.60	6.42	27.64
1910	100.00	0.76	3.38	6.68	9.52	11.34	12.32	11.79	10.23	9.13	24.85
1930	100.00	0.58	4.73	9.19	12.07	14.17	14.26	13.18	10.40	7.64	13.79
1940	100.00	4.54	5.74	12.48	15.23	16.55	14.23	10.85	7.82	5.31	7.25

APPENDIX TABLE IS.6D Household indicators 1703–1940

Census year	Mean household size						
	All house-holds	Private households			Family households		
		Iceland, Total	Rural areas	Towns	Iceland, Total	Rural areas	Towns
1703	6.15	..	..	..	6.51	..	..
1760	6.33	..	..	..	..	..	..
1801	6.38	..	..	..	..	..	..
1840	6.81	..	..	..	..	..	..
1850	6.76	..	..	..	..	..	..
1860	6.97	..	..	..	..	..	..
1870	7.50	..	..	..	..	7.68	5.95
1880	7.40	..	..	..	..	7.66	5.77
1890	6.99	..	..	..	..	7.38	5.37
1901	6.19	..	..	..	..	6.73	4.86
1910	5.78	5.75	6.45	4.67	5.97	6.61	4.92
1920	5.37	5.34	5.99	4.65	5.59	6.21	4.94
1930	5.19	5.13	5.64	4.76	5.25	5.82	4.85
1940	4.09	4.03	5.31	3.50	4.70	5.50	4.29

APPENDIX TABLE IS.7 Dates and nature of results on population structure, households/families, and vital statistics

Topic	Intro-duction	Remarks
Population		
Population at census dates	1850	Earlier censuses were conducted in 1703, 15 VIII 1769, 1 II 1801, 2 II 1835, 2 XI 1840, and 2 XI 1845.
Population by age, sex, and marital status	1850	See Hagstofa Íslands, 1997: 131–6 (Table 2.14).
Households and families		
Households (*heimili*)		
Total households	1703	Households were expressly recorded for the first time in 1703. Later counts were in 1760, 1801, 1832, 1840 (continued below): 1850: number of households. 1855: number of households. 1860: number of households. 1870: number of households. 1880: number of households. 1890: number of households. 1901: number of households. 1910: households by size. 1920: number of households. 1930: households by size and composition. 1940: households by size and composition, profession of household head. *Disaggregation*: by region.
Households by size	1860, 1870, 1910, 1930, 1940	In detailed form first time in 1910. The census of 1703 was exploited later using modern methods. Earlier with grouped data in 1860 and 1870. 1910: households by number of persons 1–20+. 1920: households by number of persons 1–10+. 1930: households by number of persons 1–15+. 1940: households by number of persons 1–10+.
Households by composition	1930, 1940	
Households by profession of household head	1940	
Families		
Families by number of children	–	

continued

APPENDIX TABLE IS.7 Dates and nature of results on population structure, households/families, and vital statistics (continued)

Topic	Intro-duction	Remarks
Population movement		
Midyear population	1850	See Hagstofa Íslands, 1997: 50ff. (Table 2.2.).
Births		
Live births	1850	
Stillbirths		
Legitimate births	1850	
Illegitimate births	1850	
Deaths		
Total deaths	1850	
Infants (under 1 year)		
Marriages		
Total marriages	1850	
Divorces and separations		
Total divorces		
Legal separations		

APPENDIX FIGURE IS.8 Population by age, sex and marital status, Iceland 1860, 1890, 1910, 1920, 1930 and 1940 (per 10,000 of total population)

Iceland, 1860

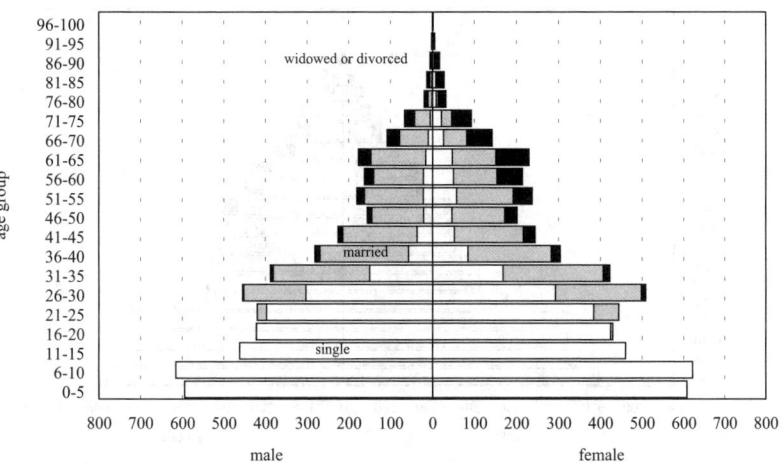

Iceland, 1890

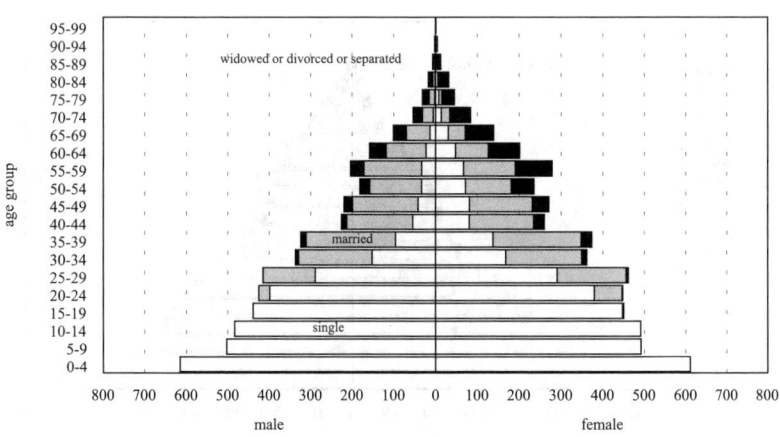

APPENDIX FIGURE IS.8 Population by age, sex and marital status, Iceland 1860, 1890, 1910, 1920, 1930 and 1940 (per 10,000 of total population) (continued)

Iceland, 1910

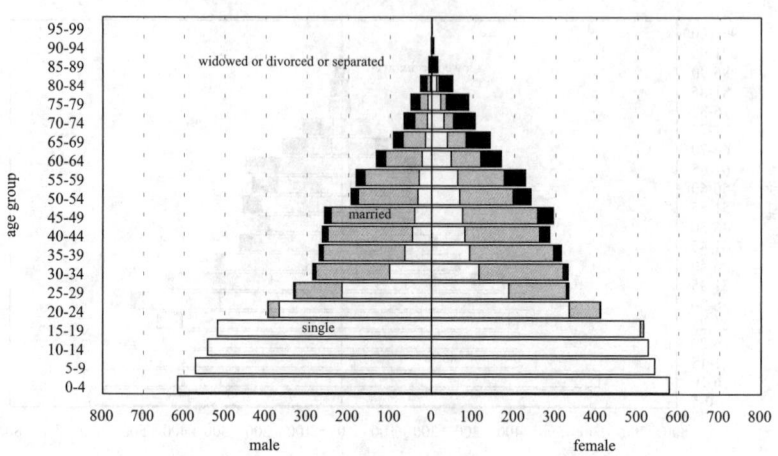

Iceland, 1920

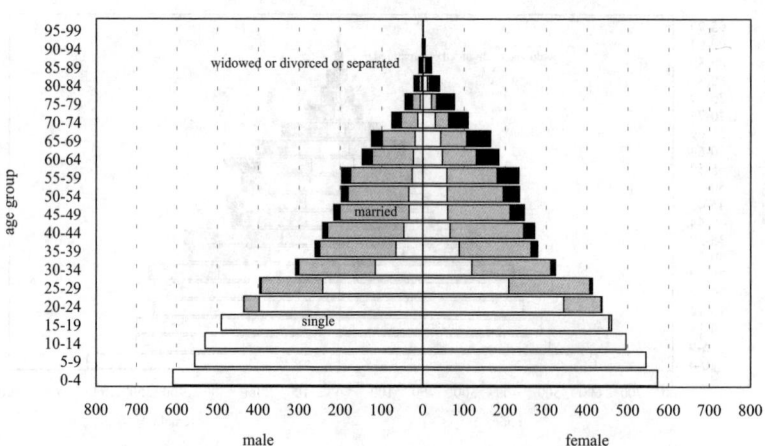

APPENDIX FIGURE IS.8 Population by age, sex and marital status, Iceland 1860, 1890, 1910, 1920, 1930 and 1940 (per 10,000 of total population) (continued)

Iceland, 1930

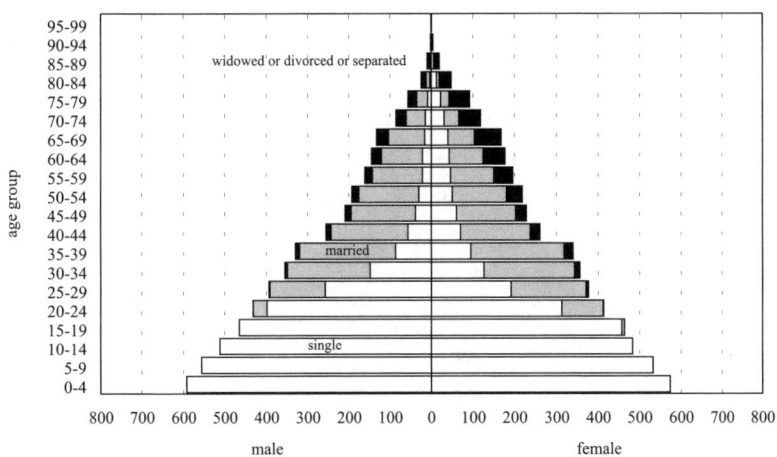

Iceland, 1940

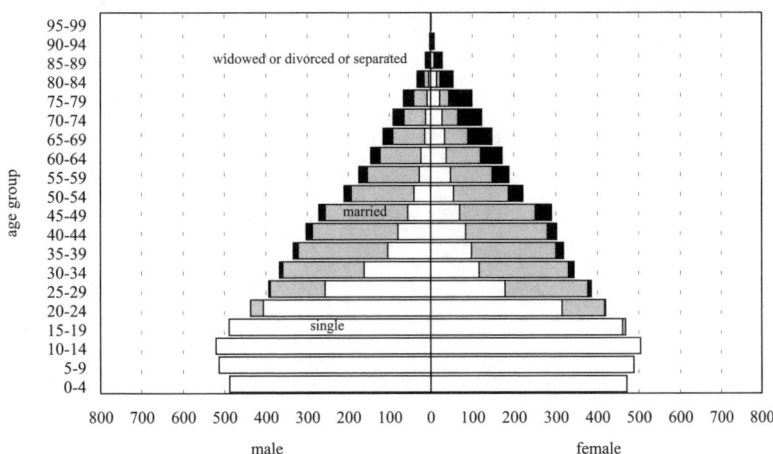

11

Ireland

Along with Wales, Scotland, and Brittany, Ireland is part of the Atlantic peripheries to which the Celtic peoples retreated when confronted with the Romans and later the Germanic tribes. In the British Isles the Anglo-Saxons began to conquer Wales and Scotland already in the ninth century; in the twelfth century the English King Henry II. invaded Ireland and claimed it for the English crown (1171 oath of allegiance of the Irish Bishops). The independence and self-sufficiency of the Irish nobility was destroyed in the centuries to come, mainly under the rule of Elizabeth I, and the island was pressed into colonial status.

James I allowed English and Scottish Protestant settlers to take possession of the north-eastern part of Ireland, the province of Ulster, thereby laying the groundwork for the division of the country which still exists today.

Further measures robbed Ireland of its last remnants of self-sufficiency. (The same was true for Scotland after it was defeated in its last battle with the English at Culloden in 1746). Finally, the creation of the United Kingdom of Great Britain and Ireland in 1801 left Ireland a mere province of the UK.

As in other European countries, in Ireland nationalist movements also spread and opposition against the English domination grew, though the country was terribly weakened by the famine between 1845 and 1850, which reduced the population by half and caused a mass exodus, mainly to the United States.

The second half of the nineteenth century saw the growth of political parties and democratization. Nationalist groups and parties advocated independence. The most radical nationalist groups saw World War I as the best chance to gain independence. On Easter 1916 they occupied public buildings and declared an independent Irish Republic. Political and public support for independence grew during the war years. Finally, on 6 December 1921 the Anglo-Irish Treaty granted Ireland Dominion status within the British Commonwealth and set up the Irish Free State. Unfortunately the six northern counties voted against membership within the new state and preferred to remain part of the United Kingdom, thus dividing the island. Further steps towards full independence of southern Ireland were the 1937 Constitution, the declaration of neutrality in World War II, and full sovereignty in 1949 when the Republic of Ireland (Eire) left the British Commonwealth (see also Chapter 21 'United Kingdom of Great Britain and Northern Ireland') (Beckett, 1991; Johnson, 1994; Bottigheimer, 1985; Clancy et al., 1995; Breen et al., 1990; Carter and Parker, 1990; Kluxen, 1991.

During the nineteenth century and up to independence of the southern provinces Ireland developed an increasingly bicephalous settlement structure: the two cities of

Belfast and Dublin grew rapidly, attracting residents from the rural areas on the west, north, and south coasts. This tendency was stronger in Belfast, and after the Republic became independent, the existing monocephalic settlement structure in Northern Ireland greatly increased. Dublin had not reached such a dominant position by 1911, but after independence it experienced major growth, mainly through migration from rural areas. In 1926 17% of the population of the Republic lived in the county of Dublin; already in 1946 nearly 22% of the population lived in the capital

Population losses were severe for several regions of Ireland, mainly those of the west and north-west coast (especially Donegal), but also the south coast and several interior regions were affected by out-migration. With the decline of agriculture and extensive animal husbandry, the economic centre of the country shifted to the west coast where good ports are located and the main shipping lines end and start. Industrialization and the rise of the service sector did not benefit the western regions and were mostly located on the shores of the Irish Sea.

POPULATION GROWTH

Already in the early nineteenth century Ireland was rather densely populated with a population of 6,802,000 in 1821. Population density, at 83 persons per square km., was higher than it is at present (Table 11.1). Due to the strong population growth until the Great Famine of 1845–1849 population density increased until the last census before the famine to 100 inhabitants per sq. km. After the Great Famine until the end of World War II population growth in Ireland was constantly negative, though with substantial variations.

Table 11.1 Population density in Ireland, 1821–1861 (inhabitants per sq. km.)

Census year	Resident population (in 1,000s)	Land area (in sq. km.)	Population density
1821	6,802	81,718	83.24
1831	7,767	81,718	95.05
1841	8,175	81,718	100.04
1851	6,552	81,718	80.18
1861	5,799	81,718	70.96

Source: Johnson, 1994: 64.

In the 1880s and 1890s a strong emigration wave set in, accelerating population decline (Figure IRL.1).[1] The declining absolute population can also be seen from the population density. From the end of the famine until the end of World War I population density declined continuously from over 80 persons per square km. in 1851 to 54 in 1911, the last census before World War I. Although fertility rates stabilized during the time of the Irish Republic (after 1921), there was no manifest population increase in the inter-war period, and population density declined, though slowly. After independence, population density in the Irish Republic was lower than in the whole of Ireland before independence, which indicates a much higher population density in Northern Ireland than in the southern provinces. In 1926 population density was only 43 inhabitants per square km. in the Republic, but 54

---

[1] All figures up to 1921 refer to the whole of Ireland; figures since 1922 refer only to the Irish Free State.

inhabitants per square km. in 1911 in the whole island (see also Courtney, 1995; Coward, 1990).

The demographic transition in Ireland deviates greatly from the transition model and the European average, at least until the inter-war period. Irish population history is usually divided into the pre-famine and the post-famine period. The Great Famine from 1845 to 1849 was the major watershed in Irish population history (Johnson, 1994) and the subsequent demographic developments cannot be understood apart from it. Before the Great Famine there was strong population growth in Ireland mainly due to natural population increase. The population increased from 6,802 million inhabitants in 1821 to 8,175 million in 1841, the year of the last census before the famine. Population increase was roughly 20%, which is very high compared with other European countries during the first half of the nineteenth century. This growth was mainly due to a large surplus of births rather than migratory gains. Immigration was low, but emigration, mainly overseas, was constant already at that time (Figure IRL.2).

The Great Famine was caused by the failure of the potato crop, which supplied the staple food of the masses of the population. Successive attacks of potato blight caused shortages of potato seed and subsequently hunger, starvation, emigration, and a large number of deaths. Between 1841 and 1851 the population declined from 8,175 million to 6,552 million, a loss of 19.85%. Demographers argue whether the Great Famine was the most important factor for this development, or whether there was a constant flow of emigration to other countries which was only enhanced by the famine. The main argument of the revisionist position is that it is unclear how many deaths should be linked to the famine and how many to related causes such as endemics and sickness.

In any case, while the population had been growing until the famine, after the famine until independence in 1921 the population permanently declined. In 1926 Ireland had only 4,229 million inhabitants.

These developments are clearly underlined by the pattern of the demographic transition, for which data are available since the 1860s. The famine greatly reduced the birth rate to a level far below the European average. The death rate was also low and below the European average; thus, there was a natural population increase. But this population surplus was not enough for an increase in the population: emigration was so strong that the population declined until the 1920s. Ireland's population development began to normalize only after the inter-war period.

During the 1860s the birth rate recovered to a level of nearly 30. Until World War I both the birth and death rates declined by tendency. During the 1880s the birth rate was lower than in the decade between 1900 and 1910. Ireland did not participate in World War I directly, but the effects of the war can also be seen in the declining birth rate and rising death rate. After independence from Britain in 1921 conditions improved and fertility decline was effectively halted; there was also major progress in reducing infant mortality. Therefore, in the 1930s the Irish birth and death rates were higher than the European rates. The Irish Republic remained neutral also during World War II, which contributed to the rise in the birth rate during the 1940s. While elsewhere in Europe the post-World War II period was marked by overall fertility decline, in Ireland the contrary was true: fertility rose so strongly that the

Figure IRL.1 Population growth and net migration 1850-1945

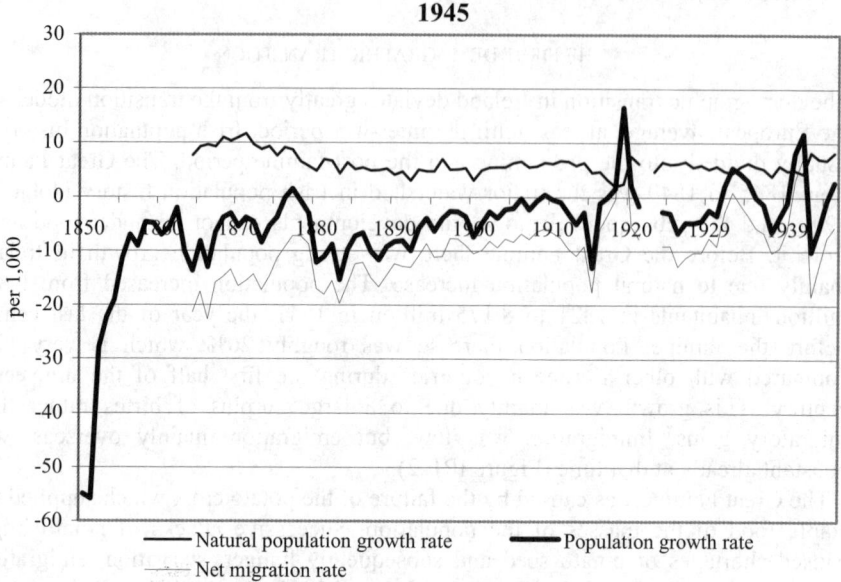

Figure IRL.2 First demographic transition 1864-1945

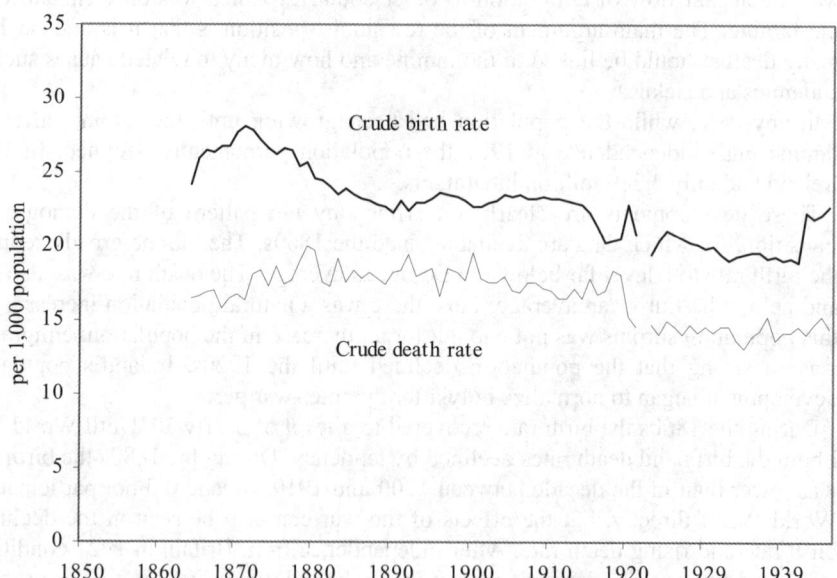

population started to increase again, after having been in decline for approximately one hundred years. Fertility remained at this very high level until the early 1980s when it started to decline. But in the 1990s there was still a considerable natural population surplus, in contrast to most other European countries with negative natural population growth. In Ireland there was therefore no clear 'first' demographic transition and also no 'second demographic transition'; these stages in the transition process were reversed.

MORTALITY AND LIFE EXPECTANCY

The infant mortality rate is defined as deaths of children aged under one year per 1,000 live births. Ireland belongs to the group of continental countries including the British Isles with a moderate infant mortality during the first half of the twentieth century. Data for the Republic of Ireland for the five-year period 1926–30 reveal a rather low infant mortality rate of 68 deaths per 1,000 live births. Ireland is singular in Western Europe for showing an increase in infant mortality in the late 1930s and during World War II. The Republic of Ireland had lower infant mortality than Northern Ireland during the inter-war period (Masuy-Stroobant, 1997) (Figure IRL.3).

Life expectancy in Ireland was on an intermediate level, not as high as in Sweden, but not as low as in Southern Europe. At the turn of the century (1900/2) life expectancy of new-born boys was 49.3 years in Ireland (Figure IRL.4) compared to 54.5 years in Sweden (1901/10; 50.9 in 1891/1900). Thus infant mortality was rather low already in 1900. While life expectancy at birth was fairly high, young adults and the elderly had a lower life expectancy than in Sweden. Around 1900 the difference for 30-year-old men was six years and for 60-year-old men five years. By the 1940s however, Ireland was able to improve life expectancy of adults and moved nearer to the Swedish level. Sex differences in life expectancy were low in Ireland around 1900 and increased only slightly until the 1940s in favour of women.

FERTILITY AND LEGITIMACY

The period after the Great Famine was characterized by low fertility, high celibacy, late age at marriage, and high permanent or temporary emigration. This situation is very similar to Portugal's during the nineteenth century. In Portugal, also a Catholic country, this situation led to the highest illegitimate fertility in Europe. In Ireland, by contrast, despite these favourable circumstances, illegitimate fertility was very low and well below the European average. It was even lower than in Switzerland and The Netherlands; only Greece had a lower rate. This low Irish level did not change from the 1860s until the 1940s. Ireland has participated in the rise in illegitimate fertility only since the 1960s, i.e. marriage has also been deinstitutionalized in Ireland to a certain extent, and its rate of illegitimate fertility has come closer to the European level (Figure IRL.5).

While illegitimate fertility was so far below the average, legitimate fertility must have been well above average; this was exactly the case in Ireland during the whole period from 1860 to 1990. When the fertility decline in Europe started in the last decades of the nineteenth century, in Ireland there was no such decline, but rather a slight increase. The legitimate fertility level was more or less constant until the 1960s when legitimate fertility began to lose ground to illegitimate fertility.

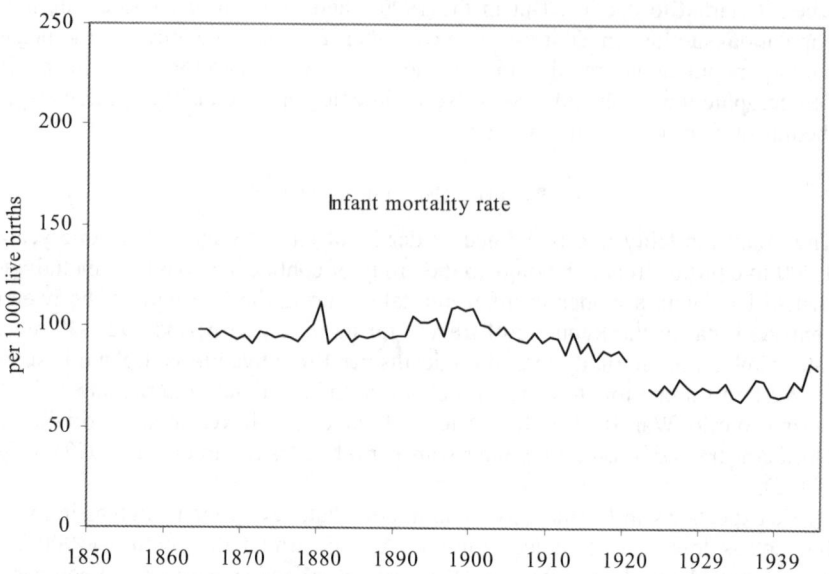

Figure IRL.3 Infant mortality 1864-1945

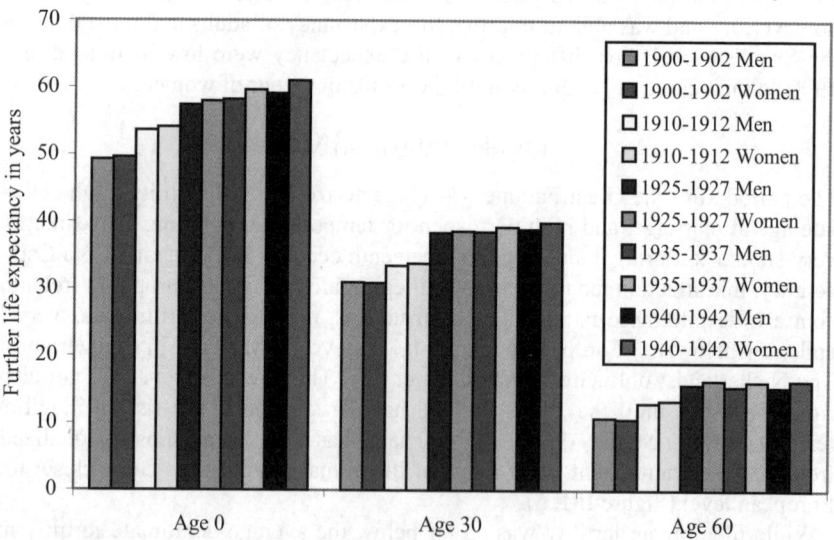

Figure IRL.4 Life expectancy 1900/02-1940/42

To sum up: during most of the nineteenth and twentieth centuries, Ireland, like Portugal, has been shaped by its position at the Atlantic periphery, creating similar conditions, but with different effects on demographic patterns. The major difference is illegitimacy, where the two countries constitute the extreme cases. Obviously religion has no influence on this family behavioural pattern.

MARRIAGE AND DIVORCE

Ireland principally belongs to the region of Europe with the *Western European marriage pattern* of late age at marriage and a high celibacy rate. But this general classification is strongly distorted by the unique situation of Ireland during the nineteenth century. The Great Famine of 1845–1849 changed demographic development so strongly that Ireland became the most extreme case of the Western European marriage pattern. As we have seen above, in the aftermath of the famine fertility was extremely low in European comparison. This phenomenon is not the result of artificial fertility reduction, but is due to other factors, including marital behaviour and emigration. As a consequence of the country's weak economy in the second half of the nineteenth century, age at marriage was the highest in Europe. We do not have data on the mean age at first marriage for this period, therefore we use the proportion of women/men married at age 20–24 as a substitute. In Ireland in 1871 this proportion was approximately 20% for women; it declined to less than 15% by 1910 and remained at this low level until the 1930s. It slowly increased after the 1940s and peaked in 1980. Compared with other European countries, age at marriage declined later and remained at a structurally lower level.

The same pattern emerges for Irish men: a decline in the proportion married at age 20–24 until 1910, constant until the 1930s and rising until 1980. The only major difference is the much lower proportion of men married, well under 10% during the whole period from 1871 to the 1970s. Irish men married latest of all male Europeans.

The high age at marriage or the low proportion of people marrying early still persisted in the post-World War II period. Women's mean age at marriage in Ireland in 1960 was the highest of all European countries. Age at marriage declined later and did not reach its lowest point until 1980, over ten years later than e.g. in Sweden; by the early 1990s this decline was not yet concluded.

The second aspect of the Western European Marriage Pattern is *marriage intensity*, measured by the *marriage rate* and the *celibacy rate*. 'Marriage intensity' refers to the availability of marriage among the population; at the same time it can be an indicator of the need to remarry after widowhood. Both indicators are strongly influenced by economic conditions—prosperity and depression. Another factor for the low fertility after the Great Famine was the high celibacy of women and men in Ireland. Together with Switzerland, Ireland had the highest celibacy rate (the proportion of never-married women aged 45–54) in Europe: 37% in 1871. The reason for this high proportion must be sought in the economic difficulties of a poor and agricultural country, with very little industry and few possibilities for work. Further, under the inheritance system in agriculture, the oldest son was the sole heir, who had to wait until his parents retired before taking over the farm. The other children had to find their own livelihood, either in Ireland or by emigrating. Emigration to England or overseas was an established pattern, and mostly young

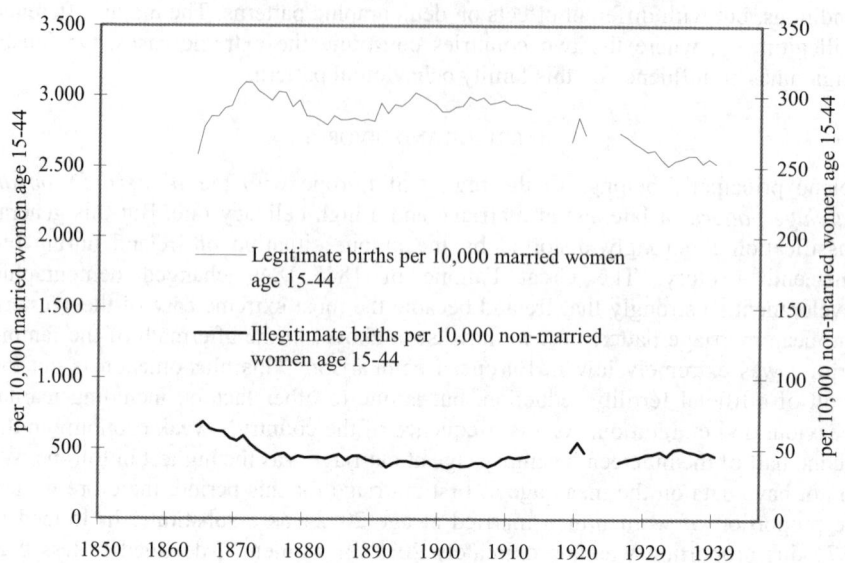

Figure IRL.5 Fertility and legitimacy 1864-1939

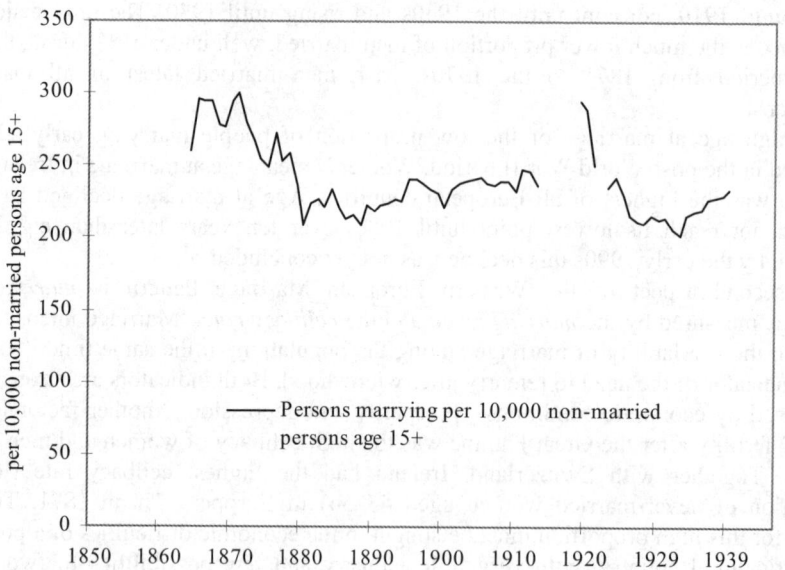

Figure IRL.6 Marriages 1864-1939

men emigrated. This likely led (as in Portugal) to a shortage of possible marriage partners for women, therefore contributing to high celibacy.

There was no substantial change in this high celibacy until 1950 (the cohorts born around 1900). Only women born after 1900 had a better chance of marrying. The trend toward universal marriage came later than in other Western European countries and remained weaker; only the birth cohorts of the 1920s and 1930s reached nearly universal marriage.

The second indicator of marriage intensity or nuptiality—the marriage rate—also reveals an extreme pattern (Figure IRL.6). The Irish marriage rate was the lowest of all European countries from the middle of the nineteenth century until the 1970s. Until 1921 there was no change in this low level, nor did nuptiality increase; this is in accordance with the celibacy rate. In the 1930s nuptiality slowly started to rise; it peaked in the early 1970s and declined again afterwards; nuptiality remained below the European average for the entire time from the 1860s to 1990.

Both indicators therefore demonstrate the low nuptiality in Ireland during the century from 1850 to 1950, resulting in low fertility. This pattern only changed after independence, though very slowly; it speeded up somewhat after World War II, when fertility and population increased. Nevertheless emigration remained an important characteristic of Irish society even after 1921.

Divorce was not allowed during the whole period from 1850 to 1945. The indissolubility of legal marriage was guaranteed by the Constitution. The only possibilities to dissolve a marriage were those few allowed by ecclesiastical law.

As a result, there are no official statistics on divorce or legal separation. But cases of *de facto* separation must have been frequent, as evidenced by permanent overseas emigration and labour migration mainly to Britain as a *social constant* in Irish life. The extent of marital breakdown was assessed by a study commissioned by the Minister for Justice (1993).

This situation has changed only recently with the introduction of the 'Judicial Separation and Family Law Reform Act 1989' extending the grounds for legal separation. Finally, the 'Draft Family Law (Divorce) Bill' of 1995 intended to introduce divorce (The Stationery Office, 1995). The bill was enacted as the 'Family Law (Divorce) Act 1997'. This legislation allows divorce in Ireland in certain circumstances (Commission on the Family, 1998: 209f; see also Kiely, 1998: 119ff.).

AGE, SEX, AND CIVIL STATUS

The age structure of Ireland until the First World War was pyramidal, although with strong irregularities (Appendix Figure IRL.8). Differences in the size of different age groups are most visible in the age structure of 1861, but also in those of 1901 and 1911. These ups and downs in the size of age groups were caused by the Great Famine and the subsequent waves of emigration. Emigration however did not affect all age groups the same way, and men's emigration was stronger than women's. The age structure of 1861 reveals this major shortage of men in the age groups of economically active persons. Men's higher mortality must have played an important role as well, given the large proportions of widowed women in 1861.

After World War I, in 1926 the age structure had become bell-shaped due to the birth decline during the war years. Birth cohorts of the late 1920s and early 1930s were again smaller than before the First World War, thus rendering the bell-shaped pattern of the Irish age structure still more clearly. In 1926 and 1936, in line with the situation in the second half of the nineteenth century, the age groups of economically active persons were reduced, mainly due to emigration.

The continuing structural problems of Ireland after the Great Famine caused a late age at marriage (higher for men) and a high proportion of celibacy among women. The economic crisis of the inter-war period did not lead to any improvement in this situation.

FAMILY AND HOUSEHOLD STRUCTURES

The demographic patterns and developments described above raise the question of how households were organized. The dominance of agriculture and the tradition of living under one roof in small settlements would favour the formation of extended families and large households. Therefore, one might expect mean household size to be large. Low urbanization and the shortage of housing *ceteris paribus* would lead to a small proportion of people living alone. The high celibacy rate, late age at marriage, and low nuptiality would lead either to a high number of single persons or very small households. The low fertility until the 1940s would lead to rather small households.

Given these assumptions, it becomes fairly clear from the data that not nuclearization, but rather the formation of large households was the main pattern in nineteenth-century Ireland. The main explanation is probably not cultural or religious, but social and economic: namely, agriculture as the basis of living, the dominance of small settlements, a low urbanization rate, and poverty.

Few statistics are available on household size and composition until the 1950s. Mean private household size can be calculated since 1821, and this indicator shows that households on average were very large in Ireland compared with other European countries. In 1821 there were 5.18 persons per private household. This proportion increased in pre-famine Ireland to 5.61 in 1831 and to 5.55 in 1841. The Great Famine reduced mean private household size: in 1851 it was merely 5.44 and by 1901 it had fallen to 4.9 persons per private household. Whereas household size dropped sharply after the Great Famine, in the first half of the twentieth century the decline was less dramatic: in 1946 mean private household size was still as high as 4.16 persons per household.

Mean family household size was even larger: the first figure, available for 1926, shows 4.80 persons per family household, compared to 4.48 persons per private household. Mean family household size surpassed mean private household size by 0.32 persons on average. If this proportion is extended to 1851, when mean private household size was 5.44 persons, then mean family household size would have been 5.76 persons. These considerations clearly show the predominance of large households in Ireland during the nineteenth and the first half of the twentieth century. This result is reinforced by the rather low proportion of one-person households from 1926 to 1946: although the proportion increased, it was only 8.28% in 1926 and 10.39% in 1946, rather low in European comparison.

The 60 years from 1851 to 1911 are covered by crude statistics on household composition by sex. The statistics distinguish between household heads and their children, visitors, and servants. Visitors probably include relatives living in the house. In 1851 there were more female than male visitors (7.8 and 6.2% of total household population, respectively; added together, this amounts to a considerable

14% of total household population). This figure probably hides many family members beyond the nuclear family and is an indication of the extended family. Up to 1911 this proportion even increased to over 17%. There were more male servants (3.6%) than female servants (3.48%) in 1851 (total 7.1%). By 1911 both proportions had declined strongly, with female servants becoming the dominant group (1.6% male vs. 2.34% female servants; total 3.9% servants). The larger proportion of male servants was also found in other countries in the early nineteenth century when male domestic positions were still common (butler, stable hand, farm labourer, coachman, etc.), but other job opportunities reduced this employment very early. Positions for female servants (maids, cooks, nannies, etc.) lasted well into the twentieth century.

THE NATIONAL SYSTEM OF DEMOGRAPHIC STATISTICS

Population Structure

Until independence in 1921 Ireland shared much of the population registration system with other parts of the United Kingdom. Regular census-taking in the United Kingdom began in 1801. Censuses were taken every ten years until 1911 with remarkable stability and regularity. After independence, censuses for Ireland were taken in 1926, 1936, and 1946 (Ireland remained neutral in World War II). Data combined by age, sex, and marital status became available in 1871, but only in very broad age groups of 10 years. This procedure was kept until the publication of the 1911 census. One-year age groups have only been published since the 1926 census.

Vital Statistics

The record of births, deaths, and marriages was introduced in the second half of the nineteenth century. Birth (also by legitimacy) and death registration started in 1864, while marriage registration started even earlier. Additional demographic variables and indicators were introduced or became available at much later dates. Data on divorces are unavailable due to the non-existence of divorce.

Households and Families

Data on *households* (*private families*) were already collected in the 1821 census (see e.g. Census Commissioners, Charlemont House, Census Office (1903: V)). But this is almost the only information about households for the entire nineteenth century. Therefore the only indicator we can derive from this information is the mean private household size. In 1901 the number of institutions (institutional households) and their respective members (inmates and personnel) was added.

In 1926, 1936, and 1946, households were counted within the housing census. This procedure may have led to an under-registration of households, because the use of the household dwelling concept underestimates the number of households, as there may be several households in one dwelling.

Private households have been analysed by size from 1 to 12 and more persons only since 1926. Thus, for the years 1926, 1936, and 1946 we have the size distribution and the number of family households and one-person households.

In 1851 a rough classification of private families according to household composition was introduced. Three different categories of household members were distinguished: heads of families and their children, visitors, and servants, classified by sex. Data for this household composition are available until 1911.

Disaggregations of the number of private families have been published for all major parts of the country, the provinces, counties, and cities.

The *household* (*private family*) was defined as a 'private family', that is, a private household. Institutions (institutional households) were published in separate chapters and not as part of 'household statistics' as for example in Germany. Private families included in principle all persons who did not live in institutions (schools, hospitals, prisons, workhouses, etc.) as inmates or personnel including family members. A private family therefore could be a one-person household or a family household with or without non-family members such as servants, boarders and lodgers, or relatives and visitors. From 1821 to 1911 private families therefore included persons living alone as well as members of a family household. From 1926 to 1946 household statistics were collected within the housing census, which implied a change in definition because now household and tenement were supposed to be identical. But if counted separately there were more households than dwellings.

Family statistics were introduced in 1946, but only marital fertility was included.

Remarks (also see introductory Table 6.1)

In the Republic of Ireland population censuses in the inter-war period were conducted in 1926 and 1937. v16–v21 have been linearly extrapolated using the growth rates of these censuses going back to 1922 and forward to 1939.

BOUNDARY CHANGES

Ireland was a kingdom until 1801 when it was united with Great Britain to form the United Kingdom of Great Britain and Ireland. In 1921 the twenty-six southern Irish counties ceded from the United Kingdom and created the Republic of Ireland. The northern provinces of Ulster remained with the United Kingdom. For regional organization see the documentation by Quick (1994) and Caramani, Flora, Kraus, and Quick (1998).

APPENDIX TABLES

APPENDIX TABLE IRL.1 Population structure at census dates 1861–1936

Census number	Census date	Census population			Marital status				Age group		
		Total	Male	Female	Single	Married	Widowed	Divorced	0-14	15-64	65+
		Absolute									
1	7–8 IV 1861	5,799,374	2,837,777	2,961,597	3,738,615	1,680,632	380,127	..	1,901,976	3,614,091	283,307
2	2–3 IV 1871	5,412,377	2,639,753	2,772,624	3,488,528	1,564,550	359,299	..	1,915,276	3,171,587	325,514
3	3–4 IV 1881	5,174,115	2,532,762	2,641,353	3,416,097	1,409,067	348,951	..	1,813,990	3,038,260	321,865
4	5–6 IV 1891	4,704,750	2,318,953	2,385,797	3,141,566	1,239,680	323,504	..	1,529,067	2,875,130	300,553
5	31 III–1 IV 1901	4,458,775	2,200,040	2,258,735	2,990,312	1,169,398	299,065	..	1,353,202	2,821,067	284,506
6	2–3 IV 1911	4,390,219	2,192,048	2,198,171	2,902,814	1,191,142	296,263	..	1,300,639	2,648,682	440,898
7	18 IV 1926	2,971,992	1,506,889	1,465,103	1,954,098	824,071	193,823	..	867,879	1,832,433	271,680
8	26 IV 1936	2,968,420	1,520,454	1,447,966	1,940,291	842,714	185,415	..	820,394	1,861,330	286,696
		Per cent									
1	7–8 IV 1861	100.00	48.93	51.07	64.47	28.98	6.55	..	32.80	62.32	4.89
2	2–3 IV 1871	100.00	48.77	51.23	64.45	28.91	6.64	..	35.39	58.60	6.01
3	3–4 IV 1881	100.00	48.95	51.05	66.02	27.23	6.74	..	35.06	58.72	6.22
4	5–6 IV 1891	100.00	49.29	50.71	66.77	26.35	6.88	..	32.50	61.11	6.39
5	31 III–1 IV 1901	100.00	49.34	50.66	67.07	26.23	6.71	..	30.35	63.27	6.38
6	2–3 IV 1911	100.00	49.93	50.07	66.12	27.13	6.75	..	29.63	60.33	10.04
7	18 IV 1926	100.00	50.70	49.30	65.75	27.73	6.52	..	29.20	61.66	9.14
8	26 IV 1936	100.00	51.22	48.78	65.36	28.39	6.25	..	27.64	62.70	9.66

APPENDIX TABLE IRL.2 Census population by region 1871–1936 (per cent)

County	1871	1881	1891	1901	1911	1926	1936	1946
Leinster	**24.74**	**24.71**	**25.25**	**25.86**	**26.47**	**38.66**	**41.11**	**43.35**
Carlow	0.96	0.91	0.87	0.85	0.82	1.14	1.15	1.15
Dublin[1]	7.48	8.10	8.91	10.05	10.87	17.03	19.78	21.52
Kildare	1.53	1.47	1.49	1.44	1.53	1.95	1.95	2.20
Kilkenny[1]	2.01	1.93	1.85	1.77	1.71	2.39	2.32	2.27
King's / Offaly[2]	1.40	1.41	1.40	1.35	1.30	1.78	1.72	1.83
Longford	1.20	1.18	1.13	1.05	1.00	1.35	1.28	1.22
Louth	1.55	1.51	1.51	1.48	1.46	2.12	2.16	2.23
Meath	1.77	1.68	1.64	1.50	1.48	2.12	2.06	2.23
Queen's / Laoighis[2]	1.48	1.41	1.38	1.28	1.25	1.75	1.68	1.69
Westmeath	1.44	1.39	1.38	1.39	1.37	1.92	1.85	1.86
Wexford	2.46	2.40	2.38	2.33	2.32	3.23	3.17	3.11
Wicklow	1.46	1.35	1.32	1.37	1.39	1.95	1.99	2.03
Munster	**25.74**	**25.72**	**24.91**	**24.13**	**23.58**	**32.64**	**31.74**	**31.03**
Clare	2.73	2.72	2.64	2.51	2.37	3.20	3.03	2.88
Cork[1]	9.55	9.58	9.31	9.08	8.93	12.31	11.99	11.64
Kerry	3.64	3.88	3.80	3.72	3.64	5.01	4.72	4.53
Limerick[1]	3.55	3.50	3.38	3.27	3.26	4.71	4.75	4.84
Tipperary	4.01	3.86	3.68	3.59	3.46	..	..	..
T. North Riding	1.74	1.66	1.62	1.53	1.44	2.02	2.02	1.96
T. South Riding	2.27	2.18	2.06	2.06	2.05	2.73	2.63	2.64
Waterford[1]	2.27	2.18	2.08	1.95	1.91	2.66	2.63	2.57
Ulster	**33.87**	**33.68**	**34.43**	**35.50**	**36.04**	**10.09**	**9.43**	**8.93**
Antrim	7.46	8.15	9.10	12.22	13.23	..	..	..
Armagh	3.31	3.15	3.04	2.80	2.73	..	..	..
Cavan	2.61	2.49	2.38	2.20	2.07	2.76	2.59	2.37
Donegal	4.03	3.98	3.95	3.90	3.85	5.15	4.78	4.60
Down	5.41	5.26	5.67	4.62	4.65	..	..	..
Fermanagh	1.72	1.64	1.57	1.46	1.41	..	..	..
(London-)Derry	3.22	3.19	3.23	3.23	3.21	..	..	..
Monaghan	2.12	1.99	1.83	1.68	1.62	2.19	2.06	1.93
Tyrone	3.99	3.83	3.63	3.39	3.26	..	..	..
Connaught	**15.63**	**15.88**	**15.41**	**14.51**	**13.92**	**18.61**	**17.69**	**16.68**
Galway[1]	4.58	4.68	4.57	4.33	4.15	5.69	5.66	5.58
Leitrim	1.77	1.74	1.68	1.55	1.46	1.88	1.72	1.52
Mayo	4.55	4.73	4.65	4.46	4.37	5.82	5.42	5.01
Roscommon	2.61	2.55	2.42	2.29	2.14	2.83	2.63	2.47
Sligo	2.12	2.16	2.08	1.88	1.80	2.39	2.26	2.10
TOTAL	**100.00**	**100.00**	**100.00**	**100.00**	**100.00**	**100.00**	**100.00**	**100.00**

Notes: [1] County and City/County Borough. [2] Renamed.

APPENDIX TABLE IRL.3 Population density by region 1871–1936 (inhabitants per sq. km.)

County	1871	1881	1891	1901	1911	1926	1936	1946
Leinster	**69**	**66**	**61**	**59**	**59**	**59**	**62**	**65**
Carlow	58	53	46	43	40	38	38	38
Dublin[1]	443	458	458	490	520	549	637	690
Kildare	49	45	41	38	40	34	34	38
Kilkenny[1]	53	49	42	39	36	34	33	32
King's / Offaly[2]	38	37	33	30	29	31	30	31
Longford	63	59	51	45	42	38	36	34
Louth	103	96	87	81	78	77	78	80
Meath	41	37	33	29	28	27	26	28
Queen's / Laoighis[2]	47	42	38	33	32	26	25	25
Westmeath	45	41	37	36	34	32	31	31
Wexford	57	53	48	45	43	41	40	39
Wicklow	39	35	31	30	30	29	29	30
Munster	**58**	**56**	**49**	**45**	**43**	**40**	**39**	**38**
Clare	48	46	40	36	33	30	28	27
Cork[1]	70	67	59	55	53	49	48	46
Kerry	42	43	38	36	34	32	30	29
Limerick[1]	72	68	59	54	53	52	52	53
Tipperary	51	47	41	38	36	..	..	..
T. North Riding	..	..	..	..	..	30	30	29
T. South Riding	..	..	..	..	..	36	35	35
Waterford[1]	67	61	53	47	46	43	42	41
Ulster	**86**	**82**	**76**	**74**	**74**	**37**	**35**	**33**
Antrim	141	147	149	190	202	..	..	..
Armagh	142	129	114	99	95	..	..	..
Cavan	77	70	61	53	49	43	41	37
Donegal	46	43	39	37	35	32	29	28
Down	119	110	108	84	83	..	..	..
Fermanagh	56	51	44	39	37	..	..	..
(London-)Derry	84	80	73	69	68	..	..	..
Monaghan	90	81	68	59	56	50	47	44
Tyrone	69	63	55	48	45	..	..	..
Connaught	**50**	**49**	**43**	**38**	**36**	**32**	**31**	**29**
Galway[1]	42	41	36	32	31	28	28	28
Leitrim	64	60	53	46	43	37	33	30
Mayo	47	46	41	38	36	32	30	27
Roscommon	60	56	49	44	38	34	32	30
Sligo	63	62	54	46	44	40	37	35
TOTAL	**66**	**63**	**58**	**55**	**54**	**43**	**43**	**43**

Notes: See Appendix Table IRL.2. Irish publications give areas in 'Statute acres' until 1971 (1 acre=0.004047 sq. km.).

APPENDIX TABLE IRL.4 Demographic developments 1850–1945 (absolute figures and rates)

Year	Mid-year population	Natural population growth rate	Population growth rate	Net migration rate	Crude birth rate	Legitimate births per 10,000 married women age 15–44	Illegitimate births per 10,000 unmarried women age 15–44	Illeg. births per 100 leg. births
1850	6,878,000	..	-55.0	..	..	..	..	..
1851	6,514,000	..	-55.9	..	..	..	..	..
1852	6,337,000	..	-27.9	..	..	..	..	..
1853	6,199,000	..	-22.3	..	..	..	..	..
1854	6,083,000	..	-19.1	..	..	..	..	..
1855	6,015,000	..	-11.3	..	..	..	..	..
1856	5,973,000	..	-7.0	..	..	..	..	..
1857	5,919,000	..	-9.1	..	..	..	..	..
1858	5,891,000	..	-4.8	..	..	..	..	..
1859	5,862,000	..	-4.9	..	..	..	..	..
1860	5,821,000	..	-7.0	..	..	..	..	..
1861	5,788,000	..	-5.7	..	..	..	..	..
1862	5,776,000	..	-2.1	..	..	..	..	..
1863	5,718,000	..	-10.1	..	..	..	..	..
1864	5,641,000	7.7	-13.7	-21.3	24.2	2,584	65	4.0
1865	5,595,000	9.3	-8.2	-17.5	25.9	2,778	69	3.9
1866	5,523,000	9.6	-13.0	-22.7	26.5	2,857	64	3.5
1867	5,487,000	9.3	-6.6	-15.8	26.3	2,854	62	3.4
1868	5,466,000	11.0	-3.8	-14.8	26.7	2,912	62	3.3
1869	5,449,000	10.3	-3.1	-13.4	26.7	2,928	57	3.0
1870	5,419,000	10.9	-5.5	-16.5	27.6	3,044	55	2.7
1871	5,398,000	11.7	-3.9	-15.6	28.0	3,095	59	2.9
1872	5,373,000	9.7	-4.7	-14.3	27.8	3,091	53	2.6
1873	5,328,000	8.8	-8.4	-17.2	27.1	3,033	49	2.5
1874	5,299,000	9.3	-5.5	-14.8	26.7	3,004	46	2.4
1875	5,279,000	7.6	-3.8	-11.4	26.2	2,968	43	2.3
1876	5,278,000	9.1	-0.2	-9.3	26.6	3,030	46	2.4
1877	5,286,000	8.7	1.5	-7.2	26.4	3,023	47	2.5
1878	5,282,000	6.5	-0.8	-7.3	25.4	2,921	42	2.4
1879	5,266,000	5.7	-3.0	-8.8	25.7	2,970	45	2.5
1880	5,203,000	4.8	-12.1	-17.0	24.6	2,858	44	2.6
1881	5,146,000	6.9	-11.1	-18.0	24.4	2,853	44	2.6
1882	5,101,000	6.7	-8.8	-15.5	24.0	2,827	44	2.7
1883	5,024,000	4.4	-15.3	-19.7	23.5	2,794	43	2.7
1884	4,975,000	6.4	-9.8	-16.2	23.9	2,861	45	2.8
1885	4,939,000	5.1	-7.3	-12.4	23.5	2,831	46	2.9
1886	4,906,000	5.4	-6.7	-12.1	23.2	2,833	42	2.7
1887	4,857,000	4.9	-10.1	-15.0	23.1	2,842	45	2.9
1888	4,801,000	4.9	-11.7	-16.6	22.8	2,827	45	3.0
1889	4,757,000	5.2	-9.2	-14.5	22.7	2,835	42	2.9
1890	4,718,000	4.1	-8.3	-12.4	22.3	2,822	41	2.8
1891	4,680,000	4.7	-8.1	-12.8	23.1	2,950	41	2.8
1892	4,634,000	3.1	-9.9	-13.0	22.5	2,877	37	2.6
1893	4,607,000	5.1	-5.9	-10.9	23.0	2,939	40	2.7
1894	4,589,000	4.8	-3.9	-8.7	23.0	2,927	41	2.8
1895	4,560,000	4.8	-6.4	-11.1	23.3	2,966	41	2.8
1896	4,542,000	7.0	-4.0	-11.0	23.7	3,024	40	2.7
1897	4,530,000	5.0	-2.6	-7.7	23.6	3,002	40	2.7

continued

APPENDIX TABLE IRL.4 Demographic developments 1850–1945 (absolute figures and rates)

Crude death rate	Infant mortality rate	Stillbirth rate	Infant mortality and stillbirth rate	Crude marriage rate	Persons marrying per 10,000 unmarried persons age 15+	Persons marrying per 10,000 unmarried persons age 15–49	Crude divorce rate	Divorces per 100 marriages	Divorces per 10,000 married persons	Year
..	..	..	..	..	..	..	..	..	..	1850
..	..	..	..	..	..	..	..	..	..	1851
..	..	..	..	..	..	..	..	..	..	1852
..	..	..	..	..	..	..	..	..	..	1853
..	..	..	..	..	..	..	..	..	..	1854
..	..	..	..	..	..	..	..	..	..	1855
..	..	..	..	..	..	..	..	..	..	1856
..	..	..	..	..	..	..	..	..	..	1857
..	..	..	..	..	..	..	..	..	..	1858
..	..	..	..	..	..	..	..	..	..	1859
..	..	..	..	..	..	..	..	..	..	1860
..	..	..	..	..	..	..	..	..	..	1861
..	..	..	..	..	..	..	..	..	..	1862
..	..	..	..	..	..	..	..	..	..	1863
16.5	..	..	..	4.9	259	326	..	..	..	1864
16.6	..	..	..	5.5	296	373	..	..	..	1865
16.8	..	..	..	5.4	295	374	..	..	..	1866
17.0	..	..	..	5.4	295	375	..	..	..	1867
15.8	..	..	..	5.1	278	355	..	..	..	1868
16.4	..	..	..	5.0	277	355	..	..	..	1869
16.7	..	..	..	5.3	295	380	..	..	..	1870
16.4	..	..	..	5.4	301	390	..	..	..	1871
18.1	..	..	..	5.0	279	361	..	..	..	1872
18.3	..	..	..	4.8	267	345	..	..	..	1873
17.4	..	..	..	4.6	255	328	..	..	..	1874
18.6	..	..	..	4.5	249	320	..	..	..	1875
17.5	..	..	..	5.0	273	350	..	..	..	1876
17.7	..	..	..	4.7	253	324	..	..	..	1877
18.9	..	..	..	4.8	258	330	..	..	..	1878
20.0	..	..	..	4.4	237	302	..	..	..	1879
19.8	..	..	..	3.9	209	266	..	..	..	1880
17.5	..	..	..	4.2	225	285	..	..	..	1881
17.3	..	..	..	4.3	227	288	..	..	..	1882
19.2	..	..	..	4.3	222	281	..	..	..	1883
17.5	..	..	..	4.5	234	297	..	..	..	1884
18.4	..	..	..	4.3	220	279	..	..	..	1885
17.8	..	..	..	4.2	213	270	..	..	..	1886
18.2	..	..	..	4.3	216	274	..	..	..	1887
17.9	..	..	..	4.2	209	264	..	..	..	1888
17.4	..	..	..	4.5	223	283	..	..	..	1889
18.2	..	..	..	4.5	218	276	..	..	..	1890
18.4	..	..	..	4.6	223	283	..	..	..	1891
19.4	..	..	..	4.6	224	284	..	..	..	1892
18.0	..	..	..	4.7	226	287	..	..	..	1893
18.2	..	..	..	4.7	225	285	..	..	..	1894
18.5	..	..	..	5.1	241	305	..	..	..	1895
16.7		..	..	5.1	241	304	..	..	..	1896
18.5		..	..	5.1	238	301	..	..	..	1897

continued

APPENDIX TABLE IRL.4 Demographic developments 1850–1945 (continued)

Year	Mid-year population	Natural population growth rate	Population growth rate	Net migration rate	Crude birth rate	Legitimate births per 10,000 married women age 15–44	Illegitimate births per 10,000 unmarried women age 15–44	Illeg. births per 100 leg. births
1898	4,518,000	5.1	-2.7	-7.8	23.4	2,972	41	2.8
1899	4,502,000	5.4	-3.6	-8.9	23.1	2,942	38	2.7
1900	4,469,000	3.1	-7.4	-10.5	22.7	2,890	38	2.7
1901	4,447,000	4.9	-4.9	-9.9	22.7	2,892	37	2.6
1902	4,435,000	5.5	-2.7	-8.2	23.0	2,924	39	2.7
1903	4,418,000	5.5	-3.8	-9.4	23.0	2,931	38	2.6
1904	4,408,000	5.5	-2.3	-7.8	23.5	2,997	38	2.6
1905	4,399,000	6.3	-2.0	-8.3	23.4	2,971	40	2.7
1906	4,398,000	6.6	-0.2	-6.8	23.5	2,992	40	2.7
1907	4,388,000	5.6	-2.3	-7.8	23.2	2,947	38	2.5
1908	4,385,000	5.7	-0.7	-6.4	23.3	2,955	39	2.6
1909	4,387,000	6.3	0.5	-5.9	23.4	2,972	43	2.8
1910	4,385,000	6.2	-0.5	-6.6	23.3	2,943	45	2.9
1911	4,381,000	6.7	-0.9	-7.6	23.2	2,942	44	2.8
1912	4,368,000	6.6	-3.0	-9.6	23.1	2,923	44	2.9
1913	4,346,000	5.8	-5.1	-10.9	23.0	2,911	45	2.9
1914	4,334,000	6.3	-2.8	-9.1	22.8	..	..	3.0
1915	4,278,000	4.5	-13.1	-17.6	22.3	..	..	3.2
1916	4,273,000	4.7	-1.2	-5.9	21.4	..	..	3.1
1917	4,273,000	3.2	0.0	-3.2	20.2	..	..	3.2
1918	4,280,000	2.0	1.6	-0.4	20.4	..	..	3.2
1919	4,352,000	2.5	16.5	14.1	20.5	2,680	48	3.4
1920	4,361,000	7.6	2.1	-5.5	22.8	2,851	55	3.4
1921	4,354,000	6.2	-1.6	-7.8	20.8	2,726	48	3.3
Republic of Ireland								
1922	3,022,000	4.7	..	..	19.5	..	..	..
1923	3,014,000	6.5	-2.7	-9.1	20.5	..	..	..
1924	3,005,000	6.1	-3.0	-9.1	21.1	..	..	..
1925	2,985,000	6.2	-6.7	-12.9	20.8	2,742	41	2.8
1926	2,971,000	6.5	-4.7	-11.3	20.6	2,712	42	2.9
1927	2,957,000	5.5	-4.7	-10.3	20.3	2,675	43	3.0
1928	2,944,000	5.9	-4.4	-10.3	20.1	2,645	44	3.1
1929	2,937,000	5.2	-2.4	-7.6	19.8	2,610	46	3.3
1930	2,927,000	5.7	-3.4	-9.1	19.9	2,622	47	3.3
1931	2,933,000	4.8	2.0	-2.8	19.5	2,559	48	3.5
1932	2,949,000	4.5	5.4	0.9	19.1	2,511	45	3.3
1933	2,962,000	5.7	4.4	-1.3	19.4	2,546	50	3.6
1934	2,971,000	6.3	3.0	-3.3	19.5	2,562	51	3.6
1935	2,971,000	5.6	0.0	-5.6	19.6	2,583	49	3.5
1936	2,967,000	5.2	-1.3	-6.6	19.6	2,584	48	3.4
1937	2,948,000	3.9	-6.4	-10.3	19.2	2,530	46	3.3
1938	2,937,000	5.7	-3.7	-9.5	19.4	2,560	48	3.4
1939	2,934,000	4.9	-1.0	-5.9	19.1	2,528	45	3.3
1940	2,958,000	5.0	8.1	3.1	19.1	..	..	3.3
1941	2,993,000	4.3	11.7	7.4	19.0	..	..	3.6
1942	2,963,000	8.3	-10.1	-18.4	22.3	..	..	3.8
1943	2,946,000	7.1	-5.8	-12.9	21.9	..	..	4.0
1944	2,944,000	6.9	-0.7	-7.6	22.2	..	..	4.1
1945	2,952,000	8.2	2.7	-5.5	22.7	..	..	4.1

APPENDIX TABLE IRL.4 Demographic developments 1850–1945 (continued)

Crude death rate	Infant mortality rate	Stillbirth rate	Infant mortality and stillbirth rate	Crude marriage rate	Persons marrying per 10,000 unmarried persons age 15+	Persons marrying per 10,000 unmarried persons age 15–49	Crude divorce rate	Divorces per 100 marriages	Divorces per 10,000 married persons	Year
18.2	..	..	..	5.0	234	296	..	..	..	1898
17.7	..	..	..	5.0	231	292	..	..	..	1899
19.6	..	..	..	4.8	221	279	..	..	..	1900
17.8	..	..	..	5.1	234	296	..	..	..	1901
17.5	..	..	..	5.2	238	302	..	..	..	1902
17.5	..	..	..	5.2	240	305	..	..	..	1903
18.0	..	..	..	5.2	241	307	..	..	..	1904
17.1	..	..	..	5.3	242	310	..	..	..	1905
16.9	..	..	..	5.2	238	306	..	..	..	1906
17.6	..	..	..	5.1	237	305	..	..	..	1907
17.5	..	..	..	5.2	239	309	..	..	..	1908
17.1	..	..	..	5.2	239	310	..	..	..	1909
17.1	..	..	..	5.0	233	303	..	..	..	1910
16.5	..	..	..	5.4	248	324	..	..	..	1911
16.5	..	..	..	5.3	247	324	..	..	..	1912
17.2	..	..	..	5.1	237	312	..	..	..	1913
16.5	..	..	..	5.5	..	..	..	..	..	1914
17.8	..	..	..	5.6	..	..	..	..	..	1915
16.7	..	..	..	5.2	..	..	..	..	..	1916
17.0	..	..	..	4.9	..	..	..	..	..	1917
18.4	..	..	..	5.3	..	..	..	..	..	1918
18.1	..	..	..	6.2	294	388	..	..	..	1919
15.3	..	..	..	6.2	289	382	..	..	..	1920
14.7	..	..	..	5.3	250	331	..	..	..	1921
Republic of Ireland										
14.7	..	..	..	5.0	235	301	..	..	..	1922
14.0	..	..	..	5.2	242	322	..	..	..	1923
15.0	..	..	..	4.9	230	306	..	..	..	1924
14.6	..	..	..	4.6	215	287	..	..	..	1925
14.0	..	..	..	4.6	212	283	..	..	..	1926
14.8	..	..	..	4.5	210	281	..	..	..	1927
14.2	..	..	..	4.7	215	288	..	..	..	1928
14.6	..	..	..	4.6	214	286	..	..	..	1929
14.2	..	..	..	4.7	214	288	..	..	..	1930
14.6	..	..	..	4.5	206	277	..	..	..	1931
14.6	..	..	..	4.4	203	273	..	..	..	1932
13.7	..	..	..	4.7	216	292	..	..	..	1933
13.2	..	..	..	4.8	219	296	..	..	..	1934
14.0	..	..	..	4.8	220	298	..	..	..	1935
14.4	..	..	..	5.0	226	307	..	..	..	1936
15.3	..	..	..	5.0	228	309	..	..	..	1937
13.6	..	..	..	5.1	230	313	..	..	..	1938
14.2	..	..	..	5.2	234	319	..	..	..	1939
14.2	..	..	..	5.1	..	..	..	..	..	1940
14.6	..	..	..	5.0	..	..	..	..	..	1941
14.1	..	..	..	5.9	..	..	..	..	..	1942
14.8	..	..	..	5.9	..	..	..	..	..	1943
15.3	..	..	..	5.7	..	..	..	..	..	1944
14.5	..	..	..	5.9	..	..	..	..	..	1945

APPENDIX TABLE IRL.5 Life expectancy by age 1900/02–1940/42[1] (in years)

Age	0	10	20	30	40	50	60	70	80
				Males					
1900–1902	49.3	50.5	42.1	31.0[2]	23.8[3]	16.9[4]	10.8[5]	5.8[6]	..
1910–1912	53.6	53.7	45.0	33.5[2]	25.9[3]	18.9[4]	13.0[5]	8.0[6]	..
1925–1927	57.37	55.20	46.40	38.39	30.43	22.67	15.75	10.20	5.81
1935–1937	58.20	55.75	46.83	38.53	30.26	22.41	15.46	9.99	6.00
1940–1942	59.10	56.25	47.24	38.92	30.58	22.53	15.37	9.60	5.68
				Females					
1900–1902	49.6	50.4	42.2	30.9[2]	23.7[3]	16.7[4]	10.6[5]	5.9[6]	..
1910–1912	54.1	53.7	45.4	33.8[2]	26.4[3]	19.2[4]	13.4[5]	8.2[6]	..
1925–1927	57.93	54.92	46.36	38.60	30.83	23.19	16.36	10.72	6.47
1935–1937	59.62	56.10	47.26	39.22	31.18	23.28	16.17	10.59	6.46
1940–1942	61.02	56.94	48.04	39.89	31.63	23.54	16.31	10.42	6.39

Notes: [1] 1900/02–1910/12 whole island; 1925/27–1940/42 Irish Republic. [2] 30–40. [3] 40–50. [4] 50–60. [5] 60–70. [6] 70–80.

APPENDIX TABLE IRL.6A Households by type 1821–1946[1] (absolute and per cent)

Census year	Household types and members									
	Total households	Private households	Family households	One-person households	Institutional households	Total household members	Private household members	Family household members	One-person household members	Institutional household members
Absolute										
1821	..	1,312,032	..	..	..	..	6,801,827	..	..	..
1831	..	1,385,066	..	..	..	..	7,767,401	..	..	..
1841	..	1,472,787	..	..	..	..	8,175,124	..	..	..
1851	..	1,204,319	..	..	..	..	6,552,385	..	..	..
1861	..	1,128,300	..	..	..	..	5,798,967	..	..	..
1871	..	1,067,598	..	..	..	..	5,412,377	..	..	..
1881	..	995,074	..	..	..	..	5,174,836	..	..	..
1891	..	932,113	..	..	..	..	4,701,750	..	..	..
1901	910,952	910,256	..	..	696	4,584,345	4,458,775	..	..	125,570
1911	..	910,748	..	..	..	..	4,390,219	..	..	..
1926	..	622,678	571,141	51,537	..	..	2,790,581	2,739,044	51,537	..
1936	..	647,362	586,792	60,570	..	..	2,791,047	2,730,477	60,570	..
1946	..	662,654	593,773	68,881	..	..	2,755,490	2,686,609	68,881	..
Per cent										
1901	100.00	99.92	..	..	0.08	100.00	97.26	..	..	2.74
1911	..	..	..	..	..	..	..	..	..	..
1926	..	100.00	91.72	8.28	..	..	100.00	98.15	1.85	..
1936	..	100.00	90.64	9.36	..	..	100.00	97.83	2.17	..
1946	..	100.00	89.61	10.39	..	..	100.00	97.50	2.50	..

Note: [1] 1821–1911 whole island; 1926–1946 Irish Republic.

APPENDIX TABLE IRL.6B Households by size and members 1926–1946 (absolute figures)

Census year	Private households total	Households by number of members											
		1 person	2 persons	3 persons	4 persons	5 persons	6 persons	7 persons	8 persons	9 persons	10 persons	11 persons	12+ persons
		Households											
1926	622,678	51,537	98,437	102,664	96,241	82,324	65,310	48,418	33,297	21,089	13,190	5,491	4,680
1936	647,362	60,570	110,988	111,509	100,118	82,910	62,764	45,793	30,962	19,669	12,230	5,350	4,499
1946	662,654	68,881	118,738	116,401	103,423	84,437	62,955	44,028	28,503	17,970	8,260	4,779	4,279
		Persons											
1926	2,790,581	51,537	196,874	307,992	384,964	411,620	391,860	338,926	266,376	189,801	131,900	60,401	58,330
1936	2,791,047	60,570	221,976	334,527	400,472	414,550	376,584	320,551	247,696	177,021	122,300	58,850	55,950
1946	2,755,490	68,881	237,476	349,203	413,692	422,185	377,730	308,196	228,024	161,730	82,600	52,569	53,204

APPENDIX TABLE IRL.6C Households by size and members 1926–1946 (per cent)

Census year	Private households total	Households by number of members											
		1 person	2 persons	3 persons	4 persons	5 persons	6 persons	7 persons	8 persons	9 persons	10 persons	11 persons	12+ persons
		Households											
1926	100.00	8.28	15.81	16.49	15.46	13.22	10.49	7.78	5.35	3.39	2.12	0.88	0.75
1936	100.00	9.36	17.14	17.23	15.47	12.81	9.70	7.07	4.78	3.04	1.89	0.83	0.69
1946	100.00	10.39	17.92	17.57	15.61	12.74	9.50	6.64	4.30	2.71	1.25	0.72	0.65
		Persons											
1926	100.00	1.85	7.05	11.04	13.80	14.75	14.04	12.15	9.55	6.80	4.73	2.16	2.09
1936	100.00	2.17	7.95	11.99	14.35	14.85	13.49	11.48	8.87	6.34	4.38	2.11	2.00
1946	100.00	2.50	8.62	12.67	15.01	15.32	13.71	11.18	8.28	5.87	3.00	1.91	1.93

APPENDIX TABLE IRL.6D Household
indicators 1821–1946

Census year	Household indicators		
	Mean private household size	Mean family household size	Mean institutional household size
1821	5.18	..	..
1831	5.61	..	..
1841	5.55	..	..
1851	5.44	..	..
1861	5.14	..	..
1871	5.07	..	..
1881	5.20	..	..
1891	5.04	..	..
1901	4.90	..	180.42
1911	4.82	..	..
1926	4.48	4.80	..
1936	4.31	4.65	..
1946	4,16	4,52	..

Note: [1] 1821–1911 whole island; 1926–1946 Irish
Republic.

APPENDIX TABLE IRL.6E Household composition 1851–1911 (absolute and per cent)

Census year	Males				Heads of families and their children	Females			Total number of males and females
	Heads of families and their children	Visitors	Servants	Total number of males		Visitors	Servants	Total number of females	
					Absolute				
1851	2.548.622	406.284	235.724	3.190.630	2.624.439	509.257	228.059	3.361.755	6.552.385
1881	2.070.028	365.278	97.971	2.533.277	2.060.068	428.794	152.697	2.641.559	5.174.836
1891	1.973.027	258.594	87.332	2.318.953	1.992.543	263.449	129.805	2.385.797	4.704.750
1901	1.816.147	310.344	73.549	2.200.040	1.822.350	322.636	113.849	2.258.735	4.458.775
1911	1.761.201	361.065	69.782	2.192.048	1.705.160	390.105	102.906	2.198.171	4.390.219
					Per cent				
1851	38,90	6,20	3,60	48,69	40,05	7,77	3,48	51,31	100,00
1881	40,00	7,06	1,89	48,95	39,81	8,29	2,95	51,05	100,00
1891	41,94	5,50	1,86	49,29	42,35	5,60	2,76	50,71	100,00
1901	40,73	6,96	1,65	49,34	40,87	7,24	2,55	50,66	100,00
1911	40,12	8,22	1,59	49,93	38,84	8,89	2,34	50,07	100,00

APPENDIX TABLE IRL.7 Dates and nature of results on population structure households/families, and vital statistics

Topic	Intro-duction	Remarks
Population		
Population at census dates	1851	Earlier censuses were conducted in 1801, 1811, 1821, 1831 and 1841. The history of the Irish census from 1801 until independence is the same as for Great Britain (see chapter 21). 1850–1921: Ireland; 1922–: Republic of Ireland.
Population by age, sex and marital status	1861	1850–1921: Ireland; 1922–: Republic of Ireland.
Households and families		
Households (private families)		
Total households	1851	Households were for the first time expressly recorded in 1851: 1851: number of households. 1861: number of households. 1871: number of households. 1881: number of households. 1891: number of households. 1901: number of households. 1911: number of households. 1926, 1936, 1946: Housing census: households by size, institutional households. *Disaggregation*: by provinces and districts.
Households by size	1926, 1936, 1946	First time in the housing census of 1926: households by number of persons 1–12+. Repeated in 1936 and 1946.
Households by composition	–	
Households by profession of household head	–	
Families (families)		
Families by number of children	1946	First special investigation of the fertility of marriages in 1946.

continued

APPENDIX TABLE IRL.7 Dates and nature of results on population structure, households/families, and vital statistics (continued)

Topic	Intro-duction	Remarks
Population movement		
Midyear population	1850	1850–1921: Ireland; 1922–: Republic of Ireland.
Births		
Live births	1864	1864–1921: Ireland; 1922–: Republic of Ireland.
Stillbirths	1960	Republic of Ireland.
Legitimate births	1864	1864–1921: Ireland; 1925–: Republic of Ireland.
Illegitimate births	1864	1864–1921: Ireland; 1925–: Republic of Ireland.
Deaths		
Total deaths	1864	1864–1921: Ireland; 1922–: Republic of Ireland.
Infants (under 1 year)	1964	Republic of Ireland.
Marriages		
Total marriages	1850	1850–1921: Ireland; 1922–: Republic of Ireland.
Divorces and separations		
Total divorces	–	No divorce law introduced.
Legal separations	–	

APPENDIX FIGURE IRL.8 Population by age, sex and marital status, Ireland 1861, 1926 and 1936 (per 10,000 of total population)

Ireland, 1861

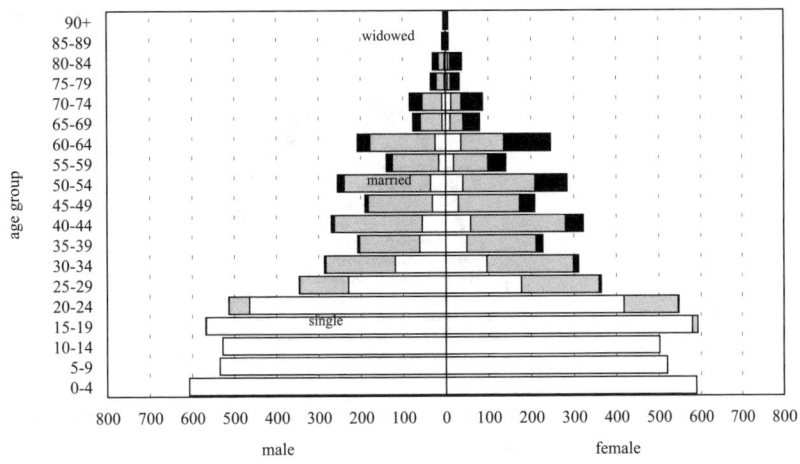

Ireland, 1926

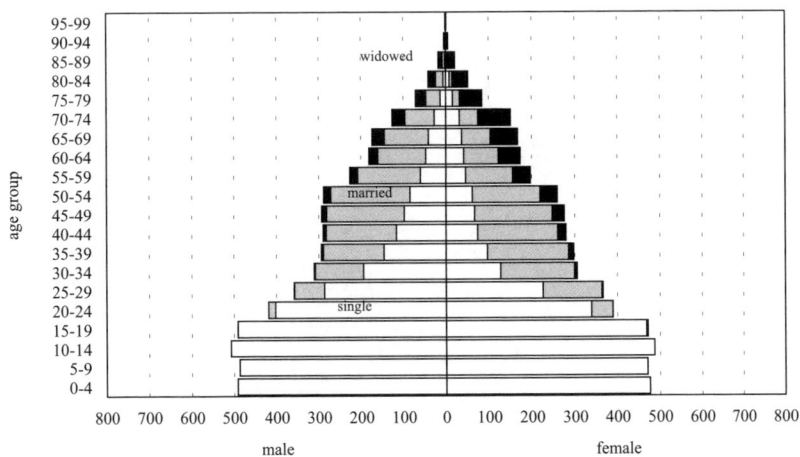

APPENDIX FIGURE IRL.8 Population by age, sex and marital status, Ireland 1861, 1926 and 1936 (per 10,000 of total population) (continued)

Ireland, 1936

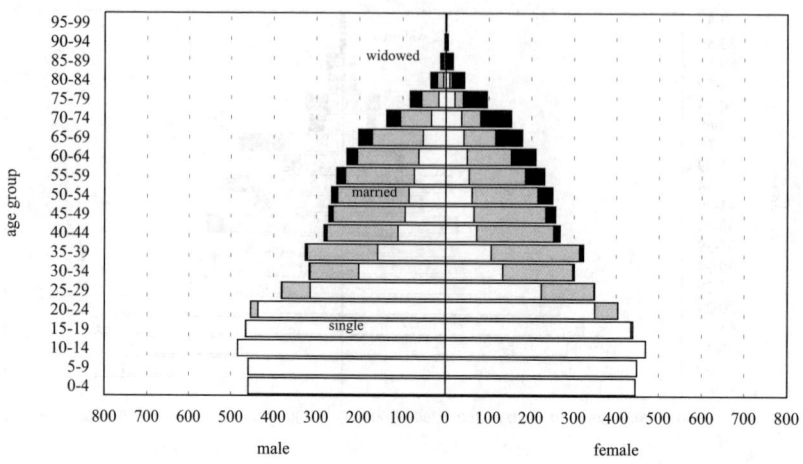

12

Italy

Italy was late in becoming a nation-state. Since the Middle Ages it was a conglomerate of different territories and city-states (republics), mainly under foreign powers, and the existence of the Papal States hindered the development of a national state. Up to the end of the eighteenth century the territories making up Italy consolidated, becoming larger and fewer in number. The main territories before the Napoleonic wars were the Republic of Venice, the Kingdom of the Two Sicilies, the Papal States, Savoy, and the territories of Milan and Tuscany. The Napoleonic wars brought an end to several of these states: Venice was conquered, and Napoleon made his brother king of Italy. With the French defeat at Waterloo and the subsequent Congress of Vienna the older territories were more or less restored and Spain, France, and Austria regained their influence. Austria managed to gain possession of Venice and Milan, and thus the main parts of northern Italy.

The movement for unification (Risorgimento) began in the first half of the nineteenth century just after the Congress of Vienna; it was part of a European movement, as countries such as Serbia, Greece, and Belgium gained their independence during the 1820s and 1830s while others (like Poland) tried but failed. In Italy, as in Germany, the impulse to unification came from the north, which was more advanced in economic, social, cultural, and political terms. Under Count Camillo Cavour's leadership, the Kingdom of Sardinia and the House of Savoy in Turin started the war for unification in 1859–60 with the support of Napoleon III. Most of the peninsula was unified, and the Kingdom of Italy was proclaimed on 14 March 1861. At that time the Veneto was still under Habsburg rule and the Papal States were still independent. The second step of unification came in 1866, when Italy won the Veneto in the war against Austria (in alliance with Prussia, which defeated Austria at Königgrätz). Finally, as a result of the war against the Holy See, Italy acquired the Papal States, reducing the papal possessions to Vatican City; it and San Marino continue to be the only remaining enclaves in Italy. This territory did not change until World War I when the Allied powers offered Italy territorial gains to fight on their side, which Italy accepted, entering the war in 1915. Austria was defeated and Trentino-Alto Adige was ceded to Italy. In the same way, Slovene and Croat territories (the Istrian Peninsula, among others) were annexed from Yugoslavia.

But nationalist aspirations went much further: the Fascist leader Benito Mussolini seized power in the crisis of 1922, and his expansionist regime sought to revive the idea of the Mediterranean as the 'mare nostrum'. Several steps were made in this direction: in 1922 the nationalist Gabriele D'Annunzio occupied Fiume/Rijeka, and in 1923 the Dodecanese Islands were taken from the defeated Ottoman Empire (Treaty of Lausanne). In 1929 Mussolini concluded the Lateran Treaty with the

Holy See: Vatican City was established as an independent state and Italy was affirmed as a catholic state. In 1935 Mussolini tried to enlarge the colonial empire on the African continent by conquering Ethiopia, after Giolotti had earlier taken Libya from the Ottoman Empire during the Italo-Turkish War of 1911–12.

At the start of World War II in 1939 Italy attacked and occupied Albania; it also attacked Greece, but was unable to occupy it without German help. In 1940 Italian troops occupied the French city of Menton. Mussolini's regime came to an end with the landing of the Allied forces on Sicily and the subsequent capitulation of the Italian troops on 8 September 1943. Italy declared war on Germany; Mussolini was arrested but later freed by German occupying troops. After the war, Italy had to give back most of the territory gained after World War I and during the 1920s and 1930s: the Dodecanese Islands were returned to Greece in 1947, and the Yugoslav territories, with the exception of Trieste, were returned to Yugoslavia. The African colonies were decolonized and later became independent states, but Italy kept the mostly German-speaking territory of South Tyrol (Seidlmayer, 1989; Procacci, 1989; Zamagni, 1993; Nanetti, 1988).

REGIONAL POPULATION STRUCTURE

Italy as a nation-state has existed only since the territories of the Italian peninsula were unified in 1861. Already when the Romans were conquering the different territories on the 'boot' of Italy, from Magna Graecia in the south, to the Etruscan lands and Gallia Cisalpina in the north, the country had no ethnic, cultural, or linguistic unity. The fall of the Roman Empire only aggravated the situation: new tribes invaded the country and brought with them new blood, culture, religion, and languages. It was not until the Middle Ages that a sort of Italian lingua franca developed, mainly through literature, and one common religion, Roman Catholicism, took hold with the decline of the Byzantine (and therefore Orthodox) influence in Italy. The formation of early states in the Middle Ages, partly in the form of city-states, partly as larger territories, split Italy into a multitude of different parts. For centuries different foreign powers, such as the German emperor, France, and Spain, exerted their influence. This system in principle came to an end with the Napoleonic era. For the first time there were attempts at unification. During the whole first half of the nineteenth century the idea of unification never diminished; it grew stronger towards the middle of the century and finally succeeded in 1861.

The new nation-state however inherited the different cultures and traditions of the older Italian states, and this heterogeneity still persists today. To some degree the territorial dimension has even grown in importance due to the shift of the economic centre of gravity to the north and north-west while the south has become increasingly peripheral. This situation was not as extreme when the country was still predominantly agricultural. Italy is probably the European country where geography is most important, due to its divided nature: part Mediterranean and part Continental.

Population density in 1861 was 85.5 inhabitants per square kilometre; it increased to 140.4 in 1936. Given the mountainous surface of Italy, population density must be considered high during the whole period. There are strong regional differences in population density. The regions of the city-states in the north-west and north-east (Liguria, Piedmont, Lombardy, Emilia-Romagna) were highly urbanized and densely settled already in 1871, when most of the central and southern regions and the islands were sparsely populated. Population growth was large for most regions, although in some regions population density did not change greatly or at all: it remained stable in Basilicata and increased only slightly in Sardinia and Umbria.

Italy's great regional heterogeneity was therefore not alleviated by population growth, but rather aggravated, at least until the late 1930s. The growing regional differences in population structure and demography are related to differences in the pace of industrialization and urbanization, which started in the north and north-west and advanced more quickly in these regions. Levels of literacy and education also rose earlier in these parts of the country. Labour migration from the south to the north caused the loss of younger and more innovative people, therefore reinforcing conservatism in the south. The significance of these factors for population structure and population growth cannot be estimated precisely, but they are assumed to have had an impact (cf. Livi-Bacci, 1977).

POPULATION GROWTH

The growth of the Italian population since unification in 1861 was high in absolute terms, but rather low in terms of growth rates. In 1861 the population was 21,777,000 inhabitants (census boundaries). In 1936 it was 42,519,000, thus nearly doubling in 75 years. But compared with other European countries, the rate of growth was not very high, never exceeding nine per thousand and usually remaining between six and eight per thousand inhabitants. In Figure I.1 we can also see the heavy negative impact of World War I on natural population growth, when the total population declined, as well as the decline in natural population growth during World War II.

One of the factors for this low population increase was high emigration. The net migration rate was constantly negative from the 1860s to the 1940s. The strongest population losses due to emigration were in the 1890s, 1900s, 1920s, and 1930s. From 1861 to 1971 about 26 million Italians emigrated (Livi-Bacci, 1977).

THE FIRST DEMOGRAPHIC TRANSITION

The demographic transition in Italy can only reasonably be studied since unification in 1861 and the introduction of a national statistical system, the first population census of 1861 and a system of vital statistics. The different states in existence before 1861 had their own statistical registration systems, but these statistics differ with regard to coverage, nature, and probably validity (cf. Livi-Bacci, 1977; Beloch, 1937, 1961, 1965 concerning population history before unification).

The available data for the first half of the nineteenth century and earlier suggest that up to the 1860s birth and death rates did not decline substantially; therefore, the entire demographic transition has occurred in the period since unification. Compared with countries such as France or England, Italy must be considered a latecomer in the demographic transition, as its birth rate only started to decline substantially in the 1890s. The death rate began to decline one to two decades earlier, thus the Italian case fits the model of the birth rate adapting to the death rate (Figure I.2).

Until World War I both the birth rate and the death rate show a rather smooth pattern without major fluctuations. The natural population surplus was high and even growing until 1914. Italy's participation in World War I greatly disturbed the demographic development, causing a major decline in the birth rate and a very sharp increase in the death rate. But interestingly, and unlike other countries during the

Figure I.1 Population growth and net migration 1862-1945

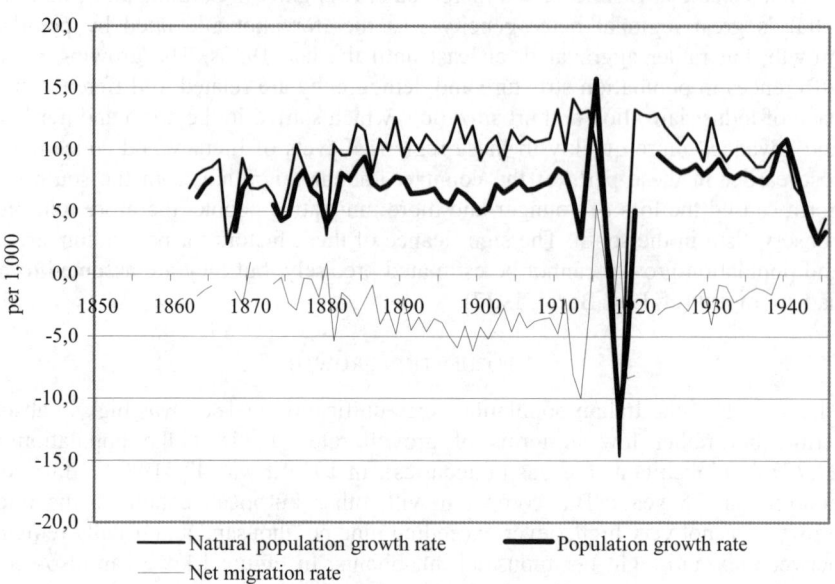

Figure I.2 First demographic transition 1862-1945

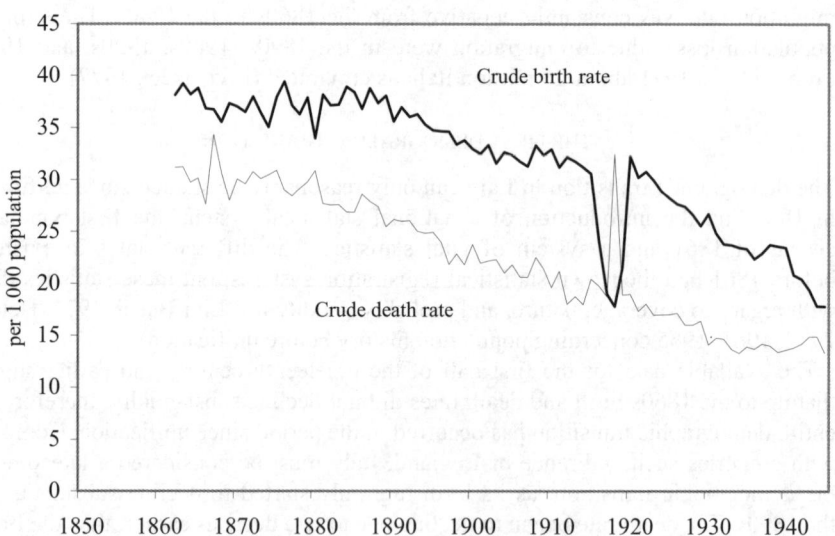

1920s and 1930s, it underwent no 'demographic crisis' in the sense of a strong fertility decline. The mortality rate continued to decline, but the birth rate remained at a rather high level. This pattern appeared again during World War II, which caused a drop in births and a loss of population of all ages as well. After 1945 the birth rate recovered, while the death rate continued to decline. Until the 1980s fertility was very high, as was natural population increase. In the 1980s a massive fertility decline set in, bringing the birth rate down to just above the death rate. Natural population increase since the 1990s has been only marginal. Italy clearly conforms to the pattern of the second demographic transition with an increase in the birth rate in the 1960s.

While mortality was rather high and above the European average from the nineteenth century until mid-twentieth century, it fell below the European average in the post-World War II period. High infant mortality contributed to the high death rate up to 1945, but a reduction of infant mortality and high emigration contributed to a low mortality afterwards.

When compared with the European demographic transition, during the nineteenth and first half of the twentieth century Italy had high and disproportional fertility, counterbalanced by high and above average mortality. The latter was mainly due to high infant mortality.

Italy's demographic history cannot be discussed without reference to the large regional differences in the country. In the nineteenth century there were some rather stable structural patterns: by tendency, fertility was higher in the south than in the north, it was lower among leading social strata such as the nobility, and it was lower in cities than in villages. The economic development of the country after unification, mainly occuring in the north-west and centre, enhanced regional differences in fertility. While fertility in the north dropped significantly, it declined only slightly in the south, causing divergent population developments and leading to massive internal migration and emigration. The mortality rate in principle reveals the same pattern as the birth rate: a faster decline in the north than the south. Thus, the effect of the widening gap between the north and the south during the transition has been the relatively high fertility level in the middle phase of the transition, the 1920s and 1930s (cf. Livi-Bacci, 1977).

MORTALITY AND LIFE EXPECTANCY

The infant mortality rate is defined as deaths of children aged under one year per 1,000 live births. Italy belongs to the group of Mediterranean countries with traditionally rather high infant mortality. It clusters with Spain and Greece, but also with Czechoslovakia and Austria. In 1901–5 the rate was 167, which was only exceeded by Spain (172), Germany (199), Austria (216), Hungary (213), and Czechoslovakia (225) (Masuy-Stroobant, 1997).

Looking a bit further back in history, in the 1880s Italy had an infant mortality rate similar to continental countries such as Switzerland and The Netherlands, with around 200 infant deaths per 1,000 live births. The main difference to these two countries is that they were able to reduce infant mortality significantly up to World War II, while Italy fell behind. Thus, up to World War II, the gap between Italy and the other two countries widened. It was only after 1945 that Italy could start to reduce its distance to more developed countries, but the gap remained until the 1980s (Van de Walle, 1986).

Pinnelli and Mancini (1997) also describe a picture of rather high infant mortality in the second half of the nineteenth century and steadily but slowly declining infant mortality. They also show that child mortality at various ages was rather high, with the same pattern of continuous but slow decline until the 1940s. Another study by Del Panta (1997) summarizes available studies and data for the old Italian states, to some extent equivalent to the modern regions, before 1861. Already in the first half of the nineteenth century there were enormous differences in infant mortality. Interestingly, southern Italy (Apulia, Calabria) had lower infant mortality rates at that time than the Veneto and Lombardy in the north. Yet longer time series from historical demographic studies for some regions (Tuscany, localities of the Veneto) show an increase in infant mortality from the seventeenth to the late eighteenth century and a declining trend only since the first decades of the nineteenth century. Thus, the regionally rather divergent trends in Italy largely explain the behaviour of the national aggregate infant mortality rate. The slow decline in infant mortality in Italy since the 1880s is due among other things to the growing divergence in infant mortality between the north and the south, as the north overtook the south in reducing infant mortality. The relative backwardness of the south continued to increase in the twentieth century, thus contributing to the high national figures for infant mortality (Figure I.3).

Life expectancy was rather low when compared with more advanced countries of the time such as Sweden. In 1876/87 life expectancy of new-born boys was 35.1 years in Italy and 45.3 in Sweden (1871/80), a difference of ten years (Figure I.4). For adults, life chances were much better than for infants, but did not match the Swedish level either. Life expectancy at birth was therefore extremely low, or, in other words, infant mortality was very high (see above). Life expectancy at birth still lagged in the 1930s, when the advantage of Swedish boys at birth was still ten years, the same as 80 years before. Nor had life expectancy at higher ages converged with the Swedish figures by the 1930s. Up to World War II Italy was unable to improve the health status of its population fast enough to catch up with the more advanced countries of Europe; the distances remained stable.

Given the low life expectancy, there were only minor sex differences in life expectancy in favour of females, though these differences increased slightly from the 1870s to the 1930s.

FERTILITY AND LEGITIMACY

Although age at marriage was average until 1945 and high afterwards, and celibacy was high, illegitimate fertility was low and below the European average. Low illegitimate fertility is a nearly constant pattern of Italian fertility during the last 150 years, and underlines the traditional concept of marriage in Italian society. It was only from the 1870s to the 1890s that illegitimate fertility in Italy was high with an increasing tendency and above the European average. But with the general fertility decline in Italy since the 1890s illegitimate fertility declined very strongly until World War I. During the inter-war period the low level of illegitimate fertility elsewhere in Europe made Italian illegitimate fertility appear relatively high. But the largest difference to the European illegitimate fertility rate can be seen during the post-war period, when Italian illegitimate fertility remained more or less constant at a very low level. Italy did not participate in the rise in out-of-wedlock births since

Figure I.3 Infant mortality 1863-1945

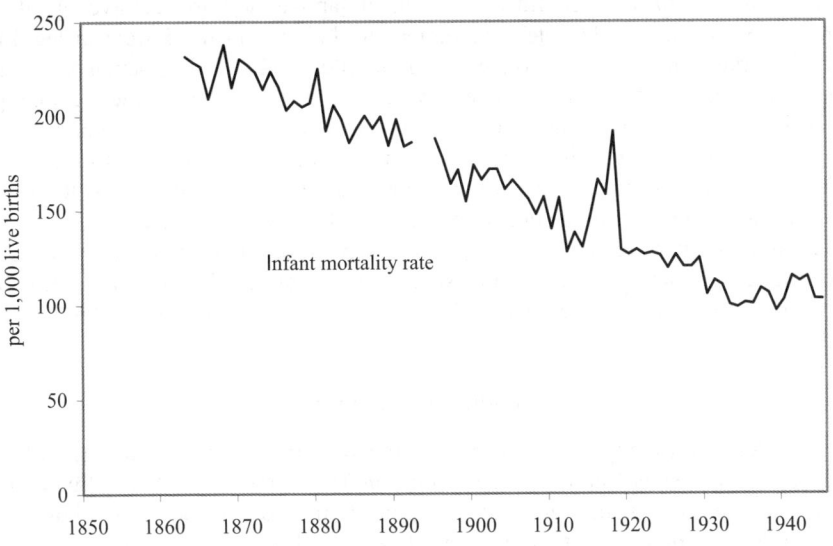

Figure I.4 Life expectancy 1876/87-1935/37

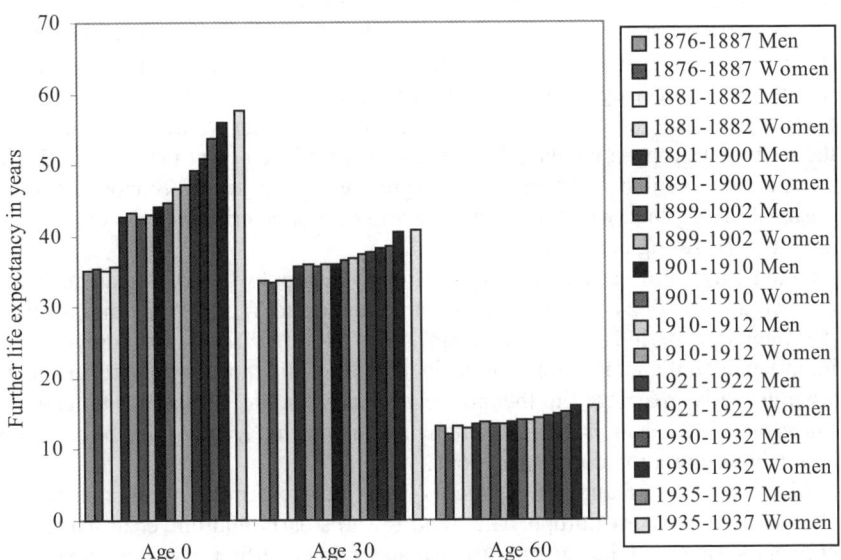

the 1980s, therefore marriage has not been deinstitutionalized to the same degree as in Western and Northern Europe (Figure I.5).

Legitimate fertility, by contrast, was high and above the European average already in the 1870s. During the inter-war period the Italian and the European legitimate fertility rates diverged, to converge again after 1945. This phenomenon again underlines how Italy's demographic pattern in the middle of the demographic transition process—as we have seen above—differs from the European pattern, with a rather high fertility still in the inter-war period. Legitimate fertility came very close to the European average in the 1960s and 1970s; since the 1980s it has been below the European average due to the very low Italian fertility rate.

To sum up, marriage in Italy has not been deinstitutionalized, at least with regard to the legitimate or illegitimate status of children. Children are still born overwhelmingly within wedlock, although people marry and have children later in life.

MARRIAGE AND DIVORCE

Italy belongs to the region of Europe with the Western European marriage pattern of *late age at marriage* and a *high celibacy rate*. But along with other Latin countries such as Spain, Portugal, France, and Belgium (with a dominant Latin culture), Italy constitutes a type different from the north-western European and continental types. Italy's situation is furthermore complicated by its strong internal heterogeneity.

Age at marriage already in the nineteenth century was lower than in continental and northern Europe. In 1890 40% of females aged 20–24 were already married, a proportion that even increased up to 1910. After World War I and until the 1940s age at marriage rose strongly: in the 1930s the proportion married declined to 30%. It was only after World War II with the marriage revolution that people again married at younger ages. But compared to other Western European countries, this tendency to early marriage was much weaker, and Italian women married later than the average European woman. The development of the age at marriage in the inter-war period is similar to Spain and is a symptom of the severe economic and social crises of these years, with the 1929–32 world economic crisis, unemployment, rising poverty, and strong emigration.

Italian men show a similar pattern. In 1890, about 10% of Italian males were married at age 20–24; this proportion increased up to World War I and declined in the inter-war period. The rise again after World War II was only of minor importance. Italian men are unique in that they did not participate in the trend towards early marriage in the post-war years, unlike northern and continental Europeans. This again is similar to Italian women. This feature must be attributed to high labour migration during the 1960s.

'Modernization of nuptiality patterns' was therefore much weaker in Italy than elsewhere in Western Europe. The trend towards early and universal marriage was not very strong, and the age of both men and women at first marriage remained well above the European average from the 1960s to the 1990s. This feature is also underlined by the low marriage rate during this period (see below).

Marriage intensity can be measured by the *marriage rate* and the *celibacy rate*. 'Intensity' means the availability of marriage, but at the same time the urgent need to remarry after widowhood ('remarriage need', Michael Mitterauer). A third component can be seen in the universality of marriage among the population. The

Figure I.5 Fertility and legitimacy 1871-1939

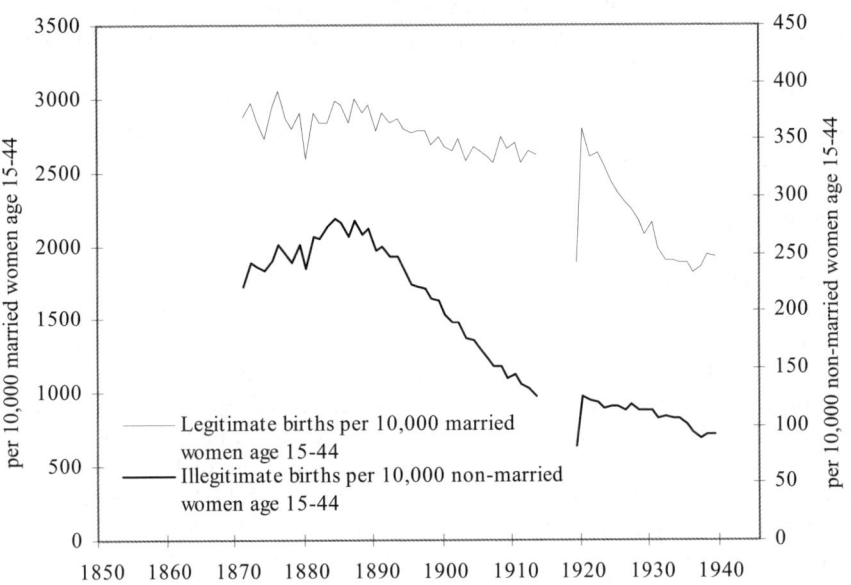

Figure I.6 Marriages 1871-1939

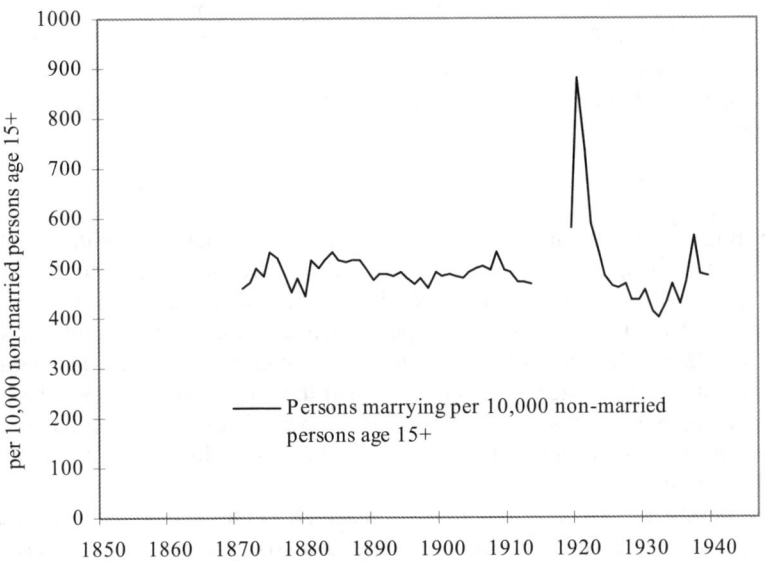

first rate refers to all marriages of unmarried persons aged 15+. In the second half of the nineteenth century this rate fluctuated around the European average (Figure I.6). In the inter-war period it was mostly below the European average, and was therefore in line with the high age at marriage during the general economic crisis. In the post-World War II period Italy had a low marriage propensity, and the marriage rate remained constantly below the European average. This is mainly the effect of the high age at marriage when in most other countries people married earlier. Since the 1970s the marriage rate has followed the European rate, although on a lower level.

Celibacy of women during the nineteenth century was high. In 1871 over 30% of women aged 45–54 had never married. While in the north-western country cluster the proportion of women remaining unmarried increased, in Italy there was a continuous though small decline up to the 1970s. The steep drop in the celibacy rate and therefore universal marriage came only for the cohorts of women born after World War I. Concerning the trend towards universal marriage, Italy is a latecomer where the nuclearization of marriage is not as strong as elsewhere.

In Italy, divorce was introduced with the divorce law of 1970, effective 1971; this law also introduced civil marriage. Divorce was permitted on the grounds of fault and marital breakdown, as evidenced by a legal separation of five years. Prior to 1971, only legal separation was permitted. Therefore, for the time before the 1970 divorce law, only figures on legal separations are available (since 1880).

Marital stability measured by the separation ratio or the divorce ratio (or the Crude Separation Rate or the Crude Divorce Rate) was higher than the European average during the last 150 years. The divorce rate since 1971 is well below the European average. The separation ratio from 1880 to the 1960s was also very low in comparative terms and only increased after the 1960s and 1970s (Figure I.6).

Divorce was still rather unpopular according to a public opinion survey in 1974 (Livi-Bacci, 1977: 214f.). Negative responses to divorce were more frequent in the south than in the north. This public sentiment reveals a clear pattern of traditionalism in Italian ideology and culture, which greatly shapes familial behaviour.

AGE, SEX, AND CIVIL STATUS

The age structure of Italy until World War I shows a pyramidal form, with a concave pattern for the youngest age groups, which became stronger during the last three decades before World War I (Appendix Figure I.8). There was no manifest birth decline until 1911; the youngest age group remained more or less stable in size. Only World War I led to a loss of births, which can be seen from the reduced proportions of the lowest age groups in 1921. During the 1920s and 1930s the birth rate recovered, but did not reach the pre-war level. Since 1921 the Italian age structure kept its bell-shaped form. In 1935 the loss of births during World War I was still apparent.

In Italy during the second half of the nineteenth century, more men remained single in higher age groups, resulting in a higher marriage age than for women. In contrast to most other European countries, in Italy the proportion of men remaining single was higher than that of women. This pattern was reversed only after World War I but then became even more accentuated until 1936. In 1871 and 1881 the proportions of widowed women were rather high, probably largely due to higher male mortality, but also to casualties during the unification wars of the 1860s. High proportions of widowhood reappeared during the inter-war period.

FAMILY AND HOUSEHOLD STRUCTURES

During the nineteenth and most of the twentieth century, Italian households were shaped by major structural differences, including the major regional differences between north and south, between the cities and rural areas, and between social classes. Household structures vary along all these lines and are not identical everywhere. But lack of detailed information on households allows us to give only a rather crude picture of the household patterns in the period from 1861 to 1931. In a long-term perspective we can only say something about the mean size of households and the main household types. The size distribution of households is given since 1901. Household composition is available only for one point in time, the year 1931.

The following presentation of household data refers to the national level and therefore conceals sometimes dramatic regional variations. Compared with other European countries, Italian households on average have been rather large: 4.86 family members per household in 1901, a number that even increased to 5.09 in 1911; in 1936 it was still at the high level of 4.62. National data prior to 1901 are only available for mean private household size, which was 4.68 in 1871. There are no national data for 1861 or for the first half of the nineteenth century, but mean household size can be estimated at well over 5.0 persons per household.

The decline of household size during the inter-war period was slow and late, as can also be seen from the proportion of small households from 1901 to 1936. The proportion of one-person households was 8.8% in 1901 and by 1936 had only increased to 9.1%. The proportion of households with two to five persons remained more or less stable from 1901 to 1936; only the proportion of households with six or more members declined. The proportion of the population living alone (as % of population) was also quite low: 1.95% in 1901 and 2.12% in 1936. Thus, the size of households did not decline to the same degree as in other European countries at that time. The causes for this phenomenon must be sought in Italy's comparatively high fertility at that time and the enduring existence of the extended family system.

The importance of the extended family can be still be shown for the year 1931, for which date household composition can be analysed. Households with only parents and relatives made up 34%, households with parents and children 58%. In any case, the proportion of relatives (grandparents, aunts living with the son or brother/sister) must have been greater than in Western European countries.

THE NATIONAL SYSTEM OF DEMOGRAPHIC STATISTICS

Population Structure

In the case of Italy the history of population data is neatly connected to the political history. Similarly to Germany, but in strong contrast to older nation-states like France, Portugal, or the Nordic countries, unification of the Italian peninsula came rather late and the formation of the Italian state was more or less finished only in 1870. The main parts of Italy were unified by 1861, but the Veneto was acquired only in 1866 and the province of Rome in 1870. Before 1861 there were no national statistics, only population statistics for the large number of different territories.

Population censuses before 1861 in the territory of the later Kingdom of Italy were conducted in the years 1800, 1816, 1825, 1833, 1844, and 1858. A historical account of the older population censuses is given in Ministero di Agricoltura, Industria e Commercio, Direzione Generale della Statistica e del Lavoro, Ufficio del Censimento (1915: 15). These population figures were later collected and integrated into a post-hoc population figure for Italy before unification. The first census for the Kingdom of Italy was held in 1861, but did not include the Veneto or the province of Rome. The first complete census was in 1871. After that, population censuses were conducted very regularly until the census of 1931, except for the 1891 census which was not held. A census was taken in 1936, but during the 1940s the war made census-taking impossible. In 1944 a partial census was conducted by the Allied powers. National data only became available after the war through the general census of 1951.

Already the census publication of 1871 presents the population by age, sex, and marital status in one-year age groups. In the censuses of 1881, 1901, 1911, and 1921 data were published for age groups only, but the census of 1931 reintroduced one-year age groups.

Vital Statistics

The record of births, deaths, and marriages was introduced after the founding of the Italian state in 1862. Before that year statistics of vital events existed only for the individual territories of the Italian peninsula. Statistical measures and indicators in addition to these three basic demographic variables were introduced step by step: births by legitimacy and infant deaths in 1863, stillbirths in 1867, and legal separations in 1880 (the number of divorces only became available in 1971, when divorce was introduced).

Households and Families

Compared with many other countries, Italian statistics from the beginning emphasized the measurement of households and families. But this is line with the still older tradition of the Italian territories before unification, which already at that time recorded the number of households. The statistics of the Kingdom of Italy maintained this emphasis on household statistics.

Data on *households* (*famiglia/e*) were already collected by the census of 1861, but not in the Veneto and the province of Rome. A historical account of these statistics up to 1881 is given in Ministero di Agricoltura, Industria e Commercio, Direzione Generale della Statistica (1883: XXIII–XXVI). In 1871 the number of private households and their respective members was published. Starting with 1881 institutional households (*convivenze*) and members in institutions were published. From 1901 onwards data are available on all major household types: family households, one-person households, and institutional households.

Starting from 1901 private households by size in a large number of size categories were published. The acquisition of South Tyrol (Alto Adige) from the former Habsburg Empire made the calculation of two different figures necessary for the 1921 census: one for the old territory and one for the new one.

In 1931 for the first time private households were published according to household types. Households were classified according to their different types of members, distinguishing between households with family members only and those including different categories of non-family members such as servants, boarders and lodgers, and different combinations of these. Furthermore, households were distinguished according to composition of the biological family.

The *definition of a household* (*famiglia*) was that of a private household, including people living alone as well as family households with and without non-family members (servants, boarders, relatives, visitors, etc.). Besides family households the category of institutions (*convivenze*) was introduced. Inmates, personnel of institutions, and their family members were counted as belonging to institutional households.

Family statistics were not collected until World War II.

Remarks (also see introductory Table 6.1)

The national age*sex*marital status data are not yet available for the most recent census of 1991. Thus the data for the variables v16, v17, and v21 have been estimated using the relative shares of the 1981 census, whereas it was possible to take the values of the variables v18–v20 from the already available age structure and the structure of marital status.

BOUNDARY CHANGES

During the wars of independence most of the Italian peninsula was unified, and the Kingdom of Italy was proclaimed on 14 March 1861. However, the Veneto was still in the Habsburgs' possession, and the Papal States were still independent. In a second step, Italy won the Veneto in the 1866 war against Austria (in alliance with Prussia, which defeated Austria at Königgrätz). Finally, as a result of the war against the Holy See, Italy acquired the Papal States, reducing the papal possessions to Vatican City; it and San Marino are the only two remaining enclaves in Italy. This territorial status remained unchanged until World War I. Participation in World War I on the side of the Allied powers brought Italy Trentino-Alto Adige, as well as Slovene and Croat territories (the Istrian Peninsula, among others) from Yugoslavia. During the 1920s and 1930s Italy tried to establish a colonial empire in the Mediterranean and on the African continent. All these non-contiguous territories were returned after World War II. Nevertheless, Italy was able to retain South Tyrol (Alto Adige). For regional organization see the documentation by Quick (1994) and Caramani, Flora, Kraus, and Quick (1998).

APPENDIX TABLE I.1 Population structure at census dates 1871–1936

Census number	Census date	Census population			Marital status				Age group		
		Total	Male	Female	Single	Married	Widowed	Divorced	0–14	15–64	65+
		Absolute									
1	31 XII 1871	26,801,105	13,472,213	13,328,892	15,490,537	9,537,694	1,772,874	..	8,702,618	16,730,102	1,368,385
2	31 XII 1881	28,459,628	14,265,383	14,194,245	16,205,371	10,361,039	1,893,218	..	9,158,457	17,843,714	1,457,457
3	10 II 1901	32,475,253	16,155,130	16,320,123	18,689,103	11,688,716	2,097,434	..	11,156,758	18,201,816	3,116,679
4	10 VI 1911	34,671,377	17,021,690	17,649,687	19,789,718	12,595,767	2,151,168	34,163	11,733,266	20,693,557	2,244,554
5	1 XII 1921	38,710,576	19,089,535	19,621,041	22,032,752	14,107,326	2,487,473	45,070	12,017,979	24,095,456	2,597,141
6	21 IV 1931	41,176,671	20,133,455	21,043,216	22,898,106	15,543,330	2,672,415	54,342	12,242,208	25,929,018	3,005,445
7	21 IV 1936	42,993,602	21,123,730	21,869,872	23,786,054	16,458,061	2,744,929	2,439	13,164,483	26,633,298	3,195,821
		Per cent									
1	31 XII 1871	100.00	50.27	49.73	57.80	35.59	6.61	..	32.47	62.42	5.11
2	31 XII 1881	100.00	50.12	49.88	56.94	36.41	6.65	..	32.18	62.70	5.12
3	10 II 1901	100.00	49.75	50.25	57.55	35.99	6.46	..	34.35	56.05	9.60
4	10 VI 1911	100.00	49.09	50.91	57.08	36.33	6.20	0.10	33.84	59.68	6.47
5	1 XII 1921	100.00	49.31	50.69	56.92	36.44	6.43	0.12	31.05	62.25	6.71
6	21 IV 1931	100.00	48.90	51.10	55.61	37.75	6.49	0.13	29.73	62.97	7.30
7	21 IV 1936	100.00	49.13	50.87	55.32	38.28	6.38	0.01	30.62	61.95	7.43

APPENDIX TABLE I.2 Census population by region 1871–1936 (per cent)

Regione	1871	1881	1901	1911	1921	1931	1936
Piemonte	10.82	10.79	10.21	9.55	8.74	8.50	8.24
Valle d'Aosta	..	..	..	..	..	..	..
Liguria	3.15	3.13	3.32	3.34	3.43	3.49	3.46
Lombardia	12.91	12.93	13.19	13.36	13.18	13.47	13.53
Trentino-Alto Adige[1]	..	..	..	..	1.67	1.60	1.62
Veneto	9.86	9.89	9.65	9.84	10.22	10.01	9.93
Friuli-Venezia Giulia[2]	..	..	..	..	2.38	2.38	2.36
Trieste	..	..	..	..	..	..	..
Emilia-Romagna[3]	7.89	7.67	7.53	7.48[4]	7.63	7.82	7.74
Toscana	8.00	7.76	7.85	7.52	7.31	7.02	6.90
Marche	3.41	3.30	3.27	3.05	2.97	2.96	2.94
Umbria	2.05	2.01	2.05	1.92	1.91	1.69	1.69
Lazio (Roma)	3.12	3.17	3.69	3.63	3.92	5.79	6.23
Abruzzi-Molise	4.79	4.63	4.44	4.02	3.70	3.64	3.64
Abruzzi	..	..	..	..	..	..	..
Molise	..	..	..	..	..	..	..
Campania	10.28	10.18	9.73	9.24	9.16	8.49	8.59
Puglia	5.30	5.58	6.04	5.94	5.93	6.04	6.15
Basilicata[5]	1.91	1.84	1.51	1.32	1.21	1.23	1.25
Calabria	4.50	4.42	4.22	3.91	3.91	4.05	4.05
Sicilia	9.64	10.29	10.87	10.24	10.49	9.46	9.26
Sardegna	2.38	2.40	2.44	2.38	2.26	2.36	2.41
TOTAL	**100.00**	**100.00**	**100.00**	**100.00**	**100.00**	**100.00**	**100.00**

Notes: [1] Named *Venezia Tridentina* prior to 1951. [2] Named *Venezia Giulia* prior to 1951. [3] Named *Emilia* prior to 1951. [4] Named *Lucania* in 1936. [5] Sum of the two compartimenti *Emilia-Ducati* (10,654 sq. km.) and *Emilia-Romagna* (10,179 sq. km.).

APPENDIX TABLE I.3 Population density by region 1871–1936 (inhabitants per sq. km.)

Regione	1871	1881	1901	1911	1921	1931	1936
Piemonte	99	105	113	117	115	119	119
Valle d'Aosta	..	..	..	..	..	..	..
Liguria	159	169	204	227	251	264	270
Lombardia	147	157	178	198	211	234	241
Trentino-Alto Adige[1]	..	..	..	..	45	48	51
Veneto	113	120	128	144	161	162	165
Friuli-Venezia Giulia[2]	..	..	..	..	100	109	112
Trieste	..	..	..	..	..	..	..
Emilia-Romagna[3]	103	106	118	129[4]	142	145	148
Toscana	89	92	106	112	117	126	128
Marche	94	97	109	113	118	126	129
Umbria	57	59	69	70	76	82	84
Lazio (Roma)	70	76	99	108	126	139	154
Abruzzi-Molise	74	76	87	87	87	97	100
Abruzzi	..	..	..	..	..	..	..
Molise	..	..	..	..	..	..	..
Campania	153	161	194	204	218	259	270
Puglia	64	72	103	111	120	129	135
Basilicata[5]	48	49	49	47	47	51	53
Calabria	70	73	91	93	100	111	114
Sicilia	88	100	137	143	158	152	153
Sardegna	26	28	33	35	36	40	43
TOTAL	**90**	**96**	**113**	**125**	**125**	**133**	**137**

Notes: See Appendix Table I.2.

APPENDIX TABLE I.4 Demographic developments 1861–1945 (absolute figures and rates)

Year	Mid-year population	Natural population growth rate	Population growth rate	Net migration rate	Crude birth rate	Legitimate births per 10,000 married women age 15–44	Illegitimate births per 10,000 unmarried women age 15–44	Illeg. births per 100 leg. births
1861	..	..	..	..	..	..	..	..
1862	21,838,000	7.0			38.1	..	..	..
1863	21,974,000	8.0	6.2	-1.8	39.2	..	..	5.2
1864	22,132,000	8.4	7.1	-1.3	38.2	..	..	5.4
1865	22,303,500	8.6	7.7	-0.9	38.8	..	..	5.3
1866[1]	23,799,500	9.2	–	–	36.8	..	..	5.5
1867[1]	25,235,500	2.4	–	–	36.7	..	..	5.9
1868	25,323,500	4.9	3.5	-1.4	35.6	..	..	6.4
1869	25,499,500	9.3	6.9	-2.4	37.3	..	..	6.4
1870	25,702,500	6.9	7.9	1.0	37.0	..	..	6.9
1871[1]	26,295,000	6.9	–	–	36.5	2,879	221	7.1
1872[1]	26,882,000	7.2	–	–	38.0	2,977	242	7.5
1873	27,032,000	6.3	5.5	-0.8	36.4	2,842	239	7.7
1874	27,149,000	4.6	4.3	-0.3	35.1	2,722	236	7.8
1875	27,277,500	7.0	4.7	-2.3	38.0	2,950	245	7.5
1876	27,485,500	10.5	7.6	-2.9	39.4	3,055	258	7.6
1877	27,718,000	8.7	8.4	-0.3	37.1	2,861	249	7.8
1878	27,906,000	7.1	6.7	-0.4	36.3	2,791	243	7.7
1879	28,081,000	8.1	6.2	-1.9	37.9	2,904	258	7.8
1880	28,193,500	3.1	4.0	0.9	34.0	2,591	237	8.0
1881	28,337,000	10.5	5.1	-5.4	38.2	2,904	265	7.9
1882	28,569,500	9.6	8.1	-1.4	37.1	2,832	264	8.1
1883	28,787,500	9.6	7.6	-2.1	37.2	2,837	274	8.4
1884	29,038,500	12.1	8.6	-3.4	38.9	2,984	281	8.2
1885	29,315,000	11.6	9.4	-2.1	38.4	2,951	278	8.2
1886	29,532,000	8.2	7.3	-0.9	36.8	2,837	266	8.1
1887	29,736,000	10.9	6.9	-4.0	38.8	3,000	279	8.1
1888	29,951,000	10.0	7.2	-2.8	37.4	2,903	267	7.9
1889	30,187,500	12.6	7.8	-4.8	38.1	2,964	272	7.9
1890	30,422,000	9.4	7.7	-1.7	35.6	2,781	253	7.9
1891	30,621,000	11.0	6.5	-4.5	37.0	2,902	256	7.6
1892	30,823,000	10.0	6.6	-3.4	36.0	2,837	248	7.5
1893	31,029,500	11.3	6.7	-4.6	36.3	2,868	248	7.5
1894	31,245,000	10.5	6.9	-3.6	35.3	2,801	236	7.3
1895	31,431,500	9.8	5.9	-3.9	34.7	2,773	223	6.9
1896	31,609,000	10.7	5.6	-5.1	34.7	2,775	221	6.9
1897	31,826,000	12.8	6.8	-5.9	34.6	2,780	220	6.8

continued

APPENDIX TABLE I.4 Demographic developments 1861–1945 (absolute figures and rates)

Crude death rate	Infant mortality rate	Stillbirth rate	Infant mortality and stillbirth rate	Crude marriage rate	Persons marrying per 10,000 unmarried persons age 15+	Persons marrying per 10,000 unmarried persons age 15–49	Crude divorce rate	Divorces per 100 marriages	Divorces per 10,000 married persons	Year
..	..	..	..	..	..	..	..	..	..	1861
31.2	..	..	..	9.1	..	..	..	..	..	1862
31.3	231.6	22.0	253.6	9.2	..	..	..	..	..	1863
29.8	228.5	16.8	245.3	9.0	..	..	..	..	..	1864
30.2	226.1	15.7	241.8	10.2	..	..	..	..	..	1865
27.6	209.3	26.8	236.1	6.0	..	..	..	..	..	1866[1]
34.4	223.4	24.2	247.6	6.8	..	..	..	..	..	1867[1]
30.7	238.0	23.7	261.7	7.2	..	..	..	..	..	1868
28.0	215.2	24.8	240.0	8.1	..	..	..	..	..	1869
30.1	230.2	25.9	256.1	7.4	..	..	..	..	..	1870
29.6	227.2	27.6	254.9	7.3	459	585	..	..	..	1871[1]
30.8	223.2	28.9	252.2	7.5	472	602	..	..	..	1872[1]
30.1	214.1	28.8	242.8	8.0	500	638	..	..	..	1873
30.5	223.7	28.4	252.0	7.7	482	616	..	..	..	1874
30.9	215.5	28.8	244.3	8.4	533	682	..	..	..	1875
29.0	203.1	30.5	233.6	8.2	518	664	..	..	..	1876
28.4	208.1	30.5	238.6	7.8	491	630	..	..	..	1877
29.2	204.8	30.9	235.7	7.2	454	583	..	..	..	1878
29.8	206.8	31.6	238.4	7.6	482	619	..	..	..	1879
30.9	225.0	31.7	256.7	7.0	444	572	..	..	..	1880
27.7	192.2	32.6	224.8	8.1	517	667	..	..	..	1881
27.6	205.7	33.3	239.0	7.8	501	647	..	..	..	1882
27.6	198.4	34.7	233.2	8.1	516	668	..	..	..	1883
26.9	185.9	33.8	219.7	8.2	530	686	..	..	..	1884
26.9	193.7	34.9	228.6	8.0	515	666	..	..	..	1885
28.6	200.1	36.1	236.2	7.9	511	662	..	..	..	1886
27.9	193.4	36.9	230.3	7.9	514	667	..	..	..	1887
27.4	199.7	37.5	237.2	7.9	515	669	..	..	..	1888
25.4	184.3	38.2	222.6	7.6	498	648	..	..	..	1889
26.2	198.3	38.9	237.2	7.3	478	622	..	..	..	1890
26.0	183.8	39.2	223.0	7.4	488	636	..	..	..	1891
26.0	186.1	40.3	226.4	7.4	488	637	..	..	..	1892
25.0	..	41.1	..	7.4	485	633	..	..	..	1893
24.8	..	41.9	..	7.4	491	641	..	..	..	1894
24.9	188.2	42.0	230.2	7.3	482	630	..	..	..	1895
24.0	177.2	42.3	219.5	7.0	469	613	..	..	..	1896
21.9	164.1	42.8	206.9	7.2	480	629	..	..	..	1897

continued

APPENDIX TABLE I.4 Demographic developments 1861–1945 (continued)

Year	Mid-year population	Natural population growth rate	Population growth rate	Net migration rate	Crude birth rate	Legitimate births per 10,000 married women age 15–44	Illegitimate births per 10,000 unmarried women age 15–44	Illeg. births per 100 leg. births
1898	32,031,000	10.5	6.4	-4.1	33.4	2,692	211	6.7
1899	32,215,500	12.0	5.7	-6.2	33.8	2,734	209	6.5
1900	32,377,000	9.2	5.0	-4.2	33.0	2,678	198	6.3
1901	32,550,000	10.5	5.3	-5.2	32.5	2,651	191	6.2
1902	32,787,000	11.2	7.2	-3.9	33.3	2,721	190	6.1
1903	33,004,000	9.3	6.6	-2.7	31.6	2,579	176	6.0
1904	33,237,000	11.6	7.0	-4.6	32.7	2,668	175	5.9
1905	33,488,500	10.6	7.5	-3.1	32.4	2,649	167	5.7
1906	33,718,000	11.1	6.8	-4.3	31.8	2,601	159	5.6
1907	33,952,000	10.7	6.9	-3.8	31.3	2,565	151	5.5
1908	34,198,000	10.8	7.2	-3.6	33.3	2,737	151	5.2
1909	34,455,000	11.0	7.5	-3.5	32.4	2,662	142	5.1
1910	34,750,500	13.3	8.5	-4.8	32.9	2,706	145	5.2
1911	35,032,500	10.0	8.0	-2.0	31.2	2,565	135	5.2
1912	35,246,000	14.1	6.1	-8.1	32.2	2,648	133	5.0
1913	35,350,500	13.0	3.0	-10.0	31.8	2,617	126	4.9
1914	35,700,500	13.2	9.8	-3.4	31.2	..	..	5.0
1915	36,270,500	10.1	15.7	5.6	30.6	..	..	4.5
1916	36,480,500	4.4	5.8	1.4	24.2	..	..	4.4
1917	36,343,000	0.2	-3.8	-4.0	19.0	..	..	5.0
1918	35,922,000	-14.6	-11.7	2.9	17.8	..	..	5.2
1919	35,716,500	2.6	-5.8	-8.4	21.6	1,889	83	4.8
1920	35,900,000	13.3	5.1	-8.2	32.3	2,798	126	4.9
1921	36,999,500	12.9	29.7	16.8	30.2	2,599	122	5.1
1922	38,196,000	12.7	31.3	18.6	30.8	2,633	120	4.9
1923	38,570,500	13.0	9.7	-3.3	29.9	2,545	115	4.8
1924	38,926,500	11.9	9.1	-2.7	28.9	2,432	117	5.0
1925	39,264,500	11.2	8.6	-2.6	28.2	2,357	117	5.2
1926	39,590,000	10.5	8.2	-2.2	27.6	2,296	113	5.1
1927	39,926,000	11.4	8.4	-3.0	27.4	2,253	118	5.4
1928	40,281,000	10.6	8.8	-1.8	26.6	2,175	114	5.3
1929	40,606,500	9.1	8.0	-1.1	25.6	2,070	113	5.5
1930	40,956,000	12.6	8.5	-4.1	26.7	2,151	113	5.3
1931	41,338,500	10.1	9.3	-0.8	24.8	1,986	107	5.4
1932	41,677,000	9.1	8.1	-1.0	23.8	1,903	107	5.5
1933	42,004,500	10.0	7.8	-2.2	23.7	1,903	107	5.4
1934	42,351,500	10.1	8.2	-2.0	23.4	1,885	106	5.3
1935	42,693,000	9.4	8.0	-1.4	23.3	1,886	101	5.0
1936	43,019,500	8.7	7.6	-1.1	22.4	1,816	93	4.7
1937	43,341,000	8.7	7.4	-1.3	22.9	1,865	90	4.3
1938	43,695,000	9.7	8.1	-1.6	23.7	1,940	93	4.2
1939	44,147,500	10.2	10.2	0.1	23.6	1,927	93	4.2
1940[2]	44,633,500	9.8	10.9	1.0	23.4	..	..	4.0
1941[2]	45,025,500	7.0	8.7	1.7	20.8	..	..	4.0
1942[2]	45,310,500	6.2	6.3	0.1	20.4	..	..	3.9
1943[2,3]	45,490,000	4.5	3.9	-0.6	19.4	..	..	3.9
1944[2,3]	45,606,000	3.0	2.5	-0.4	17.9	..	..	4.8
1945[2,3]	45,762,000	4.5	3.4	-1.1	17.8	..	..	5.4

Notes: [1] Territorial change. [2] Excluding deaths in war zones and deaths of military personnel abroad. [3] Live births refer to the postwar territory, excluding Trieste.

APPENDIX TABLE I.4 Demographic developments 1850–1945 (continued)

Crude death rate	Infant mortality rate	Stillbirth rate	Infant mortality and stillbirth rate	Crude marriage rate	Persons marrying per 10,000 unmarried persons age 15+	Persons marrying per 10,000 unmarried persons age 15–49	Crude divorce rate	Divorces per 100 marriages	Divorces per 10,000 married persons	Year
22.9	171.4	42.1	213.6	6.9	459	602	..	..	..	1898
21.8	154.6	42.2	196.7	7.3	491	644	..	..	..	1899
23.7	174.1	42.8	216.9	7.2	483	635	..	..	..	1900
22.0	166.3	43.7	210.0	7.2	486	640	..	..	..	1901
22.2	171.8	44.5	216.4	7.2	485	636	..	..	..	1902
22.3	171.9	44.8	216.7	7.2	478	625	..	..	..	1903
21.0	161.1	45.3	206.3	7.5	493	642	..	..	..	1904
21.8	166.2	45.6	211.8	7.6	502	652	..	..	..	1905
20.7	160.9	45.0	205.8	7.7	505	654	..	..	..	1906
20.6	155.9	45.2	201.1	7.7	497	642	..	..	..	1907
22.5	147.9	45.2	193.0	8.3	533	689	..	..	..	1908
21.4	157.0	45.1	202.1	7.7	495	637	..	..	..	1909
19.6	140.0	44.0	184.0	7.7	493	633	..	..	..	1910
21.2	156.7	43.4	200.1	7.4	470	602	..	..	..	1911
18.0	128.0	41.9	169.9	7.5	473	604	..	..	..	1912
18.8	138.2	41.8	180.0	7.5	468	597	..	..	..	1913
18.0	130.3	42.7	173.1	7.1	..	..	..	..	..	1914
20.4	146.8	42.6	189.4	5.1	..	..	..	..	..	1915
19.8	166.3	42.2	208.6	2.9	..	..	..	..	..	1916
18.8	158.2	43.1	201.3	2.7	..	..	..	..	..	1917
32.5	191.8	50.5	242.4	3.0	..	..	..	..	..	1918
18.9	129.1	47.3	176.5	9.3	580	733	..	..	..	1919
19.0	126.7	45.2	171.9	14.2	882	1,116	..	..	..	1920
17.4	129.3	48.1	177.4	11.9	737	933	..	..	..	1921
18.1	126.5	46.2	172.7	9.6	589	753	..	..	..	1922
17.0	127.5	45.1	172.5	8.7	533	682	..	..	..	1923
17.0	126.2	43.8	170.0	7.9	485	621	..	..	..	1924
17.1	119.4	43.9	163.2	7.5	463	593	..	..	..	1925
17.2	126.5	40.1	166.6	7.5	459	588	..	..	..	1926
16.0	120.2	38.3	158.5	7.6	466	597	..	..	..	1927
16.0	120.3	37.1	157.3	7.1	436	558	..	..	..	1928
16.4	124.8	36.8	161.6	7.1	436	559	..	..	..	1929
14.1	105.5	36.5	142.0	7.4	455	584	..	..	..	1930
14.7	112.9	35.5	148.4	6.7	411	526	..	..	..	1931
14.7	110.5	35.2	145.6	6.4	399	512	..	..	..	1932
13.7	100.1	35.4	135.6	6.9	432	557	..	..	..	1933
13.3	98.7	34.6	133.3	7.4	466	603	..	..	..	1934
13.9	101.2	34.0	135.2	6.7	429	557	..	..	..	1935
13.7	100.4	33.5	133.9	7.4	473	615	..	..	..	1936
14.2	108.8	32.9	141.6	8.7	565	736	..	..	..	1937
14.0	106.3	33.0	139.2	7.4	486	637	..	..	..	1938
13.4	97.0	32.4	129.3	7.3	482	633	..	..	..	1939
13.6	102.7	30.8	133.4	7.0	..	..	..	..	..	1940[2]
13.8	115.2	29.6	144.8	6.1	..	..	..	..	..	1941[2]
14.2	112.4	28.9	141.4	6.3	..	..	..	..	..	1942[2]
14.9	115.1	29.4	144.4	4.7	..	..	..	..	..	1943[2,3]
14.9	103.2	28.0	131.2	4.7	..	..	..	..	..	1944[2,3]
13.3	103.1	31.8	134.8	6.7	..	..	..	..	..	1945[2,3]

Notes: [1] Territorial change. [2] Excluding deaths in war zones and deaths of military personnel abroad. [3] Live births refer to the postwar territory, excluding Trieste.

Italy

APPENDIX TABLE I.5 Life expectancy by age 1876/87–1935/37 (in years)

Age	0	10	20	30	40	50	60	70	80
				Males					
1876–1887	35.1	47.1	40.4	33.6	26.3	19.5	13.1	8.0	..
1881–1882	35.16	48.16	40.58	33.81	26.44	19.47	13.18	8.16	4.99
1891–1900	42.83	51.25	43.08	35.67	28.00	20.50	13.58	7.92	4.33
1899–1902	42.59	51.21	43.02	35.68	27.94	20.42	13.47	7.74	3.98
1901–1910	44.24	51.44	43.27	35.94	28.23	20.73	13.78	8.02	4.06
1910–1912	46.57	52.48	44.15	36.70	28.88	21.23	14.10	8.15	4.15
1921–1922	49.27	53.53	45.15	37.63	29.63	21.76	14.49	8.38	4.26
1930–1932	53.76	55.46	46.75	38.58	30.39	22.45	15.16	9.05	4.85
1935–1937	..	..	..	..	..	..	..	..	..
				Females					
1876–1887	35.5	47.3	40.0	33.5	26.8	19.7	12.1	7.8	..
1881–1882	35.65	47.61	40.38	33.70	26.86	19.64	12.91	7.79	4.89
1891–1900	43.17	51.00	43.17	36.00	28.67	21.08	13.67	7.83	4.17
1899–1902	43.00	51.00	43.13	36.01	28.68	21.01	13.60	7.65	3.99
1901–1910	44.83	51.53	43.69	36.58	29.18	21.47	14.02	8.02	4.11
1910–1912	47.33	52.69	44.64	37.30	29.76	21.91	14.36	8.18	4.20
1921–1922	50.75	54.18	45.96	38.37	30.51	22.48	14.84	8.48	4.45
1930–1932	56.00	57.15	48.49	40.41	32.14	23.89	16.13	9.61	5.18
1935–1937	57.49	57.86	49.05	40.72	32.30	23.96	16.15	9.63	5.20

APPENDIX TABLE I.6A Households by type 1861–1944 (absolute and per cent)

Absolute

Census year	Household types and members									
	Total house-holds	Private house-holds	Family house-holds	One-person house-holds	Institu-tional house-holds	Total household members	Private household members	Family household members	One-person household members	Institu-tional household members
1861[1]	..	..	..	..	..	..	..	..	..	..
1871	..	5,727,536	..	..	..	..	26,801,154	..	..	..
1881	6,251,268	6,216,121	..	..	35,147	2,8459,628	27,789,754	..	..	669,874
1901	7,027,524	6,993,173	6,378,357	614,816	34,351	3,2475,253	31,590,003	30,975,187	614,816	885,250
1911	7,178,657	7,146,543	6,486,448	660,095	32,114	3,4671,377	33,668,381	33,008,286	660,095	1,002,996
1921 old[2]	8,280,311	8,250,915	7,504,221	746,694	29,396	3,7142,886	36,179,779	35,433,085	746,694	963,107
1921 new[3]	8,625,950	8,594,223	7,809,910	784,313	31,727	3,8710,576	37,679,751	36,895,438	784,313	1,030,825
1931	9,481,844	9,429,583	8,529,466	900,117	52,261	4,1176,671	39,736,021	38,835,904	900,117	1,440,650
1936	9,895,124	9,835,142	8,940,232	894,910	59,982	4,3837,477	42,215,616	41,320,706	894,910	1,621,861
1944[4]	..	..	4,441,377	..	..	..	..	18,961,828	..	..

Per cent

Census year	Total house-holds	Private house-holds	Family house-holds	One-person house-holds	Institu-tional house-holds	Total household members	Private household members	Family household members	One-person household members	Institu-tional household members
1861[1]	..	..	..	..	..	..	..	..	..	..
1871	..	..	..	..	..	..	..	..	..	..
1881	100.00	99.44	..	..	0.56	100.00	97.65	..	..	2.35
1901	100.00	99.51	90.76	8.75	0.49	100.00	97.27	95.38	1.89	2.73
1911	100.00	99.55	90.36	9.20	0.45	100.00	97.11	95.20	1.90	2.89
1921 old[2]	100.00	99.64	90.63	9.02	0.36	100.00	97.41	95.40	2.01	2.59
1921 new[3]	100.00	99.63	90.54	9.09	0.37	100.00	97.34	95.31	2.03	2.66
1931	100.00	99.45	89.96	9.49	0.55	100.00	96.50	94.32	2.19	3.50
1936	100.00	99.39	90.35	9.04	0.61	100.00	96.30	94.26	2.04	3.70
1944[4]	..	..	..	..	..	..	..	..	..	..

Notes: [1] Without *Veneto* and the *Province of Rome*. [2] Territory before 1919. [3] Territory after 1919. [4] Part of Italy only.

APPENDIX TABLE I.6B Households by size and members 1901–1936 (absolute figures)

Census year	Private households total	Households by number of members							
		1 person	2 persons	3 persons	4 persons	5 persons	6 persons	7 persons	8 persons
Households									
1901	6,993,173	614,816	1,109,697	1,129,787	1,076,179	963,705	732,584	521,806	335,749
1911	7,146,543	660,095	1,182,831	1,176,754	1,099,442	934,955	721,723	511,219	338,660
1921 old[1]	8,250,915	746,694	1,400,142	1,432,848	1,270,055	1,084,633	828,828	573,673	368,874
1921 new[2]	8,594,223	784,313	1,452,833	1,489,673	1,322,484	1,128,838	863,476	598,374	385,868
1931	9,429,583	900,117	1,603,607	1,709,587	1,599,284	1,266,684	903,529	584,254	357,413
1936	9,835,142	894,910	1,568,309	1,778,630	1,695,517	1,345,699	965,930	637,475	393,755
Persons									
1901	31,590,003	614,816	2,219,394	3,389,361	4,304,716	4,818,525	4,395,504	3,652,642	2,685,992
1911	33,668,381	660,095	2,365,662	3,530,262	4,397,768	4,674,775	4,330,338	3,578,533	2,709,280
1921 old[1]	36,179,779	746,694	2,800,284	4,298,544	5,080,220	5,423,165	4,972,968	4,015,711	2,950,992
1921 new[2]	37,679,751	784,313	2,905,666	4,469,019	5,289,936	5,644,190	5,180,856	4,188,618	3,086,944
1931	39,736,021	900,117	3,207,214	5,128,761	6,397,136	6,333,420	5,421,174	4,089,778	2,859,304
1936	42,215,616	894,910	3,136,618	5,335,890	6,782,068	6,728,495	5,795,580	4,462,325	3,150,040

Census year	Households by number of members							
	9 persons	10 persons	11 persons	12 persons	13 persons	14 persons	15 persons	16+ persons
Households								
1901	198,457	114,808	64,607	38,760	25,253	17,424	..	49,541
1911	205,469	119,333	68,331	40,119	25,060	17,459	12,691	32,402
1921 old[1]	219,594	127,271	69,848	41,213	25,263	18,265	11,271	32,443
1921 new[2]	229,682	133,077	73,096	42,973	26,178	18,939	11,544	32,875
1931	209,477	116,966	64,921	37,954	23,580	15,424	10,503	26,283
1936	229,112	129,175	72,702	41,560	25,715	16,683	11,655	28,315
Persons								
1901	1,786,113	1,148,080	710,677	465,120	328,289	243,936	..	826,838
1911	1,849,221	1,193,330	751,641	481,428	325,780	244,426	190,365	2,385,477
1921 old[1]	1,976,346	1,272,710	768,328	494,556	328,419	255,710	169,065	626,067
1921 new[2]	2,067,138	1,330,770	804,056	515,676	340,314	265,146	173,160	633,949
1931	1,885,293	1,169,660	714,131	455,448	306,540	215,936	157,545	494,564
1936	2,062,008	1,291,750	799,722	498,720	334,295	233,562	174,825	534,808

Notes: [1] Territory before 1919. [2] Territory after 1919.

APPENDIX TABLE I.6C Households by size and members 1901–1936 (per cent)

Census year	Private households total	1 person	2 persons	3 persons	4 persons	5 persons	6 persons	7 persons	8 persons
					Households				
1901	100.00	8.79	15.87	16.16	15.39	13.78	10.48	7.46	4.80
1911	100.00	9.24	16.55	16.47	15.38	13.08	10.10	7.15	4.74
1921 old[1]	100.00	9.05	16.97	17.37	15.39	13.15	10.05	6.95	4.47
1921 new[2]	100.00	9.13	16.90	17.33	15.39	13.13	10.05	6.96	4.49
1931	100.00	9.55	17.01	18.13	16.96	13.43	9.58	6.20	3.79
1936	100.00	9.10	15.95	18.08	17.24	13.68	9.82	6.48	4.00
					Persons				
1901	100.00	1.95	7.03	10.73	13.63	15.25	13.91	11.56	8.50
1911	100.00	1.96	7.03	10.49	13.06	13.88	12.86	10.63	8.05
1921 old[1]	100.00	2.06	7.74	11.88	14.04	14.99	13.75	11.10	8.16
1921 new[2]	100.00	2.08	7.71	11.86	14.04	14.98	13.75	11.12	8.19
1931	100.00	2.27	8.07	12.91	16.10	15.94	13.64	10.29	7.20
1936	100.00	2.12	7.43	12.64	16.07	15.94	13.73	10.57	7.46

Households by number of members

Census year	9 persons	10 persons	11 persons	12 persons	13 persons	14 persons	15 persons	16+ persons
				Households				
1901	2.84	1.64	0.92	0.55	0.36	0.25	..	0.71
1911	2.88	1.67	0.96	0.56	0.35	0.24	0.18	0.45
1921 old[1]	2.66	1.54	0.85	0.50	0.31	0.22	0.14	0.39
1921 new[2]	2.67	1.55	0.85	0.50	0.30	0.22	0.13	0.38
1931	2.22	1.24	0.69	0.40	0.25	0.16	0.11	0.28
1936	2.33	1.31	0.74	0.42	0.26	0.17	0.12	0.29
				Persons				
1901	5.65	3.63	2.25	1.47	1.04	0.77	..	2.62
1911	5.49	3.54	2.23	1.43	0.97	0.73	0.57	7.09
1921 old[1]	5.46	3.52	2.12	1.37	0.91	0.71	0.47	1.73
1921 new[2]	5.49	3.53	2.13	1.37	0.90	0.70	0.46	1.68
1931	4.74	2.94	1.80	1.15	0.77	0.54	0.40	1.24
1936	4.88	3.06	1.89	1.18	0.79	0.55	0.41	1.27

Notes: [1] Territory before 1919. [2] Territory after 1919.

APPENDIX TABLE I.6D Household indicators 1861–
1944

Census year	Household indicators			
	Mean total household size	Mean private household size	Mean family household size	Mean institutional household size
1861	..	..	..	..
1871	..	4.68	..	..
1881	4.55	4.47	..	19.06
1901	4.62	4.52	4.86	25.77
1911	4.83	4.71	5.09	31.23
1921 old[1]	4.49	4.38	4.72	32.76
1921 new[2]	4.49	4.38	4.72	32.49
1931	4.34	4.21	4.55	27.57
1936	4.43	4.29	4.62	27.04
1944	..	..	4.27	..

Notes: [1] Territory before 1919. [2] Territory after 1919.

APPENDIX TABLE I.6E Household composition 1931 (absolute and per cent)

Families by type and composition	House-holds absolute	Household members absolute	House-holds %	Household members %
Total households and household members	**9,429,583**	**39,736,021**	**100.00**	**100.00**
Only parents and relatives	7,813,645	35,135,299	82.86	88.42
Domestic servants	291,154	1,382,766	3.09	3.48
Journeymen	66,366	469,287	0.70	1.18
Boarders, cohabitees, and strangers	315,994	1,575,560	3.35	3.97
Servants and journeymen	7,040	51,762	0.07	0.13
Servants, cohabitees, boarders, and strangers	28,622	170,307	0.30	0.43
Journeymen, cohabitees, boarders, and strangers	4,633	38,146	0.05	0.10
Servants, journeymen, cohabitees, boarders, and strangers	1,086	9,351	0.01	0.02
Total regular and irregular persons	*8,528,540*	*38,832,478*	*90.44*	*97.73*
Irregular persons	204,140	897,428	2.16	2.26
Regular persons: total	*8,324,400*	*37,935,050*	*88.28*	*95.47*
Regular persons: only ascendants and descendants	254,524	1,498,629	2.70	3.77
Regular persons: only parents and children	5,079,317	23,089,103	53.87	58.11
Regular persons: only parents and relatives	2,990,559	13,347,318	31.71	33.59
Only strangers	926	3,426	0.01	0.01
Only one member	900,117	900,117	9.55	2.27

APPENDIX TABLE I.7 Dates and nature of results on population structure, households/families, and vital statistics

Topic	Intro-duction	Remarks
Population		
Population at census dates	1861	Before unification in 1861 earlier censuses were conducted in 1800, 1816, 1825, 1833, 1844, and 1858. The 1861 census did not include the Veneto (acquired in 1866) or the province of Rome (Papal States) acquired in 1870.
Population by age, sex, and marital status	1871	Not available for 1861.
Households and families		
Households (famiglia/e)		
Total households	1861, 1871, 1881, 1901, 1911, 1921, 1931, 1936, 1944	Households were first expressly recorded in 1861: 1861: number of households (without Veneto or province of Rome). 1871: number of households. 1881: number of households; institutional households (*convivenze*). 1901, 1911, 1921, 1931, and 1936: households by size and occupation of household head; institutional households. 1944: number of households (part of Italy only). *Disaggregation*: by provinces, etc.
Households by size	1901, 1911, 1921, 1931, 1936	First time in the housing census of 1901: households by number of persons 1–15+. Repeated in 1911, 1921, 1931, and 1936.
Households by composition	1931, 1936	Household types.
Households by profession of household head	1901, 1911, 1921, 1931, 1936	For the first time in 1901.
Families (famiglie nucleare)		
Families by number of children	–	

continued

APPENDIX TABLE I.7 Dates and nature of results on population structure, households/families, and vital statistics (continued)

Topic	Intro-duction	Remarks
Population movement		
Mid-year population	1862	
Births		
Live births	1862	
Stillbirths	1867	
Legitimate births	1863	
Illegitimate births	1863	
Deaths		
Total deaths	1862	
Infants (under 1 year)	1863	
Marriages		
Total marriages	1862	
Divorces and separations		
Total divorces	1971	
Legal separations	1880	

APPENDIX FIGURE I.8 Population by age, sex and marital status, Italy 1871, 1881, 1901, 1911, 1921 and 1936 (per 10,000 of total population)

Italy, 1871

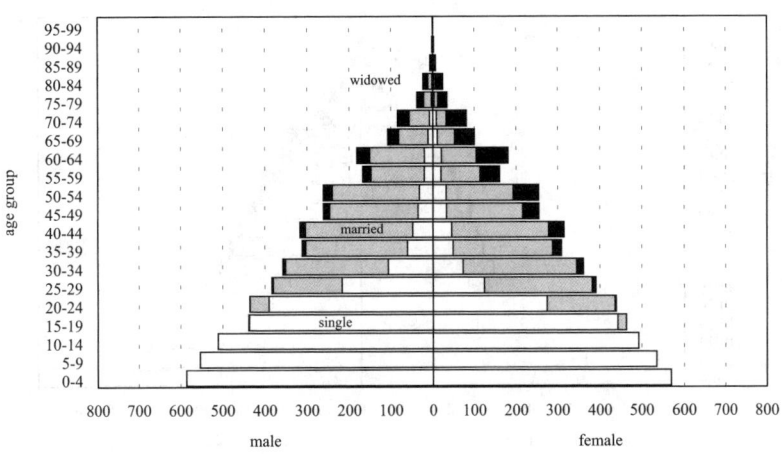

Italy, 1881

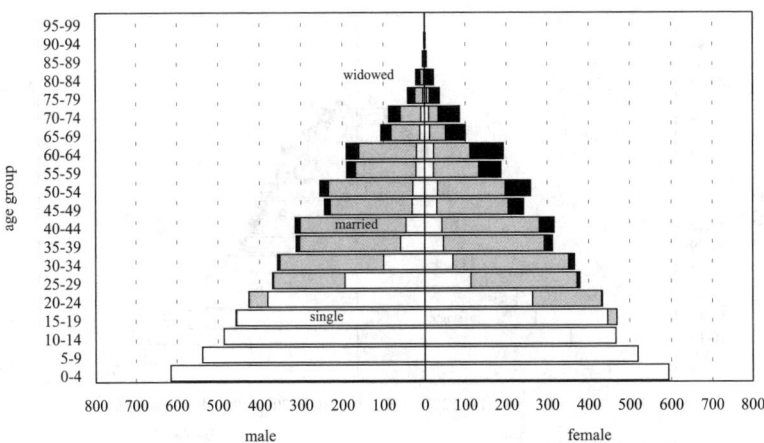

APPENDIX FIGURE I.8 Population by age, sex and marital status, Italy 1871, 1881, 1901, 1911, 1921 and 1936 (per 10,000 of total population) (continued)

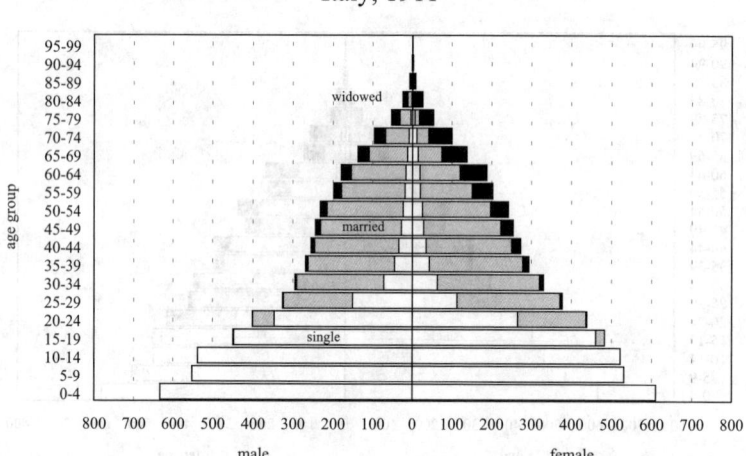

Italy, 1901

Italy, 1911

APPENDIX FIGURE I.8 Population by age, sex and marital status, Italy 1871, 1881, 1901, 1911, 1921 and 1936 (per 10,000 of total population) (continued)

Italy, 1921

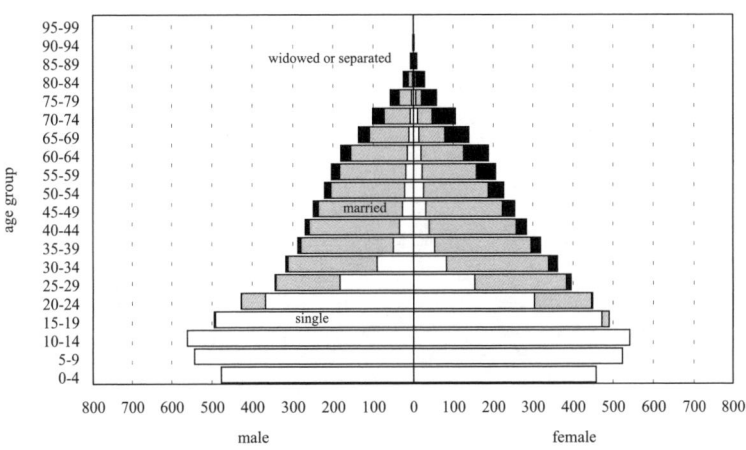

Italy, 1936

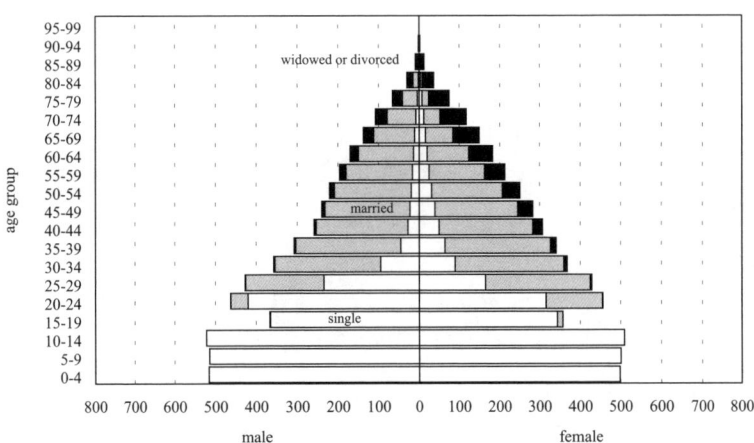

13

Luxemburg

STATE FORMATION AND TERRITORY

The territory of the old Duchy of Luxemburg was at its largest in the fourteenth century (about 10,000 sq. km.). There were three main territorial secessions in the history of Luxemburg. First, in 1649 the southern parts with the cities of Montmédy and Thionville had to be ceded to France according to the treaty of the Pyrenées. Second, in 1815 the Congress of Vienna gave Prussia the parts east of the Moselle, the Sûre, and the Our including the cities of Bitburg and Saint-Vith (about 2,280 sq. km. and 50,000 inhabitants). Finally, the major loss of territory came with the independence of Belgium in 1831 from the United Kingdom of the Netherlands. The new Belgian state acquired a large part of the Grand Duchy of Luxemburg in 1839 through the Treaty of London; the Wallonian western and north-western part of the country went to Belgium as the 'Province of Luxembourg' (about 4,320 sq. km. and 160,000 inhabitants). Since 1839 there have been no territorial changes. Luxemburg has an area of 2,586 sq. km. and its frontiers have a total length of 356 km., of which 148 km. are with Belgium, 135 with Germany, and 73 with France.

As a result of the Congress of Vienna in 1815, Luxemburg became a member of the German Federation (*Deutscher Bund*). It also became a Grand Duchy in that year. After the 1866 war between Prussia and Austria over German hegemony, in 1867 Luxemburg left the German Federation and declared its neutrality. In 1890 the Grand Duchy of Luxemburg became a sovereign state (see Als, 1989, 1991; Service Central de la Statistique et des Études Économiques, 1990a, 1990b).

REGIONAL POPULATION STRUCTURE

Since 1839 Luxemburg has been divided into three districts and 13 cantons. In 1839 the population was still relatively equally distributed over the country. Forty-two percent of all inhabitants lived in the district of Luxemburg, 33% in the district of Diekirch, and 24% in the district of Grevenmacher. A century later, in 1935, two-thirds (67%) of the population lived in the district of Luxemburg, and the population in the districts of Diekirch and Grevenmacher had declined to 20% and 13% of the total population, respectively. Thus, during the nineteenth and first half of the twentieth century urbanization and growth of the capital made the territorial structure of the population more monocephalic. This change can also be seen from the absolute population figures. While the number of inhabitants in the district of Luxemburg nearly tripled from 1839 to 1935 (71,612 to 199,635 inhabitants), there was only a small increase over the whole time period in the district of Diekirch (from 56,682 in 1839 to 59,712 in 1935). In the district of Grevenmacher the population even declined in absolute terms (from 41,571 in 1839 to 37,566 in 1935). But in the districts of Diekirch and Grevenmacher the initial population increase up to the end of the nineteenth century was followed by a decrease.

Population density follows the unequal development of the population by districts. In 1839 the population was still rather equally distributed over the country with 79 inhabitants per sq. km. in both the district of Luxemburg and of Grevenmacher. In the district of Diekirch population density was 49 inhabitants per sq. km. One hundred years later the picture had changed: population density in the district of Luxemburg was 221, in Grevenmacher 72, and in Diekirch 52 inhabitants per sq. km. Thus, population density in Grevenmacher declined, increased slightly in Diekirch, and nearly tripled in the district of Luxemburg. The canton of the city of Luxemburg alone made up 10% of the total population in 1839 and 19% in 1935. In 1839, 17% of the population lived in the two cantons Luxembourg-Ville et Campagne; in 1935 a quarter of the population did so. Population density of the whole country increased from 66 inhabitants per sq. km. in 1839 to 115 in 1935.

POPULATION GROWTH

The total population of Luxemburg was 170,000 in 1839 and increased to 297,000 in 1935; this is a total increase of 75% over the 1839 figure. Population growth therefore was not as high as in Belgium or The Netherlands. The natural population growth rate was fairly high and fluctuated around a level of 10 per 1,000 inhabitants from 1850 to 1910. World War I made the natural population growth rate negative, with deaths exceeding births. During the inter-war period natural population growth was lower than before the war with a declining tendency during the 1930s and especially the 1940s, when deaths again exceeded births (Figure L.1).

The total population growth rate followed the pattern of the natural population growth rate. Total population growth was negative—population declined—during the years of both world wars. There were also many other periods of temporary population decline due to economic crises or the excess of emigration over immigration. Economic crises were probably the main reasons for the downswing in the total population growth rate in the 1850s (recession), the late 1860s (American Civil War), the early 1870s (Franco-Prussian War of 1870/71), the late 1880s, and finally the early 1930s (world economic crisis). Such economic depressions were regularly accompanied by strong emigration movements which coincide very neatly with the business cycle and the natural population growth rate. But there were also periods of stronger immigration than emigration in the 1890s and especially the second half of the 1920s.

THE FIRST DEMOGRAPHIC TRANSITION

Demographic transition in Luxemburg finally started in the 1860s when a declining trend of the birth rate began (Figure L.2). But the birth rate did not show a continuous decline during the nineteenth century. It rose again at the end of the century, reaching a level of over 30 births per 1,000 inhabitants. But after 1900, influenced by World War I, the birth rate dropped suddenly and strongly. Although Luxemburg remained neutral during the war, it was occupied by German troops. The birth rate recovered after World War I, although on a much lower level than before the war, and declined again under the impact of the world economic depression of 1929–32. During the 1930s the natural population surplus became very small, and finally during World War II the birth rate was lower than the death rate, but mainly because of the rise in the latter.

Figure L.1 Population growth and net migration 1850-1945

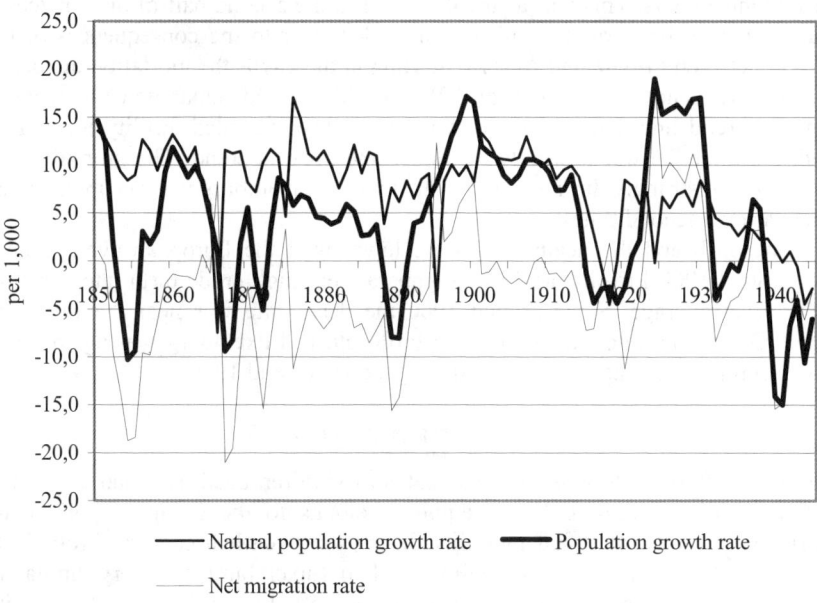

Figure L.2 First demographic transition 1850-1945

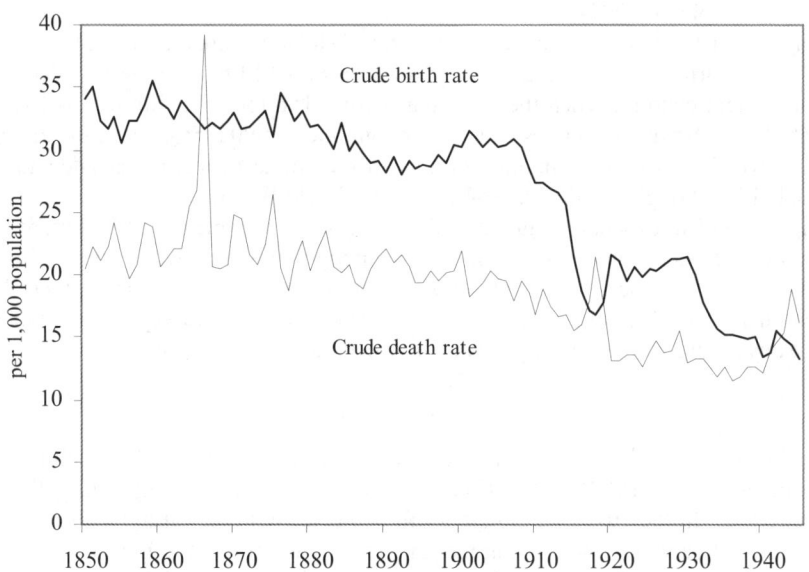

The mortality rate during the 1850s and 1860s stagnated or even increased slightly. The year 1866 saw a huge increase in the mortality rate, which peaked at 39.2 deaths per 1,000 inhabitants. This was a singular event in the second half of the nineteenth century and may be attributed either to a epidemic or to the consequences of the 1866 war between Prussia and Austria. Starting in the 1870s the mortality rate began a declining tendency, but until World War I still showed remarkable fluctuations around the trend line. During World War I mortality exceeded fertility for a short period, but after the war mortality continued the pre-war trend. The mortality rate again increased strongly during World War II when Luxemburg was occupied by the German army a second time.

Both the birth and the death rates were lower than the European average until 1900. Around 1900 Luxemburg had a comparatively high crude birth rate, equal to the European average. Since around 1900 the death rate was near the European average. During the inter-war period the birth rate in Luxemburg was again lower than the European average, especially during the 1930s and 1940s.

MORTALITY AND LIFE EXPECTANCY

The infant mortality rate is defined as deaths of children aged less than a year per 1,000 live births (Figure L.3). Luxemburg belongs to the group of continental countries with moderate infant mortality during the twentieth century. From 1900 until World War II the infant mortality level in Luxemburg was very similar to Belgium: with 159 deaths in 1901–5 it was only slightly higher than in Belgium with 154. In 1941–45 infant mortality in Luxemburg was still slightly higher than in Belgium, with 87 versus 86 infant deaths. The neighbouring countries of France and The Netherlands had lower rates than Luxemburg, while Germany had a higher rate (Masuy-Stroobant, 1997).

Figures for Luxemburg reaching back before 1900 are available for the time period 1876–80. During this period the rate was lower with 149 than in the first decade of the twentieth century, when the rate ranged from 156 to 159 infant deaths (Service Central de la Statistique et des Études Économiques, 1990a: 56). Thus, the effective and irreversible decline in infant mortality in Luxemburg came rather late and only after 1910, although this decline stalled during World War I.

Figures on life expectancy in Luxemburg are available since 1901/3 (Figure L.4). Gains in life expectancy have mainly been among new-borns, while among 40- and 60-year-olds there have been only minor improvements. In Luxemburg, there have been only small differences between the sexes concerning life expectancy, nor was there any divergence in life expectancy between the sexes over time.

FERTILITY AND LEGITIMACY

Legitimate fertility in 1900 was well above the European average, but declined very fast in the pre-World War I period, with the strong downswing during the war (Figure L.5). In the 1920s legitimate fertility was fairly high, but in the aftermath of the 1929–32 economic depression marital fertility fell below the European average. During the late 1930s and the 1940s marital fertility was still lower, with 1,000 births per 10,000 married women, while the European rate was 1,500 per 10,000 married women.

Figure L.3 Infant mortality 1901-1945

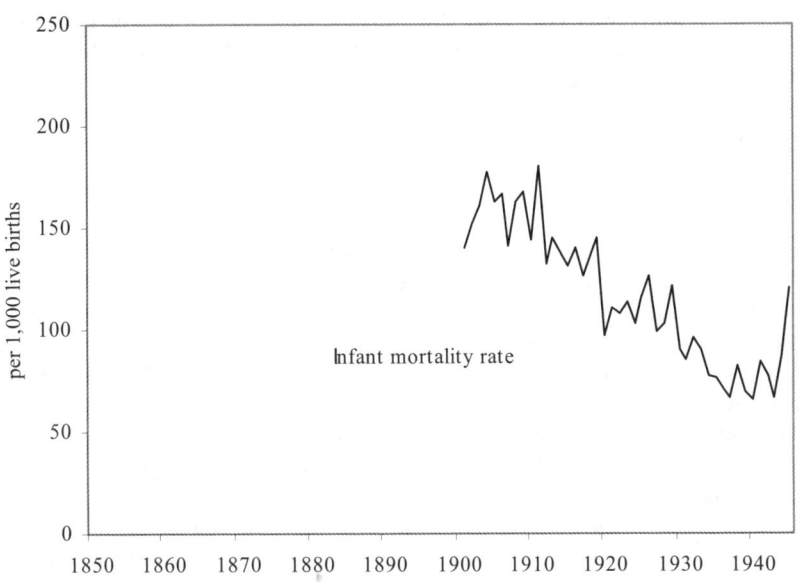

Figure L.4 Life expectancy 1901/03-1943/45

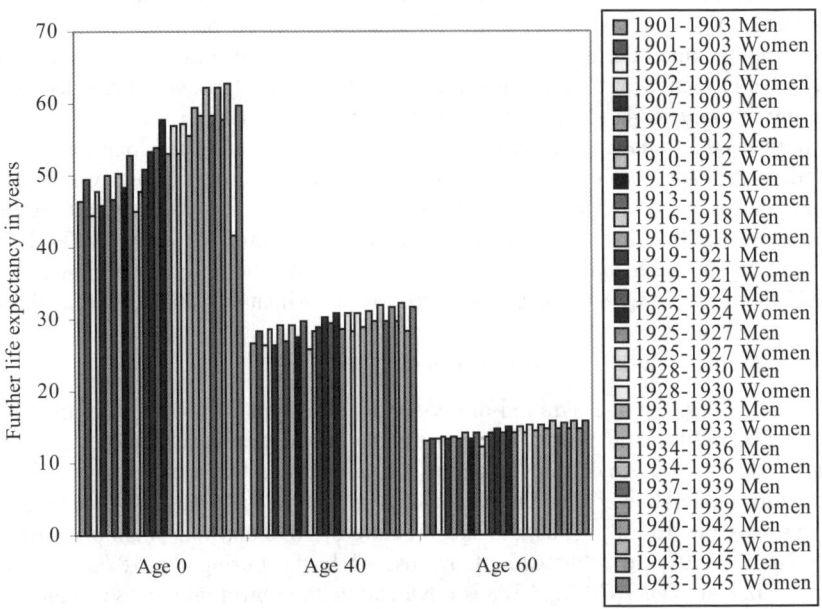

Illegitimate fertility during the whole time period was well below the European average. From 1900 to the outbreak of World War I, the illegitimate fertility rate increased, following a longer trend which originated already in the 1870s, when illegitimate fertility was very low. But with the start of World War I illegitimate fertility declined in the same way as legitimate fertility. It was also affected by the demographic crises of the 1930s and reached the very low level of approximately 50 illegitimate births per 10,000 unmarried women. In contrast to the legitimate birth rate, the illegitimate birth rate increased during World War II.

MARRIAGE AND DIVORCE

Luxemburg belongs to the region of Europe with the Western European marriage pattern of late age at marriage and a high celibacy rate. In the late nineteenth century age at marriage was high. In 1890 only 20% of women aged 20–24 were married, although until 1930 there was a continuous decline in marriage age or an increase of the proportion married at age 20–24. In 1930 this proportion had climbed to 36%. Men's age at marriage was still higher than that of women. In the late nineteenth century the proportion of men married at age 20–24 was well below 10% but showed the same increasing tendency until 1930 as for women. In 1930 the proportion peaked at 11%.

Marriage intensity can be measured by the marriage rate and the celibacy rate. The celibacy rate of women aged 45–54 ranged between 15–20% during the time period from 1890–1937 and decreased only slightly during the 1930s. Compared with other European countries, celibacy was therefore rather low. The marriage rate as a second indicator of nuptiality showed an increasing tendency from the 1890s to the 1930s (Figure L.6). World War I had a tremendous negative effect on the marriage rate, but after the war the marriage rate recovered and many people who had postponed marriage now got married. During the inter-war period marriage frequency was high, but declined during the 1920s and 1930s. Finally, World War II had the same negative influence on the marriage rate as World War I. Marriages postponed mainly during the years 1942–43 were recovered afterwards.

With regard to *marital stability*, Luxemburg participated in the long-term growth of divorces, and the level for the whole period under consideration was near the European average (Figure L.6). After World War I the divorce rate strongly increased for the first time and increased its level. Until the early 1940s divorce frequency increased only slightly. During World War II divorces declined and in 1945 there were only 8 divorces compared to approximately 100 during the 1930s.

AGE, SEX, AND CIVIL STATUS

In Luxemburg, the age pyramid did not show any signs of reduction in the lowest age group until World War I. The age structure however reveals some irregularities, partly due to the small population of the country at that time, making the age structure vulnerable to singular events such as wars, economic crises, or migration (Appendix Figure L.8). Thus, the age structure of 1890 shows a small proportion of 20–24-year-olds, probably caused by loss of births during the 1870/71 Franco-Prussian War. The 1870s and 1880s obviously led the birth rate to rise again, as the strong age groups of children (0–14) show. World War I caused a major loss of births, as can be seen in the age structure of 1927 for the 10–14-year-olds and again

Figure L.5 Fertility and legitimacy 1901-1945

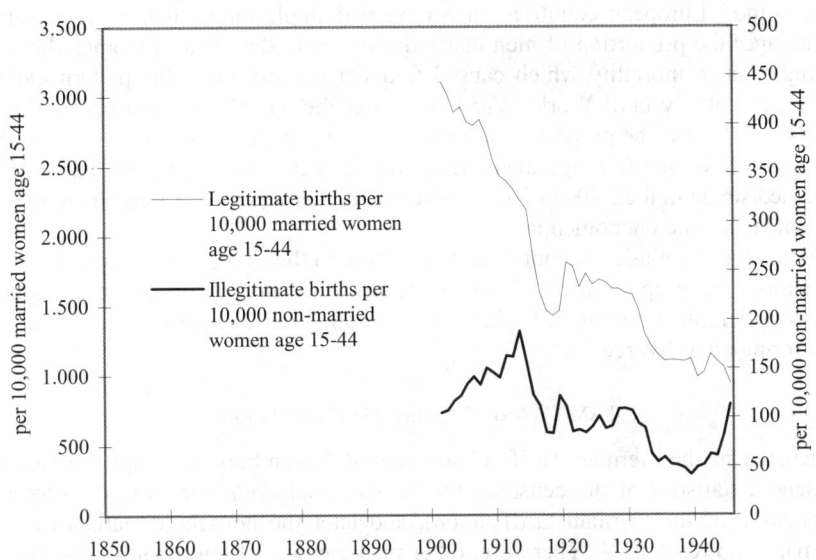

Figure L.6 Marriages and divorces 1890-1945

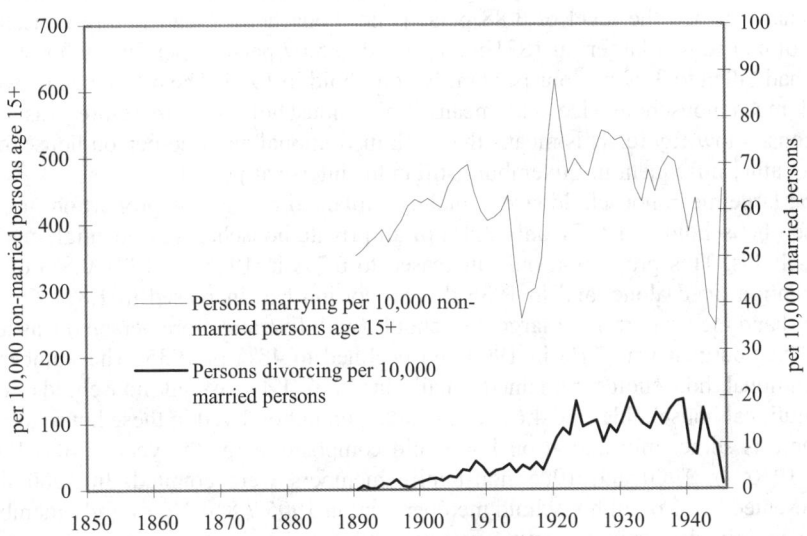

in the age structures of 1930 and 1947. The age structure of 1947 shows not only the losses of births due to World War I, but also the low birth rates of the 1930s.

As in most European countries, men remained single longer than women, but at higher ages the proportion of men married was higher than that of women, because of higher male mortality which caused frequent widowhood. This pattern did not change essentially until World War I. But after the war this pattern reversed with regard to celibacy: the proportion of men remaining single until their 30s was higher than that of women (i.e. age at marriage was higher), but more men than women remained single in their 40s to 50s. Celibacy in higher age groups thus changed from a female to a male phenomenon.

Although Luxemburg was not directly involved in the European and world wars of the period, the proportion of widowed and divorced women in higher age groups was considerable, pointing to higher male mortality and women's lower chances of remarrying after divorce.

FAMILY AND HOUSEHOLD STRUCTURES

Adherence to the German Tariff Union caused Luxemburg to adopt the German household statistics of the censuses for the so-called *Zollabrechnungsbevölkerung* (population of the German tariff union), and later the household statistics of the German Empire of 1871. Therefore, other than the size of households, few aspects of household development can be studied with these data. Mean household size was rather high in Luxemburg during the nineteenth century: in 1864 mean total household size was 5.42 persons per household. Decline in household size started already in the 1880s with the general birth decline. In 1935 mean total household size had reached the level of 3.88 persons per household. Mean family household size of course was larger: in 1871 it amounted to 5.07 persons per family household and had fallen to 3.99 persons per family household in 1935. The difference between total mean household size and mean family household size therefore was 0.11 persons, a low figure. This means that both institutional and one-person households were rather infrequent in Luxemburg still in the inter-war period.

The large mean household size is mainly explained by the low proportion of one-person households. In 1871 only 3.8% of all private households were single-person households. This proportion only increased to 6.7% in 1935. In 1871 0.8% of the population lived alone, and in 1935 this proportion had increased to 1.8%. On the other hand the proportion of large households (with five and more persons) was high in Luxemburg: it was 70% in 1900 and declined to 48% in 1935. The number of institutional households remained small: in 1910 1.4% of all households were institutional households, and 4.6% of the total population lived in these households.

There is some information on household composition for the years 1900, 1905, and 1910. In 1900 and 1905 non-family members were counted. In 1900 they represented 8.7% of all household members and in 1905 7.8%. Non-family members were mainly domestic servants, servants and farmhands, boarders, and lodgers. During this short period nuclearization in the sense of the decline of non-family members becomes visible. For the years 1905 and 1910 household composition was presented for a few categories combined with household size. The main category of non-family members was domestic servants. Domestic servants were mainly found in the large households of five or more persons and were most frequent in the category of households with 7–8 persons. The same is true for the category of 'other persons' which includes farmhands, boarders and lodgers, etc. The proportion of family members declines with household size: the larger the households, the larger the proportion of non-family members.

THE NATIONAL SYSTEM OF DEMOGRAPHIC STATISTICS

Population structure

In Luxemburg population censuses have a long tradition. Regular census-taking started already in the 1820s. The first census after the new territorial formation was taken in 1839. Luxemburg joined the German Tariff Union and became a member of the German Federation (*Deutscher Bund*). Thus, Luxemburg participated in the three annual censuses of the German Tariff Union held from 1846 to 1867. Starting from German unification in 1870/71, Luxemburg adopted the census system of the German Empire until the outbreak of World War I. At the end of the war Luxemburg's affiliation to Germany ended and France became the important neighbour. The statistical system and census-taking was therefore orientated on the French system. The quinquennial system of census-taking which dominated during the German period was given up and census-taking became rather irregular during the inter-war period due to the European political and economic turbulence.

Before 1900 Luxemburg had no official publication series for official statistics. Results from censuses were published in the law gazette, the *Mémorial du Grand-Duché de Luxembourg*. Statistical results for the nineteenth century were later published for different subjects, but unfortunately not for population censuses. Thus, there is no summary publication on historical population statistics although there are valuable general historical statistics of Luxemburg (cf. STATEC, 1990a). This title summarizes the main population statistics results. But it does not cover population by age, sex, or marital status, for example. This material is collected in this volume. This information was combined for the first time in 1890 and published in the *Mémorial*. From 1890–1905 the age was given in one-year age groups, but from 1910 to 1930 only in larger age brackets for the older ages.

Vital statistics

Annual data on births, deaths, marriages, and divorces are available since 1841. Annual data on the population on 1 January have been calculated since 1840. Disaggregations of these basic demographic variables were introduced at later stages: since 1876 births have been divided into live births and stillbirths as well as legitimate and illegitimate births. Deaths by age (under one year—infant mortality) have been registered since 1876 and neonatal mortality since 1901. Complicated measures of fertility such as the Total Period Fertility Rate (TPFR) or the cohort fertility rate are available only since the 1930s and 1940s, although age-specific fertility measures have been calculated for earlier periods, at least since 1871.

Households and families

Data on *households* (*Haushaltungen* or later *ménages*) were already collected in the censuses for the German Tariff Union since 1840. But in these censuses the mere number of households is given. With the introduction of German statistics in 1871, Luxemburg adopted the German household statistics, distinguishing between single-person households, family households, and institutional households (cf. chapter on Germany). Family households also included members co-residing with a family but who did not belong biologically to the family, such as servants, boarders, etc. (non-family household members).

Private households by size were distinguished in the census of 1900. The number of households and their respective members were distinguished for households with 1 to 11 and more persons. In 1900, 1905, and 1910 the *household composition* was published, dividing family household members into the three categories of family members, service personnel, and others.

The *definition of a household* (*Haushaltungen* or later *ménage*) during the period of the censuses for the German Tariff Union (until 1867) was that of a private household, thus it also included people living alone. From 1871 until 1910 the same definition as in the German household statistics was applied. Households were conceived as those persons who not only share one dwelling, but also have a shared household budget. Thus, in 1910 the definition for households states (Ständige Kommission für Statistik, 1911: 77):

Unter **Haushaltung** waren den Vorschriften gemäss alle zu einer wohn- und haus-wirtschaftlichen Gemeinschaft vereinigten Personen zu verstehen—sogenannte **Familien-** oder gewöhnliche **Haushaltungen**.

Einer Haushaltung gleich geachtet wurden **einzellebende Personen** mit besonderer Wohnung und eigener Hauswirtschaft—sogenannte **Einzelhaushaltungen**. Andere alleinstehende Personen wie Zimmerabmieter ohne eigene Hauswirtschaft, Chambregarnisten, Schlafgänger, waren indes derjenigen Haushaltung zuzurechnen, bei der sie wohnten und für sie die Hauswirtschaft führten, auch wenn sie in dieser Haushaltung keine Beköstigung erhielten.

The only investigation into *family statistics* was made in 1927. Family heads were classified by the number of children from 1 to 10 or more. Family heads were grouped into proprietors (*propriétaires*) of the dwelling, tenants (*locataires*), and *détenteurs de logements de service*.

Remarks (also see introductory Table 6.1)

In Luxemburg population censuses from 1890 to 1991 have been used to calculate the variables v16–v21.

BOUNDARY CHANGES

The territory of the old Duchy of Luxemburg was at its largest in the fourteenth century (about 10,000 sq. km.). There were three territorial secessions in the history of Luxemburg. In 1649 (treaty of the Pyrenees) the southern part was ceded to France, in 1815 (Congress of Vienna) the eastern parts were ceded to Prussia, and in 1839 (Treaty of London) the Wallonian part of the country went back to Belgium. The territory of the country has not changed from 1939 to the present (Als, 1991: 3ff.).

Since 1840 Luxemburg has been administratively divided into districts, cantons, and communes. In 1840 three districts were created (Luxemburg, Diekirch, and Grevenmacher). A fourth district, Mersch, comprising the cantons of Mersch and Redange, was created in 1857 and dissolved in 1867. In 1840 twelve cantons were established: Capellen, Esch, Luxemburg, Mersch, Clervaux, Diekirch, Redange,

Vianden, Wiltz, Echternach, Grevenmacher, and Remich. The number of communes was 120 in 1839 and has since changed very little; in 1920 there were 126 and in 1978 118 communes (Service Central de la Statistique et des Études Économiques, 1990a: 1–3 (with maps on pp. 1–2); see also Als, 1991: 3–7 (with map on p. 6)).

APPENDIX TABLES AND FIGURES

APPENDIX TABLE L.1 Population structure at census dates 1890–1947

Census number	Census date	Census population				Marital status				Age group		
		Total	Male	Female	Single	Married	Widowed	Divorced	0–14	15–64	65+
						Absolute						
1	1 XII 1890	211,088	105,419	105,669	130,787	66,760	13,450	91	72,500	125,299	13,289
2	2 XII 1895	217,583	109,282	108,301	134,595	69,084	13,823	81	71,515	132,243	13,825
3	1 XII 1900	235,954	121,593	114,361	145,070	76,308	14,453	123	74,711	147,036	14,207
4	1 XII 1905	246,455	126,220	120,235	149,871	81,449	14,938	197	80,080	151,716	14,659
5	1 XII 1910	259,891	134,101	125,790	156,891	87,340	15,660	..	89,571	154,738	15,582
6	1927	285,524	147,597	137,927	154,958	112,871	16,954	741	70,096	187,289	28,139
7	31 XII 1930	299,993	154,405	145,588	158,455	123,023	17,478	1,037	73,828	196,424	29,741
8	31 XII 1935	296,913	149,429	147,484	150,931	126,318	19,664	..	72,923	202,684	21,306
9	31 XII 1947	290,992	145,096	145,896	135,881	132,251	21,017	1,843	57,703	205,673	27,616
						Per cent						
1	1 XII 1890	100.00	49.94	50.06	61.96	31.63	6.37	0.04	34.35	59.36	6.30
2	2 XII 1895	100.00	50.23	49.77	61.86	31.75	6.35	0.04	32.87	60.78	6.35
3	1 XII 1900	100.00	51.53	48.47	61.48	32.34	6.13	0.05	31.66	62.32	6.02
4	1 XII 1905	100.00	51.21	48.79	60.81	33.05	6.06	0.08	32.49	61.56	5.95
5	1 XII 1910	100.00	51.60	48.40	60.37	33.61	6.03	..	34.46	59.54	6.00
6	1927	100.00	51.69	48.31	54.27	39.53	5.94	0.26	24.55	65.59	9.86
7	31 XII 1930	100.00	51.47	48.53	52.82	41.01	5.83	0.35	24.61	65.48	9.91
8	31 XII 1935	100.00	50.33	49.67	50.83	42.54	6.62	..	24.56	68.26	7.18
9	31 XII 1947	100.00	49.86	50.14	46.70	45.45	7.22	0.63	19.83	70.68	9.49

APPENDIX TABLE L.2 Census population by region 1839–1935 (per cent)

Districts/Cantons[1]	1839	1851	1865	1880	1890	1900[2]	1910	1922	1930	1935
Luxembourg	**42.16**	**42.37**	**43.11**	**46.91**	**50.83**	**56.11**	**59.69**	**62.08**	**67.51**	**67.24**
Capellen	7.94	8.02	8.11	7.73	7.34	6.68	6.15	6.14	5.61	5.64
Esch	9.02	8.56	8.77	11.71	15.90	22.08	26.48	28.41	35.01	32.99
Luxembourg-Ville	10.39	11.17	11.88	14.34	15.49	16.67	17.44	17.78	17.96	19.47
Luxembourg-Campagne	6.91	6.90	6.82	6.31	5.98	5.32	4.89	5.05	4.69	4.85
Luxembourg-Ville et Campagne	*17.30*	*18.07*	*18.71*	*20.66*	*21.47*	*21.99*	*22.33*	*22.83*	*22.65*	*24.32*
Mersch	7.90	7.72	7.53	6.80	6.12	5.37	4.74	4.71	4.24	4.28
Diekirch	**33.37**	**33.94**	**35.01**	**32.60**	**30.60**	**26.87**	**24.71**	**23.29**	**20.06**	**20.11**
Clervaux	6.78	7.17	8.02	7.34	7.03	6.41	6.12	5.83	4.89	4.92
Diekirch	9.10	9.34	9.50	9.09	8.66	7.77	7.15	6.79	5.99	5.99
Redange	8.14	8.11	8.04	7.29	7.08	6.01	5.39	4.95	4.08	4.05
Vianden	1.75	1.61	1.71	1.56	1.43	1.21	1.10	1.02	0.89	0.92
Wiltz	7.60	7.72	7.74	7.32	6.41	5.46	4.95	4.70	4.21	4.23
Grevenmacher	**24.47**	**23.69**	**21.88**	**20.49**	**18.57**	**17.02**	**15.60**	**14.63**	**12.43**	**12.65**
Echternach	7.72	7.78	7.00	6.54	5.87	5.29	4.78	4.49	3.67	3.76
Grevenmacher	8.53	8.25	7.82	7.36	6.94	6.54	6.24	5.79	5.12	5.19
Remich	8.22	7.66	7.07	6.58	5.75	5.20	4.58	4.34	3.64	3.71
Total	**100.00**	**100.00**	**100.00**	**100.00**	**100.00**	**100.00**	**100.00**	**100.00**	**100.00**	**100.00**

Notes: [1] Data refer to the actual territory of the districts and cantons. [2] Present population.

APPENDIX TABLE L.3 Population density by region 1839–1935 (inhabitants per sq. km.)

Districts/Cantons[1]	1839	1851	1865	1880	1890	1900[2]	1910	1922	1930	1935
Luxembourg	**79**	**91**	**97**	**109**	**119**	**146**	**171**	**180**	**224**	**221**
Capellen	68	78	83	82	78	79	80	81	84	84
Esch	63	69	74	102	139	213	282	306	432	403
Luxembourg-Ville	343	423	470	587	637	760	878	904	1.046	1.124
Luxembourg-Campagne	63	72	74	71	68	67	68	71	75	77
Luxembourg-Ville et Campagne	*123*	*148*	*160*	*182*	*190*	*216*	*243*	*251*	*285*	*303*
Mersch	60	67	68	64	58	56	55	55	57	57
Diekirch	**49**	**57**	**62**	**59**	**56**	**54**	**55**	**53**	**52**	**52**
Clervaux	35	42	49	47	45	45	48	46	44	44
Diekirch	65	76	81	80	76	76	77	74	75	74
Redange	52	59	61	57	56	53	52	48	46	45
Vianden	55	58	65	61	56	53	53	50	49	51
Wiltz	49	57	60	58	51	48	48	46	48	47
Grevenmacher	**79**	**88**	**85**	**82**	**75**	**76**	**77**	**73**	**71**	**72**
Echternach	71	82	77	74	67	67	67	63	59	60
Grevenmacher	69	76	75	73	69	73	76	72	73	73
Remich	109	117	113	108	95	95	93	89	85	86
Total	**66**	**75**	**79**	**81**	**82**	**91**	**100**	**101**	**116**	**115**

Notes: [1] Data refer to the actual territory of the districts and cantons. [2] Present population.

APPENDIX TABLE L.4 Demographic developments 1850–1945 (absolute figures and rates)

Year	Mid-year population	Natural population growth rate	Population growth rate	Net migration rate	Crude birth rate	Legitimate births per 10,000 married women age 15–44	Illegitimate births per 10,000 unmarried women age 15–44	Illeg. births per 100 leg. births
1850	191,150	13.6	14.6	1.1	34.1	..	..	..
1851	193,550	12.8	12.4	-0.4	35.1	..	..	..
1852	193,895	11.3	1.8	-9.5	32.4	..	..	..
1853	193,070	9.4	-4.3	-13.7	31.7	..	..	..
1854	191,100	8.4	-10.3	-18.7	32.6	..	..	..
1855	189,325	9.0	-9.4	-18.4	30.6	..	..	..
1856	189,910	12.7	3.1	-9.6	32.3	..	..	..
1857	190,245	11.6	1.8	-9.8	32.3	..	..	..
1858	190,840	9.5	3.1	-6.3	33.5	..	..	..
1859	192,630	11.7	9.3	-2.4	35.5	..	..	..
1860	194,940	13.2	11.8	-1.4	33.8	..	..	..
1861	196,985	11.9	10.4	-1.6	33.3	..	..	..
1862	198,720	10.4	8.7	-1.7	32.5	..	..	..
1863	200,710	11.9	9.9	-2.0	34.0	..	..	..
1864	202,400	7.7	8.3	0.7	33.1	..	..	..
1865	203,340	5.9	4.6	-1.3	32.5	..	..	..
1866	203,505	-7.5	0.8	8.3	31.7	..	..	..
1867	201,605	11.6	-9.4	-21.0	32.2	..	..	..
1868	199,945	11.2	-8.3	-19.5	31.7	..	..	..
1869	200,325	11.4	1.9	-9.5	32.3	..	..	..
1870	201,440	8.2	5.5	-2.7	33.0	..	..	..
1871	201,110	7.2	-1.6	-8.8	31.7	..	..	..
1872	200,085	10.3	-5.1	-15.4	31.9	..	..	..
1873	200,765	11.7	3.4	-8.3	32.5	..	..	..
1874	202,520	10.8	8.7	-2.2	33.2	..	..	..
1875	204,140	4.6	7.9	3.3	31.0	..	..	..
1876	205,325	17.0	5.8	-11.3	37.6	..	..	..
1877	206,745	14.8	6.9	-7.9	33.5	..	..	..
1878	208,090	11.2	6.5	-4.7	32.3	..	..	..
1879	209,045	10.5	4.6	-5.9	33.2	..	..	..
1880	209,975	11.5	4.4	-7.1	31.8	..	..	..
1881	210,780	9.9	3.8	-6.1	32.0	..	..	..
1882	211,670	7.6	4.2	-3.4	31.2	..	..	..
1883	212,925	9.5	5.9	-3.6	30.0	..	..	..
1884	214,025	12.1	5.1	-7.0	32.2	..	..	..
1885	214,590	9.1	2.6	-6.5	29.9	..	..	..
1886	215,180	11.3	2.7	-8.6	30.7	..	..	..
1887	215,995	11.0	3.8	-7.2	29.8	..	..	..
1888	215,625	3.9	-1.7	-5.6	24.3	..	..	..
1889	213,925	7.6	-7.9	-15.6	29.0	..	..	..
1890	212,215	6.1	-8.1	-14.2	28.2	..	..	..
1891	212,095	8.4	-0.6	-8.9	29.4	..	..	..
1892	212,930	6.5	3.9	-2.6	28.1	..	..	..
1893	213,830	8.5	4.2	-4.3	29.2	..	..	..
1894	215,220	9.1	6.5	-2.7	28.5	..	..	..
1895	216,975	-4.2	8.1	12.3	15.1	..	..	..
1896	219,240	8.4	10.3	2.0	28.6	..	..	..
1897	222,135	10.0	13.0	3.0	29.6	..	..	..

continued

APPENDIX TABLE L.4 Demographic developments 1850–1945 (absolute figures and rates)

Crude death rate	Infant mortality rate	Stillbirth rate	Infant mortality and stillbirth rate	Crude marriage rate	Persons marrying per 10,000 unmarried persons age 15+	Persons marrying per 10,000 unmarried persons age 15–49	Crude divorce rate	Divorces per 100 marriages	Divorces per 10,000 married persons	Year
20.5	..	..	..	7.5	..	..	0.0	0.1	..	1850
22.3	..	..	..	7.4	..	..	0.0	0.1	..	1851
21.1	..	..	..	6.3	..	..	0.0	0.3	..	1852
22.3	..	..	..	5.9	..	..	0.0	0.1	..	1853
24.2	..	..	..	6.0	..	..	0.0	0.1	..	1854
21.7	..	..	..	..	..	..	0.0	..	..	1855
19.6	..	..	..	6.3	..	..	0.0	0.0	..	1856
20.7	..	..	..	6.9	..	..	0.0	0.1	..	1857
24.1	..	..	..	7.0	..	..	0.0	0.0	..	1858
23.9	..	..	..	7.9	..	..	0.0	0.3	..	1859
20.6	..	..	..	7.7	..	..	0.0	0.1	..	1860
21.4	..	..	..	7.1	..	..	0.0	0.1	..	1861
22.1	..	..	..	6.5	..	..	0.0	0.0	..	1862
22.1	..	..	..	6.8	..	..	0.0	0.0	..	1863
25.4	..	..	..	6.5	..	..	0.0	0.0	..	1864
26.6	..	..	..	7.1	..	..	0.0	0.0	..	1865
39.2	..	..	..	6.7	..	..	0.0	0.0	..	1866
20.6	..	..	..	8.0	..	..	0.0	0.0	..	1867
20.5	..	..	..	6.6	..	..	0.0	0.0	..	1868
20.9	..	..	..	6.6	..	..	0.0	0.0	..	1869
24.8	..	..	..	6.5	..	..	0.0	0.0	..	1870
24.5	..	..	..	6.7	..	..	0.0	0.1	..	1871
21.6	..	..	..	6.6	..	..	0.0	0.0	..	1872
20.9	..	..	..	7.0	..	..	0.0	0.0	..	1873
22.3	..	..	..	7.5	..	..	0.0	0.1	..	1874
26.4	..	..	..	7.4	..	..	0.0	0.0	..	1875
20.5	..	..	..	6.9	..	..	0.0	0.1	..	1876
18.7	..	..	..	6.5	..	..	0.0	0.1	..	1877
21.1	..	..	..	6.6	..	..	0.0	0.0	..	1878
22.7	..	..	..	6.1	..	..	0.0	0.1	..	1879
20.3	..	..	..	6.1	..	..	0.0	0.1	..	1880
22.1	..	..	..	6.1	..	..	0.0	0.2	..	1881
23.6	..	..	..	5.6	..	..	0.0	0.0	..	1882
20.6	..	..	..	5.4	..	..	0.0	0.1	..	1883
20.1	..	..	..	6.0	..	..	0.0	0.1	..	1884
20.7	..	..	..	6.1	..	..	0.0	0.0	..	1885
19.4	..	..	..	6.5	..	..	0.0	0.1	..	1886
18.8	..	..	..	5.9	..	..	0.0	0.0	..	1887
20.4	..	..	..	5.7	..	..	0.0	0.1	..	1888
21.4	..	..	..	5.9	..	..	0.0	0.0	..	1889
22.0	..	..	..	6.0	352	457	0.0	0.0	0.0	1890
21.0	..	33.7	..	6.2	360	466	0.0	0.2	0.9	1891
21.6	..	36.3	..	6.4	372	481	0.0	0.1	0.3	1892
20.7	..	32.2	..	6.6	380	490	0.0	0.1	0.3	1893
19.4	..	34.3	..	6.8	391	503	0.0	0.3	1.5	1894
19.3	..	60.5	..	6.5	372	478	0.0	0.3	1.2	1895
20.3	..	33.6	..	6.9	391	501	0.0	0.5	2.3	1896
19.6	..	36.6	..	7.2	405	519	0.0	0.2	0.8	1897

continued

APPENDIX TABLE L.4 Demographic developments 1850–1945 (continued)

Year	Mid-year population	Natural population growth rate	Population growth rate	Net migration rate	Crude birth rate	Legitimate births per 10,000 married women age 15–44	Illegitimate births per 10,000 unmarried women age 15–44	Illeg. births per 100 leg. births
1898	225,445	8.9	14.7	5.8	29.0	..	..	..
1899	229,380	10.0	17.2	7.2	30.4	..	..	..
1900	233,230	8.3	16.5	8.2	30.2	..	..	..
1901	236,055	13.3	12.0	-1.4	31.5	3,105	105	4.0
1902	238,740	12.4	11.2	-1.1	31.1	3,018	107	4.1
1903	241,335	10.7	10.8	0.0	30.2	2,885	117	4.5
1904	243,510	10.6	8.9	-1.7	30.9	2,924	122	4.6
1905	245,510	10.5	8.1	-2.4	30.3	2,815	135	5.1
1906	247,730	10.8	9.0	-1.8	30.3	2,792	142	5.4
1907	250,380	13.0	10.6	-2.4	30.9	2,833	133	5.0
1908	253,055	10.7	10.6	-0.1	30.2	2,724	151	5.8
1909	255,665	9.8	10.2	0.4	28.4	2,539	146	6.1
1910	258,060	10.6	9.3	-1.4	27.4	2,430	141	6.1
1911	259,975	8.6	7.4	-1.2	27.4	2,394	163	7.1
1912	261,910	9.5	7.4	-2.1	26.9	2,336	162	7.2
1913	264,285	9.9	9.0	-0.9	26.5	2,259	189	8.6
1914	265,650	8.8	5.1	-3.7	25.5	2,188	156	7.3
1915	265,300	5.9	-1.3	-7.3	21.5	1,841	123	6.8
1916	264,145	2.7	-4.4	-7.1	18.8	1,595	112	7.1
1917	263,385	-0.8	-2.9	-2.1	17.1	1,466	85	5.8
1918	262,680	-4.6	-2.7	1.9	16.8	1,429	84	5.9
1919	261,525	0.0	-4.4	-4.5	17.7	1,467	122	8.3
1920	260,810	8.5	-2.7	-11.2	21.6	1,809	111	6.1
1921	260,945	7.9	0.5	-7.3	21.1	1,783	85	4.7
1922	261,520	5.9	2.2	-3.8	19.5	1,632	87	5.2
1923	264,555	7.1	11.5	4.3	20.7	1,731	84	4.7
1924	269,680	-0.2	19.0	19.2	19.9	1,651	91	5.3
1925	273,870	6.7	15.3	8.6	20.5	1,685	101	5.8
1926	278,270	5.5	15.8	10.3	20.3	1,667	89	5.1
1927	282,875	6.9	16.3	9.4	20.7	1,622	91	5.1
1928	287,295	7.3	15.4	8.1	21.3	1,622	109	5.8
1929	292,220	5.7	16.9	11.2	21.3	1,590	109	5.8
1930	297,275	8.4	17.0	8.6	21.5	1,580	107	5.5
1931	299,315	6.7	6.8	0.1	20.0	1,470	94	5.1
1932	298,150	4.5	-3.9	-8.4	17.8	1,292	89	5.5
1933	297,495	3.9	-2.2	-6.1	16.5	1,207	63	4.1
1934	297,385	3.8	-0.4	-4.2	15.7	1,148	54	3.6
1935	297,080	2.6	-1.0	-3.7	15.2	1,103	59	4.1
1936	297,490	3.6	1.4	-2.3	15.2	1,109	52	3.6
1937	299,400	3.2	6.4	3.2	15.1	1,105	51	3.6
1938	301,050	2.2	5.5	3.2	14.9	1,099	48	3.4
1939	300,165	2.4	-2.9	-5.3	15.0	1,117	41	2.9
1940	295,980	1.3	-14.1	-15.4	13.4	988	49	3.9
1941	291,615	-0.1	-15.0	-14.8	13.8	1,023	52	4.0
1942	289,645	1.0	-6.8	-7.8	15.6	1,153	63	4.3
1943	288,480	-0.6	-4.0	-3.5	14.8	1,101	61	4.4
1944	285,450	-4.5	-10.6	-6.1	14.5	1,060	82	6.2
1945	283,735	-2.9	-6.0	-3.2	13.3	948	113	9.6

APPENDIX TABLE L.4 Demographic developments 1850–1945 (continued)

Crude death rate	Infant mortality rate	Stillbirth rate	Infant mortality and stillbirth rate	Crude marriage rate	Persons marrying per 10,000 unmarried persons age 15+	Persons marrying per 10,000 unmarried persons age 15–49	Crude divorce rate	Divorces per 100 marriages	Divorces per 10,000 married persons	Year
20.2	..	36.4	..	7.6	427	546	0.0	0.1	0.6	1898
20.4	..	29.6	..	7.8	437	557	0.0	0.3	1.4	1899
21.9	..	33.0	..	7.8	432	550	0.0	0.4	1.9	1900
18.2	140.1	32.1	172.2	7.8	438	558	0.0	0.5	2.3	1901
18.7	152.0	30.6	182.6	7.6	431	548	0.0	0.6	2.6	1902
19.4	160.5	31.0	191.5	7.4	424	539	0.0	0.4	2.0	1903
20.3	177.7	26.0	203.7	7.8	456	579	0.0	0.6	3.0	1904
19.8	162.4	29.1	191.5	8.0	472	599	0.0	0.6	2.7	1905
19.6	166.7	26.6	193.3	8.3	482	613	0.1	0.9	4.3	1906
17.9	141.4	28.0	169.4	8.5	489	622	0.1	0.8	4.0	1907
19.5	162.7	30.1	192.8	7.8	447	569	0.1	1.3	6.1	1908
18.6	168.0	31.4	199.3	7.4	418	532	0.1	1.1	4.9	1909
16.7	144.4	31.7	176.1	7.2	404	515	0.1	0.7	3.0	1910
18.8	180.2	33.8	214.0	7.3	410	522	0.1	0.9	4.1	1911
17.4	132.2	29.9	162.1	7.5	418	533	0.1	1.0	4.5	1912
16.6	145.1	34.2	179.3	7.9	443	565	0.1	1.2	5.5	1913
16.7	138.5	33.8	172.2	6.0	335	427	0.1	1.1	3.7	1914
15.6	131.4	37.7	169.1	4.6	258	329	0.1	2.0	5.2	1915
16.1	140.0	40.7	180.7	5.3	295	377	0.1	1.4	4.3	1916
18.0	126.2	30.8	157.0	5.4	302	386	0.1	1.9	5.8	1917
21.4	137.3	32.9	170.2	6.2	349	446	0.1	1.2	4.3	1918
17.7	144.9	42.0	186.9	9.4	526	672	0.1	1.4	7.5	1919
13.1	96.6	34.7	131.3	11.0	617	789	0.2	1.8	11.1	1920
13.2	110.8	34.4	145.2	9.7	541	693	0.2	2.5	13.1	1921
13.5	107.8	35.7	143.5	8.5	475	608	0.2	2.5	11.8	1922
13.5	113.4	35.3	148.7	8.9	497	637	0.3	3.9	19.0	1923
20.1	103.0	38.2	141.2	8.6	483	619	0.2	2.9	13.5	1924
13.8	116.0	29.7	145.8	8.4	472	605	0.3	3.1	14.2	1925
14.7	126.1	34.6	160.7	9.1	509	653	0.3	3.0	14.9	1926
13.8	98.6	33.8	132.3	9.7	540	696	0.2	2.1	10.2	1927
14.0	102.9	36.1	139.0	9.5	536	693	0.3	2.9	13.7	1928
15.6	121.4	33.7	155.1	9.2	525	682	0.2	2.7	12.2	1929
13.0	90.5	36.4	126.9	9.1	529	690	0.3	3.5	15.6	1930
13.3	85.3	37.1	122.4	8.7	511	671	0.4	4.7	19.7	1931
13.2	95.9	37.6	133.5	7.7	454	600	0.3	4.3	15.8	1932
12.5	90.3	34.3	124.6	7.2	433	577	0.3	4.1	14.1	1933
11.9	77.4	37.7	115.1	8.0	480	646	0.3	3.5	13.1	1934
12.6	76.9	36.9	113.9	7.4	448	608	0.4	4.8	16.5	1935
11.5	70.9	30.4	101.2	8.0	483	657	0.3	3.7	14.0	1936
11.9	67.1	26.8	93.9	8.3	500	682	0.4	4.4	17.1	1937
12.7	82.3	29.2	111.5	8.2	493	674	0.4	5.0	18.9	1938
12.7	69.2	29.9	99.1	7.4	440	604	0.4	5.7	19.3	1939
12.1	65.9	28.5	94.5	6.5	387	532	0.2	3.0	9.0	1940
13.9	83.9	26.3	110.2	7.4	438	604	0.2	2.2	7.5	1941
14.6	77.7	25.3	103.0	6.0	353	488	0.4	6.5	17.5	1942
15.4	66.9	21.0	87.9	4.5	263	365	0.2	5.6	11.2	1943
18.9	87.2	24.2	111.4	4.2	246	342	0.2	5.1	9.6	1944
16.2	120.5	27.8	148.3	7.8	453	631	0.0	0.4	1.3	1945

APPENDIX TABLE L.5 Life expectancy by age 1901/3–1943/45 (in years)

Age	0	1	20	40	50	60	70	80
				Males				
1901–1903	46.3	54.8	41.4	26.6	19.6	13.0	8.1	4.3
1902–1906	44.4	53.5	41.1	26.5	19.5	13.2	7.8	4.3
1907–1909	45.8	54.6	41.6	26.4	19.3	13.2	8.0	4.3
1910–1912	46.7	55.1	42.1	26.9	19.5	13.4	7.9	4.3
1913–1915	48.2	55.8	41.9	27.5	20.0	13.4	8.1	4.4
1916–1918	45.0	51.6	40.0	25.7	18.6	12.2	7.3	4.4
1919–1921	50.7	57.5	44.7	29.0	21.1	14.1	8.4	4.4
1922–1924	54.0	60.8	45.7	29.4	21.3	14.2	8.6	4.6
1925–1927	53.0	60.0	45.0	28.7	21.3	14.3	8.6	4.6
1928–1930	53.1	59.0	44.2	28.4	20.9	14.1	8.4	4.6
1931–1933	55.6	61.0	45.5	29.0	21.3	14.5	8.7	4.8
1934–1936	58.2	62.9	46.5	29.6	21.6	14.8	8.8	4.8
1937–1939	58.4	62.8	46.6	29.7	21.8	14.7	8.9	4.8
1940–1942	57.7	62.4	46.1	29.6	21.7	14.7	8.9	4.8
1943–1945	41.6	45.3	32.3	28.4	21.2	14.6	8.9	4.8
				Females				
1901–1903	49.4	56.3	44.0	28.3	20.5	13.2	8.3	4.5
1902–1906	47.8	55.7	43.8	28.5	20.7	13.5	8.2	4.5
1907–1909	50.0	57.0	44.5	29.1	21.1	13.6	8.2	4.5
1910–1912	50.2	57.3	44.9	29.3	21.5	14.2	8.6	4.5
1913–1915	52.9	59.5	45.7	29.7	21.7	14.2	8.2	4.7
1916–1918	47.9	53.6	42.4	28.2	20.6	13.5	7.8	4.7
1919–1921	53.2	58.2	45.6	30.2	22.3	14.8	8.7	4.7
1922–1924	57.8	63.0	47.7	30.9	22.5	15.0	9.0	4.9
1925–1927	57.0	62.4	47.3	30.8	22.6	14.9	8.7	4.9
1928–1930	57.1	62.7	47.5	30.8	22.6	15.2	9.0	4.9
1931–1933	59.4	63.7	47.8	31.1	22.8	15.3	9.2	5.1
1934–1936	62.2	65.7	49.2	31.9	23.4	15.7	9.4	5.1
1937–1939	62.1	65.5	49.0	31.7	23.2	15.6	9.4	5.1
1940–1942	62.7	66.1	49.7	32.3	23.7	15.8	9.3	5.1
1943–1945	59.7	63.8	48.6	31.6	23.4	15.7	9.3	5.1

APPENDIX TABLE L.6A Households by type 1864–1935 (absolute and per cent)

Census year	Total households	Private households	Family households	One-person households	Institutional households	Total household members	Private household members	Family household members	One-person household members	Institutional household members
Absolute										
1864	37,435	..	..	..	..	202,937	..	..	..	..
1871	..	39,236	37,765	1,471	..	204,028[1]	192,773	191,302	1,471	..
1880	41,579	..	..	..	..	210,507	..	..	..	..
1885	42,460	..	..	..	..	214,633	..	..	..	..
1890	43,063	43,009	40,455	2,554	54	211,481	..	..	2,554	..
1895	44,700	44,625	41,952	2,673	75	217,716	..	..	2,673	..
1900	47,795	47,225	44,167	3,058	570	234,974	225,146	222,088	3,058	5,993
1905	51,027	50,271	47,186	3,085	756	245,888	231,197	228,112	3,085	3,268
1910	54,636	53,862	50,096	3,766	774	259,027	243,150	239,384	3,766	11,869
1916	57,926	..	..	..	..	263,490	..	..	..	..
1922	59,910	..	..	..	..	261,643	..	..	..	..
1927	67,240	67,132	63,433	3,699	..	284,702	277,438	273,739	3,699	..
1930	73,141	71,934	67,742	4,192	..	299,782	287,770	283,578	4,192	..
1935	76,604	75,783	70,692	5,091	..	296,913	287,127	282,036	5,091	..
Per cent										
1864	100.00	..	..	..	..	100.00	..	..	..	..
1871	..	100.00	96.25	3.75	..	100.00[1]	94.48	93.76	0.72	..
1880	100.00	..	..	..	..	100.00	..	..	..	..
1885	100.00	..	..	..	..	100.00	..	..	..	..
1890	100.00	99.87	93.94	5.93	0.13	100.00	..	..	1.21	..
1895	100.00	99.83	93.85	5.98	0.17	100.00	..	..	1.23	..
1900	100.00	98.81	92.41	6.40	1.19	100.00	95.82	94.52	1.30	2.55
1905	100.00	98.52	92.47	6.05	1.48	100.00	94.03	92.77	1.25	1.33
1910	100.00	98.58	91.69	6.89	1.42	100.00	93.87	92.42	1.45	4.58
1916	100.00	..	..	..	..	100.00	..	..	..	..
1922	100.00	..	..	..	..	100.00	..	..	..	..
1927	100.00	99.84	94.34	5.50	..	100.00	97.45	96.15	1.30	..
1930	100.00	98.35	92.62	5.73	..	100.00	95.99	94.59	1.40	..
1935	100.00	98.93	92.28	6.65	..	100.00	96.70	94.99	1.71	..

Note: [1] Inexact figure.

APPENDIX TABLE L.6B Households by size and members 1871–1935 (absolute figures)

Census year	Private households total	Households by number of members											
		1 person	2 persons	3 persons	4 persons	5 persons	6 persons	7 persons	8 persons	9 persons	10 persons	11+ persons
Households													
1871	39,236	1,471	:	:	:	:	:	:	:	:	:	:	:
1890	43,009	2,554	:	:	:	:	:	:	:	:	:	:	:
1900	47,225	3,058	6,422	7,454	7,504	6,788	5,419	4,091	2,668	1,597	959	1,275
1905	50,271	3,085	7,375	8,892	8,295	7,254	5,756	4,101	2,772	1,573	897	887
1910	53,862	3,766	7,807	14,087	9,067	7,869	6,205	4,244	2,751	1,606	830	825
1927	67,132	3,699	11,844	15,824	13,100	9,672	6,238	3,746	2,183	1,158	603	802
1930	71,934	4,192	13,185	17,922	14,236	10,028	6,564	3,923	1,934	1,036	517	495
1935	75,783	5,091	15,148	19,579	15,242	10,023	5,856	3,222	1,676	838	431	334
Persons													
1871	192,773	1,471	:	:	:	:	:	:	:	:	:	:	:
1890	:	2,554	:	:	:	:	:	:	:	:	:	:	:
1900	225,146	3,058	12,844	22,362	30,016	33,890	32,514	28,637	21,344	14,373	9,590	16,518
1905	231,197	3,085	14,750	24,828	33,180	36,270	34,536	28,707	22,176	14,157	8,970	10,538
1910	243,150	3,766	15,614	26,676	36,268	39,345	37,230	29,708	22,008	14,454	8,300	9,781
1927	277,438	3,699	23,688	42,261	52,400	48,360	37,428	26,222	17,464	10,422	6,030	9,464
1930	287,770	4,192	26,370	47,472	56,944	50,140	39,384	27,461	15,472	9,324	5,170	5,841
1935	287,127	5,091	30,296	53,766	60,968	50,115	35,136	22,554	13,408	7,542	4,310	3,941

APPENDIX TABLE L.6C Households by size and members 1871–1935 (per cent)

Census year	Private households total	Households by number of members										
		1 person	2 persons	3 persons	4 persons	5 persons	6 persons	7 persons	8 persons	9 persons	10 persons	11+ persons
Households												
1871	100.00	3.75	..	..	..	..	..	..	..	..	..	..
1890	100.00	5.94	..	..	..	..	..	..	..	..	..	..
1900	100.00	6.48	13.60	15.78	15.89	14.37	11.47	8.66	5.65	3.38	2.03	2.70
1905	100.00	6.14	14.67	17.69	16.50	14.43	11.45	8.16	5.51	3.13	1.78	1.76
1910	100.00	6.99	14.49	26.15	16.83	14.61	11.52	7.88	5.11	2.98	1.54	1.53
1927	100.00	5.51	17.64	23.57	19.51	14.41	9.29	5.58	3.25	1.72	0.90	1.19
1930	100.00	5.83	18.33	24.91	19.79	13.94	9.13	5.45	2.69	1.44	0.72	0.69
1935	100.00	6.72	19.99	25.84	20.11	13.23	7.73	4.25	2.21	1.11	0.57	0.44
Persons												
1871	100.00	0.76	..	..	..	..	..	..	..	..	..	..
1890	..	..	..	..	..	..	..	..	..	..	..	..
1900	100.00	1.36	5.70	9.93	13.33	15.05	14.44	12.72	9.48	6.38	4.26	7.34
1905	100.00	1.33	6.38	10.74	14.35	15.69	14.94	12.42	9.59	6.12	3.88	4.56
1910	100.00	1.55	6.42	10.97	14.92	16.18	15.31	12.22	9.05	5.94	3.41	4.02
1927	100.00	1.33	8.54	15.23	18.89	17.43	13.49	9.45	6.29	3.76	2.17	3.41
1930	100.00	1.46	9.16	16.50	19.79	17.42	13.69	9.54	5.38	3.24	1.80	2.03
1935	100.00	1.77	10.55	18.73	21.23	17.45	12.24	7.86	4.67	2.63	1.50	1.37

APPENDIX TABLE L.6D Household indicators 1864–1935

Census year	Household indicators			
	Mean total household size	Mean private household size	Mean family household size	Mean institutional household size
1864	5.42	..	..	..
1871	..	4.91	5.07	..
1880	5.06	..	..	..
1885	5.05	..	..	..
1890	4.91	..	..	..
1895	4.87	..	..	..
1900	4.92	4.77	5.03	10.51
1905	4.82	4.60	4.83	4.32
1910	4.74	4.51	4.78	15.33
1916	4.55	..	..	..
1922	4.37	..	..	..
1927	4.23	4.13	4.32	..
1930	4.10	4.00	4.19	..
1935	3.88	3.79	3.99	..

APPENDIX TABLE L.6E Household composition 1900 and 1905 (absolute and per cent)

Census year	Family households				
	Family members	Domestic servants and live-in employees	Farm workers	Other persons	Family households total
Absolute					
1900	202,797	4,097	3,406	11,782	222,082
1905	210,255	5,461	3,773	8,623	228,112
Per cent					
1900	91.32	1.84	1.53	5.31	100.00
1905	92.17	2.39	1.65	3.78	100.00

Note: Column heads in the source: *Membres de famille; Personnel de service pour les travaux domestiques et industriels; Personnel de service pour les travaux agricoles; Autres personnes; Total.*

APPENDIX TABLE L.6F Household composition by household size 1905 and 1910 (absolute and per cent)

Family households	Family members	Family members	Servants	Servants	Other persons	Other persons	Total family house-hold members	Total family house-hold members
	1905	1910	1905	1910	1905	1910	1905	1910
				Absolute				
2 persons	14,046	15,032	468	448	236	134	14,750	15,614
3 persons	23,339	25,433	731	761	758	482	24,828	26,676
4 persons	31,120	34,424	1,020	1,076	1,040	768	33,180	36,268
5 persons	33,778	37,183	1,205	1,321	1,287	841	36,270	39,345
6 persons	31,978	34,830	1,316	1,381	1,242	1,019	34,536	37,230
7 persons	46,749[1]	27,673	2,113[1]	1,189	2,021[1]	846	50,883[1]	29,708
8 persons		20,302		967		739		22,008
9 persons	20,671[2]	13,197	1,281[2]	698	1,175[2]	559	23,127[2]	14,454
10 persons		7,411		490		399		8,300
11+ persons	8,588	8,142	1,088	1,005	862	634	10,538	9,781
Total	**210,269**	**223,627**	**9,222**	**9,336**	**8,621**	**6,421**	**228,112**	**239,384**
				Column per cent				
2 persons	6.68	6.72	5.07	4.80	2.74	2.09	6.47	6.52
3 persons	11.10	11.37	7.93	8.15	8.79	7.51	10.88	11.14
4 persons	14.80	15.39	11.06	11.53	12.06	11.96	14.55	15.15
5 persons	16.06	16.63	13.07	14.15	14.93	13.10	15.90	16.44
6 persons	15.21	15.58	14.27	14.79	14.41	15.87	15.14	15.55
7 persons	22.23[1]	12.37	22.91[1]	12.74	23.44[1]	13.18	22.31[1]	12.41
8 persons		9.08		10.36		11.51		9.19
9 persons	9.83[2]	5.90	13.89[2]	7.48	13.63[2]	8.71	10.14[2]	6.04
10 persons		3.31		5.25		6.21		3.47
11+ persons	4.08	3.64	11.80	10.76	10.00	9.87	4.62	4.09
Total	**100.00**	**100.00**	**100.00**	**100.00**	**100.00**	**100.00**	**100.00**	**100.00**
				Line per cent				
2 persons	95.23	96.27	3.17	2.87	1.60	0.86	100.00	100.00
3 persons	94.00	95.34	2.94	2.85	3.05	1.81	100.00	100.00
4 persons	93.79	94.92	3.07	2.97	3.13	2.12	100.00	100.00
5 persons	93.13	94.51	3.32	3.36	3.55	2.14	100.00	100.00
6 persons	92.59	93.55	3.81	3.71	3.60	2.74	100.00	100.00
7 persons	91.88[1]	93.15	4.15[1]	4.00	3.97[1]	2.85	100.00[1]	100.00
8 persons		92.25		4.39		3.36		100.00
9 persons	89.38[2]	91.30	5.54[2]	4.83	5.08[2]	3.87	100.00[2]	100.00
10 persons		89.29		5.90		4.81		100.00
11+ persons	81.50	83.24	10.32	10.28	8.18	6.48	100.00	100.00
Total	**92.18**	**93.42**	**4.04**	**3.90**	**3.78**	**2.68**	**100.00**	**100.00**

Notes: [1] 7–8 persons. [2] 9–10 persons.

APPENDIX TABLE L.7 Dates and nature of results on population structure, households/families, and vital statistics

Topic	Intro-duction	Remarks
Population		
Population at census dates	1871	Earlier censuses were conducted as member of the German Tariff Union in 1840, 1843, 1846, 1849, 1852, 1855, 1858, 1861, 1864, 1867, 1869. From 1871 to 1910 censuses were held at the same time as in Germany (see chapter 7).
Population by age, sex, and marital status	1890	Earlier data are probably available since the census of 1871, but have not been found yet.
Households and families		
Households (*Haushaltungen* or *ménages*)		
Total households	1864	Households were recorded from 1840–1869 according to the rules of the German Tariff Union, and from 1871–1910 in line with the German censuses (see chapter 7). A distinction was made for one-person households, family households and institutional households.
		1840–1869: number of households.
		1871: number of households (3 categories).
		1875: number of households (3 categories).
		1880: number of households (3 categories).
		1885: number of households (3 categories).
		1890: number of households (3 categories).
		1895: number of households (3 categories).
		1900: number of households (3 categories), household size, household composition.
		1905: number of households (3 categories), household size, household composition.
		1910: number of households (3 categories), household size, household composition.
		1922: number of households.
		1927: number of households (3 categories), household size, household composition.
		1930: number of households (3 categories), household size.
		1935: number of households (3 categories), household size.
		1947: number of households (3 categories), household size.
		Disaggregation: by cantons.

continued

APPENDIX TABLE L.7 Dates and nature of results on population structure, households/families, and vital statistics (continued)

Topic	Intro-duction	Remarks
Households by size	1900, 1905, 1910, 1927, 1930, 1935, 1947	First time in the housing census of 1900: households by number of persons 1–11+. Repeated in 1905, 1910, 1927, 1930, 1935 and 1947.
Households by composition	1900, 1905, 1910	1900, 1905, 1910: family members, service personnel (domestics and industrial, agricultural), others.
Households by profession of household head	–	
Families (familles or Familien)		
Families by number of children	1927	First special investigation of the fertility of families in 1927. Families with 0–10/12 children.
Population movement		
Mid-year population	1850	
Births		
Live births	1850	
Stillbirths	1891	
Legitimate births	1901	
Illegitimate births	1901	
Deaths		
Total deaths	1850	
Infants (under 1 year)	1901	
Marriages		
Total marriages	1850	
Divorces and separations		
Total divorces	1850	
Legal separations	–	

APPENDIX FIGURE L.8 Population by age, sex and marital status, Luxembourg
1890, 1900, 1910 and 1947 (per 10,000 of total population)

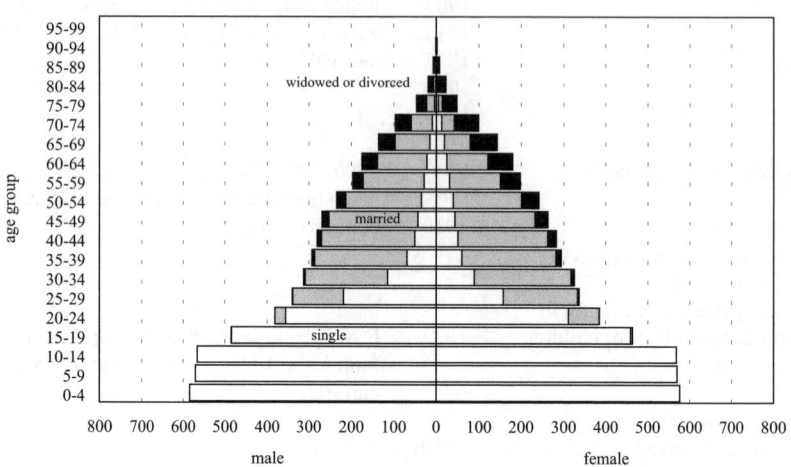

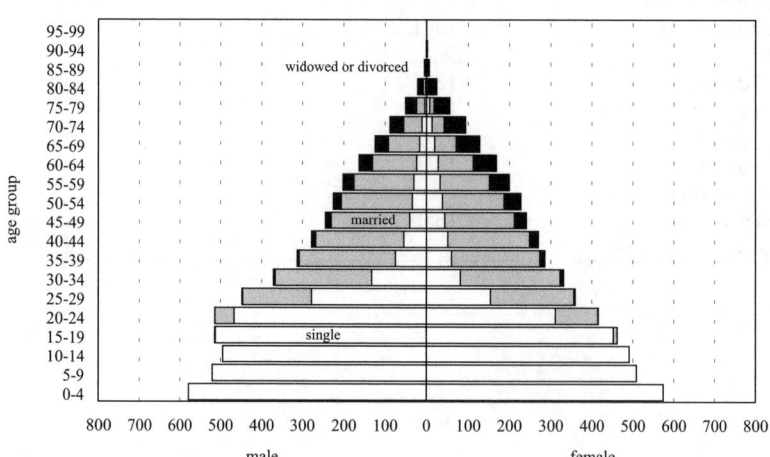

APPENDIX FIGURE L.8 Population by age, sex and marital status, Luxembourg 1890, 1900, 1910 and 1947 (per 10,000 of total population) (continued)

Luxemburg, 1910

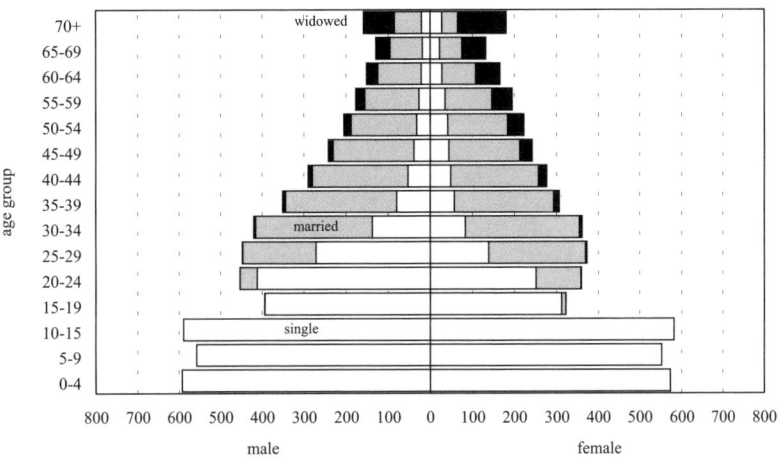

Luxemburg, 1947

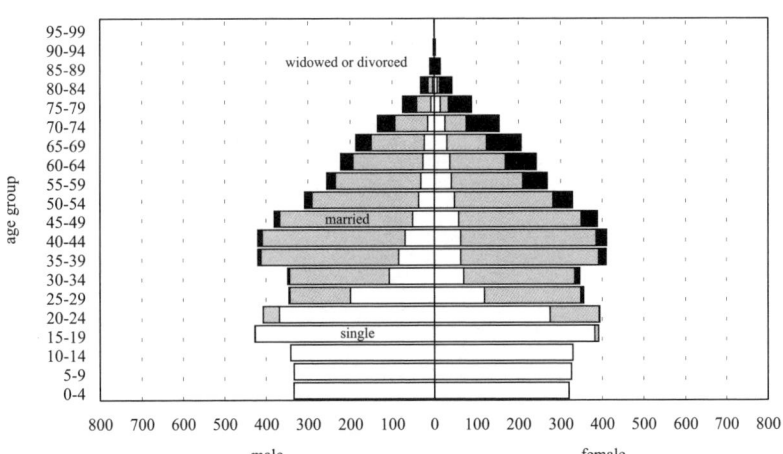

14

The Netherlands

The Netherlands are located at the north-western edge of the continent. The country was settled by Germanic tribes and only partly influenced by the Roman Empire. In the Middle Ages The Netherlands belonged to Burgundy; later they came under the rule of the Spanish Habsburgs. The major characteristics of the country started to develop in the sixteenth century: the influence of Calvinism, the building of a colonial empire, and the struggle for independence. These constellations still exert their influence on the country, as the socio-cultural segmentation and the effects of decolonization (immigration from overseas), among other things, show.

The Netherlands was one of the first countries on the European continent to develop a republican system. The Eighty Years' War for independence from Spain ended with The Netherlands being recognized as a federation composed of the seven northern provinces. This federation was the reason this system (like the Swiss cantons) was called a *consociational democracy*. The independence of the northern provinces was recognized in 1648. The southern provinces remained under the Austrian Habsburgs (and later became Belgium). Under Napoleon, the northern and southern provinces were reunited as the *Batavian Republic*. The Kingdom of the Netherlands was created in 1814/15 at the Congress of Vienna, but lost its southern provinces (Catholic and—partly—French) to Belgium in 1830. Since 1839, when the southern part of Limburg was transferred to Belgium, there have been no important boundary changes.

Formally, The Netherlands is a hereditary parliamentary monarchy. For more than a century the country has been reigned by a queen. The political system is bicameral. Politically the country has traditionally been divided into several socio-cultural milieus. Theoretical literature distinguishes between four different milieus: the Roman Catholic, the Protestant, the Socialist, and the Liberal milieu. Parties are organized according to these milieus. The segmentation of the country into these milieus has been called *pillarization* ('*verzuiling*') (Arend Lijphart). Lijphart stated that, in ideal terms, the whole society would divide itself into these separate segments. Thus, the main social organizations and groups, such as trade unions, churches, the educational system, social circles, and marriage markets organized themselves along these lines. This was true until the 1960s, but, as many studies now show, pillarization is vanishing in several fields. The Netherlands is taking part in the general trend towards secularization (the proportion of those with no religious affiliation is now higher than that of any religious group). The welfare state and the internationalization of the economy have tended to relativize differences between socio-cultural segments.

In economic terms, during its modern history The Netherlands has mainly been a nation of merchants, occupying the most important seaports of the continent, and therefore is the real 'gateway' for overseas trade to continental Europe; agriculture, fisheries, and crafts were only secondary. Thus industrialization came about rather late, after the decline of the colonial empire, and not before the end of the nineteenth century (Van Zanden, 1996).

REGIONAL POPULATION STRUCTURE

The Dutch territory was divided into eleven provinces already at the time of the first census in 1830. This structure did not change until 1986 when the twelfth province of Flevoland was created by joining the former non-provincial Zuidelijke Ijsselmeerpolders and parts of Overijssel.

The Netherlands on the whole was densely populated already in the nineteenth century, and the regional distribution of the population was rather uneven already then. The economic centre of the country was the provinces of Zuidholland, Noordholland, and Noordbrabant, where the country's major ports are located; these provinces continue to be the trading centres of the country. The other parts of the country differed in economic structure with higher proportions of agriculture, animal husbandry and milk/cheese production, fisheries, and small-scale handicrafts. Accordingly, these provinces had a much lower population density. For example, in 1869, population density in the two provinces of Zuidholland and Noordholland was twice the national average (228 and 212 inhabitants per sq. km., respectively, compared to 109). Until the mid-twentieth century, urbanization and migration from rural eastern and northern regions to the cities in the west caused a further imbalance in population density. Zuidholland's population density, for instance, climbed from twice the national average in 1869 to 2.7 times the national average in 1947, with 813 inhabitants per sq. km.. The two provinces with the largest shares of the population—Zuidholland and Noordholland—accounted for 35% of the Dutch population in 1869, increasing to 42% in 1947. These shifts in regional settlement structure reflect regional differences in economic development. The regions with the highest population density are also those where national product and incomes per capita have been highest.

POPULATION GROWTH

Already at the beginning of the nineteenth century, The Netherlands was probably the most densely populated country in Europe. At the time of the first census in 1830, the population was 2,427,000 inhabitants. In 1849 The Netherlands had 3,057,000 inhabitants, an increase of over 600,000 people in roughly twenty years. By 1947 the population had increased to 9,625,000 inhabitants. Over 120 years the population therefore nearly quadrupled, making population growth in The Netherlands one of the highest of all European countries. By comparison, Belgium's population did not quite double from 1846 to 1947. The population of most other Western European countries less than doubled during this period.

The rather high Dutch population figures are in contrast to the country's small territory: The Netherlands is one of the smallest countries in Europe in terms of territory, only 41,029 square kilometres. Population density during the nineteenth century was already high: in 1869, with 3,580,000 inhabitants, population density was already 109 persons per sq. km. With the high population growth during the demographic transition, population density in The Netherlands became the highest in Europe. In the 1990s, it ranked sixth in terms of population, while as regards population density it ranked first among the 15 countries of the European Union. The Dutch population makes up 4.1% of the total population of the European Union, while the territory of The Netherlands is only 1.3% of total EU territory.

The main factor behind the high population density in The Netherlands is the high population growth from the 1870s to the 1940s (Figure NL.1). The natural population growth rate during most of this period ranged between 10 and 15 per 1,000 and was therefore substantially higher than in most European countries at that time. The natural population growth rate increased from the 1870s until the beginning of World War I by tendency, reaching a level of over 15 per 1,000. Between World War I and World War II the natural population growth rate declined by tendency from around 15 to 10 per 1,000.

The net migration rate was structurally slightly negative: emigration therefore exceeded immigration most of the time. There were several emigration waves during the time period: in the early 1880s, around 1890, 1900, 1910, 1920, and 1940. Immigration was only higher than emigration during World War I and in the early 1930s.

THE FIRST DEMOGRAPHIC TRANSITION

The demographic transition in The Netherlands started around 1870, when the number of births and deaths began to decline continuously. While the Dutch birth rate followed the European rate very closely and was only slightly higher, the death rate increasingly dropped below the European average over time. Until World War I the demographic development was rather consistent. Although The Netherlands did not participate directly in World War I, population movement was influenced by the war in the familiar pattern of delayed births during the war and strong increase in births after the war, as well as higher mortality during the war (Figure NL.2).

The Netherlands was not affected by the demographic crisis of the 1930s as strongly as other countries; the birth rate remained high and the death rate rather low, diverging even further from the European average. Although The Netherlands declared neutrality in World War II, it was occupied by German troops and became one of the main battlefields. The drastic effects of these events can be seen in the demography, with the death rate peaking during the war and a strong recovery effect of births after the war. Although decreasing, the birth rate was rather high and well above the European average until the 1970s, when the fertility decline of the 'second demographic transition' started. The birth rate was below the European average for several years, but natural population increase was still strong because of low mortality.

The population history of The Netherlands over the last 150 years—with the exception of World War II—was less influenced by economic crises and wars than that of other countries. Nevertheless, war had an indirect influence. Although The Netherlands was not directly involved in the Franco-Prussian War of 1870/71, the death rate increased, and there was probably also a slight decrease in the birth rate with recovery in the 1870s. As the country did not participate directly in World War I, the war's influence was also moderate compared to other continental countries. Obviously, the Great Depression did not have a strong effect on the development in The Netherlands. The same is true in principle for World War II (Garssen and Harmsen, 1999).

Figure NL.1 Population growth and net migration 1850-1945

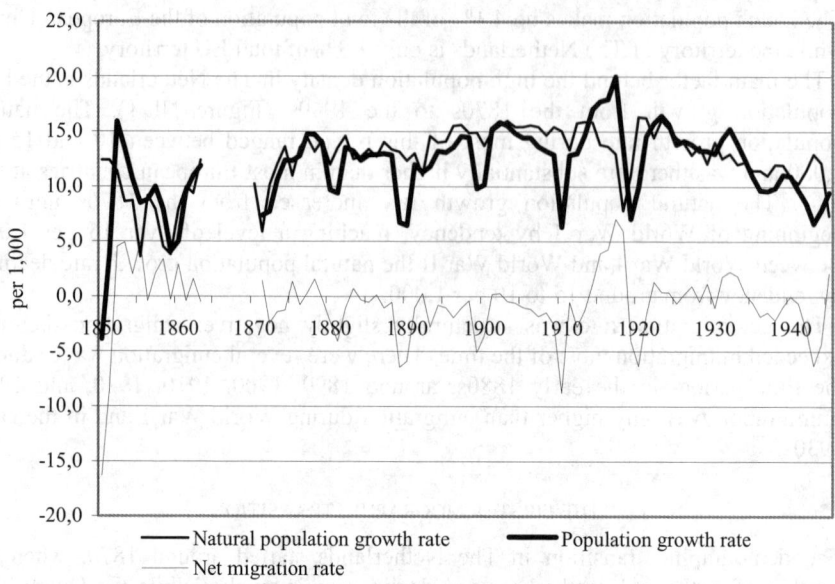

Natural population growth rate ——— Population growth rate
——— Net migration rate

Figure NL.2 First demographic transition 1850-1945

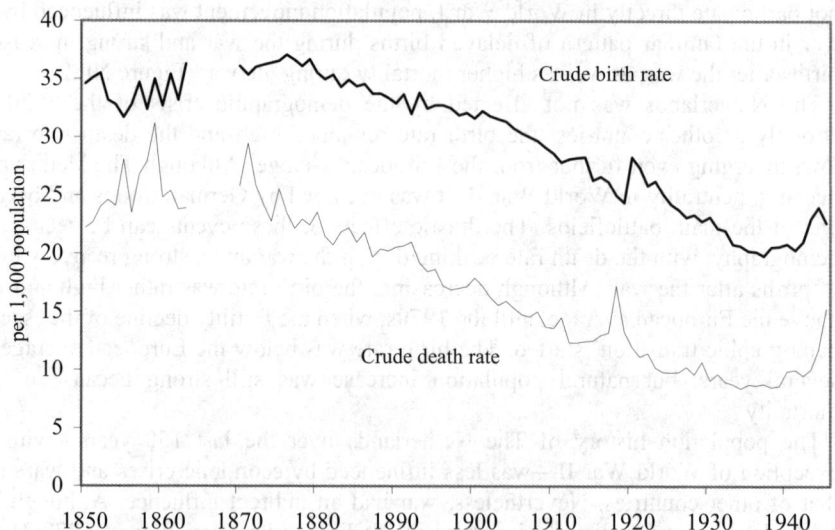

Compared with Europe as a whole, The Netherlands deviates from the 'average' European development insofar as the birth rate was higher and the death rate lower than the European average. All this led to a high natural population increase in the last 150 years, probably one of the highest in Europe. As in Belgium, child mortality was lower than elsewhere in Europe already in the nineteenth century. But in contrast to Belgium, where the birth rate was lower than the European average, in The Netherlands it was constantly higher. Nevertheless, in demographic terms The Netherlands and Belgium during this period are more similar to each other than the two countries are to France, given the very low birth rate in France until 1945. It might be posited that the Walloon demography is more similar to the French and the Flemish to the Dutch. Another hypothesis might be that the cleavage structure in The Netherlands, with its several socio-cultural milieus, led to competition between these 'pillars' in terms of fertility.

MORTALITY AND LIFE EXPECTANCY

The very low infant mortality rate of The Netherlands in the late nineteenth century is one important element of the low mortality rate (Garssen and Harmsen, 1999). The infant mortality rate is defined as deaths of children aged under one year per 1,000 live births. In nineteenth-century Europe, the Nordic countries, Switzerland, and The Netherlands had the lowest infant mortality rates, while in most of Europe infant mortality was rather high. For Masuy-Stroobant (1997: 6) this group of countries constitutes one cluster which had the lowest infant mortality rates in Europe since at least 1900. Presenting figures from 1885 to 1940, Kok, Poppel, and Kruse (1997) show that there was a large difference in infant mortality between illegitimate and legitimate births: the infant mortality of illegitimate children was 50% higher than that of legitimate children. Furthermore, the mortality of male children was constantly higher than that of female children.

Poppel and Mandemakers (1997) present a time series from 1840/44 to 1940/44 showing that infant mortality in The Netherlands increased from the 1840s to the 1870s, but decreased constantly after that time. In the 1860s the rate was 200 infant deaths per 1,000 population, which the authors call 'very high'. But international comparison (see Masuy-Stroobant, 1997: 6f.) shows that The Netherlands was a pioneer in reducing infant mortality, and that around 1900 many European countries still had levels of 200 or more infant deaths per 1,000 population (Figure NL.3).

Given the higher mortality rate of illegitimate births, it can be hypothesized that the very low illegitimacy rate (as in Switzerland) contributed to the rather low infant mortality rate in The Netherlands. This factor surely contributed to the low infant mortality rate, but the Nordic countries, also within the country cluster with low infant mortality rates, had higher illegitimacy rates than Switzerland and The Netherlands. Therefore, other factors must also have contributed to The Netherlands' lower rate.

Poppel and Mandemakers (1997) present data on infant mortality for nineteenth-century Utrecht by fathers' social status. Although the analysis is restricted to one city, the results can probably be applied to the whole country. There is a clear socio-economic differentiation in infant mortality from the upper classes to the lower classes, a result that has been obtained also from studies in other countries (see e.g. Rothenbacher, 1982; Spree, 1980). The lowest infant mortality in Utrecht is found among the upper class, followed by civil servants, lower-level professionals, and foremen. The highest infant mortality rate is found among the unskilled labourers. Between these extremes are the petty bourgeoisie, skilled workers, and farmers. Surprisingly, the petty bourgeoisie had high infant mortality rates. This variation is strongly related to the income position of these socio-economic groups, i.e. infant mortality correlates strongly with income. The authors found a characteristic development of social differences in infant mortality: social differences increased up to the end of the nineteenth century, then began to decrease. According to Smith (1991), this development is a general pattern.[1]

Another line of research has been conducted by Kok, Poppel, and Kruse (1997). They looked at differences in infant mortality according to legitimacy status and found important differences in infant mortality between legitimate and illegitimate children. The cleavage between both groups was still large in the 1880s but narrowed steadily during the health transition process with declining infant mortality. Male infants, whether legitimate or illegitimate, always had a higher risk of death, though this difference became smaller as well during the process of declining infant mortality.

The Princeton European Fertility Project is not directly addressed to the decline in infant mortality, but the development of infant mortality is one of the main features in explaining the demographic transition (see Coale and Watkins, 1986). Thus, Francine van de Walle (1986) has studied the decline in infant mortality in relation to the European demographic transition and with respect to territorial variations. Van de Walle presents a table on infant mortality in the eleven Dutch provinces from 1840–51 to 1895–99 based on Hofstee (1978). In the first half of the nineteenth century infant mortality rates in the eleven provinces were more similar; although there was under-registration, infant mortality rates began to diverge in the second half of the nineteenth century. In the economically advanced provinces of Noord- and Zuidholland infant mortality fell faster than in more backward and agricultural provinces. But on the whole the divergence between infant mortality in the eleven provinces was already rather small in 1879, compared with other European countries. The range between the province with the highest infant mortality rate and the lowest was 136 (infant deaths per 1,000 live births). Thus, the small area of the country also led to a more homogeneous pattern concerning childhood than in countries with larger territory and more heterogeneous populations (such as Germany, with a range of 313) (Van de Walle, 1986: 212).

Life expectancy was rather high compared with most other European countries, but did not reach the very high figures of the Nordic countries, such as Sweden. Life expectancy at birth was lower than in Sweden, but only by four years for boys and six years for girls (Figure NL.4). The difference between Sweden and The Netherlands progressively decreased for higher age groups. Up to World War II, the difference in life expectancy between the Dutch and the Swedish shrank, so that in the mid-twentieth century the Dutch had reached the same high level of life expectancy as the Swedes. Life expectancy of Dutch women was higher than for Dutch men. The differences between the sexes increased until the end of the nineteenth century, but by the 1940s male life expectancy had improved relative to female life expectancy.

---

[1] The Princeton European Fertility Project does not have a country study on The Netherlands.

Figure NL.3 Infant mortality 1850-1945

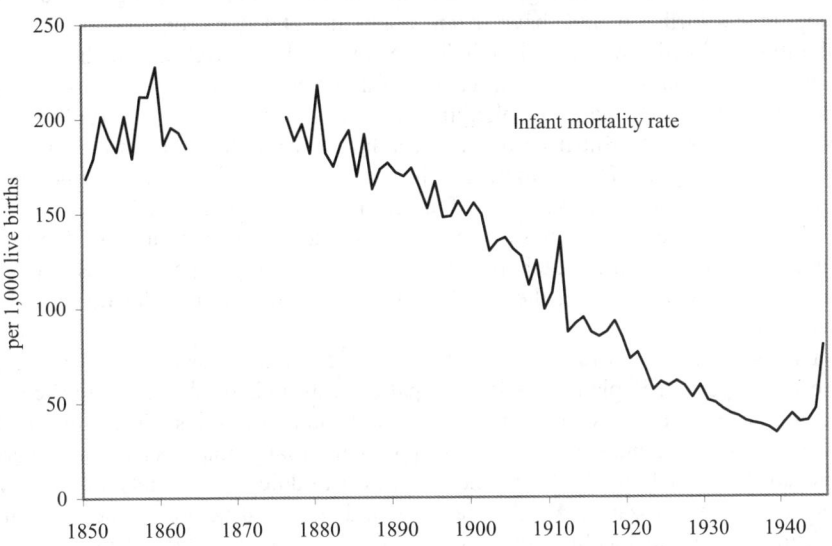

Figure NL.4 Life expectancy 1816/25-1931/40

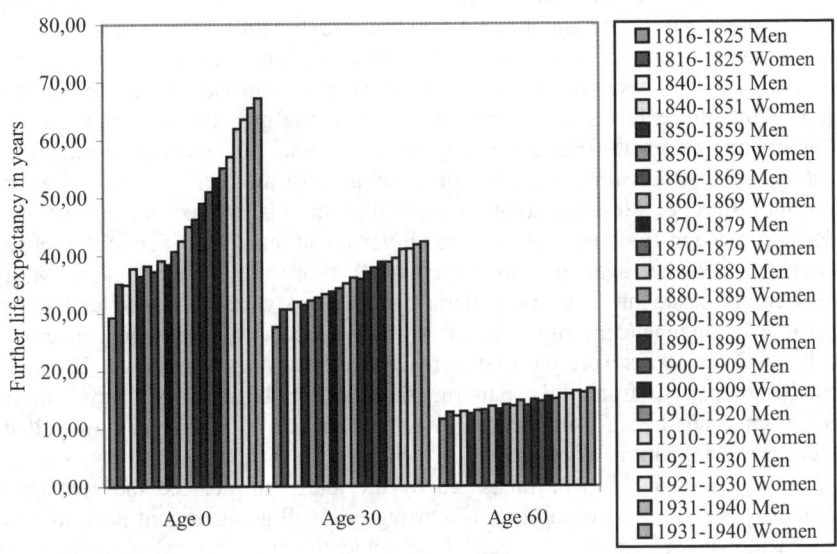

FERTILITY AND LEGITIMACY

Given the late age at marriage and the high celibacy rates, one might assume that illegitimate births would have been common. But the contrary is the case: illegitimate fertility was very low in The Netherlands and well below the European average. This situation did not change fundamentally during the last century, although the social status of illegitimacy has changed since the 1960s in The Netherlands as well. But from the nineteenth century up to the most recent fertility decline, fertility in The Netherlands has been marital fertility, and the marital fertility rate has been well above the European average (Figure NL.5).

This feature again underlines the thesis of the traditional or 'bourgeois' family and marriage model of the Dutch population. Although marriage was restricted and people married rather late, they preferred to procreate within a legally contracted marriage.

This is rather similar to Switzerland, where illegitimacy was also very low during the whole period. Explanations for this pattern can probably be found in the socio-economic structure of the country on the one hand and in the socio-cultural pattern on the other. Late industrialization did not create a large unpropertied 'proletariat'; instead, the social structure remained that of a middle-class society of merchants, fishermen, and peasants. Another factor could be the structure of the agricultural holdings or the neolocality, while a further factor might be the strong ideological and religious underpinnings of legal marital behaviour.

MARRIAGE AND DIVORCE

The Netherlands belong to the region of Europe with the Western European marriage pattern of late age at marriage and a high celibacy rate. In the nineteenth century age at marriage was one of the highest in Western Europe. Accordingly, the celibacy rate was also one of the highest in Western Europe. During the nineteenth and twentieth centuries a 'modernization of nuptiality patterns' occurred in The Netherlands as in all Western European countries. This process lasted until the 1960s, after which time we can speak of a 'post-modern' nuptiality pattern in Western Europe. Modernization of nuptiality in this context means the secular decline in age at first marriage and the universalization of marriage in the sense that marriage became available to nearly the entire adult population. Marriage restrictions based on financial criteria (pauperism) were abolished and marriage became an independent right for all without respect to economic capacity. The cohorts of the 1930s were the first to reach nearly universal marriage. The younger cohorts departed from this pattern, though not because of 'new' marriage constraints, but because of the declining importance of marriage, now called the 'deinstitutionalization' of marriage.

Marriage intensity can be measured by the marriage rate and the celibacy rate. 'Intensity' means the availability of marriage as well as the urgent need to remarry after widowhood ('remarriage need', Michael Mitterauer). A third component can be seen in the universality of marriage in the population. The first rate refers to all marriages of unmarried persons.

As in all of Europe, in The Netherlands the marriage rate since the 1860s had a rising tendency, but until World War II was more or less identical to the European average. Only since about 1950 has the marriage rate strongly deviated from the European pattern (Figure NL.6).

Female celibacy during this period was very high, as in the Nordic countries, but not as high as in Switzerland, making The Netherlands a model country for the Western European marriage pattern. Until the 1930s the celibacy rate was rather similar to the German one.

Obviously there were also strong marriage barriers in The Netherlands during the nineteenth century. This is underlined by the high age at marriage during the period, which only decreased slowly over the century.

In these respects The Netherlands differs somewhat from Belgium, but was very similar to the demographic development of Switzerland. Marriage was late and restricted, children were seldom born outside of marriage, while fertility within marriage was high. This points to a rather high social prestige of the institution of marriage. The democratization and therefore 'modernization' of marriage came only slowly and late. This particular feature of The Netherlands can likely be attributed to the late industrialization of the country, while commerce and trade played a much stronger role. Thus, the socio-economic situation is different from Belgium, where coal mining and heavy manufacturing (e.g. steel production) dominated during industrialization. It is much more similar to Switzerland, where industrialization also came rather late. The socio-economic structure therefore favoured a 'bourgeois' family structure rather than a 'proletarian' one, characterized by traditional values and behavioural models. These patterns have obviously lasted into the present.

Concerning *marital stability*, The Netherlands participated in the long-term growth of divorce. During the whole period under consideration, the divorce rate was more or less the same as the European average. The divorce rate began to rise disproportionately only in the 1970s. The rather moderate divorce rate is surprising in a country with a mixed confessional structure. It also points to a high institutionalization of marriage. To what extent empirical developments have been influenced by the divorce law remains to be determined (Figure NL.6).

From the demographic side two factors may explain the initially limited extent of divorces: age at marriage and the high status of marriage. The later people marry, the lower the propensity to get divorced. One socio-cultural factor may contribute to the low divorce rate: the cleavage structure which was based on religion and ideology and thus tended to reinforce them. This was probably most true of the Calvinists and the Catholics; due to late industrialization, the socialist ideology remained weak. Thus, in the early phase the religious pillars dominated the attitude towards marital breakdown.

AGE, SEX, AND CIVIL STATUS

In The Netherlands until World War I the age structure took a clear pyramidal shape with a concave bottom (Appendix Figure NL.8). The age structure during the second half of the nineteenth century shows great regularity without major wars or economic crises. Until 1909, the last census before World War I, there was no reduction in the size of the lowest age group of 0–4 years, indicating only minor birth decline. Only in 1920 did the concave pattern disappear, but no immediate impact of World War I on the age structure was apparent. In 1930 the age structure had become only slightly bell-shaped, because of the relatively high fertility of The Netherlands during that period (exceptional when compared with other countries).

The Netherlands

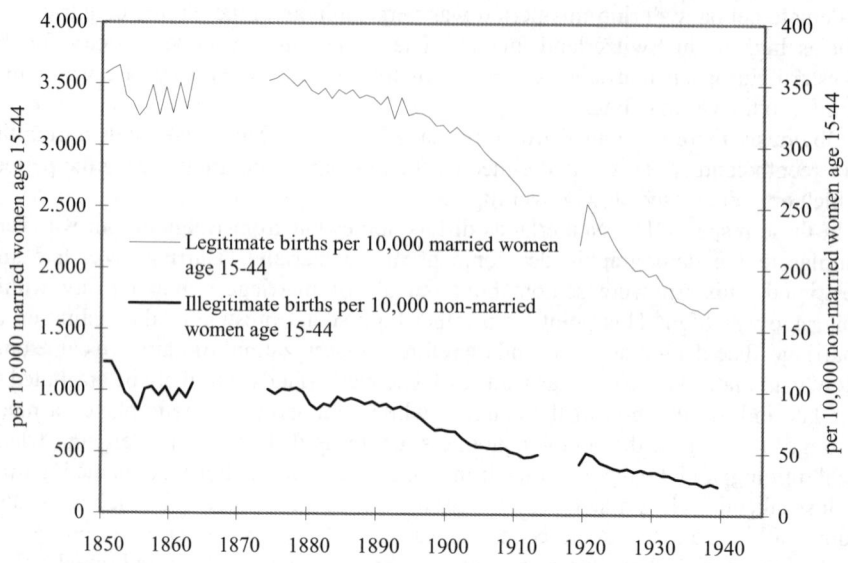

Figure NL.5 Fertility and legitimacy 1850-1939

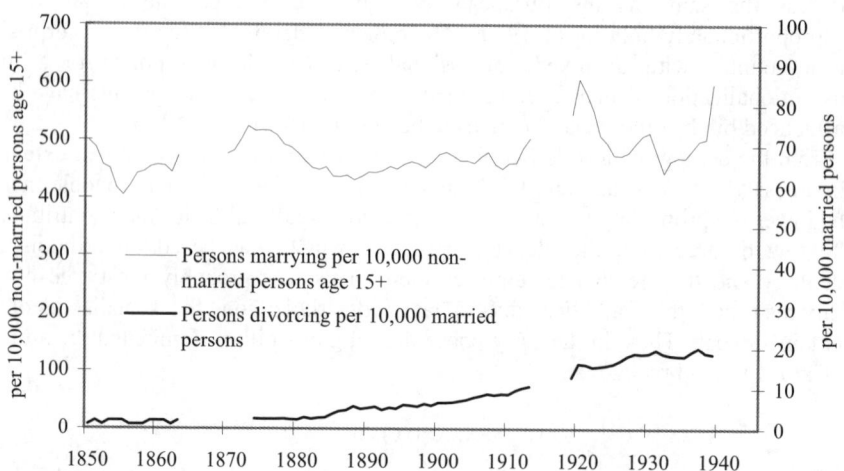

Figure NL.6 Marriages and divorces 1850-1939

World War II had an impact on the Dutch age structure, reducing the age groups born during the war years. But this loss of births was comparatively small. There were also only minor changes in the age structure of adults: male mortality and female widowhood were low in the age structure of 1947 because of Dutch neutrality (despite military occupation).

The proportion of men remaining single until their late 30s was higher than that of women, but female celibacy was more frequent from the age of 40 onwards. The proportion of women widowed or divorced was constantly higher than that of men, although low when compared to countries involved in the different wars. Only in 1947 were these proportions the same for both sexes.

FAMILY AND HOUSEHOLD STRUCTURES

For the nineteenth century and the first half of the twentieth century we have little information about households and even less on families. (Case studies like the one carried out by Janssens (1993) on Tilburg may provide deeper insights). Therefore the discussion must be restricted to some topics that are covered by the available statistics.

We have said above that The Netherlands belong to the Western European marriage pattern with a high proportion remaining unmarried and a high age at first marriage. The question arises of where all these unmarried people lived. Did they live in their own households or did they live with relatives or as servants in their employer's household? Was the extended family system the social norm or did the nuclear family combined with living alone prevail?

An initial response to these questions can be given by the mean private household size which is available as a time series since 1899. Compared with other European countries, at 4.51 persons per private household in 1899 the mean private household size was rather high and similar to Belgium. This result is in accordance with the high fertility and low mortality noted above.

On the other hand, the number of one-person households already at that time was rather high, at nearly 8% of all private households. This corresponds partly to the rather low share of servants in households, in 1899 only 4.7% of all household members. In the German Empire, for example, the respective figure was 10.9% in 1900 (Rothenbacher, 1997: 66, Table 1.4.1). Whether this result can be attributed to the agrarian structure without large estates and therefore fewer rural servants is an open question. On the other hand, the high share of persons living alone and the low share of servants living in their employers' households would indicate a rather 'modernized' family structure already at the turn of the twentieth century.

Since 1899 households and families have undergone major 'modernization': in 1971 there were only 4,000 household servants, compared to 234,000 in 1899, thus live-in servants appeared to have died out as a social arrangement. The mean private household size has declined strongly since 1899 and is now one of the lowest in Europe. This is reflected in the strong increase in one-person households, especially after World War II.

THE NATIONAL SYSTEM OF DEMOGRAPHIC STATISTICS

Population Structure

The first general population census was conducted in late 1829 and early 1830, although earlier censuses were organized in 1795 for the Batavian Republic and in 1815 at the creation of the Kingdom of the Netherlands. The two preceding centuries did not encourage census-taking due to the decentralized structure of the federation. Since 1830 population censuses have been taken decennially, but not always at the end or the beginning of each decade. The first two censuses of 1830 and 1840 were not published in separate volumes; instead, the data were included in later titles. The first census to be published in a separate volume was the 1849 census. (For a history pf Dutch population censuses see Den Dulk and Van Maarseveen, 1999). During the nineteenth century Dutch statistics were not permanently institutionalized and are characterized by great institutional diversity. A central statistical office was not established until 1899 (Van Maarseveen and Schreijnders, 1999).

Data on population by age, sex, and marital status in one-year age groups are available for the whole time span since 1830. Disaggregations by sex and type of settlement (town or rural community) are available. The later censuses introduced classification by community size.

Vital Statistics

The recording of births, deaths, and marriages was already introduced in 1804, but published data and coherent time series are available only since the 1870s. Vital statistics as historical time series were published by the CBS on the occasion of the centenary of the official Dutch statistics bureau in 1999 (Van der Bie, Dehing, and Smits (1999); see also EURODATA Newsletter no. 10, pp. 33f.; bibliographic documentation for the years 1899–1998 is available from Baarsel and Commandeur (no date)).

Households and Families

Data on households (*huishoudens*) were collected already in the 1830 census, though only the number of households and household members was given in this census. The following censuses expanded the available information on households. Disaggregations for the eleven provinces of Noordbrabant, Gelderland, Zuidholland, Noordholland, Zeeland, Utrecht, Friesland, Overijssel, Groningen, Drenthe, and Limburg were introduced as early as 1830. Later censuses distinguished between 'large communities' and 'other communities' (censuses of 1840, 1849, 1859, 1869, 1879, 1889). Households by composition were first introduced in 1869, distinguishing between related and unrelated persons, single persons, and persons in institutional households. This classification was changed in 1879 into households with household heads, children, servants, other persons, and single persons, distinguished by sex.[2] It was repeated in 1889 and constantly used until the 1971

---

[2] See Centrale Commissie voor de Statistiek (1893), p. 58, Table VII, Note 1, stating that before 1879 there are no data comparable with those of 1879 and 1889.

census.[3] Households by size (number of persons) were first published in 1909 in seven categories and combined with the number of servants in nine categories. Households by profession of household head were not published before 1960.

The definition of a household (*huishoud*, since 1930 called *gezin*) was more or less the same from 1899 until the last census of 1971. Family households were distinguished from one-person and institutional households and included all those households made up of a family nucleus, whether a married couple with or without children, an unmarried parent with child(ren), or a widowed/divorced person with children. Relatives and servants living in the household were not counted as single persons, but as household members. The reference person for statistical purposes was the household head, which was in most cases a man (the husband or father).

Family statistics did not start before the census of 1930 and were continued in 1947. The 1930 census dealt with household composition, households by number of persons, and households by number of children.

Special investigations of marital fertility were introduced in 1930 and repeated in 1947. Separate volumes for family statistics and fertility statistics have been published since 1930.

Remarks (also see introductory Table 6.1)

Data from 1930 to 1939 have been created by linear extrapolation using the growth rates of the censuses from 1920 to 1930.

BOUNDARY CHANGES

The Netherlands were established as a national state only in the aftermath of the Napoleonic period. In 1815 at the Congress of Vienna the former Belgian Low Countries (belonging to Austria from 1713 to 1797) were united with the Dutch provinces to form the United Kingdom of the Netherlands. But this construction did not last for long due to religious conflicts. Already in 1830 the southern provinces seceded from the United Kingdom of the Netherlands to form the new Kingdom of Belgium. The Conference of London in January 1831 established an independent territory of Belgium which included the province of Luxembourg. The Treaty of London (19 April 1839) transferred the southern part of the Dutch province of Limburg to Belgium. Thus, since 1839 the territory of The Netherlands has remained more or less stable. The Netherlands declared itself neutral in both World War I and World War II, though it was occupied by the German army. After World War II, minor territorial gains were made with the acquisition of the German towns Elten and Tuddern. Concerning regional organization see Quick (1994) and Caramani, Flora, Kraus, and Quick (1998).

---

[3] Centraal Bureau voor de Statistiek (1989), p. 22.

APPENDIX TABLES AND FIGURES

APPENDIX TABLE NL.1 Population structure at census dates 1849–1947

Census number	Census date	Census population			Marital status				Age group		
		Total	Male	Female	Single	Married	Widowed	Divorced	0–14	15–64	65+
		Absolute									
1	19 XI 1849	3,056,879	1,498,811	1,558,068	1,928,523	934,744	193,526	..	1,020,158	1,891,410	145,079
2	31 XII 1859	3,293,577	1,616,357	1,677,220	2,047,301	1,040,983	204,538	690	1,072,828	2,058,119	161,393
3	1 XII 1869	3,579,528	1,764,118	1,815,410	2,186,236	1,179,995	211,035	2,262[1]	1,194,769	2,186,104	197,089
4	31 XII 1879	4,012,693	1,983,164	2,029,529	2,442,464	1,344,717	222,883	2,626	1,409,069	2,384,736	218,552
5	31 XII 1889	4,511,415	2,228,487	2,282,928	2,781,602	1,479,490	246,915	3,347[1]	1,588,862	2,651,432	270,875
6	31 XII 1899	5,104,137	2,520,602	2,583,535	3,151,536	1,675,722	267,798	9,000[1]	1,777,299	3,020,186	306,541
7	31 XII 1909	5,858,175	2,899,125	2,959,050	3,577,326	1,984,162	283,004	13,578[1]	2,022,704	3,476,996	358,383
8	31 XII 1920	6,865,314	3,410,262	3,455,052	4,077,689	2,451,491	313,607	22,480[1]	2,238,194	4,223,070	404,004
9	31 XII 1930	7,935,565	3,942,676	3,992,889	4,532,234	3,029,082	335,159	39,044[1]	2,431,665	5,011,947	491,918
10	31 V 1947	9,625,499	4,791,443	4,834,056	5,124,224	3,989,710	429,776	81,789[1]	2,652,069	6,225,507	747,923
		Per cent									
1	19 XI 1849	100.00	49.03	50.97	63.09	30.58	6.33	..	33.37	61.87	4.75
2	31 XII 1859	100.00	49.08	50.92	62.16	31.61	6.21	0.02	32.57	62.49	4.90
3	1 XII 1869	100.00	49.28	50.72	61.08	32.97	5.90	0.06[1]	33.38	61.07	5.51
4	31 XII 1879	100.00	49.42	50.58	60.87	33.51	5.55	0.07	35.12	59.43	5.45
5	31 XII 1889	100.00	49.40	50.60	61.66	32.79	5.47	0.07[1]	35.22	58.77	6.00
6	31 XII 1899	100.00	49.38	50.62	61.74	32.83	5.25	0.18[1]	34.82	59.17	6.01
7	31 XII 1909	100.00	49.49	50.51	61.07	33.87	4.83	0.23[1]	34.53	59.35	6.12
8	31 XII 1920	100.00	49.67	50.33	59.40	35.71	4.57	0.33[1]	32.60	61.51	5.88
9	31 XII 1930	100.00	49.68	50.32	57.11	38.17	4.22	0.49[1]	30.64	63.16	6.20
10	31 V 1947	100.00	49.78	50.22	53.24	41.45	4.46	0.85[1]	27.55	64.68	7.77

Note: [1] Divorced and separated.

APPENDIX TABLE NL.2 Census population by region 1869–1930 (per cent)

Provincie	1869	1879	1889	1899	1909	1920	1930
Noordbrabant	11.98	11.61	11.31	10.85	10.64	10.69	11.32
Gelderland	12.09	11.64	11.35	11.11	10.93	10.63	10.45
Zuidholland	19.22	20.03	21.06	22.41	23.75	24.46	24.67
Noordholland	16.12	16.94	18.38	18.97	18.91	18.91	19.03
Zeeland	4.97	4.71	4.41	4.23	3.98	3.57	3.13
Utrecht	4.86	4.78	4.90	4.92	4.93	4.98	5.13
Friesland	8.16	8.22	7.45	6.66	6.15	5.58	5.04
Overijssel	7.09	6.83	6.54	6.52	6.54	6.39	6.57
Groningen	6.28	6.30	6.05	5.88	5.60	5.33	4.94
Drenthe	2.96	2.97	2.90	2.92	2.95	3.06	2.80
Limburg	6.26	5.96	5.68	5.53	5.67	6.41	6.94
Flevoland	..	..	..	..	..	..	..
TOTAL	**100.00**	**100.00**	**100.00**	**100.00**	**100.00**	**100.00**	**100.00**

APPENDIX TABLE NL.3 Population density by region 1869–1930
(inhabitants per sq. km.)

Provincie	1869	1879	1889	1899	1909	1920	1930
Noordbrabant	84	91	99	108	125	148	181
Gelderland	85	92	101	111	127	145	165
Zuidholland	228	266	314	380	475	572	669
Noordholland	212	245	299	346	401	470	551
Zeeland	101	106	111	120	127	134	139
Utrecht	126	139	160	182	212	251	299
Friesland	89	99	101	103	112	119	124
Overijssel	76	82	88	99	114	131	155
Groningen	98	110	119	127	144	160	171
Drenthe	40	45	49	56	65	79	83
Limburg	102	108	116	128	151	201	251
Flevoland	..	..	..	..	..	..	..
TOTAL	**109**	**122**	**137**	**154**	**180**	**211**	**244**

APPENDIX TABLE NL.4 Demographic developments 1850–1945 (absolute figures and rates)

Year	Mid-year population	Natural population growth rate	Population growth rate	Net migration rate	Crude birth rate	Legitimate births per 10,000 married women age 15–44	Illegitimate births per 10,000 unmarried women age 15–44	Illeg. births per 100 leg. births
1850	3,043,732	12.4	-3.9	-16.3	34.6	3,579	123	5.2
1851	3,055,293	12.4	3.8	-8.6	35.1	3,618	123	5.1
1852	3,103,835	11.4	15.9	4.5	35.5	3,647	112	4.7
1853	3,145,593	8.6	13.5	4.9	33.2	3,404	98	4.3
1854	3,179,289	8.7	10.7	2.0	32.8	3,353	93	4.1
1855	3,206,297	3.6	8.5	4.9	31.7	3,240	84	3.8
1856	3,234,576	9.2	8.8	-0.4	32.8	3,306	101	4.5
1857	3,267,058	7.9	10.0	2.1	34.7	3,490	103	4.3
1858	3,292,793	4.5	7.9	3.4	32.4	3,244	96	4.3
1859	3,306,252	3.8	4.1	-0.3	35.0	3,472	103	4.3
1860	3,322,778	7.9	5.0	2.9	32.7	3,261	92	4.0
1861	3,354,731	10.0	9.6	-0.4	35.4	3,508	101	4.1
1862	3,391,691	9.4	11.0	1.6	33.2	3,292	94	4.0
1863	3,431,887	12.4	11.9	-0.5	36.3	3,586	106	4.1
1864	..	..	..	..	..	..	..	..
1865	..	..	..	..	..	..	..	..
1866	..	..	..	..	..	..	..	..
1867	..	..	..	..	..	..	..	..
1868	..	..	..	..	..	..	..	..
1869	..	..	..	..	..	..	..	..
1870	3,601,146	10.3	..	..	36.1	..	..	..
1871	3,627,801	5.9	7.3	1.5	35.4	..	..	..
1872	3,655,969	10.1	7.7	-2.4	36.0	..	..	..
1873	3,695,331	12.0	10.7	-1.4	36.2	..	..	..
1874	3,741,632	13.6	12.4	-1.3	36.4	3,529	101	3.5
1875	3,788,395	11.0	12.3	1.4	36.6	3,546	98	3.3
1876	3,837,491	13.6	12.8	-0.8	37.1	3,586	101	3.3
1877	3,895,124	14.5	14.8	0.3	36.6	3,537	101	3.3
1878	3,953,339	13.2	14.7	1.6	36.1	3,482	102	3.4
1879	4,009,448	14.2	14.0	-0.2	36.7	3,535	99	3.2
1880	4,048,801	12.0	9.7	-2.3	35.5	3,450	89	3.0
1881	4,087,334	13.5	9.4	-4.1	35.0	3,420	85	2.9
1882	4,143,524	14.6	13.6	-1.0	35.3	3,469	90	3.0
1883	4,199,018	12.5	13.2	0.7	34.3	3,384	88	3.1
1884	4,251,669	12.7	12.4	-0.3	34.9	3,457	95	3.3
1885	4,307,142	13.4	12.9	-0.5	34.4	3,421	92	3.2
1886	4,363,434	12.7	12.9	0.2	34.6	3,457	94	3.3
1887	4,420,864	14.0	13.0	-1.0	33.7	3,391	92	3.3
1888	4,478,401	13.4	12.8	-0.5	33.7	3,415	90	3.2
1889	4,508,674	13.2	6.7	-6.5	33.4	3,393	92	3.4
1890	4,537,990	12.4	6.5	-5.9	32.9	3,336	88	3.3
1891	4,593,155	13.0	12.0	-1.0	33.7	3,404	90	3.3
1892	4,645,660	11.0	11.3	0.3	32.0	3,221	86	3.3
1893	4,701,243	14.6	11.8	-2.8	33.8	3,396	87	3.2
1894	4,764,279	14.0	13.2	-0.8	32.5	3,250	84	3.2
1895	4,827,549	14.1	13.1	-1.0	32.8	3,271	82	3.1
1896	4,894,055	15.5	13.6	-1.9	32.7	3,265	78	3.0
1897	4,966,431	15.6	14.6	-1.0	32.5	3,233	73	2.8

continued

APPENDIX TABLE NL.4 Demographic developments 1850–1945 (absolute figures and rates)

Crude death rate	Infant mortality rate	Stillbirth rate	Infant mortality and stillbirth rate	Crude marriage rate	Persons marrying per 10,000 unmarried persons age 15+	Persons marrying per 10,000 unmarried persons age 15–49	Crude divorce rate	Divorces per 100 marriages	Divorces per 10,000 married persons	Year
22.2	168.5	53.0	221.5	9.0	499	611	0.0	0.2	1	1850
22.7	179.2	52.8	232.0	8.8	487	595	0.0	0.3	2	1851
24.0	201.5	51.6	253.1	8.2	457	559	0.0	0.3	1	1852
24.6	190.3	52.9	243.2	7.8	451	529	0.0	0.3	2	1853
24.1	182.7	51.0	233.7	7.5	417	510	0.0	0.3	2	1854
28.1	201.4	52.8	254.2	7.3	405	490	0.0	0.3	2	1855
23.5	179.3	52.3	231.6	7.6	421	516	0.0	0.3	1	1856
26.8	211.7	53.4	265.1	7.9	442	541	0.0	0.3	1	1857
27.9	211.6	56.6	268.2	8.0	445	545	0.0	0.3	1	1858
31.2	227.4	56.4	283.8	8.2	454	556	0.0	0.3	2	1859
24.8	186.3	54.1	240.4	8.2	457	573	0.0	0.3	2	1860
25.4	195.5	53.4	248.9	8.1	456	585	0.0	0.3	2	1861
23.8	192.7	53.9	246.6	7.8	444	581	0.0	0.3	1	1862
23.9	184.4	54.6	239.0	8.3	473	634	0.0	0.4	2	1863
..	..	..	..	..	..	..	..	..	..	1864
..	..	..	..	..	..	..	..	..	..	1865
..	..	..	..	..	..	..	..	..	..	1866
..	..	..	..	..	..	..	..	..	..	1867
..	..	..	..	..	..	..	..	..	..	1868
..	..	..	..	..	..	..	..	..	..	1869
25.8	..	53.9	..	8.0	476	597	..	..	..	1870
29.5	..	56.9	..	8.0	482	605	..	..	..	1871
25.9	..	55.5	..	8.3	501	630	..	..	..	1872
24.2	..	55.0	..	8.6	524	659	..	..	..	1873
22.7	..	55.9	..	8.4	516	650	0.0	0.5	2.5	1874
25.6	..	55.2	..	8.3	517	651	0.0	0.5	2.4	1875
23.5	200.9	53.5	254.4	8.3	516	651	0.0	0.5	2.4	1876
22.2	188.3	52.4	240.7	8.1	508	642	0.0	0.5	2.4	1877
23.0	197.1	54.3	251.3	7.8	492	623	0.0	0.5	2.5	1878
22.5	181.6	54.9	236.5	7.6	488	618	0.0	0.5	2.3	1879
23.5	217.6	52.3	269.9	7.5	477	605	0.0	0.5	2.2	1880
21.5	181.9	54.0	235.9	7.3	464	588	0.0	0.6	2.7	1881
20.7	174.6	50.8	225.5	7.1	453	573	0.0	0.6	2.4	1882
21.8	186.7	53.3	240.0	7.1	449	568	0.0	0.6	2.7	1883
22.2	193.7	51.2	244.9	7.2	453	573	0.0	0.6	2.8	1884
21.0	169.4	52.6	222.1	6.9	437	553	0.1	0.9	3.7	1885
21.8	191.7	51.8	243.4	6.9	437	552	0.1	1.0	4.4	1886
19.7	162.5	52.0	214.5	7.0	439	554	0.1	1.1	4.6	1887
20.4	173.2	51.4	224.7	6.9	432	545	0.1	1.3	5.6	1888
20.2	176.6	49.4	226.0	7.0	437	551	0.1	1.1	4.9	1889
20.5	171.4	49.4	220.8	7.1	445	560	0.1	1.2	5.1	1890
20.6	169.4	47.6	217.0	7.1	444	559	0.1	1.3	5.5	1891
21.0	173.9	49.1	223.0	7.2	447	563	0.1	1.1	4.6	1892
19.2	163.7	47.4	211.1	7.3	455	571	0.1	1.2	5.2	1893
18.5	152.4	47.8	200.2	7.2	450	565	0.1	1.1	5.0	1894
18.6	166.6	48.1	214.7	7.4	458	575	0.1	1.3	6.0	1895
17.2	147.7	47.0	194.7	7.5	463	581	0.1	1.3	5.8	1896
16.9	148.3	45.7	194.0	7.4	460	576	0.1	1.2	5.5	1897

continued

APPENDIX TABLE NL.4 Demographic developments 1850–1945 (continued)

Year	Mid-year population	Natural population growth rate	Population growth rate	Net migration rate	Crude birth rate	Legitimate births per 10,000 married women age 15–44	Illegitimate births per 10,000 unmarried women age 15–44	Illeg. births per 100 leg. births
1898	5,039,418	14.9	14.5	-0.4	31.9	3,167	69	2.7
1899	5,089,380	14.9	9.8	-5.1	32.1	3,175	69	2.7
1900	5,141,633	13.7	10.2	-3.6	31.6	3,111	68	2.7
1901	5,221,180	15.0	15.2	0.2	32.2	3,159	67	2.6
1902	5,305,207	15.5	15.8	0.3	31.8	3,102	62	2.4
1903	5,389,082	16.0	15.6	-0.4	31.6	3,065	58	2.3
1904	5,470,301	15.4	14.8	-0.6	31.4	3,032	55	2.2
1905	5,550,535	15.4	14.5	-1.0	30.8	2,957	55	2.2
1906	5,631,821	15.6	14.4	-1.1	30.4	2,901	54	2.2
1907	5,709,748	15.4	13.6	-1.8	30.0	2,853	54	2.2
1908	5,786,232	14.7	13.2	-1.5	29.7	2,807	54	2.2
1909	5,861,813	15.4	12.9	-2.5	29.1	2,740	51	2.1
1910	5,898,957	15.1	6.3	-8.8	28.6	2,680	50	2.1
1911	5,975,660	13.3	12.8	-0.5	27.9	2,599	47	2.0
1912	6,054,487	15.8	13.0	-2.8	28.1	2,610	47	2.0
1913	6,144,636	15.9	14.7	-1.2	28.2	2,607	49	2.1
1914	6,251,189	15.9	17.0	1.2	28.3	..	..	2.2
1915	6,363,953	13.8	17.7	3.9	26.3	..	..	2.3
1916	6,480,142	13.7	17.9	4.3	26.6	..	..	2.2
1917	6,612,434	13.0	20.0	7.0	26.2	..	..	2.2
1918	6,704,612	7.8	13.7	6.0	25.0	..	..	2.3
1919	6,752,144	11.1	7.0	-4.0	24.4	2,199	41	2.1
1920	6,820,389	16.3	10.0	-6.3	28.3	2,536	50	2.2
1921	6,921,288	16.3	14.6	-1.7	27.4	2,439	48	2.1
1922	7,032,179	14.4	15.8	1.3	25.9	2,293	42	2.0
1923	7,149,847	16.0	16.5	0.4	26.2	2,313	40	1.9
1924	7,263,893	15.3	15.7	0.4	25.1	2,204	38	1.8
1925	7,365,732	14.4	13.8	-0.6	24.2	2,114	36	1.8
1926	7,471,512	13.9	14.2	0.2	23.8	2,059	38	1.9
1927	7,576,272	12.9	13.8	1.0	23.1	1,994	35	1.8
1928	7,678,187	13.7	13.3	-0.4	23.3	2,002	37	1.9
1929	7,781,376	12.1	13.3	1.2	22.8	1,947	35	1.8
1930	7,883,870	14.0	13.0	-1.0	23.1	1,968	35	1.8
1931	7,998,568	12.5	14.3	1.8	22.2	1,879	33	1.8
1932	8,122,482	13.0	15.3	2.3	22.0	1,854	32	1.8
1933	8,236,891	12.0	13.9	1.8	20.8	1,748	29	1.7
1934	8,341,208	12.2	12.5	0.3	20.6	1,729	29	1.7
1935	8,433,266	11.5	10.9	-0.6	20.2	1,688	27	1.6
1936	8,515,713	11.5	9.7	-1.8	20.2	1,677	26	1.5
1937	8,598,258	11.0	9.6	-1.4	19.8	1,642	24	1.4
1938	8,684,082	12.0	9.9	-2.1	20.5	1,698	25	1.5
1939	8,781,273	12.0	11.1	-0.9	20.6	1,699	23	1.3
1940	8,878,611	10.9	11.0	0.0	20.8	..	..	1.4
1941	8,965,484	10.3	9.7	-0.6	20.3	..	..	1.8
1942	9,041,989	11.5	8.5	-3.0	21.0	..	..	1.7
1943	9,102,410	13.0	6.6	-6.3	23.0	..	..	1.8
1944	9,174,432	12.2	7.9	-4.3	24.0	..	..	2.1
1945	9,262,298	7.4	9.5	2.1	22.6	..	..	3.6

APPENDIX TABLE NL.4 Demographic developments 1850–1945 (continued)

Crude death rate	Infant mortality rate	Stillbirth rate	Infant mortality and stillbirth rate	Crude marriage rate	Persons marrying per 10,000 unmarried persons age 15+	Persons marrying per 10,000 unmarried persons age 15–49	Crude divorce rate	Divorces per 100 marriages	Divorces per 10,000 married persons	Year
17.0	156.2	44.9	201.2	7.3	453	567	0.1	1.4	6.1	1898
17.2	148.5	44.7	193.2	7.5	462	578	0.1	1.3	5.8	1899
17.9	155.2	44.8	200.1	7.7	476	595	0.1	1.4	6.5	1900
17.2	149.3	43.3	192.6	7.7	480	600	0.1	1.4	6.5	1901
16.3	129.9	42.5	172.4	7.6	473	591	0.1	1.4	6.6	1902
15.6	135.1	42.4	177.5	7.4	465	580	0.1	1.5	6.9	1903
15.9	136.9	42.5	179.4	7.4	465	580	0.1	1.6	7.2	1904
15.3	130.9	42.0	172.9	7.3	461	574	0.1	1.8	7.8	1905
14.8	127.1	41.4	168.5	7.5	472	588	0.1	1.8	8.1	1906
14.6	111.9	41.8	153.7	7.6	479	597	0.1	1.9	8.6	1907
15.0	124.8	40.8	165.6	7.2	458	570	0.1	2.0	8.4	1908
13.7	99.1	41.1	140.3	7.1	451	561	0.1	2.1	8.6	1909
13.6	107.9	40.5	148.4	7.2	460	572	0.1	2.0	8.6	1910
14.5	137.2	39.9	177.1	7.2	461	572	0.2	2.2	9.5	1911
12.3	87.0	39.0	126.0	7.6	486	604	0.2	2.3	10.1	1912
12.3	91.4	38.7	130.1	7.9	503	624	0.2	2.3	10.5	1913
12.4	94.8	39.0	133.8	6.8	..	..	0.2	2.6	..	1914
12.5	86.8	39.6	126.3	6.7	..	..	0.2	2.7	..	1915
13.0	84.5	40.0	124.5	7.3	..	..	0.2	2.8	..	1916
13.2	87.1	39.2	126.3	7.5	..	..	0.2	2.7	..	1917
17.2	92.8	39.3	132.1	7.4	..	..	0.2	2.8	..	1918
13.3	84.1	36.0	120.1	8.6	545	673	0.2	2.6	12.7	1919
12.0	72.8	38.9	111.7	9.6	606	749	0.3	3.0	16.1	1920
11.1	76.2	38.8	114.9	9.2	582	720	0.3	3.1	15.9	1921
11.4	67.3	39.6	106.9	8.7	552	684	0.3	3.2	15.3	1922
10.2	56.4	28.5	84.8	8.0	509	630	0.3	3.5	15.5	1923
9.8	60.6	26.7	87.3	7.8	495	613	0.3	3.7	15.7	1924
9.8	58.4	26.1	84.5	7.4	475	588	0.3	4.0	16.1	1925
9.8	61.1	25.5	86.6	7.4	473	587	0.3	4.3	17.0	1926
10.2	58.7	26.6	85.3	7.5	479	594	0.3	4.5	18.1	1927
9.6	52.6	25.8	78.4	7.7	494	613	0.4	4.6	18.6	1928
10.7	59.0	25.3	84.4	7.9	508	630	0.4	4.5	18.5	1929
9.1	50.9	25.2	76.1	8.0	513	638	0.4	4.5	18.7	1930
9.6	49.6	25.6	75.2	7.4	479	595	0.4	5.1	19.5	1931
9.0	46.3	25.9	72.2	6.9	444	551	0.4	5.2	18.6	1932
8.8	43.9	25.7	69.6	7.2	465	578	0.4	4.9	18.2	1933
8.4	42.6	25.7	68.3	7.3	470	585	0.4	4.8	18.0	1934
8.7	40.0	25.8	65.8	7.2	469	584	0.4	4.9	17.9	1935
8.7	38.9	25.7	64.6	7.5	484	602	0.4	5.0	19.1	1936
8.8	38.1	25.8	63.9	7.7	499	621	0.4	5.2	20.1	1937
8.5	36.5	25.3	61.8	7.7	502	625	0.4	4.9	18.9	1938
8.6	33.7	25.4	59.1	9.2	598	744	0.4	4.0	18.5	1939
9.9	39.1	25.7	64.9	7.6	..	..	0.3	4.4	..	1940
10.0	43.6	21.7	65.3	7.3	..	..	0.4	5.0	..	1941
9.5	39.5	19.7	59.2	9.7	..	..	0.4	4.3	..	1942
10.0	40.1	18.8	58.9	7.2	..	..	0.5	6.9	..	1943
11.8	46.3	18.8	65.2	5.5	..	..	0.5	9.2	..	1944
15.3	79.7	19.6	99.2	7.8	..	..	0.5	6.4	..	1945

APPENDIX TABLE NL.5 Life expectancy by age 1816/25–1931/40 (in years)

Age	0	10	20	30	40	50	60	70	80
				Males					
1816–1825	29.32	40.67	32.87	27.60	21.86	16.41	11.60	7.47	4.77
1840–1851	34.94	44.39	36.86	30.71	24.06	17.98	12.14	7.22	4.02
1850–1859	36.44	45.59	37.95	31.44	24.71	18.25	12.57	7.75	4.23
1860–1869	37.2	46.7	39.2	32.7	25.8	19.2	13.2	8.1	4.6
1870–1879	38.4	48.0	40.3	33.7	26.5	19.6	13.3	8.2	4.6
1880–1889	42.5	50.4	42.3	35.1	27.6	20.5	13.9	8.5	4.7
1890–1899	46.2	51.7	43.4	35.9	28.1	20.7	14.0	8.6	4.7
1900–1909	51.0	54.3	45.7	37.8	29.5	21.8	14.7	8.9	4.9
1910–1920	55.1	55.4	46.7	38.8	30.5	22.4	15.1	9.1	5.0
1921–1930	61.9	58.7	49.7	41.0	32.1	23.5	15.9	9.6	5.2
1931–1940	65.5	60.1	50.8	41.8	32.8	24.1	16.2	9.8	5.2
1931–1940	65.7	60.3	51.0	41.9	32.9	24.1	16.3	9.8	5.2
				Females					
1816–1825	35.12	45.03	36.99	30.68	24.84	18.70	12.84	8.01	4.76
1840–1851	37.76	46.07	38.71	31.98	25.77	19.34	12.94	7.57	4.14
1850–1859	38.21	46.26	38.92	32.16	26.13	19.51	13.12	7.95	4.41
1860–1869	39.1	47.4	40.1	33.3	27.1	20.4	13.8	8.4	4.8
1870–1879	40.7	48.7	41.2	34.3	27.9	21.0	14.1	7.4	4.7
1880–1889	45.0	51.5	43.5	36.1	29.2	21.9	14.8	9.0	4.9
1890–1899	49.0	53.0	44.8	37.1	29.7	22.2	15.0	9.0	5.0
1900–1909	53.4	55.4	46.9	38.8	30.8	22.9	15.5	9.4	5.2
1910–1920	57.1	56.0	47.5	39.5	31.4	23.4	15.9	9.6	5.3
1921–1930	63.5	58.9	49.8	41.1	32.5	24.1	16.4	10.5	5.5
1931–1940	67.2	60.8	51.5	42.3	33.3	24.7	16.8	10.2	5.5
1931–1940	..	..	..	..	..	..	..	..	..

APPENDIX TABLE NL.6A Households by type 1829–1930 (absolute and per cent)

Census year	Household types and members									
	Total households	Private households	Family households	One-person households	Institutional households	Total household members	Private household members	Family household members	One-person household members	Institutional household members
					Absolute					
1829	..	538,878	..	..	..	2,613,487	..	..	..	..
1839	..	..	..	..	..	2,934,223	..	..	..	..
1849	..	639,171	..	..	..	3,056,879	..	..	..	..
1859	..	668,911	..	..	..	3,293,577	..	..	..	..
1869	..	748,732	..	..	..	3,575,080	..	..	..	..
1879	..	818,805	753,290	65,515	..	4,021,692	3,939,066	3,873,551	65,515	82,626
1889	..	1,024,277	957,292	66,985	..	4,532,394	4,430,055	4,363,070	66,985	102,339
1899	..	1,113,000	1,023,805	89,195	..	5,135,548	5,020,626	4,931,431	89,195	114,922
1909	..	1,307,000	1,181,525	125,475	..	5,889,324	5,758,967	5,633,492	125,475	130,357
1920	..	1,579,000	1,425,330	153,670	..	6,905,166	6,758,187	6,604,517	153,670	146,979
1930	1,960,891	1,958,000	1,739,544	218,456	2,891	7,998,179	7,827,907	7,609,451	218,456	170,272
					Per cent					
1879	..	100.00	92.00	8.00	..	100.00	97.95	96.32	1.63	2.05
1889	..	100.00	93.46	6.54	..	100.00	97.74	96.26	1.48	2.26
1899	..	100.00	91.99	8.01	..	100.00	97.76	96.03	1.74	2.24
1909	..	100.00	90.40	9.60	..	100.00	97.79	95.66	2.13	2.21
1920	..	100.00	90.27	9.73	..	100.00	97.87	95.65	2.23	2.13
1930	100.00	99.85	88.71	11.14	0.15	100.00	97.87	95.14	2.73	2.13

APPENDIX TABLE NL.6B　Households by size and members 1909–1930 (absolute figures)

Cen-sus year	Private house-holds total	Households by number of members							
		1 person	2 persons	3 persons	4 persons	5 persons	6–7 persons	8–9 persons	10+ per-sons
				Households					
1909	1,305,578	125,475	202,422	214,229	203,954	171,205	231,941	109,593	46,759
1920	1,579,000	153,670	..	..	..	..	..	..	..
1930	1,958,000	218,456	..	..	..	..	..	..	..
				Persons					
1909	5,758,967	125,475	404,844	642,687	815,816	856,025	2,914,120	..	..
1920	6,758,187	153,670	..	..	..	..	..	..	..
1930	7,827,907	218,456	..	..	..	..	..	..	..

APPENDIX TABLE NL.6C　Households by size and members 1909–1930 (per cent)

Cen-sus year	Private house-holds total	Households by number of members							
		1 person	2 persons	3 persons	4 persons	5 persons	6–7 persons	8–9 persons	10+ per-sons
				Households					
1909	100.00	9.61	15.50	16.41	15.62	13.11	17.77	8.39	3.58
1920	100.00	9.73	..	..	..	..	..	..	..
1930	100.00	11.16	..	..	..	..	..	..	..
				Persons					
1909	100.00	2.18	7.03	11.16	14.17	14.86	50.60	..	..
1920	100.00	2.27	..	..	..	..	..	..	..
1930	100.00	2.79	..	..	..	..	..	..	..

APPENDIX TABLE NL.6D　Household indicators 1829–1930

Census year	Household indicators			
	Mean total household size	Mean private household size	Mean family household size	Mean institutional household size
1829	..	..	4.85	..
1839	..	..	4.97	..
1849	..	..	4.78	..
1859	..	..	4.75	..
1869	..	..	..	..
1879	..	4.81	4.73	..
1889	..	4.33	4.79	..
1899	..	4.51	4.82	..
1909	..	4.41	4.77	..
1920	..	4.28	4.63	..
1930	4.08	4.00	4.37	58.90

APPENDIX TABLE NL.6E Household composition 1879–1930 (absolute and per cent)

Census year	Persons belonging to families			Family heads		Children		Servants	
	Men	Women	Total	Men	Women	Men	Women	Men	Women
	Absolute								
1879	1,916,948	1,956,603	3,873,551	713,344	105,461	995,671	917,357	68,075	145,471
1889	2,154,426	2,208,644	4,363,070	787,824	123,106	1,140,721	1,058,771	70,520	157,977
1899	2,435,783	2,495,648	4,931,431	890,347	133,930	1,307,415	1,218,813	68,260	165,312
1909	2,794,040	2,839,452	5,633,492	1,040,590	140,473	1,508,692	1,404,588	58,010	165,540
1920	3,294,712	3,309,805	6,604,517	1,272,138	153,303	1,747,184	1,621,593	41,380	157,336
1930	3,802,160	3,807,291	7,609,451	1,575,129	164,028	1,967,240	1,824,310	46,314	139,258
	Per cent								
1879	49.49	50.51	100.00	18.42	2.72	25.70	23.68	1.76	3.76
1889	49.38	50.62	100.00	18.06	2.82	26.14	24.27	1.62	3.62
1899	49.39	50.61	100.00	18.05	2.72	26.51	24.72	1.38	3.35
1909	49.60	50.40	100.00	18.47	2.49	26.78	24.93	1.03	2.94
1920	49.89	50.11	100.00	19.26	2.32	26.45	24.55	0.63	2.38
1930	49.97	50.03	100.00	20.70	2.16	25.85	23.97	0.61	1.83

continued

APPENDIX TABLE NL.6E Household composition 1879–1930 (absolute and per cent)
(continued)

Census year	Other family members		Persons living alone (single)			Population in institutions: administration		Population in institutions: inmates		Population in institutions: total
	Men	Women	Men	Women	Total	Men	Women	Men	Women	
	Absolute									
1879	139,858	788,314	24,776	40,739	11,492	39,796	31,338	44,313	38,313	
1889	155,361	868,790	26,091	40,894	20,979	47,970	33,390	56,305	46,034	
1899	169,761	977,593	34,988	54,207	23,911	54,851	42,342	60,561	54,361	
1909	186,811	1,128,883	49,792	75,683	28,426	56,584	45,347	63,951	66,406	
1920	234,010	1,377,573	58,706	94,964	38,754	57,375	50,850	66,014	80,965	
1930	213,477	1,679,695	81,778	136,678	57,930	60,863	51,479	72,762	97,510	
	Per cent									
1879	3.61	20.35	0.64	1.05	0.30	1.03	0.81	1.14	0.99	
1889	3.56	19.91	0.60	0.94	0.48	1.10	0.77	1.29	1.06	
1899	3.44	19.82	0.71	1.10	0.48	1.11	0.86	1.23	1.10	
1909	3.32	20.04	0.88	1.34	0.50	1.00	0.80	1.14	1.18	
1920	3.54	20.86	0.89	1.44	0.59	0.87	0.77	1.00	1.23	
1930	2.81	22.07	1.07	1.80	0.76	0.80	0.68	0.96	1.28	

APPENDIX TABLE NL.7 Dates and nature of results on population structure, households/families, and vital statistics

Topic	Intro-duction	Remarks
Population		
Population at census dates	1830	Introduced in 1830. Earlier censuses were conducted in 1795 and 1815, but the 1830 census was the first general census for the country and started the series of decennial population censuses.
Population by age, sex, and marital status	1830	Introduced in 1830.
Households and families		
Households (*huishouden/s*)		
Total households	1830, 1840, 1849, 1859, 1869, 1879, 1889, 1899, 1909, 1920, 1930, 1947	Households and household members. *Disaggregation*: by the eleven provinces Noordbrabant, Gelderland, Zuidholland, Noordholland, Zeeland, Utrecht, Friesland, Overijssel, Groningen, Drenthe, and Limburg. Further subdivided into 'large communities' and 'other communities' (1840, 49, 59, 69, 79, 89).
Households by size	1909, 1920, 1930, 1947	First time in 1909 in seven categories and combined with the number of servants in nine categories.
Households by composition	1859, 1869, 1879, 1889, 1899, 1909, 1920, 1930, 1947	1869: related, unrelated persons, single persons, persons in institutional households; First time in 1879, repeated in 1889; with household head, children, servants, other persons, single persons, by sex (see Centrale Commissie voor de Statistiek (1893), p. 58, Table VII, Note 1, stating that before 1879 there are no data comparable with those of 1879 and 1889.
Households by profession of household head	–	Not before 1960.
Families (*gezin/nen*)	1930, 1947	Since 1930 separate volumes for family statistics and fertility statistics.
Families by number of children	1930, 1947	Special investigation of marital fertility for the first time in 1930, repeated in 1947.

continued

APPENDIX TABLE NL.7 Dates and nature of results on population structure, households/families, and vital statistics (continued)

Topic	Intro-duction	Remarks
Population movement		
Mid-year population	1870	Calculated by using census data.
Births		
Live births	1870	
Stillbirths	1870	
Legitimate births	1874	
Illegitimate births	1874	
Deaths		
Total deaths	1870	
Infants (under 1 year)	1876	
Marriages		
Total marriages	1870	
Divorces and separations		
Total divorces	1874	
Legal separations	1874	Available for the whole period.

APPENDIX FIGURE NL.8 Population by age, sex and marital status, The Netherlands 1859, 1879, 1899, 1909, 1930 and 1947 (per 10,000 of total population)

The Netherlands, 1859

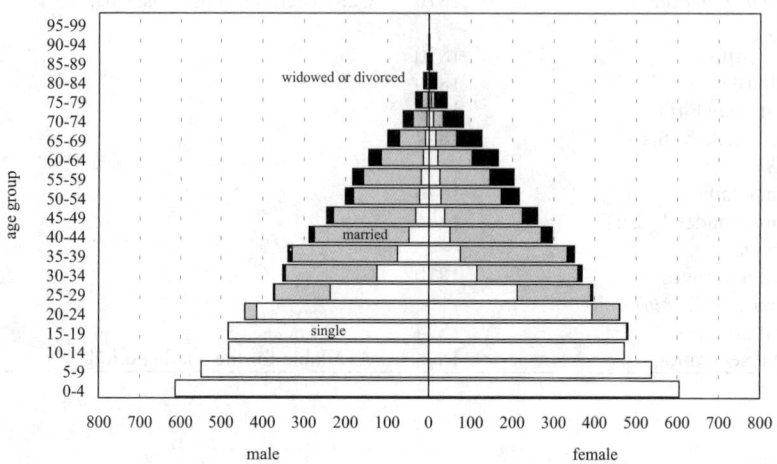

The Netherlands, 1879

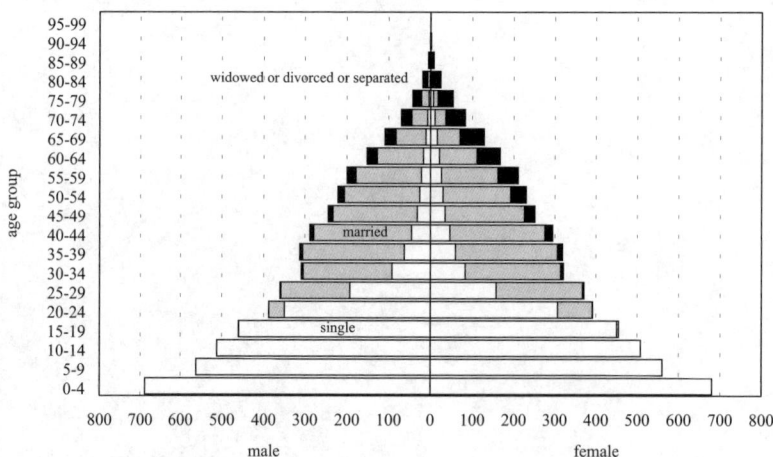

APPENDIX FIGURE NL.8 Population by age, sex and marital status, The Netherlands 1859, 1879, 1899, 1909, 1930 and 1947 (per 10,000 of total population) (continued)

The Netherlands, 1899

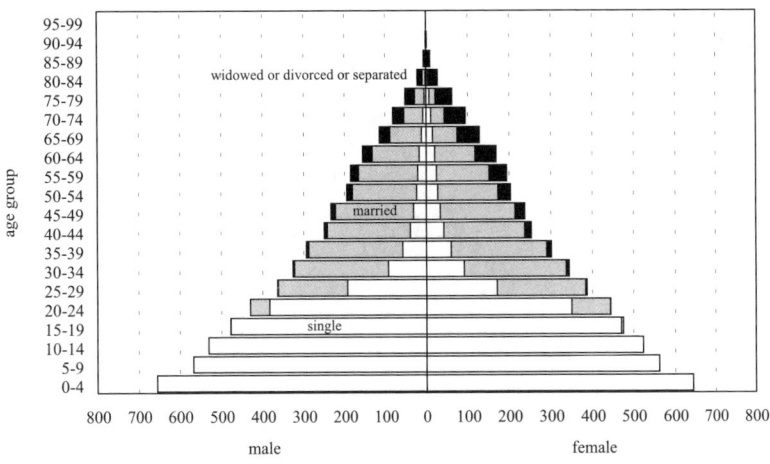

The Netherlands, 1909

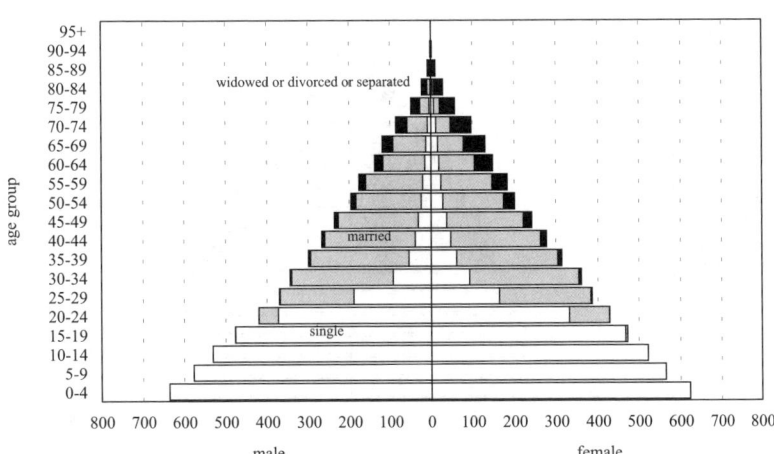

APPENDIX FIGURE NL.8 Population by age, sex and marital status, The Netherlands 1859, 1879, 1899, 1909, 1930 and 1947 (per 10,000 of total population) (continued)

The Netherlands, 1930

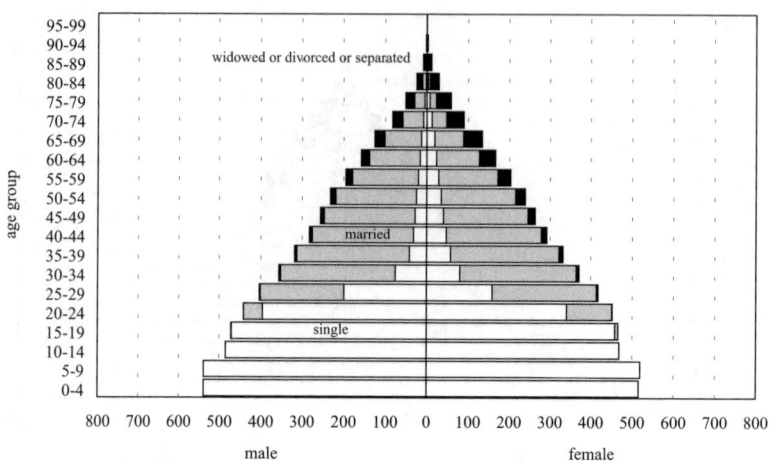

The Netherlands, 1947

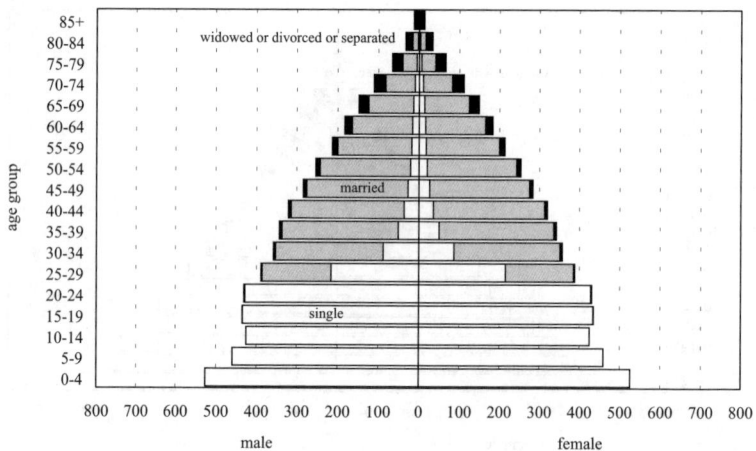

15

Norway

Norway evolved from trading posts on the shores of the North Sea. The different ports and towns on the shore were connected as the 'route to the North' which gave the country its name (*nordvegr*). Inland from the coastal settlements farmers and woodcutters settled, while along the coast fisherman and traders dominated. The geographical position of the country favoured overseas expansion. Norway expanded to the North Sea (including the Channel region—Normandy!) and later to the North Atlantic (Faeroe Islands, Iceland and Greenland, North America), as well as to other sea regions such as the Mediterranean (Norman Sicily, Epirus). In the southern part of the North Sea, however, the Norwegian expansion came into conflict with the Danish king. In 1380 Norway passed through inheritance to the Danish crown.

In 1397 Norway formed the Kalmar Union with Denmark and Sweden. Sweden left the union in the fifteenth century, which intensified the link between Norway and Denmark. In 1459, Norway gained administrative independence under the Treaty of Bergen. With the Treaty of Kiel (14 January 1814), the Great Powers annexed Norway to Sweden to punish Denmark for its alliance with Napoleon I, although Denmark's overseas territories, Greenland, Iceland, and the Faeroe Islands remained Danish. Norwegian patriots created a convention and agitated for independence under the prince of Denmark as king of Norway. A short war between Norway and Sweden ensued, but was stopped under pressure from Russia and Great Britain. The convention of the Norwegian patriots was recognized and they won rights that were rather liberal for the time.

During the nineteenth century nationalist movements were active in Norway and were organized through the liberal *Venstre* party. In the course of the nineteenth century opposition to Sweden became stronger; as an indication, the symbol of the union with Sweden figuring on the Norwegian flag was removed. Secession from Sweden and independence was achieved by a referendum on 13 August 1905; a second referendum decided in favour of the monarchy. In November 1905 the Norwegian parliament (Storting) nominated Prince Charles of Denmark to be king of Norway.

Norway was independent, but had lost to Denmark all external territories which it had originally settled in the Middle Ages. There was only one attempt to get parts of Greenland back, when the Norwegian navy occupied the eastern coast of Greenland in 1931. But the International Court of Justice in The Hague decided in favour of Denmark (Kiel, 1993; Alestalo, 1986; Alestalo and Kuhnle, 1984).

REGIONAL POPULATION STRUCTURE

It is important to note that the Norwegian population is very unevenly distributed over the country. The natural and geographic conditions alone would suggest that settlement would be concentrated in the southern part of the country, given the number of days with snow, precipitation, and frost. Only a thin coastal belt in the south has between 40 and 100 days with snow per year, while the rest of the country has 140 or more. Nearly half of the country and most of the interior regions north of the Arctic Circle have more than 180 snowy days per year. Nowhere in Norway is the climate as temperate as in Denmark, which has less than 40 days with snow annually (Alestalo and Kuhnle, 1984: 4).

Geographical and climatic conditions therefore have had a great impact on the country and its population. Arable land is very scarce due to the mountainous character of the country, and the cold climate with very short summers means a short growing season; only in the south-east are conditions better for agriculture. For this reason Norwegians developed fishing and seafaring as their main sources of income.

There are huge *regional differences* in economic development. In principle there are only two highly developed regions: the capital, Oslo (formerly Christiania), and surroundings; and the area of Bergen on the south-west coast. Generally, the coastal regions are more developed than the interior and mountainous areas, and there is a strong north–south gradient in economic development, as can be seen in the territorial distribution of GDP per capita: while in the Oslo and Bergen areas it is between 105,000–130,000 Kroner, in all central and northern provinces it is only 80,000–89,900 Kroner. Thus the interior and northern regions are peripheries within a peripheral country. These huge differences in economic resources and opportunities largely explain the country's uneven population density and settlement structure.

POPULATION GROWTH

Population density in Norway was always extremely low and still remains so compared with the European average. In 1876 there were only 5.7 inhabitants per square km. By 1910 this ratio had increased to 7.75 persons per square km., by 1920 to 8.55, and finally in 1946 it had reached 9.11 persons per square km.

Low population density might lead us to believe that population growth was low. On the contrary, it was rather high during the demographic transition (Figure N.1). The natural population growth rate from 1850 to 1910 was well above 10 per 1,000 and only declined to approximately 5 per 1,000 during the inter-war period. However, population growth was not as high as the natural population growth rate would suggest, mainly because of high emigration during the whole second half of the nineteenth century and up to the 1920s; the net migration rate did not become positive until the 1930s. There were also periods of economic crisis when emigration was very high: around 1870, in the early 1880s, and around 1905. The late 1920s again saw considerable emigration, but the main emigration wave of the nineteenth century had already passed.

The very high emigration from Norway mainly to the United States therefore reduced the absolute population increase considerably. In 1876 the total population was 1.819 million inhabitants; by 1946 the population had increased to 3.157 million inhabitants. The Norwegian population therefore increased by 74% within 70 years.

The pattern of demographic transition in Norway, Denmark, and Sweden is very similar and constitutes a special type (Figure N.2). The main features of this type are the early start of the transition process, the comparatively low birth rate, and the comparatively low death rate already in the nineteenth century. The last was due to very low infant mortality already at the end of the eighteenth century. Although the birth rate was lower than the European average, the death rate was even lower, resulting in massive natural population growth. Emigration from Scandinavia was therefore already very high during the nineteenth century, in contrast to the Mediterranean countries, where the massive population growth and thus emigration came some decades later.

Already starting in the 1860s, the birth rate showed a declining tendency in Norway, although it continued to fluctuate. The death rate fell slowly, but showed a decreasing trend from the 1860s, too. The main decline in the death rate came very much earlier in Norway. The explanation for the early decline in the death rate can probably be found, as in the other Nordic countries, in the early national population registration, which provided a unique basis of information which governments could use in combating infant mortality. Such a data base was unique to the Nordic countries; one of the main factors for the Nordic transition type has to be sought in the early introduction of population registration.

Still until the 1870s there were major fluctuations in the death and birth rates. In the 1860s and 1870s the death rate peaked twice, pointing to epidemics or famines. In the early 1870s there was a strong downswing in the birth rate, but the reasons for it are not clear. The final phase of the demographic transition is marked by the year 1900 when the birth rate started to decline very strongly; family limitation obviously became widespread around 1900. Norway was not directly involved in World War I, but nevertheless the indirect consequences were remarkable. In the early war years the birth rate declined, but recovered after the war. At the end of the war there was a strong increase in the death rate, probably largely due to an increase in infant mortality.

Like Sweden, Norway experienced a major decline in the birth rate in the 1920s and 1930s which led people to speak of a demographic crisis. Public measures were introduced to increase the birth rate. The turning point was the early 1930s. The birth rate rose up to 1940, when Norway was occupied by German troops. It continued to rise until 1948, when the second demographic transition set in. Until the 1980s the birth rate showed a declining trend, except for the years of the baby boom around 1970, which was mainly an effect of larger birth cohorts (Statistics Norway, 1994).

Norway's population history was influenced by *economic crises* and international *wars* during the last 150 years. Economic crises hit the country especially hard because of its dependence on international export markets: the main export goods were fish, ships, wood, and later oil. Norway had had a large merchant fleet throughout most of its history. Norway had to import grain and most industrial products due to its lack of industries. Thus, crises of the international trade flows had a major impact on the country. Such crises were the world economic crisis of

Figure N.1 Population growth and net migration 1850-1945

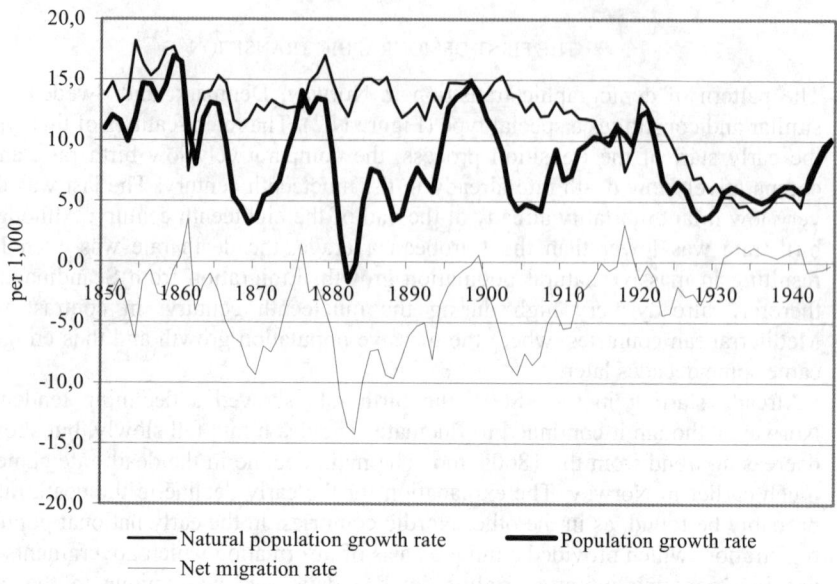

per 1,000

— Natural population growth rate   ▬ Population growth rate
— Net migration rate

Figure N.2 First demographic transition 1850-1945

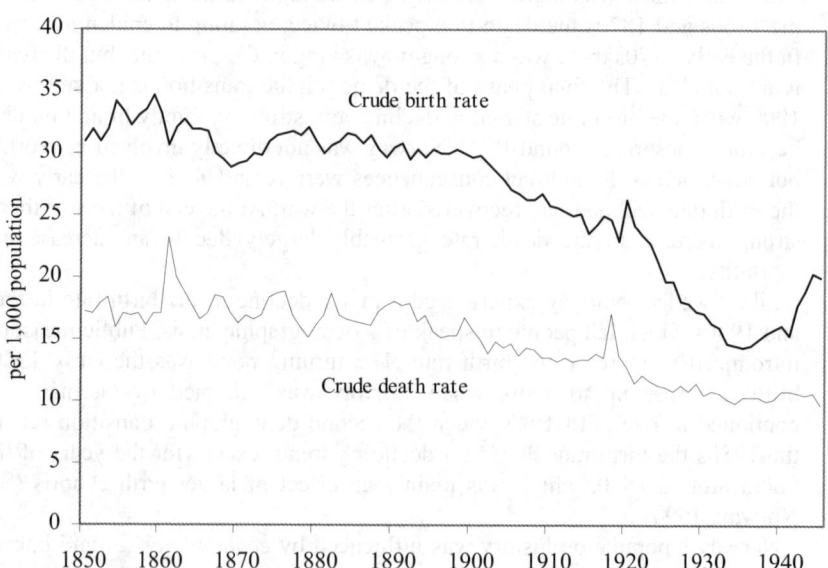

per 1,000 population

Crude birth rate

Crude death rate

the 1850s (Rosenberg, 1974), the American Civil War of the 1860s, the indirect effects of the Franco-Prussian War of 1870/71, and finally the world economic crisis of 1929–32.

Norway was only indirectly involved in wars in the last 150 years. It remained neutral in both world wars, but could not avoid being drawn into World War II and was occupied by the German army. Indirect influences were a decline in nutritional standards, therefore an increase in infant mortality, and effects on the birth rate (cf. Statistisk Sentralbyrå, 1962, 1965, and 1989).

MORTALITY AND LIFE EXPECTANCY

The infant mortality rate is defined as deaths of children aged under one year per 1,000 live births. Norway belongs to the group of countries with the lowest infant mortality, i.e. the Nordic countries (Figure N.3). Infant mortality was rather low already in 1900, at a level very similar to Sweden's. At that time it was the lowest infant mortality rate not only in Europe, but in the whole world (Masuy-Stroobant, 1997).

It is surprising to note that in 1840 Norway had an infant mortality rate very similar to Denmark's with approximately 150 infant deaths per 1,000 live births. But while Denmark's rate stagnated until 1900, Norway improved conditions for infants so much that in 1900 it became the leader in low infant mortality. It also overtook Sweden which in 1840 had had a lower infant mortality rate of roughly 120. In the period 1901–5 Norway had an infant mortality rate of 80, while Sweden's was 91. Norway was able to keep its lead until World War II, when the wartime occupation caused it to fall behind Sweden (which was not directly involved in the war). Since 1945 Norway's infant mortality rate has remained constantly higher than Sweden's (Van de Walle, 1986).

With regard to the low infant mortality already in the second half of the nineteenth century, there was a huge difference between urban and rural areas. The lower a country's infant mortality, the greater the difference between mortality in rural and urban areas. This is illustrated by the two cases of Norway and Sweden: in Norway in the decade of 1861–70 the index of urban infant mortality rate was 136 when rural areas are put at 100, and in Sweden urban infant mortality was even higher with an index value of 152. The opposite case is Germany, where infant mortality was high on the national average, but the urban/rural difference was smaller: in Prussia the index of urban infant mortality rate was 116, and in Bavaria with an extremely high infant mortality on the country average the index of urban infant mortality rate was only 104. While urban mortality was higher from the nineteenth century until the end of World War I, as a general rule it fell from the 1920s. In Norway this process was delayed until the decade of 1941–50 (Van de Walle, 1986) (for long-term changes in mortality and infant mortality see also Statistisk Sentralbyrå, 1962, 1966, and 1989).

As we could already see from the low infant mortality, life expectancy at birth was rather high in Norway and made considerable progress especially in the first half of the twentieth century (Figure N.4). Increases in life expectancy for young adults and older persons were smaller: from the 1820s to the 1940s life expectancy for 30-year-olds rose by roughly five years and for 60-year-olds by two years. Life expectancy of females was already higher than for males in the 1820s, but the differences were small: three years at birth, 1.4 years at age 30, and 0.6 years at age 60. Until the

Figure N.3 Infant mortality 1850-1945

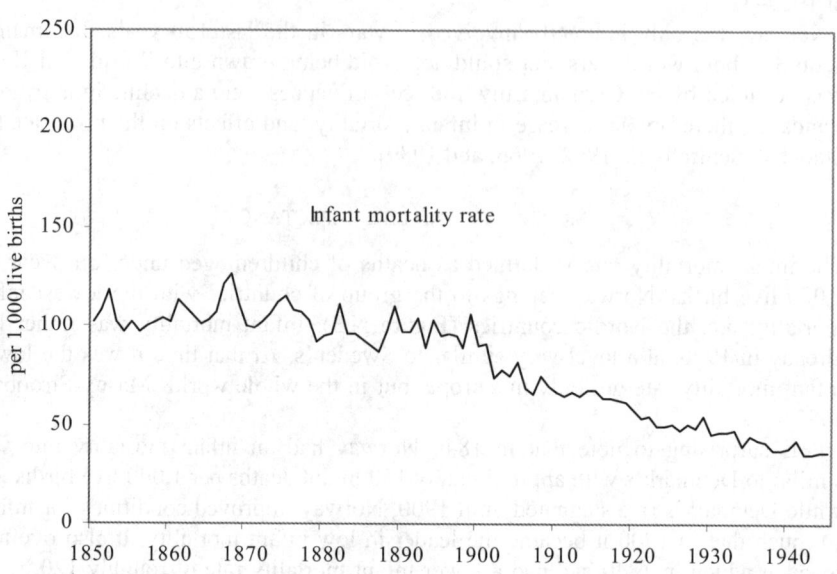

Figure N.4 Life expectancy 1821/30-1931/41

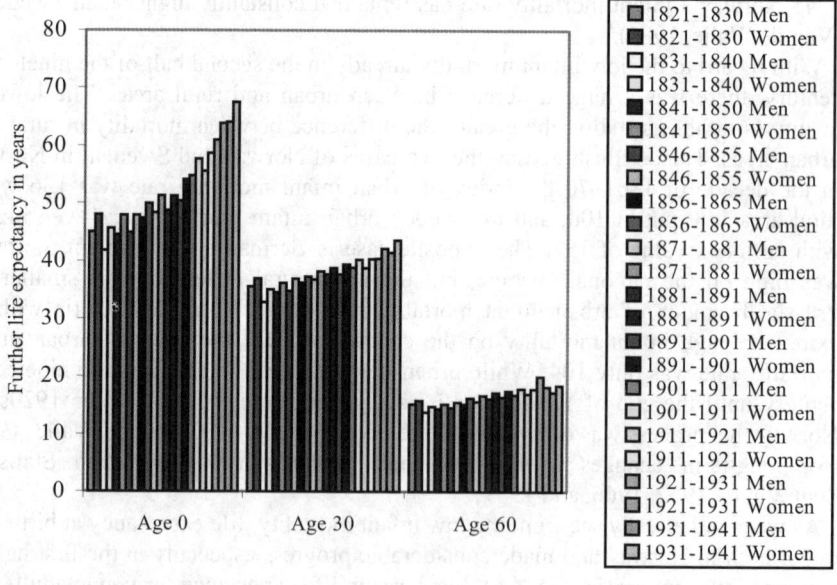

1940s the diverging tendency in life expectancy between the sexes continued, but to a very low degree. In Norway both sexes benefited more or less to the same extent from rising life expectancies.

FERTILITY AND LEGITIMACY

Norway was also a rather 'traditional' country concerning childbirth. Although it belongs to the Western European marriage pattern of late marriage and high celibacy, illegitimate births were rather rare and below the European average. This contrasts strongly with Sweden and Denmark, where the share of illegitimate births was much higher and structurally over the European average. In Norway, children were much more likely to be born within marriage than out-of-wedlock. The secular birth decline influenced both the illegitimate and the legitimate birth rate. The illegitimate birth rate decreased for nearly a century and did not increase until the 1960s. Since that time the Norwegian out-of-wedlock birth rate has been well above the European average.

The legitimate birth rate (legitimacy rate) in Norway was higher than in Europe until the demographic crisis of the 1930s, when it fell below the European average (Figure N.5). In the post-war period the legitimate birth rate has been close to the European average. When compared with the illegitimate birth rate, it becomes clear that out-of-wedlock births have increased relative to births within marriage. The relation of the illegitimate to the legitimate birth rate changed, from below the European average until the 1960s to well above it since then.

Thus, concerning legitimacy, for most of the century from 1850 to 1950 Norway was hesitant about accepting out-of-wedlock childbearing. It is only rather recently that illegitimate children have been given equal status with legitimate children and childbirth without marriage has gained social acceptance as in Denmark and Sweden.

MARRIAGE AND DIVORCE

Like its Scandinavian neighbours, Norway belongs to the European region of the Western European marriage pattern of late age at marriage and a high celibacy rate. In the nineteenth century age at marriage was one of the highest in Western Europe. This is specific for the Scandinavian countries. The developments concerning marital behaviour, namely age at marriage, marriage propensity, and celibacy were very similar for Sweden, Denmark, and Norway.

Age at marriage was very high in the second half of the nineteenth century when measured by the proportion of women married at age 20–24. In 1870 only 20% of all women in this age group were married, and this proportion increased only slightly until the 1920s. Surprisingly, and somewhat similar to Finland, the proportion of women married at this age declined during the late 1920s and early 1930s. This is indicative of the severe economic and demographic crisis in Norway as well in the inter-war period. That is the reason why the following wave of universal and early marriage in Norway was delayed (as in Finland too). This marriage revolution started in the 1950s and reached its highest point in 1970, when over 50% of women were married at age 20–24, more than twice the proportion in the late nineteenth century. The cohorts of women born since the 1950s returned to

Figure N.5 Fertility and legitimacy 1850-1939

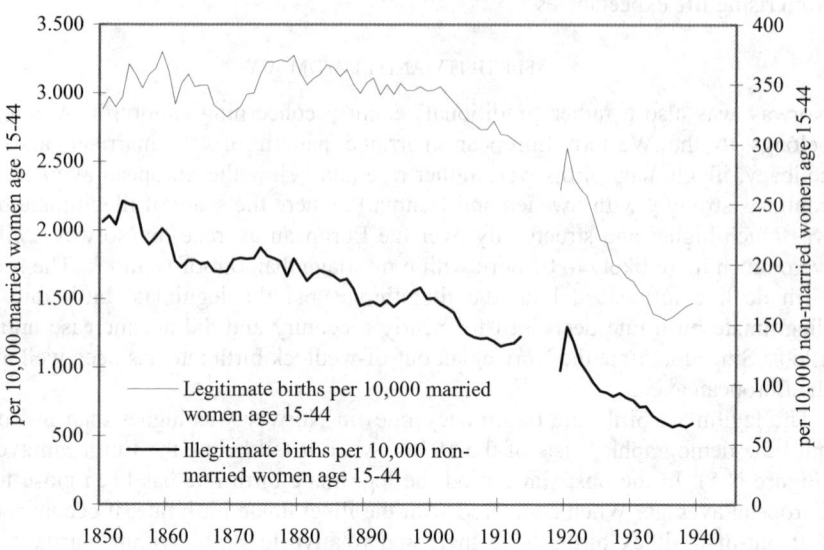

Figure N.6 Marriages and divorces 1850-1939

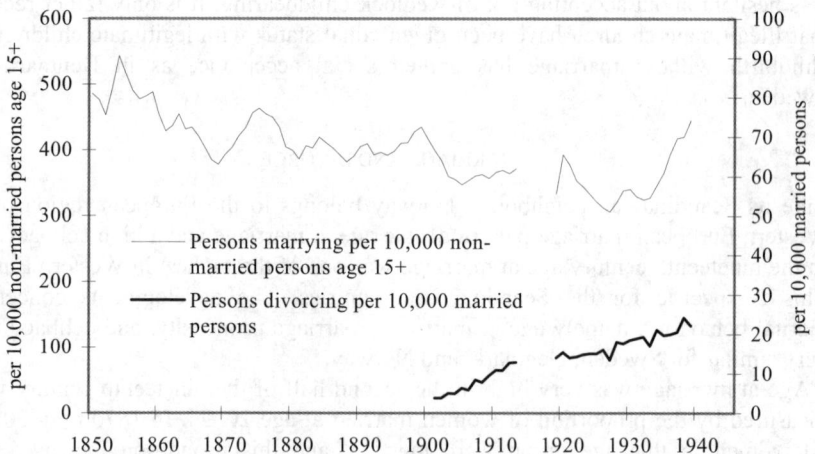

the old pattern of late and non-universal marriage, a behavioural pattern which has been labelled the 'deinstitutionalization' of marriage.

Marriage intensity can be measured by the *marriage rate* and the *celibacy rate*. 'Intensity' means the availability of marriage and the urgent need to remarry after widowhood ('remarriage need', Michael Mitterauer). A third component can be seen in the universality of marriage in the population. The marriage rate refers to all marriages of unmarried people (Figure N.6). The Norwegian marriage rate is very similar to the Swedish one, but less so to the Danish rate. Both the Swedish and the Norwegian marriage rates are well below the European average. This is a clear expression of the western marriage pattern with late age at marriage and high celibacy. There was a decline in marriage chances or nuptiality in the first half of the twentieth century in line with the small decrease in age at marriage and the proportion married at younger ages. Obviously, the economic crisis of the inter-war period also influenced marriage behaviour in a negative way: the marriage rate declined strongly. Towards the end of the 1930s and especially during the 1950s the marriage rate was high. This was the period of universalization of marriage with low age at marriage and high proportions of people marrying. There was another marriage boom around the 1970s, coinciding with the baby boom of these years. After the 1970s the marriage rate declined to its lowest level in 150 years, a clear indication of the loss of socio-legal relevance of the institution of marriage (*deinstitutionalization of marriage*).

The second indicator for marriage intensity is the celibacy rate. It indicates how many people in a population actually married. It therefore says a lot about legal and social marriage restrictions. While in the first half of the nineteenth century legal marriage restrictions very often existed or were introduced, in the second half of the nineteenth and the first half of the twentieth century these restrictions changed into social and economic ones. In Norway the development was very similar to Sweden. Women's celibacy rate (defined as women never married at age 45–54 as a percentage of all women) increased until the inter-war period: in 1870 25% of all women aged 45–54 years had never married; in 1930 this proportion had climbed to 34%. After 1930 the trend was reversed towards universal marriage, which in the 1950s culminated in a veritable marriage boom; this boom was carried by women born from the 1920s to the 1940s. Already females born in the 1950s returned to non-universal marriage, as the rise in the celibacy rate in the 1990s shows (cf. Statistisk Sentralbyrå, 1965 and 1976).

Norway reveals a very clear pattern of logistic *growth of divorces* since the late nineteenth century (Figure N.6). There was a slow growth in divorce intensity until the 1960s, when the typical acceleration set in. Until 1990 the divorce rate had not peaked. Divorce was not as common as in Sweden and Denmark in the nineteenth century and the actual level of the divorce rate (1990s) is clearly below the Swedish and Danish rates. Until the early 1970s the Norwegian divorce rate even matched the European divorce rate. Only since the 1970s has the number of divorces grown more rapidly in Norway than on the European average.

During World War II and afterwards the divorce rate showed the normal incidence pattern during economic and war crises: a declining divorce rate during the war and a strong peak after the war which subsequently normalized. There was only a small shift in the level of the divorce rate due to World War II.

In summary, Norwegian divorce law was much more restrictive for more than a hundred years until the 1960s, allowing for divorce in very few cases. Nevertheless marital breakup was much more frequent if legal separations are added. Data on these are available since 1895 and show that separations were at least as frequent as divorces (cf. Mamelund et al., 1997).

AGE, SEX, AND CIVIL STATUS

In Norway, until World War I the age structure maintained a clear pyramidal shape with strong proportions of the lowest age groups, indicating a high fertility rate and a low infant mortality rate (Appendix Figure N.8). The first signs of fertility reduction appeared between the censuses of 1900 and 1910, when the age structure at the bottom started to take on a convex shape. Until 1920 the youngest age groups continued to contract at an even pace, due to Norway's non-involvement in World War I. Nevertheless, during the 1920s a major birth decline occurred, which can be seen from the age structure of 1930, with a greatly reduced age group of 0–4-year-olds. This may have been influenced by the Great Depression. The whole 1930s were a time of low fertility, in which the respective age groups were small. Norway's occupation by German troops during World War II contributed to this major loss of births. But the 1941–46 birth cohorts were again very strong.

Like most European countries, Norway shows the pattern of men remaining single longer than women; at higher ages, however, more women than men remained unmarried. This structure did not significantly change until 1947, but celibacy tended to fall until 1910 and then rose again during the inter-war period. The proportion of widowed and divorced women in higher age groups was rather large in Norway already during the second half of the nineteenth century, due to higher male mortality and lower rates of remarriage among women.

FAMILY AND HOUSEHOLD STRUCTURES

According to the Western European marriage pattern which also prevailed in Norway, the restriction of marriage to only a segment of the population *ceteris paribus* furthered the formation of large households in the nineteenth century, because it was difficult for unmarried and widowed people with a limited income to afford living alone. We may therefore suppose that single people joined family households as servants, boarders, and lodgers, thereby constituting extended households. Therefore extended households must have existed to a considerable degree.

Unfortunately, this question cannot be answered, because until the 1950s the Norwegian household and family statistics were rather underdeveloped. Therefore we must base our description mainly on the mean household size. Households by size categories are only available serially since 1920. In 1900 an exploratory sample survey investigation into household and family statistics was undertaken, but the results and methodology of this survey do not fit into the earlier and later comprehensive statistics.

For the nineteenth century the only indicator available is mean household size and the percentage distribution of the main household categories.

Mean household size underlines the hypothesis stated above about the formation of large households, because households on average were rather large in the nineteenth century. Mean family household size in 1890 was 5.15 persons per household, a rather high figure in a European context. Mean private household size was 4.64 persons per household, indicating a large distance to the mean family household size. This difference is probably explained by the relatively large proportion of one-person households in 1875 with 12.2%; 2.6% of the population lived alone. This relatively large figure of one-person households is perhaps due to the early demographic transition. That is why, when we look further back into history, mean household size was very much larger. Unfortunately, for earlier census years we have only the total number of households rather than family households. But when we compare 1845 with 1890, mean household size had fallen from 5.00 to 4.65, a decrease of 0.35 persons per household. Assuming the same change in the size of family households, we would arrive at 5.5 persons per family household in 1845 (adding 0.35 to 5.15, the number of persons per family household in 1890).

THE NATIONAL SYSTEM OF DEMOGRAPHIC STATISTICS

Population Structure

As in all the Nordic countries, in Norway population statistics have a long tradition reaching back to the eighteenth century. Norway's long union with Denmark influenced population statistics into the first half of the nineteenth century when Norway was already in a union with Sweden. Population censuses were already conducted in the eighteenth century, beginning with the census of 1769. A second census was in 1801; from 1815 onwards there were decennial censuses in years ending with 5 until 1875. From 1890 censuses were conducted decennially in years ending with 0.

Since the census of 1865 the population has been covered by age, sex, and marital status. All the later censuses (up to the present) have collected these basic population statistics. In 1865 and 1890 age was given in grouped data for higher ages, but all other censuses give one-year age groups.

A historical account of the population censuses in Norway from 1769 to 1875 is given in Statistisk Centralbureau (1882: 1ff. and 205ff.).

Vital Statistics

In Norway the recording of births, deaths, and marriages was introduced very early, in the first half of the eighteenth century. Live births and deaths were already available in 1736, marriages from 1770–83 and again from 1795, and illegitimate births from 1770–83 and again from 1801. Stillbirths are available since 1801 and infant deaths since 1836. Divorce data became available at a much later date, in 1901, and figures on legal separations some years earlier, in 1895.

Households and Families

Data on *households* (*familier, husholdninger*) were first expressively recorded in the census of 1845. In this census only the number of households and their members were given. These household statistics were repeated in the censuses of 1855 and 1865. In 1875 one-person, family, and institutional households were distinguished. The respective members of these households were given for both sexes. The publication of these basic household types was repeated until 1910. From 1920 to

1946 households were enumerated within the housing census, which meant some change in the household statistics. A historical account of household statistics is given in Statistisk Centralbureau (1882: 31ff.).

Households by size categories were first recorded in 1900, distinguishing private households from one person to 21 and more persons. This analysis was repeated in 1920, 1930, and 1946 within the housing census.

Household composition was only analysed in the census of 1900, in which twelve different types of household members were distinguished by sex: household heads, married women, children, sons- and daughters-in-law, grandsons and grand-daughters, parents, household servants, employees, visitors, other household members, single tenants, and other persons living alone.

Households by *profession of household head* were distinguished in 1900; household heads were classified according to profession, social position, and profession combined with social position. In 1946 household data were again combined with the profession of the household head in 11 categories (Statistisk Sentralbyrå, 1952: 99ff.).

During the nineteenth century and until the 1930 census, a *household (familie, husholdning)* was defined as a *meal household*, i.e. household members had to live together and form one common budget. This household concept was last applied in Norway in the 1950 census. The *household dwelling concept*, i.e. all persons living in one dwelling were supposed to form one household, was first used in 1946 and has been used steadily since the 1960 census. Because several households can live in one dwelling, the household dwelling concept slightly underestimates the number of households (Statistics Norway, 1995: 61f.).

Family statistics were introduced in 1900 when comprehensive supplementary household statistics using the representative method were gathered for the first time. Children and grandchildren in family households were presented by age groups; family households were analysed by the number of children, from 0 to 12–15 children (Statistisk Centralbureau, 1904: 98f, 106f.).

In 1920 special statistics on the *'fertility of marriages'* were collected and published in a separate volume for the first time. This investigation explored all major aspects of marital fertility, such as the number of children by marriage duration and age of mother, childless marriages, number of children in different social classes, fertility in the different parts of Norway, and fertility decline, among others. These statistics on marital fertility were repeated in 1930 in a similar way.

Remarks (also see introductory Table 6.1)

No peculiarities.

BOUNDARY CHANGES

Norway was part of Denmark until 1814; from 1814 to 1904 it belonged to the Swedish crown. It became independent in 1905. Norway (or the territory before independence) did not change its boundaries since it was ceded to Sweden in 1814. For regional organization see the documentation by Quick (1994) and Caramani, Flora, Kraus, and Quick (1998).

APPENDIX TABLES AND FIGURES

APPENDIX TABLE N.1 Population structure at census dates 1865–1946

Census number	Census date	Census population			Marital status				Age group		
		Total	Male	Female	Single	Married	Widowed	Divorced	0–14	15–64	65+
		Absolute									
1	31 XII 1865	1,701,756	835,947	865,809	1,057,423	551,285	93,048[1]		613,410	982,268	106,078
2	31 XII 1875	1,818,853	888,571	930,282	1,132,098	583,560	101,251	1,944	625,194	1,082,471	111,188
3	31 XII 1890	1,988,674	951,290	1,037,384	1,226,063	641,501	118,973[1]		712,310	1,123,115	151,530
4	3 XII 1900	2,242,995	1,086,867	1,156,128	1,394,976	717,358	128,855	1,806[2]	790,605	1,276,654	175,736
5	1 XII 1910	2,390,402	1,151,572	1,238,830	1,491,226	760,298	136,718	2,160	832,811	1,373,948	183,643
6	1 XII 1920	2,641,242	1,281,930	1,359,312	1,625,188	851,660	155,026	8,682[2]	850,589	1,586,161	203,542
7	1 XII 1930	2,814,194	1,371,919	1,442,275	1,687,784	949,898	160,718	14,940[2]	801,549	1,777,516	233,095
8	3 XII 1946	3,146,950	1,557,278	1,589,672	1,625,676	1,309,742	176,498	30,443[2]	705,066	2,144,299	294,178
		Per cent									
1	31 XII 1865	100.00	49.12	50.88	62.14	32.40	5.47[1]		36.05	57.72	6.23
2	31 XII 1875	100.00	48.85	51.15	62.24	32.08	5.57	0.11	34.37	59.51	6.11
3	31 XII 1890	100.00	47.84	52.16	61.65	32.26	5.98[1]		35.82	56.48	7.62
4	3 XII 1900	100.00	48.46	51.54	62.19	31.98	5.74	0.08[2]	35.25	56.92	7.83
5	1 XII 1910	100.00	48.17	51.83	62.38	31.81	5.72	0.09	34.84	57.48	7.68
6	1 XII 1920	100.00	48.54	51.46	61.53	32.24	5.87	0.33[2]	32.20	60.05	7.71
7	1 XII 1930	100.00	48.75	51.25	59.97	33.75	5.71	0.53[2]	28.48	63.16	8.28
8	3 XII 1946	100.00	49.49	50.51	51.66	41.62	5.61	0.97[2]	22.40	68.14	9.35

Notes: [1] Widowed and divorced. [2] Divorced and separated.

APPENDIX TABLE N.2 Census population (per cent) and population density by region
1876–1910 (inhabitants per sq. km.)

Amt (1876–1910)[1]	1876	1891	1900	1910	1876	1891	1900	1910
	Population distribution				Population density			
Smaalenene	5.94	6.00	6.12	6.35	26	31	35	39
Akershus	6.32	4.95	5.18	5.35	22	20	24	26
Kristiana	4.23	7.55	10.18	10.12	7,700	9,438	14,250	15,125
Hedemarken	6.54	5.95	5.63	5.64	5	5	5	5
Kristians	6.38	5.40	5.18	4.97	5	4	5	5
Buskerud	5.61	5.25	5.04	5.18	7	7	8	9
Jarlsberg og Larvik	4.89	5.05	4.69	4.56	39	45	47	49
Bratsberg	4.62	4.60	4.42	4.52	6	7	7	8
Nedenæs	4.18	4.05	3.57	3.18	8	9	9	9
Lister og Mandal	4.23	3.95	3.66	3.43	12	11	12	12
Stavanger	6.27	5.85	5.71	5.89	13	13	15	16
Søndre Bergenhus	6.65	6.40	6.07	6.10	8	8	9	10
Bergen	1.87	2.70	3.21	3.22	34,000	4,154	5,538	5,923
Nordre Bergenhus	4.73	4.40	3.97	3.76	5	5	5	5
Romsdal	6.43	6.40	6.07	6.06	8	9	9	10
Søndre Trondhjem	6.43	6.20	6.03	6.19	6	7	8	8
Nordre Trondhjem	4.45	4.05	3.71	3.55	4	4	4	4
Nordland	5.66	6.60	6.79	6.90	3	4	4	4
Tromsø	2.97	3.25	3.30	3.43	2	3	3	3
Finnmarken	1.32	1.45	1.47	1.59	1	1	1	1
TOTAL	**100.00**	**100.00**	**100.00**	**100.00**	**6**	**6**	**7**	**8**

Notes: [1] Land area. Total area in 1876.

APPENDIX TABLE N.3 Census population (per cent) and population density by region
1920–1946 (inhabitants per sq. km.)

Fylke (1920–1946)[1]	1920	1930	1946	1920	1930	1946
	Population distribution			**Population density**		
Østfold	6.04	5.93	5.64	41	43	46
Akershus	6.79	8.42	9.53	36	47	60
Oslo[2]	9.74	8.99	9.06	16,125	15,813	16,824
Hedmark	5.66	5.61	5.38	6	6	6
Oppland	4.87	4.90	4.91	5	6	6
Buskerud	5.17	5.08	4.75	10	10	11
Vestfold	4.68	4.76	4.69	55	59	66
Telemark	4.72	4.55	4.18	9	9	9
Aust-Agder	2.83	2.63	2.38	9	8	9
Vest-Agder	3.13	2.88	2.98	12	12	14
Rogaland	6.26	6.15	6.40	19	20	23
Hordaland	5.89	5.83	5.96	10	11	12
Bergen	3.43	3.48	3.48	2,676	2,882	3,056
Sogn og Fjordane	3.40	3.27	3.07	5	5	5
Møre	6.00	5.86	5.80	11	11	12
Sør Trøndelag	6.30	6.22	6.15	9	10	11
Nord Trøndelag	3.36	3.41	3.36	4	5	5
Nordland	6.57	6.65	6.84	5[3]	5	6
Troms	3.43	3.45	3.61	3[3]	4	4
Finnmark	1.66	1.88	1.87	1	1	1
TOTAL	**100.00**	**100.00**	**100.00**	**9**	**9**	**10**

Notes: [1] Since 1920 named fylker. [2] Until 1920 (*Christiania*) *Kristiania*, then *Oslo*. [3] 1 January 1912: an area of 25 sq. km. with 291 inhabitants moved from *Nordland* to *Tromsø*.

APPENDIX TABLE N.4 Demographic developments 1850–1945 (absolute figures and rates)

Year	Mid-year population[1]	Natural population growth rate	Population growth rate	Net migration rate	Crude birth rate	Legitimate births per 10,000 married women age 15–44	Illegitimate births per 10,000 unmarried women age 15–44	Illeg. births per 100 leg. births
1850	1,391,941	13.7	11.0	-2.7	31.0	2,879	235	10.5
1851	1,408,903	14.8	12.0	-2.7	31.9	2,970	240	10.4
1852	1,425,472	13.1	11.6	-1.5	31.0	2,895	233	10.3
1853	1,439,755	13.6	9.9	-3.7	32.0	2,969	252	10.9
1854	1,457,020	18.2	11.8	-6.4	34.2	3,210	250	10.0
1855	1,478,722	16.3	14.7	-1.6	33.4	3,130	249	10.2
1856	1,500,612	15.3	14.6	-0.7	32.2	3,035	224	9.5
1857	1,520,744	15.9	13.2	-2.7	33.0	3,131	217	8.9
1858	1,543,195	17.4	14.5	-2.9	33.5	3,176	223	9.0
1859	1,569,801	17.7	16.9	-0.8	34.8	3,298	230	9.0
1860	1,596,089	16.1	16.5	0.4	33.3	3,155	223	9.1
1861	1,613,878	7.5	11.0	3.6	30.7	2,917	203	9.0
1862	1,626,986	12.1	8.1	-4.0	32.1	3,070	197	8.3
1863	1,646,433	13.9	11.8	-2.1	32.7	3,134	203	8.4
1864	1,668,254	14.1	13.1	-1.0	31.9	3,043	204	8.6
1865	1,690,134	15.3	12.9	-2.4	31.9	3,056	200	8.5
1866	1,706,911	14.7	9.8	-4.9	31.7	3,055	202	8.6
1867	1,716,112	11.6	5.4	-6.2	30.1	2,910	194	8.9
1868	1,723,810	11.2	4.5	-6.7	29.5	2,871	194	9.1
1869	1,729,235	11.8	3.1	-8.6	28.9	2,825	194	9.4
1870	1,735,425	12.9	3.6	-9.4	29.2	2,862	204	9.9
1871	1,744,936	12.4	5.5	-7.0	29.3	2,897	205	10.0
1872	1,755,092	13.3	5.8	-7.5	30.0	2,989	204	9.8
1873	1,766,840	12.9	6.6	-6.2	29.9	2,997	205	10.0
1874	1,783,129	12.6	9.1	-3.5	31.0	3,131	214	10.1
1875	1,803,129	12.7	11.1	-1.7	31.5	3,224	207	9.6
1876	1,828,856	12.7	14.1	1.4	31.5	3,223	205	9.5
1877	1,851,571	14.8	12.3	-2.6	31.7	3,239	202	9.3
1878	1,876,835	15.5	13.5	-2.1	31.5	3,224	190	8.7
1879	1,902,126	17.0	13.3	-3.7	32.1	3,272	205	9.2
1880	1,919,075	14.7	8.8	-5.9	30.9	3,145	195	9.1
1881	1,922,948	13.0	2.0	-11.0	30.0	3,056	186	8.9
1882	1,919,767	12.0	-1.7	-13.6	30.6	3,104	192	9.0
1883	1,919,317	14.0	-0.2	-14.2	31.0	3,134	195	9.0
1884	1,929,058	15.0	5.0	-10.0	31.6	3,203	193	8.6
1885	1,943,916	15.0	7.6	-7.4	31.5	3,186	191	8.5
1886	1,958,323	14.6	7.4	-7.3	30.9	3,118	186	8.5
1887	1,969,807	15.2	5.8	-9.4	31.4	3,169	188	8.4
1888	1,976,615	13.1	3.4	-9.7	30.4	3,064	180	8.3
1889	1,984,295	11.9	3.9	-8.0	29.6	2,997	166	7.7
1890	1,996,929	12.4	6.3	-6.1	30.4	3,073	168	7.6
1891	2,012,503	13.1	7.7	-5.3	30.8	3,109	169	7.5
1892	2,026,016	11.7	6.7	-5.0	29.6	2,985	166	7.7
1893	2,037,797	13.9	5.8	-8.1	30.3	3,061	170	7.7
1894	2,056,657	12.7	9.2	-3.5	29.6	2,989	165	7.7
1895	2,083,088	14.8	12.7	-2.1	30.4	3,068	170	7.7
1896	2,111,678	14.8	13.5	-1.2	30.0	3,017	172	7.9
1897	2,141,721	14.7	14.0	-0.7	30.0	3,017	178	8.2

continued

APPENDIX TABLE N.4 Demographic developments 1850–1945 (absolute figures and rates)

Crude death rate	Infant mortality rate	Stillbirth rate	Infant mortality and stillbirth rate	Crude marriage rate	Persons marrying per 10,000 unmarried persons age 15+	Persons marrying per 10,000 unmarried persons age 15–49	Crude divorce rate	Divorces per 100 marriages	Divorces per 10,000 married persons	Year
17.2	102.0	43.5	145.5	7.6	486	595	..	..	..	1850
17.1	107.8	42.7	150.4	7.5	476	583	..	..	..	1851
17.9	118.6	42.3	160.9	7.1	453	555	..	..	..	1852
18.3	102.5	43.4	145.9	7.8	496	607	..	..	..	1853
16.0	97.2	43.7	140.9	8.6	543	665	..	..	..	1854
17.2	102.5	43.0	145.5	8.1	515	630	..	..	..	1855
16.9	97.1	45.8	142.9	7.7	490	600	..	..	..	1856
17.1	100.3	42.6	142.9	7.5	477	584	..	..	..	1857
16.1	102.4	43.5	145.8	7.6	482	589	..	..	..	1858
17.0	104.3	41.6	145.9	7.7	488	597	..	..	..	1859
17.2	102.0	44.1	146.0	7.2	453	554	..	..	..	1860
23.2	113.2	43.0	156.2	6.8	429	524	..	..	..	1861
20.0	109.8	41.8	151.6	6.9	437	534	..	..	..	1862
18.9	105.7	39.7	145.4	7.2	455	555	..	..	..	1863
17.8	100.7	41.6	142.3	6.8	432	528	..	..	..	1864
16.6	103.2	41.3	144.5	6.9	435	531	..	..	..	1865
17.1	107.6	36.4	144.0	6.7	421	515	..	..	..	1866
18.5	121.8	38.2	160.0	6.5	404	494	..	..	..	1867
18.3	126.1	38.0	164.1	6.2	385	471	..	..	..	1868
17.1	111.4	38.5	149.9	6.2	378	463	..	..	..	1869
16.2	100.7	36.8	137.5	6.4	393	482	..	..	..	1870
16.9	98.7	39.9	138.6	6.7	403	495	..	..	..	1871
16.7	102.5	39.2	141.7	7.0	422	518	..	..	..	1872
17.0	105.9	38.9	144.7	7.3	434	533	..	..	..	1873
18.3	112.7	37.3	150.0	7.7	457	561	..	..	..	1874
18.8	114.9	37.1	152.1	7.9	463	570	..	..	..	1875
18.9	108.1	38.4	146.5	7.7	455	561	..	..	..	1876
16.9	107.2	34.8	142.0	7.6	450	557	..	..	..	1877
16.0	103.1	34.9	138.1	7.3	435	539	..	..	..	1878
15.1	91.7	35.6	127.3	6.8	405	503	..	..	..	1879
16.2	95.3	34.9	130.1	6.6	400	498	..	..	..	1880
17.0	96.6	34.4	131.0	6.4	387	484	..	..	..	1881
18.6	111.0	31.6	142.6	6.7	407	510	..	..	..	1882
17.0	96.6	30.8	127.4	6.6	403	507	..	..	..	1883
16.6	96.3	29.3	125.6	6.9	420	530	..	..	..	1884
16.5	93.1	30.1	123.2	6.7	411	521	..	..	..	1885
16.3	90.6	29.2	119.8	6.5	403	512	..	..	..	1886
16.2	87.5	27.8	115.3	6.3	392	500	..	..	..	1887
17.3	97.3	26.4	123.6	6.1	382	488	..	..	..	1888
17.8	110.0	27.5	137.5	6.3	390	501	..	..	..	1889
18.0	97.2	27.3	124.5	6.5	405	521	..	..	..	1890
17.7	96.9	28.3	125.2	6.5	410	526	..	..	..	1891
17.9	103.8	28.5	132.3	6.3	393	505	..	..	..	1892
16.5	89.1	29.8	118.9	6.4	397	510	..	..	..	1893
16.9	103.0	28.2	131.2	6.3	392	504	..	..	..	1894
15.6	95.5	25.8	121.3	6.4	398	510	..	..	..	1895
15.2	96.5	25.8	122.3	6.6	410	526	..	..	..	1896
15.3	95.6	24.7	120.3	6.6	411	527	..	..	..	1897

continued

APPENDIX TABLE N.4 Demographic developments 1850–1945 (continued)

Year	Mid-year population[1]	Natural population growth rate	Population growth rate	Net migration rate	Crude birth rate	Legitimate births per 10,000 married women age 15-44	Illegitimate births per 10,000 unmarried women age 15-44	Illeg. births per 100 leg. births
1898	2,173,807	15.0	14.8	-0.3	30.3	3,045	181	8.2
1899	2,204,083	13.2	13.7	0.6	29.9	3,015	172	7.9
1900	2,230,483	13.9	11.8	-2.0	29.7	3,020	172	7.9
1901	2,254,911	14.8	10.8	-4.0	29.8	3,046	167	7.7
1902	2,275,485	15.3	9.0	-6.3	29.2	2,988	164	7.7
1903	2,287,768	13.8	5.4	-8.5	28.6	2,933	160	7.7
1904	2,297,494	13.6	4.2	-9.4	27.9	2,878	149	7.3
1905	2,308,572	12.4	4.8	-7.6	27.1	2,804	143	7.2
1906	2,319,191	13.1	4.6	-8.5	26.8	2,776	140	7.2
1907	2,328,962	12.0	4.2	-7.8	26.3	2,734	138	7.2
1908	2,345,564	12.1	7.1	-5.0	26.3	2,737	139	7.3
1909	2,367,494	13.2	9.3	-3.9	26.7	2,796	136	7.0
1910	2,383,677	12.3	6.8	-5.5	25.8	2,699	132	7.0
1911	2,400,796	12.5	7.1	-5.4	25.7	2,693	133	7.2
1912	2,423,184	11.9	9.2	-2.6	25.3	2,656	135	7.3
1913	2,446,874	11.8	9.7	-2.1	25.0	2,621	140	7.8
1914	2,472,419	11.7	10.3	-1.3	25.1	..	..	7.8
1915	2,497,766	10.2	10.1	-0.1	23.6	..	..	7.5
1916	2,522,178	10.4	9.7	-0.7	24.2	..	..	7.7
1917	2,550,543	11.5	11.1	-0.4	25.1	..	..	7.5
1918	2,577,729	7.5	10.5	3.1	24.6	..	..	7.1
1919	2,602,869	9.1	9.7	0.6	22.9	2,292	111	7.0
1920	2,634,664	13.5	12.1	-1.5	26.3	2,601	148	8.2
1921	2,667,868	12.7	12.4	-0.3	24.2	2,384	136	8.2
1922	2,694,840	11.3	10.0	-1.3	23.3	2,307	119	7.4
1923	2,713,116	11.1	6.7	-4.4	22.8	2,246	110	7.1
1924	2,728,764	10.0	5.7	-4.2	21.3	2,092	102	7.0
1925	2,746,815	8.6	6.6	-2.0	19.7	1,929	95	7.1
1926	2,763,106	8.8	5.9	-2.9	19.6	1,914	94	7.0
1927	2,774,864	6.9	4.2	-2.6	18.1	1,752	90	7.4
1928	2,784,675	7.0	3.5	-3.5	17.9	1,723	93	7.7
1929	2,795,105	5.8	3.7	-2.1	17.3	1,660	89	7.7
1930	2,807,438	6.5	4.4	-2.1	17.0	1,629	87	7.6
1931	2,823,882	5.4	5.8	0.4	16.3	1,552	81	7.5
1932	2,841,529	5.4	6.2	0.8	16.0	1,517	82	7.7
1933	2,858,343	4.6	5.9	1.3	14.7	1,393	74	7.6
1934	2,874,206	4.7	5.5	0.8	14.6	1,374	70	7.3
1935	2,889,211	4.0	5.2	1.2	14.3	1,348	68	7.2
1936	2,903,519	4.2	4.9	0.7	14.5	1,371	65	6.8
1937	2,918,742	4.7	5.2	0.6	15.0	1,409	67	6.7
1938	2,935,803	5.5	5.8	0.3	15.4	1,448	65	6.4
1939	2,954,415	5.7	6.3	0.6	15.8	1,473	68	6.6
1940	2,973,067	5.3	6.3	0.9	16.1	..	..	6.9
1941	2,990,234	4.5	5.7	1.2	15.3	..	..	7.5
1942	3,008,883	7.0	6.2	-0.8	17.7	..	..	7.9
1943	3,032,430	8.5	7.8	-0.7	18.9	..	..	8.1
1944	3,060,216	9.7	9.1	-0.6	20.3	..	..	7.9
1945	3,091,181	10.3	10.0	-0.3	20.0	..	..	7.9

Note: [1] Mean population.

APPENDIX TABLE N.4 Demographic developments 1850–1945 (continued)

Crude death rate	Infant mortality rate	Stillbirth rate	Infant mortality and stillbirth rate	Crude marriage rate	Persons marrying per 10,000 unmarried persons age 15+	Persons marrying per 10,000 unmarried persons age 15–49	Crude divorce rate	Divorces per 100 marriages	Divorces per 10,000 married persons	Year
15.3	89.4	24.1	113.6	6.9	428	548	..	..	..	1898
16.8	106.7	25.6	132.3	7.0	435	557	..	..	..	1899
15.8	90.4	24.4	114.8	6.8	417	531	..	..	..	1900
15.0	91.1	25.5	116.6	6.5	399	509	0.1	0.9	3.8	1901
13.9	73.8	24.0	97.8	6.3	385	491	0.1	1.0	3.8	1902
14.8	77.9	25.0	102.9	5.9	360	460	0.1	1.4	5.1	1903
14.3	74.8	24.6	99.4	5.9	356	455	0.1	1.3	4.9	1904
14.7	81.5	23.3	104.8	5.7	348	445	0.1	1.8	6.4	1905
13.7	69.1	23.1	92.2	5.9	354	453	0.1	1.6	5.8	1906
14.3	65.8	23.0	88.8	6.0	361	462	0.1	2.3	8.5	1907
14.2	75.0	23.2	98.2	6.0	363	465	0.1	2.1	7.8	1908
13.6	69.5	22.9	92.4	5.9	357	458	0.2	2.5	9.5	1909
13.5	67.2	22.9	90.1	6.1	366	470	0.2	2.8	10.9	1910
13.2	64.5	22.8	87.4	6.2	370	475	0.2	2.8	10.8	1911
13.5	67.2	23.2	90.4	6.1	365	469	0.2	3.3	12.7	1912
13.3	64.3	22.3	86.6	6.2	372	479	0.2	3.3	12.9	1913
13.5	67.6	22.1	89.7	6.4	..	..	0.2	2.7	..	1914
13.4	67.3	23.2	90.5	6.4	..	..	0.2	3.5	..	1915
13.8	64.0	23.8	87.7	6.9	..	..	0.2	3.0	..	1916
13.6	64.0	22.7	86.7	7.1	..	..	0.2	3.1	..	1917
17.2	62.9	23.8	86.8	7.8	..	..	0.2	3.1	..	1918
13.8	61.7	23.3	85.0	5.9	334	425	0.2	3.9	14.1	1919
12.8	57.5	20.6	78.1	7.0	393	500	0.3	3.6	15.5	1920
11.5	53.8	18.1	71.9	6.8	378	480	0.2	3.4	14.1	1921
12.1	54.5	20.8	75.3	6.4	354	450	0.2	3.7	14.3	1922
11.6	49.5	20.8	70.3	6.3	345	439	0.2	3.9	14.9	1923
11.3	50.0	24.6	74.7	6.1	333	425	0.2	4.1	15.2	1924
11.1	50.2	25.1	75.3	5.9	322	410	0.3	4.2	15.1	1925
10.8	47.9	23.2	71.1	5.8	313	399	0.3	4.6	16.1	1926
11.2	50.7	24.4	75.1	5.7	307	392	0.2	4.0	13.5	1927
10.9	49.0	26.1	75.0	6.0	321	410	0.3	5.0	18.1	1928
11.5	54.4	26.7	81.1	6.4	339	434	0.3	4.7	17.6	1929
10.5	45.6	26.6	72.3	6.4	341	436	0.3	4.9	18.6	1930
10.9	46.3	26.9	73.2	6.3	330	422	0.3	5.1	19.0	1931
10.6	46.8	25.1	71.9	6.2	325	416	0.3	5.3	19.3	1932
10.1	47.6	26.4	74.0	6.3	328	421	0.3	4.7	17.1	1933
9.9	39.3	24.0	63.4	6.7	347	445	0.4	5.4	21.1	1934
10.3	44.2	25.0	69.2	7.1	366	470	0.3	4.8	19.7	1935
10.4	42.0	25.1	67.1	7.7	395	507	0.3	4.5	20.0	1936
10.4	42.0	22.9	64.9	8.2	418	538	0.4	4.4	20.6	1937
9.9	37.3	22.7	60.1	8.3	420	541	0.4	5.1	24.2	1938
10.1	37.2	22.4	59.7	8.8	445	573	0.4	4.4	22.2	1939
10.8	38.7	22.5	61.2	9.4	..	..	0.3	3.4	..	1940
10.8	43.0	21.1	64.0	8.8	..	..	0.4	4.2	..	1941
10.7	35.9	20.6	56.5		..	..	0.4	..	..	1942
10.4	35.4	21.1	56.5	7.9	..	..	0.4	5.4	..	1943
10.7	36.7	20.0	56.7	7.2	..	..	0.5	7.0	..	1944
9.7	36.4	20.3	56.7	7.6	..	..	0.6	8.2	..	1945

Note: [1] Mean population.

APPENDIX TABLE N.5 Life expectancy by age 1821/30–1931/41 (in years)

Age	0	10	20	30	40	50	60	70	80
				Males					
1821–1830	45.0	50.3	42.5	35.6	28.3	21.4	15.2	9.7	..
1831–1840	41.8	47.4	39.5	32.9	26.2	19.6	13.8	8.8	..
1841–1850	44.5	49.4	41.5	34.6	27.5	20.7	14.4	9.1	..
1846–1855	44.9	49.4	42.0	34.8	28.0	21.0	14.6	9.0	..
1856–1865	47.40	50.81	43.16	36.28	29.10	22.00	15.19	9.40	5.43
1871–1881	48.33	50.76	43.14	36.82	29.69	22.49	15.63	9.89	5.67
1881–1891	48.73	51.25	43.89	37.68	30.43	23.08	16.13	10.11	5.63
1891–1901	50.41	51.05	43.58	37.69	30.62	23.34	16.39	10.29	5.64
1901–1911	54.82	52.92	45.16	38.85	31.49	23.95	16.80	10.59	5.85
1911–1921	55.62	52.65	44.85	38.83	31.64	24.10	16.98	10.40	5.73
1921–1931	60.98	56.27	47.73	40.39	32.40	24.41	19.97	10.63	5.87
1931–1941	94.08	58.56	49.59	41.48	33.15	24.90	17.22	10.71	5.84
				Females					
1821–1830	48.0	52.4	44.5	29.8	29.8	22.4	15.8	10.0	..
1831–1840	45.6	50.4	42.4	28.2	28.2	21.4	14.8	9.3	..
1841–1850	47.9	51.8	43.9	29.4	29.4	22.2	15.2	9.5	..
1846–1855	47.9	52.0	44.5	29.7	29.7	22.5	15.5	9.4	..
1856–1865	49.95	52.83	45.27	30.70	30.70	23.40	16.24	10.10	6.05
1871–1881	51.30	53.10	45.39	31.14	31.14	23.84	16.67	10.55	6.05
1881–1891	31.21	53.32	45.90	31.81	31.81	24.45	17.18	10.88	6.01
1891–1901	54.14	54.11	46.54	31.31	31.31	24.86	17.46	10.97	6.14
1901–1911	57.70	55.08	47.34	32.92	32.92	25.30	17.85	11.24	6.28
1911–1921	58.71	54.98	47.19	32.96	32.96	25.28	17.78	11.15	6.19
1921–1931	63.84	58.35	49.85	34.00	34.00	25.87	18.16	11.40	6.31
1931–1941	67.55	61.25	52.12	34.89	34.89	35.00	18.38	11.38	6.22

APPENDIX TABLE N.6A Households by type 1825–1946 (absolute and per cent)

Census year	Household types and members									
	Total households	Private households	Family households	One-person households	Institutional households	Total household members	Private household members	Family household members	One-person household members	Institutional household members
	Absolute									
1825	210,390	:	:	:	:	1,051,318	:	:	:	:
1845	266,913	:	:	:	:	1,328,471	:	:	:	:
1855	304,822	:	:	:	:	1,490,047	:	:	:	:
1865	346,061	:	:	:	:	1,701,756	:	:	:	:
1875	389,611	389,448	341,806	47,642	163	1,813,424	1,808,972	1,761,330	47,642	4,452
1890	436,994	436,371	383,113	53,258	623	1,988,674	1,976,563	1,923,305	53,258	12,111
1900	524,153	522,829	429,875	92,954	1,324	2,221,477	2,196,988	2,104,034	92,954	24,489
1910	564,567	563,778	462,301	101,477	789	2,357,790	2,330,922	2,229,445	101,477	26,868
1920	577,119	574,463	520,281	54,182	2,656	2,653,131	2,594,150	2,539,968	54,182	58,981
1930	656,304	653,071	586,923	66,148	3,233	2,812,065	2,748,789	2,682,641	66,148	63,276
1946	923,060	911,472	750,399	161,073	11,588	3,095,832	2,935,606	2,774,533	161,073	160,226
	Per cent									
1825	100.00	:	:	:	:	100.00	:	:	:	:
1845	100.00	:	:	:	:	100.00	:	:	:	:
1855	100.00	:	:	:	:	100.00	:	:	:	:
1865	100.00	:	:	:	:	100.00	:	:	:	:
1875	100.00	99.96	87.73	12.23	0.04	100.00	99.75	97.13	2.63	0.25
1890	100.00	99.86	87.67	12.19	0.14	100.00	99.39	96.71	2.68	0.61
1900	100.00	99.75	82.01	17.73	0.25	100.00	98.90	94.71	4.18	1.10
1910	100.00	99.86	81.89	17.97	0.14	100.00	98.86	94.56	4.30	1.14
1920	100.00	99.54	90.15	9.39	0.46	100.00	97.78	95.73	2.04	2.22
1930	100.00	99.51	89.43	10.08	0.49	100.00	97.75	95.40	2.35	2.25
1946	100.00	98.74	81.29	17.45	1.26	100.00	94.82	89.62	5.20	5.18

APPENDIX TABLE N.6B Households by size and members 1920–1946 (absolute figures)

Census year	Households by number of members							
	Private households total	1 person	2 persons	3 persons	4 persons	5 persons	6 persons	7+ persons
	Households							
1920	574,463	54,182	84,616	93,349	88,746	75,803	60,619	117,148
1930	653,071	66,148	104,388	116,415	108,813	91,889	60,162	105,256
1946	911,472	161,073	190,150	210,015	164,210	92,028	48,575	45,421
	Persons							
1920	2,594,150	54,182	169,232	280,047	354,984	379,015	363,714	992,976
1930	2,748,789	66,148	208,776	349,245	435,252	459,445	360,972	868,951
1946	2,935,606	161,073	380,300	630,045	656,840	460,140	291,450	355,758

APPENDIX TABLE N.6C Households by size and members 1920–1946 (per cent)

Census year	Households by number of members							
	Private households total	1 person	2 persons	3 persons	4 persons	5 persons	6 persons	7+ persons
	Households							
1920	100.00	9.43	14.73	16.25	15.45	13.20	10.55	20.39
1930	100.00	10.13	15.98	17.83	16.66	14.07	9.21	16.12
1946	100.00	17.67	20.86	23.04	18.02	10.10	5.33	4.98
	Persons							
1920	100.00	2.09	6.52	10.80	13.68	14.61	14.02	38.28
1930	100.00	2.41	7.60	12.71	15.83	16.71	13.13	31.61
1946	100.00	5.49	12.95	21.46	22.37	15.67	9.93	12.12

APPENDIX TABLE N.6D Household indicators 1845–1946

Census year	Household indicators			
	Mean total household size	Mean private household size	Mean family household size	Mean institutional household size
1845	5.00	..	..	..
1855	4.98	..	..	..
1865	4.89	..	..	..
1875	4.92	..	..	..
1890	4.65	4.64	5.15	27.31
1900	4.55	4.53	5.02	19.44
1910	4.24	4.20	4.89	18.50
1920	4.18	4.13	4.82	34.05
1930	4.60	4.52	4.88	22.21
1946	4.28	4.21	4.57	19.57

APPENDIX TABLE N.6E Household composition 1900 (absolute and per cent)

Household members	Rural communities (*Bygder*)			Cities (*Byer*)			Empire (*Riget*)		
	Men	Women	Total	Men	Women	Total	Men	Women	Total
				Absolute					
Household heads present at census date	25,882	2,926	28,808	9,192	2,108	11,300	35,074	5,034	40,108
Household heads not present at census date, but within Norway	1,594	34	1,628	380	16	396	1,974	50	2,024
Household heads absent outside Norway	462	..	462	393	4	397	855	4	859
Married women	..	24,854	24,854	..	8,887	8,887	..	33,741	33,741
Children	37,952	35,140	73,092	12,914	13,434	26,348	50,866	48,574	99,440
Sons- and daughters-in-law	142	394	536	15	13	28	157	407	564
Grandsons and granddaughters	1,034	956	1,990	140	160	300	1,174	1,116	2,290
Parents	892	1,238	2,130	62	270	332	954	1,508	2,462
Household servants	58	5,746	5,804	63	3,085	3,148	121	8,831	8,952
Assistants de travail	3,486	2,940	6,426	389	288	677	3,875	3,228	7,103
Visitors	1,830	1,432	3,262	286	506	792	2,116	1,938	4,054
Other household members	4,032	4,068	8,100	1,134	1,408	2,542	5,166	5,476	10,642
Locataires seuls	2,846	1,794	4,640	1,764	929	2,693	4,610	2,723	7,333
Other persons living alone	426	452	878	293	782	1,075	719	1,234	1,953
Total permanently present: belonging to family households	75,308	79,694	155,002	24,195	30,159	54,354	99,503	109,853	209,356
Total permanently present: others	3,272	2,246	5,518	2,057	1,711	3,768	5,329	3,957	9,286
Total permanently present	78,580	81,940	160,520	26,252	31,870	58,122	104,832	113,810	218,642
Total general	159,216	163,914	323,130	53,277	63,760	117,037	212,493	227,674	440,167

continued

APPENDIX TABLE N.6E Household composition 1900 (absolute and per cent) (continued)

Household members	Rural communities (*Bygder*)			Cities (*Byer*)			Empire (*Riget*)		
	Men	Women	Total	Men	Women	Total	Men	Women	Total
				Column per cent					
Household heads present at census date	16.26	1.79	8.92	17.25	3.31	9.66	16.51	2.21	9.11
Household heads not present at census date, but within Norway	1.00	0.02	0.50	0.71	0.03	0.34	0.93	0.02	0.46
Household heads absent outside Norway	0.29	..	0.14	0.74	0.01	0.34	0.40	..	0.20
Married women	..	15.16	7.69	..	13.94	7.59	..	14.82	7.67
Children	23.84	21.44	22.62	24.24	21.07	22.51	23.94	21.33	22.59
Sons- and daughters-in-law	0.09	0.24	0.17	0.03	0.02	0.02	0.07	0.18	0.13
Grandsons and granddaughters	0.65	0.58	0.62	0.26	0.25	0.26	0.55	0.49	0.52
Parents	0.56	0.76	0.66	0.12	0.42	0.28	0.45	0.66	0.56
Household servants	0.04	3.51	1.80	0.12	4.84	2.69	0.06	3.88	2.03
Assistants de travail	2.19	1.79	1.99	0.73	0.45	0.58	1.82	1.42	1.61
Visitors	1.15	0.87	1.01	0.54	0.79	0.68	1.00	0.85	0.92
Other household members	2.53	2.48	2.51	2.13	2.21	2.17	2.43	2.41	2.42
Locataires seuls	1.79	1.09	1.44	3.31	1.46	2.30	2.17	1.20	1.67
Other persons living alone	0.27	0.28	0.27	0.55	1.23	0.92	0.34	0.54	0.44
Total permanently present: belonging to family households	47.30	48.62	47.97	45.41	47.30	46.44	46.83	48.25	47.56
Total permanently present: others	2.06	1.37	1.71	3.86	2.68	3.22	2.51	1.74	2.11
Total permanently present	49.35	49.99	49.68	49.27	49.98	49.66	49.33	49.99	49.67
Total general	100.00	100.00	100.00	100.00	100.00	100.00	100.00	100.00	100.00

continued

APPENDIX TABLE N.6E Household composition 1900 (absolute and per cent) (continued)

Household members	Rural communities (*Bygder*)			Cities (*Byer*)			Empire (*Riget*)		
	Men	Women	Total	Men	Women	Total	Men	Women	Total
				Line per cent					
Household heads present at census date	73.79	58.12	71.83	26.21	41.88	28.17	100.00	100.00	100.00
Household heads not present at census date, but within Norway	80.75	68.00	80.43	19.25	32.00	19.57	100.00	100.00	100.00
Household heads absent outside Norway	54.04	..	53.78	45.96	100.00	46.22	100.00	100.00	100.00
Married women	..	73.66	73.66	..	26.34	26.34	..	100.00	100.00
Children	74.61	72.34	73.50	25.39	27.66	26.50	100.00	100.00	100.00
Sons- and daughters-in-law	90.45	96.81	95.04	9.55	3.19	4.96	100.00	100.00	100.00
Grandsons and granddaughters	88.07	85.66	86.90	11.93	14.34	13.10	100.00	100.00	100.00
Parents	93.50	82.10	86.52	6.50	17.90	13.48	100.00	100.00	100.00
Household servants	47.93	65.07	64.83	52.07	34.93	35.17	100.00	100.00	100.00
Assistants de travail	89.96	91.08	90.47	10.04	8.92	9.53	100.00	100.00	100.00
Visitors	86.48	73.89	80.46	13.52	26.11	19.54	100.00	100.00	100.00
Other household members	78.05	74.29	76.11	21.95	25.71	23.89	100.00	100.00	100.00
Locataires seuls	61.74	65.88	63.28	38.26	34.12	36.72	100.00	100.00	100.00
Other persons living alone	59.25	36.63	44.96	40.75	63.37	55.04	100.00	100.00	100.00
Total permanently present: belonging to family households	75.68	72.55	74.04	24.32	27.45	25.96	100.00	100.00	100.00
Total permanently present: others	61.40	56.76	59.42	38.60	43.24	40.58	100.00	100.00	100.00
Total permanently present	74.96	72.00	73.42	25.04	28.00	26.58	100.00	100.00	100.00
Total general	74.93	72.00	73.41	25.07	28.00	26.59	100.00	100.00	100.00

APPENDIX TABLE N.7 Dates and nature of results on population structure,
households/families, and vital statistics

Topic	Intro-duction	Remarks
Population		
Population at census dates	1855	Earlier censuses were conducted on 15 VIII 1769, 1 II 1801, 30 IV 1815, 27 XI 1825, 29 XI 1835, and 31 XII 1845. The history of the Norwegian censuses from 1769 until 1801 is similar to the Danish censuses and from 1815 to 1900 to the Swedish censuses (see chapters 4 and 19).
Population by age, sex, and marital status	1865	Already available for 1801, but not in 1825 (only age by sex); 1835: nothing found (only sex and age); 1845 and 1855: nothing available.
Households and families		
Households (husholdninger)		
Total households	1845	Households were first expressively recorded in 1845: 1845: number of households. 1855: number of households. 1865: number of households. 1875: number of one-person, family, and institutional households; persons by sex. 1890: number of one-person, family, and institutional households; persons by sex. 1900: number of one-person, family, and institutional households; persons by sex and age; household size, household composition, number of household members. 1910: number of one-person, family, and institutional households; persons by sex. 1920: housing census: number of one-person, family, and institutional households; persons by sex; households by size. 1930: housing census: number of one-person, family, and institutional households; persons by sex; households by size. 1946: housing census: households by size, institutional households. *Disaggregation*: by provinces and districts.
Households by size	1900, 1920, 1930, 1946	First time in the population census of 1900 with a representative sample survey of 10%: households by number of persons 1–21+. Full census in 1920, 1930 and 1946.
Households by composition	1900	Representative sample survey of 10%: many different household inhabitants distinguished.

continued

APPENDIX TABLE N.7 Dates and nature of results on population structure, households/families, and vital statistics (continued)

Topic	Intro-duction	Remarks
Households by profession of household head	1900, 1920, 1930	1900: representative sample survey of 10%.
Families (familier)		
Families by number of children	1900, 1920, 1930	1900: representative sample survey of 10%; family households by number of children. 1920, 1930: special investigation into the fertility of marriages.
Population movement		
Mid-year population	1850	
Births		
Live births	1850	
Stillbirths	1850	
Legitimate births	1850	
Illegitimate births	1850	
Deaths		
Total deaths	1850	
Infants (under 1 year)	1850	
Marriages		
Total marriages	1850	
Divorces and separations		
Total divorces	1901	
Legal separations	1895	

APPENDIX FIGURE N.8 Population by age, sex and marital status, Norway 1866, 1891, 1910, 1920, 1930 and 1946 (per 10,000 of total population)

Norway, 1866

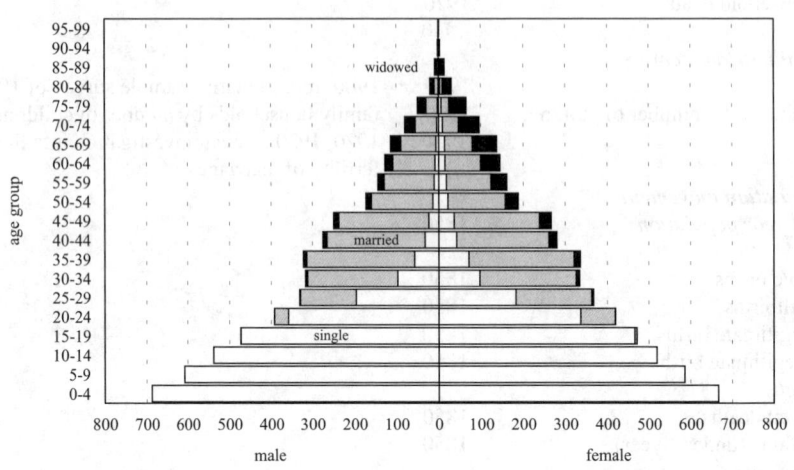

Norway, 1891

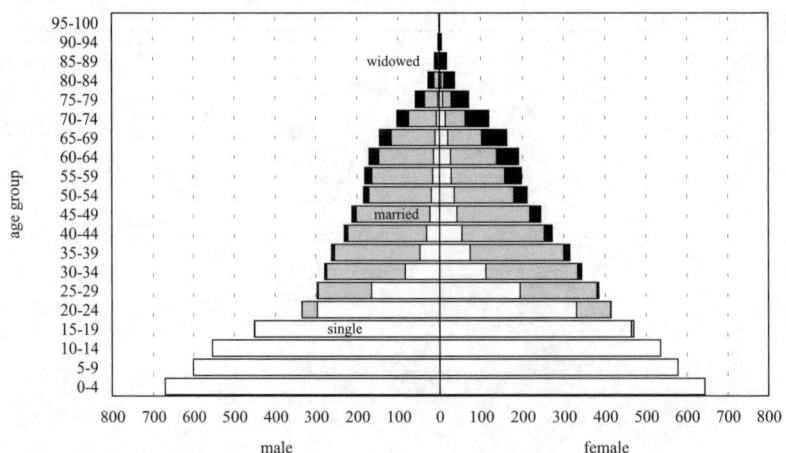

APPENDIX FIGURE N.8 Population by age, sex and marital status, Norway 1866, 1891, 1910, 1920, 1930 and 1946 (per 10,000 of total population) (continued)

Norway, 1910

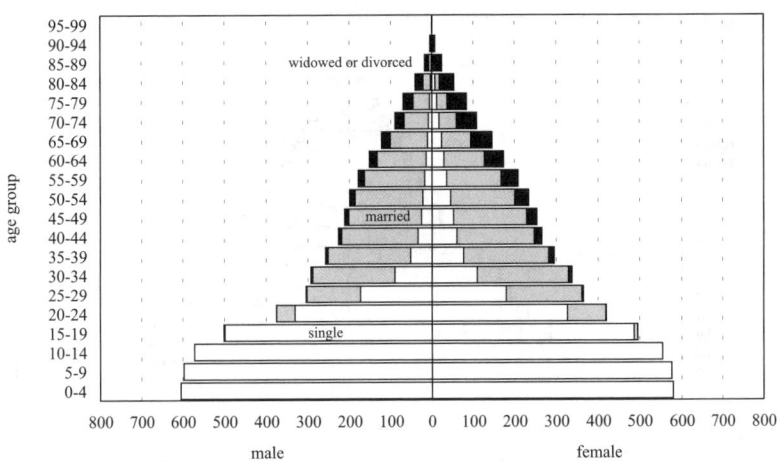

Norway, 1920

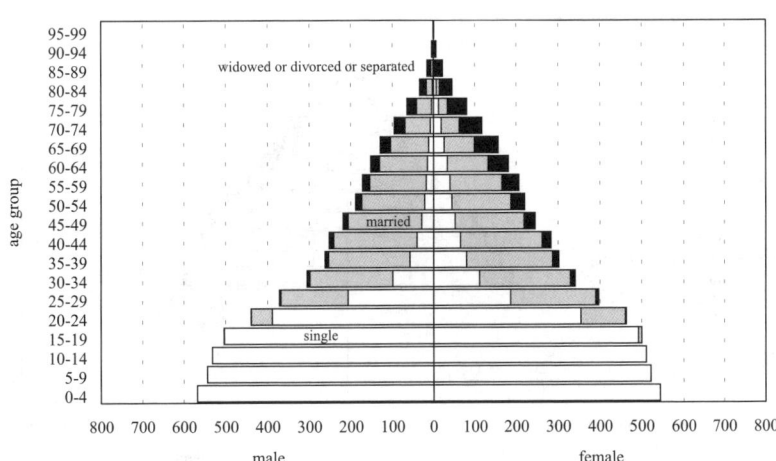

APPENDIX FIGURE N.8 Population by age, sex and marital status, Norway 1866, 1891, 1910, 1920, 1930 and 1946 (per 10,000 of total population) (continued)

Norway, 1930

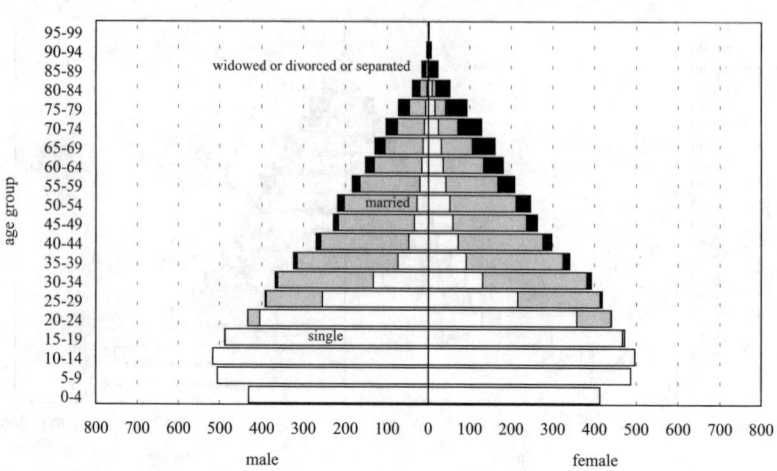

Norway, 1946

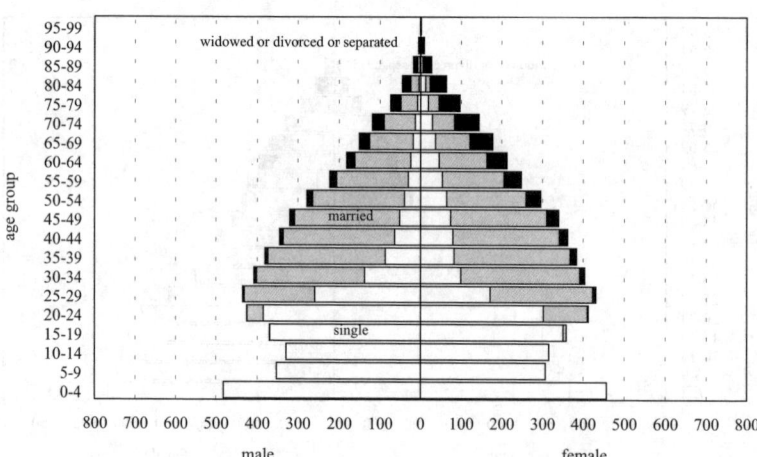

16

Poland

Poland, along with the territory of the Czechs and Slovaks, is the westernmost settlement of the Slavs. In the early Middle Ages they settled between the Germanic tribes in the west, the Baltic Sea, the Baltic tribes in the north-east, the Russians in the east, and the Hungarians in the south. Already in the high Middle Ages the country was organized as a duchy, which became the Kingdom of Poland in the late Middle Ages.

Over the centuries the Poles came under pressure from two sides: in the west German colonization began already in the thirteenth century, settling the sparsely inhabited territories east of the Elbe and Oder rivers. This colonization finally led to the formation of Prussia in north-eastern Germany. The other pressure came from the east, as the Russian empire slowly became the dominant power in Eastern Europe after the end of Mongolian domination. There were also two other powers of some importance: Sweden in the north, especially from the sixteenth to the seventeenth century, and Austria in the south, expanding its territory after the retreat of the Turks.

These pressures finally led to the dissolution of Poland in the three divisions of 1772, 1793, and 1795. Prussia and Brandenburg took over the north-western part of Poland including the cities of Danzig, Warsaw, and Posen. Russia occupied eastern Poland, while Austria occupied Galicia (with the important city of Cracow). The Congress of Vienna acknowledged the position of the great powers and did not change this constellation.

During the nineteenth century there were nationalist movements in Poland as elsewhere, but these were suppressed by its occupiers. The modern Polish state came into existence only after the defeat of Germany and Austria–Hungary in World War I. On 3 June 1918 the Allied governments recognized Polish independence. On 11 November 1918 Józef Piłsudski assumed power in Warsaw, and Poland was declared an independent republic. In June 1919 the Treaty of Versailles recognized Polish independence. Up to 1924 the territorial borders were defined in bilateral treaties with the Soviet Union and the Baltic countries. From Germany it received Posen, West Prussia, and part of Pomerania, while East Prussia and Königsberg remained German. In 1922 it received Upper Silesia from Germany as well, although the inhabitants had voted in a referendum to remain with Germany. In accordance with the 1938 Munich agreement, Teschen was transferred from Czechoslovakia. Danzig remained a free state administered by the League of Nations until 1939 when it was occupied by Germany. The new Polish state was not ethnically or linguistically homogeneous, because the territories acquired from Prussia had substantial German minorities.

World War II fundamentally changed the territory of Poland, which was reduced and shifted to the west at the expense of German territory. The Oder–Neisse line became the western border of Poland. Eastern Poland was occupied by the Soviet Union and became part of Belarus (Hoensch, 1983; Roos, 1986; Catalan, 1995; Soltys, 1995; Conze, 1993).

REGIONAL POPULATION STRUCTURE

Poland's population history is very much influenced by both world wars and the massive territorial changes afterwards. Modern Poland was founded as late as 1919. After World War II its territory fundamentally changed. That is why all population and demographic statistics in principle have to deal with two different time periods: the inter-war period and the post-World War II period.

Poland in the inter-war period was not a densely populated country. Population density in 1921 was 70 inhabitants per square kilometre, rather low when compared to Western European countries. By 1931, population density had increased to 83 inhabitants per square kilometre. The low population density nevertheless hides large regional differences in settlement structure. *Voivodships* with a high population density similar to Belgium or The Netherlands existed side by side with voivodships with less than 50 inhabitants per square kilometre. The most densely populated regions were Warsaw and its surroundings and the industrialized centres around Cracow, Lodz, Lvov, and the voivodship of Slaskie. Unequal economic development naturally affected the regional population structure via different population growth rates.

POPULATION GROWTH

After Poland's independence in 1919 the first population census of 1921 counted 27,201,000 inhabitants. By 1931 the population had increased by another five million to 32,107,000 inhabitants. This rather strong population increase was due to the high natural population growth resulting from a high birth rate and a rather low death rate. The natural population growth rate was high immediately after the end of World War I with figures exceeding 10 per 1,000 during the years 1921–23 (Figure PL.1). Although the natural population increase was rather high in the late 1920s, a declining trend set in and continued through the 1930s until the outbreak of World War II in September 1939. Overall population growth benefited from the rather low emigration, which nevertheless exceeded immigration. Emigration was very strong immediately after the war in 1921 and again during World War II. In 1938 a strong immigration wave set in, when the net migration rate reached 8.1 per 1,000 and the overall population growth rate was 11.9 per 1,000. This increase was probably due to emigration from Germany.

THE FIRST DEMOGRAPHIC TRANSITION

Poland's demographic transition can only be studied at a time point when the transition process was fully underway. National data are only available since the founding of modern Poland in 1919. It is necessary to keep in mind that the inter-war period and the post-World War II period have a totally different territorial basis; trends therefore cannot be seen as a direct continuation of older trends.

Figure PL.1 Population growth and net migration 1919-1945

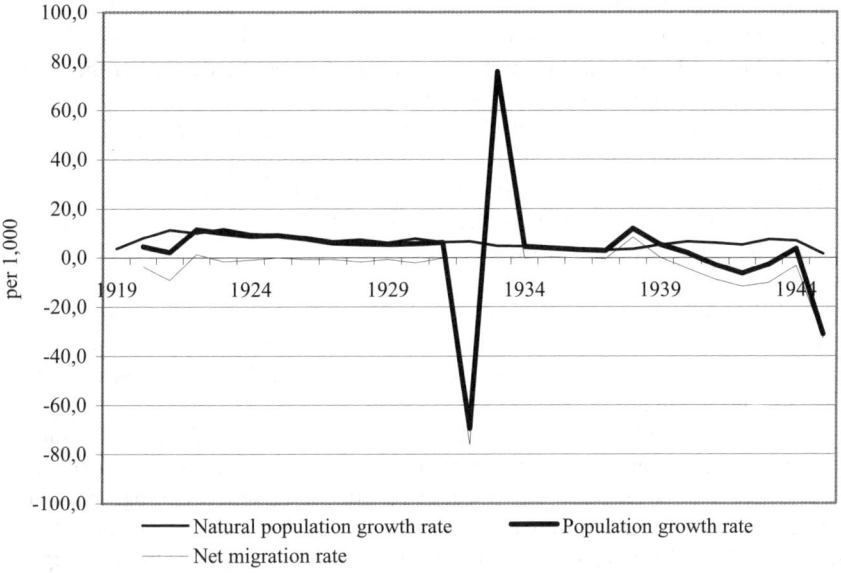

Natural population growth rate —— Population growth rate

Net migration rate

Figure PL.2 First demographic transition 1919-1938

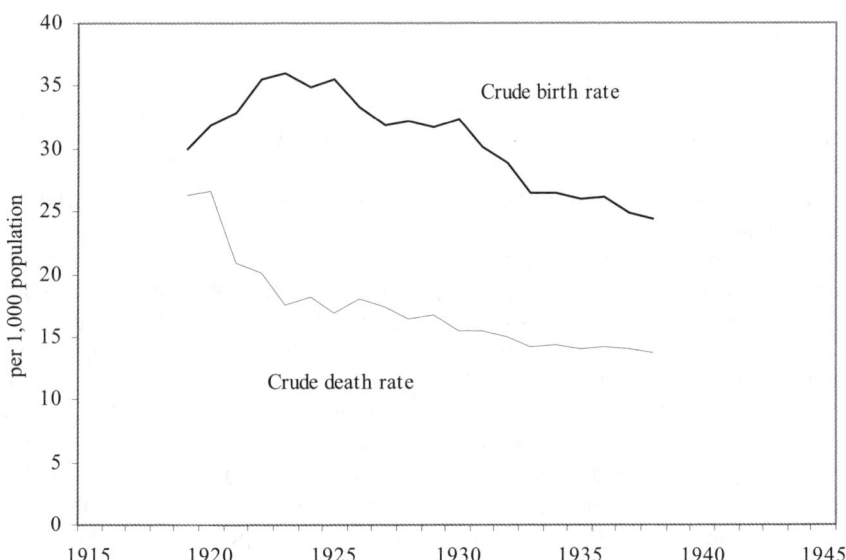

Crude birth rate

Crude death rate

After the end of World War I, Poland's birth and death rates were still strongly influenced by the effects of the war: the birth rate was still low immediately after the war and increased steeply because of recovered marriages and births. The death rate was very high and declined in the early 1920s to a 'normal' level (Figure PL.2).

From the available data it cannot be determined when the decline of the birth rate actually started, but it was likely before 1900.

In the inter-war period both the birth and the death rates declined without significant interruptions or incidences. Natural population growth was high.

After 1945—on a different state territory—postponed births and marriages were recovered, and the birth rate increased until the 1950s. But then a tremendous birth decline began, reaching its lowest level in the late 1960s. Some sort of second demographic transition occurred in the 1970s and 1980s when the birth rate rose again. After the mid-1980s the birth rate declined to a low level never seen before in Poland. The death rate increased immediately after the war (causes: famine, infant mortality), but started to decline in the 1950s. Since the 1970s the mortality rate has been on the rise again.

A comparison with the European development reveals that Poland's fertility level was above the European average for almost the entire time since 1919, except in the mid-1960s. This seems to be a constant feature of Poland's demographic history. Interestingly, the crude death rate was also rather low, and since the late 1930s approached the European level. The result of both was a high natural population growth during the whole of modern Poland's existence. Since the 1970s, the birth rate has been well above the European average while the death rate has been at the European average, indicating a high natural population increase.

MORTALITY AND LIFE EXPECTANCY

The infant mortality rate is defined as deaths of children aged under one year per 1,000 live births. Along with Bulgaria and Hungary, Poland belongs to the group of countries with the highest infant mortality. National numbers are only available since the 1920s due to the late founding of modern Poland in 1919 (Figure PL.3).

After World War I, and in the inter-war period, the level of infant mortality was rather high, amounting in the late 1920s to approximately 150. Hungary's figure in the same year was 185 and Portugal's 142. This compares with the infant mortality rate of Norway which was approximately 50 in this year. Poland's infant mortality therefore was about three times higher than that of the pioneering countries.

During the inter-war period there was only a minor reduction in infant deaths. After World War II Hungary and Portugal overtook Poland in reducing infant mortality. Poland dropped back considerably in the following decades in terms of infant mortality reduction (Masuy-Stroobant, 1997).

Life expectancy in Poland was rather low compared with the industrialized countries of Western Europe during the inter-war period. Figures are only available for 1927 and 1931/32 (Figure PL.4). In 1931/32, life expectancy of boys at birth in Poland was 48.2 years compared with 63.2 in Sweden in 1931/35, a difference in life expectancy of 15 years. For new-born girls life expectancy in Poland in 1931/32 was 51.4 years and in Sweden in 1931/35 65.3 years, a difference of 14 years. Differences in life expectancy between Poland and more advanced countries of the time were still valid for young adults (age 30) and elderly people (age 60), but these differences declined with age: the older the people, the smaller the national

Figure PL.3 Infant mortality 1927-1938

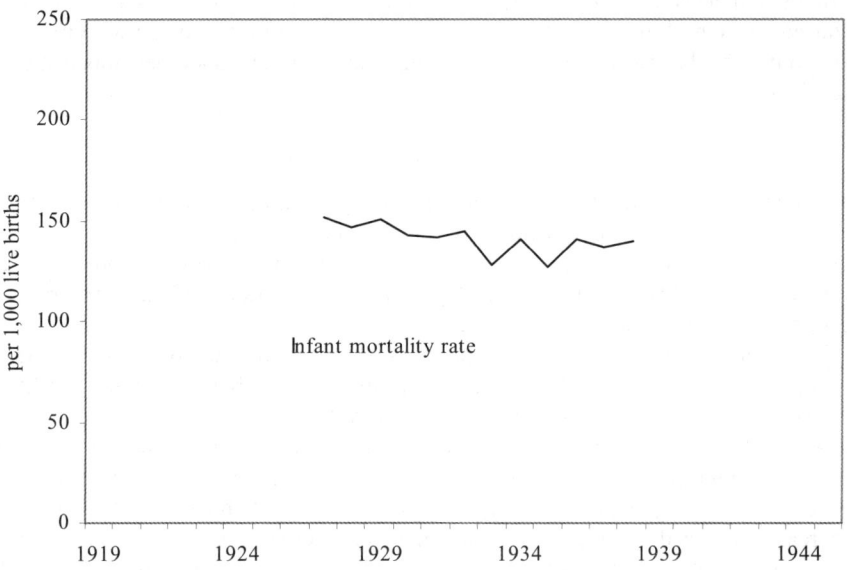

Figure PL.4 Life expectancy 1927-1931/32

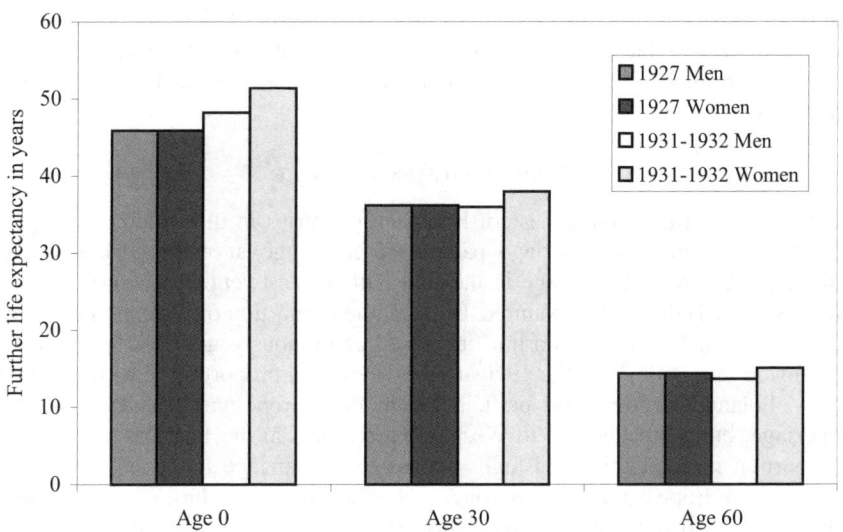

differences in life expectancy. In 1931/32 life expectancy of Polish females exceeded life expectancy of Polish males at all ages; differences were greatest for infants and least for 60-year-olds. The rather low life expectancy in Poland was caused by a multitude of factors, including the dominance of agriculture in the economy, the backward infrastructure, and the relatively underdeveloped medical services.

The Eastern European marriage pattern normally would not favour high illegitimate fertility or a large proportion of out-of-wedlock births, due to structural circumstances alone. In the case of Poland we would therefore predict a low illegitimate fertility rate and a high legitimate fertility rate, and furthermore a low proportion of out-of-wedlock births (Figure PL.5).

During the inter-war period our hypothesis is only partly true: both illegitimate and legitimate fertility were above the European average, but legitimate fertility of course was very much higher than illegitimate fertility.

After 1945 the situation was more or less anomalous. We have seen in the section on the demographic transition that there was a huge increase in the birth rate after 1945. If we disaggregate for il/legitimacy, we see that there was the same huge increase for the illegitimacy rate and the same decline afterwards. The legitimacy rate, on the other hand, increased only moderately during this time period. The unique relative increase of illegitimate fertility in the 1950s and early 1960s is also apparent in the ratio of the illegitimacy rate to the legitimacy rate.

Since the 1960s illegitimate fertility has been low and considerably below the European average. Childbirth has mainly occurred within marriage. Poland therefore did not participate in the Western European pattern of deinstitutionalization of marriage with a large increase in out-of-wedlock childbirth. Marriage remained highly institutionalized with early and universal marriage and childbirth within marriage.

MARRIAGE AND DIVORCE

Poland is one of the three Eastern European countries in this volume belonging to the Eastern European marriage pattern of early age at marriage and universal marriage. But age at marriage in the first half of the twentieth century was not as low as in the Balkans, for example. In 1921, the proportion of women married at age 20–24 was 35%. This proportion increased continuously until 1960, when nearly 60% were married. From the 1970s to the 1990s this proportion remained well over 50%. Poland therefore also participated in the Europe-wide trend towards early marriage, but the difference to Western Europe lies in the fact that since 1945 the proportion married remained high as the age at marriage remained low, while in Western Europe age at marriage started to rise during the increasing deinstitutionalization of marriage. This position is also confirmed by data on the mean age of women at first marriage which since the 1970s has been well below the European average and varied between 22 and 23 years.

Men's age at first marriage was considerably higher, and the proportion of men married at age 20–24 was lower. Still in 1921 only 13% of men were married at age 20–24. There was not such a strong tendency towards early marriage for Polish men

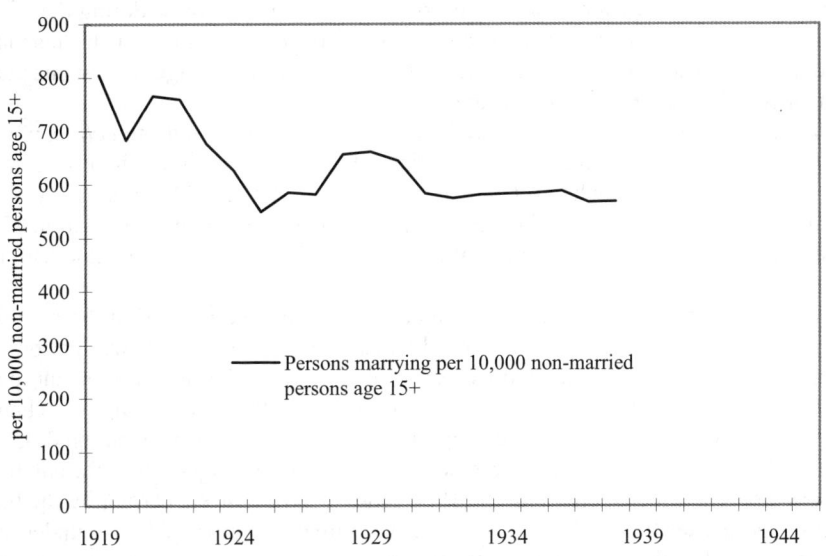

Figure PL.6 Marriages 1919-1938

as for Polish women. In 1960, nearly 30% of men were married at age 20–24, and in the 1970s and 1980s this proportion even declined, in contrast to Hungary and Czechoslovakia where men's age at marriage continued to increase during the 1970s and 1980s. Therefore, Polish men did not participate so strongly in the marriage boom of the post-World War II period. Nevertheless, men's age at first marriage remained below the European average.

Marriage intensity can be measured by the *marriage rate* and the *celibacy rate*. 'Intensity' means the availability of marriage, but at the same time the urgent need to remarry after widowhood ('remarriage need', Michael Mitterauer). A third component can be seen in the universality of marriage in the population. The marriage rate refers to all marriages of unmarried persons 15 years and older (Figure PL.6).

We have seen that with respect to age at marriage Poland developed the manifest pattern of early marriage only after World War II, while in the inter-war period age at marriage was much higher and was somewhat more similar to Western European patterns. But concerning the *universality of marriage* there was nearly no change during the twentieth century. The proportion of never-married women aged 45–54 was below 10% from 1921. There were only minor changes for different birth cohorts; only a minor increase in the 1960s and 1970s occurred, carried by the birth cohorts born after World War I. This pattern of universal marriage is also underlined by the second indicator of nuptiality, the marriage rate, which in this century was very much higher than the European average. Already in the inter-war period the marriage rate was high, and it was still higher in the decades after 1945. There was only one exception to this pattern, a massive decline in the marriage rate during the 1960s. This was the cause for the large decline in the birth rate, as we have seen when discussing the demographic transition.

In summarizing, we can say that Poland's marriage patterns clearly differ from those of Western European countries. This contrast is most evident with regard to the importance of marriage, indicated by universal marriage and a high nuptiality. In Poland, age at marriage does not seem to be strongly connected to this pattern: there was a trend from higher age at marriage in the 1920s to a very low age after 1945.

Although the country is predominantly Catholic, *divorces* in the period since 1945 have been frequent (Figure PL.6), probably an effect of socialist family legislation. This distinguishes Poland from the Catholic countries of Southern Europe such as Italy and Spain where divorces were rather infrequent or at least below the European average. Divorce rates for the inter-war period do not exist, therefore we can only discuss the period after World War II. When the European divorce rate was high in the immediate post-war years due to the war's influence on marriages, in Poland it was low. In the early 1960s the divorce rate accelerated and exceeded the European average. But from the 1970s divorce rate levelled off and fluctuated around a rather stable level. In the late 1970s and late 1980s there were major drops in the divorce rate, influenced by the economic crises of the country since the 1970s.

AGE, SEX, AND CIVIL STATUS

Appendix Figure PL.8 shows the development in the age structure of the Polish population combined with sex and marital status from 1921 to 1931, the only two censuses conducted during the inter-war period. In the age pyramid of 1921, as in Czechoslovakia, the huge loss of births during World War I and the immediate post-war years is apparent. The age cohorts of 0–4 and 5–9 years are much smaller than the age cohort 10–14, the last cohort not affected by World War I. Until 1931 Poland—in contrast to other countries—did not experience a massive birth decline: instead, the birth rate recovered, as can be seen from the rather large birth cohorts of the age groups 0–4 and 5–9 in 1931. Age at marriage was lower in 1931, and the proportion of people married—mainly at a young age—was higher in 1931 than in 1921.

FAMILY AND HOUSEHOLD STRUCTURES

Household statistics were organized in the first two Polish population censuses of 1921 and 1931. Information gathered covers the fields of main household types, households by size categories, and household composition. Mean household sizes and per cent distributions of household types, households by size, and household composition can be derived from this material.

In a European comparison, households were still very large in the inter-war period. In 1921 mean family household size was still 4.99 persons per family household and by 1931 had fallen only to 4.76 persons per family household, although averages only give an overall indication and hide distributional patterns. From the distribution of private households by size it becomes quite clear why mean household size was high. The proportion of one-person households was low: 6% in 1921 and 9% in 1931. In 1921, only 1.3% of the population lived alone; in 1931 this proportion had increased to 2.0%. The proportion of large households (five or more persons) was very high and over 50% in 1921.

Thus, the family household was the main household type, and living alone was probably only common in towns. Both the proportion of institutional households and the population living in institutional households were low. In 1921 and 1931 less than one% of the Polish population lived in institutional households.

Although official statistics do not classify households by type into nuclear or extended family households, the classification of the 1931 census may come close to such a typology: it distinguished between households comprising one person and monofamilial households (i.e. nuclear households) and polyfamilial households (i.e. extended households). The latter household type was 9.4% of all households, while the former comprised 90.6% of all households. Thus, it could reasonably be argued that approximately 10% of all households in Poland in 1931 were extended. The proportion of polyfamilial households varied by household composition. It was highest, with 14.8%, in households comprising only farm workers and apprentices or assistants in the family business; next came households with domestic servants plus farm workers and apprentices or assistants. The lowest proportion, with 4.8%, was found in households with domestic servants only. Households without any servants amounted to 9.3% and were average. Thus, there seems to be a relationship between the presence of farm workers and apprentices and the proportion of polyfamilial households. Households with only domestic servants obviously had the lowest proportion of polyfamilial households. The urban–rural dimension probably influences this distribution, rendering rural households more inclined to form polyfamilial households while the urban population tends to form nuclear households.

THE NATIONAL SYSTEM OF DEMOGRAPHIC STATISTICS

Population Structure

Poland's population statistics are largely influenced by its political history. During the nineteenth century Poland was divided between Russia, Prussia, and Austria–Hungary. Thus, population statistics before the First World War are included in these countries' statistical publications. Nevertheless, there are huge differences in amount, frequency, and detail of population statistics. Prussian statistics are very detailed, regular, and comprehensive, but for Russia there was only one well-documented population census in 1897.

Population statistics dealt with here refer to independent Poland after World War I. There were only two population censuses during the inter-war period in 1921 and 1931. During this period the territory remained rather stable. There was also a population census shortly after World War II in 1946 but with only a limited programme of questions. This census was confined to population status, but did not assess the age structure by sex and marital status and did not contain data on households.

Population by age, sex, and marital status was published for both censuses of 1921 and 1931. In 1921 age was classified in one-year age groups; in 1931 ages are given in five-year age groups beginning with 1940.

Vital Statistics

The main series of vital events such as live births, deaths, and marriages were introduced shortly after World War I. More detailed demographic statistics became available only in the 1920s. Thus, births by legitimacy and infant deaths are available since 1927. Other population statistics such as age at marriage and childbirth became available only after World War II.

Vital statistics are not comparable before and after independence and before and after World War II. Recalculations have been made by the National Statistical Institute (GUS) for the nineteenth century, but territorial changes cannot be taken into account perfectly (cf. Główny Urząd Statystycny, 1993). Thus there are inconsistencies concerning the territory before and after the war. The same situation applies after World War II, and problems of comparability of vital statistics and population census data are aggravated by the massive change in territory.

Households and Families

Data on *households* (*gospodarstwa*) were collected in the first Polish population census after independence, in 1921. This census provided basic information on households. The three elementary household types were distinguished: one-person, family, and institutional households. The respective number of persons living in these households is available as well. Furthermore, households were distinguished by number of persons. The persons living in these households was published also. These household variables were published in the 1931 census as well.

In 1921 the *composition of private households* in several categories was published. Household members were divided by sex into the following categories: single persons, persons in family households, household heads, women, sons, daughters, close relatives, distant relatives, servants (*serviteurs*), 'domestiques', boarders ('sous-locataires'), others, and finally members in institutional households.

In 1931 another way of presenting household composition was chosen: two basic *household types* were distinguished: first, households comprising a single person and monofamilial households; second, polyfamilial households. These two basic household types were further divided into four different types according the presence of domestic servants, apprentices, or farm workers.

In neither the 1921 nor the 1931 population census were households classified according to *profession* or *social status* of the household head.

The *definition of a household* (*gospodarstwo*) for the 1921 census was given in Głowny Urząd Statystyczny Rzeczypospolitei polskiej (1930: Vf.) and is in principle the same as in the German household statistics. The basic definition was the housekeeping-unit concept, meaning that a household was made up of persons who lived from the same household budget, irrespective of how many persons lived in a dwelling or even one room. Therefore boarders living in a family household but having their own budget and paying for their own meals were counted as single-person households.

In the 1931 census household statistics were collected within the framework of a housing census. The definitions deviate to some degree, especially concerning boarders, which were classified as belonging to the household only if they were related to the household head. In any other case they were counted as single-person households (Głowny Urząd Statystyczny Rzeczypospolitei polskiej, 1938: Xif.).

Family statistics in the sense of fertility statistics or as statistics of the biological nuclear family were not collected in 1921 or 1931. Such data were collected only after World War II.

Remarks (also see introductory Table 6.1)

For Poland, data on illegitimate births and divorces are missing from 1919 to 1939. The population census of 1947 was not available for interpolation of v16–v21. In the inter-war period censuses were held in 1921 and 1931. These two censuses were used for linear interpolation back to 1919 and ahead to 1945.

BOUNDARY CHANGES

During the nineteenth century Poland was divided between Germany, Austria–Hungary, and Russia. The modern Polish state came into being only after World War I with the defeat of Germany and Austria–Hungary. From Germany it received Posen, West Prussia, and part of Pomerania, while East Prussia and Königsberg remained German. In 1922 it received Upper Silesia from Germany as well. In accordance with the 1938 Munich agreement, Teschen was transferred from Czechoslovakia. Danzig remained a free state administered by the League of Nations until 1939 when it was occupied by Germany. World War II fundamentally changed the territory of Poland. The territory was reduced and shifted to the west at the expense of German territory. The Oder–Neisse line became the western border of Poland. Eastern Poland was occupied by the Soviet Union and became part of Belarus. For regional organization see the documentation by Quick (1994) and Caramani, Flora, Kraus, and Quick (1998).

APPENDIX TABLES AND FIGURES

APPENDIX TABLE PL.1 Population structure at census dates 1921–1931

Census number	Census date	Census population			Marital status				Age group		
		Total	Male	Female	Single	Married	Widowed	Divorced	0–14	15–64	65+
		Absolute									
1	30 IX 1921	25,694,700	12,417,233	13,277,467	15,329,038	8,734,596	1,585,324	25,237[1]	9,082,008	15,477,638	1,077,186
2	9 XII 1931	31,915,779	15,427,502	16,488,277	17,970,518	11,941,687	1,903,319	63,705[1]	10,726,094	19,590,005	1,572,036
		Per cent									
1	30 IX 1921	100.00	48.33	51.67	59.66	33.99	6.17	0.10[1]	35.35	60.24	4.19
2	9 XII 1931	100.00	48.34	51.66	56.31	37.42	5.96	0.20[1]	33.61	61.38	4.93

Note: [1] Divorced and separated.

APPENDIX TABLE PL.2 Census population by region
1921–1931 (per cent)

Województwa	1921	1931
M.st.Warszawskie	3.42	3.65
Warszawskie	7.76	7.88
Bialostockie	4.79	5.12
Bydgoskie	..	..
Katowickie	..	..
Kieleckie	9.32	9.14
Koszalinskie	..	..
Krakowskie	7.32[1]	7.16
Lubelskie	7.67	7.68
Lódzkie	8.28[1]	8.20
Opolskie	..	..
Pomorskie	3.45	3.36
Poznanskie	7.26[1]	6.56
Slaskie	4.14	4.03
Zielonogorskie	..	..
Lwowskie	10.00[1]	9.74
Nowogrodskie	3.02	3.29
Poleskie	3.24	3.53
Stanislawowskie	4.96	4.61
Tarnopolskie	5.25	4.98
Wilenskie and Wilna	3.61[1]	3.97
Wolynskie	5.28	6.50
Gdanskie	..	..
Olsztynskie	..	..
Rzeszowskie	..	..
Szczecinskie	..	..
Wroclawskie	..	..
TOTAL	**100.00**	**100.00**

Note: [1] Województwa and Miasta (Voivodship and City).

APPENDIX TABLE PL.3 Population density by region
1921–1931 (inhabitants per sq. km.)

Województwa	1921	1931
M.st.Warszawskie	7,694	9,686
Warszawskie	72	86
Bialostockie	40	51
Bydgoskie	..	..
Katowickie	..	..
Kieleckie	98	114
Koszalinskie	..	..
Krakowskie	114[1]	132
Lubelskie	67	79
Lódzkie	118[1]	138
Opolskie	..	..
Pomorskie	57	66
Poznanskie	74[1]	79
Slaskie	266	306
Zielonogorskie	..	..
Lwowskie	101[1]	116
Nowogrodskie	36	46
Poleskie	21	27
Stanislawowskie	73	81
Tarnopolskie	87	98
Wilenskie and Wilna	34[1]	44
Wolynskie	47	69
Gdanskie	..	..
Olsztynskie	..	..
Rzeszowskie	..	..
Szczecinskie	..	..
Wroclawskie	..	..
TOTAL	**70**	**83**

Note: [1] Województwa and Miasta (Voivodship and City).

APPENDIX TABLE PL.4 Demographic developments 1900–1945 (absolute figures and rates)

Year	Mid-year population	Natural population growth rate	Population growth rate	Net migration rate	Crude birth rate	Legitimate births per 10,000 married women age 15-44	Illegitimate births per 10,000 unmarried women age 15-44	Illeg. births per 100 leg. births
1900	25,106,000	..	..	..	..	..	..	..
1901	25,204,619	..	3.9	..	..	..	..	..
1902	25,303,238	..	3.9	..	..	..	..	..
1903	25,401,857	..	3.9	..	..	..	..	..
1904	25,500,476	..	3.9	..	..	..	..	..
1905	25,599,095	..	3.9	..	..	..	..	..
1906	25,697,714	..	3.8	..	..	..	..	..
1907	25,796,333	..	3.8	..	..	..	..	..
1908	25,894,952	..	3.8	..	..	..	..	..
1909	25,993,571	..	3.8	..	..	..	..	..
1910	26,092,190	..	3.8	..	..	..	..	..
1911	26,190,810	..	3.8	..	..	..	..	..
1912	26,289,429	..	3.8	..	..	..	..	..
1913	26,388,048	..	3.7	..	..	..	..	..
1914	26,486,667	..	3.7	..	..	..	..	..
1915	26,585,286	..	3.7	..	..	..	..	..
1916	26,683,905	..	3.7	..	..	..	..	..
1917	26,782,524	..	3.7	..	..	..	..	..
1918	26,881,143	..	3.7	..	..	..	..	..
1919	26,979,762	3.6	3.7	0.1	29.9	..	..	..
1920	27,078,381	5.2	3.6	-1.5	31.8	..	..	..
1921	27,177,000	11.9	3.6	-8.2	32.8	..	..	..
1922	27,670,000	15.5	17.8	2.3	35.5	..	..	..
1923	28,163,000	18.5	17.5	-1.0	36.0	..	..	..
1924	28,656,000	16.8	17.2	0.4	34.9	..	..	..
1925	29,149,000	18.7	16.9	-1.8	35.6	..	..	..
1926	29,642,000	15.4	16.6	1.2	33.4	..	..	..
1927	30,135,000	14.4	16.4	2.0	31.8	2,358	158	6.2
1928	30,628,000	15.6	16.1	0.5	32.1	..	..	..
1929	31,121,000	15.0	15.8	0.8	31.7	..	..	..
1930	31,614,000	16.9	15.6	-1.3	32.4	..	..	..
1931	32,107,000	14.7	15.4	0.7	30.1	..	..	..
1932	32,498,714	13.8	12.1	-1.7	28.8	..	..	..
1933	32,890,429	12.2	11.9	-0.3	26.4	..	..	..
1934	33,282,143	12.1	11.8	-0.3	26.5	..	..	..
1935	33,673,857	12.1	11.6	-0.4	26.0	..	..	..
1936	34,065,571	12.0	11.5	-0.5	26.2	..	..	..
1937	34,457,286	10.9	11.4	0.5	24.8	..	..	..
1938	34,849,000	10.6	11.2	0.6	24.4	..	..	..
1939	..	..	..	..	..	..	..	..
1940	..	..	..	..	..	..	..	..
1941	..	..	..	..	..	..	..	..
1942	..	..	..	..	..	..	..	..
1943	..	..	..	..	..	..	..	..
1944	..	..	..	..	..	..	..	..
1945	..	..	..	..	..	..	..	..

APPENDIX TABLE PL.4 Demographic developments 1900–1945 (absolute figures and rates)

Crude death rate	Infant mortality rate	Stillbirth rate	Infant mortality and stillbirth rate	Crude marriage rate	Persons marrying per 10,000 unmarried persons age 15+	Persons marrying per 10,000 unmarried persons age 15–49	Crude divorce rate	Divorces per 100 marriages	Divorces per 10,000 married persons	Year
..	..	..	..	..	..	..	..	..	..	1900
..	..	..	..	..	..	..	..	..	..	1901
..	..	..	..	..	..	..	..	..	..	1902
..	..	..	..	..	..	..	..	..	..	1903
..	..	..	..	..	..	..	..	..	..	1904
..	..	..	..	..	..	..	..	..	..	1905
..	..	..	..	..	..	..	..	..	..	1906
..	..	..	..	..	..	..	..	..	..	1907
..	..	..	..	..	..	..	..	..	..	1908
..	..	..	..	..	..	..	..	..	..	1909
..	..	..	..	..	..	..	..	..	..	1910
..	..	..	..	..	..	..	..	..	..	1911
..	..	..	..	..	..	..	..	..	..	1912
..	..	..	..	..	..	..	..	..	..	1913
..	..	..	..	..	..	..	..	..	..	1914
..	..	..	..	..	..	..	..	..	..	1915
..	..	..	..	..	..	..	..	..	..	1916
..	..	..	..	..	..	..	..	..	..	1917
..	..	..	..	..	..	..	..	..	..	1918
26.4	..	..	..	12.4	805	955	..	..	..	1919
26.6	..	..	..	10.5	683	813	..	..	..	1920
20.9	..	..	..	11.7	766	915	..	..	..	1921
20.0	..	..	..	11.5	760	910	..	..	..	1922
17.5	..	..	..	10.2	676	812	..	..	..	1923
18.1	..	..	..	9.4	627	755	..	..	..	1924
16.9	..	..	..	8.2	550	664	..	..	..	1925
18.0	..	..	..	8.7	585	709	..	..	..	1926
17.4	151.3	..	..	8.6	581	707	..	..	..	1927
16.5	146.4	..	..	9.6	656	799	..	..	..	1928
16.7	150.8	..	..	9.7	661	807	..	..	..	1929
15.5	142.7	..	..	9.4	644	789	..	..	..	1930
15.4	142.0	..	..	8.4	584	716	..	..	..	1931
15.0	144.4	..	..	8.3	575	707	..	..	..	1932
14.2	127.9	..	..	8.3	581	716	..	..	..	1933
14.4	140.6	..	..	8.3	583	720	..	..	..	1934
14.0	126.6	..	..	8.3	584	723	..	..	..	1935
14.1	141.3	..	..	8.3	588	729	..	..	..	1936
14.0	136.7	..	..	8.0	567	705	..	..	..	1937
13.8	140.0	..	..	8.0	569	708	..	..	..	1938
..	..	..	..	..	..	..	..	..	..	1939
..	..	..	..	..	..	..	..	..	..	1940
..	..	..	..	..	..	..	..	..	..	1941
..	..	..	..	..	..	..	..	..	..	1942
..	..	..	..	..	..	..	..	..	..	1943
..	..	..	..	..	..	..	..	..	..	1944
..	..	..	..	..	..	..	..	..	..	1945

APPENDIX TABLE PL.5 Life expectancy by age 1927–1931/32 (in years)

Age	0	1	15	30	45	60
Males						
1927[1]	45.9	54.6	47.7	36.2	24.9	14.4
1931–1932	48.2	56.9	47.8	36.0	24.0	13.7
Females						
1927[1]	45.9	54.6	47.7	36.2	24.9	14.4
1931–1932	51.4	58.7	49.8	38.0	26.4	15.1

Note: [1] Average data for both sexes.

APPENDIX TABLE PL.6A Households by type 1921–1931 (absolute and per cent)

Census year	Household types and members				
	Total house-holds	Private house-holds	Family house-holds	One-person households	Institutional households
Absolute					
1921	5,298,204	5,290,090	4,969,658	320,432	8,114
1931	7,167,192	7,155,284	6,510,763	644,521	11,908
Per cent					
1921	100.00	99.85	93.80	6.05	0.15
1931	100.00	99.83	90.84	8.99	0.17

continued

APPENDIX TABLE PL.6A Households by type 1921–1931 (absolute and per cent) (continued)

Census year	Household types and members				
	Total household members	Private household members	Family household members	One-person household members	Institutional household members
Absolute					
1921	25,376,175	25,134,677	24,814,245	320,432	241,498
1931	31,915,779	31,620,452	30,975,931	644,521	295,327
Per cent					
1921	100.00	99.05	97.79	1.26	0.95
1931	100.00	99.07	97.06	2.02	0.93

APPENDIX TABLE PL.6B Households by size and members 1921–1931 (absolute figures)

Census year	Private households total	Households by number of members											
		1 person	2 persons	3 persons	4 persons	5 persons	6 persons	7 persons	8 persons	9 persons	10 persons	11 persons	12+ persons
						Households							
1921	5,290,090	320,432	586,512	784,994	886,373	860,271	1,216,785[1]			569,930[2]		64,793[3]	
1931	7,155,284	644,521	854,641	1,123,621	1,258,447	1,153,246	889,096	587,390	337,284	172,251	82,861	29,863	22,063
						Persons							
1921	25,134,677	320,432	1,173,024	2,354,982	3,545,492	4,301,355	7,798,617[1]			4,884,616[2]		756,159[3]	
1931	31,620,452	644,521	1,709,282	3,370,863	5,033,788	5,766,230	5,334,576	4,111,730	2,698,272	1,550,259	828,610	328,493	243,828

Notes: [1] 6–7 persons. [2] 8–10 persons. [3] 11+ persons.

APPENDIX TABLE PL.6C Households by size and members 1921–1931 (per cent)

Census year	Private households total	Households by number of members											
		1 person	2 persons	3 persons	4 persons	5 persons	6 persons	7 persons	8 persons	9 persons	10 persons	11 persons	12+ persons
						Households							
1921	100.00	6.06	11.09	14.84	16.76	16.26	23.00[1]			10.77[2]		1.22[3]	
1931	100.00	9.01	11.94	15.70	17.59	16.12	12.43	8.21	4.71	2.41	1.16	0.42	0.31
						Persons							
1921	100.00	1.27	4.67	9.37	14.11	17.11	31.03[1]			19.43[2]		3.01[3]	
1931	100.00	2.04	5.41	10.66	15.92	18.24	16.87	13.00	8.53	4.90	2.62	1.04	0.77

Notes: [1] 6–7 persons. [2] 8–10 persons. [3] 11+ persons.

APPENDIX TABLE PL.6D Household indicators 1921–1931

Census year	Household indicators			
	Mean total household size	Mean private household size	Mean family household size	Mean institutional household size
1921	4.79	4.75	4.99	29.76
1931	4.45	4.42	4.76	24.80

APPENDIX TABLE PL.6E Household composition 1921 (absolute and per cent)

Household member	Single	Married	Widowed	Divorced / separated	Unknown	Total
		Absolute				
Present population at census date, total	15,029,555	8,716,248	1,584,820	25,213	20,339	25,376,175
Present population at census date, males	7,452,872	4,282,572	347,386	8,142	8,764	12,099,736
Present population at census date, females	7,576,683	4,433,676	1,237,434	17,071	11,575	13,276,439
Living single, total	155,883	47,835	110,669	4,142	1,903	320,432
Living single, male	91,565	30,444	25,141	2,002	1,060	150,212
Living single, female	64,318	17,391	85,528	2,140	843	170,220
Population in family households, total	14,695,441	8,625,905	1,459,116	20,746	13,037	24,814,245
Population in family households, male	7,267,702	4,223,570	318,417	6,025	4,558	11,820,272
Population in family households, female	7,427,739	4,402,335	1,140,699	14,721	8,479	12,993,973
thereof: household heads, male	154,181	3,795,613	208,891	2,936	758	4,162,379
thereof: household heads, female	69,677	153,577	576,716	6,075	1,234	807,279
thereof: wives	..	3,750,451	..	..	..	3,750,451
thereof: sons	5,901,904	182,596	6,423	1,167	776	6,092,866
thereof: daughters	5,931,049	171,259	32,611	3,920	976	6,139,815
thereof: close relatives, male	626,044	201,327	86,955	820	1,003	916,149
thereof: close relatives, female	699,792	270,017	461,482	2,234	2,828	1,436,353
thereof: distant relatives, male	156,448	14,001	4,906	277	386	176,018
thereof: distant relatives, female	205,227	29,065	26,337	756	752	262,137
thereof: *serviteurs*, male	6,282	962	387	18	32	7,681
thereof: *serviteurs*, female	183,712	7,365	16,861	788	891	209,617
thereof: *domestiques*, male	314,251	11,977	5,867	380	780	333,255
thereof: *domestiques*, female	247,889	5,999	12,148	424	792	267,252
thereof: sub-tenants, male	53,176	10,738	3,189	353	356	67,812
thereof: sub-tenants, female	31,229	6,140	8,140	329	245	46,083
thereof: other persons, male	55,416	6,356	1,799	74	467	64,112
thereof: other persons, female	59,164	8,462	6,404	195	761	74,986
Population in institutional households, total	178,231	42,508	15,035	325	5,399	241,498
Population in institutional households, male	93,605	28,558	3,828	115	3,146	129,252
Population in institutional households, female	84,626	13,950	11,207	210	2,253	112,246

continued

APPENDIX TABLE PL.6E Household composition 1921 (absolute and per cent)
(continued)

Household member	Single	Married	Widowed	Divorced / separated	Unknown	Total
		Line per cent				
Present population at census date, total	59.23	34.35	6.25	0.10	0.08	100.00
Present population at census date, males	61.60	35.39	2.87	0.07	0.07	100.00
Present population at census date, females	57.07	33.40	9.32	0.13	0.09	100.00
Living single, total	48.65	14.93	34.54	1.29	0.59	100.00
Living single, male	60.96	20.27	16.74	1.33	0.71	100.00
Living single, female	37.79	10.22	50.25	1.26	0.50	100.00
Population in family households, total	59.22	34.76	5.88	0.08	0.05	100.00
Population in family households, male	61.49	35.73	2.69	0.05	0.04	100.00
Population in family households, female	57.16	33.88	8.78	0.11	0.07	100.00
thereof: household heads, male	3.70	91.19	5.02	0.07	0.02	100.00
thereof: household heads, female	8.63	19.02	71.44	0.75	0.15	100.00
thereof: wives	..	100.00	..	..	..	100.00
thereof: sons	96.87	3.00	0.11	0.02	0.01	100.00
thereof: daughters	96.60	2.79	0.53	0.06	0.02	100.00
thereof: close relatives, male	68.33	21.98	9.49	0.09	0.11	100.00
thereof: close relatives, female	48.72	18.80	32.13	0.16	0.20	100.00
thereof: distant relatives, male	88.88	7.95	2.79	0.16	0.22	100.00
thereof: distant relatives, female	78.29	11.09	10.05	0.29	0.29	100.00
thereof: *serviteurs*, male	81.79	12.52	5.04	0.23	0.42	100.00
thereof: *serviteurs*, female	87.64	3.51	8.04	0.38	0.43	100.00
thereof: *domestiques*, male	94.30	3.59	1.76	0.11	0.23	100.00
thereof: *domestiques*, female	92.75	2.24	4.55	0.16	0.30	100.00
thereof: sub-tenants, male	78.42	15.83	4.70	0.52	0.52	100.00
thereof: sub-tenants, female	67.77	13.32	17.66	0.71	0.53	100.00
thereof: other persons, male	86.44	9.91	2.81	0.12	0.73	100.00
thereof: other persons, female	78.90	11.28	8.54	0.26	1.01	100.00
Population in institutional households, total	73.80	17.60	6.23	0.13	2.24	100.00
Population in institutional households, male	72.42	22.09	2.96	0.09	2.43	100.00
Population in institutional households, female	75.39	12.43	9.98	0.19	2.01	100.00

continued

APPENDIX TABLE PL.6E Household composition 1921 (absolute and per cent) (continued)

Household member	Single	Married	Widowed	Divorced / separated	Unknown	Total
		Column per cent				
Present population at census date, total	100.00	100.00	100.00	100.00	100.00	100.00
Present population at census date, males	49.59	49.13	21.92	32.29	43.09	47.68
Present population at census date, females	50.41	50.87	78.08	67.71	56.91	52.32
Living single, total	1.04	0.55	6.98	16.43	9.36	1.26
Living single, male	0.61	0.35	1.59	7.94	5.21	0.59
Living single, female	0.43	0.20	5.40	8.49	4.14	0.67
Population in family households, total	97.78	98.96	92.07	82.28	64.10	97.79
Population in family households, male	48.36	48.46	20.09	23.90	22.41	46.58
Population in family households, female	49.42	50.51	71.98	58.39	41.69	51.21
thereof: household heads, male	1.03	43.55	13.18	11.64	3.73	16.40
thereof: household heads, female	0.46	1.76	36.39	24.09	6.07	3.18
thereof: wives	..	43.03	..	..	..	14.78
thereof: sons	39.27	2.09	0.41	4.63	3.82	24.01
thereof: daughters	39.46	1.96	2.06	15.55	4.80	24.20
thereof: close relatives, male	4.17	2.31	5.49	3.25	4.93	3.61
thereof: close relatives, female	4.66	3.10	29.12	8.86	13.90	5.66
thereof: distant relatives, male	1.04	0.16	0.31	1.10	1.90	0.69
thereof: distant relatives, female	1.37	0.33	1.66	3.00	3.70	1.03
thereof: *serviteurs*, male	0.04	0.01	0.02	0.07	0.16	0.03
thereof: *serviteurs*, female	1.22	0.08	1.06	3.13	4.38	0.83
thereof: *domestiques*, male	2.09	0.14	0.37	1.51	3.83	1.31
thereof: *domestiques*, female	1.65	0.07	0.77	1.68	3.89	1.05
thereof: sub-tenants, male	0.35	0.12	0.20	1.40	1.75	0.27
thereof: sub-tenants, female	0.21	0.07	0.51	1.30	1.20	0.18
thereof: other persons, male	0.37	0.07	0.11	0.29	2.30	0.25
thereof: other persons, female	0.39	0.10	0.40	0.77	3.74	0.30
Population in institutional households, total	1.19	0.49	0.95	1.29	26.55	0.95
Population in institutional households, male	0.62	0.33	0.24	0.46	15.47	0.51
Population in institutional households, female	0.56	0.16	0.71	0.83	11.08	0.44

APPENDIX TABLE PL.6F Household composition 1931 (absolute and per cent)

Household type	Private households	Household head											
		1 person	2 persons	3 persons	4 persons	5 persons	6 persons	7 persons	8 persons	9 persons	10 persons	11 persons	12+ persons
Absolute													
Total households													
A	6,483,402	644,521	826,494	1,036,387	1,129,700	1,011,149	776,527	510,233	291,587	146,904	69,072	24,565	16,263
B	301,644	..	19,647	50,150	70,992	70,763	44,518	23,974	11,443	5,469	2,860	943	885
C	340,192	..	8,500	36,090	54,989	67,019	63,029	48,302	30,175	16,932	8,859	3,355	2,942
D	30,046	..	..	994	2,766	4,315	5,022	4,881	4,079	2,946	2,070	1,000	1,973
Total	7,155,284	644,521	854,641	1,123,621	1,258,447	1,153,246	889,096	587,390	337,284	172,251	82,861	29,863	22,063
Households comprising one-person and monofamilial households													
A	5,880,234	644,521	826,494	1,036,387	1,070,586	893,891	640,329	395,086	211,518	99,250	42,065	13,454	6,653
B	287,236	..	19,647	50,150	70,419	68,365	41,189	20,833	9,274	4,214	1,959	656	530
C	289,898	..	8,500	36,090	54,185	61,715	52,638	36,657	20,708	10,892	5,233	1,907	1,373
D	27,042	..	..	994	2,745	4,233	4,798	4,485	3,585	2,484	1,654	745	1,319
Total	6,484,410	644,521	854,641	1,123,621	1,197,935	1,028,204	738,954	457,061	245,085	116,840	50,911	16,762	9,875
Polyfamilial households													
A	603,168	..	..	..	59,114	117,258	136,198	115,147	80,069	47,654	27,007	11,111	9,610
B	14,408	..	..	..	573	2,398	3,329	3,141	2,169	1,255	901	287	355
C	50,294	..	..	..	804	5,304	10,391	11,645	9,467	6,040	3,626	1,448	1,569
D	3,004	..	..	..	21	82	224	396	494	462	416	255	654
Total	670,874	..	..	..	60,512	125,042	150,142	130,329	92,199	55,411	31,950	13,101	12,188

continued

APPENDIX TABLE PL.6F Household composition 1931 (absolute and per cent) (continued)

Household type	Private house-holds	Household head											
		1 person	2 persons	3 persons	4 persons	5 persons	6 persons	7 persons	8 persons	9 persons	10 persons	11 persons	12+ persons
Type per cent													
Households comprising one-person and monofamilial households													
A	90.70	100.00	100.00	100.00	94.77	88.40	82.46	77.43	72.54	67.56	60.90	54.77	40.91
B	95.22	..	100.00	100.00	99.19	96.61	92.52	86.90	81.05	77.05	68.50	69.57	59.89
C	85.22	..	100.00	100.00	98.54	92.09	83.51	75.89	68.63	64.33	59.07	56.84	46.67
D	90.00	100.00	..	100.00	99.24	98.10	95.54	91.89	87.89	84.32	79.90	74.50	66.85
Total	90.62	100.00	100.00	100.00	95.19	89.16	83.11	77.81	72.66	67.83	61.44	56.13	44.76
Polyfamilial households													
A	9.30	..	..	..	5.23	11.60	17.54	22.57	27.46	32.44	39.10	45.23	59.09
B	4.78	..	..	..	0.81	3.39	7.48	13.10	18.95	22.95	31.50	30.43	40.11
C	14.78	..	..	..	1.46	7.91	16.49	24.11	31.37	35.67	40.93	43.16	53.33
D	10.00	..	..	..	0.76	1.90	4.46	8.11	12.11	15.68	20.10	25.50	33.15
Total	9.38	..	..	..	4.81	10.84	16.89	22.19	27.34	32.17	38.56	43.87	55.24

continued

APPENDIX TABLE PL.6F Household composition 1931 (absolute and per cent) (continued)

| Household type | Private house-holds | Household head | | | | | | | | | | | |
		1 person	2 persons	3 persons	4 persons	5 persons	6 persons	7 persons	8 persons	9 persons	10 persons	11 persons	12+ persons
						Line per cent							
						Total households							
A	100.00	9.94	12.75	15.99	17.42	15.60	11.98	7.87	4.50	2.27	1.07	0.38	0.25
B	100.00	..	6.51	16.63	23.54	23.46	14.76	7.95	3.79	1.81	0.95	0.31	0.29
C	100.00	..	2.50	10.61	16.16	19.70	18.53	14.20	8.87	4.98	2.60	0.99	0.86
D	100.00	..	..	3.31	9.21	14.36	16.71	16.25	13.58	9.80	6.89	3.33	6.57
Total	100.00	9.01	11.94	15.70	17.59	16.12	12.43	8.21	4.71	2.41	1.16	0.42	0.31
						Households comprising one-person and monofamilial households							
A	100.00	10.96	14.06	17.62	18.21	15.20	10.89	6.72	3.60	1.69	0.72	0.23	0.11
B	100.00	..	6.84	17.46	24.52	23.80	14.34	7.25	3.23	1.47	0.68	0.23	0.18
C	100.00	..	2.93	12.45	18.69	21.29	18.16	12.64	7.14	3.76	1.81	0.66	0.47
D	100.00	..	..	3.68	10.15	15.65	17.74	16.59	13.26	9.19	6.12	2.75	4.88
Total	100.00	9.94	13.18	17.33	18.47	15.86	11.40	7.05	3.78	1.80	0.79	0.26	0.15
						Polyfamilial households							
A	100.00	..	..	..	9.80	19.44	22.58	19.09	13.27	7.90	4.48	1.84	1.59
B	100.00	..	..	..	3.98	16.64	23.11	21.80	15.05	8.71	6.25	1.99	2.46
C	100.00	..	..	..	1.60	10.55	20.66	23.15	18.82	12.01	7.21	2.88	3.12
D	100.00	..	..	..	0.70	2.73	7.46	13.18	16.44	15.38	13.85	8.49	21.77
Total	100.00	..	..	..	9.02	18.64	22.38	19.43	13.74	8.26	4.76	1.95	1.82

Notes: A Without domestic servants, farm workers, apprentices, etc. B With domestic servants only. C With farm workers, apprentices, etc. only. D With domestic servants, farm workers, apprentices, etc.

APPENDIX TABLE PL.7 Dates and nature of results on population structure, households/families, and vital statistics

Topic	Intro-duction	Remarks
Population		
Population at census dates	1921	After the creation of the independent state of Poland in 1918 population censuses were conducted in 1921 and 1931. Before World War II there was no further population census. The third census was conducted in 1950. Before World War I Poland, being part of Russia, Germany, and Austria-Hungary, participated in the census of these countries. Historical census data have been compiled by GUS (1993).
Population by age, sex, and marital status	1921	Available in one-year age-groups for 1921; in one-year (from 0–39) and five-year age groups (from 40–80+) in 1931 for the national level.
Households and families		
Households (gospodarstwa)		
Total households	1921, 1931	Households were first recorded in 1921 and again in 1931. 1921: housing census: family households and single persons in dwellings. Dwellings by number of household members. One-person, family, and institutional households. 1931: one-person, family, and institutional households. Households by size and type. *Disaggregation*: by towns and villages, voivodships.
Households by size	1921, 1931	1921: households by number of persons 1–501+ (for one-person, family, and institutional households) 1931: households with 1–12+ persons.
Households by composition	1921, 1931	1921: households by type of member and marital status; by type of member and confession. Household types by confession. Institutional households by number of inhabitants. 1931: *household types* by number of household members.
Households by profession of household head	–	Not available.
Families		
Families by number of children	–	Not available.

continued

APPENDIX TABLE PL.7 Dates and nature of results on population structure, households/families, and vital statistics (continued)

Topic	Intro-duction	Remarks
Population movement		
Mid-year population	1900	Data have been recalculated going back before independence.
Births		
Live births	1919	No data available from 1939–1945.
Stillbirths	1985	
Legitimate births	1927	Only data for 1927, 1970, 1980, 1985ff.
Illegitimate births	1927	Only data for 1927, 1970, 1980, 1985ff.
Deaths		
Total deaths	1919	No data available from 1939–1945.
Infants (under 1 year)	1927	
Marriages		
Total marriages	1919	No data available from 1939–1945.
Divorces and separations		
Total divorces	1946	
Legal separations	–	No calculations available.

APPENDIX FIGURE PL.8 Population by age, sex and marital status, Poland 1921 and 1931 (per 10,000 of total population)

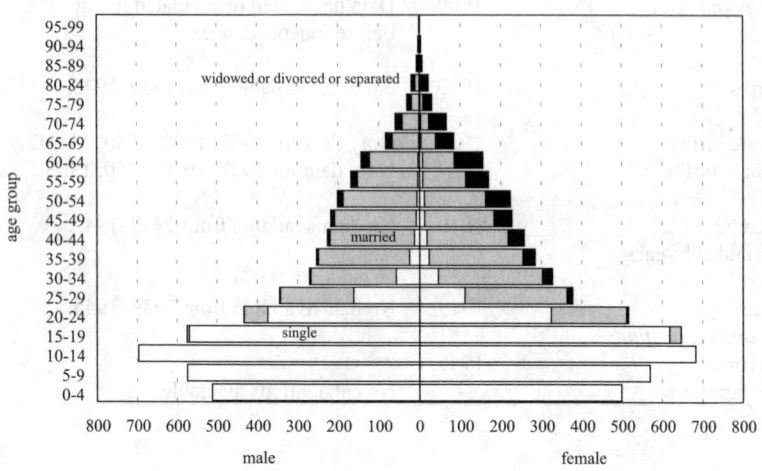

Poland, 1921

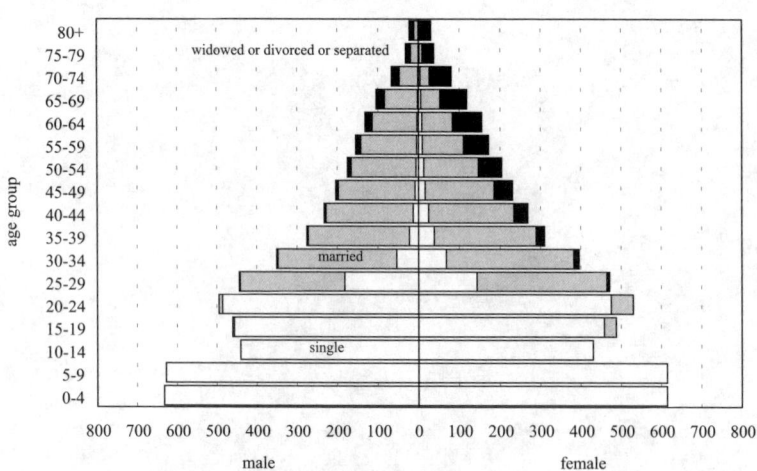

Poland, 1931

17

Portugal

STATE FORMATION AND TERRITORY

Portugal lies in the south-west corner of the European continent on its most extreme periphery. The country is nearly rectangular and has today a total area of 92,389 square kilometres, occupying about 20% of the Iberian Peninsula. The country is bordered by the Atlantic, which has for centuries shaped its orientation towards Africa, Asia, and South America. Portugal's geopolitical situation made it difficult to maintain independence from Spain in its endeavour to unite the Iberian Peninsula. Thus, only after major struggles was Portugal able to become an independent nation in 1640 with the assistance of its ally England. Portugal is thus one of the oldest nation-states in Europe, dating in principle back to 1179 (except for the Spanish interlude lasting from 1580 to 1640); in addition, its territory has remained unchanged since the Middle Ages. The occupation by the Romans brought with it language and later Christianity, which was preserved during Islamic domination. This laid the basis for a rather high socio-cultural homogeneity.

In its long history, Portugal was able to keep its monarchical system until the republican revolution of 1910. The first republic lasted only 16 years, then Salazar inaugurated his autocratic regime in 1926 which lasted until 1974. Though the British urged Portugal to enter World War I, the regime remained neutral during World War II. After Salazar's death in 1970, the revolution of 1974 finally led to the second republic with the constitution of 1975.

REGIONAL POPULATION STRUCTURE

Portugal is characterized by major economic heterogeneity dating back to the time when family farms prevailed in the north while large agricultural estates ('latifundia') were predominant in the south. Apart from agriculture, at least three factors influenced the economic structure of Portugal during the time under consideration: fishing and seafaring in the Algarve and coastal regions, and the agricultural orientation in the Centro, Alentejo, and Norte. Industry has always been underdeveloped, with signs of industrialization only in Lisbon and the north. Due to the great economic diversity of the country, the economic situation differed greatly from region to region, with Lisbon the most prosperous city, while the Alentejo and the island regions were usually the poorest.

As a result of differences in regional economic organization, the population has been very unevenly dispersed over the country; population density therefore differed tremendously. The north was densely inhabited, in contrast to the Algarve or the Alentejo. In 1878, the district of Oporto (198 inhabitants per sq. km.) had the highest population density, followed by the district of Braga in the north (117 inhabitants/sq. km.). Other districts with a high population density were Viana do Castello and Aveiro, both in the north. In 1878 Lisbon had a lower settlement density, but

urbanized rapidly until 1940, when population density nearly reached the level of
Oporto. In 1878, the Azores and Madeira were three times as populated as the
Continente (122 to 46 inhabitants per sq. km.). In 1878, the two largest towns
Oporto and Lisbon accounted for one-fifth (21%) of the total population; by 1940
this proportion had increased to one-fourth (25.7%).

POPULATION GROWTH

In the nineteenth century, Portugal was a country with a small population: 3.397
million inhabitants in 1841. This number increased to 7.755 million inhabitants in
1940, thus more than doubling within a hundred years. Natural population growth
was rather high, with figures above 10 per 1,000 from 1900 to World War I (Figure
P.1). The natural population growth rate became strongly negative during World
War I, but recovered its pre-war level in the 1920s and 1930s. World War II again
caused a downswing in the natural population growth rate, but not as strong as in the
previous war.

   Despite the high natural population growth rate, the overall population growth rate
was only modest during the demographic transition, as high emigration reduced
overall population growth. From the 1890s to the early 1930s, the net migration was
always negative, i.e. emigration was higher than immigration. Only during the 1930s
and 1940s did immigration became stronger than emigration. The largest emigratory
movement occurred from 1910 to the outbreak of World War I; a second, shorter
wave set in shortly after the war in 1920. Thus, emigration was a significant
characteristic of Portugal. Until the mid-twentieth century most emigrants went to
Brazil, although some also went to the new African colonies. Because emigration
was always male-dominated, it had tremendous negative effects on the sex and age
structure of the population, leading to a strong overrepresentation of women and the
elderly. The absence of men also had negative effects on women's chances of
marrying. Emigration also meant that many children in Portugal did not and still do
not live with their natural parents, but rather with grandparents or other relatives.

   The small size of the Portuguese population during the nineteenth century resulted
in a low average population density. In 1878 population density was only 49
inhabitants per square kilometre, in contrast to Belgium, for example, where
population density already in 1831 was 128 inhabitants per sq. km. By 1940
population density in Portugal had nearly doubled, with 85 inhabitants per sq. km.

THE FIRST DEMOGRAPHIC TRANSITION

The demographic transition in Portugal occurred later than in countries with a
stronger socio-economic development. The birth rate only began to decline after
1910. For the whole of the nineteenth century the few available data suggest that the
crude birth rate fluctuated around 33 births per 1,000 population. Although the birth
rate declined during the twentieth century as in all other Western European
countries, in Portugal this decline was slower, and the Portuguese birth rate showed
a growing divergence from the European rate. Only since the 1970s has the
Portuguese birth rate declined significantly to reach the European level. Now
Portugal, along with the other Mediterranean countries, has one of the lowest birth
rates in Europe. At least for the first decades, the death rate seems distorted by
misrepresentation of deaths at young ages and therefore seems too low up to World

War I. This finding is supported by the near stability of the crude death rate until the 1920s. Only since that time does the death rate show a significant decrease, but on a level above the European average. It is only since the 1960s that the crude death rate has converged with the European average. Natural population growth in the twentieth century in Portugal was above the European average, given the very high birth rate during that time. This is especially true for the 1930s to 1960s. Consequently, emigration was very strong during the 1950s and 1960s (Figure P.2).

In 1910 the revolution overthrew the monarchy and installed the second republic in Europe after France in 1871. The republican leader Alfonso Costa in 1917 sent an expedition corps to France and thus participated in World War I with 45,000 soldiers. Of these, 10,000 were killed or injured. In 1918 the great influenza pandemic took 60,000 lives. These two factors and the revolutionary circumstances between 1910 and 1926 (the beginning of Salazar's authoritarian regime) account for the demographic developments of that time. The major increase in the death rate was caused by the war and the influenza pandemic, but also partly by the revolution. At the start of the revolution the birth rate also declined until 1917 when Portugal ended its military engagement in France under the new dictator Sidónio Pais (Birmingham 1993: 148ff.). During World War II Portugal remained neutral, but the living conditions of the population deteriorated considerably, demonstrated by the major decline in the birth rate and the rise in the death rate. But these demographic shocks were not as dramatic as in countries participating in World War II. A strong decrease in the birth rate can also be seen in the 1890s, probably due to the conflicts between monarchists and republicans at that time. Portugal's economy was long dominated by agriculture, therefore agricultural crises exerted a much stronger influence on the business cycles than economic crises in manufacturing. Due to missing data for the nineteenth century we do not know to what extent Portugal was affected by the world economic recession of the 1850s or by various European wars such as the Crimean War and the Franco-Prussian War of 1870/71.

MORTALITY AND LIFE EXPECTANCY

During the whole period Portugal had one of the highest infant mortality rates in Europe, as high as in some economically backward countries such as Romania, Bulgaria, and parts of Yugoslavia. Only in the most recent decades was Portugal able to bring its child mortality rate down to a reasonably low level. Masuy-Stroobant's (1997: 6f.) cluster analysis of 27 European countries and territorial units groups Portugal with Romania and Yugoslavia. Infant mortality declined very late in Portugal, in the late 1940s, but child mortality has greatly improved since the 1950s, much more than in Romania and Yugoslavia. Thus, Portugal probably fits into this cluster more for the time span 1900 to 1950, while later it would fit better into a cluster with more advanced countries. In the 1990s Portugal's infant mortality rate was still above the European average (EU15), but the difference has become small (Figure P.3).

In Portugal tremendous regional differences in infant mortality continue to persist today. Traditionally infant mortality was very high in the northern regions (Minho, Tras os Montes), lower in the central and coastal regions, and higher in the Alentejo (Livi Bacci 1971: Fig. 8a, p. 116). One reason for this regional difference can be seen in different patterns of breastfeeding. It is reported that children in the Minho were weaned at only a few months of age, which contributed not only to higher

Figure P.1 Population growth and net migration 1850-1945

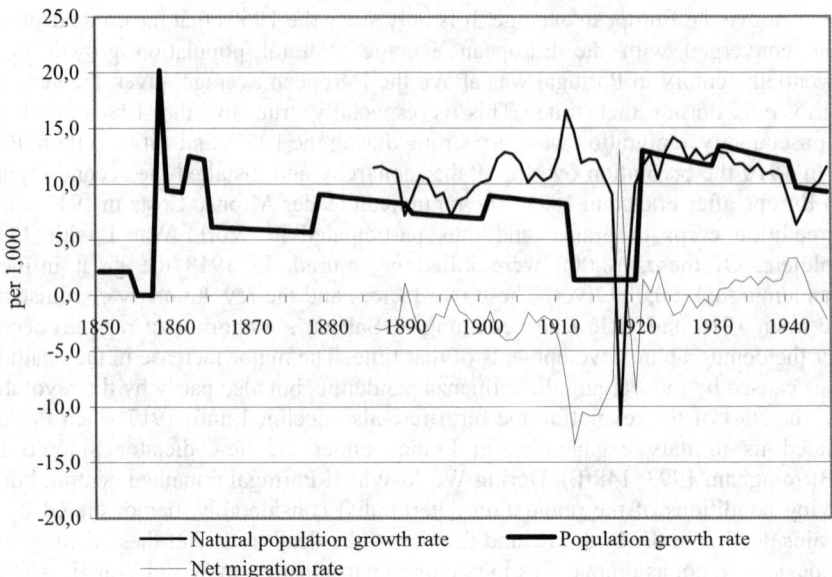

Natural population growth rate   Population growth rate
Net migration rate

Figure P.2 First demographic transition 1886-1945

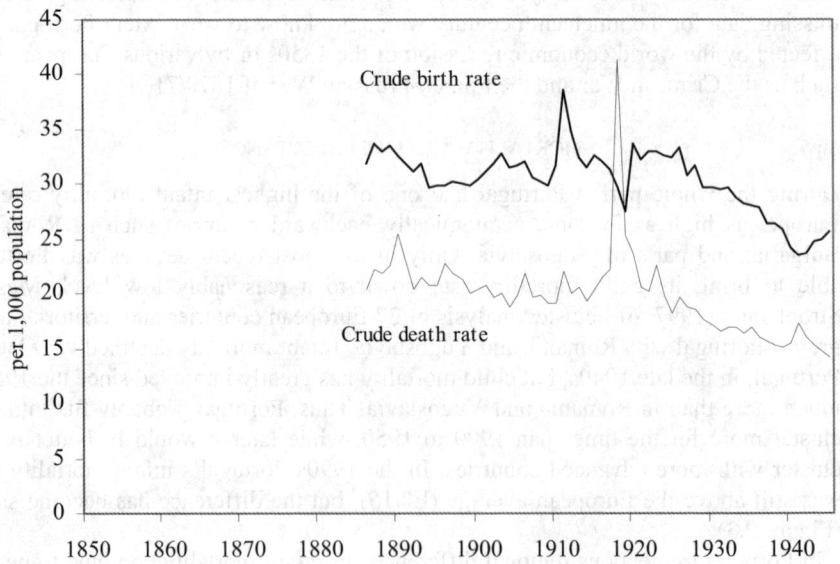

infant mortality but also to higher fertility by reducing the mean birth interval (Livi Bacci 1971: 79). Another factor seems to be the continuing lack of medical infrastructure and medical assistance at birth in the mountainous regions of the north (Livi Bacci 1971: 115 and Fig. 8b, p. 116).

Life expectancy and the health status of the population continues to be low today in a European context. The largest difference in life expectancy, when compared to more advanced countries, was for life expectancy at birth, i.e. infant mortality (see above) (Figure P.4). Life expectancy at birth in 1939/42 was 48.6 years for boys (64.3 in Sweden in 1936/40) and 52.8 for girls (66.9 in Sweden). Life expectancy in 1939/42 at the ages of 30 and 60 was also lower than in Sweden. Life expectancy was higher for women at all ages, the lower the age, the larger the difference. The sex difference in life expectancy slightly increased from 1939/42 to 1945.

FERTILITY AND LEGITIMACY

With regard to illegitimate births, Portugal is a special case within Western Europe. Moderate age at marriage and moderate celibacy rates as compared to Northern Europe would lead one to expect that illegitimacy would also have been moderate, but the opposite is the case: Portugal had one of the highest illegitimacy rates in Europe. This high illegitimacy becomes clearer if the rather small propensity to marry is taken into consideration: the marriage ratio was very low, well under the European average. How can this phenomenon be explained? To do so, we have to proceed in two steps: first, by discussing the factors that contribute to high illegitimacy on the national level, and second by discussing the regional variations. For the whole of Portugal one may speak of a certain weakness of the institution of marriage, not in the sense of a high number of dissolved marriages (through separation, divorce, etc.), but in terms of a low propensity to go through an official religious or civil marriage ceremony, especially in southern Portugal. A second factor relevant for all of Portugal is emigration, which was rather high all the time and reached tremendous levels from 1900–1920 and in the 1950s. Emigration was encouraged by the existence of the colonies in Brazil and Africa (Mozambique and Angola). As predominantly young men emigrated, there was a large surplus female population in Portugal, and many women could not find a man to marry. A third factor can be seen in the frequency of female servants in the two largest cities, Oporto and Lisbon, where there was a large number of illegitimate children. Consequently the illegitimate fertility rate in these two towns was rather high (Figure P.5).

In regional terms, illegitimacy was higher in the north than in the south, especially in Oporto and Lisbon. But this is only a question of degree rather than difference in principle. In the Alentejo, living together without a formal marriage contract was very widespread among the landless farm labourers. Therefore, births to unmarried couples and de facto families were counted as illegitimate, though they would not be considered such from a sociological perspective. In the north, one may speak of illegitimacy in the proper sense of the word, as the marriage institution was very strong, in line with Catholic values, but the economic structure in this part of the country (small farm properties) contributed to out-of-wedlock births. All over Portugal, childbirth before marriage was very common, with strong regional variations. In 1940, 12% of all illegitimate births were later legitimated by marriage, varying from 3.8% in Vila Real to 37.1% in Portalegre. When explaining

Figure P.3 Infant mortality 1913-1945

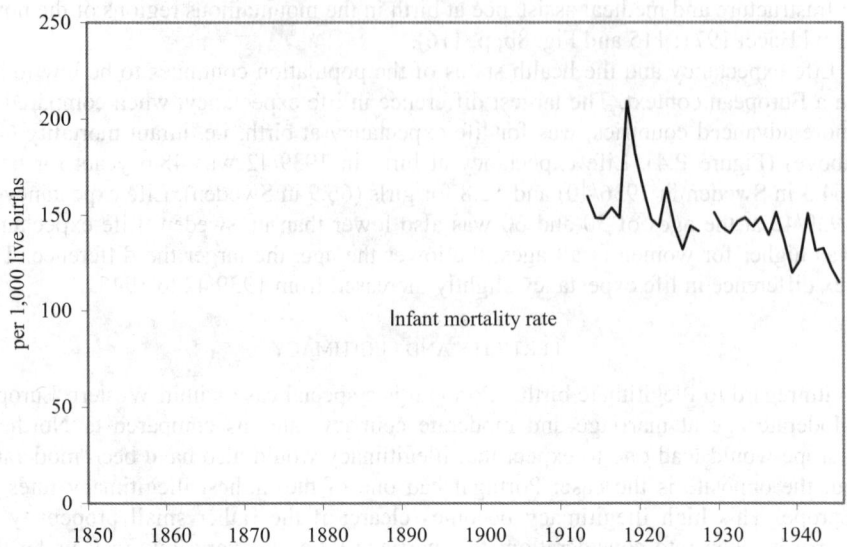

Figure P.4 Life expectancy 1939/42-1945

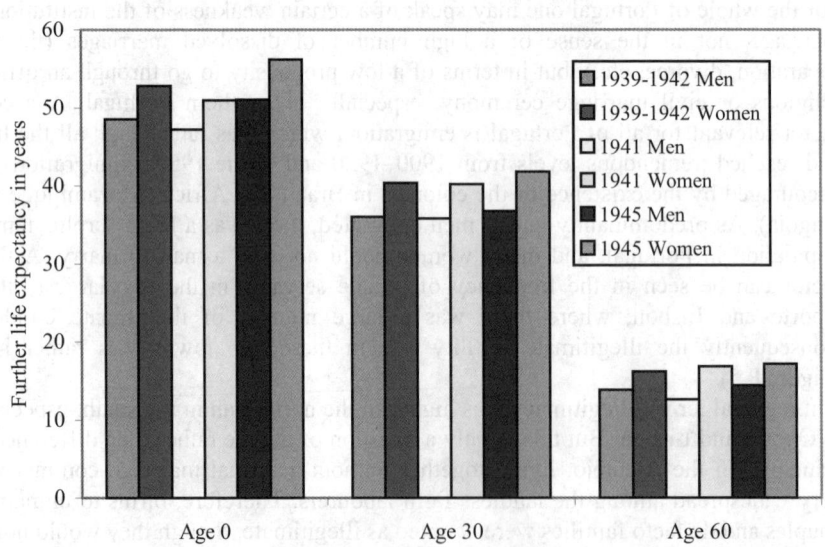

illegitimacy in Portugal, ethnologists point to a rather low degree of sexual rigidity, which is in marked contrast to the official Catholic value system. It is often said that Catholicism in Portugal is only superficial and that pre-Christian mores and rituals have survived in several regions, especially in parts of the north. To what degree the long domination of Portugal by the Moors shaped the actual behaviour and customs of the people is an open question.

Although Portugal's illegitimacy rate was always very high, it participated in the all-European trend of declining illegitimate fertility in the twentieth century. Since the 1970s the European illegitimacy rate has risen strongly due to the increasing deinstitutionalization of marriage and in the late 1980s surpassed Portugal's traditionally high rate. The renewed increase of illegitimacy and therefore the (new) process of deinstitutionalization of marriage also started in Portugal in the 1970s, but was much more moderate than in other Western European countries.

MARRIAGE AND DIVORCE

In principle, Portugal belongs to the region of Europe with the Western European marriage pattern of late age at marriage and a high celibacy rate, but this statement must be qualified. Age at marriage and the proportion of females and males married at young ages was comparatively moderate in the nineteenth century: age at marriage was not as high as in Scandinavia, but not as low as in England and Wales. Rather high age at marriage continued to prevail well into the 1930s. The decline in the age at marriage during the marriage boom of the 1960s occurred 10 to 15 years later in Portugal than in Scandinavia.

Celibacy rates were low already in the nineteenth century, and (in contrast to the Scandinavian countries, for example) declined continuously from 1850 to 1990. Only the drop in the 1960s in the phase of universal marriage in Western Europe was stronger than the previous decline. Although marriage was not historically universal, Portugal therefore diverges in this respect from the other Western European countries. There are no obvious explanations for this fact: first, emigration of young men—especially from the north—led to a surplus of (single) females in the population. Second, in the south, especially in the Alentejo, people often did not marry although they formed couples and had children. This factor would also contribute to a high celibacy rate.

Regional disaggregation shows that the proportion of females still single at age 50–54 in 1864 was higher in the north and lower in the south. Median age at first marriage (in 1950) was higher in the north and lower in the south. The regional differences in celibacy continued to shrink up to the 1960s due to the trend of universal and early marriage. Thus, in the second half of the nineteenth century the small family farms and trades in the north led to high age at marriage and a high celibacy rate. These characteristics seem to be linked with the higher fertility in the north, which was combined with high religiosity, high percentage of the labour force engaged in agriculture, high infant mortality, high emigration rates, and high illegitimacy rates.

Marriage intensity as measured by the marriage rate during the second half of the nineteenth and the first half of the twentieth century was apparently low and under the European average (Figure P.6). This can be explained by several factors: first, the 'moderate' Western European marriage pattern with moderate celibacy rate and high age at marriage; second, especially in the north the shortage of young men due

Portugal

Figure P.5 Fertility and legitimacy 1888-1939

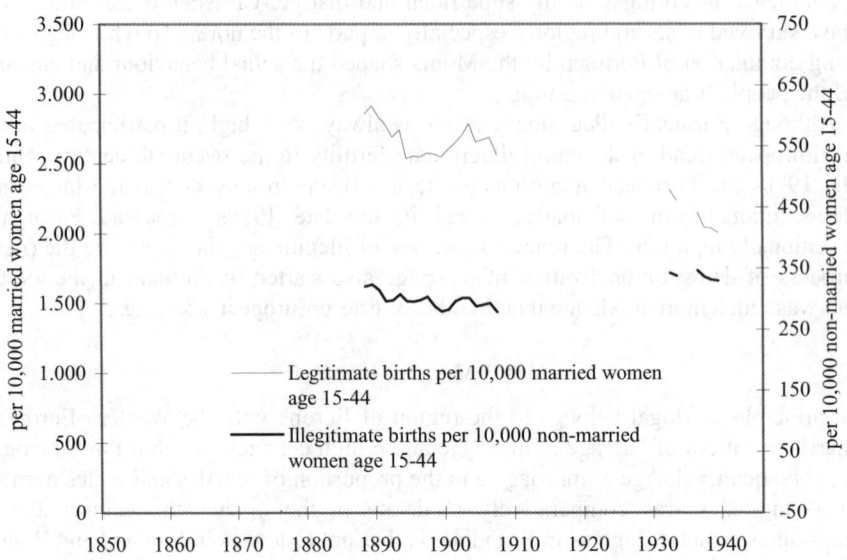

Figure P.6 Marriages and divorces 1886-1939

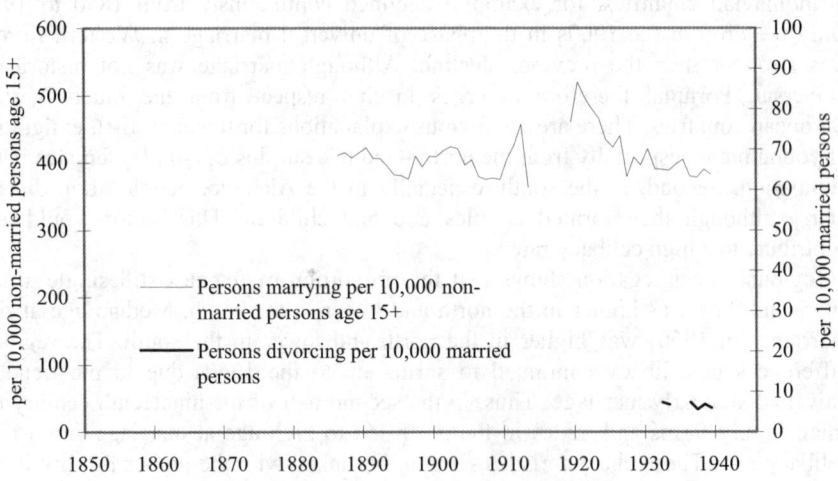

to emigration to the colonies, which led to a greater number of single women and illegitimate births; third, in the Alentejo where the latifundia system prevailed, people did not adhere to religious practices and couples often did not marry unless they had already had several children. Celibacy and illegitimacy were also widespread in the two largest cities, Oporto and Lisbon, probably related to the number of female servants and female factory workers. After the 1940s the marriage rate for the whole of Portugal increased steadily and began to converge with the European average. This rise continued until the mid-1970s when the marriage rate declined again, but remained above the European average. This means a complete change of Portuguese marriage behaviour, which has now become universal and early ten to fifteen years after the rest of Europe.

Concerning *marital stability* we only have data on divorces and legal separations (Figure P.6). Portugal was long dominated by the monarchy in coalition with the church. Divorce was only introduced by the republican regime after the revolution of 1910. Already in 1926 an authoritarian regime took over and was finally consolidated when António de Oliveira Salazar became prime minister in 1932. Divorces were only allowed for foreigners and non-Catholics. The revolution of 1974 and the introduction of democracy brought with it a modern divorce law. The liberalization of divorce can be seen in the steep increase in the divorce rate after the introduction of the new law, as couples who had waited a long time could now get a divorce. After this backlog was dealt with, the divorce rate fell again shortly after the liberalization. All in all, the level of the Portuguese divorce rate is very much lower than the European average, although with a rising tendency, a clear sign of the very different structure of the country. The figures for divorces and legal separations from the late 1920s up to the 1970s say nothing about marriage instability in Portugal and how people solved the problems of actual marriage breakdown. Legal and unofficial separation, emigration, and labour migration were all possible solutions. The lack of access to divorce probably also contributed to the high illegitimacy rates in Portugal.

AGE, SEX, AND CIVIL STATUS

In Portugal, during the whole time period from 1864 to 1940, the age structure had a pyramidal form (Appendix Figure P.8). The age structure at the bottom was concave until 1878; afterwards it became convex, indicating small reductions in fertility. But there was no fundamental change in the age composition during the whole time period. Only World War I (in which Portugal was urged to participate) caused a loss in births, which is visible in the age structure of 1920 and returns in those of 1930 and 1940. Until 1911 the age structure showed great variations between single age groups, with a large age group immediately followed by a smaller one. This is probably due to several waves of emigration to Brazil.

As in most other European countries, men remained single longer than women, but in higher age groups more females than males never married. In the second half of the nineteenth century, female celibacy in higher age groups was partly very high, probably caused by a shortage of men due to male emigration. Widowhood was also very widespread in the nineteenth century for some age groups. After World War I the Portuguese age structure became much more regular than before, as the waves of emigration came to an end.

For most of the nineteenth century the sex composition of the population was uneven, and women outnumbered men due to emigration. Especially the northern part of the country was greatly affected by emigration.

The demographic processes and migratory patterns also greatly influenced the age structure. In the north and on the islands the proportion of children was higher due to high birth rates. In the Centro and the Alentejo emigration of the young led to a high proportion of elderly people. The Algarve seems to be a special case with labour migration and obviously immigration of the elderly as well.

FAMILY AND HOUSEHOLD STRUCTURES

The development of households and families during the nineteenth century deviates strongly from the Western European countries. Assuming the data are valid, mean private household size *increased* from the 1850s to the 1920s. Only afterwards, probably due to the fertility decline and the growth in one-person households, did mean private household size decline. Portuguese household statistics are very poor until the 1960s, giving only the number of households until the 1890 census, when households by size were published (rather early compared to other countries). But there is no additional information on the household structure and no information is available on servants, boarders, or lodgers. Thus, we do not know the frequency of female servants in households, which is very important information for household, economic, and demographic structures. We do not even know if the increase in mean private household size is a real phenomenon; if so, how could it be explained? One factor could be an increase in fertility, but there is no evidence for such a thesis, because there was a rather constant birth rate before the fertility decline which did not start before 1910. A second thesis is that the number of one-person households or very small households decreased during the period. But a decrease in the number of one-person households would mean an economic decline, urging people to live in larger units. But all this is only speculation, because the size distribution of households is only available since 1890. The available data indeed show that the proportion of one-person households was rather large and declined after 1890. The proportion of 5+ person households was comparatively low and increased, as did households with four persons. Therefore, in summary, in Portugal during the end of the nineteenth century, smaller households were widespread and there were fewer larger households than in most other Western European countries. There is no clear-cut explanation for this fact, and an investigation into this special case seems to be missing, but the low nuptiality in Portugal could be one important factor. A second factor for which we have no data could be a high number of incomplete families due to emigration, out-of-wedlock births, or widowhood.

There were also regional differences with respect to family structure and family behaviour, as the number of out-of-wedlock births demonstrates: there were marked differences between the individual regions, and there was a north–south divide, with lower figures in the north than in the south (contrary to the overall European pattern with high rates in northern Europe and low ones in southern Europe).

THE NATIONAL SYSTEM OF DEMOGRAPHIC STATISTICS

Population Structure

The first modern population census was conducted as late as 1864, although census-taking partly goes back to the sixteenth century (see Appendix Table P.7). Few census statistics are available for the first half of the nineteenth century. Censuses were organized in 1801, 1821, 1835, 1841, 1854, 1858, and 1861. Only the results for the 1801 census have been published extensively. The censuses from the second half of the nineteenth century are not entirely reliable. Especially the younger age groups seem to be underrepresented, which influences all calculations taking the age structure into account (cf. Ferreira da Cunha, 1995; Sousa, 1995).

Vital Statistics

The record of live births, deaths, and marriages was also introduced rather late, only in 1886. For earlier times some vital statistics can be calculated using information from censuses and contemporary accounts and descriptions (Livi Bacci, 1971). Deaths seem to be underrepresented in the early decades, as babies, particularly girls, who died within a few days of birth were often not counted. Such cases were probably counted as stillbirths, therefore increasing the stillbirth rate, which therefore must be interpreted with caution. Data on infant deaths seem to have become available also rather late, after the turn of the century (1910). The number of stillbirths is also only available since 1900. The number of births by legitimacy is available since 1888, but obviously there are gaps in the data on illegitimacy in the 1910s and 1920s. The number of divorces was also published very late, in 1929, when divorce law was very restrictive and only foreigners were allowed to divorce. Data on legal separations are also very limited and became available very late (in 1966). Like divorces, legal separations were very restricted in Portugal until the end of the authoritarian regime in 1974. Measurement of fertility is additionally possible through the censuses of 1940 and 1950, which asked married women some questions about the number of children born to them. Cohort fertility can be measured using these data.

Households and Families

Data on households (in the nineteenth century *fogos*, later *familias*) were already collected in the census of 1732 for the continent and published continually in the later censuses with the exception of the census of 1821. Data on households for the islands (Azores and Madeira) were first collected in 1841. Thus, households for the whole of Portugal (continent and islands) are available since 1841. The first fully documented census of 1864 concerning household statistics did not present additional material to the earlier censuses: only the absolute number of households was published. In 1890 households began to be recorded by number of persons and have been ever since, with the exception of the 1930 census when households by size were not published. From 1890 to 1920 household size was presented for groups from 1 up to 7+ persons. In 1940 and 1950 the categories were extended in order to catch larger households (households with 8, 9, 10–14, 15–19, and 20+ persons). In 1911 and 1920 institutional households were included in the number of households published (see INE, *Anuário Estatístico de Portugal 1963*, 1963, vol. I: 9). A regional disaggregation of the number of households into districts was already introduced in 1864 and has been maintained since then (see INE, *Anuário Estatístico de Portugal 1980*, 1980: 23).

The definition of a household (*fogo* or *familia*) was more or less stable from 1864 until 1950. The definition included all private households: households consisting of one single person and households consisting of a family. Institutional households were not covered except in the censuses of 1911 and 1920. Institutional households were introduced in 1890 with the calculation of households by number of persons, with the exception of 1911 and 1920. Since 1890 the three household categories (one-person, family, and institutional households) can be distinguished (similar to Germany, but in contrast to Belgium). Explicit definitions of households have been given for several censuses. For the 1890 census it was stated:

Em todos os recenseamentos efféctuados tomou-se sempre *fogo* na accepção de casa ou local habitado por uma só familia; entendendo-se por familia qualquer grupo de pessoas, vivendo juntas, ou mesmo uma só pessoa vivendo independentemente.

Anteriormente ao censo de 1864, era esta a unidade de preferencia, quando não exclusivamente, adoptada para avaliar a população do paiz (Portugal. Ministerio de Fazenda. Direcção Geral da Estatística e dos Proprios Nacionaes, 1896: CI).

In 1950 it was stated:

Chef de famille. - La personne de famille qui avait la responsabilité du maintien des autres membres de la famille.

Communauté. - Tout groupement de personnes qui, d'une manière permanente ou accidentielle, vivaient en commun sous l'autorité du même chef et pour tout autre motif, en dehors de celui de la vie de famille qu'elles aient eu ou non une habitation.

Famille. - Le groupe de personnes unies par les liens de sang ou d'affinité ou par des motifs de vie ou de service domestique qui résidaient habituellement dans la même habitation, ou bien la personne qui résidait sans autre personne de famille dans une habitation séparée (Portugal. Instituto Nacional de Estatística, 1952: 9).

Family statistics did not start before the 1950 census, when families were presented by the number of children for the first time. Results have been published for married couples and unmarried women by number of children.

Remarks (also see introductory Table 6.1)

There are no data on vital statistics in Portugal from official sources before 1886 (cf. also Mitchell, 1992).

BOUNDARY CHANGES

The territory of Portugal was consolidated already in the Middle Ages. It expanded from the region of Oporto (then named Portus Cale) to the south by conquering the Arab territories and to the north. In 1250 Portugal reached the dimensions it more or less has today. Portugal lost its autonomy and was integrated into the Spanish empire from 1580 to 1640. Since the nineteenth century when the first 'modern' population censuses were conducted, Portugal's territory underwent only very minor alterations. Starting in the fourteenth century, Portugal expanded steadily overseas, to Africa, Asia, and South America. Madeira had already been discovered in the fourteenth century and was occupied by the Portuguese in 1420. The Azores were discovered about 1427; both archipelagos were settled by the end of the fifteenth century. With the decline of the Portuguese empire since the nineteenth century, of its overseas possessions only the Azores and Madeira have remained part of Portugal. Population census figures have traditionally been collected separately for the mainland and the islands. The earliest censuses only collected data for the mainland. From the first modern census in 1864 onwards the territory of continental Portugal was rather stable, amounting to roughly 89,000 square kilometres. The territorial division of the country into *distritos, concelhos* and *freguesias* has been maintained up to the present. In 1878 the number of *distritos* was 21 and only rose to 22 when the islands were given the status of a *distrito*. The number of *concelhos* was also more or less stable, but the number of *freguesias* rose due to the founding of new settlements. Concerning regional organization see also Quick (1994) and Caramani, Flora, Kraus, and Quick (1998).

APPENDIX TABLE P.1 Population structure at census dates 1864–1940

Census number	Census date	Census population			Marital status				Age group		
		Total	Male	Female	Single	Married	Widowed	Divorced	0–14	15–64	65+
					Absolute						
1	1 I 1864	4,188,410	2,005,540	2,182,870	2,620,519	1,289,847	278,044	..	1,418,348[1]	2,569,350[2]	195,034[3]
2	1 I 1878	4,550,699	2,175,829	2,374,870	2,790,761	1,471,776	288,162	..	1,535,406[1]	2,793,798[2]	215,044[3]
3	1 XII 1890	5,049,729	2,430,339	2,619,390	3,067,408	1,669,874	312,441	..	1,669,139	3,059,675	301,727
4	1 XII 1900	5,423,132	2,591,600	2,831,532	3,297,810	1,787,465	335,278	2,579[4]	1,827,541	3,273,893	309,579
5	1 XII 1911	5,960,056	2,828,691	3,131,365	3,620,121	1,971,641	360,824	7,470[5]	2,045,085	3,549,686	350,861
6	1 XII 1920	6,032,991	2,855,818	3,177,173	3,639,028	2,008,876	375,064	10,023[5]	1,966,444	3,682,412	356,405
7	1 XII 1930	6,825,883	3,255,876	3,570,007	4,016,962	2,370,106	422,757	16,058[5]	2,178,102	4,211,433	423,631
8	12 XII 1940	7,732,152	3,711,748	4,020,404	4,557,191	2,689,714	462,726	22,190[5]	2,468,218	4,742,071	498,292
					Per cent						
1	1 I 1864	100.00	47.88	52.12	62.57	30.80	6.64	..	33.86[1]	61.34[2]	4.66[3]
2	1 I 1878	100.00	47.81	52.19	61.33	32.34	6.33	..	33.74[1]	61.39[2]	4.73[3]
3	1 XII 1890	100.00	48.13	51.87	60.74	33.07	6.19	..	33.05	60.59	5.98
4	1 XII 1900	100.00	47.79	52.21	60.81	32.96	6.18	0.05[4]	33.70	60.37	5.71
5	1 XII 1911	100.00	47.46	52.54	60.74	33.08	6.05	0.13[5]	34.31	59.56	5.89
6	1 XII 1920	100.00	47.34	52.66	60.32	33.30	6.22	0.17[5]	32.59	61.04	5.91
7	1 XII 1930	100.00	47.70	52.30	58.85	34.72	6.19	0.24[5]	31.91	61.70	6.21
8	12 XII 1940	100.00	48.00	52.00	58.94	34.79	5.98	0.29[5]	31.92	61.33	6.44

Notes: [1] 0–15. [2] 16–65. [3] 66+. [4] Separated only. [5] Divorced and separated.

APPENDIX TABLE P.2 Census population by region 1878–1940 (per cent)

Distrito	1878	1890	1900	1911	1920	1930	1940
Continente	**91.41**	**92.28**	**92.51**	**92.77**	**93.19**	**93.13**	**93.09**
Aveiro	5.65	5.68	5.62	5.76	5.70	5.70	5.58
Beja	3.12	3.13	3.03	2.91	3.33	3.57	3.58
Braga	7.01	6.69	6.57	6.16	6.23	6.08	6.29
Bragança	3.71	3.56	3.40	3.35	2.82	2.75	2.76
Castello Branco	3.82	4.06	3.98	4.06	3.96	3.85	3.93
Coimbra	6.42	6.28	6.22	6.15	5.85	5.54	5.36
Evora	2.35	2.34	2.37	2.11	2.54	2.63	2.71
Faro	4.37	4.53	4.72	4.67	4.44	4.35	4.13
Guarda	5.01	4.95	4.87	4.60	4.24	3.80	3.82
Leiria	4.24	4.30	4.44	4.50	4.62	4.55	4.62
Lisboa	10.94	12.10	12.83	14.33	15.48	13.26	13.60
Portalegre	2.22	2.24	2.31	2.19	2.44	2.42	2.44
Porto	10.15	10.81	10.98	11.43	11.64	11.98	12.13
Santarem	4.86	5.05	5.20	5.50	5.50	5.55	5.49
Setubal[1]	..	..	..	..	..	3.42	3.48
Vianna do Castello	4.42	4.10	4.02	3.79	3.75	3.42	3.37
Villa Real	4.94	4.69	4.42	4.23	3.90	3.76	3.75
Vizeu	8.17	7.74	7.55	7.02	6.71	6.49	6.05
Ilhas Adjacentes	**8.57**	**7.72**	**7.47**	**7.23**	**6.81**	**6.87**	**6.92**
Acores	..	..	..	..	..	..	..
Angra do Heroismo	1.58	1.43	1.34	1.23	1.11	1.04	1.01
Horta	1.36	1.17	1.01	0.88	0.78	0.72	0.68
Ponta Delgada	2.77	2.48	2.37	2.14	1.96	1.98	2.01
Funchal (Madeira)	2.88	2.65	2.75	2.99	2.97	3.11	3.22
TOTAL	**100.00**	**100.00**	**100.00**	**100.00**	**100.00**	**100.00**	**100.00**

Note: [1] *Setúbal* was separated from *Lisboa* in the 1920s.

APPENDIX TABLE P.3 Population density by region 1878–1940 (inhabitants per sq. km.)

Distrito	1878	1890	1900	1911	1920	1930	1940
Continente	**46**	**52**	**57**	**60**	**63**	**72**	**81**
Aveiro	88	99	111	119	125	140	160
Beja	13	15	16	16	20	24	27
Braga	117	123	133	130	140	152	179
Bragança	25	27	28	29	26	29	33
Castello Branco	26	31	32	35	36	39	45
Coimbra	75	82	87	90	90	95	105
Evora	15	17	17	16	21	24	28
Faro	41	47	51	53	53	58	63
Guarda	41	45	48	48	47	47	54
Leiria	55	62	71	75	82	90	104
Lisboa	66	87	88	103	118	329	384
Portalegre	16	18	20	20	24	27	31
Porto	198	238	259	282	304	358	412
Santarem	32	37	43	47	50	57	64
Setubal[1]	..	..	..	..	..	46	53
Vianna do Castello	90	92	99	97	102	111	124
Villa Real	51	53	56	56	55	60	69
Vizeu	75	79	82	80	81	88	94
Ilhas Adjacentes	**122**	**122**	**127**	**129**	**128**	**152**	**173**
Acores	..	..	..	..	..	..	..
Angra do Heroismo	99	99	100	96	92	102	112
Horta	79	75	70	64	60	64	69
Ponta Delgada	144	143	148	140	135	160	185
Funchal (Madeira)	161	164	184	209	220	271	314
TOTAL	**49**	**55**	**59**	**62**	**66**	**74**	**85**

Note: [1] *Setúbal* was separated from *Lisboa* in the 1920s.

APPENDIX TABLE P.4 Demographic developments 1850–1945 (absolute figures and rates)

Year	Mid-year population	Natural population growth rate	Population growth rate	Net migration rate	Crude birth rate	Legitimate births per 10,000 married women age 15–44	Illegitimate births per 10,000 unmarried women age 15–44	Illeg. births per 100 leg. births
1850	3,811,191	..	2.2	..	..	..	..	..
1851	3,819,423	..	2.2	..	..	..	..	..
1852	3,827,655	..	2.2	..	..	..	..	..
1853	3,835,887	..	2.1	..	..	..	..	..
1854	3,844,119	..	2.1	..	..	..	..	..
1855	3,844,119	..	0.0	..	..	..	..	..
1856	3,844,119	..	0.0	..	..	..	..	..
1857	3,844,119	..	0.0	..	..	..	..	..
1858	3,923,410	..	20.2	..	..	..	..	..
1859	3,960,717	..	9.4	..	..	..	..	..
1860	3,998,023	..	9.3	..	..	..	..	..
1861	4,035,330	..	9.2	..	..	..	..	..
1862	4,086,357	..	12.5	..	..	..	..	..
1863	4,137,383	..	12.3	..	..	..	..	..
1864	4,188,410	..	12.2	..	..	..	..	..
1865	4,214,288	..	6.1	..	..	..	..	..
1866	4,240,166	..	6.1	..	..	..	..	..
1867	4,266,043	..	6.1	..	..	..	..	..
1868	4,291,921	..	6.0	..	..	..	..	..
1869	4,317,799	..	6.0	..	..	..	..	..
1870	4,343,677	..	6.0	..	..	..	..	..
1871	4,369,555	..	5.9	..	..	..	..	..
1872	4,395,432	..	5.9	..	..	..	..	..
1873	4,421,310	..	5.9	..	..	..	..	..
1874	4,447,188	..	5.8	..	..	..	..	..
1875	4,473,066	..	5.8	..	..	..	..	..
1876	4,498,943	..	5.8	..	..	..	..	..
1877	4,524,821	..	5.7	..	..	..	..	..
1878	4,550,699	..	5.7	..	..	..	..	..
1879	4,592,285	..	9.1	..	..	..	..	..
1880	4,633,871	..	9.0	..	..	..	..	..
1881	4,675,457	..	8.9	..	..	..	..	..
1882	4,717,042	..	8.8	..	..	..	..	..
1883	4,758,628	..	8.7	..	..	..	..	..
1884	4,800,214	..	8.7	..	..	..	..	..
1885	4,841,800	..	8.6	..	..	..	..	..
1886	4,883,386	11.5	8.5	-2.9	31.8	..	..	..
1887	4,924,972	11.6	8.4	-3.1	33.7	..	..	..
1888	4,966,557	11.2	8.4	-2.8	33.0	2,856	320	14.0
1889	5,008,143	11.0	8.3	-2.7	33.6	2,917	323	13.8
1890	5,049,729	7.1	8.2	1.1	32.6	2,833	314	13.8
1891	5,087,069	8.9	7.3	-1.6	31.9	2,777	296	13.3
1892	5,124,410	10.7	7.3	-3.4	31.1	2,689	297	13.7
1893	5,161,750	10.4	7.2	-3.2	31.8	2,741	308	13.9
1894	5,199,090	8.8	7.2	-1.7	29.6	2,536	296	14.4
1895	5,236,431	9.2	7.1	-2.0	29.9	2,554	296	14.2
1896	5,273,771	7.1	7.1	0.0	29.9	2,546	298	14.4
1897	5,311,111	8.5	7.0	-1.5	30.3	2,575	303	14.4

continued

APPENDIX TABLE P.4 Demographic developments 1850–1945 (absolute figures and rates)

Crude death rate	Infant mortality rate	Stillbirth rate	Infant mortality and stillbirth rate	Crude marriage rate	Persons marrying per 10,000 unmarried persons age 15+	Persons marrying per 10,000 unmarried persons age 15–49	Crude divorce rate	Divorces per 100 marriages	Divorces per 10,000 married persons	Year
..	..	..	..	..	..	..	..	..	..	1850
..	..	..	..	..	..	..	..	..	..	1851
..	..	..	..	..	..	..	..	..	..	1852
..	..	..	..	..	..	..	..	..	..	1853
..	..	..	..	..	..	..	..	..	..	1854
..	..	..	..	..	..	..	..	..	..	1855
..	..	..	..	..	..	..	..	..	..	1856
..	..	..	..	..	..	..	..	..	..	1857
..	..	..	..	..	..	..	..	..	..	1858
..	..	..	..	..	..	..	..	..	..	1859
..	..	..	..	..	..	..	..	..	..	1860
..	..	..	..	..	..	..	..	..	..	1861
..	..	..	..	..	..	..	..	..	..	1862
..	..	..	..	..	..	..	..	..	..	1863
..	..	..	..	..	..	..	..	..	..	1864
..	..	..	..	..	..	..	..	..	..	1865
..	..	..	..	..	..	..	..	..	..	1866
..	..	..	..	..	..	..	..	..	..	1867
..	..	..	..	..	..	..	..	..	..	1868
..	..	..	..	..	..	..	..	..	..	1869
..	..	..	..	..	..	..	..	..	..	1870
..	..	..	..	..	..	..	..	..	..	1871
..	..	..	..	..	..	..	..	..	..	1872
..	..	..	..	..	..	..	..	..	..	1873
..	..	..	..	..	..	..	..	..	..	1874
..	..	..	..	..	..	..	..	..	..	1875
..	..	..	..	..	..	..	..	..	..	1876
..	..	..	..	..	..	..	..	..	..	1877
..	..	..	..	..	..	..	..	..	..	1878
..	..	..	..	..	..	..	..	..	..	1879
..	..	..	..	..	..	..	..	..	..	1880
..	..	..	..	..	..	..	..	..	..	1881
..	..	..	..	..	..	..	..	..	..	1882
..	..	..	..	..	..	..	..	..	..	1883
..	..	..	..	..	..	..	..	..	..	1884
..	..	..	..	..	..	..	..	..	..	1885
20.4	..	..	..	6.9	411	532	..	..	..	1886
22.2	..	..	..	7.0	415	539	..	..	..	1887
21.8	..	..	..	6.8	407	530	..	..	..	1888
22.6	..	..	..	7.0	415	541	..	..	..	1889
25.5	..	..	..	7.1	422	552	..	..	..	1890
22.9	..	..	..	6.8	406	531	..	..	..	1891
20.3	..	..	..	6.8	406	531	..	..	..	1892
21.4	..	..	..	6.6	395	516	..	..	..	1893
20.8	..	..	..	6.4	382	499	..	..	..	1894
20.7	..	..	..	6.4	381	498	..	..	..	1895
22.8	..	..	..	6.3	376	491	..	..	..	1896
21.8	..	..	..	6.8	410	535	..	..	..	1897

continued

APPENDIX TABLE P.4 Demographic developments 1850–1945 (continued)

Year	Mid-year population	Natural population growth rate	Population growth rate	Net migration rate	Crude birth rate	Legitimate births per 10,000 married women age 15–44	Illegitimate births per 10,000 unmarried women age 15–44	Illeg. births per 100 leg. births
1898	5,348,451	8.8	7.0	-1.8	30.1	2,568	287	13.7
1899	5,385,792	9.7	6.9	-2.8	29.8	2,547	279	13.3
1900	5,423,132	10.1	6.9	-3.2	30.5	2,599	282	13.2
1901	5,471,943	10.4	8.9	-1.4	31.2	2,647	296	13.5
1902	5,520,755	12.3	8.8	-3.4	31.9	2,698	301	13.4
1903	5,569,566	12.8	8.8	-4.1	32.9	2,786	301	13.0
1904	5,618,377	12.7	8.7	-4.0	31.5	2,655	288	12.9
1905	5,667,188	11.8	8.6	-3.2	31.7	2,671	290	12.9
1906	5,716,000	10.1	8.5	-1.6	32.0	2,687	293	12.9
1907	5,764,811	11.0	8.5	-2.5	30.6	2,565	278	12.8
1908	5,813,622	10.3	8.4	-1.9	30.2	..	..	..
1909	5,862,433	10.6	8.3	-2.3	29.8	..	..	..
1910	5,911,245	12.5	8.3	-4.2	31.6	..	..	..
1911	5,960,056	16.6	8.2	-8.4	38.6	..	..	..
1912	5,968,160	14.8	1.4	-13.4	34.8	..	..	..
1913	5,976,264	11.9	1.4	-10.5	32.4	..	..	..
1914	5,984,368	12.2	1.4	-10.8	31.5	..	..	..
1915	5,992,472	12.1	1.4	-10.8	32.6	..	..	..
1916	6,000,575	10.6	1.4	-9.2	32.1	..	..	..
1917	6,008,679	9.0	1.3	-7.7	31.4	..	..	..
1918	6,016,783	-11.7	1.3	13.0	29.7	..	..	..
1919	6,024,887	2.2	1.3	-0.9	27.6	..	..	..
1920	6,032,991	10.0	1.3	-8.6	33.6	..	..	..
1921	6,112,280	11.6	13.0	1.4	32.2	..	..	..
1922	6,191,569	12.6	12.8	0.2	32.9	..	..	..
1923	6,270,859	10.4	12.6	2.2	33.0	..	..	..
1924	6,350,148	12.8	12.5	-0.3	32.7	..	..	..
1925	6,429,437	14.2	12.3	-1.8	32.4	..	..	..
1926	6,508,726	13.7	12.2	-1.5	33.3	..	..	..
1927	6,588,015	12.1	12.0	0.0	30.8	..	..	..
1928	6,667,305	13.1	11.9	-1.2	31.7	..	..	..
1929	6,746,594	12.2	11.8	-0.4	29.8	2,332	330	16.5
1930	6,825,883	12.6	11.6	-1.0	29.7	..	..	..
1931	6,918,337	12.8	13.4	0.5	29.5	..	..	..
1932	7,011,791	12.7	13.3	0.6	29.7	2,311	342	17.1
1933	7,104,745	11.7	13.1	1.4	28.8	2,236	338	17.3
1934	7,197,699	11.8	12.9	1.2	28.2	..	..	..
1935	7,290,653	11.1	12.7	1.7	28.0	..	..	..
1936	7,383,607	11.7	12.6	0.9	27.8	2,153	346	18.4
1937	7,476,561	10.8	12.4	1.6	26.5	2,044	336	18.7
1938	7,569,515	11.1	12.3	1.2	26.4	2,038	331	18.5
1939	7,662,469	10.8	12.1	1.3	26.0	2,007	329	18.6
1940	7,755,423	8.7	12.0	3.3	24.2	..	..	18.6
1941	7,830,905	6.3	9.6	3.3	23.5	..	..	17.8
1942	7,906,386	7.7	9.5	1.8	23.7	..	..	16.3
1943	7,981,868	9.5	9.5	-0.1	24.8	..	..	15.5
1944	8,057,350	10.2	9.4	-0.8	25.0	..	..	15.0
1945	8,132,832	11.5	9.3	-2.2	25.7	..	..	14.4

APPENDIX TABLE P.4 Demographic developments 1850–1945 (continued)

Crude death rate	Infant mortality rate	Stillbirth rate	Infant mortality and stillbirth rate	Crude marriage rate	Persons marrying per 10,000 unmarried persons age 15+	Persons marrying per 10,000 unmarried persons age 15–49	Crude divorce rate	Divorces per 100 marriages	Divorces per 10,000 married persons	Year
21.3	..	..	..	6.5	394	515	..	..	..	1898
20.1	..	..	..	6.8	409	535	..	..	..	1899
20.3	..	10.1	..	6.8	409	534	..	..	..	1900
20.9	..	10.1	..	6.9	418	546	..	..	..	1901
19.6	..	16.0	..	7.0	424	554	..	..	..	1902
20.1	..	16.8	..	6.9	421	550	..	..	..	1903
18.8	..	16.6	..	6.5	397	519	..	..	..	1904
19.9	..	16.6	..	6.6	404	528	..	..	..	1905
21.9	..	15.7	..	6.2	379	495	..	..	..	1906
19.6	..	15.6	..	6.1	375	490	..	..	..	1907
19.9	..	14.9	..	6.2	377	493	..	..	..	1908
19.2	..	15.5	..	6.1	375	490	..	..	..	1909
19.1	133.9	14.6	148.5	6.6	405	530	..	..	..	1910
22.0	..	22.6	..	6.9	427	558	..	..	..	1911
20.0	..	36.1	..	7.4	457	597	..	..	..	1912
20.6	159.6	36.9	196.5	5.9	363	475	..	..	..	1913
19.3	148.5	39.5	188.0	6.1	..	..	..	..	..	1914
20.4	148.2	40.3	188.5	6.0	..	..	..	..	..	1915
21.6	153.6	41.6	195.2	6.0	..	..	..	..	..	1916
22.3	148.4	41.4	189.8	5.6	..	..	..	..	..	1917
41.4	209.1	45.3	254.4	5.0	..	..	..	..	..	1918
25.4	181.7	42.0	223.8	7.8	460	588	..	..	..	1919
23.7	164.1	43.2	207.3	8.8	520	664	..	..	..	1920
20.7	147.7	44.8	192.5	8.4	497	635	..	..	..	1921
20.3	144.0	44.7	188.7	8.1	480	614	..	..	..	1922
22.6	164.1	44.6	208.7	7.8	466	596	..	..	..	1923
19.9	143.8	43.6	187.4	7.3	434	555	..	..	..	1924
18.3	132.1	43.7	175.8	7.1	423	541	..	..	..	1925
19.7	144.2	41.9	186.2	7.4	440	564	..	..	..	1926
18.7	141.5	41.5	183.0	6.3	379	486	..	..	..	1927
18.6	..	40.2	..	6.8	408	523	..	..	..	1928
17.6	151.2	43.1	194.4	6.6	396	508	0.1	2.0	7.8	1929
17.0	143.6	42.6	186.2	7.0	421	540	..	..	..	1930
16.7	140.6	43.3	184.0	6.5	391	501	..	..	..	1931
17.0	146.5	44.1	190.6	6.5	390	500	0.1	1.9	7.2	1932
17.0	148.5	43.8	192.3	6.5	389	499	0.1	1.8	6.7	1933
16.5	144.0	44.8	188.7	6.6	398	510	..	..	..	1934
16.9	148.7	45.0	193.7	6.7	405	520	..	..	..	1935
16.1	139.7	45.7	185.4	6.3	380	488	0.1	2.0	7.3	1936
15.7	151.4	46.6	198.0	6.3	378	486	0.1	1.5	5.5	1937
15.2	137.2	46.0	183.2	6.5	390	501	0.1	1.8	6.8	1938
15.1	119.9	45.1	165.0	6.3	383	492	0.1	1.6	5.9	1939
15.5	126.1	47.1	173.2	6.0	..	..	0.1	1.4	..	1940
17.2	150.8	47.8	198.5	7.0	..	..	0.1	1.2	..	1941
16.0	131.4	47.5	178.8	7.4	..	..	0.1	1.3	..	1942
15.3	132.6	46.4	179.1	7.3	..	..	0.1	1.6	..	1943
14.8	122.2	46.2	168.3	7.4	..	..	0.1	1.6	..	1944
14.2	114.9	42.5	157.5	7.6	..	..	0.1	1.6	..	1945

APPENDIX TABLE P.5 Life expectancy by age 1929/32–1945 (in years)

Age	0	10	20	30	40	50	60	70	80
				Males					
1929–1932[1]	49.66	54.19	45.72	38.21	29.96	22.10	14.65	8.34	..
1939–1942	48.58	52.61	44.00	36.04	28.23	20.76	13.86	8.18	4.54
1941	47.26	52.45	43.83	35.81	27.84	20.02	12.63	6.18	..
1945	51.06	53.56	44.74	36.76	28.82	21.37	14.44	8.56	..
				Females					
1929–1932[1]	49.66	54.19	45.72	38.21	29.96	22.10	14.65	8.34	..
1939–1942	52.82	56.86	48.35	40.35	32.17	23.98	16.20	9.59	5.13
1941	50.99	56.34	48.03	40.19	32.22	24.32	16.85	10.66	..
1945	56.17	58.63	59.96	41.82	33.49	25.15	17.18	10.28	..

Note: [1] Average for both sexes.

APPENDIX TABLE P.6A Households by type 1890–1940 (absolute and per cent)

Census year	Household types and members									
	Total households	Private households	Family households	One-person households	Institutional households	Total household members	Private household members	Family household members	One-person household members	Institutional household members
Absolute										
1890	..	1,248,483	1,104,999	143,484	..	..	5,049,729	4,906,245	143,484	..
1900	1,301,715	1,300,082	1,160,253	139,829	1,633	..	5,423,132	5,283,303	139,829	..
1911	..	1,411,327	1,272,760	138,567	..	..	5,960,056	5,821,489	138,567	..
1920	..	1,426,242	1,302,456	123,786	..	6,080,135	6,032,991	5,909,205	123,786	..
1930	..	1,672,000	..	..	..	..	6,825,883	..	..	..
1940	1,821,161	1,811,645	1,669,887	141,758	9,516	7,755,423	7,621,165	7,479,407	141,758	169,089
Total households per cent										
1890	..	..	..	..	..	..				
1900	100.00	99.87	89.13	10.74	0.13	100.00				
1911	..	..	..	..	..	..				
1920	..	..	..	..	..	..				
1930	..	..	..	..	..	..				
1940	100.00	99.48	91.69	7.78	0.52	100.00	98.27	96.44	1.83	2.18
Private households per cent										
1890		100.00	88.51	11.49	..		100.00	97.16	2.84	..
1900		100.00	89.24	10.76	..		100.00	97.42	2.58	..
1911		100.00	90.18	9.82	..		100.00	97.68	2.32	..
1920		100.00	91.32	8.68	..		100.00	97.95	2.05	..
1930		..	..	..	..		..	..	..	..
1940		100.00	92.18	7.82	..		100.00	98.14	1.86	..

APPENDIX TABLE P.6B Households by size and members 1890–1940 (absolute figures)

Census year	Private households total		Households by number of members					
		1 person	2 persons	3 persons	4 persons	5 persons	6 persons	7+ persons
				Households				
1890	1,248,483	143,484	217,158	223,810	201,138	162,978	121,158	178,801
1900	1,300,082	139,829	221,422	232,749	210,114	171,046	127,611	197,311
1911	1,411,327	138,567	229,026	247,887	229,110	191,401	163,523	211,813
1920	1,426,242	123,786	231,243	257,331	240,319	199,212	173,499	200,852
1940	1,811,645	141,758	294,307	352,077	321,734	251,346	179,785	270,638
				Persons				
1890	5,049,729	143,484	434,316	671,430	804,552	814,890	726,948	1,454,109
1900	5,423,132	139,829	442,844	698,247	840,456	855,230	765,666	1,680,860
1911	5,960,056	138,567	458,052	743,661	916,440	957,005	981,138	1,765,193
1920	6,032,991	123,786	462,486	771,993	961,276	996,060	1,040,994	1,676,396
1940	7,621,165	141,758	588,614	1,056,231	1,286,936	1,256,730	1,078,710	2,212,186

APPENDIX TABLE P.6C Households by size and members 1890–1940 (per cent)

Census year	Private households total		Households by number of members					
		1 person	2 persons	3 persons	4 persons	5 persons	6 persons	7+ persons
				Households				
1890	100.00	11.49	17.39	17.93	16.11	13.05	9.70	14.32
1900	100.00	10.76	17.03	17.90	16.16	13.16	9.82	15.18
1911	100.00	9.82	16.23	17.56	16.23	13.56	11.59	15.01
1920	100.00	8.68	16.21	18.04	16.85	13.97	12.16	14.08
1940	100.00	7.82	16.25	19.43	17.76	13.87	9.92	14.94
				Persons				
1890	100.00	2.84	8.60	13.30	15.93	16.14	14.40	28.80
1900	100.00	2.58	8.17	12.88	15.50	15.77	14.12	30.99
1911	100.00	2.32	7.69	12.48	15.38	16.06	16.46	29.62
1920	100.00	2.05	7.67	12.80	15.93	16.51	17.26	27.79
1940	100.00	1.86	7.72	13.86	16.89	16.49	14.15	29.03

APPENDIX TABLE P.6D Household indicators 1835–1940

Census year	Population			Fogos			Mean total household size			Mean private household size Portugal
	Portugal	Mainland	Islands	Portugal	Mainland	Islands	Portugal	Mainland	Islands	Portugal
1835	..	3,061,584	..	..	791,492	..	..	3.87	..	..
1838	..	3,224,474	..	..	827,947	..	..	3.89	..	..
1841	3,737,103	3,396,972	340,131	918,951	840,928	78,023	4.07	4.04	4.36	..
1854	3,844,119	3,499,121	344,998	999,538	919,947	79,591	3.85	3.80	4.33	..
1858	3,923,410	3,584,677	338,733	1,029,240	949,075	80,165	3.81	3.78	4.23	..
1864	4,188,410	3,829,618	358,792	1,041,238	958,201	83,037	4.02	4.00	4.32	..
1878	4,550,699	4,160,315	390,384	1,132,871	1,040,565	92,306	4.02	4.00	4.23	..
1890	5,049,729	4,660,095	389,634	1,245,720	1,151,609	94,111	4.05	4.05	4.14	4.04
1900	..	..	..	..	..	..	..	..	..	4.17
1911	..	..	..	..	..	..	..	..	..	4.22
1920	..	..	..	..	..	..	..	..	..	4.23
1940	..	..	..	..	..	..	..	..	..	4.08

APPENDIX TABLE P.7 Dates and nature of results on population structure, households/families, and vital statistics

Topic	Intro-duction	Remarks
Population		
Population at census dates	1864	The first fully published census was conducted in 1864. Earlier censuses were organized in 1801, 1821, 1835, 1841, 1854, 1858, and 1861. The censuses from 1801 to 1838 covered only the mainland and not the islands (cf. *Bibliography*, census publication for 1890, vol. I, p. LXIIf.).
Population by age, sex, and marital status	1864	
Households and families		
Households (*fogos* or *familias*)		
Total households	1864, 1878, 1890, 1900, 1911, 1920, 1930, 1940, 1950	First general census was conducted in 1864, but retrospective figures on the number of households (*fogos* or *familias*) are available also since 1835. In 1890 households by size and number of institutional households was introduced. Institutional households distinguished since 1940, earlier only one figure for *familias* or *fogos*. *Disaggregations*: regional disaggregation since 1864. For 1864– only the absolute number of private households is given. No disaggregation by sex, age, civil status, or profession of household head.
Households by size	1890, 1900, 1911, 1920, 1940, 1950	First time in 1890 in several categories. In 1900 households with 1–7+ persons; number of institutional households. Not published for 1930.
Households by composition	–	Only introduced in 1960.
Households by profession of household head	–	
Families (*familias*)		
Families by number of children	1940, 1950	The first investigation was introduced for the population census of 1940. Repeated in 1950: results are published in vol. I, pp. 288–541 (married couples and unmarried women by number of children).

continued

APPENDIX TABLE P.7 Dates and nature of results on population structure, households/families, and vital statistics (continued)

Topic	Intro-duction	Remarks
Population movement		
Mid-year population	1841	Calculated by using census data. Census data are available for all of Portugal (mainland and islands) for 1801 and starting from 1841. Population census figures for the mainland only are available far back in history for the years 1527, 1636, 1732, 1768, and 1801 and following (see above). Mid-year population for all of Portugal has been calculated since 1841 by linear interpolation. Mid-year resident population on 31 December has been published since 1941 in the Statistical Yearbook (1976, 25; 1989, 15).
Births		
Live births	1886	
Stillbirths	1900	
Legitimate births	1888	
Illegitimate births	1888	
Deaths		
Total deaths	1886	
Infants (under 1 year)	1910	
Marriages		
Total marriages	1886	
Divorces and separations		
Total divorces	1929	
Total legal separations	1966?	Of some importance until the liberalization of divorce law in 1974, because of the virtual non-existence of divorce. Divorces in 1966: 695, legal separations: 577. With the extension of divorce, legal separations dwindled. The last figure for 1979 was 76 legal separations.

APPENDIX FIGURE P.8 Population by age, sex and marital status, Portugal 1864,
1878, 1900, 1920, 1930 and 1940 (per 10,000 of total population)

Portugal, 1864

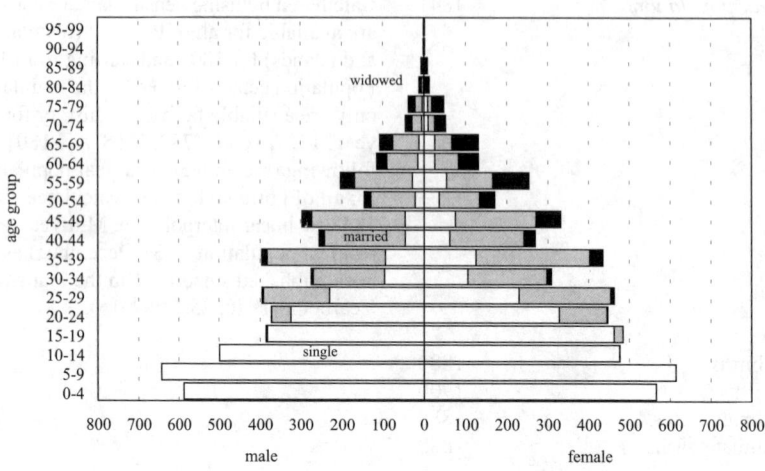

Portugal, 1878

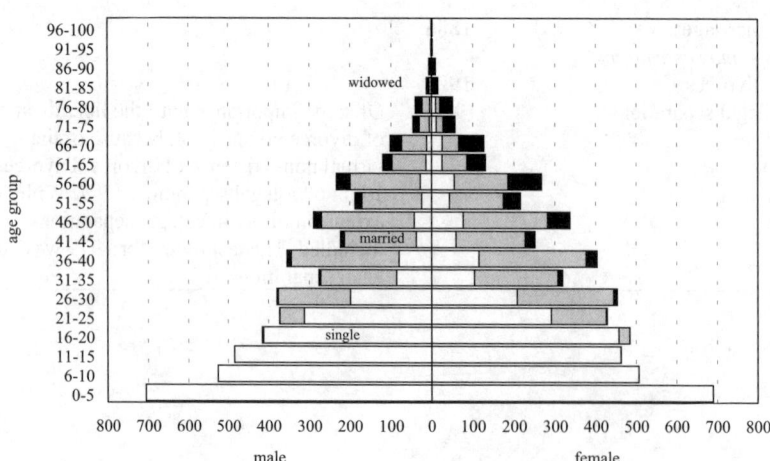

APPENDIX FIGURE P.8 Population by age, sex and marital status, Portugal 1864, 1878, 1900, 1920, 1930 and 1940 (per 10,000 of total population) (continued)

Portugal, 1900

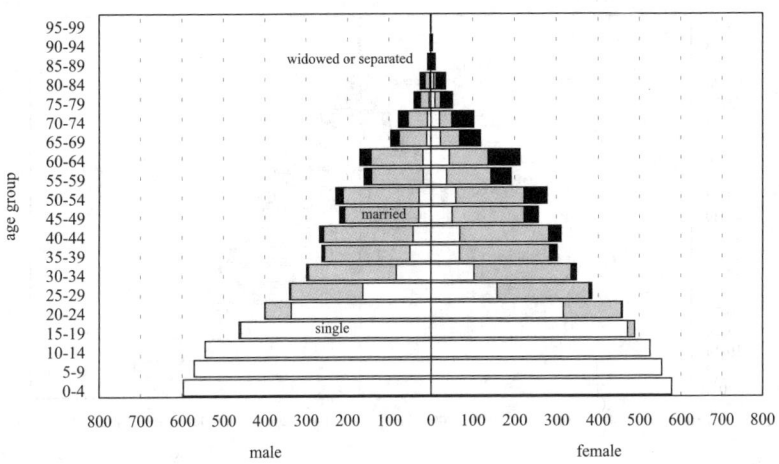

Portugal, 1920

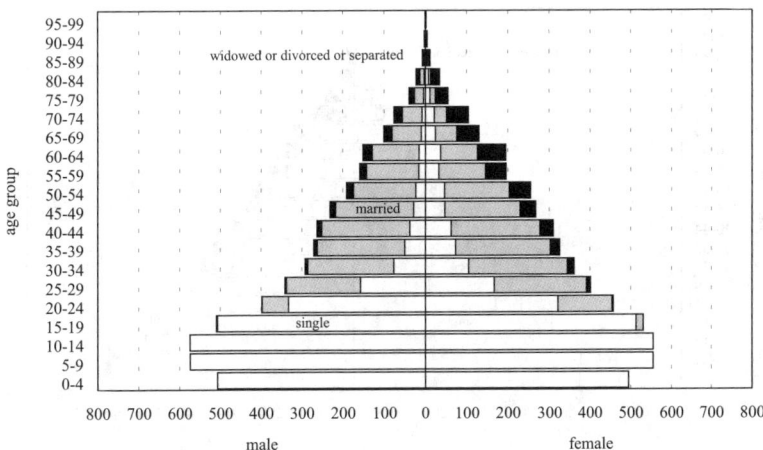

APPENDIX FIGURE P.8 Population by age, sex and marital status, Portugal 1864, 1878, 1900, 1920, 1930 and 1940 (per 10,000 of total population) (continued)

Portugal, 1930

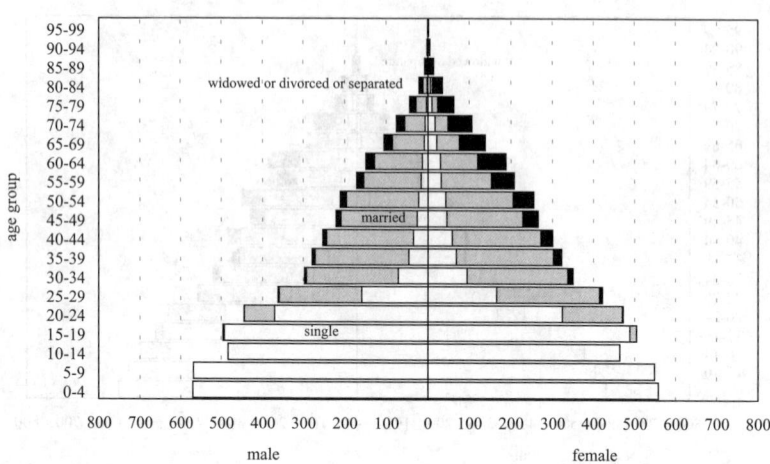

Portugal, 1940

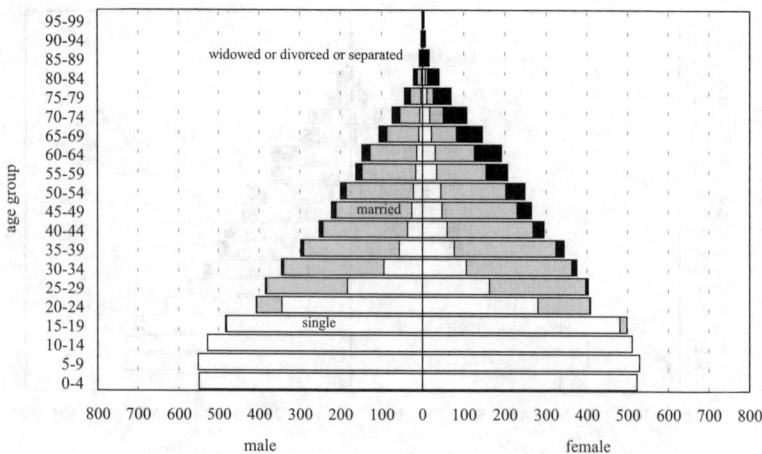

18

Spain

Due to the character of the Iberian Peninsula, Spain has undergone only minor boundary changes since the unification of the country in the fifteenth century. Nevertheless there have been two territorial questions: the first concerned the existence of Portugal and thus the unification of the Iberian Peninsula under one crown. But after the Portuguese struggle for independence in the sixteenth and early seventeenth century, there were no more Spanish attempts to regain the Portuguese territory. The other conflict concerned Catalonia, because the former Counts of Catalonia had possessions on both sides of the Pyrenees. This caused conflict with the French king, but after the seventeenth century the Pyrenees were increasingly regarded as the 'natural' border between the two countries.

Territorial changes affected the colonial empire to a much greater extent. Since the eighteenth century Spain slowly but steadily had to give up its colonies, first the European ones, and later those overseas. The war with the United States of America in 1898 ended Spain's status as a colonial power. Nevertheless, in Europe Spain was able to retain several territories off the mainland: the Canary Islands in the Atlantic Ocean, the Balearic Islands in the Mediterranean, and Ceuta and Melilla on the African continent (surrounded by Moroccan territory).

Spain declared neutrality in both World War I and World War II and was therefore not subject to any changes in territorial status (Catalan, 1995; Jurado, 1997; Reher, 1997; Carr, 1982; Pérez Moreda and Reher, 1988; Gómez Redondo, 1992; Livi-Bacci, 1968).

REGIONAL POPULATION STRUCTURE

Despite its fairly large population in European comparison and in absolute terms, Spain's large territory makes it a very sparsely populated country, at least on the national average. In 1877 there were only 33 inhabitants per square kilometre. By 1940 population density in Spain had only increased to 51 inhabitants per square kilometre. This low increase in population density during the demographic transition is mainly due to the low population growth in Spain up to World War II.

While overall population growth and density was rather low, regional differences have been very high and more or less reflect *differences in economic development*. During the nineteenth and twentieth centuries some major economic and population centres evolved: the district of the capital Madrid, Barcelona and surroundings, and the southern Mediterranean coast. Industrialization and tourism have benefited mainly the coastal regions near Barcelona and along the Mediterranean coast. On the other hand, several regions moved to a more peripheral status, in particular Galicia and the area along the Portuguese border. Strong migration from the interior to the developing centres set in, causing a growing disparity and divergence in settlement structure (cf. Jurado, 1997; Kern, 1995).

Already in 1877 the province of Castilla-La Mancha had the highest population density, amounting to 148 inhabitants per sq. km., while the national average was 33. The province of Madrid came in second in population density (74), followed by País Vasco (64). This rank order remained identical in 1940. Nevertheless, urbanization had started already during this period. The relative growth of the capital Madrid was higher than that of the province of Castilla-La Mancha. Population density in Madrid nearly tripled from 1877–1940. Average population density in the province of Cataluña also grew rapidly, driven by growth in Barcelona (from 109 inhabitants per sq. km. in 1877 to 251 in 1940). Already in the first half of the twentieth century the archipelagos of the Balearic Islands (81 persons per sq. km. in 1940) and Canary Islands (91 persons per sq. km. in 1940) developed into rather densely populated regions.

POPULATION GROWTH

In 1877 the country had 16.632 million inhabitants. By 1940 the population had increased to 25.878 million inhabitants, an absolute increase of nearly ten million inhabitants in over sixty years. Compared with northern European countries, population growth was therefore limited, as we can also see from the demographic transition with a low natural surplus population. The low population growth in Spain during the demographic transition is also apparent in Figure E.1. The natural population growth rate was well under 10 per 1,000 from the 1860s to the 1940s, with the exception of the 1920s, when the rate fluctuated around 10 per 1,000. There were only a few years in which the natural population growth rate peaked at approximately 10 per 1,000: these were 1861–62, 1903, 1908, 1912, 1915, and 1943–45. The natural population growth rate was negative in 1918, an indirect consequence of World War I, and in 1939, the last year of the Spanish civil war. Major periods of declining natural population growth rates were 1898–1900 (Spanish–American War of 1898), World War I, and most severely the years of the Spanish civil war (1936–39), especially from 1937–39. Roughly one million people died or emigrated as a result of the civil war.

Given the low natural population growth, it becomes conceivable why emigration was on average fairly low in Spain from the 1860s to the late 1930s. From the 1860s to the early 1920s emigration was stronger than immigration, with some minor exceptions: these were 1901, 1918, 1931, the late 1930s, and the years of World War II. Immigration was stronger than emigration in 1937–42, partly as a result of the civil war, and partly as a result of refugees arriving in neutral Spain during World War II. After 1939 net migration peaked again positively in 1941.

THE FIRST DEMOGRAPHIC TRANSITION

In the second half of the nineteenth century, Spain had a high level of both fertility and mortality (Figure E.2). The crude birth rate was well over 35 births per 1,000 population. The birth rate began to decline late, around 1900, after the death rate had already begun to fall. During the second half of the nineteenth century the death rate was very high—due to the high infant mortality—but around 1900 the death rate fell faster than the birth rate, thus natural population growth increased. Both the birth

Figure E.1 Population growth and net migration 1858-1945

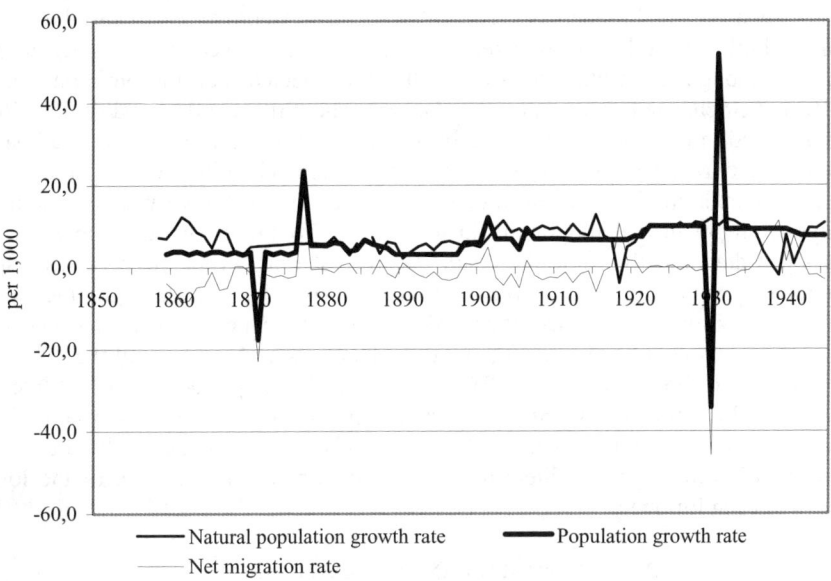

Figure E.2 First demographic transition 1858-1945

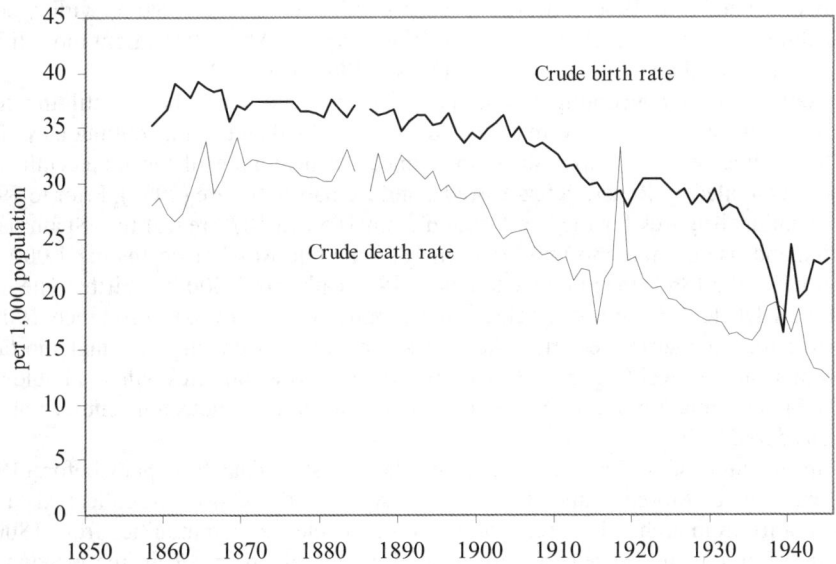

and death rates in the second half of the nineteenth century were influenced by historical events such as wars and epidemics. In the 1880s and early 1890s the death rate saw a remarkable increase. The 1898 Spanish–American War caused a decline in the birth rate followed by a recovery. World War I exerted an impact on both rates, although the death rate was much more affected than the birth rate and in effect even changed its plateau after the war. The birth rate declined during World War I, and in contrast to the strong birth decline in the rest of Europe, the Spanish birth rate during the 1920s was comparatively high. The effect was a rather strong natural population increase during the 1920s. The 1936–39 civil war was the major rupture in Spanish demographic history of the twentieth century: the birth rate dropped dramatically while the death rate rose sharply. After the civil war, Spain remained neutral during World War II; that is why the demographic curves recovered. Similar to France after 1945, Spain also experienced a long period of strong natural population growth, due to high and rising fertility until the 1980s and a low and declining death rate. The post-World War II period saw a 'real' second demographic transition in Spain, when the population increased substantially. A major decline in births began in the 1980s, affecting the country also during the 1990s. Like the other Mediterranean countries, Spain now has one of the lowest birth rates in Europe.

MORTALITY AND LIFE EXPECTANCY

The infant mortality rate is defined as deaths of children aged under one year per 1,000 live births. Spain belongs to the Mediterranean group of countries (including Austria and Czechoslovakia) which in 1900 had rather high infant mortality rates. Spain's rate from 1900 onwards is very similar to that of Austria, with a steep decline from a high level in 1900 up to World War II. After 1945 infant mortality in Spain remained on a rather high level (Masuy-Stroobant, 1997).

National data concerning infant mortality in Spain reach back until the mid-nineteenth century. They were collected from 1858–70 and again continuously since 1901. Time series for Spanish regions since the beginning of the nineteenth have been compiled by Reher, Pérez-Moreda, and Bernabeu-Mestre (1997). Prior to 1901, the national figures for the short period from 1858 to 1870 reveal that Spain had a high and rising infant mortality rate. In 1858 the rate was 171 deaths per 1,000 live births; in the 1860s the rate rose to nearly 190 deaths per 1,000 live births. The level from 1870 to 1900 probably fluctuated around this figure, because since 1901—when the time series restarts—there was a continuous decline in infant mortality from a similar level (Figure E.3). Compared with those countries with available data the Spanish infant mortality rate in the second half of the nineteenth century must be considered high.

In the light of the very fragmentary vital statistics data for Spain before 1901, Reher, Pérez-Moreda, and Bernabeu-Mestre (1997) chose to collect data on mortality from archival sources for a sample of selected communities from 1800 to 1960. The communes selected are located in central Spain and in the province of Alicante on the Mediterranean Sea. Data for central Spain show that the pretransitional level of infant mortality was very high and ranged between 200 and 250 deaths under 21 years of age per 1,000 live births. Second, infant mortality rose from the 1820s to the 1880s (a rising trend during the nineteenth century was already suggested by the national results from 1858–70) and more or less stagnated until 1900. After 1900 there was a falling trend often interrupted by upswings in the curve. During the first half of the twentieth century infant mortality declined very slowly; only after World War II did a decisive decline set in. In contrast to central Spain, the province of Alicante had much lower infant mortality, and the increase during the nineteenth century was not as steep. While infant mortality in Alicante was much lower, childhood mortality (age 1–4 years) was also as high as in central Spain, but only until the 1890s when the early childhood mortality rate of Alicante dropped rapidly, while that in central Spain declined only very slowly.

Life expectancy was low during the time period, compared with more advanced northern European countries. In 1900, life expectancy at birth was 33.9 years for boys and 35.7 years for girls, or 21 years less than for Swedish boys (1901/10: 54.5 years) and girls (1901/10: 57.0 years) (Figure E.4). Life expectancy was also rather low for young adults and for older people, although the difference to more advanced countries became smaller at higher ages. From 1900 to 1930 life expectancy increased for all ages: most for infants, and only a little for 30- and 60-year-olds. The Spanish civil war caused a decline in male life expectancy at all ages; between 1930 and 1940 life expectancy decreased most dramatically for 30-year-olds. Sex-specific differences in life expectancy were small in 1900, but increased slightly until 1930. The civil war increased this difference in women's favour: for 30-year-old women it increased from 2.9 years in 1930 to 6.0 years in 1940.

FERTILITY AND LEGITIMACY

Illegitimacy was traditionally low and under the European average in Spain. It reached its lowest level in the 1970s, due to the marriage boom in that decade with declining age at marriage. Due to the declining marriage rate and the rising age at marriage, illegitimacy began rising again around 1970 (Figure E.5).

Procreation in Spain was mainly marital procreation at a relatively high age. This can be seen in the legitimacy rate which was constantly (with minor exceptions) over the European average. Only since the major decline in births in the 1970s has legitimate fertility reached the European average. With below-average illegitimate fertility and average legitimate fertility, it is clear why Spain's total fertility in recent decades is so low compared to the European average.

Restricting procreation to married couples who married at rather high ages, thus reducing the reproductive time span considerably, did not inhibit fertility. Crude birth and crude death rates exceeded the European average for the whole demographic transition. But due to the very high mortality rate (probably due to high infant mortality) natural population growth was very low. A very high natural population growth can be seen only after World War II when mortality was greatly reduced and fertility rose. The reduction of fertility at younger ages was obviously balanced by increased fertility at higher ages. Thus, whereas women's mean age at birth of the first child was at the European level since around 1975, mean age at birth of any child was above the European average.

MARRIAGE AND DIVORCE

In general, Spain has a traditionally high age at marriage and therefore a marriage rate below the European average (Figure E.6), except from 1887 to World War I. On the other hand Spain is a country of traditionally universal marriage. At 10%, the

Figure E.3 Infant mortality 1858-1945

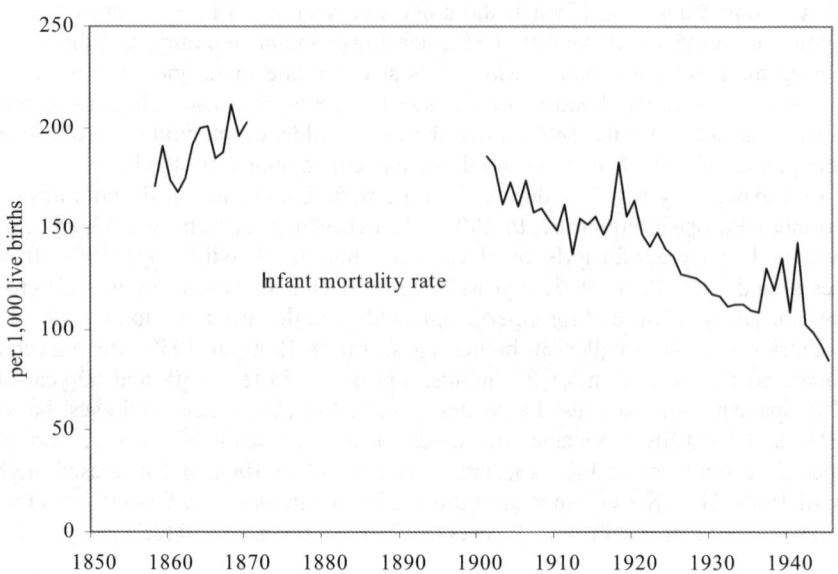

Figure E.4 Life expectancy 1900-1940

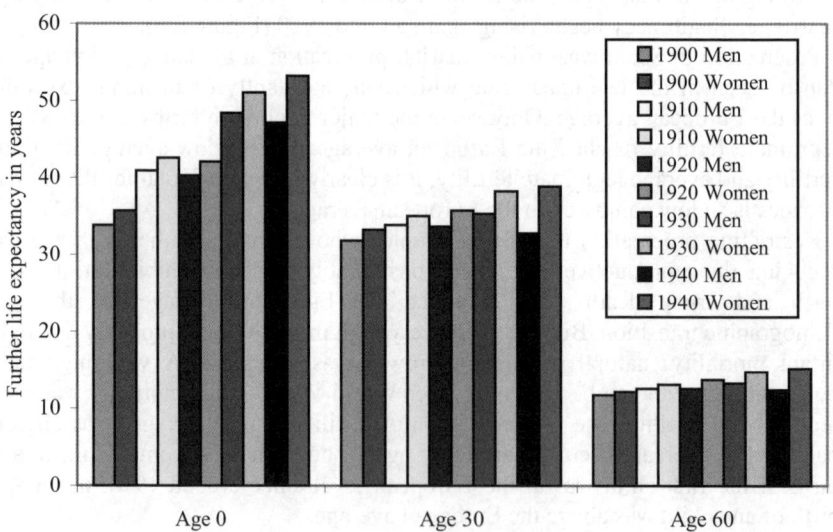

proportion of never-married women aged 45–54 until 1920 was comparable to the Eastern European countries. Spain therefore displays a *special type* of marriage pattern, combining universal and late marriage. Although age at marriage was structurally high, there were few out-of-wedlock births, thus fertility was restricted to married people. Marital fertility was therefore high historically and women continued to have children in their 30s and 40s. Premarital sexual relations were not tolerated, especially for women; virginity at marriage was extremely important, but only for women. Until they were married, women lived in the parental home, where their behaviour was supervised; after marriage they moved to the husband's house (or family). Thus, marriage was probably used as a family strategy for exchanging commodities. There is probably a common Mediterranean pattern of the marriage market, which is mainly based on the agricultural tradition of these countries, where property in land and cattle plays an important role. Thus, these marriage strategies would be the sign of a 'traditional' rather than a 'modern' society. Interestingly, the Greek case is very similar, with one exception: there, women married early, due to the custom that the sisters had to be married off before the brothers could marry. Thus, the average woman married early, and married a man who was much older than her. Obviously social or legal norms, coming from inheritance law or culture, to some degree determine the specific features of demographic behaviour. Achieving a 'modern' society is obviously pretty difficult in Spain, as the prevalence of traditional patterns and the time-lags demonstrate. The crucial variables of modernization—urbanization, deagrarization, industrialization, tertiarization, and welfare state development—explain the time-lags in Spain's demographic and social development to some extent. But there also seem to be phenomena of cultural lag, with people's value and belief systems lagging factual developments.

Mean age at marriage (no data available for this indicator) must have been high until the census of 1887, when a fundamental change occurred. This explains the low level (below the European average) of the marriage rate until 1887. From 1887 until World War I the marriage rate rose substantially. This can only be explained by a major drop in the age at marriage, perhaps because of changes in the legal marriage age in the 1880s. There were probably marriage barriers as in other continental European countries which were removed at that time. The rise in the marriage rate is therefore an empirical phenomenon and not a data error or the result of a change in registration (improvement of marriage registration could be the only reason). Age at marriage rose dramatically after World War I, which can also be seen in the decline in the marriage rate to below the European level. Starting in the 1960s, age at marriage of both sexes fell rapidly from a very high level of 28.8 years for men and 26.1 years for women to 27 resp. 24.3 years in 1974. Around 1975 there was another very steep drop until about 1980. From 1980 on, age at marriage has been rising again. The new constitution of 1978 did away with many of the restrictive features of the family law under the Franco regime, probably encouraging more young people to marry. The decline in age at marriage up to 1980 is accompanied by the steeply rising share of women and men marrying in the 20–24 age group. With regard to age at marriage and the marriage rate, Spain, which previously diverged widely from the European average, has come to match it exactly.

In Spain the right to *divorce* was only introduced shortly before 1980 (Figure E.6). There was a strong demand for divorce, as can be seen from the steeply rising

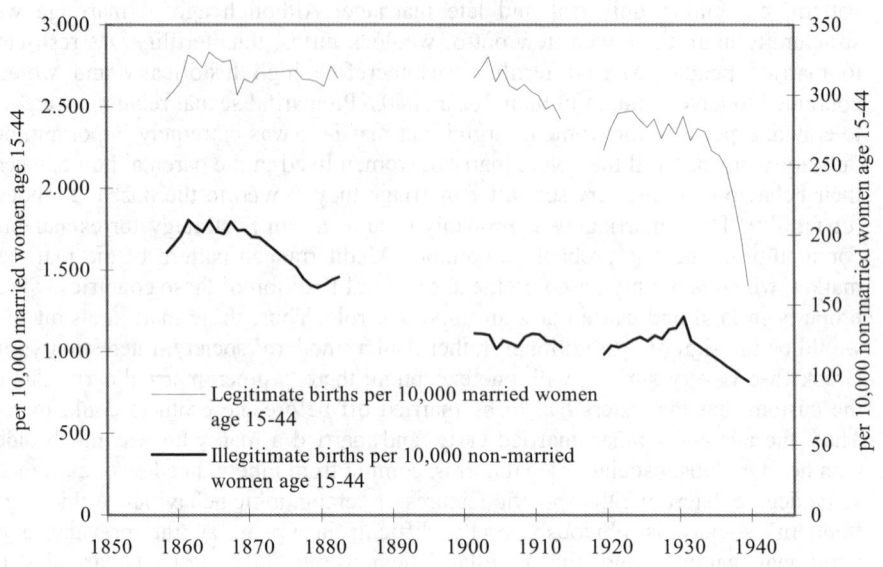

Figure E.5 Fertility and legitimacy 1858-1939

Legitimate births per 10,000 married women age 15-44

Illegitimate births per 10,000 non-married women age 15-44

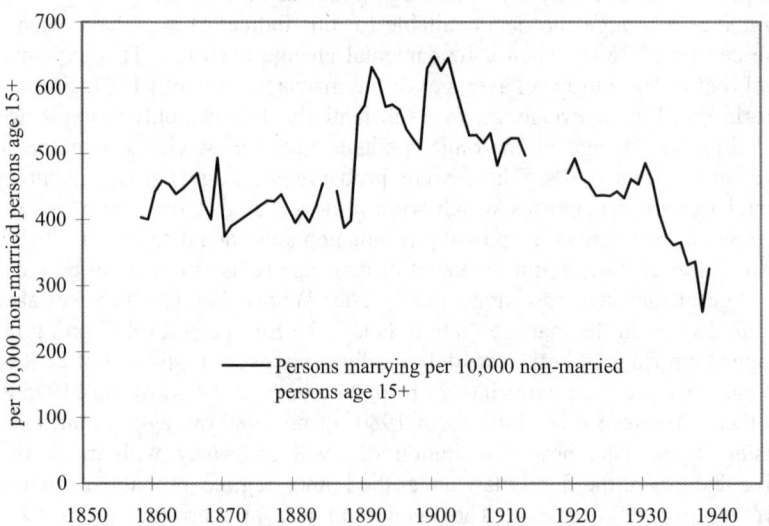

Figure E.6 Marriages 1858-1939

Persons marrying per 10,000 non-married persons age 15+

divorce rate, though still well below the European average. The non-existence of divorce is another explanation for the low illegitimacy rate in Spain, where all children born before the 1970s were considered as having been born in wedlock, even when the parents were separated. The rising divorce rate will contribute *ceteris paribus* to the rise in out-of-wedlock births.

Before the introduction of divorce, only legal separation was possible. Figures on divorce and legal separations are available since 1981. Legal separations are more frequent than divorces both before and after 1981.

Compared with the European level, both the Spanish divorce and legal separation rate are fairly low. They were even lower before 1981 during the Franco regime, when Spain clearly diverged from the developments in Western Europe. Nevertheless, marital dissolutions have been frequent since the liberalization of divorce and show strong rates of increase since the 1980s.

Besides tradition and historical influences, traditional religious (Catholic) beliefs probably continue to have a great influence on the propensity to divorce in Spain, which explains the still significant structural difference to Europe. Less industrialization and urbanization probably are not sufficient to explain this structural difference.

AGE, SEX, AND CIVIL STATUS

In Spain, a detailed age composition by sex and marital status is only available from the census of 1900 (Appendix Figure E.8). In 1900 the age structure still showed a clear pyramidal shape, but in 1910, the lowest age group of 0–4 years was smaller, pointing to a fertility decline in the late 1900s. World War I had no major impact on the Spanish age structure: Spain's demographic development was only indirectly influenced by the war. In 1930 the age structure was still quite regular, but the lowest age groups were smaller, indicating the beginning fertility decline of that time. In 1930 the age structure had become bell-shaped. The age structure of the year 1940 reveals the impact of the civil war and the loss of births, greatly reducing the lowest age group of 0–4 years. The cohorts of young men (aged 20–29) were also reduced, probably due to war losses.

The proportion of men marrying at a later age was higher than that of women. But at higher ages, celibacy among women was higher than among men, mainly due to higher mortality of men in higher age groups, which furthermore caused frequent widowhood. The proportions of widowed women were highest in 1940, probably a result of male civil war casualties.

FAMILY AND HOUSEHOLD STRUCTURES

Unfortunately, before 1960 no official household and family statistics (marital fertility statistics were published for 1920 and 1940) were published. The only possibility to gain an impression of the mean size of households is by using the number of census sheets (*cédulas récogidas*) as an indication of the number of private households. If we calculate the mean number of inhabitants per census sheet, then we get rather small figures for mean household size in the nineteenth and twentieth centuries: in 1860 4.35, in 1910 3.97, and in 1920 4.08 persons per census sheet. Although the figures are small, the data seem to reveal a decline in mean household size which of course also occurred in Spain as everywhere in Europe.

The only possibility to get more information on household and family life in Spain during 1850–1945 is therefore from special statistical studies with original census sheets or from local sources (see Reher, 1997).

THE NATIONAL SYSTEM OF DEMOGRAPHIC STATISTICS

Population Structure

Censuses in Spain were already taken in the second half of the eighteenth century, in 1768, 1787, and 1797. But afterwards there was a long break in the population statistics in Spain. The next available census dates only from the year 1857, after which census-taking became regular. Nevertheless it should be noted that coverage of Spanish censuses remained comparatively low compared with French or Prussian statistics of that time. Significant for Spanish census statistics is the very strong emphasis on the regional dimension and the lengthy presentation of data for the many provinces and subgroupings, while the presentation of data on the national level has been neglected. An historical account of the population censuses from 1768 to 1910 is included in Ministerio de Instrucción Pública y Bellas Artes. Dirección General del Instituto Geográfico y Estadístico (1916: IX–XVI).

The first three censuses of 1857, 1860, and 1877 presented the population by age groups and sex; there was no combination with marital status. This combination was introduced in 1887. The censuses from 1887 to 1920 gave the lower ages for every year of age, and the higher ages in five-year age groups. In 1930 and 1940 ages were published in one-year age groups.

Vital Statistics

Recording of vital statistics on the national level started in 1858 for most demographic series, but was discontinued after 1870. Publication of the three basic demographic variables of live births, deaths, and marriages was resumed in 1886. Many other demographic statistics were resumed only in 1900 or 1901: stillbirths in 1900, births by legitimacy and infant deaths in 1901. Divorce statistics exist only since 1981, after divorce was legalized. Synthetic fertility indices such as the total period fertility rate and the cohort fertility rate have been recalculated since 1901 and 1902, respectively.

Households and Families

In Spain, data on *households* (*familias,* later *hogares*) were not directly collected before the 1960 census. But the number of census sheets received was published already starting in 1860 and continuing until the census of 1940. For the earlier censuses the summary of sheets was given, and in the later ones the number of private households (*familias*) and institutions (*colectivas*). Thus, e.g., in 1920 received enumeration sheets for families/institutions were published (*cédulas recogidas de familia/colectivas* (Ministerio de Trabajo, Comercio e Industria. Dirección General de Estadística, 1922).

In 1960 household (*hogares*) statistics were revised, introducing households by size and the type of family. But it was only in 1970 that household and family statistics in the true sense of the word and complying with international standards began to be collected; prior to that, everything was more or less rudimentary. In

1970 households were distinguished by size and profession, and a detailed typology of family types was created.

Thus, household statistics in the strict sense did not exist in Spain until 1960. Taking the enumeration sheets as the number of households can only be a very crude substitute for the actual number of households. In principle, for 1857 to 1950 we have only one time series, the mean number of persons per enumeration sheet.

Regional disaggregations are available by provinces and districts.

There was no *definition of a household* (*familia*), because only the number of enumeration sheets was counted. In the beginning only the total of enumeration sheets was published; later this figure was split into enumeration sheets for private households (called *familias*) and for institutional households (*colectivas*).

Family statistics were introduced in the census of 1920 as *family-related fertility statistics*. The legitimate fertility of married and widowed women was investigated. The results were published in two volumes: the first classifies married and widowed women by age and the number of children, grouped as follows: 0 children (*hijos*), 1–4 children, 5–7 children, 8–10 children, and 10 or more children. The second volume presents marriage data by the age of both spouses and the number of children. The age of the spouses was cross-referenced for several age groups.

The 1940 census published a table of married and widowed women by age, duration of marriage, and the number of living children (*hijos vivientes*). Children were registered from 0–11 and more.

Remarks (also see introductory Table 6.1)

For Spain, mid-year population data for 1858–1877 have been taken from Mitchell (1992: 81). Population movement data (mid-year population, live births, deaths, marriages, (il)legitimate births) are not available from official sources for the years 1871–1877. Annual data for these variables (without mid-year population) have been created by linear extrapolation from 1871 to 1877.

The last census with detailed age*sex*civil status is the 1887 census, which gives only a very crude classification of single males by age (under 14, 15 and over) and females (under 12, 13 and over), but not married or widowed persons. Thus, only the variables v18, v19, and v20 could be calculated. It is assumed that no married or widowed males or females are under age 15 or 13, respectively.

The censuses of 1857 and 1860 include civil status only in summary form, and give the population by age groups and sex. Variables v18, v19, and v20 have been calculated under the same assumption, namely that there are no married or widowed persons under the age of 16 in either census.

In order to calculate variables v16, v17, and v21 the percentage shares of these variables for the 1887 census have been used to calculate the respective figures for the censuses of 1877, 1860, and 1857.

BOUNDARY CHANGES

Spain has undergone only minor boundary changes due to the character of the Iberian Peninsula; territorial changes affected more or less only the colonial empire. Since the eighteenth century Spain slowly but steadily had to give up its colonies, first the European ones, and later those overseas. The war with the United States of America in 1898 ended Spain's status as a colonial power. Nevertheless, in Europe

Spain was able to retain several territories off the mainland: the Canary Islands in the Atlantic Ocean, the Balearic Islands in the Mediterranean, and Ceuta and Melilla on the African continent (surrounded by Moroccan territory). Spain declared neutrality in both World War I and World War II, therefore it was subject to no changes in territorial status. For regional organization see the documentation by Quick (1994) and Caramani, Flora, Kraus, and Quick (1998).

APPENDIX TABLE E.1 Population structure at census dates 1857–1940

Census number	Census date	Census population			Marital status				Age group		
		Total	Male	Female	Single	Married	Widowed	Divorced	0–14	15–64	65+
		Absolute									
1	21 V 1857	15,464,340	7,670,933	7,793,407	8,828,619	5,574,542	1,061,179	..	5,500,116	9,108,753	855,471
2	25 XII 1860	15,673,481	7,765,508	7,907,973	8,887,369	5,721,617	1,064,262	..	5,459,386	9,316,948	897,147
3	31 XII 1877	16,634,345	8,134,331	8,500,014	9,079,344	6,450,606	1,103,581	..	..	..	..
4	31 XII 1887	17,565,632	8,612,524	8,953,108	9,588,914	6,743,757	1,232,526	..	5,857,957	10,391,559	1,316,116
5	31 XII 1900	18,618,086	9,087,821	9,530,265	10,310,425	7,021,512	1,280,081	..	6,557,979	10,698,882	1,361,225
6	31 XII 1910	19,995,686	9,725,024	10,270,662	11,255,923	7,383,484	1,342,512	..	7,151,129	11,287,874	1,556,683
7	31 XII 1920	21,389,842	10,373,382	11,016,460	12,155,227	7,722,720	1,461,028	..	7,326,283	12,356,059	1,707,500
8	31 XII 1930	23,677,794	11,565,805	12,111,989	13,468,834	8,603,361	1,569,323	..	7,483,389	14,753,661	1,440,744
9	31 XII 1940	25,877,971	12,413,777	13,464,194	14,885,165	9,107,244	1,885,562	..	7,748,951	16,438,632	1,690,388
		Per cent									
1	21 V 1857	100.00	49.60	50.40	57.09	36.05	6.86	..	35.57	58.90	5.53
2	25 XII 1860	100.00	49.55	50.45	56.70	36.51	6.79	..	34.83	59.44	5.72
3	31 XII 1877	100.00	48.90	51.10	54.58	38.78	6.63	..	..	..	..
4	31 XII 1887	100.00	49.03	50.97	54.59	38.39	7.02	..	33.35	59.16	7.49
5	31 XII 1900	100.00	48.81	51.19	55.38	37.71	6.88	..	35.22	57.46	7.31
6	31 XII 1910	100.00	48.64	51.36	56.29	36.93	6.71	..	35.76	56.45	7.79
7	31 XII 1920	100.00	48.50	51.50	56.83	36.10	6.83	..	34.25	57.77	7.98
8	31 XII 1930	100.00	48.85	51.15	56.88	36.34	6.63	..	31.61	62.31	6.08
9	31 XII 1940	100.00	47.97	52.03	57.52	35.19	7.29	..	29.94	63.52	6.53

APPENDIX TABLE E.2 Census population by region 1877–1940 (per cent)

Provincia	1877	1887	1900	1910	1920	1930	1940
Andalucia	**19.73**	**19.54**	**19.14**	**19.07**	**19.84**	**19.56**	**20.17**
Almeria	2.10	1.93	1.93	1.91	1.69	1.45	1.39
Cádiz	2.58	2.45	2.43	2.24	2.57	2.16	2.32
Córdoba	2.31	2.40	2.45	2.48	2.65	2.84	2.94
Granada	2.88	2.76	2.64	2.62	2.69	2.73	2.85
Huelva	1.26	1.45	1.40	1.56	1.55	1.51	1.42
Jaén	2.54	2.49	2.55	2.64	2.78	2.86	2.91
Málaga	3.01	2.96	2.75	2.62	2.60	2.60	2.62
Sevilla	3.05	3.10	2.98	3.00	3.30	3.42	3.72
Aragón	**5.38**	**5.19**	**4.91**	**4.78**	**3.07**	**4.38**	**4.09**
Huesca	1.52	1.45	1.32	1.24	1.18	1.03	0.90
Teruel	1.46	1.38	1.32	1.28	1.18	1.07	0.90
Zaragoza	2.41	2.36	2.27	2.25	0.70	2.27	2.30
Asturias	**3.46**	**3.39**	**3.37**	**3.44**	**3.49**	**3.36**	**3.23**
Oviedo	3.46	3.39	3.37	3.44	3.49	3.36	3.23
Baleares	**1.74**	**1.78**	**1.68**	**1.64**	**1.59**	**1.55**	**1.57**
Baleares	1.74	1.78	1.68	1.64	1.59	1.55	1.57
Canarias	**1.69**[1]	**1.66**[1]	**1.93**[1]	**2.23**[1]	**2.15**[1]	**2.36**	**2.63**
Tenerife	..	..	..	..	..	1.29	1.39
Las Palmas	..	..	..	..	..	1.07	1.24
Cantabria	**1.41**	**1.39**	**1.48**	**1.52**	**1.54**	**1.54**	**1.52**
Santander	1.41	1.39	1.48	1.52	1.54	1.54	1.52
Castilla y León	**12.81**	**12.86**	**12.37**	**11.85**	**10.97**	**10.51**	**10.41**
Avila	1.08	1.10	1.07	1.05	0.98	0.94	0.91
Burgos	2.00	1.93	1.82	1.74	1.58	1.51	1.46
León	2.10	2.17	2.07	1.98	1.93	1.88	1.91
Palencia	1.09	1.08	1.03	0.98	0.90	0.88	0.84
Salamanca	1.72	1.79	1.73	1.68	1.51	1.44	1.51
Segovia	0.90	0.88	0.85	0.84	0.78	0.74	0.73
Soria	0.93	0.87	0.81	0.78	0.71	0.66	0.62
Valladolid	1.49	1.52	1.50	1.43	1.32	1.28	1.29
Zamora	1.50	1.54	1.48	1.37	1.25	1.19	1.16
Castilla-La Mancha	**7.52**	**7.55**	**7.45**	**7.71**	**7.72**	**7.76**	**7.43**
Albacete	1.32	1.30	1.28	1.33	1.37	1.41	1.45
Ciudad Real	1.56	1.66	1.73	1.91	2.00	2.09	2.05
Cuenca	1.42	1.38	1.34	1.35	1.32	1.32	1.29
Guadalajara	1.21	1.15	1.07	1.05	0.94	0.87	0.80
Toledo	2.01	2.05	2.03	2.07	2.08	2.08	1.85
Cataluña	**10.53**	**10.50**	**10.57**	**10.46**	**11.01**	**11.85**	**11.17**
Barcelona	5.03	5.14	5.67	5.73	6.33	7.64	7.47
Gerona	1.80	1.75	1.61	1.61	1.53	1.38	1.24
Lérida	1.71	1.62	1.48	1.43	1.48	1.33	1.15
Tarragona	1.98	1.99	1.82	1.70	1.67	1.49	1.31
Comunidad Valenciana	**8.27**	**8.31**	**8.53**	**8.55**	**8.19**	**8.05**	**8.41**
Alicante	2.48	2.47	2.53	2.50	2.40	2.32	2.35
Castellón	1.71	1.66	1.67	1.62	1.44	1.31	1.21
Valencia	4.08	4.18	4.34	4.44	4.35	4.42	4.86
Extremadura	**4.45**	**4.68**	**4.74**	**4.97**	**4.95**	**4.89**	**4.85**
Badajoz	2.60	2.74	2.79	2.98	3.02	2.98	2.87
Cáceres	1.85	1.94	1.95	2.00	1.92	1.91	1.97
Galicia	**11.11**	**10.79**	**10.64**	**10.36**	**9.97**	**9.47**	**9.64**
La Coruña	3.58	3.50	3.51	3.40	3.33	3.26	3.41
Lugo	2.47	2.46	2.50	2.41	2.21	1.99	1.98
Orense	2.34	2.31	2.17	2.07	1.93	1.81	1.77
Pontevedra	2.72	2.52	2.46	2.48	2.50	2.41	2.48

continued

APPENDIX TABLE E.2 Census population by region 1877–1940 (per cent)
(continued)

Provincia	1877	1887	1900	1910	1920	1930	1940
Madrid	**3.57**	**3.89**	**4.16**	**4.41**	**5.01**	**5.87**	**6.11**
Madrid	3.57	3.89	4.16	4.41	5.01	5.87	6.11
Murcia	**2.72**	**2.80**	**3.11**	**3.09**	**3.00**	**2.74**	**2.78**
Murcia	2.72	2.80	3.11	3.09	3.00	2.74	2.78
Navarra	**1.83**	**1.73**	**1.66**	**1.57**	**1.55**	**1.47**	**1.43**
Navarra	1.83	1.73	1.66	1.57	1.55	1.47	1.43
País Vasco	**2.71**	**2.91**	**3.24**	**3.38**	**3.61**	**3.78**	**3.69**
Alava	0.57	0.53	0.52	0.49	0.46	0.44	0.44
Guipúzcoa	1.00	1.04	1.05	1.14	1.22	1.28	1.28
Vizcaya	1.14	1.34	1.67	1.76	1.92	2.06	1.97
La Rioja	**1.05**	**1.03**	**1.02**	**0.94**	**0.91**	**0.87**	**0.85**
Logroño	1.05	1.03	1.02	0.94	0.91	0.87	0.85
TOTAL	**100.00**	**100.00**	**100.00**	**100.00**	**100.00**	**100.00**	**100.00**

Note: [1] Provincia Canarias.

APPENDIX TABLE E.3 Population density by region 1877–1940 (inhabitants per sq. km.)

Provincia	1877	1887	1900	1910	1920	1930	1940
Andalucia	**37**	**39**	**41**	**43**	**48**	**53**	**60**
Almeria	40	39	41	44	41	39	41
Cádiz	58	59	62	61	75	69	82
Córdoba	28	31	33	36	41	49	55
Granada	38	38	39	41	45	51	59
Huelva	21	25	26	31	33	35	36
Jaén	31	32	35	39	44	49	55
Málaga	68	71	70	71	75	84	93
Sevilla	36	39	39	42	50	57	68
Aragón	**19**	**19**	**19**	**20**	**14**	**22**	**22**
Huesca	17	17	16	16	17	16	15
Teruel	16	16	17	17	17	17	16
Zaragoza	23	24	24	26	9	31	34
Asturias	**53**	**55**	**58**	**63**	**68**	**73**	**77**
Oviedo	53	55	58	63	68	73	77
Baleares	**58**	**62**	**62**	**65**	**68**	**73**	**81**
Baleares	58	62	62	65	68	73	81
Canarias	**39[1]**	**40[1]**	**49[1]**	**61[1]**	**63[1]**	**74**	**91**
Tenerife	..	..	..	..	..	88	105
Las Palmas	..	..	..	..	..	62	79
Cantabria	**43**	**45**	**51**	**55**	**60**	**67**	**72**
Santander	43	45	51	55	60	67	72
Castilla y León	**27**	**29**	**29**	**30**	**30**	**31**	**34**
Avila	12	13	13	14	14	15	16
Burgos	17	17	17	18	17	18	19
León	20	22	22	23	24	26	29
Palencia	15	16	16	16	16	17	18
Salamanca	19	21	21	22	21	22	25
Segovia	2	2	2	2	2	2	2
Soria	20	19	19	20	19	19	20
Valladolid	17	19	20	20	20	21	23
Zamora	16	18	18	18	17	18	19
Castilla-La Mancha	**148**	**157**	**164**	**182**	**195**	**217**	**228**
Albacete	18	18	19	21	23	27	30
Ciudad Real	38	43	47	56	63	71	76
Cuenca	23	23	24	26	27	30	32
Guadalajara	27	27	26	28	27	25	25
Toledo	32	34	36	39	42	46	45
Cataluña	**54**	**57**	**61**	**65**	**73**	**87**	**90**
Barcelona	109	117	137	148	175	234	251
Gerona	51	52	51	55	56	56	55
Lérida	23	23	23	23	26	26	24
Tarragona	51	54	52	52	55	54	52
Comunidad Valenciana	**60**	**64**	**69**	**74**	**76**	**81**	**93**
Alicante	73	77	83	88	90	94	105
Castellón	44	45	48	50	47	46	47
Valencia	63	68	75	82	86	95	115
Extremadura	**18**	**20**	**21**	**24**	**25**	**28**	**30**
Badajoz	20	22	24	27	29	32	34
Cáceres	15	17	18	20	21	23	26
Galicia	**63**	**65**	**68**	**71**	**73**	**77**	**86**
La Coruña	75	78	83	86	90	97	112
Lugo	42	44	47	49	48	47	52
Orense	56	58	58	59	59	61	66
Pontevedra	103	101	104	113	121	129	146

continued

APPENDIX TABLE E.3 Population density by region 1877–1940 (inhabitants per sq. km.) (continued)

Provincia	1877	1887	1900	1910	1920	1930	1940
Madrid	**74**	**85**	**97**	**110**	**134**	**173**	**197**
Madrid	74	85	97	110	134	173	197
Murcia	**39**	**43**	**50**	**53**	**55**	**57**	**64**
Murcia	39	43	50	53	55	57	64
Navarra	**29**	**29**	**29**	**30**	**31**	**33**	**35**
Navarra	29	29	29	30	31	33	35
País Vasco	**64**	**72**	**85**	**95**	**108**	**126**	**135**
Alava	31	31	32	32	33	34	37
Guipúzcoa	89	97	104	120	137	160	176
Vizcaya	88	109	144	162	189	224	236
La Rioja	**35**	**36**	**37**	**37**	**38**	**40**	**44**
Logroño	35	36	37	37	38	40	44
TOTAL	**33**	**35**	**37**	**39**	**42**	**47**	**51**

Note: [1] Provincia Canarias.

APPENDIX TABLE E.4 Demographic developments 1850–1945 (absolute figures and rates)

Year	Mid-year population	Natural population growth rate	Population growth rate	Net migration rate	Crude birth rate	Legitimate births per 10,000 married women age 15–44	Illegitimate births per 10,000 unmarried women age 15–44	Illeg. births per 100 leg. births
1850	..	..	..	..	..	..	..	..
1851	..	..	..	..	..	..	..	..
1852	..	..	..	..	..	..	..	..
1853	..	..	..	..	..	..	..	..
1854	..	..	..	..	..	..	..	..
1855	..	..	..	..	..	..	..	..
1856	..	..	..	..	..	..	..	..
1857	..	..	..	..	..	..	..	..
1858	15,530,000	7.2	..	..	35.2	2,546	187	5.8
1859	15,580,000	7.1	3.2	-3.8	35.9	2,594	193	5.9
1860	15,640,000	9.3	3.8	-5.5	36.7	2,650	200	6.0
1861	15,700,000	12.3	3.8	-8.5	39.0	2,816	211	5.9
1862	15,750,000	11.2	3.2	-8.0	38.5	2,789	206	5.8
1863	15,810,000	8.6	3.8	-4.8	37.8	2,737	202	5.8
1864	15,860,000	7.7	3.2	-4.5	39.2	2,834	211	5.9
1865	15,920,000	4.8	3.8	-1.0	38.6	2,798	202	5.7
1866	15,980,000	9.3	3.8	-5.5	38.3	2,772	201	5.7
1867	16,030,000	8.1	3.1	-5.0	38.5	2,784	209	5.9
1868	16,090,000	3.5	3.7	0.3	35.7	2,572	203	6.2
1869	16,140,000	2.9	3.1	0.2	37.0	2,670	204	6.0
1870	16,200,000	5.0	3.7	-1.3	36.6	2,649	199	5.9
1871	15,920,000	5.2	-17.6	-22.8	37.4	2,707	198	5.8
1872	15,980,000	5.4	3.8	-1.6	37.4	2,709	194	5.7
1873	16,030,000	5.5	3.1	-2.4	37.4	2,713	189	5.5
1874	16,090,000	5.6	3.7	-1.9	37.4	2,714	185	5.4
1875	16,140,000	5.7	3.1	-2.6	37.4	2,718	181	5.3
1876	16,200,000	5.8	3.7	-2.1	37.3	2,720	176	5.1
1877	16,590,000	5.8	23.5	17.7	36.6	2,667	169	5.0
1878	16,680,298	5.9	5.4	-0.5	36.5	2,664	164	4.9
1879	16,770,757	5.8	5.4	-0.4	36.3	2,653	162	4.8
1880	16,860,248	5.8	5.3	-0.5	36.0	2,624	164	5.0
1881	16,963,698	7.4	6.1	-1.3	37.6	2,748	168	4.8
1882	17,062,881	5.3	5.8	0.5	36.7	2,673	170	5.0
1883	17,128,283	2.9	3.8	0.9	36.0	..	..	..
1884	17,203,866	5.9	4.4	-1.5	37.0	..	..	..
1885	17,320,000	..	6.7	..	..	..	..	..
1886	17,420,000	7.4	5.7	-1.6	36.6	..	..	..
1887	17,510,000	3.3	5.1	1.8	36.1	..	..	..
1888	17,593,571	6.3	4.8	-1.5	36.4	..	..	..
1889	17,649,537	5.8	3.2	-2.6	36.7	..	..	..
1890	17,705,681	2.1	3.2	1.0	34.8	..	..	..
1891	17,762,004	3.8	3.2	-0.6	35.6	..	..	..
1892	17,818,506	5.1	3.2	-1.9	36.2	..	..	..
1893	17,875,188	5.8	3.2	-2.6	36.1	..	..	..
1894	17,932,050	4.3	3.2	-1.1	35.3	..	..	..
1895	17,989,093	6.1	3.2	-2.9	35.4	..	..	..
1896	18,046,318	6.4	3.2	-3.2	36.3	..	..	..
1897	18,103,725	5.8	3.2	-2.6	34.5	..	..	..

continued

APPENDIX TABLE E.4 Demographic developments 1850–1945 (absolute figures and rates)

Crude death rate	Infant mortality rate	Stillbirth rate	Infant mortality and stillbirth rate	Crude marriage rate	Persons marrying per 10,000 unmarried persons age 15+	Persons marrying per 10,000 unmarried persons age 15–49	Crude divorce rate	Divorces per 100 marriages	Divorces per 10,000 married persons	Year
27.9	170.9	52.6	223.5	7.3	404	660	..	..	..	1850
28.8	191.2	52.6	243.8	7.3	401	658	..	..	..	1851
27.3	173.7	..	..	8.1	443	731	..	..	..	1852
26.6	167.9	20.4	188.3	8.3	459	753	..	..	..	1853
27.3	174.7	14.6	189.3	8.2	454	739	..	..	..	1854
29.2	192.1	14.5	206.6	7.9	439	710	..	..	..	1855
31.5	199.6	13.0	212.7	8.0	448	720	..	..	..	1856
33.8	201.0	11.6	212.6	8.1	458	732	..	..	..	1857
29.0	184.5	11.9	196.4	8.3	471	747	..	..	..	1858
30.4	187.7	10.8	198.5	7.4	424	668	..	..	..	1859
32.2	211.6	9.3	220.9	6.9	401	628	..	..	..	1860
34.1	195.6	9.4	205.0	8.5	494	768	..	..	..	1861
31.6	202.6	8.0	210.6	6.4	375	579	..	..	..	1862
32.2	..	..	..	6.6	390	599	..	..	..	1863
32.0	..	..	..	6.7	398	607	..	..	..	1864
31.9	..	..	..	6.8	406	615	..	..	..	1865
31.8	..	..	..	6.9	413	622	..	..	..	1866
31.6	..	..	..	7.0	421	630	..	..	..	1867
31.5	..	..	..	7.1	429	637	..	..	..	1868
30.7	..	..	..	7.0	428	632	..	..	..	1869
30.6	..	11.8	..	7.1	438	638	..	..	..	1870
30.5	..	13.3	..	6.6	416	597	..	..	..	1871
30.1	..	13.6	..	6.2	395	559	..	..	..	1872
30.2	..	13.5	..	6.4	412	575	..	..	..	1873
31.4	..	13.7	..	6.0	396	544	..	..	..	1874
33.1	..	..	..	6.3	421	570	..	..	..	1875
31.1	..	..	..	6.7	455	607	..	..	..	1876
..	..	..	..	..	..	..	..	..	..	1877
29.3	..	..	..	6.4	444	575	..	..	..	1878
32.7	..	..	..	5.5	388	496	..	..	..	1879
30.1	..	..	..	5.6	399	509	..	..	..	1880
30.9	..	..	..	7.8	559	715	..	..	..	1881
32.6	..	..	..	8.0	574	734	..	..	..	1882
31.9	..	..	..	8.8	632	809	..	..	..	1883
31.1	..	..	..	8.5	613	786	..	..	..	1884
30.3	..	..	..	7.9	571	734	..	..	..	1885
31.0	..	..	..	7.9	575	738	..	..	..	1886
29.3	..	..	..	7.8	567	729	..	..	..	1887
29.9	..	..	..	7.4	537	692	..	..	..	1888
28.7	..	..	..	7.1	521	672	..	..	..	1889
..	..	..	..	..	..	..	..	..	..	1890
..	..	..	..	..	..	..	..	..	..	1891
..	..	..	..	..	..	..	..	..	..	1892
..	..	..	..	..	..	..	..	..	..	1893
..	..	..	..	..	..	..	..	..	..	1894
..	..	..	..	..	..	..	..	..	..	1895
..	..	..	..	..	..	..	..	..	..	1896
..	..	..	..	..	..	..	..	..	..	1897

continued

APPENDIX TABLE E.4 Demographic developments 1850–1945 (continued)

Year	Mid-year population	Natural population growth rate	Population growth rate	Net migration rate	Crude birth rate	Legitimate births per 10,000 married women age 15–44	Illegitimate births per 10,000 unmarried women age 15–44	Illeg. births per 100 leg. births
1898	18,212,698	5.1	6.0	0.8	33.6	..	..	..
1899	18,322,471	5.4	6.0	0.6	34.5	..	..	..
1900	18,433,053	4.9	6.0	1.1	34.1	..	..	..
1901	18,658,872	7.1	12.1	5.0	34.9	2,675	130	3.8
1902	18,788,477	9.5	6.9	-2.6	35.5	2,733	129	3.7
1903	18,918,982	11.4	6.9	-4.5	36.2	2,804	128	3.6
1904	19,050,395	8.6	6.9	-1.7	34.1	2,651	119	3.5
1905	19,132,718	9.4	4.3	-5.1	35.1	2,731	124	3.6
1906	19,315,961	7.8	9.5	1.7	33.7	2,629	123	3.7
1907	19,450,130	9.0	6.9	-2.1	33.2	2,603	120	3.7
1908	19,585,231	10.1	6.9	-3.2	33.6	2,636	127	3.9
1909	19,721,271	9.3	6.9	-2.4	33.0	2,592	130	4.0
1910	19,858,255	9.6	6.9	-2.7	32.6	2,568	129	4.1
1911	19,993,786	8.1	6.8	-1.3	31.4	2,486	124	4.1
1912	20,127,728	10.5	6.7	-3.9	31.7	2,514	124	4.0
1913	20,262,568	8.3	6.7	-1.7	30.5	2,426	120	4.1
1914	20,398,310	7.7	6.7	-1.1	29.8	..	..	4.1
1915	20,534,962	12.8	6.7	-6.1	29.9	..	..	4.3
1916	20,672,530	7.6	6.7	-1.0	29.0	..	..	4.7
1917	20,811,019	6.6	6.7	0.1	28.9	..	..	4.9
1918	20,950,436	-4.0	6.7	10.6	29.2	..	..	5.0
1919	21,090,787	4.9	6.7	1.8	27.8	2,231	115	5.8
1920	21,252,078	6.1	7.6	1.5	29.3	2,365	121	5.7
1921	21,410,867	9.0	7.4	-1.6	30.3	2,459	120	5.4
1922	21,627,912	9.9	10.0	0.1	30.3	2,467	122	5.4
1923	21,847,158	9.7	10.0	0.3	30.3	2,473	125	5.5
1924	22,068,626	10.1	10.0	0.0	29.6	2,417	127	5.7
1925	22,292,331	9.5	10.0	0.5	28.9	2,373	124	5.6
1926	22,518,320	10.8	10.0	-0.7	29.5	2,423	128	5.7
1927	22,746,592	9.5	10.0	0.5	28.0	2,304	126	5.8
1928	22,977,178	11.0	10.0	-1.0	29.0	2,395	133	5.8
1929	23,210,101	10.6	10.0	-0.6	28.2	2,329	134	6.0
1930	22,445,386	11.9	-34.1	-45.9	29.4	2,442	142	6.0
1931	23,674,506	10.2	51.9	41.8	27.4	2,293	125	5.8
1932	23,897,346	11.8	9.3	-2.5	28.1	2,364	121	5.5
1933	24,122,283	11.3	9.3	-2.0	27.7	2,345	117	5.5
1934	24,349,338	10.2	9.3	-0.9	26.2	2,226	114	5.7
1935	24,578,530	10.1	9.3	-0.8	25.7	2,199	110	5.7
1936	24,809,879	8.1	9.3	1.3	24.7	2,123	106	5.8
1937	25,043,405	3.7	9.3	5.6	22.6	1,941	103	6.3
1938	25,279,130	0.8	9.3	8.5	20.0	1,717	99	7.0
1939	25,517,073	-2.0	9.3	11.3	16.5	1,401	95	8.4
1940	25,757,257	7.9	9.3	1.4	24.4	..	..	5.4
1941	25,979,069	0.9	8.5	7.6	19.5	..	..	5.1
1942	26,182,451	5.5	7.8	2.3	20.2	..	..	5.7
1943	26,387,425	9.6	7.8	-1.9	22.9	..	..	6.3
1944	26,594,004	9.5	7.8	-1.7	22.5	..	..	6.7
1945	26,802,200	10.9	7.8	-3.1	23.1	..	..	6.7

APPENDIX TABLE E.4 Demographic developments 1850–1945 (continued)

Crude death rate	Infant mortality rate	Stillbirth rate	Infant mortality and stillbirth rate	Crude marriage rate	Persons marrying per 10,000 unmarried persons age 15+	Persons marrying per 10,000 unmarried persons age 15–49	Crude divorce rate	Divorces per 100 marriages	Divorces per 10,000 married persons	Year
28.5	..	..	..	6.9	507	654	..	..	..	1898
29.1	..	..	..	8.5	630	812	..	..	..	1899
29.1	..	24.4	..	8.7	648	837	..	..	..	1900
27.7	185.9	24.0	209.9	8.5	626	809	..	..	..	1901
26.0	180.5	24.7	205.2	8.7	645	833	..	..	..	1902
24.9	162.0	26.7	188.7	8.2	604	779	..	..	..	1903
25.6	172.9	26.5	199.5	7.6	564	728	..	..	..	1904
25.7	161.3	26.0	187.3	7.2	528	681	..	..	..	1905
25.8	173.7	25.4	199.1	7.2	528	682	..	..	..	1906
24.3	158.0	24.1	182.1	7.0	516	666	..	..	..	1907
23.5	159.9	25.0	184.9	7.2	531	685	..	..	..	1908
23.7	153.7	24.9	178.6	6.6	482	622	..	..	..	1909
23.0	149.3	25.0	174.3	7.0	516	665	..	..	..	1910
23.3	162.1	25.4	187.5	7.1	524	675	..	..	..	1911
21.2	137.5	26.2	163.6	7.1	524	676	..	..	..	1912
22.2	155.2	26.8	182.0	6.8	497	642	..	..	..	1913
22.1	151.8	27.6	179.4	6.6	..	..	..	..	..	1914
17.2	156.0	27.0	183.0	6.2	..	..	..	..	..	1915
21.4	146.9	27.7	174.6	6.6	..	..	..	..	..	1916
22.4	155.2	27.5	182.7	6.8	..	..	..	..	..	1917
33.2	183.0	28.4	211.4	6.7	..	..	..	..	..	1918
22.9	156.2	26.8	183.0	7.9	470	575	..	..	..	1919
23.3	164.3	26.9	191.2	8.3	493	604	..	..	..	1920
21.3	147.3	27.3	174.6	7.7	463	570	..	..	..	1921
20.4	141.7	23.7	165.4	7.6	455	562	..	..	..	1922
20.6	147.8	28.2	176.0	7.2	437	542	..	..	..	1923
19.5	140.0	29.7	169.7	7.2	437	544	..	..	..	1924
19.4	136.5	29.9	166.4	7.1	436	545	..	..	..	1925
18.7	127.5	30.4	157.9	7.2	443	555	..	..	..	1926
18.5	126.5	31.1	157.6	7.0	433	544	..	..	..	1927
18.0	125.8	31.9	157.6	7.4	461	582	..	..	..	1928
17.6	123.0	32.4	155.4	7.3	454	574	..	..	..	1929
17.6	117.1	33.0	150.1	7.8	486	617	..	..	..	1930
17.3	116.5	32.2	148.7	7.4	459	583	..	..	..	1931
16.3	111.6	32.9	144.5	6.6	408	518	..	..	..	1932
16.4	112.3	33.4	145.8	6.1	374	474	..	..	..	1933
16.0	113.1	33.2	146.2	6.0	362	459	..	..	..	1934
15.6	109.4	34.4	143.8	6.1	366	465	..	..	..	1935
16.7	108.9	32.4	141.3	5.6	331	420	..	..	..	1936
18.9	130.0	30.5	160.4	5.7	336	426	..	..	..	1937
19.2	119.7	29.3	149.0	4.5	261	330	..	..	..	1938
18.4	135.2	33.3	168.4	5.6	326	412	..	..	..	1939
16.5	108.7	30.5	139.3	8.4	..	..	..	..	..	1940
18.6	142.9	32.7	175.6	7.3	..	..	..	..	..	1941
14.7	103.2	33.4	136.6	7.2	..	..	..	..	..	1942
13.2	99.2	32.6	131.8	6.6	..	..	..	..	..	1943
13.0	93.0	32.6	125.5	7.1	..	..	..	..	..	1944
12.2	84.9	32.2	117.1	7.2	..	..	..	..	..	1945

APPENDIX TABLE E.5 Life expectancy by age 1900–1940 (in years)

Age	0	10	20	30	40	50	60	70	80
				Males					
1900	33.85	45.66	37.93	31.86	25.02	18.04	11.74	6.61	3.38
1910	40.92	49.12	41.06	33.88	26.35	19.16	12.58	7.41	3.84
1920	40.26	48.58	40.68	33.69	26.28	19.14	12.60	7.20	3.69
1930	48.38	51.55	43.11	35.34	27.50	20.05	13.30	7.83	4.06
1940	47.12	48.55	39.97	32.82	25.36	18.43	12.43	7.59	4.03
				Females					
1900	35.70	47.19	39.78	33.28	26.43	19.05	12.17	6.72	3.42
1910	42.56	50.04	42.16	35.03	27.79	20.27	13.14	7.48	3.80
1920	42.05	50.33	42.59	35.75	28.55	21.00	13.75	7.88	4.02
1930	51.06	54.32	45.94	38.26	30.38	22.38	14.80	8.54	4.31
1940	53.24	55.49	46.96	38.85	30.66	22.68	15.20	9.07	4.61

APPENDIX TABLE E.6A Households by type 1857–1940 (absolute)

Census year	Household types and members									
	Total households	Private households	Family households	One-person households	Institutional households	Total household members[1]	Private household members	Family household members	One-person household members	Institutional household members
1857	:	:	:	:	:	15,495,212	:	:	:	:
1860	3,595,668[2]	:	:	:	:	15,655,467	:	:	:	:
1877	4,236,072[2]	:	:	:	:	16,631,869	:	:	:	:
1887	:	:	:	:	:	17,560,352	:	:	:	:
1897	4,647,320[2]	:	:	:	:	:	:	:	:	:
1900	:	:	:	:	:	18,594,405	:	:	:	:
1910	5,020,304[2]	:	:	:	:	19,927,150	:	:	:	:
1920	5,227,326[2]	:	:	:	:	21,303,162	:	:	:	:
1930	:	:	:	:	:	23,563,867	:	:	:	:
1940	:	:	:	:	:	:	:	:	:	:

Notes: [1] *Población de hecho* (resident population). [2] Total enumeration sheets (*cédulas recogidas*).

APPENDIX TABLE E.6D Household indicators 1857–1940

Census year	Mean total household size
1857	:
1860	4.35
1877	3.93
1887	:
1897	:
1900	:
1910	3.97
1920	4.08
1930	:
1940	:

APPENDIX TABLE E.7 Dates and nature of results on population structure,
households/families, and vital statistics

Topic	Intro-duction	Remarks
Population		
Population at census dates	1857	Earlier censuses were conducted in 1768, 1787 and 1797 (cf. Ministerio de Instrucción Pública y Bellas Artes. Dirección General del Instituto Geográfico y Estadístico (1916: IX–XVI).
Population by age, sex and marital status	1887	1857, 1860 and 1877 no combination with marital status.
Households and families		
Households (*familias,* later *hogares*)		
Total households	1860, 1877, 1887, 1897, 1900, 1910, 1920, 1930, 1940	Households were only indirectly recorded by counting the enumeration sheets received, since 1860: 1857 and earlier: no households. 1860: private and institutional households. 1877: private and institutional households. 1887: private and institutional households. 1897: private and institutional households. 1900: private and institutional households. 1910: private and institutional households. 1920: private and institutional households (cédulas recogidas de familia/colectivas). 1930: private and institutional households. 1940: private and institutional households. *Disaggregation*: by provinces and districts.
Households by size	–	First time in the population census of 1960.
Households by composition	–	First time in the population census of 1970.
Households by profession of household head	–	
Families (*nucleos familiares*)		
Families by number of children	1920, 1940	First special investigation of the fertility of marriages in 1920. Repeated in 1940.

continued

APPENDIX TABLE E.7 Dates and nature of results on population structure, households/families, and vital statistics (continued)

Topic	Intro-duction	Remarks
Population movement		
Midyear population	1861–70, 1888–	
Births		
Live births	1858–70, 1886–	
Stillbirths	1858–70, 1900–	
Legitimate births	1858–70, 1901–	
Illegitimate births	1858–70, 1901–	
Deaths		
Total deaths	1858–70, 1886–	
Infants (under 1 year)	1858–70, 1901–	
Marriages		
Total marriages	1858–70, 1886–	
Divorces and separations		
Total divorces	1981	
Legal separations	–	

Spain

S.8 Population by age, sex and marital status, Spain 1900, 1910, 1930 and 1940 (per 10,000 of total population)

Spain, 1900

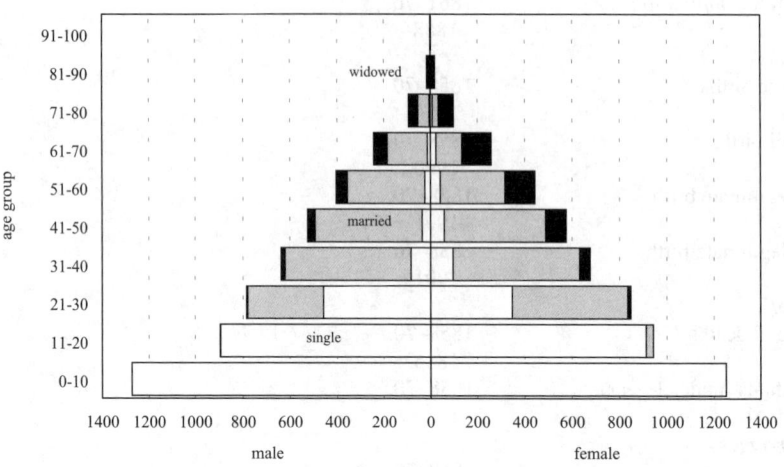

Spain, 1910

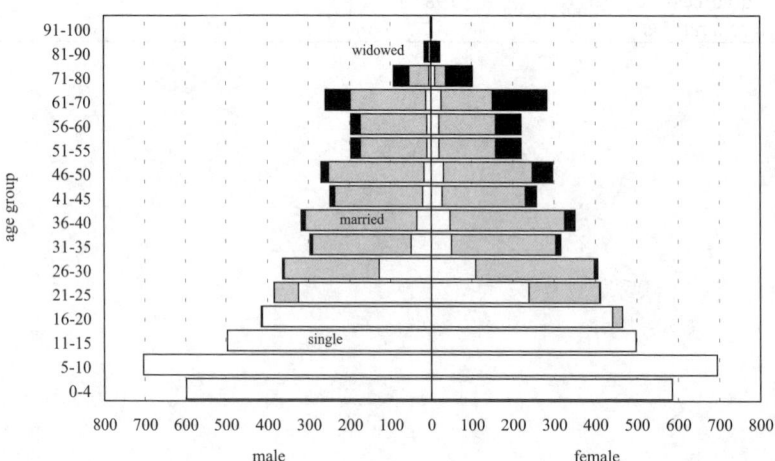

APPENDIX FIGURE S.8 Population by age, sex and marital status, Spain 1900, 1910, 1930 and 1940 (per 10,000 of total population) (continued)

Spain, 1930

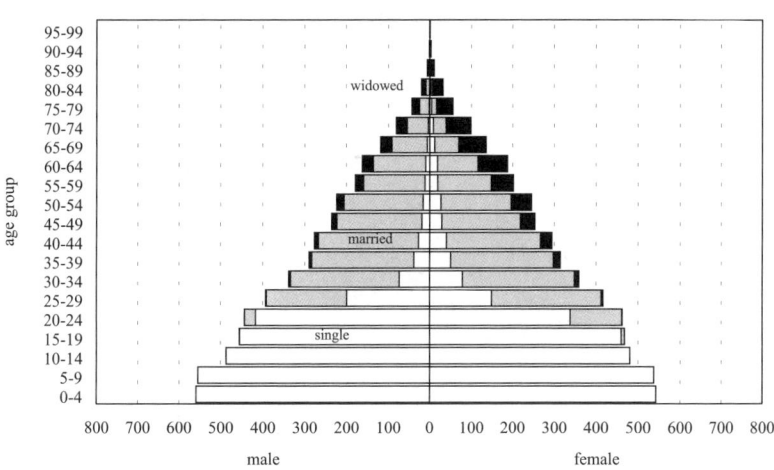

Spain, 1940

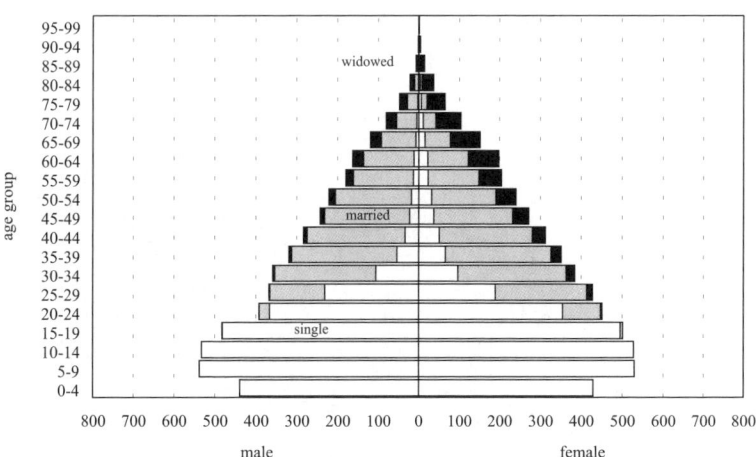

19

Sweden

STATE FORMATION AND TERRITORY

Sweden and Denmark were the two powers on the Scandinavian peninsula which shaped the region's territorial structure and cultural development, among others, to a large degree. Sweden's power position was mainly based on natural resources such as iron and wood. Very early in the Middle Ages the Swedes expanded to the neighbouring coast of Finland, where they introduced the Swedish language, culture, and later Protestantism. Finnish remained the spoken language of the people, while Swedish became the official language.

Swedish expansionism began in the sixteenth century under the Vasa dynasty. Sweden incorporated all territories on the Swedish peninsula as well as the offshore islands (Gotland, etc.). The Baltic region was incorporated and Sweden's participation in the Thirty Years' War brought gains on German territory. The rise in power of the Russian empire from the late Middle Ages following internal pacification and the end of Mongolian domination made Russia Sweden's main rival in the Baltic Sea, especially during the reign of Peter the Great in the seventeenth century. Peter the Great wanted to make Russia a sea power and therefore needed access to and domination over the Baltic Sea. Thus, at its defeat in the Nordic War in 1721, Sweden lost the Baltic territories as well as south-east Karelia and the Finnish city of Vyborg to Russia. The next main territorial conflict came during the Napoleonic period, when Sweden was defeated by Russia in 1808 and had to cede the whole of Finland to Russia. On the other hand Sweden gained Norway from Denmark following the 1813 battle of Lipsia. Norway gained its independence in 1905. The Åland Islands between Sweden and Finland were given to Finland in 1921 and remained neutral from 1921 to 1935.

By 1815 Sweden had attained the territory (apart from Norway) which it still has today. During World War I and World War II Sweden declared itself neutral and therefore did not suffer territorial changes (Alestalo, 1986; Alestalo and Kuhnle, 1984; Bengtsson, 1994; Gylfason et al., 1997; Kälvemark, 1980; Alvstam, 1995).

REGIONAL POPULATION STRUCTURE

Regional variations in population density are very large. There is a very clear north–south gradient in population density, southern Sweden being much more densely populated than the north. Centres of population density are the large towns and their surroundings, such as Göteborg, Malmö, and of course the capital, Stockholm.

Regional differences in population density reflect regional imbalances in economic development and economic structure. Agriculture is only possible in southern Sweden, while logging and wood manufacturing, fishing, mining, and metal industry are found in the northern regions. Rich natural deposits of iron in northern Sweden allowed the establishment of a Swedish automobile industry, unusual for a country of a population size under 10 million inhabitants. The service sector is highly developed, and public services in particular have attained a prominent position. Like all employment, public service employment is higher when population density is higher.

POPULATION GROWTH

Like all the Nordic countries apart from Denmark, Sweden is rather sparsely populated; population density is higher than in Norway and Finland, but lower than in Denmark. In 1870 the population was 4.169 million inhabitants; by World War I it had increased to 5.522 million, and in 1940 it was 6.371 million inhabitants. In 70 years the population had increased by 2.2 million. Population density in 1870 was 10.2 inhabitants per square km. and increased to 15.5 inhabitants per square km. 70 years later in 1940.

Natural population growth during the second half of the nineteenth century fluctuated around 10 per 1,000. From the 1880s to the 1930s natural population growth declined by tendency and fell to less than 5 per 1,000 in the mid-1930s. High natural population growth led to considerable overseas emigration mainly from the 1870s until World War I. After the war and during the inter-war period emigration stopped because of the low fertility rates, and immigration became stronger than emigration (positive net migration rate). There was a period of declining natural population growth from 1866 to 1870 as a result of the bad harvests in 1866 and 1867 (Hofsten and Lundström, 1976: 21). In combination with strong emigration, the total population growth even became negative. A second wave of strong emigration occurred in the early 1880s, but without a decline in the natural population growth rate. The late 1880s were a period of strong emigration overall, and emigration was still quite high from 1900 to 1914. Despite the strong natural population growth, there were therefore several downswings in the population growth rate, mainly caused by emigration waves, with the exception of the crisis of 1870. Although Sweden did not participate actively in World War I, both the natural and the total population growth declined, in spite of positive in-migration (Figure S.1). Taking into account the whole time period of 100 years, Swedish population growth nevertheless was rather high when compared to other European countries at that time.

THE FIRST DEMOGRAPHIC TRANSITION

Sweden's demographic transition process is similar to Norway's and Denmark's, but less so to Finland's. Demographic transition started early, already in the second half of the eighteenth century, when the infant mortality rate began to fall (Figure S.2). Both the birth rate and the mortality rate were lower than the European average. Sweden's natural population surplus was high during the second half of the nineteenth century, but less than Norway's and Denmark's. The overall transition process in Sweden was rather smooth, without very dramatic fluctuations due to wars or severe economic crises as in many continental countries. Thus, the model of the demographic transition was patterned after Sweden's development. Since the end of the wars with Russia in the eighteenth century, and the military conflicts during the Napoleonic era (1813 battle of Lipsia), Sweden has not participated in any large war in the last two centuries. It was only indirectly affected by the two

Figure S.1 Population growth and net migration 1850-1945

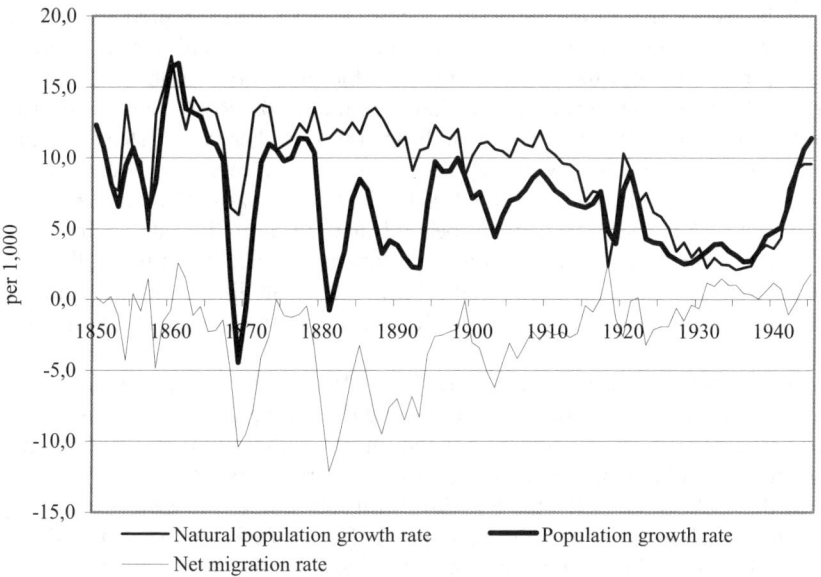

Figure S.2 First demographic transition 1850-1945

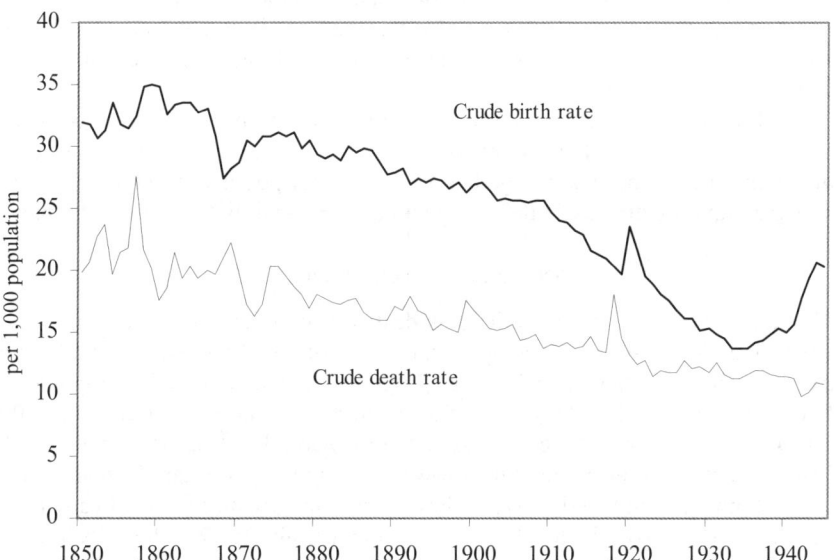

world wars in the twentieth century (Bengtsson and Ohlsson, 1994; Bernhardt, 1971; Johansson and Finnäs, 1983).

In the second half of the nineteenth century Sweden was still predominantly a rural country; therefore, epidemics and the availability of food still played a certain role, as can be seen from the ups and downs in the mortality rate in the 1850s and the 1870s. Probably the world economic crisis of the 1850s (Rosenberg, 1974) had some influence on the rising mortality rate. From 1866–70 there was a steep decline in the birth rate, accompanied by a steep decline in the mortality rate. The causes for this demographic shock were the effect of the bad harvests in 1866 and 1867 (Hofsten and Lundström, 1976: 21). It can be said that the mortality rate started to decline already in the 1850s, while the final and irreversible decline in the birth rate began in the 1860s. This later fall of the birth rate is in line with the model of the demographic transition, which posits that the birth rate adapts to the falling mortality rate.

Sweden was indirectly affected by World War I, as can be seen from declining birth figures and rising mortality before and during the war. After the war, the birth rate rose and the mortality rate dropped: many of those who had put off marrying and having children during the war now began forming families.

In the 1920s and 1930s the Swedish birth rate fell so dramatically that a public discussion about a population crisis began (*Kris i befolkningsfrågan*; Myrdal and Myrdal, 1935). This birth decline was the motor for the first population and family policy measures in Sweden. Starting in the mid-1930s the birth rate recovered, which cannot be explained by birth cohort effects (alone), but seems to be (at least partly) an effect of population and family policy. After peaking in the 1950s, the birth rate began to decline in the 'second demographic transition', only interrupted by a boom in the 1960s: this was an effect of the large birth cohorts of the 1930s and 1940s. Around 1980 the birth rate reached a historical low in Sweden and converged with the mortality rate.

In a European perspective, the demographic transition of Sweden fits very well into the Nordic type of demographic transition with an early start, low levels of births and deaths, but taken together a high natural population increase, leading to strong emigration already in the nineteenth century, mainly to the United States.

MORTALITY AND LIFE EXPECTANCY

The infant mortality rate is defined as deaths of children aged under one year per 1,000 live births. Sweden belongs to the group of countries which already in 1900 had a rather low infant mortality rate (Figure S.3). This cluster is composed of the five Nordic countries, along with The Netherlands and Switzerland. In 1900 the infant mortality rate in Sweden was at the very low level of 100 deaths per 1,000 live births; this was also one of the lowest in-group levels (Masuy-Stroobant, 1997).

Infant mortality in Sweden was so low at that time because it had already begun to decline in the early nineteenth century (Brändström, 1993). Mortality during the demographic transition in the nineteenth century was therefore rather low, causing a high population increase in Sweden. The population doubled between 1800 and 1900, from approximately 2,350,000 inhabitants to over 5,000,000. During the nineteenth century Sweden was still a predominantly agricultural country with low urbanization, few large cities, and the majority of the population living in small and scattered settlements. This pattern is perhaps one of the main causes of low infant mortality already before industrialization; it can be constantly shown that infant mortality was higher in the large cities and covaries with size of locality. Higher infant mortality in the cities is related to greater contagion due to crowded dwellings and inadequate sanitation and water supply.

As Brändström (1993) shows, there were large regional variations in infant mortality during the nineteenth century for which there is no clear-cut explanation. In principle, infant mortality was higher in the more densely populated south and in the region of the capital Stockholm, but there were also provinces in the high north with very high infant mortality rates. One main factor could be the practice of breastfeeding; others have been sought among 'cultural factors' (cf. Brändström, 1993: 27ff.; see also Brändström, 1997).

Swedish life expectancy was already quite high during the nineteenth century. Life expectancy at birth was rather high already in the 1850s, with 41 years for boys and 45 years for girls, which we could already see from the low infant mortality rate (Figure S.4). During the following 100 years newborn children gained most from mortality reduction. Their life expectancy increased by 17 years for boys and 15 years for girls. But also the 30-year-olds improved their further life expectancy considerably: 12 years for men and 10 years for women. Life expectancy for 60-year-old men and women increased by five years. Differences between the sexes in life expectancy declined in Sweden from 1850 to 1950, in contrast to most other European countries. Life expectancy of newborn girls in 1851/55 was four years higher than that of newborn boys; for 30-year-olds it was three years higher, and for 60-year-olds one year. A hundred years later, in 1941/45, the advantage of females was reduced: newborn girls had 2.7 more years life expectancy than newborn boys; 30-year-old women had 1.4 more years, and 60-year-old women 0.9 years.

FERTILITY AND LEGITIMACY

In principle, the Western European marriage pattern encourages illegitimate childbirth, because of late and non-universal marriage. Unmarried *de facto* cohabitation was common in several rural areas of Europe such as Carinthia, Bavaria, Southern Portugal, and most of Denmark and Sweden. These two countries therefore are very similar concerning the extent of illegitimate births. There are basic differences with Norway and Finland concerning the extent and structure of illegitimacy. In Norway, illegitimacy was low and below the European average. In Finland, illegitimacy was low as well, and below the European average for most of the last 150 years. But the case of Finland is less stable due to its deviating development during the first half of the twentieth century.

In Sweden, there was a slightly rising tendency in the illegitimate birth rate from 1850 to 1910 (Figure S.5). The Swedish rate continued to increase when the European rate started to decline around 1900. Sweden took part in the Europe-wide decline in the illegitimate birth rate beginning around 1900, although at a much higher level. In the 1940s the illegitimate birth rate started to rise again: this was a fundamental change in Swedish fertility behaviour, because childbirth now became overwhelmingly non-marital (pre-, post-, or extra-marital). The illegitimate birth rate increased so strongly that Sweden and Iceland presently have the highest illegitimate fertility rates in Europe.

Sweden's legitimate birth rate is again similar to Denmark's, but less similar to Finland's and Norway's. From the mid-nineteenth century until the 1920s the

Figure S.3 Infant mortality 1850-1945

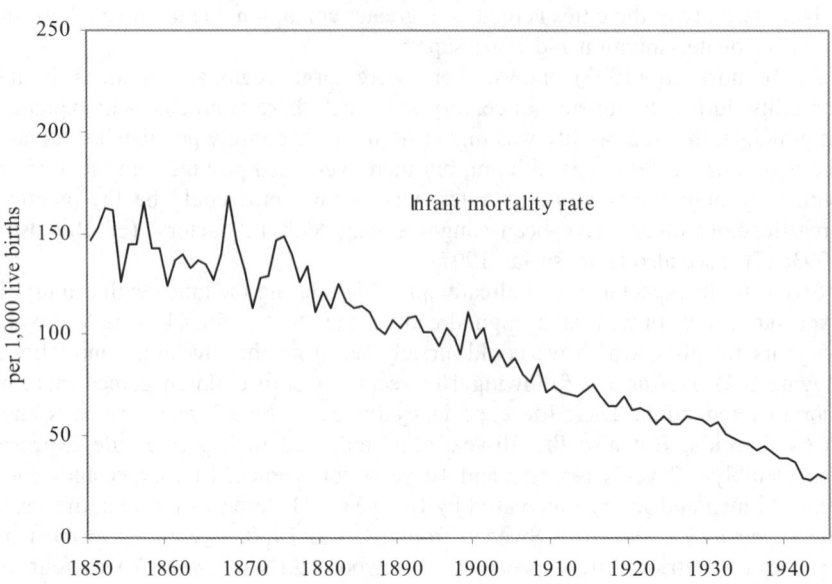

Figure S.4 Life expectancy 1851/55-1941/45

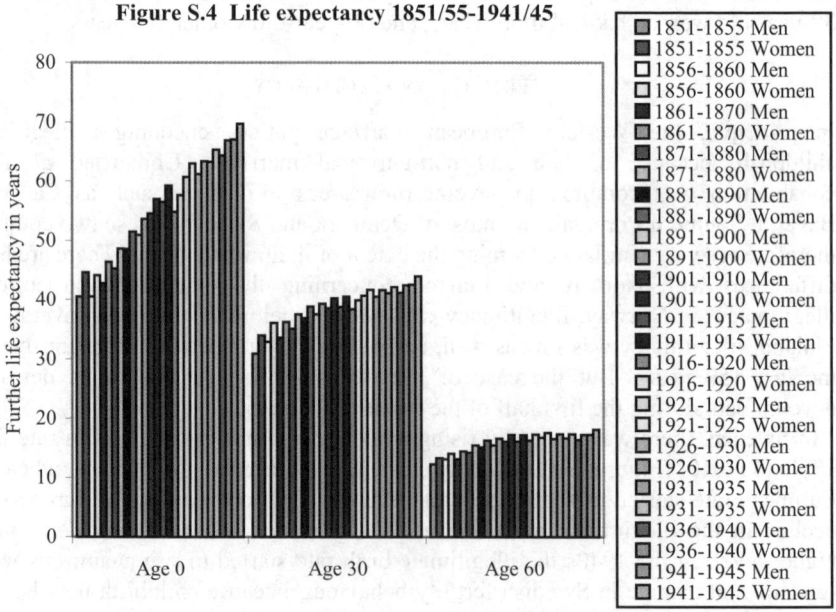

Swedish legitimate fertility rate was higher than the European average; since the 1930s this rate has been below the European average. The general tendency is that of a clearly decreasing logistic curve with the acceleration phase in the inter-war period. Since the 1940s childbearing behaviour has changed completely: giving birth within marriage has largely been superseded by out-of-wedlock childbirth. Today, approximately half of all children are born outside of legal marriage.

MARRIAGE AND DIVORCE

Sweden belongs to the region of Europe with the *Western European marriage pattern* of late age at marriage and a high celibacy rate. In the nineteenth century age at marriage was one of the highest in Western Europe. Accordingly, the celibacy rate was also one of the highest in Western Europe. Sweden's development in marital behaviour is very similar to Norway's and less so to Denmark's, while Finland again differs. In the nineteenth century age at first marriage was very high for both sexes. In 1850 less than 20% of all women at age 20–24 were married, while the figure for men was under 10%. In 1930, the proportion of women married at age 20–24 was about 20%, while the proportion of men married at age 20–24 had declined further. The marriage boom with a strongly declining age at marriage and a strongly increasing proportion married at age 20–24 started only after the 1930s and lasted until the 1970s. This boom was carried mainly by the birth cohorts of the 1920s and 1930s. Thus, in the late 1960s, for example, over 50% of all women were married already at age 20–24. In the 1960s this trend was reversed when young people began to refrain from early marriage. This is partly due to educational expansion, mainly with regard to women, but when looking at the last 150 years, the marriage boom of the 1940–50s and universal marriage seems to be rather the exception than the rule, at least in Western Europe. Thus, the process now called the evolution of the 'post-modern' nuptiality pattern and the 'deinstitutionalization' of marriage started rather early in Sweden.

Marriage intensity will be measured by the *marriage rate* and the *celibacy rate*. 'Marriage intensity' means the availability of marriage, but at the same time the urgent need to remarry after the death of a spouse ('remarriage need', Michael Mitterauer). The *marriage rate* refers to all marriages of unmarried people aged 15 and older (Figure S.6). Thus defined, the marriage rate in Sweden during the last 150 years was permanently below the European marriage rate. The development and level is very similar to Norway. The only similarity with Denmark is in the long-term development (trend) but not the level (which is higher than in Sweden and Norway). Finland is exceptional because of its deviating pattern in the first half of the twentieth century. In Sweden from 1850 to the 1930s the marriage rate was more or less at the same level, with only a small tendency to decline. The distance to the European average increased, and the Swedish rate began to diverge slightly from the European rate. This interesting fact principally points to rising economic and social obstacles to marriage. When legal marriage barriers were removed, social and economic ones took their place. The main cause is probably the strong population increase in Sweden due to high natural population surplus; the domestic economy could not support the rapidly growing population, resulting in strong emigration, mainly to the United States.

There was a drop in the marriage rate in the 1860s culminating around 1870 which corresponds to the downswing in the birth rate. Another fluctuation occurred after

World War I when postponed marriages were recovered. The historically singular rise of the Swedish marriage rate began in the 1930s, after the deep population crisis with a manifest birth decline, when population and family policy measures were initiated. It was at the same time the phase of early and universal marriage (see above). This demographic period lasted principally until the late 1960s, when the Swedes again began to marry later and to remain single longer. But before this final decline there was an earlier decline in the marriage rate immediately after 1945. The marriage and baby boom in the mid-1960s was mainly an effect of the large cohorts of the 1940s. The most recent phase in marriage behaviour—since the 1960s—is the postponement of marriage, increased celibacy, and increased out-of-wedlock births, all in all a 'deinstitutionalization' of marriage and its substitution by cohabitation before and after marriage. The Nordic countries have a long tradition of unmarried cohabitation, as we can see from history, but the influence of welfare state reforms and general increases in the standard of living must not be underestimated.

The development of the *celibacy rate* underlines what was apparent from the marriage rate. A large proportion—30%—of Swedish women aged 45–54 were never married in 1870. This high proportion even slightly increased in the following decades until the 1930s, similar to the declining marriage rate. The final turning point towards universal marriage came in 1950, that is, for the birth cohorts since 1900, but mainly of those born in the 1920s and 1930s. Women born after 1945 tendentially returned to their historically older pattern of non-universal and late marriage.

Concerning *marital stability*, for a long time Sweden did not have particularly high divorce rates. Until the end of World War I the Swedish divorce rate was at the European average. It was only after World War I that the number of divorces in Sweden increased more rapidly than in Europe (Figure S.6). This cannot be attributed to direct influences of the war, because Sweden remained neutral. A second major increase above the European level came after World War II. Again this cannot be the effect of the war, because Sweden was only indirectly involved. Besides legal changes the higher divorce rate is probably mainly due to the explosion in the number of marriages, many of which were later dissolved. In the 1960s the liberalization of the divorce law caused a very steep increase in the divorce rate until the early 1970s. In the 1970s the divorce rate fluctuated around this level, which was very high compared with the rest of Europe. Again we can see from this demographic indicator a major erosion of the social institution of marriage since the 1960s, a social trend which has been called the 'deinstitutionalization' of marriage or the trend towards a 'post-modern' marriage pattern. One final remark: the post-modern marriage pattern is very similar to the pre-modern marriage pattern, while the modern marriage pattern is very similar to the Eastern European marriage pattern.

In order to present the full picture, legal separations have to be taken into account. First data on legal separations are available from 1916 onwards. Until the late 1960s the number of legal separations was higher than the number of divorces. In the same way, the legal separation rate was higher than the divorce rate during this period. In principle, therefore, marital instability was higher in Sweden during the first half of the twentieth century than the divorce rate alone would indicate, when legal separations are added to divorces. This can only be done partially, because legal separations were often only the first stage in the divorce process. But many married

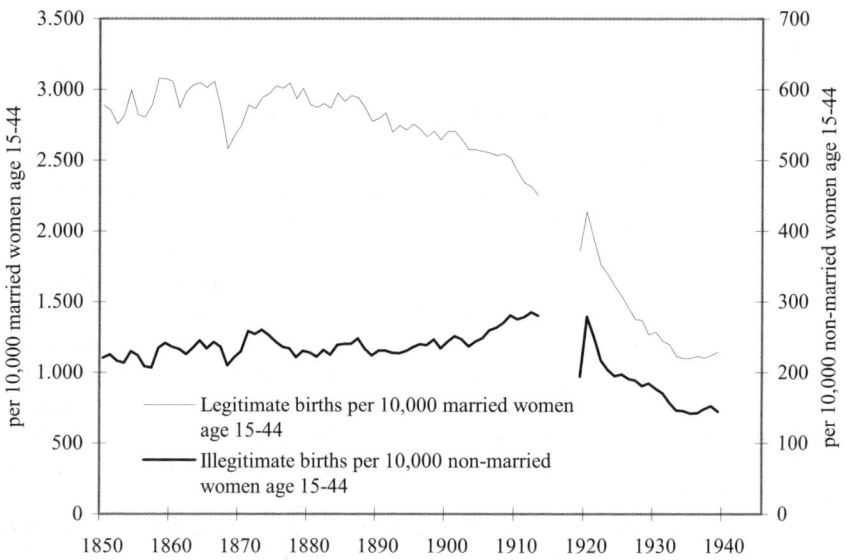

Figure S.5 Fertility and legitimacy 1850-1939

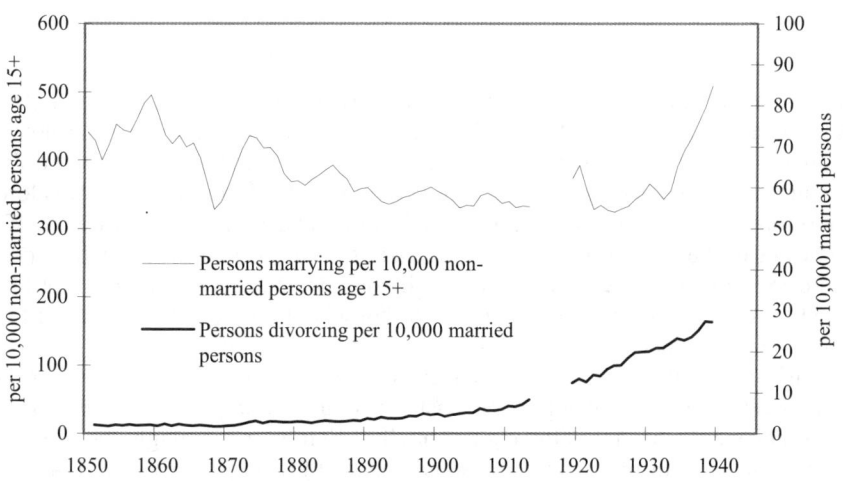

Figure S.6 Marriages and divorces 1850-1939

couples probably remained separated—at least for some time—and therefore the two rates can be added together—at least partially. In the 1970s the possibility of legal separations was abolished, and in 1977 the last case of legal separation was registered.

The Swedish age structure until World War I had a clear pyramidal shape (Appendix Figure S.8). From 1870 to 1890 the lowest age groups were very large due to high fertility and low infant mortality, making the age structure concave at the bottom. The age groups of young adults were smaller (more so for men than for women), probably caused by emigration. Between 1890 and 1900 the lowest age groups were slightly reduced, a sign of the starting fertility decline. This process continued from 1900 to 1910. Although Sweden did not participate in World War I, the age structure of 1920 shows a very strong fertility decline for the lowest two age groups 0–4 and 5–9 years. Already in 1920 the Swedish age structure assumed a bell shape. This pattern became much more pronounced in 1930 due to very strong Swedish fertility decline. It can still be seen in 1940, although the cohorts of 1936–40 were larger than those of 1926–35.

In Sweden as in most other European countries men remained single longer than women, but in higher age groups more men than women were married. This is caused by higher celibacy rates among women and higher mortality of men, leading to frequent widowhood. Until World War I the proportions of married people in younger age groups rose and celibacy in higher age groups decreased, while during the inter-war period the opposite trend set in.

FAMILY AND HOUSEHOLD STRUCTURES

The Western European marriage pattern *ceteris paribus* would favour either large households or a large number of single-person households or small households of unmarried people. Interestingly, households were very small in Sweden already in the nineteenth century, not far from the very low level of France, which was lowest in Europe because of the very early birth decline and extremely low birth rate. If the indicator of the mean private household size is used, then during the whole period from 1850 to 1990 Sweden had very small households or a very large proportion of smaller households. In 1990 mean private household size in Sweden was virtually the lowest in Europe.

This very small average is caused by a very high proportion of single-person households: during the whole of the last 150 years the proportion of single-person households in Sweden was the highest in all of Europe. Accordingly the proportion of households with five or more persons was quite low in Sweden: only France had fewer households of five and more persons. At present, Sweden has the lowest proportion of households consisting of five and more persons.

What conclusions can we draw from these meagre indicators of household development about the household organization of the Swedes? There are two possibilities: the first is methological, and the second substantive. The first explanation of the low mean private household size in Sweden could be that the definition of a private household included servants, relatives, boarders, and lodgers living in a family household. In most European countries, such persons were not counted as single-family households when they lived with the main family. But this question cannot be decided from the census definition alone. The only way to evaluate this question is to analyse original census questionnaires and compare them with printed statistics. The second explanation refers to low household size as a 'social fact' (Emile Durkheim). In this case the proportion of extended families would have been very low, widows would have lived on their own rather than with their children, and servants would not have lived with their masters. This hypothesis can only be verified by historico-demographic analyses. For the most recent time there is a methodological argument: if the household-dwelling concept is used, the number of households is smaller than if the household-keeping concept is used, because the number of dwellings is always lower than the number of households (several households can live in the same dwelling). This partly explains the small household size since 1945.

THE NATIONAL SYSTEM OF DEMOGRAPHIC STATISTICS

Population Structure

Sweden's early state formation in conjunction with the Protestant tradition contributed to the early development of population statistics, similar to Denmark, the other Nordic power centre. Population statistics of the provinces of both kingdoms, Iceland and Norway on the one hand and Finland on the other, were strongly influenced by developments in the mother country. The history of Swedish population statistics is well documented by Sundbärg (1907 (1970)) and Statistiska Centralbyrån (1969).

Already in the eighteenth century Sweden began to conduct population censuses on a regular basis and to exploit parish registers for population measurement. Censuses date back to the 1750s and became regular at the beginning of the nineteenth century. Censuses in the first half of the nineteenth century were conducted in 1805, 1810, 1820, 1830, 1840, and 1850. Since 1810 population censuses have been conducted in every year ending with zero. In 1935 additional censuses were introduced in years ending in a five, which often used a reduced question programme or applied sampling methods in order to investigate important and new social problems.

Population by age, sex, and marital status was first published in the 1870 census. Prior to this census, population figures were published by age and sex (in one-year age groups in 1860, grouped data for earlier censuses). Already in 1870 the data on ages were presented in one-year age groups. All the censuses until 1945 maintained this detailed data publication.

Vital Statistics

The main variables of vital statistics, marriages, live births, and deaths, were introduced in 1749 and are available for every year since then. Births by legitimacy are available as well since 1749. Infant deaths were recorded or can be reconstructed from the source since 1751. Annual population figures by sex (on 31 December) are also available since 1749.

Other demographic distinctions were added later: stillbirths have been recorded and published since 1851. Divorce figures are also available since 1851. Legal separations were published from 1916 until 1977 when publication stopped. Synthetic fertility measures such as the total fertility rate or the cohort fertility rate were recalculated beginning with the year 1901. Figures on the mean age at marriage have been available since the 1860s.

Households and Families

Data on *households* (*hushåll*) were first expressively recorded in 1860, but data are available since the beginning of census-taking in 1751 for the years 1805, 1810, 1820, 1830, 1840, 1850, and 1855 (cf. Statistiska Centralbyrån (1895: XXVII). Historical data on households from 1751 to 1855 are published in Statistiska Central-Byrån (1860: text pp. 34–43, table p. XXXI).

From the beginning household statistics in Sweden were rather detailed and comprehensive. Already in 1860 the three main household types of one-person households, family households, and institutional households were published. Furthermore, households were classified according to size (number of members). These household statistics were maintained in 1870 and 1880 as well. In 1890, household members were published by sex; no size distribution is available for this census. From 1900 to 1940 the classification of 1890 was published with the addition of the size distribution. In the inter-war period some special investigations were added to these basic statistics: in 1930 income and occupation of the family head was investigated; in 1935 family types were constructed and the occupation of the family head was given. Only for 1940 were no household statistics published.

Household composition became available for the first time in the 1930 census and was repeated in 1945. Different categories of household members such as children, parents, servants, etc. were distinguished. In 1935 a somewhat different typology was used, creating household types instead of calculating the number of different household members with regard to their relationship to the household head.

From 1860 to 1945 the housekeeping-unit concept formed the basis for the *definition of a household* (*hushåll*). Households were called 'person households' (*personhushåll*) in contrast to the household-dwelling concept used in the censuses from 1945 and after, when households were called 'dwelling households' (*bostadshushåll*). The definition of person households from 1860 to 1945 (and for dwelling households from 1945 to 1965) is given by Statistiska Centralbyrån (1969: 25f.). It should nevertheless be noted that household data before and after 1920 are not completely comparable:

Med personhushåll avses kosthushåll (matlagshushåll), d. v. s. hushåll vilkas medlemmar bor och äter åtminstone huvudmålet tillsammans. Till ett och samma hushåll räknas sålunda familjemedlemmar, personal i husbondens kost och inackorderingar men ej inneboende och andra hyresgäster. Dessa anses bilda egna hushåll. För definitioner se vidare SOS. Folkräkningen 1945: 7: 1, s. 2*f.

Uppgifterna från 1945 års folkräkning grundar sig på ett stickprov som omfattade ca 8 per cent av befolkningen. Tebellen innehåller tal som uppskrivits till att approximativt motsvara totalbefolkningens numerär.

I vår äldre befolkningsstatistik föreligger fr.o.m. år 1805 vissa uppgifter om hushåll. Någon modern bearbetning av tabellverkets statistik över hishåll föreligger emellertid inte.

Family statistics in the sense of fertility statistics were first investigated in 1935 after the Swedish fertility crisis of the early 1930s. At this time Swedish fertility figures had reached their lowest level in history, leading to the implementation of a national population and family policy (cf. Myrdal and Myrdal, 1935). The 1935 investigation dealt mainly with the number of children in marriages, contracted after 1900, for different social groups, distinguishing the duration of marriage and the age of the wife at marriage, taking into account the different regions, the profession and social status and the educational level of the husband, the income of the husband, and the work of the wife outside the home (Statistiska Centralbyrån, 1939: XVf.). This special investigation of marital fertility was repeated in 1945 and in all the censuses at least until 1965.

Family statistics in the modern sense as a statistics of nuclear families (*familjer*) or the biological unit only were introduced after World War II.

Remarks (also see introductory Table 6.1)

No peculiarities.

BOUNDARY CHANGES

In 1811 Sweden lost the territory of Finland to the Russian Empire. In 1814 it acquired Norway from Denmark. Norway became independent in 1905. There were no other boundary changes in Sweden. For regional organization see the documentation by Quick (1994) and Caramani, Flora, Kraus, and Quick (1998).

APPENDIX TABLE S.1 Population structure at census dates 1860–1945

Census number	Census date	Census population			Marital status				Age group		
		Total	Male	Female	Single	Married	Widowed	Divorced	0–14	15–64	65+
		Absolute									
1	31 XII 1860	3,859,730	1,874,399	1,985,331	..	..	..	..	1,292,962	2,365,658	201,110
2	31 XII 1870	4,168,565	2,016,653	2,151,912	2,552,009	1,361,499	252,503	2,554	1,419,349	2,522,506	226,710
3	31 XII 1880	4,565,668	2,215,243	2,350,425	2,780,992	1,515,586	266,031	3,059	1,488,244	2,808,414	269,010
4	31 XII 1890	4,784,981	2,317,187	2,467,794	2,892,507	1,600,076	288,510	3,888	1,593,316	2,823,927	367,738
5	31 XII 1900	5,136,441	2,506,436	2,630,005	3,133,536	1,686,251	311,108	5,546	1,666,310	3,040,297	429,834
6	31 XII 1910	5,522,403	2,698,729	2,823,674	3,376,454	1,810,685	326,986	8,278	1,751,157	3,305,176	466,070
7	31 XII 1920	5,904,489	2,898,256	3,006,233	3,558,121	1,979,220	352,053	15,095	1,728,253	3,680,045	496,191
8	31 XII 1930	6,142,191	3,020,848	3,121,343	3,531,797	2,213,585	365,090	31,719	1,525,399	4,050,833	565,959
9	31 XII 1935	6,250,506	3,090,451	3,160,055	3,445,486	2,391,026	371,447	42,547	1,383,916	4,290,908	575,682
10	31 XII 1940	6,371,432	3,160,128	3,211,304	3,273,780	2,662,484	380,703	54,465	1,300,914	4,471,103	599,415
11	31 XII 1945	6,673,749	3,319,977	3,353,772	3,225,335	2,991,174	385,740	71,500	1,441,131	4,572,246	660,372
		Per cent									
1	31 XII 1860	100.00	48.56	51.44	0.00	0.00	0.00	..	33.50	61.29	5.21
2	31 XII 1870	100.00	48.38	51.62	61.22	32.66	6.06	..	34.05	60.51	5.44
3	31 XII 1880	100.00	48.52	51.48	60.91	33.20	5.83	..	32.60	61.51	5.89
4	31 XII 1890	100.00	48.43	51.57	60.45	33.44	6.03	0.08	33.30	59.02	7.69
5	31 XII 1900	100.00	48.80	51.20	61.01	32.83	6.06	0.11	32.44	59.19	8.37
6	31 XII 1910	100.00	48.87	51.13	61.14	32.79	5.92	0.15	31.71	59.85	8.44
7	31 XII 1920	100.00	49.09	50.91	60.26	33.52	5.96	0.26	29.27	62.33	8.40
8	31 XII 1930	100.00	49.18	50.82	57.50	36.04	5.94	0.52	24.83	65.95	9.21
9	31 XII 1935	100.00	49.44	50.56	55.12	38.25	5.94	0.68	22.14	68.65	9.21
10	31 XII 1940	100.00	49.60	50.40	51.38	41.79	5.98	0.85	20.42	70.17	9.41
11	31 XII 1945	100.00	49.75	50.25	48.33	44.82	5.78	1.07	21.59	68.51	9.90

APPENDIX TABLE S.2 Census population by region 1870–1940 (per cent)

Län	1870	1880	1890	1900	1910	1920	1930	1940
Stockholms stad	3.26	3.70	5.14	5.86	6.19	7.10	8.17	9.28
Stockholms län	3.14	3.22	3.20	3.37	4.15	4.12	4.31	4.52
Uppsala	2.42	2.43	2.53	2.41	2.32	2.32	2.25	2.17
Södermanlands	3.26	3.22	3.24	3.25	3.24	3.22	3.08	3.01
Östergötlands	6.09	5.85	5.58	5.43	5.32	5.18	5.05	4.98
Jönköpings	4.32	4.29	4.05	3.95	3.88	3.86	3.78	3.80
Kronobergs	3.81	3.72	3.36	3.10	2.86	2.69	2.54	2.37
Kalmar	5.59	5.37	4.87	4.44	4.13	3.91	3.78	3.58
Gotlands	1.30	1.20	1.07	1.03	1.00	0.95	0.93	0.91
Blekinge	3.02	3.00	2.99	2.84	2.70	2.49	2.36	2.28
Kristianstads	5.33	5.06	4.64	4.26	4.13	4.08	4.01	3.89
Malmöhus	7.58	7.64	7.71	7.96	8.28	8.25	8.32	8.30
Hallands	3.05	2.96	2.84	2.76	2.66	2.52	2.44	2.39
Göteborgs och Bohus	5.56	5.72	6.23	6.56	6.90	7.20	7.44	7.63
Älvsborgs	6.69	6.33	5.77	5.45	5.22	5.08	5.10	5.16
Skaraborgs	5.85	5.65	5.16	4.69	4.36	4.13	3.94	3.75
Värmlands	6.24	5.87	5.29	4.95	4.71	4.56	4.40	4.21
Örebro	6.43	3.99	3.82	3.80	3.75	3.71	3.57	3.55
Västmanlands	2.73	2.80	2.86	2.88	2.81	2.86	2.64	2.65
Kopparbergs	4.22	4.16	4.12	4.24	4.24	4.30	4.07	3.89
Gävleborgs[1]	3.53	3.92	4.33	4.63	4.60	4.54	4.56	4.30
Västernorrlands	3.24	3.70	4.37	4.52	4.55	4.49	4.54	4.33
Jämtlands	1.68	1.84	2.09	2.16	2.14	2.27	2.20	2.18
Västerbottens	2.21	2.32	2.57	2.80	2.92	3.08	3.32	3.45
Norrbottens	1.82	1.99	2.19	2.63	2.92	3.10	3.26	3.39
TOTAL	**100.00**	**100.00**	**100.00**	**100.00**	**100.00**	**100.00**	**100.00**	**100.00**

Note: [1] Prior to 1910 spelled Gefleborgs.

APPENDIX TABLE S.3 Population density by region 1870–1940 (inhabitants per sq. km.)

Län	1870	1880	1890	1900	1910	1920	1930	1940
Stockholms stad	8,500	5,281	7,688	9,406	10,688	3,174	3,691	4,314
Stockholms län	19	20	21	23	31	33	36	39
Uppsala	20	22	24	24	25	27	27	27
Södermanlands	22	23	25	27	29	30	30	31
Östergötlands	26	27	27	28	29	31	31	32
Jönköpings	18	18	18	19	20	21	22	23
Kronobergs	18	19	18	18	18	18	18	17
Kalmar	21	22	21	21	21	21	21	21
Gotlands	19	18	16	17	18	18	18	18
Blekinge	44	47	49	50	51	51	50	50
Kristianstads	35	37	36	35	37	39	39	27
Malmöhus	67	75	78	86	97	103	108	112
Hallands	27	28	29	30	31	31	32	32
Göteborgs och Bohus	47	53	61	69	78	87	93	98
Älvsborgs	23	24	23	24	25	26	27	28
Skaraborgs	30	32	31	30	30	30	30	30
Värmlands	17	15	14	15	15	15	15	15
Örebro	32	22	22	24	25	26	26	27
Västmanlands	18	20	21	23	24	26	25	26
Kopparbergs	6	7	7	8	8	9	9	9
Gävleborgs[1]	8	10	11	13	14	15	15	15
Västernorrlands	6	7	9	10	10	11	12	12
Jämtlands	2	2	2	2	2	3	3	3
Västerbottens	2	2	2	3	3	3	4	4
Norrbottens	1	1	1	1	2	2	2	2
TOTAL	**10**	**11**	**12**	**12**	**13**	**14**	**15**	**16**

Note: [1] Prior to 1910 spelled Gefleborgs.

APPENDIX TABLE S.4 Demographic developments 1850–1945 (absolute figures and rates)

Year	Mid-year population	Natural population growth rate	Population growth rate	Net migration rate	Crude birth rate	Legitimate births per 10,000 married women age 15–44	Illegitimate births per 10,000 unmarried women age 15–44	Illeg. births per 100 leg. births
1850	3,461,914	12.1	12.3	0.2	31.9	2,891	221	10.3
1851	3,499,594	11.0	10.8	-0.3	31.7	2,859	225	10.6
1852	3,528,528	8.0	8.2	0.2	30.7	2,757	217	10.4
1853	3,551,863	7.7	6.6	-1.1	31.4	2,820	214	10.0
1854	3,585,720	13.7	9.4	-4.3	33.5	2,998	230	10.1
1855	3,624,568	10.3	10.7	0.4	31.7	2,823	225	10.4
1856	3,656,999	9.7	8.9	-0.8	31.5	2,806	209	9.6
1857	3,680,295	4.9	6.3	1.5	32.4	2,893	207	9.2
1858	3,710,921	13.1	8.3	-4.8	34.8	3,077	235	9.7
1859	3,760,987	14.9	13.3	-1.5	35.0	3,078	242	9.9
1860	3,823,732	17.2	16.4	-0.8	34.8	3,058	236	9.7
1861	3,888,534	14.1	16.7	2.6	32.6	2,872	233	10.3
1862	3,941,619	12.0	13.5	1.5	33.4	2,990	226	9.7
1863	3,994,232	14.3	13.2	-1.1	33.6	3,032	235	10.0
1864	4,046,313	13.4	12.9	-0.5	33.6	3,048	246	10.5
1865	4,092,101	13.5	11.2	-2.3	32.8	3,014	234	10.2
1866	4,137,409	13.1	11.0	-2.2	33.1	3,059	243	10.5
1867	4,178,179	11.2	9.8	-1.4	30.8	2,865	237	11.1
1868	4,184,381	6.5	1.5	-5.0	27.5	2,581	210	11.0
1869	4,165,919	6.0	-4.4	-10.4	28.2	2,674	221	11.3
1870	4,163,641	9.0	-0.5	-9.5	28.8	2,748	230	11.6
1871	4,186,351	13.2	5.4	-7.8	30.4	2,891	258	12.4
1872	4,227,295	13.8	9.7	-4.1	30.0	2,865	255	12.4
1873	4,274,192	13.6	11.0	-2.6	30.8	2,944	260	12.4
1874	4,319,766	10.5	10.6	0.0	30.8	2,969	253	12.0
1875	4,362,425	10.9	9.8	-1.1	31.2	3,025	244	11.4
1876	4,406,502	11.2	10.0	-1.2	30.8	3,010	236	11.1
1877	4,457,127	12.4	11.4	-1.0	31.1	3,047	234	11.0
1878	4,508,203	11.8	11.3	-0.4	29.8	2,936	222	10.8
1879	4,555,382	13.6	10.4	-3.2	30.5	3,008	231	11.0
1880	4,572,285	11.3	3.7	-7.6	29.4	2,894	228	11.4
1881	4,568,955	11.4	-0.7	-12.1	29.1	2,875	222	11.1
1882	4,575,680	12.0	1.5	-10.5	29.4	2,901	232	11.4
1883	4,591,350	11.6	3.4	-8.2	28.9	2,870	225	11.2
1884	4,624,022	12.5	7.1	-5.4	30.0	2,977	239	11.4
1885	4,663,609	11.7	8.5	-3.2	29.4	2,918	240	11.6
1886	4,699,979	13.2	7.7	-5.4	29.8	2,958	240	11.4
1887	4,726,045	13.5	5.5	-8.0	29.7	2,945	248	11.8
1888	4,741,579	12.8	3.3	-9.5	28.8	2,872	233	11.3
1889	4,761,333	11.7	4.1	-7.6	27.7	2,778	224	11.2
1890	4,779,695	10.8	3.8	-7.0	28.0	2,798	231	11.4
1891	4,793,866	11.5	3.0	-8.5	28.3	2,836	231	11.3
1892	4,804,808	9.1	2.3	-6.8	27.0	2,701	228	11.7
1893	4,815,508	10.5	2.2	-8.3	27.4	2,747	227	11.5
1894	4,848,667	10.7	6.8	-3.9	27.1	2,716	231	11.9
1895	4,896,221	12.3	9.7	-2.6	27.5	2,757	236	12.0
1896	4,940,914	11.5	9.0	-2.5	27.2	2,719	240	12.4
1897	4,986,100	11.3	9.1	-2.3	26.7	2,667	238	12.6

continued

APPENDIX TABLE S.4 Demographic developments 1850–1945 (absolute figures and rates)

Crude death rate	Infant mortality rate	Stillbirth rate	Infant mortality and stillbirth rate	Crude marriage rate	Persons marrying per 10,000 unmarried persons age 15+	Persons marrying per 10,000 unmarried persons age 15–49	Crude divorce rate	Divorces per 100 marriages	Divorces per 10,000 married persons	Year
19.8	146.2	..	..	7.6	441	542	..	..	..	1850
20.7	152.1	33.7	185.8	7.4	429	527	0.0	0.5	2.1	1851
22.7	162.5	32.3	194.8	6.8	400	492	0.0	0.5	1.9	1852
23.7	161.0	32.6	193.7	7.2	423	520	0.0	0.4	1.8	1853
19.8	126.2	33.2	159.4	7.7	453	557	0.0	0.4	2.1	1854
21.4	144.9	34.1	179.0	7.5	444	546	0.0	0.4	1.9	1855
21.8	144.7	33.4	178.1	7.4	441	543	0.0	0.5	2.2	1856
27.6	165.4	33.6	199.0	7.8	461	567	0.0	0.4	2.0	1857
21.7	142.7	32.8	175.5	8.1	484	595	0.0	0.4	2.0	1858
20.1	143.1	35.2	178.4	8.3	495	610	0.0	0.4	2.1	1859
17.7	123.8	32.6	156.3	7.8	469	577	0.0	0.4	1.9	1860
18.5	137.3	32.6	169.8	7.3	437	538	0.0	0.5	2.3	1861
21.4	139.3	34.2	173.5	7.1	424	523	0.0	0.4	1.8	1862
19.3	132.6	35.4	168.0	7.3	436	538	0.0	0.5	2.2	1863
20.2	136.7	34.1	170.8	7.0	419	518	0.0	0.5	2.0	1864
19.4	135.1	33.5	168.5	7.1	425	525	0.0	0.4	1.9	1865
20.0	126.9	34.4	161.3	6.7	404	500	0.0	0.5	2.0	1866
19.6	140.1	33.4	173.5	6.1	366	453	0.0	0.5	1.9	1867
21.0	168.3	33.9	202.2	5.5	328	406	0.0	0.5	1.7	1868
22.3	145.8	33.5	179.2	5.6	339	421	0.0	0.5	1.7	1869
19.8	131.9	33.4	165.3	6.0	362	449	0.0	0.5	1.9	1870
17.2	113.7	34.4	148.1	6.5	389	484	0.0	0.5	2.0	1871
16.3	128.3	32.6	160.9	7.0	417	518	0.0	0.5	2.2	1872
17.2	128.8	32.6	161.4	7.3	436	543	0.0	0.6	2.7	1873
20.3	146.7	34.4	181.1	7.3	432	539	0.1	0.7	3.0	1874
20.3	149.0	32.1	181.0	7.1	418	521	0.0	0.6	2.5	1875
19.6	140.2	32.0	172.2	7.1	418	522	0.0	0.7	2.9	1876
18.7	125.5	30.3	155.8	6.9	406	507	0.0	0.7	2.9	1877
18.1	134.2	29.2	163.3	6.5	380	475	0.0	0.7	2.7	1878
16.9	111.2	30.2	141.4	6.3	368	461	0.0	0.7	2.7	1879
18.1	120.7	30.2	150.8	6.3	370	463	0.0	0.8	2.9	1880
17.7	112.7	29.2	142.0	6.2	363	456	0.0	0.8	2.8	1881
17.4	124.6	28.0	152.6	6.3	372	469	0.0	0.7	2.6	1882
17.3	115.7	28.0	143.7	6.4	378	478	0.0	0.7	2.9	1883
17.5	113.2	27.7	140.8	6.5	386	490	0.1	0.8	3.1	1884
17.8	114.3	29.2	143.5	6.6	393	500	0.0	0.7	2.9	1885
16.6	111.2	28.3	139.5	6.4	381	487	0.0	0.8	2.9	1886
16.1	103.1	27.5	130.6	6.2	372	477	0.0	0.8	3.0	1887
16.0	100.3	27.6	127.9	5.9	354	455	0.1	0.9	3.2	1888
16.0	107.2	26.6	133.9	6.0	359	463	0.1	0.8	3.0	1889
17.1	103.1	26.6	129.7	6.0	360	466	0.1	1.0	3.7	1890
16.8	107.9	26.2	134.2	5.8	349	452	0.1	1.0	3.4	1891
17.9	109.2	25.9	135.1	5.7	339	439	0.1	1.2	3.9	1892
16.8	101.2	26.1	127.3	5.7	335	434	0.1	1.1	3.7	1893
16.4	100.9	26.3	127.2	5.7	339	439	0.1	1.0	3.6	1894
15.2	94.7	26.3	121.0	5.9	345	447	0.1	1.1	3.8	1895
15.6	103.3	26.2	129.6	5.9	348	451	0.1	1.2	4.3	1896
15.4	98.6	27.9	126.4	6.1	354	458	0.1	1.2	4.2	1897

continued

APPENDIX TABLE S.4 Demographic developments 1850–1945 (continued)

Year	Mid-year population	Natural population growth rate	Population growth rate	Net migration rate	Crude birth rate	Legitimate births per 10,000 married women age 15–44	Illegitimate births per 10,000 unmarried women age 15–44	Illeg. births per 100 leg. births
1898	5,036,275	12.0	10.0	-2.1	27.1	2,706	247	12.9
1899	5,080,160	8.7	8.6	-0.1	26.4	2,644	234	12.6
1900	5,116,722	10.2	7.1	-3.0	27.0	2,706	244	12.9
1901	5,155,835	11.0	7.6	-3.4	27.0	2,708	251	13.3
1902	5,186,990	11.1	6.0	-5.1	26.5	2,648	247	13.4
1903	5,210,022	10.6	4.4	-6.2	25.7	2,576	237	13.2
1904	5,241,051	10.5	5.9	-4.5	25.7	2,574	244	13.7
1905	5,277,848	10.0	7.0	-3.1	25.7	2,563	248	14.0
1906	5,315,970	11.3	7.2	-4.2	25.7	2,554	260	14.7
1907	5,357,384	10.9	7.7	-3.2	25.5	2,532	263	15.1
1908	5,403,657	10.8	8.6	-2.2	25.7	2,544	270	15.5
1909	5,453,021	11.9	9.1	-2.9	25.6	2,518	280	16.2
1910	5,499,422	10.6	8.4	-2.2	24.7	2,422	275	16.6
1911	5,542,101	10.2	7.7	-2.5	24.0	2,344	278	17.4
1912	5,582,996	9.6	7.3	-2.3	23.8	2,314	285	18.1
1913	5,621,388	9.5	6.8	-2.7	23.2	2,250	280	18.3
1914	5,659,095	9.0	6.7	-2.4	22.9	..	..	18.8
1915	5,696,174	6.9	6.5	-0.4	21.6	..	..	18.8
1916	5,735,153	7.7	6.8	-0.9	21.2	..	..	17.5
1917	5,779,207	7.5	7.6	0.1	20.9	..	..	17.6
1918	5,807,349	2.3	4.8	2.5	20.3	..	..	16.1
1919	5,830,444	5.3	4.0	-1.3	19.8	1,859	195	15.0
1920	5,875,763	10.3	7.7	-2.6	23.6	2,138	279	18.6
1921	5,929,403	9.1	9.0	-0.1	21.5	1,940	249	18.3
1922	5,970,918	6.8	7.0	0.2	19.6	1,763	217	17.4
1923	5,996,640	7.5	4.3	-3.2	18.9	1,696	204	16.9
1924	6,020,939	6.2	4.0	-2.1	18.1	1,612	195	16.9
1925	6,044,840	5.9	4.0	-1.9	17.6	1,540	197	17.9
1926	6,063,965	5.1	3.2	-1.9	16.8	1,457	191	18.2
1927	6,081,146	3.4	2.8	-0.6	16.1	1,377	189	18.9
1928	6,096,557	4.0	2.5	-1.5	16.1	1,369	181	18.2
1929	6,112,635	3.0	2.6	-0.4	15.2	1,268	185	19.9
1930	6,131,135	3.7	3.0	-0.6	15.4	1,285	177	18.7
1931	6,152,319	2.3	3.4	1.2	14.8	1,222	171	18.7
1932	6,176,405	3.0	3.9	0.9	14.5	1,198	157	17.2
1933	6,200,965	2.5	4.0	1.5	13.7	1,117	147	16.9
1934	6,222,328	2.4	3.4	1.0	13.7	1,101	146	16.8
1935	6,241,798	2.1	3.1	1.0	13.8	1,100	143	16.1
1936	6,258,697	2.3	2.7	0.4	14.2	1,117	143	15.1
1937	6,275,805	2.4	2.7	0.3	14.4	1,103	149	15.3
1938	6,297,468	3.4	3.4	0.1	14.9	1,121	153	14.7
1939	6,325,759	3.9	4.5	0.6	15.4	1,146	145	13.1
1940	6,356,368	3.6	4.8	1.2	15.1	..	..	12.8
1941	6,388,953	4.4	5.1	0.7	15.6	..	..	11.8
1942	6,432,337	7.8	6.7	-1.1	17.7	..	..	10.7
1943	6,490,514	9.1	9.0	-0.2	19.3	..	..	10.8
1944	6,560,088	9.6	10.6	1.0	20.6	..	..	10.6
1945	6,635,549	9.6	11.4	1.8	20.4	..	..	10.1

APPENDIX TABLE S.4 Demographic developments 1850–1945 (continued)

Crude death rate	Infant mortality rate	Stillbirth rate	Infant mortality and stillbirth rate	Crude marriage rate	Persons marrying per 10,000 unmarried persons age 15+	Persons marrying per 10,000 unmarried persons age 15–49	Crude divorce rate	Divorces per 100 marriages	Divorces per 10,000 married persons	Year
15.1	90.8	27.1	117.8	6.1	356	461	0.1	1.3	4.9	1898
17.7	111.7	26.5	138.1	6.2	361	467	0.1	1.2	4.6	1899
16.8	98.5	25.9	124.4	6.2	354	459	0.1	1.3	4.8	1900
16.1	102.9	26.0	129.0	6.1	349	452	0.1	1.1	4.2	1901
15.4	86.4	25.6	111.9	6.0	342	443	0.1	1.3	4.6	1902
15.1	92.8	25.7	118.5	5.8	330	428	0.1	1.4	4.9	1903
15.3	84.4	26.2	110.5	5.9	334	433	0.1	1.4	5.1	1904
15.6	88.3	25.2	113.5	5.9	333	432	0.1	1.5	5.2	1905
14.4	81.0	25.2	106.3	6.1	348	452	0.1	1.6	6.1	1906
14.6	76.8	25.9	102.7	6.2	352	457	0.1	1.5	5.7	1907
14.9	85.4	24.7	110.2	6.1	346	450	0.1	1.5	5.7	1908
13.7	72.2	25.0	97.1	6.0	337	437	0.1	1.6	5.9	1909
14.0	75.1	24.7	99.9	6.0	340	441	0.1	1.8	6.8	1910
13.8	72.0	25.3	97.3	5.9	331	430	0.1	1.8	6.6	1911
14.2	70.9	25.0	95.9	5.9	333	433	0.1	2.0	7.2	1912
13.6	69.7	24.7	94.4	5.9	332	432	0.1	2.3	8.4	1913
13.8	72.9	24.7	97.6	5.8	..	..	0.1	2.4	..	1914
14.7	75.8	25.2	100.9	5.8	..	..	0.1	2.6	..	1915
13.6	69.7	25.4	95.1	6.1	..	..	0.1	2.2	..	1916
13.4	64.5	23.3	87.8	6.1	..	..	0.2	2.9	..	1917
18.0	64.6	24.4	89.0	6.7	..	..	0.2	2.8	..	1918
14.5	69.6	23.1	92.8	6.9	373	483	0.2	3.0	12.4	1919
13.3	63.3	23.2	86.5	7.3	393	509	0.2	3.1	13.5	1920
12.4	64.0	25.1	89.1	6.7	357	463	0.2	3.2	12.6	1921
12.8	62.5	24.9	87.4	6.2	328	426	0.2	4.0	14.3	1922
11.4	56.2	25.1	81.3	6.3	334	434	0.2	3.8	14.0	1923
12.0	60.3	25.4	85.7	6.2	327	425	0.3	4.4	15.7	1924
11.7	55.7	24.5	80.2	6.2	324	422	0.3	4.7	16.6	1925
11.8	56.0	26.1	82.1	6.3	329	428	0.3	4.6	16.7	1926
12.7	59.8	26.1	85.8	6.4	333	433	0.3	5.1	18.4	1927
12.0	58.8	27.1	85.9	6.6	343	447	0.4	5.3	19.8	1928
12.2	58.5	27.3	85.8	6.8	351	457	0.4	5.2	20.0	1929
11.7	54.7	27.6	82.4	7.2	366	477	0.4	5.1	20.1	1930
12.5	56.6	28.9	85.6	7.0	356	465	0.4	5.5	20.9	1931
11.6	50.7	27.9	78.6	6.7	343	450	0.4	5.7	20.9	1932
11.2	49.5	27.4	76.9	7.0	355	467	0.4	5.9	22.1	1933
11.2	47.2	27.7	74.9	7.7	391	515	0.4	5.7	23.3	1934
11.7	45.9	27.6	73.4	8.2	415	548	0.4	5.3	22.8	1935
12.0	43.4	28.3	71.7	8.5	434	576	0.5	5.4	23.6	1936
12.0	45.2	29.6	74.7	8.9	456	609	0.5	5.6	25.1	1937
11.5	42.5	28.5	71.0	9.2	479	645	0.6	6.0	27.4	1938
11.5	39.5	28.0	67.5	9.7	509	689	0.6	5.8	27.3	1939
11.4	39.2	29.4	68.7	9.3	..	..	0.5	5.9	..	1940
11.3	37.0	25.1	62.1	9.1	..	..	0.5	5.9	..	1941
9.9	29.3	22.9	52.2	9.9	..	..	0.6	6.6	..	1942
10.2	28.9	22.3	51.3	9.7	..	..	0.7	7.6	..	1943
11.0	31.1	23.6	54.7	9.9	..	..	0.8	8.4	..	1944
10.8	29.9	24.6	54.5	9.7	..	..	1.0	10.1	..	1945

APPENDIX TABLE S.5 Life expectancy by age 1755/76–1941/45 (in years)

Age	0	10	20	30	40	50	60	70	80
				Males					
1755–1776	33.20	43.94	36.95	30.34	23.75	17.72	12.24	7.60	4.27
1816–1840	39.50	45.21	37.32	30.25	23.66	17.55	12.07	7.35	4.03
1841–1845	41.94	46.98	38.95	31.60	..	..	12.49	..	3.84
1846–1850	41.38	46.57	38.58	31.18	..	..	12.17	..	3.73
1851–1855	40.51	45.90	38.11	30.89	..	..	12.23	..	4.09
1856–1860	40.48	47.32	39.99	32.91	..	..	13.12	..	3.12
1861–1870	42.80	48.90	41.00	33.60	26.30	19.40	13.10	8.00	4.30
1871–1880	45.30	50.30	42.30	35.10	27.80	20.80	14.20	8.50	4.60
1881–1890	48.55	52.16	44.18	36.87	29.27	21.94	15.07	9.14	4.81
1891–1900	50.94	52.79	44.75	37.50	29.90	22.44	15.44	9.36	4.88
1901–1910	54.53	54.03	45.88	38.57	30.77	23.17	16.06	9.85	5.22
1911–1915	56.49	54.36	46.11	38.78	30.97	23.22	16.04	9.81	5.23
1916–1920	54.81	52.14	44.52	38.37	31.16	23.47	16.20	9.93	5.28
1921–1925	60.72	57.09	48.49	40.66	32.39	24.22	16.70	10.28	5.51
1926–1930	61.19	57.32	48.56	40.50	32.16	24.04	16.50	10.11	5.37
1931–1935	63.22	58.37	49.44	41.07	32.50	24.21	16.59	10.12	5.37
1936–1940	64.30	58.77	49.70	41.13	32.37	23.97	16.35	9.92	5.25
1941–1945	67.06	60.45	51.23	42.57	33.64	25.02	17.19	10.52	5.61
				Females					
1755–1776	35.70	46.25	39.15	32.17	25.21	19.26	13.08	7.91	4.47
1816–1840	43.56	48.59	40.75	33.40	26.41	19.60	13.22	8.03	4.46
1841–1845	46.60	50.52	42.60	34.95	..	..	13.77	..	4.35
1846–1850	45.59	50.10	42.21	34.48	..	..	13.41	..	4.16
1851–1855	44.64	49.39	41.57	33.95	..	..	13.28	..	4.48
1856–1860	44.15	49.99	42.60	36.06	..	..	14.04	..	4.91
1861–1870	46.40	51.80	43.90	36.20	28.70	21.30	14.40	8.80	4.70
1871–1880	48.60	52.90	45.00	37.50	30.10	22.60	15.40	9.40	5.20
1881–1890	51.47	54.22	46.40	38.82	31.28	23.64	16.25	9.96	5.40
1891–1900	53.63	54.61	46.76	39.31	31.75	24.04	16.56	10.08	5.40
1901–1910	56.98	55.58	47.66	40.20	32.53	24.74	17.19	10.53	5.64
1911–1915	59.24	56.27	48.13	40.49	32.66	24.79	17.13	10.47	5.59
1916–1920	57.62	54.45	46.70	39.89	32.55	24.78	17.24	10.59	5.75
1921–1925	62.95	58.29	49.73	41.68	33.43	25.26	17.51	10.75	5.78
1926–1930	63.33	58.43	49.73	41.60	33.25	25.01	17.29	10.56	5.67
1931–1935	65.33	59.49	50.55	42.15	33.54	25.14	17.29	10.51	5.62
1936–1940	66.92	60.46	51.27	42.48	33.67	25.12	17.19	10.37	5.49
1941–1945	69.71	62.40	53.02	44.01	34.97	26.20	18.04	11.00	5.91

APPENDIX TABLE S.6A Households by type 1860–1945 (absolute and per cent)

Census year	Household types and members									
	Total households	Private households	Family households	One-person households	Institutional households	Total household members	Private household members	Family household members	One-person household members	Institutional household members
					Absolute					
1860	..	892,497	754,014	138,483	..	3,859,728	3,817,131	3,678,648	138,483	42,597
1870	..	1,017,323	835,183	182,140	..	4,168,525	4,136,495	3,954,355	182,140	32,030
1880	..	1,152,336	921,863	230,473	..	4,565,668	4,536,036	4,305,563	230,473	29,632
1890	..	1,265,665	980,930	284,735	..	4,784,981	4,759,009	4,474,274	284,735	25,972
1900	..	1,368,304	1,044,865	323,439	..	5,136,441	5,094,109	4,770,670	323,439	42,332
1910	..	1,471,568	1,139,590	331,978	..	5,522,403	5,475,029	5,143,051	331,978	47,374
1920	..	1,607,273	1,255,741	351,532	..	5,904,489	5,852,029	5,500,497	351,532	52,460
1930	1,721,551	1,717,669	1,393,773	323,896	3,882	6,116,582	6,026,137	5,702,241	323,896	90,445
1945	..	2,361,786	1,767,337	594,449	..	6,673,688	6,607,688	6,013,239	594,449	66,000
					Total households per cent					
1930	100.00	99.77	80.96	18.81	0.23	100.00	98.52	93.23	5.30	1.48
					Private households per cent					
1860	..	100.00	84.48	15.52	..		100.00	96.37	3.63	..
1870	..	100.00	82.10	17.90	..		100.00	95.60	4.40	..
1880	..	100.00	80.00	20.00	..		100.00	94.92	5.08	..
1890	..	100.00	77.50	22.50	..		100.00	94.02	5.98	..
1900	..	100.00	76.36	23.64	..		100.00	93.65	6.35	..
1910	..	100.00	77.44	22.56	..		100.00	93.94	6.06	..
1920	..	100.00	78.13	21.87	..		100.00	93.99	6.01	..
1930	..	100.00	81.14	18.86	..		100.00	94.63	5.37	..
1945	..	100.00	74.83	25.17	..		100.00	91.00	9.00	..

APPENDIX TABLE S.6B Households by size and members 1860–1945 (absolute figures)

Census year	Private households total	Households by number of members								
		1 person	2 persons	3 persons	4 persons	5 persons	6 persons	7 persons	8 persons	9+ persons
Households										
1860	892,497	138,483	128,103	130,929	125,440	111,277	90,567	65,523	42,520	59,655
1870	1,017,323	182,140	147,625	147,097	142,837	126,627	100,859	71,455	44,508	54,175
1880	1,152,336	230,473	174,259	169,190	156,427	132,691	105,385	75,785	48,387	59,739
1890	1,265,665	284,735	..	..	..	..	..	..	..	..
1900	1,368,304	323,439	215,491	197,586	174,665	143,826	111,902	82,424	54,179	64,792
1910	1,471,568	331,978	231,110	225,784	199,577	158,767	119,097	82,924	54,992	67,339
1920	1,607,273	351,532	257,481	271,331	232,407	174,304	122,545	81,366	52,164	64,143
1930	1,717,669	323,896	313,920	339,158	272,860	186,194	118,780	72,537	42,542	47,782
1945	2,361,786	594,449	552,117	544,168	354,739	169,407	78,889	35,721	16,776	15,520
Persons										
1860	3,817,131	138,483	256,206	392,787	501,760	556,385	543,402	458,661	340,160	629,287
1870	4,136,495	182,140	295,250	441,291	571,348	633,135	605,154	500,185	356,064	551,928
1880	4,536,036	230,473	348,518	507,570	625,708	663,455	632,310	530,495	387,096	610,411
1890	4,759,009	284,735	..	..	..	..	..	..	..	..
1900	5,094,109	323,439	430,982	592,758	698,660	719,130	671,412	576,968	433,432	647,328
1910	5,475,029	331,978	462,220	677,352	798,308	793,835	714,582	580,468	439,936	676,350
1920	5,852,029	351,532	514,962	813,993	929,628	871,520	735,270	569,562	417,312	648,250
1930	6,026,137	323,896	627,840	1,017,474	1,091,440	930,970	712,680	507,759	340,336	473,742
1945	6,607,688	594,449	1,104,234	1,632,504	1,418,956	847,035	473,334	250,047	134,208	152,921

APPENDIX TABLE S.6C Households by size and members 1860–1945 (per cent)

Census year	Private households total	1 person	2 persons	3 persons	4 persons	5 persons	6 persons	7 persons	8 persons	9+ persons
					Households					
1860	100.00	15.52	14.35	14.67	14.05	12.47	10.15	7.34	4.76	6.68
1870	100.00	17.90	14.51	14.46	14.04	12.45	9.91	7.02	4.38	5.33
1880	100.00	20.00	15.12	14.68	13.57	11.51	9.15	6.58	4.20	5.18
1890	100.00	22.50	..	..	..	..	..	..	..	..
1900	100.00	23.64	15.75	14.44	12.77	10.51	8.18	6.02	3.96	4.74
1910	100.00	22.56	15.71	15.34	13.56	10.79	8.09	5.64	3.74	4.58
1920	100.00	21.87	16.02	16.88	14.46	10.84	7.62	5.06	3.25	3.99
1930	100.00	18.86	18.28	19.75	15.89	10.84	6.92	4.22	2.48	2.78
1945	100.00	25.17	23.38	23.04	15.02	7.17	3.34	1.51	0.71	0.66
					Persons					
1860	100.00	3.63	6.71	10.29	13.14	14.58	14.24	12.02	8.91	16.49
1870	100.00	4.40	7.14	10.67	13.81	15.31	14.63	12.09	8.61	13.34
1880	100.00	5.08	7.68	11.19	13.79	14.63	13.94	11.70	8.53	13.46
1890	100.00	5.98	..	..	..	..	..	..	..	..
1900	100.00	6.35	8.46	11.64	13.72	14.12	13.18	11.33	8.51	12.71
1910	100.00	6.06	8.44	12.37	14.58	14.50	13.05	10.60	8.04	12.35
1920	100.00	6.01	8.80	13.91	15.89	14.89	12.56	9.73	7.13	11.08
1930	100.00	5.37	10.42	16.88	18.11	15.45	11.83	8.43	5.65	7.86
1945	100.00	9.00	16.71	24.71	21.47	12.82	7.16	3.78	2.03	2.31

Households by number of members

APPENDIX TABLE S.6D Household indicators 1860–1945

Census year	Household indicators			
	Mean total household size	Mean private household size	Mean family household size	Mean institutional household size
1860	..	4.28	4.88	..
1870	..	4.07	4.73	..
1880	..	3.94	4.67	..
1890	..	3.76	4.56	..
1900	..	3.72	4.57	..
1910	..	3.72	4.51	..
1920	..	3.64	4.38	..
1930	3.55	3.51	4.09	23.30
1945	..	2.80	3.40	..

APPENDIX TABLE S.6E Household composition 1930 (absolute and per cent)

	House-holds	Household members	Thereof: children under 15 years	Thereof: children over 15 years	Thereof: parents	Thereof: servants	Thereof: others
Absolute	1,717,669	6,026,137	1,418,299	1,060,678	455,638	140,213	178,683
Per cent	..	100.00	23.54	17.60	7.56	2.33	2.97

APPENDIX TABLE S.6F Household composition 1935 (absolute and per cent)

Main household types	Number of households	Number of household members	Thereof: family members	Thereof: parents	Thereof: servants	Thereof: boarders and lodgers	Thereof: other household members	Household members that are children under 15 years	Household members that are temporarily present	Persons not included in households: temporarily absent	Persons not included in households: sub-tenants
					Absolute						
Matlagshushåll proper[1]	361,287	1,236,951	1,084,259	72,794	28,289	7,491	44,118	283,665	13,063	27,639	20,322
					Thereof:						
One-person households	49,078	49,078	49,078	..	..	..	..	..	251	1,700	4,911
			Multiperson households, thereof:								
Married man with wife	240,666	966,283	896,109	28,360	13,437	3,837	24,540	256,924	7,869	19,924	10,274
Single man with children	13,174	48,756	35,672	5,664	3,634	234	3,252	9,019	643	1,522	490
Single woman with children	23,817	78,614	68,829	4,691	1,174	1,290	2,630	14,223	1,382	2,380	2,463
Single man without children	22,157	63,334	22,122	23,585	7,773	553	9,301	2,914	1,501	1,451	947
Single woman without children	12,395	30,886	12,449	10,494	1,971	1,577	4,395	585	1,417	662	1,237
Sub-tenant household	16,419	18,540	17,941	332	42	1	224	701	1,841	187	..
Institutional household	1,240	20,172	20,162	..	..	..	10	919	2,949	1,349	7
Relationship unknown	332	421	360	8	..	..	53	15	2	9	..
Total	740,565	2,513,035	2,206,981	145,928	56,320	14,983	88,523	568,965	30,918	56,823	40,651
					Column per cent						
Matlagshushåll proper[1]	48.79	49.22	49.13	49.88	50.23	50.00	49.84	49.86	42.25	48.64	49.99
					Thereof:						
One-person households	6.63	1.95	2.22	0.00	0.00	0.00	0.00	0.00	0.81	2.99	12.08
			Multiperson households, thereof:								
Married man with wife	32.50	38.45	40.60	19.43	23.86	25.61	27.72	45.16	25.45	35.06	25.27
Single man with children	1.78	1.94	1.62	3.88	6.45	1.56	3.67	1.59	2.08	2.68	1.21
Single woman with children	3.22	3.13	3.12	3.21	2.08	8.61	2.97	2.50	4.47	4.19	6.06
Single man without children	2.99	2.52	1.00	16.16	13.80	3.69	10.51	0.51	4.85	2.55	2.33
Single woman without children	1.67	1.23	0.56	7.19	3.50	10.53	4.96	0.10	4.58	1.17	3.04

continued

APPENDIX TABLE S.6F Household composition 1935 (continued)

Main household types	Number of households	Number of household members	Thereof: family members	Thereof: parents	Thereof: servants	Thereof: boarders and lodgers	Thereof: other household members	Household members that are children under 15 years	Household members that are temporarily present	Persons not included in households: temporarily absent	Persons not included in households: sub-tenants
Sub-tenant household	2.22	0.74	0.81	0.23	0.07	0.01	0.25	0.12	5.95	0.33	0.00
Institutional household	0.17	0.80	0.91	0.00	0.00	0.00	0.01	0.16	9.54	2.37	0.02
Relationship unknown	0.04	0.02	0.02	0.01	0.00	0.00	0.06	0.00	0.01	0.02	0.00
Total	100.00	100.00	100.00	100.00	100.00	100.00	100.00	100.00	100.00	100.00	100.00
Line per cent											
Matlagshushall proper[1]	–	100.00	87.66	5.88	2.29	0.61	3.57	22.93	1.06	::	::
Thereof:											
One-person households	–	100.00	100.00	::			::	::	0.51	::	::
Multiperson households, thereof:											
Married man with wife	–	100.00	92.74	2.93	1.39	0.40	2.54	26.59	0.81	::	::
Single man with children	–	100.00	73.16	11.62	7.45	0.48	6.67	18.50	1.32	::	::
Single woman with children	–	100.00	87.55	5.97	1.49	1.64	3.35	18.09	1.76	::	::
Single man without children	–	100.00	34.93	37.24	12.27	0.87	14.69	4.60	2.37	::	::
Single woman without children	–	100.00	40.31	33.98	6.38	5.11	14.23	1.89	4.59	::	::
Sub-tenant household	–	100.00	96.77	1.79	0.23	0.01	1.21	3.78	9.93	::	::
Institutional household	–	100.00	99.95	::	::	::	0.05	4.56	14.62	::	::
Relationship unknown	–	100.00	85.51	1.90	::	::	12.59	3.56	0.48	::	::
Total	–	100.00	87.82	5.81	2.24	0.60	3.52	22.64	1.23	::	::

Note: [1] '*Matlagshushall*' are defined as households where household members live and eat together.

APPENDIX TABLE S.7 Dates and nature of results on population structure, households/families, and vital statistics

Topic	Intro-duction	Remarks
Population		
Population at census dates	1850	Earlier censuses were conducted starting in 1750 and are available for every five and ten years. The history of Swedish population statistics is well documented by Sundbärg (1907 and 1970) and SCB (1969).
Population by age, sex, and marital status	1870	First published for the census of 1870.
Households and families		
Households (hushåll)		
Total households	1860	Households were first expressively recorded in 1860, but data are available from 1805 onwards for the censuses of 1805, 1810, 1820, 1830, 1840, and 1850 (cf. Statistiska Centralbyrån 1895: xxvii). 1860: private households by size; number of one-person and family households; persons in institutional households. 1870: as in 1860. 1880: as in 1860. 1890: as in 1860, by sex. 1900: as in 1890. 1910: as in 1890. 1920: as in 1890. 1930: as in 1890; income and occupation of family head, number of institutional households. 1935: as in 1890; family types, occupation of family head. 1940: no household statistics. 1945: as in 1890. *Disaggregation*: by provinces and districts.
Households by size	1860, 1870, 1880, 1900, 1910, 1920, 1930, 1935, 1940, 1945	First time in the population census of 1860. Households by number of persons 1–15+. Repeated in each following census except for 1890.
Households by composition	1930, 1935, 1945	1930: household composition: different categories such as children, parents, servants, etc. 1935: household types. 1945: as in 1930.

continued

APPENDIX TABLE S.7 Dates and nature of results on population structure,
households/families, and vital statistics (continued)

Topic	Intro- duction	Remarks
Households by profession of household head	1930, 1935	Income and occupation of family head.
Families (familjer)		
Families by number of children	1935, 1945	First special investigation of the fertility of marriages in 1935. Repeated in 1945.
Population movement		
Mid-year population	1850	
Births		
Live births	1850	
Stillbirths	1851	
Legitimate births	1850	
Illegitimate births	1850	
Deaths		
Total deaths	1850	
Infants (under one year)	1850	
Marriages		
Total marriages	1850	
Divorces and separations		
Total divorces	1851	
Legal separations	1916– 1977	

APPENDIX FIGURE S.8 Population by age, sex and marital status, Sweden 1870, 1890, 1910, 1920, 1930 and 1940 (per 10,000 of total population)

Sweden, 1870

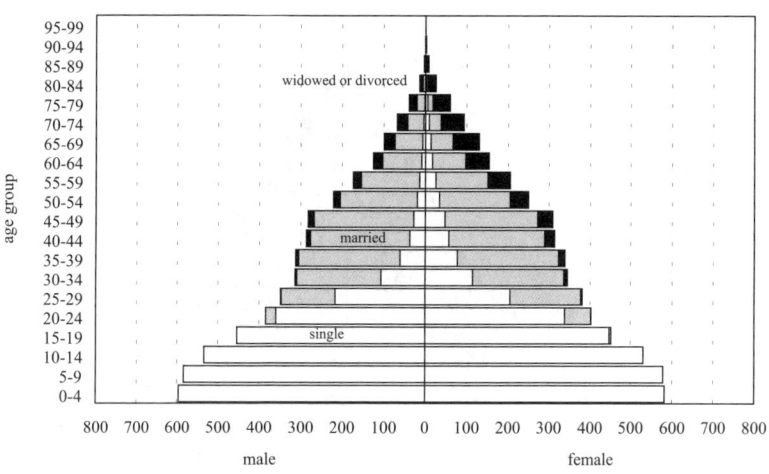

Sweden, 1890

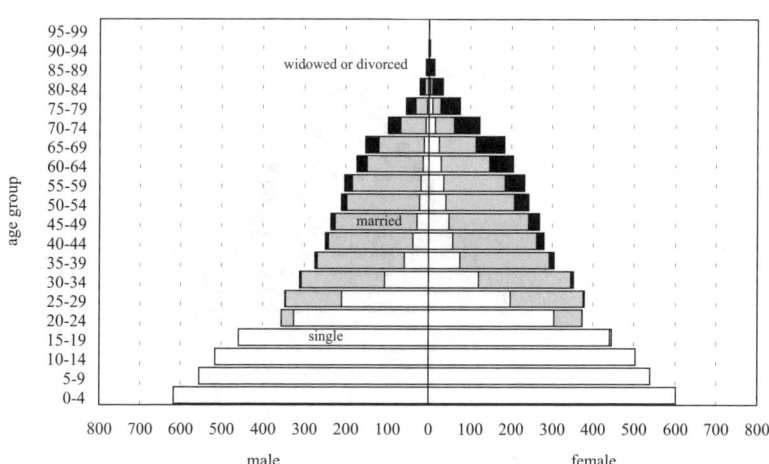

APPENDIX FIGURE S.8 Population by age, sex and marital status, Sweden 1870, 1890, 1910, 1920, 1930 and 1940 (per 10,000 of total population) (continued)

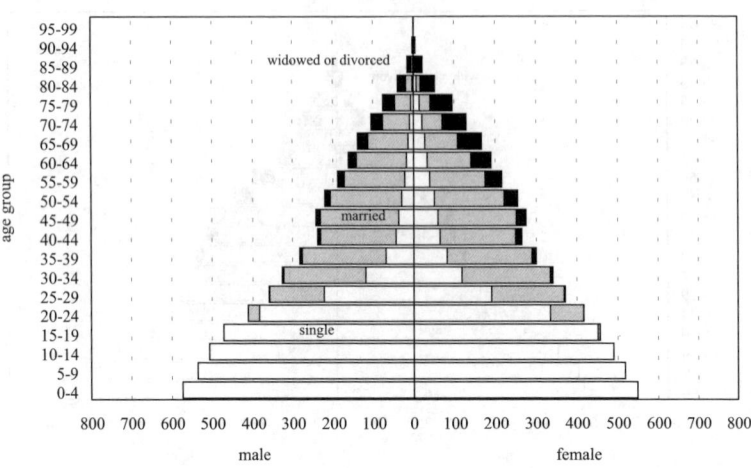

Sweden, 1910

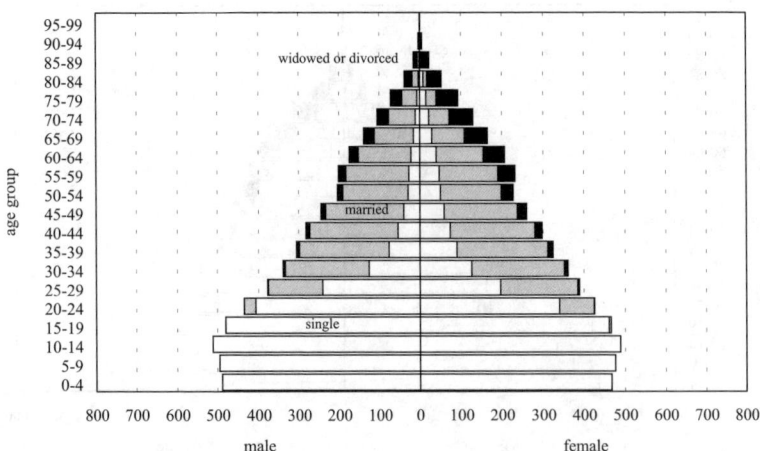

Sweden, 1920

APPENDIX FIGURE S.8 Population by age, sex and marital status, Sweden 1870,
1890, 1910, 1920, 1930 and 1940 (per 10,000 of total population) (continued)

Sweden, 1930

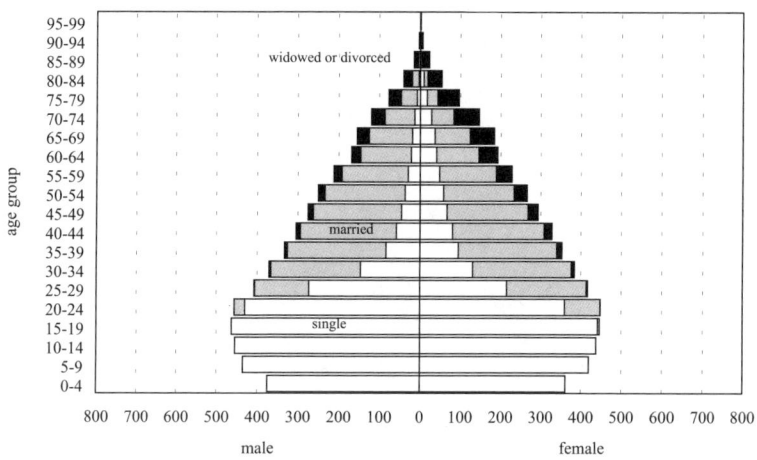

Sweden, 1940

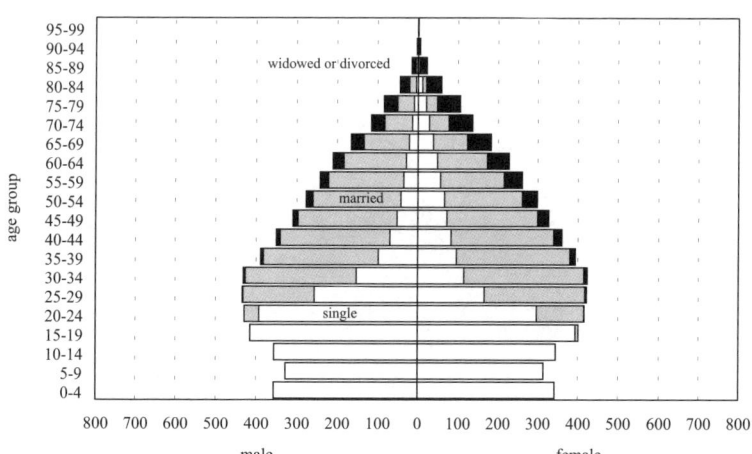

20

Switzerland

STATE FORMATION AND TERRITORY

Switzerland is a country of remarkable territorial stability through the centuries. It gained *de facto* independence from the Holy German Empire (*Heiliges Römisches Reich Deutscher Nation*) in the fourteenth century. The cantonal federation was extended until the early sixteenth century when the first territorial consolidation was reached. In 1648 the Swiss cantons gained formal independence from the Holy German Empire. In 1707 the Kingdom of Prussia took over the Principality of Neuchâtel (Fürstentum Neuenburg), which remained under Prussian sovereignty until 1848/57. The French Revolution and Napoleon I influenced the development of Switzerland to a large degree. In 1798 Napoleon I made Switzerland the Helvetian Republic. There was also a Republic of Valais, the Italian-speaking part of Switzerland. Napoleon's intention was to make Switzerland a centralized modern republic with a French administrative structure. At that time only two territories of the later Switzerland did not belong to the Helvetian Republic: the Bishopric of Basle and the Principality of Neuchâtel. The Bishopric of Basle was secularized and later joined the Swiss Federation.

The Congress of Vienna restored the old federal system of the cantons and abolished the Helvetian Republic. During the first half of the nineteenth century Switzerland formed a rather loose federation of cantons. It was more like a state federation (*Staatenbund*) than a federal state (*Bundesstaat*). The tendencies towards the nation-state also influenced Switzerland. In November 1847 the so-called *Sonderbund* war broke out which ended with the victory of the centralizing forces. A constitution was elaborated in 1848 and a federal republic was founded, consisting of 25 cantons. This construction proved to be very stable and is still in existence. In the 1970s a twenty-sixth canton (Jura) was created by splitting the canton of Berne (for general descriptions of Swiss state history, see Kästli, 1998; Im Hof, 1991 and 1997).

REGIONAL POPULATION STRUCTURE

Due to its Alpine character with large parts of the territory not suitable for settlement, population density in 1870 was still rather low with 64 inhabitants per square kilometre. By 1941, 70 years later, population density had increased to 103 persons. This low settlement density becomes clear when Swiss figures are compared with Belgian ones: in 1831 Belgium had 128 inhabitants per square kilometre and therefore had a higher population density a hundred years earlier than Switzerland.

Population growth was very uneven from 1870 to 1941. While in some cantons, such as Geneva or the city cantons of Zurich or Basle, the population (and density, because of only minor territorial changes) doubled, in other cantons such as Grisons

(Graubünden), Uri, Valais, and Ticino population size and density increased very little. Population growth therefore depended on territorial preconditions and benefited the lowlands over the disadvantaged Alpine cantons. Internal migration from the rural Alpine regions to the industrializing cities in the lowlands added to this growing imbalance. Urbanization was therefore concentrated in a few centres with cities as focal points: Basle, Zurich, and Geneva (cf. Kommission 'Bevölkerungspolitik', 1985; Höpflinger, 1986; references on population in Ritzmann-Blickenstorfer and Siegenthaler, 1996: 91; Bickel, 1947; Brüschweiler, 1948; Mattmüller, 1987; Mayer, 1952; Bundesamt für Statistik, 1988, 1992, 1993a; Fux, 2001).

POPULATION GROWTH

The population of Switzerland was still small in the nineteenth century: in 1870 there were 2,655,000 Swiss inhabitants; 70 years later, in 1941, the population had grown to 4,267,000, an absolute increase of 1.6 million inhabitants. The growth rates however were low when compared with countries such as Belgium and The Netherlands. This low population increase must be seen in the light of an absence of population losses due to wars since 1880. The main factors for the low population growth are found in the specific Swiss demographic regime, as we will see in the following section.

The low natural population growth can be seen in Figure CH.1. From 1850 to 1900 the natural population growth rate remained below 10 per 1,000, with an average of approximately 7 per 1,000. For only a few years around the turn of the century the natural population growth rate exceeded 10 per 1,000. From 1910 until the 1930s the natural population growth rate shows a steadily declining trend, falling below 5 per 1,000 in the late 1930s. This tendency was only interrupted by World War I, which caused a drop in the natural population growth rate. There were two prior downswings in the natural population growth rate, the first during the late 1850s due to economic depression and the second caused by the 1870/71 Franco-Prussian War.

Emigration from Switzerland to other countries was not as strong as from Scandinavia, for example, probably because of the lower natural population increase and therefore a smaller surplus population. Major phases of emigration were the late 1850s and the 1860s, the late 1870s and the 1880s, and the years of World War I and the early 1920s. The years around 1930 and again around 1940 were years of immigration, the latter ones partly due to refugee movements.

THE FIRST DEMOGRAPHIC TRANSITION

The secular fertility decline of Switzerland came rather late, only after 1900. In the second half of the nineteenth century the birth rate shows strong fluctuations due to national events of the 1870s (Figure CH.2). Also the death rate reacted to this national crisis with a strong increase. The death rate during the last decades of the nineteenth century and the whole twentieth century shows a remarkably continuous development with the exception of World War I. The development of the birth rate was not as stable. After the 1870s it declined by tendency, but increased again—though at a lower level—between 1900 and 1910. The result was a growing divergence in these years of the birth and death rates and therefore an increase in

Figure CH.1 Population growth and net migration 1852-1945

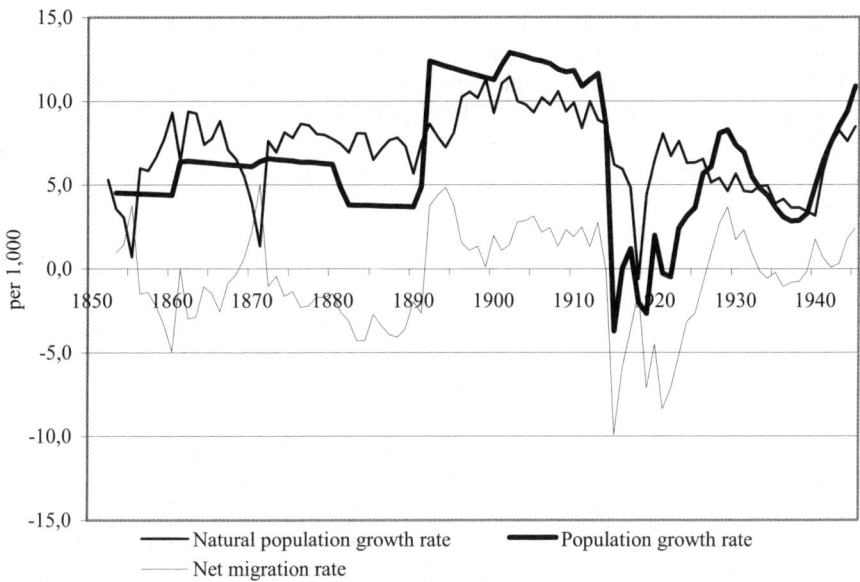

Figure CH.2 First demographic transition 1852-1945

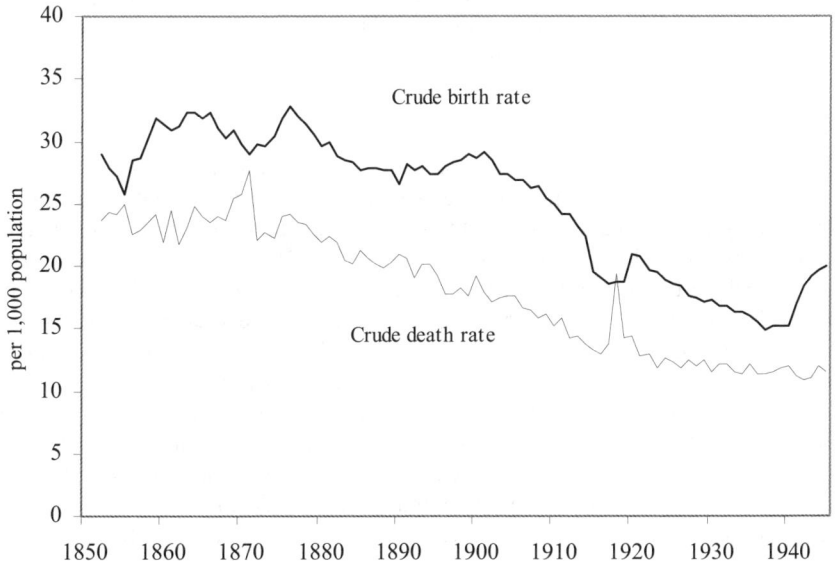

natural population growth. But the indirect influence of World War I—Switzerland was not directly involved in the war—caused a severe fertility decline.

During the inter-war period, Swiss fertility decline was strong, and the natural population surplus declined even more. Indirect influences from World War II were low (Switzerland remained neutral during the war). After World War II fertility rose strongly compared with the very low level of the inter-war period. There was also a small second demographic transition in Switzerland with the birth rate peaking around 1970. During the 1970s the birth rate declined strongly and reached a new low level, but remained above the death rate.

Switzerland's population history in the last 150 years was therefore also strongly influenced by economic crises and wars. Switzerland obviously was strongly affected by the world economic crisis of the 1850s (Rosenberg, 1974), as is shown by the declining birth rate and the rising death rate in the 1850s. Perhaps the 1870/71 Franco-Prussian War led to the strong increase in mortality and the decline in the fertility rate. The world economic depression of 1929–33 obviously had no major impact on the birth rate.

When compared with Europe as a whole, both the birth and death rates have been lower than the European average. In Switzerland, conditions such as high age at marriage, high celibacy, and inheritance law made procreation difficult and held the birth rate down. On the other hand, the death rate was also lower than the European average. This is partly an effect of a low birth rate, but it has to be emphasized that infant mortality was low; the low infant mortality again was partly caused by the low illegitimacy rate, given the fact that illegitimate births had a higher mortality rate than legitimate births.

It was only in the post-World War II period that the Swiss demographic patterns converged with the European development. The birth rate increased to the European level and the European and the Swiss death rates were very similar.

MORTALITY AND LIFE EXPECTANCY

The infant mortality rate is defined as deaths of children aged under one year per 1,000 live births. Switzerland and The Netherlands are the two continental countries that belong to the group of countries with the lowest infant mortality already around 1900, along with all five Nordic countries (Figure CH.3). Nevertheless, Switzerland was far behind the most advanced country, Norway; in 1900, with 134 infant deaths per 1,000 live births, Switzerland's infant mortality rate was similar to Finland's. The progress of infant mortality decline up to World War II was remarkable and only a little less than in Norway and Sweden (Masuy-Stroobant, 1997).

Looking at longer time series reaching back to 1880, one sees a remarkable similarity between Switzerland and The Netherlands both in the level and development of the infant mortality curve. Around 1880 infant mortality was rather high in The Netherlands and Switzerland, with 200 deaths of children under one year per 1,000 live births; at that time these two countries clearly did not belong to the group of Nordic countries with much lower rates. Thus during the nineteenth century (data do not exist before 1880) Switzerland had very high infant mortality, putting it more in a group with the continental and Southern European countries. The only difference for Switzerland and The Netherlands is the very sharp decline in infant mortality after 1880, unlike other continental countries, which brought both already in 1920 to the low level of Norway, for example (Van de Walle, 1986).

Figure CH.3 Infant mortality 1871-1945

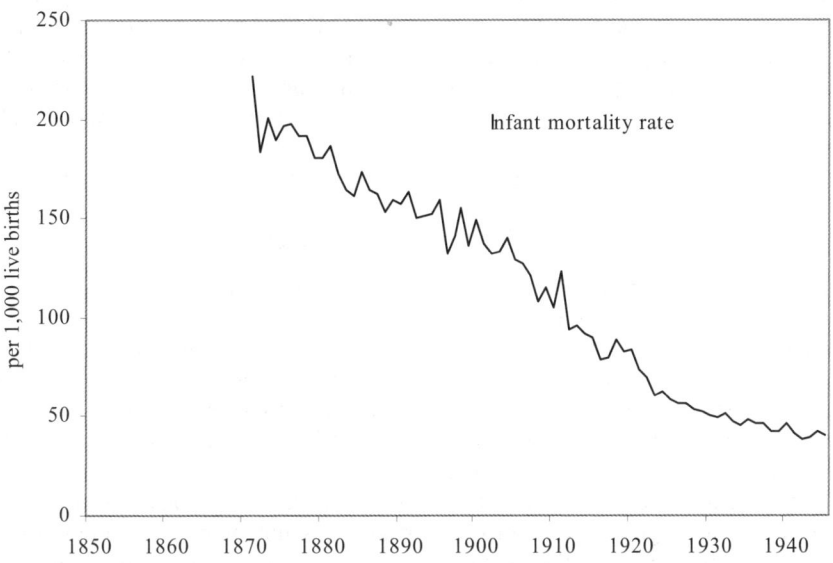

Figure CH.4 Life expectancy 1876/80-1939/44

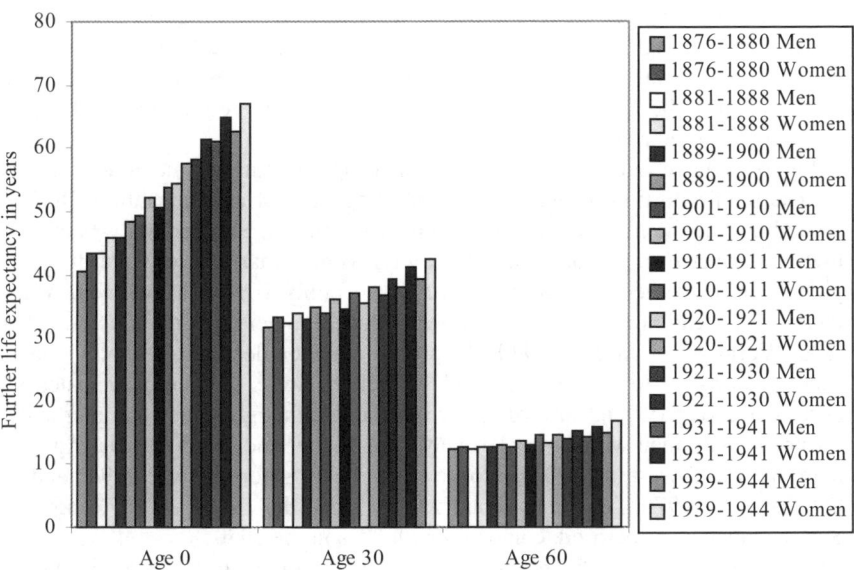

Life expectancy at birth was rather high already in 1876/80 with 41 years for boys and 43 years for girls (Figure CH.4). There were considerable gains in life expectancy at birth until 1939/44: 22 years for boys and 24 years for girls. Life expectancy for 30-year-old men during the same time period increased by seven years, and for 30-year-old women by nine years. Sixty-year-olds were still able to increase their life expectancy: 2.5 years for men and four years for women. The differences between the sexes in life expectancy therefore increased from 1880 to 1940 in favour of women: in the case of new-born children from 2.6 to 4.3 years, for 30-year-olds from 1.5 to 3.1 years, and for 60-year-olds from 0.3 to 1.9 years.

FERTILITY AND LEGITIMACY

In spite of easy divorce, marriage and childbirth within marriage continue to have a high standing in Switzerland. Out-of-wedlock births must have been regarded as undesirable and shameful, as is suggested by the very low illegitimate birth rate. Furthermore, there were no substantial changes concerning the propensity of women to give birth when unmarried. The illegitimate birth rate declined during the process of the secular birth decline until the 1940s, and increased only slightly during the time of early and universal marriage in the 1960s.

Thus, fertility was mainly marital fertility (Figure CH.5). However, due to late marriages and high celibacy, marital fertility was not high, but—compared with Europe—only average. When illegitimate and legitimate fertility are combined, it becomes clear why overall fertility in Switzerland was low.

MARRIAGE AND DIVORCE

Switzerland belongs to the region of the Western European marriage pattern with a high age at marriage and a high celibacy rate. Within the Western European group it belongs to the cluster of 'Germanic' continental countries, made up of Austria, Germany, and The Netherlands. These four countries are very similar with regard to their long-term marriage characteristics.

We do not have figures on mean age at marriage for earlier time periods, therefore we use the proportion of women married at age 20–24 as a substitute. During the second half of the nineteenth century this proportion in Switzerland was one of the lowest all over Europe, indicating that Swiss women married very late. In 1860 the proportion of women married at age 20–24 was only 16% of all women. Although there was a steady increase in the following decades, there was no structural change. After World War I until the 1940s the proportion even declined, probably due to the economic crisis during these years. Nevertheless, Swiss women participated in the post-World War II trend towards early marriage, although somewhat later and with lower intensity than women in Germany, The Netherlands, and Austria. Age at first marriage was lowest in 1970, i.e. for the birth cohorts born between 1945 and 1950, but rose after 1970, i.e. for the cohorts born since the 1950s. In 1970, 45% of all Swiss women were married, compared with 20% in the 1930s.

Concerning men, the diachronic pattern is very similar in its basic development, although age at first marriage much higher than for females. In 1860 6% of Swiss men were married at age 20–24. The proportion increased up to World War I, but in the 1930s it was the same as in 1860. The trend towards early marriage after 1945

Figure CH.5 Fertility and legitimacy 1871-1939

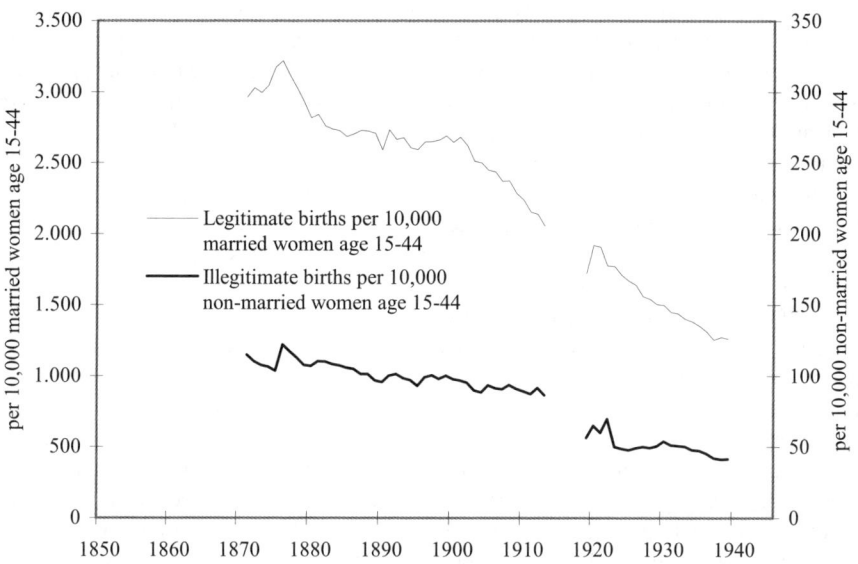

Figure CH.6 Marriages and divorces 1860-1939

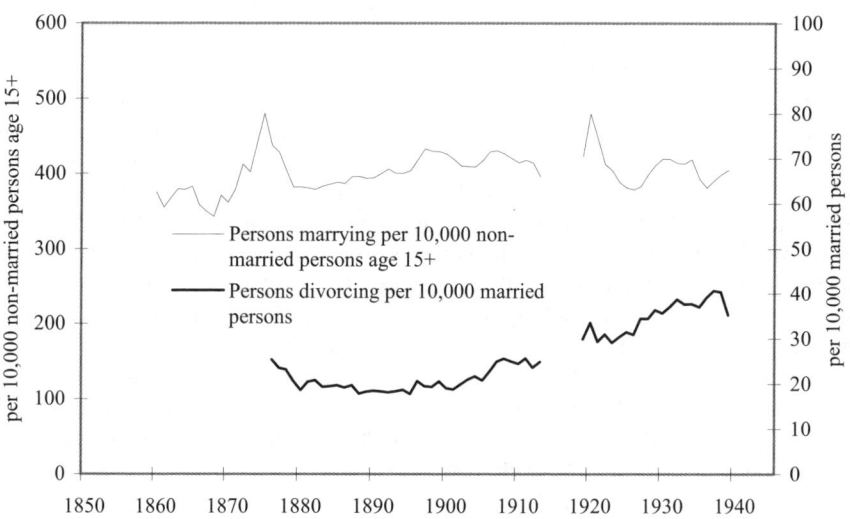

peaked in 1970 with 20% of men married at age 20–24. The birth cohorts of the 1950s again returned to late marriage.

The dimension of *marriage intensity* is composed by two indicators: the marriage rate and the celibacy rate. 'Intensity' means the availability of marriage, but at the same time the urgent need to remarry after the death of a spouse ('remarriage need', Michael Mitterauer). The Swiss marriage rate clearly confirms the picture of very late marriage in Switzerland (Figure CH.6). The marriage rate during the last 150 years was constantly well below the European average. There were only fluctuations of this rate due to economic crises and wars: the crisis in the 1870s increased the marriage rate, and World War I had the usual incidental effect on the marriage rate. The return of the Swiss to a late age at marriage after 1970 is clearly visible from the marriage rate, which declined steeply in the 1970s.

In 1860, the second indicator, the celibacy rate, was highest in Switzerland of all the 21 countries in this volume. Approximately 40% of all women aged 45–54 were never married in 1860. This high celibacy declined slowly until the 1940s, but remained among the highest in Europe, and was only exceeded by Ireland, Finland, and Austria, each of them facing singular and severe societal problems. The decline of the celibacy rate—or the growing trend towards universal marriage—started only after 1945. During the 1980s marriage had become nearly universal: only 10% of women remained unmarried during these years. The birth cohorts of 1925–34 married nearly universally. It is expected that the Swiss returned to their older pattern of non-universal marriage in the 1990s.

In contrast to the picture of marital behaviour which obviously and essentially remained 'traditional', already during the nineteenth century Switzerland had a rather *liberal divorce law*. Since the Reformation divorce was available on the grounds of fault. Divorce on the grounds of marital breakdown was introduced already in 1912. A legal separation could be obtained on the same grounds as a divorce. The early introduction of divorce on grounds of fault is probably the main explanation for the high divorce rate in Switzerland already during the nineteenth and first half of the twentieth century, well above the European average (Figure CH.6). The number of divorces and the divorce rate continued to increase from the 1880s to the 1950s with the temporary decline due to the impact of World War II. Surprisingly, the divorce rate declined in Switzerland during the period of early and universal marriage up to the 1960s. But in the late 1960s the divorce rate started to increase strongly, again reaching a level higher than in Europe. Legal separations have been few and were always less than 10% of divorces.

This increase may be due to the introduction of a liberal divorce law, but also may partly be the effect of the early and universal marriages immediately after 1945, because many of them can be assumed to have been weak relationships. Early marriage and divorce are positively correlated.

AGE, SEX, AND CIVIL STATUS

In Switzerland, the age structure remained pyramidal until World War I (Appendix Figure CH.8). From the 1860s to the 1880s the lowest age groups were large, leading to a concave pattern at the bottom of the distribution. But high infant mortality greatly reduced those large birth cohorts. In the age structure of 1860 the low birth rates of the 1850s become visible: the age groups from 5–14 years are clearly smaller. The smaller birth cohorts of these years can be detected in the age structures until 1910. Although Switzerland did not participate directly in World War I, the indirect consequences of the war are clear from the age structure of 1920. The two lowest age groups of 0–4 and 5–9 years are strongly reduced due to loss of births. Low fertility rates continued during the whole inter-war period, leading to a bell-shaped pattern in 1930 and even more clearly in 1941. In the age structure of 1930, the male age groups of 20–24 and 25–29 are very large, much larger than those of females; the causes of this phenomenon remain unclear.

The proportion of men remaining single longer than women was traditionally high in Switzerland, though in higher age groups more men than women were married, and celibacy was higher for women than for men. The proportion of widowed and divorced in higher age groups was higher for females than for males, due to higher male mortality and lower remarriage rates of women.

FAMILY AND HOUSEHOLD STRUCTURES

From 1850 to 1950, household size in Switzerland was in a middle range compared with other European countries. It was constantly less than five persons per household since 1850. In 1850 the mean size of all households was 4.93. Already in the 1870s we can see the start of the secular decline in mean household size, mainly due to fertility decline. During the inter-war period the decline in the mean household size accelerated due to the severe fertility decline in these years. In 1941, mean household size had dropped to 3.72 persons per household. Mean family household size of course was larger than the mean size of all households. The first figure available refers to 1920 and shows 4.54 family members per family household in contrast to 4.24 persons per private household and 4.38 persons per all households.

The proportion of one-person households was also in a middle field compared with other European countries until the 1930s, but increased rapidly in the following three decades. In 1960 it was 14.2%. There was even a slight decrease in the proportion of one-person households from 1900 to 1930, from 9.5% to 8.5%. Persons living alone remained stable with 2.1% in 1900 and 1930.

On the other hand, the proportion of households with five or more persons was still very high in 1900 at 43% of all households. By 1930 this proportion had declined to 33%. Persons living in households comprising five and more persons amounted to 67% in 1900, declining to 53% in 1930.

Data on household composition are available only since 1920 and collection was repeated in 1930. There was no fundamental change in the composition of households during the decade 1920–1930. The proportion of non-nuclear family members in private households was 17.3% in both 1920 and 1930. Non-nuclear family members are all those other than parents and their children and include all other persons residing in private households. While the proportion of nuclear family members remained stable at 82.7%, the proportion of members belonging to the extended family (parents and parents-in-law of household head, other relatives) actually increased from 5.5% to 6.4% of all household members. Domestic servants, boarders and lodgers, and others declined from 11.8% in 1920 to 10.9% in 1930.

Thus, household composition remained stable from 1920 to 1930; the change in household composition came in the following three decades and can be seen from the census of 1960, the first one after the war to present household composition data. The main trends in household structure of nuclearization, the decline of the extended family, and the expulsion of domestic servants, boarders, and lodgers from households came only after 1930.

Comprehensive historical statistics on Switzerland were published in 1996, edited by Heiner Ritzmann-Blickenstorfer and Hansjörg Siegenthaler. This historico-statistical compendium covers population figures for long historical periods and all Swiss cantons. It does not cover population combined by age, sex, and marital status; furthermore, data on households and families are rather sparse.

Population Structure

Censuses were conducted in the different territories of the later Helvetian Republic already in the seventeenth century (cf. Ritzmann-Blickenstorfer and Siegenthaler, 1996). After the founding of the modern Swiss Republic in 1848 a population census was held in 1850, but this census is not fully acknowledged as the first modern population census of Switzerland. The first complete census was taken in 1860. From that time onwards census-taking was a very stable and continuous task in Switzerland due to the country's lack of involvement in the wars of the late nineteenth and the twentieth centuries. It was therefore possible to hold censuses nearly every ten years at regular intervals. Only the 1890 census was held in 1888 and the 1940 census in 1941.

Population structure according to age, sex, and marital status is available since 1860 for all following population censuses. For all censuses from 1860 to 1941 data were published in one-year age groups.

Vital Statistics

The main variables of vital statistics, live births, marriages, and deaths, have been continuously recorded and published since 1851. Other demographic indicators became available at later dates: stillbirths are available since 1870, births by legitimacy since 1871, and infant deaths and divorces since 1876. The age of women and males became available rather early, in 1885. Legal separations have been published since 1897. Synthetic measures of fertility, such as the total period fertility rate and the cohort fertility rate have been calculated since 1903 and 1901, respectively.

Households and Families

During the second half of the nineteenth century until the census of 1900 household statistics in Switzerland were only developed rudimentarily. Although already the census of 1850 counted data on the number of *households* (*Haushaltungen* or *ménages*), only one figure was published for all types of households, thus combining single-person households, family households, and institutional households. In 1900 the innovation of households by size categories was introduced but without distinguishing institutional households; 1920 finally marks the beginning of new and comprehensive Swiss household statistics which were continuously gathered in later censuses. In 1920 the distinction between the three elementary household types of single persons, family households, and institutional households was introduced and applied in all following censuses. Households were classified by size, composition, profession of the household head, and number of children. The next census of 1930 maintained the household statistics of 1920, but did not present socio-economic characteristics of the households or the number of children. During World War II the 1941 census only provided the number of households, households by size, and fertility statistics.

Several summary publications present retrospective time series of household data. The number of households from 1850 to 1900 is given in Statistisches Bureau des Eidg. Departements des Innern (1904: 314f.). The census publication on households for 1970 presents data from 1920–70 (Eidgenössisches Statistisches Amt, Bureau Fédéral de Statistique, 1975), the same title of the 1980 census data for 1920–80 (Bundesamt für Statistik, Office fédéral de la statistique, Ufficio federale di statistica, 1985). The statistical abstract of Switzerland for the year 1994 (Bundesamt für Statistik (1993b) presents the data for 1920–90.

The *definition of a household* (*Haushaltung* or *ménage*) was thoroughly described in the census publication for 1920. In Switzerland the housekeeping-unit concept was applied in principle during the whole period. In 1870 the definition stated:

Als Haushaltungen werden angesehen die zu einer wohn- und hauswirtschaftlichen Gemeinschaft vereinigten Personen, die eine besondere Wohnung innehaben und eine eigene Hauswirtschaft führen; ebenso werden einzeln lebende Personen, die eine besondere Wohnung innehaben und eine eigene Hauswirtschaft führen, als Haushaltungen betrachtet. Hingegen werden andere alleinstehende Personen, wie Zimmermieter ohne eigene Hauswirtschaft, Schlafgänger u.s.w. der Haushaltung zugerechnet, bei der sie wohnen und welche für sie die Hauswirtschaft führt, auch wenn sie in dieser Haushaltung keine Beköstigung erhalten (Eidgenössisches Statistisches Bureau (1926: 5*).

In 1860 the definition of a one-person household was not as restrictive as from 1870 onwards: persons were counted as single-person households if they had a separate dwelling and provided their own meals.

In 1920 the first clear distinction between one-person, family, and institutional households was made and the three statistical terms comprehensively described. The definitions are identical to those used in German household statistics. Households have been distinguished as follows:

1. Einzelhaushaltungen, d.h. Haushaltungen einzeln lebender Personen, die eine eigene Wohnung haben und eine eigene Hauswirtschaft führen.
2. Familienhaushaltungen aus mehreren Personen bestehend, nämlich einem Vorstand, Kindern oder Verwandten, Dienstboten, Gewerbegehilfen, Zimmermietern und Schlafgängern. Zu den Gewerbegehilfen sind auch Lehrlinge gezählt worden.
3. Anstaltshaushaltungen und sonstige Haushaltungen ohne Vorstand. Als Haushaltungen ohne Vorstand kommen z.B. in Frage Arbeiter, die gemeinsam in Baracken wohnen, Dienstboten in einer Wohnung, die nicht Wohnsitz der Herrschaft ist und ähnliche seltenere Fälle (Eidgenössisches Statistisches Bureau, 1926: 5*).

Family statistics were introduced in 1920, comprising statistics of married couples and fertility statistics. Married persons living together or apart were presented by cantons, age of spouse, confession, in age combination and by age difference. Children were counted by birth years and if mother and father were still alive, by bigger towns and cantons.

In 1941 data on the fertility of married women were published: one table presents data on married women by marriage year and the number of live births from the present marriage. The second table contains the same data disaggregated by cantons and towns.

Remarks (also see introductory Table 6.1)

Data on vital statistics (resident population, live births, deaths, marriages, and stillbirths for the years 1851 to 1900 are available through Statistisches Bureau des eidg. Departements des Innern (1908: 8*–9*), with the exception of live births and stillbirths (only 1870–). From 1851 to 1869 only all births are published (live births and stillbirths).

BOUNDARY CHANGES

Since 1848, when Switzerland assumed its modern form, no major changes in the external borders have occurred. The only change was the inclusion of the Principality of Neuchâtel (Fürstentum Neuenburg) in 1848/57, which had been under the sovereignty of the Kingdom of Prussia since 1707. This corresponds with the history of the population census. The first, though experimental, census was established two years after the new Constitution, in 1850. For regional organization see the documentation by Quick (1994) and Caramani, Flora, Kraus, and Quick (1998).

APPENDIX TABLES AND FIGURES

APPENDIX TABLE CH.1 Population structure at census dates 1860–1941

Census number	Census date	Census population			Marital status				Age group		
		Total	Male	Female	Single	Married	Widowed	Divorced	0–14	15–64	65+
					Absolute						
1	10 XII 1860	2,510,504	1,236,362	1,274,142	1,575,410	738,467	155,353	41,274	740,898	1,641,779	127,827
2	1 XII 1870	2,669,147	1,304,833	1,364,314	1,648,066	799,346	172,297	49,438	835,483	1,686,577	147,087
3	1 XII 1880	2,846,102	1,394,626	1,451,476	1,736,021	919,137	181,403	9,541	908,268	1,780,428	157,406
4	1 XII 1888	2,917,754	1,417,574	1,500,180	1,782,806	935,632	187,713	11,603	940,079	1,807,789	169,886
5	1 XII 1900	3,315,443	1,627,025	1,688,418	2,013,707	1,081,715	205,597	14,424	1,028,438	2,093,739	193,266
6	1 XII 1910	3,753,293	1,845,529	1,907,764	2,259,951	1,252,876	220,580	19,886	1,173,240	2,362,275	217,778
7	1 XII 1920	3,880,320	1,871,123	2,009,197	2,281,170	1,337,653	234,334	27,163	1,083,294	2,570,064	226,962
8	1 XII 1930	4,066,400	1,958,349	2,108,051	2,258,337	1,530,068	240,791	37,204	998,421	2,828,165	239,814
9	1 XII 1941	4,265,700	2,060,399	2,205,301	2,196,754	1,748,486	264,124	56,336	943,759	2,956,904	365,037
					Per cent						
1	10 XII 1860	100.00	49.25	50.75	62.75	29.42	6.19	1.64	29.51	65.40	5.09
2	1 XII 1870	100.00	48.89	51.11	61.75	29.95	6.46	1.85	31.30	63.19	5.51
3	1 XII 1880	100.00	49.00	51.00	61.00	32.29	6.37	0.34	31.91	62.56	5.53
4	1 XII 1888	100.00	48.58	51.42	61.10	32.07	6.43	0.40	32.22	61.96	5.82
5	1 XII 1900	100.00	49.07	50.93	60.74	32.63	6.20	0.44	31.02	63.15	5.83
6	1 XII 1910	100.00	49.17	50.83	60.21	33.38	5.88	0.53	31.26	62.94	5.80
7	1 XII 1920	100.00	48.22	51.78	58.79	34.47	6.04	0.70	27.92	66.23	5.85
8	1 XII 1930	100.00	48.16	51.84	55.54	37.63	5.92	0.91	24.55	69.55	5.90
9	1 XII 1941	100.00	48.30	51.70	51.50	40.99	6.19	1.32	22.12	69.32	8.56

APPENDIX TABLE CH.2　Census population by region 1870–1941 (per cent)

Cantons[1]	1870	1880	1888	1900	1910	1920	1930	1941
Zürich	10.70	11.16	11.55	13.00	13.43	13.89	15.20	15.82
Bern	18.91	18.71	18.40	17.77	17.21	17.37	16.95	17.08
Luzern	4.97	4.77	4.63	4.43	4.45	4.56	4.65	4.85
Uri	0.60	0.85	0.58	0.60	0.59	0.62	0.57	0.63
Schwyz	1.81	1.80	1.71	1.66	1.55	1.55	1.52	1.57
Obwalden[2]	0.53	0.53	0.51	0.45	0.45	0.46	0.47	0.47
Nidwalden[2]	0.45	0.42	0.45	0.39	0.37	0.36	0.37	0.40
Glarus	1.32	1.20	1.17	0.97	0.88	0.88	0.89	0.82
Zug	0.79	0.81	0.79	0.75	0.75	0.82	0.84	0.87
Fribourg	4.14	4.06	4.08	3.86	3.73	3.69	3.52	3.56
Solothurn	2.82	2.82	2.95	3.05	3.12	3.38	3.54	3.63
Basel-Stadt[2]	1.77	2.26	2.54	3.38	3.62	3.63	3.81	3.98
Basel-Land[2]	2.03	2.08	2.12	2.05	2.03	2.11	2.29	2.20
Schaffhausen	1.43	1.34	1.30	1.27	1.23	1.29	1.25	1.27
Appenzell-AR[2]	1.85	1.84	1.85	1.66	1.55	1.42	1.21	1.05
Appenzell IR[2]	0.45	0.46	0.45	0.39	0.40	0.39	0.34	0.30
St. Gallen	7.19	7.42	7.81	7.54	8.07	7.63	7.03	6.70
Graubünden	3.47	3.32	3.26	3.17	3.12	3.09	3.10	3.00
Aargau	7.50	6.99	6.65	6.21	6.16	6.21	6.39	6.33
Thurgau	3.50	3.50	3.60	3.41	3.60	3.51	3.34	3.23
Ticino (Tessin)	4.60	4.59	4.35	4.19	4.16	3.92	3.91	3.80
Vaud (Waadt)	8.66	8.30	8.50	8.48	8.45	8.17	8.17	8.04
Valais (Wallis)	3.65	3.53	3.50	3.44	3.41	3.30	3.34	3.47
Neuchâtel (Neuenburg)	3.58	3.64	3.70	3.80	3.54	3.38	3.05	2.77
Genève (Genf)	3.35	3.53	3.63	4.01	4.13	4.41	4.21	4.10
Jura	..	..	..	..	..	..	..	..
TOTAL	**100.00**	**100.00**	**100.00**	**100.00**	**100.00**	**100.00**	**100.00**	**100.00**

Notes: [1] All changes in the area figures are due to recalculations and are not caused by border modifications. [2] Three cantons are subdivided in half-cantons, that are treated like regular cantons: *Unterwalden* is divided in *Unterwalden ob dem Wald* (or *Obwalden*) and *Unterwalden nid dem Wald* (or *Nidwalden*). *Basel* is divided in *Basel-Stadt* and *Basel-Landschaft* and *Appenzell* consists of *Appenzell-Außer-Rhoden* and *Appenzell-Inner-Rhoden*.

APPENDIX TABLE CH.3 Population density by region 1870–1941 (inhabitants per sq. km.)

Cantons[1]	1870	1880	1888	1900	1910	1920	1930	1941
Zürich	165	183	195	249	291	312	357	390
Bern	73	77	78	86	94	98	100	106
Luzern	88	90	90	99	112	119	127	139
Uri	15	22	16	19	20	22	21	25
Schwyz	53	56	55	61	64	66	68	74
Obwalden[2]	29	32	32	30	34	37	39	41
Nidwalden[2]	41	41	45	47	51	51	55	62
Glarus	51	49	49	47	48	50	53	51
Zug	88	96	96	104	117	133	142	154
Fribourg	66	69	71	77	84	86	86	91
Solothurn	96	102	110	128	148	166	182	196
Basel-Stadt[2]	1,306	1,778	2,056	3,027	3,676	3,811	4,189	4,595
Basel-Land[2]	128	140	147	159	178	192	218	220
Schaffhausen	129	129	129	141	154	168	171	181
Appenzell-AR[2]	188	199	207	227	240	227	202	185
Appenzell IR[2]	75	81	81	75	87	87	81	75
St. Gallen	95	104	113	124	150	147	142	142
Graubünden	13	13	13	15	16	17	18	18
Aargau	142	141	138	147	165	172	185	192
Thurgau	94	100	106	112	134	135	135	137
Ticino (Tessin)	43	46	45	49	55	54	57	58
Vaud (Waadt)	71	73	77	87	99	99	103	107
Valais (Wallis)	18	19	19	22	24	24	26	28
Neuchâtel (Neuenburg)	118	127	134	158	166	164	155	148
Genève (Genf)	319	358	380	472	550	606	606	621
Jura	..	..	..	..	..	..	..	..
TOTAL	**64**	**68**	**71**	**80**	**91**	**94**	**98**	**103**

Notes: [1] All changes in the area figures are due to recalculations and are not caused by border modifications. [2] Three cantons are subdivided in half-cantons, that are treated like regular cantons: *Unterwalden* is divided in *Unterwalden ob dem Wald* (or *Obwalden*) and *Unterwalden nid dem Wald* (or *Nidwalden*). *Basel* is divided in *Basel-Stadt* and *Basel-Landschaft* and *Appenzell* consists of *Appenzell-Außer-Rhoden* and *Appenzell-Inner-Rhoden*.

APPENDIX TABLE CH.4 Demographic developments 1850–1945 (absolute figures and rates)

Year	Mid-year population	Natural population growth rate	Population growth rate	Net migration rate	Crude birth rate	Legitimate births per 10,000 married women age 15–44	Illegitimate births per 10,000 unmarried women age 15–44	Illeg. births per 100 leg. births
1850	..	..	..	..	..	..	..	..
1851	..	..	..	..	..	..	..	..
1852	2,412,240	5.3	..	..	29.0	..	..	..
1853	2,423,225	3.6	4.5	1.0	27.9	..	..	..
1854	2,434,210	3.1	4.5	1.5	27.2	..	..	..
1855	2,445,195	0.7	4.5	3.8	25.7	..	..	..
1856	2,456,180	6.0	4.5	-1.5	28.5	..	..	..
1857	2,467,165	5.8	4.5	-1.4	28.7	..	..	..
1858	2,478,150	6.6	4.4	-2.2	30.2	..	..	..
1859	2,489,135	7.7	4.4	-3.3	31.9	..	..	..
1860	2,500,120	9.3	4.4	-4.9	31.3	..	..	..
1861	2,516,164	6.4	6.4	-0.1	30.9	..	..	..
1862	2,532,410	9.4	6.4	-3.0	31.2	..	..	..
1863	2,548,656	9.3	6.4	-2.9	32.2	..	..	..
1864	2,564,902	7.4	6.3	-1.1	32.3	..	..	..
1865	2,581,148	7.8	6.3	-1.5	31.8	..	..	..
1866	2,597,394	8.8	6.3	-2.6	32.3	..	..	..
1867	2,613,640	7.1	6.2	-0.9	31.0	..	..	..
1868	2,629,886	6.5	6.2	-0.4	30.2	..	..	..
1869	2,646,132	5.5	6.1	0.6	30.9	..	..	..
1870	2,662,378	3.9	6.1	2.2	29.8	..	..	..
1871	2,679,500	1.4	6.4	5.0	29.0	2,964	115	5.8
1872	2,697,200	7.6	6.6	-1.1	29.8	3,030	110	5.4
1873	2,714,900	7.0	6.5	-0.4	29.7	2,995	108	5.2
1874	2,732,600	8.1	6.5	-1.6	30.4	3,045	107	5.0
1875	2,750,300	7.8	6.4	-1.4	31.8	3,173	104	4.5
1876	2,767,900	8.7	6.4	-2.3	32.8	3,218	122	5.2
1877	2,785,600	8.6	6.4	-2.2	32.0	3,119	117	5.0
1878	2,803,300	8.0	6.3	-1.7	31.3	3,026	113	4.9
1879	2,821,000	8.0	6.3	-1.7	30.5	2,928	108	4.7
1880	2,838,700	7.7	6.2	-1.5	29.6	2,815	107	4.8
1881	2,852,500	7.4	4.8	-2.6	29.8	2,841	110	4.9
1882	2,863,400	6.9	3.8	-3.1	28.9	2,758	110	5.1
1883	2,874,300	8.1	3.8	-4.3	28.5	2,736	108	5.1
1884	2,885,200	8.1	3.8	-4.3	28.3	2,725	107	5.1
1885	2,896,100	6.5	3.8	-2.7	27.7	2,684	106	5.1
1886	2,907,000	7.1	3.7	-3.4	27.8	2,703	105	5.1
1887	2,917,900	7.7	3.7	-3.9	27.9	2,727	101	4.9
1888	2,928,800	7.8	3.7	-4.1	27.7	2,723	101	4.9
1889	2,939,700	7.3	3.7	-3.6	27.6	2,707	97	4.7
1890	2,950,600	5.7	3.7	-2.0	26.6	2,591	96	4.9
1891	2,965,100	7.6	4.9	-2.7	28.2	2,731	100	4.8
1892	3,002,300	8.6	12.4	3.7	27.7	2,665	101	5.0
1893	3,039,500	7.8	12.2	4.4	27.9	2,677	98	4.8
1894	3,076,700	7.2	12.1	4.9	27.3	2,606	97	4.8
1895	3,113,900	8.1	11.9	3.8	27.3	2,592	93	4.6
1896	3,151,100	10.3	11.8	1.5	28.1	2,646	99	4.8
1897	3,188,300	10.6	11.7	1.1	28.3	2,650	100	4.8

continued

APPENDIX TABLE CH.4 Demographic developments 1850–1945 (absolute figures and rates)

Crude death rate	Infant mortality rate	Stillbirth rate	Infant mortality and stillbirth rate	Crude marriage rate	Persons marrying per 10,000 unmarried persons age 15+	Persons marrying per 10,000 unmarried persons age 15–49	Crude divorce rate	Divorces per 100 marriages	Divorces per 10,000 married persons	Year
..	..	..	..	..	..	..	..	..	..	1850
..	..	..	..	..	..	..	..	..	..	1851
23.7	..	..	..	6.4	..	..	..	..	..	1852
24.3	..	..	..	6.3	..	..	..	..	..	1853
24.2	..	..	..	5.9	..	..	..	..	..	1854
25.0	..	..	..	5.6	..	..	..	..	..	1855
22.6	..	..	..	6.5	..	..	..	..	..	1856
22.8	..	..	..	7.1	..	..	..	..	..	1857
23.6	..	..	..	7.5	..	..	..	..	..	1858
24.1	..	..	..	7.7	..	..	..	..	..	1859
22.0	..	..	..	7.7	375	471	..	..	..	1860
24.4	..	..	..	7.2	355	447	..	..	..	1861
21.8	..	..	..	7.5	368	465	..	..	..	1862
23.0	..	..	..	7.7	379	481	..	..	..	1863
24.8	..	..	..	7.6	379	482	..	..	..	1864
24.0	..	..	..	7.6	383	489	..	..	..	1865
23.5	..	..	..	7.1	358	459	..	..	..	1866
24.0	..	..	..	6.9	350	450	..	..	..	1867
23.6	..	..	..	6.7	343	443	..	..	..	1868
25.4	..	..	..	7.2	371	481	..	..	..	1869
25.8	..	51.7	..	7.0	361	471	..	..	..	1870
27.6	221.7	51.5	273.2	7.3	379	493	..	..	..	1871
22.2	183.4	49.6	233.0	7.9	412	536	..	..	..	1872
22.7	200.2	48.7	248.9	7.6	402	523	..	..	..	1873
22.3	189.3	46.6	235.9	8.3	441	574	..	..	..	1874
24.0	196.8	48.3	245.1	9.0	481	624	..	..	..	1875
24.1	197.2	42.0	239.1	8.1	437	568	0.4	4.9	25.4	1876
23.5	191.3	40.5	231.8	7.9	428	556	0.4	4.7	23.5	1877
23.3	191.3	40.9	232.2	7.3	404	524	0.4	5.0	23.2	1878
22.6	180.9	40.8	221.7	6.9	382	496	0.3	4.8	20.7	1879
21.9	179.9	38.6	218.5	6.8	382	496	0.3	4.4	18.7	1880
22.4	186.9	39.5	226.4	6.8	381	494	0.3	4.9	20.5	1881
21.9	172.0	39.9	211.9	6.8	379	492	0.3	5.0	20.9	1882
20.4	163.9	39.3	203.2	6.9	383	498	0.3	4.6	19.4	1883
20.2	160.8	39.5	200.3	6.9	386	502	0.3	4.6	19.5	1884
21.3	173.0	40.2	213.2	6.9	388	505	0.3	4.6	19.8	1885
20.7	164.3	41.8	206.2	6.9	387	503	0.3	4.5	19.3	1886
20.2	162.1	41.5	203.6	7.1	396	516	0.3	4.5	19.8	1887
19.9	153.0	41.3	194.3	7.1	396	516	0.3	4.1	17.9	1888
20.3	159.1	38.2	197.3	7.0	394	513	0.3	4.2	18.3	1889
20.9	156.9	39.1	196.1	7.1	394	513	0.3	4.2	18.5	1890
20.6	162.9	37.4	200.2	7.2	400	520	0.3	4.1	18.4	1891
19.0	149.7	37.8	187.5	7.3	406	527	0.3	4.0	18.2	1892
20.1	151.6	37.7	189.4	7.2	400	519	0.3	4.1	18.4	1893
20.1	152.7	37.7	190.4	7.2	400	519	0.3	4.2	18.7	1894
19.2	159.2	37.8	196.9	7.3	404	523	0.3	4.0	17.8	1895
17.8	132.3	36.7	169.0	7.5	418	540	0.3	4.4	20.7	1896
17.7	141.1	36.5	177.6	7.8	433	559	0.3	4.1	19.5	1897

continued

APPENDIX TABLE CH.4 Demographic developments 1850–1945 (continued)

Year	Mid-year population	Natural population growth rate	Population growth rate	Net migration rate	Crude birth rate	Legitimate births per 10,000 married women age 15–44	Illegitimate births per 10,000 unmarried women age 15–44	Illeg. births per 100 leg. births
1898	3,225,500	10.2	11.5	1.3	28.5	2,660	98	4.7
1899	3,262,700	11.3	11.4	0.1	29.0	2,690	100	4.7
1900	3,299,900	9.3	11.3	2.0	28.6	2,643	98	4.7
1901	3,340,600	11.1	12.2	1.1	29.0	2,679	97	4.5
1902	3,384,200	11.5	12.9	1.4	28.5	2,622	95	4.5
1903	3,428,000	10.0	12.8	2.8	27.4	2,510	90	4.4
1904	3,471,900	9.8	12.6	2.8	27.3	2,501	89	4.4
1905	3,515,800	9.3	12.5	3.1	26.9	2,447	93	4.7
1906	3,559,900	10.2	12.4	2.2	26.9	2,437	91	4.6
1907	3,604,000	9.8	12.2	2.5	26.2	2,369	91	4.6
1908	3,647,400	10.6	11.9	1.3	26.4	2,375	94	4.7
1909	3,690,700	9.4	11.7	2.3	25.5	2,286	91	4.7
1910	3,734,800	9.9	11.8	1.9	25.0	2,239	89	4.7
1911	3,775,900	8.4	10.9	2.5	24.2	2,155	87	4.8
1912	3,819,000	10.0	11.3	1.3	24.1	2,141	92	5.0
1913	3,864,000	8.9	11.6	2.8	23.2	2,056	86	4.9
1914	3,897,300	8.6	8.5	-0.1	22.4	..	..	5.2
1915	3,882,800	6.2	-3.7	-9.9	19.5	..	..	4.8
1916	3,882,900	5.9	0.0	-5.9	19.0	..	..	4.6
1917	3,887,500	4.8	1.2	-3.6	18.5	..	..	4.9
1918	3,879,600	-0.6	-2.0	-1.4	18.7	..	..	5.1
1919	3,869,200	4.4	-2.7	-7.1	18.6	1,721	56	4.5
1920	3,876,900	6.5	2.0	-4.5	20.9	1,921	65	4.6
1921	3,875,800	8.1	-0.3	-8.4	20.8	1,908	60	4.3
1922	3,873,900	6.7	-0.5	-7.2	19.7	1,775	70	5.3
1923	3,883,300	7.6	2.4	-5.2	19.5	1,770	50	3.8
1924	3,895,500	6.3	3.1	-3.2	18.9	1,707	49	3.8
1925	3,909,700	6.3	3.6	-2.7	18.6	1,670	48	3.8
1926	3,931,900	6.5	5.6	-0.9	18.3	1,639	49	3.9
1927	3,955,900	5.1	6.1	0.9	17.6	1,558	50	4.2
1928	3,988,200	5.4	8.1	2.7	17.4	1,540	49	4.1
1929	4,021,500	4.6	8.3	3.7	17.2	1,504	50	4.3
1930	4,051,400	5.7	7.4	1.7	17.2	1,499	54	4.6
1931	4,079,700	4.6	6.9	2.3	16.7	1,447	51	4.4
1932	4,102,200	4.6	5.5	0.9	16.7	1,440	51	4.3
1933	4,121,900	4.9	4.8	-0.2	16.4	1,400	50	4.3
1934	4,140,000	4.9	4.4	-0.6	16.3	1,384	48	4.1
1935	4,155,200	3.9	3.7	-0.2	16.0	1,352	47	4.1
1936	4,168,000	4.2	3.1	-1.1	15.6	1,314	45	4.0
1937	4,179,800	3.6	2.8	-0.8	14.9	1,254	42	3.8
1938	4,191,800	3.6	2.9	-0.8	15.2	1,271	41	3.6
1939	4,205,600	3.4	3.3	-0.1	15.2	1,261	41	3.6
1940	4,226,400	3.2	4.9	1.8	15.2	..	..	4.0
1941	4,253,700	5.8	6.4	0.6	16.9	..	..	3.9
1942	4,286,000	7.5	7.5	0.1	18.4	..	..	3.6
1943	4,323,000	8.2	8.6	0.3	19.2	..	..	3.3
1944	4,364,000	7.6	9.4	1.8	19.6	..	..	3.3
1945	4,412,000	8.5	10.9	2.4	20.1	..	..	3.6

APPENDIX TABLE CH.4 Demographic developments 1850–1945 (continued)

Crude death rate	Infant mortality rate	Stillbirth rate	Infant mortality and stillbirth rate	Crude marriage rate	Persons marrying per 10,000 unmarried persons age 15+	Persons marrying per 10,000 unmarried persons age 15–49	Crude divorce rate	Divorces per 100 marriages	Divorces per 10,000 married persons	Year
18.3	155.0	36.9	191.9	7.8	430	554	0.3	4.1	19.4	1898
17.7	136.5	36.2	172.7	7.8	429	553	0.3	4.3	20.6	1899
19.3	149.7	35.8	185.5	7.7	426	548	0.3	4.0	19.1	1900
18.0	137.2	37.2	174.4	7.6	419	539	0.3	4.0	18.8	1901
17.1	131.7	36.4	168.1	7.4	410	527	0.3	4.4	19.9	1902
17.4	133.3	35.1	168.4	7.4	409	526	0.3	4.7	21.0	1903
17.5	140.1	36.2	176.3	7.3	409	524	0.4	4.9	21.7	1904
17.6	128.8	36.0	164.8	7.5	417	535	0.3	4.6	20.8	1905
16.6	126.7	35.3	162.0	7.7	429	549	0.4	4.9	22.8	1906
16.4	121.0	33.7	154.8	7.7	430	551	0.4	5.4	25.0	1907
15.8	107.6	33.5	141.0	7.6	426	545	0.4	5.6	25.6	1908
16.1	114.9	33.8	148.7	7.4	420	536	0.4	5.6	25.0	1909
15.1	105.0	33.7	138.7	7.3	414	529	0.4	5.6	24.5	1910
15.8	123.4	31.4	154.8	7.4	418	533	0.4	5.8	25.7	1911
14.2	93.8	32.3	126.1	7.3	414	528	0.4	5.4	23.7	1912
14.3	96.0	31.7	127.7	6.9	396	504	0.4	6.0	24.9	1913
13.8	91.5	32.0	123.5	5.7	..	..	0.4	6.5	..	1914
13.3	90.0	31.6	121.6	5.0	..	..	0.4	7.5	..	1915
13.0	78.5	30.2	108.7	5.7	..	..	0.4	7.0	..	1916
13.7	79.2	28.6	107.7	6.0	..	..	0.4	7.1	..	1917
19.3	88.2	30.6	118.8	6.7	..	..	0.4	6.5	..	1918
14.2	82.4	28.8	111.3	7.9	423	538	0.5	6.4	29.9	1919
14.4	83.7	30.0	113.7	9.0	480	611	0.6	6.4	33.5	1920
12.8	74.0	29.3	103.3	8.4	447	571	0.5	6.1	29.4	1921
13.0	69.6	29.4	99.1	7.8	412	527	0.5	7.0	31.0	1922
11.8	60.5	28.4	88.9	7.6	404	518	0.5	6.8	29.2	1923
12.6	62.0	28.0	90.0	7.3	388	498	0.5	7.4	30.4	1924
12.2	58.4	26.7	85.1	7.2	381	490	0.6	7.9	31.5	1925
11.8	56.5	25.6	82.1	7.1	378	488	0.6	7.9	31.0	1926
12.4	56.8	25.2	82.0	7.2	383	494	0.6	8.7	34.5	1927
12.1	53.6	25.0	78.6	7.5	399	516	0.6	8.5	34.5	1928
12.5	52.1	24.8	76.9	7.8	411	533	0.7	8.7	36.4	1929
11.6	50.8	24.3	75.1	7.9	419	545	0.7	8.5	35.7	1930
12.1	49.4	23.5	72.9	7.9	419	546	0.7	8.9	37.1	1931
12.2	51.0	23.5	74.4	7.8	414	542	0.7	9.5	38.8	1932
11.4	47.8	23.6	71.4	7.8	413	543	0.7	9.4	37.7	1933
11.3	45.7	22.0	67.7	7.8	419	553	0.7	9.3	37.7	1934
12.1	47.9	22.3	70.2	7.3	392	520	0.7	9.9	37.1	1935
11.4	46.5	22.1	68.6	7.1	381	507	0.8	10.9	39.1	1936
11.3	46.7	20.9	67.6	7.3	391	522	0.8	11.1	40.7	1937
11.6	42.8	21.4	64.2	7.4	399	535	0.8	10.9	40.4	1938
11.8	42.6	22.2	64.8	7.5	404	546	0.7	9.5	35.3	1939
12.0	46.2	20.9	67.1	7.7	..	..	0.7	9.5	..	1940
11.1	41.1	18.9	60.0	8.5	..	..	0.7	8.5	..	1941
10.9	38.3	16.8	55.1	8.6	..	..	0.7	8.7	..	1942
11.0	39.8	16.8	56.6	8.3	..	..	0.7	9.0	..	1943
12.0	42.2	16.7	58.9	8.0	..	..	0.7	9.0	..	1944
11.6	40.7	16.3	57.1	8.1	..	..	0.8	10.5	..	1945

APPENDIX TABLE CH.5 Life expectancy by age 1876/80–1939/44 (in years)

Age	0	10	20	30	40	50	60	70	80
				Males					
1876–1880	40.6	46.9	38.8	31.7	24.8	18.1	12.2	7.4	4.1
1881–1888	43.3	47.9	39.6	32.2	25.1	18.4	12.4	7.4	4.2
1889–1900	45.7	49.0	40.5	32.9	25.5	18.6	12.5	7.6	4.1
1901–1910	49.25	50.34	41.70	33.80	26.03	18.90	12.73	7.78	4.27
1910–1911	50.65	51.07	42.37	34.32	26.48	19.18	12.81	7.83	4.32
1920–1921	54.48	52.53	43.85	35.56	27.47	19.89	13.26	8.01	4.34
1921–1930	58.15	54.13	45.16	36.76	28.34	20.52	13.76	8.30	4.57
1931–1941	60.93	55.75	46.66	38.10	29.47	21.34	14.29	8.63	4.64
1939–1944	62.68	57.08	47.92	39.26	30.42	22.08	14.75	8.85	4.75
				Females					
1876–1880	43.2	48.2	40.3	33.2	26.3	19.1	12.5	7.5	4.2
1881–1888	45.7	49.0	41.0	33.8	26.7	19.4	12.7	7.5	4.2
1889–1900	48.5	50.3	42.2	34.7	27.3	19.8	13.0	7.7	4.2
1901–1910	52.15	51.98	43.69	36.10	28.43	20.71	13.67	8.15	4.51
1910–1911	53.89	63.17	44.74	36.88	28.91	21.13	14.61	8.18	4.12
1920–1921	57.50	54.48	45.85	37.79	29.66	21.71	14.40	8.39	4.20
1921–1930	61.41	56.54	47.63	39.31	30.86	22.60	15.12	9.01	4.89
1931–1941	64.84	58.94	49.73	41.03	32.26	23.73	15.95	9.52	5.09
1939–1944	66.96	60.62	51.28	42.32	33.35	24.65	16.65	9.97	5.32

APPENDIX TABLE CH.6A Households by type 1850–1941 (absolute and per cent)

Census year	Household types and members									
	Total house-holds	Private house-holds	Family house-holds	One-person house-holds	Institu-tional house-holds	Total household members	Private household members	Family household members	One-person household members	Institu-tional house-hold members
Absolute										
1850	485,087	:	:	:	:	2,392,740	:	:	:	:
1860	528,105	:	:	:	:	2,510,494	:	:	:	:
1870	557,018	:	:	:	:	2,655,001	:	:	:	:
1880	607,725	:	:	:	:	2,831,787	:	:	:	:
1888	638,064	:	:	:	:	2,917,754	:	:	:	:
1900	728,920	:	:	:	:	3,315,443	:	:	:	:
1910	829,009	:	:	:	:	3,753,293	:	:	:	:
1920	886,874	883,346	807,835	75,511	3,528	3,880,320	3,743,318	3,667,807	75,511	137,002
1930	1,002,915	994,587	910,024	84,563	8,328	4,065,974	3,903,688	3,819,125	84,563	162,286
1941	:	1,147,029	:	:	:	4,265,703	:	:	:	:
Per cent										
1920	100.00	99.60	91.09	8.51	0.40	100.00	96.47	94.52	1.95	3.53
1930	100.00	99.17	90.74	8.43	0.83	100.00	96.01	93.93	2.08	3.99

APPENDIX TABLE CH.6B Households by size and members 1900–1930 (absolute figures)

Census year	Private households total	Households by number of members											
		1 person	2 persons	3 persons	4 persons	5 persons	6 persons	7 persons	8 persons	9 persons	10 persons	11 persons	12+ persons
		Households											
1900	728,920[1]	69,468	112,491	119,603	114,189	96,747	74,210	52,477	34,632	21,880	13,521	7,562	12,140
1920	883,346	75,511	147,844	164,972	155,102	121,501	83,532	54,192	33,138	19,934	11,754	6,715	9,151
1930	994,587	84,563	196,449	208,361	182,511	128,045	194,658	..	..	..	..	..	..
		Persons											
1900	3,315,443[2]	69,468	224,982	358,809	456,756	483,735	445,260	367,339	277,056	196,920	135,210	83,182	216,726
1920	3,743,318	75,511	295,688	494,916	620,408	607,505	501,192	379,344	265,104	179,406	117,540	73,865	132,839
1930	3,903,688	84,563	392,898	625,083	730,044	640,225	1,430,875	..	..	..	..	..	..

Notes: [1] All households. [2] Total population.

APPENDIX TABLE CH.6C Households by size and members 1900–1930 (per cent)

Census year	Private households total	Households by number of members											
		1 person	2 persons	3 persons	4 persons	5 persons	6 persons	7 persons	8 persons	9 persons	10 persons	11 persons	12+ persons
		Households											
1900	100.00[1]	9.53	15.43	16.41	15.67	13.27	10.18	7.20	4.75	3.00	1.85	1.04	1.67
1920	100.00	8.55	16.74	18.68	17.56	13.75	9.46	6.13	3.75	2.26	1.33	0.76	1.04
1930	100.00	8.50	19.75	20.95	18.35	12.87	19.57	..	..	..	..	..	..
		Persons											
1900	100.00[2]	2.10	6.79	10.82	13.78	14.59	13.43	11.08	8.36	5.94	4.08	2.51	6.54
1920	100.00	2.02	7.90	13.22	16.57	16.23	13.39	10.13	7.08	4.79	3.14	1.97	3.55
1930	100.00	2.17	10.06	16.01	18.70	16.40	36.65	..	..	..	..	..	..

Notes: [1] All households. [2] Total population.

APPENDIX TABLE CH.6D Household indicators 1850–1941

Census year	Household indicators			
	Mean total household size	Mean private household size	Mean family household size	Mean institutional household size
1850	4.93	::	::	::
1860	4.75	::	::	::
1870	4.77	::	::	::
1880	4.66	::	::	::
1888	4.57	::	::	::
1900	4.55	::	::	::
1910	4.53	::	::	::
1920	4.38	4.24	4.54	38.83
1930	4.05	3.92	4.20	19.49
1941	3.72[1]	::	::	::

Note: [1] Total population per private household.

APPENDIX TABLE CH.6E Household composition 1920–1930 (absolute and per cent)

Census year	Persons in private households total	Household head	Wife/husband of household head	Children of household head	Parents of household head	Parents-in-law of household head	Other relatives of household head	Domestic servants	Other employees	Boarders and lodgers	Other persons
	Absolute										
1920	3,743,318	883,346	621,702	1,591,715		205,773[1]		95,118	109,379	186,262	50,023
1930	3,903,688	994,587	720,857	1,514,787	87,101		162,232[2]	107,752	105,569	172,051	38,752
	Per cent										
1920	100.00	23.60	16.61	42.52		5.50[1]		2.54	2.92	4.98	1.34
1930	100.00	25.48	18.47	38.80	2.23		4.16[2]	2.76	2.70	4.41	0.99

Notes: [1] Parents, parents-in-law and other relatives. [2] Includes also other relatives.

APPENDIX TABLE CH.7 Dates and nature of results on population structure,
households/families, and vital statistics

Topic	Intro-duction	Remarks
Population		
Population at census dates	1850	Earlier censuses conducted since the seventeenth century (cf. Ritzmann-Blic??kenstorfer and Siegenthaler (1996)).
Population by age, sex, and marital status	1860	
Households and families		
Households (Haushaltungen or ménages)		
Total households	1850	Households first expressively recorded in 1850 (cf. Statistisches Bureau des Eidgenössischen Departement des Innern 1892: 40*): 1850: number of households (one-person, family, and institutional households combined in only one category). 1860: as in 1850. 1870: as in 1850. 1880: as in 1850. 1888: as in 1850. 1900: as in 1850; in addition: households by size. 1910: as in 1850. 1920: number of households (one-person, family, and institutional); households by size, composition, profession, number of children. 1930: as in 1920, but no profession or number of children. 1941: only number of households. *Disaggregation*: by cantons and districts.
Households by size	1900, 1920, 1930, 1941	First time in the population census of 1900: households by number of persons 1–12+. First extensive household statistics in 1920. Repeated in 1930 and 1941.
Households by composition	1920, 1930	Family and non-family members.
Households by profession of household head	1920, 1930	Socio-professional position.
Families (Familien)		
Families by number of children	1920, 1941	First special investigation of families by number of children in 1920. Married women by number of children born 1941.

continued

APPENDIX TABLE CH.7 Dates and nature of results on population structure, households/families, and vital statistics (continued)

Topic	Intro-duction	Remarks
Population movement		
Mid-year population	1852	
Births		
Live births	1851	
Stillbirths	1870	
Legitimate births	1871	
Illegitimate births	1871	
Deaths		
Total deaths	1851	
Infants (under 1 year)	1876	
Marriages		
Total marriages	1851	
Divorces and separations		
Total divorces	1876	
Legal separations	1897	

APPENDIX FIGURE CH.8 Population by age, sex and marital status, Switzerland
1860, 1880, 1900, 1920, 1930 and 1941 (per 10,000 of total population)

Switzerland, 1860

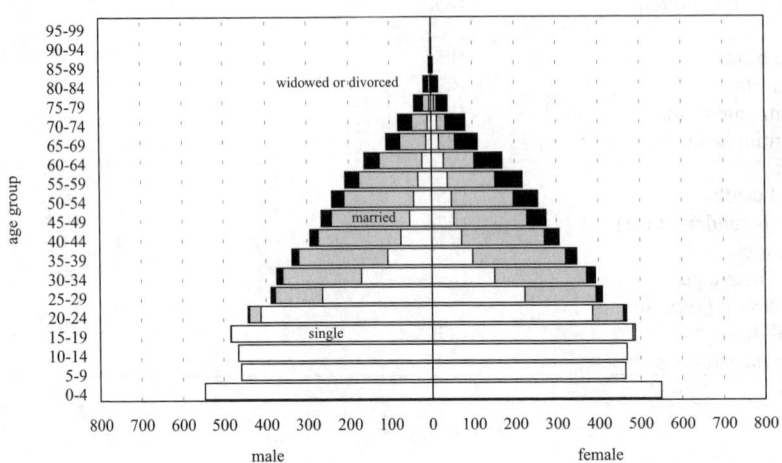

Switzerland, 1880

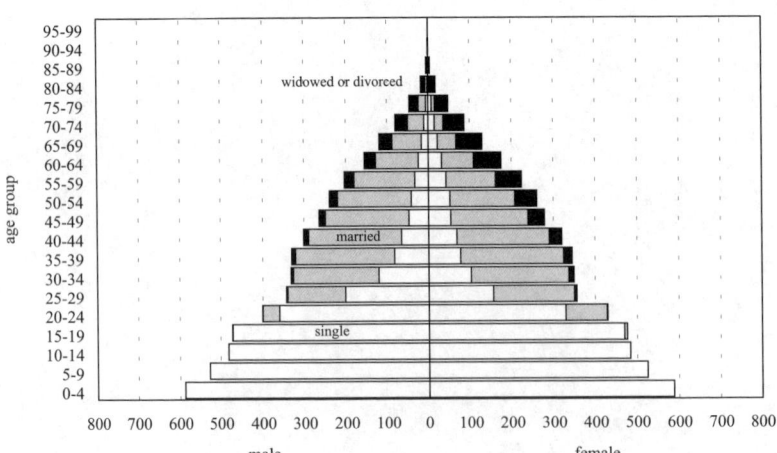

APPENDIX FIGURE CH.8 Population by age, sex and marital status, Switzerland
1860, 1880, 1900, 1920, 1930 and 1941 (per 10,000 of total population) (continued)

Switzerland, 1900

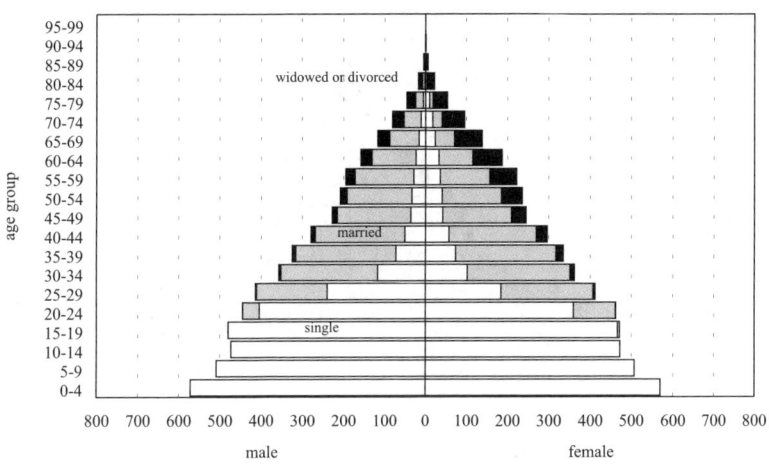

Switzerland, 1920

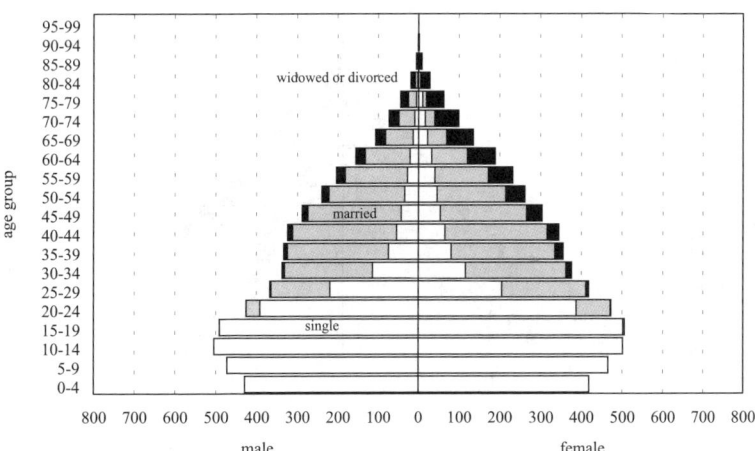

APPENDIX FIGURE CH.8 Population by age, sex and marital status, Switzerland
1860, 1880, 1900, 1920, 1930 and 1941 (per 10,000 of total population) (continued)

Switzerland, 1930

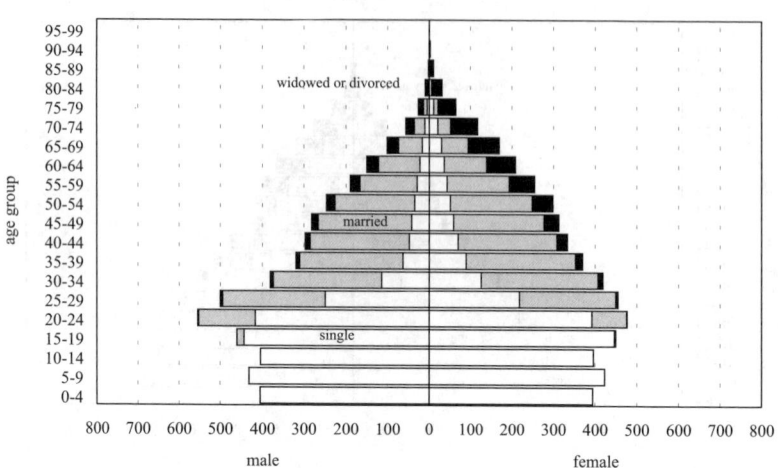

Switzerland, 1941

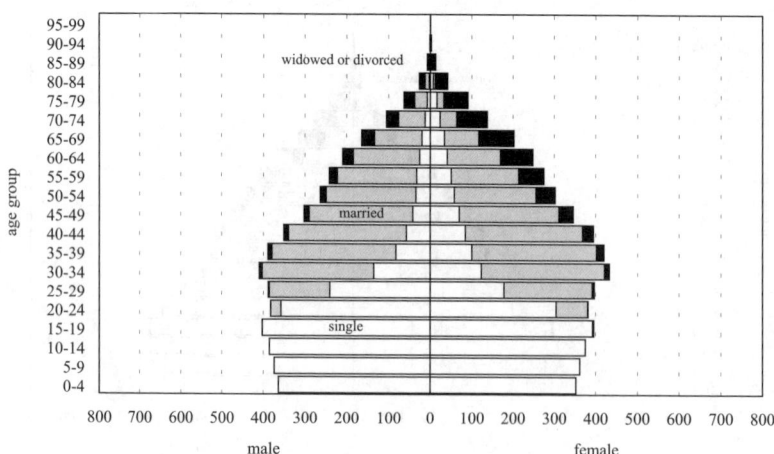

21

United Kingdom of Great Britain and Northern Ireland

The United Kingdom is composed of Great Britain and Northern Ireland. Great Britain itself is composed of three different parts: England, Wales, and Scotland. The United Kingdom of Great Britain and Ireland was originally established in 1801, when Ireland formally became part of the country. (As Ireland is treated in a separate chapter, we only deal here with Great Britain and Northern Ireland. Concerning Ireland and the Irish Republic see also the chapter on Ireland). The United Kingdom therefore consists of four parts: England, Wales, Scotland, and Ireland (since 1921 Northern Ireland).

Attempts to unify the British Isles under one crown date back to the high Middle Ages. The power centre of the country always lay in the south at the river Thames, near the merchant cities of the continent (Belgium, The Netherlands) and the mouth of the Rhine River. The conquest of the country therefore started from the Anglo-Saxon world. Already in 1277 Wales lost independence and was formally dissolved by the Tudor family. Scotland remained formally independent until 1707 when a union between England and Scotland was concluded. But insurgency persisted and the last battle between the English and Scottish was fought as late as 1746 (Culloden). Ireland was integrated into the United Kingdom in 1801. In 1921 Southern Ireland gained independence, while Northern Ireland remained part of the United Kingdom.

All four parts of the kingdom kept some sort of home rule although the UK is not a federal state. But the administration of the four parts of the country differs due to tradition, history, and local conditions. This is also apparent with regard to statistics (general literature includes Wende, 1995; Niedhart, 1996; Kamerman and Kahn, 1997; Ringen, 1997; Laslett and Wall, 1972; Teitelbaum, 1984; Coleman and Salt, 1992; Joshi, 1989; Wall, Robin, and Laslett, 1983; Wrigley and Schofield, 1981).

Already during the nineteenth century the UK was one of the most densely populated countries in Europe. In 1871 there were 121 inhabitants per square kilometre, and by 1931 population density had increased to 197 inhabitants per square km. The population is very unequally distributed over the four parts of the UK: England more or less constantly makes up three-fourths of the total population, Wales around 5%, Scotland roughly 10%, and Northern Ireland (since 1921) less than 3%. Unequal distribution of the population over the territory is reflected in uneven population density. Population density in England was always higher than in other parts of the country. Wales was second, Northern Ireland third, and Scotland last. This pattern remained stable in the one hundred years from 1850 to 1950. Population density of England and Wales increased faster and much more strongly than that of Northern Ireland and Scotland. Obviously, strong internal migration is one characteristic of the time period.

Regions with major population agglomerations in *England* are the counties of York West Riding, Lancaster, and Greater London. These three counties account for over 35% of the population of England and their population density is the highest in England: population density in Greater London has been over 10,000 since 1891, the county of York city had a population density of over 5,000 inhabitants in 1931, and the county of Lancaster a population density of over 1,000 inhabitants in 1931.

Wales had a very uneven population structure. Already in 1871 33% of the population lived in the county of Glamorgan, rising to 47% in 1931. The county of Monmouth was second, accounting for 17% of total population in 1931. Taken together, these two counties alone accounted for two-thirds of the Welsh population in 1931 and had the highest population density as a consequence. In Glamorgan it was 580 inhabitants per sq. km. in 1931, and in Monmouth 310.

In *Scotland* the city of Glasgow accounted for one-fifth of the total Scottish population already in the nineteenth century. Urbanization increased this proportion to 33% by 1931. Second in population size came the county of Edinburgh (Midlothian), amounting to approximately 11% in 1931. Both of these two counties of course also had the highest population density. Significant for Scotland are the large regional differences in population density and their remarkable stability over time.

Northern Ireland, finally, reveals a highly urbanized pattern. In the inter-war period Belfast already accounted for one-third of the population of Northern Ireland. Over two-thirds of the population resided in only three counties—Belfast C.B., County Down, and County Antrim—in 1937.

POPULATION GROWTH

Natural population growth in the UK during the second half of the nineteenth century was constantly high with values well over 10 per 1,000. Natural population growth from the 1860s until World War I were remarkably stable and show no major fluctuations due to economic crises or military conflicts. During the second half of the nineteenth century there was a constant flow of emigration from the British Isles. The net migration rate was always negative, fluctuating between 2 and 5 per 1,000. Only the 1880s were a period of stronger emigration (Figure UK.1).

World War I changed this rather stable and continuous development. The natural population growth rate declined in the last war years, reaching its lowest level in 1918 with only 1.8 per 1,000. After the war, from 1920–1 natural population growth reached pre-war levels, but after that time during the whole inter-war period natural population growth was substantially lower than before World War I. The declining population surplus caused emigration to cease. While during the 1920s emigration was still higher than immigration, the pattern was reversed during the 1930s. In the 1930s Britain changed from a traditional country of emigration to a country of immigration. The low birth rates of the 1930s therefore could partly be compensated by immigration. Nevertheless, the total population growth rate during the inter-war period was only half what it had been in the second half of the nineteenth century.

THE FIRST DEMOGRAPHIC TRANSITION

The demographic transition of the UK is a somewhat artificial subject: first, the country's borders changed with the independence of the Irish Republic. Second, the country is composed of four parts that differ significantly in various ways: territory, population size, population structure, etc. But here it is argued that England alone, which in 1951 accounted for 79% of the total population of the UK, is large enough to be representative of the whole UK.

Due to the great differences between the different countries of the UK, we will sometimes refer to developments in individual parts such as England. During most of the demographic transition the UK had a rather high natural population growth (Figure UK.2). In the 1860s the birth rate was rather high, and the death rate was very low and below the European average, resulting in a strong natural population growth. During the second half of the nineteenth century both the birth and the death rates showed no major irregularities apart from increases in the death rate, probably mainly due to epidemics. The first major distortion of the demographic development during the transition phase came with World War I, which caused a massive postponement of births and a major increase in the death rate. Although births were made up after the war, the birth decline accelerated because of the economic depression of the late 1920s and early 1930s. The 1930s in particular were a time of political, social, and economic instability with consequences for demographic behaviour. During the 1930s the natural population increase dropped off sharply. World War II made the birth rate decline further and the death rate rise. Immediately after the war there was a jump in the birth rate, probably partly a cohort effect from the post-World War I period. The birth rate declined in the 1950s, whereas during the 1960s the 'second demographic transition' began with a rise in fertility and a subsequent decline. In the mid-1970s population growth became zero when the birth rate converged with the death rate. Natural population growth in the 1980s was very low, due to the low fertility level.

When the demographic transition of the UK is compared with that of Europe, it is apparent that already in the nineteenth century the UK birth and death rates were lower than in Europe. But in the UK the death rate was so low—thanks to low infant mortality—that the natural population increase was high. But the consequences of two world wars in the twentieth century brought an end to these high growth rates. In particular, the crisis in the inter-war period brought British fertility below the European level. And also the post-World War II demographic development was shaped by lower natural population growth than the European average. Thus, the British Isles experienced high population growth earlier than most European countries —already in the eighteenth century—due to an early decline in mortality. This pattern survived until the end of the nineteenth century. The consequence of the early population growth—especially in England—was a high population density already in the first half of the nineteenth century.

MORTALITY AND LIFE EXPECTANCY

The infant mortality rate is defined as deaths of children aged under one year per 1,000 live births. The whole United Kingdom and its constituent parts of (Northern) Ireland, Scotland, England, and Wales shared very similar patterns of infant mortality. All these territories fit into the same intermediate cluster of moderate

Figure UK.1 Population growth and net migration, United Kingdom 1864-1945

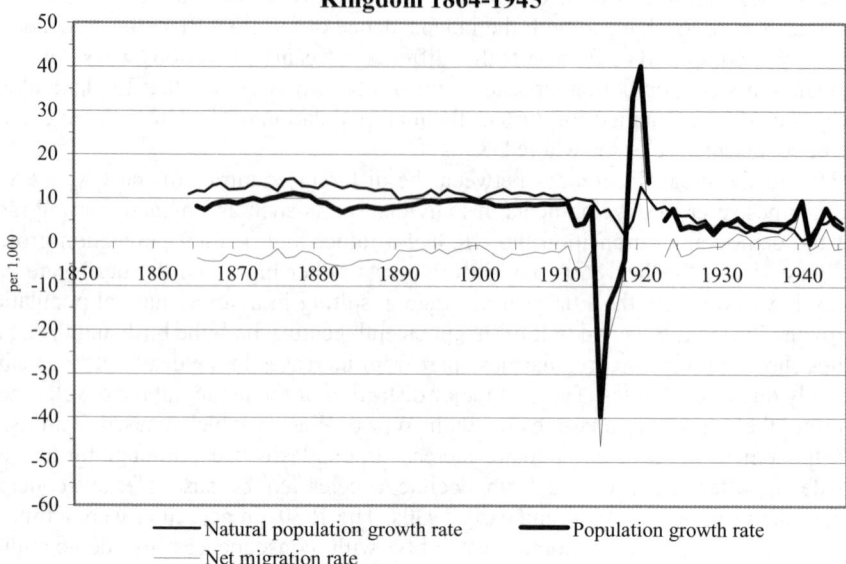

— Natural population growth rate   — Population growth rate
— Net migration rate

Figure UK.2 First demographic transition, United Kingdom 1864-1945

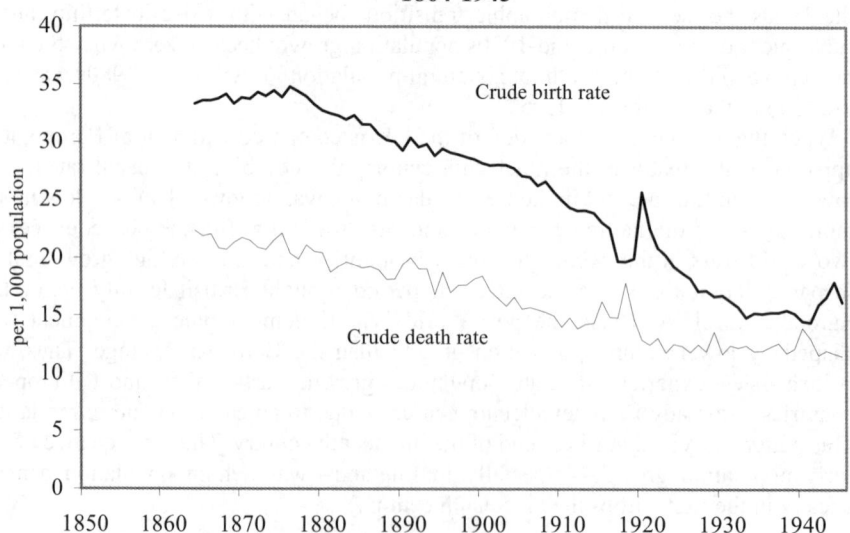

infant mortality, lying between the positive extreme of the Nordic countries and the negative one of the Mediterranean and Eastern European countries. Most of the continental countries belong to this country cluster as well (Masuy-Stroobant, 1997). There are nevertheless differences between these parts of the British Isles. Around 1900 Scotland had a much lower infant mortality rate than England and Wales. In the five-year period 1926–30 Scotland lost its position and instead had the highest infant mortality rate in the entire UK. England and Wales together with the Republic of Ireland had the lowest rate, followed by Northern Ireland, and finally Scotland (Figure UK.3).

Reasons for these differences are not easy to find. In the case of England there are long time series on infant mortality (cf. Woods, Williams and Galley, 1993; Woods, 1997a), which could shed light on historical preconditions. In England and Wales (annual data available since the 1840s) there was no clear-cut trend in infant mortality during the nineteenth century. There was a declining tendency until the 1880s, but afterwards the curve went up until 1900, when the final and very steep decrease in mortality set in. Obviously the increase in the infant mortality rate in the last two decades of the nineteenth century is only due to Wales; in England infant mortality had been steadily declining already since the 1750s (Woods, Williams, and Galley, 1993: 37). In Wales living conditions must have greatly deteriorated during the second half of the nineteenth century, while in England there was obviously a constant improvement.

Infant mortality in the different parts of the UK is strongly shaped by differing degrees of urbanization and industrialization. Already in the Middle Ages England was a highly urbanized country with many autonomous cities. Urbanization was lower in the western and northern peripheries of the kingdom. Infant mortality was much higher in urban regions, especially the large cities, than in rural areas and small settlements. This may explain the difference between England and Wales and Scotland around 1900. As Woods, Williams, and Galley (1993: 41) show, in the major cities, infant mortality was always higher than the average for England and Wales. But obviously the years after 1900 were the decisive period in infant mortality in the United Kingdom: there must have been drastic reforms with an impact on mortality rates in order to produce such a sharp decline. A persuasive explanation for this turning point around 1900 has not yet been proposed, but should be sought in the policies of the large towns concerning sanitation and water supply, among other things, because in the large cities in particular, infant mortality declined sharply, and already at that time a large proportion of the population was urbanized. The introduction of national health insurance and other social security provisions after 1900 may also have had an impact (1908 Old Age Pension Act) (cf. also Woods, 1997b; Reid, 1997).

Life expectancy in the largest part of the United Kingdom—in England and Wales—during the nineteenth century was already rather favourable. When compared with Sweden, life expectancy in the 1850s was partly higher in England and Wales than in Sweden. Around 1850, life expectancy at birth in both countries was high and at a comparable level, at 40 years for new-born boys. At age 30 and age 60 English men had a higher life expectancy than Swedish men of that time, though the difference was only one or two years. But by the 1930s, England and Wales had lost their favourable position relative to Sweden: in the former, life expectancy of new-born boys was 58.7 years; in Sweden it was 63.2 years, a difference of 4.5 years. Swedish men also had a higher life expectancy at the age of 30 and 60 (Figure EW.4). Sex differences in life expectancy in England and Wales were small during the nineteenth century, but increasingly diverged until the 1930s: the difference in life expectancy between the sexes in favour of women doubled between the 1850s and the 1930s.

FERTILITY AND LEGITIMACY

Although female celibacy was high in the UK during the nineteenth century and age at marriage was late, illegitimate fertility was low. It was very much lower than the European average (Figure UK.5). The illegitimate fertility rate showed a declining trend during the 100 years from 1850 to 1950, with a temporary increase in the 1890s. The decline in illegitimate births began earlier than that of legitimate births. World War II caused a fundamental change in the illegitimacy pattern in the United Kingdom. During and after the war the illegitimate fertility rate rose, but declined during the 1950s with the marriage boom. In the 1960s another change occurred when illegitimate fertility in the UK exceeded the European rate for the first time. A fundamental change in fertility values must have occurred during that time. In the 1970s there was a wave of illegitimacy with a subsequent decline in the 1980s. After that illegitimate fertility increased strongly and now shows a pattern similar to the Nordic countries.

More or less the opposite can be said of the development of legitimate fertility. It was higher than in Europe during the nineteenth century but lower after World War I. But the development of legitimate fertility follows the European pattern rather closely. The birth decline mainly affected legitimate fertility, which declined strongly during the demographic transition, while illegitimate fertility declined much less.

Thus during the last 150 years the UK has undergone a fundamental change from low illegitimacy to high illegitimate fertility. Behind this change in demographic behaviour is a fundamental change in the concept of marriage and childbirth. After World War II, childbirth before and without marriage became a socially accepted fact.

MARRIAGE AND DIVORCE

The UK belongs to the region of the Western European marriage pattern with late and non-universal marriage. Nevertheless, it must be emphasized that the pattern was not as extreme as in countries such as Switzerland, Austria, and later Finland.

The following discussion is mainly based on data from England and Wales. Calculations for the UK have not been made for the indicators on the proportion married at age 20–24. From the 1850s to the 1870s the proportion of women married at age 20–24 was rather high, at over 30%, a figure which puts England closer to countries like France and Italy than to the Nordic countries, where this proportion was only 20%. This means that in England, age at marriage was already low in the mid-nineteenth century. Although the proportion of women married at age 20–24 declined after 1870 and remained on a lower level until the 1930s, the national level was still higher than in the Nordic countries. In other words, age at marriage increased and was especially high during the inter-war period. Starting in the 1930s age at marriage started to fall and the proportion of women married at age 20–24

Figure EW.3 Infant mortality, England and Wales 1850-1945

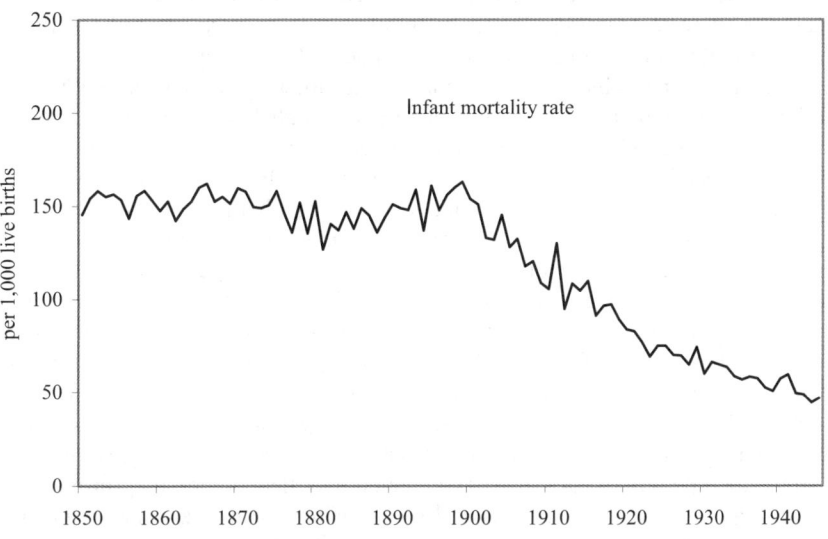

Figure EW.4 Life expectancy, England and Wales 1841-1930/32

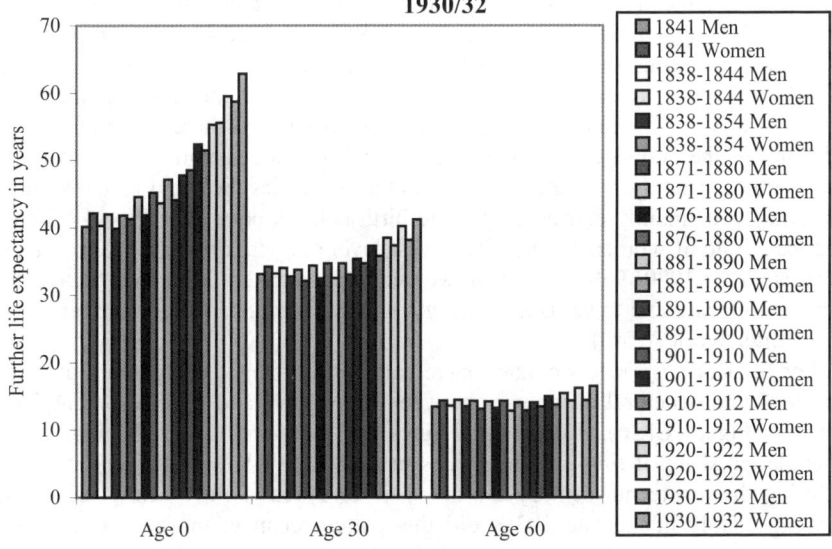

increased, peaking at around 1970 with nearly 60% of women married in their early 20s. This proportion is the highest ever in all Western European countries. The postponement of marriage after this wave of early marriage started later in England than in the Nordic countries. Thus, structural traits in English society favoured early marriage in the nineteenth century and continue to do so today.

The pattern for English men is similar to that for English women, with the main difference being that the marriage pattern of English men deviated even more strongly from that of men in other European countries. In the 1870s, 20% of English men were married at the early age of 20–24 years. In most Nordic countries this proportion was only about 10%, and even in Southern European countries the proportion was lower. The tendency of English men to marry early is exceptional in European demographic history. As for English women, age at marriage increased after the 1870s and reached its highest level in the 1930s; but even at this time English men married earlier than men in most other Western European countries. Since the early 1930s English men increasingly favoured early marriage, and in 1970 the proportion of men married at age 20–24 peaked at 38%. Along with the Belgians, English men married earliest of all Europeans. As for English women, the subsequent postponement of marriage started later also for English men. They retained their pattern of early marriage much longer than other male Europeans.

Marriage intensity can be measured by the *marriage rate* and the *celibacy rate*. 'Intensity' means the availability of marriage, but at the same time the urgent need to remarry after widowhood. The high celibacy rate of English women in the mid-nineteenth century clearly places England within the country group with the Western European marriage pattern. But there are important differences when compared with the demographically most similar countries, the Nordic countries. In the 1870–90s roughly 30% of English women were never married at age 45–54, a proportion very similar to countries such as Sweden, Norway, and Finland. But what distinguishes England from the Nordic countries is the early decline in the celibacy rate at a time when it was still increasing in those countries. In England there was already a slight decline in the celibacy rate after 1900, which continued until World War II and accelerated strongly after the war. As in other countries the trend towards universal marriage was mainly carried by female birth cohorts born after World War I. The celibacy rate of women reached its lowest level at approximately 5% in the 1980s, that is, in the 1980s 95% of English women had married at least once by age 45–54. In the 1990s a trend towards increasing celibacy started, carried by the birth cohorts born after World War II.

For the *marriage rate* we again have data for the United Kingdom, but there are basically no structural differences between UK figures and figures for England and Wales (Figure UK.6). The basic features are the same, given the impact of the population share of England and Wales in the whole UK, which was 83% in 1931. During the nineteenth century the marriage rate was slightly below the European average. Only in the late 1930s did this pattern change: the rate rose above the European average and remained at this level also in the second half of the twentieth century. Already in the nineteenth century, then, the UK was influenced by the Western European pattern of late and non-universal marriage. The country changed its position during the twentieth century. When compared with the Nordic countries, where marriage had a low standing in society (as revealed by demographic indicators), in the UK people married earlier, more frequently, and a larger

Figure UK.5 Fertility and legitimacy, United Kingdom 1864-1939

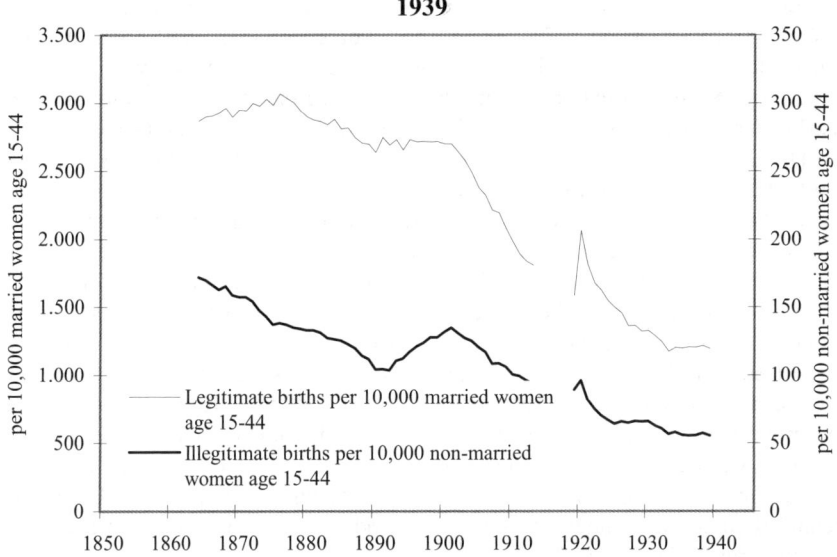

Figure UK.6 Marriages and divorces, United Kingdom 1864-1939

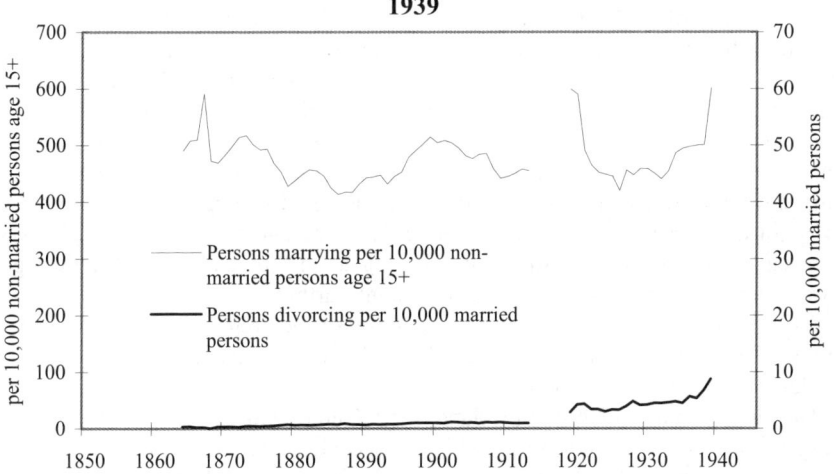

proportion of the population married. It is often asked whether this feature can be attributed mainly to a high degree of industrialization and urbanization in the United Kingdom versus the predominance of peasant societies in the Nordic countries.

Marital stability, when measured by the divorce rate, was very high during the nineteenth century and fell only slightly during the first half of the twentieth century (Figure UK.6). A first major upswing in the divorce rate came as a consequence of World War II, when many marriages broke down. The divorce rate peaked in 1945–50. Divorces declined during the 1950s, when the marriage boom set in. In the 1960s the divorce rate started its secular increase, first obviously due to structural causes, but in the late 1960s a major liberalization of the divorce law was enacted. The consequence was a tremendous increase in divorces, and the divorce rate now exceeds the European divorce rate for the first time since the nineteenth century.

The low divorce rate in the United Kingdom until the post-war years is mainly explained by the restrictive divorce law. In England and Wales divorce was only introduced in 1859; before that only legal separation existed and to a limited extent divorce by a private Act of Parliament. The act of 1859 introduced civil marriage and divorce on grounds of fault. In 1923, men and women obtained equal status in divorce law, and in 1937 the grounds were extended considerably. Finally, in 1971 divorce on the sole condition of marital breakdown was introduced. In Northern Ireland divorce on grounds of fault was introduced as late as 1937 in accordance with the English law of 1937.

AGE, SEX, AND CIVIL STATUS

Appendix Figures GB.8, EW.8, SC.8 and NI.8 present the age structure for the different parts of the United Kingdom from 1851 to 1931 and from 1926 to 1936 for Northern Ireland. The differences between the age structure of England and Wales and that of Great Britain are marginal. Because of more detailed data available for England and Wales, we refer here to England and Wales. Until 1911 the age structure of England and Wales remained rather regular but was already tending to move from a pyramidal to a bell shape due to the starting fertility decline. The impact of World War I on the decline of the lowest two age groups (0–4 and 5–9) was not as great as in France and Germany, as the age structure for 1921 reveals. The age structure of 1931 shows that during the 1920s and especially during the Great Depression the lowest age cohorts shrank further.

As in most European countries the proportion of men remaining single longer was higher than that of women. But female celibacy in higher age groups was more widespread, as was widowhood.

The age structure of Northern Ireland in 1926 and 1936 was very similar to that of England and Wales at that time, with the exception that the youngest age groups were much larger in Northern Ireland due to higher Irish fertility.

FAMILY AND HOUSEHOLD STRUCTURES

Official statistics unfortunately give only a few hints about the basic social group of families and households. There is little information on the number and size of households. If we take mean family household size as a summary characteristic of household structures, mean household size in England and Wales lay somewhere in the middle of all European countries, with a mean value of well below 5.0 persons per household. In 1801 mean household size was 4.69; it fluctuated during the nineteenth century, but the decrease in mean household size only began with the birth decline at the end of the century. Before World War I, mean size had fallen to 4.51 in 1911 and in 1931 to 3.91 persons per household.

Mean household size is strongly influenced by the proportion of people living alone. This proportion again was in the middle between the Nordic countries with a high proportion and the Southern European countries with a low proportion of one-person households. The proportion of large households (with five or more persons) was also in a middle field between the extremes.

The different parts of the United Kingdom demonstrate interesting differences concerning the size of households. In England and Wales households were smallest, in Scotland they were of medium size, and in Northern Ireland they were the largest households, at least in the 1920s and 1930s.

Obviously, factors like industrialization and urbanization play an important role in determining household size, most visible in England and Wales with rather small households. The larger households in Northern Ireland are probably due to the Catholic population with higher fertility and lower industrialization and urbanization.

THE NATIONAL SYSTEM OF DEMOGRAPHIC STATISTICS

The availability of data has to be described separately for the territories which make up the United Kingdom: England and Wales, Scotland, and Ireland/Northern Ireland. Wales is the fourth historically distinguished territory but is usually combined with England in census publications. Data availability is described for the United Kingdom without Ireland until the independence of the Irish Free State in 1921 and including Northern Ireland after 1921. For data on Ireland for the whole period, see the chapter on Ireland.

Population Structure

The United Kingdom of Great Britain and Ireland provided a stable state structure for more than a century, which was the basis for early and very regular census-taking. Decennial censuses began already in 1801 and have been carried out with outstanding regularity up to the present. They have been conducted every decade ending in '1' following the first census of 1801. Censuses were thus taken in the years 1801, 1811, 1821, 1831, 1841, 1851, 1861, 1871, 1881, 1891, 1901, 1911, 1921, and 1931. During World War II no census was held. When Ireland separated from the United Kingdom this regularity in census-taking was interrupted for the northern provinces of Ireland: during the inter-war years censuses were organized in 1926 and 1937. The regular census of 1921 could not be carried out due to the political circumstances.

Population data by age, sex, and marital status are available since 1851, but have been presented during the nineteenth century in highly grouped form. For England and Wales and Scotland data are available in five- or ten-year age groups from 1851 to 1901. One-year age groups were published only from 1901 to 1931. For Northern Ireland the censuses of 1926 and 1937 presented data on one-year age groups.

Vital Statistics

In contrast to the censuses, the collection of vital statistics began at different times in the three parts of the United Kingdom. In *England and Wales* the record of births, deaths, and marriages was introduced already in 1838. Infant deaths are available since 1839. Births by legitimacy are available since 1841/45. Data on divorces (decrees for dissolution) are available since 1858, and data on stillbirths have been collected since 1928.

In *Scotland* vital statistics registration came much later. Births, deaths, marriages, legitimate births, and infant deaths have been recorded since 1855. Data on divorces and Nullity Decrees are available since 1855 as well. Data on stillbirths have been published since 1939.

In *Northern Ireland* most vital statistics time series start in 1922, after separation from the southern provinces. This is the case for live births, marriages, deaths, legitimate births, and infant deaths. Data on divorces are available since 1939 and data on stillbirths since 1962.

Households and Families

Data on *households* (*private families*) were already collected in the census of 1801 and continuously in all the subsequent censuses. Household statistics are identical for England and Wales and for Scotland. But household statistics remained at this low level of detail, and no really comprehensive household statistics were established before World War II. During the nineteenth century households were given the term '*private families*' in contrast to '*institutions*'. Private families comprised single persons and family households and are more or less identical to the modern definition of a private household. Institutional households were clearly distinguished already in the nineteenth century; the number of these was published only sporadically in favour of the number of personnel and inmates of these different institutions. Nevertheless, statistics on institutions in the nineteenth century are fairly comprehensive compared with other countries. There is detailed information on different types of institutions, their personnel and inmates. For the nineteenth century the only indicator that can be derived from the British household statistics is mean household size.

The only extension in household statistics made until World War II was the distinction of private families by size. In *England and Wales* this disaggregation was introduced in 1901 and repeated in every census until 1931. Household members were distinguished from 1 to 15 or more members.

In *Scotland* data on households by size were published earlier, already for the census of 1861 and repeated in every census until 1931.

In *Northern Ireland* households by size are available for both censuses of 1926 and 1937. In 1926 households were distinguished by members from 1 to 15 or more; in 1937 from 1 to 10 or more members.

Households (*private families*) were defined by official statistics in contrast to institutional households. 'Private families' were private households with at least one household member ('one-person family'). Before the 1950 census, British statistics used 'family' instead of 'household'.

Family statistics in the sense of fertility statistics of married women developed differently in the different parts of the UK. In *England and Wales* data on families by the number of children were first collected in 1911. A separate Volume XIII was published on the 'Fertility of Marriage' (no author given, 1917, 1923). An investigation into fertility was also conducted in 1921 but on a smaller scale (no author given, 1927: 175ff.).

For *Scotland* no such data were published.

In *Northern Ireland* the first special investigation of the fertility of marriages was produced in 1926.

Remarks (also see introductory Table 6.1)

The data for the UK refer to the territory of the United Kingdom as it was set up in 1801, that is, including Great Britain and Ireland from 1801 to 1921, and Great Britain and Northern Ireland only from 1922 to 1990. Data are also available for the constituent parts of the UK, that is, England and Wales, Scotland, Great Britain, Ireland from 1801–1921, and Eire from 1922 to the present.

BOUNDARY CHANGES

The United Kingdom of Great Britain and Ireland was created in 1801 by merging the Kingdom of Ireland with England/Wales and Scotland. In 1921 the United Kingdom lost the territory of the Republic of Ireland. Apart from this loss there have been only minor territorial changes in the last two centuries. This becomes clear when remembering that the territory consists of islands and therefore has natural boundaries. A second point is that since the Norman invasion in 1066 no other foreign power has succeeded in invading the British Isles. For regional organization see the documentation by Quick (1994) and Caramani, Flora, Kraus, and Quick (1998).

APPENDIX TABLE GB.1 Population structure at census dates, Great Britain 1851–1931

Census number	Census date	Census population			Marital status				Age group		
		Total	Male	Female	Single	Married	Widowed	Divorced	0–14	15–64	65+
		Absolute									
1	30–31 III 1851	22,887,636	10,638,454	12,249,182	13,850,106	7,685,440	1,352,090	..	7,912,004	13,867,827	1,107,805
2	7–8 IV 1861	23,128,518	11,226,107	11,902,411	14,002,570	7,826,164	1,299,784	..	8,253,195	13,794,289	1,081,034
3	2–3 IV 1871	26,072,284	12,662,077	13,410,207	15,766,743	8,827,136	1,478,405	..	9,434,532	15,389,006	1,248,746
4	3–4 IV 1881	29,710,012	14,439,377	15,270,635	18,135,373	9,923,262	1,651,377	..	10,834,197	17,501,204	1,374,611
5	5–6 IV 1891	33,028,172	15,995,618	17,032,554	20,229,092	10,961,590	1,837,490	..	11,604,460	19,848,014	1,575,698
6	31 III–1 IV 1901	36,999,946	17,902,368	19,097,578	22,258,388	12,696,675	2,044,883	..	12,040,841	23,224,895	1,734,210
7	2–3 IV 1911	40,831,396	19,754,447	21,076,949	23,951,932	14,632,652	2,244,724	2,088[1]	12,587,504	26,108,142	2,135,750
8	19–20 VI 1921	42,769,196	20,422,881	22,346,315	23,450,772	16,742,904	2,555,444	19,100	11,940,167	28,246,017	2,583,012
9	26–27 IV 1931	44,795,357	21,458,533	23,336,824	23,103,213	18,856,084	2,798,510	36,432	10,825,072	30,655,571	3,314,714
		Per cent									
1	30–31 III 1851	100.00	46.48	53.52	60.51	33.58	5.91	..	34.57	60.59	4.84
2	7–8 IV 1861	100.00	48.54	51.46	60.54	33.84	5.62	..	35.68	59.64	4.67
3	2–3 IV 1871	100.00	48.57	51.43	60.47	33.86	5.67	..	36.19	59.02	4.79
4	3–4 IV 1881	100.00	48.60	51.40	61.04	33.40	5.56	..	36.47	58.91	4.63
5	5–6 IV 1891	100.00	48.43	51.57	61.25	33.19	5.56	..	35.14	60.09	4.77
6	31 III–1 IV 1901	100.00	48.38	51.62	60.16	34.32	5.53	..	32.54	62.77	4.69
7	2–3 IV 1911	100.00	48.38	51.62	58.66	35.84	5.50	0.01[1]	30.83	63.94	5.23
8	19–20 VI 1921	100.00	47.75	52.25	54.83	39.15	5.97	0.04	27.92	66.04	6.04
9	26–27 IV 1931	100.00	47.90	52.10	51.58	42.09	6.25	0.08	24.17	68.43	7.40

Note: [1] Unknown.

APPENDIX TABLE EW.1 Population structure at census dates, England and Wales 1851–1931

Census number	Census date	Census population			Marital status				Age group		
		Total	Male	Female	Single	Married	Widowed	Divorced	0–14	15–64	65+
		Absolute									
1	30–31 III 1851	19,998,894	9,262,975	10,735,919	11,967,540	6,852,795	1,178,559	..	6,883,194	12,145,660	970,040
2	7–8 IV 1861	20,066,224	9,776,259	10,289,965	12,032,157	6,917,395	1,116,672	..	7,150,024	11,984,393	931,807
3	2–3 IV 1871	22,712,266	11,058,934	11,653,332	13,603,001	7,831,890	1,277,375	..	8,202,041	13,435,482	1,074,743
4	3–4 IV 1881	25,974,439	12,639,902	13,334,537	15,725,739	8,814,860	1,433,840	..	9,468,591	15,317,204	1,188,644
5	5–6 IV 1891	29,002,525	14,052,901	14,949,624	17,625,028	9,768,197	1,609,300	..	10,172,235	17,457,688	1,372,602
6	31 III–1 IV 1901	32,527,843	15,728,613	16,799,230	19,402,188	11,328,918	1,796,737	..	10,545,739	20,464,351	1,517,753
7	2–3 IV 1911	36,070,492	17,445,608	18,624,884	20,963,807	13,126,070	1,980,615	..	11,050,867	23,141,299	1,878,326
8	19–20 VI 1921	37,886,699	18,075,239	19,811,460	20,540,890	15,065,058	2,264,069	16,682	10,500,455	24,988,001	2,398,243
9	26–27 IV 1931	39,952,377	19,133,010	20,819,367	20,324,878	17,093,411	2,501,373	32,715	9,520,198	27,468,970	2,963,209
		Per cent									
1	30–31 III 1851	100.00	46.32	53.68	59.84	34.27	5.89	..	34.42	60.73	4.85
2	7–8 IV 1861	100.00	48.72	51.28	59.96	34.47	5.56	..	35.63	59.72	4.64
3	2–3 IV 1871	100.00	48.69	51.31	59.89	34.48	5.62	..	36.11	59.16	4.73
4	3–4 IV 1881	100.00	48.66	51.34	60.54	33.94	5.52	..	36.45	58.97	4.58
5	5–6 IV 1891	100.00	48.45	51.55	60.77	33.68	5.55	..	35.07	60.19	4.73
6	31 III–1 IV 1901	100.00	48.35	51.65	59.65	34.83	5.52	..	32.42	62.91	4.67
7	2–3 IV 1911	100.00	48.37	51.63	58.12	36.39	5.49	..	30.64	64.16	5.21
8	19–20 VI 1921	100.00	47.71	52.29	54.22	39.76	5.98	0.04	27.72	65.95	6.33
9	26–27 IV 1931	100.00	47.89	52.11	50.87	42.78	6.26	0.08	23.83	68.75	7.42

APPENDIX TABLE SC.1 Population structure at census dates, Scotland 1851–1931

Census number	Census date	Census population			Marital status				Age group		
		Total	Male	Female	Single	Married	Widowed	Divorced	0–14	15–64	65+
		Absolute									
1	30–31 III 1851	2,888,742	1,375,479	1,513,263	1,882,566	832,645	173,531	..	1,028,810	1,722,167	137,765
2	7–8 IV 1861	3,062,294	1,449,848	1,612,446	1,970,413	908,769	183,112	..	1,103,171	1,809,896	149,227
3	2–3 IV 1871	3,360,018	1,603,143	1,756,875	2,163,742	995,246	201,030	..	1,232,491	1,953,524	174,003
4	3–4 IV 1881	3,735,573	1,799,475	1,936,098	2,409,634	1,108,402	217,537	..	1,365,606	2,184,000	185,967
5	5–6 IV 1891	4,025,647	1,942,717	2,082,930	2,604,064	1,193,393	228,190	..	1,432,225	2,390,326	203,096
6	31 III–1 IV 1901	4,472,103	2,173,755	2,298,348	2,856,200	1,367,757	248,146	..	1,495,102	2,760,544	216,457
7	2–3 IV 1911	4,760,904	2,308,839	2,452,065	2,988,125	1,506,582	264,109	..	1,536,637	2,966,843	257,424
8	19–20 VI 1921	4,882,497	2,347,642	2,534,855	2,909,882	1,677,846	291,375	2,418	1,439,712	3,150,878	291,907
9	26–27 IV 1931	4,842,980	2,325,523	2,517,457	2,778,335	1,762,673	297,137	3,717	1,304,874	3,184,872	353,234
		Per cent									
1	30–31 III 1851	100.00	47.62	52.38	65.17	28.82	6.01	..	35.61	59.62	4.77
2	7–8 IV 1861	100.00	47.35	52.65	64.34	29.68	5.98	..	36.02	59.10	4.87
3	2–3 IV 1871	100.00	47.71	52.29	64.40	29.62	5.98	..	36.68	58.14	5.18
4	3–4 IV 1881	100.00	48.17	51.83	64.51	29.67	5.82	..	36.56	58.46	4.98
5	5–6 IV 1891	100.00	48.26	51.74	64.69	29.64	5.67	..	35.58	59.38	5.05
6	31 III–1 IV 1901	100.00	48.61	51.39	63.87	30.58	5.55	..	33.43	61.73	4.84
7	2–3 IV 1911	100.00	48.50	51.50	62.76	31.64	5.55	..	32.28	62.32	5.41
8	19–20 VI 1921	100.00	48.08	51.92	59.60	34.36	5.97	0.05	29.49	64.53	5.98
9	26–27 IV 1931	100.00	48.02	51.98	57.37	36.40	6.14	0.08	26.94	65.76	7.29

United Kingdom

APPENDIX TABLE NI.1 Population structure at census dates, Northern Ireland 1926–1937

Census number	Census date	Census population			Marital status				Age group		
		Total	Male	Female	Single	Married	Widowed	Divorced	0–14	15–64	65+
		Absolute									
1	18–19 IV 1926	1,256,561	608,088	648,473	788,137	389,561	78,863	..	364,405	790,331	101,825
2	28 II–1 III 1937	1,279,745	623,154	656,591	776,325	424,119	79,301	..	346,905	817,212	115,628
		Per cent									
1	18–19 IV 1926	100.00	48.39	51.61	62.72	31.00	6.28	..	29.00	62.90	8.10
2	28 II–1 III 1937	100.00	48.69	51.31	60.66	33.14	6.20	..	27.11	63.86	9.04

APPENDIX TABLE UK.2 Census population by region, United Kingdom
1871–1931 (per cent)

County	1871	1881	1891	1901	1911	1921	1931
England	76.92	77.91	78.71	79.19	78.73	76.68	77.82
Wales	4.35	4.31	4.35	4.42	5.66[1]	5.78	5.40
Scotland	12.03	11.83	11.53	11.50	11.14	10.63	10.09
Northern Ireland	..	..	..	..	..	2.74[2]	2.67[3]
TOTAL	**100.00**	**100.00**	**100.00**	**100.00**	**100.00**	**100.00**	**100.00**
Great Britain	**93.30**	**94.05**	**94.58**	**95.11**	**95.53**	**93.08**	**93.31**

Notes: [1] Incl. Monmouthshire. Until 1901 Monmouthshire was counted to England,
since 1911 together with Wales. [2] 1926. [3] 1937.

APPENDIX TABLE UK.3 Population density by region, United
Kingdom 1871–1931 (inhabitants per sq. km.)

County	1871	1881	1891	1901	1911	1921	1931
England	163	187	209	234	255	270	287
Wales	63	71	79	89	117[1]	128	125
Scotland	44	48	52	58	62	63	63
Northern Ireland	..	..	..	..	..	93[2]	94[3]
TOTAL	**121**	**137**	**152**	**169**	**185**	**188**	**197**
Great Britain	**114**	**130**	**145**	**162**	**178**	**187**	**196**

Notes: [1] Incl. Monmouthshire. Until 1901 Monmouthshire was counted to England,
since 1911 together with Wales. [2] 1926. [3] 1937.

APPENDIX TABLE EL.2 Census population by region, England 1871–1931 (%)

County[1]	1871	1881	1891	1901	1911	1921	1931
Bedford	0.68	0.61	0.59	0.56	0.58	0.58	0.59
Berks	0.91	0.89	0.86	0.82	0.81	0.84	0.83
Buckingham	0.82	0.72	0.67	0.64	0.65	0.67	0.73
Cambridgeshire[2]	0.87	0.76	0.68	0.60	0.59	0.58	0.58
Isle of Ely	..	..	0.23	0.21	0.21	0.21	0.21
Chester/Cheshire	2.61	2.62	2.71	2.68	2.84	2.91	2.91
Cornwall	1.68	1.34	1.18	1.05	0.97	0.91	0.85
Cumberland	1.02	1.02	0.97	0.87	0.79	0.77	0.70
Derby	1.77	1.88	1.90	1.98	2.03	2.03[a]	2.03
Devon	2.80	2.45	2.30	2.15	2.08	2.02	1.96
Dorset	0.91	0.78	0.71	0.66	0.66	0.65	0.64
Durham	3.19	3.52	3.70	3.85	4.07	4.20	3.98
Essex	2.17	2.34	2.85	3.52	4.01	4.17	4.70
Gloucester	2.49	2.32	2.35	2.33	2.19	2.15	2.10
Hampshire / Hants[3]	2.53	2.41	2.51	2.60	2.83	2.85	2.95
Isle of Wight	..	..	0.29	0.27	0.26	0.27	..
Hereford	0.58	0.49	0.42	0.37	0.34	0.32	0.30
Hertford	0.90	0.82	0.82	0.84	0.92	0.95	1.07
Huntingdon (and Peterborough)	0.30	0.24	0.20	0.18	0.17	0.16	0.15
Kent	3.95	3.97	2.94	3.12	3.11	3.24	3.26
Lancaster	13.12	14.03	14.22	14.24	14.17	13.99	13.49
Leicester	1.25	1.30	1.36	1.42	1.42	1.40	1.45
Lincoln	2.03	1.91	1.72	1.62	1.68	1.71	1.67
Parts of Holland	..	..	0.28	0.25	0.25	0.24	0.25
Parts of Kesteven	..	..	0.39	0.34	0.33	0.31	0.29
Parts of Lindsey	..	..	1.06	1.03	1.10	1.16	1.13
(Greater) London	..	..	15.40	14.73	13.44	12.73	11.77
Middlesex	11.82	11.86	2.04	2.57	3.35	3.56	4.39
Monmouth	0.91	0.86	0.94	0.97	..	..	..
Norfolk	2.04	1.81	1.70	1.55	1.48	1.43	1.35
Northampton	1.14	1.11	1.09	1.09	1.04	0.99	0.97
Soke of Petersborough	..	..	0.13	0.13	0.13	0.13	0.14
Northumberland	1.80	1.76	1.84	1.96	2.07	2.12	2.03
Nottingham	1.49	1.59	1.62	1.67	1.79	1.82	1.91
Oxford	0.83	0.73	0.69	0.60	0.59	0.54	0.56
Rutland	0.10	0.09	0.08	0.06	0.06	0.05	0.05
Salop/Shropshire	1.15	1.01	0.86	0.78	0.73	0.69	0.65
Somerset	2.15	1.91	1.60	1.41	1.36	1.32	1.27
Stafford	3.99	3.99	3.96	4.02	4.01	3.83	3.83
Suffolk	1.62	1.45	1.32	1.21	1.17	1.14	1.07
East Suffolk	..	..	0.88	0.83	0.82	0.83	..
West Suffolk	..	..	0.44	0.38	0.35	0.31	0.28
Surrey	5.07	5.84	1.90	2.12	2.51	2.64	3.16
Sussex	1.94	1.99	2.00	1.95	1.97	2.07	2.06
East Sussex	..	..	1.48	1.46	1.45	1.51	1.46
West Sussex	..	..	0.51	0.49	0.52	0.56	0.60
Warwick	2.95	2.99	3.05	3.05	3.09	3.95	4.11
Westmorland	0.30	0.26	0.24	0.21	0.19	0.19	0.17
Wilts	1.20	1.05	0.96	0.88	0.85	0.83	0.81
Worcester	1.58	1.54	1.40	1.47	1.56	1.15	1.12
York East Riding	1.26	1.28	1.24	1.25	1.29	1.31	1.29
York North Riding	1.36	1.41	1.31	1.22	1.25	1.29	1.26
York West Riding	8.52	8.84	8.90	8.93	9.05	9.03[4]	9.20
York City	0.20	0.20	0.24	0.25	0.24	0.24	0.23
TOTAL	**100.00**	**100.00**	**100.00**	**100.00**	**100.00**	**100.00**	**100.00**

Notes: [1] 1 1871–81 'ancient' counties; 1891–1931 *Administrative Counties* (with associated *County Boroughs*). [2] Including the *Isle of Ely*. [3] Named Southampton until 1871. [4] On 1 April 1929 *York West Riding* gained an area of 10 sq. km. with 28 inhabitants from *Derby*.

APPENDIX TABLE EL.3 Population density by region, England 1871–1931
(inhabitants per sq. km.)

County[1]	1871	1881	1891	1901	1911	1921	1931
Bedford	122	125	133	140	159	168	180
Berks	107	117	126	135	145	16	166
Buckingham	93	91	96	102	113	122	140
Cambridgeshire[2]	88	88	84	83	88	91	97
Isle of Ely	..	..	66	66	73	77	81
Chester/Cheshire	196	242	281	312	360	385	412
Cornwall	102	95	92	92	93	91	91
Cumberland	54	64	68	68	68	69	67
Derby	143	173	196	231	259	272[a]	289
Devon	90	90	94	98	103	105	108
Dorset	77	75	76	80	88	90	95
Durham	272	331	388	452	522	563	565
Essex	109	144	197	273	341	371	444
Gloucester	164	180	200	220	226	232	241
Hampshire / Hants[3]	126	141	164	188	223	236	258
Isle of Wight	..	..	209	215	231	249	..
Hereford	58	56	53	52	52	52	51
Hertford	122	124	137	158	190	203	245
Huntingdon (and Peterborough)	69	64	58	57	59	58	59
Kent	202	243	205	243	265	289	309
Lancaster	571	706	803	906	986	1,019	1,037
Leicester	129	155	175	203	221	229	251
Lincoln	61	66	69	73	82	87	91
Parts of Holland	..	..	74	73	76	80	84
Parts of Kesteven	..	..	56	55	59	57	59
Parts of Lindsey	..	..	75	81	94	104	107
(Greater) London	..	..	13,875	14,974	14,924	14,802	14,512
Middlesex	3,483	3,978	929	1,316	1,870	2,081	2,723
Monmouth	131	141	184	211	..	..	..
Norfolk	80	81	88	90	94	95	95
Northampton	96	107	116	130	135	135	140
Soke of Petersborough	..	..	162	190	208	218	241
Northumberland	77	83	97	115	133	143	145
Nottingham	150	184	204	235	276	293	326
Oxford	93	92	87	96	102	10	108
Rutland	57	55	56	51	51	46	43
Salop/Shropshire	74	73	68	69	71	70	70
Somerset	109	110	104	104	109	111	113
Stafford	291	324	358	410	447	45	479
Suffolk	91	93	94	97	103	104	104
East Suffolk	..	..	107	113	123	129	..
West Suffolk	..	..	77	75	74	69	67
Surrey	562	734	280	350	453	498	631
Sussex	110	130	145	160	176	193	204
East Sussex	..	..	190	211	227	248	255
West Sussex	..	..	87	93	108	120	137
Warwick	278	322	358	401	443	57	607
Westmorland	33	32	33	31	31	32	32
Wilts	73	74	74	77	82	84	87
Worcester	177	199	198	234	271	22	232
York East Riding	87	104	113	127	143	152	159
York North Riding	53	63	65	68	76	83	85
York West Riding	265	304	341	384	424	443[4]	478
York City	4,000	6,250	4,467	5,200	5,467	5,600	5,667
TOTAL	**163**	**187**	**209**	**234**	**255**	**270**	**287**

Notes: See Appendix Table EL.2.

APPENDIX TABLE W.2 Census population by region, Wales 1871–1931 (per cent)

County	1871	1881	1891	1901	1911	1921	1931
Anglesey	4.19	3.75	3.29	2.96	2.11	1.96	1.89
Brecon/Brecknock	4.93	4.26	3.36	3.14	2.44	2.30	2.24
Cardigan	6.00	5.14	4.15	3.54	2.48	2.30	2.12
Carmarthen	9.62	9.18	8.62	7.84	6.61	6.59	6.90
Carnarvon	8.72	8.74	7.70	7.32	5.16	4.93	4.67
Denbigh	8.55	8.23	7.83	7.67	5.99	5.84	6.09
Flint	6.25	5.95	5.07	4.71	3.84	4.03	4.36
Glamorgan	32.57	37.55	45.23	49.97	46.30	47.14	47.28
Merioneth	3.87	3.82	3.23	2.85	1.90	1.69	1.66
Monmouth	..	..	..	..	16.36	16.98	16.78
Montgomery	5.59	4.85	3.82	3.20	2.19	1.92	1.85
Pembroke	7.57	6.76	5.79	5.11	3.72	3.46	3.36
Radnor	2.06	1.76	1.45	1.34	0.95	0.90	0.81
TOTAL	**100.00**	**100.00**	**100.00**	**100.00**	**100.00**[1]	**100.00**	**100.00**

Note: [1] Incl. *Monmouthshire*. Until 1901 *Monmouthshire* was counted to England, since 1911 together with Wales.

APPENDIX TABLE W.3 Population density by region, Wales 1871–1931
(inhabitants per sq. km.)

County	1871	1881	1891	1901	1911	1921	1931
Anglesey	65	65	70	71	71	73	69
Brecon/Brecknock	32	31	27	28	31	32	31
Cardigan	41	39	35	34	33	34	31
Carmarthen	48	52	55	57	67	73	75
Carnarvon	71	80	80	85	85	89	82
Denbigh	67	65	69	77	84	89	91
Flint	102	124	116	123	140	161	170
Glamorgan	179	244	328	410	529	591	579
Merioneth	30	33	28	29	27	26	25
Monmouth	..	..	..	..	282	321	310
Montgomery	35	33	28	27	26	25	23
Pembroke	57	58	55	55	57	58	55
Radnor	23	21	18	19	19	20	17
TOTAL	**63**	**71**	**79**	**89**	**117**[1]	**128**	**125**

Note: [1] Incl. *Monmouthshire*. Until 1901 *Monmouthshire* was counted to England, since 1911 together with Wales.

APPENDIX TABLE SC.2 Census population by region, Scotland 1871–1931 (%)

'County'	1871[1]	1881[1]	1891[1]	1901	1911	1921	1931
Aberdeen	7.29	7.17	7.05	6.80	6.55	6.17	6.19
Aberdeen City[a]	..	..	..	..	..	..	..
Angus (Forfar)	7.08	7.12	6.91	6.35	5.90	5.55	5.58
Dundee City	..	..	..	..	..	..	..
Argyll	2.26	2.03	1.84	1.65	1.49	1.58	1.30
Ayr	5.98	5.84	5.61	5.68	5.63	6.12	5.88
Banff	1.85	1.69	1.54	1.36	1.28	1.17	1.14
Berwick	1.07	0.94	0.79	0.69	0.63	0.57	0.56
Bute	0.51	0.48	0.45	0.42	0.38	0.70	0.39
Caithness	1.19	1.04	0.92	0.76	0.67	0.57	0.54
Clackmannan	0.71	0.70	0.82	0.72	0.65	0.68	0.66
Dumbarton	1.76	2.01	2.43	2.55	2.94	3.09	3.06
Dumfries	2.23	2.03	1.84	1.63	1.53	1.54	1.67
East Lothian (Haddington)	1.13	1.04	0.92	0.87	0.90	0.96	0.97
Fife	4.79	4.60	4.72	4.90	5.63	6.00	5.70
Inverness	2.62	2.41	2.24	2.01	1.83	1.68	1.69
Kincardine	1.01	0.91	0.87	0.92	0.86	0.86	0.83
Kinross	0.21	0.19	0.17	0.16	0.17	0.16	0.14
Kirkcudbright	1.25	1.12	0.99	0.87	0.80	0.76	0.62
Lanark	22.77	24.20	27.47	29.94	30.39	31.52	32.75
Glasgow City	..	..	..	..	..	..	..
Midlothian (Edinburgh)	9.76	10.41	10.78	10.93	10.67	10.36	10.86
Edinburgh City	..	..	..	..	..	..	..
Moray (Elgin)	1.28	1.18	1.07	1.01	0.90	0.86	0.85
Nairn	0.30	0.27	0.22	0.20	0.19	0.18	0.17
Orkney	0.92	0.86	0.75	0.65	0.55	0.49	0.45
Peebles	0.36	0.37	0.37	0.34	0.32	0.31	0.31
Perth	3.81	3.45	3.03	2.75	2.60	2.58	2.50
Renfrew	6.46	7.04	5.74	6.02	6.62	6.12	5.97
Ross and Cromary	2.41	2.11	1.96	1.70	1.62	1.45	1.30
Roxburgh	1.46	1.42	1.34	1.10	0.99	0.92	0.95
Selkirk	0.57	0.70	0.70	0.51	0.53	0.47	0.47
Stirling	2.92	3.00	2.93	3.18	3.38	3.32	3.43
Sutherland	0.71	0.62	0.55	0.47	0.42	0.37	0.33
West Lothian (Linlithgow)	1.22	1.18	1.32	1.48	1.68	1.72	1.67
Wigtown	1.16	1.04	0.89	0.74	0.67	0.63	0.60
Zetland (Shetland)	0.95	0.80	0.72	0.63	0.59	0.53	0.43
TOTAL	**100.00**	**100.00**	**100.00**	**100.00**	**100.00**	**100.00**	**100.00**

Note: [1] Same area like in 1901 supposed.

APPENDIX TABLE SC.3 Population density by region, Scotland 1871–1931
(inhabitants per sq. km.)

'County'	1871[1]	1881[1]	1891[1]	1901	1911	1921	1931
Aberdeen	48	52	56	60	61	59	59
Aberdeen City[a]	..	..	..	..	..	..	..
Angus (Forfar)	105	118	123	125	124	120	119
Dundee City	..	..	..	..	..	..	..
Argyll	9	9	9	9	9	10	8
Ayr	69	74	77	87	91	102	97
Banff	38	39	38	37	37	35	34
Berwick	30	30	27	26	25	24	23
Bute	30	32	32	34	32	60	34
Caithness	23	22	21	19	18	16	15
Clackmannan	170	184	234	227	220	234	227
Dumbarton	93	118	154	179	220	238	234
Dumfries	27	27	27	26	26	27	29
East Lothian (Haddington)	55	56	53	56	62	68	68
Fife	123	132	145	168	205	224	211
Inverness	8	8	8	8	8	8	8
Kincardine	34	34	35	42	41	42	40
Kinross	33	33	33	33	38	38	33
Kirkcudbright	18	18	17	17	16	16	13
Lanark	336	397	486	588	635	674	686
Glasgow City	..	..	..	..	..	..	..
Midlothian (Edinburgh)	346	410	458	516	536	534	555
Edinburgh City	..	..	..	..	..	..	..
Moray (Elgin)	35	36	35	36	35	34	33
Nairn	24	24	21	21	21	21	19
Orkney	32	33	31	30	27	25	23
Peebles	13	16	17	17	17	17	17
Perth	20	20	19	19	19	20	19
Renfrew	349	424	372	433	507	488	491
Ross and Cromary	10	10	10	10	10	9	8
Roxburgh	28	31	31	28	27	26	27
Selkirk	27	38	41	33	36	33	33
Stirling	84	96	101	121	138	139	142
Sutherland	5	4	4	4	4	3	3
West Lothian (Linlithgow)	132	141	170	212	257	270	260
Wigtown	31	31	29	26	25	25	23
Zetland (Shetland)	22	21	20	20	20	18	15
TOTAL	**44**	**48**	**52**	**58**	**62**	**63**	**63**

Note: [1] Same area like in 1901 supposed.

APPENDIX TABLE NI.2 Census population by region, Northern Ireland 1926–1937 (per cent)

County / C. Borough	1926	1937
Antrim	15.27	15.39
Armagh	8.75	8.52
Belfast C.B.	33.02	34.22
Down	16.63	16.48
Fermanagh	4.61	4.30
Londonderry	11.14[1]	7.42
Londonderry C.B.	..	3.75
Tyrone	10.58	10.00
TOTAL	**100.00**	**100.00**

Note: [1] County and County Borough.

APPENDIX TABLE NI.3 Population density by region, Northern Ireland 1926–1937 (inhabitants per sq. km.)

County / C. Borough	1926	1937
Antrim	68	69
Armagh	87	86
Belfast C.B.	6,917	7,065
Down	85	86
Fermanagh	34	33
Londonderry	67[1]	46
Londonderry C.B.	..	5,333
Tyrone	42	41
TOTAL	**93**	**94**

Note: [1] County and County Borough.

APPENDIX TABLE UK.4 Demographic developments, United Kingdom 1850–1945
(absolute figures and rates)

Year	Mid-year population	Natural population growth rate	Population growth rate	Net migration rate	Crude birth rate	Legitimate births per 10,000 married women age 15–44	Illegitimate births per 10,000 unmarried women age 15–44	Illeg. births per 100 leg. births
1850	..	..	..	..	..	..	..	..
1851		..	..	..	..	..	..	..
1852		..	..	..	..	..	..	..
1853		..	..	..	..	..		..
1854		..	..	..	..	..		..
1855		..	..	..	..	..		..
1856		..	..	..	..	..	..	..
1857		..	..	..	..	..		..
1858		..	..	..	..	..	..	..
1859		..	..	..	..	..	..	..
1860		..	..	..	..	..	..	..
1861		..	..	..	..	..	..	..
1862		..	..	..	..	..	..	..
1863		..	..	..	..	..	..	..
1864	29,680,437	11.0	..	..	33.3	2,868	172	6.9
1865	29,925,177	11.7	8.2	-3.6	33.6	2,898	170	6.7
1866	30,147,755	11.6	7.4	-4.2	33.6	2,906	166	6.5
1867	30,409,132	12.9	8.6	-4.3	33.8	2,927	163	6.3
1868	30,689,977	13.4	9.2	-4.3	34.2	2,962	165	6.3
1869	30,978,278	12.0	9.3	-2.7	33.3	2,896	159	6.2
1870	31,256,535	12.1	8.9	-3.2	33.8	2,949	157	6.0
1871	31,555,699	12.3	9.5	-2.8	33.7	2,941	157	6.0
1872	31,874,184	13.4	10.0	-3.5	34.3	2,999	154	5.8
1873	32,177,551	13.3	9.4	-3.8	34.0	2,979	148	5.6
1874	32,501,517	12.9	10.0	-3.0	34.5	3,030	143	5.3
1875	32,838,758	11.8	10.3	-1.5	33.9	2,985	137	5.2
1876	33,199,993	14.4	10.9	-3.5	34.8	3,071	138	5.1
1877	33,575,940	14.5	11.2	-3.3	34.4	3,038	137	5.1
1878	33,943,773	12.9	10.8	-2.0	34.0	3,003	135	5.1
1879	34,304,037	12.7	10.5	-2.2	33.3	2,943	134	5.2
1880	34,622,930	12.3	9.2	-3.1	32.8	2,899	133	5.2
1881	34,934,476	13.8	8.9	-4.9	32.5	2,875	133	5.3
1882	35,206,616	13.1	7.7	-5.3	32.3	2,864	131	5.3
1883	35,449,721	12.3	6.9	-5.5	32.0	2,840	127	5.2
1884	35,724,229	12.9	7.7	-5.2	32.3	2,879	126	5.1
1885	36,015,501	12.4	8.1	-4.4	31.6	2,809	126	5.3
1886	36,313,581	12.3	8.2	-4.1	31.5	2,816	123	5.2
1887	36,599,143	11.7	7.8	-3.9	30.7	2,744	120	5.2
1888	36,881,271	12.1	7.6	-4.4	30.2	2,703	114	5.1
1889	37,178,928	11.9	8.0	-3.9	30.0	2,698	112	5.0
1890	37,484,763	9.9	8.2	-1.7	29.3	2,636	104	4.8
1891	37,802,440	10.3	8.4	-1.9	30.4	2,745	105	4.7
1892	38,134,110	10.5	8.7	-1.8	29.6	2,689	104	4.6
1893	38,490,333	10.8	9.3	-1.5	29.8	2,729	111	4.7
1894	38,859,067	12.0	9.5	-2.5	28.8	2,654	112	4.7
1895	39,221,109	10.7	9.2	-1.5	29.4	2,730	117	4.6
1896	39,599,072	12.1	9.5	-2.6	29.1	2,713	121	4.6
1897	39,987,294	11.3	9.7	-1.6	28.9	2,717	124	4.5

continued

APPENDIX TABLE UK.4 Demographic developments, United Kingdom 1850–1945 (absolute figures and rates)

Crude death rate	Infant mortality rate	Stillbirth rate	Infant mortality and stillbirth rate	Crude marriage rate	Persons marrying per 10,000 unmarried persons age 15+	Persons marrying per 10,000 unmarried persons age 15–49	Crude divorce rate	Divorces per 100 marriages	Divorces per 10,000 married persons	Year
..	..	..	..	..	..	..	..	..	..	1850
..	..	..	..	..	..	..	..	..	..	1851
..	..	..	..	..	..	..	..	..	..	1852
..	..	..	..	..	..	..	..	..	..	1853
..	..	..	..	..	..	..	..	..	..	1854
..	..	..	..	..	..	..	..	..	..	1855
..	..	..	..	..	..	..	..	..	..	1856
..	..	..	..	..	..	..	..	..	..	1857
..	..	..	..	..	..	..	..	..	..	1858
..	..	..	..	..	..	..	..	..	..	1859
..	..	..	..	..	..	..	..	..	..	1860
..	..	..	..	..	..	..	..	..	..	1861
..	..	..	..	..	..	..	..	..	..	1862
..	..	..	..	..	..	..	..	..	..	1863
22.3	..	..	..	7.8	490	607	0.0	0.1	0.3	1864
21.9	..	..	..	8.0	508	629	0.0	0.1	0.4	1865
22.1	..	..	..	8.0	510	632	0.0	0.0	0.2	1866
20.8	..	..	..	9.3	591	734	0.0	0.0	0.2	1867
20.7	..	..	..	7.4	473	588	0.0	0.0	0.1	1868
21.3	..	..	..	7.3	469	584	0.0	0.1	0.3	1869
21.8	..	..	..	7.5	483	602	0.0	0.1	0.3	1870
21.5	..	..	..	7.7	498	622	0.0	0.1	0.3	1871
20.9	..	..	..	8.0	514	641	0.0	0.1	0.3	1872
20.7	..	..	..	8.0	517	644	0.0	0.1	0.5	1873
21.5	..	..	..	7.8	501	623	0.0	0.1	0.4	1874
22.1	..	..	..	7.7	492	612	0.0	0.1	0.4	1875
20.4	..	..	..	7.7	494	613	0.0	0.1	0.5	1876
19.9	..	..	..	7.3	469	581	0.0	0.1	0.5	1877
21.1	..	..	..	7.1	453	561	0.0	0.1	0.6	1878
20.5	..	..	..	6.7	428	529	0.0	0.2	0.7	1879
20.4	..	..	..	6.8	438	542	0.0	0.2	0.6	1880
18.7	..	..	..	7.0	449	533	0.0	0.2	0.7	1881
19.3	..	..	..	7.2	457	564	0.0	0.1	0.6	1882
19.6	..	..	..	7.2	455	561	0.0	0.2	0.7	1883
19.4	..	..	..	7.1	446	549	0.0	0.2	0.8	1884
19.1	..	..	..	6.8	425	523	0.0	0.2	0.8	1885
19.2	..	..	..	6.6	414	510	0.0	0.2	0.7	1886
19.0	..	..	..	6.7	418	513	0.0	0.2	0.9	1887
18.1	..	..	..	6.8	417	513	0.0	0.2	0.7	1888
18.1	..	..	..	7.0	433	531	0.0	0.2	0.7	1889
19.4	..	..	..	7.2	443	544	0.0	0.1	0.7	1890
20.0	..	..	..	7.3	444	545	0.0	0.2	0.8	1891
19.0	..	..	..	7.3	447	551	0.0	0.2	0.7	1892
19.0	..	..	..	6.9	432	533	0.0	0.2	0.8	1893
16.8	..	..	..	7.1	446	552	0.0	0.2	0.8	1894
18.7	..	..	..	7.1	453	562	0.0	0.2	0.8	1895
17.0	..	..	..	7.5	479	597	0.0	0.2	0.9	1896
17.6	..	..	..	7.6	491	613	0.0	0.2	1.0	1897

continued

APPENDIX TABLE UK.4 Demographic developments, United Kingdom 1850–1945 (continued)

Year	Mid-year population	Natural population growth rate	Population growth rate	Net migration rate	Crude birth rate	Legitimate births per 10,000 married women age 15–44	Illegitimate births per 10,000 unmarried women age 15–44	Illeg. births per 100 leg. births
1898	40,380,792	11.1	9.7	-1.3	28.7	2,712	128	4.5
1899	40,774,296	10.4	9.7	-0.7	28.5	2,715	128	4.3
1900	41,154,646	9.8	9.2	-0.5	28.2	2,699	132	4.3
1901	41,538,211	10.9	9.2	-1.7	28.0	2,699	135	4.2
1902	41,892,680	11.5	8.5	-3.1	28.0	2,640	131	4.2
1903	42,246,591	12.2	8.4	-3.8	28.0	2,577	127	4.2
1904	42,611,375	11.1	8.6	-2.6	27.7	2,491	125	4.4
1905	42,980,788	11.5	8.6	-2.9	27.1	2,377	120	4.4
1906	43,361,077	11.3	8.8	-2.5	27.0	2,321	117	4.4
1907	43,737,834	10.7	8.6	-2.1	26.3	2,212	109	4.3
1908	44,128,819	11.3	8.9	-2.4	26.6	2,195	109	4.4
1909	44,519,454	10.7	8.8	-2.0	25.7	2,080	106	4.5
1910	44,915,934	11.0	8.8	-2.1	25.0	1,982	101	4.5
1911	45,324,425	9.5	9.0	-0.5	24.4	1,893	99	4.7
1912	45,508,243	10.2	4.0	-6.2	24.1	1,838	96	4.7
1913	45,713,370	9.8	4.5	-5.4	24.1	1,807	94	4.7
1914	46,089,249	9.6	8.2	-1.4	23.9	..	..	4.7
1915	44,333,000	6.9	-39.6	-46.5	23.1	..	..	4.8
1916	43,710,000	7.7	-14.3	-22.0	22.6	..	..	5.1
1917	43,280,000	4.9	-9.9	-14.8	19.7	..	..	5.9
1918	43,116,000	1.8	-3.8	-5.6	19.7	..	..	6.5
1919	44,599,000	5.2	33.3	28.1	19.9	1,585	89	6.3
1920	46,472,000	12.8	40.3	27.5	25.7	2,064	96	5.1
1921	47,123,000	10.1	13.8	3.8	22.6	1,812	82	5.0
1922[1]	44,331,000	7.8	–	–	20.9	1,675	75	4.9
1923	44,563,000	8.4	5.2	-3.2	20.2	1,623	70	4.7
1924	44,915,000	6.7	7.8	1.1	19.3	1,545	67	4.7
1925	45,059,000	6.3	3.2	-3.1	18.7	1,498	64	4.6
1926	45,232,000	6.4	3.8	-2.6	18.2	1,457	66	4.8
1927	45,388,000	4.6	3.4	-1.2	17.1	1,362	65	5.0
1928	45,577,000	5.3	4.1	-1.1	17.2	1,365	66	5.1
1929	45,673,000	3.0	2.1	-0.9	16.7	1,321	66	5.2
1930	45,866,000	5.1	4.2	-0.9	16.8	1,327	66	5.2
1931	46,074,000	3.8	4.5	0.7	16.3	1,287	63	5.0
1932	46,335,000	3.5	5.6	2.1	15.8	1,245	61	5.0
1933	46,520,000	2.4	4.0	1.6	14.9	1,174	57	4.9
1934	46,666,000	3.3	3.1	-0.2	15.3	1,203	58	4.9
1935	46,869,000	3.2	4.3	1.1	15.2	1,198	56	4.7
1936	47,081,000	3.0	4.5	1.5	15.3	1,206	55	4.6
1937	47,288,700	2.7	4.4	1.7	15.3	1,205	56	4.6
1938	47,494,500	3.7	4.3	0.6	15.5	1,218	57	4.7
1939	47,761,400	3.0	5.6	2.5	15.2	1,196	56	4.6
1940	48,225,900	0.6	9.6	9.0	14.6	..	..	4.8
1941	48,216,000	1.4	-0.2	-1.6	14.4	..	..	5.8
1942	48,399,700	4.3	3.8	-0.5	16.0	..	..	6.1
1943	48,788,900	4.6	8.0	3.4	16.6	..	..	6.9
1944	49,016,400	6.1	4.6	-1.5	17.9	..	..	7.9
1945	49,182,300	4.7	3.4	-1.3	16.2	..	..	10.0

Note: [1] Territorial change.

APPENDIX TABLE UK.4 Demographic developments, United Kingdom 1850–1945 (continued)

Crude death rate	Infant mortality rate	Stillbirth rate	Infant mortality and stillbirth rate	Crude marriage rate	Persons marrying per 10,000 unmarried persons age 15+	Persons marrying per 10,000 unmarried persons age 15–49	Crude divorce rate	Divorces per 100 marriages	Divorces per 10,000 married persons	Year
17.7	..	..	..	7.7	503	630	0.0	0.2	1.0	1898
18.2	..	..	..	7.8	515	647	0.0	0.2	1.0	1899
18.4	..	..	..	7.6	505	637	0.0	0.2	1.0	1900
17.1	..	..	..	7.5	509	643	0.0	0.2	1.0	1901
16.5	..	..	..	7.6	505	638	0.0	0.3	1.2	1902
15.8	..	..	..	7.5	496	625	0.0	0.3	1.2	1903
16.6	..	..	..	7.3	482	606	0.0	0.2	1.0	1904
15.6	..	..	..	7.3	476	599	0.0	0.2	1.1	1905
15.7	..	..	..	7.5	484	607	0.0	0.2	1.0	1906
15.5	..	..	..	7.6	485	608	0.0	0.3	1.1	1907
15.3	..	..	..	7.2	458	573	0.0	0.3	1.1	1908
15.0	..	..	..	7.0	442	552	0.0	0.3	1.1	1909
14.0	..	..	..	7.1	445	555	0.0	0.3	1.0	1910
14.8	..	..	..	7.3	450	561	0.0	0.2	1.0	1911
13.9	..	..	..	7.5	458	569	0.0	0.2	1.0	1912
14.3	..	..	..	7.5	456	566	0.0	0.2	1.0	1913
14.4	..	..	..	7.7	..	..	0.0	0.3	..	1914
16.2	..	..	..	9.5	..	..	0.0	0.2	..	1915
14.9	..	..	..	7.6	..	..	0.0	0.4	..	1916
14.8	..	..	..	7.2	..	..	0.0	0.3	..	1917
17.8	..	..	..	8.0	..	..	0.0	0.5	..	1918
14.8	..	..	..	9.9	599	760	0.1	0.6	2.9	1919
12.9	..	..	..	9.8	590	753	0.1	0.9	4.3	1920
12.5	..	..	..	8.1	491	628	0.1	1.0	4.4	1921
13.1	..	..	..	7.7	464	596	0.1	0.9	3.4	1922[1]
11.8	..	..	..	7.5	452	582	0.1	0.9	3.4	1923
12.6	78.2	..	..	7.5	449	580	0.1	0.8	3.0	1924
12.4	77.3	..	..	7.5	446	578	0.1	0.9	3.4	1925
11.9	72.3	..	..	7.0	420	546	0.1	1.0	3.3	1926
12.5	72.4	..	..	7.7	456	596	0.1	1.1	4.0	1927
11.9	68.0	..	..	7.5	447	586	0.1	1.3	4.8	1928
13.6	76.3	..	..	7.7	459	603	0.1	1.1	4.2	1929
11.7	63.1	..	..	7.8	459	605	0.1	1.1	4.2	1930
12.5	68.5	..	..	7.6	450	596	0.1	1.2	4.5	1931
12.3	68.3	..	..	7.5	441	586	0.1	1.3	4.5	1932
12.5	66.4	..	..	7.7	455	606	0.1	1.3	4.6	1933
12.0	61.4	..	..	8.3	487	651	0.1	1.2	4.8	1934
12.0	60.4	..	..	8.5	495	664	0.1	1.2	4.5	1935
12.3	62.1	..	..	8.5	498	670	0.1	1.4	5.7	1936
12.6	61.1	..	..	8.6	500	675	0.1	1.4	5.4	1937
11.8	55.5	..	..	8.6	501	678	0.1	1.7	6.8	1938
12.2	53.5	..	..	10.4	601	817	0.2	1.9	8.7	1939
14.0	61.0	..	..	11.1	..	..	0.2	1.6	..	1940
13.0	63.3	..	..	9.3	..	..	0.1	1.6	..	1941
11.6	52.9	..	..	8.9	..	..	0.2	2.0	..	1942
12.0	51.9	..	..	7.1	..	..	0.2	3.3	..	1943
11.8	47.6	..	..	7.1	..	..	0.3	4.1	..	1944
11.5	48.8	..	..	9.3	..	..	0.4	3.9	..	1945

Note: [1] Territorial change.

APPENDIX TABLE EW.4 Demographic developments, England and Wales 1850–1945 (absolute figures and rates)

Year	Mid-year population[1]	Natural population growth rate	Population growth rate	Net migration rate	Crude birth rate	Legitimate births per 10,000 married women age 15–44	Illegitimate births per 10,000 unmarried women age 15–44	Illeg. births per 100 leg. births
1850	17,773,000	12.6	11.7	-0.9	33.4	..	..	7.3
1851	17,982,849	12.3	11.7	-0.6	34.2	2,854	188	7.3
1852	18,193,206	11.9	11.6	-0.4	34.3	2,854	188	7.3
1853	18,404,368	10.4	11.5	1.1	33.3	2,773	175	6.9
1854	18,616,310	10.6	11.4	0.8	34.1	2,837	177	6.9
1855	18,829,000	11.1	11.3	0.2	33.7	2,803	176	6.9
1856	19,042,412	14.0	11.2	-2.8	34.5	2,862	182	6.9
1857	19,256,516	12.6	11.1	-1.5	34.4	2,847	182	6.9
1858	19,471,291	10.6	11.0	0.5	33.7	2,775	182	7.1
1859	19,686,701	12.7	10.9	-1.7	35.0	2,887	186	6.9
1860	19,902,713	13.1	10.9	-2.3	34.4	2,830	180	6.8
1861	20,119,314	13.0	10.8	-2.2	34.6	2,846	181	6.8
1862	20,371,013	13.6	12.4	-1.2	35.0	2,877	184	6.8
1863	20,625,855	12.3	12.4	0.1	35.3	2,893	190	6.9
1864	20,883,889	11.7	12.4	0.6	35.4	2,910	190	6.8
1865	21,145,151	12.2	12.4	0.2	35.4	2,908	185	6.6
1866	21,409,684	11.8	12.4	0.5	35.2	2,900	179	6.4
1867	21,677,525	13.7	12.4	-1.4	35.4	2,924	176	6.2
1868	21,948,713	14.0	12.4	-1.6	35.8	2,954	180	6.3
1869	22,223,299	12.5	12.4	-0.2	34.8	2,871	172	6.1
1870	22,501,316	12.3	12.4	0.0	35.2	2,909	171	6.0
1871	22,788,594	12.4	12.6	0.2	35.0	2,890	170	5.9
1872	23,096,495	14.4	13.3	-1.1	35.8	2,962	167	5.7
1873	23,408,556	14.4	13.3	-1.1	35.4	2,945	159	5.5
1874	23,724,834	13.8	13.3	-0.5	36.0	3,002	156	5.3
1875	24,045,385	12.6	13.3	0.7	35.4	2,957	146	5.0
1876	24,370,267	15.5	13.3	-2.2	36.4	3,052	146	4.9
1877	24,699,539	15.7	13.3	-2.4	36.0	3,013	146	5.0
1878	25,033,259	14.1	13.3	-0.7	35.6	2,988	144	5.0
1879	25,371,489	14.0	13.3	-0.6	34.7	2,911	142	5.0
1880	25,714,288	13.7	13.3	-0.4	34.3	2,878	141	5.1
1881	26,046,142	15.0	12.7	-2.3	33.9	2,848	141	5.1
1882	26,334,942	14.1	11.0	-3.2	33.8	2,837	139	5.1
1883	26,626,959	13.8	11.0	-2.8	33.5	2,819	135	5.0
1884	26,922,192	14.0	11.0	-3.0	33.7	2,843	132	4.9
1885	27,220,706	13.6	11.0	-2.7	32.9	2,776	130	5.0
1886	27,522,532	13.3	11.0	-2.3	32.8	2,778	128	5.0
1887	27,827,706	12.8	11.0	-1.8	31.9	2,699	124	5.0
1888	28,136,258	13.1	11.0	-2.1	31.3	2,656	117	4.9
1889	28,448,239	12.9	11.0	-2.0	31.1	2,651	115	4.8
1890	28,763,673	10.7	11.0	0.3	30.2	2,581	107	4.6
1891	29,085,819	11.2	11.1	-0.1	31.4	2,692	106	4.4
1892	29,421,392	11.5	11.4	-0.1	30.5	2,604	101	4.4
1893	29,760,842	11.6	11.4	-0.2	30.7	2,609	103	4.4
1894	30,104,201	13.0	11.4	-1.6	29.6	2,498	100	4.5
1895	30,451,528	11.6	11.4	-0.2	30.3	2,549	99	4.4
1896	30,802,858	12.6	11.4	-1.2	29.7	2,490	97	4.4
1897	31,158,245	12.2	11.4	-0.8	29.6	2,467	95	4.3

continued

APPENDIX TABLE EW.4 Demographic developments, England and Wales 1850–1945 (absolute figures and rates)

Crude death rate	Infant mortality rate	Stillbirth rate	Infant mortality and stillbirth rate	Crude marriage rate	Persons marrying per 10,000 unmarried persons age 15+	Persons marrying per 10,000 unmarried persons age 15–49	Crude divorce rate	Divorces per 100 marriages	Divorces per 10,000 married persons	Year
20.8	145.6	..	..	8.6	..	..	..	..	..	1850
22.0	154.1	..	..	8.6	549	664	..	..	..	1851
22.4	158.3	..	..	8.7	561	678	..	..	..	1852
22.9	155.2	..	..	8.9	577	697	..	..	..	1853
23.5	156.5	..	..	8.6	556	672	..	..	..	1854
22.6	153.5	..	..	8.1	525	635	..	..	..	1855
20.5	143.6	..	..	8.4	546	660	..	..	..	1856
21.8	155.7	..	..	8.3	541	654	..	..	..	1857
23.1	158.4	..	..	8.0	527	637	0.0	0.0	0.1	1858
22.4	153.1	..	..	8.5	562	680	0.0	0.1	0.3	1859
21.2	147.6	..	..	8.5	566	685	0.0	0.1	0.3	1860
21.6	152.8	..	..	8.1	541	654	0.0	0.1	0.6	1861
21.4	142.2	..	..	8.1	536	650	0.0	0.1	0.4	1862
23.0	148.6	..	..	8.4	561	681	0.0	0.1	0.4	1863
23.7	152.6	..	..	8.6	577	702	0.0	0.1	0.5	1864
23.2	160.2	..	..	8.8	587	715	0.0	0.1	0.5	1865
23.4	162.2	..	..	8.8	588	718	0.0	0.1	0.3	1866
21.7	152.6	..	..	8.3	555	679	0.0	0.1	0.3	1867
21.9	155.1	..	..	8.1	543	664	0.0	0.0	0.1	1868
22.3	151.6	..	..	8.0	537	659	0.0	0.1	0.4	1869
22.9	159.7	..	..	8.1	545	670	0.0	0.1	0.4	1870
22.6	157.8	..	..	8.3	564	695	0.0	0.1	0.4	1871
21.3	149.6	..	..	8.7	589	725	0.0	0.1	0.3	1872
21.0	149.2	..	..	8.8	594	730	0.0	0.1	0.5	1873
22.2	150.7	..	..	8.5	576	707	0.0	0.1	0.5	1874
22.7	158.3	..	..	8.4	566	694	0.0	0.1	0.5	1875
20.9	146.3	..	..	8.3	560	687	0.0	0.1	0.5	1876
20.3	136.0	..	..	7.9	532	652	0.0	0.1	0.6	1877
21.6	152.1	..	..	7.6	513	628	0.0	0.2	0.7	1878
20.7	135.5	..	..	7.2	485	593	0.0	0.2	0.8	1879
20.6	152.8	..	..	7.5	504	617	0.0	0.1	0.6	1880
18.9	126.7	..	..	7.6	512	625	0.0	0.2	0.7	1881
19.6	140.6	..	..	7.8	521	637	0.0	0.1	0.6	1882
19.6	137.2	..	..	7.8	518	632	0.0	0.2	0.7	1883
19.7	147	..	..	7.6	504	615	0.0	0.2	0.8	1884
19.2	138	..	..	7.3	480	585	0.0	0.2	0.9	1885
19.5	149	..	..	7.1	468	570	0.0	0.2	0.7	1886
19.1	145	..	..	7.2	471	573	0.0	0.2	0.9	1887
18.2	136	..	..	7.2	471	573	0.0	0.2	0.7	1888
18.2	144	..	..	7.5	486	591	0.0	0.2	0.7	1889
19.5	151	..	..	7.8	499	606	0.0	0.1	0.6	1890
20.2	149	..	..	7.8	498	605	0.0	0.2	0.8	1891
19.0	148	..	..	7.7	492	597	0.0	0.1	0.7	1892
19.2	159	..	..	7.3	466	566	0.0	0.2	0.8	1893
16.6	137	..	..	7.5	475	576	0.0	0.2	0.7	1894
18.7	161	..	..	7.5	471	571	0.0	0.2	0.8	1895
17.1	148	..	..	7.9	493	598	0.0	0.2	0.9	1896
17.4	156	..	..	8.0	497	604	0.0	0.2	0.9	1897

continued

APPENDIX TABLE EW.4 Demographic developments, England and Wales 1850–1945 (continued)

Year	Mid-year population[1]	Natural population growth rate	Population growth rate	Net migration rate	Crude birth rate	Legitimate births per 10,000 married women age 15–44	Illegitimate births per 10,000 unmarried women age 15–44	Illeg. births per 100 leg. births
1898	31.517.725	11.8	11.4	-0.4	29.3	2,433	93	4.3
1899	31,881,365	10.9	11.4	0.5	29.1	2,413	89	4.2
1900	32,249,187	10.5	11.4	0.9	28.7	2,372	86	4.1
1901	32,612,022	11.6	11.1	-0.5	28.5	2,344	84	4.1
1902	32,950,909	12.3	10.3	-2.0	28.5	2,342	84	4.1
1903	33,293,321	13.0	10.3	-2.7	28.5	2,333	85	4.1
1904	33,639,287	11.8	10.3	-1.5	28.1	2,296	85	4.2
1905	33,988,844	12.0	10.3	-1.8	27.3	2,230	83	4.2
1906	34,342,040	11.8	10.3	-1.5	27.2	2,217	83	4.2
1907	34,698,905	11.3	10.3	-1.1	26.5	2,152	79	4.1
1908	35,059,484	12.0	10.3	-1.7	26.8	2,177	82	4.2
1909	35,423,805	11.2	10.3	-0.9	25.8	2,089	81	4.3
1910	35,791,902	11.6	10.3	-1.3	25.1	2,025	78	4.3
1911	36,189,685	9.8	11.0	1.2	24.3	1,960	80	4.5
1912	36,382,456	10.6	5.3	-5.3	24.0	1,929	79	4.5
1913	36,606,226	10.3	6.1	-4.2	24.1	1,934	80	4.5
1914	36,960,684	9.8	9.6	-0.2	23.8	..	..	4.4
1915	35,358,896[2]	7.1	..	..	23.0	..	..	4.7
1916	34,642,000[2]	8.0	..	..	22.7	..	..	5.0
1917	34,197,000[2]	5.0	..	..	19.5	..	..	5.9
1918	34,024,000[2]	1.5	..	..	19.5	..	..	6.7
1919	35,427,000[2]	5.3	..	..	19.5	1,519	91	6.4
1920	37,247,000[2]	12.0	..	..	24.5	1,924	93	5.2
1921	37,932,000	10.3	..	..	22.4	1,761	79	4.8
1922	38,205,000	7.7	7.1	-0.5	20.4	1,607	70	4.6
1923	38,449,000	8.1	6.3	-1.8	19.7	1,553	64	4.3
1924	38,795,000	6.6	8.9	2.3	18.8	1,481	62	4.3
1925	38,935,000	6.1	3.6	-2.5	18.3	1,435	59	4.2
1926	39,114,000	6.2	4.6	-1.6	17.8	1,391	60	4.4
1927	39,286,000	4.3	4.4	0.1	16.7	1,300	59	4.6
1928	39,483,000	5.1	5.0	-0.1	16.7	1,303	60	4.7
1929	39,600,000	2.8	3.0	0.1	16.3	1,264	60	4.8
1930	39,801,000	4.9	5.1	0.2	16.3	1,266	60	4.8
1931	39,988,000	3.5	4.7	1.2	15.8	1,227	57	4.7
1932	40,201,000	3.2	5.3	2.1	15.3	1,185	55	4.6
1933	40,350,000	2.1	3.7	1.6	14.4	1,115	52	4.6
1934	40,467,000	3.0	2.9	-0.1	14.8	1,143	53	4.5
1935	40,645,000	3.0	4.4	1.4	14.7	1,141	51	4.4
1936	40,839,000	2.7	4.8	2.1	14.8	1,147	51	4.3
1937	41,031,000	2.5	4.7	2.2	14.9	1,149	52	4.3
1938	41,215,000	3.5	4.5	1.0	15.1	1,162	54	4.4
1939[3]	41,460,000	2.8	5.9	3.1	14.8	1,142	52	4.3
1940[3]	41,862,000[4]	0.2	9.6	..	14.1	..	..	4.5
1941[3]	41,748,000[4]	1.1	-2.7	..	13.9	..	..	5.7
1942[3]	41,897,000[4]	4.1	3.6	..	15.6	..	..	5.9
1943[3]	42,259,000[4]	4.3	8.6	..	16.2	..	..	6.8
1944[3]	42,449,000[4]	6.1	4.5	..	17.7	..	..	7.9
1945[3]	42,636,000[4]	4.5	4.4	..	15.9	..	..	10.3

Notes: [1] Estimated midyear home population for the whole time series. [2] Figures are for civilians only. [3] From 3 September 1939 to 31 December 1949, for males, and from 1 June 1941 to 31 December 1949, for females, mortality rates are based upon civilian deaths only; but, as in other years, the number of deaths include those of non-civilians registered in the United Kingdom. [4] Total population, i.e. including members of H.M. Forces overseas.

APPENDIX TABLE EW.4 Demographic developments, England and Wales 1850–1945 (continued)

Crude death rate	Infant mortality rate	Stillbirth rate	Infant mortality and stillbirth rate	Crude marriage rate	Persons marrying per 10,000 unmarried persons age 15+	Persons marrying per 10,000 unmarried persons age 15-49	Crude divorce rate	Divorces per 100 marriages	Divorces per 10,000 married persons	Year
17.5	160	..	..	8.1	502	609	0.0	0.2	0.9	1898
18.2	163	..	..	8.2	507	616	0.0	0.2	0.8	1899
18.2	154	..	..	8.0	490	595	0.0	0.2	0.9	1900
16.9	151	..	..	8.0	486	590	0.0	0.2	0.8	1901
16.3	133	..	..	7.9	485	590	0.0	0.2	1.0	1902
15.5	132	..	..	7.8	478	583	0.0	0.2	1.0	1903
16.3	145.3	..	..	7.7	467	570	0.0	0.2	0.9	1904
15.3	128.2	..	..	7.7	467	571	0.0	0.2	1.0	1905
15.5	132.5	..	..	7.9	479	586	0.0	0.2	0.9	1906
15.1	117.6	..	..	8.0	485	594	0.0	0.2	1.0	1907
14.8	120.4	..	..	7.6	459	564	0.0	0.2	1.0	1908
14.6	108.7	..	..	7.4	447	549	0.0	0.3	1.1	1909
13.5	105.4	..	..	7.5	454	559	0.0	0.2	0.9	1910
14.6	130.1	..	..	7.6	461	568	0.0	0.2	0.9	1911
13.4	94.8	..	..	7.8	473	584	0.0	0.2	0.9	1912
13.8	108.4	..	..	7.8	474	586	0.0	0.2	0.9	1913
14.0	104.6	..	..	8.0	..	..	0.0	0.3	..	1914
15.9	109.7	..	..	10.2	..	..	0.0	0.4	..	1915
14.7	91.2	..	..	8.1	..	..	0.0	0.4	..	1916
14.6	96.5	..	..	7.6	..	..	0.0	0.3	..	1917
18.0	97.2	..	..	8.4	..	..	0.0	0.4	..	1918
14.2	89.1	..	..	10.4	645	817	0.0	0.4	2.4	1919
12.5	83.9	..	..	10.2	629	800	0.1	0.8	4.2	1920
12.1	82.8	..	..	8.5	520	664	0.1	1.1	4.7	1921
12.7	77.1	..	..	7.8	481	616	0.1	0.9	3.4	1922
11.6	69.4	..	..	7.6	465	598	0.1	0.9	3.4	1923
12.2	75.1	..	..	7.6	466	602	0.1	0.8	2.9	1924
12.1	75.0	..	..	7.6	462	599	0.1	0.9	3.3	1925
11.6	70.2	..	..	7.2	434	564	0.1	0.9	3.2	1926
12.3	69.7	39.8	109.5	7.8	475	620	0.1	1.0	3.9	1927
11.7	65.1	41.8	106.8	7.7	464	607	0.1	1.3	4.9	1928
13.4	74.4	41.7	116.1	7.9	476	626	0.1	1.1	4.1	1929
11.4	60.0	42.5	102.5	7.9	476	627	0.1	1.1	4.2	1930
12.3	66.4	42.6	109.0	7.8	467	618	0.1	1.2	4.4	1931
12.0	65.0	43.1	108.2	7.6	457	606	0.1	1.3	4.5	1932
12.3	63.7	43.2	106.9	7.9	470	626	0.1	1.3	4.6	1933
11.8	58.6	42.2	100.8	8.5	503	672	0.1	1.3	4.9	1934
11.7	56.9	40.8	97.7	8.6	510	684	0.1	1.2	4.6	1935
12.1	58.5	41.4	99.9	8.7	514	691	0.1	1.5	5.7	1936
12.4	57.6	40.6	98.2	8.8	517	697	0.1	1.4	5.4	1937
11.6	52.7	39.8	92.5	8.8	517	700	0.2	1.7	6.8	1938
12.1	50.8	39.6	90.3	10.6	623	847	0.2	1.9	8.9	1939[3]
13.9	57.4	38.6	96.0	11.2	..	..	0.2	1.6	..	1940[3]
12.8	59.7	36.0	95.7	9.3	..	..	0.2	1.6	..	1941[3]
11.5	49.5	34.4	83.9	8.8	..	..	0.2	2.1	..	1942[3]
11.9	48.9	31.1	79.9	7.0	..	..	0.2	3.4	..	1943[3]
11.6	44.5	28.4	72.9	7.1	..	..	0.3	4.1	..	1944[3]
11.4	47.0	28.4	75.4	9.3	..	..	0.4	3.9	..	1945[3]

Notes: [1] Estimated midyear home population for the whole time series. [2] Figures are for civilians only. [3] From 3 September 1939 to 31 December 1949, for males, and from 1 June 1941 to 31 December 1949, for females, mortality rates are based upon civilian deaths only; but, as in other years, the number of deaths include those of non-civilians registered in the United Kingdom. [4] Total population, i.e. including members of H.M. Forces overseas.

APPENDIX TABLE SC.4 Demographic developments, Scotland 1850–1945 (absolute figures and rates)

Year	Mid-year population[1]	Natural population growth rate	Population growth rate	Net migration rate	Crude birth rate	Legitimate births per 10,000 married women age 15–44	Illegitimate births per 10,000 unmarried women age 15–44	Illeg. births per 100 leg. births
1850	2,873,000	..	8.4	..	..	..	..	..
1851	2,896,000	..	7.9	..	..	..	..	..
1852	2,918,000	..	7.5	..	..	..	..	..
1853	2,939,000	..	7.1	..	..	..	..	..
1854	2,959,000	..	6.8	..	..	..	..	..
1855	2,978,000	10.5	6.4	-4.1	31.3	2,911	170	8.5
1856	2,996,000	14.5	6.0	-8.4	34.0	3,129	202	9.3
1857	3,012,000	13.8	5.3	-8.5	34.3	3,146	213	9.8
1858	3,028,000	13.3	5.3	-8.1	34.3	3,143	215	9.8
1859	3,042,000	14.7	4.6	-10.1	35.0	3,195	225	10.0
1860	3,055,000	12.2	4.3	-8.0	34.6	3,149	224	10.1
1861	3,069,000	14.5	4.6	-10.0	34.9	3,170	229	10.2
1862	3,098,000	12.9	9.4	-3.5	34.6	3,131	239	10.8
1863	3,127,000	12.1	9.3	-2.8	35.0	3,163	250	11.1
1864	3,156,000	12.0	9.2	-2.8	35.6	3,223	255	11.1
1865	3,185,000	13.2	9.1	-4.1	35.5	3,219	257	11.1
1866	3,215,000	13.2	9.3	-3.8	35.4	3,201	265	11.5
1867	3,245,000	13.8	9.2	-4.6	35.1	3,203	250	10.8
1868	3,275,000	14.0	9.2	-4.9	35.3	3,217	254	10.8
1869	3,306,000	11.3	9.4	-2.0	34.3	3,132	248	10.9
1870	3,337,000	12.3	9.3	-3.1	34.6	3,173	245	10.5
1871	3,369,000	12.3	9.5	-2.8	34.5	3,167	243	10.5
1872	3,405,000	12.8	10.6	-2.2	34.9	3,214	241	10.2
1873	3,441,000	12.4	10.5	-2.0	34.8	3,207	237	10.0
1874	3,478,000	12.4	10.6	-1.7	35.6	3,316	216	8.8
1875	3,515,000	11.9	10.5	-1.4	35.2	3,251	231	9.6
1876	3,552,000	14.8	10.4	-4.3	35.6	3,295	233	9.5
1877	3,590,000	14.7	10.6	-4.1	35.3	3,282	220	9.0
1878	3,628,000	13.8	10.5	-3.3	35.0	3,239	223	9.2
1879	3,667,000	14.3	10.6	-3.6	34.3	3,174	221	9.3
1880	3,706,000	13.3	10.5	-2.8	33.6	3,110	217	9.3
1881	3,743,000	14.4	9.9	-4.5	33.7	3,125	213	9.1
1882	3,771,000	14.1	7.4	-6.7	33.5	3,109	212	9.2
1883	3,799,000	12.5	7.4	-5.2	32.8	3,058	202	8.9
1884	3,827,000	14.1	7.3	-6.8	33.8	3,162	206	8.8
1885	3,856,000	13.4	7.5	-5.8	32.7	3,060	208	9.3
1886	3,885,000	14.0	7.5	-6.5	32.9	3,099	201	8.9
1887	3,914,000	12.7	7.4	-5.3	31.8	2,993	197	9.1
1888	3,944,000	13.2	7.6	-5.6	31.3	2,962	188	8.8
1889	3,973,000	12.5	7.3	-5.2	30.9	2,941	182	8.7
1890	4,003,000	10.6	7.5	-3.1	30.4	2,907	169	8.2
1891	4,036,000	10.5	8.2	-2.3	31.2	2,995	176	8.3
1892	4,079,000	12.1	10.5	-1.6	30.6	2,936	165	7.9
1893	4,122,000	11.5	10.4	-1.1	30.8	2,932	168	8.1
1894	4,166,000	12.8	10.6	-2.2	29.9	2,830	159	7.9
1895	4,210,000	10.6	10.5	-0.1	30.0	2,832	158	7.8
1896	4,254,000	13.8	10.3	-3.4	30.4	2,847	160	7.8
1897	4,299,000	11.6	10.5	-1.1	30.0	2,804	152	7.6

continued

APPENDIX TABLE SC.4 Demographic developments, Scotland 1850–1945 (absolute figures and rates)

Crude death rate	Infant mortality rate	Stillbirth rate	Infant mortality and stillbirth rate	Crude marriage rate	Persons marrying per 10,000 unmarried persons age 15+	Persons marrying per 10,000 unmarried persons age 15–49	Crude divorce rate	Divorces per 100 marriages	Divorces per 10,000 married persons	Year
..	..	..	..	..	..	..	..	..	..	1850
..	..	..	..	..	..	..	..	..	..	1851
..	..	..	..	..	..	..	..	..	..	1852
..	..	..	..	..	..	..	..	..	..	1853
..	..	..	..	..	..	..	..	..	..	1854
20.8	125	..	..	6.6	377	468	0.0	0.1	0.3	1855
19.5	118	..	..	6.9	396	492	0.0	0.1	0.4	1856
20.6	118	..	..	7.1	408	509	0.0	0.1	0.4	1857
21.0	121	..	..	6.5	375	468	0.0	0.1	0.3	1858
20.3	108	..	..	7.0	403	504	0.0	0.1	0.5	1859
22.3	127	..	..	6.9	403	505	0.0	0.1	0.5	1860
20.3	111	..	..	6.8	397	499	0.0	0.1	0.6	1861
21.7	117	..	..	6.6	388	488	0.0	0.1	0.6	1862
22.9	120	..	..	7.1	415	522	0.0	0.0	0.2	1863
23.6	126	..	..	7.2	422	530	0.0	0.0	0.0	1864
22.3	125	..	..	7.4	435	547	0.0	0.0	0.1	1865
22.2	122	..	..	7.4	434	545	0.0	0.0	0.1	1866
21.3	119	..	..	7.0	410	516	0.0	0.0	0.1	1867
21.2	118	..	..	6.7	395	496	0.0	0.1	0.3	1868
23.0	129	..	..	6.7	395	497	0.0	0.0	0.1	1869
22.2	123	..	..	7.2	424	533	0.0	0.1	0.3	1870
22.2	130	..	..	7.1	423	532	0.0	0.0	0.2	1871
22.1	124	..	..	7.5	446	560	0.0	0.0	0.2	1872
22.3	125	..	..	7.8	460	578	0.0	0.1	0.5	1873
23.2	125	..	..	7.6	450	565	0.0	0.1	0.7	1874
23.2	132	..	..	7.4	439	550	0.0	0.1	0.6	1875
20.9	121	..	..	7.5	444	556	0.0	0.2	0.8	1876
20.6	115	..	..	7.2	426	533	0.0	0.1	0.5	1877
21.2	123	..	..	6.7	399	498	0.0	0.3	1.2	1878
20.0	108	..	..	6.4	380	474	0.0	0.2	1.0	1879
20.3	125	..	..	6.6	392	488	0.0	0.3	1.5	1880
19.3	113	..	..	6.9	411	512	0.0	0.3	1.3	1881
19.4	118	..	..	7.1	417	518	0.0	0.3	1.2	1882
20.2	119	..	..	7.1	417	519	0.0	0.2	1.2	1883
19.6	118	..	..	6.8	400	497	0.0	0.3	1.5	1884
19.3	121	..	..	6.6	384	477	0.0	0.3	1.3	1885
18.9	116	..	..	6.3	368	457	0.0	0.4	1.7	1886
19.0	122	..	..	6.4	370	459	0.0	0.3	1.4	1887
18.1	113	..	..	6.4	372	461	0.0	0.4	1.8	1888
18.4	121	..	..	6.6	383	474	0.0	0.4	1.7	1889
19.7	131	..	..	6.9	396	490	0.0	0.3	1.5	1890
20.7	128	..	..	6.9	399	493	0.0	0.4	1.8	1891
18.5	117	..	..	7.0	403	498	0.0	0.4	1.9	1892
19.3	136	..	..	6.6	375	463	0.0	0.4	1.8	1893
17.1	117	..	..	6.6	377	465	0.0	0.4	1.9	1894
19.5	133	..	..	6.7	383	471	0.0	0.4	1.9	1895
16.6	115	..	..	7.1	403	495	0.0	0.4	2.1	1896
18.4	138	..	..	7.2	408	501	0.0	0.5	2.2	1897

continued

APPENDIX TABLE SC.4 Demographic developments, Scotland 1850–1945
(continued)

Year	Mid-year population[1]	Natural population growth rate	Population growth rate	Net migration rate	Crude birth rate	Legitimate births per 10,000 married women age 15–44	Illegitimate births per 10,000 unmarried women age 15–44	Illeg. births per 100 leg. births
1898	4.345.000	12.1	10.6	-1.5	30.1	2.808	147	7.3
1899	4,391,000	11.6	10.5	-1.2	29.8	2,769	139	7.0
1900	4,437,000	11.1	10.4	-0.7	29.6	2,740	137	6.9
1901	4,479,000	11.6	9.4	-2.3	29.5	2,718	135	6.9
1902	4,507,000	12.0	6.2	-5.8	29.4	2,705	131	6.7
1903	4,536,000	12.7	6.4	-6.3	29.4	2,711	131	6.6
1904	4,564,000	12.0	6.1	-5.8	29.1	2,658	141	7.3
1905	4,593,000	12.4	6.3	-6.1	28.6	2,611	142	7.4
1906	4,621,000	12.2	6.1	-6.1	28.6	2,603	145	7.6
1907	4,650,000	11.1	6.2	-4.8	27.7	2,528	136	7.3
1908	4,680,000	11.4	6.4	-5.0	28.1	2,557	140	7.4
1909	4,709,000	11.5	6.2	-5.3	27.3	2,476	144	7.9
1910	4,739,000	11.0	6.3	-4.6	26.2	2,370	139	7.9
1911	4,751,000	10.6	2.5	-8.0	25.7	2,314	140	8.2
1912	4,741,000	10.6	-2.1	-12.7	25.9	2,340	138	7.9
1913	4,728,000	10.0	-2.7	-12.8	25.5	2,307	131	7.6
1914	4,747,000	10.6	4.0	-6.6	26.1	..	..	7.6
1915	4,771,000	6.8	5.0	-1.8	23.9	..	..	7.4
1916	4,795,000	8.2	5.0	-3.2	22.9	..	..	7.6
1917	4,810,000	5.8	3.1	-2.7	20.2	..	..	8.1
1918	4,812,000	4.2	0.4	-3.8	20.5	..	..	8.7
1919	4,820,000	6.5	1.7	-4.8	22.1	1,956	111	7.6
1920	4,864,000	14.1	9.0	-5.0	28.1	2,478	151	8.1
1921	4,882,000	11.7	3.7	-8.0	25.2	2,236	130	7.7
1922	4,898,000	8.6	3.3	-5.3	23.5	2,088	117	7.4
1923	4,888,000	9.9	-2.0	-12.0	22.9	2,038	112	7.2
1924	4,862,000	7.5	-5.3	-12.9	22.0	1,957	107	7.1
1925	4,867,000	7.9	1.0	-6.9	21.4	1,906	102	7.0
1926	4,864,000	7.9	-0.6	-8.6	21.1	1,870	106	7.3
1927	4,853,000	6.4	-2.3	-8.6	19.9	1,762	106	7.8
1928	4,848,000	6.5	-1.0	-7.5	20.0	1,764	108	7.9
1929	4,832,000	4.6	-3.3	-7.9	19.2	1,689	111	8.4
1930	4,828,000	6.3	-0.8	-7.1	19.6	1,728	106	7.9
1931	4,843,000	5.8	3.1	-2.7	19.0	1,683	102	7.7
1932	4,883,000	5.1	8.2	3.1	18.6	1,648	100	7.7
1933	4,912,000	4.4	5.9	1.5	17.6	1,563	91	7.3
1934	4,934,000	5.1	4.5	-0.6	18.0	1,595	94	7.4
1935	4,953,000	4.6	3.8	-0.7	17.7	1,579	87	6.9
1936	4,966,000	4.5	2.6	-1.8	17.9	1,594	87	6.9
1937	4,977,000	3.8	2.2	-1.6	17.6	1,575	83	6.6
1938	4,993,000	5.1	3.2	-1.9	17.7	1,585	83	6.5
1939[2]	5,007,000	4.5	2.8	..	17.4	1,553	80	6.4
1940[2]	5,065,000[3]	2.7	..	..	17.1	..	..	6.3
1941[2]	5,160,000[3]	3.3	18.4	..	17.4	..	..	7.0
1942[2]	5,174,000[3]	5.0	2.7	..	17.5	..	..	7.7
1943[2]	5,189,000[3]	5.4	2.9	..	18.3	..	..	8.2
1944[2]	5,210,000[3]	6.0	4.0	..	18.4	..	..	8.6
1945[2]	5,187,000[3]	4.7	-4.4	..	16.8	..	..	9.4

Notes: [1] Estimated midyear home population for the whole time series. [2] From 3 September 1939 to 31 December 1949, for males, and from 1 June 1941 to 31 December 1949, for females, mortality rates are based upon civilian deaths only; but, as in other years, the number of deaths include those of non-civilians registered in the United Kingdom. [3] Total population, i.e. including members of H.M. Forces overseas.

APPENDIX TABLE SC.4 Demographic developments, Scotland 1850–1945
(continued)

Crude death rate	Infant mortality rate	Stillbirth rate	Infant mortality and stillbirth rate	Crude marriage rate	Persons marrying per 10,000 unmarried persons age 15+	Persons marrying per 10,000 unmarried persons age 15–49	Crude divorce rate	Divorces per 100 marriages	Divorces per 10,000 married persons	Year
18.0	134	..	..	7.4	415	509	0.0	0.4	2.1	1898
18.1	131	..	..	7.5	421	516	0.0	0.5	2.6	1899
18.5	128	..	..	7.3	407	499	0.0	0.4	2.1	1900
17.9	129	..	..	7.0	390	477	0.0	0.5	2.3	1901
17.3	113	..	..	7.1	393	482	0.0	0.6	2.9	1902
16.8	118	..	..	7.1	397	487	0.0	0.6	2.8	1903
17.1	123	..	..	7.1	393	483	0.0	0.6	2.6	1904
16.2	116	..	..	6.8	378	466	0.0	0.5	2.3	1905
16.4	115	..	..	7.2	398	490	0.0	0.5	2.4	1906
16.6	110	..	..	7.2	397	491	0.0	0.6	2.8	1907
16.6	121	..	..	6.8	375	463	0.0	0.6	2.6	1908
15.8	108	..	..	6.4	355	439	0.0	0.6	2.6	1909
15.2	108	..	..	6.5	362	448	0.0	0.7	3.0	1910
15.1	112	..	..	6.7	371	461	0.0	0.7	3.1	1911
15.3	105	..	..	6.9	380	472	0.1	0.8	3.3	1912
15.5	110	..	..	7.1	396	493	0.1	0.7	3.3	1913
15.5	111	..	..	7.4	..	..	0.1	1.0	..	1914
17.1	126	..	..	7.6	..	..	0.1	0.7	..	1915
14.7	97	..	..	6.5	..	..	0.1	0.9	..	1916
14.4	107	..	..	6.3	..	..	0.1	1.0	..	1917
16.3	100	..	..	7.2	..	..	0.1	1.4	..	1918
15.6	102	..	..	9.1	508	643	0.2	1.9	10.1	1919
14.0	92	..	..	9.6	533	678	0.2	1.7	9.3	1920
13.6	90	..	..	8.0	444	567	0.1	1.3	6.0	1921
14.9	101	..	..	7.0	388	497	0.1	1.1	4.5	1922
13.0	80	..	..	7.2	397	511	0.1	1.0	4.3	1923
14.5	98	..	..	6.6	366	473	0.1	1.4	5.2	1924
13.5	91	..	..	6.7	367	476	0.1	1.4	5.3	1925
13.1	83	..	..	6.4	352	458	0.1	1.4	4.9	1926
13.6	88.7	..	..	6.7	368	481	0.1	1.5	5.5	1927
13.5	85.7	..	..	6.8	372	487	0.1	1.5	5.8	1928
14.7	86.8	..	..	6.8	374	492	0.1	1.6	6.0	1929
13.3	83.1	..	..	6.9	377	497	0.1	1.4	5.4	1930
13.3	81.8	..	..	6.8	368	488	0.1	1.7	6.5	1931
13.5	86.2	..	..	6.8	370	493	0.1	1.5	5.5	1932
13.2	81.1	..	..	7.0	379	506	0.1	1.5	5.6	1933
12.9	77.7	..	..	7.5	406	545	0.1	1.3	5.1	1934
13.2	76.8	..	..	7.7	416	560	0.1	1.3	5.4	1935
13.5	82.3	..	..	7.6	414	558	0.1	1.7	6.9	1936
13.9	80.3	..	..	7.7	417	566	0.1	1.7	6.9	1937
12.6	69.6	..	..	7.8	419	570	0.2	2.0	8.3	1938
12.9	68.5	44.1	112.6	9.2	498	680	0.2	1.9	9.3	1939[2]
14.4	78.3	44.0	122.3	..	..	..	0.2	1.5	..	1940[2]
14.1	82.8	41.2	124.0	..	..	..	0.1	1.6	..	1941[2]
12.5	69.3	39.7	109.0	..	..	..	0.2	2.1	..	1942[2]
12.9	65.2	36.9	102.1	..	..	..	0.3	3.4	..	1943[2]
12.5	65.0	33.6	98.6	..	..	..	0.3	4.7	..	1944[2]
12.1	56.3	33.9	90.2	..	..	..	0.4	4.6	..	1945[2]

Notes: [1] Estimated midyear home population for the whole time series. [2] From 3 September 1939 to 31 December 1949, for males, and from 1 June 1941 to 31 December 1949, for females, mortality rates are based upon civilian deaths only; but, as in other years, the number of deaths include those of non-civilians registered in the United Kingdom. [3] Total population, i.e. including members of H.M. Forces overseas.

APPENDIX TABLE NI.4 Demographic developments, Northern Ireland 1922–1945
(absolute figures and rates)

Year	Mid-year population	Natural population growth rate	Population growth rate	Net migration rate	Crude birth rate	Legitimate births per 10,000 married women age 15–44	Illegitimate births per 10,000 unmarried women age 15–44	Illeg. births per 100 leg. births
1922	1,269,000	7.6	..	..	23.2	2,495	66	4.2
1923	1,259,000	9.1	-7.9	-17.0	23.9	2,545	72	4.5
1924	1,258,000	6.5	-0.8	-7.3	22.7	2,401	67	4.4
1925	1,257,000	6.3	-0.8	-7.1	22.0	2,319	67	4.5
1926	1,254,000	7.4	-2.4	-9.8	22.5	2,347	73	4.8
1927	1,250,000	6.8	-3.2	-10.0	21.4	2,214	74	5.1
1928	1,247,000	6.4	-2.4	-8.8	20.9	2,155	68	4.8
1929	1,240,000	4.4	-5.6	-10.1	20.5	2,103	69	5.0
1930	1,237,000	7.0	-2.4	-9.5	20.9	2,131	75	5.3
1931	1,243,000	6.2	4.8	-1.4	20.7	2,095	75	5.3
1932	1,251,000	5.8	6.4	0.6	20.1	2,020	75	5.5
1933	1,258,000	5.1	5.6	0.5	19.6	1,964	69	5.1
1934	1,265,000	6.2	5.5	-0.7	20.1	2,001	75	5.4
1935	1,271,000	4.8	4.7	-0.1	19.4	1,934	69	5.1
1936	1,276,000	5.9	3.9	-2.0	20.3	2,014	69	4.9
1937	1,281,000	4.8	3.9	-0.9	19.8	1,958	69	5.0
1938	1,286,000	6.3	3.9	-2.4	20.0	1,972	63	4.5
1939	1,295,000	5.9	6.9	1.0	19.5	1,909	63	4.6
1940	1,299,000	4.9	3.1	-1.8	19.6	..	..	5.0
1941	1,308,000	5.2	6.9	1.7	20.6	..	..	5.1
1942	1,329,000	9.1	15.8	6.7	22.3	..	..	5.0
1943	1,341,000	10.3	8.9	-1.3	23.5	..	..	5.7
1944	1,357,000	10.2	11.8	1.5	22.8	..	..	5.8
1945	1,359,000	9.3	1.5	-7.8	21.3	..	..	5,8

APPENDIX TABLE NI.4 Demographic developments, Northern Ireland 1922–1945
(absolute figures and rates)

Crude death rate	Infant mortality rate	Stillbirth rate	Infant mortality and stillbirth rate	Crude marriage rate	Persons marrying per 10,000 unmarried persons age 15+	Persons marrying per 10,000 unmarried persons age 15–49	Crude divorce rate	Divorces per 100 marriages	Divorces per 10,000 married persons	Year
15.6	77	..	..	6.4	318	423	..	..	..	1922
14.9	77	..	..	6.4	317	422	..	..	..	1923
16.1	85	..	..	6.0	298	397	..	..	..	1924
15.8	86	..	..	6.1	306	409	..	..	..	1925
15.1	85	..	..	5.7	287	384	..	..	..	1926
14.6	78	..	..	5.8	288	386	..	..	..	1927
14.4	78	..	..	5.9	293	393	..	..	..	1928
16.0	86	..	..	6.0	299	402	..	..	..	1929
13.9	68	..	..	6.1	304	409	..	..	..	1930
14.5	73	..	..	6.0	299	402	..	..	..	1931
14.2	83	..	..	5.6	281	379	..	..	..	1932
14.5	80	..	..	6.0	303	410	..	..	..	1933
13.8	70	..	..	6.5	326	441	..	..	..	1934
14.6	86	..	..	6.9	348	472	..	..	..	1935
14.4	77	..	..	7.1	359	487	..	..	..	1936
15.1	78	..	..	6.7	338	460	..	..	..	1937
13.7	75	..	..	6.7	337	459	..	..	..	1938
13.5	71	..	..	7.1	358	489	0.0	0.3	1.4	1939
14.6	86	..	..	7.5	..	..	0.1	1.1	..	1940
15.4	77	..	..	9.2	..	..	0.1	0.6	..	1941
13.2	76	..	..	8.8	..	..	0.1	1.0	..	1942
13.2	78	..	..	7.6	..	..	0.1	1.2	..	1943
12.5	67	..	..	7.0	..	..	0.1	1.4	..	1944
12.1	68	..	..	7.7	..	..	0.1	1.7	..	1945

APPENDIX TABLE EW.5 Life expectancy by age, England and Wales 1841–1930/32
(in years)

Age	0	10	20	30	40	50	60	70	80
				Males					
1841	40.19	47.08	39.88	33.13	26.56	20.02	13.50	8.51	4.92
1838–1844	40.36	47.47	39.99	33.21	26.46	19.87	13.60	8.55	4.97
1838–1854	39.91	47.05	39.48	32.76	26.06	19.54	13.53	8.45	4.93
1871–1880	41.35	47.60	39.40	32.10	25.30	18.93	13.14	8.27	4.79
1876–1880	41.92	48.16	39.86	32.47	25.59	19.14	13.31	8.44	4.96
1881–1890	43.66	49.00	40.27	32.52	25.42	18.82	12.88	8.04	4.52
1891–1900	44.13	49.63	41.02	33.07	25.64	18.90	12.93	8.05	4.62
1901–1910	48.53	51.81	43.01	34.76	26.96	19.76	13.49	8.39	4.86
1910–1912	51.50	53.08	44.21	35.81	27.74	20.29	13.78	8.53	4.90
1920–1922	55.62	54.64	45.78	37.40	29.19	21.36	14.36	8.75	4.93
1930–1932	58.74	55.79	46.81	38.21	29.62	21.60	14.43	8.62	4.74
				Females					
1841	42.18	47.81	40.81	34.25	27.72	21.07	14.40	9.03	5.20
1838–1844	42.04	47.86	40.65	34.06	72.50	20.84	14.49	9.12	5.34
1838–1854	41.85	47.67	40.29	33.81	27.34	20.75	14.34	9.02	5.26
1871–1880	44.62	49.76	41.66	34.41	27.46	20.68	14.24	8.95	5.20
1876–1880	45.25	50.32	42.10	34.75	27.68	20.80	14.32	9.08	5.38
1881–1890	47.18	51.10	42.42	34.76	27.60	20.56	14.10	8.77	5.00
1891–1900	47.77	51.97	43.44	35.39	27.82	20.64	14.10	8.78	5.05
1901–1910	52.38	54.53	45.77	37.36	29.37	21.81	15.01	9.25	5.36
1910–1912	55.35	53.91	47.10	38.54	30.30	22.51	15.48	9.58	5.49
1920–1922	59.58	57.53	48.73	40.26	31.86	23.69	16.22	9.95	5.56
1930–1932	62.88	58.87	49.88	41.22	32.55	24.13	16.50	10.02	5.46

APPENDIX TABLE SC.5 Life expectancy by age, Scotland 1861/70–1930/32 (in years)

Age	0	10	20	30	40	50	60	70	80
				Males					
1861–1870	40.33	46.10	38.75	32.20	..	..	13.30	..	4.59
1871–1880	40.95	46.07	38.68	32.05	..	..	13.18	..	4.68
1881–1890	43.92	47.10	40.19	33.06	..	..	13.52	..	5.00
1891–1900	44.41	48.60	40.43	33.02	25.71	18.91	13.12	8.28	4.91
1910–1912	50.10	51.86	43.27	35.17	27.25	19.91	13.54	8.38	4.94
1920–1922	53.08	53.55	44.82	36.52	28.43	20.68	13.82	8.40	4.78
1930–1932	56.0	54.9	46.0	37.4	29.1	21.3	14.1	8.4	4.6
				Females					
1861–1870	43.85	48.26	41.05	34.26	..	..	14.38	..	4.89
1871–1880	43.80	48.19	40.94	34.25	..	..	14.48	..	5.16
1881–1890	46.33	49.54	41.93	34.95	..	..	14.82	..	5.46
1891–1900	47.47	50.39	42.41	34.92	27.83	20.74	14.33	9.19	5.26
1910–1912	53.18	53.83	45.35	37.22	29.48	21.91	15.17	9.38	5.51
1920–1922	56.35	55.53	46.82	38.63	30.68	22.79	15.64	9.65	5.36
1930–1932	59.5	57.2	48.3	39.8	31.4	23.3	18.9	9.6	5.2

APPENDIX TABLE NI.5 Life expectancy by age, Northern Ireland 1911–1936/38 (in years)

Age	0	10	20	30	40	50	60	70	80
				Males					
1911	50.7	51.5	43.2	31.9[1]	24.4[2]	17.6[3]	12.1[4]	8.0[5]	..
1925–1927	55.42	54.42	45.63	37.46	29.28	21.55	14.79	9.36	5.43
1936–1938	57.8	55.4	46.4	33.6[1]	25.4[2]	18.0[3]	11.6[4]	7.0[5]	..
				Females					
1911	51.0	50.7	42.8	31.9[1]	24.7[2]	18.1[3]	12.8[4]	8.5[5]	..
1925–1927	56.11	53.73	45.22	37.42	29.65	22.18	15.55	10.20	6.25
1936–1938	59.2	56.1	47.1	34.6[1]	26.4[2]	18.8[3]	12.4[4]	7.6[5]	..

Notes: [1] 30–40. [2] 40–50. [3] 50–60. [4] 60–70. [5] 70–80.

APPENDIX TABLE EW.6A Households by type, England and Wales 1801–1931 (absolute and per cent)

Census year	Household types and members									
	Total house-holds	Private house-holds	Family house-holds	One-person house-holds	Institu-tional house-holds	Total household members	Private household members	Family household members	One-person household members	Institu-tional household members
Absolute										
1801	..	1,896,723	..	..	..	8,892,536	..	..	..	..
1811	..	2,142,147	..	..	..	10,164,256	..	..	..	..
1821	..	2,493,423	..	..	..	12,000,236	..	..	..	..
1831	..	2,911,874	..	..	..	13,896,797	..	..	..	..
1841	..	..	..	..	..	15,914,148	..	..	..	..
1851	3,714,048	3,712,290	..	..	1,758	17,927,609	..	..	..	271,006
1861	4,493,208	4,491,524	..	..	1,684	20,066,224	..	..	..	311,793
1871	5,051,495	5,049,016	..	..	2,479	22,712,266	..	..	..	417,579
1881	..	5,633,192	..	..	..	25,974,439	..	..	..	..
1891	..	6,131,001	..	..	..	29,002,525	..	..	..	466,210
1901	..	7,036,868	..	..	..	32,527,843	..	..	..	..
1911	..	7,943,137	7,519,955	423,182	..	35,179,511	34,606,173	34,182,991	423,182	573,338
1921	8,753,897	8,739,197	8,212,341	526,856	14,700	37,034,829	36,179,946	35,653,090	526,856	854,883
1931	10,248,103	10,233,139	9,544,437	688,702	14,964	38,932,898[1]	38,042,464	37,353,762	688,702	890,434
Per cent all households										
1851	100.00	99.95	..	..	0.05	100.00	..	..	..	1.51
1861	100.00	99.96	..	..	0.04	100.00	..	..	..	1.55
1871	100.00	99.95	..	..	0.05	100.00	..	..	..	1.84
1881	100.00	..	..	..	..	100.00	..	..	..	..
1891	100.00	..	..	..	..	100.00	..	..	..	1.61
1901	100.00	..	..	..	..	100.00	..	..	..	..
1911	100.00	..	..	..	..	100.00	98.37	97.17	1.20	1.63
1921	100.00	99.83	93.81	6.02	0.17	100.00	97.69	96.27	1.42	2.31
1931	100.00	99.85	93.13	6.72	0.15	100.00	97.71	95.94	1.77	2.29
Per cent private households										
1911	..	100.00	94.67	5.33	..	100.00	100.00	98.78	1.22	1.66
1921	100.00	100.00	93.97	6.03	..	100.00	100.00	98.54	1.46	2.36
1931	100.00	100.00	93.27	6.73	..	100.00	100.00	98.19	1.81	2.34

Note: [1] Total enumerated population: 39,952,377.

APPENDIX TABLE EW.6B Households by size and members, England and Wales 1911–1931 (absolute figures)

Cen-sus year	Households by number of members							
	Private households total	1 person	2 persons	3 persons	4 persons	5 persons	6 persons	7 persons
	Households							
1911	7,943,137	423,182	1,283,582	1,531,412	1,439,519	1,145,619	823,028	551,217
1921	8,739,197	526,856	1,546,948	1,823,619	1,625,292	1,213,464	818,448	520,074
1931	10,233,139	688,702	2,239,817	2,459,879	1,980,533	1,271,474	746,614	421,833
	Persons							
1911	34,606,173	423,182	2,567,164	4,594,236	5,758,076	5,728,095	4,938,168	3,858,519
1921	36,179,946	526,856	3,093,896	5,470,857	6,501,168	6,067,320	4,910,688	3,640,518
1931	38,042,464	688,702	4,479,634	7,379,637	7,922,132	6,357,370	4,479,684	2,952,831

continued

APPENDIX TABLE EW.6B Households by size and members, England and Wales 1911–1931 (absolute figures) (continued)

Cen-sus year	Households by number of members							
	8 persons	9 persons	10 persons	11 persons	12 persons	13 persons	14 persons	15+ persons
	Households							
1911	344,844	200,742	106,126	51,784	23,429	10,110	4,490	4,053
1921	314,771	179,344	98,251	40,503	17,646	7,400	3,361	3,220
1931	214,353	112,028	54,382	24,592	10,726	4,386	1,841	1,979
	Persons							
1911	2,758,752	1,806,678	1,061,260	569,624	281,148	131,430	62,860	66,981
1921	2,518,168	1,614,096	982,510	445,533	211,752	96,200	47,054	53,330
1931	1,714,824	1,008,252	543,820	270,512	128,712	57,018	25,774	33,562

APPENDIX TABLE EW.6C Households by size and members, England and Wales
1911–1931 (per cent)

Cen-sus year	Households by number of members							
	Private househol ds total	1 person	2 persons	3 persons	4 persons	5 persons	6 persons	7 persons
	Households							
1911	100.00	5.33	16.16	19.28	18.12	14.42	10.36	6.94
1921	100.00	6.03	17.70	20.87	18.60	13.89	9.37	5.95
1931	100.00	6.73	21.89	24.04	19.35	12.43	7.30	4.12
	Persons							
1911	100.00	1.22	7.42	13.28	16.64	16.55	14.27	11.15
1921	100.00	1.46	8.55	15.12	17.97	16.77	13.57	10.06
1931	100.00	1.81	11.78	19.40	20.82	16.71	11.78	7.76

continued

APPENDIX TABLE EW.6C Households by size and members, England and Wales
1911–1931 (per cent) (continued)

Cen-sus year	Households by number of members							
	8 persons	9 persons	10 persons	11 persons	12 persons	13 persons	14 persons	15+ persons
	Households							
1911	4.34	2.53	1.34	0.65	0.29	0.13	0.06	0.05
1921	3.60	2.05	1.12	0.46	0.20	0.08	0.04	0.04
1931	2.09	1.09	0.53	0.24	0.10	0.04	0.02	0.02
	Persons							
1911	7.97	5.22	3.07	1.65	0.81	0.38	0.18	0.19
1921	6.96	4.46	2.72	1.23	0.59	0.27	0.13	0.15
1931	4.51	2.65	1.43	0.71	0.34	0.15	0.07	0.09

APPENDIX TABLE EW.6D Household indicators, England and Wales 1801–1931

Census year	Household indicators						
	Families or separate occupiers	Total present population	Total present population to families or separate occupiers	Mean total house-hold size	Mean private house-hold size	Mean family house-hold size	Mean institu-tional house-hold size
1801	1,896,723	8,892,536	4.69	..	..	..	..
1811	2,142,147	10,164,256	4.74	..	..	..	..
1821	2,493,423	12,000,236	4.81	..	..	..	..
1831	2,911,874	13,896,797	4.77	..	..	..	..
1841	..	15,914,148	..	..	..	..	..
1851	3,712,290	17,927,609	4.83	..	..	..	..
1861	4,491,524	20,066,224	4.47	..	..	..	..
1871	5,049,016	22,712,266	4.50	..	..	..	..
1881	5,633,192	25,974,439	4.61	..	..	..	..
1891	6,131,001	29,002,525	4.73	..	..	..	..
1901	7,036,868	32,527,843	4.62	..	..	..	..
1911	8,005,290	36,070,492	4.51	..	4.36	4.55	..
1921	..	..	..	4.23	4.14	4.34	58.16
1931	..	..	..	3.80	3.72	3.91	59.51

APPENDIX TABLE SC.6A Households by type, Scotland 1801–1931 (absolute and per cent)

Census year	Total house-holds	Private house-holds	Family house-holds	One-person house-holds	Institutional house-holds	Total household members	Private household members	Family household members	One-person household members	Institutional household members
Absolute										
1801	..	..	..	..	..	1,608,420	..	..	..	..
1811	..	..	..	..	..	1,805,864	..	..	..	..
1821	..	..	..	..	..	2,091,521	..	..	..	..
1831	..	..	..	..	..	2,364,386	..	..	..	..
1841	..	..	..	..	..	2,620,184	..	..	..	..
1851	..	..	..	..	..	2,888,742	..	..	..	..
1861	678,584	666,786	606,330	60,456	..	3,062,294	..	..	60,456	..
1871	..	..	..	..	..	3,360,018	..	..	..	..
1881	..	810,699	735,991	74,708	..	3,735,573	..	..	74,708	..
1891	876,029	874,007	790,585	83,422	..	4,025,647	..	..	83,422	73,669
1901	967,200	964,940	883,938	81,002	..	4,472,103	..	..	81,002	96,028
1911	..	1,010,531	947,886	62,645	..	4,760,904	4,601,070	4,538,425	62,645	..
1921	..	1,057,609	989,264	68,345	..	4,882,497	4,699,266	4,630,921	68,345	..
1931	..	1,146,852	1,067,571	79,281	..	4,842,980	4,683,189	4,603,908	79,281	133,618
Per cent all households										
1861	100.00	98.26	89.35	8.91	..	100.00	..	..	1.97	..
1891	..	..	..	..	..	100.00	..	..	..	..
1901	..	..	..	..	..	100.00	..	..	2.00	..
1911	100.00	99.77	90.25	9.52	..	100.00	..	..	2.07	1.83
1921	100.00	99.77	91.39	8.37	..	100.00	..	..	1.81	2.15
1931	..	..	..	..	..	100.00	96.64	95.33	1.32	..
Per cent private households										
1861	..	100.00	90.93	9.07	..	..	..	..	..	..
1891	..	100.00	90.78	9.22	..	..	..	..	..	..
1901	..	100.00	90.46	9.54	..	..	..	..	..	..
1911	..	100.00	91.61	8.39	..	..	..	..	..	..
1921	..	100.00	93.80	6.20	..	..	..	..	..	..
1931	..	..	..	..	..	100.00	100.00	98.64	1.36	..

APPENDIX TABLE SC.6B Households by size and members, Scotland 1861–1931
(absolute figures)

Cen-sus year	Private house-holds total	Households by number of members						
		1 person	2 persons	3 persons	4 persons	5 persons	6 persons	7 persons
					Households				
1861	666,786	60,456	98,794	103,680	100,899	90,252	74,579	55,437
1881	810,699	74,708	124,741	123,718	118,472	106,280	88,886	67,706
1891	874,007	83,422	136,902	133,984	125,220	111,405	93,324	71,899
1901	964,940	81,002	147,304	155,394	146,791	127,959	104,134	78,122
1911	1,010,531	62,645	149,807	172,206	167,992	144,194	112,861	81,123
1921	1,057,609	68,345	159,726	188,798	182,727	150,992	113,008	77,817
1931	1,146,852	79,281	204,789	237,269	214,485	158,313	105,054	65,658
					Persons				
1861	3,062,294[1]	60,456	197,588	311,040	403,596	451,260	447,474	388,059
1881	3,735,573[1]	74,708	249,482	371,154	473,888	531,400	533,316	473,942
1891	4,025,647[1]	83,422	273,804	401,952	500,880	557,025	559,944	503,293
1901	4,472,103[1]	81,002	294,608	466,182	587,164	639,795	624,804	546,854
1911	4,601,070	62,645	299,614	516,618	671,968	720,970	677,166	567,861
1921	4,699,266	68,345	319,452	566,394	730,908	754,960	678,048	544,719
1931	4,683,189	79,281	409,578	711,807	857,940	791,565	630,324	459,606

continued

APPENDIX TABLE SC.6B Households by size and members, Scotland 1861–1931
(absolute figures) (continued)

Cen-sus year	Households by number of members							
	8 persons	9 persons	10 persons	11 persons	12 persons	13 persons	14 persons	15+ persons
				Households					
1861	36,437	21,220	11,487	5,809	3,136	1,670	1,009	1,921
1881	46,764	28,478	15,132	7,662	3,663	1,688	948	1,853
1891	51,388	31,767	17,472	8,572	3,919	1,835	808	2,090
1901	54,381	33,585	18,661	9,071	4,077	1,747	774	1,938
1911	54,220	32,426	17,769	8,499	3,817	1,543	694	735
1921	50,098	30,200	17,241	8,088	3,873	1,859	907	3,930
1931	38,700	21,608	11,506	5,146	2,552	1,113	532	846
				Persons					
1861	291,496	190,980	114,870	63,899	37,632	21,710	14,126	68,108
1881	374,112	256,302	151,320	84,282	43,956	21,944	13,272	82,495
1891	411,104	285,903	174,720	94,292	47,028	23,855	11,312	97,113
1901	435,048	302,265	186,610	99,781	48,924	22,711	10,836	125,519
1911	433,760	291,834	177,690	93,489	45,804	20,059	9,716	11,876
1921	400,784	271,800	172,410	88,968	46,476	24,167	12,698	19,137
1931	309,600	194,472	115,060	56,606	30,624	14,469	7,448	14,809

Note: [1] Total population.

APPENDIX TABLE SC.6C Households by size and members, Scotland 1861–1931
(per cent)

Cen-sus year	Private house-holds total	Households by number of members						
		1 person	2 persons	3 persons	4 persons	5 persons	6 persons	7 persons
				Households				
1861	100.00	9.07	14.82	15.55	15.13	13.54	11.18	8.31
1881	100.00	9.22	15.39	15.26	14.61	13.11	10.96	8.35
1891	100.00	9.54	15.66	15.33	14.33	12.75	10.68	8.23
1901	100.00	8.39	15.27	16.10	15.21	13.26	10.79	8.10
1911	100.00	6.20	14.82	17.04	16.62	14.27	11.17	8.03
1921	100.00	6.46	15.10	17.85	17.28	14.28	10.69	7.36
1931	100.00	6.91	17.86	20.69	18.70	13.80	9.16	5.73
				Persons				
1861	100.00[1]	1.97	6.45	10.16	13.18	14.74	14.61	12.67
1881	100.00[1]	2.00	6.68	9.94	12.69	14.23	14.28	12.69
1891	100.00[1]	2.07	6.80	9.98	12.44	13.84	13.91	12.50
1901	100.00[1]	1.81	6.59	10.42	13.13	14.31	13.97	12.23
1911	100.00	1.36	6.51	11.23	14.60	15.67	14.72	12.34
1921	100.00	1.45	6.80	12.05	15.55	16.07	14.43	11.59
1931	100.00	1.69	8.75	15.20	18.32	16.90	13.46	9.81

continued

APPENDIX TABLE SC.6C Households by size and members, Scotland 1861–1931
(per cent) (continued)

Cen-sus year	Households by number of members							
	8 persons	9 persons	10 persons	11 persons	12 persons	13 persons	14 persons	15+ persons
				Households				
1861	5.46	3.18	1.72	0.87	0.47	0.25	0.15	0.29
1881	5.77	3.51	1.87	0.95	0.45	0.21	0.12	0.23
1891	5.88	3.63	2.00	0.98	0.45	0.21	0.09	0.24
1901	5.64	3.48	1.93	0.94	0.42	0.18	0.08	0.20
1911	5.37	3.21	1.76	0.84	0.38	0.15	0.07	0.07
1921	4.74	2.86	1.63	0.76	0.37	0.18	0.09	0.37
1931	3.37	1.88	1.00	0.45	0.22	0.10	0.05	0.07
				Persons				
1861	9.52	6.24	3.75	2.09	1.23	0.71	0.46	2.22
1881	10.01	6.86	4.05	2.26	1.18	0.59	0.36	2.21
1891	10.21	7.10	4.34	2.34	1.17	0.59	0.28	2.41
1901	9.73	6.76	4.17	2.23	1.09	0.51	0.24	2.81
1911	9.43	6.34	3.86	2.03	1.00	0.44	0.21	0.26
1921	8.53	5.78	3.67	1.89	0.99	0.51	0.27	0.41
1931	6.61	4.15	2.46	1.21	0.65	0.31	0.16	0.32

Note: [1] Total population.

APPENDIX TABLE SC.6D   Household indicators, Scotland 1861–1931

Census year	Household indicators		
	Mean total household size	Mean private household size	Mean family household size
1861	4.51	:	:
1871	:	:	:
1881	:	:	:
1891	4.60	:	:
1901	4.62	:	:
1911	:	4.55	4.79
1921	:	4.44	4.68
1931	:	4.08	4.31

APPENDIX TABLE NI.6A   Households by type, Northern Ireland 1926–1937 (absolute and per cent)

Census year	Household types and members									
	Total households	Private households	Family households	One-person households	Institutional households	Total household members	Private household members	Family household members	One-person household members	Institutional household members
	Absolute									
1926	273,789	273,668	252,341	21,327	121	1,205,180[1]	1,192,887	1,171,560	21,327	12,293
1937	302,774	302,631	276,850	25,781	143	1,242,667[2]	1,228,991	1,203,210	25,781	13,676
	Per cent all households									
1926	100.00	99.96	92.17	7.79	0.04	100.00	98.98	97.21	1.77	1.02
1937	100.00	99.95	91.44	8.51	0.05	100.00	98.90	96.82	2.07	1.10
	Per cent private households									
1926	..	100.00	92.21	7.79	0.04	..	100.00	98.21	1.79	1.03
1937	..	100.00	91.48	8.52	0.05	..	100.00	97.90	2.10	1.11

Notes: [1] Total population 1,256,561. [2] Total population 1,279,745.

APPENDIX TABLE NI.6B Households by size and members, Northern Ireland 1926–
1937 (absolute figures)

Cen-sus year	Households by number of members							
	Private house-holds total	1 person	2 persons	3 persons	4 persons	5 persons	6 persons	7 persons
				Households				
1926	273,668	21,327	45,001	47,967	44,652	37,248	28,393	20,014
1937	302,631	25,781	57,259	58,939	51,923	39,013	27,590	17,911
				Persons				
1926	1,192,887	21,327	90,002	143,901	178,608	186,240	170,358	140,098
1937	1,228,991	25,781	114,518	176,817	207,692	195,065	165,540	125,377

continued

APPENDIX TABLE NI.6B Households by size and members, Northern Ireland 1926–
1937 (absolute figures) (continued)

Cen-sus year	Households by number of members							
	8 persons	9 persons	10 persons	11 persons	12 persons	13 persons	14 persons	15+ persons
				Households				
1926	13,244	7,862	4,528	1,896	910	384	150	92
1937	11,126	6,554	3,698	1,594	744	326	109	64
				Persons				
1926	105,952	70,758	45,280	20,856	10,920	4,992	2,100	1,495
1937	89,008	58,986	36,980	17,534	8,928	4,238	1,526	1,001

APPENDIX TABLE NI.6C Households by size and members, Northern Ireland 1926–1937 (per cent)

Census year	Private households total	1 person	2 persons	3 persons	4 persons	5 persons	6 persons	7 persons
				Households				
1926	100.00	7.79	16.44	17.53	16.32	13.61	10.37	7.31
1937	100.00	8.52	18.92	19.48	17.16	12.89	9.12	5.92
				Persons				
1926	100.00	1.79	7.54	12.06	14.97	15.61	14.28	11.74
1937	100.00	2.10	9.32	14.39	16.90	15.87	13.47	10.20

continued

APPENDIX TABLE NI.6C Households by size and members, Northern Ireland 1926–1937 (per cent) (continued)

Census year	8 persons	9 persons	10 persons	11 persons	12 persons	13 persons	14 persons	15+ persons
				Households				
1926	4.84	2.87	1.65	0.69	0.33	0.14	0.05	0.03
1937	3.68	2.17	1.22	0.53	0.25	0.11	0.04	0.02
				Persons				
1926	8.88	5.93	3.80	1.75	0.92	0.42	0.18	0.13
1937	7.24	4.80	3.01	1.43	0.73	0.34	0.12	0.08

APPENDIX TABLE NI.6D Household indicators, Northern Ireland 1926–1937

Census year	Mean total household size	Mean private household size	Mean family household size	Mean institutional household size
1926	4.40	4.36	4.64	101.60
1937	4.10	4.06	4.35	95.64

APPENDIX TABLE UK.7 Dates and nature of results on population structure, households/families, and vital statistics

Topic	Intro-duction	Remarks
Population		
Population at census dates	1851	Earlier censuses were conducted 9–10 III 1801, 26–27 V 1811, 27–28 V 1821, 29–30 V 1831, and 6–7 VI 1841. The history of the census of Great Britain from 1801 until 1911 is the same as for Ireland (see Chapter 11).
Population by age, sex, and marital status	1851	
Households and families		
Households (*private families* or *households*)		
Total households	1851, 1861, 1871, 1881, 1891, 1901, 1911, 1921, 1926, 1931, 1937	Households were recorded by each census from 1801: 1851: *England and Wales*: number of households. *Scotland*: number of households. 1861: *England and Wales*: number of households. *Scotland*: number of households, households by size. 1871: *England and Wales*: number of households. *Scotland*: number of households. 1881: *England and Wales*: number of households. *Scotland*: number of households. 1891: *England and Wales*: number of households. *Scotland*: number of households, households by size. 1901: *England and Wales*: number of households, households by size. *Scotland*: number of households, households by size. 1911: *England and Wales*: number of households, households by size. *Scotland*: number of households, households by size. 1921: *England and Wales*: number of households, households by size. *Scotland*: number of households, households by size. 1926: *Northern Ireland*: number of households, households by size. 1931: *England and Wales*: number of households, households by size. *Scotland*: number of households, households by size. 1937: *Northern Ireland*: number of households, households by size. *Disaggregation*: by provinces and districts.

continued

APPENDIX TABLE UK.7 Dates and nature of results on population structure, households/families, and vital statistics (continued)

Topic	Intro-duction	Remarks
Households by size	1861, 1891, 1911, 1921, 1926, 1931, 1937	*England and Wales*: 1901: 1–15+, 1911: 1–15+, 1921: 1–15+, 1931: 1–15+ persons. *Scotland*: 1861, 1881, 1891, 1901, 1911, 1921, 1931. *Northern Ireland*: first time in the census of 1926: households by number of persons 1–15+. Repeated in 1937: 1–10+ persons.
Households by composition	–	
Households by profession of household head	–	
Families (families)		
Families by number of children	1911, 1921, 1926	*England and Wales*: 1911, 1921 *Scotland*: – *Northern Ireland*: First special investigation of the fertility of marriages in 1926.
Population movement		
Mid-year population	1850–, 1864–	UK: 1864–; EW: 1850–; SC: 1850–; NI: 1922–.
Births		
Live births	1850–, 1864–	UK: 1864–; EW: 1850–; SC: 1855–; NI: 1922–.
Stillbirths	1928–, 1960–	UK: 1960–; EW: 1928–; SC: 1939–; NI: 1962–.
Legitimate births	1850–	UK: 1850–; EW: 1850–; SC: 1855–; NI: 1922–.
Illegitimate births	1850–	UK: 1850–; EW: 1850–; SC: 1855–; NI: 1922–.
Deaths		
Total deaths	1850–, 1864–	UK: 1864–; EW: 1850–; SC: 1855–; NI: 1922–.
Infants (under 1 year)	1850–, 1924–	UK: 1924–; EW: 1850–; SC: 1951–; NI: 1955–.
Marriages		
Total marriages	1850–, 1855–	UK: 1855–; EW: 1850–; SC: 1855–; NI: 1922–.
Divorces and separations		
Total divorces	1858–, 1864–	UK: 1864–; EW: 1858–; SC: 1855–; NI: 1939–.
Legal separations	–	

APPENDIX FIGURE GB.8 Population by age, sex and marital status, Great Britain
1911, 1921 and 1931 (per 10,000 of total population)

Great Britain, 1911

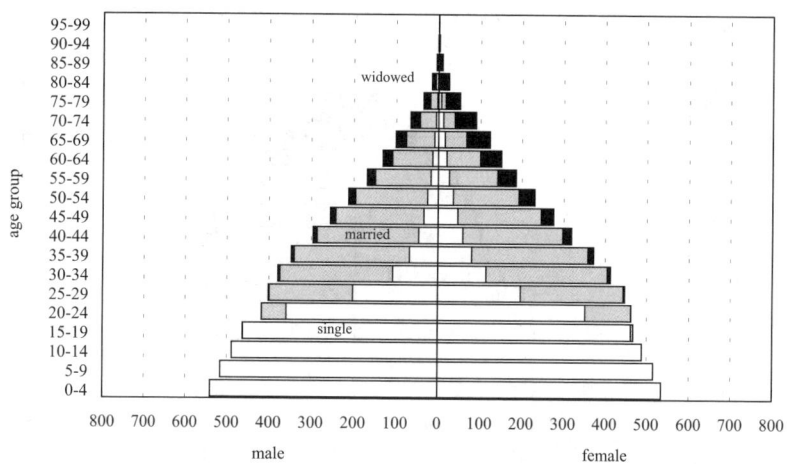

Great Britain, 1921

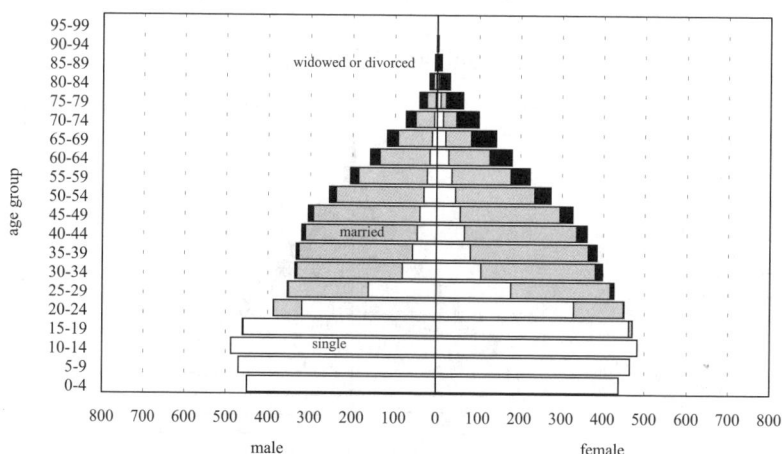

APPENDIX FIGURE GB.8 Population by age, sex and marital status, Great Britain
    1911, 1921 and 1931 (per 10,000 of total population) (continued)

Great Britain, 1931

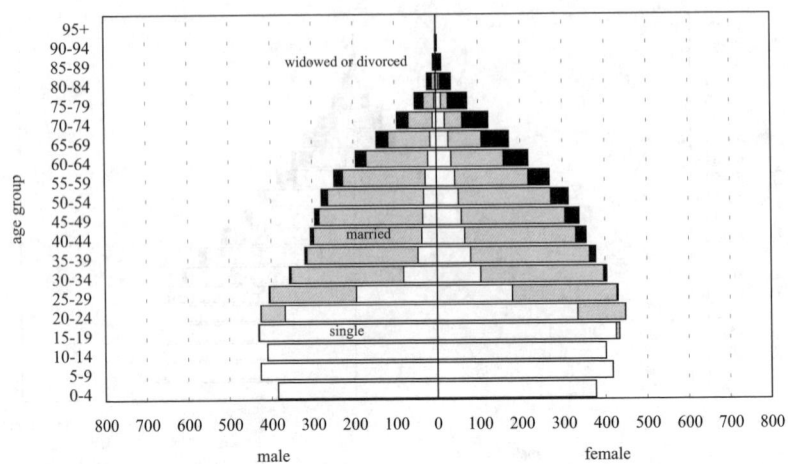

APPENDIX FIGURE EW.8 Population by age, sex and marital status, England and
    Wales 1911, 1921 and 1931 (per 10,000 of total population)

England and Wales, 1911

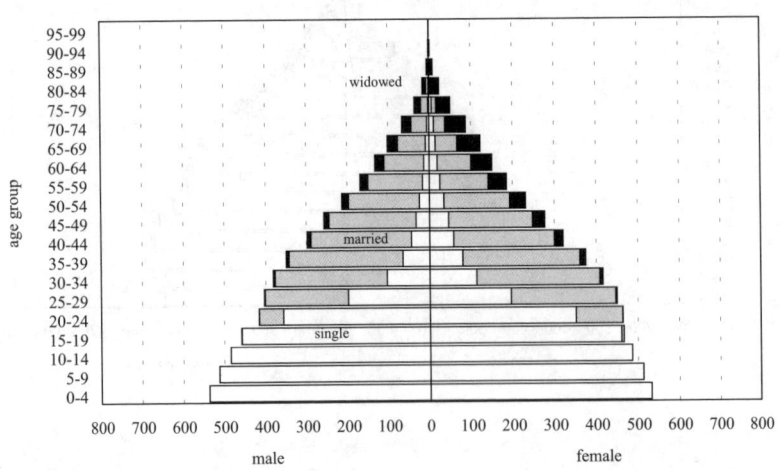

APPENDIX FIGURE EW.8 Population by age, sex and marital status, England and
Wales 1911, 1921 and 1931 (per 10,000 of total population) (continued)

England and Wales, 1921

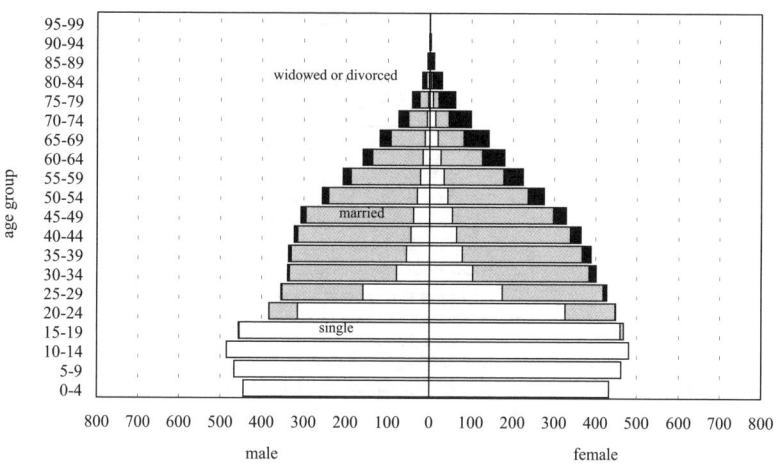

England and Wales, 1931

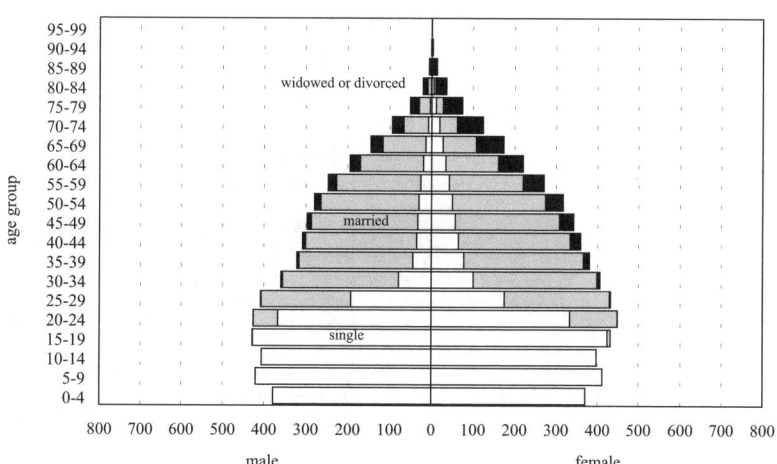

APPENDIX FIGURE SC.8 Population by age, sex and marital status, Scotland 1861, 1871, 1901, 1911, 1921 and 1931 (per 10,000 of total population)

Scotland, 1861

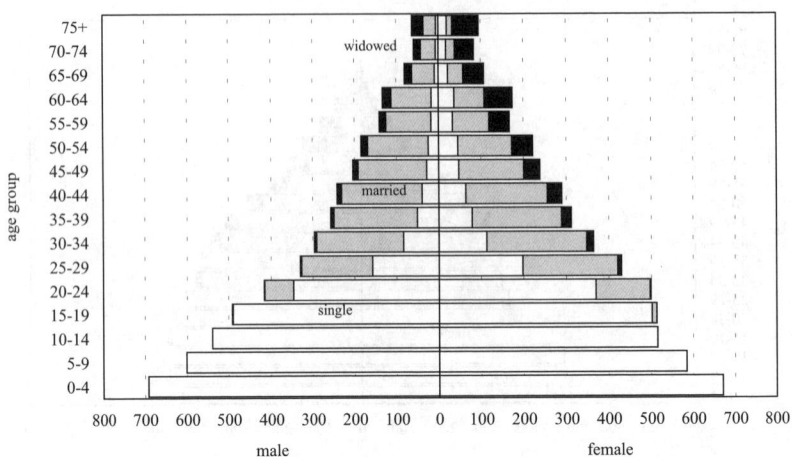

Scotland, 1871

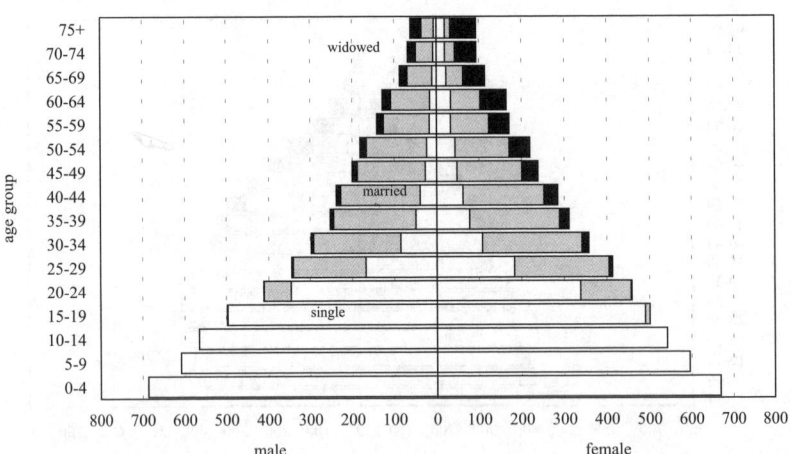

APPENDIX FIGURE SC.8 Population by age, sex and marital status, Scotland 1861, 1871, 1901, 1911, 1921 and 1931 (per 10,000 of total population) (continued)

Scotland, 1901

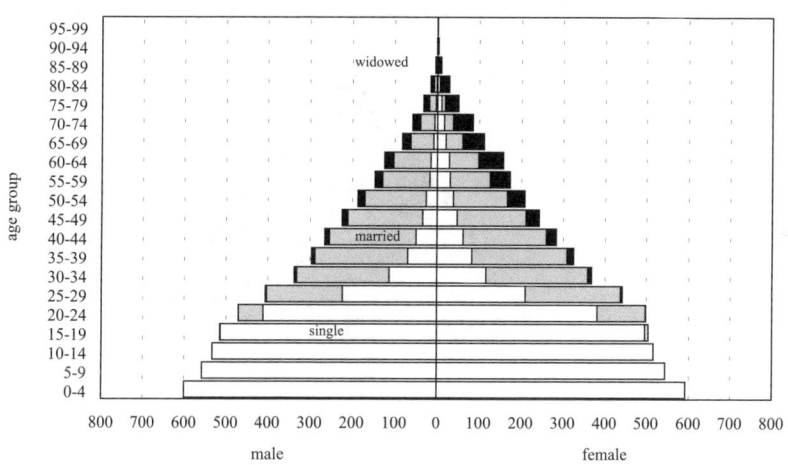

Scotland, 1911

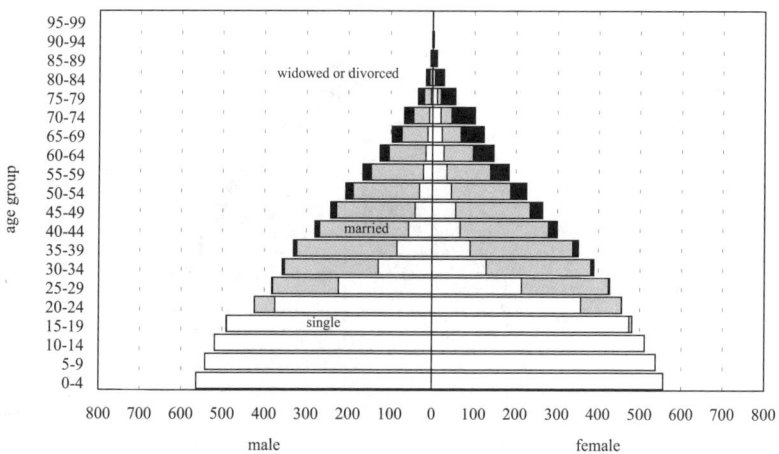

APPENDIX FIGURE SC.8 Population by age, sex and marital status, Scotland 1861, 1871, 1901, 1911, 1921 and 1931 (per 10,000 of total population) (continued)

Scotland, 1921

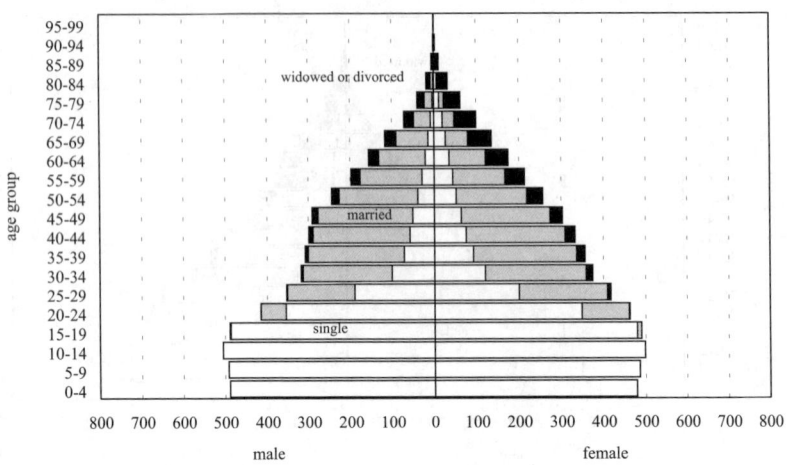

Scotland, 1931

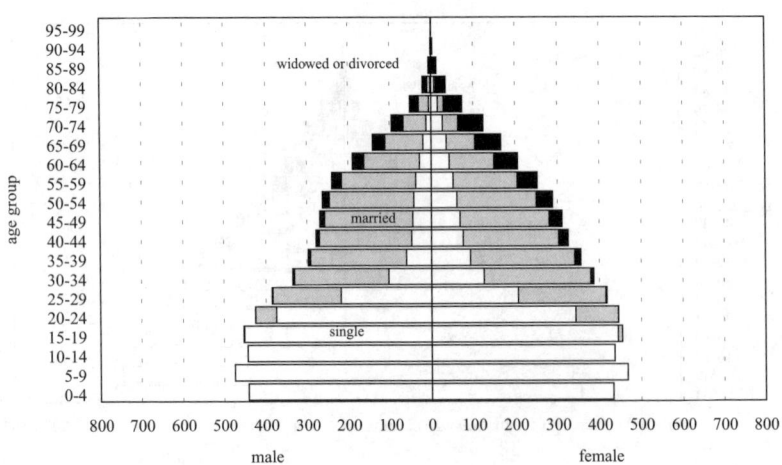

APPENDIX FIGURE NI.8 Population by age, sex and marital status, Northern Ireland 1926 and 1937 (per 10,000 of total population)

Northern Ireland, 1926

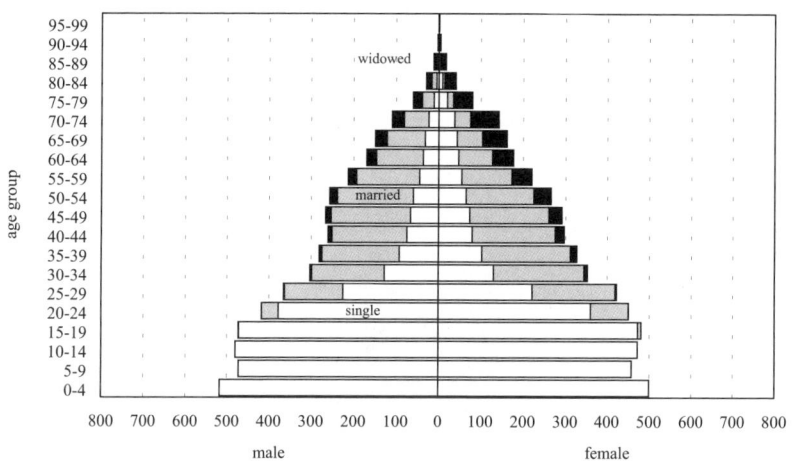

Northern Ireland, 1937

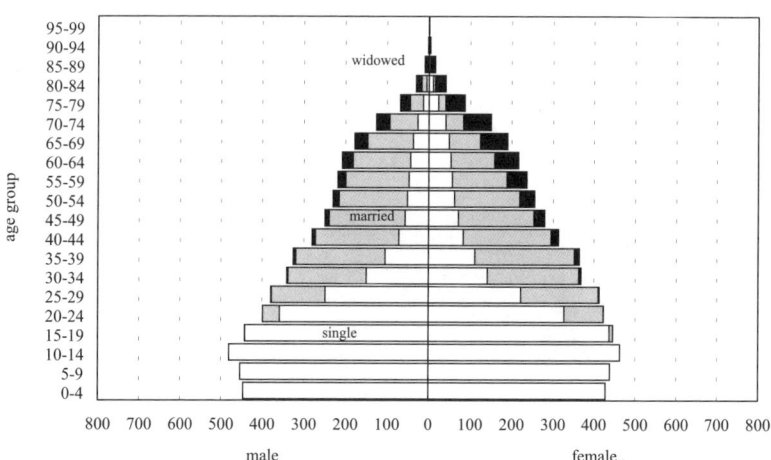

Part III
Appendices

1

A Note on the CD-ROM

Acknowledgements

The country tables were compiled by the author with the help of many librarians and students; their contribution is gratefully recognized in the Preface to this volume. The data collection was partly founded on an older database which is as well acknowledged in the Preface. The author developed the structure of the data base and collected the data. The author furthermore designed the basic structure of the CD-ROM, developed its content, and constructed its databases. I thank Birgit Becker for programming the interface.

As a supplement to the handbook, the CD-ROM provides data for further analyses of demographic developments, population and household structures in Western and East-Central Europe. The CD-ROM includes not only the printed country tables in computerized form, it also contains additional data tables with basic data on demographic developments and the population by age, sex and marital status for one-year age groups that may be used for specific research purposes and statistical analyses. Thus, with the help of the CD-ROM, the reader can study population questions with respect to main trends in demographic developments, the population by size and composition according to region, sex, age and marital status, shifts in the population structure and the composition of households—for individual countries or comparatively.

Before using the CD-ROM, the reader should first consult the handbook. The General Introduction (Chap. I.1) presents the background and history of the project and outlines the overall structure of the handbook. Especially, the introductory chapter Demographic Measures and Demographic Statistics (Chap. I.6) presents the main concepts and methods used for the collection and analysis of demographic data covered in the tables and the graphs. Four introductory chapters on Population and Territory, Population Growth and Demographic Transition, Marriage, Legitimacy, Divorce, and Households and Families (Chap. I.2–I.5), examine the main trends from 1850–1945 and cross-national differences between European population movements, as well as providing comparative tables. For analyses of particular countries, the handbook's Country Profiles (Chap. II.1–II.21) introduce the reader to nation state formation and territorial changes, population structures and movements, and the systems of national demographic statistics. Statistical sources and relevant literature are listed in one Bibliography at the end of the volume. All tables of the individual country profiles are included on the CD-ROM, but graphs are presented in the book only. Finally, we have standardized the numbering, indicators, and presentation of the Country Tables and Figures.

A Note on the CD-ROM

TABLE 1.1 Tables and time series on CD-ROM (Excel)

Country	Code	Table 1	Table 2	Table 3	Table 4	Table 5	Table 6
Austria - Empire	A	1869– 1910	1866– 1910	—	1850– 1913	1870/80– 1906/10	1869– 1910
Austria - Republic	A	1920–39	—	1923–51	1871– 1945	1930/33	1920–34
Belgium	B	1846– 1947	1846– 1947	1846– 1947	1850– 1945	1881/90– 1918/32	1846– 1947
Czechoslovakia	CS	1921–30	1921–50	1921–50	1919–45	1920/22– 37	1921–50
Denmark	DK	1855– 1940	1870– 1901	1911–40	1850– 1945	1835/44– 1941/45	1840– 1940
Finland	SF	1865– 1940	1875– 1940	1875– 1940	1850– 1945	1881/90– 194145	1865– 1900
France	F	1851– 1946	1872– 1946	1872– 1946	1850– 1945	1817/31– 1933/38	1851– 1946
Germany	D	1871– 1939	1871– 1933	1871– 1933	1850– 1945	1871/81– 1932/34	1871– 1939
Greece	GR	1907–28	1870– 1947	1870– 1940	1850– 1945	1879– 1940	1861– 1951
Hungary - Empire	H	1880– 1910	1870– 1910	—	1865– 1918	—	1870– 1910
Hungary - Kingdom	H	1920–41	1920–30	1930—49	1869– 1945	1900/01– 1941	1920–41
Iceland	IS	1840– 1940	1901–40	1901–40	1850– 1945	1841/50– 1941/50	1703– 1940
Ireland/Irish Republic	IRL	1861– 1936	1871– 1946	1871– 1946	1850– 1945	1900/2– 1940/42	1821– 1946
Italy	I	1871– 1936	1871– 1936	1871– 1936	1861– 1945	1876/87– 1935/37	1871– 1944
Luxemburg	L	1890– 1947	1839– 1935	1839– 1935	1850– 1945	1901/03– 1943/45	1864– 1935
The Netherlands	NL	1849– 1947	1869– 1930	1869– 1930	1850– 1945	1871/81– 1932/34	1829– 1930
Norway	N	1865– 1946	1876– 1910	1920– 1946	1850– 1945	1821/30– 1931/41	1825– 1946
Poland	PL	1921–31	1921–31	1921–31	1900–45	1927– 31/32	1921–31
Portugal	P	1864– 1940	1878– 1940	1878– 1940	1850– 1945	1929/32– 45	1835– 1940
Spain	E	1857– 1940	1877– 1940	1877– 1940	1850– 1945	1900–40	1857– 1940
Sweden	S	1860– 1945	1870– 1940	1870– 1940	1850– 1945	1755/76– 1941/45	1860– 1945
Switzerland	CH	1860– 1941	1870– 1941	1870– 1941	1850– 1945	1876/80– 1939/44	1850– 1941
United Kingdom	UK	—	1871– 1931	1871– 1931	1850– 1945	—	—
Great Britain	GB	1851– 1931	—	—	—	—	—
England and Wales	EW	1851– 1931	—	—	1850– 1945	1841– 1930/32	1801– 1931
England	EL	—	1871– 1931	1871– 1931	—	—	—
Wales	W	—	1871– 1931	1871– 1931	—	—	—
Scotland	SC	1851– 1931	1871– 1931	1871– 1931	1850– 1945	1861/70– 1930/32	1801– 1931
Northern Ireland	NI	1926–37	1926–37	1926–37	1922–45	1911– 1936/38	1926–37

The handbook provides important background information for the use of the data contained on the CD-ROM. To make proper use of the electronic tables and databases included, users of the electronic version are asked to consult the handbook, in particular the sections 'State Formation and Territory', 'The National

System of Demographic Statistics' and 'Boundary Changes'. The CD-ROM thus complements, but does not substitute for the handbook, while it also includes a wealth of supplementary data. Besides the computer-readable tables which are included in the handbook, additional tables on population developments and structure that could not be published due to space limitations are included on the CD-ROM. The data comprise first: the absolute values used for calculating the demographic indicators (annual data for mid-year population, live births, deaths, marriages, divorces, etc.); second: the absolute values on the population by age, sex and marital status in one-year age groups for each population census. It is important to note that these latter data have been included for the time period 1850 to 1990. These additional databases allow further analysis by the reader, be it research on the demographic development of one individual country, or new comparative analyses of some selected variables.

I. Coverage

The handbook and CD-ROM cover all Western European countries, plus the East-Central European countries of Czechoslovakia, Hungary and Poland. Thus, it includes all of the European Union member states. For most countries, data are available from 1850 until 1945. For Czechoslovakia and Poland, data series start after the end of World War I. In Italy, national data became available in the 1860s after unification. As regards Austria and Hungary, data are available for two different territorial states: for the larger territory until World War I, and the retrospectively recalculated figures for the territory of the republic resp. kingdom. In contrast to statistics in other fields, population statistics in Europe remained national until 1945; there was no equivalent to 'European population statistics', which began to be compiled with the foundation of the European Union after the war. Thus only national data are presented in the handbook and on the CD-ROM. On the CD-ROM, users will find easy access to these national areas by clicking on the left banner:

Country   Countries covered (1850–1945): Belgium, Denmark, Finland, France, Germany, Greece, Iceland, Ireland, Luxemburg, The Netherlands, Norway, Portugal, Spain, Sweden, Switzerland, United Kingdom, England and Wales, and Scotland; Austrian Empire (1850–1913); Austrian Republic (1871–1945); Czechoslovakia (1919–45); Hungarian Empire (1865–1918); Hungarian Kingdom (1869–1945); Italy (1861–1945); Poland (1900–45); Northern Ireland (1922–45).

II. Type of information

The CD-ROM provides information on four main aspects of population structure and development for each country, or at the regional level.

Population structure and density   Development of national population structures by population size, sex, marital status and age according to population censuses (with the age being given as detailed as possible, mostly in one-year age groups).
Development of population distribution and population density

	by regions according to population censuses.
Vital statistics	Annual series on mid-year population, population growth and net migration, fertility, legitimacy and illegitimacy, general and infant mortality, nuptiality and divortiality.
Life expectancy	For each country one table on life expectancy by sex for selected ages.
Households and families	Basic data and indicators for the years of the population censuses on households by type, members, size, composition, in some cases also by region and profession of household head.

TABLE 1.2 Variable names and variable description for the Additional Table II on 'Age, Sex, and Civil Status' on CD-ROM (Excel)

Variable name	Variable description	Variable name	Variable description
AGE	Year of age (or age group)		
YEAR	Census year (or year of population registration)		
COUN	Numerical country code		
CODE	Alphanumerical country code		
M_TOT	Males total	F_TOT	Females total
M_SGL	Males single	F_SGL	Females single
M_MAR	Males married (Iceland: ... and living with wife)	F_MAR	Females married (Iceland: ... and living with husband)
M_WID	Males widowed	F_WID	Females widowed
M_SEP	Males separated	F_SEP	Females separated
M_SEP_DF	Males separated de facto	F_SEP_DF	Females separated de facto
M_DIV	Males divorced	F_DIV	Females divorced
M_UNK	Males unknown	F_UNK	Females unknown
M_WDS	Males widowed or divorced or separated	F_WDS	Females widowed or divorced or separated
M_MAS	Males married, but separated	F_MAS	Females married, but separated
M_DIS	Males divorced or separated	F_DIS	Females divorced or separated
M_WD	Males widowed or divorced	F_WD	Females widowed or divorced
M_LTG	Males living together	F_LTG	Females living together
M_MAR_T	Males married total (Iceland)	F_MAR_T	Females married total (Iceland)
		F_MAR_US	Females married to the U.S. Defence Force who are included in the National Registry (Iceland)
M_SEP_LE	Males legally separated (Iceland)	F_SEP_LE	Females legally separated (Iceland)
M_SWD	Males single, widowed and divorced	F_SWD	Females single, widowed and divorced
M_MA1	Males married	F_MA1	Females married
M_MA2	Males remarried	F_MA2	Females remarried
M_MAR_LG	Males legally married	F_MAR_LG	Females legally married
M_MAR_DF	Males non-legally married	F_MAR_DF	Females non-legally married

TABLE 1.3 Value labels for the variables of the Additional Table II on 'Age, Sex, and Civil Status' on CD-ROM (Excel)

Variable	Value Label	Description (sorted)	Value Label (sorted)	Description
AGE	100+, 101+, etc.	100 years and more, etc.		
	199	Unknown		
	200	Total		
COUN	301	Austrian Empire	200	United Kingdom
	305	Austrian Republic	202	England and Wales
	211	Belgium	203	Scotland
	315	Czechoslovakia	204	Ireland
	390	Denmark	205	Irish Republic
	375	Finland	206	Northern Ireland
	220	France	208	Great Britain
	255	German Empire	210	The Netherlands
	260	Federal Republic of Germany	211	Belgium
	350	Greece	212	Luxemburg
	311	Hungarian Empire	220	France
	310	Hungarian Kingdom	225	Switzerland
	395	Iceland	230	Spain
	204	Ireland	235	Portugal
	205	Irish Republic	255	German Empire
	325	Italy	260	Federal Republic of Germany
	212	Luxemburg	290	Poland
	210	The Netherlands	301	Austrian Empire
	385	Norway	305	Austrian Republic
	290	Poland	310	Hungarian Kingdom
	235	Portugal	311	Hungarian Empire
	230	Spain	315	Czechoslovakia
	380	Sweden	325	Italy
	225	Switzerland	350	Greece
	200	United Kingdom	375	Finland
	208	Great Britain	380	Sweden
	202	England and Wales	385	Norway
	203	Scotland	390	Denmark
	206	Northern Ireland	395	Iceland

III. Types of data

The following types of data are available on this CD-ROM; they allow browsing, printing, and/or further computation depending on the data format:

Tables   Handbook appendix tables (1–6) (PDF and Excel formats)
                       Additional tables (I–II) (PDF and Excel formats)

Documentation   Country chapter section on 'The national system of demographic statistics' with information on the history and organization of population statistics and a definition of statistical concepts (PDF format).

Handbook appendix table (7) (PDF format) on the availability of demographic statistics.

The complete 'Bibliography', comprising full documentation of the statistical sources used for compiling the tables and databases (PDF format).

The CD-ROM brochure explains how to install and run the programmes on the CD-ROM, and how to launch the menu-driven (hyperlinks) interface that leads users through the different options. Links allow easy access to the different types of information and files. We hope that the CD-ROM fosters further in-depth comparative or individual country analyses, and can be easily amended and updated for future research by users.

2

BIBLIOGRAPHY

SOURCES

AUSTRIA

1. Vital statistics

Bolognese-Leuchtenmüller, B. (1978), *Bevölkerungsentwicklung und Berufs-struktur, Gesundheits- und Fürsorgewesen in Österreich 1750–1918.* Wirtschafts- und Sozialstatistik Österreich-Ungarns, vol. 1; Materialien zur Wirtschafts- und Sozialgeschichte, vol. 1. Munich: Oldenbourg.

Österreichisches Statistisches Zentralamt (ÖSTAT) (1923–), *Statistisches Handbuch für die Republik Österreich 19...* Vienna: Österreichisches Statistisches Zentralamt.

2. Population structure by age, sex, and marital status

1869   K. K. Statistische Central-Commission (1871), *Bevölkerung und Viehstand der im Reichsrathe vertretenen Königreiche und Länder, dann der Militärgränze nach der Zählung vom 31. December 1869. Heft I. Bevölkerung nach Geschlecht, Religion, Stand und Aufenthalt.* Vienna: Kaiserlich-Königliche Hof- und Staatsdruckerei, pp. 302–3.

K. K. Statistische Central-Commission (1871), *Bevölkerung und Viehstand der im Reichsrathe vertretenen Königreiche und Länder, dann der Militärgränze nach der Zählung vom 31. December 1869. Heft III. Bevölkerung nach dem Alter.* Vienna: Kaiserlich-Königliche Hof- und Staatsdruckerei, pp. 446–61.

1880   K. K. Direction der Administrativen Statistik (1882), *Die Bevölkerung der im Reichsrathe vertretenen Königreiche und Länder nach Alter und Stand. 4. Heft der 'Ergebnisse der Volkszählung und der mit derselben verbundenen Zählung der häuslichen Nutzthiere vom 31. December 1880'.* Vienna: Kaiserlich Königliche Hof- und Staatsdruckerei (Oesterreichische Statistik, hrsg. von der K. K. Statistischen Central-Commission, Bd. II, Heft 1), pp. 547 and 565.

1890   Bureau der K. K. Statistischen Central-Commission (1893), *Die Ergebnisse der Volkszählung vom 31. December 1890 in den im Reichsrathe vertretenen Königreichen und Ländern. 3. Heft. Die Bevölkerung nach Grössenkategorien der Ortschaften, Stellung zum Wohnungsinhaber, Geschlecht, Alter und Familienstand, Confession, Umgangssprache, Bildungsgrad, Gebrechen.* Vienna: Kaiserlich Königliche Hof- und Staatsdruckerei (Oesterreichische Statistik, hrsg. von der K. K. Statistischen Central-Commission, Bd. XXXII, Heft 3), pp. 60–1.

1900   Bureau der K. K. Statistischen Zentral-Kommission (1903), *Die Ergebnisse der Volkszählung vom 31. Dezember 1900 in den im Reichsrate vertretenen Königreichen und Ländern. 2. Band. 3. Heft. Die Alters- und Familienstandsgliederung, die Bevölkerung nach Altersklassen und der*

Aufenthaltsdauer innerhalb der Grössenkategorien der Ortschaften, die Umgangssprache in Verbindung mit der sozialen Gliederung der Wohnparteien, mit der Alters- und Familienstandsgliederung, mit dem Bildungsgrade nach Altersklassen, mit der Konfession. Vienna: Kaiserlich Königliche Hof- und Staatsdruckerei (Österreichische Statistik, hrsg. von der K. K. Statistischen Zentral-Kommission, Bd. LXIII, Heft 3), p. 33.

1910   Bureau der K. K. Statistischen Zentral-Kommission (1903), *Die Ergebnisse der Volkszählung vom 31. Dezember 1910 in den im Reichsrate vertretenen Königreichen und Ländern. 1. Band. 3. Heft. Die Alters- und Familienstandsgliederung und Aufenthaltsdauer.* Vienna: Kaiserlich Königliche Hof- und Staatsdruckerei (Österreichische Statistik, hrsg. von der K. K. Statistischen Zentral-Kommission, Neue Folge Bd. 1, Heft 3), pp. 38–9.

1920   Statistische Zentralkommission (1921), *Ergebnisse der ausserordentlichen Volkszählung vom 31. Jänner 1920. Alter und Familienstand der Wohnparteien.* Vienna: Österreichische Staatsdruckerei (Beiträge zur Statistik der Republik Österreich, hrsg. von der Statistischen Zentralkommission, Heft 6), p. 49.

1923   No data published.

1934   Bundesamt für Statistik (1935), *Die Ergebnisse der österreichischen Volkszählung vom 22. März 1934. Bundesstaat. Tabellenheft.* Vienna: Österreichische Staatsdruckerei (Statistik des Bundesstaates Österreich, hrsg. vom Bundesamt für Statistik, Heft 2), pp. 8–10.

1939   Statistisches Reichsamt (1941), *Volks-, Berufs- und Betriebszählung vom 17. Mai 1939. Volkszählung. Die Bevölkerung des Deutschen Reichs nach den Ergebnissen der Volkszählung 1939. Heft 2: Geschlecht, Alter und Familienstand der Bevölkerung des Deutschen Reichs. Tabellenteil.* Berlin: Verlag für Sozialpolitik, Wirtschaft und Statistik. Paul Schmidt, pp. 2/6–7, 2/24–5, 2/70–81 (Statistik des Deutschen Reichs, vol. 552,2).

1869–   Helczmanovski, H., ed. (1973), *Beiträge zur Bevölkerungs- und Sozialgeschichte*
1971   *Österreichs. Nebst einem Überblick über die Entwicklung der Bevölkerungs- und Sozialstatistik.* Im Auftrag des Österr. Statist. Zentralamtes hrsg. von H. Helczmanovski. Vienna: Österreichisches Statistisches Zentralamt.

1750–   Bolognese-Leuchtenmüller, B. (1978), *Bevölkerungsentwicklung und Berufs-*
1918   *struktur, Gesundheits- und Fürsorgewesen in Österreich 1750–1918.* (Wirtschafts- und Sozialstatistik Österreich-Ungarns, vol. 1; Materialien zur Wirtschafts- und Sozialgeschichte, vol. 1). Munich: Oldenbourg.

1829–   Österreichisches Statistisches Zentralamt (1979b), *Geschichte und Ergebnisse der*
1979   *zentralen amtlichen Statistik in Österreich 1829–1979. Tabellenanhang.* Beiträge zur Österreichischen Statistik, Vol. 550A. Vienna: Österreichisches Statistisches Zentralamt.

3. Population census results on households and families

1869   K. K. Statistische Central-Commission (1872), *Bevölkerung und Viehstand der im Reichsrathe vertretenen Königreiche und Länder, dann der Militärgränze nach der Zählung vom 31. December 1869. Heft VI. Wohnorte. - Erläuterungen zu den Viehstandstabellen.* Vienna: Kaiserlich-Königliche Hof- und Staatsdruckerei, pp. 42–3 and 48–9 (only for the 5 large towns: Vienna, Graz, Trieste, Prague, and Brünn).

1880   Bureau der K. K. Statistischen Central-Commission (1884), *Die Ergebnisse der Volkszählung vom 31. Dezember 1880 in den im Reichsrath vertretenen Königreichen und Ländern in analytischer Bearbeitung. 6. Heft der 'Ergebnisse der Volkszählung und der mit derselben verbundenen Zählung der häuslichen Nutzthiere vom 31. December 1880'.* Vienna: Kaiserlich Königliche Hof- und Staatsdruckerei (Oesterreichische Statistik, hrsg. von der K. K. Statistischen

Central-Commission, Bd. V, Heft 3), pp. XXX–XXXVIII and 24.

1890   Bureau der K. K. Statistischen Central-Commission (1893), *Die Ergebnisse der Volkszählung vom 31. December 1890 in den im Reichsrathe vertreten Königreichen und Ländern. 4. Heft. Die Wohnungsverhältnisse in den grösseren Städten und ihren Vororten.* Vienna: Kaiserlich Königliche Hof- und Staatsdruckerei (Oesterreichische Statistik, hrsg. von der K. K. Statistischen Central-Commission, Bd. XXXII, Heft 4), pp. XVff. and 2–9.

1900   Bureau der K. K. Statistischen Zentral-Kommission (1904), *Die Ergebnisse der Volkszählung vom 31. Dezember 1900 in den im Reichsrate vertreten Königreichen und Ländern. 1. Heft. Erweiterte Wohnungsaufnahme.* Vienna: Kaiserlich Königliche Hof- und Staatsdruckerei (Österreichische Statistik, hrsg. von der K. K. Statistischen Zentral-Kommission, Bd. LXV, Heft 1).

       Bureau der K. K. Statistischen Zentral-Kommission (1903), *Die Ergebnisse der Volkszählung vom 31. Dezember 1900 in den im Reichsrate vertreten Königreichen und Ländern. 2. Heft. Beschränkte Wohnungsaufnahme.* Vienna: Kaiserlich Königliche Hof- und Staatsdruckerei (Österreichische Statistik, hrsg. von der K. K. Statistischen Zentral-Kommission, Bd. LXV, Heft 2).

       Bureau der K.K. Statistischen Zentral-Kommission (1905), *Die Ergebnisse der Volkszählung vom 31. Dezember 1900 in den im Reichsrate vertreten Königreichen und Ländern. 5. Heft. Die Haushaltungs- und Familienstatistik in den Grosstädten.* Vienna: Kaiserlich Königliche Hof- und Staatsdruckerei (Österreichische Statistik, hrsg. von der K. K. Statistischen Zentral-Kommission, Bd. LXV, Heft 5).

       Bureau der K. K. Statistischen Zentral-Kommission (1905), *Die Ergebnisse der Volkszählung vom 31. Dezember 1900 in den im Reichsrate vertreten Königreichen und Ländern. 6. Heft (Supplement). Die erweiterte Wohnungsaufnahme und die Aufnahme der Häuser in der Stadt Prag und den Vorortgemeinden.* Vienna: Kaiserlich Königliche Hof- und Staatsdruckerei (Österreichische Statistik, hrsg. von der K. K. Statistischen Zentral-Kommission, Bd. LXV, Heft 6 (Supplement)).

1910   Bureau der K. K. Statistischen Zentralkommission (1918), *Die Ergebnisse der Volkszählung vom 31. Dezember 1910 in den im Reichsrate vertreten Königreichen und Ländern. 4. Band. 3. Heft. Haushaltungsstatistik.* Vienna: Kaiserlich Königliche Hof- und Staatsdruckerei (Österreichische Statistik, hrsg. von der K. K. Statistischen Zentral-Kommission, Neue Folge Bd. 4, Heft 3).

1920   Statistische Zentralkommission (1921), *Ergebnisse der ausserordentlichen Volkszählung vom 31. Jänner 1920. Alter und Familienstand, Wohnparteien.* Vienna: Österreichische Staatsdruckerei (Beiträge zur Statistik der Republik Österreich, hrsg. von der Statistischen Zentralkommission, Heft 6).

1923   Bundesamt für Statistik (1923), *Vorläufige Ergebnisse der Volkszählung vom 7. März 1923.* Vienna: Österreichische Staatsdruckerei (Beiträge zur Statistik der Republik Österreich, hrsg. vom Bundesamte für Statistik, Heft 12).

1934   Bundesamt für Statistik (1935), *Die Ergebnisse der österreichischen Volkszählung vom 22. März 1934. Bundesstaat. Textheft.* Vienna: Österreichische Staatsdruckerei (Statistik des Bundesstaates Österreich, hrsg. vom Bundesamt für Statistik, Heft 1), pp. 74–80 (Familienstatistik), pp. 80–4 (Haushaltungsstatistik).

       Bundesamt für Statistik (1935), *Die Ergebnisse der österreichischen Volkszählung vom 22. März 1934. Bundesstaat. Tabellenheft.* Vienna: Österreichische Staatsdruckerei (Statistik des Bundesstaates Österreich, hrsg. vom Bundesamt für Statistik, Heft 2), pp. 396–401 (Familienstatistik), pp. 401–5 (Haushaltungsstatistik).

1939   Statistisches Reichsamt (1944), *Volks-, Berufs- und Betriebszählung vom 17. Mai 1939. Die Haushaltungen im Deutschen Reich.* Berlin: Verlag für Sozialpolitik,

Wirtschaft und Statistik. Paul Schmidt (Statistik des Deutschen Reichs, vol. 553). Statistisches Reichsamt (1943), *Volks-, Berufs- und Betriebszählung vom 17. Mai 1939. Die Familien im Deutschen Reich. Die Ehen nach der Zahl der geborenen Kinder.* Berlin: Verlag für Sozialpolitik, Wirtschaft und Statistik. Paul Schmidt (Statistik des Deutschen Reichs, vol. 554).

1869–
1971
Helczmanovski, H., ed. (1973), *Beiträge zur Bevölkerungs- und Sozialgeschichte Österreichs. Nebst einem Überblick über die Entwicklung der Bevölkerungs- und Sozialstatistik.* Im Auftrag des Österr. Statist. Zentralamtes hrsg. von H. Helczmanovski. Vienna: Österreichisches Statistisches Zentralamt.

1750–
1918
Bolognese-Leuchtenmüller, B. (1978), *Bevölkerungsentwicklung und Berufsstruktur, Gesundheits- und Fürsorgewesen in Österreich 1750–1918.* (Wirtschafts- und Sozialstatistik Österreich-Ungarns, vol. 1; Materialien zur Wirtschafts- und Sozialgeschichte, vol. 1). Munich: Oldenbourg.

1829–
1979
Österreichisches Statistisches Zentralamt (1979b), *Geschichte und Ergebnisse der zentralen amtlichen Statistik in Österreich 1829–1979. Tabellenanhang.* Beiträge zur Österreichischen Statistik, vol. 550A. Vienna: Österreichisches Statistisches Zentralamt.

BELGIUM

1. Vital statistics

Institut National de Statistique (1–, 1870–), *Annuaire Statistique de la Belgique.* Brussels: INS.

—— (1–, 1936–), *Bulletin de Statistique.* Brussels: INS.

—— (1965), *Climatologie–Territoire–Démographie et Santé Publique–Enseignement 1900–1961.* Brussels: INS.

2. Population structure by age, sex, and marital status

1846
Ministre de l'Intérieur (1849), *Statistique de la Belgique. Population. Recensement Général (15 Octobre 1846).* Brussels, p. 434.

1856
Ministre de l'Intérieur (1861), *Statistique de la Belgique. Population. Recensement Général (31 Décembre 1856).* Brussels, p. 210.

1866
Ministre de l'Intérieur (1870), *Statistique de la Belgique. Population. Recensement Général (31 Décembre 1866).* Brussels, p. 472.

1880
Ministre de l'Intérieur (1884), *Statistique de la Belgique. Population. Recensement Général (31 Décembre 1880).* Brussels, pp. 910–1.

1890
Ministre de l'Intérieur et de l'Instruction Publique (1893), *Statistique de la Belgique. Population. Recensement Général du 31 Décembre 1890.* Vol. II. Brussels, pp. 288–9.

1900
Ministre de l'Intérieur et de l'Instruction Publique (1903), *Statistique de la Belgique. Population. Recensement Général du 31 Décembre 1900.* Vol. II. Brussels, pp. 358–9.

1910
Ministre de l'Intérieur (1913), *Statistique de la Belgique. Population. Recensement Général du 31 Décembre 1910.* Vol. III. Brussels, pp. 588–9.

1920
Ministre de l'Intérieur et de l'Hygiène (1926), *Statistique de la Belgique. Population. Recensement Général du 31 Décembre 1920.* Vol. III. Brussels, pp. 228–9.

1930
Royaume de Belgique. Ministère de l'Intérieur. Office Central de Statistique (1937), *Population. Recensement Général au 31 Décembre 1930, Tome IV.* Brussels, pp. 108–9.

1947
Royaume de Belgique. Ministère des Affaires Économiques et des Classes Moyennes. Institut National de Statistique (1951), *Recensement Général de la*

Population, de l'Industrie et du Commerce au 31 Décembre 1947. Vol. V: *Répartition de la Population par Âge*. Brussels, pp. 78–81.

3. Population census results on households and families

1846   Ministre de l'Intérieur (1849), *Statistique de la Belgique. Population. Recensement Général (15 Octobre 1846)*. Brussels, pp. XXVI–XXVIII and 249.

1856   Ministre de l'Intérieur (1861), *Statistique de la Belgique. Population. Recensement Général (31 Décembre 1856)*. Brussels, pp. XIV–XV and 158–9.

1866   Ministre de l'Intérieur (1870), *Statistique de la Belgique. Population. Recensement Général (31 Décembre 1866)*. Brussels, pp. XVIII–XIX, 172–3 and 190.

1880   Ministre de l'Intérieur (1884), *Statistique de la Belgique. Population. Recensement Général (31 Décembre 1880)*. Brussels, pp. XX–XXI and 172–3.

1890   Ministre de l'Intérieur et de l'Instruction Publique (1893), *Statistique de la Belgique. Population. Recensement Général du 31 Décembre 1890*. Vol. I. Brussels, pp. XVIII–XIX and 174–5.

1900   Ministre de l'Intérieur et de l'Instruction Publique (1903), *Statistique de la Belgique. Population. Recensement Général du 31 Décembre 1900*. Vol. I. Brussels, pp. XXIV–XXVI and 184–5.

1910   Ministre de l'Intérieur (1916, 1912), *Statistique de la Belgique. Population. Recensement Général du 31 Décembre 1910*. Vol. I (1916). Brussels, pp. 167–70, 234–8; Vol. II (1912), pp. 186–7.

1920   Ministre de l'Intérieur et de l'Hygiène (1926, 1925), *Statistique de la Belgique. Population. Recensement Général du 31 Décembre 1920*. Vol. I. Brussels, pp. 37–40, 87–92 and 109–17; Vol. II (1925), pp. 92–3.

1930   Royaume de Belgique. Ministère de l'Intérieur. Office Central de Statistique (1934), *Recensement Général au 31 Décembre 1930*. Vol. I (1934) *Population*. Brussels, pp. 6 and 158–66; Vol. VI (1937) *Population*; Vol. VIII (1938) *Recensement des Familles*.

1947   Royaume de Belgique. Ministère des Affaires Économiques et des Classes Moyennes. Institut National de Statistique (1951), *Recensement Général de la Population, de l'Industrie et du Commerce au 31 Décembre 1947*. Vol. VI: *Recensement des Ménages*. Brussels.

       Royaume de Belgique. Ministère des Affaires Économiques et des Classes Moyennes. Institut National de Statistique (1951), *Recensement Général de la Population, de l'Industrie et du Commerce au 31 Décembre 1947*. Vol. VII: Recensement *des Familles*. Brussels.

1900–   Institut National de Statistique (1965), *Climatologie–Territoire–Démographie et*
1961   *Santé Publique–Enseignement 1900–1961*. Brussels: INS, pp. 18–9.

CZECHOSLOVAKIA

1. Vital statistics

Czech Statistical Office (19..–), *Czech Statistical Yearbook 19...* Prague: Central Statistical Office (CSO).

—— (1998), *Czech Demographic Handbook*. Prague: Central Statistical Office (CSO), Population Statistics Division.

Český statistický úřad (CSU) (1997), *Fakta o Sociální Situaci v Česke Republice*. (Facts on the Social Situation in the Czech Republic). Prague: CSU.

Federální Statistický Úřad (FSU) (1985), *Historická Statistická Ročenka ČSSR*. (Historical Statistics of the CSSR). Prague: SNTL.

2. Population structure by age, sex, and marital status

1921 Státni Úrad Statistický (1924), *Predbezne vysledky sčitáni lidu z 15. unora 1921. Recensement de la Population dans la République Tchécoslovaque le 15 février 1921 (Census of population in the Republic of Czechoslovakia, February 15, 1921). (La statistique Tchécoslovaque, VIe série, recensement de la population).* Tome I. Prague, pp. 196–207.

1930 Státni Úrad Statistický (1934), *Sčitáni Lidu v Republice Československé ze dne 1. Prosince 1930. Díl I. Růst, koncentrace a hustota obyvatelstva, pohlaví, věkové rozvrstvení, rodinný stav, státní příslušnost, národnost, náboženské vyznání.* Prague: Státni Tiskarna v Praze, pp. 135–44.

1921– Federální Statistický Úřad (FSU) (1985), *Historická Statistická Ročenka ČSSR.*
1950 Prague: SNTL.

1921– Czech Statistical Office (1998), *Czech Demographic Handbook.* Prague: Central
1991 Statistical Office (CSO), Population Statistics Division, pp. 35ff., 128–39.

3. Population census results on households and families

1921 Státni Úrad Statistický (1927), *Predbezne vysledky sčitáni lidu z 15. unora 1921. Recensement de la Population dans la République Tchécoslovaque le 15 février 1921 (Census of population in the Republic of Czechoslovakia, February 15, 1921). (La statistique Tchécoslovaque, VIe série, recensement de la population).* Vol. III. Prague.

1930 Státni Úrad Statistický (1938), *Sčitáni Lidu v Republice Československé ze dne 1. Prosince 1930. Díl IV. Část 2. Domácnosti a rodiny.* Prague: Státni Tiskarna v Praze.

1921– Federální Statistický Úřad (FSU) (1985), *Historická Statistická Ročenka ČSSR.*
1950 Prague: SNTL, pp. 66, 433, 634.

1921– Czech Statistical Office (1998), *Czech Demographic Handbook.* Prague: Central
1991 Statistical Office (CSO), Population Statistics Division, pp. 127, 145–6.

DENMARK

1. Vital statistics

Danmarks Statistik (1–, 1896–), *Statistisk årbog.* Copenhagen: Danmarks Statistik.

—— (1985), *Danske byers folketal 1801–1981.* Copenhagen: Danmarks Statistik.

—— (1964a), *Folketal, areal og klima 1901–60.* Statistiske Undersøgelser no. 10. Copenhagen: Danmarks Statistik.

—— (1964b), *Spædbørnsdødeligheden i Danmark 1931–60.* Statistiske Undersøgelser no. 11. English ed. 1965. Copenhagen: Danmarks Statistik.

—— (1965a), *Nyere tendenser i dødeligheden.* Statistiske Undersøgelser no. 15. Copenhagen: Danmarks Statistik.

—— (1965b), *Fertilitetsforskelle i Danmark.* Statistiske Undersøgelser no. 18. Copenhagen: Danmarks Statistik.

—— (1966), *Befolkningsudvikling og sundhedsforhold 1901–60.* Statistiske Undersøgelser no. 19. Copenhagen: Danmarks Statistik.

—— (1968), *Fertiliteten udenfor ægteskab.* Statistiske Undersøgelser no. 21. Copenhagen: Danmarks Statistik.

Johansen, H. (1985), *Dansk økonomisk statistik 1814–1980.* Danmarks historie, vol. 9. Copenhagen: Gyldendal.

Statens Statistiske Bureau (1905), *Befolkningsforholdene i Danmark i det 19. Aarhundrede. La population du Danemark pendant le 19ᵉ siècle.* Udgivet af Statens Statistiske Bureau. Publié par le Bureau de Statistique de l'État. Statistisk Tabelværk Femte Række, Litra A, Nr. 5. Copenhagen: Bianco Lunos Bogtrykkeri.

2. Population structure by age, sex, and marital status

1855   Statistisk Bureau (1856), *Tabeller over Folkemængden efter Kjön, ugift eller gift og Alder i Kongeriget Danmark, Hertugdömmet Slesvig og Hertugdömmerne Holsteen og Lauenborg, den 1ˢᵗᵉ Februar 1855.* Copenhagen (Statistisk Tabelværk. Ny Række, Tolvte Bind (Statistical Tables, New Series, vol. 12)), pp. 132–33.

1860   Statistisk Bureau (1863), *Tabeller over Folkemængden i Kongeriget Danmark, Hertugdömmet Slesvig, Hertugdömmet Holsteen og Hertugdömmet Lauenborg, efter Alder, Kjön og æteskabelig Stilling samt efter Næringsvei og Stilling den 1ˢᵗᵉ Februar 1860.* Copenhagen (Statistisk Tabelværk. Tredie Række, Attende Bind (Statistical Tables, Series 3, vol. 8)), pp. 46–7.

1870   Statistisk Bureau (1871), *Tabeller over Folkemængden i Kongeriget Danmark den 1ˢᵗᵉ Februar 1870.* Copenhagen (Statistisk Tabelværk. Tredie Række, Förste Bind (Statistical Tables, Series 3, vol. 1)), pp. 66–7.

1880   Statistisk Bureau (1883), *Folkemængden i Kongeriget Danmark den 1ˢᵗᵉ Februar 1880.* Copenhagen (Danmarks Statistik. Statistisk Tabelværk. Fjerde Række, Litra A. Nr. 3 (Statistical Tables, Series 4, Letter A. Nr. 1)), pp. 87 and 89.

1890   Statistisk Bureau (1893), *Tabellariske Oversigter over Folkemængdens Fordeling efter Alder, Kjøn, ægteskabelig Stilling, Troessamfund og Næringsveje m.m. samt Arealet og Antallet af Gaarde og Huse i Kongeriget Danmark den 1ˢᵗᵉ Februar 1890 (Tableaux de la population du Royaume de Danemark le 1ᵉʳ février 1890 par âge, par sexe, par état civil, par confession, par profession etc. ainsi que de la superficie et des maisons).* Copenhagen (Danmarks Statistik. Statistisk Tabelværk. Fjerde Række, Litra A. Nr. 8, b (Statistical Tables, Series 4, Letter A. Nr. 8, b)), pp. 136–7.

1901   Statistisk Departement (1903), *Folketællingen i Kongeriget Danmark den 1. Februar 1901. Første Del (Population du Royaume de Danemark le 1ᵉʳ Février 1901. Première partie).* Copenhagen: Bianco Lunos Bogtrykkeri (Danmarks Statistik. Statistisk Tabelværk. Femte Række, Litra A. Nr. 3 (Statistical Tables, Series 5, Letter A. Nr. 3)), pp. 96–7.

1911   Statistisk Departement (1913), *Folketællingen i Kongeriget Danmark den 1. Februar 1911. Første Del (Population du Royaume de Danemark le 1ᵉʳ Février 1911. Première partie).* Copenhagen (Danmarks Statistik. Statistisk Tabelværk. Femte Række, Litra A. Nr. 9 (Statistical Tables, Series 5, Letter A. Nr. 9)), pp. 98–9.

1921   Statistisk Departement (1925), *Folketællingen i Kongeriget Danmark den 1. Februar 1921 (Recensement Général de la Population du Danemark le 1ᵉʳ Février 1921).* Copenhagen: H. H. Thieles Bogtrykkeri (Danmarks Statistik. Statistisk Tabelværk. Femte Række, Litra A. Nr. 16 (Statistical Tables, Series 5, Letter A. Nr. 16)), pp. 22–3.

1930   Statistisk Departement (1935), *Folketællingen i Kongeriget Danmark den 5. November 1930 (Recensement Général de la Population du Danemark 5 Novembre 1930).* Copenhagen: Bianco Lunos Bogtrykkeri (Danmarks Statistik. Statistisk Tabelværk. Femte Række, Litra A. Nr. 20 (Statistical Tables, Series 5, Letter A. Nr. 20)), pp. 22–3.

1940   Statistiske Departement (1944), *Folketællingen den 5. November 1940 og Befolningens Bevægelser 1931–40 (Recensement Général de la Population du*

Danemark 5 Novembre 1940 et Mouvement de la Population 1931–40). Copenhagen: Bianco Lunos Bogtrykkeri (Danmarks Statistik. Statistisk Tabelværk. Femte Række, Litra A. Nr. 22 (Statistical Tables, Series 5, Letter A. Nr. 22)), pp. 28–9.

1800– Statens Statistiske Bureau (1905), *Befolkningsforholdene i Danmark i det 19.*
1901 *Aarhundrede (La population du Danemark pendant le 19ᵉ siècle)*. (Statistisk Tabelværk 5. Ser., Letter A, no. 5). Copenhagen: Bianco Lunos Bogtrykkeri.

1901– Danmarks Statistisk (1966), *Befolkningsudvikling og sundhedsforhold 1901–60.*
1960 Statistiske Undersøgelser no. 19. Copenhagen: Danmarks Statistik.

1814– Johansen, H. (1985), *Dansk økonomisk statistik 1814–1980.* (Danmarks historie,
1980 vol. 9). Copenhagen: Gyldendal.

3. Population census results on households and families

1834 No household data available.

1840 *Statistisk Tabelværk, udgivet af den dertil allernaadigst anordnede Commission. Siette Hæfte, indeholdene an detailleret Fremstilling af Folkemængden i Kongeriget Danmark d. 1ste Februar 1840, summariske Tabeller over Folkemængden til samme Tid i Hertugdommerne Slesvig, Holsteen og Lauenborg, en detailleret tabellarisk Fremstilling af Folkemængden paa Færøerne, i Island og Grønland samt i de Danske Besiddelser in Vestindien, deels i 1834 og deels i 1835, endelig Tabeller over Antallet af Ægteviede, Fodte og Døde i Danmark, med Færøerne og Island, for Aarene 1834 til 1839.* Copenhagen: Trykt i unos Bogtrykkeri, 1842, pp. IV–V.

1845 *Statistisk Tabelværk, udgivet af den dertil allernaadigst anordnede Commission. Tiende Hæfte, indeholdene an detailleret Fremstilling af Folkemængden i Kongeriget Danmark den 1ste Februar 1845, summariske Tabeller over Folkemængden til samme Tid i Hertugdommerne Slesvig, Holsteen og Lauenborg, en detailleret tabellarisk Fremstilling af Folkemængden paa Færøerne, i Island, Grønland og de Danske Besiddelser in Vestindien, deels i 1840 og deels i 1841, samt Tabeller over Antallet af Ægteviede, Fodte og Døde i Danmark, med Færøerne og Island, for Aarene 1840 til 1841.* Copenhagen: Trykt i unos Bogtrykkeri, 1846, pp. V–VI.

1850 No household data available.

1855 Statistisk Bureau (1857), *Tabeller over Folkemængden efter Kjön, ugift eller gift og Alder i Kongeriget Danmark, Hertugdömmet Slesvig og Hertugdömmerne Holsteen og Lauenborg, den Iˢᵗᵉ Februar 1855.* Copenhagen (Statistisk Tabelværk. Ny Række, Tolvte Bind (Statistical Tables, New Series, vol. 12)), pp. XXIV–XXIX.

1860 Statistisk Bureau (1863), *Tabeller over Folkemængden i Kongeriget Danmark, Hertugdömmet Slesvig, Hertugdömmet Holsteen og Hertugdömmet Lauenborg, efter Alder, Kjön og æteskabelig Stilling samt efter Næringsvei og Stilling den Iˢᵗᵉ Februar 1860.* Copenhagen (Statistisk Tabelværk. Tredie Række, Attende Bind (Statistical Tables, Series 3, vol. 8)), pp. 16–9.

1870 Statistisk Bureau (1871), *Tabeller over Folkemængden i Kongeriget Danmark den Iˢᵗᵉ Februar 1870.* Copenhagen (Statistisk Tabelværk. Tredie Række, Attende Bind (Statistical Tables, Series 3, vol. 8)), pp. IX–X.

1880 Statistisk Bureau (1883), *Folkemængden i Kongeriget Danmark den Iˢᵗᵉ Februar 1880.* Copenhagen (Danmarks Statistik. Statistisk Tabelværk. Fjerde Række, Litra A. Nr. 3 (Statistical Tables, Series 4, Letter A. Nr. 3)), pp. LXVII–LXXI.

1890 Statistisk Bureau (1894), *Hovedresultaterne af Folketællingen i Kongeriget Danmark den 1ˢᵗᵉ Februar 1890, med tilhørende Befolkningskaart. (Résultats généraux du recensement en Danemark le 1ᵉʳ Février 1890, avec deux cartes démographiques).* Copenhagen: Bianco Lunos Kgl. Hof-Bogtrykkeri (Danmarks

Statistik. Statistisk Tabelværk. Fjerde Række, Litra A. Nr. 8, a (Statistical Tables, Series 4, Letter A. Nr. 8, a)), pp. CXXXVff.

1901   Statistisk Departement (1903), *Folketællingen i Kongeriget Danmark den 1. Februar 1901. Første Del (Population du Royaume de Danemark le 1ᵉʳ Février 1901. Première partie)*. Copenhagen: Bianco Lunos Bogtrykkeri (Danmarks Statistik. Statistisk Tabelværk. Femte Række, Litra A. Nr. 3 (Statistical Tables, Series 5, Letter A. Nr. 3)), pp. 33*–7* and 120–4.

1911   Statistisk Departement (1913), *Folketællingen i Kongeriget Danmark den 1. Februar 1911. Første Del (Population du Royaume de Danemark le 1ᵉʳ Février 1911. Première partie)*. Copenhagen (Danmarks Statistik. Statistisk Tabelværk. Femte Række, Litra A. Nr. 9 (Statistical Tables, Series 5, Letter A. Nr. 9), pp. 68*–73* and 123–7.

1921   Statistisk Departement (1925), *Folketællingen i Kongeriget Danmark den 1. Februar 1921 (Recensement Général de la Population du Danemark le 1ᵉʳ Février 1921)*. Copenhagen: H. H. Thieles Bogtrykkeri (Danmarks Statistik. Statistisk Tabelværk. Femte Række, Litra A. Nr. 16 (Statistical Tables, Series 5, Letter A. Nr. 16), pp. 67*–73* and 66–73.

1930   Statistisk Departement (1935), *Folketællingen i Kongeriget Danmark den 5. November 1930 (Recensement Général de la Population du Danemark 5 Novembre 1930)*. Copenhagen: Bianco Lunos Bogtrykkeri (Danmarks Statistik. Statistisk Tabelværk. Femte Række, Litra A. Nr. 20 (Statistical Tables, Series 5, Letter A. Nr. 20)), pp. 38*–42* and 52–63.

1940   Nothing found for this year. Households by size must have been published (cf. Danmarks Statistik 1966).

1800–   Statens Statistiske Bureau (1905), *Befolkningsforholdene i Danmark i det 19.*
1901   *Aarhundrede (La population du Danemark pendant le 19ᵉ siècle)*. (Statistisk Tabelværk 5. Ser., Letter A, no. 5). Copenhagen: Bianco Lunos Bogtrykkeri.

1901–   Danmarks Statistisk (1966), *Befolkningsudvikling og sundhedsforhold 1901–60.*
1960   Statistiske Undersøgelser no. 19. Copenhagen: Danmarks Statistik. (private households by size and members)

1814–   Johansen, H. (1985), *Dansk økonomisk statistik 1814–1980*. (Danmarks historie,
1980   vol. 9). Copenhagen: Gyldendal.

1901–   Danmarks Statistik (1976), *Levevilkår i Danmark 1976*. Copenhagen: Danmarks
1970   Statistik and the National Institute of Social Research (Socialforskningsinstituttet).

FINLAND

1. Vital statistics

Central Statistical Office (n.s. 1–, 1903–), *Suomen tillastollinen vuosikirja/Statistisk årsbok för Finland/Statistical Yearbook of Finland*. Helsinki: CSO.

—— (1–, 1924–), *Bulletin of Statistics*. Helsinki: CSO. Quarterly.

—— (1979), *Population by Industry and Commune in 1880–1975*. Statistical Surveys, No. 63. Helsinki: CSO.

—— (1987), *Population in Finland: Past, Present, Future*. Helsinki: CSO.

Kannisto, V. (1986), *Geographic Differentials in Infant Mortality in Finland 1871–1983*. Studies, No. 126. Helsinki: CSO.

—— (1990), *Mortality of the Elderly in the Late 19th- and Early 20th-Century Finland*. Studies No. 175. Helsinki: CSO.

Kolari, R. (1980), *Cohort Mortality in Finland from 1851*. Studies, No. 57. (Summary in English). Helsinki: CSO.

Myrskylä, P. (1978), *Development and Regional Differences of Fertility in Finland.* Studies, No. 36. (Summary in English). Helsinki: CSO.

Statistics Finland, International Business Statistics (1999), *Trends. Ten-Year Review.* Helsinki: Statistics Finland, International Business Statistics (IBS).

Suomenmaan Virallinen Tilasto (1902), *Pääpiirteet Suomen väestötilastosta vuosina 1750–1890. II. Väestön muutokset* (Éléments démographiques principaux de la Finlande pour les années 1750–1890. II. Mouvement de la population). Suomenmaan Virallinen Tilasto, Väkiluvun-Tilastoa VI, 33/Official Statistics of Finland ser. VI population statistics, vol. 33. Helsingissä: Keisarillisen Senaatin Kirjapainossa.

—— (1909), *Pääpiirteet Suomen väestötilastosta vuosina 1750–1890. III. Esitys* (Éléments démographiques principaux de la Finlande pour les années 1750–1890. III. Texte). Suomenmaan Virallinen Tilasto, Väkiluvun-Tilastoa VI, 41/Official Statistics of Finland ser. VI population statistics, vol. 41. Helsingissä: Keisarillisen Senaatin Kirjapainossa.

Tilastollinen päätoimisto (1958), *Vuoden 1950 yleinen väestölaskenta. 1950 population census.* Volume IX. English Summary. Suomen virallinen tilasto. VI, Väestötilastao: C 102. Helsinki:Valtioneuvoston lkirjapaino.

Vattula, K. (1983), *Suomen taloushistoria 3. Historiallinen tilasto.* (The economic history of Finland 3. Historical statistics). Helsinki: Kustannusosakeyhtiö Tammi.

2. *Population structure by age, sex, and marital status*

1865   Tilastollinen päätoimisto (1870), *Befolknings-statistik. Första häftet. Finlands befolkning den 31 December 1865.* Helsingfors: å Kejserliga Senatens tryckeri (Bidrag till Finlands Officiela Statistik, VI Befolknings-statistik; No. 1), pp. 32–3 (text) and XIV–XV (tables).

1870   Census was only conducted in the large cities.

1875   Tilastollinen päätoimisto (1880), *Befolknings-statistik. Finlands folkmängd den 31 December 1875 samt öfversigt af folkmändsförändringarna åren 1975–1877.* Helsingfors: å Kejserliga Senatens tryckeri (Bidrag till Finlands Officiela Statistik, VI Befolknings-statistik; No. 5), pp. 5–9 (text) and 14–53 (tables).

1880   Tilastollinen päätoimisto (1882), *Finlands folkmängd den 31 December 1880. 1:sta häftet. Population de la Finlande au 31 Décembre 1880. Première partie.* Helsingfors: å Kejserliga Senatens tryckeri (Bidrag till Finlands Officiela Statistik, VI Befolknings-statistik, No. 9), pp. 36–40.

1890   Tilastollinen päätoimisto (1894), *Finlands folkmängd den 31 December 1890. Population de la Finlande au 31 Décembre 1890.* Helsingfors: Finska Litteratur-Sällskapets tryckeri (Bidrag till Finlands Officiela Statistik, VI Befolknings-statistik), pp. 16ff. (text) and 43–6 (tables).

1900   Tilastollinen päätoimisto (1905), *Öfversikt af Finlands folkmängd den 31 December 1900. Jämte upgifter från Föregående Allmänna Folkräkningar i Landet. Aperçu de la Population de la Finlande au 31 Décembre 1900 et données tirées des recensements généraux précédents.* Helsingfors: Kejserliga Senatens tryckeri (Bidrag till Finlands Officiella Statistik, VI Befolkningsstatistik, 37), pp. 35ff. (text) and 44ff. (tables).

1910   Tilastollinen päätoimisto (1915), *Finlands folkmängd den 31 December 1910 (Enligt Församlingarnas Kyrkoböcker). I Delen: Folkmängden samt befolkningens fördelning efter kön, ålder, civilstånd, trossamfund, bildningsgrad och födelseort jämte den frånvarande befolkningens fördelning efter vistelseort.*

Population de la Finlande au 31 Décembre 1920 (selon les régistres ecclésiastiques). Tome II: Nombre de la population, répartition par le sexe, l'âge, l'état civil, la langue, la confession, le degré d'instruction, le lieu de naissance ainsi que le domicile de la population absente. Helsingfors: Kejserliga Senatens tryckeri (Bidrag till Finlands Officiella Statistik, VI Befolkningsstatistik, 45), pp. 60ff. (text) and 136–9 (tables).

1920 Tilastollinen päätoimisto (1923), *Finlands folkmängd den 31 December 1920 (Enligt Församlingarnas Kyrkoböcker). II Delen: Fördelning efter kön, ålder, civilstånd, språk, trosbekännelse, bildningsgrad och födelseort äfvensom den franvarande befolkningens fördelning efter vistelseort. Population de la Finlande au 31 Décembre 1920 (selon les régistres ecclésiastiques). Tome I: Répartition par le sexe, l'âge, l'état civil, la confession, le degré d'instruction, le lieu de naissance ainsi que le domicile de la population absente.* Helsingfors: Statsrådets tryckeri (Finlands Officiella Statistik, VI Befolkningsstatistik, 56:2), pp. 16ff. (text) and 2–4 (tables).

1930 Tilastollinen päätoimisto (1933), *Suomen väestö joulukuun 31 p:nä 1930 (Seurakunnankirjojen ja sivilirekisterin mukaan). II Nide: Ryhmitys sukupuolen, iän, siviilisäädyn, uskontokunnan, sivistyskannan ja syntymäpaikan mukaan ynnä poissaolevan väestön joitus olinpaikan mukaan. Population de la Finlande au 31 Décembre 1930 (selon les régistres ecclésiastiques et le régistre civil). Tome II: Répartition par le sexe, l'âge, l'état civil, la confession, le degré d'instruction, le lieu de naissance ainsi que le domicile de la population absente.* Helsinki: Valtioneuvoston Kirjapaino (Suomen Virallinen Tilasto - Finlands Officiella Statistik, VI Väestötilastoa - Befolkningsstatistik, 76: 2), pp. 17ff. (text) and 2–4 (tables).

1940 Tilastollinen päätoimisto (1945), *Suomen väestö joulukuun 31 p:nä 1940 (Seurakunnankirjojen ja sivilirekisterin mukaan). I Nide: Väkiliku ja kielisuhteet, ryhmitys sukupuolen, iän, siviilisäädyn, uskontokunnan ja syntymäpaikan mukaan ynnä poissaolevan väestön jaoitus olinpaikan mukaan. Population de la Finlande au 31 Décembre 1940 (selon les régistres ecclésiastiques et le régistre civil). Tome I: Nombre de la population, répartition par la langue, le sexe, l'âge, l'état civil, la confession, le lieu de naissance ainsi que le domicile de la population absente.* Helsinki: Valtioneuvoston Kirjapaino (Suomen Virallinen Tilasto - Finlands Officiella Statistik, VI Väestötilastoa - Befolkningsstatistik, 98: 1), pp. 34ff. (text) and 28–9 (tables).

1750– Suomenmaan Virallinen Tilasto (1899), *Pääpiirteet Suomen väestötilastosta*
1890 *vuosina 1750–1890. I. Väestön tila (Éléments démographiques principaux de la Finlande pour les années 1750–1890. I. État de la population)* (Suomenmaan Virallinen Tilasto, Väkiluvun-Tilastoa VI, 29 (Official Statistics of Finland ser. VI population statistics, vol. 29)). Helsinki.

1750– Suomenmaan Virallinen Tilasto (1909), *Pääpiirteet Suomen väestötilastosta*
1890 *vuosina 1750–1890. III. Esitys (Éléments démographiques principaux de la Finlande pour les années 1750–1890. III. Texte)* (Suomenmaan Virallinen Tilasto, Väkiluvun-Tilastoa VI, 41 (Official Statistics of Finland ser. VI population statistics, vol. 41)). Helsinki.

3. Population census results on households and families

1865 Tilastollinen päätoimisto (1870), *Befolknings-statistik. Första häftet. Finlands befolkning den 31 December 1865.* Helsingfors: å Kejserliga Senatens tryckeri (Bidrag till Finlands Officiela Statistik, VI Befolknings-statistik; No. 1), pp. 22–3 (text, nothing in tables).

1870 Tilastollinen päätoimisto (1874), *Befolknings-statistik. Folkräkningen i Mars 1870 i städerna Helsingfors, Åbo, Wiborg och Uleåborg.* Helsingfors: å Kejserliga

Senatens tryckeri (Bidrag till Finlands Officiela Statistik, VI Andra Serien), pp. XX–XXVI (text only). (Census was only conducted in the large cities).

1875 Tilastollinen päätoimisto (1880), *Befolknings-statistik. Finlands folkmängd den 31 December 1875 samt öfversigt af folkmändsförändringarna åren 1975–1877.* Helsingfors: å Kejserliga Senatens tryckeri (Bidrag till Finlands Officiela Statistik, VI Befolknings-statistik; No. 5) (nothing available).

1880 Tilastollinen päätoimisto (1885), *Finlands folkmängd den 31 December 1880. Senare häftet. Population de la Finlande au 31 Décembre 1880. Deuxième partie.* Helsingfors: å Kejserliga Senatens tryckeri (Bidrag till Finlands Officiela Statistik, VI Befolknings-statistik, No. 11), pp. 1–2 (text) and 2–3 (table).

1890 Tilastollinen päätoimisto (1894), *Finlands folkmängd den 31 December 1890. Population de la Finlande au 31 Décembre 1890.* Helsingfors: Finska Litteratur-Sällskapets tryckeri (Bidrag till Finlands Officiela Statistik, VI Befolknings-statistik), pp. 34–5 (text) and 84–5 (tables).

1900 Tilastollinen päätoimisto (1905), *Öfversikt af Finlands folkmängd den 31 December 1900. Jämte upgifter från Föregående Allmänna Folkräkningar i Landet. Aperçu de la Population de la Finlande au 31 Décembre 1900 et données tirées des recensements généraux précédents.* Helsingfors: Kejserliga Senatens tryckeri (Bidrag till Finlands Officiella Statistik, VI Befolkningsstatistik, 37), pp. 147ff. (text) and 203ff. (tables).

1910 Tilastollinen päätoimisto (1915), *Finlands folkmängd den 31 December 1910 (Enligt Församlingarnas Kyrkoböcker). I Delen: Folkmängden samt befolkningens fördelning efter kön, ålder, civilstånd, trossamfund, bildningsgrad och födelseort jämte den frånvarande befolkningens fördelning efter vistelseort. Population de la Finlande au 31 Décembre 1920 (selon les régistres ecclésiastiques). Tome II: Nombre de la population, répartition par le sexe, l'âge, l'état civil, la langue, la confession, le degré d'instruction, le lieu de naissance ainsi que le domicile de la population absente.* Helsingfors: Kejserliga Senatens tryckeri (Bidrag till Finlands Officiella Statistik, VI Befolkningsstatistik, 45) (no data given).

1920 Tilastollinen päätoimisto (1923), *Finlands folkmängd den 31 December 1920 (Enligt Församlingarnas Kyrkoböcker). II Delen: Fördelning efter kön, ålder, civilstånd, språk, trosbekännelse, bildningsgrad och födelseort äfvensom den franvarande befolkningens fördelning efter vistelseort. Population de la Finlande au 31 Décembre 1920 (selon les régistres ecclésiastiques). Tome I: Répartition par le sexe, l'âge, l'état civil, la confession, le degré d'instruction, le lieu de naissance ainsi que le domicile de la population absente.* Helsingfors: Statsrådets tryckeri (Finlands Officiella Statistik, VI Befolkningsstatistik, 56: 2) (no data given).

1930 Tilastollinen päätoimisto (1933), *Suomen väestö joulukuun 31 p:nä 1930 (Seurakunnankirjojen ja sivilirekisterin mukaan). II Nide: Ryhmitys sukupuolen, iän, siviilisäädyn, uskontokunnan, sivistyskannan ja syntymäpaikan mukaan ynnä poissaolevan väestön joitus olinpaikan mukaan. Population de la Finlande au 31 Décembre 1930 (selon les régistres ecclésiastiques et le régistre civil). Tome II: Répartition par le sexe, l'âge, l'état civil, la confession, le degré d'instruction, le lieu de naissance ainsi que le domicile de la population absente.* Helsinki: Valtioneuvoston Kirjapaino (Suomen Virallinen Tilasto - Finlands Officiella Statistik, VI Väestötilastoa - Befolkningsstatistik, 76: 2) (no data given).

1940 Tilastollinen päätoimisto (1945), *Suomen väestö joulukuun 31 p:nä 1940 (Seurakunnankirjojen ja sivilirekisterin mukaan). I Nide: Väkiliku ja kielisuhteet, ryhmitys sukupuolen, iän, siviilisäädyn, uskontokunnan ja syntymäpaikan mukaan ynnä poissaolevan väestön jaoitus olinpaikan mukaan. Population de la Finlande au 31 Décembre 1940 (selon les régistres ecclésiastiques et le régistre civil).*

Tome I: Nombre de la population, répartition par la langue, le sexe, l'âge, l'état civil, la confession, le lieu de naissance ainsi que le domicile de la population absente. Helsinki: Valtioneuvoston Kirjapaino (Suomen Virallinen Tilasto - Finlands Officiella Statistik, VI Väestötilastoa - Befolkningsstatistik, 98:1) (no data given).

1750–
1890 Suomenmaan Virallinen Tilasto (1899), *Pääpiirteet Suomen väestötilastosta vuosina 1750–1890. I. Väestön tila (Éléments démographiques principaux de la Finlande pour les années 1750–1890. I. État de la population)* (Suomenmaan Virallinen Tilasto, Väkiluvun-Tilastoa VI, 29 (Official Statistics of Finland ser. VI population statistics, vol. 29)). Helsinki, pp. 264–8.

1750–
1890 Suomenmaan Virallinen Tilasto (1909), *Pääpiirteet Suomen väestötilastosta vuosina 1750–1890. III. Esitys (Éléments démographiques principaux de la Finlande pour les années 1750–1890. III. Texte)* (Suomenmaan Virallinen Tilasto, Väkiluvun-Tilastoa VI, 41 (Official Statistics of Finland ser. VI population statistics, vol. 41)). Helsinki.

FRANCE

1. Vital statistics

Bureau de la Statistique Générale (1–56, 1878–1940/45), *Annuaire Statistique de la France 1966.* Paris: Imprimérie Nationale.

—— (1–39, 1911–1949), *Bulletin de la Statistique Générale de la France.* Paris: Imprimérie Nationale.

Institut National de la Statistique et des Études Économiques (INSEE) (57–, 1946–), *Annuaire Statistique de la France.* Paris: INSEE.

—— (1949–), *Bulletin Mensuel de Statistique.* Paris: INSEE.

—— (1966), *Annuaire Statistique de la France 1966. Résumé Rétrospectif.* Vol. 72. n.s. No. 14. Paris: INSEE.

Villa, P. (1994), *Un Siècle de Données Macro-économiques.* INSEE Résultats, no. 303–4. Paris: INSEE.

2. Population structure by age, sex, and marital status

1851 Ministre de l'Agriculture, du Commerce et des Travaux Publics (1855), *Statistique de la France. Deuxième Série: Territoire et Population.* Vol. II. Paris: Imprimerie Impériale, pp. 260–1.

1856 Bureau de la Statistique Générale (1859), *Statistique de la France. Deuxième Série. Tome IX. Résultats du dénombrement de la population en 1856.* Paris, Strasburg: Imprimerie Administrative de Veuve Berger-Levrault, pp. 12–3.

1861 Bureau de la Statistique Générale (1864), *Statistique de la France. I°: Résultats généraux du dénombrement de 1861 comparé aux cinq dénombrements antérieurs. II°: Recensement spécial des communautés religieuses.* Strasburg: Imprimerie Administrative de Veuve Berger-Levrault, pp. 96–7.

1866 Bureau de la Statistique Générale (1869), *Statistique de la France. Deuxième Série. Tome XVII: Population. Résultats généraux du dénombrement de 1866.* Strasburg: Imprimerie Administrative de Veuve Berger-Levrault, pp. 8–9.

1872 Bureau de la Statistique Générale (1873), *Statistique de la France. Deuxième Série. Tome XXI: Résultats généraux du dénombrement de 1872.* Strasburg: Imprimerie Nationale, p. 8.

1876 Bureau de la Statistique Générale (1878), *Statistique de la France. Résultats généraux du dénombrement de 1876. France. Algérie. Colonies.* Paris: Imprimerie Nationale, p. 7.

1881   Ministère du Commerce. Service de la Statistique Générale (1883), *Résultats statistiques du dénombrement de 1881. France et Algérie.* Paris: Imprimerie Nationale, p. 93.

1886   République Française. Ministère du Commerce et de l'Industrie (Division de la Compatabilité et de la Statistique) (1888), *Statistique Générale de la France. Résultats statistiques du dénombrement de 1886. Ire partie.–France.* Paris, Nancy: Berger-Levrault et Cie, pp. 86–7.

1891   République Française. Ministère du Commerce, de l'Industrie, des Postes et des Télégraphes. Direction du Travail (1899), *Statistique Générale de la France. Résultats statistiques du dénombrement de 1896.* Paris: Imprimerie Nationale, p. 414.

1896   République Française. Ministère du Commerce, de l'Industrie, des Postes et des Télégraphes. Office du Travail (1894), *Statistique Générale de la France. Résultats statistiques du dénombrement de 1891.* Paris: Imprimerie Nationale, pp. 58–61 (text), 299–363 (tables).

1901   République Française. Ministère du Travail et de la Prévoyance Sociale. Statistique Générale de la France (1915), *Résultats statistiques du recensement de la population effectué le 5 Mars 1911. Tome I. Deuxième partie. Population présente totale.* Paris: Imprimerie Nationale, pp. 86–7.

1906   République Française. Ministère du Travail et de la Prévoyance Sociale. Statistique Générale de la France (1910), *Résultats statistiques du recensement de la population effectué le 4 Mars 1906. Tome I. Deuxième partie. Population présente totale. Population active et établissements.* Paris: Imprimerie Nationale, pp. 18–25 (text), 153 and 166–9 (tables).

1911   République Française. Ministère du Travail et de la Prévoyance Sociale. Statistique Générale de la France (1915), *Résultats statistiques du recensement de la population effectué le 5 Mars 1911. Tome I. Deuxième partie. Population présente totale.* Paris: Imprimerie Nationale, pp. 86–7.

1921   République Française. Ministère du Travail, de l'Hygiène, de l'Assistance, et de la Prévoyance Sociale. Statistique Générale de la France (1927), *Résultats statistiques du recensement général de la population effectué le 6 Mars 1921. Tome I. Deuxième partie. Population présente totale.* Paris: Imprimerie Nationale, p. 26.

1926   République Française. Présidence du Conseil. Sous-Secrétariat d'État de l'Économie Nationale. Statistique Générale de la France (1930), *Résultats statistiques du recensement général de la population effectué le 7 Mars 1926. Tome I. Deuxième partie. Population présente totale.* Paris: Imprimerie Nationale, pp. 78–81.

1931   République Française. Présidence du Conseil. Statistique Générale de la France (1935), *Résultats statistiques du recensement général de la population effectué le 8 Mars 1931. Tome I. Deuxième partie. Population présente totale.* Paris: Imprimerie Nationale, p. 36.

1936   État Français. Ministère des Finances. Service National des Statistiques. Direction de Statistique Générale (1942), *Résultats statistiques du recensement général de la population effectué le 8 Mars 1936. Tome I. Deuxième partie. Population présente totale.* Paris: Imprimerie Nationale, pp. 82–5.

1946   République Française. Ministère des Finances et des Affaires Économiques. Institut National de la Statistique et des Études Économiques. Direction de la Statistique Générale (1953), *Résultats statistiques du recensement général de la population effectué le 10 Mars 1946. Volume II: Population présente totale.* Paris: Imprimerie Nationale; Presses Universitaires de France, pp. 4–7.

1851– INSEE (1966), *Annuaire Statistique de la France 1966. Résumé Rétrospectif.*
1962   Paris: INSEE (vol. 72. n.s. no. 14), p. 58f.

3. Population census results on households and families

1851   Ministre de l'Agriculture, du Commerce et des Travaux Publics (1855), *Statistique de la France. Deuxième Série. Territoire et Population*. Vol. II. Paris: Imprimerie Impériale, pp. XX (text) and 120–1 (table).

1856   Bureau de la Statistique Générale (1859), *Statistique de la France. Deuxième Série. Tome IX. Résultats du dénombrement de la population en 1856*. Paris: Imprimerie Impériale, pp. XXII–XXIV (text) and 6–9 (table).

1861   Bureau de la Statistique Générale (1864), *Statistique de la France. I°: Résultats généraux du dénombrement de 1861 comparé aux cinq dénombrements antérieurs. II°: Recensement spécial des communautés religieuses*. Strasburg: Imprimerie Administrative de Veuve Berger-Levrault, pp. XXXVI–XL and 70–3.

1866   Bureau de la Statistique Générale (1869), *Statistique de la France. Deuxième Série. Tome XVII: Population. Résultats généraux du dénombrement de 1866*. Strasburg: Imprimerie Administrative de Veuve Berger-Levrault, pp. XIX–XXII, 5 and 74–5.

1872   Bureau de la Statistique Générale (1873), *Statistique de la France. Deuxième Série. Tome XXI: Résultats généraux du dénombrement de 1872*. Strasburg: Imprimerie Nationale, pp. XXII–XXIII, 5 and 18–9.

1876   Bureau de la Statistique Générale (1878), *Statistique de la France. Résultats généraux du dénombrement de 1876. France. Algérie. Colonies*. Paris: Imprimerie Nationale, pp. XXIX–XXXII, 4–5 and 76–9.

1881   Ministère du Commerce. Service de la Statistique Générale (1883), *Résultats statistiques du dénombrement de 1881. France et Algérie*. Paris: Imprimerie Nationale, pp. XXXV–XXXVII, 90–1 and 100–1.

1886   République Française. Ministère du Commerce et de l'Industrie (Division de la Comptabilité et de la Statistique). Statistique Générale de la France (1886), *Résultats statistiques du dénombrement de 1886. Première partie. - France*. Paris, Nancy: Berger-Levrault, pp. 53–64 (text/households), 121–32 (text/families), 84 and 92–3 (table/households) and 170–9 (table/families).

1891   République Française. Ministère du Commerce, de l'Industrie, des Postes et des Télégraphes. Office du Travail. Statistique Générale de la France (1894), *Résultats statistiques du dénombrement de 1891*. Paris: Imprimerie Nationale, pp. 105–8 (text/households), 245–66 (text/families), 408–9 (table/households) and 415 (table/families).

1896   République Française. Ministère du Commerce, de l'Industrie, des Postes et des Télégraphes. Direction du Travail. Statistique Générale de la France (1899), *Résultats statistiques du dénombrement de 1896*. Paris: Imprimerie Nationale, pp. 52–3 (text/households), 89–93 (text/families), 196–7 and 214–7 (table/households) and 203 (table/families).

1901   République Française. Ministère du Travail et de la Prévoyance Sociale. Direction du Travail. Service du Recensement (1907), *Résultats statistiques du recensement de la population effectué le 24 Mars 1901. Tome V. Enquêtes annexes. Familles - aveugles et sourds-muets - habitations - forces motrices*. Paris: Imprimerie Nationale (habitation, families, and households).

1906   No data on households available.

1911   No published data found (statistics included in publication for 1921).

1921   République Française. Ministère du Travail, de l'Hygiène, de l'Assistance, et de la Prévoyance Sociale. Statistique Générale de la France (1928), *Résultats statistiques du recensement général de la population effectué le 6 Mars 1921. Tome I. Première partie. Introduction. Population légale ou de résidence habituelle*. Paris: Imprimerie Nationale, pp. 62 (text/households) and 108 (table/households); 64–5 (text and table/institutional households).

République Française. Ministère du Travail, de l'Hygiène, de l'Assistance, et de la

Prévoyance Sociale. Statistique Générale de la France (1927), *Résultats statistiques du recensement général de la population effectué le 6 Mars 1921. Tome I. Deuxième partie. Population présente totale*. Paris: Imprimerie Nationale, pp. 62 (text) and 108 (table); 64–5 (text/institutional households) and 76–88 (table/institutional households).

1926 République Française. Présidence du Conseil. Sous-Secrétariat d'État de l'Économie Nationale. Statistique Générale de la France (1928), *Résultats statistiques du recensement général de la population effectué le 7 Mars 1926. Tome I. Première partie. Population légale ou de résidence habituelle*. Paris: Imprimerie Nationale, pp. 66–7 (text/households) and 112 (table/households); 60–1 (text/institutional households) and 72–81 (table/institutional households).

République Française. Présidence du Conseil. Sous-Secrétariat d'État de l'Économie Nationale. Statistique Générale de la France (1930), *Résultats statistiques du recensement général de la population effectué le 7 Mars 1926. Tome I. Deuxième partie. Population présente totale*. Paris: Imprimerie Nationale, pp. 65 (text/households) and 100 (table/households); 11–4 (text and table/institutional households).

République Française. Présidence du Conseil. Sous-Secrétariat d'État de l'Économie Nationale. Statistique Générale de la France (1932), *Résultats statistiques du recensement général de la population effectué le 7 Mars 1926. Tome IV. Infirmités - Habitations - Ménages et logements*. Paris: Imprimerie Nationale, pp. 31ff. (text) and 91ff. (table).

République Française. Présidence du Conseil. Sous-Secrétariat d'État de l'Économie Nationale. Statistique Générale de la France (1932), *Statistiques des familles en 1926*. Paris: Imprimerie Nationale.

1931 République Française. Présidence du Conseil. Statistique Générale de la France (1933), *Résultats statistiques du recensement général de la population effectué le 8 Mars 1931. Tome I. Première partie. Introduction. Population légale ou de résidence habituelle. Appendice: Population des Colonies et des Pays Étrangers*. Paris: Imprimerie Nationale, pp. 64 (text/households) and 110 (table/households); 55–6 (text/institutional households) and 65–74 (table/institutional households).

République Française. Ministère de l'Économie Nationale. Statistique Générale de la France (1939), *Recensement de 1931. Statistique des Familles. Productivité des Mariages. Habitants recensés d'après l'année de naissance*. Paris: Imprimerie Nationale.

1936 République Française. Ministère de l'Économie. Direction de la Statistique Générale et de la Documentation (1938), *Résultats statistiques du recensement général de la population effectué le 8 Mars 1936. Tome I. Première partie. Population légale ou de résidence habituelle. Appendice: Population des Territoires Français d'Outre-Mer et des Pays Étrangers*. Paris: Imprimerie Nationale, pp. 44 (text/households) and 92 (table/households); 37–8 (text/institutional households) and 46–55 (table/institutional households).

République Française. Ministère de l'Économie Nationale. Service National des Statistiques. Direction de la Statistique Générale (1945), *Statistique des Familles en 1936*. Paris: Imprimerie Nationale.

1946 République Française. Ministère des Finances et des Affaires Économiques. Institut National de la Statistique et des Études Économiques. Direction de la Statistique Générale (1948), *Résultats statistiques du recensement général de la population effectué le 10 Mars 1946. Volume I. Population légale ou de résidence habituelle. Appendice: Population des Territoires Français d'Outre-Mer et des Pays Étrangers*. Paris: Imprimerie Nationale, Presses Universitaires de France, pp. 74–5 (text/households) and 136 (table/households); 67 (text/institutional households) and 138–41 (table/institutional households).

République Française. Ministère des Finances et des Affaires Économiques. Institut National de la Statistique et des Études Économiques. Direction de la Statistique Générale (1953), *Résultats statistiques du recensement général de la population effectué le 10 Mars 1946. Volume IV: Familles*. Paris: Imprimerie Nationale; Presses Universitaires de France.

République Française. Ministère des Finances et des Affaires Économiques. Institut National de la Statistique et des Études Économiques. Direction de la Statistique Générale (1953), *Résultats statistiques du recensement général de la population effectué le 10 Mars 1946. Volume VI: Habitations. Première partie. Immeubles*. Paris: Imprimerie Nationale; Presses Universitaires de France, p. 56.

République Française. Ministère des Finances et des Affaires Économiques. Institut National de la Statistique et des Études Économiques. Direction de la Statistique Générale (1949), *Résultats statistiques du recensement général de la population effectué le 10 Mars 1946. Volume VI: Habitations. Deuxième partie. Ménages et Logements*. Paris: Imprimerie Nationale; Presses Universitaires de France, pp. 3ff. and 389.

1801–1962	INSEE (1966), *Annuaire Statistique de la France 1966. Résumé Rétrospectif*. Paris: INSEE (vol. 72. n.s. no. 14). p. 22 (households 1861–1962).
1946–1988	INSEE (1988), *Annuaire Statistique de la France 1988*. Paris: INSEE, p. 50 (households 1946–1988).

GERMANY

1. Vital statistics

Kraus, A. (1980), *Quellen zur Bevölkerungs-, Sozial- und Wirtschaftsstatistik Deutschlands 1815–1875. Vol. 1: Quellen zur Bevölkerungsstatistik Deutschlands 1815–1875*. Compiled by A. Kraus. Series ed. W. Köllmann. Forschungen zur deutschen Sozialgeschichte, vol. 2/I. Boppard am Rhein: Harald Boldt.

Rothenbacher, F. (1997), *Historische Haushalts- und Familienstatistik von Deutschland 1815–1990*. Frankfurt/New York: Campus Verlag.

Statistisches Bundesamt, ed. (1972), *Bevölkerung und Wirtschaft 1872–1972*. Stuttgart/Mainz: Kohlhammer.

Statistisches Reichsamt (1–59, 1880–1942), *Statistisches Jahrbuch für das Deutsche Reich*. Berlin: Puttkammer & Mühlbrecht, later Reimar Hobbing, finally Verlag für Sozialpolitik, Wirtschaft und Statistik, Paul Schmidt.

—— (1–24, 1921–1944), *Wirtschaft und Statistik*. Berlin: Reimar Hobbing, later Verlag für Sozialpolitik, Wirtschaft und Statistik, Paul Schmidt.

2. Population structure by age, sex, and marital status

1871	Kaiserliches Statistisches Amt (1875), *Die Volkszählung im Deutschen Reich vom 1. Dezember 1871, Vierteljahrshefte zur Statistik des Deutschen Reichs*, vol. 3, no. 3, section 3. Berlin: Puttkammer & Mühlbrecht, pp. VI.34–VI.35, VI.82–VI.91 (Statistik des Deutschen Reichs, vol. 14, no. 3, section 3).
1875	Kaiserliches Statistisches Amt (1878), *Die Volkszählung im Deutschen Reiche vom 1. Dezember 1875, Monatshefte zur Statistik des Deutschen Reichs vol. 1878*. Berlin: Puttkammer & Mühlbrecht (Statistik des Deutschen Reichs, series I, vol. 30, no. 4).
1880	Kaiserliches Statistisches Amt (1883), *Die Volkszählung im Deutschen Reich am 1. Dezember 1880*. Berlin: Puttkammer & Mühlbrecht, pp. 104–6, 180–97 (Statistik des Deutschen Reichs, vol. 57).

1885   Kaiserliches Statistisches Amt (1888), *Die Volkszählung im Deutschen Reich am*
        1. Dezember 1885. Berlin: Puttkammer & Mühlbrecht, pp. 110–2, 172–88
        (Statistik des Deutschen Reichs, new series, vol. 32).
1890   Kaiserliches Statistisches Amt (1894), *Die Volkszählung am 1. Dezember 1890 im*
        Deutschen Reich. Tabellen mit Erläuterungen und graphischen Darstellungen.
        Berlin: Puttkammer & Mühlbrecht, pp. 92–111 (Statistik des Deutschen Reichs,
        new series, vol. 68).
1895   Age structure in one-year age groups not published for this year.
1900   Kaiserliches Statistisches Amt (1903), *Die Volkszählung am 1. Dezember 1900 im*
        Deutschen Reich. Erster Teil. Berlin: Puttkammer & Mühlbrecht, pp. 154–73
        (Statistik des Deutschen Reichs, vol. 150).
1905   Age structure in one-year age groups not published for this year.
1910   Kaiserliches Statistisches Amt (1915), *Die Volkszählung im Deutschen Reiche am*
        1. Dezember 1910. Berlin: Puttkammer & Mühlbrecht, pp. 201–3 (Statistik des
        Deutschen Reichs, vol. 240).
1925   Statistisches Reichsamt (1928), *Volks-, Berufs- und Betriebszählung vom 16. Juni*
        1925. Volkszählung. Die Bevölkerung des Deutschen Reichs nach den
        Ergebnissen derVolkszählung 1925. Teil I: Einführung in die Volkszählung 1925.
        Tabellenwerk. Berlin: Reimar Hobbing, p. 174 (Statistik des Deutschen Reichs,
        vol. 401,I).
1933   Statistisches Reichsamt (1936), *Volks-, Berufs- und Betriebszählung vom 16. Juni*
        1933. Volkszählung. Die Bevölkerung des Deutschen Reichs nach den
        Ergebnissen der Volkszählung 1933. Heft 2: Geschlecht, Alter und Familienstand
        der Bevölkerung des Deutschen Reich. Berlin: Verlag für Sozialpolitik, Wirtschaft
        und Statistik, Paul Schmidt, pp. 2/70–1 (Statistik des Deutschen Reichs, vol.
        451,1).
1939   Statistisches Reichsamt (1941), *Volks-, Berufs- und Betriebszählung vom 17. Mai*
        1939. Volkszählung. Die Bevölkerung des Deutschen Reichs nach den
        Ergebnissen derVolkszählung 1939. Heft 2: Geschlecht, Alter und Familienstand
        der Bevölkerung des Deutschen Reichs. Tabellenteil. Berlin: Verlag für
        Sozialpolitik, Wirtschaft und Statistik, Paul Schmidt, pp. 2/6–7, 2/24–5, 2/70–81
        (Statistik des Deutschen Reichs, vol. 552,2).
1871–   Statistisches Bundesamt, ed. (1972), *Bevölkerung und Wirtschaft 1872–1972.*
1939   Stuttgart/Mainz: Kohlhammer, pp. 95–6.

3. Population census results on households and families

1871   Kaiserliches Statistisches Amt (1874–75), *Die Volkszählung im Deutschen Reich*
        vom 1. Dezember 1871.
        Part 1: Vierteljahrshefte zur Statistik des Deutschen Reichs für das Jahr 1873,
        vol. 1, no. 2, section 1. Berlin: Puttkammer & Mühlbrecht, 1874 (Statistik des
        Deutschen Reichs, series 1, vol. 2, no. 2, section 1).
        Part 2: Vierteljahrshefte zur Statistik des Deutschen Reichs für das Jahr 1875,
        vol. 3, no. 3, section 3. Berlin: Puttkammer & Mühlbrecht, 1875 (Statistik des
        Deutschen Reichs, series 1, vol. 14, no. 3, section 3).
1875   Kaiserliches Statistisches Amt (1877–78), *Die Volkszählung im Deutschen Reiche*
        vom 1. Dezember 1875.
        Monatshefte zur Statistik des Deutschen Reichs vol. 1877, July–Dec. Berlin:
        Puttkammer & Mühlbrecht, 1877 (Statistik des Deutschen Reichs, series I, vol.
        25, no. 2).
        Monatshefte zur Statistik des Deutschen Reichs vol. 1878 April. Berlin:
        Puttkammer & Mühlbrecht, 1878 (Statistik des Deutschen Reichs, series I, vol.
        30, no. 4).
1880   Kaiserliches Statistisches Amt (1883), *Die Volkszählung im Deutschen Reich am*

  1. Dezember 1880. Berlin: Puttkammer & Mühlbrecht (Statistik des Deutschen Reichs, vol. 57).

1885 Kaiserliches Statistisches Amt (1888), *Die Volkszählung im Deutschen Reich am 1. Dezember 1885*. Berlin: Puttkammer & Mühlbrecht (Statistik des Deutschen Reichs, new series, vol. 32).

1890 Kaiserliches Statistisches Amt (1894), *Die Volkszählung am 1. Dezember 1890 im Deutschen Reich. Tabellen mit Erläuterungen und graphischen Darstellungen.* Berlin: Puttkammer & Mühlbrecht (Statistik des Deutschen Reichs, new series, vol. 68).

1895 Kaiserliches Statistisches Amt (1897–98), *Die Volkszählung am 1. Dezember 1895, Vierteljahrshefte zur Statistik des Deutschen Reichs*, vol. 6, 1895, no. I–IV; vol. 7, 1898, no. I–II. Berlin: Puttkammer & Mühlbrecht.

1900 Kaiserliches Statistisches Amt (1903), *Die Volkszählung am 1. Dezember 1900 im Deutschen Reich. Erster Teil.* Berlin (Statistik des Deutschen Reichs, vol. 150); *Zweiter Teil.* Berlin: Puttkammer & Mühlbrecht (Statistik des Deutschen Reichs, vol. 151).

1905 Kaiserliches Statistisches Amt (1906–08), *Die Volkszählung am 1. Dezember 1905, Vierteljahrshefte zur Statistik des Deutschen Reichs*, vol. 15, 1906, no. IV; vol. 16, 1907, no. I–IV; vol. 17, 1908, no. I. Berlin: Puttkammer & Mühlbrecht.

1910 Kaiserliches Statistisches Amt (1915), *Die Volkszählung im Deutschen Reiche am 1. Dezember 1910*. Berlin: Puttkammer & Mühlbrecht (Statistik des Deutschen Reichs, vol. 240).

1925 Statistisches Reichsamt (1930), *Volks-, Berufs- und Betriebszählung vom 16. Juni 1925. Volkszählung. Die Bevölkerung des Deutschen Reichs nach den Ergebnissen der Volkszählung 1925. Die Haushaltungen und Familien nach ihrer beruflichen und sozialen Gliederung.* Berlin: Reimar Hobbing (Statistik des Deutschen Reichs, vol. 407).

1933 Statistisches Reichsamt (1936–37), *Volks-, Berufs- und Betriebszählung vom 16. Juni 1933. Volkszählung. Die Familien und Haushaltungen nach den Ergebnissen der Volks- und Berufszählung 1933.* Berlin: Verlag für Sozialpolitik, Wirtschaft und Statistik, Paul Schmidt, 1937.
  Die Haushaltungen im Deutschen Reich. Berlin: Verlag für Sozialpolitik, Wirtschaft und Statistik, Paul Schmidt, 1936 (Statistik des Deutschen Reichs, vol. 452, no. 3).

1939 Statistisches Reichsamt (1944), *Volks-, Berufs- und Betriebszählung vom 17. Mai 1939. Die Haushaltungen im Deutschen Reich.* Berlin: Verlag für Sozialpolitik, Wirtschaft und Statistik, Paul Schmidt (Statistik des Deutschen Reichs, vol. 553).
  Statistisches Reichsamt (1943), *Volks-, Berufs- und Betriebszählung vom 17. Mai 1939. Die Familien im Deutschen Reich. Die Ehen nach der Zahl der geborenen Kinder.* Berlin: Verlag für Sozialpolitik, Wirtschaft und Statistik, Paul Schmidt (Statistik des Deutschen Reichs, vol. 554).

1871– Rothenbacher, F. (1997), *Historische Haushalts- und Familienstatistik von*
1939 *Deutschland 1815–1990.* Frankfurt/New York: Campus.

1871– Statistisches Bundesamt, ed. (1972), *Bevölkerung und Wirtschaft 1872–1972.*
1939 Stuttgart/Mainz: Kohlhammer, p. 98.

GREECE

1. Vital statistics

National Statistical Service of Greece (1–, 1929–; n.s. 1–, 1956–), *Monthly Statistical Bulletin.* Athens: NSSG. (in Greek/English).

—— (1–, 1930–; n.s. 1–, 1954–), *Statistical Yearbook of Greece*. Athens: NSSG (in Greek/English).

—— (1–, 1956–), *Mouvement Naturel de la Population de la Grèce en 19...* Athens: NSSG (in Greek/French).

2. Population structure by age, sex, and marital status

1870   Ipourgeion Esoterikon (1872), *Statistiki tis Ellados. Plithismos 1870*. En Athinais [Athens]: Ethniko Tipographio, pp. κα΄–κδ΄ (text) and 88–135 (tables) (Age structure by sex available, but not combined by civil status).

1879   Ipourgeion Esoterikon (1881), *Statistiki tis Ellados. Plithismos 1879*. En Athinais: Ek tou tipographeiou S. Vlastou, pp. 28–32, esp. pp. 28–9 (Age structure by sex and civil status available, but only in relative form).

1889   Ministère de l'Intérieur, Section d'Économie Publique et de Statistique (1891), *Statistique de la Grèce. Population. Recensement général à la date 15-16 Avril 1889*. 3 parts. Athens: Imprimerie Nationale. (Data not included in part 3, parts 1 and 2 not available).

1896   Royaume de Grèce, Ministère de l'Intérieur, Section d'Économie Publique et de Statistique (1897), *Résultats statistiques du recensement de la population de 17-18 octobre 1896*. 2 parts. Athens: Imprimerie Nationale. (Data not included in part 2, part 1 is not available).

1907   Royaume de Grèce, Ministère de l'Intérieur, Service du Recensement (1909), *Résultats statistiques du recensement général de la population effectué le 27 Octobre 1907 par Dr. Georges Chomatianos*. Vol. I. Athens: Imprimerie Nationale, pp. 156–7.

1920   République Héllénique, Ministère de l'Économie Nationale (1928), *Statistique Générale de la Grèce. Recensement de la population de la Grèce au 19 Décembre 1920/1 Janvier 1921. Résultats statistiques généraux. A. Population. B. Familles.* Athens: Imprimerie Nationale, p. 10.

1928   Royaume de Grèce, Ministère de l'Économie Nationale (1935), *Statistique Générale de la Grèce. Résultats statistiques du recensement de la population de la Grèce du 15-16 Mai 1928. II. Âge - État matrimonial - Instruction.* Athens: Imprimerie Nationale, pp. 3–4.

1940   Census results have never been fully published; respective data are not available.

1870–   National Statistical Service of Greece (1960), *Demographic Trends and*
1961   *Population Projections of Greece*. Athens: NSSG, p. 14 (age structure).

1928–   National Statistical Service of Greece (1980), *The Population of Greece in the*
1971   *Second Half of the twentieth Century*. Athens: NSSG, p. 21 (age structure).

3. Population census results on households and families

1870   Ipourgeion Esoterikon (1872), *Statistiki tis Ellados. Plithismos 1870*. En Athinais: Ethniko Tipographio, pp. ιδ'–ιζ' (text) and 56–70 (tables).

1879   Ipourgeion Esoterikon (1881), *Statistiki tis Ellados. Plithismos 1879*. En Athinais: Ek tou tipographeiou S. Vlastou, pp. 24–6 (text) and 94–107 (tables).

1889   Ministère de l'Intérieur, Section d'Économie Publique et de Statistique (1891), *Statistique de la Grèce. Population. Recensement général à la date 15-16 Avril 1889*. 3 parts. Athens: Imprimerie Nationale (data not included in part 3, parts 1 and 2 not available).

1896   Royaume de Grèce, Ministère de l'Intérieur, Section d'Économie Publique et de Statistique (1897), *Résultats statistiques du recensement de la population de 17–18 octobre 1896*. 2 parts. Athens: Imprimerie Nationale (data not included in part 2, part 1 is not available).

1907 Royaume de Grèce, Ministère de l'Intérieur, Service du Recensement (1909), *Résultats statistiques du recensement général de la population effectué le 27 Octobre 1907 par Dr. Georges Chomatianos*. Vols. I and II. Athens: Imprimerie Nationale (no household data published in both vols.).

1920 République Héllénique, Ministère de l'Économie Nationale (1928), *Statistique Générale de la Grèce. Recensement de la population de la Grèce au 19 Décembre 1920/1 Janvier 1921. Résultats statistiques généraux. A. Population. B. Familles.* Athens: Imprimerie Nationale, pp. 94–112 (Greek numbers) (text), CVIII–CXXII and 265–424 (tables).

1928 Royaume de Grèce, Ministère de l'Économie Nationale (1935), *Statistique Générale de la Grèce. Résultats statistiques du recensement de la population de la Grèce du 15-16 Mai 1928. II. Âge - État matrimonial - Instruction.* Athens: Imprimerie Nationale (no household data published).

1940 Census results have never been fully published; data on number of households are available by '*Journal Officiel du Gouvernement,* no. 29, fascicule A, du 2 février 1946', and '*Population de la Grèce au Recensement du 16 octobre 1940.* Athens 1950.'

1861– Royaume de Grèce, Office National de Statistique de Grèce (1961), *Résultats du*
1951 *recensement de la population effectué le 7 Avril 1951. Voume I: Aperçu historique–Rapport méthodologique–Analyse des résultats–Tableaux par superficie et altitude.* Athens: Imprimerie Nationale, pp. IX–XV history of population censuses 1821–1951, comparative table of published variables) and CXC–CXCVIII (concerns the years 1861, 1870, 1879, 1920, 1940 and 1951).

1920– National Statistical Service of Greece (1988), *Statistical Yearbook of Greece*
1981 *1987.* Athens: NSSG, p. 33.

HUNGARY

1. Vital statistics

Hungarian Central Statistical Office (1992), *Time Series of Historical Statistics 1867–1992. Volume I: Population—Vital Statistics.* Budapest: Hungarian Central Statistical Office.

Központi Statisztikai Hivatal (1996), *Magyarország népessége és gazdasága. Múlt és jelen* (Population and economy of Hungary. Past and present). Budapest: Központi Statisztikai Hivatal (KSH).

2. Population structure by age, sex, and marital status

1870 Census publication not available for inclusion.

1880 Az Orszagos Magyar Kir. Statisztikai Hivatal (1882), *A Magyar Korona országaiban az 1881. Év elején végrehajtott népszámlálás eredmenyei némely hasznos názi állatok kimutatásával együtt. I. Köt. Ergebnisse der in den Ländern der Ungarischen Krone am Anfange des Jahres 1881 vollzogenen Volkszählung sammt Nachweisung einiger nutzbaren Hausthiere. Band I.* Budapest: Az Athenaeum R. Társulat Konyvnyamdaja, pp. 248ff.

1890 Königlich Ungarisches Statistisches Bureau (1893), *Ergebnisse der in den Ländern der Ungarischen Krone am Anfange des Jahres 1891 durchgeführten Volkszählung. I. Theil. Allgemeine Demographie.* Budapest: Pester Buchdruckerei Actien-Gesellschaft (Ungarische Statistische Mitteilungen, Neue Folge, Band I), pp. 116ff.

1900 Office Central de Statistique du Royaume de Hongrie (1907), *Dénombrement de la population des pays de la sainte couronne Hongroise en 1900. Troisième partie: Démographie détaillée.* Budapest: Société anonyme d'imprimerie de Pest (Publications Statistiques Hongroises, Nouvelle série, vol. 5), pp. 242ff.

1910 Magyar Kir. Központi Statisztikai Hivatal (1916), *A Magyar Szent Korona Országainak 1910 évi Népszamlálása. Ötödik Rész: Részletes Demografia.* Budapest: Pesti könyvnyomda Részvénytársaság (Magyar Statisztikai közlemenyek, uj Sorozat, 61. Kötet).
Office Central de Statistique du Royaume de Hongrie (1916), *Recensement général de la population des pays de la sainte couronne Hongroise en 1910. Cinquième partie: Démographie détaillée.* Budapest: Société anonyme d'imprimerie de Pest (Publications Statistiques Hongroises, Nouvelle série, vol. 61), pp. 170ff.

1920 Office Central Royal Hongrois de Statistique (1928), *Recensement de la population en 1920. Cinquième partie: Démographie détaillée.* Budapest: Société anonyme d'imprimerie de Pest (Publications Statistiques Hongroises, Nouvelle série, vol. 73), pp. 54ff.

1930 Office Central Royal Hongrois de Statistique (1936), *Recensement général de la population en 1920. IVe partie. Les professions exercées par la population, combinés avec les principales données démographiques et les conditions de propriétés bâties et foncières de la population. V^e partie. Démographie détaillée et données sur les maisons d'habitation et les logements.* Budapest: Imprimerie Stephaneum Société Anonyme (Publications Statistiques Hongroises, Nouvelle série, vol. 96), pp. 244ff.

1941 No data available.

1867– Hungarian Central Statistical Office (1992), *Time Series of Historical Statistics*
1992 *1867–1992. Volume I: Population–Vital Statistics.* Budapest: Hungarian Central Statistical Office.

3. Population census results on households and families

1870 Königlich Ungarisches Statistisches Bureau (1871), *Ergebnisse der in den Ländern der Ungarischen Krone am Anfange des Jahres 1870 vollzogenen Volkszählung sammt Nachweisung der nutzbaren Hausthiere. Im Auftrage des Königl. Ungarischen Ministers für Landwirtschaft, Gewerbe und Handel verfasst und herausgegeben durch das ...* Pest: Druckerei des Athenaeum, pp. 1–5 (historical introduction on censuses), 4–5 and 7 (text 'Wohnparteien'), 9–19 (table 'Wohnparteien'), 549ff. (housing conditions).

1880 Az Orszagos Magyar Kir. Statisztikai Hivatal (1882), *A Magyar Korona országaiban az 1881. Év elején végrehajott népszámlálás eredmenyei némely hasznos názi állatok kimutatásával együtt. I. Köt. Ergebnisse der in den Ländern der Ungarischen Krone am Anfange des Jahres 1881 vollzogenen Volkszählung sammt Nachweisung einiger nutzbaren Hausthiere. Band I.* Budapest: Az Athenaeum R. Társulat Konyvnyamdaja, pp. 1, 5–6 (text) and 12–22 (tables).

1890 Az Orszagos Magyar Kir. Statisztikai Hivatal (1893), *A Magyar Korona országaiban az 1891. Év elején végrehajott népszámlálás eredmenyei. I. Rész. Általános népleirás (Magyar Statisztikai közlemenyek, uj Folyam, I. Kötet). – Königlich Ungarisches Statistisches Bureau (1893), Ergebnisse der in den Ländern der Ungarischen Krone am Anfange des Jahres 1891 durchgeführten Volkszählung. I. Theil. Allgemeine Demographie* (Ungarische Statistische Mittheilungen, Neue Folge, Band I). Budapest: Pesti Jönyvnyomda-Részvény-Társaság, Pester Buchdruckerei Actiengesellschaft, pp. 43*–9* (text) and 2–10 (tables).

1900 Office Central de Statistique du Royaume de Hongrie (1907), *Dénombrement de la population des pays de la sainte couronne Hongroise en 1900. Troisième partie: Démographie détaillée.* Budapest: Société anonyme d'imprimerie de Pest

(Publications Statistiques Hongroises, Nouvelle série, vol. 5), pp. XI–XII (translation of table heads), 6–9 and 20–5 (tables).

1910   Magyar Kir. Központi Statisztikai Hivatal (1916), *A Magyar Szent Korona Országainak 1910 évi Népszamlálása. Ötödik Rész: Részletes Demografia. Budapest: Pesti könyvnyomda Részvénytársaság (Magyar Statisztikai közlemenyek, uj Sorozat, 61. Kötet). – Office Central de Statistique du Royaume de Hongrie (1916), Recensement général de la population des pays de la sainte couronne Hongroise en 1910. Cinquième partie: Démographie détaillée.* Budapest: Société anonyme d'imprimerie de Pest (Publications Statistiques Hongroises, Nouvelle série, vol. 61), pp. VI–VII (translation of table heads), 6–9 and 11 (tables).

1920   Office Central Royal Hongrois de Statistique (1928), *Recensement de la population en 1920. Cinquième partie: Démographie détaillée.* Budapest: Société anonyme d'imprimerie de Pest (Publications Statistiques Hongroises, Nouvelle série, vol. 73), pp. without page number (translation of table heads), 5, 7 (tables on households and institutions) and 266–97 (marital fertility).

1930   Office Central Royal Hongrois de Statistique (1936), *Recensement général de la population en 1920. IVe partie. Les professions exercées par la population, combinés avec les principales données démographiques et les conditions de propriétés bâties et foncières de la population. V^e partie. Démographie détaillée et données sur les maisons d'habitation et les logements.* Budapest: Imprimerie Stephaneum Société Anonyme (Publications Statistiques Hongroises, Nouvelle série, vol. 96), pp. XXX–XXXI (translation of table heads) and 374–7 (tables).

1941   No data available.

1867–   Hungarian Central Statistical Office (1992), *Time Series of Historical Statistics*
1992   *1867–1992. Volume I: Population – Vital Statistics.* Budapest: Hungarian Central Statistical Office, pp. 75–8 (tables) and 343–4 (definitions) (data for 1949/60–90).

ICELAND

1. Vital statistics

Hagstofa Íslands/Statistics Iceland (1997), *Hagskinna. Sögulegar Hagtölur um Ísland/Icelandic Historical Statistics.* Reykjavík: Hagstofa Íslands.

Hagstofa Íslands (1991–), *Landshagir. Statistical Abstract of Iceland 1991.* Reykjavík: Hagstofa Íslands.

Hagstofu Íslands (1967, 1976, 1984), *Toelfraedihandbok 1967, 1974, 1984. Statistical Abstract of Iceland.* Reykjavík: Hagstofu Íslands.

Nordic Statistical Secretariat, ed. (1–, 1963–), *Yearbook of Nordic Statistics 1962–.* Copenhagen: Nordic Council of Ministers.

Statens Statistiske Bureau i Danmark (ed.), *Sammendrag af statistiske oplysninger om Island. Statistical Abstract of Iceland.* 1, 1907. Series Statistiske Meddelelser. Copenhagen: Statens Statistiske Bureau.

2. Population structure by age, sex and marital status

1850   Det Statistiske Bureau (1855), *Meddelelser fra det Statistiske Bureau.* 2. Samling. Copenhagen.
       Hansen, S. (s.a.), *Skýrslur um landshagi á Islandi.* Volume I, pp. 38–9.

1855   Det Statistiske Bureau (1858), *Meddelelser fra det Statistiske Bureau.* 1. Række, 4. Samling. Copenhagen.
       Hansen, S. (1858), *Skýrslur um landshagi á Islandi.* Fjrsta bindi. Kaupmannhöfn, pp. 470–1.

1860   Det Statistiske Bureau (1865), *Statistiske Meddelelser*. 2de Række, vol. 4
        (Communications Statistiques, 2me série, tome 4). Copenhagen: Bianco Lunos
        Bogtrykkeri ved F.S. Mule.
        Hansen, S. (1866), *Skýrslur um landshagi á Islandi*. Pridja bindi. Kaupmannhöfn,
        pp. 152–3.

1870   Det Statistiske Bureau (1883), *Statistiske Meddelelser*. 3de Række, vol. 6
        (Communications Statistiques, 3me série, tome 6, 1re livraison). Copenhagen:
        Bianco Lunos Bogtrykkeri.

1880   Det Statistiske Bureau (1883), *Statistiske Meddelelser*. 3de Række, vol. 6
        (Communications Statistiques, 3me série, tome 6, 1re livraison). Copenhagen:
        Bianco Lunos Bogtrykkeri.

1890   Statens Statistiske Bureau (1892), *Folketællingen paa Island den 1ste November
        1890. Population de l'Islande du 1er novembre 1890*. Copenhagen: Bianco Lunos
        Bogtrykkeri (Danmarks Statistik. Statistiske Meddelelser, 3de Række, vol. 12, 2
        (Communications Statistiques, 3me série, tome 12, 2me livraison)), pp. 194–5.

1901   Statens Statistiske Bureau (1904), *Folketællingen paa Island den 1. November
        1901. Population de l'Islande du 1er Novbr. 1901*. Copenhagen: Bianco Lunos
        Bogtrykkeri (Danmarks Statistik. Statistiske Meddelelser, Fjerde Række,
        Fjortende Bind, Andet Hælfte (Communications Statistiques, 4me série, tome 14,
        2me livraison)), pp. 27–9.

1910   Stjornarrádi Íslands - Ministère de l'Islande (1913), *Manntal á Íslandi 1.
        Desember 1910. Recensement de la population de l'Islande le 1er Décembre 1910*.
        Reykjavik: Prentsmiðjan Gutenberg, pp. 46–8.

1920   Hagstofu Íslands - Bureau de Statistique de l'Islande (1926), *Manntal á Íslandi 1.
        Desember 1920. Recensement de la population de l'Islande le 1er Décembre 1920*.
        Reykjavik: Prentað í Prentsmiðjunni Gutenberg, pp. 24–7.

1930   Hagstofu Íslands - Bureau de Statistique de l'Islande (1937), *Manntal á Íslandi 2.
        Desember 1930. Recensement de la population de l'Islande le 2 Décembre 1930*
        (Hagskyrslur Íslands - Statistique de l'Islande, 92). Reykjavik: Prentað í
        Ríkisprentsmiðjan Gutenberg, pp. 24–7.

1940   Hagstofu Íslands - Bureau de Statistique de l'Islande (1949), *Manntal á Íslandi 2.
        Desember 1940. Recensement de la population de l'Islande le 2 Décembre 1940*
        (Hagskyrslur Íslands - Statistique de l'Islande, 122). Reykjavik: Prentað í
        Ríkisprentsmiðjunni Gutenberg, pp. 11–4.

1801–   *Sammendrag af statistiske Oplysninger*, Nr. 4 and 6–11. København 1874–1893;
1890   *Statistisk Aarbog*, I–VIII. København 1896–1903 (main results of censuses 1801–
        1890).

1703–   Hagstofa Íslands/Statistics Iceland (1997), *Hagskinna. Sögulegar Hagtölur um
1990   Ísland/Icelandic Historical Statistics*. Reykjavík: Hagstofa Íslands, pp. 131–6
        (table 2.14).

3. Population census results on households and families

1850   Det Statistiske Bureau (1855), *Meddelelser fra det Statistiske Bureau*. 2. Samling.
        Copenhagen, pp. 85–95.

1855   Det Statistiske Bureau (1858), *Meddelelser fra det Statistiske Bureau*. 1. Række,
        4. Samling. Copenhagen, pp. 3–4 (text) and 22–33 (table).

1860   Det Statistiske Bureau (1865), *Statistiske Meddelelser*. 2de Række, vol. 4
        (Communications Statistiques, 2me série, tome 4). Copenhagen: Bianco Lunos
        Bogtrykkeri ved F. S. Mule, pp. 18–29.

1870   Det Statistiske Bureau (1883), *Statistiske Meddelelser*. 3de Række, vol. 6
        (Communications Statistiques, 3me série, tome 6, 1re livraison). Copenhagen:
        Bianco Lunos Bogtrykkeri.

1880   Det Statistiske Bureau (1883), *Statistiske Meddelelser*. 3de Række, vol. 6

(Communications Statistiques, 3me série, tome 6, 1re livraison). Copenhagen: Bianco Lunos Bogtrykkeri.

1890   Statens Statistiske Bureau (1892), *Folketællingen paa Island den 1ste November 1890. Population de l'Islande du 1er novembre 1890.* Copenhagen: Bianco Lunos Bogtrykkeri (Danmarks Statistik. Statistiske Meddelelser, 3de Række, vol. 12, 2 (Communications Statistiques, 3me série, tome 12, 2me livraison)), pp. 224–5 (text).

1901   Statens Statistiske Bureau (1904), *Folketællingen paa Island den 1. November 1901. Population de l'Islande du 1er Novbr. 1901.* Copenhagen: Bianco Lunos Bogtrykkeri (Danmarks Statistik. Statistiske Meddelelser, Fjerde Række, Fjortende Bind, Andet Hælfte (Communications Statistiques, 4me série, tome 14, 2me livraison)), pp. 5–13 (tables) and 73 (text).

1910   Stjornarrádi Íslands - Ministère de l'Islande (1913), *Manntal á Íslandi 1. Desember 1910. Recensement de la population de l'Islande le 1er Décembre 1910.* Reykjavik: Prentsmiðjan Gutenberg, pp. 130–3 (tables) and 192–4 (text).

1920   Hagstofu Íslands - Bureau de Statistique de l'Islande (1926–1928), *Manntal á Íslandi 1. Desember 1920. Recensement de la population de l'Islande le 1er Décembre 1920* (Hagskyrslur Íslands - Statistique de l'Islande, 46a). Reykjavik: Prentað í Prentsmiðjunni Gutenberg, pp. 30*–1* (text).
       Hagstofu Íslands - Bureau de Statistique de l'Islande (1926), *Manntal á Íslandi 1. Desember 1920. Recensement de la population de l'Islande le 1er Décembre 1920* (Hagskyrslur Íslands - Statistique de l'Islande, 46b). Reykjavik: Prentað í Prentsmiðjunni Gutenberg, pp. 62–4, 151–3 (tables).

1930   Hagstofu Íslands - Bureau de Statistique de l'Islande (1937), *Manntal á Íslandi 2. Desember 1930. Recensement de la population de l'Islande le 2 Décembre 1930* (Hagskyrslur Íslands - Statistique de l'Islande, 92). Reykjavik: Prentað í Ríkisprentsmiðjan Gutenberg, pp. 34*–9* (text) and 1–8, 66–73, 160 (tables).

1940   Hagstofu Íslands - Bureau de Statistique de l'Islande (1949), *Manntal á Íslandi 2. Desember 1940. Recensement de la population de l'Islande le 2 Décembre 1940* (Hagskyrslur Íslands - Statistique de l'Islande, 122). Reykjavik: Prentað í Ríkisprentsmiðjunni Gutenberg, pp. 27*–30* (text) and 64–9 (tables).

1801–   *Sammendrag af statistiske Oplysninger*, Nr. 4 and 6–11. København 1874–1893;
1890   *Statistisk Aarbog*, I–VIII. Copenhagen1896–1903 (main results of censuses 1801–1890).

1703–   Hagstofa Íslands/Statistics Iceland (1997), *Hagskinna. Sögulegar Hagtölur um*
1993   *Ísland/Icelandic Historical Statistics*. Reykjavík: Hagstofa Íslands, tables 2.15–2.19, pp. 137–40 (households since 1703)

IRELAND

1. Vital statistics

Board of Trade (1–83, 1840/53–1924/38), *Statistical Abstract for the United Kingdom*. London: Her Majesty's Stationery Office.

Central Statistics Office (1–, 1931–), *Annual Abstract of the Irish Free State*. Dublin: CSO.

—— (1–, 1926–), *Irish Trade Journal and Statistical Bulletin* (later: *Statistical Bulletin*). Dublin: CSO.

Vaughan, W., and A. Fitzpatrick, eds. (1978), *Irish Historical Statistics. Population, 1821–1971*. A New History of Ireland, vol. II. Dublin: Royal Irish Academy.

2. Population structure by age, sex, and marital status

1851   No author given (1855), *The Census of Ireland for the Year 1851. Part IV. Report on Ages and Education*. Dublin: Alexander Thom and Sons, p. 188 (only age and sex in one-year age groups).
No author given (1856), *The Census of Ireland for the Year 1851. Part VI. General Report*. Dublin: Alexander Thom and Sons, pp. 663–4 (only age and sex in one-year age groups).

1861   No author given (1876), *Census of Ireland, 1871. Part II. General Report, with Illustrative Maps and Diagrams. Summary Tables and Appendix*. Dublin: Alexander Thom, pp. 53–62 (text) and 220 (table).

1871   No author given (1876), *Census of Ireland, 1871. Part II. General Report, with Illustrative Maps and Diagrams. Summary Tables and Appendix*. Dublin: Alexander Thom, pp. 53–62 (text) and 220 (table).

1881   No author given (1882), *Census of Ireland, 1881. Part II. General Report, with Illustrative Maps and Diagrams*. Dublin: Alexander Thom, p. 107.

1891   No author given (1892), *Census of Ireland, 1891. Part II. General Report, with Illustrative Maps, Tables and Appendix*. Dublin: Her Majesty's Stationery Office, p. 111.

1901   Census Commissioners, Charlemont House, Census Office (1903), *Census of Ireland, 1901. Summary Tables*. Dublin: His Majesty's Stationery Office, p. 8.

1911   Census Office, Charlemont House, Dublin (1913), *Census of Ireland, 1911. Area, Houses and Population: Also the Ages, Civil or Conjugal Condition, Occupations, Birthplaces, Religion, and Education of the People*. Dublin: Stationery Office, p. 101.

1926   Department of Industry and Commerce (1929), *Census of Population 1926. Volume V. Part I. Ages, Orphanhood and Conjugal Conditions. Classified by Areas Only*. Dublin: Stationery Office, pp. 42–3.

1936   Department of Industry and Commerce (1939), *Ireland. Census of Population 1936. Volume V. Part I. Ages, Orphanhood and Conjugal Conditions. Classified by Areas Only*. Dublin: Stationery Office, pp. 42–3.

1946   Central Statistics Office (1950), *Census of Population of Ireland 1946. Volume V. Part I. Ages, Orphanhood and Conjugal Conditions. Classified by Areas Only*. Dublin: The Stationery Office, pp. 54–5.

1821– Vaughan, W., and A. Fitzpatrick, eds. (1978), *Irish Historical Statistics.*
1971   *Population, 1821–1971*. Dublin: Royal Irish Academy. (A New History of Ireland, vol. II), pp. 78ff.

3. Population census results on households and families

1851   No author given (1856), *The Census of Ireland for the Year 1851. Part VI. General Report*. Dublin: Alexander Thom and Sons, pp. XXVII–XXXV (text) and 620–3 (table).

1861   No author given (1876), *Census of Ireland, 1871. Part II. General Report, with Illustrative Maps and Diagrams. Summary Tables and Appendix*. Dublin: Alexander Thom (publication not available).

1871   No author given (1876), *Census of Ireland, 1871. Part II. General Report, with Illustrative Maps and Diagrams. Summary Tables and Appendix*. Dublin: Alexander Thom, pp. 14–5 (text) and 203 (table).

1881   No author given (1882), *Census of Ireland, 1881. Part II. General Report, with Illustrative Maps and Diagrams*. Dublin: Alexander Thom, pp. 7–8 and 76–7, 138–9 and 380–4 (table).

1891   No author given (1892), *Census of Ireland, 1891. Part II. General Report, with Illustrative Maps, Tables and Appendix*. Dublin: Her Majesty's Stationery Office, pp. 9–10 and 75 (text), 167 and 530–3 (tables).

1901 Census Commissioners, Charlemont House, Census Office (1902), *Census of Ireland, 1901. Part II. General Report, with Illustrative Maps and Diagrams, Tables and Appendix*. Dublin: His Majesty's Stationery Office, pp. 11–2 and 75 (text), 580–3 (table).

Census Commissioners, Charlemont House, Census Office (1903), *Census of Ireland, 1901. Summary Tables*. Dublin: His Majesty's Stationery Office, pp. V and VIII (text), 5 (table).

1911 Census Office, Charlemont House, Dublin (1913), *Census of Ireland, 1911. Area, Houses and Population: Also the Ages, Civil or Conjugal Condition, Occupations, Birthplaces, Religion, and Education of the People. General Report with Tables and Appendix*. Dublin: Stationery Office, pp. XX–XXXIII (text) and 294–7 (table).

1926 Department of Industry and Commerce (1929), *Census of Population 1926. Volume IV. Housing*. Dublin: Stationery Office, pp. 14–22 (tables).

Department of Industry and Commerce (1934), *Census of Population 1926. Volume X. General Report*. Dublin: Stationery Office, pp. 58–75 (text).

1936 Department of Industry and Commerce (1940), *Census of Population 1936. Volume IV. Housing*. Dublin: Stationery Office, pp. 22–42 (tables).

1946 Central Statistics Office (1954), *Census of Population of Ireland 1946. Volume IV. Part I. Housing. Part 2. Social Amenities*. Dublin: Stationery Office, pp. 16–24 (tables).

Central Statistics Office (1953), *Census of Population of Ireland 1946. Volume IX. Fertility of Marriage*. Dublin: Stationery Office.

1821– Vaughan, W., and A. Fitzpatrick, eds. (1978), *Irish Historical Statistics.*
1971 *Population, 1821–1971*. Dublin: Royal Irish Academy. (A New History of Ireland, vol. II) (no data on households).

ITALY

1. Vital statistics

Direzione Generale della Statistica (publisher varies: since 1922 Instituto Centrale di Statistica (series 1, 1–13, 1878–1905/07 (1908); series 2, 1–9, 1911 (1912)–1922/25 (1926); series 3, 1–7, 1927–1933; series 4, 1–10, 1934–1943)), *Annuario statistico italiano*. Roma.

Istituto Centrale di Statistica (1968), *Sommario di statistiche storiche dell'Italia 1861–1965*. Rome: ISTAT.

—— (1985), *Popolazione residente e presente dei Comuni. Censimenti dal 1861 al 1981*. Rome: ISTAT.

—— (1986), *Sommario di statistiche storiche 1926–1985*. Rome: ISTAT.

2. Population structure by age, sex, and marital status

1861 Ministro d'Agricoltura, Industria e Commercio (1866), *Statistica del Regno d'Italia. Popolazione. Censimento generale (31 dicembre 1861)*. Vol. III. Florence: Tipografia Letteraria e degli Ingegneri (only data on age by sex).

1871 Ministero di Agricoltura, Industria e Commercio, Ufficio Centrale di Statistica (1875), *Popolazione classificata per età, sesso, stato civile ed istruzione elementare. Censimento 31 dicembre 1871*. Vol. II. Rome: Tipografia Cenniniana, pp. 301–4.

1881 Ministero di Agricoltura, Industria e Commercio, Direzione Generale della Statistica (1883), *Censimento della popolazione del regno d'Italia al 31 dicembre*

1881. Vol: II: *Popolazione classificata per età, sesso, stato civile e istruzione elementare*. Rome: Tipografia Bodoniana, p. 584.

1901   Ministero di Agricoltura, Industria e Commercio, Direzione Generale della Statistica (1903), *Censimento della popolazione del regno d'Italia al 10 febraio 1901*. Vol. II: *Numere delle famiglie e numere degli abitanti classificati secondo la qualità della dimora, il luogo di nascita, il sesso, l'età, lo stato civile e l'istruzione. – Ciechi e sordo-muti - Stranieri - Lingue parlate*. Rome: Tipografia Nazionale di G. Bertero, p. 337.

1911   Ministero di Agricoltura, Industria e Commercio, Direzione Generale della Statistica e del Lavoro, Ufficio del Censimento (1914), *Censimento della popolazione del regno d'Italia al 10 giugno 1911*. Vol. II: *Popolazione presente per sesso, età, stato civile ed istruzione (Tav. IV)*. Rome: Tipografia Nazionale di G. Bertero, p. 638.

1921   Presidenza del Consiglio dei Ministri, Istituto Centrale di Statistica (1928), *Censimento della popolazione del regno d'Italia al 1° dicembre 1921. XIX Relazione generale*. Rome: Stabilimento Poligrafico per l'Amministrazione dello Stato, pp. 166ff. (text) and 111* (table).

1931   Istituto Centrale di Statistica del Regno d'Italia (1935), *VII Censimento generale della popolazione 21 aprile 1931*. Vol. IV: *Relazione generale. Parte seconda - Tavole*. Rome: Tipografia I. Failli, pp. 66–9 (table).

1936   Istituto Centrale di Statistica del Regno d'Italia (1938), *VIII Censimento generale della popolazione 21 aprile 1936 - XIV*. Vol. III: *Regno. Popolazione - Territorio - Famiglie - Convivenze - Sesso - Stato civile - Età - Stranieri. Parte prima - Relazione*. Rome: Tipografia Ippolito Failli, pp. 118–21 (table).

        Istituto Centrale di Statistica del Regno d'Italia (1937), *VIII Censimento generale della popolazione 21 aprile 1936 - XIV*. Vol. III: *Regno. Popolazione - Territorio - Famiglie - Convivenze - Sesso - Stato civile - Età - Stranieri. Parte seconda - Tavole*. Rome: Tipografia Ippolito Failli, pp. 118–21 (table).

1861–   Istituto Centrale di Statistica (1968), *Sommario di statistiche storiche dell'Italia*
1965   *1861–1965*. Rome: ISTAT.

1861–   Istituto Centrale di Statistica (1985), *Popolazione residente e presente dei*
1981   *Comuni. Censimenti dal 1861 al 1981*. Rome: ISTAT.

1926–   Istituto Centrale di Statistica (1986), *Sommario di statistiche storiche 1926–1985*.
1985   Rome: ISTAT.

3. Population census results on households and families

1861   Direzione della Statistica Generale del Regno (1867), *Statistica d'Italia. Popolazione. Parte I. Censimento generale (31 Dicembre 1861)*. Florence: Tipografia di G. Barbèra, pp. 26–30 (text) and 162–73 (table).

        Ministro d'Agricoltura, Industria e Commercio (1866), *Statistica del Regno d'Italia. Popolazione. [Parte I]. Censimento generale (31 dicembre 1861)*. Vol. III. Florence: Tipografia Letteraria e degli Ingegneri, pp. VII–VIII (text) and 74–5 (table) (household heads by professions).

1871   Direzione Generale della Statistica (s.a.), *Censimento 31 dicembre 1871. Volume I. Popolazione di fatto e popolazione stabile e mutabile*. Rome, pp. VI–XI (text) and 405–18 (table).

1881   Ministero di Agricoltura, Industria e Commercio, Direzione Generale della Statistica (1883), *Censimento della popolazione del regno d'Italia al 31 dicembre 1881. Volume I - (Parte II). Popolazione secondo la qualità della dimora degli abitanti nei comuni - assenti - famiglie o convivenze sociali - abitazioni - nati all'estero e cittadini stranieri - numero dei ciechi, dei sordo-muti e degli idioti e dei cretini*. Rome: Tipografia Eredi Botta, pp. 1–129 and 137–52 (tables).

        Ministero di Agricoltura, Industria e Commercio, Direzione Generale della

Statistica (1883), *Censimento della popolazione del regno d'Italia al 31 dicembre 1881. [Volume IV] Relazione generale e confronti internazionali.* Rome: Tipografia Eredi Botta, pp. XXIII–XXXIII (text), 94 and 100 (tables).

1901   Ministero di Agricoltura, Industria e Commercio, Direzione Generale della Statistica (1903), *Censimento della popolazione del regno d'Italia al 10 febraio 1901. Volume II. Numere delle famiglie e numere degli abitanti classificati secondo la qualità della dimora, il luogo di nascita, il sesso, l'età, lo stato civile e l'istruzione. – Ciechi e sordo-muti - Stranieri - Lingue parlate.* Rome: Tipografia Nazionale di G. Bertero, pp. 3–138 and 384–7 (tables).

Ministero di Agricoltura, Industria e Commercio, Direzione Generale della Statistica (1904), *Censimento della popolazione del regno d'Italia al 10 febraio 1901. Volume IV. Popolazione presente di ciascun compartimento e del Regno classificata per sesso, età e professione unica o principale. - Professioni accessorie. - Lavoro a domicilio. - Famiglie classificate secondo il numero dei componenti e secondo la professione del capo. - Convivenze in alberghi, collegi, ospedali, ecc. - Temporaneamente disoccupati. - Proprietari di beni immobili. - Religioni.* Rome: Tipografia Nazionale di G. Bertero, pp. 190–249 (tables).

Ministero di Agricoltura, Industria e Commercio, Direzione Generale della Statistica (1904), *Censimento della popolazione del regno d'Italia al 10 febraio 1901. Volume V. Relazione sul metodo di esecuzione e sui risultati del censimento, raffrontati con quelli dei censimenti italiani precedenti e di censimenti esteri.* Rome: Tipografia Nazionale di G. Bertero, pp. XXXII–XXXVII (text), 71 and 154–6 (tables).

1911   Ministero di Agricoltura, Industria e Commercio, Direzione Generale della Statistica e del Lavoro, Ufficio del Censimento (1915), *Censimento della popolazione del regno d'Italia al 10 giugno 1911. Volume VI. Popolazione presente classificata secondo la religione - Popolazione presente classificata secondo il luogo di nascita - Proprietari di beni immobili - Ciechi - Sordomuti - Popolazione presente di età superiore a novanta anni - Stranieri - Famiglie - Convivenze non famigliare.* (Tav. VII a XVII). Rome: Tipografia Nazionale di G. Bertero, pp. 383–487 (tables).

Ministero di Agricoltura, Industria e Commercio, Direzione Generale della Statistica e del Lavoro, Ufficio del Censimento (1915), *Censimento della popolazione del regno d'Italia al 10 giugno 1911. Vol. VII. Relazione.* Rome: Tipografia Nazionale Bertero, pp. 29–39 (text) and 60*–71*, 110*–41* (tables).

1921   Presidenza del Consiglio dei Ministri, Istituto Centrale di Statistica (1928), *Censimento della popolazione del regno d'Italia al 1° dicembre 1921. XIX Relazione generale.* Rome: Stabilimento Poligrafico per l'Amministrazione dello Stato, pp. 149–65 (text) and 46*–82* (tables).

1931   Istituto Centrale di Statistica del Regno d'Italia (1935), *VII Censimento generale della popolazione 21 aprile 1931. Volume IV. Relazione generale. Parte prima - Testo.* Rome: Tipografia I. Failli, pp. 26*–38* (text).

Istituto Centrale di Statistica del Regno d'Italia (1935), *VII Censimento generale della popolazione 21 aprile 1931. Volume IV. Relazione generale. Parte seconda - Tavole.* Rome: Tipografia I. Failli, pp. 12–65 (tables).

1936   Istituto Centrale di Statistica del Regno d'Italia (1938), *VIII Censimento generale della popolazione 21 aprile 1936 - XIV. Volume III. Regno. Popolazione - Territorio - Famiglie - Convivenze - Sesso - Stato civile - Età - Stranieri. Parte prima - Relazione.* Rome: Tipografia Ippolito Failli, pp. 40*–69* (text), 115*–3* (appendix tables).

Istituto Centrale di Statistica del Regno d'Italia (1937), *VIII Censimento generale della popolazione 21 aprile 1936 - XIV. Volume III. Regno. Popolazione - Territorio - Famiglie - Convivenze - Sesso - Stato civile - Età - Stranieri. Parte seconda - Tavole*. Rome: Tipografia Ippolito Failli, pp. 20–91 (tables).

1944   Commissione Alleata e Presidenza del Consiglio dei Ministri - Istituto Centrale di Statistica (1945), *Censimenti e Indagini per la Ricostruzione Nazionale eseguiti nel Settembre 1944. Dati Provvisori: 1ᵃ edizione*. Rome, Febraio 1944, pp. 31–4 (text), 56–7 (table).

1861–   Istituto Centrale di Statistica (1968), *Sommario di statistiche storiche dell'Italia*
1965   *1861–1965*. Rome: ISTAT.

1861–   Istituto Centrale di Statistica (1985), *Popolazione residente e presente dei*
1981   *Comuni. Censimenti dal 1861 al 1981*. Rome: ISTAT.

1926–   Istituto Centrale di Statistica (1986), *Sommario di statistiche storiche 1926–1985*.
1985   Rome: ISTAT.

LUXEMBURG

1. Vital statistics

Service Central de la Statistique et des Études Économiques (1–, 1949–), *Annuaire Statistique du Luxembourg*. Luxemburg: STATEC. (Initially published irregularly, now annually. The 1949, 1955, 1960 and 1973 issues are retrospective.)

—— (1988), *La Mortalité au Luxembourg 1901–1995*. By G. Trausch. Cahiers Économiques, no. 88. Luxemburg: STATEC.

—— (1990a), *Statistiques Historiques 1839–1989*. Luxemburg: STATEC.

—— (1990b), *1839–1989: Histoire Quantitative—Commentaire des Tableaux et Graphiques de l'Annuaire Historique*. Cahiers Économiques, Série D, no. 81. Luxemburg: STATEC.

2. Population structure by age, sex, and marital status

1890   No author given (1891), *Allgemeine Volkszählung im Großherzogthum Luxemburg aufgestellt am 1. Dezember 1890, in Gemäßheit des Beschlusses des Regierungsconseils vom 14. Oktober 1890, und nach Maßgabe der Beschlüsse des Bundesraths des Deutschen Reichs, etc.* Luxemburg: Druck der Hofbuchdruckerei B. Buck, Leon Buck, Nachfolger, pp. 80–4.

1895   Grand-Duché de Luxembourg (1896), *Mémorial du Grand-Duché de Luxembourg*. Année 1896. Nᵒˢ 1 à 72. *Memorial des Großherzogthums Luxemburg*. Jahr 1896. Nr. 1–72. Hier N° 10 de 1896: *Allgemeine Volkszählung im Großherzogthum Luxemburg aufgestellt am 2. Dezember 1895, in Gemäßheit des Beschlusses des Regierungsconseils vom 13. September 1895, und nach Maßgabe der Beschlüsse des Bundesraths des Deutschen Reichs, etc.* Luxemburg: Imprimerie de la Cour V. Bück (L. Bück, Succ.), pp. 82–5.

1900   Commission Permanente de Statistique (1903), *Grand-Duché de Luxembourg. Publications de la Commission Permanente de Statistique. 2ᵉ Fascicule. État de la Population dans le Grand-Duché d'après les résultats du recensement du 1ᵉʳ décembre 1900. Première partie*. Luxemburg: Imprimerie P. Worré-Mertens, pp. 85–6.

1905   Commission Permanente de Statistique (1906), *Grand-Duché de Luxembourg. Publications de la Commission Permanente de Statistique. 11ᵉ Fascicule. État de la Population dans le Grand-Duché d'après les résultats du recensement du 1ᵉʳ décembre 1905. Première partie*. Luxemburg: Imprimerie P. Worré-Mertens, pp. 56–8 (text) and 82*ff. (table).

1910   Ständige Kommission für Statistik (1911), *Grossherzogtum Luxemburg. Publikationen der Ständigen Kommission für Statistik. Heft XXXVI. Ergebnisse der Volkszählung vom 1. Dezember 1910 nebst Ortschaftsverzeichnis.* Luxemburg: Charles Beffort, pp. 33–4 and 46–7.

1922 Office de Statistique (1923), *Grand-Duché de Luxembourg. Publications de l'Office de Statistique. Fascicule 46. Résultats du recensement de la population du 1ᵉʳ décembre 1922 et Chiffres de la population de résidence habituelle au 31 décembre 1922, avec la Nomenclature alphabétique des localités, villes, bourgs, villages, hameaux, châteaux, fermes, moulins et maisons isolées.* Luxemburg: Imprimerie M. Huss (no data available).
See also Office de Statistique (1929), pp. 24* (age: 0–15, 15–70+ in 5-year age groups without sex division in relative numbers).

1927 Office de Statistique (1929), *Grand-Duché de Luxembourg. Publications de l'Office de Statistique. Fascicule 55. Résultats du recensement de la population du 1ᵉʳ décembre 1927, et Chiffres de la population de résidence habituelle au 31 décembre 1927, avec la Nomenclature alphabétique des localités, villes, bourgs, villages, hameaux, châteaux, fermes, moulins et maisons isolées.* Luxemburg: Imprimerie Art. Luxbg. S.A., Anc. Dʳ M. Huss, Luxbg., pp. 16* and 23*.

1930 Office de Statistique (1932), *Grand-Duché de Luxembourg. Publications de l'Office de Statistique. Fascicule 62. Résultats du recensement de la population du 1ᵉʳ décembre 1930, avec la Nomenclature alphabétique des localités, villes, bourgs, villages, hameaux, châteaux, fermes, moulins et maisons isolées.* Luxemburg: Imprimerie de la Cour Victor Buck, pp. 18* and 25–6*.

1935 Office de Statistique (1938), *Grand-Duché de Luxembourg. Publications de l'Office de Statistique. Fascicule 69. Résultats du recensement de la population du 31ᵉʳ décembre 1935. Tome I.* Luxemburg: Imprimerie Ch.-Léon Beffort, pp. 29 and 55.

1839– Als, G. (1989), *Population et Économie du Luxembourg 1839–1989. Réalités et*
1989 *Perspectives 1989/5* (ed. by Banque Générale du Luxembourg).

1839– Als, G. (1991), *Histoire Quantitative du Luxembourg 1839–1990.* Luxemburg:
1990 STATEC, 1991 (Cahiers Économiques, Série D, no. 79).

1839– Service Central de la Statistique et des Études Économiques (1990a), *Statistiques*
1989 *Historiques 1839–1989.* Luxemburg: STATEC.

1839– Service Central de la Statistique et des Études Économiques (1990b), *1839–1989:*
1989 *Histoire Quantitative - Commentaire des Tableaux et Graphiques de l'Annuaire Historique.* Luxemburg: STATEC (Cahiers Économiques, Série D, no. 81).
Service Central de la Statistique et des Études Économiques (various years), *Annuaire Statistique du Luxembourg.* 1–, 1949–. (Initially published irregularly, now annually. The 1949, 1955, 1960 and 1973 issues are retrospective.)

3. Population census results on households and families

1890 No author given (1891), *Allgemeine Volkszählung im Großherzogthum Luxemburg aufgestellt am 1. Dezember 1890, in Gemäßheit des Beschlusses des Regierungsconseils vom 14. Oktober 1890, und nach Maßgabe der Beschlüsse des Bundesraths des Deutschen Reichs, etc.* Luxemburg: Druck der Hofbuchdruckerie B. Buck, Leon Buck, Nachfolger, pp. 2–11 (table).

1895 Grand-Duché de Luxembourg (1896), *Mémorial du Grand-Duché de Luxembourg. Année 1896.* Nᵒˢ 1 à 72. *Memorial des Großherzogthums Luxemburg. Jahr 1896.* Nr. 1–72. Hier Nᵒ 10 de 1896: *Allgemeine Volkszählung im Großherzogthum Luxemburg aufgestellt am 2. Dezember 1895, in Gemäßheit des Beschlusses des Regierungsconseils vom 13. September 1895, und nach Maßgabe der Beschlüsse des Bundesraths des Deutschen Reichs, etc.* Luxemburg: Imprimerie de la Cour V. Bück (L. Bück, Succ.).

1900 Commission Permanente de Statistique (1903), *Grand-Duché de Luxembourg. Publications de la Commission Permanente de Statistique. 2ᵉ Fascicule. État de la*

Population dans le Grand-Duché d'après les résultats du recensement du 1er décembre 1900. Première partie. Luxemburg: Imprimerie P. Worré-Mertens, pp. 50–64 and 149–57 (text).

Commission Permanente de Statistique (1903), *Grand-Duché de Luxembourg. Publications de la Commission Permanente de Statistique. 3e Fascicule. État de la Population dans le Grand-Duché d'après les résultats du recensement du 1er décembre 1900. Deuxième partie.* Luxemburg: Imprimerie P. Worré-Mertens, pp. 2–81 and 305–23.

1905   Commission Permanente de Statistique (1906), *Grand-Duché de Luxembourg. Publications de la Commission Permanente de Statistique. 11e Fascicule. État de la Population dans le Grand-Duché d'après les résultats du recensement du 1er décembre 1905. Première partie.* Luxemburg: Imprimerie P. Worré-Mertens, pp. 86–99.

Commission Permanente de Statistique (1907), *Grand-Duché de Luxembourg. Publications de la Commission Permanente de Statistique. 13e Fascicule. État de la Population dans le Grand-Duché d'après les résultats du recensement du 1er décembre 1905. Deuxième partie.* Luxemburg: Imprimerie P. Worré-Mertens, pp. 142–52 (text) and 89*–103* (tables).

1910   Ständige Kommission für Statistik (1911), *Grossherzogtum Luxemburg. Publikationen der Ständigen Kommission für Statistik. Heft XXXVI. Ergebnisse der Volkszählung vom 1. Dezember 1910 nebst Ortschaftsverzeichnis.* Luxemburg: Charles Beffort, pp. 76–80 (text) and 2*–65* (table).

1922   Office de Statistique (1923), *Grand-Duché de Luxembourg. Publications de l'Office de Statistique. Fascicule 46. Résultats du recensement de la population du 1er décembre 1922 et Chiffres de la population de résidence habituelle au 31 décembre 1922, avec la Nomenclature alphabétique des localités, villes, bourgs, villages, hameaux, châteaux, fermes, moulins et maisons isolées.* Luxemburg: Imprimerie M. Huss, pp. 2–65 (table).

1927   Office de Statistique (1929), *Grand-Duché de Luxembourg. Publications de l'Office de Statistique. Fascicule 55. Résultats du recensement de la population du 1er décembre 1927, et Chiffres de la population de résidence habituelle au 31 décembre 1927, avec la Nomenclature alphabétique des localités, villes, bourgs, villages, hameaux, châteaux, fermes, moulins et maisons isolées.* Luxemburg: Imprimerie Art. Luxbg. S.A., Anc. Dr M. Huss, Luxbg., pp. 31*–40* (text) and 2–65 (table).

1930   Office de Statistique (1932), *Grand-Duché de Luxembourg. Publications de l'Office de Statistique. Fascicule 62. Résultats du recensement de la population du 1er décembre 1930, avec la Nomenclature alphabétique des localités, villes, bourgs, villages, hameaux, châteaux, fermes, moulins et maisons isolées.* Luxemburg: Imprimerie de la Cour Victor Buck, pp. 50*–2* (text) and 2–65 (table) (for data on household size see Office de Statistique (1938: 103).

1935   Office de Statistique (1938), *Grand-Duché de Luxembourg. Résultats du recensement de la population du 31er décembre 1935. Tome I.* (Publications de l'Office de Statistique. Fascicule 69). Luxemburg: Imprimerie Ch.-Léon Beffort, pp. 96–106 (text).
Tableau général. Superficies, nombre des constructions habités et inhabités, nombre des appartements inhabités, nombre des ménages, population présente et absente, population de résidence habituelle et population politique d'après le recensement du 31 décembre 1935, pp. 2–3.

1947   Office de la Statistique Génèrale (1948?), *Grand-Duché de Luxembourg. Ministère des Affaires Économiques. Statistique Générale. Résultats du recensement de la population du 31er décembre 1947. Premiers Résultats et Liste Alphabétique des Localités.* (Publications de l'Office de la Statistique Générale,

Fascicule 78). Esch-sur-Alzette: Imprimerie-Reluire Henry Ney-Etcher, p. 12.

1839– Als, G. (1989), *Population et Économie du Luxembourg 1839–1989*. Réalités et
1989 Perspectives 1989/5 (ed. by Banque Générale du Luxembourg).

1839– Als, G. (1991), *Histoire Quantitative du Luxembourg 1839–1990*. Luxemburg:
1990 STATEC, 1991 (Cahiers Économiques, Série D, no. 79), pp. 75–9.

1839– Service Central de la Statistique et des Études Économiques (1990a), *Statistiques*
1989 *Historiques 1839–1989*. Luxemburg: STATEC, pp. 69 and 73–4.

1839– Service Central de la Statistique et des Études Économiques (1990b), 1839–1989:
1989 *Histoire Quantitative - Commentaire des Tableaux et Graphiques de l'Annuaire*
Historique. Luxemburg: STATEC (Cahiers Économiques, Série D, no. 81).

Service Central de la Statistique et des Études Économiques (various years),
Annuaire Statistique du Luxembourg. 1–, 1949–. (Initially published irregularly,
now annually. The 1949, 1955, 1960 and 1973 issues are retrospective.)

THE NETHERLANDS

1. Vital statistics

Bureau voor de Statistiek (CBS) (1–90, 1906–1995), *Maandschrift van het Centraal
Bureau voor de Statistiek (CBS)*. s'Gravenhage: Staatsuitgeverij.

Centraal Bureau voor de Statistiek (CBS) (1–, 1953–), *Maandstatistiek van de
Bevolking*. Voorburg and Heerlen: CBS.

—— (CBS) (1–, 1969/70–), *Statistical Yearbook of the Netherlands*. Voorburg and
Heerlen: CBS.

—— (CBS) (1970), *Zeventig jaren statistiek in tijdreksen 1899–1969*. The Hague:
Staatsuitgeverij.

—— (CBS) (1975), *75 jaar statistiek van Nederland*. The Hague: Staatsuitgeverij
(time series from 1900–1974).

Société de Statistique des Pays-Bas (1882), *Resumé statistique pour le Royaume des
Pays-Bas, 1850–1883*. La Haye: H. L. Smits.

—— (1883–), *Jaarcijfers/Annuaire Statistique des Pays Bas*. La Haye: H. L. Smits
(Title and publisher varies).

Van der Bie, R., P. Dehing, and J.P. Smits, red. (1999), *Tweehonderd jaar statistiek
in tijdreeksen, 1800–1999*. Voorburg and Heerlen: CBS / Amsterdam: Stichting
beheer IISG.

Vereeniging voor de Statistiek in Nederland (1–19, 1881–1897), *Jaarcijfers over
18.. en vorige Jaren omtrent Bevolking, Landbouw, Handel, Belastingen,
Onderwijs enz*. The Hague: Ter Drukkerij van H. L. Smits.

2. Population structure by age, sex, and marital status

1830 No author given (1864), *Uitkomsten der vierde tienjarige volkstelling in het
Koningrijk der Nederlanden op den een en dertigsten December 1859*. The
Hague, pp. 414–9, esp. p. 419.

1840 No author given (1864), *Uitkomsten der vierde tienjarige volkstelling in het
Koningrijk der Nederlanden op den een en dertigsten December 1859*. The
Hague, pp. 420–1.

1849 No author given (1852), *Uitkomsten der derde tienjarige volkstelling in het
Koningrijk der Nederlanden op den Negentienden November 1849*. The Hague:
Algemene Landsdrukkerij, p. 8.

1859 No author given (1864), *Uitkomsten der vierde tienjarige volkstelling in het
Koningrijk der Nederlanden op den een en dertigsten December 1859*. The

Hague, pp. 184–54.

1869 No author given (1875), *Uitkomsten der vijfde tienjarige volkstelling in het Koningrijk der Nederlanden op den eersten December 1869, tweede deel.* The Hague, pp. 48–9.

1879 Departement van Binnenlandsche Zaken (1881), *Uitkomsten der zesde tienjarige volkstelling in het Koningrijk der Nederlanden op den dertigsten December 1879.* The Hague, pp. 69–71.

1889 Centrale Commissie voor de Statistiek (1893), *Uitkomsten der zevende tienjaarlijksche volkstelling in het Koninkrijk der Nederlanden op den een en dertigsten December 1889 (met uitzondering van de beroepstelling). Overzicht van de uitkomsten.* The Hague, p. 81 (only 5-year age groups).
There is no summary table for one-year age groups whether on the level of the Rijk or for the provinces. For each of the 11 provinces there is a single volume, containing the data in one-year age groups, but only for each of the communes, without a summary table for the province. Therefore the data were requested from the CBS and were kindly supplied by Marleen van Os from the Population Department of Statistics Netherlands on July 17, 1997.

1899 Centraal Bureau voor de Statistiek (1901), *Uitkomsten der achtste tienjaarlijksche Volkstelling in het Koningrijk der Nederlanden gehouden op den een en dertigsten December 1899 (met uitzondering van de beroepstelling en de woningstatistiek), twaalfde deel: Het Rijk.* The Hague, pp. 114–7 (Bijdragen tot de Statistiek van Nederland, nieuwe volgreeks No. 3).

1909 Centraal Bureau voor de Statistiek (1911), *Uitkomsten der negende tienjaarlijksche Volkstelling in het Koningrijk der Nederlanden gehouden op den een en dertigsten December 1909, tweede deel: Het Rijk.* The Hague, pp. 375–8 (Bijdragen tot de Statistiek van Nederland, nieuwe volgreeks No. CXLIV).

1920 Centraal bureau voor de statistiek (CBS) (1922), *Volkstelling 31 December 1920. Leeftijd, burgerlijke staat, samenwoning, geboorteplats, nationaliteit.* The Hague, pp. 247–9 (Statistiek van Nederland, No. 352).

1930 Centraal bureau voor de statistiek (CBS) (1933), *Volkstelling 31 December 1930. Deel II: Leeftijd, burgerlijke staat, samenwoning, geboorteplats, nationaliteit.* The Hague, pp. 258–60 (Statistiek van Nederland).

1947 Centraal bureau voor de statistiek (CBS) (1954), *12^e Volkstelling, annex woningtelling 31 Mei 1947. Serie A. Rijks- en provinciale cijfers. Deel 1: Belangrijkste uitkomsten der eigenlijke Volkstelling.* Utrecht, pp. 58–9.

1830– Centrale Commissie voor de Statistiek (1893), *Uitkomsten der zevende*
1889 *tienjaarlijksche volkstelling in het Koninkrijk der Nederlanden op den een en dertigsten December 1889 (met uitzondering van de beroepstelling). Overzicht van de uitkomsten.* The Hague, pp. 79–81.

1830– Centraal bureau voor de statistiek (CBS) (1924), *Volkstelling 31 December 1920.*
1920 *Inleiding tot de uitkomsten der tiende algemeene volkstelling.* The Hague, esp. pp. 86–9.

1830– Centraal bureau voor de statistiek (CBS) (1970), *Bevolking van Nederland naar*
1969 *geslacht, leeftijd en burgerlijke staat 1830–1969.* The Hague: Staatsuitgeverij, esp. pp. 82–94.

3. Population census results on households and families

1830 No author given (1864), *Uitkomsten der vierde tienjarige volkstelling in het Koningrijk der Nederlanden op den een en dertigsten December 1859. Tweede deel.* The Hague, pp. 407–21.

1840 No author given (1852), *Uitkomsten der derde tienjarige volkstelling in het Koningrijk der Nederlanden op den Negentienden November 1849.* The Hague: Algemeene Landsdrukkerij, pp. V–VII (text).

1849   No author given (1852), *Uitkomsten der derde tienjarige volkstelling in het Koningrijk der Nederlanden op den Negentienden November 1849.* The Hague: Algemeene Landsdrukkerij, pp. V–VII (text), 2–3 (table).

1859   No author given (1863), *Uitkomsten der vierde tienjarige volkstelling in het Koningrijk der Nederlanden op den een en dertigsten December 1859. Eerste deel.* The Hague: van Weelden en Mingelen, pp. IX–XI (text), 1–133, 165–223 (tables).
No author given (1864), *Uitkomsten der vierde tienjarige volkstelling in het Koningrijk der Nederlanden op den een en dertigsten December 1859. Tweede deel.* The Hague: van Weelden en Mingelen, pp. 407–21 (data for 1830 and 1840).

1869   No author given (1873), *Uitkomsten der vijfde tienjarige volkstelling in het Koningrijk der Nederlanden op den eersten December 1869, eerste deel.* The Hague: van Weelden en Mingelen, pp. VIII–X (text); 1–253 and 255–84 (tables).

1879   Departement van Binnenlandsche Zaken (1881), *Uitkomsten der zesde tienjarige volkstelling in het Koningrijk der Nederlanden op den dertigsten December 1879.* The Hague: van Weelden en Mingelen, pp. 10–2 (text) .

1889   Centrale Commissie voor de Statistiek (1893), *Uitkomsten der zevende tienjaarlijksche volkstelling in het Koninkrijk der Nederlanden op den een en dertigsten December 1889 (met uitzondering van de beroepstelling). Overzicht van de uitkomsten.* The Hague, pp. 57–9 (table VII) (no summary for the country, but data for each province in separate volumes available).

1899   Centraal Bureau voor de Statistiek (1904), *Inleiding tot de uitkomsten der achtste algemeene tienjaarlijksche Volkstelling van een en dertig December 1899 en daaraan verbonden Beroepstelling en Woningstatistiek, in vergelijking zooveel mogelijk met de uitkomsten van vroegere tellingen. Aflevering I. Uitkomsten der eigenlijke Volkstelling* (1903), pp. 55–61; *Aflevering II. Uitkomsten der beroepstelling en der woningstatistiek (1904),* pp. 355–74. The Hague: Gebrs. Belinfante (Bijdragen tot de Statistiek van Nederland, nieuwe volgreeks No. XXXII).
Centraal Bureau voor de Statistiek (1901), *Uitkomsten der achtste tienjaarlijksche Volkstelling in het Koningrijk der Nederlanden gehouden op den een en dertigsten December 1899 (met uitzondering van de beroepstelling en de woningstatistiek), twaalfde deel: Het Rijk.* The Hague, pp. 25–7 (Bijdragen tot de Statistiek van Nederland, nieuwe volgreeks No. 3).

1909   Centraal Bureau voor de Statistiek (1913), *Inleiding tot de uitkomsten der Negende Algemeene Tienjaarlijksche Volkstelling met daaraan verbonden Woning- en Beroepstelling. Introduction des resultats du Neuvième recensement général et du dénombrement des demeures habitées et des professions.* The Hague: Gebrs. Belinfante, pp. 55–65 (Bijdragen tot de Statistiek van Nederland, nieuwe volgreeks No. 184).
Centraal Bureau voor de Statistiek (1911), *Uitkomsten der Negende Tienjaarlijksche Volkstelling in het Koninkrijk der Nederlanden gehouden op den een en dertigsten December 1909. Résultats du neuvième recensement de la population du Royaume des Pays-Bas au 31 décembre 1909. Derde Deel. Troisième Partie.* The Hague: Gebrs. Belinfante, pp. 215–24 and 245–77 (tables) (Bijdragen tot de Statistiek van Nederland, nieuwe volgreeks No. CXLIV).

1920   Centraal bureau voor de statistiek (CBS) (1924), *Volkstelling 31 December 1920. Inleiding tot de uitkomsten der tiende algemeene volkstelling.* The Hague: N. V. Boekh. V. H. Gebr. Belinfante, pp. 47–55 (text) (Statistiek van Nederland, No. 378).
Centraal bureau voor de statistiek (CBS) (1922), *Volkstelling 31 December 1920. Leeftijd, burgerlijke staat, samenwoning, geboorteplats, nationaliteit.* The Hague: N. V. Boekh. V. H. Gebr. Belinfante, pp. 251–3 (table) (Statistiek van Nederland,

No. 352).

1930 Centraal bureau voor de statistiek (CBS) (1933), *Volkstelling 31 December 1930. Deel II: Leeftijd, burgerlijke staat, samenwoning, geboorteplats, nationaliteit.* The Hague, pp. 261–3 (Statistiek van Nederland).
Centraal bureau voor de statistiek (CBS) (1933), *Volkstelling 31 December 1930. Deel IV: Woningstatistiek en gezinsstatistiek.* The Hague, pp. 65–153 (Statistiek van Nederland).
Centraal bureau voor de statistiek (CBS) (1934), *Volkstelling 31 December 1930. Deel IX: Inleiding tot de uitkomsten der elfde algemeene volkstelling, van de woningstatistiek en gezinsstatistiek, van de statistiek der huwelijksvruchtbaarheid en van de statistiek der academisch gegradueerden. Uitkomsten van de statistiek der huwelijksvruchtbaarheid en van die der academisch gegradueerden (absolute cijfers).* The Hague, pp. 25–33 (introduction), 97–117 (family statistics), 118–59 (statistics on marital fertility) (Statistiek van Nederland).

1947 Centraal bureau voor de statistiek (CBS) (1954), *12^e Volkstelling, annex woningtelling 31 Mei 1947. Serie A. Rijks- en provinciale cijfers. Deel 1: Belangreijkste uitkomsten der eigenlijke Volkstelling.* Utrecht: Uitgeversmaatschappij W. de Haan N. V., pp. 34–8 (definitions), 68–72 (Tables 2A and 2B).
Centraal bureau voor de statistiek (CBS) (1951), *12^e Volkstelling, annex woningtelling 31 Mei 1947. Serie A. Rijks- en provinciale cijfers. Deel 3: Woning- en gezinstelling.* Utrecht: Uitgeversmaatschappij W. de Haan N. V., pp. 17–20 (definitions); pp. 61–2 and 70–82 (text), 88–91 (tables).
Centraal bureau voor de statistiek (CBS) (1951), *12^e Volkstelling, annex woningtelling 31 Mei 1947. Serie A. Rijks- en provinciale cijfers. Deel 4: Statistiek der bestaande huwelijken en van de vruchtbaarheid dezer huwelijken.* Utrecht: Uitgeversmaatschappij W. de Haan N. V.
Centraal bureau voor de statistiek (CBS) (1949), *12^e Volkstelling, annex woningtelling 31 Mei 1947. Serie B. Voornamste cijfers per gemeente. Deel 2: Woning- en gezinstelling.* The Hague: Staatsdrukkerij - en uitgeverijbedrijf.

1795– Centraal Bureau voor de Statistiek (compiled by J. Jonker, J. van Maarseveen, and
1871, T. Vreugdenhil), and NIWI (P. Doorn) (1999), Part 1. *Data en publicatie*
1899 *Volkstelling 1899.* 2 CD-ROMs. Voorburg/Heerlen: CBS; Part 2. *Publicaties Volkstellingen 1795–1971.* 5 CD-ROMs. Voorburg/Heerlen: CBS.

1899– Centraal Bureau voor de Statistiek (CBS) (1970), *Zeventig jaren statistiek in*
1960 *tijdreksen 1899–1969.* The Hague: Staatsuitgeverij, p. 13.

1899– Centraal Bureau voor de Statistiek (CBS) (1989), *Negentig jaren statistiek in*
1988 *tijdreeksen 1899–1989.* The Hague: sdu/uitgeverij/cbs-publikaties, p. 22.

1899– Centraal Bureau voor de Statistiek (CBS) (1994), *Vijfennegentig jaren statistiek in*
1993 *tijdreeksen 1899–1994.* The Hague: sdu/uitgeverij/cbs-publikaties, p. 20.

NORWAY

1. Vital statistics

Mamelund, S., H. Brunborg, and T. Noack (1997), *Skilsmisser i Norge 1886–1995 for kalenderår og ekteskapskohorter. Divorce in Norway 1886–1995 by Calendar Year and Marriage Cohort.* Reports, no. 97/19. Oslo-Kongsvinger: Statistisk Sentralbyrå–Statistics Norway.

Statistics Norway (1995), *Historisk statistikk 1994.* NOS C 188. Oslo-Kongsvinger: Statistisk Sentralbyrå–Statistics Norway.

Statistisk Sentralbyrå (SSB) (1–, 1880–), *Statistisk Årbok 19...* Oslo: Statistisk Sentralbyrå.

—— (1962), *Dødeligheten og dens årsaker i Norge 1856–1955*. (Mortality Trends and Causes of Death in Norway). SØS, no. 10. Oslo: Statistisk Sentralbyrå.

—— (1965), *Ekteskap, fødsler og vandringer i Norge 1856–1960*. (Marriages, Births and Migration in Norway). SØS, no. 13. Oslo: Statistisk Sentralbyrå.

—— (1966), *Dødelighet blant spedbarn i Norge 1901–1963*. (Infant Mortality in Norway). SØS, no. 17. Oslo: Statistisk Sentralbyrå.

—— (1969), *Historisk statistikk 1968*. NOS ser. 12 no. 245. Oslo: Statistisk Sentralbyrå.

—— (1976), *Ekteskap og barnetal–ei gransking av fertilitetsutviklinga i Norge 1920–1970*. (Marriages and Number of Children: An Analysis of Fertility Trends in Norway). Articles. Oslo: Statistisk Sentralbyrå.

—— (1978), *Historisk statistikk 1978*. NOS ser. XII vol. 291. Oslo: Statistisk Sentralbyrå.

—— (1989), *Fruktbarhet og dødelighet i Norge 1771–1987*. (Fertility and mortality in Norway). Reports, no. 89/17. Oslo: Statistisk Sentralbyrå.

2. Population structure by age, sex, and marital status

1865   Departementet for det indre (1868), *Resultaterne af Folketællingen i Norge i Januar 1866. Første hefte, indeholdene Tabeller over folkemængde med mere i rigets forskjellige jurisdiktioner samt folkemængde fordelt efter alder, kjøn og ægteskabelig stilling den 31te december 1865* (Norges Officielle Statistik, C.No.1). Christiania: Trykt i det Steenske Bogtrykkeri, p. 60.

1875   Statistisk Centralbureau (1879), *Resultaterne af Folketællingen i Norge i Januar 1876. 2^det hefte, indeholdene Opgaver over de beboede Huse og Husholdninger samt Folkemængden fordelt efter Kjøn, Alder og ægteskabelig Stilling* (Norges Officielle Statistik, C.No.1). Christiania: Trykt i det Steenske Bogtrykkeri, pp. 136–7.

1890   Statistisk Centralbureau (1895), *Folketællingen i Kongeriget Norge i Januar 1891. Beboede Huse og Husholdninger samt Folkemængde fordelt efter Kjøn, Alder og ægteskabelig Stilling. (Recensement du 1er Janvier: Maisons habitées et ménages. Population classé par sexe, par âge et par état civil.)* (Norges Officielle Statistik, Tredie Række No. 229). Christiania: I Kommission hos H. Aschehoug, pp. 106–7 and 174–93.

1900   Statistisk Centralbureau (1903), *Folketællingen i Kongeriget Norge 3 December 1900. Andet Hefte. Folkemængde fordelt efter Kjøn, Alder og ægteskabelig Stilling. (Recensement du 3 Décembre 1900: Population classé par sexe, par âge et par état civil.)* (Norges Officielle Statistik, Fjerde Række No. 73). Christiania: I Kommission hos H. Aschehoug, pp. 214–7.

        Statistisk Centralbureau (1906), *Folketællingen i Kongeriget Norge 3 December 1900. Hovedoversigt. (Recensement du 3 Décembre 1900: Aperçu général.)* (Norges Officielle Statistik, V. 4.). Christiania: I Kommission hos H. Aschehoug, pp. 23–33.

1910   Statistisk Centralbyraa (1914), *Folketællingen i Norge 1 December 1910. Femte Hefte. Folkemængde fordelt efter Kjøn, Alder og egteskabelig Stilling samt Fødesteder. Fremmede Staters Undersaatter. (Recensement du 1 Décembre 1910: Population classé par sexe, par âge, par état civil et par lieu de naissance. - Sujets étrangers.)* (Norges Officielle Statistik, VI.8). Christiania: I Kommission hos H. Aschehoug, pp. 130–2.

        Statistisk Centralbureau (1916), *Folketællingen i Kongeriget Norge 1 December 1910. Hovedoversigt. (Recensement du 1 Décembre 1910: Aperçu général.)* (Norges Officielle Statistik, VI. 77). Christiania: I Kommission hos H.

Aschehoug, pp. 21–40.

1920   Statistisk Centralbyrå (1923), *Folketællingen i Norge 1 Desember 1920. Tredje Hefte. Folkemengden fordelt efter kjønn, alder og ekteskapelig stilling. (Recensement du 1 Décembre 1920: III. Population répartie par le sexe, l'âge et l'état civil.)* (Norges Offisielle Statistikk, VII.76). Christiania: I Kommisjon hos H. Aschehoug, pp. 144–51.

1930   Statistisk Centralbyrå (1934), *Folketellingen i Norge 1 Desember 1930. Femte hefte. Folkemengden fordelt efter kjønn, alder og ekteskapelig stilling. (Recensement du 1er Décembre 1930: V. Population répartie par le sexe, l'âge et l'état civil.)* (Norges Offisielle Statistikk, IX.24). Oslo: I Kommisjon hos H. Aschehoug, pp. 2–44.

1946   Statistisk Sentralbyrå (1951), *Folketellingen i Norge 3. Desember 1946. Fjerde hefte. Folkemengden etter kjønn, alder og ekteskapelig stilling. Riket og fylkene. Fremmede statsborgere. (Recensement de la population le 3 décembre 1946: IV. Population par sexe, âge et état civil. Royaume et préfectures. Sujets étrangers.)* (Norges Offisielle Statistikk XI.50.). Oslo: I Kommisjon hos H. Aschehoug, pp. 2–15 (0–14 one-year age groups, otherwise grouped data); pp. 2–3 and 37–47 (one-year age groups).

1801–
1960   Statistisk Sentralbyrå (1969), *Historisk statistikk 1968* (NOS ser. 12 no. 245). Oslo: Statistisk Sentralbyrå.

1801–
1975   Statistisk Sentralbyrå (1978), *Historisk statistikk 1978* (NOS ser. XII vol. 291). Oslo: Statistisk Sentralbyrå.

1801–
1990   Statistics Norway (1995), *Historisk statistikk 1994* (NOS C 188). Oslo-Kongsvinger: Statistisk Sentralbyrå–Statistics Norway.

3. Population census results on households and families

1825   Departementet for det Indre (1874), *Tabeller Vedkommende Folketællingerne i Aarene 1801 og 1825.* (Norges Officielle Statistik, C.No.1). Christiania: Trykt i Ringvolds Bogtrykkeri, pp. 67–76.

1855   Departementet for det Indre (1857), *Statistiske Tabeller for Kongeriget Norge, udgivne efter Foranstaltning af Departementet for det Indre. Sextende Række, indeholdene Tabeller over Folkemængden i Norge den 31te December 1855 samt over de i Tidsrummet 1846–1855 Ægteviede, Fodte og Døde.* Christiania: Trykt hos W. C. Fabritius, pp. IV–IX.

1865   Departementet for det Indre (1868), *Resultaterne af Folketællingen i Norge i Januar 1866. Første hefte, indeholdene Tabeller over folkemængde med mere i rigets forskjellige jurisdiktioner samt folkemængde fordelt efter alder, kjøn og ægteskabelig stilling den 31te december 1865* (Norges Officielle Statistik, C.No.1). Christiania: Trykt i det Steenske Bogtrykkeri, pp. 3–10 and 11–5.

1875   Statistisk Centralbureau (1879), *Resultaterne af Folketællingen i Norge i Januar 1876. 2det hefte, indeholdene Opgaver over de beboede Huse og Husholdninger samt Folkemængden fordelt efter Kjøn, Alder og ægteskabelig Stilling* (Norges Officielle Statistik, C.No.1). Christiania: Trykt i det Steenske Bogtrykkeri, pp. 73–86, 93–4 (tables).
        Statistisk Centralbureau (1882), *Bidrag til Tabeller indeholdene Resultaterne af Folketællingen i Norge i Januar 1876.* (Norges Officielle Statistik. Ny Række. Udgiven i aaret 1882. C.No.1). Christiania: Trykt i Ringvolds Bogtrykkeri, pp. 1–4 and 205–10 (historical account on population censuses); 31–5 (text on households).

1890   Statistisk Centralbureau (1895), *Folketællingen i Kongeriget Norge i Januar 1891. Beboede Huse og Husholdninger samt Folkemængde fordelt efter Kjøn, Alder og ægteskabelig Stilling. (Recensement du 1er Janvier: Maisons habitées et ménages. Population classé par sexe, par âge et par état civil.)* (Norges Officielle

Statistik, Tredie Række No. 229). Christiania: I Kommission hos H. Aschehoug, pp. 72–105, 234–5 (tables).

Statistisk Centralbureau (1898), *Oversigt over de vigtigste Resultater af de statistiske Tabeller vedkommende Folketællingen i Kongeriget Norge 1 Januar 1891. (Aperçu général du recensement du 1ᵉʳ Janvier 1891.)* (Norges Officielle Statistik, Tredie Række No. 284). Christiania: I Kommission hos H. Aschehoug, pp. 25–7 (text).

1900   Statistisk Centralbureau (1904), *Folketællingen i Kongeriget Norge 3 December 1900. Tredie Hefte. Beboede Huse og Husholdninger. (Recensement du 3 Décembre 1900: Maisons habitées et ménages.)* (Norges Officielle Statistik, Fjerde Række No. 82). Christiania: I Kommission hos H. Aschehoug, pp. 54–87 (tables), 90–149 (representative data).

Statistisk Centralbureau (1906), *Folketællingen i Kongeriget Norge 3 December 1900. Hovedoversigt. (Recensement du 3 Décembre 1900: Aperçu général.)* (Norges Officielle Statistik, V. 4.). Christiania: I Kommission hos H. Aschehoug, pp. 19–22 (text).

1910   Statistisk Centralbyraa (1913), *Folketællingen i Norge 1 December 1910. Tredje Hefte. Bebodde Hus og Husholdninger. (Recensement du 1 Décembre 1910: Maisons habitées et ménages.)* (Norges Officielle Statistik, V.188). Christiania: I Kommission hos H. Aschehoug, pp. 66–100 (tables).

Statistisk Centralbureau (1916), *Folketællingen i Kongeriget Norge 1 December 1910. Hovedoversigt. (Recensement du 1 Décembre 1910: Aperçu général.)* (Norges Officielle Statistik, VI. 77.). Christiania: I Kommission hos H. Aschehoug, pp. 22–3 (text).

1920   Statistisk Centralbyrå (1923), *Folketællingen i Norge 1 Desember 1920. Sjette Hefte. Barnetallet i norske ektskap. (Census of 1ˢᵗ December 1920: VI. Fertility of Marriages.)* (Norges Offisielle Statistikk, VII.97). Christiania: I Kommisjon hos H. Aschehoug.

Statistisk Centralbyrå (1923), *Folketællingen i Norge 1 Desember 1920. Syvende Hefte. Boligstatistikk. – Byer. (Recensement du 1ᵉʳ Décembre 1920: VII: Statistique d'habitation. - Villes.)* (Norges Offisielle Statistikk, VII.98). Christiania: I Kommisjon hos H. Aschehoug, pp. 10–1*, 67*–8* (text); 78, 201–8 (tables) (household census at the same time).

Statistisk Centralbyrå (1924), *Folketællingen i Norge 1 Desember 1920. Ottende Hefte. Boligstatistikk. – Bygder. (Recensement du 1ᵉʳ Décembre 1920: VIII: Statistique d'habitation. - Districts ruraux.)* (Norges Offisielle Statistikk, VII.144.). Christiania: I Kommisjon hos H. Aschehoug, pp. 10*–1*, 57*–61* (text); 62–87, 118–32 (tables) (at the same time household census).

1930   Statistisk Centralbyrå (1935), *Folketællingen i Norge 1. desember 1930. Niende Hefte. Barnetallet i norske ekteskap. (Census of December 1ˢᵗ 1930: IX. Fertility of Marriages.)* (Norges Offisielle Statistikk, IX.62). Christiania: I Kommisjon hos H. Aschehoug.

Statistisk Centralbyrå (1935), *Folketællingen i Norge 1. desember 1930. Tiende Hefte. Boligstatistikk. (Recensement du 1ᵉʳ décembre 1930: X: Statistique d'habitation.)* (Norges Offisielle Statistikk, IX.63). Christiania: I Kommisjon hos H. Aschehoug, pp. 5*ff. (text); 8ff. and 72ff. (tables) (at the same time household census).

1946   Statistisk Sentralbyrå (1952), *Folketellingen i Norge 3. desember 1946. Femte Hefte. Boligstatistikk. (Recensement du 3 décembre 1946: V: Statistique d'habitation.)* (Norges Offisielle Statistikk, XI.99). Christiania: I Kommisjon hos H. Aschehoug, pp. 28*–35* and 40*–7* (text), 100–58 and 188–230 (tables) (at the same time household census).

–   Statistisk Sentralbyrå (1969), *Historisk statistikk 1968* (NOS ser. 12 no. 245).

Oslo: Statistisk Sentralbyrå (no household or dwelling data).
- Statistisk Sentralbyrå (1978), *Historisk statistikk 1978* (NOS ser. XII vol. 291). Oslo: Statistisk Sentralbyrå (only housing data).
1920–46 Statistics Norway (1995), *Historisk statistikk 1994* (NOS C 188). Oslo-Kongsvinger: Statistisk Sentralbyrå–Statistics Norway (private households and their members by size 1920–46, pp. 99–100).

POLAND

1. Vital statistics

Główny Urząd Statystycny (1993), *Historia Polski W Liczbach. Ludność. Terytorium.* Warsaw: GUS.

Główny Urząd Statystycny Rzeczypospolitej Polskiej, Office Central de Statistique de la République Polonaise (1-, 1920/21–), *Rocznik statystyki Rzeczypospolitej Polskiej/Annuaire Statistique de la République Polonaise.* Warszawa/Varsovie: Nakladem Głównego Urzędu Statystycnego.

2. Population structure by age, sex, and marital status

1921   Głowny Urząd Statystyczny (1927), *Pierwszy roszechny spis Rzeczypospolitej Polskiej z dnia 30 wresnia 1921 roku. Mieszkania ludność. Stosunki zawodowe. Tablice państwowe. Le premier recensement général de la République Polonaise du 30 Septembre 1921. Logements. Population. Professions. Tableaux relatifs à la Pologne entière.* Warsaw: Nakładem Głownego Urzędu Statystycznego *(*Statystyka Polski. *Statistique de la Pologne publiée par l'Office Central de Statistique de la République Polonaise, Tome XXXI)*, pp. 38–9.

1931   Głowny Urząd Statystyczny (1937), *Drugi powszechny spis ludności z dn. 9. XII. 1931 r. Mieszkania i gospodarstwa domowe. Ludność. Stosunki zawodowe. Deuxième recensement général de la population du 9. XII. 1931. Logements et ménages. Professions.* Zeszyt 62. Polska (dane skrócone). Pologne (données abrégées). Warsaw: Nakładem Głownego Urzędu Statystycznego (Statystyka Polski Seria C, Part 62), pp. 32–3.

Główny Urząd Statystyczny (1938), *Zeszyt 94a. Mieszkania i gospodarstwa domowe. Ludność. Logements et ménages. Population.* Warsaw: Nakładem Głownego Urzędu Statystycznego (Statystyka Polski Seria C, Part 94a), p. 40.

1921–   Główny Urząd Statystycny (1993), *Historia Polski W Liczbach. Ludność.*
1990   *Terytorium.* Warsaw: GUS, pp. 122ff.

3. Population census results on households and families

1921   Głowny Urząd Statystyczny Rzeczypospolitei polskiej (1926), *Pierwszy powszechny spis Rzeczypospolitej Polskiej z dnia 30 września 1921 roku. Mieszkania ludność. Stosunki zawodowe. Tablice państwowe. Le premier recensement général de la République Polonaise du 30 Septembre 1921. Logements. Population. Professions. Tableaux relatifs à la Pologne entière.* Warsaw: Nakładem Głownego Urzędu Statystycznego (Statystyka Polski. Statistique de la Pologne publiée par l'Office Central de Statistique de la République Polonaise, Tome XXXI), pp. VI–VII (text), 12–4 (tables).

Głowny Urząd Statystyczny Rzeczypospolitei polskiej (1932), *Mieszkania. Analiza Wyników spisu Mieszkań z 30.IX. 1991. Logements. Analyse des résultats du recensement des logements du 30. IX 1921.* Warsaw: Nakładem Głownego Urzędu Statystycznego (Statystyka Polski. Statistique de la Pologne publiée par l'Office Central de Statistique de la République Polonaise, Tome XXXII), pp. 46–

50 (text).
Głowny Urząd Statystyczny Rzeczypospolitei polskiej (1930), *Pierwszy powszechny spis Rzeczypospolitej Polskiej z dnia 30 września 1921 roku. Gospodarstwa Domowe. Tablice. Le premier recensement général de la République Polonaise du 30 Septembre 1921. Ménages. Tableaux.* Warsaw: Nakładem Głownego Urzędu Statystycznego (Statystyka Polski. Statistique de la Pologne publiée par l'Office Central de Statistique de la République Polonaise, Tome XXXV).

1931 Głowny Urząd Statystyczny Rzeczypospolitei polskiej (1937), *Drugi powszechny spis ludności z dn. 9. XII. 1931 r. Mieszkania i gospodarstwa domowe. Ludność. Stosunki zawodowe. Deuxième recensement général de la population du 9. XII. 1931. Logements et ménages. Professions.* Zeszyt 62. Polska (dane skrócone). Pologne (données abrégées). Warsaw: Nakładem Głownego Urzędu Statystycznego (Statystyka Polski Seria C, Part 62), pp. XIX–XXII (text), 2–21 (tables).
Głowny Urząd Statystyczny Rzeczypospolitei polskiej (1938), *Drugi powszechny spis ludności z dn. 9. XII. 1931 r. Mieszkania i gospodarstwa domowe. Ludność. Polska. Logements et ménages. Population. Pologne.* Warsaw: Nakładem Głownego Urzędu Statystycznego (Statystyka Polski Seria C, Zeszyt 94a), pp. X–XII (text), 2–14 (tables).

1946 Głowny Urząd Statystyczny Rzeczypospolitei polskiej (1947), *Powszechny sumaryczny spis ludności z dn. 14. II. 1946 r. General summarized population census on February the 14ᵗʰ 1946.* Warsaw: Nakładem Głownego Urzędu Statystycznego (Statystyka Polski, Seria D, Zeszyt 1). (no data on households)

1921– Główny Urząd Statystycny (1993), *Historia Polski W Liczbach. Ludność.*
1990 *Terytorium.* Warsaw: GUS, pp. 122ff.

PORTUGAL

1. Vital statistics

Instituto Nacional de Estatística (INE) (1–, 1875–), *Anuário Estatístico de Portugal.* Lisbon: INE (Continues the '*Annuário Estatístico* ...')
—— (INE) (1–, 1862–), *Estatísticas Demográficas.* Lisbon: Instituto Nacional de Estatística (INE).
Ministerio das Obras Publicas, Commercio e Industria. Repartação de Estatistica (1–, 1875–), *Annuário Estatístico do Reino de Portugal.* (Ed. and title changed: *Annuário Estatístico de Portugal*). Lisbon: publisher varies.

2. Population structure by age, sex, and marital status

1864 No editor given (1868), *Estatistica de Portugal. População. Censo no 1.° de Janeiro 1864.* Lisbon: Imprensa Nacional, pp. 305f.

1878 No editor given (1881), *Estatistica de Portugal. População. Censo no 1.° de Janeiro 1878.* Lisbon: Imprensa Nacional, p. 427.

1890 Portugal. Ministerio da Fazenda. Direcção Geral da Estatistica e dos Proprios Nacionaes (1900), *Censo da População do Reino de Portugal no 1.° de Dezembro de 1890. Volume II: População de Facto Agrupada Segunda as Idades, Distinguindo o Sexo, o Estado Civil e a Instrucção Elementar.* Lisbon: Imprensa Nacional, pp. 2f.

1900 Portugal. Ministerio dos Negocios da Fazenda. Direcção Geral da Estatistica e dos Proprios Nacionaes (1906), *Censo da População do Reino de Portugal no 1.° de Dezembro de 1900 (Quarto recenseamento geral da população). Volume*

II: População de Facto Agrupada Segunda as Idades, Distinguindo o Sexo, o Estado Civil e a Instrucção Elementar. População Segundo a Religião. Lisbon: Typographia da 'A Editora', pp. 2f.

1911   Portugal. Ministerio das Finanças. Direcção Geral da Estatística - 4.º Reparticão (1913), *Estatística Demográfica. Censo da População de Portugal no 1.º de Dezembro de 1911 (5.º recenseamento geral da população). (Recensement de la Population de Portugal au 1er Décembre 1911). Parte II: População de Facto Agrupada por Idades, Distinguindo Sexo, Estado Civil e Instrução. Quadros comparativos. (Population de fait d'après les âges, en distinguant le sexe, l'état civil et l'instruction. Tableax comparatifs).* Lisbon: Imprensa Nacional, pp. 4f.

1920   República Portuguesa. Ministério das Finanças. Direcção Geral da Estatística (1925), *Censo da População de Portugal no 1.º de Dezembro de 1920 (6.º recenseamento geral da população). (Recensement de la Population de Portugal au 1er Décembre 1920). Volume II: População de Facto Agrupada por Idades, Distinguindo Sexo, Estado Civil e Instrução. (Population de fait d'après les âges, en distinguant le sexe, l'état civil et l'instruction).* Lisbon: Imprensa Nacional, pp. 2f.

1930   República Portuguesa. Direcção Geral da Estatística (1934), *Censo da População de Portugal no 1.º de Dezembro de 1930 (7.º recenseamento geral da população). (Recensement de la Population de Portugal au 1er Décembre 1930). Volume II: População de Facto Agrupada por Idades, Distinguindo Sexo, Estado Civil e Instrução. (Population de fait d'après les âges, en distinguant le sexe, l'état civil et l'instruction).* Lisbon: Imprensa Nacional, pp. 4f.

1940   Portugal. Instituto Nacional de Estatística (1945), *VIII Recenseamento Geral da População no Continente e Ilhas Adjacentes em 12 Dezembro de 1940. Volume I: Portugal (Continente e Ilhas Adjacentes).* Lisbon: Imprensa Nacional de Lisbon, pp. 65–75.

1950   Portugal. Instituto Nacional de Estatística (1952), *IX Recenseamento Geral da População no Continente e Ilhas Adjacentes em 15 de Dezembro de 1950. Tomo II: Idade e Instrução.* Lisbon: Tipografia Portuguesa, LDA., pp. 11–3.

3. Population census results on households and families

1864   No editor given (1868), *Estatistica de Portugal. População. Censo no 1.º de Janeiro 1864.* Lisbon: Imprensa Nacional, pp. VII, XII–XIII (text), 305 (table).

1878   No editor given (1881), *Estatistica de Portugal. População. Censo no 1.º de Janeiro 1878.* Lisbon: Imprensa Nacional, pp. VIII–X, XVII–XVIII (text), 427 (table).

1890   Portugal. Ministerio da Fazenda. Direcção Geral da Estatistica e dos Proprios Nacionaes (1896), *Censo da População do Reino de Portugal no 1.º de Dezembro de 1890. Volume I: Fogos - População de Residencia Habitual e População de Facto; Sexo, Naturalidade, Estado civil e Instrucção (Feux - Population de sejour habituel et population de fait; sexe, naturalité, état civil et instruction).* Lisbon: Imprensa Nacional, pp. CI–CII (text retrospective household statistics 1835–90), 2–27 and 43–272 (tables).

Portugal. Ministerio da Fazenda. Direcção Geral da Estatistica e dos Proprios Nacionaes (1900), *Volume III: População de Facto, Classificada Segundo as Grandes Divisões profissionais por Sexos e grupos de idades; numero e composição das familias.* Lisbon: Imprensa Nacional, parte IV, pp. 241–50 (tables).

1900   Portugal. Ministerio dos Negocios da Fazenda. Direcção Geral da Estatistica e dos Proprios Nacionaes (1905), *Censo da População do Reino de Portugal no 1.º de Dezembro de 1900 (Quarto recenseamento geral da população). Volume I:*

Fogos. População de Residencia Habitual e População de Facto, Distinguindo o Sexo, Naturalidade, Estado Civil e Instrução Elementar. Lisbon, Quadro I–4, pp. 2–29.

Portugal. Ministerio dos Negocios da Fazenda. Direcção Geral da Estatistica e dos Proprios Nacionaes (1906), *Volume III: População de Facto, Classificada Segundo as Grandes Divisões profissionais por Sexos e grupos de idades; cegos, surdos-mudos, idiotas e alienados; numero e composicão das familias.* Lisbon: Imprensa Nacional, parte IV, pp. 195–202.

1911   Portugal. Ministerio das Finanças. Direcção Geral da Estatística - 4.º Reparticão (1913), *Estatística Demográfica. Censo da População de Portugal no 1.º de Dezembro de 1911 (5.º recenseamento geral da população). (Recensement de la Population de Portugal au 1ᵉʳ Décembre 1911). Parte I: Fogos. População de Residencia Habitual e População de Facto, Distinguindo Sexo, Nacionalidade, Naturalidade, Estado Civil e Instrução.* Lisbon: Imprensa Nacional, pp. IX–XI (text on households 1890–1911), 4–285, 317–26 and 348–9 (tables).

Portugal. Ministerio das Finanças. Direcção Geral da Estatística - 4.º Reparticão (1917), *Estatística Demográfica. Censo da População de Portugal no 1.º de Dezembro de 1911 (5.º recenseamento geral da população). (Recensement de la Population de Portugal au 1ᵉʳ Décembre 1911). Parte VI: Censo das Povoações. Fogos. População de Facto Clasificada por 'Distritos', 'Concelhos', 'Freguesias' e Povoações. (Recensement des Peuplades. Ménages. Population de fait classifiée par 'distritos', 'concelhos', 'freguesias' et peuplades).* Lisbon: Imprensa Nacional, pp. 4–378 (tables).

1920   República Portuguesa. Ministério das Finanças. Direcção Geral da Estatística (1923), *Censo da População de Portugal no 1.º de Dezembro de 1920 (6.º recenseamento geral da população). (Recensement de la Population de Portugal au 1ᵉʳ Décembre 1920). Volume I: Fogos. População de Residencia Habitual e População de Facto, Distinguindo Sexo, Nacionalidade, Naturalidade, Estado Civil e Instrução. (Ménages. Population résidente et population de fait, d'après le sexe, la nationalité, le lieu de naissance, l'état civil et l'instruction).* Lisbon: Imprensa Nacional, pp. 2–223 (tables) and 251–7 (tables on households by size).

1930   República Portuguesa. Direcção Geral da Estatística (1933), *Censo da População de Portugal no 1.º de Dezembro de 1930 (7.º recenseamento geral da população). (Recensement de la Population de Portugal au 1ᵉʳ Décembre 1930). Volume I: Famílias. População de Residência Habitual e População de Facto, Distinguindo Sexo, Nacionalidade, Naturalidade, Estado Civil e Instrução. (Ménages. Population résidente et population de fait, d'après le sexe, la nationalité, le lieu de naissance, l'état civil et l'instruction).* Lisbon: Imprensa Nacional, pp. 4–235 (tables).

1940   Portugal. Instituto Nacional de Estatística (1942), *VIII Recenseamento Geral da População no Continente e Ilhas Adjacentes em 12 Dezembro de 1940. Resultados provisórios nos distritos, concelhos e freguesias do continente e ilhas relativos ao número de famílias e à população presente por sexos.* Lisbon: Imprensa Nacional de Lisboa, pp. 5–61 (tables).

Portugal. Instituto Nacional de Estatística (1945), *VIII Recenseamento Geral da População no Continente e Ilhas Adjacentes em 12 Dezembro de 1940. Volume I: Portugal (Continente e Ilhas Adjacentes).* Lisbon: Imprensa Nacional de Lisboa, pp. XIV–XV (text in Portuguese), 2–25 (tables on households), 28–35 (tables on couples with children), pp. 488–9 (text in French).

1950   Portugal. Instituto Nacional de Estatística (1952), *IX Recenseamento Geral da População no Continente e Ilhas Adjacentes em 15 de Dezembro de 1950. Tomo I: População Residente e Presente, Familias, Casais, Mulheres Casadas, Convivências, Estrangeiros, Cegos, Surdos-mudos e Órfãos.* Lisbon: Tipografia

Portuguesa, LDA., pp. 14–5 (comparative table of census contents 1864–1950); 18–303 (households); 304–541 (married couples and unmarried women by number of children); 542–75 (institutional households).

1835–90 See 1890 in this table.

1940–60 Portugal. Instituto Nacional de Estatística (1964), *X Recenseamento Geral da População no Continente e Ilhas Adjacentes (As 0 horas de 15 de Dezembro de 1960). Tomo I Volume 1. Prédios e Fogos: População - Dados Retrospectivos (Distritos, Concelhos e Freguesias). Tome I Volume Ier. Immeubles et Feux; Population - Données Rétrospectives (Districts, 'Concelhos' et 'Freguesias').* Lisbon, pp. 3–10 (table).

Portugal. Instituto Nacional de Estatística (1964), *X Recenseamento Geral da População no Continente e Ilhas Adjacentes (As 0 horas de 15 de Dezembro de 1960). Tomo I Volume 2.° Prédios e Fogos: População - Dados Retrospectivos (Lugares). Tome I Volume 2.ème. Immeubles et Feux; Population - Données Rétrospectives (Hameaux).* Lisbon, pp. 3–613 (table).

SPAIN

1. Vital statistics

Comisión de Estadística General del Reino (1–, 1858–), *Anuario Estadístico de España*. Madrid: Imprenta Nacional.

Garcia Fernandez, P. (s.a., 1985?), *Poblacion de los Actuales Terminos Municipales 1900–1981: Poblaciones de Hecho segun los Censos*. Madrid: INE.

Instituto Nacional de Estadística (1–, 1901–), *Movimiento Natural de la Población*. Madrid: INE.

—— (1–, 1917–), *Boletín de Estadística*. Madrid: INE.

—— (1987), *Poblaciones de Hecho de los Municipios Españoles según los Censos Oficiales de 1900 a 1981*. Madrid: INE.

Presidencia del Gobierno, Instituto Nacional de Estadística (1952), *Principales Actividades de la Vida Española en la Primera Mitad del Siglo XX. Síntesis Estadística*. Madrid: INE.

2. Population structure by age, sex, and marital status

1857 Comision de Estadística General del Reino (1858), *Censo de la Población de España según el Recuento Verificado en 21 de Mayo de 1857*. Madrid: Imprenta Nacional, pp. 860–1. (Only age groups and sex, no combination with marital status published.)

1860 Junta General de Estadística (1863), *Censo de la Población de España según el Recuento Verificado en 25 de Diciembre de 1860*. Madrid: Imprenta Nacional, pp. 698–9. (Only age groups and sex, no combination with marital status published.)

1877 Dirección General del Instituto Geográfico y Estadístico (1883), *Censo de la Población de España según el Empadronamiento hecho en 31 Diciembre de 1877*. Vol. I. Madrid: Imprenta de la Dirección General del Instituto Geográfico y Estadístico, pp. XXVI and 746. (Only age groups and sex, no combination with marital status published.)

1887 Dirección General del Instituto Geográfico y Estadístico (1892), *Censo de la Población de España según el Empadronamiento hecho en 31 Diciembre de 1887*. Vol. II. Madrid: Imprenta de la Dirección General del Instituto Geográfico y Estadístico, pp. 444–5.

1897 Not available.

1900 Ministerio de Instrucción Pública y Bellas Artes. Dirección General del Instituto

Geográfico y Estadístico (1907), *Censo de la población de España según el empadronamiento hecho en la península e islas adyacentes en 31 de diciembre de 1900*. Vol. III. Madrid: Imprenta de la Dirección General del Instituto Geográfico y Estadístico, pp. 296–7.

1910   Ministerio de Instrucción Pública y Bellas Artes. Dirección General del Instituto Geográfico y Estadístico (1917), *Censo de la población de España según el empadronamiento hecho en la península e islas adyacentes el 31 de diciembre de 1910*. Vol. III. Madrid: Talleres del Instituto Geográfico y Estadístico, pp. 402–3.

1920   Ministerio de Trabajo, Comercio e Industria. Jefatura Superior de Estadística (1926), *Censo de la población de España según el empadronamiento hecho en la península e islas adyacentes el 31 de diciembre de 1920*. Vol. III. Madrid: Imprenta de los Hijos de M. G. Hernández, pp. 276–7.

1930   Ministerio de Trabajo. Dirección General de Estadística (s.a.), *Censo de la población de España según el empadronamiento hecho en la península e islas adyacentes el 31 de diciembre de 1920*. Vol. III. Madrid: Masanava, S. L., pp. 3–4.

1940   Presidencia del Gobierno. Instituto Nacional de Estadística (s.a.), *Censo de la población de España según la inscripción de 31 de diciembre de 1940. Resumen Nacional. De las clasificaciones por sexo, edad, instrucción elemental, fecundidad y profesión de la población presente (HECHO), correspondientes a los totales de las provincias, de las capitales y de los municipios no capitales mayores de 20.000 habitantes*. Madrid: Barranco, pp. 3–6.

1900–   Almarcha, A., et al. (1975), *Estadisticas Basicas de España 1900–1970*. Madrid:
1970   Confederacion Española de Cajas de Ahorras (only age in 1-year age groups by sex for censuses from 1900–1965, pp. 20–5).

1901–   Presidencia del Gobierno, Instituto Nacional de Estadística (1952), *Principales*
1951   *Actividades de la Vida Española en la Primera Mitad del Siglo XX. Síntesis Estadística* (Main activities of people in Spain in the first half of the twentieth century. Statistical synthesis). Madrid: INE (no age by sex or marital status).

3. Population census results on households and families

1857   Comision de Estadística General del Reino (1858), *Censo de la Población de España según el Recuento Verificado en 21 de Mayo de 1857*. Madrid: Imprenta Nacional (no household data).

1860   Junta General de Estadística (1863), *Censo de la Población de España según el Recuento Verificado en 25 de Diciembre de 1860*. Madrid: Imprenta Nacional, pp. 696–9.

1877   Dirección General del Instituto Geográfico y Estadístico (1883), *Censo de la Población de España según el Empadronamiento hecho en 31 Diciembre de 1877*. Vol. I. Madrid: Imprenta de la Dirección General del Instituto Geográfico y Estadístico, pp. 2ff. (for each province and *ayuntamiento*).

Dirección General del Instituto Geográfico y Estadístico (1879), *Resultados Generales del Censo de la Población de España según el Empadronamiento hecho en 31 Diciembre de 1877*. Madrid: Establecimiento Tipografico de R. Labaios, pp. 552–3.

1887   Dirección General del Instituto Geográfico y Estadístico (1891), *Censo de la Población de España según el Empadronamiento hecho en 31 Diciembre de 1887*. Vol. I. Madrid: Imprenta de la Dirección General del Instituto Geográfico y Estadístico, pp. 728–31.

1897   Dirección General del Instituto Geográfico y Estadístico (1899), *Resultados Provisionales del Censo de la población de España según el empadronamiento hecho en la península é islas adyacentes el 31 de diciembre de 1897*. Madrid: Imprenta de la Dirección General del Instituto Geográfico y Estadístico, pp. 322–3

(table).
1900   Ministerio de Instrucción Pública y Bellas Artes. Dirección General del Instituto
       Geográfico y Estadístico (1902), *Censo de la población de España según el
       empadronamiento hecho en la península e islas adyacentes en 31 de diciembre de
       1900*. Vol. I. Madrid: Imprenta de la Dirección General del Instituto Geográfico y
       Estadístico, p. 323.
1910   Ministerio de Instrucción Pública y Bellas Artes. Dirección General del Instituto
       Geográfico y Estadístico (1913), *Censo de la población de España según el
       empadronamiento hecho en la península e islas adyacentes el 31 de diciembre de
       1910*. Vol. I. Madrid: Imprenta de la Dirección General del Instituto Geográfico y
       Estadístico, p. 339.
1920   Ministerio de Trabajo, Comercio e Industria. Dirección General de Estadística
       (1922), *Censo de la población de España según el empadronamiento hecho en la
       península e islas adyacentes el 31 de diciembre de 1920*. Vol. I. Madrid: Talleres
       de la Dirección General del Instituto Geográfico, Imprenta de los Hijos de M. G.
       Hernández, p. 339.
       Ministerio de Trabajo, Comercio e Industria. Servicio General de Estadística
       (1928), *Censo de población de 1920. Tomo IV. Clasificación de las mujeres y
       viudas por la edad y el número de sus hijos*. Madrid: Imprenta de los Hijos de M.
       G. Hernández.
       Ministerio de Trabajo y Previsión, Servicio General de Estadística (1929), *Censo
       de población de 1920. Tomo VI. Clasificación de los matrimonios por la edad de
       los esposos en combinación con el número de sus hijos*. Madrid: Imprenta de los
       Hijos de M. G. Hernández.
1930   Presidencia del Consejo de Ministros, Dirección General del Instituto Geográfico,
       Catastral y de Estadística (1932), *Censo de la población de España según el
       empadronamiento hecho en la península e islas adyacentes y posesiones del norte
       y costa occidental de África en 31 de diciembre de 1930*. Vol. I. Madrid: Talleres
       del Instituto Geográfico y Catastral, pp. 333–49 (tables)
1940   Ministerio de Trabajo. Dirección General de Estadística (1943), *Censo de la
       población de España según el empadronamiento hecho de en la península e islas
       adyacentes y posesiones del norte y costa occidental de África el 31 de diciembre
       de 1940*. Vol. I. Madrid: no publisher, pp. 310–1 (table).
       Presidencia del Gobierno, Instituto Nacional de Estadística (1946), *Censo de la
       población de España según la inscripción de 31 diciembre de 1940. Resumen
       nacional de las clasificaciones por sexo, edad, instrucción elelmental, fecundidad
       y profesión de la población presente (HECHO), correspondientes a los totales de
       las provincias, de las capitales y de los municipios no capitales mayores de
       20.000 habitantes*. Madrid: Barranco, pp. 7–8 (fertility).
1900–70 Almarcha, A., et al. (1975), *Estadisticas Basicas de España 1900–1970*. Madrid:
       Confederacion Española de Cajas de Ahorras (no household data).
1901–51 Presidencia del Gobierno, Instituto Nacional de Estadística (1952), *Principales
       Actividades de la Vida Española en la Primera Mitad del Siglo XX. Síntesis
       Estadística* (Main activities of people in Spain in the first half of the twentieth
       century. Statistical synthesis). Madrid: INE (no household data).

SWEDEN

1. Vital statistics

Statistiska Centralbyrån (1–, 1914–), *Statistisk årsbok för Sverige*. Stockholm: SCB.
—— (1–, 1918–), *Statistical Yearbook of Administrative Districts of Sweden*.
   Stockholm: SCB.

—— (1969), *Historisk statistik för Sverige. Del 1: Befolkning.* 2nd rev. and extended ed. Stockholm: SCB.

—— (1977), *Levnadsförhållanden–utveckling och nuläge enligt tillgänglig statistik 1976.* Levnadsförhållanden, rapport, vol. 6. Stockholm: SCB.

Sundbärg, G. (1903a), 'Rikets folkmängd åren 1750–1900, fördelad after ålder och kön'. *Statistisk Tidskrift* No. 2: 139–221.

—— (1903b), 'Rikets folkmängd åren 1750–1900, fördelad åldersvis efter civilstånd'. *Statistisk Tidskrift* No. 2: 118–85.

—— (1907 (1970)), *Bevölkerungsstatistik Schwedens 1750–1900.* Urval: Skriftserie. With preface and terminology in English. Stockholm: SCB.

2. *Population structure by age, sex, and marital status*

1860   Statistiska Central-Byrån (1865), *Statistiska Centralbyråns underdånige berättelse för åren 1856–1860. Tredje och sista afdelningen: Innehållande. Folkmängden den 31 December 1860 efter ålder, födelseort, stamskilnad och yrken, antalet sinnessjuka, blinda och döfstumma, samt dödlighets- och lifslängdstabeller.* (Bidrag till Sveriges Officiela Statistik. A) Befolknings-Statistik. Ny följd. II: 3). Stockholm: Tryckt hos P. A. Norstedt & Söner, Kungl. Bogtryckare, p. 13.

1870   Statistiska Central-Byrån (1874), *Statistiska Centralbyråns underdånige berättelse för år 1870. Tredje och sista afdelningen: Innehållande. Folkmängden den 31 December 1870 efter ålder, födelseort, stamskilnad och yrken; antalet sinnessjuke, döfstumme och blinde, samt dödlighets- och lifslängdstabeller, jemte 6 diagram.* (Bidrag till Sveriges Officiela Statistik. A) Befolknings-Statistik. Ny följd. XII: 3). Stockholm: P. A. Norstedt & Söner, Kungl. Bogtryckare, p. 52.

1880   Statistiska Centralbyrån (1885), *Statistiska Centralbyråns underdånige berättelse för år 1880. Tredje och sista afdelningen: Folkmängden den 31 December 1880 efter ålder, födelseort, stamskilnad och yrken; antalet sinnessjuke, döfstumme och blinde, samt dödlighets- och lifslängdstabell.* (Bidrag till Sveriges Officiela Statistik. A) Befolkningsstatistik. Ny följd. XXII: 3). Stockholm: Kungl. Bogtryckeriet, P. A. Norstedt & Söner, pp. 14–7.

1890   Statistiska Centralbyrån (1895), *Statistiska Centralbyråns underdånige berättelse för år 1890. Tredje och sista afdelningen: Folkmängden församlingsvis åren 1860–1890; Folkmängden år 1890 efter kön, ålder, civilstand, hushåll, födelseort, stamskilnad och yrken; antalet sinnessjuke, döfstumme och blinde; frånvarande personer och qvarstående obefintlige; dödlighets- och lifslängdstabeller för åren 1881–1890* (Bidrag till Sveriges Officiela Statistik. A) Befolkningsstatistik. Ny följd. XXXII: 3). Stockholm: Kungl. Bogtryckeriet, P. A. Norstedt & Söner, pp. 77–9.

1900   Statistiska Centralbyrån (1907), *Statistiska Centralbyråns underdånige berättelse för år 1900. Tredje afdelningen: Folkmängden år 1900 efter kön, ålder, civilstånd, hushåll, födelseort, stamskillnad och yrken; lyten; frånvarande personer samt obefintliga.* (Bidrag till Sveriges Officiela Statistik. A) Befolkningsstatistik. Ny följd. XLII: 3). Stockholm: Kungl. Bogtryckeriet, P. A. Norstedt & Söner, pp. 64–7.

1910   Kungl. Statistiska Centralbyrån (1913), *Folkräkningen den 31 December 1910 av Kungl. Statistiska Centralbyrån. II. Folkmängdens fördelning efter kön, ålder och civilstånd.* (Sveriges Officiela Statistik. Folkmängden och dess Förändringar). Stockholm: Kungl. Bogtryckeriet, P. A. Norstedt & Söner, pp. 2 and 4.

1920   Kungl. Statistiska Centralbyrån (1926), *Folkräkningen den 31 December 1920 av Kungl. Statistiska Centralbyrån. III. Folkmängden efter ålder, kön, civilstånd och födelseort. Äktenskapen efter varaktighet och efter makarnas ålder.* (Sveriges Officiela Statistik. Folkmängden och dess Förändringar). Stockholm: Kungl. Bogtryckeriet, P. A. Norstedt & Söner, pp. 2–7.

1930   Statistiska Centralbyrån (1936), *Folkräkningen den 31 December 1930 av Statistiska Centralbyrån. II. Bygdeindeling. Folkmängden efter ålder, kön och civilstånd. Inrikes omflyttning (inkl. fördelning efter födelseort).* (Sveriges Officiela Statistik. Folkmängden och dess Förändringar). Stockholm: Kungl. Bogtryckeriet, P. A. Norstedt & Söner, pp. 8–11.

1935   Statistiska Centralbyrån (1937), *Särskilda Folkräkningen 1935/36 av Statistiska Centralbyrån. II. Allmänna folkräkningen den 31 december 1935: Folkmängden i ettårs-och femårsklasser efter kön och civilstånd.* (Sveriges Officiela Statistik. Folkmängden och dess Förändringar). Stockholm: Kungl. Bogtryckeriet, P. A. Norstedt & Söner, pp. 2–4.

1940   Statistiska Centralbyrån (1942), *Folkräkningen den 31 December 1940 av Statistiska Centralbyrån. I. Areal och folkmängd inom särskilda förvaltningsområden m. m. befolkningsagglomerationer.* (Sveriges Officiela Statistik. Folkmängden och dess Förändringar). Stockholm: Kungl. Bogtryckeriet, P. A. Norstedt & Söner, pp. 2–4.

1945   Statistiska Centralbyrån (1950), *Folkräkningen den 31 December 1945 av Statistiska Centralbyrån. VI. Totala räkningen. Folkmängden efter ålder, kön och civilstand. Dödlighets- och livlängstabeller.* (Sveriges Officiela Statistik. Folkmängden och dess Förändringar). Stockholm: Kungl. Bogtryckeriet, P. A. Norstedt & Söner, pp. 2–4.

1750–   Hofsten, E., and H. Lundström (1976), *Swedish Population History. Main Trends*
1970   *from 1750 to 1970.* Stockholm: SCB. (Urval: Skriftserie)
1720–   Statistiska Centralbyrån (1969), *Historisk statistik för Sverige. Del 1. Befolkning.*
1967   2nd rev. and extended ed. Stockholm: SCB.
1750–   Sundbärg, G. (1907 (1970)), *Bevölkerungsstatistik Schwedens 1750–1900.* With
1900   preface and terminology in English. Stockholm: SCB. (Urval: Skriftserie)

3. Population census results on households and families

1855   Statistiska Central-Byrån (1859), *Statistiska Centralbyråns underdånige berättelse för åren 1851 med 1855. Andra afdelningen: Innehållande. Folkmängden den 31 December 1855 i rikets särskilda administrativa fördelningar. (Utgörande fortsättning af Tabell-Kommissionens underdånige berättelse för åren 1851–1855, första afdelningen, afgifven år 1857).* (Bidrag till Sveriges Officiela Statistik. A) Befolknings-Statistik. Ny följd. II. 2.). Stockholm: P. A. Norstedt & Söner, Kongl. Bogtryckare, pp. I–LXXXVI (table).

Statistiska Central-Byrån (1860), *Statistiska Centralbyråns underdånige berättelse för åren 1851 med 1855. Tredje och sista afdelningen: Innehållande. Folkmängden den 31 December 1855 efter kön, ålder, civilstånd, hushåll, ståndsklasser, lefnadsyrken, och näringar m. m., jemte dödlighets- och lifslängdstabeller.* (Bidrag till Sveriges Officiela Statistik. A) Befolknings-Statistik. Ny följd. II. 3.). Stockholm: P. A. Norstedt & Söner, Kongl. Bogtryckare, pp. 33–41 (text: historical data on households 1751–1855), XXXI (table).

1860   Statistiska Central-Byrån (1864), *Statistiska Centralbyråns underdånige berättelse för åren 1856 med 1860. Andra afdelningen: Innehållande. Folkmängden den 31 December 1860 inom särskilda administrativa områden, samt efter hushåll eller matlag, kön och civilstånd, jemte vigde par, lefvande födde och aflinde, 1856–1860, församlingsvis.* (Bidrag till Sveriges Officiela Statistik. A) Befolknings-Statistik. Ny följd. II: 2). Stockholm: P. A. Norstedt & Söner, Kungl. Bogtryckare, pp. XXXV–XLI (text), 1–85 (table).

1870 Statistiska Central-Byrån (1873), *Statistiska Central-Byråns underdånige berättelse för år 1870. Andra afdelningen: Innehållande. Folkmängden den 31 December 1870 inom serskilda administrativa, judiciela och kyrkliga områden, samt efter kön, civilstånd och hushåll eller matlag, jemte vigda par, lefvande födde och aflinde, 1861–1870, församlingsvis.* (Bidrag till Sveriges Officiela Statistik. A) Befolknings-Statistik. Ny följd. XII: 2). Stockholm: P. A. Norstedt & Söner, Kungl. Bogtryckare, pp. XVI–XXIV (text), 1–107 (table).

1880 Statistiska Centralbyrån (1883), *Statistiska Centralbyråns underdånige berättelse för år 1880. Andra afdelningen: Areal och folkmängd för särskilda administrativa, judiciela och ecklesiastika områden jemte folkmängd fördelning efter kön och civilstånd samt hushåll församlingsvis år 1880, åfvensom antalet vigde, födde och döde församlingsvis åren 1871–1880 samt folkmängd församlingsvis åren 1805–1880 och länsvis åren 1751–1880.* (Bidrag till Sveriges Officiela Statistik. A) Befolkningsstatistik. Ny följd. XXII: 2). Stockholm: Kungl. Bogtryckeriet, P. A. Norstedt & Söner, pp. XIII–XV (text), 1–108 (tables).

1890 Statistiska Centralbyrån (1895), *Statistiska Centralbyråns underdånige berättelse för år 1890. Tredje och sista afdelningen: Folkmängden församlingsvis åren 1860–1890; Folkmängden år 1890 efter kön, ålder, civilstand, hushåll, födelseort, stamskilnad och yrken; antalet sinnessjuke, döfstumme och blinde; frånvarande personer och qvarstående obefintlige; dödlighets- och lifslängdstabeller för åren 1881–1890.* (Bidrag till Sveriges Officiela Statistik. A) Befolkningsstatistik. Ny följd. XXXII: 3). Stockholm: Kungl. Bogtryckeriet, P. A. Norstedt & Söner, pp. XXV–XXVIII (text), 1–55 (tables).

1900 Statistiska Centralbyrån (1907), *Statistiska Centralbyråns underdånige berättelse för år 1900. Tredje afdelningen: Folkmängden år 1900 efter kön, ålder, civilstånd, hushåll, födelseort, stamskillnad och yrken; lyten; frånvarande personer samt obefintliga.* (Bidrag till Sveriges Officiela Statistik. A) Befolkningsstatistik. Ny följd. XLII: 3). Stockholm: Kungl. Bogtryckeriet, P. A. Norstedt & Söner, pp. XXI–XXIV (text), 1–60 and 62–3 (tables).

1910 Kungl. Statistiska Centralbyrån (1914), *Folkräkningen den 31 December 1910 av Kungl. Statistiska Centralbyrån. I. Areal och Folkmängd för särskilda förvaltningsområden.* (Sveriges Officiella Statistik. Folkmängden och dess Förändringar). Stockholm: Kungl. Bogtryckeriet, P. A. Norstedt & Söner, pp. 1–126 (tables).

Kungl. Statistiska Centralbyrån (1918), *Folkräkningen den 31 December 1910 av Kungl. Statistiska Centralbyrån. IV. Folkmängdens fördelning efter hushåll, trosbekännelse, födelseort m. m.* (Sveriges Officiella Statistik. Folkmängden och dess Förändringar). Stockholm: Kungl. Bogtryckeriet, P. A. Norstedt & Söner, pp. 2*–6* (text), 2–5 (tables).

1920 Kungl. Statistiska Centralbyrån (1923), *Folkräkningen den 31 December 1920 av Kungl. Statistiska Centralbyrån. I. Areal och Folkmängd för särskilda förvaltningsområden. Folkmängdens fördelning efter hushåll.* (Sveriges Officiela Statistik. Folkmängden och dess Förändringar). Stockholm: Kungl. Bogtryckeriet, P. A. Norstedt & Söner, pp. 37*–42* (text), 84–95 and 196–9 (tables).

Kungl. Statistiska Centralbyrån (1926), *Folkräkningen den 31 December 1920 av Kungl. Statistiska Centralbyrån. III. Folkmängden efter ålder, kön, civilstånd och födelseort. Äktenskapen efter varaktighet och efter makarnas ålder.* (Sveriges Officiela Statistik. Folkmängden och dess Förändringar). Stockholm: Kungl. Bogtryckeriet, P. A. Norstedt & Söner, pp. 53*–6* (text), 81–95 (tables).

1930 Statistiska Centralbyrån (1935), *Folkräkningen den 31 December 1930 av Statistiska Centralbyrån. I. Areal, Folkmängd och Hushåll inom Särskilda Förvaltningsområden m. m. Befolkningsagglomerationer.* (Sveriges Officiela Statistik. Folkmängden och dess Förändringar). Stockholm: Kungl. Bogtryckeriet,

P. A. Norstedt & Söner, pp. 45*–7* (text), 1–121 and 142–5 (tables).
Statistiska Centralbyrån (1937), *Folkräkningen den 31 December 1930 av Statistiska Centralbyrån. VI. Hushåll. Skolbildning. Yrkesväxling. Biyrke m. m.* (Sveriges Officiela Statistik. Folkmängden och dess Förändringar). Stockholm: Kungl. Bogtryckeriet, P. A. Norstedt & Söner, pp. 1–26 (text historical data 1860–1930); 80–121, 158–9 and 206–9 (tables).
Statistiska Centralbyrån (1939), *Folkräkningen den 31 December 1930 av Statistiska Centralbyrån. IX. Äktenskap och Barnantal. Marriages and the number of children.* (Sveriges Officiela Statistik. Folkmängden och dess Förändringar). Stockholm: Kungl. Bogtryckeriet, P. A. Norstedt & Söner.

1935/36 Statistiska Centralbyrån (1938), *Särskilda Folkräkningen 1935/36 av Statistiska Centralbyrån. III. Partiella folkräkningen I mars 1936: Specialundersökning av bostadsförhållandena i 100 landskommuner. Recensement de la population en 1935/36 par le Bureau Central de Statistique. III. Le recensement partiel de la population en Mars 1936: Enquête spécial des conditions d'habitations dans 100 communes rurales.* (Sveriges Officiela Statistik. Folkmängden och dess Förändringar). Stockholm: Kungl. Bogtryckeriet, P. A. Norstedt & Söner.
Statistiska Centralbyrån (1939), *Särskilda Folkräkningen 1935/36 av Statistiska Centralbyrån. VI. Partiella folkräkningen I mars 1936: Barnantal och döda barn i äktenskapen. Recensement de la population en 1935/36 par le Bureau Central de Statistique. Le recensement partiel de la population en Mars 1936: Nombre d'enfants et enfants décédés dans les mariages.* (Sveriges Officiela Statistik. Folkmängden och dess Förändringar). Stockholm: Kungl. Bogtryckeriet, P. A. Norstedt & Söner.
Statistiska Centralbyrån (1940), *Särskilda Folkräkningen 1935/36 av Statistiska Centralbyrån. VII. Partiella folkräkningen I mars 1936: Familjer. Matlagshushåll. Bostads-hushåll och bostäder. Recensement de la population en 1935/36 par le Bureau Central de Statistique. Le recensement partiel de la population en Mars 1936: Familles. Ménages. Habitations.* (Sveriges Officiela Statistik. Folkmängden och dess Förändringar). Stockholm: Kungl. Bogtryckeriet, P. A. Norstedt & Söner.

1940   No household statistics gathered.

1945   Statistiska Centralbyrån (1949), *Folkräkningen den 31 December 1945 av Statistiska Centralbyrån. V. Totala räkningen. Folkmängden kommunvis efter ålder och kön samt efter yrke m. m. Recensement total. Population par âge et par sexe, par branches d'activité économique etc. dans les divisions communales.* (Sveriges Officiela Statistik. Folkmängden och dess Förändringar). Stockholm: Kungl. Bogtryckeriet, P. A. Norstedt & Söner.
Statistiska Centralbyrån (1950), *Folkräkningen den 31 December 1945 av Statistiska Centralbyrån. VII:1. Partiella undersökningar (Tolvtedelssamplingen). Behandlar delar av Familjestatistiken. Enquêtes partielles (Échantillon de 8 %) Traitant certaines partie de la statistique des familles.* (Sveriges Officiela Statistik. Folkmängden och dess Förändringar). *Stockholm: K. L. Beckmans Bogtryckeri.*
Statistiska Centralbyrån (1954), Folkräkningen den 31 December 1945 av Statistiska Centralbyrån. VII:2. Partiella undersökningar (Tolvtedelssamplingen). Behandlar delar av Familjestatistiken. Enquêtes partielles (Échantillon de 8 %) Traitant certaines partie de la statistique des familles. (Sveriges Officiela Statistik. Folkmängden och dess Förändringar). Stockholm: K. L. Beckmans Bogtryckeri.

1750–   Hofsten, E., and H. Lundström (1976), *Swedish Population History. Main Trends*
1970   *from 1750 to 1970.* Stockholm: SCB. (Urval: Skriftserie)
1720–   *Statistiska Centralbyrån (1969), Historisk statistik för Sverige. Del 1. Befolkning.*

1967   2nd rev. and extended ed. Stockholm: SCB, pp. 84–5.
1860–   Statistiska Centralbyrån (1977), *Levnadsförhållanden - utveckling och nuläge*
1975   *enligt tillgänglig statistik 1976*. Stockholm: SCB, pp. 48–9 (Central Bureau of
        Statistics, Levnadsförhållanden, rapport, vol. 6).
1750–   Sundbärg, G. (1907 (1970)), *Bevölkerungsstatistik Schwedens 1750–1900*. With
1900   preface and terminology in English. Stockholm: SCB (Urval: Skriftserie).

SWITZERLAND

1. Vital statistics

Bundesamt für Statistik (1–, 1891–), *Statistisches Jahrbuch der Schweiz*. Berne: BFS.

Eidgenössisches Volkswirtschaftsdepartement (1–, 1928–), *Die Volkswirtschaft. Das Magazin für Wirtschaftspolitik*. Berne: Eidgenössisches Volkswirtschafts-departement.

Ritzmann-Blickenstorfer, H., ed.; under the supervision of H. Siegenthaler (1996), *Historische Statistik der Schweiz/Statistique historique de la Suisse/Historical Statistics of Switzerland*. Zurich: Chronos.

2. Population structure by age, sex, and marital status

1860   Statistisches Bureau des Eidgenössischen Departement des Innern, Bureau de
        Statistique du Département fédéral de l'Intérieur (1866), *Eidgenössische
        Volkszählung. Recensement fédéral 10 Décembre 1860. III. Lieferung. IIIᵉ
        Livraison. Alter, Geschlecht und Familienstand. Age, Sexe et Etat-civil.*
        (Schweizerische Statistik. Statistique de la Suisse. Bevölkerung. Population).
        Berne: Verlag von Orell, Füssli & Cⁱᵉ in Zurich, pp. 204–5.

1870   Statistisches Bureau des Eidgenössischen Departement des Innern, Bureau de
        Statistique du Département fédéral de l'Intérieur (1874), *Eidgenössische
        Volkszählung vom 1. December 1870. Recensement Fédéral du 1ᵉʳ Décembre
        1870. Zweiter Band. Deuxième volume. Die Bevölkerung nach Alter, Geschlecht
        und Familienstand. Age, Sexe et État-civil de la Population.* (Schweizerische
        Statistik. Statistique de la Suisse). Berne: Verlag von Orell, Füssli & Cⁱᵉ in Zurich,
        pp. 408–9.

1880   Statistisches Bureau des Eidgenössischen Departement des Innern, Bureau de
        Statistique du Département fédéral de l'Intérieur (1883), *Eidgenössische
        Volkszählung vom 1. Dezember 1880. Zweiter Band. Die Bevölkerung nach Alter,
        Geschlecht und Familienstand. Recensement Fédéral du 1ᵉʳ décembre 1880.
        Deuxième volume. Age, Sexe et État-civil de la Population.* (Schweizerische
        Statistik Band LVI). Berne: Verlag von Orell, Füssli & Co. in Zurich, pp. 2–3.

1888   Statistisches Bureau des Eidgenössischen Departement des Innern (1892), *Die
        Ergebnisse der Eidgenössischen Volkszählung vom 1. Dezember 1888. Zweiter
        Band. Die Unterscheidung der Bevölkerung nach dem Geschlechte, nach dem
        Familienstande und nach dem Alter.* (Schweizerische Statistik 88. Lieferung).
        Berne: Art. Institut Orell Füssli in Zurich, pp. 2–3.

1900   Statistisches Bureau des Eidg. Departements des Innern (1905), *Die Ergebnisse
        der Eidgenössischen Volkszählung vom 1. Dezember 1900. Zweiter Band. Die
        Unterscheidung der Bevölkerung nach dem Geschlechte, nach dem
        Familienstande und nach dem Alter.* (Schweizerische Statistik 145. Lieferung).
        Berne: Buchdruckerei Gustav Grunau, in Kommission bei A. Francke, Berne, pp.
        6–9.

1910   Statistisches Bureau der Schweiz. Finanzdepartement (1917), *Die Ergebnisse der*

Eidgenössischen Volkszählung vom 1. Dezember 1910. Zweiter Band. Die Unterscheidung der Bevölkerung nach dem Geschlechte, nach dem Familienstande und nach dem Alter. Konfessions- und Altersverhältnisse der zusammenlebenden Ehepaare. (Schweizerische Statistik 204. Lieferung). Bümpliz-Berne: Buchdruckerei Benteli A.-G., in Kommission bei A. Francke, Berne, pp. 6–9.

1920   Eidgenössisches Statistisches Bureau (1925), *Eidgenössische Volkszählung vom 1. Dezember 1920. Zusammenfassende Darstellung für die Schweiz. Erstes Schlussheft. Allgemeine Ergebnisse.* (Schweizerische Statistische Mitteilungen, hg. vom Eidgenössisches Statistisches Bureau VII. Jg. 1925, 6. Heft). Berne-Bümpliz: Buchdruckerei Benteli A.-G., in Kommission bei A. Francke A.-G., Berne, pp. 70–3.

1930   Eidgenössisches Statistisches Amt (1935), *Eidgenössische Volkszählung vom 1. Dezember 1930. Band 21: Schweiz. Tabellenteil.* (Statistische Quellenwerke der Schweiz, hg. vom Eidgenössischen Statistischen Amt, Heft 66). Berne: (no publisher given), pp. 70–3.

1941   Eidgenössisches Statistisches Amt, Bureau Fédéral de Statistique (1948), *Eidgenössische Volkszählung vom 1. Dezember 1941. Recensement Fédéral de la Population 1941. Band 21 - 21e Volume. Schweiz-Suisse. Tabellenteil I - Tableaux Ire partie.* (Statistische Quellenwerke der Schweiz, Heft 198, Statistiques de la Suisse, 198me Fascicule. Reihe Ab 4 - Série Ab 4). Berne: (no publisher given), pp. 72–5.

1860–   Ritzmann-Blickenstorfer, H., ed.; under the supervision of H. Siegenthaler (1996),
1990   *Historische Statistik der Schweiz/Statistique historique de la Suisse/Historical Statistics of Switzerland.* Zurich: Chronos, pp. 118–29.

3. Population census results on households and families

1860   Statistisches Bureau des Eidgenössischen Departement des Innern (1862), *Bevölkerung. Eidgenössische Volkszählung 10. Décember 1860. I. Lieferung. Schweizerische Statistik.* Berne: Druck von Walder & Schiller in Zurich, pp. 422–3 (tables).

1870   Statistisches Bureau des Eidgenössischen Departement des Innern (1872), *Eidgenössische Volkszählung vom 1. December 1870. Erster Band. Die Bevölkerung nach Geschlecht, Civilstand, Heimath, Aufenthalt, Religion, Gebrechen, Sprachverhältnissen, nebst der Zahl der Haushaltungen, der Wohnhäuser und bewohnbaren Räume.* (Schweizerische Statistik). Berne: Verlag von Orell, Fuessli & Cie. in Zurich, pp. VII–XV, esp. X–XII (definitions), 212–3 and 217 (tables).

1880   Statistisches Bureau des Eidgenössischen Departement des Innern, Bureau de Statistique du Département fédéral de l'Intérieur (1881), *Eidgenössische Volkszählung vom 1. Dezember 1880. Erster Band. Die Bevölkerung nach Geschlecht, Altersperioden, Civilstand, Heimath, Aufenthalt, Konfession und Sprache, nebst der Zahl der Haushaltungen und der bewohnten Häuser und Räumlichkeiten. Recensement Fédéral du 1er décembre 1880. Premier volume. Population répartie selon le sexe, l'âge, l'état civil, l'origine, le séjour, la confession et la langue, et nombre des ménages, des maisons habitées et des locaux habités.* (Schweizerische Statistik vol. LI). Berne: Verlag von Orell, Füssli & Co. in Zurich, pp. XLI–XLVI (text), 208 (table).

1888   Statistisches Bureau des Eidgenössischen Departement des Innern (1892), *Die Ergebnisse der Eidgenössischen Volkszählung vom 1. Dezember 1888. Erster Band. Zahl der Häuser, der Haushaltungen, der Gesammtbevölkerung, letztere unterschieden nach dem Heimatsverhältnisse, dem Geburtsort, nach der Confession und der Muttersprache.* (Schweizerische Statistik 84. Lieferung).

Berne: Art. Institut Orell Füssli in Zurich, pp. 40*–2* (text) and 2–182 (tables).

1900   Statistisches Bureau des Eidg. Departements des Innern (1904), *Die Ergebnisse der Eidgenössischen Volkszählung vom 1. Dezember 1900. Erster Band. Zahl der Häuser, der Haushaltungen, der Bevölkerung; Unterscheidung der Wohnbevölkerung nach Heimat, Geburtsort, Geschlecht, Konfession und Muttersprache; Die Schweizerbürger nach Heimatkanton und Heimatgemeinde.* (Schweizerische Statistik 140. Lieferung). Berne: Buchdruckerei Lack & Grunau, in Kommission bei A. Francke, Berne, pp. 2–193, 314–41 (tables, retrospective results 1860–1900).

1910   Statistisches Bureau der Schweiz. (1915), *Die Ergebnisse der Eidgenössischen Volkszählung vom 1. Dezember 1910. Erster Band. Zahl der Häuser und der Haushaltungen, der ortsanwesenden Bevölkerung und der Wohnbevölkerung. Unterscheidung der Wohnbevölkerung nach Heimat, Geburtsort, Geschlecht, Konfession und Muttersprache; Unterscheidung der Schweizerbürger nach dem Heimatkanton und der Heimatgemeinde.* (Schweizerische Statistik 195. Lieferung). Bümpliz-Berne: Buchdruckerei Benteli A.-G., in Kommission bei A. Francke, Berne, pp. 27*–9* (text); 2–287 and 297–8 (tables) (households 1870, 1880, 1888, 1900, 1910 by canton).

1920   Eidgenössisches Statistisches Bureau (1925), *Eidgenössische Volkszählung vom 1. Dezember 1920. Zusammenfassende Darstellung für die Schweiz. Erstes Schlussheft. Allgemeine Ergebnisse.* (Schweizerische Statistische Mitteilungen, hg. vom Eidgenössischen Statistischen Bureau VII. Jg. 1925, 6. Heft). Berne-Bümpliz: Buchdruckerei Benteli A.-G., in Kommission bei A. Francke A.-G., Berne, pp. 10*–1* (text), 2–31 (tables) (pp. 2–3 households 1850–1920), 48–69 and 138–47 (family statistics).

      Eidgenössisches Statistisches Bureau (1926), *Eidgenössische Volkszählung vom 1. Dezember 1920. Zusammenfassende Darstellung für die Schweiz. Drittes Schlussheft. Haushaltungsstatistik.* (Schweizerische Statistische Mitteilungen, hg. vom Eidgenössischen Statistischen Bureau VIII. Jg. 1926, 1. Heft). Winterthur: Verlagsanstalt Buchdruckerei Konkordia, in Kommission bei A. Francke A.-G., Berne.

1930   Eidgenössisches Statistisches Amt (1935), *Eidgenössische Volkszählung vom 1. Dezember 1930. Band 21: Schweiz. Tabellenteil.* (Statistische Quellenwerke der Schweiz, hg. vom Eidgenössischen Statistischen Amt, Heft 66). Berne: (no publisher given), pp. 7–11 (introduction), 15 (table households 1850–1930).

1941   Eidgenössisches Statistisches Amt, Bureau Fédéral de Statistique (1948), *Eidgenössische Volkszählung vom 1. Dezember 1941. Recensement Fédéral de la Population 1941. Band 21 - 21ᵉ Volume. Schweiz-Suisse. Tabellenteil I - Tableaux Iᵉʳᵉ partie.* (Statistische Quellenwerke der Schweiz, Heft 198, Statistiques de la Suisse, 198ᵐᵉ Fascicule. Reihe Ab 4 - Série Ab 4). Berne: (no publisher given), pp. 11*–9* (introduction), 3 (table, households 1850–1941).

      Eidgenössisches Statistisches Amt, Bureau Fédéral de Statistique (1948), *Eidgenössische Volkszählung 1. Dezember 1941. Recensement Fédéral de la Population 1941. Band 22 - 22ᵉ Volume. Schweiz-Suisse. Tabellenteil II - Tableaux IIᵐᵉ partie.* (Statistische Quellenwerke der Schweiz, Heft 215, Statistiques de la Suisse, 215ᵐᵉ Fascicule. Reihe Ab 5 - Série Ab 5). Berne: (no publisher given), pp. 164–5 (married women by number of children).

1920–70 Eidgenössisches Statistisches Amt, Bureau Fédéral de Statistique (1975), *Eidgenössische Volkszählung 1970. Recensement fédéral de la population 1970. Band 8 - 8ᵉ volume. Schweiz 5 - Suisse 5. Haushaltungen - Ménages.* Berne: Bundesamt für Statistik/Bureau Fédéral de Statistique (Statistische Quellenwerke der Schweiz, Heft 561, Statistiques de la Suisse, 561e fascicule), pp. 16–9 (households 1920–70).

1920–80 Bundesamt für Statistik, Office fédéral de la statistique, Ufficio federale di statistica (1985), *Eidgenössische Volkszählung 1980. Schweiz: Haushaltungen, Familien, Band 12. Recensement fédéral de la population 1980. Suisse. Ménages, Familles, Volume 12*. Berne: Bundesamt für Statistik. (Statistische Quellenwerke der Schweiz, Heft 712), pp. 179–82 (households 1920–80).

1920–90 Bundesamt für Statistik (1993b), *Statistisches Jahrbuch der Schweiz 1994*. Zurich: Verlag Neue Zürcher Zeitung, pp. 32–9 (households 1920–90).

1860– Ritzmann-Blickenstorfer, H., ed.; under the supervision of H. Siegenthaler (1996),
1990 *Historische Statistik der Schweiz/Statistique historique de la Suisse/Historical Statistics of Switzerland*. Zurich: Chronos, pp. 98–9.

UNITED KINGDOM OF GREAT BRITAIN AND NORTHERN IRELAND

1. Vital statistics

Board of Trade (1–83, 1840/53–1924/38), *Statistical Abstract for the United Kingdom*. London: Her Majesty's Stationery Office (HMSO).

Central Statistical Office (84–88, 1935/46–1938/1950), *Annual Abstract of Statistics*. London: CSO.

Mitchell, B. (1988), *British Historical Statistics*. Cambridge: Cambridge University Press.

——, with P. Deane (1971), *Abstract of British Historical Statistics*. University of Cambridge, Department of Applied Economics. Monographs, no. 17. Cambridge: Cambridge University Press.

——, and H. Jones (1971), *Second Abstract of British Historical Statistics*. University of Cambridge, Department of Applied Economics. Monographs, no. 18. Cambridge: Cambridge University Press.

Office of Population Censuses and Surveys (New annual series 1–31, 1921 (1923)– 1951 (1953)), *The Registrar General's Statistical Review of England and Wales*. London: HMSO.

—— (1990), *Marriage and Divorce Statistics. Historical Series on Marriages and Divorces in England and Wales, 1837–1983*. (Series FM2 no. 16). London: HMSO.

—— (1992), *Mortality Statistics. Serial Tables. Review of the Registrar General on Deaths in England and Wales, 1841–1990*. (Series DH1 no. 25). London: HMSO.

Registrar General of Birth, Death, and Marriages in England (1–83, 1837/38 (1839)– 1920 (1922)), *Annual Report of the Registrar General of Birth, Death, and Marriages in England*. London: HMSO.

Registrar General of Births, Deaths, and Marriages in Scotland (1–56, 1902–1910 (1912)), *Detailed Annual Report of the Registrar-General of Births, Deaths, and Marriages in Scotland: Abstracts for ... ; presented to Parliament by command of His Majesty*. London: HMSO.

Registrar General for Northern Ireland (1–, 1922–), *(no.) Annual Report of the Registrar General (year)*. Belfast: The General Register Office.

Registrar General for Scotland (57–, 1911–), *Annual Report of the Registrar General of Births, Deaths and Marriages for Scotland (year)*. Edinburgh: General Register Office for Scotland.

2. Population structure by age, sex, and marital status

1851   *England and Wales*: No author given (1854), *Census of Great Britain, 1851. Population Tables. II. Ages, Civil Condition, Occupations, and Birth-Place of the People: with the numbers and ages of the blind, deaf-and-dumb, and the inmates of workhouses, prisons, lunatic asylums, and hospitals. Vol. I.* London: George Edward Eyre and William Spottiswoode, p. CCI.
       Scotland: ibidem.

1861   *England and Wales*: No author given (1863), *Census of England and Wales for the Year 1861. Population Tables. Vol. II. Ages, Civil Condition, Occupations, and Birth-Places of the People: with the ages and occupations of the blind, of the deaf-and-dumb, and of the inmates of certain public institutions.* London: George Edward Eyre and William Spottiswoode, p. XX.
       Scotland: Scotland. Census Office (1864), *Census of Scotland 1861. Population tables and report. Vol. II. Ages, civil or conjugal condition, occupations, and birth places of the people in Scotland with the number and ages of the blind, the deafdumb, and the inmates of poorhouses, prisons, lunatic asylums, and hospitals.* Edinburgh, 1864.

1871   *England and Wales*: No author given (1873), *Census of England and Wales, 1871. Population Abstracts. Ages, Civil Condition, Occupations, and Birth-Places of the People. Vol. III.* London: George Edward Eyre and William Spottiswoode, p. XXIV.
       Scotland: Scotland. Census Office (1872), *Eighth Decennial Census of the Population of Scotland Taken 3d April 1871, With Report. Vol. I. Report and Scotland in Civil Counties and Parishes, Showing the Number of Families, Persons, Houses, Rooms with Windows, and of Children 5–13 Years of Age in the Receipt of Education, in 1871, and Corresponding Particulars in 1861.* Edinburgh: Neill & Company.

1881   *England and Wales*: No author given (1883), *Census of England and Wales. (43 & 44 Vict. c. 37). 1881. Volume III. Ages, Condition as to Marriage, Occupations, and Birth-Places of the People.* London: Eyre and Spottiswoode, p. V.
       Scotland: No author given (1883), *Ninth Decennial Census of the Population of Scotland Taken 4th April 1881, With Report. Vol. II. (Ages, Education, Civil Condition, Birthplaces, Occupations, General Index).* Edinburgh: Neill & Company, p. 142.

1891   *England and Wales*: No author given (1893), *Census of England and Wales. (53 & 54 Vict. c. 61). 1891. Ages, Condition as to Marriage, Occupations, Birth-Places and Infirmities. Vol. III.* London: Printed for Her Majesty's Stationery Office by Eyre and Spottiswoode, p. V.
       Scotland: No author given (1893), *Tenth Decennial Census of the Population of Scotland Taken 5th April 1891, With Report. Vol. II. Part I.* Edinburgh: Printed for Her Majesty's Stationery Office by Neill & Co., p. 120.

1901   *England and Wales*: No author given (1903), *Census of England and Wales. 1901. (63 Vict. c. 4). Summary Tables. Area, Houses and Population; also Population Classified by Ages, Condition as to Marriage, Occupations, Birthplaces, and Infirmities.* London: Printed for His Majesty's Stationery Office by Love & Malcolmson, p. 172.
       Scotland: No author given (1903), *Eleventh Decennial Census of the Population of Scotland Taken 5th April 1901, With Report. Vol. II.* Glasgow: Printed for His Majesty's Stationery Office by James Hedderwick & Sons, p. 34.

1911   *England and Wales*: No author given (1915), *Census of England and Wales. 1911. (10 Edward 7 and George 5, Ch. 27). Summary Tables. Area, Families or Separate Occupiers and Population; also Population Classified by Ages, Condition as to Marriage, Occupations, Tenements, Birthplaces, and Infirmities.*

London: Printed under the Authority of His Majesty's Stationery Office by Harrison and Sons, pp. 90–1.

Scotland: No author given (1913), *Census of Scotland, 1911. Report on the Twelfth Decennial Census of Scotland. Volume II.* London: His Majesty's Stationery Office, pp. 224–6.

1921   *England and Wales*: No author given (1925), *Census of England & Wales 1921. General Tables Comprising: Population, Housing, Institutions, Ages and Marital Conditions, Education, Birthplace and Nationality, Welsh Language.* London: His Majesty's Stationery Office, pp. 90–1.

Scotland: No author given (1923), *Census of Scotland, 1921. Report on the Thirteenth Decennial Census of Scotland. Volume II.* Edinburgh: His Majesty's Stationery Office, pp. 171–2.

1926   *Northern Ireland*: Government of Northern Ireland (1929), *Census of Population of Northern Ireland 1926. General Report. Printed and presented pursuant to the provisions of 15 and 16 Geo. V., ch. 21.* Belfast: H. M. Stationery Office, pp. 12–3.

1931   *England and Wales*: No author given (1935), *Census of England & Wales 1931. General Tables Comprising: Population, Institutions, Ages and Marital Conditions, Birthplace and Nationality, Welsh Language.* London: His Majesty's Stationery Office, pp. 141–2.

Scotland: No author given (1923), *Census of Scotland, 1931. Report on the Fourteenth Decennial Census of Scotland. Volume II. Populations, Ages and Conjugal Conditions, Birthplaces, Gaelic-Speaking and Housing.* Edinburgh: His Majesty's Stationery Office, pp. 79–80.

1937   *Northern Ireland*: Government of Northern Ireland (1940), *Census of Population of Northern Ireland 1937. General Summary. Printed and presented pursuant to the provisions of 26 Geo. 5 and 1 Edw. 8, Chap. 25.* Belfast: His Majesty's Stationery Office, pp. 10–1.

1851–   Mitchell, B., with P. Deane (1971), *Abstract of British Historical Statistics.*
1951   Cambridge: Cambridge University Press (University of Cambridge, Department of Applied Economics. Monographs, no. 17).

1851–   Mitchell, B., and H. Jones (1971), *Second Abstract of British Historical Statistics.*
1961   Cambridge: Cambridge University Press (University of Cambridge, Department of Applied Economics. Monographs, no. 18).

1851–   Mitchell, B. (1988), *British Historical Statistics.* Cambridge: Cambridge
1981   University Press.

3. Population census results on households and families

1851   *England and Wales*: No author given (1852), *Census of Great Britain, 1851. Population Tables. I. Number of the Inhabitants in the Years 1801, 1811, 1821, 1831, 1841 & 1851. Vol. I.* London: Printed by W. Clowes and Sons for Her Majesty's Stationery Office, pp. XXXIV–XLIV (text); XCV–CIII (England and Wales), CXX (Scotland) (tables).

Scotland: ibidem.

1861   *England and Wales*: No author given (1863), *Census of England and Wales for the Year 1861. Vol. III. General Report.* London: George Edward Eyre and William Spottiswoode, pp. 7–11 (text), 79–80, 88–90 and 94–9 (tables).

Scotland: No author given (1862), *Census of Scotland - 1861. Population Tables and Report. Number of the Inhabitants, Families, Children at School, Houses, and Rooms with Windows, in the Civil Counties and Parishes, Registration Counties and Districts, Burghs, Towns, Villages, and Islands of Scotland: Also a Classification of Families According to their Sizes, the Number of Persons they Contain, and their Relative House Accommodation.* Edinburgh: Printed by Murray and Gibb for Her Majesty's Stationery Office, pp. XVI, XXV–XXVI (text); XLVIII–XLIX, 2–101, 164ff. (tables).

1871   *England and Wales*: No author given (1873), *Census of England and Wales. For the Year 1871. General Report. Vol. IV*. London: Printed by George Edward Eyre and William Spottiswoode, pp. XX–XXI (families), XXIX–XXXI (houses) (text); 3, 8, 10–1 (tables).

     Scotland: Scotland. Census Office (1872), *Eighth Decennial Census of the Population of Scotland Taken 3d April 1871, With Report. Vol. I. Report and Scotland in Civil Counties and Parishes, Showing the Number of Families, Persons, Houses, Rooms with Windows, and of Children 5–13 Years of Age in the Receipt of Education, in 1871, and Corresponding Particulars in 1861*. Edinburgh: Neill & Company.

1881   *England and Wales*: No author given (1883), *Census of England and Wales. (43 & 44 Vict. c. 37). 1881. Volume IV. General Report*. London: Eyre and Spottiswoode, pp. 13–4 (text), 77 (tables).

     Scotland: Scotland. Registrar General's Office (1882), *Ninth Decennial Census of the Population of Scotland Taken 4th April 1881, With Report. Vol. I*. Edinburgh: Neill & Company, pp. XV–XVI (text); 285–321 (tables).

1891   *England and Wales*: No author given (1893), *Census of England and Wales. (53 & 54 Vict. c. 61). 1891. Volume IV. General Report with Summary Tables and Appendices*. London: Printed for Her Majesty's Stationery Office by Eyre and Spottiswoode, pp. 19–25, 77–81 (text), 95 (tables).

     Scotland: No author given (1892), *Tenth Decennial Census of the Population of Scotland Taken 5th April 1891, With Report. Vol. I*. Edinburgh: Printed for Her Majesty's Stationery Office by Neill & Co., pp. XV–XVI (text); XX–XXI, 192–206, 304–42 (tables).

1901   *England and Wales*: No author given (1904), *Census of England and Wales. 1901. (63 Vict. c. 4). General Report with Appendices*. London: Printed for His Majesty's Stationery Office by Darling & Son, pp. 36–43, 160–4 (text), 193–4 (tables).

     No author given (1903), *Census of England and Wales. 1901. (63 Vict. c. 4). Summary Tables. Area, Houses and Population; also Population Classified by Ages, Condition as to Marriage, Occupations, Birthplaces, and Infirmities*. London: Printed for His Majesty's Stationery Office by Love & Malcolmson, pp. 1 and 136 (tables).

     Scotland: No author given (1902), *Eleventh Decennial Census of the Population of Scotland Taken 31st March 1901, With Report. Vol. I*. Glasgow: Printed for His Majesty's Stationery Office by James Hedderwick & Sons, pp. XVII–XXI (text), XXVI–XXVIII, 294–309 (tables public institutions) and 324–76 (tables).

1911   *England and Wales*: No author given (1912), *Census of England and Wales. 1911. (10 Edward 7 and George 5, Ch. 27). Area, Families or Separate Occupiers and Population. Vol. I. Administrative Areas. Counties, Urban and Rural Districts*. London: printed for His Majesty's Stationery Office by Harrison and Sons, pp. XI (text), 1, 3, 7 (tables).

     No author given (1913), *Census of England and Wales. 1911. (10 Edward 7 and George 5, Ch. 27). Vol. VIII. Tenements in Administrative Counties and Urban and Rural Districts*. London: Printed under the Authority of His Majesty's Stationery Office by Harrison and Sons, pp. III–XXIV, esp. III–VIII (text), 1–665, esp. p. 2.

     No author given (1917, 1923), *Census of England and Wales. 1911. (10 Edward 7 and George 5, Ch. 27). Vol. XIII. Fertility of Marriage. Part I and II*. London: Printed under the Authority of His Majesty's Stationery Office by Harrison and Sons.

No author given (1915), *Census of England and Wales. 1911. (10 Edward 7 and George 5, Ch. 27). Summary Tables. Area, Families or Separate Occupiers and Population; also Population Classified by Ages, Condition as to Marriage, Occupations, Tenements, Birthplaces, and Infirmities.* London: Printed under the Authority of His Majesty's Stationery Office by Harrison and Sons, pp. 1 and 72 (tables).

No author given (1917), *Census of England and Wales. 1911. (10 Edward 7 and George 5, Ch. 27). General Report with Appendices.* London: Printed under the Authority of His Majesty's Stationery Office by Harrison and Sons, pp. 21, 24, 169–92 (text).

Scotland: No author given (1913), *Census of Scotland, 1911. Report on the Twelfth Decennial Census of Scotland. Volume II.* London: His Majesty's Stationery Office, pp. C–CIII (text on housing and households), 524–68, esp. 520–30 (tables on housing and households).

1921   *England and Wales*: No author given (1925), *Census of England & Wales 1921. General Tables Comprising: Population, Housing, Institutions, Ages and Marital Conditions, Education, Birthplace and Nationality, Welsh Language.* London: His Majesty's Stationery Office, pp. 82–126, 171–3 (tables on housing, families and institutions).

No author given (1927), *Census of England & Wales 1921. General Report with Appendices.* London: His Majesty's Stationery Office, pp. 34–60 (text on housing and families), 160–83 (text on dependency, orphanhood and fertility).

Scotland: No author given (1923), *Census of Scotland, 1921. Report on the Thirteenth Decennial Census of Scotland. Volume II. Report.* Edinburgh: His Majesty's Stationery Office, pp. XXXVIII–XLV (text on housing), 224–71, esp. 228–9 (tables on housing conditions).

No author given (1924), *Census of Scotland, 1921. Report on the Thirteenth Decennial Census of Scotland. Volume IV. Dependent Children.* Edinburgh: His Majesty's Stationery Office.

1926   *Northern Ireland*: Government of Northern Ireland (1929), *Census of Population of Northern Ireland 1926. General Report. Printed and presented pursuant to the provisions of 15 and 16 Geo. V., ch. 21.* Belfast: H. M. Stationery Office, pp. XX, XXII–XXIII, XXX–XXXIV, LI–LVI (definitions and text); 5–6 and 58–62 (tables).

1931   *England and Wales*: No author given (1935), *Census of England & Wales 1931. General Tables Comprising: Population, Institutions, Ages and Marital Conditions, Birthplace and Nationality, Welsh Language.* London: His Majesty's Stationery Office, pp. 112–24, 175–7 (tables on institutions).

No author given (1935), *Census of England & Wales 1931. Housing. Report and Tables.* London: His Majesty's Stationery Office (includes household statistics).

Scotland: No author given (1933), *Census of Scotland, 1931. Report on the Fourteenth Decennial Census of Scotland. Volume II. Populations, Ages and Conjugal Conditions, Birthplaces, Gaelic-Speaking and Housing.* Edinburgh: His Majesty's Stationery Office, pp. XLI–L (text) and 130–86 (tables, mainly housing).

1937   *Northern Ireland*: Government of Northern Ireland (1940), *Census of Population of Northern Ireland 1937. General Summary. Printed and presented pursuant to the provisions of 26 Geo. 5 and 1 Edw. 8, Chap. 25.* Belfast: His Majesty's Stationery Office, pp. V (definition) and 5–6 (tables).

1851–   Mitchell, B., with P. Deane (1971), *Abstract of British Historical Statistics.*
1951   Cambridge: Cambridge University Press (University of Cambridge, Department of Applied Economics. Monographs, no. 17) (no household and family statistics).

1851–   Mitchell, B., and H. Jones (1971), *Second Abstract of British Historical Statistics.*

1961   Cambridge: Cambridge University Press (University of Cambridge, Department of Applied Economics. Monographs, no. 18) (no household and family statistics).

1851– Mitchell, B. (1988), *British Historical Statistics*. Cambridge: Cambridge
1981   University Press (no household and family statistics).

REFERENCES

Alderson, M. (1981), *International Mortality Statistics*. New York: Facts on File.

Alestalo, M. (1986), *Structural Change, Classes and the State: Finland in an Historical and Comparative Perspective*. Research Reports, 33. Helsinki: University of Helsinki

——, and S. Kuhnle (1984), *The Scandinavian Route: Economic, Social, and Political Developments in Denmark, Finland, Norway and Sweden*. Research Reports, 31. Helsinki: University of Helsinki.

——, R. Andorka, and I. Harcsa (1987), *Agricultural Population and Structural Change: A Comparison of Finland and Hungary*. Research Reports, 34. Helsinki: University of Helsinki.

Als, G. (1989), *Population et Économie du Luxembourg 1839–1989*. Réalités et Perspectives 1989/5 (ed. by Banque Générale du Luxembourg).

—— (1991), *Histoire Quantitative du Luxembourg 1839–1990*. Cahiers Économiques, Série D, no. 79. Luxemburg: STATEC.

Alvstam, C., ed. (1995), *National Atlas of Sweden: Manufacturing and Services*. Stockholm: SNA Publishing.

Andorka, R., and I. Harcsa (1990), 'Modernization in Hungary in the Long and Short Run Measured by Social Indicators'. *Social Indicators Research* 21: 1–199.

Armengaud, A., and A. Fine (1988), *La population française au XXe siècle*. Paris: Presses Universitaires de France.

Az Orszagas Magyar Kir. Statiszikai Hivatal (1882), see Sources, Hungary, part 3.

Bairoch, P., J. Batou, and P. Chèvre (1988), *La Population des Villes Européennes, 800–1850. Banque de Données et Analyse Sommaire des Résultat*s. Publications du Centre d'Histoire Économique Internationale de l'Université de Genève, 2. Geneva: Librairie Droz.

Barbieri, M. (1998), 'La mortalité infantile en France'. *Population* 53(4): 813–38.

Baum, M., and A. Westerkamp (1931), *Rhythmus des Familienlebens: Das von einer Familie täglich zu leistende Arbeitspensum*. Forschungen über Bestand und Erschütterung der Familie in der Gegenwart, vol. 5. Berlin: Herbig Verlagsbuchhandlung.

Becker, G. (1993), *A Treatise on the Family*. Enlarged ed. Cambridge, MA: Harvard University Press.

Beckett, J. (1991), *Geschichte Irlands*. Bis zur Gegenwart fortgeführt von K. Metz. 3rd extended ed. Stuttgart: Alfred Kröner Verlag.

Beloch, K. (1937, 1961, 1965), *Bevölkerungsgeschichte Italiens*. Vols. I, II and III. Berlin: Walter de Gruyter.

Bengtsson, T., ed. (1994), *Population, Economy, and Welfare in Sweden*. Berlin: Springer Verlag.

——, and R. Ohlsson (1994), 'The Demographic Transition Revised'. In Bengtsson, 13–36.

Bernhardt, E. (1971), *Trends and Variations in Swedish Fertility: A Cohort Study*. Urval: Skriftserie utgiven av Statistiska Centralbyrån, no. 5. Stockholm: SCB.

Bickel, W. (1947), *Bevölkerungsgeschichte und Bevölkerungspolitik der Schweiz: Seit dem Ausgang des Mittelalters*. Zurich: Buechergilde Gutenberg.

Bideau, A., B. Desjardins, and H. Pérez Brignoli, eds. (1997), *Infant and Child Mortality in the Past*. International Studies in Demography. Oxford: Clarendon Press.

Birmingham, D. (1993), *A Concise History of Portugal*. Cambridge: Cambridge University Press.

Blasius, D. (1987), *Ehescheidung in Deutschland 1794–1945. Scheidung und Scheidungsrecht in historischer Perspektive*. Göttingen: Vandenhoeck & Ruprecht.

Bossert, G. (1891), 'Die Visitationsprotokolle der Diözese Konstanz von 1574–1581'. *Blätter für württembergische Kirchengeschichte* 6: 1–5, 9–14, 17–9, 28–30, 36–8, 43–6, 51–3, 59–62.

Bottigheimer, K. (1985), *Geschichte Irlands*. Stuttgart: W. Kohlhammer.

Bourdelais, P., and M. Demonet (1997), 'Infant Mortality in French Cities in the Mid-Nineteenth Century'. In Corsini and Viazzo, 95–108.

Brändström, A. (1993), 'Infant Mortality in Sweden, 1750–1950: Past and Present Research into its Decline'. In Corsini and Viazzo, 19–34.

——, (1997), 'Life Histories of Lone Parents and Illegitimate Children in Nineteenth-Century Sweden'. In Corsini and Viazzo, 173–91.

Breen, R., et al. (1990), *Understanding Contemporary Ireland: State, Class and Development in the Republic of Ireland*. London: Macmillan.

Brüschweiler, C. (1948), *Bevölkerungsentwicklung und Strukturwandlungen nach Heimatgruppen in den Kantonen 1850–1941*. Berne: Direktion des Armenwesens.

Bundesamt für Statistik, Office Fédéral de la Statistique, Ufficio Federale di Statistica (1985), see Sources, Switzerland, part 3.

—— (1988), *Die Bevölkerung der Schweiz um 1800*. Berne: BFS.

—— (1992), *Eidgenössische Volkszählung 1990. Bevölkerungsentwicklung 1850–1990. Die Bevölkerung der Gemeinden. Recensement fédéral de la population 1990. Evolution de la population 1850–1990. La population des communes*. Berne: BFS.

—— (1993a), *Eidgenössische Volkszählung 1990. Zur Geschichte der eidgenössischen Volkszählung*. Berne: BFS.

—— (1993b), see Sources, Switzerland, part 3.

Bureau de la Statistique Générale (1864), see Sources, France, part 3.

Bureau der K.K. Statistischen Zentralkommission (1918), see Sources, Austria, part 3, population census 1910.

Caramani, D., F. Kraus, P. Flora, and M. Quick (1998), *European Regions 1870–1990. The Territorial Units of Official Statistics*. Mannheim (unpublished manuscript).

Carr, R. (1982), *Spain, 1808–1975*. Oxford: Clarendon Press.

Carter, R., and A. Parker (1990), *Ireland: Contemporary Perspectives on an Land and its People*. London: Routledge.

Caselli, G. (1994), *Long-term Trends in European Mortality*. English translation of a paper presented at the European Population Conference. Paris, 21–25 October 1991: London: HMSO (Studies on Medical and Population Subjects, No. 56).

Catalan, J. (1995), *The Development of Two European Peripheral Economies in the Long Term: Poland and Spain, 1450–1990*. MZES, Working Paper, Research

Department III/No. 13. Mannheim: Mannheim Centre for European Social Research.

Census Commissioners, Charlemont House, Census Office (1903), see Sources, Ireland, part 3.

Centraal Bureau voor de Statistiek (1989), see Sources, The Netherlands, part 3.

—— (compiled by J. Jonker, J. van Maarseveen, and T. Vreugdenhil), and NIWI (P. Doorn) (1999), see Sources, The Netherlands, part 3.

Centrale Commissie voor de Statistiek (1893), see Sources, The Netherlands, part 3.

Chesnais, J.-C. (1992), *The Demographic Transition*. Oxford: Oxford University Press.

Chouliarakis, M. (1973–76), *Demographic, Administrative, and Population Development of Greece, 1821–1971*. 3 vols. in 4 parts. Athens: National Centre for Social Research (EKKE) (in Greek).

—— (1975a), *The Statistical Measurement of the Population of Greece, 1821–1900*. Athens: no publisher given (in Greek).

—— (1975b), *History of Population Censuses in Relation to Greece, 1900–1971*. Athens: no publisher given (in Greek).

—— (1988), *Development of the Population in the Rural Regions of Greece, 1920–1981*. Athens: National Centre for Social Research (EKKE) (in Greek).

Clancy, P., S. Drudy, K. Lynah, and L. O'Dowd, eds. (1995), *Irish Society: Sociological Perspectives*. Dublin: Institute of Public Administration.

Clogg, C., M. Massagli, and S. Eliason (1989), 'Population Undercount and Social Science Research'. *Social Indicators Research* 21: 559–98.

Clogg, R. (1992), *A Concise History of Greece*. Cambridge: Cambridge University Press.

Coale, A., and S. Watkins, eds. (1986), *The Decline of Fertility in Europe. The Revised Proceedings of a Conference on the Princeton European Fertility Project*. Princeton, New Jersey: Princeton University Press.

Coleman, D., and J. Salt (1992), *The British Population: Patterns, Trends and Processes*. Oxford: Oxford University Press.

Commaille, J., and F. de Singly, eds. (1996), *La Question Familiale en Europe*. Paris: L'Harmattan.

Commission on the Family (1998), *Strengthening Families for Life: Final Report of the Commission on the Family to the Minister for Social, Community and Family Affairs*. Dublin: The Stationery Office.

Conze, W. (1993), *Ostmitteleuropa: Von der Spätantike bis zum 18. Jahrhundert*. Edited and with an afterword by K. Zernack. Munich: Beck.

Corsini, C., and P. Viazzo, eds. (1993a), *The Decline of Infant Mortality in Europe–1850–1950–Four National Case Studies*. Florence, Italy: UNICEF.

——, and P. Viazzo (1993b), 'The Historical Decline of Infant Mortality: An Overview'. In Corsini and Viazzo, 9–17.

——, and P. Viazzo, eds. (1997), *The Decline of Infant and Child Mortality: The European Experience: 1750–1990*. The Hague: Nijhoff.

Council of Europe (1978–), *Recent Demographic Developments in Council of Europe Member States 1978–*. Strasburg: Council of Europe.

—— (1990), *Household Structures in Europe. Report of the Select Committee of Experts on Household Structures*. Population Studies, No. 22. Strasbourg: Council of Europe.

Courtney, D. (1995), 'Demographic Structure and Change in the Republic of Ireland and Northern Ireland'. In P. Clancy et al., eds. *Irish Society: Sociological Perspectives*. Dublin: Institute of Public Administration in association with The Sociological Association of Ireland, 39–89.

Coward, J. (1990), 'Irish Population Problems'. In R. Carter and A. Parker, eds. *Ireland: Contemporary Perspectives on a Land and its People*. London and New York: Routledge, 55–86.

Cross, M., and S. Perry, eds. (1997), *Population and Social Policy in France*. London and Washington: Pinter.

Croze, M. (1987), 'Les statistiques démographiques'. In J. Affichard, ed. *Pour une Histoire de la Statistique. Tome 2: Matériaux*. Paris: INSEE; Paris: Economica, 21–34.

Daktoglou, P. (1980), 'Verfassung und Verwaltung'. In K.-D. Grothusen, ed. *Griechenland*. Südosteuropa-Handbuch, vol. 3. Göttingen: Vandenhoeck & Ruprecht, 13–53.

Danmarks Statistik (1964b, 1965a), see Sources, Denmark, part 1.

Del Panta, L. (1997), 'Infant and Child Mortality in Italy, Eighteenth to Twentieth Century: Long-Term Trends and Territorial Differences'. In Bideau, Desjardins, and Brignoli, 7–21.

Den Dulk, K., and J. van Maarseveen (1999), 'The Population Censuses in the Netherlands'. In J. van Maarseveen and M. Gircour, eds., *A Century of Statistics: Counting, Accounting and Recounting in the Netherlands*. Voorburg: CBS/Amsterdam: Stichting beheer IISG, 303–34.

Dupâquier, J. (1988), *Histoire de la population française*. Vol. 3: De 1789 à 1914; Vol. 4: De 1914 à nos jours. Paris: Presses Universitaires de France.

Durdik, C. (1973), 'Bevölkerungs- und Sozialstatistik in Österreich im 18. und 19. Jahrhundert'. In Helczmanovski, 225–66.

Easterlin, R. (1968), *Population, Labor Force, and Long Swings in Economic Growth: The American Experience*. New York: Columbia Univ. Press (National Bureau of Economic Research (New York, NY): General series; 86).

—— (1987), *Birth and Fortune: The Impact of Numbers on Personal Welfare*. 2nd ed. Chicago: University of Chicago Press.

——, and E. Crimmins (1985), *The Fertility Revolution: A Supply-Demand Analysis*. 1st ed. Chicago: University of Chicago Press.

Eidgenössisches Statistisches Amt, Bureau Fédéral de Statistique (1975), see Sources, Switzerland, part 3.

Eidgenössisches Statistisches Bureau (1926), see Sources, Switzerland, part 3.

Elklit, J. (1978), 'Household Structure in Denmark 1769–ca. 1890'. In S. Åkerman, H. Johansen, and D. Gaunt, eds. *Chance and Change: Social and Economic Studies in Historical Demography in the Baltic Area*. Odense: Odense University Press, 109–21.

Etemad, B. (1990), *Les Sources Statistiques Rétrospectives Internationales et Nationales du XIXe et du XXe Siècles*. University of Geneva, Centre for International Economic History, Monograph 4. Geneva: Centre d'Histoire Economique Internationale.

EUROSTAT (1977–), *Demographic Statistics 1960–76ff*. Luxemburg: Office for Official Publications of the European Communities.

Ferreira da Cunha, Adrião Simões (1995), *O Sistema Estatístico Nacional. Algumas notas sobre a evolução dos seus princípios orientadores: de 1935 ao presente.* Lisbon: Instituto Nacional de Estatística (INE).

Festy, P. (1985), 'Evolution contemporaine du mode de formation des familles en Europe occidentale'. *European Journal of Population* 1(1): 179–205.

Fircks, A. Freiherr von (1898), *'Bevölkerungslehre und Bevölkerungspolitik'.* Leipzig: C. L. Hirschfeld.

Flora, P. (1975), 'Quantitative Historical Sociology. A Trend Report and Bibliography'. *Current Sociology* XXIII(2).

——, F. Kraus, and W. Pfenning (1987), *State, Economy, and Society in Western Europe. A Data Handbook in Two Volumes. Vol. II: The Growth of Industrial Societies and Capitalist Economies.* Frankfurt: Campus Verlag; London: Macmillan Press; Chicago: St. James Press.

Fux, B. (2001, forthcoming), 'Switzerland'. In P. Flora and T. Bahle, eds. *Family Change and Family Policies in Belgium, The Netherlands, and Switzerland.* Oxford: Clarendon Press.

Garssen, J., and C. Harmsen (1999), 'De toegenomen dynamiek van huishoudens'. In R. van der Bie and P. Dehing, eds. (1999), *National goed. Feiten en cijfers over onze samenleving–(ca.) 1800–1999.* Voorburg and Heerlen: CBS/Amsterdam: Stichting beheer IISG, 219-31.

Glendon, M. (1989), *The Transformation of Family Law. State, Law, and Family in the United States and Western Europe.* Chicago and London: The University of Chicago Press.

Główny Urząd Statystycny (1993), see Sources, Poland, part 1.

Głowny Urząd Statystyczny Rzeczypospolitei polskiej (1930), see Sources, Poland, part 3.

—— (1938), see Sources, Poland, part 3.

Gómez Redondo, R. (1992), *La mortalidad infantil española en el siglo XX.* Madrid: Centro de Investigaciones Sociológicas.

Goody, J. (1983), *The Development of the Family and Marriage in Europe.* Cambridge: Cambridge University Press.

Gröwer, K. (1998), ''Wilde Ehen' in den hansestädtischen Unterschichten: 1814–1871'. *Archiv für Sozialgeschichte* 38: 1–22.

—— (1999), *Wilde Ehen im 19. Jahrhundert: Die Unterschichten zwischen städtischer Bevölkerungspolitik und polizeilicher Repression; Hamburg, Bremen, Lübeck.* Berlin/Hamburg: Reimer.

Gylfason, T., et al. (1997), *The Swedish Model under Stress. A View from the Stands.* Stockholm: SNS Förlag.

Hagstofa Íslands/Statistics Iceland (1997), *Hagskinna. Sögulegar Hagtölur um Ísland/Icelandic Historical Statistics.* Reykjavík: Hagstofa Íslands.

Hajnal, J. (1965), 'European Marriage Patterns in Perspective'. In D. Glass and D. Eversley, eds. *Population in History. Essays in Historical Demography.* London: Arnold, 101–43.

Helczmanovski, H., ed. (1973), *Beiträge zur Bevölkerungs- und Sozialgeschichte Österreichs. Nebst einem Überblick über die Entwicklung der Bevölkerungs- und Sozialstatistik.* By order of the Österreichischen Statistischen Zentralamtes, ed. by H. Helczmanovski. Vienna: Österreichisches Statistisches Zentralamt.

Hindelang, H. (1909), *Die eheliche und uneheliche Fruchtbarkeit mit besonderer Berücksichtigung Bayerns. Mit graphischen Darstellungen.* Beiträge zur Statistik Bayerns, ed. by the Königliches Statistisches Landesamt, vol. 71. Munich: Lindauer.

Hionidou, V. (1997), 'Infant Mortality in Greece, 1859–1959: Problems and Research Perspectives'. In Corsini and Viazzo, 155–72.

Höpflinger, F. (1986), *Bevölkerungswandel in der Schweiz. Zur Entwicklung von Heiraten, Geburten, Wanderungen und Sterblichkeit.* Grüsch: Verlag Rüegger.

—— (1997), 'Haushalts- und Familienstrukturen im intereuropäischen Vergleich'. In S. Hradil and S. Immerfall, eds. *Die westeuropäischen Gesellschaften im Vergleich.* Opladen: Leske + Budrich, 97–138.

Hoensch, J. (1983), *Geschichte Polens.* Stuttgart: Eugen Ulmer.

—— (1984), *Geschichte Ungarns 1867–1983.* Stuttgart: Verlag W. Kohlhammer.

—— (1992), *Geschichte Böhmens. Von der slawischen Landnahme bis ins 20. Jahrhundert.* 2nd rev. and expanded ed. Munich: Beck.

Hoesch, E. (1993), *Geschichte der Balkanländer. Von der Frühzeit bis zur Gegenwart.* Munich: Beck.

Hoffmann-Nowotny, H.-J. (1996), 'Partnerschaft—Ehe—Familie: Ansichten und Einsichten'. *Zeitschrift für Bevölkerungswissenschaft* 21(2): 111–30.

Hofstee, E. (1978), *De Demografische Ontwikkeling van Nederland in de Eerste Helft van de Negentiende Eeuw: Een Historisch-Demographische en Sociologische Studie.* Deventer: Van Loghum Slaterus.

Hofsten, E., and H. Lundström (1976), *Swedish Population History. Main Trends from 1750 to 1970.* Urval: Skriftserie. Stockholm: SCB.

Hungarian Central Statistical Office (1992), see Sources, Hungary, part 1.

Ilbery, B. (1986), *Western Europe: A Systematic Human Geography.* 2nd ed. Oxford: Oxford University Press.

Imhof, A. (1978), 'The Computer in Social History: Historical Demography in Germany'. *Computers and the Humanities* 32: 227–36.

Im Hof, U. (1991), *Mythos Schweiz. Identität—Nation—Geschichte 1291–1991.* Zurich: Verlag Neue Zürcher Zeitung.

—— (1997), *Geschichte der Schweiz.* 6th ed. Stuttgart: Kohlhammer.

Institut National de la Statistique et des Études Économiques (INSEE) (1966), see Sources, France, part 1.

Instituto Nacional de Estatística (1984), *Estatisticas Demograficas 1980–1982.* Lisbon: INE.

—— (1985), *Instituto Nacional de Estatística 50 anos, Portugal 1935–1985.* Lisbon: INE.

—— (1995), *Estatisticas Demograficas 1994.* Lisbon: INE.

Janssens, A. (1993), *Family and Social Change. The Household as a Process in an Industrializing Community.* Cambridge Studies in Population, Economy and Society in Past Time, vol. 21. Cambridge: Cambridge University Press.

Johansen, H. (1987), *The Danish Economy in the Twentieth Century.* New York: St. Martin's Press.

Johansson, L., and F. Finnäs (1983), *Fertility of Swedish Women Born 1927–1960.* Urval: Skriftserie utgiven av Statistiska Centralbyrån, no. 14. Stockholm: SCB.

Johnson, J. (1994), *The Human Geography of Ireland.* New York: John Wiley & Sons.

Joshi, H., ed. (1989), *The Changing Population of Britain*. Oxford: Basil Blackwell.

Jurado, T. (1997), 'Spain'. *EURODATA Newsletter* No. 6: 27–31.

Kälvemark, A. (1980), *More Children of Better Quality? Aspects on Swedish Population Policy in the 1930s*. Stockholm: Almqvist & Wiksell.

Kästli, T. (1998), *Die Schweiz—eine Republik in Europa. Geschichte des Nationalstaats seit 1798*. Zurich: Verlag Neue Zürcher Zeitung.

Kamerman, S., and A. Kahn, eds. (1997), *Family Change and Family Policies in Great Britain, Canada, New Zealand, and the United States*. Family Change and Family Policies in the West, vol. 1. Oxford: Clarendon Press.

Kaufmann, F.-X. (1990), 'Familie und Modernität'. In Lüscher et al., 391–415.

—— (1995), *Zukunft der Familie im vereinten Deutschland: Gesellschaftliche und politische Bedingungen*. Munich: Beck.

Kern, R. (1995), *The Regions of Spain: A Reference Guide to History and Culture*. Westport/London: Greenwood Press.

Keyfitz, N., and W. Flieger (1968), *World Population: An Analysis of Vital Data*. 2nd ed. 1970. Chicago and London: The University of Chicago Press.

——, and W. Flieger (1990), *World Population Growth and Aging: Demographic Trends in the Late Twentieth Century*. Chicago and London: The University of Chicago Press.

Kiel, A. (1993), *Continuity and Change. Aspects of Contemporary Norway*. Oslo: Scandinavian University Press.

Kielly, G. (1998), 'Ireland'. In J. Ditch, H. Barnes, and J. Bradshaw, eds. *European Observatory on National Family Policies. Developments in National Family Policies in 1996*. York: Social Policy Research Unit (SPRU)/Commission of the European Communities., 113-30.

Klinger, A. (1993), *The Demographic Situation of Hungary in Europe*. Population Studies, No. 27. Strasburg: Council of Europe Press.

Kluxen, K. (1991), *Geschichte Englands. Von den Anfängen bis zur Gegenwart*. 4th ed. Stuttgart: Alfred Kröner (Kröners Taschenausgabe Band 374).

Knodel, J. (1974), *The Decline of Fertility in Germany 1871–1939*. Princeton, New Jersey: Princeton University Press.

Kok, J., F. van Poppel, and E. Kruse (1997), 'Mortality Among Illegitimate Children in Mid-Nineteenth-Century The Hague'. In Corsini and Viazzo, 193–211.

Kommission 'Bevölkerungspolitik', ed. (1985), *Sterben die Schweizer aus? Die Bevölkerung der Schweiz: Probleme, Perspektiven, Politik*. Berne/Stuttgart: Verlag Paul Haupt.

Kraus, A. (1979), '"Antizipierter Ehesegen' im 19. Jahrhundert. Zur Beurteilung der Illegitimität unter sozialgeschichtlichen Aspekten'. *Vierteljahresschrift für Wirtschafts- und Sozialgeschichte* 66: 174–215.

—— (1980), *Quellen zur Bevölkerungs-, Sozial- und Wirtschaftsstatistik Deutschlands 1815–1875. Vol. 1: Quellen zur Bevölkerungsstatistik Deutschlands 1815–1875*. Compiled by A. Kraus. Series ed. W. Köllmann. Forschungen zur deutschen Sozialgeschichte, vol. 2/I. Boppard am Rhein: Harald Boldt.

Kuhnle, S. (1989), 'Statistikkens historie i Norden'. In Nordiska Statistiska Sekretariatet, ed. *Norden för och nu. Ett sekel i statistisk belysning*. Stockholm: Norstedts Tryckeri, 21–45.

Kytir, J., and R. Münz (1993), 'Infant Mortality in Austria, 1820–1950: Trends and Regional Patterns'. In Corsini and Viazzo, 71–86.

Lacy, T. (1998), *Ring of Seasons: Iceland – Its Culture and History*. Ann Arbor: The University of Michigan Press.

Ladstätter, J. (1973), 'Wandel der Erhebungs- und Aufarbeitungsziele der Volkszählungen seit 1869'. In Helczmanovski, 267–94.

Laslett, P., and R. Wall, eds. (1972), *Household and Family in Past Time: Comparative Studies in the Size and Structure of the Domestic Group over the Last Three Centuries*. Cambridge: Cambridge University Press.

Leridon, H. (1989), 'Naissance du premier enfant et devenir des unions consensuelles'. In P. L'Hardy and C. Thélot, eds. *Les ménages: mélanges en l'honneur de Jacques Desabie*. Paris: INSEE, 265–81.

Lesthaeghe, R. (1977), *The Decline of Belgian Fertility, 1800–1970*. Princeton, New Jersey: Princeton University Press.

Leyland, J., et al. (1990), *The Economist Book of Vital World Statistics. A Complete Guide to the World in Figures*. London: Hutchinson Business Books.

Liesner, T. (1985), *Economic Statistics 1900–1983: United Kingdom, United States of America, France, Germany, Italy, Japan*. London: The Economist Publications.

Livi-Bacci, M. (1968), 'Fertility and Nuptiality Changes in Spain from the Late 18th to the Early 20th Century'. *Population Studies* 22, part 1 (March): 83–102, and part 2 (July): 211–34.

—— (1971), *A Century of Portuguese Fertility*. Princeton, New Jersey: Princeton University Press.

—— (1977), *A History of Italian Fertility during the Last Two Centuries*. Princeton, New Jersey: Princeton University Press.

—— (1986), 'Social-Group Forerunners of Fertility Control in Europe'. In Coale and Watkins, 182–200.

Loth, W. (1987), *Geschichte Frankreichs im 20. Jahrhundert*. Stuttgart: Kohlhammer.

Lüscher, K., F. Schultheis and M. Wehrspaun, eds. (1990), *Die 'postmoderne' Familie. Familiale Strategien und Familienpolitik in einer Übergangszeit*. Konstanz: Universitätsverlag.

Lutz, W. (1987), *Finnish Fertility since 1772: Lessons from an Extended Decline*. Helsinki: Population Research Institute/Väestöntutkimuslaitos Väestöliitto.

Mamelund, Brunborg, and Noack (1997), see Sources, Norway, part 1.

Malthus, T. (1992, 1798), *An Essay on the Principle of Population, or, a View of its Past and Present Effects on Human Happiness: With an Inquiry into our Prospects Respecting the Future Removal or mitigation of the Evils which it Occasions*. Cambridge: Cambridge University Press.

Marcuse, M. (1907), 'Heiratsbeschränkungen'. *Zeitschrift für Socialwissenschaft* 10: 225–97.

Masuy-Stroobant, G. (1997), 'Infant Health and Infant Mortality in Europe: Lessons from the Past and Challenges for the Future'. In Corsini and Viazzo, 1–34.

Mattmüller, M., et al. (1987), *Bevölkerungsgeschichte der Schweiz. Part I: Die frühe Neuzeit 1500–1700. Vol. I Darstellung*. Basler Beiträge zur Geschichtswissenschaft, vol. 154. Basle: Helbing & Lichtenhahn.

Matz, K.-J. (1980), *Pauperismus und Bevölkerung: Die gesetzlichen Ehebeschränkungen in den süddeutschen Staaten während des 19. Jahrhunderts.* Industrielle Welt, vol. 31. Stuttgart: Klett.

Mayer, K. (1952), *The Population of Switzerland.* New York: Columbia University Press.

Meyer, T. (1993), 'Der Monopolverlust der Familie: Vom Teilsystem Familie zum Teilsystem privater Lebensformen'. *Kölner Zeitschrift für Soziologie und Sozialpsychologie* 45: 23–40.

The Minister for Justice (1993), *Marital Breakdown: A Review and Proposed Changes.* Dublin: The Stationery Office.

Ministerio de Instrucción Pública y Bellas Artes. Dirección General del Instituto Geográfico y Estadístico (1916), *Censo de la población de España según el empadronamiento hecho en la península e islas adyacentes el 31 de diciembre de 1910.* Vol. II. Madrid: Talleres del Instituto Geográfico y Estadístico.

Ministero di Agricultura, Industria e Commercio, Direzione Generale della Statistica (1883), see Sources, Italy, part 3.

——, Direzione Generale della Statistica e del Lavoro, Ufficio del Censimento (1915), see Sources, Italy, part 3.

Ministerio de Trabajo, Comercio e Industria. Dirección General de Estadística (1922), see Sources, Spain, part 3.

Mitchell, B. (1980/1981), *European Historical Statistics 1750–1975,* 2nd rev. ed. London and Basingstoke: The Macmillan Press/New York: Facts on File.

—— (1992), *European Historical Statistics 1750–1988,* 3rd ed. London and Basingstoke: Macmillan Publishers.

Mitterauer, M. (1979), 'Familienformen und Illegitimität in ländlichen Gebieten Österreichs'. *Archiv für Sozialgeschichte* 19: 123–88.

—— (1983), *Ledige Mütter: Zur Geschichte illegitimer Geburten in Europa.* Munich: Beck.

—— and R. Sieder (1982), *The European Family. Patriarchy to Partnership from the Middle Ages to the Present.* Chicago: The University of Chicago Press; Oxford: Blackwell (revised translation of *Vom Patriarchat zur Partnerschaft: Zum Strukturwandel der Familie.* Munich: Beck, 1977).

Müller, G., with V. Bornschier (1988), *Comparative World Data: A Statistical Handbook for Social Science.* Frankfurt: Campus Verlag; Baltimore and London: The Johns Hopkins University Press.

Münz, R. (1984), *Familienpolitik: Gestern, heute, morgen.* Salzburg: Amt der Salzburger Landesregierung.

Myrdal, A., and G. Myrdal (1935), *Kris i befolkningsfrågan.* 7th ed. Stockholm: Bonnier.

Nanetti, R. (1988), *Growth and Territorial Policies: The Italian Model of Social Capitalism.* London and New York: Pinter Publishers.

National Centre for Social Research (1972), *Statistical Works 1821–1971. Statistics During the 150 Years of Rebirth of Greece,* by M. Chouliarakis, E. Gritsopoulos, M. Gevetsis, and A. Agiopetritis. Athens: National Centre for Social Research (EKKE) (in Greek).

National Statistical Service of Greece (1960), *Mouvement naturel de la Grèce en 1956.* Athènes. Imprimerie Nationale (in Greek/French).

—— (1966), *Demographic Trends and Population Projections of Greece*. Athens: NSSG.

——, Centre for Planning and Economic Research (1974), *Urban–Rural Population Dynamics of Greece 1950–1995*. Athens: NSSG.

—— (1980), *The Population of Greece in the Second Half of the 20th Century*. Athens: NSSG.

—— (1994), *Résultats du recensement de la population et des habitations effectué le 5 avril 1981. Vol. 1: Population par divisions géographiques et administratives*. Athènes: NSSG:

Niedhart, G. (1996), *Geschichte Englands im 19. und 20. Jahrhundert*. Munich: Verlag C. H. Beck.

Nieminen, M. (1999), *Väestötilastoja 250 vuotta. Katsaus väestötilaston historiaan vuosina 1749–1999*. Suomen virallinen tilasto (SVT)–Finlands Officiella Statistik–Official Statistics of Finland, Väestö–Befolkning–Population 1999:8. Helsinki: Tilastokeskus.

No author given (1917, 1923, 1927), see Sources, United Kingdom, part 3.

Oberschall, A. (1920), *Das Volkszählungsgesetz vom 8. April 1920 nebst der Durchführungsverordnung vom 30. Oktober 1920*. Reichenberg: Gebrüder Stiepel.

Österreichisches Statistisches Zentralamt (ÖSTAT) (1979a), *Geschichte und Ergebnisse der zentralen amtlichen Statistik in Österreich 1829–1979. Festschrift aus Anlaß des 150jährigen Bestehens der zentralen amtlichen Statistik in Österreich*. Beiträge zur Österreichischen Statistik, Vol. 550. Vienna: Österreichisches Statistisches Zentralamt.

—— (1979b), *Geschichte und Ergebnisse der zentralen amtlichen Statistik in Österreich 1829–1979. Tabellenanhang*. Beiträge zur Österreichischen Statistik, Vol. 550A. Vienna: Österreichisches Statistisches Zentralamt.

Peacock, A., J. Wiseman, and J. Veverka (1967), *The Growth of Public Expenditure in the United Kingdom*. 2nd rev. ed. London: Allen & Unwin.

Pérez Moreda, V., and D. Reher (1988), *Demografía histórica en España*. Madrid: Ediciones El Arquero.

Perrenoud, A. (1997), 'Child Mortality in Francophone Europe: State of Knowledge'. In Bideau, Desjardins, and Brígnoli, 22–37.

Pinelli, A., and P. Mancini (1997), 'Gender Mortality Differences from Birth to Puberty in Italy, 1887–1940'. In Corsini and Viazzo, 73–93.

Pitkänen, K. (1983), 'Infant Mortality Decline in a Changing Society'. *Yearbook of Population Research in Finland*, Vol. XXI. Helsinki: Väestöntutkimuslaitos Väestöliitto.

Poppel, F. van, and K. Mandemakers (1997), 'Differential Infant and Child Mortality in the Netherlands, 1812–1912: First Results of the Historical Sample of the Population of the Netherlands'. In Bideau, Desjardins, and Brígnoli, 276–300.

Portugal. Ministerio da Fazenda. Direcção Geral da Estatística e dos Proprios Nacionaes (1896), see Sources, Portugal, part 3.

——. Instituto Nacional de Estatística (1952), see Sources, Portugal, part 3.

Pounds, N. (1979), *An Historical Geography of Europe, 1500–1840*. Cambridge: Cambridge University Press.

Price, R. (1993), *A Concise History of France*. Cambridge: Cambridge University Press.

Prinzing, F. (1902), 'Die Wandlungen der Heiratshäufigkeit und des mittleren Heiratsalters'. *Zeitschrift für Socialwissenschaft* 5: 656–74.

Procacci, G. (1989), *Geschichte Italiens und der Italiener*. Munich. Beck Verlag.

Puntila, L. (1980), *Politische Geschichte Finnlands 1809–1977*. Helsinki: Kustannusosakeyhtiö Otava.

Quick, M. (1994), *Regional Territorial Units in Western Europe Since 1945*. MZES/EURODATA Working Paper No. 5. Mannheim: Mannheim Centre for European Social Research (MZES).

Reher, D. (1997), *Perspectives on the Family in Spain: Past and Present*. Oxford: Clarendon Press.

——, V. Pérez-Moreda, and J. Bernabeu-Mestre (1997), 'Assessing Change in Historical Contexs: Childhood Mortality Patterns in Spain during the Demographic Transition'. In Corsini and Viazzo, 35–56.

République Française. Ministère du Commerce et de l'Industrie (1888), see Sources, France, part 2.

——. Ministère des Finances et des Affaires Économiques. Institut National de la Statistique et des Études Économiques. Direction de la Statistique Générale (1949, 1953), see Sources, France, part 3.

République Héllénique, Ministère de l'Économie Nationale (1928), see Sources, Greece, part 3.

Reid, A. (1997), 'Locality or Class? Spatial and Social Differentials in Infant and Child Mortality in England and Wales, 1895–1911'. In Corsini and Viazzo, 129–54.

Ringen, S., ed. (1997), 'Great Britain'. In Kamerman and Kahn, 29–102.

Ritzmann-Blickenstorfer, H., and H. Siedenthaler (1996), see Sources, Switzerland, part 1.

Rokkan, S. (1999), *State Formation, Nation-Building, and Mass Politics in Europe: The Theory of Stein Rokkan*. Based on his collected works. P. Flora with S. Kuhnle and D. Urwin, eds. Oxford: Oxford University Press.

Rollet, C. (1997a), 'Childhood Mortality in High-Risk Groups: Some Methodological Reflections Based on French Experience'. In Corsini and Viazzo, 213–25.

——, (1997b), 'The Fight Against Infant Mortality in the Past: An International Comparison'. In Bideau, Desjardins, and Brignoli, 38–60.

——, and P. Bourdelais (1993), 'Infant Mortality in France, 1750–1950: Evaluation and Perspectives'. In Corsini and Viazzo, 51–70.

Roos, H. (1986), *Geschichte der polnischen Nation 1918–1985. Von der Staatsgründung im Ersten Weltkrieg bis zur Gegenwart*. 4th rev. and expanded ed. Stuttgart: W. Kohlhammer.

Rosenberg, H. (1974), *Die Weltwirtschaftskrise 1857–1859*. Göttingen: Vandenhoeck & Ruprecht.

Rostow, W. (1998), *The Great Population Spike and After. Reflections on the 21st Century*. New York/Oxford: Oxford University Press.

Rothenbacher, F. (1982), 'Zur Entwicklung der Gesundheitsverhältnisse in Deutschland seit der Industrialisierung'. In E. Wiegand and W. Zapf, eds.

Wandel der Lebensbedingungen in Deutschland: Wohlfahrtsentwicklung seit der Industrialisierung. Frankfurt/New York: Campus, 335–424.

—— (1989), *Soziale Ungleichheit im Modernisierungsprozeß des 19. und 20. Jahrhunderts.* Frankfurt/New York: Campus.

—— (1995), 'Household and Family Trends in Europe: From Convergence to Divergence'. *EURODATA Newsletter* No. 1, Spring 1995: 3–9.

—— (1996), 'European Family Indicators'. *EURODATA Newsletter* No. 3, Spring 1996: 19–23.

—— (1997a), *Historische Haushalts- und Familienstatistik von Deutschland 1815– 1990.* Frankfurt/New York: Campus Verlag.

—— (1997b), 'Familienberichterstattung *in* und *für* Europa'. In H.-H. Noll, ed. *Sozialberichterstattung in Deutschland: Konzepte, Methoden und Ergebnisse für Lebensbereiche und Bevölkerungsgruppen.* Weinheim and Munich: Juventa Verlag, 93–123.

—— (1998a), *Statistical Sources for Social Research on Western Europe 1945– 1995. A Guide to Social Statistics.* Europe in Comparison, vol. 6. Opladen: Leske + Budrich.

—— (1998b), 'Social Change in Europe and its Impact on Family Structures'. In J. Eekelaar and T. Nhlapo, eds. *The Changing Family: International Perspectives on the Family and Family Law.* Oxford: Hart Publishing, 3–31.

—— (1998c), 'France'. *EURODATA Newsletter* No. 7, Spring 1998: 29–33.

——, and F. Putz (1987), *Die Haushalts- und Familienstatistik im Deutschen Reich und in der Bundesrepublik Deutschland.* Wiesbaden: Bundesinstitut für Bevölkerungsforschung (Materialien zur Bevölkerungswissenschaft, no. 51).

Roussel, L. 1992: 'La famille en Europe occidentale: divergences et convergences'. *Population* 47(1): 133–52.

Royaume de Grèce. Ministère de l'Intérieur, Service du Recensement (1909), see Sources, Greece, part 2.

Schofield, R., D. Reher, and A. Bideau, eds. (1991), *The Decline of Mortality in Europe.* Oxford: Clarendon Press.

Schultheis, F. (1988), *Sozialgeschichte der französischen Familienpolitik.* Frankfurt/New York: Campus Verlag.

Schwenger, H. (1999), 'Austria'. *EURODATA Newsletter,* No. 9, Spring 1999: 17– 23.

Seidlmayer, M. (1989), *Geschichte Italiens. Vom Zusammenbruch des Römischen Reiches bis zum ersten Weltkrieg.* 2nd expanded ed. Stuttgart: Alfred Kröner Verlag.

Service Central de la Statistique et des Études Économiques (1990a, 1990b), see Sources, Luxemburg, part 1.

Shorter, E., J. Knodel, and E. van de Walle (1971), 'The Decline of Non-marital Fertility in Europe, 1880–1940'. *Population Studies* 25: 375–93.

Shoup, P. (1981), *The East European and Soviet Data Handbook: Political, Social, and Developmental Indicators, 1945–1975.* New York: Columbia University Press.

Sieburg, Heinz-Otto (1995), *Geschichte Frankreichs.* 5th expanded ed. Stuttgart: Kohlhammer.

Simon, E. (1925), 'Der Kampf gegen die Entvölkerung Frankreichs'. *Zeitschrift des Preußischen Statistischen Landesamts* 65: 53–68.

Skilling, G., ed. (1991), *Czechoslovakia 1918–88. Seventy Years from Independence*. London: Macmillan.

Smith, D. (1991), 'Mortality Differentials before the Health Transition. *Health Transition Review* 1: 235–37.

Soltys, S. (1995), *Der polnische Arbeitsmarkt im Umbruch*. Frankfurt/New York: Campus.

Spree, R. (1980), 'Die Entwicklung der differentiellen Säuglingssterblichkeit in Deutschland seit der Mitte des 19. Jahrhunderts. (Ein Versuch zur Mentalitätsgeschichte)'. In A. Imhof, ed. *Mensch und Gesundheit in der Geschichte: Vorträge eines internationalen Colloquiums in Berlin vom 20. bis zum 23. Sept. 1978*. Husum: Matthiesen, 251–78.

Ständige Kommission für Statistik (1911), see Sources, Luxemburg, part 3.

Statens Statistiske Bureau (1905), see Sources, Denmark, part 1.

Stationery Office (1995), *The Right to Remarry: A Government Information Paper on the Divorce Referendum*. Dublin: The Stationery Office.

Statistics Norway (1994), *Social Survey 1993. Summary with Tables and Graphs*. Oslo-Kongsvinger: Statistics Norway.

—— (1995), see Sources, Norway, part 1.

Statistik Österreich (2000), *Demographisches Jahrbuch Österreichs 1998*. Wien: Statistik Österreich.

Statistisches Bureau des Eidg. Departements des Innern (1904), see Sources, Switzerland, part 3.

—— (1908), *Ehe, Geburt und Tod in der schweizerischen Bevölkerung während der zehn Jahre 1891–1900. Erster Teil: Die Eheschliessungen und Ehelösungen.* (Schweizerische Statistik 158. Lieferung). Bern: Kommissionsverlag A. Francke. Buchdruckerei 'Effingerhof', Brugg.

Statistisk Bureau (1857, 1894), see Sources, Denmark, part 3.

—— (1871, 1883), see Sources, Denmark, part 2.

Statistisk Centralbureau (1882), see Sources, Norway, part 3.

Statistisk Sentralbyrå (1962, 1965, 1966, 1976 and 1989), see Sources, Norway, part 1.

—— (1904, 1952), see Sources, Norway, part 3.

Statistiska Centralbyrån (1939, 1895), see Sources, Sweden, part 3.

—— (1969), see Sources, Sweden, part 1.

Statistiska Central-Byrån (1860), see Sources, Sweden, part 3.

Sugar, P., P. Hanák, and T. Frank, eds. (1990), *A History of Hungary*. Bloomington and Indianapolis: Indiana University Press.

Sundbärg, G. (1907 (1970)), see Sources, Sweden, part 1.

—— (1908), *Aperçus Statistiques Internationaux*. (Reprinted by Gordon and Breach Science Publishers, New York, London and Paris. Demographic Monographs, Vol. 4). Stockholm: Imprimerie Royale.

Suomenmaan Virallinen Tilasto (1899, 1902, 1909), see Sources, Finland, part 1.

Taylor, C., and D. Jodice (1983), *World Handbook of Political and Social Indicators*. 2 vols. 3rd ed. New Haven and London: Yale University Press.

Teitelbaum, M. (1984), *The British Fertility Decline*. Princeton, New Jersey: Princeton University Press.

Thorsteinsson, T. (1948), 'Grundlaget for befolkningsstatistikken i Island'. In *Det 18de Nordiske Statistiske Mote*. Reykjavik.

Tillastollinen päätoimisto (1870), see Sources, Finland, part 3.

Todorova, M. (1993), *Balkan Family Structure and the European Pattern: Demographic Developments in Ottoman Bulgaria.* Washington, D.C.: The American University Press.

Tyrell, H. (1990), 'Ehe und Familie—Institutionalisierung und Deinstitutionalisierung'. In Lüscher et al., 145–56.

Ungern-Sternberg, R. von (1937a), 'Wirtschaftliche Konjunktur und Geburtenfrequenz'. *Jahrbücher für Nationalkökonomie und Statistik* 145: 471–87.

—— (1937b), *Die Ursachen neuzeitlicher Ehezerrüttung.* Berlin: Stilke.

United Nations, Department for Economic and Social Information and Policy Analysis, Statistics Division (1949–), *Demographic Yearbook 1948–.* New York: United Nations.

——, Department of International Economic and Social Affairs, Statistical Office (1979), *Demographic Yearbook/Annuaire Démographique. Special issue 1978: Historical Supplement.* New York: United Nations.

U.S. Department of Commerce/Bureau of the Census (1975), *Historical Statistics of the United States: Colonial Times to 1970. 2 Parts. Bicentennial Edition.* Washington, DC: U.S. Government Printing Office.

Van Baarsel, G., and W. Commandeur, compilers (no date), *Honderd jaar cijfers in drieduizend publicaties. Bibliografie van de CBS-publicaties 1899–1998.* This bibliography can be searched over the Internet: http://www.cbs.l/nl/bibliotheek/bibliografie.htm.

Van Maarseveen, J., M. Gircour, and R. Schreijnders, eds. (1999), *A Century Rounded Up: Reflections on the History of the Central Bureau of Statistics in the Netherlands.* Voorburg: CBS/Amsterdam: Stichting beheer IISG.

Van de Walle, E. (1974), *The Female Population of France in the Nineteenth Century. A Reconstruction of 82 Départements.* Princeton, New Jersey: Princeton University Press.

Van de Walle, F. (1986), 'Infant Mortality and the European Demographic Transition'. In Coale and Watkins, 201–33.

Van der Bie, R., P. Dehing, and J. Smits, eds. (1999), see Sources, The Netherlands, part 1.

Van Zanden, J., ed. (1996), *The Economic Development of The Netherlands since 1870.* (The Economic Development of Modern Europe Since 1870, vol. 7). Cheltenham, UK/Brookfield, US: Edward Elgar Publishing.

Vaughan, W., and A. Fitzpatrick (1978), *Irish Historical Statistics. Population, 1821–1971.* Dublin: Royal Irish Academy.

Viazzo, P. (1997), 'Alpine Patterns of Infant Mortality in Perspective'. In Corsini and Viazzo, 61–73.

Vögele, J. (1997), 'Urbanization, Infant Mortality and Public Health in Imperial Germany'. In Corsini and Viazzo, 109–25.

Wall, R. (1997), 'Zum Wandel der Familienstrukturen im Europa der Neuzeit'. In J. Ehmer, T. Hareven, and R. Wall, eds. *Historische Familienforschung: Ergebnisse und Kontroversen.* Frankfurt/New York: Campus, 255–82.

—— (1998), 'Characteristics of European Family and Household Systems'. *Historical Social Research* 23(1/2): 44–66.

——, J. Robin, and P. Laslett, eds. (1983), *Family Forms in Historic Europe.* Cambridge: Cambridge University Press.

Watkins, S. (1991), *From Provinces into Nations: Demographic Integration in Western Europe, 1870–1960.* Princeton, New Jersey: Princeton University Press.

Weinberger, M. (1994), 'Recent Trends in Contraceptive Use'. *Population Bulletin of the United Nations* 36: 55–80.

Wende, P. (1995), *Geschichte Englands.* 2nd revised and extended ed. Stuttgart: Kohlhammer.

Woods, R. (1997a), 'Infant Mortality in Britain: A Survey of Current Knowledge on Historical Trends and Variations'. In Bideau, Desjardins and Pérez Brignoli, 74–88.

—— (1997b), 'Differential Mortality Patterns Among Infants and Other Young Children: The Experience of England and Wales in the Nineteenth Century'. In Corsini and Viazzo, 57–72.

——, N. Williams, and C. Galley (1993), 'Infant Mortality in England, 1550–1950: Problems in the Identification of Long-Term Trends, Geographical and Social Variations'. In Bideau, Desjardins and Pérez Brignoli, 35–50.

The World Bank (1978–), *World Development Report.* New York, N.Y.: Oxford University Press.

Wrigley, E., and R. Schofield (1981), *The Population History of England 1541–1871: A Reconstruction.* London: Arnold.

Zamagni, V. (1993), *The Economic History of Italy 1860–1990.* Oxford: Clarendon Press.

Zapf, W. (1995), 'Wandel, sozialer'. In B. Schäfers, ed. *Grundbegriffe der Soziologie.* 4th improved and enlarged ed. Uni-Taschenbücher, vol. 1416. Opladen: Leske & Budrich, 427–32.

——, et al. (1987), Individualisierung und Sicherheit: Untersuchungen zur Lebensqualität in der Bundesrepublik Deutschland. Munich: Verlag C. H. Beck.